Lecture Notes in Computer Science 7405

Commenced Publication in 1973
Founding and Former Series Editors:
Gerhard Goos, Juris Hartmanis, and Jan van Leeuwen

Xinbing Wang   Rong Zheng   Tao Jing
Kai Xing (Eds.)

Wireless Algorithms, Systems, and Applications

7th International Conference, WASA 2012
Yellow Mountains, China, August 8-10, 2012
Proceedings

 Springer

Volume Editors

Xinbing Wang
Shanghai Jiao Tong University
Department of Electronic Engineering
800 Dongchuan Rd., Minhang District, Shanghai, 200240, China
E-mail: xwang8@sjtu.edu.cn

Rong Zheng
University of Houston, Department of Computer Science
4800 Calhoun Rd., 565 Philip G. Hoffman Hall, Houston, TX 77204-3010, USA
E-mail: rzheng@uh.edu

Tao Jing
Beijing Jiaotong University
School of Electronics and Information Engineering
3 Shangyuan Village, Haidian District, Beijing, 100044, China
E-mail: tjing@bjtu.edu.cn

Kai Xing
University of Science and Technology of China
School of Computer Science and Technology
P.O. Box 4, USTC West Campus, Hefei, Anhui, 230027, China
E-mail: kxing@ustc.edu.cn

ISSN 0302-9743   e-ISSN 1611-3349
ISBN 978-3-642-31868-9   e-ISBN 978-3-642-31869-6
DOI 10.1007/978-3-642-31869-6
Springer Heidelberg Dordrecht London New York

Library of Congress Control Number: 2012942191

CR Subject Classification (1998): F.1, F.2, D.1-2, D.4, C.2.4, C.2, C.4, H.4

LNCS Sublibrary: SL 1 – Theoretical Computer Science and General Issues

Typesetting: Camera-ready by author, data conversion by Scientific Publishing Services, Chennai, India

Printed on acid-free paper

Springer is part of Springer Science+Business Media (www.springer.com)

Preface

Over the past few years, wireless communications and networks have enjoyed tremendous growth, driven by 3G/4G cellular technologies, the wide deployment of WiFi access points, and the proliferation of smart personal mobile devices. At the same time, end users are accustomed to bandwidth-hungry applications such as online video streaming, online gaming, e-mails with multimedia attachment, etc. Emergence of multimedia networking requires next-generation wireless networks to provision for not only basic Internet access but also quality of service guarantee, with seamless roaming across heterogeneous networks. Scalable solutions are crucial to handle large amount of mobile users; and they give rise to new challenges for both industry and academia with regard to resource allocation and scheduling, mobility management, distributed algorithms, cooperative networking, dynamic spectrum sharing, security and privacy, as well as scalable and energy-efficient network protocols.

The annual International Conference on Wireless Algorithms, Systems, and Applications (WASA) provides a forum for theoreticians, system and application designers, protocol developers, and practitioners to exchange ideas, share new findings, and discuss challenging issues for the current and next-generation wireless networks. Past WASA conferences were held in Xian (2006), Chicago (2007), Dallas (2008), Boston (2009), Beijing (2010), and Chendu (2011). The 7th WASA conference took place at the Yellow Mountains during August 8–10, 2012. The conference received 116 full submissions, out of which 32 were invited papers for six special topic sessions [Cognitive Radio Networks (CRN), Cyber-Physical Network Systems (CPNS), Mobile Handset Networking Systems (MHNS), Underwater and Radar Wireless Networks (URWN), and Wireless and Mobile Security (WMS)]. Among the remaining 84 submissions, 24 were accepted as regular papers, with an acceptance ratio of 28.6%. Each submission was rigorously reviewed by at least three Program Committee members.

We thank all the authors for submitting their papers to the conference. We also thank all the members of the Technical Program Committee and external referees for their help in completing the reviewing process under the tight time constraints. We especially thank Special Session Chairs Jun-Hong Cui, Qilian Liang, Xue Liu, Xiuzhen Chen, Dong Xuan, and Yanchao Zhang for inviting high-quality papers. We are grateful to the members of the Steering Committee and Organizing Committee for their involvement throughout the process. WASA 2012 was a true teamwork. Finally, many other people contributed to the success of WASA 2012, whose names cannot be listed here due to space limitation. However, we owe them our gratitude.

August 2012

Xinbing Wang
Rong Zheng
Tao Jing

Organization

WASA 2012 was organized by Beijing Jiaotong University, China, in cooperation with NSFC.

Steering Committee

Xiuzhen Cheng   The George Washington University, USA(Co-chair)
Peng-Jun Wan   Illinois Institute of Technology, USA(Co-chair)

Executive Committee

Honorary General Co-chairs

Ness Shroff   The Ohio State University, USA
Jianghong Han   Hefei University of Technology, China

General Chair

Tao Jing   Beijing Jiaotong University, China

TPC Co-chairs

Rong Zheng   University of Houston, USA
Xinbing Wang   Shanghai Jiaotong University, China

Local Organization Co-chairs

Xiaofang Tang   Beijing Jiaotong University, China
Yan Huo   Beijing Jiaotong University, China
Na Xia   Hefei University of Technology, China

Publicity Co-chairs

Habib M. Ammari   University of Michigan, Dearborn, USA
Xiaohua Tian   Shanghai Jiaotong University, China

Publication Chair

Kai Xing   University of Science and Technology of China

Registration Chair

Yan Huo   Beijing Jiaotong University, China

Technical Program Committee

Costas Busch	Louisiana State University, USA
Jiannong Cao	Hong Kong Polytechnic University, SAR China
Jen-Yeu Chen	National Dong-Hwa University, Taiwan
Yong Cui	Tsinghua University, China
Hongwei Du	Harbin Institute of Technology, China
Amitabha Ghosh	Princeton University, USA
Maleq Khan	Virginia Tech, USA
Jangwon Lee	Yonsei University, South Korea
Wonjun Lee	Korea University, South Korea
Deying Li	Renmin University of China
Minming Li	City University of Hong Kong, SAR China
Qun Li	College of William and Mary, USA
XiaoJun Lin	Purdue University, USA
Benyuan Liu	University of Massachusetts - Lowell, USA
Jia Liu	Ohio State University, USA
Wei Lou	Polytechnic University of Hong Kong, SAR China
Kejie Lu	University of Puerto Rico at Mayaguez
Jelena Misic	Ryerson University, USA
Srinivasan Parthasarathy	IBM Research
Jian Qiu	Hangzhou Dianzi University, China
Yun Rui	Shanghai Advanced Research Institute, Chinese Academy of Sciences
Michael Segal	Ben-Gurion University of the Negev, Israel
Jian Tan	IBM T.J. Watson Research, USA
Xiaohu Tang	Southwest Jiaotong University, China
Xiaohua Tian	Shanghai Jiaotong University, China
Pengjun Wan	Illinois Institute of Technology, USA
Amy Yuexuan Wang	Tsinghua University, China
Yu Wang	University of North Carolina at Charlotte, USA
Kui Wu	University of Victoria, Canada
Guoliang Xing	Michigan State University, USA
Chi-Wei Yi	National Chiao Tung University, Taiwan
Yung Yi	KAIST, Korea
Junshan Zhang	Arizona State University, USA

External Reviewers

Changqing Bu	University of Electronic Science and Technology of China
Zhipeng Cai	Georgia State University, USA
Xianghui Cao	Zhejiang University, China
Adam Champion	The Ohio State University, USA
Xi Chen	McGill University, Canada

Jinxue Zhang	Arizona State University, USA
Rui Zhang	Arizona State University, USA
Shuo Zhang	University of Science and Technology of China
Zhongyuan Zhao	Beijing University of Posts and Telecommunications, China
Guanbo Zheng	University of Houston, USA
Huan Zhou	Zhejiang University, China

Sponsorship

National Natural Science Foundation of China (NSFC), China
Beijing Jiaotong University, China

Table of Contents

Throughput and Delay with Network Coding in Hybrid Mobile Ad Hoc Networks: A Global Perspective

Jian Li[1,3], Luoyi Fu[1], Xinbing Wang[1], Changliang Xie[1], Xiaohua Tian[1],
Yongsheng Zhang[2], and Xiaoli Wang[2]

[1] Department of Electronic Engineering, Shanghai Jiao Tong University
[2] DoCoMo Beijing Communications Laboratories, China
[3] The State Key Laboratory of Integrated Services Networks, Xidian University, China
{fighting0818,yiluofu,xwang8,xcl_sjtu,xtian}@sjtu.edu.cn
{zhangy,wangxl}@docomolabs-beijing.com.cn

Abstract. In this paper, we study throughput and delay scaling laws of wireless networks with network coding under different mobility models. Specifically, we consider 2-hop and multi-hop schemes with n nodes and k original packets for each pair of source-destination. We consider two ad hoc network mobility models- hybrid random walk models (HRWM) and discrete random direction models (DRDM). For the hybrid random walk models, we divide the unit square into $n^{2\beta}$ cells with an area of $1/n^{2\beta}$, where $0 \le \beta \le 1/2$, each cell is further divided into $n^{1-2\beta}$ subcells. For the discrete random direction models, the unit square is divided into $n^{2\alpha}$ cells with an area of $1/n^{2\alpha}$, where $0 \le \alpha \le 1/2$. At the beginning of each time slot, every node moves from its current cell to the adjacent cell. We find that (1) under 2-hop relay scheme with network coding, there is a $\log n$ gain on delay only when the mobility model is random walk model; (2) under multi-hop relay scheme, there is a turning point and a critical turning point for delay in these two models. For hybrid random walk models, we take $k = \Theta(n^{\beta})$, and obtain that the delay is halved by the turning point $\beta = 1/4$. Compared to the network without network coding, our results show that there is a critical turning point $\beta = 1/5$, which means when $0 \le \beta < 1/5$, the delay will be better without network coding for the network, and when $1/5 \le \beta \le 1/2$, network coding helps decrease the delay. The same results also hold in discrete random direction models. At last, we propose the network model with network coding and infrastructure mode together. And in this mode, we obtain the results of throughput and delay.

1 Introduction

The research on wireless network transmission throughput and delay has been carried out since P. Gupta and P. R. Kumar [1] first came up with the notation of "capacity" for wireless ad hoc networks. They proposed a protocol interference unicast mode and found the capacity of a random wireless network with static nodes scales as $\Theta(\frac{1}{\sqrt{n\log n}})$. In order to improve the throughput of wireless networks, Grossglauser and Tse [2] proposed a 2-hop relaying algorithm in which the nodes are allowed to move, and obtained the throughput of $\Theta(1)$. Although this algorithm leads to the higher throughput, it also increases the delay to $\Omega(n)$ [3],[4].

X. Wang et al. (Eds.): WASA 2012, LNCS 7405, pp. 1–19, 2012.

In previous studies, discussed above, all nodes conduct packet transmission through the conventional store-and-forward mode. After these "pure" wireless networks with nodes mobility and transmission algorithms, researchers began to think about more approaches to improve the throughput and delay [16]. Network coding, which allows not only packets replication and forwarding but also packets mixing at the intermediate nodes, is thought to be a promising operation. Ahlswede et al. [5] first proposed network coding, and then, Li et al. [6] proposed a linear network coding algorithm to achieve the optimal max-flow. In [7], [8], a more practical network coding approach called Random Linear Coding(RLC) was proposed to mix the packets independently and randomly. Later, Tracey et al. [9] presented the RLC approach for multicast scheme, and Ghaderi et al. [10] analyzed the network coding performance against automatic repeat request scheme for reliable multicast transmission. Recently, Liu et al.[11],[12] demonstrated that there is no order change of throughput but a constant amplitude gain in static networks with network coding. In mobile networks, Zhang et al. [13] first showed that there is a $\log n$ gain in delay tolerant networks.

As most of the previous works are based on specific models such as i.i.d. mobility model, some challenging questions still remain open:

- How representative are these specific models in the study and in the industry application?
- Can the throughput-delay relationship be significantly different under some other reasonable mobility models?
- What is the impact of network coding on these models?

In this paper, we present a study considering throughput and delay for mobile ad hoc networks with network coding under two general mobility models, and focus on how the restricted parameter of the mobility model influences the throughput and delay. We introduce two forms of mobility models, first studied by Sharma et al.[14], i.e., hybrid random walk models and discrete random direction models with constraint parameter β and α, respectively.

Our observation shows that under 2-hop relay scheme, the delay is unrelated to β and α. While under multi-hop relay scheme, the delay varies as β and α increases, and there is a turning point for delay both under hybrid random walk models and discrete random direction models. Moreover, we find there is a critical turning point which determines the usefulness of adopting network coding in the network.

Our main contributions are summarized as follows:

- In 2-hop relay scheme, under hybrid random walk models and discrete random direction models with network coding, the throughput is $\Theta(1)$ and the delay is $\Theta(n)$. Thus there is a $\log n$ gain on delay only when the mobility model is random walk model.
- In multi-hop relay scheme, there are two significant points for delay, i.e., the turning point 1/4 and the critical turning point 1/5 under hybrid random walk models and discrete random direction models, as shown in Figures 1 and 2. It is interesting to see that these two models have the same turn point and critical turning point, this is because the difference between these two models is the duration of a time slot, which has no impact on the results.

- The critical turning point determines the usefulness of adopting network coding in the network. In our work, the number of original packets k has a strong influence on the motion of relay nodes. Compared with [14], the transmission time, which dominates in whole delay without network coding, will be shorter for $\beta, \alpha < 1/5$, thus it is useless to use network coding; for $1/5 \leq \beta, \alpha \leq 1/2$, the transmission delay will be shorter with network coding due to the increase of original packets $k = \Theta(n^\beta)$ and $k = \Theta(n^\alpha)$, respectively.
- The turning point divides the network coding delay into two cases depending on β and α. The whole delay is composed of three parts: the time for source node to send $m = (1 + \epsilon)k$ coded packets, the time for coded packets to be delivered between relay nodes and the time for destination node to collect at least k coded packets. For $0 < \beta, \alpha \leq 1/4$, the time for coded packets to be delivered between relay nodes dominates in the whole delay; for $1/4 \leq \beta, \alpha \leq 1/2$, the time for source node to send m coded packets dominates in the whole delay due to the increase of original packets k.

The rest of the paper is organized as follows. In Section 2, we describe the hybrid random walk models and discrete random direction models, and discuss the interference model and some notations. We introduce the network coding operation and RLC relay schemes, and give out the main results in Section 3. We analyze the delay and throughput under hybrid random walk models with network coding in Section 4, and under discrete random direction models in Section 5. We propose a new network mode with base stations and introduce the network models in Section 6. The corresponding results and analysis with network coding is provided in Section 7. A discussion about delay and throughput in previous sections is provided in Section 8. Finally, we end our paper with some conclusions in Section 9.

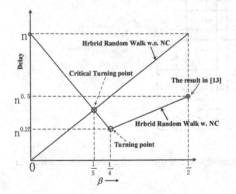

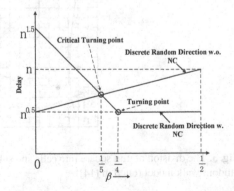

Fig. 1. The delay obtained in hybrid random walk models with and without RLC in multi-hop scheme

Fig. 2. The delay obtained in discrete random direction models with and without RLC in multi-hop scheme

2 The Model

We consider an ad hoc network consisting of n mobile nodes, distributed uniformly on a unit square S. The square is assumed to be a $torus^2$, i.e., which means the top and bottom edges, the left and right edges are assumed to touch each other. All the nodes in the network generate traffic at the same rate. And we take 2-hop relay scheme and multi-hop relay scheme into consideration.

2.1 Hybrid Random Walk Models

A parameter β, which takes values between 0 and 1/2, is used to define these models. First, we divide the unit square into $n^{2\beta}$ square cells with an area of $1/n^{2\beta}$ each, resulting in a discrete torus of size $n^\beta \times n^\beta$. Then, each cell is further divided into $n^{1-2\beta}$ square subcells with an area of $1/n$ each, as shown in Figure 3. Time is divided into slots of equal duration. At each time slot, a node is assumed to be in any subcell. Initially, all nodes are distributed uniformly and independently on the unit square. At the beginning of a time slot, a node moves from its current subcell to another subcell in the adjacent cells. Here we have an explanation for adjacent cells: Let a node be in cell (i,j), where $i, j = 0, 1, 2, ..., n^\beta - 1$ at time slot t, then, at time slot $t + 1$, the node is equally likely to be in the same cell (i,j) or any of the four adjacent cells (i-1,j),(i+1,j),(i,j-1),(i,j+1), where the addition and subtraction operations are performed modulo n^β. Specifically, for $\beta = 0$, the above mobility model is i.i.d. model and for $\beta = 1/2$, it is random walk model.

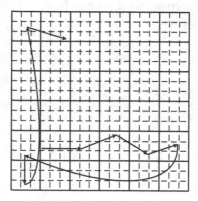

Fig. 3. The division of unit square into cells and subcells; and the motion of a node under a hybrid random walk model (cited in [14])

2.2 Discrete Random Direction Models

A parameter α, which takes values between 0 and 1/2, is used to define these models. We divide the unit square S into $n^{2\alpha}$ square cells, with an area of $1/n^{2\alpha}$ each, resulting in a discrete torus of size $n^\alpha \times n^\alpha$. Initially, all the nodes are distributed uniformly and independently on the unit square. The motion of a node is divided into multiple trips. At the beginning of a trip, the node chooses a direction θ uniformly between $[0, 2\pi]$, and moves a distance of $n^{-\alpha}$ in that direction at a speed of v_n. Here we choose $v_n = \Theta(\frac{1}{\sqrt{n}})$ because we keep the network area fixed and let the number of nodes increase to infinity, which means that the average neighborhood size scales as $\Theta(\frac{1}{\sqrt{n}})$. Time is divided into slots of equal duration, and at the beginning of a time slot, each node moves from its current cell to one of the four adjacent cells or stay at the current cell with equal probability. In our models, the duration of a slot should be $\Theta(n^{1/2-\alpha})$.

2.3 Model for Successful Transmission

In our work, we take the interference model into consideration, which ensures the success or failure of a transmission between a pair of nodes. We use the protocol model of [1]. Let W be the bandwidth of the system in bits per second and X_t^i denote the position of node i, for $i = 1...n$, at time t. Under the protocol model, node i can communicate directly with node j at a rate of W bits per second at time t, if and only if, the following interference constraint is satisfied:

$$d(X_t^k, X_t^j) \geq (1 + \delta)d(X_t^i, X_t^j)$$

for every other node $k \neq i, j$ that is simultaneously transmitting. Here $d(x, y)$ is the distance between nodes x and y, and δ is a positive constant independent of n.

2.4 Network Performance Metrics

Definition of throughput: Let $\lambda_i(t)$ be the total number of packets delivered from the source node i to the destination node in t time slots, then the throughput is defined as

$$\lambda(n) = \liminf_{t \to \infty} \frac{1}{t}\lambda_i(t)$$

Note that when network coding is utilized, $\lambda_i(t)$ is the number of successfully decoded packets received by the destination node of S-D pair i in t time slots.

Definition of delay: The delay in the network coding scheme is the time for the source node to send the coded packets to the destination and the destination to successfully decode all the original packets, we denote it as $D(n)$.

3 Throughput and Delay with Network Coding: Schemes and Results

We first review the network coding operation which is the same as that in [9]. Then we introduce the schemes used to analyze throughput and delay with network coding. At last, main results for the hybrid random walk models and discrete random direction models with RLC are presented.

3.1   Network Coding Operation

Random linear coding (RLC for short) [9] is applied to a finite set of k original packets, $M = \{m_1, m_2, \cdots, m_k\}$, which is called a generation. We assume that all the k packets in M are linearly independent. In the RLC protocol, destination node collects several linear combinations of the packets in M. Once the destination node has k independent linear combinations of the packets, it can recover all the packets successfully. Let f_l denote one of the encoded packets. Then f_l has the form $f_l = \sum_{i=1}^{k} a_i \cdot m_i$, where a_i is the RLC vector known to the destination. For decoding purpose, the transmitting nodes also send the random coding vectors as overhead within each packet. Each node v collects the coding vectors for the packets it receives in a decoding matrix G_v. A received packet is said to be innovative if its coding vector increases the rank of the matrix G_v.

3.2   RLC-Based Relay Schemes

In this subsection, we describe the RLC-based relay schemes with 2-hop and multi-hop routing strategies, which will be used in the later analysis of network coding in mobile ad hoc networks.

Proposition 1: In the description of RLC-based relay schemes, we use the concept of "generation". In the following, a generation means the source has k original packets that wants to send to the destination, and the source node will group these k packets into one generation and use the RLC schemes to encode them. The destination node will recover all the original packets after it has collected enough coded packets from this generation.

Schemes 1: 2-hop Relay with RLC

(1) k original packets in each source node will be grouped into one generation. Each source will send $m = (1 + \epsilon)k$ coded packets for each generation, where ϵ is a constant.

(2) When the relay node has received the coded packet, it will store it in the buffer which has infinite capacity and wait encoding and transmission. After all the nodes have received the coded packet from the source, it will be deleted from the buffer.

(3) Each subcell will become active once in every ψ time slots, the value of ψ will be discussed later.

(4) For an active subcell with at least two nodes, randomly assign a node as sender and independently choose another node in the subcell as receiver. The transmission is scheduled to operate in either "Source-to-Relay" or "Relay-to-Destination" mode with equal probability of 1/2, described as follows:

– Source to Relay transmission: If the sender has a new encoded packet that has never been transmitted before, send the packet to the receiver and delete it from the buffer. As for the receiver which is a relay node, it collects packets from the sender and stores them in a buffer of infinite capacity in order to await encoding and transmission.

– Relay to Destination transmission: If the sender has a new encoded packet for the receiver, transmit it. Before a relay transmits a packet to its destined destination, it has to undergo RLC encoding again, on all the packets in its buffer for the same destination. The receiver that is the destination node must receive enough innovative packets to achieve the rank k of the decoding matrix G_v so that it can recover the original packets.

Schemes 2: Multi-hop Relay with RLC

(1) k original packets in each source node will be grouped into one generation. Each source will send $m = (1 + \epsilon)k$ coded packets for each generation, where ϵ is a constant.
(2) When the relay node has received the coded packet, it will store it in the buffer which has infinite capacity and wait encoding and transmission. After all the nodes have received the coded packet from the source, it will be deleted from the buffer.
(3) Each subcell will become active once in every ψ time slots, the value of ψ will be discussed later.
(4) For an active subcell with at least two nodes, suppose one is the source node, the other one is the relay node. Then the source node sends the coded packet to the relay node. At next time slot, the relay node moves from the current cell to the adjacent cell or stays at the current cell as illustrated in the mobility model with the same probability. If the relay node moves to an adjacent cell, it will carry the coded packet and move around until it meets another relay node and passes the coded packet to the relay node. Thus, a coded packet will be passed at least once and at most twice when it goes through any cell.

Proposition 2: In multi-hop relay scheme, when a relay node holding the coded packet goes through a cell, it will hold the coded packet until it meets another relay node and then forwards the coded packet to the relay node. The relay node will forward its coded packet to another relay node only once in one cell, which means a coded packet will be passed at least once and at most twice(at the beginning from the source node) when it goes through any cell.

Proposition 3: Under the protocol model, we take the interference model into consideration, therefore each subcell in a cell will become active regularly once in ψ time slots. From [15], we take $\psi = (4\lceil 1 + \Delta \rceil + 3)^2$, here ψ only depends on Δ, and is independent of n. Note that, $\lceil x \rceil$ is the ceiling function of x, which returns the smallest integer not smaller than x, or formally,

$$\lceil x \rceil = \min \{n \in \mathbb{Z} | n \geq x\},$$

where $\mathbb{Z}$ is the set of real numbers.

3.3 Main Results for RLC-Based Schemes

In this subsection, we summarize the main results of RLC-based schemes under hybrid random walk models and discrete random direction models. Here, we focus on presenting these results, the proofs of these results will be analyzed in the following section.

Theorem 1: Under the hybrid random walk models in 2-hop relay scheme with RLC used, for $0 < \beta \leq 1/2$, we take $k = \Theta(n^{2\beta})$, and obtain $T(n) = \Theta(1)$, $D(n) = \Theta(n)$; for $\beta = 0$, it is the i.i.d. model, we take $k = \Theta(n)$, and have $T(n) = \Theta(1)$, $D(n) = \Theta(n)$.

Remark 1: Note that our results for $\beta = 0$ and $\beta = 1/2$ are in agreement with the corresponding results for fast mobility model and slow mobility model in [13]. This means that our models and schemes are representative.

Theorem 2: Under the hybrid random walk models in multi-hop relay scheme with RLC used, for $\beta = 0$, we take $k = \Theta(\log n)$, and have $T(n) = \Theta(1/n)$, $D(n) = \Theta(\log n)$; for $0 < \beta < 1/4$, we take $k = \Theta(n^{\beta})$, and obtain $T(n) = \Theta(n^{\beta-1})$, $D(n) = \Theta(n^{1-3\beta} \log n)$; for $1/4 \leq \beta \leq 1/2$, we take $k = \Theta(n^{\beta})$, and have $T(n) = \Theta(n^{\beta-1})$, $D(n) = \Theta(n^{\beta})$.

Remark 2: For the two extreme choices of β, i.e., $\beta = 0, 1/2$, our results yield with those in [13].

Theorem 3: Under the discrete random direction models in 2-hop relay scheme with RLC adopted, for $0 \leq \alpha < 1/2$, we take $k = \Theta(n^{2\alpha})$, and obtain $T(n) = \Theta(1)$, $D(n) = \Theta(n)$; for $\alpha = 1/2$, we take $k = \Theta(n)$, and have $T(n) = \Theta(1)$, $D(n) = \Theta(n)$.

Theorem 4: Under the discrete random direction models in multi-hop relay scheme with RLC adopted, for $0 \leq \alpha < 1/4$, we take $k = \Theta(n^{\alpha})$, and obtain $T(n) = \Theta(n^{\alpha-1})$, $D(n) = \Theta(n^{3/2-4\alpha} \log n)$; for $1/4 \leq \alpha \leq 1/2$, we take $k = \Theta(n^{\alpha})$, and have $T(n) = \Theta(n^{\alpha-1})$, $D(n) = \Theta(n^{1/2})$.

4   Throughput and Delay with Network Coding under Hybrid Random Walk Models: Analysis

In this section, we present details of proofs for results on RLC-based scheme under hybrid random walk models which are discussed in the previous section.

4.1   Preliminaries

To make the analysis more apparent and easy, we first recall some notations for hybrid random walk models: first hitting time, first return time [14], minimal flooding delay and minimal 2-hop delay [13], and inter-meeting time.

Definition of First Hitting Time: The first hitting time for the set of states $A \subset S_X$ is given by $\tau_H^A = \inf \{t \geq 0 : X(t) \in A\}$ with $X(0)$ being distributed according to Π_X.

Definition of First Return Time: The first return time for the set of states $A \subset S_X$ is given by $\tau_H^A = \inf \{t > 0 : X(t) \in A\}$ with $X(0) \in A$.

Definition of Minimal 2-hop Delay: Whenever a source node encounters a relay node, it will send a coded packet to the relay node. The minimal 2-hop delay is the time for the source to encounter k different nodes in the network, here k is the number of original packets.

Definition of Minimal flooding Delay: Whenever a node that has coded packets encounters a relay node, it will send the coded packets to the relay node. Then the corresponding time is called minimal flooding delay.

Now, we recall the results concerning the first hitting time and first return time for a single state in case of a 2-D torus of size $n^\beta \times n^\beta$, for $0 < \beta \leq 1/2$.

Lemma 41. *Let H denote the first hitting time for a single state on a 2-D torus of size $n^\beta \times n^\beta$, then $\mathbb{E}\{H\} = \Theta(n^{2\beta} \log n)$.*

Lemma 42. *Let H denote the first return time for a single state on a 2-D torus of size $n^\beta \times n^\beta$, then $\mathbb{E}\{H\} = \Theta(n^{2\beta})$.*

Next we present the results for minimal 2-hop delay and minimal flooding delay.

Lemma 43. *The minimal 2-hop delay under hybrid random walk models is $\Theta(n^{2\beta})$ for $0 < \beta \leq 1/2$, and $\Theta(n)$ for $\beta = 0$.*

Proof. Under the hybrid random walk models for $\beta = 0$, it is the i.i.d. mobility model, the corresponding minimal 2-hop delay is $\Theta(n)$, which is proved in [13]. When $0 < \beta \leq 1/2$, the joint position of two nodes due to independent hybrid random walks can be viewed as a difference random walk relative to the position one node. Then the inter-meeting times are just the inter-visit times of cell $(1, 1)$ for the difference random walk on a torus of $n^\beta \times n^\beta$, which is shown in the following lemma.

Lemma 44. *Let τ be the random variable representing the inter-meeting time for two nodes in the same cell of a random walk mobility model on a 2-D torus of size $n^\beta \times n^\beta$, we have*

$$\mathbb{E}[\tau] = \Theta(n^{2\beta}) \quad and \quad \mathbb{E}[\tau^2] = \Theta(n^{4\beta} \log n)$$

Proof. The proof is presented in technical report [20].

Let N be the number of distinct nodes the source node has met in $n^{2\beta}$ time slots. Based on the previous results, we can obtain that $\mathbb{E}[N] = (1 - \epsilon)n^{2\beta}$, where $0 < \epsilon < 1$ is a constant, and $\sigma_N = O(n^{2\beta} \log n)$. By the Chebyshev inequality, for any $0 < \kappa < 1$, we have

$$\mathbf{P}\{\mathbf{N} \leq (1 - \kappa)\mathbb{E}[\mathbf{N}]\} \leq \frac{\sigma_{\mathbf{N}}}{\kappa^2 \mathbb{E}[\mathbf{N}]^2} = \mathbf{O}(\frac{\log \mathbf{n}}{\mathbf{n}^{2\beta}}) \to 0$$

Here $0 < \beta \leq 1/2$, which means that $N = \Theta(n^{2\beta})$, w.h.p.

Lemma 45. *The minimal flooding delay under hybrid random walk model is $\Theta(n^\beta)$ for $0 < \beta \leq 1/2$ and $\Theta(\log n)$ for $\beta = 0$.*

Proof. We cite the following important result about rumor spreading on torus: Theorem 3 in [15] states that following the flooding rule mentioned above, at time slot t, there exists a sub-torus of size $\sqrt{t} \times \sqrt{t}$, where for each cell in this sub-torus, there exists at least one node holding the packet delivered by the source node. Therefore, in $\Theta(n^{\beta})$ time slots, where $0 < \beta \leq 1/2$ we can cover the whole torus of size $n^{\beta} \times n^{\beta}$ *w.h.p.* When $\beta = 0$, the mobility model is i.i.d., the minimal flooding delay is $\Theta(\log n)$, which is presented in [13].

Lemma 46. *Any subcell has at least two nodes with positive constant probability for any* $0 < \beta \leq 1/2$.

Proof. The proof is presented in technical report [20].

4.2   Proof Outline for 2-Hop Relay with RLC (Theorem 1)

First, we prove the case for 2-hop relay scheme. We want to know how many time slots the destination node needs to receive $\Theta(k)$ coded packets, then based on the RLC scheme, it can recover the original packets *w.h.p.* From *Lemma 43* we know that, after $N_1 = \Theta(n^{2\beta})$ time slots, the source node has already delivered coded packets to $m_1 = \Theta(n^{2\beta})$ different nodes. From [17], we can infer that for a simple random walk on a torus of size $n^{\beta} \times n^{\beta}$, the mixing time will also be $\Theta(n^{2\beta})$. Therefore, these m_1 nodes with coded packets are uniformly distributed in the torus *w.h.p.* after $N_2 = \epsilon n^{2\beta}$ time slots, where ϵ is a constant. From *Lemma 46* we know that each node in the network meets a node with coded packets with a constant probability. Then after $N_1 + N_2$ time slots, the destination node begins to collect coded packets instead of doing that immediately. We are interested in estimating the time it takes the destination node to collect $k = \Theta(n^{2\beta})$ coded packets, which means it can recover the original packets *w.h.p.* Let us denote this time by N_3. As all the nodes with coded packets are uniformly and independently distributed in the network, according to the network models, the probability for two nodes to be in the same subcell is $n^{2\beta-1}$.

Observe that

$$N_3 = \tau_1 n^{2\beta-1} + ... + (\tau_1 + \tau_2 + ... + \tau_i)(1 - n^{2\beta-1})^{i-1} n^{2\beta-1} + ...$$

Here τ_i for $i \geq 1$ are the inter-meeting times which are the same order of first return time of a hybrid random walk on a 2-D torus of size $n^{\beta} \times n^{\beta}$, which is known as $\Theta(n^{2\beta})$. Therefore, we have $\mathbb{E}\{\tau_i\} = \Theta(n^{2\beta})$, for $i \geq 1$. Taking the expectations on both sides of the above equation and performing some simple algebraic manipulations, we obtain

$$\mathbb{E}\{N_3\} = \Theta(n) \quad for \quad 0 < \beta \leq 1/2$$

Therefore the total delay for 2-hop scheme is $N = N_1 + N_2 + N_3 = \Theta(n^{2\beta}) + \epsilon n^{2\beta} + \Theta(n) = \Theta(n)$, for $0 < \beta \leq 1/2$. And when $\beta = 0$, the mobility model is i.i.d. model and the minimal 2-hop delay is $\Theta(n)$, thus the whole delay is $\Theta(n)$.

In our work, the key point is to increase the redundancy to improve the probability for the destination node to meet the coded packets. In 2-hop relay scheme, the redundancy is only the number of replications. Then based on the throughput equation

$c = \Theta(\frac{1}{nmr^2})$(see [18]), where r is the transmission range that is $\Theta(n^{-\beta})$ in the hybrid random walk models, and m is the redundancy, we obtain that the throughput for 2-hop relay scheme is $\Theta(n\frac{1}{nn^{2\beta}(n^{-\beta})^2})=\Theta(1)$.

4.3   Proof Outline for Multi-hop Relay with RLC (Theorem 2)

Here, we compute the lower bound of delay for the destination node to get $\Theta(k)$ coded packets. The key problem is that how many time slots it costs the destination node to get $\Theta(k)$ coded packets. We suppose that after D time slots, the destination node gets $\Theta(k)$ coded packets, then based on the RLC scheme, the destination node has enough coded packets to recover k original packets $w.h.p.$

From the definition of hybrid random walk models, we know that when $0 < \beta \leq 1/2$, the transmission speed is much faster than the speed of node mobility, so in the following analysis, we ignore the transmission time of the packets.

In multi-hop relay with RLC scheme, the source node firstly sends $m = (1 + \epsilon)k$ coded packets to the network, here we choose $k = \Theta(n^\beta)$, for $0 < \beta \leq 1/2$. Then the relay nodes deliver these coded packets to the destination node, the procedure is shown in Figure 4. From the definition of minimal flooding delay, we know, after $\Theta(n^\beta)$ time slots, we denote it as D_1, $m = (1 + \epsilon)k$ coded packets are sent to $\Theta(n)$ nodes, we call them the first relay nodes, therefore we can regard the network as a scenario with many nodes holding the useful coded packets for the destination, which is similar to the broadcast session for each time slot. Each first relay node will forward the coded packets to other nodes in a sequential fashion as illustrated in Figure 4. Thus the delay D_2 for the destination node to receive a coded packet is composed of three parts: The time needed for the first relay node to send the coded packets to other relay nodes, the time for the coded packets to be delivered between relay nodes in multi-hop scheme and the time for the destination node to receive the coded packets from the relay nodes.

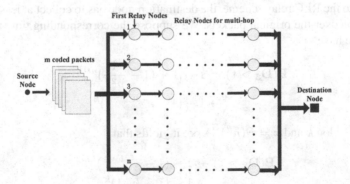

Fig. 4. A more dedicated view of multi-hop relay scheme. The source node sends the coded packets to more than k nodes, which is similar to a broadcast session. For each first relay nodes, it operates in a sequential fashion.

Let D_s be the time needed for the first relay node to send the coded packets to other relay nodes. In the hybrid random walk models, the network is divided into a 2-D torus of size $n^{1/2-2\beta} \times n^{1/2-2\beta}$. Then from *Lemma 41*, the expectation of D_s, denoted by $\mathbb{E}[D_s]$, is

$$\mathbb{E}[D_s] = \Theta(n^{1-4\beta} \log n)$$

Let D_r be the time spent by the relay nodes to deliver coded packets between each other, and $\mathbb{E}[D_r]$ is the expectation of D_r. Similarly we have

$$\mathbb{E}[D_r] = \Theta(n^{1-4\beta} \log n)$$

Finally, let D_d be the time for the destination node to get coded packets from the relay nodes and $\mathbb{E}[D_d]$ is the expectation. As we assume the mobility of nodes is independent and the arrival of packets is independent of node mobility, the destination node is uniformly and independently distributed in the network. Thus, we have

$$\mathbb{E}[D_d] = \Theta(n^{1-4\beta} \log n)$$

For the hybrid random walk models, the average distance between the source node and the destination node is $\Theta(1)$, and the transmission range in a cell is $\Theta(\sqrt{2}n^{-\beta})$. We assume the relay node has to go through H cells before it meets the destination node, and $\mathbb{E}[H]$ is the expectation. Therefore we have

$$\mathbb{E}[H] = \Theta(\frac{1}{\sqrt{2}n^{-\beta}}) = \Theta(n^{\beta})$$

Thus we obtain that

$$\begin{aligned} \mathbb{E}[D_2] &= \mathbb{E}[D_s] + \mathbb{E}[H]\mathbb{E}[D_r] + \mathbb{E}[D_d] \\ &= \Theta(n^{1-3\beta} \log n) \end{aligned}$$

According to the RLC relay scheme, the destination node has to collect at least k coded packets to recover the original packets. We suppose the corresponding time to be D_3, therefore we have

$$\mathbf{P}(\mathbf{D_3} > \mathbf{t}) = 1 - [1 - (1 - \frac{1}{n^{2\beta}})^{nt}]^k$$
$$\to 1 - (1 - e^{-n^{1-2\beta}t})^k$$

Let $t = n^{2\beta-1} \log k$ and $k = \Theta(n^{\beta}) \to \infty$, it yields that

$$\mathbf{P}(\mathbf{D_3} > \mathbf{t}) \to 1 - (1 - e^{-\log k})^k$$
$$\to 1 - (1 - k-1)^k$$
$$\to 1 - e^{-1}$$

Thus, the delay for the destination node to collect k coded packets is $n^{2\beta-1} \log k$, as we take $k = \Theta(n^{\beta})$, then the corresponding delay expectation becomes $\Theta(n^{2\beta-1} \log n)$.

Therefore, the delay D and the expectation $\mathbb{E}[D]$ for multi-hop relay scheme under hybrid random walk models is

$$\mathbb{E}[D] = \mathbb{E}[D_1] + \mathbb{E}[D_2] + \mathbb{E}[D_3]$$
$$= \mathbb{E}[D_1] + \mathbb{E}[D_s] + \mathbb{E}[H]\mathbb{E}[D_r] + \mathbb{E}[D_d] + \mathbb{E}[D_3]$$
$$= \Theta(n^\beta) + \Theta(n^{1-3\beta} \log n) + \Theta(n^{2\beta-1} \log n)$$

Thus, for $0 < \beta < 1/4$, we have $\mathbb{E}[D] = \Theta(n^{1-3\beta} \log n)$; and for $1/4 \leq \beta \leq 1/2$, we have $\mathbb{E}[D] = \Theta(n^\beta)$.

When $\beta = 0$, the mobility model becomes i.i.d. model, we take $k = \Theta(\log n)$ and the minimal flooding delay is $\Theta(\log n)$. For i.i.d. model, the delay for the transmission rate can be ignored. Since $\Theta(n)$ nodes in the network have coded packets, therefore, the delay for the destination node to collect k coded packets is $\Theta(\log n)$ because every transmission will be helpful for decoding $w.h.p.$ Thus the delay for $\beta = 0$ is $\Theta(\log n)$, which is the same with the result in [13].

As for the throughput, in multi-hop relay scheme, the redundancy has two parts: the number of hops and the number of packet replications. The average number of hops for multi-hop relay scheme is proved in the above analysis, which is $\mathbb{E}[H] = \Theta(n^\beta)$. And in our work we assume $k = \Theta(n^\beta)$, which is the same with that is [13], when β equals to 0 and 1/2 respectively. Therefore, based on the throughput equation $c = \Theta(\frac{1}{nmr^2})$, we obtain that the throughput is $c = \Theta(\frac{1}{nn^\beta(n^{-\beta})^2}) = \Theta(n^{\beta-1})$.

5   Throughput and Delay with Network Coding under Discrete Random Direction Models: Analysis

In this section, we present details of proofs for the results on RLC-based scheme under discrete random direction models which are discussed in the previous section.

5.1   Proof Outline for 2-Hop Relay with RLC (Theorem 3)

Lemma 51. *The minimal flooding delay under discrete random direction models is* $\Theta(n^{1/2})$.

Proof. The proof is presented in technical report [20].

Here we adopt the same analysis method as that in Section IV-B. From the definition of discrete random direction models and hybrid random walk models, we can see that the time slot is different, which are $\Theta(n^{1/2-\alpha})$ and $\Theta(1)$ respectively. Then we have $N_1 = \Theta(n^{2\alpha})\Theta(n^{1/2-\alpha}) = \Theta(n^{1/2+\alpha})$, $N_2 = \epsilon n^{1/2+\alpha}$. However, the key point is the delay for the destination node to receive $\Theta(k)$ coded packets which is defined as N_3, from the equation in the previous proof, we still have $N_3 = \Theta(n)$. Therefore the 2-hop delay for the discrete random direction models is $N = N_1 + N_2 + N_3 = \Theta(n^{1/2+\alpha}) + \epsilon n^{1/2+\alpha} + \Theta(n) = \Theta(n)$. Under the discrete random direction models, the transmission range r is $\Theta(n^{-\alpha})$, thus the throughput for 2-hop relay scheme is $\Theta(n\frac{1}{nn^{2\alpha}(n^{-\alpha})^2}) = \Theta(1)$.

5.2 Proof Outline for Multi-hop Relay with RLC (Theorem 4)

Here, we adopt the same analysis method as that in Section IV-C. The definitions for D_s, D_r, D_d and their expectations $\mathbb{E}[D_s]$, $\mathbb{E}[D_r]$, $\mathbb{E}[D_d]$ are not changed. Thus we have $\mathbb{E}[D_s] = \mathbb{E}[D_r] = \mathbb{E}[D_d] = \Theta(n^{1-4\alpha} \log n)\Theta(n^{1/2-\alpha}) = \Theta(n^{3/2-5\alpha} \log n)$.

The number of hops for relay nodes is still $\mathbb{E}[H] = \Theta(n^\alpha)$, and $\mathbb{E}[D_3] = \Theta(n^{2\alpha-1})$ $\Theta(n^{1/2-\alpha}) = \Theta(n^{\alpha-1/2})$, therefore the delay D and its expectation $\mathbb{E}[D]$ for the discrete random direction models is

$$\begin{aligned}\mathbb{E}[D] &= \mathbb{E}[D_1] + \mathbb{E}[D_2] + \mathbb{E}[D_3]\\ &= \Theta(n^{1/2}) + \Theta(n^{3/2-4\alpha} \log n) + \Theta(n^{\alpha-1/2})\end{aligned}$$

Thus, for $0 \leq \alpha < 1/4$, we have $\mathbb{E}[D] = \Theta(n^{3/2-4\alpha} \log n)$; and for $1/4 \leq \alpha \leq 1/2$, we have $\mathbb{E}[D] = \Theta(n^{1/2})$.

For the throughput under discrete random direction models, we assume k to be $\Theta(n^\alpha)$, and the number of hops is $\mathbb{E}[H] = \Theta(n^\alpha)$ as proved in the above analysis. Then based on the throughput equation $c = \Theta(\frac{1}{nmr^2})$, we obtain that the throughput is $c = \Theta(\frac{1}{nn^\alpha(n^{-\alpha})^2}) = \Theta(n^{\alpha-1})$.

6 Network Model with Base Stations and RLC

From this section, we will adopt a new scheme to analyze the throughput and delay for ad hoc network. We regularly allocate the base stations in the network and propose the 2-hop relay algorithm to deduce the throughput and delay.

6.1 Network Model with Base Stations

Cell Partitioned Network Model With Base Stations: The whole network is cell partitioned as previous hybrid random walk models. Then $m = n^b (0 \leq b \leq 1)$ base stations are regularly distributed in $n^{2\beta}$ cells. All the base stations are connected by wires so that they can communicate in $\Theta(1)$ delay. The base station locates at the center position of one cell, and the cell includes $n^{1-2\beta}$ subcells. A base station can communicate with all the nodes in the same cell, while a node can only deliver packets to the base station when it is in the same subcell as the destined base station. In other words, base station has enough transmission power to cover the whole cell. What's more, we assume uplink and downlink use different frequencies to avoid interference. This means when a base station is transmitting packets, all the other transmissions between two nodes or one node and a base station can still go on without any problems. The node transmission schemes are the same as previous hybrid random walk models. To make the analysis clearly, here we assume the k packets to have the order of $k = n^d$ where $0 \leq d \leq 1$.

6.2 2-Hop Relay Algorithm under Hybrid Random Walk Models with Base Stations

When we introduce the base stations into the network, there are two conditions in a subcell now: it has a base station or not. When a node moves into a new subcell in a time slot, if the subcell doesn't have a base station, the node acts in the same way as described in the previous section, otherwise the node will act as follows:

- Source to base station transmission: If the nodes in the subcell have packets to transmit, randomly choose such a node as the source, and send the packet to the base station within the subcell. If no such node exists, stay idle.
- Base station tó base station transmission: As defined above, in $\Theta(1)$ time, the base station will broadcast the received packet to all the other base stations via wires.
- Base station to destination transmission: In the last step, the base station sends the packet to the destination node within its corresponding cell. The transmission ends.

7 Throughput and Delay under 2-Hop Relay Algorithm with Network Coding in Hybrid Random Walk Models with Base Stations

In this section, we present the main results under 2-hop relay algorithm with RLC when base stations are added to the network and give the detailed proofs as well.

7.1 Preliminaries

First, we will present some important lemmas in the hybrid random walk models with base stations.

Lemma 71. When $k = \Omega(m)$, the input rate of each queue in the base stations is $\Theta(\frac{1}{m})$; and when $k = o(m)$ the input rate of each queue in the base stations is $\Theta(\frac{1}{k})$.

Proof. Since input rate of each queue in base station is not changed by the mobility pattern of mobile nodes, thus the input rate of each queue in the base station is $\Theta(\frac{1}{m})$ for $k = \Omega(m)$ and $\Theta(\frac{1}{k})$ for $k = o(m)$, respectively, which are proved in [19].

In the hybrid random walk models, the motion of nodes on a 2-D torus of size $n^\beta \times n^\beta$ with m base stations regularly distributed is equivalent of motion on a 2-D torus of size $\frac{n^\beta}{\sqrt{m}} \times \frac{n^\beta}{\sqrt{m}}$ with a single base station.

From the definition of first hitting time and first return time in Section IV-A and *Lemma 41* in [14], we can derive the results for the 2-D torus of size $\frac{n^\beta}{\sqrt{m}} \times \frac{n^\beta}{\sqrt{m}}$.

Lemma 72. *Let H denote the first hitting time for a single state on a 2-D torus of size* $\frac{n^\beta}{\sqrt{m}} \times \frac{n^\beta}{\sqrt{m}}$, *then* $\mathbb{E}\{H\} = \Theta(\frac{n^{2\beta}}{m} \log n)$.

Lemma 73. *Let H denote the first return time for a single state on a 2-D torus of size* $\frac{n^\beta}{\sqrt{m}} \times \frac{n^\beta}{\sqrt{m}}$, *then* $\mathbb{E}\{H\} = \Theta(\frac{n^{2\beta}}{m})$.

Next we analyze the throughput and delay under 2-hop relay scheme without network coding in hybrid random walk models with base stations.

Lemma 74. *When* $k = \Omega(m)$, *the delay is* $D = \Theta(n^{2\beta})$ *and the throughput is* $\lambda = \Theta(\frac{1}{n})$.

Proof. The successful transmitting of packets from the nodes to a base station needs two procedures: The source node is to transmit the packet to the base station and the base station is ready to receive the packet. The probability that the source node is scheduled to transmit the packet to the base station is $\frac{1}{mq}$, where q is the density of nodes in the network. According to *Lemma 72* and *Lemma 73*, the first hitting time of a cell with a base station is $\Theta(\frac{n^{2\beta}}{m} \log n)$, and the first return time of a cell with a base station is $\Theta(\frac{n^{2\beta}}{m})$. Thus the delay is $D = \Theta(\frac{n^{2\beta}}{m} \log n) + \Theta(\frac{n^{2\beta}}{m})(\frac{1}{mq})^{-1} = \Theta(n^{2\beta})$.

From *Lemma 71*, we know the input rate of each queue in base stations is $\Theta(\frac{1}{m})$, during the time interval [0,T], the total number of packets sent to base stations is $\Theta(\frac{1}{m}) \times Tm$. To guarantee a stable network, the throughput of whole network cannot exceed the packets that base stations are able to serve in time interval [0,T]. Thus we have $\lambda Tm \leq \Theta(\frac{1}{m}) \times Tm$, that is $\lambda \leq \Theta(\frac{1}{n})$. Therefore, the throughput in 2-hop relay algorithm with base stations is $\Theta(\frac{1}{n})$.

Lemma 75. *When $k = o(m)$, the delay is $D = \Theta(n^{2\beta+d-b})$ and the throughput is $\lambda = \Theta(n^{b-d-1})$.*

Proof. The proof is presented in technical report [20].

7.2   Results and Analysis

Theorem 5: In the network with base stations, under 2-hop relay algorithm with network coding, when $k = \Omega(m)$, that is $0 \leq b \leq d \leq 1$, we obtain the throughput is $\Theta(\frac{1}{n})$; the delay is $\Theta(n)$, for $0 \leq b < 1$ and $\Theta(n^{2\beta})$, for $b = 1$, where $k = n^d$ and $m = n^b$.

Proof. The proof is presented in technical report [20].

Theorem 6: In the network with base stations, under 2-hop relay algorithm with network coding, when $k = o(m)$, that is $0 \leq d \leq b \leq 1$, we obtain the throughput is $\Theta(n^{2b-d-2})$ for $2b - d - 1 \geq 0$ and $\Theta(n^{-1})$ for $2b - d - 1 < 0$, and the delay is $\Theta(n)$, where $k = n^d$ and $m = n^b$.

Proof. The proof is presented in technical report [20].

8   Discussion

We summarize the results with network coding under hybrid random walk models and discrete random direction models in 2-hop and multi-hop schemes and make a comparison with the results in [14], in Table I and Table II respectively. Furthermore, the delay in multi-hop relay scheme with network coding under hybrid random walk models and discrete random direction models are shown in Figures 1 and 2.

From above results we can see that in 2-hop relay scheme, there is a $\log n$ gain on delay only when the mobility model is random walk model. For the hybrid random walk models in multi-hop scheme, when $\beta = 1/2$, the mobility model is random walk model, we take $k = \Theta(\sqrt{n})$, and obtain $D(n) = \Theta(\sqrt{n})$; when $\beta = 0$, it is i.i.d.

Table 1. Comparison for throughput and delay in 2-hop relay with network coding algorithms

Scheme	Condition	Throughput	Delay
HRWM w.o. NC. for 2-hop [14]	$\beta < 1/2$	$\omega(1/\sqrt{n})$	$\Theta(n)$
HRWM w.o. NC. for 2-hop [14]	$\beta = 1/2$	$\omega(1/\sqrt{n})$	$\Theta(n \log n)$
HRWM w. NC. for 2-hop	$k = \Theta(n)\ \beta = 0$	$\Theta(1)$	$\Theta(n)$
HRWM w. NC. for 2-hop	$k = \Theta(n^{2\beta})\ 0 < \beta \le 1/2$	$\Theta(1)$	$\Theta(n)$
DRDM w.o. NC. for 2-hop [14]	$0 \le \alpha < 1/2$	$\omega(1/\sqrt{n})$	$\Theta(n)$
DRDM w.o. NC. for 2-hop [14]	$\alpha = 1/2$	$\omega(1/\sqrt{n})$	$\Theta(n \log n)$
DRDM w. NC. for 2-hop	$k = \Theta(n^{2\alpha})\ 0 \le \alpha < 1/2$	$\Theta(1)$	$\Theta(n)$
DRDM w. NC. for 2-hop	$k = \Theta(n)\ \alpha = 1/2$	$\Theta(1)$	$\Theta(n)$

Table 2. Comparison for throughput and delay in multi-hop relay with network coding algorithms

Scheme	Condition	Throughput	Delay
HRWM w.o. NC. for multi-hop [14]	$0 \le \beta \le 1/2$	$\omega(1/\sqrt{n})$	$\Theta(n^{2\beta} \log n)$
HRWM w. NC. for multi-hop	$k = \Theta(n^{\beta})\ 0 < \beta < 1/4$	$\Theta(n^{\beta-1})$	$\Theta(n^{1-3\beta} \log n)$
HRWM w. NC. for multi-hop	$k = \Theta(n^{\beta})\ 1/4 \le \beta \le 1/2$	$\Theta(n^{\beta-1})$	$\Theta(n^{\beta})$
DRDM w.o. NC. for multi-hop [14]	$0 \le \alpha \le 1/2$	$\omega(1/\sqrt{n})$	$\Theta(n^{\alpha+1/2} \log n)$
DRDM w. NC. for multi-hop	$k = \Theta(n^{\alpha})\ 0 \le \alpha < 1/4$	$\Theta(n^{\alpha-1})$	$\Theta(n^{3/2-4\alpha} \log n)$
DRDM w. NC. for multi-hop	$k = \Theta(n^{\alpha})\ 1/4 \le \alpha \le 1/2$	$\Theta(n^{\alpha-1})$	$\Theta(n^{1/2})$

model, we take $k = \Theta(\log n)$, and the delay is $\Theta(\log n)$. These results are the same with those in [13]. Specifically in our work, we choose $k = \Theta(n^{\beta})$ for $0 < \beta \le 1/2$ and $k = \Theta(\log n)$ for $\beta = 0$, there is a jump at $\beta = 0$. It is because as $\beta \to 0$, the number of original packets $k = \Theta(n^{\beta}) \to \Theta(1)$, which is a constant, as the key purpose of network coding is to increase the redundancy for the network, therefore it will be useless to use network coding for a constant number of original packets. Thus we take $k = \Theta(\log n)$ for $\beta = 0$ as [13].

Furthermore, we obtain that there is a turning point for delay at $\beta = 1/4$ as shown in Figure 1. For $0 < \beta \le 1/4$, we take $k = \Theta(n^{\beta})$, the time for the coded packets to be delivered between first relay nodes and destination node dominates in the whole delay, which is $\Theta(n^{1-3\beta} \log n)$; for $1/4 \le \beta \le 1/2$, we take $k = \Theta(n^{\beta})$, the minimal flooding delay $\Theta(n^{\beta})$ dominates in the whole delay. Thus, the delay is halved by β.

An interesting insight provided by our results is that when $\beta < 1/5$, the delay will be better for the network without network coding; and when $1/5 \le \beta \le 1/2$, network coding will get a shorter delay. We name this point $\beta = 1/5$ as critical turning point. For our work, the number of original packets has a strong influence on the motion of relay nodes. From the proof in Section IV-C, we know that when $\beta < 1/5$, the time $\Theta(n^{1-3\beta} \log n)$ for multi-hop relay is dominant in the whole delay, while the delay for the network without network coding is $\Theta(n^{2\beta} \log n)$ in [14]. Therefore, for $\beta < 1/5$, the transmission time for multi-hop relay without network coding will be shorter than that with network coding, thus it is useless to use network coding in this situation. While when $1/5 \le \beta \le 1/2$, as the number of original packets increase, network coding will obtain a shorter relay time than that without network coding. Thus, we call $\beta = 1/5$ a critical turning point for the network.

As for the discrete random direction models, from the analysis in Section V, it can be derived that the dominant delays are in the same order as those in the hybrid random walk models, therefore, it is no surprise that the turning point and the critical turning point are the same as those of hybrid random walk models.

At last, we combine the network coding technique and the infrastructure mode technique together in one network model, and calculate the throughput and delay performance in such network. We obtain that under 2-hop relay algorithm with network coding, when $k \doteq \Omega(m)$, the throughput is $\Theta(\frac{1}{n})$ and the delay is $\Theta(n)$ for $0 \leq b < 1$ and $\Theta(n^{2\beta})$ for $b = 1$. And when $k = o(m)$, we achieve that the throughput $\Theta(n^{2b-d-2})$ for $2b - d - 1 \geq 0$ and $\Theta(n^{-1})$ for $2b - d - 1 < 0$, and the delay $\Theta(n)$, here $k = n^d$ and $m = n^b$.

9   Conclusion

We propose two techniques to improve the network performance including throughput and delay in this paper. We study two mobility models-hybrid random walk models and discrete random direction models and adopt two-hop relay scheme and multi-hop relay scheme respectively. In such network coding models, we conclude that there is a $\log n$ gain on delay under 2-hop relay scheme only when the mobility model is random walk model. And in multi-hop relay scheme, we find there is a turning point $\beta = 1/4$ for hybrid random walk models and $\alpha = 1/4$ for discrete random direction models. Furthermore, compared to the scheme without network coding, it can be derived that whether to use network coding in hybrid random walk models and discrete random direction models or not depends on the mobility model parameter β and α, which means there is a critical turning point $\beta = 1/5$ and $\alpha = 1/5$ for two mobility models respectively in consideration of the delay with network coding or without network coding. Then, we study the infrastructure mode and finally we propose the network model with network coding and infrastructure mode together. And in this mode, we obtain the results of throughput and delay.

Acknowledgment. This paper is supported by National Fundamental Research Grant (No. 2010CB731803); NSF China (No. 60832005); China Ministry of Education New Century Excellent Talent (No. NCET-10-0580); China Ministry of Education Fok Ying Tung Fund (No. 122002); Qualcomm Research Grant; Shanghai Basic Research Key Project (No. 11JC1405100); National key project of China (2012ZX03001009, 2010ZX03003-001-01); China Postdoctoral Science Foundation Grant (No. 2011M500774).

References

1. Gupta, P., Kumar, P.R.: The Capacity of Wireless Networks. IEEE Transactions on Information Theory 46(2), 388–404 (2000)
2. Grossglauser, M., Tse, D.N.C.: Mobility increases the capacity of ad-hoc wireless networks. Proc. IEEE/ACM Transactions on Networking 10, 477–486 (2002)
3. Neely, M., Modiano, E.: Capacity and delay tradeoffs for ad hoc mobile networks. IEEE Transactions on Information Theory 51(6), 1917–1937 (2005)

4. El Gammal, A., Mammen, J., Prabhakar, B., Shah, D.: Throughput-delay trade-off in wireless networks. In: Proc. IEEE INFOCOM, Hong Kong, China, vol. 1 (March 2004)
5. Ahlswede, R., Cai, N., Li, S.-Y.R., Yeung, R.W.: Network Information Flow. IEEE Transactions on Information Theory 46(4), 1204–1216 (2000)
6. Li, S.-Y.R., Yeung, R.W., Cai, N.: Linear Network Coding. IEEE Transactions on Information Theory 49(2), 371–381 (2003)
7. Jaggi, S., Chou, P.A., Jain, K.: Low complexity optimal algebraic multicast codes. In: Proc. of IEEE International Symposium on Information Theory, Yokohama, Japan (June-July 2003)
8. Ho, T., Koetter, R., Medard, M., Karger, R.D., Effros, M.: The benefits of coding over routing in a randomized setting. In: Proc. of IEEE International Symposium on Information Theory, Yokohama, Japan (June-July 2003)
9. Ho, T., Medard, M., Koetter, R., Karger, D.R., Effros, M., Shi, J., Leong, B.: A Random Linear Network Coding Approach to Multicast. IEEE Transactions on Information Theory 52(10), 4413–4430 (2006)
10. Ghaderi, M., Towsley, D., Kurose, J.: Network Coding Performance for Reliable Multicast. In: Proc. IEEE MILCOM 2007, Orlando, Florida, USA, pp. 1–7 (October 2007)
11. Liu, J., Goeckel, D., Towsley, D.: The Throughput Order of Ad Hoc Networks Employing Network Coding and Broadcasting. In: Proc. of IEEE MILCOM 2006, Washington DC, Alaska, USA, pp. 1–7 (October 2006)
12. Liu, J., Goeckel, D., Towsley, D.: Bounds on the Gain of Network Coding and Broadcasting in Wireless Networks. In: Proc. IEEE INFOCOM, Anchorage, Alaska, USA, pp. 724–732 (May 2007)
13. Zhang, C., Fang, Y., Zhu, X.: Throughput-Delay Tradeoffs in Large-Scale MANETs with Network Coding. In: Proc. IEEE INFOCOM, Rio de Janeiro, Brazil, pp. 199–207 (April 2009)
14. Sharma, G., Mazumdar, R., Shroff, N.B.: Delay and capacity trade-offs in mobile ad hoc networks: a global perspective. IEEE/ACM Transactions on Networking, 981–992 (October 2007)
15. Li, P., Fang, Y., Li, J., Huang, X.: Smooth Trade-offs Between Throughput and Delay in Mobile Ad Hoc Networks. IEEE Transactions on Mobile Computing 11(3), 427–438 (2012)
16. Li, P., Zhang, C., Fang, Y.: The Capacity of Wireless Ad Hoc Networks Using Directional Antennas. IEEE Transactions on Mobile Computing 10(10), 1374–1387 (2011)
17. Aldous, D., Fill, J.: Reversible markov chains and random walks on graphs, http://www.stat.berkeley.edu/~adlous/RWG/book.html
18. Xinbing Wang, Y., Bei, Q., Fu, P.L.: Speed Improves Delay-Capacity Trade-Off in Motion-Cast. IEEE Transactions on Parallel and Distributed Systems, 729–742 (2011)
19. Fu, L., Li, J., Guo, J., Wang, X., Zhang, Y., Wang, X., Zhao, Q.: Multicast Capacity-Delay Tradeoff with Network Coding in MANETs. In: Cheng, Y., Eun, D.Y., Qin, Z., Song, M., Xing, K. (eds.) WASA 2011. LNCS, vol. 6843, pp. 72–83. Springer, Heidelberg (2011)
20. Li, J., Wang, X., Fu, L., Xie, C., Tian, X., Zhang, Y., Wang, X.: Throughput and Delay with Network Coding in Hybrid Mobile Ad Hoc Network: A Global perspective. Technical Report (2011), http://iwct.sjtu.edu.cn/Personal/xwang8/paper/NC-capacity.pdf

HERO – A Home Based Routing in Pocket Switched Networks*

Shengling Wang[1], Min Liu[1], Xiuzhen Cheng[2,4], Zhongcheng Li[1],
Jianhui Huang[3], and Biao Chen[4]

[1] Institute of Computing Technology, Chinese Academy of Sciences, China
[2] Department of Computer Science, The George Washington University, USA
[3] IBM China
[4] Department of Computer Information Science, University of Macau, China

Abstract. Pocket switched networks (PSNs) take advantage of human mobility to distribute data. Investigations on real-world trace data indicate that human mobility follows a simple reproducible pattern: a human being usually visits a few places at high frequencies. These most frequently visited places form the *home* of a node, which is exploited in this paper to design two HomE based ROuting (HERO) algorithms. In the basic HERO, the first encountered relay whose home contains the place where the destination resides is selected to deliver the data. The enhanced HERO, on the other hand, continuously selects a better relay that visits the destination place at a higher frequency. In both algorithms, each node only needs to maintain and exchange its relatively stable home information and/or the corresponding visiting frequencies; therefore no global networking information and no frequent information update are needed, resulting in a low burden on the network due to its low communication and storage overheads. Moreover, HERO involves only simple arithmetic operations, thus causing little computation overhead at the mobile nodes. The simulation results indicate that both HERO algorithms outperform the state-of-the art.

Keywords: Pocket switched networks, routing, Human mobility.

1 Introduction

PSN is a new networking paradigm that makes use of human mobility to provide occasional contact opportunities for mobile devices to deliver data. It falls into the category of delay/disruption tolerant networks (DTNs). PSNs inherit some traits from DTNs such as intermittent connectivity, limited network capacity, and energy and storage constraints of the participants. These traits require PSN

---

* This work has been supported by the National Basic Research Program of China (No. 2011CB302702, No.2011CB302800), the Beijing Nova Program, the National Natural Science Foundation of China (No. 61120106008, No. 61132001, No. 61133015, No. 60803140, No. 60970133, No. 61070187, and No. 61003225), the National Science Foundation of the US (CNS-0831852), and the NPST program by King Saud University Project No. 10-INF1184-02.

X. Wang et al. (Eds.): WASA 2012, LNCS 7405, pp. 20–30, 2012.
© Springer-Verlag Berlin Heidelberg 2012

applications to be delay/disruption tolerant and make *store-carry-forward* the mainstream communication mode for data delivery. In a typical PSN, mobile nodes[1] serve as relays to physically carry the data and forward it opportunistically upon contacting with others. Hence, relay selection is a key problem, which directly affects the efficiency of PSN data delivery.

Whether a node is a good relay in a PSN depends on the connectivity between the node and the destination. Nevertheless, it is a challenge to measure such a connectivity because node mobility makes it nondeterministic and dynamic. Moreover, relay selectors in a PSN are regular nodes with limited resources (storage, computation capability, battery power, etc.), and hence the burden of a selector for computing or comparing the connectivity with the nodes it contacts increases with the rapidly growing number of portable devices in the network. Therefore an effective and efficient routing strategy should place a low burden on the nodes and should be scalable. To achieve this goal, the routing strategy should satisfy the following three design requirements: i) no global knowledge maintained at each node; ii) no frequent information update at each node; and iii) low computation and storage overheads on each node. As indicated in Section 2, none of the existing routing strategies designed for PSNs could simultaneously satisfy all these three requirements.

In fact, the traits of PSNs are rooted from human mobility, which can simplify the routing decision. Our investigation [1] on the real world data reveals that human mobility has an important characteristic, namely, *a high degree of spatial regularity*. To be specific, each node has a significant probability of returning to a few highly frequently visited places. Taking into account the spatial regularity of human mobility, we propose two HomE based ROuting (HERO) algorithms for PSNs, with each placing at most one copy of a data in the network at any instant of time. Our algorithms introduce a concept of *home*, which is a set of places a node often visits. Because the probability that a node comes back home is high, the node can successfully deliver the data to the destination at a high probability if its home includes the place where the destination resides.

The basic HERO relies on the first encountered relay whose home contains the place where the destination resides to deliver the data. The enhanced HERO continuously changes the relay if a new one with a higher visiting frequency to the destination place is met. These two HERO algorithms have the following characteristics, which demonstrate that they do scale well, and do cause low burden on the network.

1) HERO requires no global networking knowledge maintained at each node, which results in low storage and communication overheads. Existing routing schemes such as [2–5] force each node maintain an entry for every other node in the network, while [6, 7] require each node to keep the global routing information and update it whenever the network topology changes. Compared to them, HERO orchestrates the spatial regularity of human mobility to determine the relay based on the local information, i.e, the most frequently visited places, which incurs little overhead.

---

[1] In our paper, a node refers to a human being.

2) HERO requires no frequent information update. In HERO, each node maintains the list of the most frequently visited places, which is relatively stable in a dynamic network environment. Moreover, this maintained information is relatively integral and precise, which results in infrequent updates. In some DTN routing algorithms such as those proposed in [6, 7], each node infers the global routing table (made up of a series of relays) from its local observations. Due to the locality constraint of each node, the global routing table may not be integral, correct, or consistent. As a result, the nodes may respond differently or even improperly.

3) HERO owns the distributed trait. Many existing PSN routing schemes such as those proposed in [8–10] employ a central node to bridge different communities, which may become the potential bottleneck. In HERO, no central role is involved. Hence, HERO is distributed in nature.

4) HERO is simple and effective. HERO involves only simple algebraic operations, resulting in low computation overhead. Moreover, HERO does not rely on any complicated or unrealistic human mobility model. For example, it does not require nodes to have strict repetitive motions such as in [11] or require the inter-contact time between two nodes to follow a specific distribution. Our simulation study based on the Dartmouth College mobility trace data validates its effectiveness and practicability.

It is worth noting that though the basic and enhanced HERO algorithms are presented as single-copy data delivery techniques for PSNs, their relay selection rules can be generalized naturally to get multi-copy versions. In this paper, we investigate the relay selection rules for single-copy data delivery because we want to clearly demonstrate how *home* can help to improve the efficiency of data delivery without relying on the redundancies caused by multiple copy data delivery.

The rest of the paper is organized as follows. Section 2 presents the related work while Section 3 elaborates on our HERO model. The basic and enhanced HERO algorithms are detailed in Section 4. Our conclusions are presented in Section 6.

2   Related Work

PSNs fall into the DTN category. Hence we first briefly review the major DTN routing algorithms in this section. Following that we address the popular routing algorithms designed for PSNs.

Existing DTN routing algorithms are classified into two categories: *deterministic* and *stochastic*. Deterministic approaches [12, 11, 13, 14] provide deterministic routing decisions assuming that some kinds of network connectivity information are known *a priori*. Jain *et al.* [12] modify Dijkstra's algorithm to compute the DTN routes (made up of a series of relays) when the network connectivity patterns are known. DHR [11] is a hierarchical routing framework based on the assumption that nodes in a network are either static or with strict repetitive motions. Conan *et al.* [13] minimize the delivery time given that the inter-contact interval between every pair of nodes is known. Gao *et al.* [14] formulate the problem of routing for multicast in DTNs as a unified knapsack problem assuming that the contact rate between any two nodes in the network is given.

Due to the uncertainty and dynamism of a DTN, it is challenging to obtain the network connectivity information. Hence, deterministic approaches are hard to implement in practical applications. This stirs the research of stochastic approaches [2, 3, 5, 15, 7, 16, 10].

PROPHET [2] uses the past encounters to predict the delivery probability. In FRESH [3], a node needs to keep a record of its most recent time meeting with each of the other nodes. Any node that encounters the destination more recently than the source can be selected as a relay. Gao *et al.* [5] exploit the transit contact pattern for each node, through which a node with a higher contact chance is selected as a relay. Liu and Wu [15] model the network as a probabilistic time-space graph and propose an expected minimum delay algorithm.

MaxProp [7] determines which data is transmitted or deleted from the buffer according to the delivery likelihood, whose computation requires each node i to keep track of f_j^i, the probability of the next meeting node being j. Dang and Wu [10] propose a cluster-based routing algorithm, in which nodes within the same cluster communicate directly while two nodes belonging to different clusters utilize gateways to relay the data.

Epidemic [16] selects relays randomly. It disseminates a large number of copies of each data in order to enhance the delivery ratio, which incurs a heavy communication overhead. To trade off between the communication overhead and the delivery ratio, a utility-based spraying method is proposed in [4], which requires each node i to maintain a utility function $U_i(j)$ for every other node j in the network and selects relays according to the utilities of the nodes.

Because PSNs are formed by human beings, their data delivery efficiency can be greatly enhanced by taking advantage of the traits of human behaviors. According to the traits of human behaviors an algorithm employs, social-based and location-based approaches are proposed, with the former making use of the sociality of human beings while the latter utilizing the spatial characteristics of human mobility to select relays.

BUBBLE [8], SimBet[9], SocialCast [17], user-centric dissemination [18], and SANE [19], are social-based mechanisms, where a more popular person has a higher chance to be utilized as a relay. MobySpace [20] is a location-based approach. It selects a node with a similar mobility pattern to the destination as the relay. The mobility pattern of a node is characterized by its probabilities of visiting all locations in the network.

3   The HERO Model

In this section, we introduce the HERO model in detail.

HERO divides the whole PSN area, denoted by Ω, into multiple zones Z_i, with $\cup Z_i = \Omega$ and $\cap Z_i = \emptyset$. These zones can have any shape. Each zone Z_i is identified by its center coordinates (x_i, y_i).

HERO can employ various methods for its nodes to figure out the center coordinates of a zone. For example, the center coordinates of a zone can be broadcasted by the access points or access routers in an infrastructure-based network; or they can be determined based on a mapping function if the node is aware of its own physical location.

As we have articulated earlier, human mobility follows a simple reproducible pattern: *one usually visits one or a few zones at a high frequency.* These frequently visited zones form the *home* of a node:

Definition 1 (Home). *The home of a node i, denoted by H_i, is the set of zones it usually visits.*

Home is the base of HERO. Thus it is critical to determine the home for each node. There exist two simple strategies: i) a node can statically configure the zones it usually visits as its home; and/or ii) it can dynamically add a zone to its home once the visiting frequency of the zone is larger than a given threshold. Similarly, a zone can be deleted from a node's home either statically or dynamically.

We assume that any two nodes located at the same zone can communicate directly with each other. In our HERO algorithms, once two nodes contact, they exchange their home information. A relay can be selected according to the distances between the zones of its home and that of the destination. Some related definitions are given as follows:

Definition 2 (Neighbor set). *The neighbor set of node i, denoted by N_i, is the set of nodes that can communicate directly with i.*

Based on our assumption, all the nodes covered by the zone where i resides belong to N_i. More generally, N_i includes the nodes in a neighboring zone that can communicate with i directly. Note that $i \notin N_i$.

Definition 3 (Destination zone). *The zone the destination currently resides is the* destination zone, *denoted by Z_d.*

Definition 4 (Distance between home and destination). *The distance between the home of node i, H_i, and the destination zone Z_d is the minimum distance between Z_d and any zone in H_i, i.e., $\|H_i - Z_d\| = \min\{\|Z_i - Z_d\| \mid Z_i \in H_i\}$.*

Definition 5 (Home node). *Node i is called a* home node *of a data with destination zone Z_d if $\|H_i - Z_d\| = 0$.*

4   HERO Algorithms

In this section, we propose the basic and enhanced HERO algorithms.

4.1   The Basic HERO Algorithm

When the source cannot directly communicate with the destination, the basic HERO algorithm selects a home node of the data as a relay. This relay is the only one for the data: once the relay receives the data, it never delivers to other nodes except the destination. The process of the basic HERO is given in Algorithm 1, where the function $send(B, i)$ indicates that the data B is sent to node i.

Algorithm 1. The Basic HERO Algorithm

Require: N_s: the neighbor set of the source s; Z_d: the destination zone; H_i: the home of node i.

1: **repeat**
2:     Update N_s
        ▷ If destination d is in the neighborhood, deliver directly;
3:     **for** each node $i \in N_s$ **do**
4:         **if** $i = d$ **then**
5:             $send(B, i)$, **return**
6:         **end if**
7:     **end for**
        ▷ If the source is a relay, no other relay node needs to be selected;
8:     **if** $\|H_s - Z_d\| = 0$ **then**
        return
9:     **end if**
        ▷ If locating a home node of the data in the neighborhood, selects this node as a relay;
10:     **if** $\exists i \in N_s, s.t. \|H_i - Z_d\| = 0$ **then**
11:         $send(B, i)$, **return**
12:     **end if**
13: **until** the data expires

4.2 The Enhanced HERO Algorithm

The basic HERO is simple and naive. Based on it, many variants can be produced to enhance the efficiency of data delivery. In this subsection, we elaborate an enhanced HERO algorithm that takes into account the visiting frequency of a node to a zone. As the visiting frequencies to the zones in a home are different, we introduce the concept of *visiting intensity* to depict this trait:

Definition 6 (Visiting intensity). *The visiting intensity of zone Z_j by node i, denoted as V_{ij}, is the visiting frequency of node i to zone Z_j within a unit time.*

The enhanced HERO is a single-copy multi-relay mechanism based on the concept of home. In this algorithm, once two nodes contact, they exchange their home and visiting intensity information. The main idea of the enhanced HERO is to continuously find the relay whose probability to visit the destination zone is higher than that of the node currently carrying the data. When a source cannot communicate with the destination directly, it delivers the data to a home node in its neighborhood whose visiting intensity is the highest. If this node meets another home node whose visiting intensity is higher than other neighboring home nodes and itself, it delivers the data to this home node and discards the data itself. The detailed description of the enhanced HERO is shown in Algorithm 2.

Algorithm 2. The Enhanced HERO Algorithm

Require: N_i: the neighbor set of node i; Z_d: the destination
zone; S_{Hi}: the set of home nodes met by the node i; V_{ij}:
the visiting intensity of node i to zone Z_j.

1: **repeat**
2:      Update N_i ▷ Node i may be the source or a relay;
3:      **for** each node $j \in N_i$ **do**
4:         **if** $j = d$ **then**
5:            $send(B, j)$, **return**
6:         **end if**
7:         Update N_j
8:      **end for**
9:      $S_{Hi} \leftarrow \{j \in N_i \mid \|H_j - Z_d\| = 0\}$
10:    **if** $S_{Hi} \neq \emptyset$ **then**
          ▷ Select the neighbor k with the highest visiting
intensity to Z_d;
11:       **if** $\exists k \in S_{Hi} \wedge (V_{kZ_d} > V_{iZ_d}) \wedge (V_{kZ_d} \geq V_{hZ_d}$ for
$\forall h \in S_{Hi} \backslash \{k\})$ **then**
12:          $send(B, k)$, **return**
13:       **end if**
14:    **end if**
15: **until** the data expires

Note that both the basic HERO and the enhanced HERO are inherently based
on the following assumption: the destination stays at Z_d during the process of
data delivery. This assumption is reasonable especially when nodes connected
through WiFi, the most mainstream wireless technology used in PSNs, because
many real world trace records such as [21, 22] indicate that the mobility pattern
of WiFi nodes is quasi-static in a sense that the clients tend to stay in the
same location for a long time. However, if this assumption does not hold, our
algorithms can still work by slightly changing their ways of usage. For example,
the data can be delivered to each zone in the destination's home in light of the
routing policy of our algorithms. Even though the destination is not located at
any zone of its home, the data can still be delivered to the infrastructure or a
static node in the zones of the destination's home, from which the data can be
retrieved when the destination comes back home.

5   Performance Validation

In this section, we evaluate the performance of HERO with the Dartmouth
College mobility trace data [23]. We choose the data collected from 09/21/2003
to 10/20/2003 because in this period the records are integral and the nodes'
behaviors are regular.

In our simulation study, each AP is represented as a zone. As described above, by changing the ways of utilizing our algorithms, the data can be delivered to a destination with high mobility. Hence, in this simulation, we keep the basic assumption that the destination stays at Z_d during the process of data delivery. We randomly choose 100 mobile nodes as the sources and randomly assign one of the APs to each source as its destination. Thus, there are in total 100 communication pairs, which remains unchanged in our simulation study.

Because the running time increases rapidly as the number of mobile nodes increases, we limit the number of nodes to a manageable size, a common measure taken by [6, 20, 4], which also use the Dartmouth College trace data. To construct the simulation scenarios, we first randomly select 200 mobile nodes and add the 100 sources selected before to get a 300-node scenario. Then we add 100 randomly selected new mobile nodes to the 300-node scenario to get a 400-node scenario. Repeat this process we obtain the 500-node and 600-node scenarios. For each network scenario, we repeat 10 times and the averaged results are reported to enhance the confidence level. For simplicity, we denote by $U = x$ the x-node scenario, where U is the network size. Because 300~600 nodes represent about 5.4~10.8% of the total mobile nodes in the trace, which contains 5543 mobile nodes, the performance is worse than that obtained from the whole set of trace date for each scheme investigated in this simulation study.

Let the number of zones in a home be the home size. Through extensive tests we found that when the largest home size is limited to 10% of the zones in the network, namely the average home size is about 10, a good trade-off between quality and quantity of relays can be obtained.

In this simulation, we compare the performance of HERO with that of MobySpace [20], the most related research that selects a relay with a similar mobility pattern as the destination, and that of Epidemic [16], a flooding algorithm

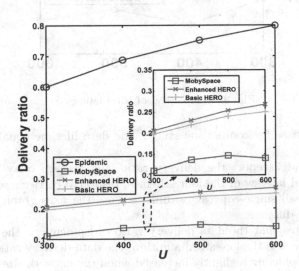

Fig. 1. Comparison of delivery ratio

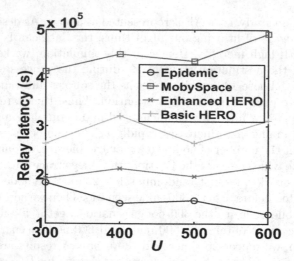

Fig. 2. Comparison of relay latency

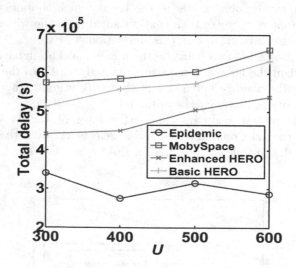

Fig. 3. Comparison of total latency

serving as the base for comparison study. The data lifetime equals simulation duration.

Figs. 1, 2 and 3 report the delivery ratio, the average relay latency, and the average total latency of the four schemes, respectively. Because HERO and Mobyspace are all single-copy algorithms, we use the axes graph in Fig. 1 to emphasize their difference.

Fig. 1 indicates that the data delivery ratio of Epidemic is the highest and that of MobySpace is the lowest. In addition, the data delivery ratio of all algorithms except Epidemic is slightly increased when the network size U increases. These observations can be justified as follows. Since Epidemic adopts a flooding policy, it can make a better use of the network connectivity, which is enhanced significantly when U increases. However, in HERO and Mobyspace, no matter how many mobile nodes exist, there is at most one copy of the to-be-delivered data in the network at any instant of time. As a result, though the probability of finding a good relay is increased when U increases, the enhancement of the network connectivity only slightly impacts on the performance of HERO and Mobyspace. This is the reason why the delivery ratio of Epidemic is increased faster than those of HERO and Mobyspace.

From Figs. 2 and 3, we observe that the average relay latency and the average total latency of Epidemic are the shortest, while those of Mobyspace are the longest and those of HERO algorithms are in-between. In addition, their average relay latencies and average total latencies are susceptible to the relay latencies and total latencies of the newly added successful communication pairs when U increases. Hence, when U increases, their average relay latencies and average total latencies either increase or decrease.

Based on the above analysis, we conclude that the performance of Epidemic in terms of the data delivery ratio, relay latency, and total latency is better than that of the enhanced HERO, which is better than that of the basic HERO. The performance of MobySpace is the worst.

6   Conclusion

In this paper, we propose two home-based routing (HERO) algorithms, the basic HERO and the enhanced HERO, which make use of the spatial regularity of human mobility to select relays. The basic HERO is a single-copy single-relay algorithm while the enhanced one is a single-copy multi-relay algorithm. Both algorithms rely on the concept of *home*, which is the set of places a node often visits. We use the Dartmouth college trace data to validate the performance of both HERO algorithms in terms of data delivery ratio, relay latency, and end-to-end delay, and compare them with two relevant research, MobySpace and Epidemic. Our simulation results indicate that both HERO algorithms outperform Mobyspace but are worse than Epidemic, which provides an upper bound on the delivery ratio and a lower bound on the delivery latency. However, the transmission cost of Epidemic in terms of the number of relays is much higher than those of the HERO algorithms.

References

1. Wang, S., Liu, M., Cheng, X., Song, M.: Routing in Pocket Switched Networks. IEEE Wireless Communications 19(2), 67–73 (2012)
2. Lindgren, A., Doria, A., Scheln, O.: Probabilistic routing in intermittently connected networks. In: MobiHoc, Annapolis Maryland, USA (2003)
3. Dubois-Ferriere, H., Grossglauser, M., Vetterli, M.: Age matters: efficient route discovery in mobile Ad hoc networks using encounter ages. In: MobiHoc, Annapolis, Maryland, USA (2003)

4. Spyropoulos, T., Turletti, T., Obraczka, K.: Routing in Delay-Tolerant Networks comprising heterogeneous node populations. IEEE Transactions on Mobile Computing 8(8), 1132–1147 (2009)
5. Gao, W., Cao, G.: On exploiting transient contact patterns for data forwarding in delay tolerant networks. In: ICNP, Kyotp, Japan (2010)
6. Jones, E., Li, L., Schmidtke, J., Ward, P.: Practical Routing in delay tolerant networks. IEEE Transactions on Mobile Computing 6(8), 943–959 (2007)
7. Burgess, J., Gallagher, B., Jensen, D., Levine, B.: MaxProp: routing for vehicle-based disruption-tolerant networks. In: INFOCOM, Piscataway, USA (2006)
8. Hui, P., Crowcroft, J., Yoneki, E.: BUBBBLE Rap: social-based forwarding in delay tolerant networks. In: MOBIHOC, Hong Kong, China (2008)
9. Daly, E., Haahr, M.: Social network analysis for routing in disconnected delay-tolerant MANETs. In: MOBIHOC, Montreal, CA (2007)
10. Dang, H., Wu, H.: Practical Clustering and cluster-based routing protocol for delay-tolerant mobile networks. IEEE Transactions on Wireless Communication 9(6), 1874–1881 (2010)
11. Liu, C., Wu, J.: Scalable routing in delay tolerant networks. In: MOBIHOC, Montreal, CA (2007)
12. Jain, S., Fall, K., Patra, R.: Routing in a delay tolerant network. In: SIGCOMM, New York, USA (2004)
13. Conan, V., Leguay, J., Friedman, T.: Fixed point opportunistic routing in delay tolerant networks. IEEE Journal on Selected Areas in Communications 26(5), 773–781 (2008)
14. Gao, W., Li, Q., Zhao, B., Cao, G.: Multicasting in delay tolerant networks: a social network perspective. In: MOBIHOC, New Orleans, USA (2009)
15. Liu, C., Wu, J.: Routing in a cyclic Mobispace. In: MOBIHOC, Hong Kong, China (2008)
16. Vahdat, A., Becker, D.: Epidemic routing for partially connected ad hoc networks. Technical Report CS-200006, Duke University (2000)
17. Costa, P., Mascolo, C., Musolesi, M., Picco, G.: Socially-aware routing for publish-subscribe in delay-tolerant mobile Ad hoc networks. IEEE Journal on Selected Areas in Communications 26(5), 748–760 (2008)
18. Gao, W., Cao, G.: User-centric data dissenmination in disruption tolerant networks. In: INFOCOM, Shanghai, China (2011)
19. Alessandro Mei, A., Morabito, G., Santi, P., Stefa, J.: Social-aware stateless forwarding in pocket switched networks. In: INFOCOM, Shanghai, China (2011)
20. Leguay, J., Friedman, T., Conan, V.: Evaluating mobility pattern space routing for DTNs. In: INFOCOM, Barcelona, Catalunya, SPAIN (2006)
21. Balachandran, A., Voelker, M., Bahl, P., Rangan, P.: Characterizing user behavior and network performance in a public wireless LAN. In: ACM SIGMETRICS International Conference on Measurement and Modeling of Computer Systems, Marina Del Rey, California (2002)
22. Balazinska, M., Castro, P.: Characterizing mobility and network usage in a corporate wireless local-area network. In: MobiSys 2003, San Francisco, California (2003)
23. Henderson, T., Kotz, D., Abyzov, I., Yeo, J.: CRAWDAD trace set dartmouth/campus/movement (v.2005-03-08) (2005),
   http://crawdad.cs.dartmouth.edu/dartmouth/campus/movement

Routing for Information Leakage Reduction in Multi-channel Multi-hop Ad-Hoc Social Networks

Wei Cheng[1], Dengyuan Wu[2], Xiuzhen Cheng[2], and Dechang Chen[3]

[1] Department of Computer Science,
University of California, Davis, Davis CA, USA
[2] Department of Computer Science,
The George Washington University, Washington DC, USA
[3] Department of Preventive Medicine and Biometrics,
Uniformed Services University of the Health Sciences
weicheng@ucdavis.edu
{andrewwu,cheng}@gwu.edu
dchen@usuhs.mil

Abstract. This paper investigates the routing problem for information leakage reduction in multi-channel ad-hoc networks. In particular, we focus on two routing models: Trusted Group Multicast (TGM) and Confidential Unicast (CU). In TGM, a group member shares the information with all other group members; while in CU, a group member may only want to share the information with a few selected group members. In both cases, the sender would like to transmit the information through a route with a minimal probability of being overheard by non-destination users. To achieve this objective, we propose a routing algorithm to reduce the information leakage. The performance of our design is evaluated through simulation studies.

1 Introduction

The routing problem in wireless networks has been extensively studied with the objectives of improving either the networking performance such as end-to-end delay and throughput, or robustness, reliability, and security. However, a fundamental problem of preventing information leakage to unwelcome users, who should not but can overhear the transmissions over the air, has never been addressed in literature. Although wireless transmissions can be secured by cryptographic primitives, reducing the probability of being overheard by unwelcome users is still critical as security mechanisms could be broken and the exposure of the information to malicious users may cause wreak havoc to certain applications (such as military applications). We therefore target on studying the routing problem to reduce the probability of information leakage in wireless networks.

This problem can be generally defined as follows. Given an information source and the corresponding sets of destinations and unwelcome users, computing a

X. Wang et al. (Eds.): WASA 2012, LNCS 7405, pp. 31–42, 2012.

routing path satisfying the following three requirements with decreasing priorities: i) the information can successfully reach all destinations; ii) the probability of information leakage to unwelcome users is minimized; and ii) the probability of information leakage to non-destination users is minimized. This problem is NP-hard as a special case, the well-known Steiner tree problem which asks for the minimum number of non-destination nodes in forming a routing path, is NP-Complete.

Instead of considering the general problem defined above, this paper investigates two special instances focusing on reducing the information leakage in social networking applications, in which users share their information with others who may also be interested through ad-hoc multi-hop transmissions. There are two types of users in a social network: the members of a common interest group and the non-group users. The two instances of the general routing problem for information leakage reduction respectively adopt the following two routing models: the *Trusted Group Multicast (TGM)* model and the *Confidential Unicast (CU)* model. In TGM, a user is willing to share its information with all members in its common interest group; thus the objective of TGM is to minimize the non-group user's probability of overhearing the information. In CU, a user may only want to share its information with a certain subset of members. As non-destination group members may even be more harmful than non-group users since the former may have more interests in and more knowledge about the information, the objectives of CU must first minimize the non-destination group member's overhearing probability and then minimize the probability of information leakage to non-group users. In such a case, the non-destination group members are unwelcome users.

We assume that the multi-hop ad hoc social network under our consideration can make use of multiple channels for wireless transmissions. We further assume that each user is aware of its available channels and the network topology, which can be obtained during the common interest group construction. Our intention is to design a routing algorithm that can select a path satisfying the design objectives of TGM and CU. The contributions of the paper are quad-fold:

- We propose a general problem, the routing problem for information leakage reduction in wireless networks. This problem has never been addressed in literature.
- We analyze the objectives of two novel routing models (TGM and CU), which defines two special instances of the general problem in social networks, and propose a general graph model that can cover both TGM and CU.
- We propose a routing algorithm for information leakage reduction in social networks based on the general graph model.
- Simulation studies demonstrate that our proposed algorithm outperforms the Breadth-First Search (BFS) based routing algorithm in terms of the information leakage probability.

In the rest of the paper, we briefly summarize the related work in the area of ad-hoc networks in Section 2. Our general graph model for both TGM and CU is presented in Section 3. A routing algorithm for information leakage reduction, denoted by RILR, is proposed in Section 4. A simulation study to validate the performance of the RILR algorithm is reported in Section 5. Finally, we conclude the paper and discuss our future research in Section 6.

2   Related Work

Routing problems have been extensively studied in wireless ad-hoc networks and sensor networks. The objectives of the prior research are either to improve the transmission performance such as delay, throughput, and energy consumption, or to enhance the robustness of the network when malicious attacks targeting on the transmissions exist. Various routing schemes have been proposed in the literature, including the classic AODV algorithm [1], the secure routing mechanism [2], and the recent cooperative relay selection algorithm [3], just to name a few. But none of them takes into account the objective of reducing the information leakage to non-destination users, which is the focus of this paper.

Existing multicast routing algorithms for information sharing [4–7] are studied mainly based on graph theory. Steiner tree based routing is considered in [4] and [5] with different objectives: [4] aims to minimize the path length and the energy consumption while [5] intends to reduce the computation overhead and the number of transmissions. On the other hand, Spanning trees are also exploited for multicast routing algorithm design [6, 7]. In particular, [6] selects the relays from a minimal spanning tree that is constructed based on an energy consumption metric while [7] targets on reducing the retransmissions caused by interference during the spanning tree construction.

Inspired by the opportunity of utilizing multiple channels for highly crowded wireless transmissions, a number of routing algorithms have been proposed to achieve the traditional routing objectives [9–13]. In [9], a shortest path routing algorithm is developed based on a weighted graph, where the assigned weights are utilized to avoid the interference among adjacent links. In [10], the links with the highest channel availability are selected to relay the data to the destination. A cross-layer opportunistic spectrum access and dynamic routing algorithm is proposed in [11] to maximize the network throughput by performing joint routing, dynamic spectrum allocation, scheduling, and transmit power control. Routing algorithms for route robustness enhancement in terms of the degree of connectivity are studied in [12, 13].

In this paper, we study the routing problem to reduce the information leakage for information sharing among common interest group members in social networks. This problem has never been addressed in any type of wireless networks. Two novel routing models are proposed and a routing algorithm that can reduce the information leakage for both models is investigated.

3   Problem Formulation

In order to model the routing problem for information leakage reduction in social networks, we first analyze the objectives of TGM and CU in this section.

Then, a general mathematical model that can realize all the objectives of both TGM and CU is proposed. At the end of this section, we discuss the metrics for evaluating the performance of a routing algorithm in terms of the information leakage probability.

3.1   Objectives

In social networks, Trusted Group Multicast and Confidential Unicast both involve three types of users: *destinations*, *unwelcome users*, and *outsiders*. In TGM, all the members within the common interest group are destinations and the set of unwelcome users contains the unauthorized users that are interested in the group information but do not have the right to joint the group. In CU, the destination(s) is (are) one (a few) of the members within the common interest group and the unwelcome users include both the unauthorized non-group users and the non-destination group members. The outsiders for both TGM and CU include users in the network that are neither destinations nor unwelcome users. Generally speaking, a user needs to deliver the information to its destinations, parry the unwelcome users, and minimize the probability of information being overheard by unwelcome users and outsiders in both models. Correspondingly, we can employ the following common objectives to summarize those of TGM and CU in descending order of priorities.

1. Ensure successful information deliveries to the destinations.
2. If possible, do not employ unwelcome users as information relays.
3. Minimize the probability of being overheard by unwelcome users.
4. Minimize the number of outsiders as information relays.
5. Minimize the probability of being overheard by outsiders.
6. Minimize the transmission time in terms of the number of hops to reach all the destinations.

We model these six objectives by a graph, in which the destinations, the unwelcome users, and the outsiders are the vertices. Since TGM and CU both have the same three types of nodes and the same design objectives for information leakage reduction, a common graph model suffices.

   If only considering the objective of successful and fast information delivery, we can construct a routing topology by employing the Breadth-First Search algorithm (BFS). However, BFS does not consider information leakage reduction, which is addressed by the 2nd-5th objectives. The problem of information leakage reduction is non-trivial when all the six objectives are considered. In the rest of this section, we formally present the graph model along with the performance evaluation metrics.

3.2   A General Graph Model for Information Leakage Reduction

We assume that an information source is aware of the network topology that contains all the common interest group members and the set of unwelcome users for a specific information sharing session. We also assume that the source and all its destinations are connected, which can be ensured during the common interest group construction procedure. We model the network topology by a weighted graph $G(V, E)$, where V is the set of users, and E is the set of edges. There exists an edge between two users if they can overhear each other. We assign a weight $w_{i,j}$ to each edge $e_{i,j} \in E$, where $w_{i,j}$ denotes the probability for v_j to detect v_i's transmissions. The value of $w_{i,j}$ is set according to the network topology and the available channels. Note that edges can be directed, and that $w_{i,j} = 0$ if the edge $e_{i,j}$ does not exist. Without loss of generality, we denote by v_0 the information source itself. The set of destinations, the set of unwelcome users, and the set of outsiders are denoted as V_D, V_A, and V_O, respectively. Note that $V_D \bigcup V_A \bigcup V_O = V$ and $|V_D| + |V_A| + |V_O| = |V|$. Let V_R be the set of users that are on v_0's information sharing routes and can actively relay the information. Thus $v_0 \in V_D$ and $v_0 \in V_R$. Let $I(v_i) = \{v_j | (v_i, v_j) \in E\}$ represent the set of users that are within v_i's transmission range, where $0 \leq i, j \leq |V|$ and $i \neq j$. Denote by $G_R(V', E')$ the derived graph of V_R such that $V' = \{v_i | v_i \in V_R \text{ or } v_i \in I(v_j), \text{ where } v_j \in V_R\}$ and $E' = \{e_{j,i} | v_j \in V_R \text{ and } v_i \in I(v_j)\}$. Note that G_R is a subgraph of G that includes all the users who may overhear or obtain the information, and that there is no edge between any two non-relay users in G_R. For each user $v_i \in V'$, we calculate its probability of overhearing the interested information, denoted as $P'_{ro}(v_i)$, according to the following formula.

$$P'_{ro}(v_i) = \begin{cases} 0, V_R = \Phi \\ 1, v_i \in V_R \bigcup V_D \\ 1 - \prod_{v_j \in V_R} (1 - w_{j,i}), \text{otherwise} \end{cases} \tag{1}$$

Note that $P'_{ro}(v_i) \in [0,1]$ increases with the increase of the number of relays that include v_i in their communication ranges. We utilize $P'_{ro}(v_i)$ as v_i's weight.

Let $D(v_0, V_D)$ represent the maximum hop distance from v_0 to the destinations in G_R. Note that $D(v_0, V_D) = +\infty$ if V_D is not connected in G_R. The notations used in this model are summarized in Table 1. Also note that we use '*node*' to substitute '*source*', '*outsider*', '*relay*' and '*destination*' in the following graph-based modeling and analysis.

Given a graph G, v_0, V_D, V_A, and V_O, our goal is to find a V_R, such that the following six objectives can be achieved in a descending order of priorities:

1. $G_R \supseteq V_D$ and V_D is connected in G_R: all the nodes in V_D are in G_R, and they are connected.
2. $V_R \bigcap V_A = \Phi$: V_R does not include any node in V_A.
3. $min(\max\{P'_{ro}(v_i) | v_i \in V_A\})$: the maximum node weight in V_A is minimized.
4. $min(|V_O \bigcap V_R|)$: the number of nodes in the intersection of V_R and V_O is minimized.
5. $min(\max\{P'_{ro}(v_i) | v_i \in V_O \setminus V_R\})$: the maximum node weight in $V_O \setminus V_R$ is minimized.
6. $min(D(v_0, V_D))$: the maximum hop distance from v_0 to the nodes in V_D is minimized.

Table 1. Notations and their semantic meanings

Notations	Meanings
V_D	The set of destinations
V_A	The set of unwelcome users
V_O	The set of outsiders
V_R	The set of relays
G_R	The derived graph of V_R
$I(v_i)$	v_i's one-hop directed neighbors
$w_{i,j}$	v_j's probability of detecting v_i's transmissions
$P'_{ro}(v_i)$	v_i's probability of overhearing the information
$D(v_0, V_D)$	Maximum hop distance from the source to the destinations

3.3 Performance Metrics

The layout of the proposed graph model is illustrated in Fig. 1(a). According to the objectives, the performance of a feasible V_R should be evaluated based on the following criteria in descending order of priorities:

1. $\boldsymbol{max}\,P'_{ro}(A)$: the maximum node weight in V_A.
2. $\mathbf{N}_{ro} = |V_O \bigcap V_R|$: the number of outsider relays.
3. $\boldsymbol{max}\,P'_{ro}(O \setminus R)$: the maximum node weight in $V_O \setminus V_R$.
4. $\boldsymbol{max}\mathbf{D}$: the maximum hop distance between v_0 and the nodes in V_D.

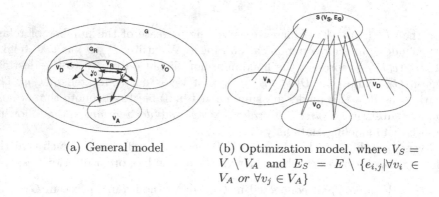

(a) General model

(b) Optimization model, where $V_S = V \setminus V_A$ and $E_S = E \setminus \{e_{i,j} | \forall v_i \in V_A \text{ or } \forall v_j \in V_A\}$

Fig. 1. The graph model for Information leakage reduction

4   Routing Algorithm for Information Leakage Reduction

In this section, we present a routing algorithm for information leakage reduction in social networks based on the proposed general graph model shown in Fig. 1(a). In order to check the existence of feasible solutions to achieve the first two objectives, we first remove the nodes in V_A from the graph G. We then check whether there exists a connected subgraph that contains all the nodes in V_D in the residual graph. This checking process can be finished in a polynomial time by employing the BFS algorithm starting from the node v_0.

In the rest of this section, we assume there always exist feasible solutions so that we can focus on the optimization problem of achieving the last four objectives. In order to solve the problem, we construct a graph shown in Fig. 1(b), where S is the residual graph constructed by removing V_A and all the edges associated with the nodes in V_A from G, based on the general model in Fig. 1(a). The edges that connect two nodes in V_A and V_S, in V_O and V_S, and in V_D and V_S, represent the edges in E. Note that all the nodes in V_O and V_D are also in V_S, and that each pair of these duplicated nodes is connected by an edge.

During the routing algorithm design, we assume that the channel availability information is known, that the selected relays only broadcast the information once, and that all the selected receivers can receive the information successfully from the relays. The $w_{i,j}$ is set as the reciprocal of the number of available channels.

In Fig. 1(b), to achieve the third objective, we need to find a connected subgraph S' of S such that all the nodes in V_D can be dominated by the nodes in S', and that the maximum P'_{ro} value among the dominated nodes in V_A is minimized. Note that $V_R = V_{S'}$ is a candidate solution, and that there may exist multiple candidate solutions. As the objectives are listed in descending priority orders, the next step is to choose a candidate solution that should satisfy the following conditions with decreasing order of priorities: i) it should include the minimum number of outsiders, ii) it should minimize the maximum P'_{ro} value, which is less than 1, among the dominated nodes in V_O, and iii) it should minimize the maximum hop distance from v_0 to the destination nodes.

According to the above analysis, we propose a greedy routing algorithm, which is illustrated in Algorithm 1, to find a feasible solution based on the graph model shown in Fig. 1(b). The notations used in the algorithm are summarized in Table 2.

In the algorithm, we select the relay nodes and add them to V_R one by one. The algorithm consists of three phases. In the first phase, we set $\{v_0\}$ as V_R, and calculate P'_{ro} for all the nodes (line 4). We then construct a set of dominating relays from V_S in the second phase, so that all the nodes in V_D can be dominated.

Table 2. Algorithm notations

Notations	Meanings
$Info(v_i)$	Whether v_i can obtain the information
w_i^A	v_i's aggregated probability of being overheard by unwelcome users (3)
w_i^O	v_i's aggregated probability of being overheard by outsiders (4)
$\overline{V_D}$	The set of nodes that can directly reach V_D (2)
V_R^E	The set of dominating relays

Finally, we add nodes from V_S to the set of selected dominating relays so that all the relays can be connected in the third phase.

In the dominating relay selection process, we first construct a set of nodes, denoted by $\overline{V_D}$, which can directly send information to at least one of the destinations according to (2).

$$\overline{V_D} = V_D \bigcup \{v_j \in V \setminus V_A | e_{j,i} \in E \text{ and } v_i \in V_D\} \tag{2}$$

We iteratively select nodes from $\overline{V_D}$ one by one to construct the dominating relay set until all the destinations are dominated by the selected nodes. At each selection iteration, we first remove the unnecessary nodes, which can not send information to more destinations, from $\overline{V_D}$ (*Line 10-14*). Then, we find a set of nodes in $\overline{V_D}$, which can minimize the accumulated probability of being overheard by the unwelcome users if they are selected as relays (*Line 15-16*). The accumulated probability is calculated according to (3).

$$w_i^A = \max\{1 - (1 - P'_{ro}(v_j))(1 - w_{i,j}) | v_j \in V_A\} \tag{3}$$

Similarly, we define a node v_i's impact on the accumulated probability of being overheard by the outsiders in (4).

$$w_i^O = \max\{1 - (1 - P'_{ro}(v_j))(1 - w_{i,j}) | v_j \in V_O \setminus V_R\} \tag{4}$$

Based on the priority order of the 4th and the 5th objectives, we select a node from the smallest w_i^A node set according to *Line 17-22*. Then, we add the selected node to V_R. It follows from (1) that $P'_{ro}(v_i)$ depends on the nodes in V_R. Thus, it should be recalculated at each iteration (*Line 24*).

As the constructed dominating relay set (*Line 27*) may not be connected, we iteratively add nodes to V_R until it is connected (*Line 30-34*). In order to achieve the 3rd-5th objectives, the connecting node selection process is in a way similar to the process of dominating relay selection, and the selection is not based on the nodes' connectivity. As a result, there may exist redundant nodes in V_R. Therefore, jointly considering the last objective, the final route is calculated by employing the BFS algorithm on the selected V_R with the branch cut procedure (*Line 35-36*), which can remove the branches that do not contain any destination node.

Note that the algorithm's complexity is polynomial as the selection process, the BFS algorithm, the connectivity checking, and the branch cut procedure, can all be finished in a polynomial time.

5   Simulations

In this section, we use Matlab to evaluate the performance of the proposed algorithm (denoted as RILR) by comparing its performance with that of the BFS based algorithm. For fairness, we revise the BFS algorithm by skipping the unwelcome users and giving priority to the destinations during the route

---

Algorithm 1. Routing for Information Leakage Reduction

1: **Phase I: Initialization**
2: $V_R = \{v_0\}$, $Info(v_0) = 1$;
3: $Info(v_i) = 1$, for $\forall v_i \in I(v_0) \bigcap V_D$;
4: Calculate $P'_{ro}(v_i)$ for $\forall v_i \in V$ according to Eq. (1);
5: $\forall v_i \in V_D \setminus I(v_0)$, $Info(v_i) = 0$;
6:
7: **Phase II: Relay Selection**
8: Construct $\overline{V_D}$ according to Eq. (2);
9: **while** $\exists v_i \in V_D$ s.t. $Info(v_i) == 0$ **do**
10:     **for** $\forall v_j \in \overline{V_D}$ **do**
11:         **if** $\forall v_k \in I(v_j) \bigcap V_D$, s.t. $Info(v_k) == 1$ **then**
12:             Remove v_j from $\overline{V_D}$;
13:         **end if**
14:     **end for**
15:     Calculate w_j^A for $\forall v_j \in \overline{V_D}$ according to Eq. (3);
16:     Find a set of nodes with the smallest w_j^A in $\overline{V_D}$;
17:     Calculate w_j^O for all the nodes in the set according to Eq. (4);
18:     **if** the set includes nodes in V_D **then**
19:         Pick a node v_j, which has the smallest w_j^O, from the intersection of the set and V_D;
20:     **else**
21:         Pick a node v_j, which has the smallest w_j^O, from the set;
22:     **end if**
23:     Add v_j to V_R;
24:     Recalculate $P'_{ro}(v_i)$ for $\forall v_i \in V$ according to Eq. (1);
25:     $\forall v_k \in I(v_j) \bigcap V_D$, set $Info(v_k) = 1$;
26: **end while**
27: $V_R^E = V_R$;
28:
29: **Phase III: Connected Rout Construction**
30: **while** V_R^E is not connected **do**
31:     Calculate w_j^A for $\forall v_j \in V_S \setminus V_R$ according to Eq. (3);
32:     Find a set of nodes with the smallest w_j^A in $V_S \setminus V_R$;
33:     Repeat *Line 17-24*;
34: **end while**
35: Construct a BFS tree in V_R starting from v_0;
36: Remove the subtrees that do not contain the nodes in V_R^E, from V_R;
37: Recalculate $P'_{ro}(v_i)$ for $\forall v_i \in V$ according to Eq. (1);
38:
39: **Outputs:**
40: Output the smallest BFS tree containing V_R^E, $\boldsymbol{max}P'_{ro}(A)$, $\mathbf{N}_{ro}$, $\boldsymbol{max}P'_{ro}(O \setminus R)$, and $\boldsymbol{max}\mathbf{D}$;

---

construction. This means that the revised BFS algorithm does not choose un-welcome users as relays but selects the destinations as relays when destinations and outsiders are in the same level.

In the simulation study, 100 nodes are randomly deployed in a 100×100 area. The source node v_0 are deployed in the center of the area. 10 nodes are randomly selected as the destinations, and another set of 10 nodes are randomly selected as the unwelcome users. We assume that all the nodes have the same communication range and the same set of available channels. The number of available channels varies between 4 and 11. We set the edge weight $w_{i,j}$ as the reciprocal of the number of available channels. The average node degree is controlled by the communication range, which is set as 20. As a result, the average node degree varies between $9.8 - 12.5$ in the simulations. Note that we only consider the simulated networks containing routes that can connect the sources and the destinations without the help of the unwelcome users, during the performance evaluation. Each reported result in Fig. 2(a), Fig. 2(b), and Fig. 3 is the mean of $100,000$ instances.

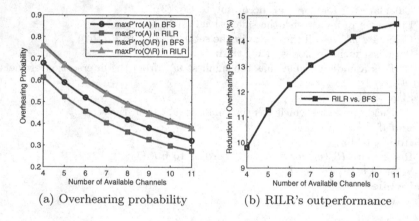

(a) Overhearing probability   (b) RILR's outperformance

Fig. 2. Simulation results

Fig. 2(a) reports the performance of RILR in terms of the maximum overhearing probabilities of the unwelcome users and the outsiders. We can conclude that increasing the number of available channels can help to reduce the overhearing probabilities. This indicates that we can effectively reduce the probability of information leakage to non-destination users by take the advantage of multi available channels. Moreover, the proposed routing algorithm always outperforms the revised BFS algorithm in terms of overhearing probability. Regarding the unwelcome users' overhearing probability, which is the most important concern in confidential information sharing, RILR can achieve an average of 12% reduction in information leakage compared with the revised BFS algorithm as shown in Fig. 2(b). Note that the outperformance of RILR increases along with the increase of the number of available channels. The costs of the reduction include the increase in route length and the increase of the number of outsider relays as shown in Fig. 3.

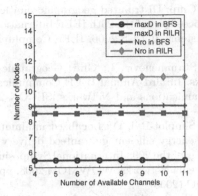

Fig. 3. Number of nodes in the route

6 Conclusion and Future Research

In this paper, we propose a routing algorithm to reduce the probability of information leakage during the wireless transmissions in social networks. Two routing models, Trusted Group Multicast and Confidential Unicast, are considered in this paper. Through the simulations, the proposed RILR routing algorithm always yields a lower overhearing probability compared with the BFS based routing algorithm.

In our future work, we will study the routing problem of information leakage reduction in more complex environments. For example, retransmissions, which can increase the overhearing probability and can affect the values of $w_{i,j}$, w_i^A, and w_i^O, will be considered during the algorithm design. We will also add thresholds to w_i^A and w_i^O during the relay selection so that the maximum overhearing probability can be controlled. Moreover, the scheme that can handle the case with dynamic available channels will be proposed for the routing algorithm design.

Acknowledgments. The research was partially supported by the US NSF under grants CNS-0963957 and CNS-0964060.

References

1. Perkins, C.E., Royer, E.M.: Ad-hoc on-demand distance vector routing. In: Proceedings of the 2nd IEEE Workshop on Mobile Computing Systems and Applications, pp. 90–100 (1997)
2. Karlof, C., Wagner, D.: Secure routing in wireless sensor networks: attacks and countermeasures. In: Proceedings of the First IEEE International Workshop on Sensor Network Protocols and Applications, pp. 113–127 (May 2003)
3. Li, Y., Wang, P., Niyato, D., Zhuang, W.: A dynamic relay selection scheme for mobile users in wireless relay networks. In: INFOCOM, 2011 Proceedings IEEE, pp. 256–260 (April 2011)

4. Wu, S., Candan, K.S.: Gmp: Distributed geographic multicast routing in wireless sensor networks. In: Proceedings of the 26th IEEE International Conference on Distributed Computing Systems, ICDCS 2006. IEEE Computer Society, Washington, DC (2006)
5. Sanchez, J., Ruiz, P., Stojmnenovic, I.: Gmr: Geographic multicast routing for wireless sensor networks. In: 3rd Annual IEEE Communications Society on Sensor and Ad Hoc Communications and Networks, SECON 2006, vol. 1, pp. 20–29 (September 2006)
6. Frey, H., Ingelrest, F., Simplot-Ryl, D.: Localized minimum spanning tree based multicast routing with energy-efficient guaranteed delivery in ad hoc and sensor networks. In: Proceedings of the 2008 International Symposium on a World of Wireless, Mobile and Multimedia Networks, WOWMOM 2008, pp. 1–8. IEEE Computer Society, Washington, DC (2008)
7. Johansson, T., Osipov, E., Carr-Motyčková, L.: Interference Aware Construction of Multi- and Convergecast Trees in Wireless Sensor Networks. In: Balandin, S., Moltchanov, D., Koucheryavy, Y. (eds.) NEW2AN 2008. LNCS, vol. 5174, pp. 72–87. Springer, Heidelberg (2008)
8. Liu, Y., Liang, W.: Energy-Efficient Multiple Routing Trees for Aggregate Query Evaluation in Sensor Networks. In: Harju, J., Heijenk, G., Langendörfer, P., Siris, V.A. (eds.) WWIC 2008. LNCS, vol. 5031, pp. 201–212. Springer, Heidelberg (2008)
9. Xin, C., Xie, B., Shen, C.C.: A novel layered graph model for topology formation and routing in dynamic spectrum access networks. In: 2005 First IEEE International Symposium on New Frontiers in Dynamic Spectrum Access Networks, DySPAN 2005, pp. 308–317 (November 2005)
10. Pefkianakis, I., Wong, S., Lu, S.: Samer: spectrum aware mesh routing in cognitive radio networks. In: Cognitive Radio Networks, 3rd IEEE Symposium on New Frontiers in Dynamic Spectrum Access Networks, DySPAN 2008, pp. 1–5 (2008)
11. Ding, L., Melodia, T., Batalama, S., Matyjas, J., Medley, M.: Cross-layer routing and dynamic spectrum allocation in Cognitive Radio Ad hoc Networks. IEEE Transactions on Vehicular Technology 59(4), 1969–1979 (2010)
12. Shih, C.F., Liao, W., Chao, H.L.: Joint routing and spectrum allocation for multihop cognitive radio networks with route robustness consideration. IEEE Transactions on Wireless Communications 10(9), 2940–2949 (2011)
13. Abbagnale, A., Cuomo, F.: Gymkhana: A connectivity-based routing scheme for cognitive radio ad hoc networks. In: INFOCOM IEEE Conference on Computer Communications Workshops, pp. 1–5 (March 2010)

AMPLE: A Novel Incentive Approach to Adaptive-Width Channel Allocation in Multi-hop, Non-cooperative Wireless Networks*

Chunyang Wu[1], Fan Wu[1,**], Guihai Chen[1], and Bo Sheng[2]

[1] Shanghai Key Laboratory of Scalable Computing and Systems,
Department of Computer Science and Engineering,
Shanghai Jiao Tong University
[2] Department of Computer Science, University of Massachusetts Boston
chunyang506@sjtu.edu.cn, {fwu,gchen}@cs.sjtu.edu.cn,
shengbo@cs.umb.edu

Abstract. Due to the limitation of radio spectrum resource and fast deployment of wireless devices, careful channel allocation is of great importance for mitigating the performance degradation caused by interference among different users in wireless networks. Most of existing work focused on fixed-width channel allocation. However, latest researches have demonstrated that it is possible to combine contiguous channels for better utilizing the available channels. In this paper, we study the problem of adaptive-width channel allocation in multi-hop, non-cooperative wireless networks from a game-theoretic point of view. We first present a strategic game model for this problem and demonstrate the existence of Nash Equilibrium (NE) in an anarchical scenario. Since a NE is not an ideal solution, we then propose AMPLE, a novel incentive approach to guarantee the system performance at high level. Since the problem of channel allocation in multiple collision domains is NP-complete, we first present an approximate algorithm that gives an allocation with good system performance. We then design a charging scheme that guarantees the system to converge to a Dominant Strategy Equilibrium (DSE), in which it is to the best interest of each node to follow the computed channel allocation, regardless how the others behave. Numerical results verify that AMPLE does prevent nodes' misbehavior, and achieves much higher average system throughputs than anarchical NEs.

1 Introduction

Due to historical reasons, radio spectrum is manually divided into communication channels, and each channel is assigned to a specific application in a geographic area. For instance, the commonly used IEEE 802.11 standard specifies several orthogonal channels (*e.g.*, 3 in IEEE 802.11b/g and 12 in IEEE 802.11a). Such static channelization prevents the limited radio spectrum from being used efficiently [11, 15, 18]. Furthermore,

* This work was supported in part by China NSF grant 61170236 and 61133006. The opinions, findings, conclusions, and recommendations expressed in this paper are those of the authors and do not necessarily reflect the views of the funding agencies or the government.
** Corresponding author.

X. Wang et al. (Eds.): WASA 2012, LNCS 7405, pp. 43–59, 2012.

the United States has completed its transition to fully digital television broadcasting on June 12, 2009, and opened up unlicensed use of TV whitespaces that span 100-250 MHz of spectrum [1]. This raises the need for dynamic spectrum allocation.

Ranveer Chandra et al. [6] proposed that the width of IEEE 802.11-based communication channels can be changed adaptively in software by using commodity Wi-Fi hardware. For example, two contiguous 20 MHz channels can be combined into a 40 MHz channel to provide higher bit-rate. Furthermore, the emergence of cognitive radio makes it more convenient to adaptively utilize available radio spectrum. Although the problem of channel allocation has been extensively studied in the literature, the feature of adaptive-width channel has not been fully considered [22].

Since nodes equipped with cognitive radio can easily adapt themselves to operate in any part of radio spectrum spaces, we can no longer assume that the nodes in the network would follow the prescribed spectrum allocation protocol faithfully. The most rational strategy for an individual node is to tune its wireless interface to the available spectrum (channel), in which it can get the best payoff. However, such selfish behavior may degrade the networks performance, due to inefficient channel allocation. In this paper, we consider the problem of adaptive-width channel allocation in non-cooperative wireless networks, where the participating nodes are always selfish and pursue their own objectives. Wu *et al.* [22] presented an incentive scheme to guarantee the system to converge to a state, in which system-wide throughput is optimized. However, their work only applies to a single-hop network, wherein all transmissions on the same channel will collide with each other. This limits the practical usage of the proposed incentive scheme, because spatially well separated transmissions can work on the same channel simultaneously. For example, in a large building, two well separated access points can serve wireless users using the same channel. Therefore, we will study the problem of adaptive-width channel allocation in multi-hop, non-cooperative wireless networks, and propose our strong and practical solution.

To understand the impact of participating nodes' selfish behavior, we first model the problem of adaptive-width channel allocation as a strategic game, and study the Nash equilibrium (NE) the system converge to, when there is no exogenous factor to influence the nodes' behavior. We introduce a simple algorithm to simulate selfish nodes' behaviors, and to compute a NE the system may converge to. Although the algorithm cannot enumerate all the possible NEs, its outputs provide us the following understanding of the NE:

1. NE is not a strong equilibrium for all the players to comply with. In a NE scenario, only under the assumption that all other players kept their equilibrium strategies would a player of the game have incentives to keep its equilibrium strategy. Thus NE does not provide strong incentives for the game player.
2. NE is usually not globally efficient, which means that the maximized system-wide performance is not always achieved. So, even if the system converged to one of the NEs, some player might benefit at the cost of system-wide performance degradation.
3. Although our algorithm finishes in $O(nc)$ steps, where n is the number of nodes in the network and c is the number of available channels, the convergence may take extremely long time in practice.

Therefore, NE is not an ideal solution to the problem of adaptive-width channel allocation, and we need to seek stronger solutions that can guarantee the system performance at high level.

To achieve strong incentives and to maintain high system performance, we propose an incentive scheme, namely AMPLE, that can guarantee the system converging to a Dominant Strategy Equilibrium (DSE), a novel incentive approach to Adaptive-width channel allocation in Multi-hop, non-cooPerative wireLess nEtworks. In game theory, DSE is a solution much stronger than NE. For each node, instead of going through a complicated decision process, simply picking its corresponding strategy in the DSE is the best strategy, regardless of the others' strategies. In the meanwhile, the system-wide performance achieved in the DSE is guaranteed to be high.

The major contributions of this paper are as follows:

1. First, to our knowledge, we are the first to study the problem of adaptive-width channel allocation in multi-hop, non-cooperative wireless networks. Our solution is strong and practical.
2. Second, we present an algorithm to simulate the selfish behavior of the nodes. The results of the algorithm show that there exist multiple NEs the system may converge to. More importantly, NE is not a perfect solution concept to the problem studied in this paper.
3. Third, we propose an incentive scheme that can guarantee the convergence of the system to a Dominant Strategy Equilibrium (DSE), in which the system-wide performance achieved in the DSE is guaranteed to be high.

The rest of the paper is organized as follows. In Section 2, we present our system model, game model and some necessary concepts. In Section 3, we show the existence of NE in anarchy. In Section 4, we propose AMPLE, as our solution to the problem. In Section 5, we report the evaluation results. In Section 6, we give a brief review of the related work. Finally, in Section 7, we conclude this paper and put forward potential future work.

2 Preliminaries

2.1 System Model

In this paper we consider a static wireless network with some access points. Each access point is equipped with a radio interface and can provide data service within its coverage area. Define $N \triangleq \{1, 2, 3, ..., n\}$. Figure 1(a) illustrates a proper example. There are three access points (AC) A, B and C. The dotted circles are the coverage areas of those ACs. In this scenario, A conflicts with C while not with B.

Given a set of channels donated by $C \triangleq \{1, 2, ..., c\}$, we assume that the channels are contiguous, orthogonal (non-interfering), and homogenous. Since the access points need the channels to provide services to their customers, we want to efficiently allocate the channels to the access points. Due to service quality requirement, we require that the access points do not have any channel conflict with each other. By treating each access point as a node in the graph, we set up a conflict graph $G \triangleq (N, E)$, where E represents the conflict edge set, $e = (i, j) \in E$ means that j and i conflict with each other.

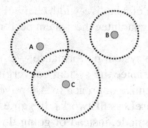 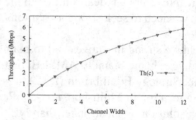

(a) An example showing conflic-   (b) Properties of the effective aggregate
tion between access points.   throughput $Th(c)$.

Fig. 1.

For any access point $i \in N$, We denote its allocated channel set by $\mathbb{C}(i)$.

We require that the channels allocated to an access point must be contiguous. An AC
can obtain a higher throughput by combining contiguous channels into a wider on Let
$Th(c)$ represent the effective aggregated throughput of a channel with the bandwidth of
c original channels. As shown in [4], $Th(c)$ is a concave non-decreasing function of c.
Figure 1(b) illustrates these properties of $Th(c)$.

For a particular AC, it is able to combine contiguous channels, which are not conflicting with its neighbors. Thus its throughput is that of the combined channel.

Definition 1 (Longest Contiguous Segment (LCS)). *Given an integer set A, a contiguous segment is subset that requires the elements are contiguous. We define $LCS(A)$
as the longest contiguous segment in A.*

Based on this definition, we formulate the throughput of AC i as

$$T_i(s) = Th(|LCS(\mathbb{C}[i])|).$$

2.2 Game Model

We model the adaptive-width channel allocation as a strategic game. In this game, we
treat the access points as players. We assume the players are rational and do not collude
or cooperate with each other. The strategy of player $i \in N$ is its allocated channel set:

$$s_i \triangleq \mathbb{C}(i).$$

In the rest of this paper, we use s_i and $\mathbb{C}(i)$ interchangeably.

The strategy profile s is a vector composed of all the players' strategies,

$$s \triangleq (s_1, s_2, ..., s_n)^T.$$

Conventionally, s_{-i} represents the strategy profile of the other players except player i.

For a strategy profile s, let's denote the throughput of player i by $T_i(s)$. As mentioned
previously, the allocated channels of one player should be contiguous. If it selects some
separated channels that can not be combined, it can not fully utilize them.

We then define a player's utility. As in the literature (*e.g.* [8, 20, 26–28]), we assume that there exists some kind of virtual currency in the system. In this paper, we define the utility of player i as

$$u_i(s) \triangleq \alpha T_i(s) - \mathcal{P}_i(s), \tag{1}$$

where α is a coefficient and $\mathcal{P}_i(s)$ represents the charge to player i for using channels. Since a player cannot guarantee the quality of the service provided to its customers, we let $u_i(s) \triangleq -\mathcal{P}_i(s)$, when the player collide with one of its conflicting neighbors.

We then review some solution concepts from game theory used in this paper.

Definition 2 (Nash Equilibrium [17]). *A strategy profile s^* is a Nash Equilibrium of a strategic game, if for any player $i \in N$ and for any strategy $s_i \neq s_i^*$,*

$$u_i(s_i^*, s_{-i}^*) \geq u_i(s_i, s_{-i}^*). \tag{2}$$

Definition 3 (Dominant Strategy Equilibrium [10, 17]). *A strategy profile s^* is a dominant strategy equilibrium of a strategy game, if for any player $i \in N$, any strategy $s \neq s^*$ and any strategy profile of the other players s_{-i},*

$$u_i(s_i^*, s_{-i}) \geq u_i(s_i, s_{-i}). \tag{3}$$

3 Anarchical Nash Equilibrium

In this section, we show the existence of Nash Equilibrium (NE) in anarchy, when there is no external factor to influence the players' behaviors. Each player's objective is to maximize its own throughput and hence the utility of the player is

$$u_i(s) = \alpha T_i(s), \tag{4}$$

if it does not collide with its conflicting neighbors; otherwise

$$u_i(s) = 0. \tag{5}$$

3.1 Computing NE

The pseudo-code for computing a NE is showed in Algorithm 1. We first successively allocate each node a random available channel (Line 1-7). We denote the set of adjacent nodes to a node as

$$Adj[i] \triangleq \{j|(i,j) \in E\}.$$

Then, we check each node and update its allocated channel(s) if it can get its throughput improved with the new allocation (Line 8-12). We repeat the above process until no node can improve its throughput by jumping to another set of contiguous channels. We denote the set of adjacent nodes to a node as

$$Adj[i] \triangleq \{j|(i,j) \in E\}.$$

Algorithm 1. Computing a NE

Require: A conflict graph $G = (N, E)$, a set of channels $C = \{0, 1, \ldots, c - 1\}$.
Ensure: Channel allocation $\mathbb{C}[i]$ for any node i in N.
1: $\forall i \in N, \mathbb{C}[i] = \Phi$
2: **for** $i \in N$ **do**
3:     **if** $C \setminus \bigcup\limits_{j \in Adj[i]} \mathbb{C}[j] \neq \Phi$ **then**
4:         $x :=$ a random channel in $C \setminus \bigcup\limits_{j \in Adj[i]} \mathbb{C}[j]$
5:         $\mathbb{C}[i] := \{x\}$
6:     **end if**
7: **end for**
8: **repeat**
9:     **for** $i \in N$ **do**
10:         $\mathbb{C}[i] := LCS \left(C \setminus \bigcup\limits_{j \in Adj[i]} \mathbb{C}[j] \right)$
11:     **end for**
12: **until** No $\mathbb{C}[i]$ can be changed.
13: **return** $\mathbb{C}[i], i \in N$

3.2 Analysis

We prove the channel allocation strategy profile s^* determined by $\mathbb{C}[i], i \in N$, which is computed by Algorithm 1, is a NE.

Theorem 1. *The channel allocation strategy profile s^* computed by Algorithm 1 is a NE.*

Proof. Since conflicting access points can not share any channel, the throughput of each conflicting ones will be zero if they share some channels. Hence for any strategy profile s and any player i in N, $u_i(s) = 0$ if $\mathbb{C}[i] \cap \bigcup\limits_{j \in Adj[j]} \mathbb{C}[j] \neq \Phi$.

If for a node i, we choose another $\mathbb{C}'[i]$. Denote this new strategy by s_i. Let $s = (s_i, s^*_{-i})$. We distinguish two cases:

1. $\mathbb{C}'[i] \cap \bigcup\limits_{j \in Adj[j]} \mathbb{C}[j] \neq \Phi$. This happens when Player i collides with its neighbors.
   In this case, it is not able to utilize the channel, so $u_i(s) = 0 \leq u_i(s^*)$.
2. $\mathbb{C}'[i] \cap \bigcup\limits_{j \in Adj[j]} \mathbb{C}[j] = \Phi$. This means that Player i combines another set of channels.
   Let $D = C \setminus \bigcup\limits_{j \in Adj[i]} \mathbb{C}[j]$. On one hand, Algorithm 1 ensures $\mathbb{C}[i] = LCS(D)$.
   On the other hand, $\mathbb{C}'[i] \subseteq D$. So, $|LCS(\mathbb{C}'[i])| \leq |LCS(D)| = |\mathbb{C}[i]|$. Therefore $u_i(s) \leq u_i(s^*)$.

We can conclude that for any player i and for any strategy profile $s = (s_i, s^*_{-i})$,

$$u_i(s) \leq u_i(s^*).$$

The result computed by Algorithm 1 is a NE.   □

4   Design of AMPLE

NE is not an ideal solution concept. As we have mentioned, given a particular network topology, there may exist many NEs and the global performance might vary in a wide range in different NEs. Figure 2 illustrates an example of comparing two NEs.

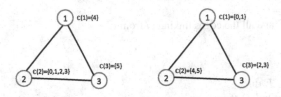

Fig. 2. An example of comparing two NEs. The right one gives a better global throughput than the left one, when there are 6 channels and 3 access points.

In this section, to cope with the weakness of NE, we propose our carefully designed incentive scheme AMPLE. AMPLE consists of two components. One is an approximate algorithm that gives an allocation with good system performance. To stimulate the access points to follow this allocation, the other part is a charging scheme to guarantee that following the computed channel allocation is the dominant strategy of each access point. Thus AMPLE guarantees the system to converge to a Dominant Strategy Equilibrium (DSE).

4.1   Channel Allocation

We now introduce our channel allocation algorithm. Our procedure can be divided into two phases. The first phase (Algorithm 2) converts the original conflict graph $G \triangleq (N, E)$ into a directed acyclic graph $\tilde{G} \triangleq (N, \tilde{E})$. Based on $\tilde{G}$, the second phase (Algorithm 3) specifies the channels allocated to each node.

Constructing $\tilde{G}$. In this phase, we convert G into a directed acyclic graph $\tilde{G} = (N, \tilde{E})$. The pseudo-code is listed in Algorithm 2.

Based on nodes' degrees, we divide N into several independent sets and give each node an order to represent which set it is in (Line 1-9). Let $Ord(i)$ represent the order of node i. The loop iteratively finds a node i of maximal degree, remove i and its edges. If i's degree is equal to that of last node j, indicating that i and j do not share an edge (or j is not with maximal degree), then let $Ord(i) := Ord(j)$. Otherwise, let $Ord(i) := Ord(j) + 1$. We record the maximal order as $\mathcal{O}$. Next we construct the directed acyclic graph $\tilde{G} = (N, \tilde{E})$ based on the nodes' orders (Line 10-17). For any edge (i, j) in E, if $Ord(i) < Ord(j)$ then we add $\langle j, i \rangle$ to $\tilde{E}$; otherwise we add $\langle i, j \rangle$ to $\tilde{E}$.

Algorithm 2. Converting the original conflict graph G into a directed acyclic graph $\tilde{G}$

Require: $G = (N, E)$
Ensure: $\tilde{G} = (N, \tilde{E}), \mathcal{O}, \{Ord(i)|i \in N\}$
1: $\mathcal{O} := 0$
2: **while** $G \neq \Phi$ **do**
3:    $\mathcal{O} := \mathcal{O} + 1$
4:    $d :=$ the degree of G
5:    **while** G contains a node ω of degree d **do**
6:        $Ord(\omega) = \mathcal{O}$
7:        Remove ω and all the edges linking ω from G
8:    **end while**
9: **end while**
10: $\tilde{E} := \Phi$
11: **for** $e := (i, j) \in E$ **do**
12:    **if** $Ord(i) < Ord(j)$ **then**
13:        $\tilde{E} := \tilde{E} \cup \{\langle j, i \rangle\}$
14:    **else**
15:        $\tilde{E} := \tilde{E} \cup \{\langle i, j \rangle\}$
16:    **end if**
17: **end for**
18: **return** $\tilde{G} = (N, \tilde{E}), \mathcal{O}, \{Ord(i)|i \in N\}$

Allocating Channels. We then show the details in Algorithm 3, which computes the channel allocation.

For any node $i \in N$, we define

$$prev(i) \triangleq \{s \in \tilde{N}|\langle s, i \rangle \in \tilde{E}\}. \tag{6}$$

We first initialize $\mathcal{L}(i)$ (Line 1-9). Here $\mathcal{L}(i)$ is a label which we subsequently use to identify its channels. We give each node a label as the minimal element in $N\backslash \bigcup_{j \in prev(i)} \{\mathcal{L}(j)\}$. In the loop, we record the maximal $\mathcal{L}(i)$ as $\mathscr{L}$ (Line 6).

In line 10-18, we give each node an original set of channels based on $\mathcal{L}(i)$. If $|C| < \mathscr{L} + 1$, we give each node that satisfies $\mathcal{L}(i) < |C|$ one channel (Line 12). Otherwise we give each node $\lfloor \mathcal{L}(i)|C|/(\mathscr{L} + 1) \rfloor$ channels (Line 16).

Similar to Algorithm 1, we then amend the allocation and try to broaden the nodes' channels (Line 19-23).

We show an example of the allocation algorithm in Figure 3.

Time Complexity. For Algorithm 2, constructing $\tilde{G}$ takes $O(|N||E|)$ time. In Algorithm 3, calculating $\mathcal{L}(i)$ takes $O(|N|)$ time; computing the original channels takes $O(|N|)$ time; in the worst situation, amending the channels takes $O(|N||C|)$ time. In sum the upper bound of the time complexity is $O(|N||E| + |N||C|)$.

4.2   Design of Charging Scheme

As we have mentioned, NE does not provide a perfect solution to the problem of adaptive width channel allocation. In this section, we propose a charging scheme to make the

---

Algorithm 3. Computing the allocation

Require: $C, \tilde{G} = (N, \tilde{E}), \mathcal{O}, \{Ord(i)|i \in N\}$
Ensure: $\{\mathbb{C}(i)|i \in N\}$
 1: $\mathcal{L} := 0$
 2: **for** $k := \mathcal{O}$ downto 1 **do**
 3:     **for** $i \in N$ s.t. $Ord(i) = k$ **do**

 4:         $\mathcal{L}(i) := \min \left\{ N\backslash \bigcup_{j \in prev(i)} \{\mathcal{L}(j)\} \right\}$

 5:         **if** $\mathcal{L}(i) > \mathcal{L}$ **then**
 6:             $\mathcal{L} := \mathcal{L}(i)$
 7:         **end if**
 8:     **end for**
 9: **end for**
10: **if** $|C| < \mathcal{L} + 1$ **then**
11:     **for** $i \in N$ s.t. $\mathcal{L}(i) < |C|$ **do**
12:         $\mathbb{C}(i) := \{\mathcal{L}(i)\}$
13:     **end for**
14: **else**
15:     **for** $i \in N$ **do**
16:         $\mathbb{C}(i) := \{\lfloor \frac{\mathcal{L}(i)|C|}{\mathcal{L}+1} \rfloor, \ldots, \lfloor \frac{(\mathcal{L}(i)+1)|C|}{\mathcal{L}+1} \rfloor - 1\}$
17:     **end for**
18: **end if**
19: **repeat**
20:     **for** $i := 0$ to $n - 1$ **do**
21:         $\mathbb{C}[i] := LCS(C\backslash \bigcup_{j \in Adj[i]} \mathbb{C}[j])$

22:     **end for**
23: **until** No $\mathbb{C}[i]$ is changed.
24: **return** $\{\mathbb{C}(i)|i \in N\}$

---

system converge to an equilibrium state, called Dominant Strategy Equilibrium (DSE). This scheme is proposed for two objectives:

1. The charging scheme surely triggers the system's convergence to a DSE, which is a stable state that all the players follows the allocation proposed computed by AMPLE.
2. The charge should be rational and as little as possible. This is because a big or even tremendous charge or punishment would lead no player join the scheme. Exactly as a forfeit of one million dollars for a small mistake like not handling the homework on time is not adopted in real life. An unreasonable charge scheme would strip the significance of the scheme.

Donate the strategy profile determined in Algorithm 3 by s^*. We next introduce a charging formula, which is a virtual currency [8, 20, 26–28] to incentive the players' behaviors.

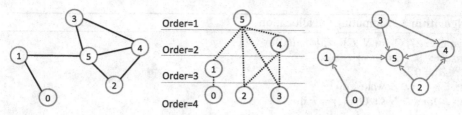

(a) The original conflict graph (b) Divide the nodes into 4 (c) Construct $\tilde{G} = (N, \tilde{E})$.
$G = (N, E)$.   independent sets. Here dotted This step constructs the di-
                                  lines are the edges in E. (Line rected edges from nodes
                                  1-9 in Algorithm 2)   in higher order to nodes in
                                                                lower order (Line 10-17 in
                                                                Algorithm 2)

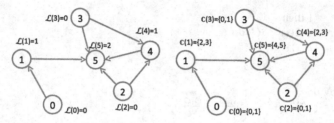

(d) Calculate $\mathcal{L}(i)$ to each node. (e) Calculate $\mathbb{C}(i)$ to each node
(Line 1-9 in Algorithm 3)   (Line 10-23 in Algorithm 3).

Fig. 3. An example of the allocation algorithm for 6 access points and 6 channels. ($N = \{0, 1, 2, 3, 4, 5\}, C = \{0, 1, 2, 3, 4, 5\}$)

Definition 4 (Charging formula). *For any player i and any strategy profile $s = (s_i, s_{-i})$, the charge of player i is*

$$\mathcal{P}_i(s) \triangleq \alpha \left(T_i(s_i^*, s_{-i})/2 + Th(|s_i^* \backslash s_i|) + A \right), \tag{7}$$

where

$$A = \frac{|s_i \backslash s_i^*| Th^2(|s_i|)}{4(T_i(s_i^*, s_{-i}) + Th(|s_i^* \backslash s_i|))}. \tag{8}$$

For $\mathcal{P}_i(s)$, the first term $T_i(s_i^*, s_{-i})/2$ is an essential part of charge. The second term $Th(|s_i^* \backslash s_i|)$ and the third term A together forms an external part of charge. This external part treats as a punishment, an additional charge. When the player obeys s_i^*, this part is zero, which means no penalty is imposed. However, when it does not obey s_i^* and behave s_i, this part varies and increase higher than the additional utility obtained by s_i.

Then, we prove the strategy profile s^* is a DSE.

Theorem 2. *The channel allocation strategy profile s^* computed by Algorithm 3 is a DSE under the charging scheme.*

Proof. For any profile $s = (s_i, s_{-i})$, the utility of player i, $u_i(s_i, s_{-i})$ is

$$u_i(s_i, s_{-i}) = \alpha(T_i(s_i, s_{-i}) - \mathcal{P}_i(s)). \tag{9}$$

If i chooses s_i^* as its strategy,

$$u_i(s_i^*, s_{-i}) = \alpha\left(T_i(s_i^*, s_{-i})/2\right). \tag{10}$$

Omitting the coefficient α,

$$
\begin{aligned}
&1/\alpha(u_i(s_i^*, s_{-i}) - u_i(s_i, s_{-i})) \\
=& T_i(s_i^*, s_{-i}) - T_i(s_i, s_{-i}) + Th(|s_i^* \backslash s_i|) + A \\
=& T_i(s_i^*, s_{-i}) - T_i(s_i, s_{-i}) + Th(|s_i^* \backslash s_i|) + \frac{|s_i \backslash s_i^*| Th^2(|s_i|)}{4(T_i(s_i^*, s_{-i}) + Th(|s_i^* \backslash s_i|))} \\
\geq& -T_i(s_i, s_{-i}) + 2\sqrt{\frac{(T_i(s_i^*, s_{-i}) + Th(|s_i^* \backslash s_i|))Th^2(|s_i|)}{4(T_i(s_i^*, s_{-i}) + Th(|s_i^* \backslash s_i|))}} \\
=& -T_i(s_i, s_{-i}) + Th(|s_i|) \\
\geq& 0,
\end{aligned}
\tag{11}
$$

we have

$$u_i(s_i^*, s_{-i}) \geq u_i(s_i, s_{-i}). \tag{12}$$

Therefore we conclude that s^* is DSE.   □

5   Numerical Results

We implement AMPLE and evaluate its performance using network simulations. The objective of our simulations is twofold. One is to test the performance of our channel allocation algorithm's outputs, which is the system-wide throughput. Since no proper existing works are comparable to our system, this evaluation compares the system-wide throughput achieved by anarchical NE and AMPLE's DSE. The other one is to verify that the system indeed converge to the DSE when AMPLE is used.

5.1   Simulation Methodology

In the simulation experiments, we use a basic CSMA/CA protocol with binary slotted exponential back-off as the MAC layer protocol. Following [22], the parameters used for the experiments are listed in Table 1.

Metrics: We evaluate two quantitative values as metrics in this paper:

1. Utility: Utility is the difference between the player's valuation on throughput and charge for using the channels. This metric reflects the impacts of a player's behavior on its own.
2. System-wide throughput: It is the sum of all the players' throughputs. This metric is used to measure the effectiveness of our design on the performance of the channel allocation game.

Table 1. Parameters used to obtain numerical results

Packet Payload	1450 bytes
PHY&MAC Header	50 bytes
ACK Packet Size	30 bytes
Minimum Contention Window	32
Number of Backoff Stages	5
Original Channel Bit Rate	1 Mbps
Propagation Delay	1 μs
Slot Time	50 μs
SIFS	28 μs
DIFS	128 μs
ACK Timeout	300 μs

5.2   Performance

In this set of simulations, we evaluate the system-wide throughput of AMPLE and an-archical NE.

In the first simulation, we assume there are 20 access points and 12 channels. We set the degree of each point ranges from 3 to 5 and obeys a binomial distribution ($\sim Bin(20, 0.2)$), in which the average degree is 4. The first simulation is repeated 10^4 times. In each run, we generate a conflict graph, execute and record the system-wide throughputs of AMPLE and anarchical NE. Due to the limitation of space, we show the results of the first 50 runs in Figure 4. From Figure 4, we can observe that AMPLE gives relatively higher throughput than anarchical NE. Although anarchical NE gets higher throughput some times (almost twice every 25 runs), the average system-wide throughput of AMPLE is better than that of the anarchical NE. From this evaluation, the average ratio of the system-wide throughputs between AMPLE and anarchical NE is 1.1457, showing that AMPLE achieves an average of 15% higher throughput than that of anarchical NE.

In the second evaluation, we fix the number of access points at 20, and vary the number of channels among 3, 6, 8, and 12. Other settings are the same as the first evaluation. In this evaluation, we repeat each simulation until the convergence level 10^{-4} is reached.

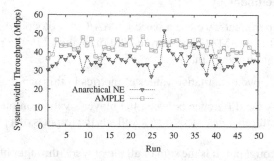

Fig. 4. The result of the first 50 runs of the simulation measuring the system-wide throughputs of AMPLE and anarchical NE. In each run, there are 20 access points and 12 channels.

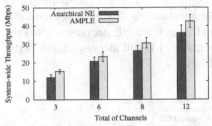

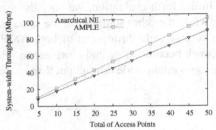

(a) The results of system-wide throughput achieved by AMPLE and anarchical NE when there are 3, 6, 8, and 12 channels and 20 access points. The height of the bar show the average throughput, and the error-bar shows the standard deviation of the measured results.

(b) The results of system-wide throughput achieved by AMPLE and anarchical NE when the total of access points varies from 5 to 50. The number of channels is 12.

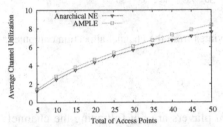

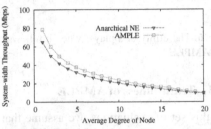

(c) The results of channel utilization achieved by AMPLE and anarchical NE when the total of access points varies from 5 to 50. The number of channels is 12.

(d) The results of system-wide throughput achieved by AMPLE and anarchical NE when node degree varies from 1 to 20.

Fig. 5. Experiment results for the first to the forth evaluations

Figure 5(a) illustrates the results. We can see that AMPLE always achieves higher system-wide throughput than anarchical NE does. At the same time, the standard deviations of AMPLE's results are also relatively smaller, which shows that the performance of AMPLE is more stable.

In the third evaluation, we vary the number of access points, while fixing the number of channels at 12. We simulate the number of access points from 5 to 50. Other settings are the same as the first simulation. In this evaluation, we also repeat each simulation until the convergence level 10^{-4} is reached.

Figure 5(b) shows that both the system-wide throughput of AMPLE and anarchical NE increase with the number of access points. However, AMPLE's throughput is larger than that of anarchical NE, and the gap between AMPLE and anarchical NE grows with the number of nodes.

We also record the average utilization of a channel in the third evaluation. Here, channel utilization means the average number of access points allocated to each channel. Figure 5(c) shows that the channel utilization of AMPLE is always higher than that of anarchical NE.

In the forth evaluation, we vary the average degree of the access points from 1 to 20, while the other settings are the same as the first simulation. Figure 5(d) shows that the system-wide throughput of both AMPLE and anarchical NE decreases when the network become more and more denser. However, AMPLE still always achieve better average system-wide throughput than anarchical NE.

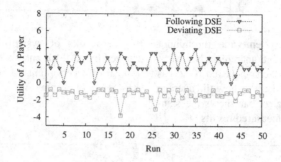

Fig. 6. The utility of a player when it follows or deviates from the channel allocation computed by AMPLE

5.3 Truthfulness of AMPLE

In this set of evaluations, we assume that 20% players are not following the channel allocation computed by AMPLE. We assume there are 12 channels, 20 players, and the average degree of the access points is 4. In each run, we randomly pick 4 misbehaving access points and let them deviate from the channel allocation computed by AMPLE. Then we record the utility got by a fifth access point in 50 runs.

Figure 6 shows that the utility of a player when it follows or deviates from the channel allocation computed by AMPLE. We can observe that following the computed channel allocation is always no worse than that of deviating from it. Besides, the utility when following the scheme is always positive while the utility when deviating it is usually negative. So when AMPLE is used, the incentives for following the computed channel allocation is always guaranteed, no matter what the other players do. This result verifies that players cannot benefit by deviating from the channel allocation computed by AMPLE, when our charging scheme is used. Therefore, the convergence to the DSE is guaranteed on our charging scheme.

6 Related Work

In this section, we review the related work in this field. Felegyhazi et al. [9] first proposed a game model for the static multi-radio multi-channel allocation. Wu et al. [24] later put forward a mechanism to converge the multi-radio multi-channel allocation game to the strongly dominant strategy equilibrium (SDSE). They both only considered the problem in a single collision domain which is different from the scenario we consider in this paper. Recently, a number of strategy-proof auction-based spectrum allocation mechanisms (*e.g.*, TRUST [30], SMALL [23], and VERITAS [29]) have been proposed to solve the problem in multiple collision domain. An important relevant work on channel allocation game is [12], in which the authors modeled it as a graph coloring problem and discussed the price of anarchical state under various topology conditions. However, none the the above work considers adaptive-width channels. A latest work by Wu et al. [22] discussed the allocation in adaptive-width channels. However, it is only valid in a single collision domain as well.

In wireless networks, the game theory is also applied to study problems such as media access. For example, MacKenzie et al. [14] studied the behaviors of selfish nodes in Aloha networks. Later, Cagalj et al. [5] and Konorski [13] utilized game-theoretic approaches to investigate the media access problem of selfish behavior in CSMA/CA networks. Nie and Comaniciu [16] proposed a game theoretic framework to study the behavior of cognitive radios for distributed adaptive spectrum allocation in cognitive radio networks. Some other relevant works on incentive-compatibility in wireless networks are [2, 3, 7, 8, 19–21, 25–28].

7 Conclusion and Future Work

In this paper, we proposed an approach for adaptive-width channel allocation in multi-hop, non-cooperative wireless networks. We first gave an algorithm to compute an efficient channel allocation, and then presented a charging scheme to guarantee that it is to the best interest of each player to follow the computed channel allocation. Evaluation results showed that our approach achieved good performance. As for future work, there can be several potential directions. One of the possible direction is to consider the case, in which the access points can be carefully to partially overlapping channels.

References

1. Second rep. and order and memorandum opinion and order, http://hraunfoss.fcc.gov/edocs_public/attachmatch/FCC-08-260A1.pdf
2. Anderegg, L., Eidenbenz, S.: Ad hoc-VCG: a truthful and cost-efficient routing protocol for mobile ad hoc networks with selfish agents. In: Proceedings of the Ninth International Conference on Mobile Computing and Networking (MobiCom), San Diego, CA (September 2003)
3. Ben Salem, N., Buttyan, L., Hubaux, J.P., Jakobsson, M.: A charging and rewarding scheme for packet forwarding in multi-hop cellular networks. In: Proceedings of the Fourth ACM Symposium on Mobile Ad Hoc Networking and Computing (MobiHoc), Annapolis, MD (June 2003)
4. Bianchi, G.: Performance analysis of the IEEE 802.11 distributed coordination function. IEEE Journal on Selected Areas in Communications 18(3), 535–547 (2000)
5. Čagalj, M., Ganeriwal, S., Aad, I., Hubaux, J.-P.: On selfish behavior in CSMA/CA networks. In: Proceedings of 24th Annual IEEE Conference on Computer Communications (INFOCOM), Miami, FL (April 2005)
6. Chandra, R., Mahajan, R., Moscibroda, T., Raghavendra, R., Bahl, P.: A case for adapting channel width in wireless networks. In: Proceedings of ACM SIGCOMM 2008 Conference on Applications, Technologies, Architectures, and Protocols for Computer Communications, Seattle, USA (August 2008)

7. Deek, L.B., Zhou, X., Almeroth, K.C., Zheng, H.: To preempt or not: Tackling bid and time-based cheating in online spectrum auctions. In: INFOCOM, pp. 2219–2227 (2011)
8. Eidenbenz, S., Resta, G., Santi, P.: Commit: A sender-centric truthful and energy-efficient routing protocol for ad hoc networks with selfish nodes. In: Proceedings of the 19th International Parallel and Distributed Processing Symposium (IPDPS), Denver, CO (April 2005)
9. Félegyházi, M., Čagalj, M., Bidokhti, S.S., Hubaux, J.-P.: Non-cooperative multi-radio channel allocation in wireless networks. In: Proceedings of 26th Annual IEEE Conference on Computer Communications (INFOCOM), Anchorage, AK (May 2007)
10. Fudenberg, D., Tirole, J.: Game Theory. MIT Press (1991)
11. Gummadi, R., Balakrishnan, H.: Wireless networks should spread spectrum based on demands. In: Proceedings of ACM Hotnets, Calgary, Canada (October 2008)
12. Halldórsson, M.M., Halpern, J.Y., Li, L.E., Mirrokni, V.S.: On spectrum sharing games. In: Proceedings of the 23rd Annual ACM SIGACT-SIGOPS Symposium on Principles of Distributed Computing (PODC), St. John's, Canada (July 2004)
13. Konorski, J.: Multiple Access in Ad-Hoc Wireless LANs with Noncooperative Stations. In: Gregori, E., Conti, M., Campbell, A.T., Omidyar, G., Zukerman, M. (eds.) NETWORKING 2002. LNCS, vol. 2345, pp. 1141–1146. Springer, Heidelberg (2002)
14. MacKenzie, A.B., Wicker, S.B.: Stability of multipacket slotted Aloha with selfish users and perfect information
15. Moscibroda, T., Chandra, R., Wu, Y., Sengupta, S., Bahl, P., Yuan, Y.: Load-aware spectrum distribution in wireless lans. In: Proceedings of the 16th International Conference on Network Protocols (ICNP) (October 2008)
16. Nie, N., Comaniciu, C.: Adaptive channel allocation spectrum etiquette for cognitive radio networks. In: Proceedings of the First IEEE International Symposium on New Frontiers in Dynamic Spectrum Access Networks (DySPAN), Baltimore Harbor, MD (November 2005)
17. Osborne, M.J., Rubenstein, A.: A Course in Game Theory. MIT Press (1994)
18. Rahul, H., Edalat, F., Sodini, D.K.C.: Frequency-aware rate adaptation and mac protocols. In: Proceedings of The Fourteenth International Conference on Mobile Computing and Networking (MobiCom), San Francisco, CA (September 2009)
19. Srinivasan, V., Nuggehalli, P., Chiasserini, C.-F., Rao, R.: Cooperation in wireless ad hoc networks
20. Wang, W., Eidenbez, S., Wang, Y., Li, X.-Y.: Ours–optimal unicast routing systems in non-cooperative wireless networks. In: Proceedings of The Twelfth International Conference on Mobile Computing and Networking (MobiCom), Los Angeles (September 2006)
21. Wang, W., Li, X.-Y., Wang, Y.: Truthful multicast in selfish wireless networks. In: Proceedings of the Tenth International Conference on Mobile Computing and Networking (MobiCom), Philadelphia, PA (September 2004)
22. Wu, F., Singh, N., Vaidya, N., Chen, G.: On adaptive-width channel allocation in non-cooperative, multi-radio wireless networks. In: Proceedings of 30th Annual IEEE Conference on Computer Communications (INFOCOM), Shanghai, China (April 2011)
23. Wu, F., Vaidya, N.: Small: A strategy-proof mechanism for radio spectrum allocation. University of Illinois at Urbana-Champaign, Tech. Rep. (2010)
24. Wu, F., Zhong, S., Qiao, C.: Globally optimal channel assignment for non-cooperative wireless networks. In: Proceedings of 27th Annual IEEE Conference on Computer Communications (INFOCOM), Phoenix, AZ (April 2008)
25. Xu, P., Xu, X., Tang, S., Li, X.-Y.: Truthful online spectrum allocation and auction in multi-channel wireless networks. In: INFOCOM, pp. 26–30 (2011)

26. Zhong, S., Li, L.E., Liu, Y.G., Yang, Y.R.: On designing incentive-compatible routing and forwarding protocols in wireless ad-hoc networks–an integrated approach using game theoretical and cryptographic techniques. In: Proceedings of The Eleventh International Conference on Mobile Computing and Networking (MobiCom), Cologne, Germany (September 2005)
27. Zhong, S., Chen, J., Yang, Y.R.: Sprite, a simple, cheat-proof, credit-based system for mobile ad-hoc networks
28. Zhong, S., Wu, F.: On designing collusion-resistant routing schemes for non-cooperative wireless ad hoc networks. In: Proceedings of The Thirteenth International Conference on Mobile Computing and Networking (MobiCom), Montreal, Canada (September 2007)
29. Zhou, X., Gandhi, S., Suri, S., Zheng, H.: ebay in the sky: Strategy-proof wireless spectrum auctions. In: Proceedings of The Fourteenth International Conference on Mobile Computing and Networking (MobiCom), San Francisco, CA (September 2008)
30. Zhou, X., Zheng, H.: Trust: A general framework for truthful double spectrum auctions. In: Proceedings of 28th Annual IEEE Conference on Computer Communications (INFOCOM), Rio de Janeiro, Brazil (April 2009)

Characterizing Home Network Traffic: An Inside View

Kuai Xu[1], Feng Wang[1], Lin Gu[2], Jianhua Gao[3], and Yaohui Jin[4,5]

[1] Arizona State University
[2] Hong Kong University of Science and Technology
[3] Wuhan University
[4] Shanghai Jiaotong University
[5] State Key Laboratory of Advanced Optical Communication Systems and Networks

Abstract. The rapid spread of residential broadband connections and Internet-capable consumer devices in home networks has changed the landscape of Internet traffic. To gain a deep understanding of Internet traffic for home networks, this paper develops a traffic monitoring platform that collects and analyzes home network traffic via programmable home routers and traffic profiling servers. Using traffic data captured from real home networks, we present traffic characteristics in home networks, and then apply principal component analysis to uncover temporal correlations among application ports. To the best of our knowledge, this paper is the first study to characterize network traffic of Internet-capable devices from inside home networks.

1 Introduction

In recent years, the rapid growth of Internet-capable devices in the home and residential broadband access has driven the rising adoptions of home networks. The availability of home networks not only creates new application opportunities such as remote health care and Internet television, but also changes the distribution of Internet traffic, e.g., a recent study shows that video streaming via Netflix accounts for 32.7% of peak downstream traffic in United States [1]. As home networks become an important part of the Internet ecosystem, it is very crucial to understand network traffic between the Internet and home networks as well as the traffic exchanged within home devices.

Most home users lack technical expertise to manage the increasingly complicated home networks, and an extensive body of research have focused on how to simplify network management tasks for home users [2–6]. Several recent studies have been devoted to understanding traffic characteristics of home networks using aggregated and sampled traffic collected from edge routers in Internet service providers [7–9]. However, these measurement studies stand from the perspective of outside home networks, thus lack the visibility of *what is happening in home networks*. The in-depth understanding of home network traffic could aid home users in effectively securing and managing home networks.

X. Wang et al. (Eds.): WASA 2012, LNCS 7405, pp. 60–71, 2012.

In this paper we focus on understanding traffic characteristics in home networks. Towards this end, we first develop a traffic monitoring platform that collects network flow streams via traffic profiling servers and programmable home routers that connect home networks and the Internet via home gateways such as DSL or cable modems. Using traffic data collected from real home networks, we analyze traffic patterns of connected devices in home networks, and characterize the volume, behavior and temporal features of home network traffic.

Our findings on temporal characteristics of application ports lead us to explore principal component analysis (PCA) to uncover temporal correlations among these ports. The experiment results show that there indeed exist several application port clusters in home networks with each cluster exhibiting distinct traffic patterns. For example, one cluster consists of major canonical applications including 80/TCP (HTTP), 443/TCP (HTTPS), 53/UDP (DNS), while another cluster contains a group of unknown ports with all traffic sent to temporary servers running on Amazon Elastic Compute Cloud (Amazon EC2). Closer examinations reveal that all the traffic in the latter cluster are associated with suspicious activities.

The contributions of this paper are two-fold. First, we develop a traffic monitoring platform that automatically collects, analyzes and makes sense of network traffic for Internet-capable devices in home networks. Secondly, we present traffic characteristics of home networks, and apply principal component analysis to uncover temporal correlations among application ports. To the best of our knowledge, this paper is the first study to characterize traffic patterns of Internet-capable home devices from the inside perspective.

The remainder of this paper is organized as follows. Section 2 describes the traffic monitoring platform we developed for home networks, while Section 3 presents the basic characteristics of home network traffic, and applies principal component analysis to uncover temporal correlations of application ports in home network traffic. Section 4 discusses related work, and Section 5 concludes this paper and outlines the future work.

2   Traffic Monitoring Platform for Home Networks

To understand what is happening in home networks, we develop a real-time behavior monitoring platform to collect and analyze network traffic for Internet-capable devices in the home [10]. The monitoring platform captures network traffic via programmable home routers, which connect home networks with the Internet through home gateways such as cable or DSL modems. Using a Linux distribution for embedded devices, OpenWrt [11], we configure a programmable home router and export network flows traversing through all the interfaces of the router to a traffic profiling server running in the same home network. The continuous network flows, aggregated from IP packets, contain a number of important features for our traffic analysis including the start and end time-stamps, source IP address (srcIP), destination IP address (dstIP), source port number (srcPort), destination port number (dstPort), and protocol, packets and bytes.

Many host-based monitoring systems are also able to collect these traffic flows on individual devices, e.g., Windows and Linux machines, however such host-based approaches are very difficult to deploy across all the possible devices due to the high heterogeneity of Internet-capable devices in the home.

Compared with incoming and outgoing traffic of home networks, the overhead of transferring flow data from programmable home routers to traffic profiling servers is not significant. Figure 1 shows the overhead of collecting traffic data from programmable home routers (top figure), the bandwidth usages of outgoing traffic (middle figure) and incoming traffic (bottom figure) of one home network that deploys the platform. As shown in the top figure, the network flow data exported by home routers consumes less than 4Kbps bandwidth, which is much smaller than outgoing and incoming traffic illustrated in the middle and bottom graphs. In general, the network bandwidth usage of incoming traffic towards home networks is larger than that of outgoing traffic, as most of Internet activities in these home networks are Web browsing, email communications, and video streaming.

The availability of the traffic monitoring platform makes it possible for us to analyze data traffic exchanged between home devices and Internet end hosts, as well as data traffic exchanged among home network devices. Making sense of these traffic could not only assist home users in understanding *what is happening in home networks*, but also help detect anomalous traffic towards home networks or originating from compromised home devices. In the next section, we will use traffic data collected from real home networks that deploy the traffic monitoring platform to characterize network traffic of Internet-capable home devices from a

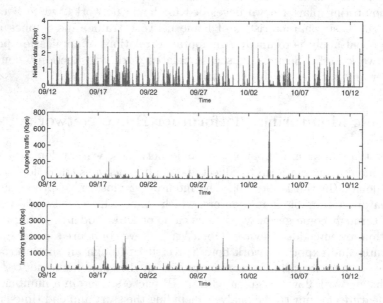

Fig. 1. Bandwidth usage of data collection (top figure), outgoing traffic (middle figure) and incoming traffic (bottom figure) of home networks

variety of traffic information including *volume features* measured by the numbers of flows, packets and bytes, *social features* through analyzing IP addresses and application ports, and *temporal dynamics* of these traffic. Each of these traffic features captures the behavior of home devices from a unique perspective. Combined together, they provide a broad picture of home network traffic, and more importantly, reveal interesting traffic activities in home networks.

3   Characterizing Home Network Traffic

In this section, we first describe data-sets used in this study and present the general characteristics of home network traffic. Subsequently, we explore principal component analysis to analyze temporal correlations among application ports for uncovering clusters of application ports sharing significant temporal patterns in network traffic.

3.1   Datasets

The traffic data used in this study is collected from two home networks (home network A and home network B) that deploy our traffic monitoring platform during one-month time span from 09/12/2011 to 10/12/2011. The numbers of total devices in home networks A and B are 6 and 3, respectively. Figure 2 shows the number of *online* devices in home network A over time. As illustrated in Figure 2, the number of *online* devices in home network A observed during 5-min time bins varies from 0 to 6, reflecting Internet usage patterns of these devices during this one-month time period. Note that the number of home devices remaining above 1 between 09/12 and 09/28 is due to a probing program continuously running on one home device to measure end-to-end performance to

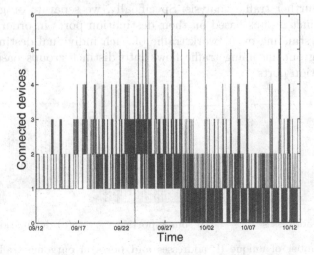

Fig. 2. The number of *online* devices in the home network A over time

a number of distributed servers. These devices collectively have communicated with over 4,800 unique end hosts on the Internet from 529 different autonomous systems (ASes) during this period. Similarly, the devices in home network B collectively communicate with over 4,400 end hosts from 726 ASes.

3.2   Traffic Characteristics

We study the traffic characteristics of home networks by firstly examining IP addresses and application ports over time, since they reflect *whom do home devices communicate with* and *what applications do home devices use.* Figures 3[a-c] illustrate the numbers of unique destination IP addresses, unique source ports and unique destination ports for the outgoing traffic during 5-min time bins over time, respectively.

Our first interesting observation lies in the large number of unique destination IP addresses during 5-min time bins, as shown in Figure 3[a]. Closer examination revealed that a single visit to a major content-rich Web portal could trigger tens of TCP connections to different Web servers, and the large number of destination IP addresses actually correspond to legitimate Web servers visited by home users. For example, our empirical experiment of visiting the front page of www.cnn.com with a Firefox browser finds that loading the entire page requires the browser to talk with 18 different IP addresses from a variety of Internet service and content providers including Facebook (social network site), Google (search engine), Limelight Networks (content deliver network), Rackspace Hosting (cloud service provider), Valueclick (online advertising), and cnn itself.

The second observation from Figure 3 is that the number of unique destination ports for outgoing traffic in home networks is far less than that of unique source ports. The small number of destination ports in outgoing traffic provides a simple and natural classification on home network traffic, thus we follow a port-driven approach for further traffic analysis. Specifically, we separate outgoing traffic flows into distinct groups based on their destination ports in order to gain an in-depth understanding on network traffic of each individual destination port. Similarly, we group incoming traffic flows into distinct groups based on their source destination ports.

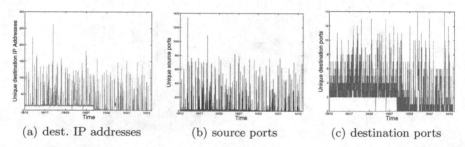

(a) dest. IP addresses   (b) source ports   (c) destination ports

Fig. 3. The number of unique IP addresses and ports in outgoing traffic for home network A over time

Figures 4[a][b] illustrate the temporal frequency of all destination ports for home network A and B during one-month time period, respectively. It is interesting to find three types of temporal patterns among these ports. The first type of destination ports are consistently observed during all days. For example, port 80/TCP is observed in all days during the one-month period in both networks. The second type of ports are observed during several days, while the last type includes ports that are only observed in one or two days suggesting these infrequent ports might be associated with unusual or anomalous traffic. Similar observations hold for the source ports in the incoming traffic towards home networks. More interestingly, Figures 4[a][b] also reveal temporal correlations among groups of applications ports that consistently show up around approximately the same times. This observation motivates us to explore correlation analysis techniques to understand the reasons behind such temporal correlations.

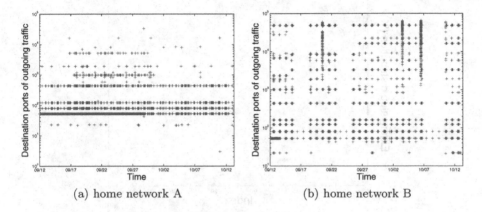

(a) home network A   (b) home network B

Fig. 4. Time-series observations of destination ports in outgoing traffic

3.3   Temporal Correlation Analysis of Application Ports

To explore temporal correlation among application ports in home networks, we propose to use principal component analysis (PCA) to analyze traffic patterns of network applications. PCA is a widely used technique in network traffic analysis [12, 13] due to its ability of analyzing multivariate data and locating interrelated variables [14].

Let p and t denote the total number of ports observed in the data and the total number of time bins. Our initial step is to construct a $p \times t$ matrix X, where $x_{i,j}$ denotes the total number of network flows for the destination port i ($i = 1, 2, \ldots, p$) in the outgoing traffic (or the source port i in the incoming traffic) during the j-th ($j = 1, 2, \ldots, t$) time period. The vector x_i^T reflects a time-series of observations for the application port i. Next we obtain the covariance matrix S, p non-decreasing ordered eigenvalues, $\lambda_1, \lambda_2, \ldots, \lambda_p$, and the corresponding eigenvectors $\alpha_1, \alpha_2, \ldots, \alpha_p$, where where s_{ab} is the covariance of two application ports a and b, and $S\alpha_i = \lambda_i \alpha_i$, for $1 \le i \le p$.

The p principal components of the matrix X can be derived by projecting the matrix onto the p eigenvectors, i.e., $PC_i = \alpha_i^T X$, $i = 1, 2, \ldots, p$. As $var(PC_i) = var(\alpha_i^T X) = \alpha_i^T X \cdot X^T \alpha_i = \alpha_i^T S\alpha_i = \lambda\alpha_i^T \alpha_i = \lambda_i$, the variance captured by the i-th principal component is essentially the i-th eigenvalue λ_i.

PCA transforms the space of the p observed variables in the original matrix X into a new space of p principal components $\{PC_i\}$, $i = 1, 2, \ldots, p$. Figure 5 shows the distribution of the eigenvalues using the matrix constructed with the one-month traffic data from home network A. As shown in Figure 5, a few largest eigenvalues account for the majority of the variance in the original matrix, suggesting that the corresponding top principal components capture most variances.

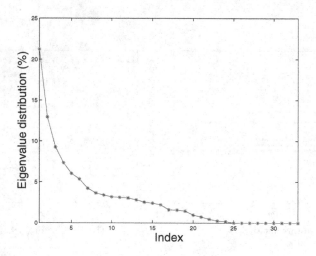

Fig. 5. Eigenvalue distribution of the matrix constructed with the one-month traffic data for home network A

Thus, the final step of the PCA process is to project the original data-set onto a subspace with a smaller dimensionality to get approximate representations while retaining the majority of the variance in the original data-set. Specifically, we require that the largest m eigenvalues that are larger than a fixed threshold such that each selected principal component captures a non-trivial variance in the original data-sets. In the experiment, we use 5% of the total variances as the threshold for determining the value of m.

The principal component PC_i can also be represented as: $PC_i = \alpha_i^T X = [\alpha_{i1}x_1 + \ldots + \alpha_{ip}x_p]^T = [\sum_{j=1}^{p} \alpha_{ij}x_j]^T$, where α_{ij}, $j = 1, \ldots, p$, is the coefficient of x_j for PC_i. The coefficient value α_{ij} reflects the contribution or influence of the application port j to the variance obtained by the i-th component. Such relationship between principal components and observed variables leads to the discovery of a cluster of application ports that contribute similar influence towards the same principal components because of the inherent temporal correlations among these ports. As a result, we group the application ports that contribute similar high influence towards the variance of each of the top principal components into a distinct `srcPort` cluster for incoming traffic (or a `dstPort` cluster for outgoing traffic). In other words, PCA discovers the clusters of application ports that exhibit significant correlations in the temporal traffic patterns.

Table 1 lists the membership of the 6 `dstPort` clusters discovered via the principal component analysis using one-month traffic data collected in home network A. $Cluster_1$ includes port 43/TCP and consecutive ports 33435-33440/UDP. The in-depth analysis shows that the flows associated with 43/TCP are legitimate *whois* traffic towards *Team Cymru IP to AS mapping service*, while all traffic associated with ports 33435-33440/UDP were sent towards an unknown server and failed to get response from the server. The legitimate traffic on port 43/TCP and suspicious traffic on 33435-33440/UDP were observed during the same time window, which explain these seven ports to be grouped as a single `dstPort` cluster. Although $Cluster_1$ includes a service port 43/TCP, the majority of ports, 33435-33440/UDP, does reflect anomalous traffic activity from one home network device. $Cluster_2$ includes four canonical ports (i.e., DNS, HTTP, HTTPS, and NTP), which are used by home network devices on a daily basis and thus naturally form a `dstPort` cluster.

$Cluster_3$ includes three consecutive ports 16384-16386/UDP, which was sent by the FaceTime video calling application on an iPhone device. This cluster indicates that many user-installed applications or vendor-installed applications could use non-traditional ports for data communications with end hosts on the Internet. Such practices make it more challenging to differentiate anomalous or legitimate traffic on unusual ports. $Cluster_4$ includes three ports, i.e., 843/TCP, 1200-1201/TCP. Closer examinations reveal that a Windows laptop communicated with seven different instances in Amazon EC2 Cloud on these three ports *simultaneously* during 9 different days over the first two weeks. As home users are not aware of any application involving these ports and servers, these traffic is likely sent by a malware on the compromised laptop. $Cluster_5$ includes two ports 1863/TCP and 7001/UDP used by Windows MSN messenger, while $Cluster_6$ includes two ports 993/TCP and 5223/TCP, which are used by GMail and Apple Push Notification service running on the iPhone device that connects to the home network over Wi-Fi.

These experiment results with real home network traffic confirm that there indeed exist a variety of `dstPort` clusters that group applications ports with strong temporal correlations. Some of these clusters, e.g., $Cluster_1$ and $Cluster_4$ in Table 1, even lead to surprising findings on suspicious network traffic originating from home network devices that might be compromised by Internet malwares. Therefore, characterizing network traffic for Internet-capable devices in the home could not only provide valuable insight on behavior patterns of these connected devices, but also help improve the security and management of home networks.

Table 1. dstPort clusters discovered via PCA on temporal correlation

dstPort Cluster	Port Number	Application	User-aware
1	43/TCP	whois	Yes
	33435/UDP	unknown	No
	33436/UDP	unknown	No
	33437/UDP	unknown	No
	33438/UDP	unknown	No
	33439/UDP	unknown	No
	33440/UDP	unknown	No
2	53/UDP	DNS	Yes
	80/TCP	Web/HTTP	Yes
	123/UDP	NTP	Yes
	443/TCP	Web/HTTPS	Yes
3	16384/UDP	FaceTime	Yes
	16384/UDP	FaceTime	Yes
	16386/UDP	FaceTime	Yes
4	843/TCP	unknown	No
	1200/TCP	unknown	No
	1201/TCP	unknown	No
5	1863/TCP	MSN	Yes
	7001/UDP	MSN	Yes
6	993/TCP	IMAP over SSL	Yes
	5223/TCP	AppPush Notification Service	Yes

4 Related Work

Unlike enterprise networks which have dedicated network professionals to manage and operate the networks, securing home networks has been a considerable challenge, as most home users do not have sufficient technical expertise and knowledge to manage and secure the networks [15]. As a result, connected devices in home networks are targets and victims of virus, worms, and botnets, and become a major source of spams and a part of botnets. In [16], Feamster proposes to outsource the management and operations of home networks to a third party that has expertise of network operations and security management. In [17], Yang et al. study network management tools that are currently deployed in home networks via interviewing 25 home networks users, and report user experiences of these network management tools. To aid in troubleshooting and managing home networks, [18] proposes to build a home network data recorder system as a general-purpose logging platform to record what is happening in home networks. Many researches have also focused human computer interactions in home networks [2–4], troubleshooting and diagnosis [5, 6], and broadband network sharing among different Internet service providers [19].

Home network performance has recently drawn significant attentions from the research community. A recent work [20] performs controlled experiments in a lab environment for evaluating the impact of home networks on end-to-end performance of end systems. In addition, several commercial or open source tools have been developed for measuring and diagnosing Internet properties of end users. For example, Netalyze [21], a network measurement and diagnosis service, tests a wide variety of functionalities at network, transport and application layers for end users' Internet connectivity in edge networks such as home networks. Kermit, a network probing tool, was developed in [22] to visualize the broadband speed and bandwidth usage for home users. [23] measures and analyzes the behavior characteristics of a variety of home gateways such as DSL and cable modems, including NAT binding timeout, throughput, and protocol support, and their influence on network performance and user experience. A recent work [24] measures network access link performance directly from home gateway devices, and has inspired us to characterize network traffic from inside home networks through programmable home routers.

As residential broadband users continue to grow, many studies have been devoted to measure and characterize residential broadband networks [7–9]. However, all of these studies stand from outside home networks, and lack the visibility of the home networks, such as home network architecture, diversity of end hosts. For example, [7] examines the growth of residential user-to-user traffic in Japan, a country with a high penetration rate of residential broadband access, and studies the impact of these traffic on usage patterns and traffic engineering of commercial backbone networks. In addition, [8] studies several properties of broadband networks, including link capacities, round-trip times, jitter, and packet loss rates using active TCP and ICMP probes, while [9] passively collects packet-level traffic data of residential networks at aggregated routers of a large Internet service provider, and analyzes dominant characteristics of residential traffic including network and transport-level features, prominent applications, and network path dynamics. Different from these prior work, this paper leverages the availability of traffic flows exported from programmable home routers, and presents the first study of traffic characteristics of Internet-capable devices in home networks.

5 Conclusions and Future Work

In light of the rapid growth of home networks, this paper develops a traffic monitoring platform to collect and analyze network traffic for Internet-capable devices in home networks. Relying on programmable home routers that connect home networks to the Internet, we first collect network flow streams to traffic profiling servers. Subsequently, we analyze traffic characteristics of home networks, and use principal component analysis to uncover distinct clusters of application ports with temporal correlation. We are currently developing privacy-preserving data collection capacity into the traffic monitoring platform, so that we could deploy the platform into a large number of home networks to demonstrate its benefits in managing and securing home networks.

Acknowledgment. This research is supported in part by China 973 program under grant 2010CB328200, the Key Laboratory of Advanced Optical Communication Systems and Networks in Shanghai, and ASU New College SRCA grants.

References

1. CNN, Netflix takes up 32.7 of Internet bandwidth, http://www.cnn.com/2011/10/27/tech/web/netflix-internet-bandwith-mashable/index.html
2. Grinter, R., Edwards, K., Newman, M., Ducheneaut, N.: The Work to Make a Home Network Work. In: Proceedings of European Conference on Computer-Supported Cooperative Work (ECSCW) (September 2005)
3. Grinter, R., Edwards, K., Chetty, M., Poole, E., Sung, J., Yang, J., Crabtree, A., Tolmie, P., Rodden, T., Greenhalgh, C., Benford, S.: The ins and outs of home networking: the case for useful and usable domestic networking. ACM Transactions on Computer-Human Interaction 16(2) (2009)
4. Yang, J., Edwards, W.K., Haslem, D.: Eden: Supporting Home Network Management Through Interactive Visual Tools. In: Proceedings of ACM Symposium on User Interface Software and Technology (October 2010)
5. Poole, E., Edwards, K., Jarvis, L.: The Home Network as a Sociotechnical System: Understanding the Challenges of Remote Home Network Problem Diagnosis. Journal of Computer-Supported Cooperative Work Special Issue on CSCW, Technology, and Diagnostic Work (2009)
6. Aggarwal, B., Bhagwan, R., Das, T., Eswaran, S., Padmanabhan, V., Voelker, G.: NetPrints: Diagnosing Home Network Misconfigurations Using Shared Knowledge. In: Proceedings of USENIX Symposium on Networked System Design and Implementation (NSDI) (May 2009)
7. Cho, K., Fukuda, K., Esaki, H., Kato, A.: The Impact and Implications of the Growth in Residential User-to-User Traffic. In: Proceedings of ACM SIGCOMM (September 2006)
8. Dischinger, M., Haeberlen, A., Gummadi, K.P., Saroiu, S.: Characterizing Residential Broadband Networks. In: Proceedings of Internet Measurement Conference (October 2007)
9. Maier, G., Feldmann, A., Paxson, V., Allman, M.: On Dominant Characteristics of Residential Broadband Internet Traffic. In: Proceedings of Internet Measurement Conference (November 2009)
10. Xu, K., Wang, F., Lee, M.: HomeTPS: Uncovering What is Happening in Home Networks (Demo). In: Proceedings of IEEE Consumer Communications and Networking Conference (January 2012)
11. OpenWrt, OpenWrt: a Linux distribution for embedded devices, https://openwrt.org/
12. Lakhina, A., Crovella, M., Diot, C.: Diagnosing Network-Wide Traffic Anomalies. In: Proceedings of ACM SIGCOMM (2004)
13. Lakhina, A., Papagiannaki, K., Crovella, M., Diot, C., Kolaczyk, E., Taft, N.: Structural Analysis of Network Traffic Flows. In: Proceedings of ACM SIGMETRICS (June 2004)
14. Jolliffe, I.T.: Principal Component Analysis, 2nd edn. Spinger Series in Statistics (2002)
15. Edwards, W., Grinter, R., Mahajan, R., Wetherall, D.: Advancing the State of Home Networking. Communications of the ACM 54(6), 62–71 (2011)
16. Feamster, N.: Outsourcing Home Network Security. In: Proceedings of ACM SIGCOMM Workshop on Home Networks (HomeNets) (Septèmber 2010)
17. Yang, J., Edwards, W.K.: A Study on Network Management Tools of Householders. In: Proceedings of ACM SIGCOMM Workshop on Home Networks (HomeNets) (September 2010)

18. Calvert, K., Edwards, W.K., Feamster, N., Grinter, R.E., Deng, Y., Zhou, X.: Instrumenting Home Networks. In: Proceedings of ACM SIGCOMM Workshop on Home Networks (HomeNets) (September 2010)
19. Yiakoumis, Y., Yap, K., Katti, S., Parulkar, G., McKeown, N.: Slicing Home Networks. In: Proceedings of ACM SIGCOMM Workshop on Home Networking (August 2011)
20. DiCioccio, L., Teixeira, R., Rosenberg, C.: Impact of Home Networks on End-to-End Performance: Controlled Experiments. In: Proceedings of ACM SIGCOMM Workshop on Home Networks (September 2010)
21. Kreibich, C., Weaver, N., Nechaev, B., Paxson, V.: Netalyzr: Illuminating The Edge Network. In: Proceedings of Internet Measurement Conference (November 2010)
22. Chetty, M., Haslem, M., Baird, A., Ofoha, U., Sumner, B., Grinter, R.: Why Is My Internet Slow?: Making Network Speeds Visible. In: Proceedings of ACM Conference on Computer-Human Interaction (May 2011)
23. Hatonen, S., Nyrhinen, A., Eggert, L., Strowes, S., Sarolahti, P., Kojo, M.: An Experimental Study of Home Gateway Characteristics. In: Proceedings of ACM Internet Measurement Conference (November 2010)
24. Sundaresan, S., de Donato, W., Feamster, N., Teixeira, R., Crawford, S., Pescape, A.: Broadband Internet Performance: A View From the Gateway. In: Proceedings of ACM SIGCOMM (August 2011)

SHIELD: A Strategy-Proof and Highly Efficient Channel Auction Mechanism for Multi-radio Wireless Networks*

Zuying Wei, Tianrong Zhang, Fan Wu**, Guihai Chen, and Xiaofeng Gao

Shanghai Key Laboratory of Scalable Computing and Systems
Department of Computer Science and Engineering
Shanghai Jiao Tong University, China
{zu_ying_hi,ztr1211,wu-fan,gchen,gao-xf}@sjtu.edu.cn

Abstract. Due to users' fast-growing demands, wireless spectrum is becoming a more and more scarce resource. However, the state of spectrum usage shows that while large chunks of spectrum are left idle at many places, many emerging wireless applications cannot get enough spectrum to provide their services. In contrast to existing truthful mechanisms for channel redistribution, which achieve strategy-proofness at the price of lowered system performance, we propose SHIELD, which not only guarantees strategy-proofness in the process of channel redistribution, but also achieves high system performance. Our evaluation results show that SHIELD outperforms the existing mechanisms, in terms of spectrum utilization and user satisfaction ratio. Here, channel utilization represents the average number of radios allocated to channels, and buyer satisfaction ratio shows the percentage of buyers who get at least one channel in the auction.

Keywords: Wireless Network, Channel Allocation, Mechanism DesignWireless Network, Channel Allocation, Mechanism Design.

1 Introduction

As the fast development of the communication technologies, the spectrum is becoming a more and more scarce resource. It is expected that global mobile data traffic will increase 26-fold between 2010 and 2015 [5]. To adapt the fast growth of data traffic over wireless links, next generation wireless applications need more spectrum to carry their services. However, traditional spectrum management makes new wireless network applications face the plight of increasingly scarce spectrum resources. Currently, almost every country has a specific department for regulating spectrum usage, e.g. Federal Communications Commission (FCC) [11] in the US and Radio Administration Bureau(RAB) in China [28]. FCC and RAB divide available wireless spectrum into a number of bands, and grants the right of using each band within a specified geographical area to a particular business organization or wireless application. Traditional static spectrum allocation has been unable to meet the growing demand for wireless

---

* This work was supported in part by China NSF grant 61170236 and 61133006. The opinions, findings, conclusions, and recommendations expressed in this paper are those of the authors and do not necessarily reflect the views of the funding agencies or the government.
** Corresponding author.

X. Wang et al. (Eds.): WASA 2012, LNCS 7405, pp. 72–87, 2012.

broadband services [12]. On one hand, frequency bands for wireless communications have almost been fully allocated [10]. On the other hand, already allocated spectrum is not fully utilized. For example, measurement results show that in downtown Berkeley, the utilization of spectrum up to 3GHz is only about 32%, while for the spectrum of 3-5GHz the utilization is less than 1% [45]. Therefore, to improve the spectrum utilization, we need to find a more efficient mechanism to redistribute the idle spectrum to the wireless applications that need the spectrum resource.

A usual way to implement spectrum redistribution is to use auction, by which the spectrum owner (seller) gets profit through leasing idle spectrum to the wireless applications (buyers) who need the spectrum. In the literature, there are a number of auction mechanisms proposed for dynamic spectrum/channel redistribution, e.g., [39, 50–52]. These auction mechanisms target at guaranteeing strategy-proofness of the spectrum auction. Intuitively, an auction mechanism is strategy-proof, if it is the best strategy for each buyer to truthfully report her valuation of the good as the bid, no matter what the others do, and nobody's individual rationality is hurt. Two commonly used metrics for evaluating the efficiency of a spectrum auction mechanism are spectrum utilization and buyer satisfaction ratio. Here, spectrum utilization captures the average number of buyers (or radios if the buyers have multiple radios) correspond to each channel, and buyer satisfaction ratio represents the percentage of buyers who get at least one channel in the auction. Although most of existing channel auction mechanisms achieve strategy-proofness, they provide low guarantee for the allocation efficiency in terms of spectrum utilization and buyer satisfaction ratio.

In this paper, we propose SHIELD, which is a $\underline{S}$trategy-proof and $\underline{HI}$ghly $\underline{E}$fficient channe$\underline{L}$ auction mechanism for multi-ra$\underline{D}$io wireless networks. SHIELD not only guarantees strategy-proofness, but also achieves high performance compared with existing mechanisms. SHIELD divides the buyers into non-conflicting groups, in which every pair of buyers are well separated and can do the transmission on the same channel simultaneously, and gives larger groups higher precedence to be allocated a channel. In this paper, we make the following key contributions.

– First, we model the problem of channel redistribution as a sealed-bid auction, and propose a simple but efficient channel auction mechanism, namely SHIELD.
– Second, we prove that SHIELD is a strategy-proof channel auction mechanism.
– Third, we do extensive simulations to compare the performance of SHIELD with existing representative channel auction mechanisms, such as SMALL and VERITAS. Evaluation results verify that SHIELD guarantees strategy-proofness, and show that SHIELD outperforms existing representative channel auction mechanisms in terms of spectrum utilization and user satisfaction ratio.

We organize the rest of this paper as follows. In Section 2, we present the game model for the problem of channel redistribution and review some important solution concepts from game theory. In Section 3, we give the detailed description of SHIELD. In Section 4, we illustrate simulation results of our auction mechanism. In Section 5, we discuss related works. In Section 6, we conclude the paper and point out potential directions for future work.

2 Preliminaries

In this section, we show our game-theoretic model, and review some closely related solution concepts from game theory.

2.1 Game-Theoretic Model

We model the problem of channel redistribution as a sealed-bid auction, in which there are a spectrum seller and a number of buyers. The seller holds m idle wireless channels, denoted by $C = \{c_1, c_2, \ldots, c_m\}$. The seller wants to lease her idle channels to buyers to get some profit. A channel can be leased to multiple buyers, who are not conflicting with each other according to an adequate Signal to Interference and Noise Ratio (SINR). Buyers, such as WiFi access points, desperately need the channels to serve their customers. Suppose there are n buyers, denoted by $N = \{1, 2, \ldots, n\}$. Each buyer has a private valuation of a channel, denoted by $v = \{v_1, v_2, \ldots, v_n\}$. Each buyer may equip with a single radio or multiple radios, so a buyer may bid for one or multiple channels. We assume that each channel is of the same value to each buyer. Therefore, we require that each buyer bid equally for each channel she requests. We also assume that the buyers do not cheat about the number of radios she has. Each buyer $i \in N$ has a per-channel valuation v_i. The per-channel valuation can be the revenue gained by the buyer for serving her customers. The channel valuation v_i is private information to the buyer i. In the auction, each buyer i submits her sealed per-channel bid b_i together with the number of radios r_i she has to the seller/auctioneer. The seller/auctioneer will decide auction result based on the buyers' bids. Then, we can represent the buyers' bid vector as $b = (b_1, b_2, \ldots, b_n)$, and demand vector as $r = (r_1, r_2, \ldots, r_n)$.

The seller/auctioneer use a deterministic channel allocation algorithm to determine determines the channel allocation $y = (y_1, y_2 \ldots, y_n)$ based on the bids. Here, y_i means that buyer i gets y_i channels in the auction. Then the kth ($k \leq y_i$) radio of buyer i can work on the kth channel allocated to i. Each buyer i should pay for the channels she won in the auction with price $p_i = \sum_{k=1}^{y_i} p_i^k$. Here, p_i^k represents the charge to buyer i's kth channel. The utility u_i of buyer i is defined as the difference between her valuation of allocated channels and the charge of using the channels:

$$u_i = \sum_{k=1}^{y_i} u_i^k = \sum_{k=1}^{y_i} (v_i - p_i^k) = v_i \cdot y_i - p_i.$$

Here, u_i^k represents the utility of buyer i gets on the kth channel. We assume that the buyers are rational, and always want to maximize their own utilities. In contrast to an individual buyer's objective, our auction mechanism aims to achieve high channel allocation efficiency, in terms of spectrum utilization and buyer satisfaction ratio.

Here, we use an example to show that traditional VCG auction model [6, 15, 33] cannot guarantee strategy-proofness for spectrum auction. VCG auction model sorts the bidders in non-increasing order, and then allocate the channels to the bidders one by one using lowest indexed channel in each bidder's available channel set. The charge to bidder i is the bid of the bidder who would get the channel if bidder i is absent. We model the interference among bidders using a conflict graph, which means that two bidders cannot use the same channel simultaneously if there is an edge between each other. Fig. 1 shows a simple example to illustrate that the VCG auction violates strategy-proofness. We assume that there are two channels waiting to be leased out. In Fig. 1(a), all the bidders bid truthfully and in Fig. 1(b) bidder E bids untruthfully. Table 1 shows the utilities of all the bidders when E bids truthfully and untruthfully. We can see that when E bids $b_E = v_E = 4$, he loses in the auction and get utility of 0. When he bids $b_E = 6 \neq v_E$, he wins in the auction and gets the utility of 2. The bidder E can increase his utility by bidding untruthfully. We can see that the traditional VCG auction model cannot guarantee strategy-proofness.

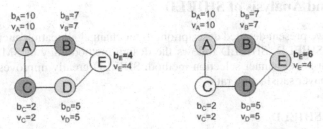

(a) User A, B, C, D get the channel. (b) User A, B, D, E get the channel.

Fig. 1. A simple example which shows that traditional VCG auction model violates strategy-proofness

Table 1. Utilities of all the bidders when E bids truthfully and untruthfully

Fig. 1(a)	Fig. 1(b)
$v_A = 10, b_A = 10, u_A = 6$	$v_A = 10, b_A = 10, u_A = 8$
$v_B = 7, b_B = 7, u_B = 3$	$v_B = 7, b_B = 7, u_B = 7$
$v_C = 2, b_C = 2, u_C = 2$	$v_C = 2, b_C = 2, u_C = 0$
$v_D = 5, b_D = 5, u_D = 1$	$v_D = 5, b_D = 5, u_D = 3$
$v_E = 4, b_E = 4, \mathbf{u_E = 0}$	$v_E = 4, \mathbf{b_E = 6}, \mathbf{u_E = 2}$

In Section 3.1, we will present our strategy-proof channel auction mechanism—SHIELD.

2.2 Solution Concepts

We review two important solution concepts from game theory in this section.

Definition 1 (Dominant Strategy [14, 26])
A strategy s_i is player i's dominant strategy, if for any $s'_i \neq s_i$ and any strategy profile of the other players s_{-i}, her utility satisfies:

$$u(s_i, s_{-i}) \geq u(s'_i, s_{-i}).$$

In our game model, each buyer is a player, and s_i is a buyer i's bid.

A dominant strategy of a player is one that maximizes her utility regardless of what strategies the other players choose. Before defining *strategy-proofness*, we review the definition of *incentive-compatibility* and *individual-rationality*. An auction mechanism is *incentive-compatible* if it is one's dominant-strategy for bidding real valuation. *Individual-rationality* means that the buyers can always achieves at least as much utility from participating in the auction as staying outside.

Definition 2 (Strategy-Proof Mechanism [24, 31])
A mechanism is strategy-proof if it satisfies both incentive-compatibility and individual-rationality.

3   Design and Analysis of SHIELD

In this section, we present detailed description of our channel allocation auction mechanism, namely SHIELD. SHIELD follows the design methodology of SMALL [39]. However, with a novel winner selection method, SHIELD greatly improves spectrum utilization and buyer satisfaction ratio.

3.1   Design of SHIELD

We now present the design of SHIELD. SHIELD works in three steps: buyer grouping, winner selection, and charge determination.

When a buyer i is equipped with r_i radio(s), we use r_i elementary buyer(s) to represent the buyer i(e.g., Fig. 2). We use N' to denote the set of elementary buyers. Therefore, each elementary buyer requests only one channel. Actually, a buyer who is equipped with one radio is an elementary buyer herself. Similar to [39,51], SHIELD groups the buyers in a bid-independent way. SHIELD models the interference among buyers using a conflict graph. Each node in the graph is an elementary buyer. For each radio equipped by a buyer, we use an elementary buyer to represent it. Each edge in the graph represents that the two elementary buyers who interfere with each other. Since the radios belonging to the same buyer have interference between each other, we connect the nodes/elementary buyers of the same buyer with each other to indicate the confliction. There are also conflicts across nodes/elementary buyers belonging to different buyers, we connect them with each other to represent the conflicts. Then SHIELD divides all the elementary buyers into non-conflicting groups based on the conflict graph. We can use existing graph coloring algorithms (e.g., [38]) to figure out the grouping.

Fig. 2 shows a toy example. In Fig. 2, buyer A is equipped with two radios. Node A^1 and A^2 represent the two elementary buyers of buyer A. Similarly, B^1 and B^2 represent the two elementary buyers of buyer B, C^1 and C^2 represent the two elementary buyers of buyer C. There are seven elementary buyers. There are many possible grouping results, for example $g_1 = \{A^1, C^2\}$, $g_2 = \{A^2, B^1, D\}$ and $g_3 = \{B^2, C^1\}$.

Without loss of generality, we assume that the elementary buyers have been divided into x non-conflicting groups by a given graph coloring algorithm:

$$G : \{g_1, g_2, \ldots, g_x\}.$$

Next, we discuss the very important step—winner selection. SHIELD sorts the buyer groups according to group size in non-increasing order as follows:

$$G' : |g'_1| \geq |g'_2| \geq \ldots \geq |g'_x|.$$

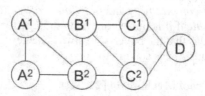

Fig. 2. A simple conflict graph

In case of a tie, each tied group has an equal probability of being ordered prior to the others. SHIELD chooses the first m (or x, if $x < m$) groups as winning groups. Furthermore, SHIELD sets the elementary buyers except the one with the smallest bid in each winning group as winners. In case of a tie, each tied elementary buyer has an equal probability of being selected as a winner. Algorithm 1 shows the pseudo code for the winner selection process.

Algorithm 1. Winner Selection

Input: A set of elementary buyers N', a vector of channel demands r, a vector of bids b, a set of the idle channels C, the number of idle channels m.
Output: A set of winners W, an allocated matrix of channels T.
1: $sum\_r = \sum_{i=1}^{n} r_i$.
2: $T = 0^{sum\_r, m}$.
3: $(G, x) = Grouping(N')$.
4: $nc = \min\{m, x\}$.
5: $G' = Sort(G)$ based on group size.
6: **for all** $g'_j \in G'$ **do**
7:    **if** $nc \geq 0$ **then**
8:       $nc = nc - 1$.
9:       **for all** $i \in g'_j$ **do**
10:          $T_{ij} = 1$.
11:       **end for**
12:       $WS = g'_j - \{argmin_{l \in g'_j}(b_l)\}$.
13:       $W = W \cup WS$.
14:    **end if**
15: **end for**
16: **return** $W and T$.

We note that to achieve strategy-proofness, SHIELD sacrifices a buyer in each winning group. No matter how large the set of buyers is, the number of sacrificed buyers is bounded by m, which is the number of channels for leasing.

Finally, we determine the charges to the winners. The winners in each group are charged equally and the charge is the smallest bid in that group. For each winner $l \in g'_j$, the payment of her is $min\{b_q | q \in g'_j\}$. Then the charge p_i to a buyer $i \in N$ is the sum of charges to her winning elementary buyers. We note that since each elementary buyer will not be charged more than her bid. The seller's income is the payments of all the buyers who get the channels:

$$Income = \sum_{i=1}^{n} p_i.$$

3.2 Analysis

In this section, we prove that SHIELD is strategy-proof, which means that reporting one's truthful per-channel valuation as a bid is the best strategy of each buyer.

Lemma 1. *When SHIELD is used, it is a dominant-strategy for each buyer to truthfully report her per-channel valuation as the bid.*

Proof. SHIELD use a bid-independent grouping method to group the elementary buyers. The bid of buyer i will not affect the winning group selection method. Next, we will show that no matter how a buyer bids, she can not increase her utility by bidding untruthfully. In other words, a buyer can not increase her utility by misreporting.

If buyer i bids truthfully(i.e., $b_i = v_i$) and gets y_i channel. Then her utility is

$$u_i = \sum_{k=1}^{y_i} u_i^k = \sum_{k=1}^{y_i} (v_i - p_i^k).$$

Let t be the kth one of the elementary buyers generated from buyer i. Suppose $t \in g_j'$. If g_j' is not a winning group, then t cannot be a winner no matter how buyer i bids. We then analyze the case, in which g_j' is a winning group. We prove that buyer i can not increase her utility get from elementary buyer t by bidding untruthfully. We distinguish two cases:

- If $b_i = v_i = \min\{b_s | s \in g_j\}$ when bidding truthfully. In this case, the elementary buyer t would lose in auction or win with a charge equal to her valuation. So $u_i^k = 0$. Let's see the utility get from the elementary buyer t if buyer i bids untruthfully. We further distinguish two cases:
  If the bid $b_i' < b_i$, t will also lose in the auction and result in the utility $u_i^k = 0$.
  If the bid $b_i' > b_i$, the utility on t is 0 when t still loses in the auction. If t wins in the auction, her utility will be $u_i'^k = v_i - p_i'^k$. That means the new lowest bid of the group $\min\{b_s | s \in g_j \setminus \{t\}\} \geq b_i = v_i$.

$$\begin{aligned} u_i'^k &= v_i - p_i'^k \\ &= v_i - \min\{b_s | s \in g_j \setminus \{t\}\} \\ &\leq v_i - b_i \\ &= 0. \end{aligned}$$

  The utility on t will be non-positive. We can get that, if $b_i = v_i = \min\{b_s | s \in g_j\}$, no matter how i bids, she can not improve her utility got on t and her utility on t will be no more than 0.
- If $b_i = v_i > \min\{b_s | s \in g_j \setminus \{t\}\}$, buyer t would win in the auction and get the utility $u_i^k = b_i - p_i^k = b_i - \min\{b_s | s \in g_j \setminus \{t\}\}$ if i reports her bid truthfully. If i bids untruthfully, the utility of the buyer will be also u_i^k or will become 0.
  Assume i bids $b_i' > \min\{b_s | s \in g_j\}$, t will win in the auction. Her utility will not change and is still $u_i'^k = v_i - \min\{b_s | s \in g_j \setminus \{t\}\} = u_i^k$ because the lowest bid of the group has not changed. But if she loses the auction her utility will be 0.

We can see that for an elementary buyer t, she can not improve her utility no matter how i bids , which can be indicated as: $u_i^k \geq u_i'^k$. As we supposed above, the elementary buyer t is the kth one generated from buyer i. For buyer i, her utility is

$$u_i = \sum_{k=1}^{y_i} u_i^k \geq \sum_{k=1}^{y_i} u_i'^k = u_i'.$$

$\square$

We can get the conclusion from the above analysis that bidding truthfully is the buyers' dominant strategy when participating in the auction.

Theorem 1. *SHIELD satisfies incentive-compatibility.*

We next show that SHIELD satisfies individual-rationality.

Lemma 2. *SHIELD satisfies individual-rationality.*

Proof. For an elementary buyer t, she can get 0 or higher utility through participating in the auction truthfully. So the utility of the buyer who is equipped with more than one radios can get 0 or higher utility too. That is to say: truthfully participating in the auction is not worse than staying outside, which can be indicated as follows:

$$u_i^k \geq 0 (1 \leq k \leq y_i),$$

$$u_i = \sum_{k=1}^{y_i} u_i^k \geq 0.$$

Then the allocation mechanism satisfies individual-rationality.   □

Since SHIELD satisfies both incentive-compatibility and individual-rationality, we can draw the following conclusion.

Theorem 2. *SHIELD is a strategy-proof channel auction mechanism.*

4 Evaluation Results

In this section, we show the evaluation results. We compare the performance of SHIELD with that of SMALL and VERITAS.

4.1 Metrics

We use the following three metrics to evaluate the performance of the channel auction mechanisms.

- Utility: Utility is defined as the difference between a buyer's channel valuation and charge. As we mentioned in Sect. 3.2, a buyer may bid truthfully or untruthfully. The utility reflect the impacts of buyers' behaviors including bidding truthfully and untruthfully. We use this metric in our evaluations to verify that no buyer can increase her utility by misreporting.
- Spectrum utilization: Average number of radios allocated to each channel.
- Buyer satisfaction ratio: Buyer satisfaction ratio is the percentage of the buyers who get at least one channel in the auction. Buyer satisfaction ratio and spectrum utilization reflect the performance of a channel auction mechanism.

4.2   Evaluation Setup

We now show the settings of the evaluation: we use a greedy graph coloring algorithm [37] to implement SHIELD. We assume that there are 6, 12, or 24 idle channels available and evaluate the cases in which every buyer has a single radio or 3 radios. We vary the number of buyers from 20 to 400. The sized terrain area can be 1000×1000, 1500×1500, or 2000×2000 meters. The interference range of each node is set to 425 meters. We assume that buyers' valuation per channel are randomly distributed in (0,1].

4.3   Evaluation Results

In our first set of evaluations, we show that, SHIELD ensures that no buyer can increase her utility by misreporting the per-channel valuation. We set the number of buyers to 200. We randomly choose a buyer to show the results of honest reporting and misreporting. Since the utilities of the buyers when bidding truthfully and untruthfully is the same in most of the cases, to illustrate clearly, we just show the cases in which these two utilities are different. The simulation is repeated more than 1000 times. Fig. 3 shows

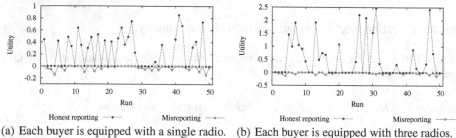

(a) Each buyer is equipped with a single radio.   (b) Each buyer is equipped with three radios.

Fig. 3. Utilities of buyer 55 if she bids truthfully and untruthfully when each buyer is equipped with a single radio or three radios in a terrain area of 2000×2000 meters

the results of buyer 55. Evaluation results of other nodes are similar to that of buyer 55 when bidding truthfully and untruthfully. When the two utilities are different, buyer 55 can always get a much higher utility when bidding truthfully. In Fig. 3, we can also get that when buyer 55 bids truthfully, the utility is always non-negative, while bidding untruthfully can lead to negative utility. Therefore, a buyer can not increase his utility by misreporting.

In our second set of evaluations, we compare the performance of SHIELD with SMALL and VERITAS, in terms of spectrum utilization and buyer satisfaction ratio. Our evaluation results show that SHIELD performs better than SMALL and VERITAS. When the buyers are extremely sparse, SHIELD performs a little bit worse than VERITAS. The reason for this is that SHIELD sacrifices a buyer in each winning group. As the number of buyers increases SHIELD performs better than VERITAS. SHIELD always outperforms SMALL regardless of the number of buyers and the size of terrain area.

Fig. 4 shows spectrum utilizations of SHIELD, SMALL and VERITAS under the condition that there are 6, 12, and 24 idle channels available. In this evaluation, we set

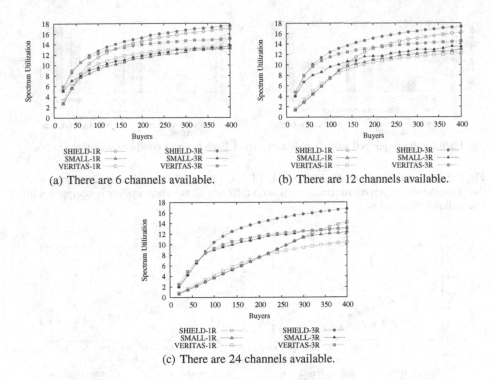

(a) There are 6 channels available.   (b) There are 12 channels available.

(c) There are 24 channels available.

Fig. 4. Spectrum utilizations of SHIELD, SMALL, and VERITAS when there are 6, 12, and 24 channels provided. Each buyer is equipped with one radio or three radios, in a terrain area of 2000×2000 meters.

the terrain area to 2000×2000 meters. We can see from Fig. 4 that when the number of buyers is small, SHIELD achieves a little bit lower spectrum utilization than VERITAS. This is because VERITAS does not need to sacrifice any buyer. When the number of buyers is more than a critical value(e.g. 120 in Fig. 4(a)), SHIELD outperforms VER-ITAS. This is because non-grouping based algorithm used in VERITAS fails to fully consider the whole network topology. Fig. 4(b) and Fig. 4(c) show that, when each is equipped with three radios and the number of buyers is more than 80, SHIELD performs much better than SMALL and VERITAS. SHIELD outperforms better than SMALL in most of the cases.

Fig. 5 shows the spectrum utilizations of SHIELD, SMALL, and VERITAS in different terrain areas with the same buyer density when each buyer is equipped with a single radio or three radios. We assume there are 80, 180, and 320 buyers that are randomly distributed in the terrain areas when the size of terrain area is 1000×1000, 1500×1500, and 2000×2000 meters, respectively. We can see from Fig. 5 that SHIELD always performs not worse than SMALL and VERITAS. Especially when the terrain area is relatively large(1500×1500, and 2000×2000 meters), SHIELD performs much better than SMALL and VERITAS.

Fig. 6 shows the buyer satisfaction ratios of SHIELD, SMALL and VERITAS. In Fig. 6(a), Fig. 6(b) and Fig. 6(c), there are 6, 12, and 24 idle channels available, respectively. In each figure, we show the simulation results when each buyer requests only one radio

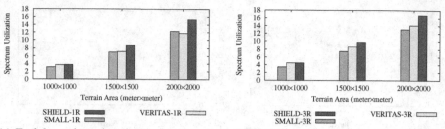

(a) Each buyer is equipped with a single radio.   (b) Each buyer is equipped with three radios.

Fig. 5. Spectrum utilizations of SHIELD, SMALL and VERITAS for auctioning 12 channels with the same density of buyers in terrain areas with different sizes, when a buyer is equipped with one radio or three radios

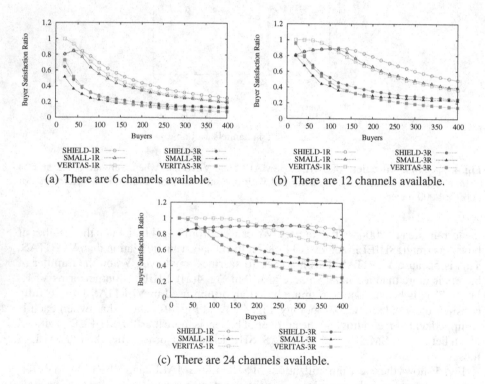

Fig. 6. Buyer satisfaction ratios of SHIELD, SMALL and VERITAS when there are 6, 12, and 24 channels provided. Each buyer is equipped with one radio or three radios, in a terrain area of 2000×2000 meters.

or three radios in 2000×2000 meters terrain area. We can see from Fig. 6 that when the number of buyers is very small, SHIELD performs a little worse than VERITAS. The reason for this is that SHIELD sacrifices a buyer in each winning group. When the number of buyers is a little larger, SHIELD and SMALL outperforms VERITAS. When each buyer is equipped with a single radios, Fig. 6(b) and Fig. 6(c) shows that

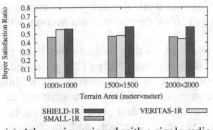
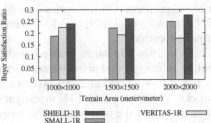

(a) A buyer is equipped with a single radio.   (b) A buyer is equipped with three radios.

Fig. 7. Buyer satisfaction ratios of SHIELD, SMALL and VERITAS for auctioning 12 channels with the same buyers density in terrain areas of different sizes, when a buyer is equipped with one radio or three radios

SHIELD and SMALL get nearly the same buyer satisfaction ratios when the number of buyers is less than 125 and 310, respectively. This is because SHIELD and SMALL use the same method of winner selection in one winning group. When each buyer is equipped with three radios, Fig. 6(a) and Fig. 6(b) show that SHIELD achieves higher buyer satisfaction ratios than SMALL and VERITAS in most of the cases. Fig. 6(a) and Fig. 6(b) also show that when the number of buyers is very large, SHIELD and SMALL achieves more closer buyer satisfaction ratio and they both outperforms VERITAS.

Fig. 7 shows the buyer satisfaction ratios of SHIELD, SMALL, and VERITAS for auctioning 12 channels in the same density of buyers in different terrain areas, when a buyer is equipped with one or three radios. We assume there are 80, 180, and 320 when the terrain area is 1000×1000, 1500×1500, and 2000×2000 meters, respectively. The buyers are randomly distributed in the terrain area. We can see from Fig. 7 that SHIELD always performs not worse than SMALL and VERITAS. Especially when the terrain area is relatively large (1500×1500, and 2000×2000 meters), SHIELD performs much better than SMALL and VERITAS.

5   Related Works

In this section, we review the related works on channel allocation with cooperative participants and non-cooperative participants.

5.1   Existing Works with Cooperation Participants

Generally, channel assignment schemes in cellular networks can be categorized as fixed channel assignment (FCA), dynamic channel assignment (DCA), and hybrid channel assignment (HCA), which is a combination of FCA and DCA. Many works have been done for wireless LANs(WLANs). For example, Mishra et al. [25] explored the use of channel hopping to improve the fairness and performance of overlapping 802.11 network deployments.

Many works about the channel allocation problems have also been done in wireless mesh networks. For instance, Kodialam and Nandagopal [20, 21] considered the problem of optimal channel assignment, scheduling and routing using a linear programming technique. Rad et al. [27] formulated joint channel allocation, interface assignment, and MAC problem. On the optimal problem of the network throughput, Alicherry et al. [2], Raniwala et al. [29], and Kodialam et al. [21] took the routing into account with channel allocation.

The spectrum allocation problem and improvement on this problem has been researched in many other wireless networks too. Kyasanur and Vidya [22] proposed a flow based routing and channel assignment approach for a single interface in ad-hoc networks. Vedantham et al. [32] investigated the granularity of channel assignment decisions that gives the best trade-off in terms of performance and complexity in ad-hoc networks. Ding et al. [8]studied distributed routing, relay selection, and spectrum allocation in cognitive and cooperative ad hoc networks. Authors in [19, 46] study the spectrum management problem in use of cognitive radio.

5.2   Existing Works with Non-cooperative Participants

The related works showed in above section requests the users to cooperate with each other. While an another category of works consider the case with non-cooperative participants. Related works in this section can be divided into two sub-categories including static auction and online auction.

Static Auction. Felegyhazi et al. [13] studied Nash Equilibria in static multi-radio multi-channel allocation game. After that, Wu et al. [41] proposed a strongly dominant strategy equilibrium to improve the performance of channel allocation, and the scheme achieves the optimal system throughput in single-hop wirelwss networks. Han et al. [18] presented a distributed algorithms for simultaneous channel allocation of individual links and packet-scheduling, in Software-Defined Radio (SDR) wireless networks.

In recent years, Zhou et al. proposed TRUST [51] and VERITAS [50], which are based on spectrum auction and achieve truthfulness. TRUST is a general framework for truthful double spectrum auction, which takes both buyers and sellers into account and achieves good performance. VERITAS focuses on the buyers and the circumstances, under which buyers request multiple channels. The most closely related work is SMALL [39], which also focuses on the buyers except that it lets the seller to set reserve price to protect her interest.

Xu et al. [42] designed an efficient channel allocation algorithm in different cases, such that the the social efficiency can be approximately maximized. Xu et al. also designed a polynomial time approximation scheme to maximize the social efficiency. Mahmoud and Gupta [1] designed a polynomial-time truthful spectrum auction that offers a performance guarantee on the expecter revenue for Bayesian setting. Yang et al. [44] designed a truthful auction mechanism for the cooperative communication, named TASC. TASC is individually rational and budget-balanced, where wireless node can trade relay services. Wu et al. [40] studies the problem of adaptive-width channel allocation from a game-theoretic perspective and achieve higher system-wide throughput than that when system is in NE.

Online Auction. Many works have been done for online auctions. Hajiaghayi et al. [16] considered online auctions with a limited supply and presented value- and time-strategyproof mechanisms with constant efficiency- and revenue-competitiveness. Hajiaghayi et al. [17] gave a characterization for the online allocation rules that are truthfully implementable. Recently, Li [23] used a game theoretic model to increase the rebate incentive mechanism. Wang et al. [34] proposed TODA which is a truthful online double auction for spectrum allocation in wireless networks. Xu et al. [43] designed an efficient spectrum channel allocation and auction method for online wireless channel scheduling to decide whether to grant each user's exclusive usage and how much will be charged. Deek et al. [7] proposed a truthful online spectrum auction design called Topaz. Topaz can distribute spectrum efficiently while discouraging bidders from misreporting their bids or time report.

Game theoretic methods are also used in studying the media access problems in wireless networks and there are also other works on strategy-proofness in wireless networks. There are many examples including ad hoc networks [3, 4, 9, 30, 35, 36, 47–49].

6   Conclusion and Future Work

In this section, we draw our conclusion and discuss the future work. In this paper, we have proposed SHIELD, which is a strategy-proof and highly efficient channel auction mechanism for multi-radio wireless networks. We have proven its strategy-proofness and have implemented SHIELD. Our evaluation results have shown that SHIELD can achieve higher performance compared with existing channel auction mechanisms. For future work, it will be interesting to investigate the problem of the collusion resistance in designing wireless channel auction mechanisms.

References

1. Al-Ayyoub, M., Gupta, H.: Truthful spectrum auctions with approximate revenue. In: Proceedings of 30th Annual IEEE Conference on Computer Communications (INFOCOM), Shanghai, China, pp. 2813–2821 (April 2011)
2. Alicherry, M., Bhatia, R., Li, L.: Joint channel assignment and routing for throughput optimization in multi-radio wireless mesh networks. In: Proceedings of The Eleventh International Conference on Mobile Computing and Networking (MobiCom), Cologne, Germany (September 2005)
3. Anderegg, L., Eidenbenz, S.: Ad hoc-VCG: a truthful and cost-efficient routing protocol for mobile ad hoc networks with selfish agents. In: Proceedings of the Ninth International Conference on Mobile Computing and Networking (MobiCom), San Diego, CA (September 2003)
4. Ben Salem, N., Buttyan, L., Hubaux, J.P., Jakobsson, M.: A charging and rewarding scheme for packet forwarding in multi-hop cellular networks. In: Proceedings of the Fourth ACM Symposium on Mobile Ad Hoc Networking and Computing (MobiHoc), Annapolis, MD (June 2003)
5. Cisco Visual Networking Index, Global mobile data traffic forecast update, 2010-2015, February1 (2011)
6. Clarke, E.H.: Multipart pricing of public good. Public Choice 11(1), 17–33 (1971)
7. Deek, L.B., Zhou, X., Almeroth, K.C., Zheng, H.: To preempt or not: Tackling bid and time-based cheating in online spectrum auctions. In: Proceedings of 30th Annual IEEE Conference on Computer Communications (INFOCOM), Shanghai, China, pp. 2219–2227 (April 2011)
8. Ding, L., Melodia, T., Batalama, S.N., Matyjas, J.D.: Distributed routing, relay selection, and spectrum allocation in cognitive and cooperative ad hoc networks. In: Proceedings of the Seventh Annual IEEE Communications Society Conference on Sensor, Mesh and Ad Hoc Communications and Networks SECON, Boston, Massachusetts, USA, June 21-25, pp. 484–492 (2010)
9. Eidenbenz, S., Resta, G., Santi, P.: Commit: A sender-centric truthful and energy-efficient routing protocol for ad hoc networks with selfish nodes. In: Proceedings of the 19th International Parallel and Distributed Processing Symposium (IPDPS), Denver, CO (April 2005)

10. FCC Online Table of Frequency Allocations, November 18 (2008)
11. Federal Communications Commission (FCC), http://www.fcc.gov/
12. Federal Communications Commission Spectrum Policy Task Force, Report of the spectrum efficiency working group, November 15 (2002)
13. Félegyházi, M., Čagalj, M., Bidokhti, S.S., Hubaux, J.-P.: Non-cooperative multi-radio channel allocation in wireless networks. In: Proceedings of 26th Annual IEEE Conference on Computer Communications (INFOCOM), Anchorage, AK (May 2007)
14. Fudenberg, D., Tirole, J.: Game Theory. MIT Press (1991)
15. Groves, T.: Incentives in teams. Econometrica 41(4), 617–631 (1973)
16. Hajiaghayi, M.T., Kleinberg, R., Parkes, D.C.: Adaptive limited-supply online auctions. In: Proceedings of the ACM Symposium on Electronic Commerce (EC) (October 2004)
17. Hajiaghayi, M.T., Kleinberg, R.D., Mahdian, M.: Online auctions with reusable goods. In: Proceedings of the ACM Symposium on Electronic Commerce (EC) (October 2005)
18. Han, B., Kumar, V.S.A., Marathe, M.V., Parthasarathy, S., Srinivasan, A.: Distributed strategies for channel allocation and scheduling in software-defined radio networks. In: Proceedings of 28th Annual IEEE Conference on Computer Communications (INFOCOM), Rio de Janeiro, Brazil (April 2009)
19. Hou, Y.T., Shi, Y., Sherali, H.D.: Optimal spectrum sharing for multi-hop software defined radio networks. In: Proceedings of 26th Annual IEEE Conference on Computer Communications (INFOCOM), Anchorage, AK (May 2007)
20. Kodialam, M., Nandagopal, T.: Characterizing achievable rates in multi-hop wireless mesh networks with orthogonal channels. IEEE/ACM Transaction on Networking 13(4), 868–880 (2005)
21. Kodialam, M., Nandagopal, T.: Characterizing the capacity region in multi-radio multi-channel wireless mesh networks. In: Proceedings of The Eleventh International Conference on Mobile Computing and Networking (MobiCom), Cologne, Germany (September 2005)
22. Kyasanur, P., Vaidya, N.: A routing protocol for utilizing multiple channels in multi-hop wireless networks with a single transceiver. In: Proceedings of the Second International Conference on Quality of Service in Heterogeneous Wired/Wireless Networks (QShine), Orlando, FL (August 2005)
23. Li, L.I.: Reputation, trust, and rebates: How online auction markets can improve their feedback mechanisms. Journal of Economics & Management Strategy 19(2), 303–331 (2010)
24. Mas-Colell, A., Whinston, M.D., Green, J.R.: Microeconomic Theory. Oxford Press (1995)
25. Mishra, A., Shrivastava, V., Agrawal, D., Banerjee, S., Ganguly, S.: Distributed channel management in uncoordinated wireless environments. In: Proceedings of The Twelfth International Conference on Mobile Computing and Networking (MobiCom), Los Angeles (September 2006)
26. Osborne, M.J., Rubenstein, A.: A Course in Game Theory. MIT Press (1994)
27. Rad, A.H.M., Wong, V.W.: Joint channel allocation, interface assignment and mac design for multi-channel wireless mesh networks. In: Proceedings of 26th Annual IEEE Conference on Computer Communications (INFOCOM), Anchorage, AK, pp. 1469–1477 (May 2007)
28. Radio Administration Bureau(RAB), http://wgj.miit.gov.cn/
29. Raniwala, A., Gopalan, K., Cker Chiueh, T.: Centralized channel assignment and routing algorithms for multi-channel wireless mesh networks. ACM SIGMOBILE Mobile Computing and Communications Review (MC2R) 8(2), 50–65 (2004)
30. Srinivasan, V., Nuggehalli, P., Chiasserini, C.-F., Rao, R.: Cooperation in wireless ad hoc networks. In: Proceedings of 22nd Annual IEEE Conference on Computer Communications (INFOCOM), San Francisco, CA (April 2003)
31. Varian, H.: Economic mechanism design for computerized agents. In: USENIX Workshop on Electronic Commerce (1995)
32. Vedantham, R., Kakumanu, S., Lakshmanan, S., Sivakumar, R.: Component based channel assignment in single radio, multi-channel ad hoc networks. In: Proceedings of The Twelfth International Conference on Mobile Computing and Networking (MobiCom), Los Angeles (September 2006)

33. Vickrey, W.: Counterspeculation, auctions and competitive sealed tenders. Journal of Finance 16(1), 8–37 (1961)
34. Wang, S., Xu, P., Xu, X., Tang, S., Li, X., Liu, X.: Toda: Truthful online double auction for spectrum allocation in wireless networks. In: Proceedings of the First IEEE International Symposium on New Frontiers in Dynamic Spectrum Access Networks, DySPAN (2010)
35. Wang, W., Eidenbez, S., Wang, Y., Li, X.-Y.: Ours–optimal unicast routing systems in non-cooperative wireless networks. In: Proceedings of The Twelfth International Conference on Mobile Computing and Networking (MobiCom), Los Angeles (September 2006)
36. Wang, W., Li, X.-Y., Wang, Y.: Truthful multicast in selfish wireless networks. In: Proceedings of the Tenth International Conference on Mobile Computing and Networking (MobiCom), Philadelphia, PA (September 2004)
37. Welsh, D.J.A., Powell, M.B.: An upper bound for the chromatic number of a graph and its application to timetabling problems. The Computer Journal 10(1), 85–86 (1967)
38. West, D.B.: Introduction to Graph Theory, 2nd edn. Prentice Hall (1996)
39. Wu, F., Vaidya, N.: Small: A strategy-proof mechanism for radio spectrum allocation. In: Proceedings of 30th Annual IEEE Conference on Computer Communications (INFOCOM), Shanghai, China (April 2011)
40. Wu, F., Singh, N., Vaidya, N.H., Chen, G.: On adaptive-width channel allocation in non-cooperative, multi-radio wireless networks. In: Proceedings of 30th Annual IEEE Conference on Computer Communications (INFOCOM), Shanghai, China, pp. 2804–2812 (April 2011)
41. Wu, F., Zhong, S., Qiao, C.: Globally optimal channel assignment for non-cooperative wireless networks. In: Proceedings of 27th Annual IEEE Conference on Computer Communications (INFOCOM), Phoenix, AZ (April 2008)
42. Xu, P., Li, X.-Y., Tang, S., Zhao, J.: Efficient and strategyproof spectrum allocations in multichannel wireless networks. IEEE Trans. Computers 60(4), 580–593 (2011)
43. Xu, P., Xu, X., Tang, S., Li, X.-Y.: Truthful online spectrum allocation and auction in multichannel wireless networks. In: Proceedings of 30th Annual IEEE Conference on Computer Communications (INFOCOM), Shanghai, China (April 2011)
44. Yang, D., Fang, X., Xue, G.: Truthful auction for cooperative communications. In: Proceedings of The Eleventh ACM Symposium on Mobile Ad Hoc Networking and Computing (MobiHoc). ACM, Paris (2011)
45. Yang, J.: Spatial channel characterization for cognitive radios. Master's thesis, University of California, Berkeley (2004)
46. Zheng, H., Peng, C.: Collaboration and fairness in opportunistic spectrum access. In: Proceedings of IEEE International Conference on Communications(ICC) (September 2005)
47. Zhong, S., Li, L.E., Liu, Y.G., Yang, Y.R.: On designing incentive-compatible routing and forwarding protocols in wireless ad-hoc networks–an integrated approach using game theoretical and cryptographic techniques. In: Proceedings of The Eleventh International Conference on Mobile Computing and Networking (MobiCom), Cologne, Germany (September 2005)
48. Zhong, S., Chen, J., Yang, Y.R.: Sprite, a simple, cheat-proof, credit-based system for mobile ad-hoc networks. In: Proceedings of 22nd Annual IEEE Conference on Computer Communications (INFOCOM), San Francisco, CA (April 2003)
49. Zhong, S., Wu, F.: On designing collusion-resistant routing schemes for non-cooperative wireless ad hoc networks. In: Proceedings of The Thirteenth International Conference on Mobile Computing and Networking (MobiCom), Montreal, Canada (September 2007)
50. Zhou, X., Gandhi, S., Suri, S., Zheng, H.: ebay in the sky: Strategy-proof wireless spectrum auctions. In: Proceedings of The Fourteenth International Conference on Mobile Computing and Networking (MobiCom), San Francisco, CA (September 2008)
51. Zhou, X., Zheng, H.: Trust: A general framework for truthful double spectrum auctions. In: Proceedings of 28th Annual IEEE Conference on Computer Communications (INFOCOM), Rio de Janeiro, Brazil (April 2009)
52. Zhou, X., Zheng, H.: Breaking bidder collusion in large-scale spectrum auctions. In: Proceedings of The Eleventh ACM Symposium on Mobile Ad Hoc Networking and Computing (MobiHoc), Chicago, IL (June 2010)

A Nonparametric Bayesian Approach for Opportunistic Data Transfer in Cellular Networks

Nam Tuan Nguyen[1], Yichuan Wang[2], Xin Liu[2], Rong Zheng[3], and Zhu Han[1]

[1] ECE Department, University of Houston, TX
[2] University of California, Davis, CA
[3] CS Department, University of Houston, TX

Abstract. The number of mobile Internet users is growing rapidly, as well as the capability of mobile Internet devices. As a result, the enormous amount of traffic generated everyday on mobile Internet is pushing cellular services to their limits. We see great potential in the idea of scheduling the transmission of delay tolerant data towards times when the network condition is better. However, such scheduling requires good network condition prediction, which has not been effectively tackled in previous research. In this paper, we propose a Dynamic Hidden Markov Model (DHMM) to model the time dependent and location dependent network conditions observed by individual users. The model is dynamic since transition matrix and states are updated when new observations are available. On the other hand, it has all the properties of a Hidden Markov Model. DHMM can predict precisely the next state given the current state, hence can provide a good prediction of network condition. DHMM has two layers, the top layer is Received Signal Strength (RSS) and the bottom layer consists of states, defined as a mixture of location, time and the signal strength itself. Since the state is defined as a mixture, it is hidden and the number of states is also not known a priori. Thus, the Nonparametric Bayesian Classification is applied to determine the hidden states. We show through simulations that when combined with a Markov decision process, the opportunistic scheduling can reduce transmission costs up to 50.34% compared with a naive approach.

1 Introduction

Based on Cisco's estimate, mobile Internet traffic will grow to 6.3 exabyte (10^6 terabytes) in 2015 [1]. All wireless service providers are facing paramount challenges in serving the increasing traffic on cellular networks. However, *not all traffic is created equally*. While many applications, such as voice call and on-line gaming, demand real-time service, there exists an increasingly large number of applications that are delay tolerant times-scale, called *delay-tolerant* data. In addition, data from a large cellular network shows that there exists a significant lag between content generation and user-initiated upload time, more that 55% uploaded content on mobile network is at least 1 day old [2]. In addition to existing delay-tolerant data, service providers are also considering dynamic pricing

X. Wang et al. (Eds.): WASA 2012, LNCS 7405, pp. 88–99, 2012.
© Springer-Verlag Berlin Heidelberg 2012

to incentize certain applications and users to be more flexible in transmissions time. Such flexibility can be leveraged to improve network resource utilization through opportunistically schedules when network resource is abundant.

The delay tolerance of such jobs varies from subseconds to hours. For example, web browser and Multimedia Messaging Service (MMS) messages can tolerate subseconds to seconds of delay. Emails can tolerate seconds to tens of seconds of delay. Content update, such as Facebook, Twitter, and Rich Site Summary feeds, can tolerate hundreds of seconds of delay. Content precaching and uploading can tolerate minutes to hours of delay. OS/application updates can endure even longer delay. However, current cellular networks more or less treat all traffic as equal, which results in performance degradation during peak load period.

The idea of opportunistic transmission schedule for delay-tolerant application is first explored in [3], where a simple histogram-based predictor is employed. The performance of the opportunistic transmission scheme clearly depends on how well the future network can be predicted. In this paper, we develop a more elaborate model that better captures inherent user profile and provides more accurate estimation of future network condition. The proposed model is motivated by the predicability of human mobility patterns [4,5]. Since network conditions location and time dependent, user experienced quality of service is predictable as well. However, building a user profile is inherently hard. Though the observations of network condition can be collected, we do not know how many states there are and which state (or cluster) the observations reside in. Even for a given location, network condition is dynamic due to small scale fading and network dynamics (e.g., load). Furthermore, there are distinctive modes in human mobility, e.g., human behaves totally different during weekdays and during weekends.

To address these challenges, we propose a dynamic hidden Markov model to model the user experienced network condition as the result of user mobility, available access networks, and time-varying nature of the wireless channel. A Nonparametric Bayesian Classification (NBC) method is used to determine the state space. Observations in the Dynamic Hidden Markov Model (DHMM) consist of three features: time, location and signal strength. Since users normally follows a stable schedule, their locations are closely correlated with time and duration they are at the locations. Moreover, even within the same coarse grained location such as in a building, their mobilities or the background noises have a strong correlation over time. As a result, signal strength also has a strong correlation with location and time. NBC can be applied efficiently in this scenario to locate closely related observations and group them into corresponding clusters. Each cluster is associated with a state in our DHMM. Among many variations of NBC, the Infinite Gaussian Mixture Model (IGMM) is the most widely applicable model due to its robustness to many types of distribution as well as its high performance in classifying the observations. IGMM is a generative model describing the way the observations are created. With the DHMM, opportunistic scheduling decision can be made based on the predicted network condition and requirements of the application.

Our contributions are summarized as follows.

1. We present a Dynamic Hidden Markov Model to capture user network condition profiles. The model is dynamic because the states and transition matrix are updated each time new observations are obtained. This is necessary to accommodate the situation when users move to new locations, we need to determine the states in the model to reflect the new change. If the state is not recognized, the DHMM simply does not operate since one requirement of DHMM is the complete knowledge of states.
2. We develop a non-parametric Bayesian approach to unsupervised clustering with an unbounded number of mixtures to determine the state space of user profile. Specifically, we define a prior over the likelihood of devices using the Dirichlet distribution [6]. Based on the properties of the Dirichlet distribution, we derive a Gibbs sampling algorithm that can be used to sample from the posterior distribution, and determine the number of clusters.
3. Based on the developed DHMM model, we apply the Markov Decision Process (MDP) to decide the optimal schedule of user transmission subject to a delay requirement.

It is worth mentioning that DHMM model is general and not limited to the opportunistic scheduling. Other potential applications include location-based advertisements where the payoff not only depends on location but also on other contextual information (such as preferences and past behavior). The effectiveness of the proposed method is validated using synthetic data and the results show great improvement over a naive method.

This paper is organized as follows. In Section 2, we discuss related work. Opportunistic data transmission mechanism is described in Section 3. Section 4 introduces the DHMM system model. Next, in Section 5, we investigate the NBC approach to cluster the feature space. To evaluate the proposed framework, simulation results are presented in Section 6. And finally, conclusions are drawn in Section 7.

2   Literature Review

User profile, the history one's network condition can be used to predict his own future network condition. In [4,5], the authors point out that individual human travel patterns are highly predictable. Since network condition experienced by a user, such as available networks and signal strength, is location dependent, it also has predictability. While network condition is predictable for individual users, it may differ across different users. Hence individual user profile is crucial to obtain a good estimation of future network condition.

The idea of leveraging delay tolerant data in resource management has been studied in the literature. In [7], the authors exploit delay tolerant data for energy saving on mobile phones by choosing from different network interfaces (cellular, WiFi) if available. An online link selection algorithm based on the Lyapunov framework is proposed. In [8], the authors propose to use WiFi network whenever possible to offload data from 3G connections. They propose to use recent WiFi availability to predict the future availability. In both papers, simple first-order predictors that utilize past observations to predict future network connectivity or link transmission rate in near future.

The Markov (or hidden Markov) model is a powerful tool for prediction, and many recent works have employed it for the mobility prediction. In [9], the vehicular position location prediction is performed by the hidden Markov models (HMMs) trained with prediction data to model the strength of the received signals for particular areas. In [10], location context is used in the creation of a predictive model of users future movements based on the Markov models. In [11], by investigating the mobility problem in a cellular environment, a Markov model is constructed to predict future cells of a user.

Recently, there has been some works using nonparametric Bayesian classification. For example, in [12], the authors proposed a Nonparametric Bayesian Hidden Markov Model to build a static HMM for speech recognition, . In contrast, our work considers a dynamic HMM, and users' profiles are utilized to schedule effectively users' access. Several recent works apply the Bayesian nonparametric schemes in different applications. In [13], spectrum access in cognitive radio networks is modeled as a repeated auction game subject to monitoring and entry costs. A Bayesian nonparametric belief update scheme is devised based on the Dirichlet process. In [14], an approach is proposed that enables a number of cognitive radio devices which are observing the availability pattern of a number of primary users. The cognitive radios then cooperate and use the Bayesian nonparametric techniques to estimate the distributions of the primary users activity pattern, assumed to be completely unknown.

In this paper, the proposed DHMM is different from other works in the following aspects. In DHMM, the states are not solely determined by the location. They are combinations of time, location, and signal strength. By collecting experiment data from wireless users, we observe that even within the same location, signal strength may still vary significantly. Thus, additional information other than the location information is necessary to achieve better signal prediction. Another important contribution lies in the dynamic nature of the model, the states and transition matrix are incrementally updated to reflect the recent trend of users. Finally, different from the previous schemes, in this paper, we employ the nonparametric Bayesian approach to determine the states of the DHMM for scheduling transmission in wireless network.

3   Opportunistic Scheduling

In this section, we briefly discuss the mechanism to make scheduling decisions for an instance of data transmission given its deadline. We assume time is slotted. When delay tolerant data becomes available, the protocol is started at time slot 1. A deadline is specified by the application layer. The data has to be transmitted before the deadline, otherwise user experience will be harmed. In our framework, we call this deadline *horizon M*. The goal of the opportunistic scheduling is to

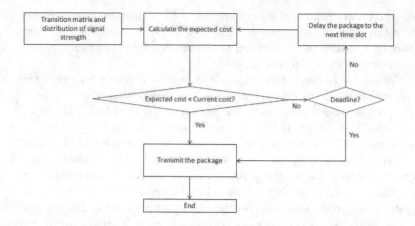

Fig. 1. Decision making process

minimize the network resource usage, while bounding the delay of data transmission. In each time slot, we make a decision whether to transmit right away or further delay the transmission based on the current network condition (e.g., RSS_i), time until deadline, and user network profile. If the deadline is imminent M, the data needs to be transmitted regardless of the network condition. Transmission at any time slot incurs an instantaneous network resource cost, which is a function of the network condition at that time, notated as L_i. The expected cost when using the optimal policy is C. The cost at a time slot i is defined as $1/RSS$ where RSS is the signal strength. The reward function is defined as the signal strength. Hence, the more the signal strength we gain by rescheduling, the more the reward we receive and the less the cost we have to pay. The notations are summarized as follows:

- M: Horizon, deadline for data transmission.
- L_i: Network resource consumption (cost) for transmitting the job at time slot i, calculated based on RSS_i.
- $C_i(S_i)$: Expected network resource cost from time slot i on using an optimal policy given current state is S_i.

If a Markov model for RSS_i is given, we can use the standard MDP technique to decide the optimal transmission time. Because MDP is a mature and well-known technique, we only sketch the main steps here due to space limitation. At each step, the action at time slot i can be decided by

$$\text{Action} = \begin{cases} \text{Transmit,} & L_i \leq C_{i+1}(S_i); \\ \text{Delay,} & L_i > C_{i+1}(S_i). \end{cases} \tag{1}$$

The decision process is illustrated on Figure 1. To find $C_i(S_i)$ for each time slot, we use the backward induction. Starting from the last time slot, if we are at the time slot M, due to the deadline, we have to transmit regardless, the expected cost is the expectation of resource cost at that time slot is $E(RSS_M|RSS_i)$. In this process, it is critical to estimate future network conditions. To address this challenging issue, we propose the DHMM model and NBC approach in the subsequent sections.

4   Dynamic Hidden Markov Model

HMM is widely used in the literature for signal strength prediction. The states are normally defined as locations that are inherently limited as mentioned in Section 2. In our work, we base on the predictability of signal strength and its strong correlation with location and time to build our model, the DHMM.

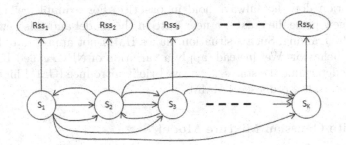

Fig. 2. Dynamic hidden markov model

Figure 2 illustrates the model. The bottom layer consists of the hidden states of the model, notated by S_i. Each state is defined as a multivariate joint distribution of time, location and signal strength. Although each state consists of a set of observations, it is still hidden because from the observations, we cannot differentiate which state generates the observations. The signal strength, location and time associated with a state are strongly correlated. Hence, they tend to be grouped together in a small cluster. User movement, including time of arrival and departure as well as visited locations, is predictable. As a result, the state, which comprises the two features, is predictable. In the model, states are associated with a cluster of observations, hence, the two concepts can be used exchangeably depending on the context.

The top layer is the RSS value, notated by RSS_i. Since each state generates its own distribution of RSS, prediction of the next state leads to the prediction of RSS following the respective distribution. In the context of scheduling user access, a distribution of the next possible states is input to a standard MDP to calculate the expected value of reward until the deadline. From the MDP result, if it is more beneficial to wait then the transmission will be delayed until we receive higher rewards. Otherwise, it will be transmitted immediately. In the next Section, we describe a procedure to determine the states of DHMM as well as the current state of an observation. We note that historical network conditions are readily available locally on mobile devices, and thus collecting this information incurs little extra cost.

At this point, the states are defined, however there are two questions left. The first question is how to determine the states and the number of the states given the observations. It is important to emphasize that the number of states or clusters are not known, hence, traditional clustering algorithms are not appropriate. And the second question is how to determine the current state of a user. Only by inferring about the current state can we calculate the transition probability and expected reward. The NBC is the best solution the questions since it does not require prior knowledge about the number of clusters to be known as a priori.

5   Nonparametric Bayesian Classification

In an HMM, it is required that the number of states is known a priori. However, this assumption does not always hold in practice. For example, when a user comes to a new place, he creates a new state in the model and this new state is not known by training. Such a situation makes HMM not appropriate for modeling a user behavior. We, instead, apply a variation of NBC, called IGMM, to dynamically determine the states. Next, we briefly introduce IGMM highlighting its connection to the proposed DHMM.

5.1   Infinite Gaussian Mixture Model

IGMM is a generating model following which we believe the observations are created. Intuitively, we assume that there are an unbounded number of joint distributions, each distribution generates a cluster of observations. One observation here in our application includes three parameters, time, location and signal strength. In IGMM, it is assumed that the number of clusters is infinite, but only a limited number of clusters are observed. The number of clusters can grow as large as needed when more data is obtained. Figure 3 shows a graphical representation of the IGMM, and a formal definition of IGMM is given below:

Definition 1. *Infinite Gaussian Mixture Model.*

$$\boldsymbol{w}|\alpha \sim Stick(\alpha); z_i|\boldsymbol{w} \sim Multinomial(\cdot|\boldsymbol{w}); \boldsymbol{\theta}_k \sim \boldsymbol{H};$$
$$\boldsymbol{x}_i|(z_i = k, \Sigma_k, \boldsymbol{\mu}_k) \sim G(\cdot|\boldsymbol{\mu}_k, \Sigma_k), \tag{2}$$

where $\boldsymbol{\theta}_j \sim \boldsymbol{H}$ stands for:

$$\Sigma_k \sim Inverse\ Wishart_{v0}(\Lambda_0); \boldsymbol{\mu}_k \sim G(\boldsymbol{\mu}_0, \Sigma_k/K_0), \tag{3}$$

and $\boldsymbol{w}|\alpha \sim Stick(\alpha)$ is a shorthand of:

$$w'_k|\alpha \sim Beta(1, \alpha); w_k = w'_k \prod_{l=1}^{K-1}(1 - w'_k); K \to \infty. \tag{4}$$

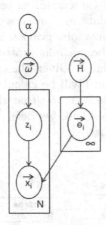

Fig. 3. Infinite gaussian mixture model

Figure 3 and the above definition fully describe the IGMM. The $Stick(\alpha)$ is a *stick breaking process* [6] used to generate an infinite number of weights, $\boldsymbol{w}$, that sum up to 1. $\boldsymbol{w}$ is the mixing weight vector, which defines the contributions of each distribution in the observations set. $z_i = k$ indicates that $\boldsymbol{x}_i$ belongs to cluster k with probability $p(z_i = k) = w_k$. and $\boldsymbol{X} = [\boldsymbol{x}_1, \boldsymbol{x}_2, ..., \boldsymbol{x}_N]$ is the data set of N observations. The observations are assumed to follow k joint Gaussian distributions which can be represented by $\boldsymbol{\theta}_k$, a parameter set of a cluster. Specifically, $\boldsymbol{\theta}_k$ includes a set of mean vector and covariance matrix for each cluster. The mean vector and the covariance matrix in turn are assumed to follow a Gaussian distribution and Inverse Wishart distribution, $\boldsymbol{H}$, respectively.

Specifically, the generative model can be explained in our scenario as follow. A user can travel to many locations and each location has a different signal strength profile at different time of the day. As a result, a combination of location, signal strength, and time forms a cluster, which follows a distribution represented by $\boldsymbol{\theta}_k$, where k is the index of the cluster. The arrival time and departure time of the user at a specific location and the signal strength at that location can be reasonably assumed to follow Gaussian distributions. The parameter vector includes two components, $\boldsymbol{\mu}_k$ and Σ_k. $\boldsymbol{\mu}_k$ can be understood as an aggregate of the means of the four dimensions. The same interpretation applies to Σ_k as the variance. The mean vector, α represents our confidence on the model. The larger the α, the stronger our confidence about choosing the base distribution, $\boldsymbol{H}$, and the more concentrated the distributions of $\boldsymbol{\theta}_k$'s around that base distribution.

5.2   Determining the States

Given the model and the observations, infer the model parameters using the inference algorithm in [15] [16]. A Gibbs sampling algorithm [15] is implemented to sample the indicators from their posterior distributions. The indicators here in our application are the labels of the states. To this end, we are now in the position to outline the opportunistic scheduling based on DHMM as illustrated in Figure 4. First, the training data are processed, and states are determined by the Gibbs sampler. When a new observation is available, we run the Gibb sampler again to determine the observations' states. After identifying the states, the transition matrix will be updated. Given the current state and the updated transition matrix, the future reward will be calculated until the deadline. If the cost of transfer in the current state is greater than the expected cost in the future and the deadline has not been reached, we defer the transmission. Otherwise, data will be transmitted immediately.

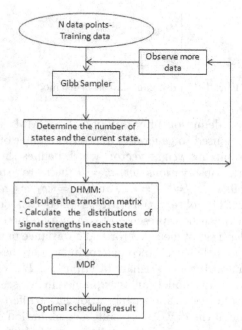

Fig. 4. Opportunistic scheduling framework

As we can see, the states in DHMM are dynamically updated as more observations becomes available. This property is a significant improvement since we are able to determine the current state associated with the observation and incorporate the new observation into the model when the user moves to a location that has never been recorded. Given the current states, one can easily update the transition matrix in the DHMM model to reflect the recent dynamics.

6   Simulation Results

To evaluate the proposed method, we generate synthetic data as follows. A random number of locations were selected, each location is specified by a two-tuple of longitude and latitude. Every day, the user follows a schedule and stays in each location for a Normal distributed random length of time. Totally, there are 14 locations. The longitude and latitude means for the locations are chosen randomly in the range of [0, 14] with variance in each location set to 1. Signal strength mean in each location is selected randomly in the range of [0, 30] and has a standard deviation of 1.55dBm. Deadline is chosen to be 20. After generating the synthetic data, we divide it into two parts, a training part and an online part. Transmission cost is defined as the inverse of the signal strength. Figure 5 shows the output of the Gibbs sampler. Since we can only show a 3D picture, latitude, time and RSS were chosen. Observations within a rectangle are from the same location while those within an eclipse are classified as one cluster or state by the Gibbs sampler. Although there are only 10 locations, Gibbs sampler outputs 14 states since at the same location, there can be more than one signal strength profiles over the time.

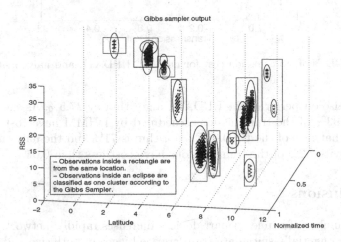

Fig. 5. Clustering result

The Gibbs sampler has high clustering accuracy and agility when new observations are present. As shown in Figure 5, although there are only three observations marked by "x", they are grouped together to form a new state. Thus, whenever a user enters a new new location, the DHMM will be immediately updated with the new state.

Each scenario is run 800 times using traces from the online part of the synthetic profile to make the results statistically meaningful. Performance of the DHMM is compared with that of two other methods. The first method is a naive approach, which simply transmits data immediately regardless of future rewards. The second method is the UPDATE algorithm in [3]. Every time, all three algorithms are used to schedule the transmission on the same synthetic trace, and the total transmission cost of each test is collected. In Figure 6, we show the Cumulative Distribution Function (CDF) of the transmission costs in all the tests run. CDF is used to show the distribution of transmission cost among all the tests. An average reduction of 50.34% of network cost is achieved when applying the DHMM and MDP compared to the naive one. Our proposed

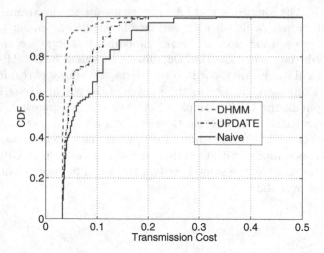

Fig. 6. CDFs of transmission cost for DHMM, UPDATE and naive methods

framework also outperforms the UPDATE algorithm by 27.5%. As shown in the figure, over 93% of the transmissions scheduled by DHMM have cost less than 0.04, while that rate of the UPDATE algorithm is 71% and the naive method is even worse with 52% of the transmissions have cost less than 0.04.

7   Conclusions

When the number of wireless smart devices increases rapidly, network load also increases exponentially since data transfers are bigger in both size and quantity. However, not all traffic are created equally. In this paper, we propose to exploit the delay-tolerance of certain data transfers to opportunistically schedule such jobs to times when the network condition is more favorable. To achieve this goal, we proposed an DHMM model and the NBC approach to build an adaptive model of user profiles based on observations. Through simulations, we showed that the proposed scheme improves over the naive method by 50.34%. The results presented in this paper demonstrated the promises of exploiting user and application characteristics in better resource management in cellular data networks. As future work, we plan to collect real-world measurement data from mobile users to test the proposed framework.

References

1. Cisco visual networking index: Global mobile data traffic forecast update, 20102015 (2010), http://www.cisco.com/en/US/solutions/collateral/ns341/ns525/ns537/ns705/ns827/white_paper_c11-520862.html
2. Trestian, A.K.I., Ranjan, S., Nucci, A.: Taming user-generated content in mobile networks via drop zones. In: Proc. of IEEE INFOCOM 2011 (April 2011)

3. Wang, Y., Liu, X.: UPDATE: User-Profile-Driven Adaptive Transfer preprint, http://www.cs.ucdavis.edu/~liu/preprint/Update.pdf
4. Gonzalez, M.C., Hidalgo, C.A., Barabasi, A.L.: Understanding individual human mobility patterns. Nature 453(7196), 779–782 (2008)
5. Song, C., Qu, Z., Blumm, N., Barabsi, A.-L.: Limits of predictability in human mobility. Science 327(5968), 1018–1021 (2010)
6. Teh, Y.W.: Dirichlet processes. Encyclopedia of Machine Learning. Springer, New York (2007)
7. Ra, M.-R., Paek, J., Sharma, A., Govindan, R., Krieger, M.H., Neely, M.J.: Energy-delay tradeoffs in smartphone applications. In: Banerjee, S., Keshav, S., Wolman, A. (eds.) MobiSys, pp. 255–270. ACM (2010)
8. Balasubramanian, A., Mahajan, R., Venkataramani, A.: Augmenting mobile 3g using WiFi. In: MobiSys 2010: Proceedings of the 8th International Conference on Mobile Systems, Applications, and Services, pp. 209–222. ACM, New York (2010)
9. Mangold, S., Kyriazakos, S.: Applying pattern recognition techniques based on hidden Markov models for vehicular position location in cellular networks. In: IEEE Vehicular Technology Conference (1999)
10. Ashbrook, D., Starner, T.: Using GPS to learn significant locations and predict movement across multiple users. Personal and Ubiquitous Computing 7(5), 275–286 (2003)
11. Bhattacharya, A., Das, S.K.: LeZi-Update: An information-theoretic framework for personal mobility tracking in PCS networks. Wireless Networks 8(2/3), 121–135 (2002)
12. Ding, N., Ou, Z.: Variational nonparametric Bayesian Hidden Markov Model. In: The Proceedings of IEEE International Conference on Acoustics, Speech, and Signal Processing (ICASSP), Dallas, TX, USA (2010)
13. Han, Z., Zheng, R., Poor, V.H.: Repeated auctions with Bayesian nonparametric learning for spectrum access in cognitive radio networks. IEEE Transactions on Wireless Communications 10(3), 890–900 (2011)
14. Saad, W., Han, Z., Poor, H.V., Basar, T., Song, J.B.: A cooperative Bayesian nonparametric framework for primary user activity monitoring in cognitive radio Networks. IEEE Journal on Selected Areas in Communications, special issue on Cooperative Network (accepted)
15. Wood, F., Black, M.J.: A nonparametric bayesian alternative to spike sorting. Journal of Neuroscience Methods 173(1), 1–12 (2008)
16. Nguyen, N.T., Zheng, G., Han, Z., Zheng, R.: Device fingerprinting to enhance wireless security using nonparametric Bayesian method. In: IEEE Annual IEEE Conference on Computer Communications INFOCOM, Shanghai (April 2011)

Online Protocol Verification in Wireless Sensor Networks via Non-intrusive Behavior Profiling

Yangfan Zhou[1,2], Xinyu Chen[1], Michael R. Lyu[1,2], and Jiangchuan Liu[3]

[1] Shenzhen Research Institute, The Chinese U. of Hong Kong, Shenzhen, China
[2] Dept. of Comp. Sci. and & Eng., The Chinese U. of Hong Kong, Shatin, Hong Kong
[3] School of Computing Sci., Simon Fraser U., Burnaby, BC, Canada

Abstract. Wireless communication protocols are centric to Wireless Sensor Network (WSN) applications. However, WSN protocols are prune to defects, even after their field deployments. A convenient tool that can facilitate the detection of post-deployment protocol defects is of great importance to WSN practitioners. This paper presents Probe-I (sensor network Protocol behavior Inspector), a novel tool to obtain, visualize, and verify the behaviors of WSN protocols after their field deployments. Probe-I collects the protocol behaviors in a non-intrusive manner, *i.e.*, via passively listening to the packet exchanges in the target network. Then with a role-oriented behavior modeling approach, Probe-I models the protocol behaviors node by node based on the sniffed packets, which well reflects how the target protocol performs in each node. This allows the WSN practitioners to readily see if the target protocol behaves as intended by simply verifying the correctness of the behavior metrics in a simple, baseline test. Finally, the verified metrics allow Probe-I to automatically check the protocol behaviors from time to time during the network lifetime. The suggested behavior discrepancy can unveil potential protocol defects. We apply Probe-I to verify two WSN data collection protocols, and find their design defects. It shows that Probe-I can substantially facilitate WSN protocol verification.

1 Introduction

Wireless communication protocols are centric to wireless sensor networks (WSNs) in reporting the physical information of interest. The successful application of a WSN largely relies on whether its protocols can work as intended. However, recent publications have reported that various protocol defects are frequently encountered in field deployments, leading to their failures [1,2]. Trustworthy protocol remains a critical concern towards the extensive deployments of WSNs. Unfortunately, discovering protocol defects after deployment is a very challenging task. It is hard to identify the subtle symptoms of a defect before it causes notable problems that may lead to fatal system failures.

This paper presents Probe-I (sensor network Protocol behavior Inspector), a novel tool to unveil post-deployment protocol defects in WSNs. A WSN practitioner can load Probe-I into a mobile device and carry it to the deployment field.

X. Wang et al. (Eds.): WASA 2012, LNCS 7405, pp. 100–111, 2012.

`Probe-I` can then profile the runtime of a protocol, learn its behavior models, and automatically produce alarms when suspicious protocol defect symptoms are found. To this end, `Probe-I` incorporates two key components: a *non-intrusive* mechanism to collect the protocol runtime data and accurately model the protocol behaviors, and an anomalous behavior detection approach that can identify protocol defect symptoms from the tremendous behavior data.

Key to `Probe-I` in modeling protocol behaviors is that the packet exchanging profiles of a protocol can well reflect its behaviors, since packet exchanging is centric to WSN protocols in nature. Hence, leveraging on the broadcasting nature of wireless communications, `Probe-I` equips a wireless interface (*e.g.*, that on a compatible sensor node) compatible with that adopted in the target network, and passively eavesdrops the packets in the air. A profiling approach specifically tailored for WSN protocols is then employed to model the behaviors of the target protocol based on the sniffed packets. Thus, unlike instrumentation-based tools (*e.g.*, EnviroLog [3] and Declarative Tracepoints [4]) that will inevitably intrude the executions of the target protocol, `Probe-I` requires no modifications to both the software and hardware of the target sensor nodes. Most importantly, it will not alter the original executions of the target protocol. This provides it nice fidelity and no overhead in capturing the protocol behaviors.

Although the protocol behaviors can be profiled, manually inspecting the data to identify the potential defect symptoms becomes a daunting task, which may be extremely labor intensive. `Probe-I` addresses this challenge with a two-step approach. First, it allows a WSN practitioner to perform a baseline test, where the protocol behaviors are easy to be verified. After the correctness of the protocol is confirmed in the baseline test, `Probe-I` saves the *verified* behavior data to the mobile device. During the system runtime, the WSN practitioner can from time to time bring the device again to the network field. The newly collected protocol behavior data will be compared with the verified data obtained in the baseline test. The discrepancy of the two set of data indicates suspicious protocol behaviors. `Probe-I` will then issue an alert, suggesting further inspection of the protocol implementation.

The rest of the paper is organized as follows. We overview the design of `Probe-I` in Section 2. Section 3 elaborates how `Probe-I` collects the protocol runtime data of a WSN protocol and models its behaviors. In Section 4, we discuss the details on detecting defect symptoms in `Probe-I`. Two case studies are provided in Section 5 to demonstrate the effectiveness of `Probe-I`. Section 6 presents the related work. We conclude this paper in Section 7.

2   Overview of Probe-I

Figure 1 shows the concept of our mobile device assisted non-intrusive approach, namely, `Probe-I`, to discover post-deployment protocol defects. The packet exchanges of the target WSN can be eavesdropped with a compatible wireless interfacing device, namely, a *sniffer*, connected to a more powerful mobile device (*e.g.*, a tablet computer). A convenient choice of such a sniffer is a compatible

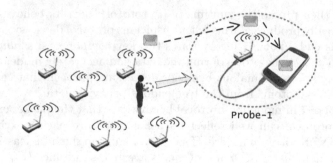

Fig. 1. Probe-I concept

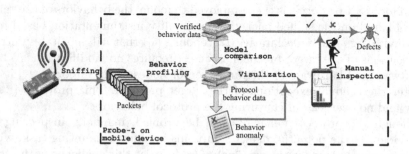

Fig. 2. System overview of Probe-I

sensor node. Exploiting the computational and visualization capabilities of the mobile device, Probe-I models and shows the protocol behaviors. Suspicious behaviors can be detected, which help discover post-deployment protocol defects.

Such a new conceptual design is feasible with the recent advancement in mobile computing. For example, the current version of Android [5] enables mobile devices to connect through a USB (Universal Serial Bus) cable to a peripheral device via the on-the-go (OTG) mode or the host mode. It is convenient to connect a mobile device to a sniffer to obtain the packets it has captured.

Figure 2 overviews the Probe-I design. Probe-I can collect the protocol behaviors in a simple test scenario and plot them. A WSN practitioner can then readily examine whether the protocol behaves as intended. We call such a verification process a *baseline test*. If the correctness of the protocol in the baseline test is verified, the behavior data can be saved in the mobile device for further verification processes, namely, the *runtime tests*: During the network lifetime, the WSN practitioner can from time to time carry the mobile device into the network field to verify the protocol. Each time when a node is accessed, Probe-I can collect its behaviors, and compare them with those collected in the baseline test. The discrepancy means that the protocol behaviors are different from the baseline test unexpectedly, which, as a result, indicates potential defect symptoms. Hence, such discrepancy will be shown to the WSN practitioner.

Next, we will discuss how Probe-I collects and models the protocol behaviors in Section 3, and how Probe-I finds behavior discrepancy in Section 4.

3   Protocol Behavior Profiling and Modeling

3.1   Profiling Protocol Behaviors

When a protocol defect is triggered, it will change the correct behaviors of the protocol, resulting in a malfunction or a performance degradation. Since packet exchanges are centric to a protocol, the malfunction or performance degradation of a protocol will generally cause the packet exchanging behaviors to deviate from the normal. Examples include packet loss, large packet delay, and low packet throughput. Hence, we can verify the protocol via a "black box" approach, *i.e.*, by monitoring the packet exchanging behaviors.

Note that it is possible that the sniffer successfully receives a packet intended to a node, while the node *per se* fails to receive the packet, or *vice versa*. Such inconsistency will make the sniffer get distorted knowledge of the protocol. To avoid it, `Probe-I` focuses on one node at a time (namely, the *target node u*) by putting the sniffer close to u. Thus, it can obtain high-fidelity packet receiving events of the target node. In this way, `Probe-I` observes the behaviors of the protocol running on u by monitoring the packets that involve u (*i.e.*, those intended for u and those sent by u).

Fig. 3. Typical packet structure of WSNs

To do this, `Probe-I` should be packet content-aware. It obtains the sender and receiver information by analyzing the packet header. Figure 3 shows the typical packet structure of WSNs, where a packet p consists of a header and a payload. Let $p.data$ denote the payload. In the header, the *sender ID* is the node that sends the packet (*i.e.*, the *sender*). The *receiver ID* is its intended recipient (*i.e.*, the *receiver*). When a node sends or relays a packet, it will update the *sender ID* to its own ID, and the *receiver ID* to its next-hop neighbor. Let $p.src$ and $p.dest$ denote the sender and receiver of p. Note that such a packet structure is generally adopted in typical WSN protocols. For example, the *Active Message* packet format bears such a structure, which is generally used in the protocols for TinyOS applications [6] (*e.g.*, Collection Tree Protocol (CTP) [7]).

Provided the packet format information, `Probe-I` can then parse the packets it has eavesdropped during t. For a sniffed packet p, if either $p.src$ or $p.dest$ is node u, `Probe-I` will save p (together with the capturing time, denoted by $p.time$). Thus, during the monitoring period t, `Probe-I` can obtain a sequence of packets that are sent to or sent by u in a chronological order of their capturing time. Let $\mathcal{P}_t(u)$ denote such a sequence. `Probe-I` then models the protocol behaviors running on u during t based on $\mathcal{P}_t(u)$, which is illustrated next.

3.2 Role-Oriented Protocol Behavior Modeling

Data packet flows in a WSN typically follow two types, data collection and data dissemination. The former is generally for obtaining the readings from the sensor nodes, while the latter for distributing information to the sensor nodes. Considering the major purpose of WSNs is typically for obtaining the sensor readings, we focus on modeling the behaviors of data collection protocols in this paper. Data dissemination can be deemed as the reverse traffic of data collection, and therefore can be modeled with a similar approach.

There are three kinds of nodes involved in a typical data collection protocol, specifically, *source*, *sink*, and *relay*, as shown in Figure 4. A source node generates a packet (*e.g.*, a packet carrying the sensor readings of the node), a sink node is the intended final destination of the packet, and a relay is an intermediate node that helps forward the packet to its next-hop neighbor towards the sink.

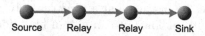

Source   Relay   Relay   Sink

Fig. 4. A simple scenario where three roles of nodes are shown

Probe-I identifies that a target node u is a source if it captures packets from u which are not previously received by u. We say such a packet p is *generated* by node u. A target node u is a sink if Probe-I captures packets intended for u which will not again be sent out by u. We say such a packet p is *collected* by node u. Finally, Probe-I can know that a target node u is a relay if it captures packets intended for u which is again sent out by u. We say such a packet p is *relayed* by node u. The above notions are formally described as follows.

source - if $\exists\, p \in \mathcal{P}_t(u)$ with $p.src = u$ and $\nexists\, q$ with $q.dest = u$ and $q.data = p.data$
sink   - if $\exists\, p \in \mathcal{P}_t(u)$ with $p.dest = u$ and $\nexists\, q$ with $q.src = u$ and $q.data = p.data$
relay - if $\exists\, p$ and $q \in \mathcal{P}_t(u)$ with $p.dest = u$, $q.src = u$, and $q.data = p.data$

Naturally, nodes with different roles (*i.e.*, source, sink, or relay) have different protocol behavior specifics, which should be modeled separately. What follows discusses our role-oriented behavior modeling considerations.

1) Source: For a source node, an important consideration is the number of packets it has generated in a given period of time. In this regard, Probe-I divides the monitoring period into many disjoint time intervals, each with a fix length τ. Then it considers the packets g_i ($i = 1, 2, ..., \lfloor \frac{t}{\tau} \rfloor$) generated by u in every time interval as the metrics that reflect the behaviors of the protocol running at u.

2) Sink: For a sink node, the number of packets it can collect in a given period of time is an important parameter. Hence, similarly, Probe-I also divides the monitoring period into disjoint time intervals, each with length τ. Then it considers the packets c_i ($i = 1, 2, ..., \lfloor \frac{t}{\tau} \rfloor$) collected by u in every time interval as the metrics that reflect the protocol behaviors at u.

Moreover, if packet sequence number is available in the packet structure (see Figure 3), it is then feasible to check the end-to-end packet loss rate. Again, packet loss rate is measured in each of the intervals with length τ.

3) Relay: Critical to a packet relay process is how long a packet has been staying in the relay node. This indicates the hop-by-hop delay, and contributes in sum to the end-to-end delay of the packet. Therefore, `Probe-I` obtains the time between when a packet arrives at node u and when the packet leaves the node. Specifically, consider packets p and q in $\mathcal{P}_t(u)$ with $p.dest=q.src=u$ and $q.data=p.data$. Then the relay delay is $q.time-p.time$. `Probe-I` uses such delays of all forwarded packets in t to model the protocol behaviors in t.

Note that it is possible that a packet p may be resent if the packet cannot be successfully delivered. Hence, in the above considerations, q is the packet with the largest $q.time$ in all packets with source field src identical to u and payload field $data$ identical to $p.data$. In other words, we only consider the last (successful) relay attempt of a packet.

Moreover, to describe such *retransmissions*, for the source and the relay nodes, `Probe-I` records the number of transmission attempts for each packet being sent. This metric can capture the link quality.

Finally, `Probe-I` also measures the *protocol overhead* for all nodes. Specifically, it divides the monitoring period into disjoint time intervals, each with length τ, and calculates the ratio between the number of data packets and that of control packets in each interval.

4   Detecting the Anomalous Protocol Behaviors

Now we discuss how `Probe-I` compares the verified behaviors (*i.e.*, those collected in the baseline test) with those collected in a runtime test. The protocol behaviors of a node may change in two aspects, *i.e.*, role or behavior metrics discussed in Section 3. We illustrate them as follows.

4.1   Role Changes

We consider the role change of a node because it may reflect dramatic changes of the protocol behaviors. For example, when a node recognized as a relay in the baseline test is found to be a sink in a runtime test, it means that the node has not relayed some received packets as it should have done. This indicates unexpected packet drops for the relay node. Hence, such a model violation should be presented to the WSN practitioner.

Finally, note that it is straightforward to detect the role change of a node with the role identification approach described in Section 3.2.

4.2   Discrepancy in Behavior Data

`Probe-I` compares the protocol behaviors in terms of their data distributions. Specifically, given each protocol behavior metric, we suggest that for the two sets of corresponding behavior data $\mathcal{B}$ and $\mathcal{R}$ collected in the baseline test and the runtime test respectively, their distributions should be compared. If their distributions have no significant difference, `Probe-I` considers that the protocol behaviors in the runtime test is similar to those in the baseline test. As a result, the protocol functions correctly in the runtime test.

`Probe-I` detects the discrepancy of the behavior data in $\mathcal{B}$ and $\mathcal{R}$ with a statistical hypothesis test approach as follows. First, `Probe-I` assigns the samples in $\mathcal{B}$ into k different bins according to their values. We consider two cases: 1) The data of the performance metric are continuous; 2) They are discrete. The relay delay is an example of the first case, while the transmission times is an example of the second case.

1) The data are continuous: Suppose b_{max} and b_{min} are the samples with largest and smallest values in $\mathcal{B}$ respectively. Then, $(-\infty, +\infty)$ is divided into k intervals, where $[b_{min} + \frac{b_{max}-b_{min}}{2(k-1)}, b_{max} - \frac{b_{max}-b_{min}}{2(k-1)}]$ is divided into k-2 intervals with equal size $\frac{b_{max}-b_{min}}{k-1}$, and two tail intervals are $(-\infty, b_{min} + \frac{b_{max}-b_{min}}{2(k-1)}]$ and $(b_{max} - \frac{b_{max}-b_{min}}{2(k-1)}, +\infty)$. A bin is then assigned to each interval. A sample is put into a bin if the value of the sample falls into the corresponding interval of the bin. Figure 5(a) shows an example of how to divide $(-\infty, +\infty)$ into k=5 intervals, while Figure 5(b) shows the resulting bins corresponding to the intervals.

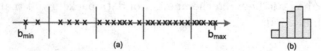

(a)   (b)

Fig. 5. An example showing how to put the samples (each denoted by a 'x') into 5 bins

2) The data are discrete: Suppose there are k different values of the samples in $\mathcal{B}$. A bin is then assigned to each value. A sample is put into a bin if the value of the sample is equal to the corresponding value of the bin.

Thus, for either case, all the samples in $\mathcal{B}$ can be put into the bins. Let B_1, B_2, ..., B_k denote the number of samples in the bins respectively. Then, for all the samples in $\mathcal{R}$ collected in the runtime test, they will also be put into k bins, according to the same value intervals as those for $\mathcal{B}$ (for the continuous data case), or according to the same values as those for $\mathcal{B}$ (for the discrete data case). Let R_1, R_2, ..., R_k denote the number of samples in the bins respectively.

Note that for the discrete-data case, it is possible that a sample in $\mathcal{R}$ cannot be put into any of the k bins. In other words, its value does not match the values of any samples in $\mathcal{B}$. In this case, such a sample is an outlier. This indicates an anomaly in the protocol behaviors in the runtime test, comparing with the baseline test. Hence, `Probe-I` will report such discrepancy in behavior data immediately and suggest further inspection of the protocol implementation.

Otherwise (*i.e.*, all the samples in $\mathcal{R}$ can be put into the bins), let us suppose the number of the data samples in $\mathcal{R}$ is n. If the data samples in $\mathcal{R}$ follow the distribution of the data samples in $\mathcal{B}$, the *expected* number of the samples in each bin i, denoted by $\overline{R}_i$, should be:

$$\overline{R}_i = \frac{B_i}{\sum_{i=1}^{k} B_i} \cdot n \tag{1}$$

If the expected number of samples in any bin in either tail is less than 5, the bin is pooled with a neighboring bin, until the count in each extreme bin is at least 5. Suppose in the end, there are m resulting bins. Let R'_1, R'_2, ..., R'_m denote the numbers of samples in $\mathcal{R}$ that are put in the m bins respectively, and $\overline{R}'_1$, $\overline{R}'_2$, ..., $\overline{R}'_m$ denote the expected numbers of samples in $\mathcal{R}$ that should be in the bins respectively.

Probe-I then adopts Pearson's chi-squared (χ^2) hypothesis test to test the goodness of fit of the two sets of data (*i.e.*, $[R'_1, R'_2, ..., R'_m]$ and $[\overline{R}'_1, \overline{R}'_2, ..., \overline{R}'_m]$) in terms of their distributions [8]. Its *null hypothesis* is that the distribution of $[R'_1, R'_2, ..., R'_m]$ is consistent with the expected distribution, *i.e.* that of $[\overline{R}'_1, \overline{R}'_2, ..., \overline{R}'_m]$, while the *alternative hypothesis* is that it is not.

For the χ^2 test, the value of the test-statistic is calculated as [8]:

$$\chi^2 = \sum_{i=1}^{m} \frac{(R'_i - \overline{R}'_i)^2}{\overline{R}'_i} \tag{2}$$

The χ^2 statistic can then be used to calculate a *p-value* by comparing the value of the statistic to a χ^2 distribution with the number of degrees of freedom equal to $m-1$. The p-value represents the uncertainty in the claim that the null hypothesis is false. Probe-I considers that when the p-value is larger than 0.1, a conventional significance level threshold, the null hypothesis will not be rejected. In other words, we will consider that the protocol behaviors in the baseline test are different from those in the runtime test if the difference in the distributions of $\mathcal{B}$ and $\mathcal{R}$ is statistically significant, *i.e.*, the probability that the alternative hypothesis is true is larger than 90%. In this case, Probe-I will output such a protocol behavior anomaly detected in the runtime test, and suggest further inspection of the protocol implementation.

Finally, note that the statistical hypothesis test is non-parametric, which does not require any *a priori* knowledge of the distribution. This fits our problem domain since we do not know how a performance metric should actually distribute for the target protocol.

5   Evaluation

To show the effectiveness of Probe-I in modeling and verifying WSN protocols, we provide two representative case studies in this section. We will examine how protocol behavior anomalies caused by design defects can be conveniently identified with Probe-I. The target WSN protocols in these two case studies are based on the codes distributed with TinyOS [6].

We implement Probe-I with Java. Such a platform independent implementation makes it convenient to port it to various mobile devices. In our experimental studies, for convenience consideration, we use a laptop computer as the mobile device and a sensor node as the sniff to eavesdrop the packets exchanged in our target WSNs. The computer is connected with the sniff with a USB cable.

5.1   Case Study I: Data Forwarding

In our first case study, we verify a lightweight multi-hop packet forwarding protocol based on `BlinkToRadio` distributed with TinyOS [6]. The target WSN contains three sensor nodes. The correct behaviors of the target protocol are simple: Node 2 will generate 25 packets per second, and send each packet to node 1. Node 1, upon receiving a packet from node 2, will forward the packet immediately to node 0. Node 0 will collect the packets intended for itself. In other words, node 0 is a sink, node 1 is a relay, and node 2 is a source.

After the network is deployed, we perform a baseline test. The sniff is put close the three nodes one by one. Since the baseline test should be a simple verifiable test, for each target node, the monitoring period is short (nearly 30 seconds). `Probe-I` then collects the packets sent to or sent by each target node, and models the protocol behaviors running on each node. τ is set 1 second. `Probe-I` then identify the role of each node successfully. For each node, the corresponding behavior metrics are also consistent with our design purpose. Hence, the correctness of the protocol is confirmed in the baseline test.

We then again access the network with `Probe-I` to perform a runtime test. This time we let `Probe-I` monitor each node for a longer period of time (nearly 3 minutes). `Probe-I` finds no behavior anomaly for the sink node and the source node. Also, for the relay node, `Probe-I` does not find the data of the behavior metrics (*i.e.*, the relay delay and the transmission attempts) collected in both tests have significant discrepancy. However, it issues an alert showing that node 1 has two roles: a new but unintended role *sink*, in addition to its designed role *relay*. This is obviously a fault, which means node 1 must have received some packets and have not sent them out.

We then inspect the protocol implementation for the relay node. Starting from the codes that handle a packet receiving event, we instantly find that a received packet can be actively dropped in function `AMSend.send` due to a busy flag. The flag is set when the node is in the process of sending a packet. This means before a previously-received packet has been sent, another packet arrives unexpectedly, causing the protocol to drop the new arrival packet. To correct this fault, the protocol should employ a buffer to cache packets until the previously-received packet has been sent.

Note that such a fault is only triggered occasionally, and causes an occasional packet loss, which tends to be neglected. We have shown that `Probe-I` can however effectively model the protocol behaviors and successfully detect such a subtle protocol defect via identifying role changes of sensor nodes.

5.2   Case Study II: Collection Tree Protocol

In this case study, we test a more sophisticated routing protocol CTP (Collection Tree Protocol) [9]. CTP is frequently employed to transfer sensor readings to sinks. We intend to examine whether CTP performs well in mobile networks. The target WSN contains four sensor nodes. One is the sink, while three are sources that will generate one packet per second. The packets from the sources will be conveyed to the sink possibly via other sensor nodes. Hence, a source node may also serve as a relay. Since the packet rate is low, we set τ 10 seconds in our tests, and let `Probe-I` monitor each sensor node for nearly 3 minutes.

In our baseline test, all nodes are stationary. `Probe-I` correctly identifies the node roles. The behavior metrics are also correct. The baseline test has passed.

We then start a runtime test, where the sink and two nodes close to the sink are stationary (which may serve as relays) and the rest one node is mobile. CTP should be able to find another relay when the previous relay for the mobile node cannot be reached due to its mobility. `Probe-I` reports that the distributions of the number of packet transmission attempts and the overhead are inconsistent with the baseline test. In particular, `Probe-I` shows that the number of packet transmission attempts has a new value 30, *i.e.*, some packets are retransmitted for 30 times. By inspecting the CTP design, we find that a route is considered broken only when a packet cannot be successfully transmitted after 30 attempts. This may not be proper for mobile networks.

`Probe-I` reveals that CTP may not be a good choice for mobile networks, since routes may be reestablished frequently, incurring larger overhead and transmission failures (and packet loss). The route reestablishing procedure should be improved to cope with node mobility, which confirms the findings in [10].

This case study demonstrates how `Probe-I` can greatly facilitate the verification of a protocol in a new network scenario. Note that without such a tool, it would be quite labor-intensive to manually inspect the design of CTP to justify whether it is applicable in the new mobile scenario.

6   Related Work

Various research efforts have been put to enhance the reliability of WSN protocols. Many techniques, including simulation-based testing and troubleshooting approaches, network monitoring mechanisms, and debugging tools are proposed, which are surveyed in what follows.

TOSSIM [11] and Avrora [12] are two widely-adopted simulation tools for WSNs. Before field-deploying a protocol, WSN practitioners can resort to such simulation platforms to confirm its correct behavior. But a comprehensive simulation will generate tremendous protocol behavior data. Verifying the correctness of the protocol behavior largely depends on manual efforts, which is labor-intensive. T-Check [13] and KleeNet [14] are two simulation-based approaches that can find WSN bugs by exploring program states extensively. Sentomist [15] locates bug symptoms via finding outliers in application behaviors collected via simulations. However, high-fidelity simulation remains difficult, given the complexity of the real world and the unexpected working scenarios [16]. As a result, protocol defects may still escape from being detected in simulation platforms. `Probe-I`, in contrast, focuses on detecting protocol defects in deployed networks.

SNTS [17] deploys many additional sensor nodes in the target network field to collect the packets of the target WSN. These sensor nodes have to be collected manually to retrieve their collected packets. It only suits small experimental network. PAD [18] attaches logs in regular data packets to help the base station diagnose network problems. The logging and piggyback mechanisms will inevitably disturb the original protocol behaviors.

Sympathy [19] introduces a diagnosis agent in the target sensor nodes to collects their run-time data, and transmitting them to the base station. Tools based on instrumentation (*e.g.*, EnviroLog [3] and Declarative Tracepoints [4]) have also been proposed to log the protocol behaviors in a sensor node during its runtime. PDA [20] inserts state hypotheses into the WSN codes. If they do not hold during runtime, alerts can be issued. These tools can help detect protocol defects. However, as real-time systems, WSN programs are sensitive to timing. Running on the same hardware, such behavior data collection and verification mechanisms will inevitably intrude the executions of the original codes. As a result, a defect may hide when such a mechanism turns on, but can still be triggered when it is disabled. Hence, these tools are still not adequate to eliminating protocol defects, not to mention the human efforts in reprogramming an existing WSN application to incorporate such tools. Probe-I avoids such inadequacy via a non-intrusive protocol behavior data collection approach.

7   Conclusion

This paper presents Probe-I (sensor network Protocol behavior Inspector), a mobile device assisted tool that can unveil post-deployment protocol defects in WSNs. Probe-I collects the protocol behaviors by passively listening to the packet exchanges with a mobile device equipped with a compatible wireless interface (*i.e.*, a USB-connected sensor node). Such a behavior data collection mechanism is non-intrusive, *i.e.*, it will not change the execution of the original WSN protocols. This can provide Probe-I nice fidelity in obtaining the real protocol behaviors, since the executions of WSN codes are sensitive to timing.

Probe-I then employs a node-by-node role-oriented approach to model the protocol behaviors based on the sniffed packets. Hence, it focuses on the protocol defects that can cause packet exchanges to deviate from the normal. With Probe-I, a WSN practitioner can verify whether a protocol works as well in field as it does in a simple baseline test. It can illustrate potential protocol defect symptoms, *i.e.*, the behavior discrepancy found in a runtime test. This can facilitate manual inspection of the protocol implementation to locate the root cause of such discrepancy. We successfully employs Probe-I to detect protocol design defects in two WSN data collection protocols, which shows its effectiveness.

Acknowledgements. This work was substantially supported by the National Natural Science Foundation of China (Project No. 61100077), the National Basic Research Program of China (973 Project No. 2011CB302603), the Research Grants Council of the Hong Kong Special Administrative Region, China (Project Nos. CUHK 415311 and N_CUHK405/11). J. Liu's work was supported by a Canadian NSERC Discovery Grant, a Discovery Accelerator Supplements Award, an NSERC Engage Grant, a MITACS Project Grant, and a China NSFC Major Program of International Cooperation Grant (61120106008).

References

1. Barrenetxea, G., Ingelrest, F., Schaefer, G., Vetterli, M.: The hitchhiker's guide to successful wireless sensor network deployments. In: Proc. of ACM SenSys (2008)
2. Werner-Allen, G., Lorincz, K., Johnson, J., Lees, J., Welsh, M.: Fidelity and yield in a volcano monitoring sensor network. In: Proc. of OSDI (2006)
3. Luo, L., He, T., Zhou, G., Gu, L., Abdelzaher, T.F., Stankovic, J.A.: Achieving repeatability of asynchronous events in wireless sensor networks with EnviroLog. In: Proc. of the IEEE INFOCOM (2006)
4. Cao, Q., Abdelzaher, T., Stankovic, J., Whitehouse, K., Luo, L.: Declarative trace-points: A programmable and application independent debugging system for wireless sensor networks. In: Proc. of ACM SenSys (2008)
5. Google Inc.: Android operating system, http://www.android.com
6. TinyOS Community Forum: TinyOS: An open-source OS for the networked sensor regime, http://www.tinyos.net
7. Gnawali, O., Fonseca, R., Jamieson, K., Moss, D., Levis, P.: Collection tree protocol. In: Proc. of the ACM SENSYS, pp. 1–14 (November 2009)
8. Greenwood, P.E., Nikulin, M.S.: A Guide to Chi-Squared Testing. Wiley (1996)
9. Gnawali, O., Fonseca, R., Jamieson, K., Moss, D., Levis, P.: Collection tree protocol. In: Proc. of ACM SenSys (2009)
10. Chipara, O., Lu, C., Bailey, T.C., Roman, G.C.: Reliable clinical monitoring using wireless sensor networks: Experiences in a step-down hospital unit. In: Proc. of ACM SenSys (2010)
11. Levis, P., Lee, N., Welsh, M., Culler, D.: TOSSIM: Accurate and scalable simulation of entire tinyos applications. In: Proc. of the ACM SenSys (2003)
12. Titzer, B., Lee, D., Palsberg, J.: Avrora: Scalable sensor network simulation with precise timing. In: Proc. of the IEEE IPSN, pp. 477–482 (May 2005)
13. Li, P., Regehr, J.: T-Check: Bug finding for sensor networks. In: Proc. of IPSN (2010)
14. Sasnauskas, R., Landsiedel, O., Alizai, M.H., Weisez, C., Kowalewskiz, S., Wehrle, K.: KleeNet: Discovering insidious interaction bugs in wireless sensor networks before deployment. In: Proc. of the ACM/IEEE IPSN (2010)
15. Zhou, Y., Chen, X., Lyu, M., Liu, J.: Sentomist: Unveiling transient sensor network bugs via symptom mining. In: Proc. of the IEEE ICDCS (2010)
16. Stojmenovic, I.: Simulations in wireless sensor and ad hoc networks: matching and advancing models, metrics, and solutions. IEEE Comm. 46(12), 102–107 (2008)
17. Khan, M.M.H., Luo, L., Huang, C., Abdelzaher, T.: SNTS: Sensor network troubleshooting suite. In: Proc. of the IEEE DCOSS (2007)
18. Liu, K., Li, M., Liu, Y., Li, M., Guo, Z., Hong, F.: Passive diagnosis for wireless sensor networks. In: Proc. of the ACM SENSYS (2008)
19. Ramanathan, N., Chang, K., Kapur, R., Girod, L., Kohler, E., Estrin, D.: Sympathy for the sensor network debugger. In: Proc. of the ACM SENSYS (2005)
20. Rmer, K., Ma, J.: PDA: Passive distributed assertions for sensor networks. In: Proc. of IPSN (2009)

SPSA Based Packet Size Optimization Algorithm in Wireless Sensor Networks

Na Xia[1,2], Ruji Feng[1], and Lina Xu[1]

[1] School of Computer and Information,
Hefei University of Technology, Hefei 230009, China
[2] Engineering Research Center of Safety Critical Industrial Measurement
and Control Technology, Ministry of Education of China,
Hefei 230009, China

Abstract. During the data aggregation in wireless sensor networks, the size of transmitted data packet is an important parameter which will influence the energy consumption efficiency (ECE) of sensor nodes directly. Therefore, it is a key topic to optimize the packet size to maximize ECE. In this paper, a novel model is set up to describe the relationship between ECE and the packet size, wireless transceivers, communication protocols and channels. Then a Simultaneous Perturbation Stochastic Approximation (SPSA) theory based packet size optimization algorithm is proposed in two communication models, and we demonstrate the validity of algorithm compared with the method of numerical analysis in extensive simulation experiments.

Keywords: WSNs, packet size, SPSA, energy efficiency.

1 Introduction

Wireless Sensor Networks (WSNs) is composed of numerous energy constrained sensor nodes scattered in surveillance field. Due to its wide applications in military, industry, environment protection, etc, it has attracted extensive attention from many countries and research institutions, and has become a hot issue [1,2,3]. In most applications, sensor nodes are powered by batteries, which are difficult to be replaced or recharged. Consequently, the energy efficiency of WSNs is always the research focus.

Several methods have been presented to solve the problem [4,5]. Energy consumption efficiency model was proposed in literature [4]. The research only considered the impact of channel encoding and then found the optimal packet size to maximize the energy consumption efficiency. Another similar ECE model was proposed in literature [5], in which the author considered the impact of MAC protocols to sensor nodes' energy consumption efficiency, then achieved the optimal packet size.

In the previous research, the optimal packet size is always obtained by the method of numerical analysis, which is a kind of traversal method with low efficiency. So it is difficult to be applied to compute the optimal packet size in real-time and dynamic communication environment.

X. Wang et al. (Eds.): WASA 2012, LNCS 7405, pp. 112–119, 2012.

In this paper, we propose a packet size optimization algorithm based on Simultaneous Perturbation Stochastic Approximation (SPSA), by which the ECE of sensor nodes can be maximized in real-time. Then, the limited energy of each senor node can be used to transmit as much data as possible.

The remainder of the paper is organized as follows: In section 2, ECE model of single hop communication is described. Packet size optimization algorithm based on SPSA is proposed in section 3. The metrics of performance are defined in section 4, with the simulation result analysis. Section 5 is our conclusion and consideration about the future work.

2   ECE Model

The link layer packet is the basic communication unit between neighboring sensor nodes in WSNs. It consists of a header field with α bits long, payload with l bits long and a trailer with τ bits. The header field generally includes an event/location/attribute identifier and hence, α is expected to be only a few bytes. The payload contains information bits and the trailer is composed of parity bits for error control.

Based on this packet format, we can express the energy required to communicate (transmit and receive) one bit of information across a single hop as

$$E_b = E_t + E_r + \frac{E_{dec}}{l} \tag{1}$$

where E_t and E_r are the energy consumption of the transmitter and receiver respectively. E_{dec} represents the decoding energy per packet. For a t error correcting binary BCH code, E_{dec} is given in [4]. Hence, they are as follows.

$$E_t = \frac{[(P_{te} + P_o)\frac{(\alpha+l+\tau)}{R} + P_{tst}T_{tst}]}{l}$$

$$E_r = \frac{[P_{re}\frac{(\alpha+l+\tau)}{R} + P_{rst}T_{rst}]}{l}$$

$$E_{dec} = (2nt + 2t^2)(E_{add} + E_{mult}) \tag{2}$$

where, $P_{te/re}$ is the power consumed in the transmitter/receiver electronics; $P_{tst/rst}$ is the start-up power consumed in the transmitter or receiver; $T_{tst/rst}$ is the start-up time of transceivers; P_o is the output transmit power; R is the data rate; n is the packet length, $n = \alpha + l + \tau$; E_{add} is the energy consumption in the addition of decoding and E_{mult} is the energy consumption in the multiplication of decoding.

Formula (1) can be simplified in terms of radio parameters k_1 and k_2 as

$$E_b = k_1\frac{\alpha + \tau + l}{l} + \frac{k_2 + E_{dec}}{l} \tag{3}$$

where k_1 and k_2 are given by

$$k_1 = [(P_{te} + P_o) + P_{re}]/R$$

$$k_2 = P_{tst}T_{tst} + P_{rst}T_{rst}$$

Hence, two important parameters k_1 and k_2 are achieved, and they are constants for a given radio transceiver and data rate. k_1 can be considered as the consumed energy in the communication of one bit, and k_2 represents the start-up energy consumption. For the RFM-TR1000 transceiver, k_1 and k_2 are calculated to be $1.85\mu J/bit$ and $24.86\mu J$, respectively.

Take CSMA/CA protocol into account, and the communication mechanism is as follows. When N bits data are transmitted in total, the data will be divided into $\lceil N/l \rceil$ data packets. Before transmitting the data, transmitter will send a request packet RTS towards receiver and transmit the data packet after receiving the CTS from receiver. Transmitter will not transmit the next data packet until receiving ACK, which is sent from receiver after each packet is received. Let's define that RTS, CTS, ACK are the control packets, and the size of them are all q bits. Consequently, there are $\lceil N/l \rceil$ data packets and ($\lceil N/l \rceil + 2$) control packets in total.

According to the meanings of k_1 and k_2, the energy consumption for transmitting the control packets is as follows

$$E_{control} = (\left\lceil \frac{N}{l} \right\rceil + 2)[(\alpha + q + \tau_1)k_1 + k_2 + E_{dec1}] \tag{4}$$

the energy consumption for transmitting the data packets is as follows

$$E_{data} = \left\lceil \frac{N}{l} \right\rceil [(\alpha + l + \tau_2)k_1 + k_2 + E_{dec2}] \tag{5}$$

where E_{dec1} and E_{dec2} are the energy consumption for decoding the control packets and the data packets, respectively. τ_1 and τ_2 are the parity bits of control packets and data packets, respectively.

The total energy consumption is as follows:

$$\begin{aligned}
E &= E_{control} + E_{data} \\
&= (\left\lceil \frac{N}{l} \right\rceil + 2)[(\alpha + q + \tau_1)k_1 + k_2 + E_{dec1}] \\
&\quad + \left\lceil \frac{N}{l} \right\rceil [(\alpha + l + \tau_2)k_1 + k_2 + E_{dec2}] \\
&= k_1[\left\lceil \frac{N}{l} \right\rceil (2\alpha + q + l + \tau_1 + \tau_2) + 2(\alpha + q + \tau_1)] \\
&\quad + k_2(2\left\lceil \frac{N}{l} \right\rceil + 2) + (\left\lceil \frac{N}{l} \right\rceil + 2)E_{dec1} + \left\lceil \frac{N}{l} \right\rceil E_{dec2} \tag{6}
\end{aligned}$$

As far as we know, in the process of transmitting data, a packet tends to be in error in the presence of one or more bit errors. Assuming independent bit errors,

the probability [4] that the packet will be correctly received without error control
is given by

$$PER = (1 - p)^{\alpha + l} \tag{7}$$

where p is the bit error rate (BER). And on the other hand, for a given reliability,
the effect of encoding is to allow greater payload length (l). Taking binary BCH
scheme as an example, decoding failures are detectable, but they are as bad as
packet errors since no retransmission schemes are in use. Hence, the probability
[4] that the packet will be correctly received is given by

$$PER = \sum_{j=0}^{t} \binom{n}{j} p^j (1 - p)^{n-j} \tag{8}$$

where t is the error correcting capability of BCH scheme and is further related
to the number of parities τ, $\tau \geq \log_2 \sum_{j=0}^{t} \binom{n}{j}$.

Above all, when transmitting N bits, the ECE of single hop communication
between two sensor nodes is as follows

$$\eta = \frac{Nk_1}{E} PER \tag{9}$$

$$s.t \quad l = 8\epsilon, \quad \epsilon = 1, 2, \ldots \tag{10}$$

What we aim at is that achieving the optimal payload length l^* so as to maximize
η in (9). Constraint condition in (10) means that the unit of payload length in
the packet format is byte.

3   Packet Size Optimization Algorithm

3.1   Basic Idea of the Algorithm

Simultaneous Perturbation Stochastic Approximation (SPSA) algorithm is a
stochastic optimization method introduced by Spall in 2003 [6]. The central focus
with SPSA is the stochastic setting where only measurements of the objective
function are available without any gradient information.

In recent years, SPSA algorithm is successfully applied in many theoretical
researches and practical applications of different fields [7,8]. Hence, the paper
introduces SPSA algorithm to get the optimal payload length so as to maximize
the ECE of sensor node.

Because SPSA algorithm is used for the problem of minimizing the objective
function, the objective function of this paper is converted as follows:

$$Y = \frac{E}{Nk_1 PER} \tag{11}$$

Now, the basic idea of using SPSA algorithm to get the optimal payload length
is as follows.

First, the initial iterative point l_0 is chosen randomly in $[0,N]$. Then the simultaneous perturbation scalar $\triangle_k$ is generated by using a Bernoulli ± 1 distribution with probability of $1/2$. And the simultaneous perturbation amplitude c_k is as follows

$$c_k = \frac{c}{(k+1)^\gamma}, k = 0, 1, 2, \ldots \tag{12}$$

where c is a positive constant and its value usually relates to the concrete application. Here, we set $c = 50$ after lots of experiments. 0.101 is effectively the lowest allowable subject of γ to satisfy the theoretical conditions. And k is the current number of iterations.

Then, two values of the objective function which are corresponding to the two perturbation points can be computed as $Y(l_k + c_k \triangle_k)$ and $Y(l_k - c_k \triangle_k)$. And the gradient which is determined by the two perturbation points is approximately the estimated gradient of the current iterative point l_k.

$$g_k = \frac{Y(l_k + c_k \triangle_k) - Y(l_k - c_k \triangle_k)}{2c_k \triangle_k}, k = 0, 1, 2 \ldots \tag{13}$$

Then the iterative point can be updated by using the factor of step a_k, and a_k is given by

$$a_k = \frac{a}{(k + A + 1)^\lambda}, k = 0, 1, 2 \ldots \tag{14}$$

where a is a positive constant. 0.602 is effectively the lowest allowable subject of λ to satisfy the theoretical conditions. A is a positive scalar and is 10 percent or less of the maximum number of expected/allowed iterations (I_{max}), as $A \leq 10\% I_{max}$.

The updated iterative point l_{k+1} is given by

$$l_{k+1} = l_k - a_k g_k, k = 0, 1, 2, \ldots \tag{15}$$

Terminate the algorithm if there is little change (≤ 0.1 bit) in several successive iterations or the maximum allowable number of iterations I_{max} has been reached. Otherwise, iteration should be continued.

The constant a can be achieved as follows. Assume that $U(l_1 - l_0 = U)$ is the initial step range. According to formula (15), $| a_0 g_0 |= U$, and according to formula (13), g_0 can be achieved. Then based on formula (14), $a = | U(A + 1)^\lambda / g_0 |$.

3.2   Implementation of the Algorithm

The pseudo code based on SPSA is shown in algorithm 1.

4   Simulation

4.1   Performance Metrics

Definition 1. *(Computation Efficiency)* Assume that the total data to be transmitted are N bits, and r sets of experiments are conducted. The actual numbers of iterations for achieving the optimal payload length based on SPSA are

$I_{b1}, I_{b2}, \ldots, I_{br}$, respectively. And the average value of them is $\overline{I_b}$. That means the objective function value is computed $2 \times \overline{I_b}$ times averagely. On the other hand, according to the constraint condition, the computing times of objective function value is $\lceil N/8 \rceil$ using numerical analysis method.

Then the computation efficiency of SPSA is defined as follows.

$$\beta = 1 - \frac{2 \times \overline{I_b}}{\lceil N/8 \rceil} \tag{16}$$

Definition 1 reflects the efficiency of SPSA, compared with numerical analysis method. If β is positive, SPSA has better solving efficiency than numerical analysis method; then, if β equals 0, the performance of the two methods are similar; otherwise, SPSA is proved to be with lower efficiency than numerical analysis method.

---

input : the total data N, the initial payload length l_0, the initial step
$\quad\quad\quad U(l_1 - l_0 = U)$, the initial perturbation amplitude c, the expected total
$\quad\quad\quad$ iterations I_{max}, A, the encoding symbol i
output: the optimal payload length l^*

Initialization: $k_1 = 1.85$, $k_2 = 24.86$, $\alpha = 16$, $q = 16$, $p = 0.0003$, $k = 0$,
$\lambda = 0.602$, $\gamma = 0.101$
Achieve the corresponding τ_1, τ_2, E_{dec1}, E_{dec2} and PER according to the
encoding symbol i;
Get $\triangle_0$ according to Bernoulli ± 1 distribution with probability of $1/2$; /* get
the initial perturbation direction */
Get $Y(l_0 + c_0\triangle_0)$ and $Y(l_0 - c_0\triangle_0)$. Get g_0 according to equation (13);
Get the constant a according to equation (14) and (15), then $l_1 = l_0 - a_0g_0$;
$k = k + 1$;
while $k \leq I_{max}$ **do**
$\quad$ According to i, get the corresponding τ_1,τ_2, E_{dec1}, E_{dec2} and PER;
$\quad$ Get a_k and c_k ;   /* update a_k and c_k */
$\quad$ Achieve $\triangle_k$ according to Bernoulli ± 1 distribution with probability of $1/2$;
$\quad$ /* update the perturbation direction for each iteration */
$\quad$ Get $Y(l_k + c_k\triangle_k)$ and $Y(l_k - c_k\triangle_k)$, and according to equation (13), get
$\quad$ g_k; then $l_{k+1} = l_k - a_kg_k$; $k = k + 1$;
$\quad\quad$ /* update the iterative point and the number of iterations */
$\quad$ **if** $\mid l_k - l_{k-1} \mid \leq 0.1$ **then**
$\quad$ | break;
$\quad$ **end**
end

Algorithm 1. SPSA based packet size optimization algorithm

4.2   Experiment Results Analysis

We implemented the algorithm and performed the simulation on Matlab 7.1 platform. BCH scheme is used for the channel encoding, so energy consumption in the addition and multiplication during decoding the packet is as follows, respectively.

$$E_{add} = 3.3 \times 10^{-5} m (mW/MHz)$$
$$E_{mult} = 3.7 \times 10^{-5} m^3 (mW/MHz)$$

where $m = \lfloor \log_2 n + 1 \rfloor$.

What' more, the simulation experiment is conducted under two conditions, one is with BCH scheme and the other without it. Under each condition, we conduct three sets of experiments with different total data amount (N=640bits, 1000bits and 2000bits). And $N/2$ is selected to be the initial iterative point l_0. In each set of experiments, we use ten different initial iterative steps $U = \{\max\{N - l_0, l_0\} \times \xi/10, \xi = 1, 2, \cdots, 10\}$ to achieve the optimal payload length.

(1) Packet without BCH scheme

These experiments are conducted without BCH scheme, and the parameters setting and experiment results are listed in table 1.

Table 1. The parameters setting and performance evaluation

Set	N	c	I_{max}	A	$\overline{l_s}$	$\overline{\eta_s}$	$\overline{I_b}$	l_v	η_v	β
1	640	50	100	10	432	0.6646	14.8	432	0.6646	0.63
2	1000	50	100	10	448	0.6916	32.1	448	0.6916	0.4864
3	2000	50	100	10	456	0.7175	16.6	456	0.7175	0.8672

Table 1 depicts that in each set of experiment, every average ECE achieved by SPSA absolutely equals to the one achieved by numerical analysis method, that's to say, every average ECE reaches max, which means the optimal payload length is found accurately by SPSA. What's more, the β is positive, which demonstrates that SPSA is more efficient to compute the optimal solution than numerical analysis method.

(2) Packet with BCH scheme ($t = 2$)

These sets of experiments are conducted with BCH scheme, and the error correcting capability $t=2$, which will determine the length of parities τ. The simulation parameters and results are listed in table 2.

Table 2. The performance evaluation with BCH scheme

Set	N	c	I_{max}	A	i	$\overline{l_s}$	$\overline{\eta_s}$	$\overline{I_b}$	l_v	η_v	β
1	640	50	100	10	2	640	0.7283	13.7	640	0.7283	0.6575
2	1000	50	100	10	2	998.4	0.8045	17.9	1000	0.8047	0.7136
3	2000	50	100	10	2	1888	0.8723	356.4	1888	0.8723	0.5488

From table 2, we can see that in each set of experiments every average ECE achieved by SPSA almost reach the one achieved by numerical analysis method, which represents the algorithm obtains the optimal payload length with maximal ECE. Furthermore, the computation efficiency in three sets of experiments are 0.6575, 0.7136, and 0.5488, which demonstrates the fast convergence of SPSA algorithm and the superiority to numerical analysis method.

5   Conclusion and Future Work

In this paper, we investigated the packet size optimization in WSNs, and an ECE model of single hop communication is set up to take the channel coding and MAC layer protocol into account. A SPSA based algorithm is proposed to achieve the optimal payload length to maximize the ECE. By theoretical analysis and extensive simulation, we demonstrate its validity in quality of solution and computation efficiency compared with numerical analysis method.

For future work, we will apply the algorithm to practical sensors and networks to test its feasibility and propose a channel sensing strategy to realize the dynamic packet size optimization, so that the limited energy of each senor node can be used to transmit as much data as possible.

References

1. Le-Trung, Q., Taherkordi, A., Skele, T.: Information Storage, Reduction and Dissemination in Sensor Networks: A Survey. In: IEEE Consumer Communications and Networking Conference, pp. 1–6. IEEE Press, Las Vegas (2009)
2. Kulkarni, V.R., Rster, A., Venayagamoorthy, K.G.: Computational Intelligence in Wireless Sensor Networks: A Survey. In: IEEE Communications Survey & Tutorials, pp. 68–96. IEEE Press (2011)
3. Isaac, J.S., Hancke, P.G., Madhoo, H.: A survey of wireless sensor networks applications from a power utility's distribution perspective. In: IEEE AFRICON, pp. 1–5. IEEE Press (2011)
4. Sankarasubramaniam, Y., Akyildiz, I.F., Mclaughlin, S.W.: Energy Efficiency Based Packet Size Optimization in Wireless Sensor Networks. In: IEEE International Workshop on Sensor Network Protocols and Applications, pp. 1–8. IEEE Press, Anchorage AK (2003)
5. Zhao, T., Yang, W.G.: Energy Efficiency Based Packet Size Optimal Design in Wireless Sensor Networks. Journal of the Graduate School of the Chinese Academy of Sciences 25, 161–166 (2008)
6. Spall, J.C.: Introduction to Stochastic Search and Optimization. John Wiley & Sons, Incorporated, Hoboken (2003)
7. Zhang, H.J., Zhao, J., Geng, T.: The improved convergence of SPSA and its application in drive system. In: IEEE Conference on Industrial Electronics and Applications, pp. 662–666. IEEE Press (2009)
8. Steenis, R., Rivera, E.D.: Plant-friendly signal generation for system identification using a modified SPSA methodology. In: IEEE Conference on Decision and Control, pp. 470–475. IEEE Press (2009)

Lower Bounds on Data Collection Time
in Sensor Networks

Xianwei Sun[1], Scott C.-H. Huang[2], and Minming Li[1]

[1] City University of Hong Kong, Kowloon, Hong Kong SAR
[2] National Tsing Hua University, Hsinchu, Taiwan ROC

Abstract. We study the time complexity of data collection in sensor networks. A simple mathematical model for sensor networks regarded as lines, multi-lines and trees is defined and corresponding optimal schedules are provided. A lower bound of data collection time on general graph networks is also derived.

Furthermore, we discuss the data collection problem where each node can transmit arbitrary hops per time slot. An optimal schedule is derived where each node can transmit 2 hops. We also prove the schedule is nearly optimal if each node can transmit k ($k > 2$) hops (with constant error).

1 Introduction

In the area of general ad hoc networks, as well as sensor webs, researchers have focused on routing [12], medium access control (MAC) [1], [9], and physical layer [11]. References [13] and [8] are protocol suites specifically designed for sensor webs. Furthermore, theoretical results regarding capacity of general static ad hoc networks first appeared in [7]. Finally, most relevant to our research is the so-called packet routing problem, which consists of moving packets of data from one location to an other as quickly as possible in a network and has been studied in conjunction with wire line and wireless network models(see, for example, [10], [6], [5],and [2]). In this paper, we derive new results specific to sensor networks, where in particular, nonuniform data distribution over the network is assumed. We describe optimal strategies to perform data collection under various assumptions and derive corresponding time performances with respect to a simple discrete mathematical model for a sensor network. In this model, the amount of data accumulated at each sensor node(characterized by a number of unit data packets) after some given observation period is assumed finite and determined. Furthermore,we distinguish between two phases of operation in a sensor network. In the first phase or observation/measuring phase, area monitoring results in an accumulation of data at each sensor node. In the second phase or data transfer, the collected data is transmitted to some processing center located within the sensor network. In this paper, we investigate the efficiency limits with respect to time of such data transfers. This paper is organized as follows. In Section 2, we define our sensor network model. Then we present the optimal results of data collection time in tree sensor networks and a lower bound on data collection time in any connected graph in Section 3 . In Section 4 and 5, we discuss the data collection problem where each node can transmit arbitrary hops per time slot.

X. Wang et al. (Eds.): WASA 2012, LNCS 7405, pp. 120–131, 2012.
© Springer-Verlag Berlin Heidelberg 2012

2   Network Model and Problem Statement

In this section, we give the definitions of a sensor network and the data collection time problem. A sensor network is defined as a collection of n nodes $\{N_1, \ldots, N_n\}$, for $1 \leq i \leq n$. Each node is associated with a nonnegative integer that represents the number of data packets stored at this node at the end of transmit/receive processing. We use v_i to denote the number of data packets stored at node N_i for $1 \leq i \leq n$. There is one special node N_0 (the processing center) which we will refer to as the *base station* (BS). Let $\mathcal{V} = \{N_0, N_1, \ldots, N_n\}$. All the nodes including the BS have a common transmission range r and an interference range $r' = mr$, $m \geq 1$, $m \in \mathbb{Z}$. In other words, a transmission from N_i to N_j (where $i, j \geq 0$) is successful if and only if their Euclidean distance $dist(N_i, N_j)$ is less than r and for every other simultaneously transmitting node N_k $(k \geq 0)$ we have $dist(N_k, N_j) \geq r'$. This model is a generalization of the problem described in [4], [3]. In [4] and [3], interference range r' is equal to the transmission range r. In practice, m is often between 2 and 3. So it is important to solve the problem when the ratio of interference range and transmitting range is a general integer.

We also assume that time is slotted and one-hop transmission takes one time slot (TS). The network is further assumed to be fully synchronized. A node can only transmit/receive one data packet per time slot. Concurrent transmissions may occur in the network in this interference model if they are separated far enough. Our network may be represented as a weighted graph $\{\mathcal{V}, \mathcal{E}, \boldsymbol{v}_n\}$ where $\mathcal{V} = \{N_0, \ldots, N_n\}$ represents the set of nodes, $\mathcal{E}$ represents the set of links, and $\boldsymbol{v}_n = (v_1, \ldots, v_n)$ represents the number of data packets to be transmitted at $N_1, \ldots, N_n$.

In this graph model, the base station (BS) or N_0 is the root of network and an edge represents a wireless connection (a link) between two nodes. The general data collection problem in a given sensor network refers to the problem of routing all the data collected by the sensor nodes to the BS as efficiently as possible with respect to time and energy. However, in this paper, we shall focus on the time efficiency alone of the data collection task on directional antenna systems. As discussed in [3], the results of directional antenna systems over a single line network can be extended to omnidirectional antenna systems. Conclusions and their proofs on omnidirectional antenna systems follow similar arguments as those of directional antenna systems. So we just discuss the data collection time on directional antenna systems here.

If a schedule of transmission of the data collection task in the sensor network has the smallest time slots, we call it an optimal schedule. In this paper, we omit some proofs due to space limit.

3   Data Collection in Sensor Networks

In this section, we mainly discuss the data collection time problem in the sensor networks when a node can only transmit data to its immediate neighbor in the network. We first consider the case where the sensor network is a line (an example is given in Fig 1). In this type of network, all sensor nodes are assumed to be evenly located along a line with N_0 placed at one end and N_n placed at the other end. The distance between any two nodes is denoted by d. Assume that all nodes are equipped with directional antenna allowing transmissions over a distance r, where $r = (1 + \delta)d, \delta > 0$. We further assume that $\delta < \frac{1}{m}$ for some given integer m. Assume N_i is situated exactly at distance i from the BS. A transmission from N_i to N_{i+1} is denoted by $i \to i+1$. Prior to finding an optimal schedule of a line network with general m, we first estimate the time performance of the optimal schedule. Let $T(\boldsymbol{v})$ be the minimum data collection time defined as the minimum time duration over all possible data collection schedules with the number of data packets $\boldsymbol{v} = (v_1, \ldots, v_n)$. Then, according to [3], the following theorem holds.

Theorem 1. *If $\boldsymbol{v} = (v_1, \ldots, v_n)$ and $v_i = 0 \; \forall i > n$, we have*

$$T(\boldsymbol{v}) = \max_i \left(i - 1 + \sum_{j=i}^{i+m-2} (j - i + 1)v_j + m \sum_{j \geq i+m-1} v_j \right), \qquad (1)$$

Here we study the data collection time in line networks and design appropriate data collection schedules. Our goal is to determine the minimum duration of the collection phase and an associated optimal communication strategy. We consider the following converse problem (distribution problem) first. Instead of nodes sending packets to the BS, we assume the BS is to send packets to nodes. This problem is of separate interest in sensor networks. The collection problem has the same time performance as the distribution problem when they have the same network and packets. We propose the following simple algorithm to determine BS actions of the distribution problem.

Algorithm 1 determines the BS action at each time step: BS remains idle (i.e. `action[step]` = 0) or transmits data packet (`action[step]` = 1). The result is stored in a vector `action[]`. The procedure is illustrated in the example of Figure 1, where $\mathcal{V} = \{0, 1, 2, 3, 4\}$, $E = \{(i, i+1), 0 \leq i \leq 3\}$, $\boldsymbol{v} = (0, 1, 0, 1, 1)$, $m = 3, r = (1+\delta)d, \delta < \frac{1}{3}$. The schedule of transmissions according to Algorithm 1 is completed in $7 \; TS$. Next we determine its performance in general. Let T_i be the last busy time slot at N_i ($1 \leq i \leq n$) in the execution of Algorithm 1 (i.e. in the previous example, we have $T_1 = 7, T_2 = 6, T_3 = 6, T_4 = 4$). Clearly, Algorithm 1 runs in $\max_{1 \leq i \leq n} T_i$.

We now return to the data collection problem. The construction of a schedule here is based on the symmetric operations of distribution. Note that if we can consider the operation of transmitting specific packets from the BS to other nodes individually, this problem can actually be viewed as the "reverse operation" of the data collection problem and the optimal time is the same as the optimal time of the data collection problem. In the data collection problem, each node other than the BS has a number of packets to be sent to the BS. Correspondingly, in the *reverse problem*, each node other than the BS has a number of packets

---

rule 1. Optimal Actions in Line Networks

Input: $n, v_1, \ldots, v_n$

             /* $v_i \in \mathbb{N} \cup \{0\}$, v_i **represents the number of packets at** $\mathbf{N}_i$ */

Output: action[], step $\leftarrow$ 1, legal $\leftarrow$1, packets_left $\leftarrow \sum_{i=1}^{n} v_i$, i $\leftarrow$ n,

  while packets_left $\neq 0$ do

    if $i > m - 1$ then

      action[step] $\leftarrow$ 1

      step $\leftarrow$ step $+ m$

    else

      action[step] $\leftarrow$ 1

      step $\leftarrow$ step $+ i$

    end if

    packets_left $\leftarrow$ packets_left $- v_i$

    $i \leftarrow i - 1$

  end while

  step action[]

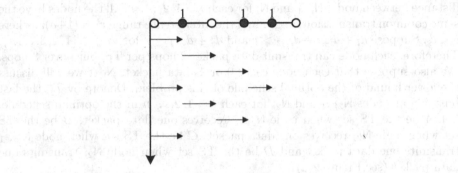

Fig. 1. Optimal distribution schedule on a line network. The job is performed in 7 TS.

to be *received from* the BS. Since the solution to one problem corresponds to the solution to the other, we only consider the distribution problem from now on.

Similar to the result of [3], we can obtain an optimal schedule when the networks are trees.

Next, we consider the data collection problem in general networks. We propose a schedule which performs within a factor of m of an optimal strategy on general networks. The proposed schedule consists of two sub procedures.

- Extract a shortest path spanning tree τ_{SP}
- Apply the optimal schedule on tree networks to τ_{SP}.

One can show that shortest path spanning trees always exist by using Dijkstra's algorithm. We obtain the minimum data collection time of the spanning tree (τ_{SP}) applying the result of tree networks. Then we demonstrate that τ_{SP} is an m-approximate of an optimal strategy on general graphs.

Theorem 2. *For any (connected) graph G, and any shortest path spanning tree τ_{SP}, we have*

$$\frac{T(\tau_{SP})}{m} \leq T(G) \leq T(\tau_{SP}) \qquad (2)$$

Proof. We define $t_1(G)$ as the minimum distribution time when transmission and reception are simultaneously allowed in a TS at any given node. Clearly, $t_1(G) \leq T(G)$. By the conclusion of Corollary 1.4 in Appendix I of [3], we also have $t_1(G) = t_1(\tau_{SP})$. Besides, for any connected graph A the following inequality holds $T(A) \leq mt_1(A)$. Choose $A = \tau_{SP}$, then $T(\tau_{SP}) \leq mt_1(\tau_{SP})$. Therefore $T(G) \geq t_1(G) = t_1(\tau_{SP}) \geq \frac{T(\tau_{SP})}{m}$, which implies the first inequality. The second inequality obviously holds.   □

4   Extension to 2 Hops

The extended model is defined below. The sensor network is a line and d_i is the distance between nodes N_{i-1} and N_i for each $i = 1, 2, \ldots n$. All the nodes have the same common transmission range r and the interference range $r' = (1+\delta)r$, where $\delta < \frac{1}{2}$. Suppose $d_i + d_{i+1} + d_{i+2} > r$ and $d_j + d_{j+1} \leq r$ for $\forall i, j \in \{1, 2, 3, \ldots n\}$. Therefore, each node can transmit data packet 2 hops per TS, but never 3 hops. We also suppose that each node carry 0 or 1 data packet. Next we will discuss the lower bound of the optimal schedule of this problem. Denote by $T_{2i}^{\star}$ the last busy TS at nodes N_{2i-1} and N_{2i} for each $i = 1, 2, \ldots n$ in the optimal schedule. Let A be the TS set when node N_{2i-1} receives one data packet, B be the TS set when node N_{2i} receives one data packet, C be the TS set when node N_{2i-1} transmits one data packet and D be the TS set when node N_{2i} transmits one data packet (see Figure 2(a)).

Let $|A| = x$, $|B| = y$, $|C| = z$, $|D| = w$, $|A \cap D| = m$, $|B \cap C| = h$, we obtain the following relations.

$$\begin{cases} x = z + v_{2i-1} \\ y = w + v_{2i} \\ z + w - h = \sum_{j>2i} v_j \end{cases}$$

Then

$$\begin{aligned} T_{2i}^{\star} &= T(A) + T(B) + T(C) + T(D) - T(A \cap D) - T(B \cap C) + i - 1 \\ &= x + y + z + w - h - m + i - 1 = 2(z+w) + v_{2i-1} + v_{2i} - h - m + i - 1 \\ &= 2\sum_{j>2i} v_j + 2h + v_{2i-1} + v_{2i} - h - m + i - 1 = 2\sum_{j>2i} v_j + v_{2i-1} + v_{2i} + h - m + i - 1. \end{aligned}$$

Since $m \leq x$ and $m \leq w$, we get $2m \leq x + w = z + w + v_{2i-1} = \sum_{j>2i} v_j + h + v_{2i-1}$.

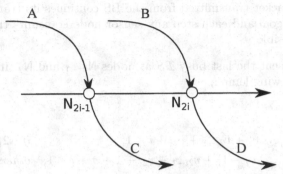

(a) The receiving /transmitting processes of nodes N_{2i-1} and N_{2i}.

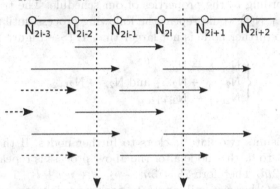

(b) Transmissions in the schedule produced by our schedule.

Fig. 2.

Therefore:

$$T_{2i}^{\star} = 2\sum_{j>2i} v_j + v_{2i-1} + v_{2i} + h - m + i - 1$$

$$\geq \frac{3}{2}\sum_{j>2i} v_j + v_{2i-1} + v_{2i} + \frac{1}{2}(h - v_{2i-1}) + i - 1 \geq \frac{3}{2}\sum_{j>2i} v_j + \frac{1}{2}v_{2i-1} + v_{2i} + i - 1.$$

We denote $\lceil \frac{3}{2}\sum_{j>2i} v_j + \frac{1}{2}v_{2i-1} \rceil + v_{2i} + i - 1$ by S_{2i} as a lower bound of $T_{2i}^{\star}$. Next, we construct a schedule to solve the problem. Its main idea is as follows:

1. BS transmits the first data packet to the furthest node, transmits the second data packet to the second furthest node,...transmit the $i - th$ data packet to the $i - th$ furthest node.
2. If the BS can transmit a data packet (to node N_1 or N_2), then BS transmits one data packet as far as possible.

3. Each data packet transmitted from the BS continues its transmission until reaching its goal and each step any sensor node transmits the data packet as far as possible.

Use T_{2i} to represent the last busy TS at nodes N_{2i-1} and N_{2i} in our schedule, we have the following lemma:

Lemma 1

$$T_{2i} = \begin{cases} \frac{3}{2}\sum_{j>2i} v_j + v_{2i-1} + v_{2i} + i - 1, & \text{if } 2\left|\sum_{j>2i} v_j;\right. \\ \frac{3}{2}(\sum_{j>2i} v_j - 1) + v_{2i-1} + v_{2i} + 1 + \sigma + i - 1,^1 & \text{otherwise.} \end{cases}$$

Proof. BS needs $i - 1$ TS to transmit a data packet to the node segment (N_{2i-1}, N_{2i}). According to the properties of our schedule. The transmissions in the segment (N_{2i-1}, N_{2i}) would repeat the following process until the number of the data packet to further node is not larger than 1: (See Figure 2(b))

$$\begin{cases} N_{2i-2} \rightarrow N_{2i} \\ N_{2i-3} \rightarrow N_{2i-1} \text{ and } N_{2i} \rightarrow N_{2i+2} \\ N_{2i-1} \rightarrow N_{2i+1} \end{cases}$$

□

Each process transmits two data packets to further nodes. If there is no data packet to transmit to further node after the above process is repeated $m-$times, then $\sum_{j>2i} v_j = 2m$. Therefore $T_{2i} = 3m + v_{2i-1} + v_{2i} + i - 1 = \frac{3}{2}\sum_{j>2i} v_j + v_{2i-1} + v_{2i} + i - 1$. Otherwise, still one data packet needs to transmit to further node, we need 2 TS to transmit the data packet (the first two steps in the process), then we get $\sum_{j>2i} v_j = 2m + 1$. If $v_{2i-1} \geq 1$, N_{2i-1} can receive a data packet at the same time N_{2i} transmit a data packet to N_{2i+2} (or N_{2i+1}), then $T_{2i} = 3m + 2 + v_{2i-1} - 1 + v_{2i} + i - 1 = \frac{3}{2}(\sum_{j>2i} v_j - 1) + v_{2i-1} + v_{2i} + 1 + i - 1$. If $v_{2i-1} = 0$, $T_{2i} = 3m + 2 + v_{2i} + i - 1 = \frac{3}{2}(\sum_{j>2i} v_j - 1) + v_{2i-1} + v_{2i} + 2 + i - 1$.

Theorem 3. *For each $i = 1, 2, \ldots n$, our schedule has $T_{2i} = S_{2i}$.*

Proof. There are two cases we need to prove according to the parity of $\sum_{j>2i} v_j$.

1. $\sum_{j>2i} v_j$ is even. If $v_{2i-1} = 0$, then $S_{2i} = \frac{3}{2}\sum_{j>2i} v_j + v_{2i} + i - 1 = \frac{3}{2}\sum_{j>2i} v_j + v_{2i-1} + v_{2i} + i - 1 = T_{2i}$. If $v_{2i-1} = 1$, $S_{2i} = \lceil \frac{3}{2}\sum_{j>2i} v_j + \frac{1}{2} \rceil + v_{2i} + i - 1 = \frac{3}{2}\sum_{j>2i} v_j + 1 + v_{2i} + i - 1 = \frac{3}{2}\sum_{j>2i} v_j + v_{2i-1} + v_{2i} + i - 1 = T_{2i}$.

2. $\sum_{j>2i} v_j$ is odd. If $v_{2i-1} = 0$, then $S_{2i} = \lceil \frac{3}{2}\sum_{j>2i} v_j \rceil + v_{2i} + i - 1 = \frac{3}{2}(\sum_{j>2i} v_j - 1) + 2 + v_{2i} + i - 1 = T_{2i}$. If $v_{2i-1} = 1$, then $S_{2i} = \lceil \frac{3}{2}\sum_{j>2i} v_j + \frac{1}{2} \rceil + v_{2i} + i - 1 = \frac{3}{2}(\sum_{j>2i} v_j - 1) + 2 + v_{2i} + i - 1 = T_{2i}$.

□

---

^{1} Here if $v_{2i-1} \geq 1$, $\sigma = 0$, otherwise $\sigma = 1$.

Our schedule is not always optimal if some nodes carry more than 1 data packets. We show an example that our schedule needs two more TS than the optimal one. See Figure 3 for example, in which the left is our schedule and the right is the optimal schedule.

5   Extension to k Hops ($k \geq 3$)

We continue the discussion of the special case in last section. However, this section we assume that for each $i = 1, 2, \ldots n - 1$, node N_i can transmit data packet r_i hops per TS, but never $r_i + 1$ hops. Also we suppose that each node carries 0 or 1 data packet. Next we will focus on the lower bound of optimal schedule of this problem. Let H_i be the first busy TS at node N_i and T_j be the last busy TS at node N_j for each $i, j \in \{1, 2, \ldots n\}$ in the optimal schedule. Formally, we make the following definitions.

Definition 1. $T_{ij}^\star$: the last busy time when node N_j transmit the $(\sum_{l \geq i} v_l) - th$ data packet farther in the optimal schedule.

Definition 2. $m_i \stackrel{def}{=} \min \{r_j | 0 \leq j \leq i\}$

Let $D_{ij} = T_{ij}^\star - H_j$, we will prove the following inequality.

Lemma 2. For any $1 \leq j \leq i$, $D_{ii} \geq D_{ij} - 1$.

Next, we will calculate a lower bound of D_{ij} using $\sum_{l \geq i} v_l$ and r_{m_i}. Let $m_i = j$, considering the region $(j, j + r_j]$, there are $\sum_{l \geq i} v_l$ data packets passing through node j. The lower bound of D_{ij} can be derived in the following way. We need to transmit $\sum_{l \geq i} v_l$ data packets into the region and transmit x data packets out of the region. The process of transmitting into the region and transmitting out of the region may be in the same time with some demands.

Lemma 3. For each $1 \leq j \leq i$, if $j + r_j < i$, we have $D_{ij} \geq \lceil (1 + \frac{1}{r_j}) \sum_{l \geq i} v_l \rceil$. Otherwise we have $D_{ij} \geq \lceil (1 + \frac{1}{r_j}) \sum_{l \geq i} v_l \rceil - \sum_{l=i}^{j+r_j} v_l$.

Proof. We need to transmit $\sum_{l \geq i} v_l$ data packets through region $(j, j + r_j]$. There are three cases in the transmissions of this region.

1. Transmitting a data packet into the region: This case needs one TS per data packet.
2. Transmitting a data packet(data A) into the region and transmit another data(data B) packet out of the region simultaneously: This case has the same time performance as the following process I. Data B is sent to the further node of the region and data A move to left at least one node. I needs one TS per data packet.
3. Transmitting a data packet out of the region: This case needs one TS per data packet.

Suppose the number of the data packets in cases $(1), (2), (3)$ are x_1, x_2, and x_3, respectively. Then $\sum_{l \geq i} v_l = x_1 + x_2$. If $i < j + r_j$, let x_4 be the number of data packets that would be stored at the nodes between N_{j+r_j} and N_i. Suppose $x_4 = 0$. We have $\sum_{l \geq i} v_l = x_2 + x_3 + x_4$. Therefore we get $x_1 = x_3 + x_4$. In case 2, each data packet in the region can move to left at most $r_j - 1$ times, since it was transmitted into the region in the very beginning. Otherwise there will be one more data packet in case 1. Therefore, we have $x_2 \leq x_1(r_j - 1)$. Since $D_{ij} = x_1 + x_2 + x_3 = 2x_1 + x_2 - x_4$, $\sum_{l \geq i} v_l = x_1 + x_2$, and $x_2 \leq x_1(r_j - 1)$, we get $x_1 \geq \lceil \frac{1}{r_j} \sum_{l \geq i} v_l \rceil$, which means $D_{ij} = \sum_{l \geq i} v_l + x_1 \geq \lceil (1 + \frac{1}{r_j}) \sum_{l \geq i} v_l \rceil$ (if $j + r_j < i$) or $D_{ij} = \sum_{l \geq i} v_l + x_1 \geq \lceil (1 + \frac{1}{r_j}) \sum_{l \geq i} v_l \rceil - \sum_{l \geq i}^{j+r_j} v_l$ (if $j + r_j \geq i$).
$\square$

If all r_is are the same, our schedule has an excellent time performance. We can prove our schedule is nearly optimal except some constant TS error (at most two TS).

Lemma 4. *For each $r_i = k$, suppose $T_i(x)$ be the last busy time when the x-th data packet is transmitted out from N_i (including pass through N_i) with $x \leq \sum_{j > i} v_j$ and $0 \leq i \leq k - 1$, we get $T_i(x) = x + \lceil \frac{x - (k-i)}{k} \rceil$.*

Lemma 5. $T_{i+k}(x) = T_i(x) + 1$ *for each $i = 0, 1, 2, \ldots$ and $x \leq \sum_{j > i} v_j$.*

Theorem 4. $T_{i+ak} = T_i(\sum_{j > i+ak} v_j) + a + v_{i+ak}$ *for each $a \geq 0, 0 \leq i \leq k - 1$.*

Let $S_y = T_{yy}^\star$ be a lower bound of $T_y^\star$. The following Theorem is obtained.

Theorem 5. $T_y \leq S_y + 2$.

6   Comparison with Other Algorithms

In this section, we will compare our schedule with other two transmitting methods (transmitting nearer first and transmitting randomly). Two groups of results are showed in the following figures with different variables. For group 1 horizontal axis represents the number of nodes in the network; For group 2, horizontal axis represents the hops each node can transmit. Vertical axis represents the time slots used in all the groups.

- In group 1, n is from 10 to 100 and $v_1 = v_2 = \ldots v_n = 1$, Figure 4(a)(b)(c) shows the case where $k = 3, 4$, and 5, respectively.
- In group 2, $k = 2$ to 10 and $n = 100$. Figure 5(a) shows the case where $v_1 = 100, v_2 = \ldots = v_{99} = 0, v_{100} = 1$ Figure 5(b) shows the case where $v_1 = v_2 = \ldots = v_{100} = 1$. Figure 5(c) shows the case where $v_i = 101 - i$ for each $i = 1, 2, \ldots, 100$.
- We use 'Farther' to represent Farther Algorithm (our algorithm), 'Nearer' to represent the algorithm which transmits nearer first and 'Random' to represent the algorithm which transmits randomly.

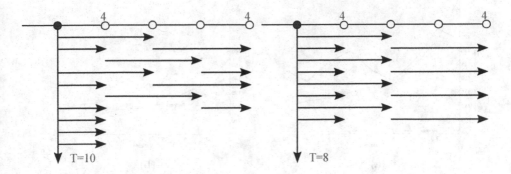

Fig. 3. An example where our method can not get the optimal schedule

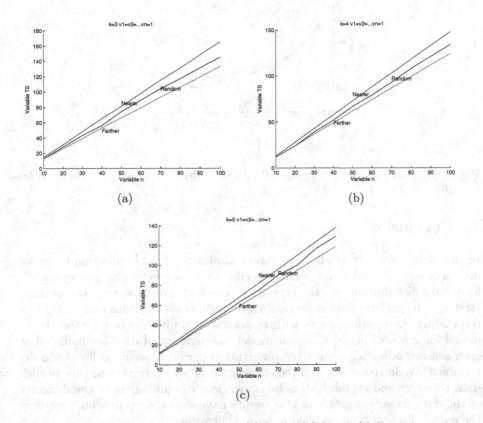

Fig. 4. $v_1 = v_2 = \ldots v_n = 1$, (a) $k = 3$, (b) $k = 4$, (c) $k = 5$

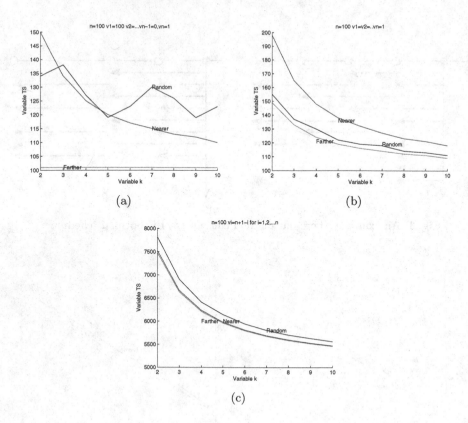

Fig. 5. (a) $v_1 = 100, v_2 = \ldots = v_{99} = 0, v_{100} = 1$, (b) $v_1 = v_2 = \ldots = v_{100} = 1$, (c) $v_i = 101 - i , \forall\, i = 1, \ldots, 100$

7   Conclusion

In this paper, we have studied the time complexity of data collection in sensor networks and derived novel results specific to sensor networks where nonuniform data distribution over the network is assumed. We have described optimal strategies to perform data collection under various assumptions and derive corresponding time performances with respect to a simple discrete mathematical model for a sensor network. In our model, the amount of data accumulated at each sensor node after some given observation period is assumed finite and determined. We have investigated the efficiency limits with respect to time of such data transfers and established useful upper/lower bounds despite the difficulty of the data collection problem. Our results have shown deep insights regarding the data collection time problem in sensor networks.

References

1. Bharghavan, V., Demers, A., Shenker, S., Zhang, L.: MACAW: a media access protocol for wireless LAN's. In: Proceedings of the Conference on Communications Architectures, Protocols and Applications, pp. 212–225. ACM (1994)
2. Chlebus, B.S., Gasieniec, L., Gibbons, A., Pelc, A., Rytter, W.: Deterministic broadcasting in ad hoc radio networks. Distributed Computing 15(1), 27–38 (2002)
3. Florens, C., Franceschetti, M., McEliece, R.J.: Lower bounds on data collection time in sensory networks. IEEE Journal on selected Areas in Communications, 22(6) (2004)
4. Florens, C., McEliece, R.: Scheduling algorithms for wireless ad-hoc sensor networks. In: GLOBECOM, NewYork, vol. 1, pp. 6–10 (2002)
5. Fraigniaud, P.: Approximation Algorithms for Minimum-Time Broadcast under the Vertex-Disjoint Paths Mode. In: Meyer auf der Heide, F. (ed.) ESA 2001. LNCS, vol. 2161, pp. 440–451. Springer, Heidelberg (2001)
6. Fraigniaud, P.: Minimum-time broadcast under edge-disjoint paths modes. In: International Conference on Fun with Algorithm, Citeseer (2001)
7. Gupta, P., Kumar, P.R.: The capacity of wireless networks. IEEE Transactions on Information Theory 46(2), 388–404 (2000)
8. Intanagonwiwat, C., Govindan, R., Estrin, D.: Directed diffusion: A scalable and robust communication paradigm for sensor networks. In: Proceedings of the 6th Annual International Conference on Mobile Computing and Networking, pp. 56–67. ACM (2000)
9. Ju, J.H., Li, V.O.K.: TDMA scheduling design of multihop packet radio networks based on latin squares. IEEE Journal on Selected Areas in Communications 17(8), 1345 (1999)
10. Leighton, F.T., Maggs, B.M., Rao, S.B.: Packet routing and job-shop scheduling inO (congestion+ dilation) steps. Combinatorica 14(2), 167–186 (1994)
11. Pursley, M.B.: The role of spread spectrum in packet radio networks. NASA STI/Recon Technical Report N, 88, 11929 (1987)
12. Royer, E.M., Toh, C.K.: A review of current routing protocols for ad hoc mobile wireless networks. IEEE Personal Communications 6(2), 46–55 (1999)
13. Sohrabi, K., Gao, J., Ailawadhi, V., Pottie, G.J.: Protocols for self-organization of a wireless sensor network. IEEE (see also IEEE Wireless Communications) Personal Communications 7(5), 16–27 (2000)

Minimum Total Communication Power Connected Dominating Set in Wireless Networks*

Deying Li[1], Donghyun Kim[2,**], Qinghua Zhu[1], Lin Liu[1], and Weili Wu[3]

[1] School of Information, Renmin University of China, Beijing 100872, China
{deyingli,qinghuazhu,spl}@ruc.edu.cn
[2] Dept. of Mathematics and Computer Science,
North Carolina Central University 1801 Fayetteville St. Durham NC 27707, USA
donghyun.kim@nccu.edu
[3] Dept. of Computer Science,
University of Texas at Dallas, Richardson, TX, 75080, USA
weiliwu@utdallas.edu

Abstract. A virtual backbone of a wireless network is a connected subset of nodes responsible for routing messages in the network. A node in the subset is likely to be exhausted much faster than the others due to its heavy duties. This situation can be more aggravated if the node uses higher communication power to form the virtual backbone. In this paper, we introduce the *minimum total communication power connected dominating set (MTCPCDS)* problem, whose goal is to compute a virtual backbone with minimum total communication power. We show this problem is NP-hard and propose two distributed algorithms. Especially, the first algorithm, MST-MTCPCDS, has a worst case performance guarantee. A simulations is conducted to evaluate the performance of our algorithms.

1 Introduction

A *virtual backbone (VB)* of a wireless network is a connected subset of nodes such that each node outside the subset is adjacent to a node in the subset. It is well-known that the substructure can be exploited to improve efficiency of wireless networks. A VB causes less overhead and becomes more effective if its size is small. The *minimum connected dominating set (MCDS)* problem is to

---

* This work was supported in part by the NSFC under Grants No. 61070191 and 91124001, the Fundamental Research Funds for the Central Universities,and the Research Funds of Renmin University of China 12XNH179, and Research Fund for the Doctoral Program of Higher Education of China No. 20100004110001. This work was also supported in part by US National Science Foundation (NSF) CREST No. HRD-0833184 and by US Army Research Office (ARO) No. W911NF-0810510. This work was partially supported by the NSF under Grant No. HRD-0833184, IIS-0513669, CCF-0621829, and CNS-0524429.
** Corresponding Author.

X. Wang et al. (Eds.): WASA 2012, LNCS 7405, pp. 132–141, 2012.
© Springer-Verlag Berlin Heidelberg 2012

find a connected subset of nodes such that all nodes outside the subset has a neighbor in the subset, and frequently used to compute a quality VB. Since it is NP-hard, several approximation algorithms [1–3] and a full polynomial-time approximation scheme (FPTAS) [4] are introduced for MCDS in unit disk graph (UDG). In [5–7], the authors introduced distributed algorithms for MCDS. In [8], Kim et al. studied MCDS in unit ball graph (UBG). In [9], Thai et al. studied MCDS in disk graph (DG). The minimum node-weight dominating set (or connected dominating set) problem is also extensively studied [10–13].

Due to their heavy duties, the nodes in a VB are likely to be exhausted much faster than the other nodes. In addition, this situation can be further aggravated if the nodes use higher communication power to form the VB. Based on this observation, we claim a VB with smaller total (or equivalently average) communication power to form a CDS is more energy-efficient. In the literature, topology control of a wireless network via communication power adjustment is frequently used to improve the energy-efficiency of a protocol running over the network without compromising its performance [14–17]. To the best of our knowledge, however, no effort has been made to find a CDS in a wireless network of nodes with adjustable communication power, and *our work is the first one making an effort toward this direction*. In fact, it has been implicitly assumed that every node of a wireless network has a fixed transmission power when computing a VB.

In this paper, we introduce the *minimum total communication power connected dominating set (MTCPCDS)* problem, whose goal is to find a CDS of a wireless network such that the sum of communication power of the nodes in the CDS becomes minimum. The formal definition of MTCPCDS is in Definition 1. Note that MTCPCDS problem can be considered as a generalization of the problem models in [10–13]. The summary of the contributions is as follow. First, we propose MTCPCDS and show it is NP-hard. Second, we introduce a simple distributed approximation algorithm, *a minimum spanning tree (MST) based distributed algorithm for MTCPCDS (MST-MTCPCDS)*, prove its performance ratio, and analyze its time and message complexities. Third, we introduce *a new greedy heuristic algorithm for MTCPCDS (GREEDY-MTCPCDS)*, and analyze its time and message complexities. At last, we study the average performance of the proposed algorithms via simulation.

The rest of this paper is organized as follows. Section 2 presents the notations, definitions, and important assumptions. Section 3 and Section 4 introduce MST-MTCPCDS and GREEDY-MTCPCDS, respectively. Our simulation result and corresponding discussions are given in Section 5. Finally, Section 6 concludes this paper.

2   Notations, Assumptions, and Problem Definition

In this paper, V is the set of the nodes in a given wireless network and n is the number of the nodes. Given V and corresponding communication power assignment of the nodes, $G[V]$ is the communication graph induced by the nodes.

For simplicity, we will use $G = (V, E)$ to represent the communication graph. Therefore, the meaning of G is highly dependent on the context. $G(V, E)$ is a communication graph with a node set V and an edge set E. In many cases, a graph in this paper is edge-weighted and we use $w_E(u, v)$ to represent the edge weight between two nodes $u, v \in V$. Each node u can adjust its communication power $p(u)$ such that $0 \leq p(u) \leq p_{max}(u)$, where $p_{max}(u)$ is the maximum communication power of u. $P_{max} = \bigcup_{u \in V} p_{max}(u)$.

As like [15–17], we assume the energy $\mathcal{E}$ consumed to transmit a bit of message is $\mathcal{E} = \beta \cdot d^{\alpha}$, where d is the travel distance of the message, α is a power attenuation factor, a constant between 2 and 5, and β is some constant. $Hopdist(u, v)$ and $Eucdist(u, v)$ are the hop and euclidean distance between u and v, respectively.

Definition 1 (MTCPCDS). *Given a pair $\langle V, P_{max} \rangle$, MTCPCDS is to determine the communication power of each node and find a subset $D \subseteq V$ such that 1) each node is either in D or is (bidirectionally) connected to a node in D, 2) $G[D]$ is connected, and 3) the total communication power assigned to D is minimum. More formally, it is to find $\langle D \subseteq V, \{p(u)|u \in D\} \rangle$ such that 1) $\forall u \in D$, $0 < p(u) \leq p_{max}(u)$, 2) both of $G(D, E_1)$ and $G(V, E_1 \cup E_2)$ are bidirectionally connected, where $E_1 = \{(u, v)| \min\{p(u), p(v)\} \geq \beta \cdot Eucdist(u, v)^{\alpha}, \forall u, v \in D\}$, and $E_2 = \{(u, v)| \min\{p(u), p_{max}(v)\} \geq \beta \cdot Eucdist(u, v)^{\alpha}, \forall u \in D, v \notin D\}$, and 3) $\sum_{v \in D} p(v)$ is minimum, respectively.*

Theorem 1. *The MTCPCDS problem is NP-hard.*

Proof. Imagine a grid graph such that the euclidean distance between any two neighbors is exactly 1. Clearly, such grid graph is a special case of UDG. Next, consider a subclass of MTCPCDS defined over the grid graph such that 1) $p_{max}(v) = 1$ for all $v \in V$. In such grid graph, the subclass of MTCPCDS is equivalent to MCDS since the power level of each node in an optimal solution of the subclass has to be either 0 or 1. (the power level of a node is 0 means the node is not in the CDS. Otherwise, it is in the CDS.) By [18], MCDS is still NP-hard even in such grid graph. Therefore, the subclass of MTCPCDS is also NP-hard. As a result, MTCPCDS without the constraint on the maximum power level of each node is NP-hard in general UDGs.

3   A MST Based Approximation Algorithm for MTCPCDS (MST-MTCPCDS)

Now, we introduce MST-MTCPCDS. Given $\langle V, P_{max} \rangle$, the algorithm performs the following steps in a sequential order.

1. Constructs an edge-weighted auxiliary graph $G_{aux}^{EW} = (V_{aux}^{EW}, E_{aux}^{EW})$ such that for any two node pair u and v in V, (u, v) is in E_{aux}^{EW} if and only if $d^{\alpha}(u, v) \leq \min\{p_{max}(v_i), p_{max}(v_j)\}$. Also, $w_E(u, v) = d^{\alpha}(u, v)$ is assigned as the edge weight of (u, v). Note that such construction can be done in a fully distributed (localized) manner by letting each node exchange a "hello" message with its neighbors.

2. Finds an MST T_{mst} of G_{aux}^{EW} using an existing distributed MST algorithm such as Kruskal's algorithm. Suppose D is the set of non-leaf nodes in T_{mst}. Clearly, D is a CDS of G_{aux}^{EW} since $G_{aux}^{EW}[D]$ is connected and all nodes in $V \setminus D$ is adjacent to at least one node in D.

3. Assign the communication power of each node as follows: i) For each $v \in D$, we set $p(v)$ to the maximum edge weight between v and any u such that v and u are adjacent in T_{mst}, and ii) for each node $w \in V \setminus D$, we need to adjust w's power properly so that it can send a message to at least one node in D.

Theorem 2. *The running time of MST-MTCPCDS is $O(n^2)$.*

Proof. The first step takes $O(n^2)$ time to construct G_{aux}^{EW} and assign a weight on each edge of it. The second step takes $O(n^2)$ time to compute an MST T_{mst} using Kruskal's algorithm and find a set D of non-leaf nodes of T_{mst}. The last step takes $O(|D| \cdot \Delta)$ time to determine the communication power level of each node in D by observing its neighbors, where Δ is the maximum degree of G_{aux}^{EW}. As a result, the running time of MST-MTCPCDS is $O(n^2)$.

Theorem 3. *The approximation ratio of MST-MTCPCDS is 2Δ for the MTCPCDS problem.*

Proof. Suppose T is any spanning tree in G_{aux}^{EW}. Let $NL(T)$ be the set of non-leaf nodes in T and $E(T)$ be the edges in T. We denote the weight of an edge e and the communication power level of node v by $w_E(e)$ and $p(v)$, respectively. Since each edge is connecting two end points, $w_E(e)$ can be included in $\sum_{v \in NL(T)} p(v)$ at most two times. Therefore, we have $\sum_{v \in NL(T)} p(v) \leq 2 \sum_{e \in E(T)} w_E(e)$, and $\sum_{e \in E(T)} w_E(e) \leq \Delta \sum_{v \in NL(T)} \max_{\{(v,u) \in T | \forall u \in V\}} d^\alpha(v,u) = \Delta \sum_{v \in NL(T)} p(v)$, where Δ is the maximum degree of G_{aux}^{EW}.

Now, suppose D^* is an optimal solution of the MTCPCDS problem. Then, there should be a spanning tree T^* of D^* on G_{aux}^{EW}. Also, suppose D is an output of our algorithm given an input G_{aux}^{EW}, and T is a corresponding spanning tree of D. Then, we can observe 1) in MST-MTCPCDS, T is an MST of G_{aux}^{EW}. Since T^* is a spanning tree, we have $\sum_{e \in E(T)} w_E(e) \leq \sum_{e \in E(T^*)} w_E(e)$, and 2) D^* has to be a set of non-leaf nodes of T^*. Otherwise, we can remove a leaf node from D^* which contradicts to our assumption that D^* is optimal. Therefore, we have $\sum_{v \in NL(T^*)} p(v) = \sum_{v \in D^*} p(v)$. As a result, $\sum_{v \in D} p(v) \leq 2 \sum_{e \in E(T)} w_E(e) \leq 2 \sum_{e \in E(T^*)} w_E(e) \leq 2\Delta \sum_{v \in NL(T^*)} p(v) = 2\Delta \sum_{v \in D^*} p(v)$, and the theorem holds true.

4 GREEDY-MTCPCDS: A New Greedy Heuristic Algorithm for MTCPCDS

GREEDY-MTCPCDS consists of two distinct phases. In the first phase, given a MTCPCDS problem instance, the algorithm computes a G_{aux}^{EW} in a distributed manner as MST-MTCPCDS does. Therefore, no node needs to keep the global information of G_{aux}^{EW}. In the second phase, it applies a distributed greedy strategy to G_{aux}^{EW}. At the beginning of the second phase, the color of each node is white, but later becomes gray or black. At the end, the set of black nodes forms a CDS.

Given a node $v_i \in V$ and its current communication power $p(v_i)$, the cost to increase its communication power to $p_{new}(v_i)$ is defined as

$$Cost(p(v_i), p_{new}(v_i)) = (p_{new}(v_i) - p(v_i))/(|N[p_{new}(v_i)]|),$$

where $N[p_{new}(v_i)]$ is the set of white nodes in G_{aux}^{EW} dominated by v_i using the new communication power $p_{new}(v_i)$. In case that $|N[p_{new}(v_i)]| = 0$, which implies that v_i cannot reach any white neighbor even using its maximum communication power, $Cost(p(v_i), p_{new}(v_i))$ returns -1. Intuitively, this cost function is representing the cost-efficiency of increasing the communication power of v_i from $p(v_i)$ to $p_{new}(v_i)$.

The second phase consists of multiple rounds. Each round is initiated by a current root r_c. The very first round is started by electing a new current root r_c with minimum $Cost_{best}(r_c)$, where

$$Cost_{best}(r_c) = \min_{p(r_c) < p_{new}(r_c) \le p_{max}(r_c)} \{Cost(p(r_c), p_{new}(r_c))\}.$$

Once elected, the r_c increases its communication power to $Cost_{best}(r_c)$. Note that for any r_c, the effective number of choices for $p_{new}(r_c)$ is bounded by Δ, which is the maximum degree of G_{aux}^{EW}. Then, r_c becomes a black node and each (white) node to which r_c can send a signal using the new communication power $p_{new}(r_c)$ becomes gray. Note that those gray nodes are some of the neighbors of r_c in G_{aux}^{EW}. Next, r_c constructs a node set X of the gray nodes, selects the node $v_i \in X$ with minimum $Cost_{best}(v_i)$ value, and sends an invitation to v_i with X and $W = \bigcup_{v_j \in X} Cost_{best}(v_j)$.

On receiving the invitation, v_i becomes a new r_c and repeats the round. Generally speaking, after a new r_c is elected, followings are performed in a sequential order.

1. r_c becomes a black node, adjusts its communication power to $p_{new}(r_c)$ such that $Cost_{best}(r_c)$ can be achieved. All of white neighbors reachable from r_c using the new communication power become gray. Then, r_c calculates X' and W', where X' is the set of gray nodes at most two hops far from r_c and W' is the set of $Cost_{best}(v_i)$ for each $v_i \in X'$. Then, merges those with old X and W which inherited from the previous root (i.e. $X \leftarrow X \bigcup X'$ and $W \leftarrow W \bigcup W'$). While merging, any new information overwrites its old version. To optimize the size of X and W, for each $v_j \in X$, if $Cost_{best}(v_j) = -1$, we can remove v_j from X and $Cost_{best}(v_j)$ from W since v_j does not have any reachable white node anymore.

2. Once the merged, the new r_c picks a node $v \in X$ with the minimum $Cost_{best}(v)$ value (which can be found from W within a linear time) as the next r_c. If X is empty, then all nodes should be either black or gray, and thus r_c terminates this phase. Otherwise, r_c sends an invitation message to another node $v \in X$ with minimum $Cost_{best}(v)$ value.

After the second phase, the set of black nodes and its corresponding power assignments will be a CDS of G_{aux}^{EW}. Now, we analyze the time and message complexities of GREEDY-MTCPCDS.

Theorem 4. *Both the time and message complexities of GREEDY-MTCPCDS are $O(|V|\Delta^2)$.*

Proof. It take $O(n^2)$ time to obtain G_{aux}^{EW} in the first phase. Now, we discuss about the second phase. In each round, r_c needs to collect the cost information from every black and gray node within two hops. In detail, r_c first sends the query message to its direct neighbors using one broadcasting message and this incurs $O(1)$ time and takes $O(1)$ messages. For each direct neighbor v_i of r_c, v_i needs to spend $O(1)$ time and incur $O(1)$ messages to broadcast the query to its direct neighbors. Also, v_i will take $O(\Delta)$ time and incur $O(\Delta)$ messages to collect the cost information from its direct neighbors. To send this to the r_c, it will take $O(1)$ time and generate $O(1)$ messages. Therefore, both the time and message complexities of one round is $O(1) + O(\Delta) \cdot O(1 + \Delta + 1) = O(\Delta^2)$. Since we can have at most $|V|$ rounds, the time and message complexities of GREEDY-MTCPCDS are $O(|V|\Delta^2)$.

5   Simulation Results and Analysis

To the best of our knowledge, there is no CDS computation algorithm adjusting the communication power of each node. Therefore, we compare the average performance of our algorithms with CDS-BD-D in [7], a typical MCDS algorithm. The simulations are conducted over a 100×100 2-D space. We compare the total communication power and the size of CDSs generated by the three algorithms under different parameter settings. For each parameter setting, we obtain an averaged result from 100 trials. In each trial, we randomly place n nodes over the terrain. If the induced G_{aux}^{EW} by the nodes is disconnected, we simply discard it and generate a new one.

As we mentioned, the power model to send a message over a distance d is $E = \beta \cdot d^\alpha$. For simplicity, we normalize $\beta = 1$. We assume that the signal is moving in the air and set α to 2. Then, the remaining tunable parameters in the simulations are as follows:

1. The number of nodes n. We vary n from 80 to 200 to check the scalability of the algorithms.
2. The interval of maximum power of each node $[a, b]$. In the simulation, the maximum power of each node is generated from a normal distribution with mean equal to $\frac{a+b}{2}$ and standard deviation equal to $\frac{b-a}{4}$.

In Figure 1, we compare the averaged total communication power of CDSs generated by the three approaches. In Figure 1(a), 1(b), and 1(c), the maximum communication power of each node is from $[100, 400]$, $[100, 900]$, and $[400, 900]$, respectively. For each interval, we vary the number of nodes from 80 to 200. From this simulation results, we can clearly see both of MST-MTCPCDS and

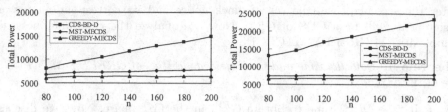

(a) The maximum power of each node is randomly chosen between 100 to 400.

(b) The maximum power of each node is randomly chosen between 100 to 900.

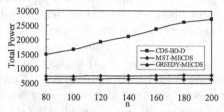

(c) The maximum power of each node is randomly chosen between 400 to 900.

Fig. 1. Averaged total communication power of CDSs generated by CDS-BD-D, MST-MTCPCDS, and GREEDY-MTCPCDS

GREEDY-MTCPCDS outperform CDS-BD-D in terms of the averaged total communication power of CDSs. This is natural since CDS-BD-D was designed for MCDS, not for MTCPCDS. We can also observe, while we did not prove the worst case performance of GREEDY-MTCPCDS, GREEDY-MTCPCDS works better than MST-MTCPCDS on average. Therefore, they are in a trade-off relationship.

In Figure 2, we compare the performance of the three approaches using the average size of CDSs, which is a traditional quality measurement for CDS. From the simulation results, we can see that on average, the size of CDSs computed by GREEDY-MTCPCDS is even better than that of CDSs generated by CDS-BD-D, which is an approximation algorithm for the MCDS problem. Meanwhile, we can observe that CDS-BD-D works better than MST-MTCPCDS, but this is understandable since MST-MTCPCDS is an approximation algorithm for MTCPCDS, not for MCDS.

In conclusion, the three algorithms are in a very interesting trade-off relationship. CDS-BD-D is an approximation algorithm for MCDS and has a worst case performance guarantee. MST-MTCPCDS is an approximation algorithm for MTCPCDS and has a worst case performance guarantee. CDS-BD-D is better than MST-MTCPCDS for MCDS, but MCDS is better than CDS-BD-D for MTCPCDS. On the other hand, GREEDY-MTCPCDS is not an approximation algorithm for any of the problems and has no worst case performance guarantee, but on average, it outperforms the other two algorithms in both performance metrics, the size and the total communication power.

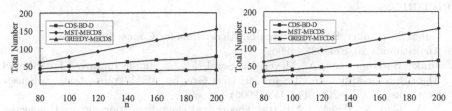

(a) The maximum power of each node is randomly chosen between 100 to 400.   (b) The maximum power of each node is randomly chosen between 100 to 900.

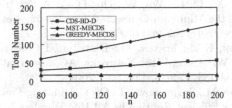

(c) The maximum power of each node is randomly chosen between 400 to 900.

Fig. 2. Averaged size of CDSs generated by CDS-BD-D, MST-MTCPCDS, and GREEDY-MTCPCDS

6   Conclusions and Future Work

In this paper, we proposed the minimum total communication power connected dominating set (MTCPCDS) problem. In detail, given n nodes and their maximum communication powers, MTCPCDS is to determine each node's communication power and to find a CDS of the network. We proved this problem is NP-hard and proposed two distributed approaches. The first approach exploits an existing distributed approximation algorithm for MST to solve MTCPCDS and has a worst case performance guarantee. The second one is a simple greedy algorithm and theoretically runs faster than the first one in a sparse graph. In the extensive simulations, we saw that they are in a very interesting trade-off relationship and produce quality solutions for MTCPCDS.

In [19], the authors studied a problem similar to MTCPCDS, but did not consider the maximum communication power level of each node, and thus is less realistic. In such a case, a constant factor approximation can be easily obtained. However, for MTCPCDS with the maximum communication power level constraint, we were only able to obtain a $O(\Delta)$ approximation. Therefore, obtaining a constant factor approximation of MTCPCDS is still open.

In this paper, we mostly focused on establishing a theoretical foundation of the problem and its solutions. As a future work, we are interested in taking the remaining energy level of each node into the consideration and try to improve our approach so that it can actually help to extend the lifetime of CDS based wireless networks.

References

1. Guha, S., Khuller, S.: Approximation Algorithms for Connected Dominating Sets. Algorithmica 20, 374–387 (1996)
2. Funke, S., Kesselman, A., Meyer, U., Segal, M.: A Simple Improved Distributed Algorithm for Minimum CDS in Unit Disk Graphs. ACM Transactions on Sensor Networks (TOSN) 2(3), 444–453 (2006)
3. Li, X., Gao, X., Wu, W.: A Better Theoretical Bound to Approximate Connected Dominating Set in Unit Disk Graph. In: Li, Y., Huynh, D.T., Das, S.K., Du, D.-Z. (eds.) WASA 2008. LNCS, vol. 5258, pp. 162–175. Springer, Heidelberg (2008)
4. Cheng, X., Huang, X., Li, D., Wu, W., Du, D.-Z.: A Polynomial-Time Approximation Scheme for the Minimum-Connected Dominating Set in Ad Hoc Wireless Networks. Networks 42(4), 202–208 (2003)
5. Wan, P.-J., Alzoubi, K.M., Frieder, O.: Distributed Construction of Connected Dominating Set in Wireless Ad Hoc Networks. ACM Journal on Mobile Networks and Applications (MONET) 9(2), 141–149 (2004)
6. Wu, J., Dai, F., Gao, M., Stojmenovic, I.: On Calculating Power-Aware Connected Dominating Sets for Efficient Routing in Ad Hoc Wireless Networks. IEEE/KICS Journal of Communications and Networks 4, 59–70 (2002)
7. Kim, D., Wu, Y., Li, Y., Zou, F., Du, D.-Z.: Constructing Minimum Connected Dominating Sets with Bounded Diameters in Wireless Networks. IEEE Transactions on Parallel and Distributed Systems (TPDS) 20(2), 147–157 (2009)
8. Kim, D., Zhang, Z., Li, X., Wang, W., Wu, W., Du, D.-Z.: A Better Approximation Algorithm For Computing Connected Dominating Sets in Unit Ball Graphs. IEEE Transactions on Mobile Computing (TMC) 9(8), 1108–1118 (2010)
9. Thai, M.T., Wang, F., Liu, D., Zhu, S., Du, D.-Z.: Connected Dominating Sets in Wireless Networks with Different Transmission Ranges. IEEE Transactions on Mobile Computing (TMC) 6(7), 721–730 (2007)
10. Guha, S., Khuller, S.: Improved Methods for Approximating Node Weighted Steiner Trees and Connected Dominating Sets. Information and Computation 150(1), 57–74 (1999)
11. Gao, X., Huang, Y., Zhang, Z., Wu, W.: $(6 + \epsilon)$-Approximation for Minimum Weight Dominating Set in Unit Disk Graphs. In: Hu, X., Wang, J. (eds.) COCOON 2008. LNCS, vol. 5092, pp. 551–557. Springer, Heidelberg (2008)
12. Huang, Y., Gao, X., Zhang, Z., Wu, W.: A Better Constant-Factor Approximation for Weighted Dominating Set in Unit Disk Graph. Journal of Combinatorial Optimization (JOCO) 18(2), 179–194 (2009)
13. Dai, D., Yu, C.: A $(5+\epsilon)$-Approximation Algorithm for Minimum Weighted Dominating Set in Unit Disk Graph. Theoretical Computer Science (TCS) 41(8-10), 756–765 (2009)
14. Clementi, A., Crescenzi, P., Penna, P., Rossi, G., Vocca, P.: On the Complexity of Computing Minimum Energy Consumption Broadcast Subgraphs. In: Ferreira, A., Reichel, H. (eds.) STACS 2001. LNCS, vol. 2010, pp. 121–131. Springer, Heidelberg (2001)
15. Wan, P.J., Calinescu, G., Li, X.Y., Frieder, O.: Minimum-energy Broadcasting in Static Ad Hoc Wireless Networks. Wireless Networks 8(6), 607–617 (2002)
16. Ambühl, C.: An Optimal Bound for the MST Algorithm to Compute Energy Efficient Broadcast Trees in Wireless Networks. In: Caires, L., Italiano, G.F., Monteiro, L., Palamidessi, C., Yung, M. (eds.) ICALP 2005. LNCS, vol. 3580, pp. 1139–1150. Springer, Heidelberg (2005)

17. Flammini, M., Klasing, R., Navarra, A., Perennes, S.: Improved Approximation Results for the Minimum Energy Broadcasting Problem. Algorithmica 49(4), 318–336 (2007)
18. Clark, B.N., Colbourn, C.J., Johnson, D.S.: Unit Disk Graphs. Discrete Mathematics 86, 165–177 (1990)
19. Carmi, P., Katz, M.J., Segal, M., Shpungin, H.: Fault-Tolerant Power Assignment and Backbone in Wireless Networks. Ad Hoc & Sensor Wireless Networks 4(4), 355–366 (2007)

Supporting Multi-level Quality of Services in Data Broadcast Systems

Jingsong Lv[1], Victor C.S. Lee[2], Minming Li[2], and Enhong Chen[1]

[1] School of Computer Science and Technology,
University of Science and Technology of China, Hefei, P.R. China
[2] Department of Computer Science,
City University of Hong Kong, Hong Kong, P.R. China
ljs11433@mail.ustc.edu.cn, {csvlee,minming.li}@cityu.edu.hk,
cheneh@ustc.edu.cn

Abstract. Data broadcasting becomes a popular approach to disseminating information to a large population of mobile clients. Although there are lots of research efforts on addressing the scheduling in data broadcast systems, little attention has been paid to the QoS (Quality of Service) issue, which is crucial to any information dissemination application. To support different levels of QoS, data items could be allocated to multiple logical channels with speeds commensurate with respective QoS levels. Therefore, an online EDF (Earliest Deadline First)-based dispatcher is devised to dispatch data items scheduled in the multi-channel allocation to the single physical channel in data broadcast systems. We prove that no data item dispatched by the dispatcher will be delayed with respect to their subscribed QoS levels. In addition, we prove that, under certain conditions, the EDF-based dispatcher is also applicable in the presence of gaps between data items allocated in a QoS level.

Keywords: broadcast schedule, channel allocation, data dissemination, multi-level QoS, rounding method.

1 Introduction

With the advances in telecommunications, interconnectivity, and mobile computing, data broadcasting through wireless channels is preferable to unicasting in disseminating information to large numbers of mobile terminals with common interests, as broadcasting can efficiently satisfy all pending requests for the same data item with a single response.

In mobile communication and wireless networks, data broadcasting has been used for sending public information, (including weather, news, sports, traffic, elections and so on), personalized information (including stocks, lottery, horoscopes, health care and so on) and emergency information to intelligent mobile terminals, such as smart watches and mobile phones. In satellite networks, it has been used for updating car navigation systems, GPS timing and positioning. Data broadcasting has also been widely applied commercially, such as StarBand, Hughes

X. Wang et al. (Eds.): WASA 2012, LNCS 7405, pp. 142–153, 2012.

Network, Intel Intercast System, T-DMB System and STiMi (Satellite-Terrestrial Interactive Multi-service Infrastructure)-based CMMB (China Mobile Multimedia Broadcasting) System. Recently, due to the development of 3G network (such as OFDMA-based mobile Wimax [1]) and the convergence of networks including broadcasting cable network, telecom network and computer network, both the available bandwidth for broadcasting and the demand for information dissemination services (such as SMS group sending) have been rapidly increasing.

In data broadcast systems, a large group of clients retrieve data items maintained by a server. The server broadcasts data items based on a scheduling algorithm through a high-speed downlink channel. The clients monitor the channel for data items of their interest. Conventionally, scheduling data items for broadcasting at the server side has been regarded as the key to good performance in data broadcast systems. In the literature, a significant amount of the research effort has been put on studying different scheduling approaches to meeting a variety of performance objectives such as improving broadcast efficiency and reducing data access latency [2–8]. However, most, if not all, of these studies did not support multi-level quality of services (QoS), which is a feature commonly found in many information systems to accommodate applications or users with diverse performance requirements [9]. For example, layered multicast [10] support multi-level video quality. Among the very few studies on multi-level QoS, in [11], an MULS framework is introduced to provide multiple levels of service quality in terms of average data access latency by tuning control parameters, such as number of samples, number of iterations. To translate higher-level QoS representations into lower-level representations, some QoS mapping schemes have been introduced in DiffServ (Differentiated Services) networks for unicast flows [12]. Our study will focus on translating multi-level QoS from multi-channel allocation into single-channel allocation in data broadcast systems through QoS mapping.

Recently, the simulation results from [13] show that the real-time performance of single-channel scheduling in terms of request deadline miss ratio is better than the one of multi-channel scheduling under the condition of the same total bandwidth. To compare the two scheduling, a multi-channel allocation structure is constructed as follows. We partition the physical bandwidth of the high-speed downlink channel into multiple low-speed logical channels. Each of these logical channels can be used to support applications or users subscribing a certain QoS level. In other words, data items are logically transmitted on a channel with speed commensurate with the subscribed QoS level. Given a logical channel, any existing scheduling algorithm can be used to determine the service order for data items in the channel. Based on this structure, we propose an online algorithm to map data items in a multi-channel allocation onto a single-channel allocation. As a result, data items in the single-channel allocation can be transmitted through the high-speed downlink channel for broadcasting.

Our paper makes three main contributions. First, based on a multi-channel allocation structure, which consists of a set of logical channels, each of which represents a QoS level, we devise an online EDF-based dispatcher to map data items in the multi-channel allocation onto a single-channel allocation for subsequent transmission. We prove that no data item will be delayed with the dispatcher. In other words, the EDF-based dispatcher guarantees the QoS committed by the initially allocated logical channels. Second, based on the EDF-based dispatcher, we prove that the average turnaround time of the output single-channel allocation is smaller than that of the input multi-channel allocation. This result can provide system architects a solid theoretical view of the two alternative design configurations, namely, single-channel and multi-channel architectures. Third, we prove that, under certain conditions, the EDF-based dispatcher is also applicable in the presence of gaps between data items on a logical channel. This relaxed restriction further improves the practicality of the EDF-based dispatcher.

The remainder of the paper is organized as follows. In Section 2, we present the problem description and assumptions. In Section 3, an EDF-based dispatcher is proposed to map all items in multi-channel allocation onto a single physical channel without violating the stipulated time constraints. In Section 4, it is proved that the dispatcher can be applied to gapless problem, namely the adjacent data items in multi-channel allocation have no gap. After that, in Section 5, we prove that the dispatcher is applicable to the problem of *integral gaps between slotted items* in multi-channel allocation. Finally, we conclude the paper in Section 6.

2   Problem Description

In this study, we present a multi-channel allocation structure to represent multiple QoS (Quality of Service) levels on the server side. The structure consists of a set of logical channels, each of these logical channels can be used to support applications or users subscribing a certain QoS level. In other words, data items are logically transmitted on a channel with speed commensurate with the subscribed QoS level. Given a logical channel, any existing scheduling algorithm proposed in the literature can be adopted to determine the service order for data items in the channel. Based on this structure, we devise an online dispatcher to map data items in the multi-channel allocation onto a single physical channel for transmission in data broadcast systems. Note that the dispatcher does not change the service order of data items in a logical channel, which is determined by the adopted scheduler. The structure of the high-speed physical channel and the multiple low-speed logical channels are described by Assumptions (i)-(vi) which are shown as follows.

(i) The bandwidth of the single physical channel is $B_s \in \mathbf{R}^+$;
(ii) There are $K \geq 2$ QoS levels. Each of these levels is represented by a logical channel and the bandwidth of the I_{th} logical channel is $B_I = \frac{B_s}{g_I}$, where $g_I \in \mathbf{R}^+$, $I \in \{1, 2, 3, \ldots, K\}$ and $1 < g_1 \leq g_2 \leq g_3 \leq \ldots \leq g_K$;
(iii) The two above have the same total bandwidth, namely $B_s = \sum_{I=1}^{K} \frac{B_s}{g_I} \Rightarrow$ $\sum_{I=1}^{K} \frac{1}{g_I} = 1$;

(iv) A unit time or a time slot, is defined as the time taken to transmit one unit-sized item on the single physical channel. Note that it is always possible to split a non-unit-sized item into multiple unit-sized pages. Hence, g_I denotes the time taken to transmit one item on the I_{th} logical channel. Specifically, if $g_I \in \mathbf{N}^+$, g_I denotes the number of time slots to transmit one item on the I_{th} logical channel;

(v) There is no gap between adjacent items allocated on a logical channel. We also assume that the first items on the logical channels are aligned synchronously at time 0. The gaps will be further discussed in Section 5;

(vi) The J_{th} ($J \in \mathbf{N}^+$) item on the I_{th} ($I \in \{1, 2, 3, \ldots, K\}$) logical channel is represented as a tuple: $\langle t_{L(I,J)}, t_{L(I,J)} + g_I \rangle = \langle (J-1) * g_I, J * g_I \rangle$, where $t_{L(I,J)}$ is the beginning time of the item and $(t_{L(I,J)} + g_I)$ is the end time.

Note that these timings of a data item in Assumption (vi) are hypothetical. They are determined by the adopted scheduling algorithm which is also responsible for ensuring that the end time of a data item is earlier than the deadlines of associated requests, if any. The actual beginning and end times of a data item are known only when it has been dispatched onto the single physical channel for transmission.

Based on this structure, the problem is to find a method to map all items in the multi-channel allocation onto a single-channel allocation without causing any delay. Specifically, for any item $\langle t_{L(I,J)}, t_{L(I,J)} + g_I \rangle$ in the multi-channel allocation to be mapped to a time slot with beginning time t_x ($t_x \in \mathbf{N}$) on the single physical channel, it must satisfy the following time constraint in order to guarantee the QoS committed by the respective logical channel.

$$t_{L(I,J)} \leq t_x \leq t_{L(I,J)} + g_I - 1 \tag{1}$$

For any given mapped item in the single-channel allocation, the lower bound of the time constraint specifies that its actual beginning time must be no earlier than the hypothetical beginning time of the same item in the multi-channel allocation and the upper bound specifies that its actual end time must be no later than the hypothetical end time of the same item in the multi-channel allocation.

3 An EDF-Based Dispatcher

To satisfy Constraint (1), we devise an EDF-based dispatcher in Algorithm 1, which maps one of the items from K logical channels to the current time slot of the single physical channel at the beginning of every time slot. Suppose the current time is t_x, which is the beginning time of a particular time slot. Firstly, the dispatcher moves items whose beginning times are not later than the current time ($t_{L(I,J)} \leq t_x$) from the K logical channels to a temporary priority queue, which is kept in order of the end time ($t_{L(I,J)} + g_I$). The dispatcher resembles traditional EDF if the beginning time and end time are respectively regarded as arrival time and deadline. In the case of a tie, the item with smaller channel number has higher priority. This step ensures that all items in the temporary priority queue satisfy the lower bound of Constraint (1). The EDF-based dispatcher removes all infeasible items, if any, in the temporary priority queue. An item becomes infeasible if it is impossible to broadcast the item completely before its end time, i.e., $t_{L(I,J)} + g_I < t_x + 1$. This step ensures that all items in the temporary priority queue satisfy the upper bound of Constraint (1). Altogether, the two steps ensure that all items kept in the temporary priority queue satisfy Constraint (1). Lastly, the item at the head of the temporary priority queue, if any, is moved to the current time slot of the single physical channel for broadcasting and the remaining items are kept in the temporary priority queue for the next iteration.

Algorithm 1. EDF-based dispatcher

Input: M : a buffer of items $(\langle t_{L(I,J)}, t_{L(I,J)} + g_I \rangle)$ on logical channel $I = 1, 2, \ldots, K$;

Output: S : an array of sequenced items on the single physical channel;

1 /* Q: a temporary priority queue kept in order of item end time   */
2 **for** *each item* $\langle t_{L(I,J)}, t_{L(I,J)} + g_I \rangle$ *in* M **do**
3   /* move items whose beginning time is not later than the current time to Q */
4   **if** $t_{L(I,J)} \leq t_x$ **then**
5          $Q \leftarrow Q \cup \{\langle t_{L(I,J)}, t_{L(I,J)} + g_I \rangle\}$;
6          $M \leftarrow M - \{\langle t_{L(I,J)}, t_{L(I,J)} + g_I \rangle\}$;

7 **for** *each item* $\langle t_{L(I,*)}, t_{L(I,*)} + g_I \rangle$ *in* Q **do**
8   /* drop all infeasible items   */
9   **if** $t_{L(I,*)} + g_I < t_x + 1$ **then**
10         $Q \leftarrow Q - \{\langle t_{L(I,*)}, t_{L(I,*)} + g_I \rangle\}$;

11 /* output the first item in Q for broadcasting if Q is not empty, otherwise skip   */
12 **if** $Q \neq \emptyset$ **then**
13     $S[t_x] \leftarrow$ Extract_Min(Q);

---

4   Gapless Mapping

Based on the EDF-based dispatcher, any mapped items satisfy Constraint (1). However, just as shown in lines 8–10 of Algorithm 1, infeasible items are removed from the temporary priority queue. So, the removed items cannot be mapped onto the single physical channel. Now, we rule out this possibility by proving the following theorem.

Theorem 1. *The EDF-based dispatcher can map all continuous items on multiple logical channels onto a single physical channel with the same total bandwidth without violating Constraint (1).*

Proof. Assume that the EDF-based dispatcher could not map all items to the time slots of the single physical channel. Then there should be a time t_x, i.e. the beginning time of some time slot, when the time slot is blank due to empty priority queue or competitive for at least two items of only $(1+\varepsilon)$ remaining time before end time, where $0 \leq \varepsilon < 1$. Here, "competitive" means a state for which the dispatcher will remove at least one item from the current priority queue for the next time slot in lines 8–10. Next, using mathematical induction, we will prove that the two cases never happen at any time t_x.

Firstly, when time $t_x = 0$, there are K items added to the priority queue and no item is removed from the priority queue, as the end time $g_I > 1$ for any item on logical channel $I = 1, 2, 3, \ldots, K$ shown in Assumption (ii). So the current time slot will not be blank. Suppose that it is a competitive time slot. Then the first two items in the current priority queue should satisfy $g_1 = 1 + \varepsilon_1 < 2$ and $g_2 = 1 + \varepsilon_2 < 2$, where $0 \leq \varepsilon_1 \leq \varepsilon_2 < 1$. So $\frac{1}{g_1} + \frac{1}{g_2} > \frac{1}{2} + \frac{1}{2} = 1$, which contradicts Assumption (iii). Hence competitive time slot is also not possible. Summing up the above, neither of the two cases happens at time 0.

Secondly, assume that the two cases never happen at any time $t_x < k$. Now we will prove that the two cases do not happen at time $t_x = k$.

Suppose that at least one of the two cases happens at time $t_x = k$. If it is the case of blank time slot, the end time of the last mapped or removed item for any of the multiple logical channels will be greater than t_x. We set it as $(t_x + \varepsilon_I)$ for the item on logical channel I, where $\varepsilon_I > 0$. So the number of the mapped or removed items is at least $\sum_{I=1}^{K} \frac{t_x + \varepsilon_I}{g_I} \geq t_x + \lceil \min\{\varepsilon_I | 1 \leq I \leq K\} \rceil \geq t_x + 1$. However, there are at most t_x items mapped onto the single physical channel until time t_x. So there must be at least 1 time slot that is competitive before time t_x. It is a contradiction to the inductive hypothesis on time $t_x < k$. Therefore, the case of blank time slot does not happen at time $t_x = k$.

If it is the case of competitive time slot, the end times of competitive items should be $(t_x + 1 + \varepsilon_1)$, $(t_x + 1 + \varepsilon_2)$, $(t_x + 1 + \varepsilon_3)$, $\ldots$, $(t_x + 1 + \varepsilon_m)$, where $0 \leq \varepsilon_1, \varepsilon_2, \varepsilon_3, \ldots, \varepsilon_m < 1$ and $2 \leq m \leq K$. We set $\varepsilon = \max\{\varepsilon_1, \varepsilon_2, \varepsilon_3, \ldots, \varepsilon_m\}$, where $0 \leq \varepsilon < 1$. Then the number of the mapped or removed items is at most $\sum_{I=1}^{K} \left\lfloor \frac{t_x + 1 + \varepsilon}{g_I} \right\rfloor - m \leq \left\lfloor \sum_{I=1}^{K} \frac{t_x + 1 + \varepsilon}{g_I} \right\rfloor - m = \lfloor t_x + 1 + \varepsilon \rfloor - m = t_x + 1 - m$. However, there are t_x time slots available for mapping items onto the single physical channel. So there must be at least $m - 1 \geq 1$ time slots that are blank before time t_x. It is also a contradiction to the inductive hypothesis on time $t_x < k$. Therefore the case of competitive time slot does not happen at time $t_x = k$.

Since the two above steps have been proved, it has now been proved by mathematical induction that the two cases never happen at any time. So the initial assumption is false. Theorem 1 holds.   □

To sum up, the EDF-based dispatcher can map *all* items from multiple logical channels onto a single physical channel without violating Constraint (1). Based on this result, we further prove the following Property 1. Note that the turnaround time is the interval of time between the submission of an item (arrival time) and its end time and, therefore, the beginning time of an item must be later than or equal to its arrival time.

Property 1. The average turnaround time of the output single-channel allocation mapped by the EDF-based dispatcher is smaller than that of the input multi-channel allocation.

Proof. The proof is divided into two parts. (1) Given any item in multi-channel allocation, according to Theorem 1, the end time of the mapped item in single-channel allocation is not later than that in multi-channel allocation. Additionally, the arrival time of the item is fixed upon its arrival. So the turnaround time of each mapped item in single-channel allocation is not larger than that in multi-channel allocation. (2) For at least one item, its end time $(t_x + 1)$ in single-channel allocation is earlier than the end time $(t_{L(I,J)} + g_I)$ in multi-channel allocation. Otherwise, we have $t_x + 1 = t_{L(I,J)} + g_I = J * g_I$ for all items on channel $I = 1, 2, 3, \ldots, K$, where $t_x \in \mathbf{N}$ and $J \geq 1$. However, when $t_x = 0$, we have $J * g_I = t_x + 1 = 1 \Rightarrow g_I \leq 1$ which contradicts Assumption (ii). Hence the turnaround time of at least one mapped item in single-channel allocation is smaller than that in multi-channel allocation.

To conclude, the average turnaround time of the output single-channel allocation mapped by the EDF-based dispatcher is smaller than that of the input multi-channel allocation. So Property 1 is proved.   □

5   Gap Problem

In practice, due to various reasons such as unpredictable and dynamic data access behavior of clients, gaps may be introduced between adjacent items allocated on a logical channel. In this section, we consider the problem of having gaps between adjacent items in multi-channel allocation. To the best of our knowledge, no existing solution including the EDF-based dispatcher proposed in Section 2 can perform the mapping with gaps of arbitrary sizes. For example, consider $K = 2$, $g_1 = g_2 = 2$, and suppose that there is a gap of size $\frac{1}{2}$ at the beginning of the two logical channels. That is, on both channels, the beginning time and end time of the first item are respectively $\frac{1}{2}$ and $2\frac{1}{2}$. In this case, only the second time slot on the single physical channel can satisfy Constraint (1) but it is impossible to map both items onto the same time slot. Here, we take the first step to prove that, under certain conditions, the EDF-based dispatcher is also applicable in the presence of gaps. To make this mapping feasible, the gaps must be aligned with time slot boundaries. Recall that a time slot is defined as the time taken to transmit one item on the single physical channel. In other words, the size of gaps must be a multiple of the time slot. Accordingly, the beginning time of any item in multi-channel allocation is also aligned with time slot boundary. That is, g_I in Assumption (ii) becomes an integral value, namely, $g_I \in \mathbf{N}^+$. Otherwise, it may be impossible to map all items from multiple logical channels to a single physical channel without violating Constraint (1). With the restriction that the size of gaps must be a multiple of the time slot and the beginning times and end times of items in multi-channel allocation are all aligned with time slot boundaries, we call the problem *integral gaps between slotted items.*

Next, we prove the following theorem.

Theorem 2. *The EDF-based dispatcher can map all items from multiple logical channels with integral gaps between slotted items onto a single physical channel without violating Constraint (1).*

The basic idea of the proof is to associate each item in multi-channel allocation fractionally to all time slots in single-channel allocation without violating Constraint (1). Next, the associations are iteratively eliminated until the item is associated with only one of the time slots. At the end of the iterative process, if it can be guaranteed that every item is associated with only one time slot and every time slot is associated with at most one item, a mapping is found.

To facilitate explanation of the proof, a bipartite graph $G = (D, T, S)$ is constructed. There are two types of vertices in the graph. One side of the bipartite graph consists of item vertices $D = \{d^* : \text{all items in multi-channel allocation}\}$. The other side consists of slot vertices $T = \{t_x : \text{all time slots in single-channel allocation}\}$. To associate an item d^* to a time slot with beginning time t_x, the corresponding vertices are connected by an edge $(d^*, t_x) \in S$ and a weight $s_{t_x}^{d^*}$ is assigned to the edge. Specifically, for an item $d^* =< t_{L(I,J)}, t_{L(I,J)} + g_I >$ on logical channel I $(1 \leq I \leq K)$ in multi-channel allocation, it is associated with g_I time slots in single-channel allocation between the slot with beginning time $t_{L(I,J)}$ and the slot with beginning time $(t_{L(I,J)} + g_I - 1)$ and an initial weight of $\frac{1}{g_I}$ is assigned to each of the g_I edges. If t_x is the beginning time of an associated time slot, we have $t_{L(I,J)} \leq t_x \leq t_{L(I,J)} + g_I - 1$ and $s_{t_x}^{d^*} = \frac{1}{g_I}$. Based on the construction of the bipartite graph described above, we can observe the following invariants of the graph.

$$\sum_{t_x = t_{L(I,J)}}^{t_{L(I,J)} + g_I - 1} s_{t_x}^{d^*} = 1 \; \forall d^* \tag{2}$$

$$\sum_{d^*} s_{t_x}^{d^*} \leq \sum_{I=1}^{K} \frac{1}{g_I} = 1 \; \forall t_x \tag{3}$$

Invariant (2) implies that the summation of weight values of all edges from a given item to any time slots is 1. Invariant (3) implies that the summation of weight values of all edges from any items to a given time slot is at most 1. It is because there is at most one item from each of the K channels connected to a given time slot.

Next, a rounding process similar to [14] in respect of keeping satisfying constraints is applied to eliminate the edges until every item vertex is connected to only one slot vertex and every slot vertex is connected by at most one item vertex. In this case, this mapping can assign all items in multi-channel allocation to different time slots in single-channel allocation. The rounding process is iteratively executed in time order of the slot vertices. In each iteration, a slot vertex that has the earliest beginning time among the slot vertices that have never been selected to be current slot vertices in past iterations is selected to be current slot vertex. If the current slot vertex has no connective edge incident to any item vertex, it is eliminated from the graph and this iteration terminates. Otherwise, the weight value of the connective edge of the current slot vertex incident to the item vertex that represents the item with the earliest end time is rounded to one. Meanwhile, the weight values of all the edges incident to these two vertices are rounded to zero. Finally, the weight values of other edges in the graph are adjusted accordingly. To be specific, for any item vertex (excluding the item vertex that represents the item with the earliest end time) adjacent to the current slot vertex, the weight of its connective edge incident to the current slot vertex is distributed to its connective edges incident to other slot vertices. An edge of weight 1 means that the item is mapped to the time slot. On the other hand, an edge of weight 0 is eliminated.

As shown in Fig. 1, suppose t_x is the current slot vertex, d^* is the adjacent item vertex of t_x that represents the item with the earliest end time, and $d_1, d_2, ..., d_k$ ($k \geq 1$) are also adjacent item vertices of t_x, if any. t_n is the latest adjacent slot vertex of d^* and t_m is the latest one of the latest adjacent slot vertices of $d_1, d_2, ..., d_k$. Consider d^* in the current iteration of the rounding process, $s_{t_x}^{d^*}$ is increased to 1 and the weight values of the other edges, if any, incident to d^* are decreased to 0. For any other item vertex d_i ($1 \leq i \leq k$), $s_{t_x}^{d_i}$ is decreased to 0 and $s_{t_j}^{d_i}$ is increased by $s_{t_x}^{d_i} * \dfrac{s_{t_j}^{d^*}}{\sum\limits_{l=1}^{n} s_{t_l}^{d^*}}$ for any $j \in \{1, 2, \ldots, n\}$. At the end of this iteration, item d^* is mapped to the time slot with beginning time t_x.

Additionally, choosing item d^* that has the earliest end time to be mapped to the current time slot is to ensure that weight adjustment is feasible for the edges incident to other item vertices. Otherwise, suppose that another item d_i ($1 \leq i \leq k$) that has end time later than the earliest one is chosen to be mapped to the earliest time slot, and the latest slot vertex without violating Constraint (1) for item vertex d_i is $t_{n'}$ ($t_n < t_{n'} \leq t_m$). The weight adjustment is infeasible for the edges incident to item vertices that have latest slot vertices earlier than $t_{n'}$, such as d^*. For example, the value of $s_{t_j}^{d^*}$ for any $j \in \{n+1, n+2, \ldots, n'\}$ cannot be adjusted as no edge is connected from d^* to

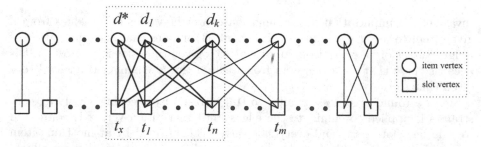

Fig. 1. A bipartite graph at the beginning of an iteration of the rounding process

$t_{n+1}, t_{n+2}, \ldots, t_{n'}$. That is why the item that has the earliest end time is chosen to be mapped to the earliest time slot.

Based on the construction of the bipartite graph, Invariants (2) and (3) hold initially. Next, we prove the following property.

Property 2. Invariants (2) and (3) hold at the end of each iteration of the rounding process.

Proof. As Invariants (2) and (3) do not change in an iteration when the current slot vertex is an isolated vertex, it is sufficient to prove it only for the iterations when the current slot vertex is not an isolated vertex.

Firstly, we prove Invariant (2). For item vertex d^*, $s_{t_x}^{d^*}$ is increased to 1 and any other edge incident to the item vertex is deleted. So Invariant (2) holds for item vertex d^*. For any other item vertex that is adjacent to t_x, i.e., d_i ($1 \le i \le k$), if any, $s_{t_x}^{d_i}$ is decreased to 0 (by $s_{t_x}^{d_i}$). However, for the connective edges of item d_i incident to slot vertices $t_1, t_2, \ldots, t_n$, their weight values are totally increased by $\sum_{j=1}^{n} s_{t_x}^{d_i} * \dfrac{s_{t_j}^{d^*}}{\sum_{l=1}^{n} s_{t_l}^{d^*}} = s_{t_x}^{d_i}$. So the summation of weight values of all edges incident to any other adjacent item vertex of t_x does not change. As Invariant (2) holds initially based on the construction of the bipartite graph, Invariant (2) still holds for the other adjacent item vertices. For the item vertices that are not adjacent to t_x, no weight value of connective edge is altered during the iteration. Therefore, Invariant (2) also holds.

Secondly, we prove Invariant (3). For slot vertex t_x, $s_{t_x}^{d^*}$ is increased to 1 and any other edge incident to the slot vertex is eliminated after its weight value is decreased to 0. So the summation of the weight values of all edges incident to slot vertex t_x is still less than or equal to 1. Namely, Invariant (3) holds for slot vertex t_x. For any other slot vertex that is adjacent to d^*, i.e., t_j ($1 \le j \le n$), edge (d^*, t_j) has its weight value decreased by $s_{t_j}^{d^*}$ (to 0). And any other edges incident to this slot vertex have their weight values totally increased by at most

$$\Delta s = \sum_{i=1}^{k} s_{t_x}^{d_i} * \dfrac{s_{t_j}^{d^*}}{\sum_{l=1}^{n} s_{t_l}^{d^*}} = s_{t_j}^{d^*} * \dfrac{\sum_{i=1}^{k} s_{t_x}^{d_i}}{\sum_{l=1}^{n} s_{t_l}^{d^*}}.$$ Because Invariant (2) holds for item vertex

d^* and Invariant (3) holds for slot vertex t_x, initially, that is, $\sum_{l=1}^{n} s_{t_l}^{d^*} + s_{t_x}^{d^*} = 1$

and $\sum_{i=1}^{k} s_{t_x}^{d_i} + s_{t_x}^{d^*} \le 1$ hold. So we get $\sum_{i=1}^{k} s_{t_x}^{d_i} \le \sum_{l=1}^{n} s_{t_l}^{d^*}$. Therefore, $\Delta s \le s_{t_j}^{d^*}$. That is, for the summation of the weight values of edges incident to any given slot vertex t_j, the increased value due to the eliminated edges incident to slot vertex t_x is less than or equal to the decreased value due to the eliminated edge (d^*, t_j). That is, Invariant (3) holds for slot vertex t_j ($1 \le j \le n$). For the slot vertices that are not adjacent to d^*, Invariant (3) clearly holds as no weight value of edge incident to these slot vertices is altered during iteration.   □

In fact, each iteration of the rounding process corresponds to each mapping of the EDF-based dispatcher and the outcomes are the same, i.e., the item (item vertex) with the earliest end time is broadcast (mapped) at the current time slot (current slot vertex). In other words, the mapping produced by the rounding process is in fact in earliest-end-time-first order which is, in principle, the same as the mapping generated by the EDF-based dispatcher. Note that it is possible that a slot vertex is not connected to any item vertex. It happens when the temporary priority queue is empty at some current time slot. In this case, no item is broadcast (or mapped). So Theorem 2 can be proved as follows.

Proof (of Theorem 2). As Property 2 holds, no more than one edge incident to the current slot vertex have their weight values rounded to 1, namely no more than one items are competitive for the current time slot. So Theorem 2 holds.   □

6   Conclusion

In this paper, to support multi-level QoS, we devise an EDF-based dispatcher to map all items from multiple logical channels with speeds commensurate with the respective QoS levels onto a single physical channel without causing delay. We show that the output single-channel allocation mapped by the EDF-based dispatcher outperforms the input multi-channel allocation in terms of average turnaround time. As an extension, for the problem of *integral gaps between slotted items* in multi-channel allocation, we prove that the EDF-based dispatcher can also be applied by constructing a bipartite graph to associate all items in multi-channel allocation to different time slots in single-channel allocation.

References

1. Jiang, T., Xiang, W., Chen, H.H., Ni, Q.: Multicast broadcast services support in OFDMA-based WiMAX systems (Advances in mobile multimedia). IEEE Communications Magazine 45(8), 78–86 (2007)
2. Ardizzoni, E., Bertossi, A., Pinotti, M., Ramaprasad, S., Rizzi, R., Shashanka, M.: Optimal skewed data allocation on multiple channels with flat broadcast per channel. IEEE Transactions on Computers 54(5), 558–572 (2005)
3. Anticaglia, S., Barsi, F., Bertossi, A., Iamele, L., Pinotti, M.: Efficient heuristics for data broadcasting on multiple channels. Wireless Networks 14(2), 219–231 (2008)
4. Liaskos, C., Petridou, S., Papadimitriou, G., Nicopolitidis, P., Pomportsis, A.: On the analytical performance optimization of wireless data broadcasting. IEEE Transactions on Vehicular Technology 59(2), 884–895 (2010)
5. Chen, C., Lee, C., Wang, S.: On optimal scheduling for time-constrained services in multi-channel data dissemination systems. Information Systems 34(1), 164–177 (2009)
6. Liu, K., Lee, V.: On-demand broadcast for multiple-item requests in a multiple-channel environment. Information Sciences 180(22), 4336–4352 (2010)
7. Acharya, S., Franklin, M., Zdonik, S.: Balancing push and pull for data broadcast. ACM SIGMOD Record 26(2), 194 (1997)
8. Hu, C., Chen, M.: Adaptive multi channel data dissemination: support of dynamic traffic awareness and push-pull time balance. IEEE Transactions on Vehicular Technology 54(2), 673–686 (2005)

9. Jin, J., Nahrstedt, K.: QoS specification languages for distributed multimedia applications: A survey and taxonomy. IEEE MultiMedia Magazine 11(3), 74–87 (2004)

10. McCanne, S., Jacobson, V., Vetterli, M.: Receiver-driven layered multicast. In: ACM SIGCOMM, pp. 117–130 (1996)

11. Hung, H.P., Chen, M.S.: MULS: A General Framework of Providing Multilevel Service Quality in Sequential Data Broadcasting. IEEE Transactions on Knowledge and Data Engineering 19(10), 1433–1447 (2007)

12. Shin, J., Kim, J.W., Kuo, C.C.J.: Quality-of-service mapping mechanism for packet video in differentiated services network. IEEE Transactions on Multimedia 3(2), 219–231 (2001)

13. Lv, J., Lee, V., Li, M., Chen, E.: Profit-based scheduling and channel allocation for multi-item requests in real-time on-demand data broadcast systems. Data & Knowledge Engineering 73, 23–42 (2012)

14. Gandhi, R., Khuller, S., Parthasarathy, S., Srinivasan, A.: Dependent rounding and its applications to approximation algorithms. Journal of the ACM (JACM) 53(3), 324–360 (2006)

Maximizing Network Topology Lifetime Using Mobile Node Rotation

Fatme El-Moukaddem, Eric Torng, and Guoliang Xing

Department of Computer Science and Engineering,
Michigan State University,
East Lansing, MI 4 8824, U.S.A.
{elmoukad,torng,glxing}@cse.msu.edu

Abstract. One of the key challenges facing wireless sensor networks (WSNs) is extending network lifetime due to sensor nodes having limited power supplies. Extending WSN lifetime is complicated because nodes often experience differential power consumption. For example, nodes closer to the sink in a given routing topology transmit more data and thus consume power more rapidly than nodes farther from the sink. Inspired by the huddling behavior of emperor penguins where the penguins take turns on the cold extremities of a penguin "huddle", we propose mobile node rotation, a new method for using low-cost mobile sensor nodes to address differential power consumption and extend WSN lifetime. Specifically, we propose to rotate the nodes through the high power consumption locations. We propose efficient algorithms for single and multiple rounds of rotations. Our extensive simulations show that mobile node rotation can extend WSN topology lifetime by more than eight times on average in a which is significantly better than existing alternatives.

1 Introduction

In the past decade, wireless sensor networks (WSNs) have been deployed in wide range of applications such as habitat monitoring [1], environment monitoring [2,3], and surveillance systems [4]. Many of these applications need to gather a large amount of data and transmit it to the sink where it can be analyzed. Moreover, these networks must remain operational for a long period of time on limited power supplies (such as batteries). On the other hand, they are often deployed in remote or inaccessible environments, making it extremely difficult for any manual maintenance like battery replacement. As a result, one of the main challenges faced by data intensive WSNs is managing the power consumption of nodes to maximize the lifetime of the WSN.

Recently, the *controlled mobility* of sensors has been exploited to improve the energy efficiency of WSNs. For instance, by relocating mobile sensors, the communication topology of a network can be dynamically configured to reduce power consumption. Moreover, mobile sensors can physically carry large chunks of data to reduce energy consumption in wireless transmissions [5]. Such approaches become increasingly attractive due to the emergence of numerous low-cost mobile sensor prototypes such as Robomote [6], Khepera [7], and FIRA [8].

X. Wang et al. (Eds.): WASA 2012, LNCS 7405, pp. 154–165, 2012.

However, many applications have constraints which make existing approaches infeasible. We identify three key constraints. The first is that the location of the nodes and the communication topology of the network may not be mutable. For example, in a surveillance or environment monitoring application, the exact placement of sensor nodes may not be adjusted without compromising the operation of the system. The second is that all nodes have equal, typically limited, capabilities. This rules out approaches that require a few nodes with extra capabilities and the ability to perform complex motion planning. The third is that nodes face differential power consumption where some nodes consume significantly more power than other nodes. For example, nodes closer to the sink in a given routing topology often have to transmit more data and thus consume more power than nodes farther from the sink in the given topology.

To address these three constraints that limit existing techniques, we propose a new approach that we call *mobile node rotation* which is inspired by the huddling and rotation behavior of emperor penguins that help them breed in the fierce arctic winter. Penguins on the outside of the huddle face temperatures as low as $-45\,°C$ and strong winds while those on the inside of the huddle enjoy warm ambient temperatures as high as $37\,°C$ and significant wind protection. Emperor penguins rotate positions to share the burden of being on the outside [9]. In mobile node rotation, we propose to rotate the physical positions of mobile sensors to share the burden of any high power consumption location. We observe that mobile node rotation is particularly suitable for mobile sensor platforms with limited mobility as we can impose mobility constraints on individual nodes. For example, we can model the constraints of the NIMS sensors [10] that are only capable of moving along fixed cables by only allowing such sensors to exchange with other sensors on the same set of cables. Likewise, mobile node rotation does not require powerful nodes capable of performing complex motion planning calculations or developing new mobility-aware routing topologies since all movements are to known positions and the topology does not change.

We make the following contributions in this paper. (1) We present a new problem, *Max-lifetime Node Rotation (MaxLife)*, that models maximizing the lifetime of a WSN using rounds of mobile node rotation. MaxLife can incorporate any energy consumption model for both wireless communication and node movement. (2) We efficiently solve the one round MaxLife problem by reducing it to the assignment problem. (3) We propose an efficient distributed algorithm for the general multiple round MaxLife problem. (4) We prove upper bounds on the lifetime improvement ratio of mobile node rotation approaches. (5) We conduct extensive simulations based on energy models obtained from existing mobile sensor platforms. We show that our algorithms can significantly increase the network lifetime. With just one rotation round, we can almost double the network lifetime. With multiple rounds, we can increase network lifetime by factors exceeding eight and seven using the centalized and distributed implementations respectively.

2   Related Work

Three general approaches, mobile base stations, data mules, and mobile relays, have been proposed to use the mobility of nodes to extend WSN lifetime. In mobile station approaches, a powerful mobile base station node moves around the WSN and collects data from other nodes through one or multiple hops transmissions [11,5,12,13,14]. The goal is to mitigate differential power consumption by rotating the set of nodes that are close to the base station. These approaches usually incur high latency because of the low speed of the mobile stations. In data mule approaches [15,16,17], one or multiple mobile nodes, called mules, visit all the nodes in the network to collect the data and then physically carry the data to the sink. Similar to the base station approaches, these approaches incur high latencies since nodes have to wait for a mule to pass by to be able to transmit the data. In mobile relay approaches, the mobile nodes in the network relocate to different positions to reduce the communication distances between nodes. In [18], the authors propose an iterative algorithm in which each node moves to the midpoint of its neighbors. This algorithm minimizes the total power consumption of WSN, but it ignores the power consumed by mobility. The approaches in [19,20] refine the algorithm in [18] by taking into account the mobility power consumption. However, their objective is to reduce the total power consumption; they do not necessarily lead to greater WSN lifetime because they may save energy at the wrong nodes. The approach in [21] targets critical nodes in the network. However, it considers WSNs that are mostly static with a small number of mobile relays. Finally, none of the mobile relay approaches can be applied in settings where the exact positions of the WSN nodes must not change.

3   Problem Definition

We consider WSNs consisting of many wireless mobile sensor nodes and a single static sink. The sensor nodes gather data from their surroundings and transmit the data through one or multiple hops to the sink forming a directed routing tree. We divide time into intervals. In each interval, each sensor node transmits the data it gathered as well as the data it received from its children to its parent along the routing tree. The goal is to maximize the lifetime of the WSN, i.e. the number of time intervals until the first node dies. We use this definition of lifetime assuming that all nodes are needed in their exact positions in order to not compromise the operation of the system.

One of the main reasons limiting the lifetime of such networks is differential power consumption; nodes closer to the sink usually transmit a large amount of data and consequently consume more power than nodes further away from the sink. As a result, the lifetime of the WSN is substantially reduced even though the WSN still contains nodes rich in energy. Mobile base stations mitigate differential power consumption by having a powerful mobile sink move around the WSN. We propose a new solution, mobile node rotation, that uses multiple low-cost mobile nodes rotate or swap positions and roles allowing nodes to share the burden of high consumption locations and the benefits of low consumption locations. We formally define the problem as follows.

Definition 1 (One-Round Max-Lifetime Node Rotation (1-MaxLife))
Input Instance:

- $S = (s_1, \ldots, s_n)$, *a list of sensor nodes*
- u, *the network sink, and* p_u, *its position*
- $P = (p_1, \ldots, p_n)$, *a list of positions such that node* s_i *starts at position* p_i
- $E = (e_1, \ldots, e_n)$, *a list of initial energies for nodes in* S
- T, *a directed routing tree represented as a set of non-zero values* t_{ij} *for every arc* (p_i, p_j) *in the tree corresponding to the amount of energy consumed when transmitting one data unit from* p_i *to* p_j
- K, *a set of values* k_{ij} *for every pair of positions* p_i *and* p_j, *corresponding to the amount of energy consumed by a node when it moves between* p_i *and* p_j
- $\Lambda = (\lambda_1, \ldots, \lambda_n)$, *the amount of data gathered at each position per time interval*

Output Instance: A matching M of nodes in S to locations in P, and two durations r_1 and r_2 such that nodes transmit data from their original positions for r_1 time intervals, relocate to their new position according to M, then generate and transmit data for r_2 time intervals such that the total duration $(r_1 + r_2)$ is maximized and no node's energy goes to 0 before $r_1 + r_2$.

We define the **Max-Lifetime Node Rotation (MaxLife)** problem to be the general version where nodes can switch positions any number of times.

4 Node Rotation Algorithms

In this section, we first present our centralized node rotation algorithm NR1 to the 1-MaxLife problem. Then, we present CNR, a centralized algorithm for the general MaxLife problem. Finally, we present a practical distributed algorithm DNR for the general MaxLife problem that uses only local information and reduces the number of node movements. All algorithms begin by having nodes compute the load l_j at each position p_j in P which is the total energy consumed in transmitting all the data gathered in one time interval from the subtree rooted at p_j to its parent. More formally, $l_j = t_{jq} \cdot \sum_{i \in T(p_j)} \lambda_i$ where $T(p_j)$ is the subtree rooted at p_j and p_q is the position of the parent of p_j in the tree.

Algorithm NR1. NR1 transforms the input instance into an instance of the assignment problem [22], a combinatorial optimization problem in which we are given n people and n tasks and an efficiency c_{ij} for each person performing each task and the goal is to assign each task to a person to optimize some efficiency measure. We first assume we know the optimal length of the first time interval r_1. To compute the optimal matching M of sensor nodes to positions, we transform the instance I into an instance of the maximum bottleneck assignment problem I' for the given r_1 as follows. Each mobile node s_i corresponds to a person and each location p_j in P corresponds to a task. The efficiency c_{ij} of a person s_i performing task p_j corresponds to the total lifetime of s_i after transmitting for a period r_1 from its original position p_i, then moving to p_j where it transmits until its energy is depleted; that is, $c_{ij} = r_1 + \frac{e - l_i r_1 - k_{ij}}{l_j}$. The optimal solution for the maximum bottleneck assignment instance I' corresponds to an optimal matching M for the given r_1.

We now need to compute the best duration r_1. We observe that we can express r_2 as a function $L_2(r_1)$ that decreases as r_1 increases since there is less energy for the second round. We can then define the total network lifetime as a function $L(r_1) = r_1 + L_2(r_1)$. We use golden ratio search to find the best r_1. When $L(r_1)$ is unimodal, golden ratio search yields an optimal r_1 that maximizes $L(r_1)$. To start the golden ratio search algorithm, we first compute $L(I) = \min_{j=1}^{n} e_j / l_j$ which is an upper bound on r_1. Our algorithm NR1 runs in $O(\log L(I) n^{2.5})$ time because golden ratio search has $O(\log L(I))$ time complexity and each assignment problem has $O(n^{2.5})$ time complexity.

Centralized Algorithm CNR(r, l_{cr}, f). One solution to the general MaxLife problem is to extend NR1 to run in multiple rounds such that in each round, nodes are matched to positions using an optimal matching for that round. We use this algorithm (CNR-B) for comparison purposes only, as it has a large overhead and results in unnecessary movements.

We propose the following algorithm, CNR, as a more practical and effective solution. The main idea is that in each round, only critical nodes, *i.e.* nodes at locations with a high power consumption rate, relocate to lower consumption positions. Each critical node tries to find a low power consumption rate node to swap positions with. First, a node is selected to be the controller. The controller collects energy and location information from all the other nodes once and computes an initial list of critical nodes L_{cr} such that $s_i \in L_{cr}$ if $l_i > l_{cr}$. Then, it proceeds in rounds of fixed length r. At the end of the round, the controller computes the target position of each node in L_{cr}, informs the corresponding nodes which then relocate to their new positions, and then updates L_{cr}. The target positions of nodes in L_{cr} are computed as follows. First, nodes in L_{cr} are considered in descending order of their current consumption rate. For each critical node s, the controller considers all noncritical nodes that are still available for switching. For each candidate node c, the controller computes $L_1(c)$, the minimum of s's and c's expected lifetime without swapping, and $L_2(c)$, the minimum of s's and c's expected lifetime if they swap positions. The controller selects candidate c^* as target for s if and only if c^* has the maximum value $L_2(c^*)$ and $L_2(c^*)/L_1(c^*) \geq f$. This last condition is eliminates swaps that increase the network lifetime by negligible amounts. At this point c^* becomes unavailable for other critical nodes in the round. After nodes relocate, a new round starts and the process is repeated until the first node dies.

Distributed Algorithm DNR. Our practical multiple rotation round algorithm is $DNR(r, h, l_{cr}, f)$ which is based on CNR but requires only local information. As with CNR, all rounds will have duration r. In each round, each critical node s_i finds a noncritical node to swap with as follows: s_i collects the position, load, and current energy level from descendants that are at most h hops away and have not committed to switch with other critical nodes. Then s_i selects the candidate c^* with maximum value $L2(c)$ satisfying $L_2(c)/L_1(c) \geq f$. At this point c^* commits to switch with s_i. We note that this distributed implementation only requires loose synchronization between nodes as critical nodes send messages to their descendants and parent at the beginning of each round only, stating that a new round is about to start. The overhead of this synchronization is moderate, as opposed to the regular time sync schemes where nodes have to ping each other all the time to keep their clocks in sync.

5   Upper Bounds on Lifetime Improvement Ratio

We now prove some upper bounds on lifetime improvement ratios for any node rotation algorithms. We first consider the 1-MaxLife problem. We then consider the general MaxLife problem. We use the following notation in our analysis. For any node rotation algorithm A and input instance I, let $L(A, I)$ denote the lifetime achieved using algorithm A on I, $L(I)$ the lifetime without node rotation, and $R_A(I) = \min_I L(A, I)/L(I)$ the lifetime improvement ratio (LIR) of A on I. Finally, let $EV(I) = \max_{i=1}^n e_i / \min_{j=1}^n e_j$ be the initial energy variance of I.

Theorem 1. *For any one round node rotation algorithm A and any input instance I $R_A(I) \leq 1 + EV(I)$.*

Proof. Let s_i denote the bottleneck node in I that determines $L(I)$; that is, $L(I) = e_i/l_i$. Clearly, $r_1 \leq L(I)$. We now observe that $r_2 \leq EV(I) \cdot L(I)$ because the node that moves to position p_i can have at most energy $EV(I) \cdot e_i$. Thus, $r_1 + r_2 \leq (1 + EV(I))L(I)$ and $R_A(I) \leq 1 + EV(I)$.   □

This leads to two corollaries, one for the special case where all nodes have the same initial energy and one for multiple round rotation algorithms.

Corollary 1. *For any one round node rotation algorithm A and any input instance I with $EV(I) = 1$, $R_A(I) \leq 2$.*

Corollary 2. *For any j round node rotation algorithm A and any input instance I, $R_A(I) \leq 1 + (j - 1)EV(I)$.*

We note that although our one round solution NR1 is optimal for 1-MaxLife only when $L(r_1)$ is unimodular, our simulations (Section 6) show that NR1's LIR is usually very close to the upper bound of 2 for input instances I with $EV(I) = 1$. Moreover, for input instances I where $EV(I) > 1$, NR1's LIR is often better than 2.

We now prove upper bounds on the $R_A(I)$ for inputs I corresponding to balanced trees of degree $d + 1$ using a multiple rotation round algorithm.

Theorem 2. *For any node rotation algorithm A and any input I where T represents a balanced tree of degree $d+1$ and $t_{ij} = t$ for all non-zero t_{ij}, h is the lowest level of the tree where the root is at level 0, and for $1 \leq i \leq n$, $e_i = e$ and $\lambda_i = 1$, then*

$$R_A(I) \leq \frac{(d^{h+1} - 1)^2}{(h(d-1) + d - 2)d^{h+1} + 1}$$

Proof. To prove this upper bound, we ignore the energy consumed by movement. The best solution is to then have all nodes equally share the transmission of all data. We first compute $L(I)$ which is constrained by the bottleneck node at level 0 that transmits data from the entire tree to the sink. The total number of nodes $n = \sum_{j=0}^{h} d^j$ as there are d^j nodes at level j. It follows that

$$L(I) = \frac{e}{nt} = \frac{d-1}{d^{h+1} - 1} \frac{e}{t}$$

We next compute the lifetime L^* of the WSN if we are able to perfectly share the transmission of all data among all n sensor nodes. A node at level i is the root of a subtree of size $D_i = \sum_{j=0}^{h-i} d^j$. Thus, the total amount of data transmitted each time interval is

$$D = \sum_{i=0}^{h} d^i D_i = \sum_{i=0}^{h} d^i \sum_{j=0}^{h-i} d^j = \frac{d^{h+1}(h(d-1) + d - 2) + 1}{(d-1)^2}$$

This implies that $L^* = \dfrac{ne}{Dt} = \dfrac{(d^{h+1})(d-1)}{(h(d-1) + d - 2)d^{h+1} + 1} \dfrac{e}{t}$.
Dividing L^* by $L(I)$ gives us the result.   □

Table 1 displays some of the upper bounds for different values of d and h. The improvement ratio starts at a factor of 1.8 for a tree with 3 nodes and rapidly increases with both the degree and the level.

Table 1. Upper Bounds on Lifetime Improvement Ratios in Balanced Trees

d / h	1	2	3	4	5
2	1.80	2.88	4.59	7.45	12.36
3	2.29	4.97	11.27	26.77	66.08
4	2.78	7.74	23.08	72.99	240.82
5	3.27	11.17	41.53	164.37	679.26

6   Simulation Results

In this section, we evaluate the performance of NR1, CNR, and DNR algorithms through simulations. For comparison purposes, we also evaluate the performance of the baseline CNR-B algorithm. We generated 100 networks each consisting of 100 nodes placed uniformly at random in a 150m by 150m area with the sink node chosen uniformly at random. We set the maximum communication distance to 35m, which was shown in [23] to lead to a high packet reception ratio for TelosB motes in outdoor environments. For each network, we constructed the routing tree from the sources to the sink using greedy geographic routing in which each node forwards its data to the neighbor that is closest to the sink. We note that our algorithms are applicable to network topologies generated by any routing algorithms. We set the t_{ij} and the k_{ij} values based on the energy models in [23,21] since they are based on realistic platforms; any other energy model for communication or mobility could be used without any algorithmic change. We usually set each node's e_i to the same value typically ranging from half full to full, though in some simulations different nodes have different e_i values. For our distributed algorithm DNR, we set the local improvement factor f to 1.25 and the critical consumption rate threshold l_{cr} to 10% of the range of ratios in the network. We describe our choices for r and h below. We assess the performance of algorithms using several criteria. The main criteria is *lifetime improvement ratio*. We also assess the number of rounds required, the number of nodes that move per round, and the number of movements per node over the network lifetime.

6.1   Single Rotation Round

We first evaluate the performance of NR1 for the 1-MaxLife problem in trees. For all 100 inputs, $1.91 \leq R_{NR1}(I) \leq 1.99$, and the average value of $R_{NR1}(I) = 1.95$. We observe that the results are very close to the theoretical upper bound of 2 from Corollary 1. When we varied the starting energy level of the nodes between half full and completely full, the average lifetime improvement ratio of NR1 increased to 2.3. We also observe that most of the nodes change their positions; on average 86 nodes relocate to new positions and 14 nodes remain at their original location. This is not too expensive since only a single rotation is performed which means the network's activity is interrupted only once.

6.2   Multiple Rotation Rounds

Round Duration. We now evaluate the performance of CNR and DNR with $h = 2$ for the general MaxLife problem using our CNR-B algorithm as a baseline. We first study the effect of varying r on the performance of both algorithms. Figure 1 shows the average lifetime improvement ratios for both algorithms as we increase r denoted as a fraction of the static lifetime $L(I)$. We see that both CNR and DNR outperform CNR-B for all values of r but especially smaller r. For $r \leq 4L(I)/5$, $R_{CNR}(I) \geq 2.5 + R_{CNRB}(I)$. For $r \leq 3L(I)/5$, $R_{DNR}(I) \geq 2.5 + R_{CNRB}(I)$. At $r = L(I)/2$, the difference in lifetime improvement ratio is 3.5 and 2.5 for CNR and DNR respectively. One notable feature of CNR and DNR's performance is that the LIR decreases slowly for $L(I)/5 \leq r \leq 7L(I)/10$; CNR takes on a maximum value of 9.1 and DNR a maximum value of 8.2. Both are reached for $r = L(I)/5$. When r is too large, the LIR of both algorithms drops because nodes stay at high consumption positions for too long.

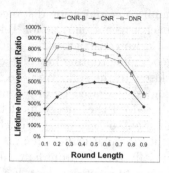

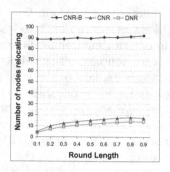

Fig. 1. Average lifetime improvement ratios of CNR(r) and DNR as a function of r plotted as a fraction of $L(I)$

Fig. 2. Average number of relocations of CNR(r) and DNR as a function of r plotted as a fraction of $L(I)$

For most of the remaining simulations, we set $r = L(I)/2$. This almost maximizes the LIR while maximizing r which minimizes the number of disruptions to the network.

Node Relocations. We next compare all three algorithms with respect to how much the sensor nodes move. We first consider the number of relocations per round. As we can see from Fig. 2, both CNR and DNR outperform CNR-B again. In particular, with CNR-B, more than 90% of the nodes relocate in each round whereas with CNR and DNR, the average number of relocating nodes stays below 14% and 17% respectively. These nodes are usually different in each round as 96% of the nodes move between 0 and 3 times overall and the remaining 4% move up to 6 times during their lifetime. For DNR, most of the energy available at each node is consumed by communication rather than movement: 85% of the nodes spend at least 80% of their energy on communication and no node spends more than 35% of its energy on movement. We observe that node relocations increase only slightly for both CNR and DNR as round duration r increases because more nodes become critical in each round due to more time at high consumption locations.

Distributed Approach and Hop Distance Parameter h. We now analyze the effect of the hop distance parameter h on the performance of DNR. We plot the complementary cumulative distribution function (CCDF) of the LIR for DNR with h set to 1, 2, and 4 in Fig. 3. The CCDF gives us the probability that the lifetime improvement ratio exceeds a given threshold. For comparison, we also plot the CCDF of CNR and CNR-B. From this data, we see that setting $h = 2$ is sufficient to achieve excellent performance as the CCDF for $h = 2$ is almost identical to that of $h = 4$. In both cases, 93% of the topologies have lifetime improvement ratios of at least 420% and more than 50% of topologies have lifetime improvement ratios over 700%. With $h = 1$, DNR is much less effective; the number of nodes taking turns transmitting from the high consumption position may be too low. In the remaining simulations, we set $h = 2$ for DNR.

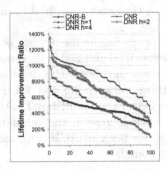

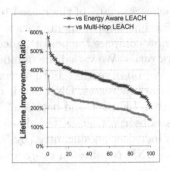

Fig. 3. CCDF of LIR of CNR and DNR with $r = L(I)/2$ and $h = 1$, 2, and 4

Fig. 4. CCDF of LIR of DNR versus LEACH and multihop LEACH

Lifetime Improvement Ratio Increase per Round We now assess how much effect each round has on the LIR. Specifically, if we stop node rotations after round n, what will the lifetime be? All three algorithms, CNR-B, CNR and DNR, result in a LIR that is essentially linear in the number of rounds with each round increasing the lifetime improvement ratio by between 40 and 50%. This analysis shows that these algorithms are effective in increasing the LIR but that CNR and DNR are more effective than CNR-B in minimizing distance moved and maintaining a reserve of energy rich nodes for later rounds. This is why CNR and DNR outperform CNR-B which moves 93% of the nodes in each round.

Comparison with Existing Approaches. In this section, we compare DNR to existing approaches. We consider only approaches that do not change the positions of where nodes are placed. This rules out existing mobile relay approaches and leaves us with non-mobility approaches like LEACH [24] that rotate the roles of different nodes by periodically changing the topology of the network but not modifying any node positions. Specifically, we compare DNR with LEACH [24] as it serves as the base for several other clustering algorithms that seek to increase network lifetime and (2) multihop LEACH [25], an improved variation that uses multihop transmissions between cluster heads. Both LEACH approaches assume that data is compressed before being transmitted while DNR does not. To compare all approaches in a similar setting, we run them all without data compression.

We compare DNR to LEACH and multihop LEACH on an input instance I by computing the *lifetime comparison ratio* $R_{DNR}(I)/R_A(I)$ where A is either LEACH or multihop LEACH. Figure 4 shows the complementary cumulative distribution function of both lifetime comparison ratios. First, we note that DNR outperforms both LEACH variations for every topology, attaining lifetimes between 2 and 5.75 times better than LEACH and between 1.4 and 3.7 times better than multihop LEACH. Additionally, we observe that DNR needs many fewer rounds than both LEACH variations. On average, DNR needs 8 rounds of rotations whereas the average number of rounds is 1800 for LEACH and 2000 for multihop LEACH. We also note that the round duration r used for the LEACH approaches was 20% of the r used by DNR as using the same r resulted in much lower lifetime improvements ratios for LEACH.

We now compare the performance of all three approaches as the density of the network varies. We varied the number of nodes between 60 and 200 in increments of 10. We observe that both average LIRs decrease slowly as the density of the network increases. DNR attains average lifetimes between 3.3 and 4.0 times better than LEACH, and between 2 and 2.3 times better than multihop LEACH. We also observe that as the density of the network increases, the number of rounds increases significantly (by 50% and 100%) for both LEACH approaches whereas DNR requires on average only two more rounds.

7   Conclusion

In this paper, we considered the problem of maximizing the lifetime of mobile WSNs. We exploited the mobility of nodes to mitigate differential power consumption by having nodes take turns in high power consumption positions without modifying the existing communication topology. We present efficient algorithms for both the single round and the general multiple round MaxLife problem. This approach is very different than other schemes such as data mules in that all nodes expend relatively little energy on movement and move only a few times during the network lifetime. Our simulations show that our node rotation approach can improve average lifetime by more than a factor of eight and that our algorithms outperform existing non-mobility approaches for mitigating differential power consumption to prolong network lifetime.

References

1. Szewczyk, R., Mainwaring, A., Polastre, J., Anderson, J., Culler, D.: An analysis of a large scale habitat monitoring application. In: SenSys, pp. 214–226 (2004)
2. Suzuki, M., Saruwatari, S., Kurata, N., Morikawa, H.: A high-density earthquake monitoring system using wireless sensor networks. In: Proceedings of the 5th International Conference on Embedded Networked Sensor Systems, ser. SenSys 2007, pp. 373–374 (2007)
3. Filipponi, L., Santini, S., Vitaletti, A.: Data Collection in Wireless Sensor Networks for Noise Pollution Monitoring. In: Nikoletseas, S.E., Chlebus, B.S., Johnson, D.B., Krishnamachari, B. (eds.) DCOSS 2008. LNCS, vol. 5067, pp. 492–497. Springer, Heidelberg (2008)
4. Luo, L., Cao, Q., Huang, C., Abdelzaher, T.F., Stankovic, J.A., Ward, M.: Enviromic: Towards cooperative storage and retrieval in audio sensor networks. In: ICDCS, p. 34 (2007)
5. Somasundara, A.A., Ramamoorthy, A., Srivastava, M.B.: Mobile element scheduling with dynamic deadlines. IEEE Transactions on Mobile Computing 6(4), 395–410 (2007)
6. Dantu, K., Rahimi, M., Shah, H., Babel, S., Dhariwal, A., Sukhatme, G.S.: Robomote: enabling mobility in sensor networks. In: IPSN, pp. 404–409 (2005)
7. http://www.k-team.com/robots/khepera/index.html

8. Kim, J.-H., Kim, D.-H., Kim, Y.-J., Seow, K.-T.: Soccer Robotics. Springer (2004)
9. Zitterbart, D., Wienecke, B., Butler, J., Fabry, B.: Coordinated movements prevent jamming in an emperor penguin huddle. PLoS one 6(6), e20260 (2011)
10. Pon, R., Batalin, M., Gordon, J., Kansal, A., Liu, D., Rahimi, M., Shirachi, L., Yu, Y., Hansen, M., Kaiser, W., Srivastava, M., Sukhatme, G., Estrin, D.: Networked infomechanical systems: a mobile embedded networked sensor platform. In: Fourth International Symposium on Information Processing in Sensor Networks, IPSN, pp. 376–381 (April 2005)
11. Luo, J., Hubaux, J.-P.: Joint mobility and routing for lifetime elongation in wireless sensor networks. In: INFOCOM, pp. 1735–1746 (2005)
12. Gu, Y., Bozdag, D., Ekici, E.: Mobile element based differentiated message delivery in wireless sensor networks. In: WoWMoM, pp. 83–92 (2006)
13. Kansal, A., Jea, D.D., Estrin, D., Srivastava, M.B.: Controllably mobile infrastructure for low energy embedded networks. IEEE Transactions on Mobile Computing 5(8), 958–973 (2006)
14. Xing, G., Wang, T., Xie, Z., Jia, W.: Rendezvous planning in mobility-assisted wireless sensor networks. In: RTSS 2007: Proceedings of the 28th IEEE International Real-Time Systems Symposium, pp. 311–320 (2007)
15. Jea, D., Somasundara, A., Srivastava, M.B.: Multiple Controlled Mobile Elements (Data Mules) for Data Collection in Sensor Networks. In: Prasanna, V.K., Iyengar, S.S., Spirakis, P.G., Welsh, M. (eds.) DCOSS 2005. LNCS, vol. 3560, pp. 244–257. Springer, Heidelberg (2005)
16. Jain, S., Shah, R., Brunette, W., Borriello, G., Roy, S.: Exploiting mobility for energy efficient data collection in wireless sensor networks. MONET 11(3), 327–339 (2006)
17. Ooi, C.-C., Schindelhauer, C.: Minimal energy path planning for wireless robots. In: ROBOCOMM, p. 2 (2007)
18. Goldenberg, D.K., Lin, J., Morse, A.S.: Towards mobility as a network control primitive. In: MobiHoc, pp. 163–174 (2004)
19. Tang, C., McKinley, P.K.: Energy optimization under informed mobility. IEEE Trans. Parallel Distrib. Syst. 17(9), 947–962 (2006)
20. El-Moukaddem, F., Torng, E., Xing, G., Kulkarni, S.: Mobile relay configuration in data-intensive wireless sensor networks. In: IEEE MASS, pp. 80–89 (2009)
21. El-Moukaddem, F., Torng, E., Xing, G.: Maximizing data gathering capacity of wireless sensor networks using mobile relays. In: IEEE MASS, pp. 312–321 (2010)
22. Burkard, R.E.: Selected topics on assignment problems. Discrete Applied Mathematics, 257–302 (2002)
23. Sha, M., Xing, G., Zhou, G., Liu, S., Wang, X.: C-mac: Model-driven concurrent medium access control for wireless sensor networks. In: INFOCOM, pp. 1845–1853 (2009)
24. Handy, M., Haase, M., Timmermann, D.: Low energy adaptive clustering hierarchy with deterministic cluster-head selection. In: International Workshop on Mobile and Wireless Communications Network, pp. 368–372 (2002)
25. Liu, Y., Luo, Z., Xu, K., Chen, L.: A reliable clustering algorithm base on leach protocol in wireless mobile sensor networks. In: International Conference on Mechanical and Electrical Technology (ICMET), pp. 692–696 (2010)

Joint Beamforming and Power Allocation Algorithm for Cognitive MIMO Systems via Game Theory

Feng Zhao, Bin Li, and Hongbin Chen

Key Laboratory of Cognitive Radio and Information Processing,
(Guilin University of Electronic Technology), Ministry of Education, Guilin 541004, China

Abstract. Cognitive radio (CR) has been recently proposed as a promising technology to achieve efficient use of the frequency resources by allowing the coexistence of primary users (PUs) and secondary users (SUs) in the same frequency band. In this paper, a joint beamforming and power allocation algorithm based on game theory is proposed for cognitive MIMO systems. The objective is to maximize the sum rate of SUs subject to the transmit power constraint and the PU interference constraint. The design of the cognitive system is formulated as a non-cooperative game, where the SUs compete with each other over the resources made available by the PUs. Nash equilibrium is considered as the solution of this game. Simulation results show that the proposed algorithm can converge to a locally optimal pair of power vector and beamforming vector.

Keywords: Cognitive radio, MIMO, game theory, beamforming, power allocation, Nash equilibrium.

1   Introduction

With the rapid deployment of various wireless systems, the limited radio spectrum is becoming increasingly crowded. On the other hand, it is evident that most of the allocated spectrum experience low utilization. As a novel approach to enhancing the utilization efficiency of the scarce radio spectrum, cognitive radio (CR) has attracted tremendous interests recently [1]. A key feature of the CR network is to allow a SU to simultaneously share a licensed spectrum as long as the secondary transmission does not interfere with the primary link. As a result, the challenge of the CR network is to protect the PUs from harmful interference induced by the SUs as well as to meet the quality of service (QoS) demands of PUs. Multiple-input multiple-output (MIMO) technique, with its significantly increased channel capacity, has become a dominating technique in the future-generation wireless systems. It is thus quite natural to combine these two techniques to achieve higher spectral efficiency. This technological combination results in the so-called cognitive MIMO radio [2].

Beamforming and power control are two well-known approaches that can mitigate co-channel interference (CCI) and thus enhance the system capacity. Recently, joint beamforming and power control has been widely studied for the CR network as a quite

X. Wang et al. (Eds.): WASA 2012, LNCS 7405, pp. 166–177, 2012.
© Springer-Verlag Berlin Heidelberg 2012

promising interference suppression technique in [3]-[6]. For such a system, it has additional challenge of keeping the operation of SUs such that the received interference at the PUs remains below a tolerable limit. In [4], the joint beamforming and power allocation for a single-input multiple-output (SIMO) multiple access channels in CR networks is considered. The problem of joint beamforming and power control for SUs when they are allowed to transmit simultaneously with PUs is studied in [5]. The objective is to optimize the network sum rate under the interference constraints of PUs, which is a non-convex problem. Iterative dual subgradient algorithm is proposed to solve such problems. In [6], the authors considered the downlink of CR systems with multiple SUs and multiple PUs. Precoding and power allocation are performed at the cognitive base station to maximize the throughput of the secondary network. It is difficult to solve due to its non-convex properity, then the authors convert it into a convex optimization problem.

Game theory is suitable for analyzing conflict and cooperation among rational decision makers. Because of the inherently competitive nature of multiuser CR networks, in recent years, game theory has been applied to solve the problem of power control [7] for providing the maximum throughput in CR networks. The authors in [8] further considered both power and rate control using a game   theoretical approach, where the SUs are only considered as active players in the game. The extension to the cognitive MIMO system is considered in [2][9][10]. Therein, both theoretic analysis and algorithm are carefully investigated. However, the problem of joint beamforming and power allocation for the cognitive MIMO systems is different from the traditional radio networks and to the best of our knowledge, no studies have been performed to look at this problem in a cognitive MIMO radio environment via game theory.

Comparing with previous work on joint beamforming and power allocation in CR, in this paper, we study the problem of joint beamforming and power allocation in cognitive MIMO downlink under a game-theoretic framework. The aim is to maximize the sum rate of SUs by optimizing the beamforming vectors and the power allocation among the secondary users jointly when the channel state information is known at the transmitter. We consider a cognitive radio environment where a PU is allocated with a licensed radio spectrum and the utilization of which could be improved by sharing it with the SUs. In this case, the SUs who compete for the spectrum offered by the PU and the cost of the spectrum is determined by using a pricing function. A non-cooperative game is used to analyze this situation and the Nash equilibrium is considered as the solution of this game. Even though the main objective of this non-cooperative game formulation is to maximizè the profit of all SUs, based on the equilibrium adopted by all SUs, the revenue of the primary user/service provider can be maximized as well.

2   System Model and Problem Formulation

We consider a CR network which shares the spectrum resource with a primary network, as illustrated in Fig. 1. Similar system models have been considered in [11]. The primary network consists of a primary base station (PBS) that transmits signals to a single PU. The secondary network has a single cognitive base station (CBS), equipped with M antennas, serving K SUs. Throughout this paper, we assume that the PBS and the PU are equipped with a single antenna. Due to the sharing of the same frequency band, the received signal at the PU is interfered by the signals transmitted from CBS. Similarly, the received signals at the SUs are interfered by the signal transmitted from the PBS. Without loss of generality, each SU equips only one antenna. The transmit signal is compactly written by

$$\mathbf{X} = \sqrt{P}\mathbf{FS} \tag{1}$$

where $\mathbf{S} = [s_1, s_2, \cdots, s_K]^T$ denotes the ($K \times 1$) transmit signal vector, in which s_k ($\Omega = \{1, \cdots, K\}, k \in \Omega$) is the desired signal for the k-th SU. $\mathbf{F} = [\mathbf{f}_1, \mathbf{f}_2, \cdots, \mathbf{f}_K]$ denotes the transmit beamforming matrix, with $\mathbf{f}_k$ being a ($M \times 1$) beamforming vector for the k-th SU, normalized to unit power $\|\mathbf{f}_k\| = 1$. Likewise, $p = diag\{\sqrt{p_1}, \sqrt{p_2}, \cdots, \sqrt{p_K}\}$ accounts for power allocation matrix. p_k is the allocated power to the k-th SU. For simplicity, this paper assumes that all the SUs are homogeneous and experience independent fading.

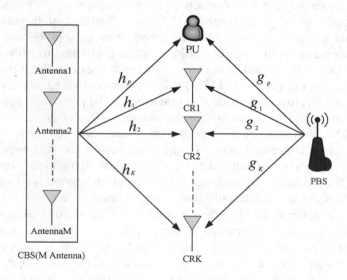

Fig. 1. Cognitive MIMO system

The received signal at the k-th SU is given by

$$\begin{aligned}
y_k &= \mathbf{h}_k^T \mathbf{X} + \sqrt{p_p} g_k x + n_k \\
&= \sqrt{p_k} \mathbf{h}_k^T \mathbf{f}_k s_k + \mathbf{h}_k^T \sum_{i=1, i \neq k}^{K} \sqrt{p_i} \mathbf{f}_i s_i + \sqrt{p_p} g_k x + n_k
\end{aligned} \tag{2}$$

where $\mathbf{h}_k$ denotes the ($M \times 1$) channel vector from the CBS to the k-th SU, it is i.i.d., complex Gaussian, with zero mean and unit variance; P_p denotes the transmit power of the PU, g_k represents the channel coefficient vector between the PBS and the k-th SU, x represents the transmitted signal from the PBS, n_k is a vector of additive noise whose entries are i.i.d., complex Gaussian, with zero mean and variance σ_k^2.

The received signal at the primary user is given by

$$y_p = \sqrt{P_p} g_p x + \mathbf{h}_p^T \sum_{i=1}^{K} \sqrt{p_i} \mathbf{f}_i s_i + n_p \tag{3}$$

where g_p denotes the channel between the PU and the PBS, $\mathbf{h}_p$ is a ($M \times 1$) vector representing the channel between the CBS and the PU, n_p denotes the additive noise and is assumed to be i.i.d., complex Gaussian, with zero mean and variance σ_p^2.

Then, the signal to interference plus noise ratio (SINR) of the k-th cognitive user is

$$SINR_k = \frac{p_k |\mathbf{h}_k^T \mathbf{f}_k|^2}{\sum_{i=1,i \neq k}^{K} p_i |\mathbf{h}_k^T \mathbf{f}_i|^2 + p_p |g_k|^2 + \sigma_k^2} \tag{4}$$

In order to allow the SUs to share the spectrum with the primary user, we should investigate appropriate power and beamforming weights to distribute them among the users so that the sum throughput of SUs is maximized, and the interference created to the PU is as small as possible. Thus, the optimization problem can be formally stated as follows:

$$C = \max \sum_{k=1}^{K} \log_2(1 + SINR_k)$$

$$\text{subject to} \quad \begin{cases} \sum_{k=1}^{K} p_k |\mathbf{h}_p^T \mathbf{f}_k|^2 \leq I_{th} \\ \sum_{k=1}^{K} p_k \leq p_T \\ SINR_k \geq \gamma_{\min,k} \end{cases} \tag{5}$$

where $I_{th}, \gamma_{\min,k}$, and p_T are the given values with respect to the interference power, $SINR$, and the total transmit power, respectively. Our objective is to consider the joint optimization of beamforming and power allocation in order to maximize the sum rate of the secondary system with the following three constraints. The first constraint restricts the interference power to the PBS. The second constraint is to guarantee the total transmission power from the CSB is bounded by a certain limit. In the third constraint, the *SINR* requirement for each SU is ensured.

3   Non-cooperative Game

3.1   Game-Theoretic Formulation

Game theory is an effective tool to analyze competitive optimization problems. For the cognitive MIMO system, each SU's transmission is a source of interference for the others. When a SU selfishly chooses a strategy to increase its own utility, it may increase the interference of some other SUs. Thereby, the strategies chosen by different SUs depend on each other. Based on the system model described above, a non-cooperative game can be formulated as follows [12]:

$$G = \{\Omega, \{\mathbf{f}_k, p_k\}_{k \in \Omega}, \{u_k\}_{k \in \Omega}\} \tag{6}$$

The players in this game are the SUs. The strategy of each of the players is the beamforming weights and transmit power (denoted by $\mathbf{f}_k$ and p_k for secondary user k), which is non-negative. The utility for each player is the profit (i.e., revenue minus cost) of SU (denoted by u_k) in sharing the spectrum with the PU and other SUs. *SINR* can be taken as the optimization variable. Consequently, the utility function can be designed based on the mutual information

$$u_k = \log_2(1 + SINR_k) \tag{7}$$

Due to greediness, a payoff function based on (7) leads to an inefficient outcome, *i.e.*, each player focuses on the forming of its own beam without nulling the interference to the PU. To prevent this selfish behavior, pricing has been used as an effective tool to give distributed players incentives to cooperate for resource usages. Therefore, the payoff function should consist of revenue and cost. Specifically, the new utility function of the k-th SU with pricing is rewritten as follows:

$$u_k = \log_2(1 + SINR_k) - \lambda p_k \mid \mathbf{h}_p^T \mathbf{f}_k \mid^2 \tag{8}$$

where λ is a positive scalar as the pricing factor and has an effect to reflect the potential interference to the PU. Thus, a non-cooperative game is formulated as:

$$\max \quad \sum_{k=1}^{K} u_k$$

$$\text{subject to} \begin{cases} \sum_{k=1}^{K} p_k \mid \mathbf{h}_p^T \mathbf{f}_k \mid^2 \le I_{th} \\ \sum_{k=1}^{K} p_k \le p_T \\ SINR_k \ge \gamma_{\min,k} \end{cases} \tag{9}$$

where $k \in \Omega$ is the set of players, and $\mathbf{f}_k$ and p_k is the set of admissible strategies of the k-th player, defined as $B = \{\mathbf{f}_1, \mathbf{f}_2, \cdots, \mathbf{f}_K, p_1, p_2, \cdots, p_K\}$. Here, each SU competes against the others by choosing its beamforming vector $\mathbf{f}_k$ and power p_k to maximize its own utility function.

3.2   Existence of Nash Equilibrium

To analyze the outcome of the game, the achievement of a Nash equilibrium is a well-known optimality criterion. In a Nash equilibrium point, every player is unilaterally optimal and no player can increase its utility alone by changing its own strategy. According to the fundamental game theory result, the strategic non-cooperative game admits at least one Nash equilibrium point if, for all $k \in \Omega$: 1) the feasible set $\mathbf{f}_k$ and p_k are a nonempty compact convex subset of a Euclidean space, and 2) the utility function $u_k(\cdot)$ is continuous and quasi-concave on $B_k = \{\mathbf{f}_k, p_k\}$.

By taking the first derivative of $u_k(\cdot)$ with respect to p_k and $\mid \mathbf{f}_k \mid^2$ respectively, it can be seen that

$$\frac{\partial u_k}{\partial p_k} = \frac{1}{\ln 2} \frac{\mid \mathbf{h}_k^T \mathbf{f}_k \mid^2}{\sum_{i=1, i \ne k}^{K} p_i \mid \mathbf{h}_k^T \mathbf{f}_i \mid^2 + p_p \mid g_k \mid^2 + \sigma_k^2 + p_k \mid \mathbf{h}_k^T \mathbf{f}_k \mid^2} - \lambda \mid \mathbf{h}_p^T \mathbf{f}_k \mid^2 \tag{10}$$

$$\frac{\partial u_k}{\partial \mid \mathbf{f}_k \mid^2} = \frac{1}{\ln 2} \frac{p_k \mid \mathbf{h}_k^T \mid^2}{\sum_{i=1, i \ne k}^{K} p_i \mid \mathbf{h}_k^T \mathbf{f}_i \mid^2 + p_p \mid g_k \mid^2 + \sigma_k^2 + p_k \mid \mathbf{h}_k^T \mathbf{f}_k \mid^2} - \lambda p_k \mid \mathbf{h}_p^T \mid^2 \tag{11}$$

Then by setting these first derivatives to zero, we get

$$p_k = \frac{\dfrac{\mid \mathbf{h}_k^T \mid^2}{\lambda \ln 2 \mid \mathbf{h}_p^T \mid^2} - [\sum_{i=1, i \ne k}^{K} p_i \mid \mathbf{h}_k^T \mathbf{f}_i \mid^2 + p_p \mid g_k \mid^2 + \sigma_k^2]}{\mid \mathbf{h}_k^T \mathbf{f}_k \mid^2} \tag{12}$$

$$|\mathbf{f}_k|^2 = \frac{\dfrac{|\mathbf{h}_k^T|^2}{\lambda \ln 2 \, |\mathbf{h}_p^T|^2} - [\sum_{i=1,i \neq k}^{K} p_i \, |\mathbf{h}_k^T \mathbf{f}_i|^2 + p_p \, |g_k|^2 + \sigma_k^2]}{p_k \, |\mathbf{h}_k^T|^2} \tag{13}$$

Moreover, by finding the second derivative of $u_k(\cdot)$ with respect to p_k and $|\mathbf{f}_k|^2$ respectively, we get

$$\frac{\partial^2 u_k}{\partial p_k^2} = -\frac{1}{\ln 2} \frac{|\mathbf{h}_k^T \mathbf{f}_k|^4}{[\sum_{i=1,i \neq k}^{K} p_i \, |\mathbf{h}_k^T \mathbf{f}_i|^2 + p_p \, |g_k|^2 + \sigma_k^2 + p_k \, |\mathbf{h}_k^T \mathbf{f}_k|^2]^2} \tag{14}$$

$$\frac{\partial^2 u_k}{\partial [|\mathbf{f}_k|^2]^2} = -\frac{1}{\ln 2} \frac{p_k^2 \, |\mathbf{h}_k^T|^4}{[\sum_{i=1,i \neq k}^{K} p_i \, |\mathbf{h}_k^T \mathbf{f}_i|^2 + p_p \, |g_k|^2 + \sigma_k^2 + p_k \, |\mathbf{h}_k^T \mathbf{f}_k|^2]^2} \tag{15}$$

As $|\mathbf{h}_k^T \mathbf{f}_k|^4 \geq 0$ and $p_k^2 \, |\mathbf{h}_k^T|^4 \geq 0$, it is easy to check that $\dfrac{\partial^2 u_k}{\partial p_k^2} \leq 0$ and $\dfrac{\partial^2 u_k}{\partial [|\mathbf{f}_k|^2]^2} \leq 0$.

Consequently, the utility functions of SUs satisfy all the required conditions for the existence of at least one NE based on the non-cooperative game with pricing scheme.

3.3   Joint Beamforming and Power Allocation Algorithm

In this section, we present an iterative algorithm that repeats the beamforming and the power allocation steps until convergence [13]. The algorithm has two parts: First, the power allocation part operates for a certain specified number of iterations N, using some initial beamforming matrix, and computes a power vector which may not be the optimal because the algorithm stops without necessarily converging. Then, for this power vector, the generalized eigenvalue solver finds the optimal beamforming matrix. This set of power allocation and beamforming steps is repeated, using the power in each round and then the beamforming vectors that are calculated from the previous round, until convergence is achieved to a locally optimal pair of power and beamforming vectors. The algorithm is proposed so as to maximize the sum rate of SUs, while not degrading QoS for the primary link.

The iterative algorithm is summarized as follows:

Set $n := 0$, Initialize powers $p_k^{(0)}$ and beamforming vectors $\mathbf{f}_k^{(0)}$, $k \in \Omega$.

Step1: At each iteration, set $n_0 := n$, $k \in \Omega$. Repeat{

For each user $k \in \Omega$ calculate the interference

$$I_k^{(n)} = \sum_{i \in \Omega, i \neq k}^{K} p_i^{(n)} \, |\mathbf{h}_k^T \mathbf{f}_i^{(n)}|^2 + p_p^{(n)} \, |g_k|^2 + \sigma_k^2 \tag{16}$$

For each user $k \in \Omega$ update power

$$p_k^{(n+1)} = \frac{\dfrac{|\mathbf{h}_k^T|^2}{\lambda \ln 2 |\mathbf{h}_p^T|^2} - I_k^{(n)}}{|\mathbf{h}_k^T \mathbf{f}_k^{(n)}|^2} \tag{17}$$

Set $n := n+1$; $\mathbf{f}_k^{(n)} := \mathbf{f}_k^{(n-1)}$ for each $k \in \Omega$.

} until $n = n_0 + N$.

Step2: For each user $k \in \Omega$ compute the beamforming vector, these are generalized eigenvalue problems as

$$\mathbf{f}_k^{(n)} = \arg\max_{|x|=1} \frac{x^H M_k^S x}{x^H M_k^I x} \tag{18}$$

where $M_k^S = p_k^{(n)} |\mathbf{h}_k^T|^2$ and $M_k^I = \sum_{i \in \Omega, i \neq k}^{K} p_i^{(n)} |\mathbf{h}_k^T|^2 + (p_p^{(n)} |g_k|^2 + \sigma_k^2) \mathbf{I}$

Step3: Repeat steps 1 and 2 until convergence.

3.4   Convergence of the Algorithm

For any fixed $\lambda > 0$, $p_k^{(n+1)} = \dfrac{\dfrac{|\mathbf{h}_k^T|^2}{\lambda \ln 2 |\mathbf{h}_p^T|^2} - I_k^{(n)}}{|\mathbf{h}_k^T \mathbf{f}_k^{(n)}|^2}$. If $\lambda_1 > \lambda_2$, then the

corresponding optimal solutions $\hat{p}(\lambda_1)$ and $\hat{p}(\lambda_2)$ are obtained , satisfying

$\hat{p}(\lambda_1) < \hat{p}(\lambda_2)$ regardless of the initial values. The algorithm can be implemented to obtain the fixed point of equation (17). We assume the order of power allocation is from SU1 to SU K, The process of step1 could be regarded as a power game with a coordinate utility function, as the power allocation strategy of each SU is the best response of the utility function, so the convergence and optimality of step 1 can be guaranteed.

The beamforming and power updates algorithm can be interpreted as best-responses in a beamforming and power allocation game. Concerning the algorithm, note that power updates and the beamforming updates result in an increase of the objective function. That is, the total utility function $U(p^{(n+1)}, \mathbf{F}^{(n+1)}) \geq U(p^{(n)}, \mathbf{F}^{(n)})$, for $n = 0, 1$, … … .The locally optimization of $\mathbf{F}$ and p are implemented alternatingly until the total utility of CR network converges to a stable value.

4   Simulation Results

In this section, we provide numerical results to show the convergence properties of joint beamforming and power allocation algorithm with respect to beamforming weight and transmit power for each link. For simplicity, we consider a CR scenario with two SUs and a single PU when all channel knowledge is perfectly known in the system. In the following results, we choose pricing factor λ=0.25, the noise power σ^2 =3e-3W, the PU transmit power p_p =0.1W, the SU maximum transmit power p_{max} = 10 W, the interference threshold I_{th} =100, the k-th SU minimum SINR constraint $\gamma_{min,k}$ = 5 dB, respectively. The channel coefficients are drawn from the Rayleigh distribution.

In what follows, we examine the convergence of the joint beamforming and power allocation algorithm with respect to transmit power level and beamforming weight. Fig. 2 shows the convergence of power level of each secondary link, in which the power initialization for each secondary link is the same as 0, it is observed that the transmit power converges in a few iterations due to the preceding update of the beamforming array. Fig. 3 depicts the beamforming weight allocated for each secondary link when transmit powers converge to the optimal levels. While the initialization of beamforming weights is set to be 1 for each secondary link. Fig. 4 plots the sum utility of the SUs when the interference to PU caused by SUs is restricted. Moreover, Fig. 5 plots the sum utility of the SUs versus the pricing factor λ. As observed from Figs. 4 and 5, the sum utility of the SUs converges and decreases as λ increases.

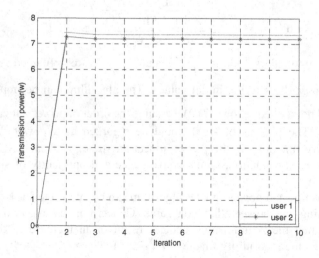

Fig. 2. Convergence of power for each user

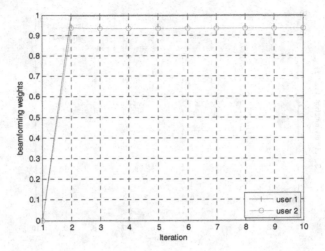

Fig. 3. Convergence of beamforming weights for each user

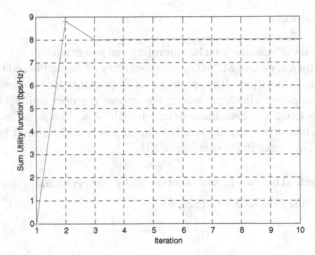

Fig. 4. Fig. 4. The achievable sum utility

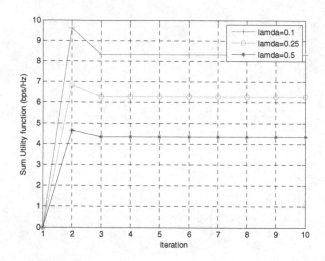

Fig. 5. The achievable sum utility for different λ

5   Conclusions

In this paper, we investigate the joint beamforming and power allocation problem based on game theory for a cognitive MIMO system consisting of single PU and multiple SUs sharing the same spectrum. The problem is formulated as a non-cooperative beamforming and power allocation game. We choose a proper utility function with pricing to characterize the data transmission for all SUs. Moreover, we propose a distributed algorithm that compute locally optimal power and transmit beamforming vectors, in an effort to maximize sum rate of SUs.

Acknowledgment. This work was supported by the National Natural Science Foundation of China (61172055, 61162008).

References

1. Mitola, J.: Cognitive radio for flexible mobile multimedia communication. In: Proc. IEEE Int. Workshop on Mobile Multimedia Commun. (MoMuC), San Diego, CA, pp. 3–10 (1999)
2. Scutari, G., Palomar, D.P., Barbarossa, S.: Coginitive MIMO radio. IEEE Signal Process. Maga., 546–592 (2008)
3. Islam, H., Liang, Y.C., Hoang, A.T.: Joint power control and beamforming for cognitive radio networks. IEEE Trans. Wireless Commun. 7(7), 2415–2419 (2008)
4. Zhang, L., Liang, Y.C., Xin, Y.: Joint beamforming and power control allocation for multiple access channels in cognitive radio networks. IEEE J. Sel Areas Commun. 26(1), 38–51 (2008)

5. Wang, F.G., Wang, W.B.: Sum rate optimization in interference channel of cognitive radio network. In: Proc. IEEE Int. Conference on Commun. (ICC), pp. 1–5 (2010)
6. Jiang, D., Zhang, H., Yuan, D.: Linear precoding and power allocation in the downlink of cognitive radio networks. In: Proc. IEEE Int. Conference on Communications, Circuits and Systems (ICCCAS), pp. 68–72 (2010)
7. Li, H., Gai, Y., He, Z., Niu, K., Wu, W.: Optimal power control game algorithm for cognitive radio networks with multiple interference temperature limits. In: Proc. IEEE Vehicular Technology Conference (VTC Spring), pp. 1554–1558 (2008)
8. Zhou, P., Yuan, W., Liu, W., Cheng, W.G.: Joint power and rate control in cognitive radio networks: a game-theoretical approach. In: Proc. IEEE Int. Conference on Commun., pp. 3296–3301 (2008)
9. Scutari, G., Palomar, D.P.: MIMO cognitive radio: a game theoretical approach. IEEE Trans. Signal Process. 58(2), 761–780 (2010)
10. Zhong, W., Xu, Y.Y., Tianfield, H.: Game-theoretic opportunistic spectrum sharing strategy selection for cognitive MIMO multiple access channels. IEEE Trans. Signal Process. 59(6), 2745–2759 (2011)
11. Hamdi, K., Zhang, W., Letaief, K.B.: Opportunistic spectrum sharing in cognitive MIMO wireless networks. IEEE Trans. Wireless Commun. 8(8), 4098–4109 (2009)
12. Niyato, D., Hossain, E.: Competitive spectrum sharing in cognitive radio networks: a dynamic game approach. IEEE Trans. Wireless Commun. 7(7), 2651–2660 (2008)
13. Chrisanthopoulou, M.-P., Tsoukatos, K.P.: Joint beamforming and power control for CDMA uplink throughput maximization. In: Proc. IEEE Int. Symposium on Personal, Indoor and Mobile Radio Communications, pp. 1–5 (2007)

Bit Allocation Scheme with Primary Base Station Cooperation in Cognitive Radio Network

Xiaorong Xu[1,2], Aiping Huang[1], Jianwu Zhang[2], and Baoyu Zheng[3]

[1] Institute of Information and Communication Engineering,
Zhejiang University, Hangzhou, China
xuxr@hdu.edu.cn, Aiping.huang@zju.edu.cn
[2] College of Telecommunication Engineering, Hangzhou Dianzi University, Hangzhou, China
jwzhang@hdu.edu.cn
[3] Institute of Signal Processing and Transmission,
Nanjing University of Posts and Telecommunications, Nanjing, China
zby@njupt.edu.cn

Abstract. Bit allocation scheme for cognitive OFDM with base station cooperation (BSC) in primary network is discussed in this correspondence. Under this circumstance, the optimization problem is formulated to minimize the interference to the primary BSC network, in order to guarantee the fixed rates for cognitive user transmission. With the knowledge of channel state information (CSI) in the interference channel, the optimal solutions can be solved by Lagrange optimum methods. Furthermore, bit assignment and access ability of cognitive users are analyzed in BSC model. Relationship of primary interference power and secondary allocated bits are presented. Simulation results indicate that, the access ability of cognitive user is significantly enhanced by BSC in comparison with non-cooperative primary network scenario, and the corresponding interference power could be reduced significantly with the proposed optimal bit assignment scheme.

Keywords: Cognitive radio network, Primary base station cooperation, Bit allocation, Channel state information.

1   Introduction

Radio spectrum is regarded as one of the most precious resources in wireless communications. Currently, the fixed spectrum allocation to licensed networks leads to serious spectrum underutilization. According to a research by FCC, there exists an immense waste in the usage of licensed spectrum in the dimensions of time, space and frequency [1]. The goal of changing spectrum allocation policy is to take advantage of the technological advance in radios to make spectrum more efficient and flexible. One innovative solution is the notion of cognitive radio that senses its outside spectrum surroundings while causes little interference to primary user even at moderate to high transmit powers. This concept of exploiting the underutilized spectrum was firstly proposed by Mitola on the basis of software radios [2].

X. Wang et al. (Eds.): WASA 2012, LNCS 7405, pp. 178–186, 2012.

On one hand, original cognitive radio can enhance overall spectrum efficiency of cognitive user by opportunistic spectrum access. On the other hand, transmission from cognitive users usually plays a part of harmful interference to primary users on the same spectrum. This motivates our goal of constraining cognitive users' transmitting power with fixed rates for cognitive user guaranteed service on maintaining primary users' performance. For this consideration, secondary users must execute "cognition" process that adjust their transmit power adaptively, that is, both satisfying their signal interference noise ratio (SINR) and maintaining primary users' SINR constraint. This transmission power restriction is equivalent to "interference temperature" in dynamic spectrum access [2],[3].

Base stations cooperation (BSC) has been recently proposed as a new method to increase cellular system capacity, which is equivalent to reduce mutual interference [4]. On the assumption of full BSC, different base stations in separated cells can be considered as a single base station with multiple spatial independent antennas. This approach introduces significant performance improvement while accepting complexity tradeoff. Therefore, only adjacent base stations cooperation becomes a more practical strategy [4],[5].

Since BSC increases primary users' capacity in cellular system, it's necessary for us to investigate cognitive users' uplink channel capacity and bit allocation scheme in this situation. The rest of the paper is organized as follows. System model is introduced in Section II. Solutions of sub-carrier bit allocation for cognitive users are discussed in Section III. In Section IV, we compare their performance of bit assignment and analyze the access ability of cognitive users with BSC model. Finally, conclusions are drawn in Section V.

2   System Model

We consider the uplink cognitive OFDM channel scenario that is depicted in Fig. 1, where BS_i denotes the i-th primary receiver using licensed spectrum corresponding with primary users in the BSC cellular system, while secondary user transmitter (SUT) wants to transmit its information to its corresponding secondary user receiver (SUR) over the same spectrum.

We define sub-channels from SUT to SUR as cognitive channel, whereas sub-channels from SUT to BS_i as interference channel. We also specify g_{ik} as the interference channel gains for the k-th sub-carrier to the i-th primary base station and channel gain h_k corresponding with the cognitive channel for the k-th sub-carrier, over Rayleigh fading channels with mean $E[g_{ik}]$ and $E[h_k]$ respectively. Therefore, cognitive users must adjust its transmitting power P_k adaptively on the k-th sub-carrier, for the interference constraint of all BSC working over the same spectrum under specific knowledge of CSI g_{ik} and h_k.

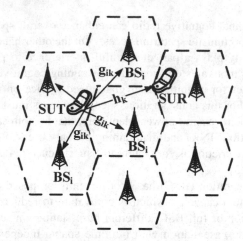

Fig. 1. Cognitive OFDM channel scenario in BSC

Interference temperature describes the interference power on the specific spectrum, which is denoted as a metric for interference analysis from SUT to BS_i [2],[3]. It is given by

$$T\left(f_c, B\right) = P_I\left(f_c, B\right)/(Q \cdot B) \tag{1}$$

where $P_I\left(f_c, B\right)$ is the average interference power on the spectrum with bandwidth B and central frequency f_c, Q is the Boltzmann constant with value 1.38×10^{-23} J/K.

Since the interference temperature is directly determined by interference power, for convenience, we define T as the interference power limit on bandwidth B, which denotes the interference upper-bound of primary user receiver (i.e., primary base stations). In cognitive OFDM system, for the i-th single cell, total cognitive interference must keep below a threshold, hence

$$\sum_k T_i\left(f_{c,k}, B\right) \leq T \tag{2}$$

where k indicates the k-th sub-carrier. While in primary BSC system, for each "co-operative base stations group", primary user combiner outputs the signal received by the base station with highest SINR. This combination process is similar to selection ratio combination (SRC) method, which yields to $P_T = \overline{\text{SINR}} \sum_i 1/i$ [5]. Owing to the gain $\sum_i 1/i$, primary BSC can equivalently endure more interference from cognitive users. Hence, the total cognitive transmitter interference power can be written as

$$P_T = \sum_i \sum_k T_i\left(f_{c,k}, B\right) \leq T \cdot \sum_i \frac{1}{i} \tag{3}$$

Therefore, bit allocation is the problem of optimal assignment bits in the k-th sub-carrier under SUT power constraint, which minimizes the interference power with a threshold given by primary BS. The optimal problem can be written as

$$\arg \min \sum_i \sum_k \sum_m \rho_{i,k} \left| g_{ik} \right|^2 P_{i,k,m} \tag{4}$$

The above optimization problem is subjected to the following conditions

$$R_{\text{total}} = \sum_i \sum_k \rho_{i,k} B \log_2 \left[1 + \frac{h_k P_{i,k}}{(N_0 B)_{i,k}} \right] \tag{5}$$

$$\sum_{i=1}^{I} \rho_{i,k} = 1, \ \rho_{i,k} = \{0,1\}, \ k = 1, 2, \cdots, K \tag{6}$$

$$R_1 : R_2 : \cdots : R_I = r_1 : r_2 : \cdots : r_I \tag{7}$$

$$P_k \geq 0, \ k = 1, 2, \cdots, K \tag{8}$$

$$R_i \geq 0, \ i = 1, 2, \cdots, I \tag{9}$$

where $(N_0 B)_{i,k}$ denotes interference power of the k-th sub-carrier at the i-th primary BS. It is remarkable that, optimal target in Eq. (4) can be seen as bit allocation problem, where bits are allocated in sub-carriers with the purpose of rate constraint, and interference power should achieve the minimum value in this condition, as Eq. (5) indicated. It is illustrated that, in cognitive OFDM with primary BSC, SUT transmitting power should be controlled to eliminate interference to primary BSC receivers, as well as bit allocation scheme should be applied to minimize total interference power.

3   Bit Allocation Scheme with Primary BS Cooperation

In CRN with BSC, assume Rayleigh fading is implemented in cognitive channel and interference channel, the optimal problem is described as Eq. (4)-(9), which still needs two kinds of CSI knowledge, namely, interference channel CSI g_{ik} and cognitive channel CSI h_k. Hence, we consider the solution of bit allocation problem with full CSI which is expressed as follows.

To find the optimal bit allocation for the k-th sub-carrier at the i-th primary BS, we define the function $P_{i,k}(b_{i,k}) = \sum_{m=1}^{b_{i,k}} \Delta P_{i,k,m}$, where $\Delta P_{i,k,m}$ indicates the additional required power to transmit one additional bit through the k-th sub-carrier at the i-th primary BS, when the number of bit loaded on the sub-carrier is $(m-1)$. Hence, the Lagrange optimum problem can be written as

$$J(P_k) = \sum_i \sum_k \sum_m \rho_{i,k} |g_{i,k}|^2 \Delta P_{i,k,m} - \lambda \sum_i \sum_k \rho_{i,k} B \log_2 \left(1 + \frac{h_k P_{i,k}}{(N_0 B)_{i,k}}\right) \tag{10}$$

Eq. (10) is nonlinear optimization problem that could not be solved numerically. Hence, we consider another solution method. Refer to classical Hughes-Hartogs bit allocation algorithm, we propose an improved scheme that the required power to one bit $\Delta P_{i,k,m}$ can be acted as geometric progression through the k-th sub-carrier [11],[12]. Hence, $\Delta P_{i,k,m}$ can be expressed as

$$\Delta P_{i,k,m} = \frac{(f(m) - f(m-1))}{|h_k|^2} \tag{11}$$

where $f(b_{i,k}) = \frac{N_0}{3} \left[Q^{-1} \left(\frac{Pr_b}{4} \right) \right]^2 \left(2^{b_{i,k}} - 1 \right)$ indicates the required power for transmitting $b_{i,k}$ bits through the k-th sub-carrier at the i-th primary BS, with the guaranteed BER Pr_b for MQAM modulation [5],[6],[11].

Hence, the sequences $|g_{i,k}|^2 \Delta P_{i,k,1}$, $|g_{i,k}|^2 \Delta P_{i,k,2}$,....., $|g_{i,k}|^2 \Delta P_{i,k,b_{i,k}}$ is the geometric progression with the initial term $|g_{i,k}|^2 \frac{f(1)}{|h_{i,k}|^2}$ and common ration 2. If the last term approaches to minimization, it is said that the total interference power can achieve its minimum value [11]. To find the minimum value of $\sum_{k=1}^{K_i} |g_{i,k}|^2 \Delta P_{i,k,b_{i,k}}$, we apply the Arith-metric Geo-metric (AM-GM) means inequality, and obtain the optimal allocated bits at the k-th sub-carrier with the i-th primary BS, expressed as

$$b_{i,k} = \frac{2}{K_i} \sum_{k=1}^{K_i} \log_2 \frac{|g_{i,k}|}{|h_{i,k}|} + \frac{R_i}{K_i} - 2 \log_2 \frac{|g_{i,k}|}{|h_{i,k}|} \tag{12}$$

where $R_i = \sum_{k=1}^{K_i} b_{i,k}$, $i = 1, 2, \cdots, I, k = 1, 2, \cdots, K_i$. I is the number of primary BSC and K_i denotes the allocated sub-carrier number at the i-th primary BS.

If $b_{i,k}$ is not an integer in Eq. (12), it needs to round off as an integer, namely, if $R_l = R_i - \sum_{k=1}^{K_i} \hat{b}_{i,k} \neq 0$, the steps of bit rounding procedure can be expressed as follows.

1) $R_l = 0$, bit rounding procedure is not needed.
2) $R_l > 0$, select R_l sub-carriers based on a descending order of the bit difference $b_{i,k} - \hat{b}_{i,k}$, and add one bit to each sub-carrier.

3) $R_l < 0$, select $|R_l|$ sub-carriers based on a ascending order of the bit difference $b_{i,k} - \hat{b}_{i,k}$, and subtract one bit from each sub-carrier.

Therefore, the intuition behind this bit allocation scheme is to take advantage of good cognitive access conditions: when cognitive channel is good (h_k large) and interference channel is low (g_{ik} small), less bits would be allocated to the k-th sub-carrier due to better channel quality guarantees low bit rate transmission; on the contrary, as cognitive quality degrades, more bits should be allocated to this sub-carrier, in order to satisfy BER requirement for cognitive network.

4   Simulation Results and Analysis

Our simulation is implemented by Matlab simulation tool with numerical analysis. In our simulations, we assume BSC OFDM system with total bandwidth $B = 5\text{MHz}$ and $K = 64/128$ sub-carriers. Suppose system BER requirement is $\text{Pr}_b = 10^{-4}$, and the assigned total bits range from 32bits to 256bits. Noise power on each cognitive sub-channel is supposed to be $\sigma^2 = 0.01$. Hexagonal cell is also assumed, moreover, primary BSC contains 3 nearest base stations to the primary user in primary BS cooperation group, hence, $i = 1, 2, 3, 4$.

Fig. 2 depicts the relationship of allocated bits and primary interference power for the improved Hughes-Hartogs bit allocation scheme with different BSC and sub-carrier numbers. It is apparent that the proposed algorithm with more sub-carrier outperforms the less one, and interference power could be suppressed obviously. When the cooperative primary BS is 4 and total allocated bits are 150, interference power could reduce about 6dB for 128 sub-carriers. It is indicated that bits assignment for each sub-carrier is reduced because the corresponding cognitive channel becomes better to guarantee low bit rate transmission. On the other hand, the increasing of BSC could guarantee low interference power in smaller sub-carrier number scenario, i.e., for 64 sub-carriers range from 32bits to 96bits, 4 BSC performs better than 2 BSC, however, for 128 sub-carriers, 4 BSC and 2 BSC have the same interference power. Hence, the increasing of BSC could improve cooperative diversity for primary network, and cognitive user dynamic spectrum access (DSA) would be influenced in smaller assigned bits scenario. For higher sub-carrier number, the effect is not apparent.

Fig. 3 shows the three dimensional relationships between cognitive channel spectral efficiency C/B and average channel gains. It is indicated that, spectral efficiency rises up when $E[h_k]$ increases. Just as expected that, cognitive capacity could be enhanced with the improving of cognitive channel condition. By contrast, spectral efficiency declines as the interference channel gain $E[g_{ik}]$ increases. The reason can be explained that, when the interference channel becomes better, cognitive user has to reduce its transmitting power so as to protect primary receivers, namely, the cooperative BS has to restrain cognitive access ability. Actually, BSC improved the

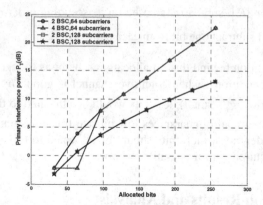

Fig. 2. Relationship of allocated bits and primary interference power

anti-interference performance for primary users through cooperative diversity, which also depends on the performance of SU. Hence, the tradeoff between cognitive access ability and BSC complexity should be investigated.

We mainly consider 4 cases of BSC: no BSC (i.e. traditional cellular system without cooperation), 2 BSC (only the most adjacent BS for cooperation), 3 BSC, and 4 BSC (square cells are assumed). Simulation results are depicted in Fig. 4. It is obviously that, the cognitive access ability increases with the number of primary BSC, but the trend is not linearly. The highest gain is obtained from no BSC to three BSC. Increasing the number of cooperative base stations from three to four provides less gain than that from no BSC to two BSC, as well as from two BSC to three BSC. We emphasize that the relationship between SU accessing ability and primary BSC numbers would keep this trend in general, which indicates that only a few number of BSC ought to be sufficient for cognitive user.

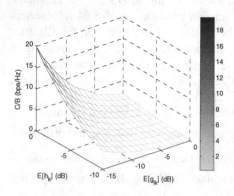

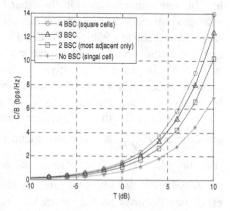

Fig. 3. Cognitive channel spectral efficiency and average channel gains

Fig. 4. Cognitive channel spectral efficiency for different BSC numbers

5   Conclusions

Bit allocation and cognitive channel spectral efficiency reflect the access ability for cognitive user in CRN. In this correspondence, we proposed an improved Hughes-Hartogs bit allocation strategy in primary BS cooperation scenario. Optimization problem is formulated to minimize the interference power in order to guarantee the fixed rates for cognitive user transmission. The solution is given by the improved scheme. Moreover, the increasing of BSC could improve cooperative diversity for primary network, and the increasing of sub-carrier number could guarantee low bit rate transmission, hence cognitive access ability would be enhanced. In addition, it is also indicated that cognitive user access ability increases with the increment of inter-ference temperature upper-bound, the growth of cognitive channel gains, as well as the number of primary BSC. Therefore, many factors influence the cognitive spectral efficiency, the proposed bit allocation scheme provides an efficient strategy for prac-tical primary BS cooperation scenario.

Acknowledgements. This work is partly supported by National Natural Science Foundation of China (Grant No. 61102066, 60972058, 60972039), China Postdoctoral Science Foundation entitled "Research on Key Technologies of Multi-user Resource Allocation and Cooperative Transmission in Cognitive Radio Networks" (Grant No. 2012M511365), and Scientific Research Project of Zhejiang Provincial Education Department (Grant No. Y201119890).

References

1. FCC: Spectrum Policy Task Force Report. FCC 02-155 (2002)
2. Mitola, J.: Cognitive Radio: An Integrated Agent Architecture for Software Defined Ra-dio. Royal Institution Technology, Stockholm (2000)
3. Haykin, S.: Cognitive Radios: Brain-Empowered Wireless Communication. IEEE Journal on Selected Aeras in Communications 23(2), 12–18 (2005)
4. Shamai, S., Somekh, O., Zaidel, B.: Multi-cell Communications: an Information Theoretic Perspective. In: Proceedings of Internation Joint Workshop on Communications and Cod-ing, Donnini (Florence), Italy (2004)
5. Goldsmith, A.: Wireless Communications, pp. 208–209. Cambridge University Press (2005)
6. Biglieri, E., Proakis, J., Shamai, S.: Fading Channels: Information-Theoretic and Commu-nications Aspects. IEEE Transactions on Information Theory 44(6), 2619–2692 (1998)
7. Babai, A., Saltzberg, B., Ergen, M.: Multi-carrier Digital Communications-Theory and Applications of OFDM, 2nd edn. Springer, New York (2004)
8. Patzold, M.: Mobile Fading Channels. Wiley, New York (2002)
9. Erceg, V., et al.: An Empirically Based Path Loss Model for Wireless Channels in Subur-ban Environments. IEEE Journal on Selected Aeras in Communications, 1205–1211 (1999)

10. Saad, W., Han, Z., Basar, T., Hjorungnes, A., et al.: Hedomic Coalition Formation Games for Secondary Base Station Cooperation in Cognitive Radio Networks. In: Proceedings of 2010 IEEE Wireless Communications and Networking Conference (WCNC 2010), pp. 1–6 (2010)

11. Sun, D.W., Zheng, B.Y.: A Novel Resource Allocation Algorithm in Multi-media Heterogeneous Cognitive OFDM System. KSII Transactions on Internet and Information Systems 4(5), 691–708 (2010)

12. Li, L., Zheng, B.Y.: A Time-Sharing Resource Allocation Method in Heterogeneous Cognitive OFDM Networks. In: Proceedings of 2010 IEEE Wireless Communications and Signal Processing (WCSP 2010), pp. 1–5 (2010)

13. Lee, C.W., Jeon, G.J.: Low Complexity Bit Allocation Algorithm for OFDM Systems. International Journal of Communication Systems 21, 1171–1179 (2008)

14. Kang, X., Liang, Y.C., Nallanathan, A., Garg, H.K.: Optimal Power Allocation for Fading Channels in Cognitive Radio Networks: Ergodic Capacity and Outage Capacity. IEEE Transactions on Wireless Communications 8(2), 940–950 (2009)

15. Li, L., Zheng, B.Y.: Power Allocation for Cognitive OFDM with Separated Interference Limits. In: Proceedings of IET 3rd International Conference on Wireless, Mobile and Multimedia Networks (ICWMMN 2010), pp. 187–190 (2010)

Optimal Spectrum Sharing for Contention-Based Cognitive Radio Wireless Networks

Manish Wadhwa[1], Chunsheng Xin[2], Min Song[3], Norou Diawara[4],
Yanxiao Zhao[5], and Komalpreet Kaur[5]

[1] Department of Information Technology, South University, Virginia Beach, USA
[2] Department of Computer Science, Norfolk State University, Norfolk, USA
[3] Department of Electrical and Computer Engineering, University of Toledo, Toledo, USA
[4] Department of Mathematics and Statistics, Old Dominion University, Norfolk, USA
[5] Department of Electrical and Computer Engineering, Old Dominion University, Norfolk, USA

Abstract. Fixed spectrum assignment policy lead to the need for a more dynamic approach to spectrum access. This paper analyzes the optimal dynamic spectrum sharing possibilities among primary and secondary users in cognitive radio networks, where the channel access for both primary and secondary users in the same channel is contention-based. We assume slotted time. Fixed and random allocations of primary users in the channels are considered for contention-based study. This means that in a fixed allocation, the number of primary users is fixed in a specific channel; their number may vary in different channels. Random allocation on the other hand considers primary users randomly allocated in different channels in each time slot. Given the number of channels and primary users, we find the optimal number of secondary users that obtains maximum throughput in spectrum sharing with primary users. The results obtained provide low complexity solutions for implementation in practical systems.

Keywords: Cognitive radio network, spectrum management, spectrum sharing, optimization.

1   Introduction

Spectrum scarcity and low utilization lead to *dynamic spectrum access (DSA)* [1–3]. DSA has been studied under three main classes: 1) open access, 2) hierarchical access, and 3) dynamic exclusive use [4–6]. Open access allows access similar to industrial,science, and medicine (ISM) bands. The hierarchical access is further subdivided into underlay, overlay and interweave [4–7]. The dynamic exclusive use allows secondary users to have access to the bands based on conditional exclusive usage provided by primary users. Dynamic spectrum leasing (DSL) has been studied by various researchers in which the spectrum licensees are granted the rights to sell or trade their spectrum to third party [8–11]. The model developed in this paper may be applied to these classes of DSA with some modifications, we are presenting this work more specifically for hierarchical interweave model.

Under interweave dynamic spectrum sharing, also called *opportunistic spectrum access* in the literature, primary users (PU) have the privilege to use their licensed spectrum band, and secondary users (SU) are allowed to access the band only when primary

X. Wang et al. (Eds.): WASA 2012, LNCS 7405, pp. 187–196, 2012.

users are not using it. This is the approach taken in interweave networks [4], where SU keeps monitoring the spectrum, temporarily (opportunistically) accesses it when PU ceases using it, and gives up the band upon the resurgence of PU signal. The sensing requirements may be stringent with interweave model especially when sensing opportunities are changing quickly, as the SUs must be able to sense the arriving PU signal and immediately leave the band, and if available, jump to another band. The study related to sensing is beyond the scope of this paper, and we assume that there is seamless sensing of the available bands. Whenever there is PU arrival, SU hops to another band or goes into waiting state.

Finding optimal spectrum sharing possibilities has been studied in past [12, 13]. This problem of finding optimal secondary usage further shows that dynamic spectrum access saves a lot of spectrum wastage. By abiding to the FCC rules and regulations regarding dynamic spectrum access, new spectral resources can be created. We provide upper bounds on the optimal number of secondary users. Theoretical bounds present an important understanding into the behavior of systems. Regulation authorities can make regulations by studying these upper bounds. The main contributions of this paper are as follows. This paper derives a set of formulations for finding the optimal number of secondary users for fixed and random allocations. Low complexity solutions are developed that have lower demands on processing for practical systems.

The rest of the paper is organized as follows. Section 2 presents the network model for fixed and random allocations of primary users. Section 3 deals with finding optimal solutions for the two allocations considered. In section 4, we present numerical results and then conclude the paper in section 5.

2   Network Model and Throughput Analysis

The network model we consider consists of primary and secondary users with all the users independent of each other (e.g., see [13–15]). This model maps well with the interweave model [4]. The spectrum opportunities for interweave model are determined based on the primary user usage requirements. The secondary users access a specific spectrum band at 8 AM because they find the band to be idle. However, at 9 AM, primary users need the band. The secondary users have to give it up and search for a new band. This is the model we are using in this paper, where the secondary user activity is based on this ON/OFF model.

With the assumption of slotted time, secondary users dynamically detect the available accessible channels. Furthermore, in each time slot, every primary/secondary user generates data to transmit with a probability p. The number of primary users and secondary users are denoted N and $\tilde{N}$, respectively. The licensed spectrum of primary users is partitioned into M channels. The N primary users are allocated into the M channels. For random allocation X_i ($1 \leq i \leq M$, $X_i \geq 0$) denote the number of primary users allocated to channel i. Also, we define a random variable Y_i such that $Y_i = 1$ if channel i is available for secondary users and 0 otherwise. h denotes the number of available channels for secondary usage.

PU throughput is independent of SU throughput. The overall throughput of primary and secondary users can be optimized if secondary user throughput is optimized, since

Table 1. Definitions of the variables used in the network model

Variable	Definition
N	Number of Primary Users
$\tilde{N}$	Number of Secondary Users
M	Number of Channels
X_i	Number of primary users allocated to channel i
T_s	Secondary User Throughput
h	Number of available channels in each time slot for secondary usage.
Y_i	Random variable that attains value 1, if channel i is available for secondary users and 0 otherwise
V	$= \sum_{i=1}^{M} Y_i$, Number of accessible channels for secondary users.
S	$= \{x_1, \ldots, x_M \mid \sum_{i=1}^{M} x_i = N\}$, is the set containing the number of primary users in each channel for random allocation
f_V	$= f_{Y_1} * \cdots * f_{Y_M}$, probability mass function (pmf) to determine whether a channel is available to secondary users or not

primary users are independent in using the channels while secondary users are dependent upon how primary users use the channels. Based on the model considered, secondary users are only opportunistically using the channels and hence cannot have any impact on primary user throughput. Thus, in order to optimize the overall throughput, it is sufficient to optimize the secondary user throughput. In the network model, we just model the SU throughput in the following subsections. Before we go ahead and present the network models for fixed and random allocations, Table 1 presents the definitions of variables used.

2.1 Fixed Allocation

In the fixed allocation, the number of primary users allocated to channels is fixed over all time slots. These primary users have traffic generation probability of p. These primary users use the channels and produce total primary user throughput over a time slot, while secondary users opportunistically access these channels and optimize their performance opportunistically. As discussed earlier, the throughput of SUs is required to be optimized to give optimal overall throughput. Before finding the optimal number of secondary users we need to look at the overall SU throughput which is given as follows.

$$T_s = \sum_{h=1}^{M} f_V(h) \cdot T_s(h). \tag{1}$$

where $T_s(h)$ [13] is the secondary user throughput for given h available channels,

$$T_s(h) = \tilde{N} \cdot p \cdot (1 - \frac{p}{h})^{\tilde{N}-1}. \tag{2}$$

2.2 Random Allocation

In the random allocation, the primary users are randomly allocated access to the channels. These primary users access these channels with traffic generation probabilities of p. Similar to fixed allocation, we find the secondary user throughput for random allocation, denoted as $T_s'(M, N, \tilde{N}, p)$, as follows.

$$T'_s(M, N, \tilde{N}, p) = \sum_{\{n_1, \dots, n_M\} \in \mathcal{S}} f_{\mathbf{X}}(n_1, \dots, n_M; N, \tfrac{1}{M}) \times T_s(n_1, \dots, n_M; M, N, \tilde{N}, p).$$

(3)

where the pmf for a multinomial distribution $\mathbf{X} = [X_1, \dots, X_M]$ is

$$f_{\mathbf{X}}(n_1, \dots, n_M; N, \tfrac{1}{M}) = \tfrac{N!}{n_1! \cdots n_M!} \left(\tfrac{1}{M}\right)^N.$$

Here $n_1, \dots, n_M$ are the numbers representing randomly alloacted primary users in each channel. Also, similar to $T_s(h)$ for fixed allocation, $T_s(n_1, \dots, n_M; M, N, \tilde{N}, p)$ gives the secondary user throughput for random allocation for each random case.

3 Optimal Solution

Let $\tilde{N}^*$ denote the optimal number of secondary users that maximizes the total through-put. The $\tilde{N}^*$ can be numerically computed. That is, given N, M, p, we compute a set of throughputs T for varying $\tilde{N}$, and then we identify the maximum throughput. The $\tilde{N}^*$ is the $\tilde{N}$ corresponding to the maximum throughput.

3.1 Fixed Allocation

For finding $\tilde{N}^*$, we take the derivative of Eq.2. Finding the partial derivative of Eq. (2) with respect to $\tilde{N}$ and equating it to zero, we get

$$\tilde{N} = \tfrac{-1}{\log(1 - \frac{p}{h})}.$$

(4)

$\tilde{N}$ is dependent upon p and h, thus for a given p, we need to find the value of h that gives optimal number of secondary users and hence optimal performance. In order to find the value of h that optimizes $\tilde{N}$, we need to take a look at the distribution of h. Since h is random, we perform Monte Carlo Simulations by performing the experiment over $10,000$ random samples. It must be noted that the number $10,000$ was chosen such that the number is large enough for performing such kind of simulations. These sim-ulations are performed for fixed and random allocations where the number of primary and secondary users was kept same while traffic generation probabilities were varied. In other set of simulations, for a fixed traffic generation probability, simulations were performed by varying the number of primary and secondary users.

We thus find the distribution of h as shown in Fig. 1 for $p = 0.2$, Fig. 2 for $p = 0.4$, and Fig. 3 for $p = 0.9$ when $M = 10$ and $N = 30$. After performing simulations with many other values of M, N and p, it is found that the distribution of h is heavily con-centrated around the mean of h, i.e., the probability of occurrence of available channels around the mean value of h is highest. Thus optimal number of secondary users, $\tilde{N}^*$, can be found by taking the mean of h as the number of accessible channels.

To find the expected number of available channels, we determine the probability of availability of each channel and then add all these probabilities as follows.

$$\overline{h_f} = \sum_{i=1}^{M} (1 - p)^{X_i}.$$

(5)

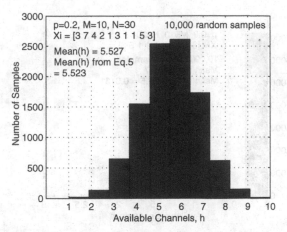

Fig. 1. Monte Carlo Simulations for M = 10, N = 30, p = 0.2

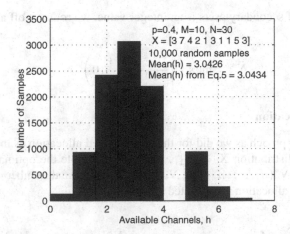

Fig. 2. Monte Carlo Simulations for M = 10, N = 30, p = 0.4

It is obvious that the channel availability depends on the traffic generation probability. The higher the p, the lower the number of channels available for secondary usage and hence lower the mean. We can notice from Fig. 1, Fig. 2 and Fig. 3 that as the p increases from 0.2 to 0.4 to 0.9, the number of available channels shrink more and more towards 0. Since the traffic generation probability is same over each channel, the number of primary users in each channel is the determining factor. Thus Eq.(5) determines the mean number of available channels. The logical conclusion from this is that the optimal number of secondary users that can have access to the available channels depends mainly on the mean number of available channels as the probability of occurrence of available channels for a large set of random samples around the mean is highest.

Thus, we can write Eq. (4) as follows.

$$\tilde{N}^* = \frac{-1}{\log\left(1 - \frac{p}{h_f}\right)}$$

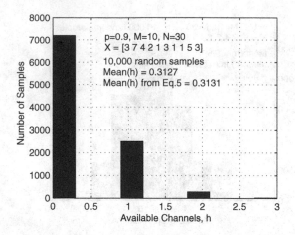

Fig. 3. Monte Carlo Simulations for M = 10, N = 30, p = 0.9

Since the number of secondary users is an integer value, we round it off and write $\tilde{N}^*$ as follows.

$$\tilde{N}^* = \max \left(\left\lceil \frac{-1}{\log(1-\frac{p}{h_f})} \right\rceil, 0 \right) \tag{6}$$

3.2 Random Allocation

We take a similar approach as we did for the case of fixed allocation as in Eq. (6). For a specific random distribution $\mathbf{X} = [n_1, \ldots, n_M]$, we denote the optimal number of secondary users as $\tilde{N}^*(n_1, \ldots, n_M; M, N, p)$. Then the optimal number of secondary users under random allocation is computed as follows.

$$\tilde{N}^* = \sum_{\{n_1,\ldots,n_M\}\in\mathcal{S}} f_{\mathbf{X}}(n_1, \ldots, n_M; N, \tfrac{1}{M}) \times \tilde{N}^*(n_1, \ldots, n_M; M, N, p). \tag{7}$$

Since the number of available channels is a random number based on the random distribution, we can get the optimal solution by finding the expected number of available channels, denoted as $\overline{h_r}$, as follows:

$$\overline{h_r} = \sum_{j=1}^{C} \left(\sum_{i=1}^{M} (1-p)^{X_{ij}} \right) \cdot f_X(j), \tag{8}$$

where

$$f_X(j) = \frac{N!}{n_{1j}! \cdots n_{Mj}!} \left(\frac{1}{M} \right)^N$$

Here $f_X(j)$ represents the probability mass function of jth configuration out of total C configurations possible for a given M and N, where the value of C can be calculated using the method of finding the combinations with repetitions as follows.

$$C = \binom{N+M-1}{N}$$

Since the problem of finding optimal solution for random allocation is similar to the one for fixed allocation, we can write the optimal solution for random allocation as follows.

$$\tilde{N}^* = \max\left(\left\lceil \frac{-1}{\log(1-\frac{p}{h_r})} \right\rceil, 0\right) \tag{9}$$

We note that the formulations obtained in this paper have less complexity as compared to the ones derived in [13]. For fixed allocation, the optimal solution in [13] has a complexity of $O(M^2)$. The solution provided by this paper, as seen from Eqs. (5) and (6), has a complexity of $O(M)$. For random allocation, the optimal solution in [13] has a complexity of $O(M^2C)$. In this paper, on the other hand, there is only one nested loop inside the main loop as given by Eqs. (8) and (9). Thus the complexity of the solution provided in this paper is $O(MC)$.

4   Numerical Results

Under the fixed allocation scheme, we illustrate the optimal number of secondary users versus the traffic generation probability with $M = 10$, $N = 5$ (Fig. 4), $M = 10$, $N = 10$ (Fig. 5), and $M = 10$, $N = 40$ (Fig. 6). The optimal number of secondary users given by Eq. (6) follows very closely with the one obtained through numerical computation. It can be observed from Fig. 4, Fig. 5 and Fig. 6 that the results given by Eq. (6) and the results obtained through numerical approach match very well for the worst, best and average case configurations.

In Fig. 7 and Fig. 8, we plot the optimal number of secondary users versus the traffic generation probability with $M = 10$, $N = 5$ and 15 (Fig. 7) and $M = 10$, $N = 10$ and 30 (Fig. 8), under the random allocation scheme. The plots obtained for optimal solution

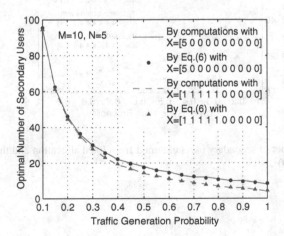

Fig. 4. Optimal number of secondary users obtained from fixed allocation and that from Eq. (6), when M=10 and N=5

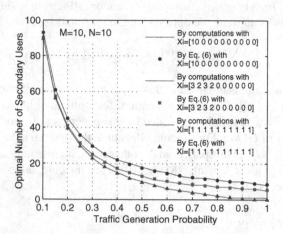

Fig. 5. Optimal number of secondary users obtained from fixed allocation and that from Eq. (6), when M=10 and N=10

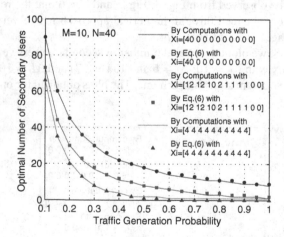

Fig. 6. Optimal number of secondary users obtained from fixed allocation and that from Eq. (6), when M=10 and N=40

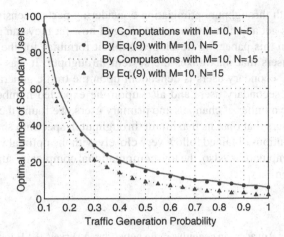

Fig. 7. Optimal number of secondary users obtained from random allocation and that from Eq.(9), when M=10 and N=5, and 15

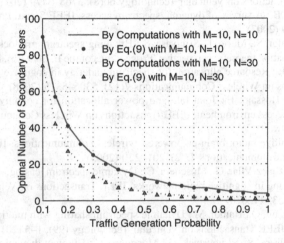

Fig. 8. Optimal number of secondary users obtained from random allocation and that from Eq. (9), when M=10 and N=10, and 30

follow very closely with the plots obtained through numerical computation. Based on the results of various other experiments with varying M, N and p, we conclude that Eq. (9) is a good estimation for the optimal number of secondary users that maximizes the total throughput.

5   Conclusions

The importance of dynamic spectrum access is well established in the engineering community. Researchers have invested a great deal in the throughput optimization problem.

Our paper deals with throughput optimization considering perfect sensing. Regulation authorities can thus get a qualitative understanding of how far they can give access for secondary usage. In this paper, we developed explicit formulas for the optimal number of secondary users that maximizes the system throughput. It was found that the optimal number of secondary users is dependent upon the traffic generation probability of primary and secondary users and also upon the expected number of available channels. Given the number of channels and primary users, we found the optimal number of secondary users that obtains maximum throughput in spectrum sharing with primary users. The solutions obtained follow very closely with the optimal values obtained using numerical computation. Also, the low computational complexity supports its practical implementation.

References

1. Wang, B., Liu, K.: Advances in cognitive radio networks: A survey. IEEE Journal of Selected Topics in Signal Processing 5(1), 5–23 (2011)
2. Stotas, S., Nallanathan, A.: Enhancing the capacity of spectrum sharing cognitive radio networks. IEEE Transactions on Vehicular Technology 60(8), 3768–3779 (2011)
3. Zhao, Q., Sadler, B.: A survey of dynamic spectrum access. IEEE Signal Processing Magazine 24(3), 79–89 (2007)
4. Goldsmith, A., Jafar, S., Maric, I., Srinivasa, S.: Breaking spectrum gridlock with cognitive radios: An information theoretic perspective. Proceedings of the IEEE 97(5), 894–914 (2009)
5. Le, L., Hossain, E.: Resource allocation for spectrum underlay in cognitive radio networks. IEEE Transactions on Wireless Communications 7(12), 5306–5315 (2008)
6. Kim, D., Le, L., Hossain, E.: Joint rate and power allocation for cognitive radios in dynamic spectrum access environment. IEEE Transactions on Wireless Communications 7(12), 5517–5527 (2008)
7. Haykin, S.: Cognitive radio: brain-empowered wireless communications. IEEE Journal on Selected Areas in Communications 23(2), 201–220 (2005)
8. Jayaweera, S., Vazquez-Vilar, G., Mosquera, C.: Dynamic spectrum leasing: A new paradigm for spectrum sharing in cognitive radio networks. IEEE Transactions on Vehicular Technology 59(5), 2328–2339 (2010)
9. Lin, P., Jia, J., Zhang, Q., Hamdi, M.: Dynamic spectrum sharing with multiple primary and secondary users. IEEE Transactions on Vehicular Technology (99), 1–5 (2010)
10. Hakim, K., Jayaweera, S., El-howayek, G., Mosquera, C.: Efficient dynamic spectrum sharing in cognitive radio networks: centralized dynamic spectrum leasing (c-dsl). IEEE Transactions on Wireless Communications 9(9), 2956–2967 (2010)
11. El-Howayek, G., Jayaweera, S.: Distributed dynamic spectrum leasing (d-dsl) for spectrum sharing over multiple primary channels. IEEE Transactions on Wireless Communications 10(1), 55–60 (2011)
12. Srinivasa, S., Jafar, S.: How much spectrum sharing is optimal in cognitive radio networks? IEEE Transactions on Wireless Communications 7, 4010–4018 (2008)
13. Wadhwa, M., Xin, C., Song, M., Park, E.: Throughput Analysis for a Contention-Based Dynamic Spectrum Sharing Model. IEEE Transactions on Wireless Communications 9(4), 1426–1433 (2010)
14. Chang, N., Liu, M.: Competitive analysis of opportunistic spectrum access strategies. In: Proc. IEEE Infocom, pp. 1535–1542 (2008)
15. Huang, S., Liu, X., Ding, Z.: Opportunistic spectrum access in cognitive radio networks. In: Proc. IEEE Infocom, pp. 1427–1435 (2008)

Fast Group Communication Scheduling in Duty-Cycled Multihop Wireless Sensor Networks*

Xiaohua Xu[1], Jiannong Cao[2], and Peng-Jun Wan[1]

[1] Illinois Institute of Technology, Chicago IL 60616, USA
[2] Hong Kong Polytechnic University, Kowloon, Hong Kong

Abstract. We study group communication scheduling in duty-cycled multi-hop wireless sensor networks. Assume that time is divided into time-slots and we group multiple consecutive time-slots into periods. Each node can transmit data at any time-slot while it only wakes up at its active time-slot of every period and thus be allowed to receive data. Under the protocol interference model, we investigate four group communication patterns, *i.e.*, broadcast, data aggregation, data gathering, and gossiping. For each pattern, we develop a delay efficient scheduling algorithm which greatly improve the current state-of-the-art algorithm. Additionally, we propose a novel and efficient design to coherently couple the wireless interference requirement and duty cycle requirement.

1 Introduction

The emergence of *wireless sensor networks (WSNs)* ushers in a period of prosperous control applications. Contingent on user requests, the control applications usually require efficient delivery of sensory data. The process of streaming data from given source nodes to given destination nodes is termed as *group communication*. Depending on the number of source nodes and destination (or sink) nodes, there are generally four group communication patterns in WSNs:

Broadcast: a source node sends a common packet to all other nodes.

Data Aggregation: a sink node collects a packet from every other node and every intermediate node combines all received packets with its own packet into a single packet of fixed-size according to some aggregation function such as *sum* and *variance* [16].

Data Collection: a sink node collects a raw packet from every other node. Data collection differs from data aggregation in the sense that no in-network processing is allowed for data collection. Thus, each node needs to transmit its raw data and relay all received data towards the sink.

Gossiping: every node broadcasts a packet to all other nodes. Gossiping is also called as all-to-all broadcast in the sense that a gossiping task can be divided into n broadcast task, *i.e.*, each of these n nodes broadcasts its own data once to all other nodes. Here n is the number of nodes in the network. From another viewpoint, a gossiping task consists

* This work was supported in part by the National Science Foundation of USA under grant CNS-0916666 and by National Natural Science Foundation of P. R. China under grant 61128005.

X. Wang et al. (Eds.): WASA 2012, LNCS 7405, pp. 197–205, 2012.

of n data collection tasks, *i.e.*, each of these n nodes collects a raw packet from every other node.

The group communication tasks often come with stringent delay constraints imposed by control applications. Here, the *delay (or latency)* for finishing a group communication task can be interpreted as the duration from the time when the first node transmits for this task, to the time when the destination node(s) receive all required data for this task. One promising way of minimizing the delay is to maximize the network throughput which is subject to the intrinsic wireless interference. A well accepted wireless interference model is the protocol interference model [5], which can serve as a useful abstraction of WSNs. A number of protocols have been proposed in the literature for group communication scheduling such as [2, 4, 6–10, 16, 18, 20]. However, those work omit the practical duty-cycling scenario where wireless nodes switch between the active state and the dormant state. In this work, we will study delay efficient group communication scheduling in duty-cycled WSNs under the protocol interference model. For each group communication task, we will develop a fast scheduling algorithm and prove that it can achieve an approximation bound that greatly improves the previous best result. Let P be the period of the given duty-cycled network, *i.e.*, the length of time it takes for the wireless nodes to go through a complete on/off cycle, we have

- For broadcast scheduling, we can achieve an approximation bound on latency of $(1 + o(1)) \cdot |P|$ while the previous best approximation bound is $17|P|$ in [11].
- For data aggregation scheduling, we can achieve an upper bound on latency of $(6\Delta + 3R + O(\log R) \cdot |P|$ while the previous best upper bound is $(\Delta + 15R - 3) \cdot |P|$ in [12]. Here R and Δ are the graph radius and the maximum node degree of the communication graph respectively.
- For data collection scheduling, we can achieve an approximation ratio of $10|P|$.
- For gossiping, we can achieve an approximation bound of $10|P|$.

For any uncoordinated duty-cycled WSN, if all nodes's active time-slots in a period are the same (the network has an utilization of at most $\frac{1}{|P|}$), each transmission costs one period. In this case, the lower-bound on the delay of finishing any group communication task is $\Omega(|P|)$. However, if nodes's active time-slots in a period are not random, we may improve the network performances by determining each node's active time-slot in advance based on its geographical locations.

The rest of the paper is organized as follows. Section 2 formulates the group communication scheduling problem in WSNs. In Section 3, we construct a universal routing tree for group communication scheduling. Section 4, 5, 6 and 7 are devoted to scheduling algorithm design for broadcast, data aggregation, data collection, and gossiping respectively. We present an energy-efficient unified framework for coupling the addressing of wireless interference and duty-cycling requirement in Section 8. We review the related results in Section 9 and conclude the paper in Section 10.

2 Network Model

Consider a WSN modeled as a communication graph $G = (V, E)$ in a two-dimensional Euclidean plane, where V is the set of all sensor nodes and E is the set of communication links. A node $u \in V$ can transmit data to another node $v \in V$ if v lies within the transmission range of node u. We assume uniform transmission range normalized to one. Thus, the communication graph turns out to be a unit disk graph G, *i.e.*, a communication link exists between any pair of nodes if and only if their distance is at most one. We will focus on the Protocol Interference Model (PrIM) [5]: each node u has an *interference range* ρ such that any node v will be interfered by the signal from u if $\|uv\| \leq \rho$ and node v is *not* the intended receiver of the transmission from u. Similar to most of the existing work such as [16], [20], we assume that $\rho = 1$ for simplicity.

In a duty-cycled scenario, time is divided into time-slots and every consecutive $|P|$ time-slots are grouped into a period. Each node chooses one active time-slot in P randomly and independently. Each node can transmit data at any time-slot while it only wakes up at its active time-slot of every period and thus be allowed to receive data.

Given a group communication task (*i.e.*, broadcast, aggregation, collection, or gossiping) under this duty-cycled scenario, the objective is to design routing and a *transmission schedule* to finish this task with minimum delay. Here the transmission schedule specify the node activities and can be interpreted as an assignment of the transmission time-slots to all nodes, *i.e.*, a mapping $V \mapsto 2^N$. Then a valid communication schedule in $G(V, E)$ with delay L can be defined as a sequence of sender sets $S_1, S_2, \cdots, S_L$ such that if all nodes transmit according to this sequence, this group communication task can be finished successfully. The scheduling problem for broadcast, data aggregation and gossiping in the duty-cycled scenario has been proven to be NP-hard in [11], [12] and [14] respectively.

3 Routing Tree

The construction of routing tree relies on a concept of Connected Dominating Set (CDS). Please refer to a recent survey [1] and references therein on CDS. In a graph $G = (V, E)$, a subset V' of V is a dominating set (DS) if each node in V is either in V' or adjacent to some node in V'. Nodes in V' are called *dominators*, whereas nodes not in V' are called *dominatees*. A subset C of V is a CDS if C is a dominating set and C induces a connected subgraph.

The routing tree rooted at a node u is constructed as follows. Starting from u, we perform *breadth-first-search (BFS)* over G to build the BFS tree T_{BFS}; We next select the *maximal independent set (MIS)* of T_{BFS} by an existing approach [15], and use this MIS as dominating set; We connect MIS by using some nodes (*i.e.* connectors) to form a CDS G_c of G; For each dominatee v not in G_c, we connect it to G_c by adding a link from v to one of its neighboring dominators. The about operations result in a routing tree T. It is easy to verify that the depth of T is at most $R_u + 1$, where R_u is the hop distance between the root u and and its farthest node.

We will associate the tree T with *ranks* of the nodes by using the method in [9, 16]. We proceed ranking layer-by-layer in the bottom-up manner. Initially, $rank(v) = 0$ for each node v in the bottom layer. For each layer i from R down to 1, for each node u in level i, we assign the ranks as follows: if u has no child, $rank(u)$ is set to zero; if u has at least one child, let r be the maximum rank of its children. If u has only one child of rank r, then $rank(u)$ is set to r; otherwise $rank(u)$ is set to $r + 1$. As observed in [9, 16], each node has rank no more than its parent in T, and for each node $v \in V$, we have $rank(v) = O(\log |V|)$.

4   Broadcast Scheduling

We first construct a routing tree rooted at the source node and ranks of nodes. Then, the broadcast scheduling process consists of two phases: (1) broadcast data to all nodes in the CDS, (2) broadcast data from dominators to dominatees.

In the first phase, for each integer $0 \leq i < R$ (node level) and $0 \leq j < r$ (rank) where R is the depth of the routing tree and r is the rank of the distinguished source node, set V_{ij} to be the set of nodes in layer i with rank j, and V'_{ij} to be the set of their children. We perform scheduling for the pair of node subsets (V_{ij}, V'_{ij}) as follows. Let W_0 be the set of parents of nodes in V'_{ij} with rank j. We apply the algorithm ILBS in [9] to generate a $(V_{ij}, V'_{ij} \setminus Inf(W_0))$-schedule $(W_1, W_2, \cdots, W_{16})$ where $Inf(W_0)$ is the set of nodes in $V \setminus W_0$ each of which has exactly one neighbor in W_0. Then, for each $0 \leq k \leq 16$, all nodes in W_k transmit in the $(i + 51(r - j) + 3k)$-th period when their children are awake.

In the second phase, we schedule the transmissions by the dominators as follows: partition the set V' of dominators into 2-*independent sets* $\{V'_i : 1 \leq i \leq 12\}$ [9]. Here 2-independent set means that the pairwise distance of nodes in this set are all greater than 2. The dominators in V'_i transmit in the i-th period when their children are awake.

Next, we analyze the performance of our broadcast scheduling algorithm.

Theorem 1. *The proposed algorithm for broadcast scheduling produces a correct broadcast schedule of latency $(R + \log R)|P|$ where R is the graph radius of the communication graph and P is a period in a duty-cycled network.*

Proof. The correctness proof involves two arguments: (1) any pair of concurrent transmitting nodes will not conflict with each other, (2) any node will receive the data before it transmits. Both arguments are similar to [9].

In the first phase, each node in the CDS needs $|P|$ to transmit its message to all the children, thus this phase costs at most $(R + 51r)|P|$. By the folklore area argument, we have that the size of the CDS is bounded by $O(R^2)$. This implies that $r = O(\log R)$. Thus, this phase has latency at most $(R + O(\log R)) \cdot |P|$. In the second phase, the broadcast schedule takes at most $12|P|$ time-slots. Thus, the theorem follows.

The lower bound for the broadcast scheduling problem is R. The lower bound can be achieved when the network topology is a chain and the active time-slot of any node is exactly one time-slot after that of its parent in the routing tree. Thus, we have the following theorem.

Theorem 2. *The proposed algorithm for broadcast scheduling can achieve $(1 + o(1)) \cdot |P|$-approximation bound where P is a period in a duty-cycled network.*

5   Data Aggregation Scheduling

We first construct a routing tree (inward-arborescence) rooted at the sink node and ranks of nodes. Then, the data aggregation scheduling process consists of two phases: (1) dominatees transmit data to dominators, (2) dominators route data towards the root.

The first phase consists of one-hop data transmissions from dominatees to dominators. We will split this phase into multiple rounds. In each round, for every dominator u, we first select a link $\overrightarrow{vu}$ from one of its neighboring dominatees to itself. Assume all selected links form a set $\mathcal{L}$. We then transmit links in $\mathcal{L}$. It is easy to verify that each round costs at most $6|P|$ time-slots, where P is the period. Since each dominator has at most Δ neighboring dominatees, there are at most Δ rounds. Thus, the first phase costs at most $6\Delta \cdot |P|$ time-slots.

In the second phase, we will perform data transmissions in a pipelined manner. For each node u, let i be its level, let j be its rank, and let a be its active time-slot in a period, l is the label received by the link $\overrightarrow{uv}$ by the algorithm IMC in [16]. If u is a dominator, we will assign a time-slot of $2((R - i) + 44j + 4(l - 1)) \cdot |P| + a$ to transmit; If u is connector, we will assign a time-slot of $2((R - i) + 44j + 4(l - 1)) \cdot |P| + |P| + a$ to transmit. In our method, all dominators transmit at even periods only, and all connectors transmit at odd periods only; the time-disjoint property can avoid conflicts between nodes from different groups. It is easy to prove that our method can avoid interference (similar to [16]) and this phase costs at most $(2R + O(\log R)) \cdot |P|$ time-slots.

Theorem 3. *The proposed algorithm for data aggregation scheduling produces an aggregation schedule of latency at most* $(6\Delta + 3R + O(\log R)) \cdot |P|$.

6   Data Collection Scheduling

We first construct a routing tree T rooted at the sink node. Our algorithm then relies on a labeling of the edges of T. We first order all nodes in V in the decreasing order of depth in T. Ties are broken arbitrarily. Assume the resulting sequence is:

$$\sigma \longleftarrow < v_1, v_2, \cdots, v_n > .$$

We assign the j-th edge in the tree path from the sink node to v_i with a label $2(i-1)+j$. For an edge connecting v_i and its parent, the number of assigned labels is equal to the number of descendants of v_i in T. If v_i is connector (dominator), all labels received by the edge between v_i and its parent are odd (even). The edges across two consecutive layers of the dominating tree receive distinct labels. Considering a node v_i, let h be the length of the path from the sink node to v_i. The maximum label assigned to the edges in the path from the sink node to v_i is $2(i - 1) + h$. It is sufficient to show that $2(i - 1) + h \leq 2n - 3$, *i.e.*, the largest label is $2n - 3$.

For each number k, let E_k denote the set of edges of T which contains a label k, and A_k denote the links in the inward s-arborescence oriented from the edges in E_k. Here s denotes the sink node. Then, if k is odd (respectively, even), all the receiving (respectively, transmitting) endpoints of links in A_k are dominators. Moreover, every dominator is incident to at most one link in A_k.

Then, the transmission schedule are partitioned into $2n - 3$ rounds. The k-th round ($1 \leq k \leq 2n - 3$) is scheduled as follows. We color all dominators such that for each non-dominating node, all its one-hop neighboring dominators receive distinct colors. Since at most 5 dominators can be adjacent to a common node, the number of colors used is at most 5. For each link, assume its dominator endpoint receives the i-th color and the active time-slot for duty cycling of the corresponding sender is a, then this link is scheduled in the $i \cdot |P| + a$-th time-slot of the k-th round. Thus, each round takes at most $5|P|$ time-slots. It is easy to verify the correctness of this transmission schedule, in addition, the schedule has a delay of at most $5(2n - 3) \cdot |P|$.

As $n - 1$ is a trivial lower bound on the delay for data collection, the approximation ratio of the transmission schedule presented is at most $10|P|$.

Theorem 4. *The proposed scheduling algorithm for data collection achieves an approximation bound of* $10|P|$.

Unbounded Packet-Size Model: Since the packet-size can be arbitrarily large, we can adopt our transmission schedule for data aggregation (described in Section 5 to finish this data collection task under the unbounded packet-size model.

7 Data Gossiping Scheduling

Let the *graph center* of the network be a node v_c such that the hop distance of the path from node v_c to the node farthest from v_c in the network reaches minimum. We will use v_c as the root to construct a routing tree. The gossiping scheduling process consists of two phases. In the first phase, the graph center v_c collects data from all the other nodes. We will apply our transmission scheduling for data collection presented in Section 6. In the second phase, the graph center broadcasts all data one by one to all other nodes.

We first color all dominators such that for each non-dominating node, all its one-hop neighboring dominators receive distinct colors. The coloring can ensure that all dominators with the monotone color can transmit (or receive) data concurrently without conflict. Since at most 5 dominators can be adjacent to a common node, the number of colors used is at most 5. By proper renumbering of the colors, we assume that v_c has the first color. We group the time-slots into $10|P|$-slot frames. In each frame, the first $5|P|$ slots form a dominator sub-frame, and the remaining $5|P|$ slots form a connector subframe. Only dominators (respectively, connectors) are allowed to transmit in the dominator (respectively, connector) subframe in each frame. The node v_c transmits one packet in each frame. Upon receiving a packet in a dominator subframe, for each connector, assume the color of its child dominator is i $(0 \le i < 5)$, assume the active time-slot of its child dominator is i in a period is a, this connector transmits the received packet in the time-slot of $(5+i) \cdot |P| + a$; clearly, this transmission occurs in a connector subframe. Upon receiving a packet in a connector subframe, for each dominator with color i $(0 \le i < 5)$, assume the active time-slot of its child dominator is i in a period is a, then this dominator transmits in the time-slot of $i \cdot |P| + a$. Clearly, this transmission occurs in a dominator subframe.

It is easy to verify the correctness of the above schedule. We then bound the delay of the second phase. After $n - 1$ frames, v_c transmits the last packet. After another $R + 1$ frames where R is the graph radius, the last packet reaches all nodes. Therefore, the total number of time-slots takes by the second phase is at most

$$10|P| \cdot ((n-1) + (R+1)) = 10(n+R) \cdot |P|.$$

The first phase takes at most $5(2n - 3) \cdot |P|$ time-slots. Hence, the total number of time-slots taken by the two phases is at most

$$10(n + R)|P| + 5(2n - 3) \cdot |P| = (20n + 10R - 15) \cdot |P|.$$

Theorem 5. *The proposed scheduling algorithm for gossiping can achieve an upper bound on delay of* $(20n + 10R - 15) \cdot |P|$.

Clearly, the minimum gossiping latency of G is at least $n - 1 + R$ where R is the graph radius of G, thus we have:

Theorem 6. *The proposed scheduling algorithm for gossiping can achieve an approximation bound of* $20|P|$.

Unbounded Packet-Size Model: Under this model, we can just perform broadcast only once instead of n times where n is the number of nodes. The broadcast phase, the graph center will transmit the combined data of the packets from all nodes only once.

8 Coupling Duty Cycle Requirement and Interference Requirement

In Section 1, we have showed that for any uncoordinated wireless networks, if all nodes's active time-slots in a period are the same, then the network has an utilization of at most $\frac{1}{|P|}$. Thus, when $|P|$ becomes large, the duty cycle requirement will cause the network performance to be very bad. On the other hand, wireless interference requirement also limits the network performance. We will propose a novel design that can address both challenges simultaneously and greatly improve the network performances such as energy-efficiency and delay. Our design will couple interference requirement and duty cycle requirement tightly.

Let $|P|$ be the length of a period. Let $K = \lceil \sqrt{|P|} \rceil$. We will employ a grid partition of the deployment plane. The vertical lines $x = i \cdot \ell$ for $i \in \mathbb{Z}$ and horizontal lines $y = j \cdot \ell$ for $j \in \mathbb{Z}$ partition the planes into half-open and half-closed grids of side ℓ (here $\mathbb{Z}$ represents the integer set):

$$\{[i\ell, (i+1)\ell) \times [j\ell, (j+1)\ell) : i, j \in \mathbb{Z}\}.$$

Next, we color the grids such that one grid among every K^2 grids is assigned with the same color. Each node will determine its active time-slot of a duty-cycled scheduling period based on its geographical locations. At the same time, if at most one node from every grid with a monotone color transmits simultaneously, the transmissions are interference-free subject to the wireless interference requirement.

We then index the colors and denote σ_g as the color of grid g ($\sigma_g \in \{0, 1, \cdots, K^2 - 1\}$). Note that a number of methods have been proposed in the literature to approximate the geometric locations of nodes. For each node $u \in V$, let σ_g be the color index of the grid g where p lies, we then assign σ_g as an active time-slot in each duty cycle period for this node u. For each of the above group communications, we can perform a partition-based scheduling and the delay will be greatly reduced.

9   Related Work

We first conduct literature review on delay efficient group communication scheduling in WSNs. For broadcast scheduling, Chlamtac and Kutten [3] proved the NP-hardness of finding a minimum makespan collision-free broadcast scheduling for general graphs, even in the absence of wireless interference. Gandhi *et al.* [4] studied the broadcast scheduling problem for multi-hop wireless networks with bounded transmission range. They present a simple algorithm which guarantees the makespan and the number of retransmissions to be within 468 times their respective optimal values. Huang*et al.* [9] proposed three approximation algorithms for the broadcast scheduling problem.

Data Aggregation/Collection Scheduling with minimum delay has been proven to be NP-hard [2] and well studied in [10, 16, 18–20].

Huang *et al.* [7], [8] studied minimum-latency gossiping in multi-hop wireless networks. Wan *et al.* [17] studied gossiping scheduling under the approximated physical interference model. Jiao *et al.* [13, 14] studied minimum-latency gossiping in duty-cycle wireless networks.

There are some most recent work on group communication scheduling in uncoordinated duty-cycled wireless networks such as [11] for broadcast scheduling, [12] for data aggregation scheduling and [14] for gossiping scheduling in the duty-cycled scenario respectively.

10   Conclusion

We proposed a suite of efficient scheduling algorithms for fast group communication in duty-cycled multi-hop wireless networks under the protocol interference model. The proposed algorithms can achieve the best constant approximation bounds compared to the existing work. We also proposed a novel design to coherently couple the interference requirement and duty cycle requirement which can greatly improve the network performance. As future work, it will be interesting to modify our scheduling algorithms to some other wireless interference models.

References

1. Blum, J., Ding, M., Thaeler, A., Cheng, X.: Connected dominating set in sensor networks and manets. In: Handbook of Combinatorial Optimization, pp. 329–369 (2005)
2. Chen, X., Hu, X., Zhu, J.: Minimum Data Aggregation Time Problem in Wireless Sensor Networks. In: Jia, X., Wu, J., He, Y. (eds.) MSN 2005. LNCS, vol. 3794, pp. 133–142. Springer, Heidelberg (2005)
3. Chlamtac, I., Kutten, S.: On broadcasting in radio networks–problem analysis and protocol design. IEEE Transactions on Communications, 1240–1246 (2002)
4. Gandhi, R., Mishra, A., Parthasarathy, S.: Minimizing broadcast latency and redundancy in ad hoc networks. IEEE/ACM Transactions on Networking, 840–851 (2008)
5. Gupta, P., Kumar, P.: The capacity of wireless networks. IEEE Transactions on Information Theory 46(2), 388–404 (2000)
6. Hong, J., Cao, J., Li, W., Lu, S., Chen, D.: Sleeping schedule-aware minimum latency broadcast in wireless ad hoc networks. In: IEEE ICC, pp. 1–5. IEEE (2009)

7. Huang, S., Du, H., Park, E.: Minimum-latency gossiping in multi-hop wireless networks. In: ACM MobiHoc, pp. 323–330 (2008)
8. Huang, S., Wan, P., Du, H., Park, E.: Minimum latency gossiping in radio networks. IEEE TPDS, 790–800 (2010)
9. Huang, S., Wan, P., Jia, X., Du, H., Shang, W.: Minimum-latency broadcast scheduling in wireless ad hoc networks. In: IEEE INFOCOM, pp. 733–739 (2007)
10. Huang, S., Wan, P., Vu, C., Li, Y., Yao, F.: Nearly Constant Approximation for Data Aggregation Scheduling in Wireless Sensor Networks. In: IEEE INFOCOM, pp. 366–372 (2007)
11. Jiao, X., Lou, W., Ma, J., Cao, J., Wang, X., Zhou, X.: Duty-cycle-aware minimum latency broadcast scheduling in multi-hop wireless networks. In: IEEE ICDCS, pp. 754–763 (2010)
12. Jiao, X., Lou, W., Wang, X., Cao, J., Xu, M., Zhou, X.: Data aggregation scheduling in uncoordinated duty-cycled wireless sensor networks under protocol interference model. In: Ad Hoc and Sensor Wireless Networks
13. Jiao, X., Lou, W., Wang, X., Ma, J., Cao, J., Zhou, X.: Interference-Aware Gossiping Scheduling in Uncoordinated Duty-Cycled Multi-hop Wireless Networks. In: Pandurangan, G., Anil Kumar, V.S., Ming, G., Liu, Y., Li, Y. (eds.) WASA 2010. LNCS, vol. 6221, pp. 192–202. Springer, Heidelberg (2010)
14. Jiao, X., Lou, W., Wang, X., Ma, J., Cao, J., Zhou, X.: On interference-aware gossiping in uncoordinated duty-cycled multi-hop wireless networks. In: Ad Hoc Networks (2011)
15. Wan, P.-J., Alzoubi, K.M., Frieder, O.: Distributed construction of connected dominating set in wireless ad hoc networks. In: IEEE INFOCOM (2002)
16. Wan, P., Huang, S., Wang, L., Wan, Z., Jia, X.: Minimum-latency aggregation scheduling in multihop wireless networks. In: ACM MobiHoc, pp. 185–194 (2009)
17. Wan, P., Wang, L., Frieder, O.: Fast group communications in multihop wireless networks subject to physical interference. In: IEEE MASS, pp. 526–533 (2009)
18. Xu, X., Li, X.Y., Mao, X., Tang, S., Wang, S.: An improved approximation algorithm for data aggregation in multi-hop wireless sensor networks. IEEE TPDS (2011)
19. Xu, X., Li, X.Y., Wan, P.J., Tang, S.: Efficient Scheduling for Periodic Aggregation Queries in Multihop Sensor Networks. To Appear in IEEE/ACM Transactions on Networking
20. Yu, B., Li, J., Li, Y.: Distributed Data Aggregation Scheduling in Wireless Sensor Networks. In: INFOCOM (2009)

Reliable Cooperative Sensing
in Cognitive Networks
(Invited Paper)

Mai Abdelhakim, Jian Ren, and Tongtong Li*

Department of Electrical & Computer Engineering,
Michigan State University, East Lansing, MI 48824, USA
{abdelhak,renjian,tongli}@egr.msu.edu

Abstract. In this paper, we consider reliable cooperative spectrum sensing in cognitive networks under the Spectrum Sensing Data Falsification (SSDF) attacks. One effective method to mitigate the SSDF attacks is the q-out-of-m fusion scheme, where the final decision is based on q sensing reports from m polled users. In this paper, first, we derive the asymptotic behavior of the fusion scheme as the network size increases. It is found that the false alarm rate decreases exponentially as the network size increases, even if the percentage of malicious users remains fixed. Second, we propose an iterative approach to obtain the best scheme parameters that minimizes the false alarm rate and enforces the miss detection constraint. Third, we discuss different attack scenarios and propose a malicious user detection method to further improve the performance. It is shown that by exploiting the malicious user detection scheme, the system performance is improved significantly under various attacks.

Keywords: cognitive networks, cooperative sensing, malicious attack, data fusion.

1 Introduction

Spectrum is the most precious resource for communication networks. Due to the wide range of existing and emerging applications, spectrum scarcity has become an urgent problem. Meanwhile, according to the Federal Communication Commission FCC, the utilization of the licensed spectrum bands in space and time has shown to be between 15% and 85% [1]. The spectrum scarcity and underutilization issues have motivated the development of a new paradigm based on dynamic spectrum access and known as cognitive networks [2]. In cognitive networks the spectrum is used opportunistically by secondary users when it is not utilized by the licensed (primary) users. To do this, the spectrum is sensed and the spectrum holes are identified prior to transmissions.

In order to improve the accuracy of the spectrum sensing process, cooperative spectrum sensing was proposed [3], where multiple cognitive radios share their

---

* Corresponding author.

X. Wang et al. (Eds.): WASA 2012, LNCS 7405, pp. 206–217, 2012.
© Springer-Verlag Berlin Heidelberg 2012

sensing information with the fusion center, which makes the final decision accordingly. However, the reliability of the cooperative sensing is threatened by the presence of malicious attacks. One serious threat is the Spectrum Sensing Data Falsification attack (SSDF) [4]. In the SSDF attack, some authenticated users are compromised and intentionally report false sensing information. This would lead to a low spectrum utilization and/or high interference to the primary system. In order to mitigate the SSDF attack several approaches has been proposed in [5–9]. In [5–7], the sensing reports (energy levels) are weighted according to a certain weighting functions, and the weights are updated based on the radios instantaneous behavior.

In [8, 9], we proposed a simple, yet effective, hard fusion rule based on the q-out-of-m scheme. In the q-out-of-m scheme, the final decision is based on q sensing reports out of m polled users. In [9], we presented a linear approach to obtain the scheme parameters, which significantly reduces the computational complexity of the optimal exhaustive search. In this paper, first, the asymptotic performance of the linear approach is analyzed and the effect of the network size on the detection accuracy is derived. It is found that the false alarm rate decreases exponentially as the network size increases, even if the percentage of malicious users is unchanged. Second, we extend our work by proposing a modified linear approach that provides near-optimal solution. As opposed to the direct-linear approach, the modified approach enforces the miss detection constraint through an iterative method. The convergence of the modified linear approach has shown to be fast. Third, we present different attack strategies and propose a scheme to detect malicious users. With malicious node detection, the system performance is improved significantly under various attacks. Several simulation examples are carried out to demonstrate the effectiveness of the proposed schemes.

2   Problem Formulation

We assume that the network consists of n active users including k malicious users. We refer to n as the network size. We first assume that malicious users can detect the primary signal with no errors and always report false information. More general attack strategies will be discussed in Section 4. The percentage of malicious users k/n is denoted by α. Each node in the network performs spectrum sensing and reports its one bit hard decision result to a central node (fusion center) through a control channel. The control channel is assumed to be error free. The sensing result is either '1' which means that the primary user is present, or '0' which means that the band is not used by the primary. All users experience independent and identically distributed (i.i.d) fading with the same average signal to noise ratio (SNR), such that each user has a probability of false alarm P_f, and a probability of detection P_d.

The fusion center is then responsible for making the final decision based on the received sensing reports from all users. α is assumed to be known, or can be estimated, at the fusion center. The q-out-of-m scheme is an effective hard fusion rule that can mitigate the SSDF attacks, as will be illustrated in the next subsection.

2.1   q-out-of-m Fusion Scheme

Among the hard fusion rules, the q-out-of-m scheme can achieve a good compromise between minimizing the false alarm rate and satisfy the miss detection constraint. The fusion center uses the q-out-of-m rule to decide whether the band is idle or busy based on the sensing reports. In the q-out-of-m scheme, the fusion center randomly polls m out of n users and relies on q-out-of-m rule for final decision making (the fusion center decides that a primary is present if q or more out of the m polled users report '1') [8]. The main objective is to minimize the overall false alarm rate (Q_f) while keeping the overall miss detection (Q_m) below a certain predefined value β. Hence, it is desired to get the optimum parameters m and q that can achieve the objectives. The problem can be formulated as follows:

$$\min_{m,q} Q_f(m,q); \tag{1}$$
$$s.t. \ \ Q_m(m,q) \leq \beta;$$
$$s.t. \ \ 1 \leq q \leq m \leq n; \ \ q, m \in \mathbb{N}.$$

In order to obtain a closed form expressions for Q_f and Q_m, we define $P_{k,n-k}^{d,m-d}$ as the probability of polling $m-d$ out of $n-k$ benign users and d out of k malicious users. That is, $P_{k,n-k}^{d,m-d} = \frac{\binom{k}{d}\binom{n-k}{m-d}}{\binom{n}{m}}$

According to our system model, the false alarm rate is expressed in (2), where three different scenarios are implied [8]:

$$Q_f = \begin{cases} \displaystyle\sum_{\substack{d=\max(0,\\ m+k-n)}}^{k} P_{k,n-k}^{d,m-d} \sum_{i=q-d}^{m-d} \binom{m-d}{i} P_f^i (1-P_f)^{(m-d-i)}, & k \leq q; \\[4mm] 1, & m+k-n > q; \\[4mm] \displaystyle\sum_{d=q}^{\min(k,m)} P_{k,n-k}^{d,m-d} + \sum_{\substack{d=\max(0,\\ m+k-n)}}^{q-1} P_{k,n-k}^{d,m-d} \sum_{i=q-d}^{m-d} \binom{m-d}{i} P_f^i (1-P_f)^{m-d-i}, & \substack{k>q \ and \\ m+k-n \leq q}. \end{cases} \tag{2}$$

Scenario 1: $k \leq q$. When the number of malicious users is less than or equal to q (consequently $k \leq m$), there would be some benign users involved, among the m polled users, in the final decision making. If the m polled users contain d out of the k malicious users, then the false alarm occurs when there are $q-d$ or more benign users sending false alarms.

Scenario 2: $m+k-n > q$. When the number of malicious users is large enough to make $m+k-n > q$ (Since $m-n \leq 0$, this implies $k > q$), there are so few benign users such that among m polled users, there are at least $m-(n-k) > q$ malicious users. In this case, false alarm happens with probability 1, leading to spectrum waste. This is because the secondary user will not use the channel even if there is a white space. Thus, q should not be too small.

Scenario 3: $k > q$ but $m + k - n \leq q$. When the number of malicious users is moderate, the false alarm probability depends on how many malicious users are polled. If among m polled users, there are at least q malicious users included, then the secondary system is jammed regardless of the behavior of other benign users. Otherwise, if there are $d < q$ malicious users polled, then false alarm occurs when there are at least $q - d$ benign users reporting erroneous results.

The miss detection probability Q_m can be expressed in terms of the detection probability Q_d, such that $Q_m = 1 - Q_d$. In q-out-of-m scheme, Q_d can be expressed as follows:

$$Q_d = \begin{cases} 0, & \text{if } n - k < q; \\ \\ \displaystyle\sum_{\substack{d=\max(0, \\ m+k-n)}}^{\min(k,m-q)} P_{k,n-k}^{d,m-d} \sum_{i=q}^{m-d} \binom{m-d}{i} P_d^i (1 - P_d)^{m-d-i}, \\ \quad \text{if } n - k \geq q. \end{cases} \tag{3}$$

It is shown from (3) that if q is greater than the number of benign users, then the primary signal will never be detected (i.e. $Q_d = 0$). This case will result in severe interference to the primary system. Thus, q should not be too large. In the case that the number of benign users is greater than q, then at least there should be q users reporting the presence of the primary signal in order to be able to detect it. The number of malicious users $d = max(0, m+k-n)$ indicates that when the number of users being polled, m, is greater than that of the benign users, then there are at least $m - (n - k)$ copies of malicious reports received by the fusion center.

3   Simplified Collaborative Sensing Schemes

In this section, first, we highlight the motivation to the simplified collaborative sensing schemes. Then, we discuss two simplified approaches to obtain the q-out-of-m scheme parameters, namely: the linear approach, and the modified linear approach. The asymptotic performance of the linear approaches is also derived.

3.1   Motivation

We aim at obtaining the best scheme parameters for large network sizes and derive the asymptotic performance of the q-out-of-m scheme as the network size increases. In the optimal q-out-of-m scheme, exhaustive search is conducted to obtain the scheme parameters (m and q). The complexity of the optimal approach is $O(n^2)$. Therefore, it is computationally unfeasible to get the optimal m and q for large network sizes using the optimal exhaustive approach. However, when we search for the optimal parameters at relatively small network sizes with $\beta = 0.01$, the following two main observations are made [9]:

Observation 1: The optimal m is almost independent of the percentage of malicious users. In fact, it is equal or very close to n, as shown in Figure 1(a). One intuitive interpretation for this is that since the polling is random, it is better to know the decisions of all the users.

Observation 2: The optimal value of q, denoted by q_o, also follows an approximately linear function of n with different slopes depending on the percentage of the malicious users, as shown in Figure 1(b).

Motivated by these observations, we propose simplified approaches to obtain the q-out-of-m parameters for large network sizes. This will be illustrated in the following subsection.

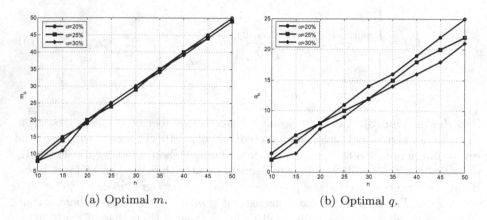

(a) Optimal m.   (b) Optimal q.

Fig. 1. The optimal parameters m and q obtained using exhaustive search

3.2   A Linear Approach

We showed in the previous subsection that the optimal m and q can be approximated as linear functions of n, with m almost equals to n. We exploit these observations by setting $m = n$ and using the following linear function of n to obtain q [9]:

$$\hat{q}_{n,\alpha} = \lceil q_{n_0,\alpha} + S_o(\alpha)(n - n_0) \rceil, \tag{4}$$

where $S_o(\alpha)$ is the slope of the optimal q_o versus n curve given that the percentage of the malicious users is α, $\hat{q}_{n,\alpha}$ is the suboptimal q value at a network size n, and $q_{n_o,\alpha}$ is the optimal q value at a relatively small network size n_0 and it serves as a reference point. Both $\hat{q}_{n,\alpha}$ and $q_{n_o,\alpha}$ are at α percent of malicious users. $\lceil x \rceil$ is the smallest integer larger than or equal to x.

We can get the optimal scheme parameters at relatively small network sizes, and use them as reference points. These optimal (m, q) pairs for the different network sizes and α ratios, can be obtained and stored in a look-up table, then used to get the suboptimal scheme parameters for large network sizes. It is worth mentioning that if the channel conditions change, the individual P_f and P_m would change and consequently the optimal scheme parameters will be different.

In this case, the slope and the reference points would change, and the simplified approach should be applied with the new settings. In practical situations, a periodically update of the reference points and related slopes would be required.

3.3   Performance Analysis of the Linear Approach

In this subsection, we show that the performance of the linear q-out-of-m scheme improves almost exponentially as the network size increases. We also formulate the change in the overall miss detection probability when the simplified approach is employed as compared to the optimal q-out-of-m scheme.

Proposition: For a fixed and a relatively low malicious users ratio α, the overall false alarm rate using the linear q-out-of-m approach diminishes exponentially as the network size n goes to infinity. More Specifically, as n is large enough, we can choose q such that $P_f < \frac{q-k}{n-k} \leq 2P_f$, then $Q_f \leq exp\left(-\frac{(Bn+C)^2}{An}\right)$, where A, B and C are constants.

In order to prove the statement above, we consider the simplified approach where we set $m = n$, then it follows that $d = k$ and the term $P_{k,n-k}^{d,m-d}$ is equal to one. In the case where $q \geq k$, the false alarm probability Q_f can be expressed as:

$$Q_f = \sum_{i=q-k}^{n-k} \binom{n-k}{i} P_f^i (1 - P_f)^{n-k-i}. \tag{5}$$

It is clear that Q_f is the summation over a binomial probability density function with parameters P_f and $n - k$, where the random variable is the number of benign users having false alarm. Recall that the Chernoff bound [10] states that if X is a binomial random variable with mean μ, then:

$$Pr\left(X \geq (1 + \delta)\mu\right) < e^{-\mu\delta^2/3} \qquad \text{for } 0 < \delta \leq 1. \tag{6}$$

Let the random variable X be the number of benign users sending false alarm, then $\mu = (n-k)P_f$. Therefore, $Q_f = Pr(X > q-k)$. By setting $(1+\delta)\mu = q-k$, we get $\delta = \frac{q-k}{(n-k)P_f} - 1$. When $P_f < \frac{q-k}{n-k} \leq 2P_f$, we have $0 < \delta \leq 1$. It then follows from (6) that:

$$Q_f \leq \exp\left[-\left(\frac{q-k}{P_f(n-k)} - 1\right)^2 (n-k)\frac{P_f}{3}\right] \tag{7}$$

Let $q = \hat{q}_{n,\alpha}$ and $\hat{q}_{n,\alpha} = q_{n_o,\alpha} + (n - n_o)S_o(\alpha)$ and assuming that the percentage of the malicious users is fixed, Q_f can be bounded as follows:

$$Q_f \leq \exp\left[-\frac{[q_{n_o,\alpha} - n_oS_o(\alpha) + n(S_o(\alpha) - P_f(1-\alpha)) - k]^2}{3P_fn(1-\alpha)}\right] \tag{8}$$

Let $A = 3P_f(1 - \alpha)$, $B = S_o(\alpha) - P_f(1 - \alpha) - \alpha$ and $C = q_{n_o,\alpha} - n_o S_o(\alpha)$, then (8) can be rewritten as:

$$Q_f \leq \exp\left[-\frac{(C + nB)^2}{An}\right],\tag{9}$$

where A, B and C are constants. That proves the proposition.

Remark: When the network size $n \to \infty$, then it follows from (9) that $Q_f \to 0$, which implies that for a fixed α, we can improve the performance significantly by increasing the network size.

In addition to the low false alarm rate, the simplified approach should also ensure low miss detection probability. If $q_{n_1,\alpha}$ is the optimal parameter obtained by exhaustive search at large network size n_1. Again, $q_{n_1,\alpha}$ is unfeasible to be obtained and a suboptimal $\hat{q}_{n_1,\alpha}$ is used instead as mentioned earlier. For a fixed malicious users ratio α and network size n_1, we consider possible increase in the miss detection probability as a result of using the simplified approach. The miss detection probabilities obtained using the linear and optimal q-out-of-m schemes are denoted by Q_{m_s} and Q_{m_o}, respectively. By setting $m = n_1$, we get:

$$Q_{m_s} = 1 - \sum_{i=q_{n_1,\alpha}+\Delta q_{n_1,\alpha}}^{n_1-\alpha n_1} \binom{n_1 - \alpha n_1}{i} P_d^i (1 - P_d)^{n_1-\alpha n_1-i},\tag{10}$$

and

$$Q_{m_o} = 1 - \sum_{i=q_{n_1,\alpha}}^{n_1-\alpha n_1} \binom{n_1 - \alpha n_1}{i} P_d^i (1 - P_d)^{n_1-\alpha n_1-i},\tag{11}$$

where $\Delta q_{n_1,\alpha} = \hat{q}_{n_1,\alpha} - q_{n_1,\alpha}$. Knowing that Q_{m_o} satisfies the problem constraint, we define $\Delta Q_m = Q_{m_s} - Q_{m_o}$ as the increase in the miss detection probability. Therefore, ΔQ_m is expressed as:

$$\Delta Q_m = \sum_{i=q_{n_1,\alpha}}^{q_{n_1,\alpha}+\Delta q_{n_1,\alpha}-1} \binom{n_1 - \alpha n_1}{i} P_d^i (1 - P_d)^{n_1-\alpha n_1-i}.\tag{12}$$

ΔQ_m is required to be as small as possible to keep the miss detection below the predefined limit. It is noted that if $\Delta q_{n_1,\alpha} \to 0$, $\Delta Q_m \to 0$ and $Q_{m_s} \to Q_{m_o}$. However, it is hard to obtain ΔQ_m, since $q_{n_1,\alpha}$ does not have a closed form expression. We modify the linear approach to enforce the miss detection constraint as will be illustrated in the next subsection.

3.4   Modification on the Linear Approach

To ensure that the scheme parameter $\hat{q}_{n,\alpha}$, obtained using the linear approximation, results in the lowest false alarm rate and satisfies the miss detection

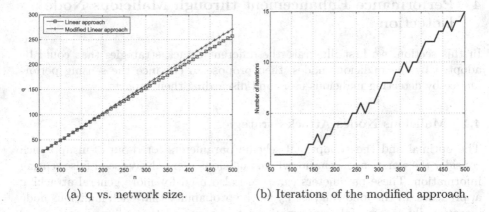

(a) q vs. network size.   (b) Iterations of the modified approach.

Fig. 2. The modified linear approach at $\alpha = 25\%$

constraint in (1), we propose to modify the linear approach using an iterative method to find $\hat{q}_{n,\alpha}$. This algorithm works as follows:

1. Set $m = n$ and use the linear approximation in (4) as an initial value for $\hat{q}_{n,\alpha}$.
2. Calculate the miss detection probability using (3).
3. Increase $\hat{q}_{n,\alpha}$ to $\hat{q}_{n,\alpha} + 1$ if the miss detection is below the predefined β. Then, go to step 2.
4. Decrease $\hat{q}_{n,\alpha}$ to $\hat{q}_{n,\alpha} - 1$ if the miss detection is above the predefined β. Then, go to step 2.
5. Terminate the iterations when the largest $\hat{q}_{n,\alpha}$ that meets the miss detection constraint is obtained.

The approach above guarantees that the linear approximation will satisfy the miss detection constraint. This modification provides a near-optimal solution, since it obtains the highest value for q that satisfies the problem constraint. Note that, higher values of q lower the false alarm rate. The sub-optimal q (that is $\hat{q}_{n,\alpha}$) obtained using the linear approach, with and without the modification procedure, is shown in Figure 2(a). It is shown that the linear relationship between q and n is also valid after the modification; therefore, with modified values for the reference points and/or the slope $S_o(\alpha)$, the asymptotic performance derived in Subsection 3.3 also applies for the modified linear approach. Thus, it can also be concluded that using the modification procedure, the false alarm rate decreases exponentially as the network size increases, even at a fixed percentage of malicious users. In Figure 2(b), the number of iterations required in the modified approach is plotted versus the network size. It is shown that the modified approach has fast convergence property, and thus it is significantly less computationally intensive than the optimal exhaustive search.

4   Performance Enhancement through Malicious Node Detection

In this section, we first illustrate the different attack strategies that could be adopted by the malicious nodes, then propose to enhance the sensing performance by detecting malicious users and discarding their reports.

4.1   Malicious Nodes Attack Strategies

The optimal and the suboptimal scheme parameters for q-out-of-m approach consider the worst case scenario, where malicious users always send false sensing information. These parameters (m, q) are also used for more general attacking approaches. In the following, let P_a be the probability that each malicious node intentionally reports false information. It is assumed that all malicious users have the same probability of attack in a particular sensing period. We consider three different attacking strategies:

– *Strategy 1:* In this strategy $P_a = 1$. That is, malicious users always report false sensing information.
– *Strategy 2:* In this strategy, the malicious users send false data with an arbitrary probability P_a that is fixed, with $0 < P_a < 1$.
– *Strategy 3:* In this strategy, dynamic attack is adopted by the malicious users by changing P_a after each attacking block, which is composed of T sensing periods. More specifically,

$$P_{a_n} = P_{a_{n-1}} + \Delta_1 x - \Delta_2(1 - x), \tag{13}$$

where P_{a_n} is the probability that a malicious user attacks in the nth attacking block, x is a Bernoulli random variable characterized by the probability P_x, Δ_1 and Δ_2 are the increment and decrement step size, respectively.

Denote the false alarm and miss detection probabilities of the malicious users as $\tilde{P}_f$ and $\tilde{P}_m$. Then, the overall attacking probability in the nth attacking block is:

$$P_{attack} = \begin{cases} P_{a_n}(1 - \tilde{P}_m) + (1 - P_{a_n})\tilde{P}_m, & \text{primary user present,} \\ P_{a_n}(1 - \tilde{P}_f) + (1 - P_{a_n})\tilde{P}_f, & \text{primary user absent.} \end{cases} \tag{14}$$

4.2   Malicious Node Detection Approach

We propose a simple, yet effective, method to detect malicious users and improve the overall performance. In the proposed approach, we use two counters for each node at the fusion center. These counters are updated after each sensing period by comparing the final decision (using the q-out-of-m rule) with the individual sensing reports. The first counter for node i is denoted by $T_{i,o}$, and it represents the number of times node i sends '0' when the final decision is '1'. The second counter $T_{i,1}$ represents the number of times node i sends '1' when the final decision is '0'.

If the observation time is N sensing periods, then when $N \geq N_{th}$, $\frac{T_{i,o}}{N}$ and $\frac{T_{i,1}}{N}$ would be approximate indications for the benign users' miss detection probability and false alarm rate, respectively, where N_{th} is the minimum observation interval required to collect sufficient information about the users behvior. Hence, if $\frac{T_{i,o}}{N}$ is greater than $P_m + \delta$ or $\frac{T_{i,1}}{N}$ is greater than $P_f + \delta$, where δ is a considerably small value, then the corresponding user's report is discarded from the next decision process, but its counter will continue to be updated in the next observation period. In case $\frac{T_{i,o}}{N}$ is greater than $P_m + \delta_1$ or $\frac{T_{i,1}}{N}$ is greater than $P_f + \delta_2$, where δ_1 and δ_2 are relatively large, then the corresponding user will be discarded from the spectrum sensing process and its counter will no longer be calculated. The proposed malicious node detection method can also be used to determine the percentage of malicious users.

It is noted that the detection of the dynamic attacks is more difficult and takes longer time than that of static attacks. Simulations will show that this simple malicious detection approach improves the performance significantly for all attack strategies.

5   Simulation Results

In our numerical analysis, we assume that the miss detection limit is $\beta = 0.01$ and the individual sensing probabilities are $P_f = 0.1$ and $P_d = 0.775$. At different values for α, $S_o(\alpha)$ is calculated using points at $n = 20$ and $n = 35$. The reference points are at $n_o = 35$. We evaluate the performance in the following examples:

Example 1: Modified Linear Approach. In this example, the performance of the linear and modified linear approaches are evaluated in terms of the miss detection probability. We assume that the malicious users can detect the primary signal perfectly and always report false information (i.e. $P_{attack} = 1$). The miss detection of both approaches are shown in Figure 3. It is clear from Figure 3(a) that using the linear approach a slight increase in the miss detection over β happens at $\alpha = 15\%$ and 25%. This problem is solved by enforcing the modification procedure discussed in section 3.4 as shown in Figure 3(b).

Example 2: Malicious Detection Scheme. We assume that $\alpha = 25\%$, and the malicious users have $\tilde{P}_f = P_f$ and $\tilde{P}_m = 1 - P_d$. We use the modified linear q-out-of-m approach for fusion and investigate the performance under different attacking strategies. For the second attack strategy, we set $P_a = 0.7$, and for the third attach strategy we set $\Delta_1 = \Delta_2 = 0.2$, $P_{a_1} = 0.7$, $T = 10$ and $P_x = 0.5$.

When the malicious detection approach is not employed, it is shown in Figure 4 that the performance is worst under the first attack strategy, where malicious users always report false information. It is also clear from the figure that the false alarm rate improves as the network size increases, even under the same percentage of malicious users.

Using the proposed malicious node detection algorithm with $N_{th} = 100$, $\delta = 0.05$, $\delta_1 = 0.4$ and $\delta_2 = 0.3$, the overall false alarm is also shown in Figure 4. No prior knowledge of the attack strategy is assumed at the fusion center. It is clear

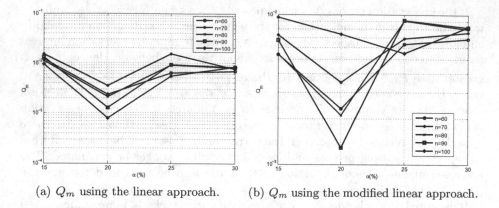

(a) Q_m using the linear approach.   (b) Q_m using the modified linear approach.

Fig. 3. Example 1: The miss detection probability using the linear and modified approaches

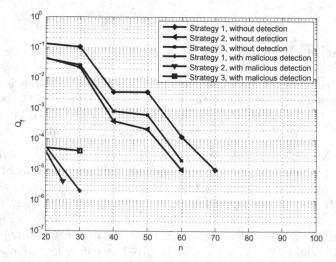

Fig. 4. Example 2: False alarm rate vs. network size with and without employing malicious node detection

that the malicious detection approach improved the performance significantly for the different kinds of attack, however dynamic attacks take longer time to be detected as compared to static attacks.

6   Conclusions

In this paper, we used the q-out-of-m fusion rule for cooperative spectrum sensing in cognitive networks to mitigate the SSDF attacks. We proposed an iterative approach to obtain the near-optimal q-out-of-m scheme parameters and enforce the miss detection constraint. The proposed approach has fast convergence and can be easily applied to large-scale networks, where optimal exhaustive search would be infeasible. It is shown that the false alarm rate of the proposed scheme decreases almost exponentially as the network size increases, even if the percentage of malicious users remains the same. In addition, we discussed different attack scenarios and proposed a malicious user detection scheme that has shown to improve the performance significantly under the different SSDF attack strategies.

References

1. Commission, F.C.: Spectrum policy task force. Technical Report 02 - 155 (November 2002)
2. Haykin, S.: Cognitive radio: brain-empowered wireless communications. IEEE Journal on Selected Areas in Communications 23(2), 201–220 (2005)
3. Cabric, D., Mishra, S., Brodersen, R.: Implementation issues in spectrum sensing for cognitive radios. In: Conference Record of the Thirty-Eighth Asilomar Conference on Signals, Systems and Computers, vol. 1, pp. 772–776 (November 2004)
4. Chen, R., Park, J.M., Hou, Y., Reed, J.: Toward secure distributed spectrum sensing in cognitive radio networks. IEEE Communications Magazine 46(4), 50–55 (2008)
5. Hu, F., Wang, S., Cheng, Z.: Secure cooperative spectrum sensing for cognitive radio networks. In: IEEE Military Communications Conference, pp. 1 –7 (October 2009)
6. Zhao, T., Zhao, Y.: A new cooperative detection technique with malicious user suppression. In: IEEE International Conference on Communications, pp. 1–5 (June 2009)
7. Kaligineedi, P., Khabbazian, M., Bhargava, V.: Secure cooperative sensing techniques for cognitive radio systems. In: IEEE International Conference on Communications, ICC 2008, pp. 3406–3410 (May 2008)
8. Wang, H., Lightfoot, L., Li, T.: On phy-layer security of cognitive radio: Collaborative sensing under malicious attacks. In: 2010 44th Annual Conference on Information Sciences and Systems (CISS), pp. 1–6 (March 2010)
9. Abdelhakim, M., Zhang, L., Ren, J., Li, T.: Cooperative sensing in cognitive networks under malicious attack. In: IEEE International Conference on Acoustics, Speech and Signal Processing (ICASSP) pp. 3004 –3007 (May 2011)
10. Mitzenmacher, M., Upfal, E.: Probability and computing randomized algorithms and probabilistic analysis. Cambridge Univ. Press (2009)

Heterogeneous Multicast Networks
with Wireless Helping Networks

Xuanyu Cao[1,2], Jinbei Zhang[1], Guanglin Zhang[1], Luoyi Fu[1], and Xinbing Wang[1]

[1] Department of Electronic Engineering, Shanghai Jiao Tong University, China
[2] The State Key Laboratory of Integrated Services Networks, Xidian University, China

Abstract. Previously, it has been shown that wired infrastructures such as optical networks can improve the capacity of ad hoc wireless networks significantly. However, sometimes these wired infrastructures are too expensive or even infeasible. In this paper, we use wireless helping networks to enhance the throughput performance of ad hoc networks. We focus on heterogeneous multicast networks with wireless helping networks. The heterogeneity refers to the inhomogeneity of the distribution of the nodes. The helping networks are neither the sources nor the destinations of data flow. They only serve as relays of the data. The wireless helping networks can be regularly placed or randomly uniformly distributed or mobile. We derive achievable throughput for all these three cases. We also make a comparison between them and pure ad hoc networks without helping networks to see the contribution of wireless helping networks.

1 Introduction

There have been great interests in the scaling laws of wireless networks since the seminal work [1]. In that paper, Gupta and Kumar show that a throughput of $\Theta(1/n\sqrt{\log n})$ is achievable. In [2], Franceschetti et.al show us a throughput of $\Theta(1/\sqrt{n})$ is achievable via percolation theory.

Besides unicast, multicast is also considered in the literature[3]. Heterogeneity is also considered in wireless networks. For instance, [4] and [5] study the capacity of wireless networks with Inhomogeneous Poisson Process (IPP) distribution and give the upper bound and lower bound for the networks respectively. The impact of mobility on wireless networks is first discussed in [13]. In that paper, Grossglauser and Tse show that mobility can significantly increase the throughput capacity of wireless networks to $\Theta(1)$ at the cost of large delay. Garetto et.al [15][16] combine mobility and heterogeneity and derive the upper and lower bound for throughput capacity of mobile heterogeneous networks. The delay capacity tradeoff is considered in [18][17] and generally capacity can only increase at the cost of large delay. Li et.al [19] and Zhang et.al [20][21] study the impact of directional antennas on capacity and delay of wireless ad hoc networks.

In the above works, all nodes are assumed to share one common communication channel and one same wireless channel bandwidth. However, the corresponding capacity scaling for these kind of pure ad hoc wireless networks are pessimistic. The per node throughput usually goes to zero as the number of nodes goes to infinity. Although mobility can somehow increase the network capacity, it will also incur the large delay.

X. Wang et al. (Eds.): WASA 2012, LNCS 7405, pp. 218–234, 2012.

Thus, a kind of *hybrid wireless networks* is proposed. The hybrid networks consist of both wireless ad hoc networks and wired base stations. In [11], Kozat and Tassiulas study the throughput capacity of hybrid wireless networks where both normal ad hoc nodes and access points are randomly distributed. In [9], Zemlianov and Veciana study the hybrid wireless networks with random ad hoc nodes and fixed base stations. In [8], Liu et.al show that under the k-nearest-cell strategy, if the number of base stations is $\Omega(\sqrt{n})$, then the network throughput will gain a significant enhance. In [12], Li et.al consider hybrid networks with so called L-maximum-hop strategy and show that [8] is actually a special case for that. Zhang et.al [10] consider hybrid wireless networks with directional antennas. Li et.al [7] consider the hybrid networks with asymmetric traffic patterns and network areas. Mao et.al [14] take multicast into consideration for hybrid networks.

However, this kind of hybrid wireless networks will need wired infrastructures which are very costly and even infeasible under some conditions. For example, in the battle field, constructing wired infrastructures previously is impossible. As a result, some scholars suggest to replace the wired infrastructures with wireless helping networks with large bandwidth (related with the number of nodes). For example, Li et.al [6] derive an achievable throughput of the asymmetric networks with wireless helping networks. This kind of wireless helping network is more realistic and less costly compared to wired base stations. The wireless helping network is neither sources of data nor destinations of data. They only serve as relay for transmissions. In addition, they are usually equipped with large bandwidth and thus more powerful than normal nodes. There is no doubt that the existence of these powerful wireless helping nodes will enhance the capacity performance of the original ad hoc network significantly.

So far, some works have been done about the multicast in hybrid networks with wired infrastructures or wired networks. But, to the best of our knowledge, few previous works have taken heterogeneous multicast with wireless helping networks into consideration. For wireless helping network, although its bandwidth will scale with the number of nodes, it is still finite. In contrast, the bandwidth of wired base stations is infinite. This is an essential difference since the transmission on the wireless helping networks will also take time. Besides, unlike [14], the multicast considered in this paper is heterogeneous i.e. the cluster clients (destinations) are more likely to be located nearby their corresponding cluster heads (sources).

In this paper, we will study the achievable throughput of heterogeneous multicast network with wireless helping network. The wireless helping network is assumed to have a large bandwidth (scales with n). The network area is a rectangle and thus asymmetric. We consider three cases: the wireless helping network is (i) regularly placed (ii) randomly distributed (iii) mobile. We derive achievable throughput for all the three cases respectively, which are the main results of this paper. We attempt to find out the extra throughput a heterogeneous multicast network can gain with the help of powerful wireless helping networks. We will also make a comparison between the three cases and pure ad hoc network without helping networks under a special case.

The rest of this paper is organized as follows. In Section 2, we describe the system model, including network topology and interference model. In Section 3 and Section 4, we describe the routing strategy and derive the corresponding achievable throughput for heterogeneous multicast network with regular wireless helping network and heterogeneous multicast network with random wireless helping network, respectively. In Section 5, we describe the transmission scheme and achievable throughput of heterogeneous multicast network with mobile wireless helping network. In Section 6 we show an achievable throughput for pure heterogeneous multicast networks without helping networks. In Section 7, we compare the results in previous sections and discuss (i)whether the wireless helping network will improve the throughput or not (ii)whether the mobility of helping network will improve the throughout or not . Finally, we conclude the paper in Section 8.

2 System Model

2.1 Network Model

We consider a heterogeneous multicast network to be the normal network. Specifically, there are $n^h (h > 0)$ cluster heads in the network. Those heads are served as sources of data flows. Each head has $n^c (c > 0)$ clients which are the destinations of the data from this head. The network area is a rectangle with width n^{a_1} and length n^{a_2}, where $a_2 \geq a_1 > 0$. In the following, we denote the direction of the short side of the rectangle as the direction of x axis and the direction of the long side of the rectangle as the direction of y axis. We denote the network as A. The n^h cluster sessions are independently distributed on the network area. Each head is uniformly distributed on the area. Once a head is distributed on the position ξ, all the clients of this head will be distributed independently around it with probability density fuction (PDF) $f(z, \xi)$. The function $f(z, \xi)$ induces heterogeneity into the network model and is achieved in the following way:

$$f(z, \xi) = \frac{s(|z - \xi|)}{\int_A s(|z - \xi|)dz}$$

where $s()$ is a positive, monotonically decreasing, continuous function defined on the interval $[0, \infty)$. We further assume $s()$ satisfy the property: $\lim_{\rho \to \infty} \rho^{2+\varepsilon} s(\rho) = c_1$, where c_1 and ε are two positive constants. Since we have:

$$\int_A s(|z - \xi|)dz \leq \int_{\mathbb{R}^2} s(|z|)dz = 2\pi \int_0^\infty \rho s(\rho)d\rho$$

and

$$\int_A s(|z - \xi|)dz \geq \int_0^1 \frac{1}{4} 2\pi \rho d\rho s(\rho) \geq \frac{\pi}{2} \int_0^1 \rho s(\rho)d\rho$$

we can say that $f(z, \xi)$ and $s(|z - \xi|)$ are of the same order i.e. there exists two positive constants $\underline{c}$ and $\overline{c}$ such that for all z and ξ in the network area, we have: $\underline{c}s(|z - \xi|) \leq f(z, \xi) \leq \overline{c}s(|z - \xi|)$.

In addition, there are $m = n^b (b > 0)$ helping nodes in the network area. These helping nodes can be either regularly placed on the network area or randomly distributed on the network area. If they are regularly placed, we call the corresponding network **heterogeneous multicast network with regular wireless helping network**, which will be discussed in Section 3. If the helping nodes are uniformly and independently distributed on the network area, we call the corresponding network **heterogeneous multicast network with random wireless helping network**, which will be discussed in Section 4. Since the distribution of random wireless helping network is uniform, we will see that the analysis is very similar to regular wireless helping network.

The wireless helping network can also be mobile. We call this model **heterogeneous multicast network with mobile wireless helping network**. This is specified as follows. Among the m helping nodes, each will have a home point. The m home points are regularly placed in the network area. Then each helping node will move within a circle centered at its home point independently. The radius of these circles are all n^r. In each circle, the probability density of the corresponding helping node is assumed to be uniform. The movement of each helping node is a stationary ergodic random process. This model will be discussed in Section 5.

2.2 Definition of Gaussian Channel Model[1]

The maximum transmission rate from transmitter X_i to its receiver X_j is given by:

$$R_{ij} = W \log(1 + SINR_{ij})$$

where W is the bandwidth of the channel and $SINR_{ij}$ is the signal to noise and interference ratio i.e. $SINR_{ij} = \frac{P_i/d_i^\gamma}{N + \sum_{k \neq i} P_k/d_k^\gamma}$. P_i is the transmission power of each transmitter. d_k is the distance from any simultaneously active transmitter to the receiver X_j. γ is the attenuation exponent. As usual, we assume $\gamma > 2$.

2.3 Definition of Protocol Model[1]

Nodes are assumed to employ a common transmission range, R. Then node i will transmit data successfully to node j iff:

(i) The distance between node i and j is no more than R, i.e., $d_{ij} \leq R$
(ii) For any other simultaneously active transmitters k, $d_{kj} \geq (1 + \triangle)R$

where $\triangle$ is a positive constant.

In the following sections, we will use Gaussian Channel Model to analyze static wireless helping networks in Section 3, Section 4 and Section 6. However, in Section 5, we will use Protocol Model to analyze the mobile helping network for simplicity. In fact, since Protocol Model has some kind of feasibility under Gaussian Channel Model, our analysis for mobile wireless helping networks can be easily extended to Gaussian Channel Model. Protocol Model is only for analysis convenience.

3 Achievable throughput of Heterogeneous Multicast Network with Regular Wireless Helping Network

In this section, we study the achievable throughput of heterogeneous multicast network with regular wireless helping network. We assume the bandwidth of the normal network to be W_1, a positive constant. This bandwidth is used for either the communications between normal nodes or the communications between normal nodes and helping nodes. However, the bandwidth of the helping network is W_2, an variable related with n. This bandwidth is only used for communications between helping nodes. Then we transmit the data flow from the cluster heads to their corresponding clients with the help of helping nodes. Firstly, we transmit the data from the heads to a nearby help node. Secondly, we transmit the data from this help node to a help node near the destined clients. Thirdly, we transmit the data from that help node to the corresponding clients. The first step is called uplink while the third one is called downlink. We further divide the bandwidth of normal nodes into uplink bandwidth W_3 and downlink bandwidth W_4, where W_3 and W_4 are two positive constants i.e. $W_1 = W_3 + W_4$. This will ensure that there is no interference between uplink transmissions and downlink transmissions.

We first derive the achievable throughput for the network under the assumption $b > a_2 - a_1$ carefully. After this, we will show that another achievable throughput can also be gained via a similar way of analysis for the case $b \leq a_2 - a_1$.

We tessellate the network area into small squares (cells) with side length $l = \sqrt{\frac{n^{a_1+a_2}}{n^b}} = n^{\frac{a_1+a_2-b}{2}}$. The constraint $b + a_1 > a_2$ will guarantee the feasibility of this tessellation. Then we just put the n^b helping nodes at the center of each cell such that one cell has exactly one helping node.

By using a TDMA transmission scheme and an equal power for every normal nodes and an equal power for every helping nodes, every cell can achieve a $\Theta(1)$ transmission rate at uplink (first step) or downlink (third step) and a $\Theta(W_2)$ transmission rate at the second step. In Step I and III, we only allow transmission within the same cell. In Step II, we allow transmission between adjacent cells. This concluded as the following lemma. The proof can be found in [6].

Lemma 3.1. *Every cell can achieve a $\Theta(1)$ transmission rate at the first step and third step. Every cell can achieve a $\Theta(W_2)$ transmission rate at the second step.*

Now we are ready to derive the throughput of the step I (uplink), step II, and step III (downlink), respectively. The lowest one among these three will be the bottleneck of the overall multicast transmission and is therefore the throughput of the whole network.

Step I: From the heads (sources) to the helping network.

In Step I, for every head, it must be located in a cell. We transmit the data from this head to the helping node belonging to this cell.In order to derive an achievable throughput for Step I, we need an upper bound for the number of heads in each cell. This is stated in the following lemma.

Lemma 3.2. *For every cell, there are at most $\Theta(\max\{n^{h-b}, \log n\})$ heads inside it w.h.p.*

Proof. The proof is a standard application of Chernoff bound.

For any particular cell, denote X the number of heads inside it. Then for any positive sequence x_n, we have:

$$\mathbb{P}(X \geq x_n) \leq \frac{\mathbb{E}(e^X)}{e^{x_n}} \leq \frac{(1 + (e-1)n^{-b})^{n^h}}{e^{x_n}} \leq \exp((e-1)n^{h-b} - x_n)$$

The last step uses the fact that $1 + x \leq e^x$. Denote event E_1 as {There exists a cell such that the number of heads inside it is larger than x_n}. Then we have:

$$\mathbb{P}(E_1) \leq \frac{n^{a_1 + a_2}}{l^2} \exp((e-1)n^{h-b} - x_n) = n^b \exp((e-1)n^{h-b} - x_n)$$

If $h > b$, then $x_n = \Theta(n^{h-b})$ will ensure that $\mathbb{P}(E_1) \to 0$. Else, $h \leq b$, then $x_n = \Theta(\log n)$ will also ensure that $\mathbb{P}(E_1) \to 0$. Thus we complete the proof.

Hence, we get an achievable throughput for Step I (uplink):

$$\lambda_1 = \Theta \left(\min \left\{ n^{b-h}, \frac{1}{\log n} \right\} \right)$$

Step II: Helping network relay.

In this Step II, we transmit the data through helping network in the following way. This routing strategy is the same as [6]. Suppose there is a head client pair. The coordinate of the cell the head lies in is (x_1, y_1) and the coordinate of the cell the client lies in is (x_2, y_2). Every coordinate can also represent a helping node. Firstly, we transmit the data from (x_1, y_1) to (x_1, y_2) through the line parallel to the y axis. Then we transmit the data from (x_1, y_2) to (x_2, y_2) though the line parallel to the x axis. Each time, we only allow the transmission between two adjacent helping nodes. And by using multihop and TDMA, we can transmit the data successfully.

In order to get an achievable throughput for Step II, we need to get an upper bound on the number of data flows that go across each cell. This is done by the following lemma.

Lemma 3.3. *For every cell, the number of data flows that go across it is at most w.h.p.:*

$$\Theta(\min\{n^h, \max\{n^{c+h+\frac{a_1-a_2-b}{2}}, n^{h+\frac{a_2-a_1-b}{2}}, \log n\}\})$$

Proof. One can refer to [22] for a technical proof.

Therefore, we've got an achievable throughput for Step II.

$$\lambda_2 = \Theta \left(W_2 \max \left\{ n^{-h}, \min \left\{ n^{-c-h+\frac{a_2+b-a_1}{2}}, n^{-h+\frac{a_1+b-a_2}{2}}, \frac{1}{\log n} \right\} \right\} \right)$$

Step III: From the helping network to clients (destinations).

In order to derive an achievable throughput of Step III, for every cell, we need an upper bound for the number of cluster sessions which have at least one client inside it. This is got by the following lemma.

Lemma 3.4. *For every cell, the number of cluster sessions which have at least one client inside it is no more than w.h.p.:*

$$\Theta \left(\min\{n^h, \max\{\log n, n^{c+h-b}\}\} \right)$$

Proof. One can refer to [22] for a technical proof.

Therefore, an achievable throughput of Step III is :

$$\lambda_3 = \Theta\left(\max\left\{n^{-h}, \min\left\{\frac{1}{\log n}, n^{b-c-h}\right\}\right\}\right)$$

Now we've finished the discussion of the throughput of all the steps and we arrive at one main result:

Theorem 3.1 *When $b > a_2 - a_1$, an achievable throughput for heterogeneous multicast networks with regular wireless helping networks is:*

$$\lambda = \Theta(\min\{\lambda_1, \lambda_2, \lambda_3\})$$

where

$$\lambda_1 = \min\left\{n^{b-h}, \frac{1}{\log n}\right\}$$

$$\lambda_2 = W_2 \max\left\{n^{-h}, \min\left\{n^{-c-h+\frac{a_2+b-a_1}{2}}, n^{-h+\frac{a_1+b-a_2}{2}}, \frac{1}{\log n}\right\}\right\}$$

$$\lambda_3 = \max\left\{n^{-h}, \min\left\{\frac{1}{\log n}, n^{b-c-h}\right\}\right\}$$

Now we consider the case $b \leq a_2 - a_1$. The analysis is quite similar to the case $b > a_2 - a_1$.

When $b \leq a_2 - a_1$, similar to [6], we tessellate the long side n^{a_2} into n^b intervals of length n^{a_2-b}. In this way, we get n^b small rectangles (cells) of which the length is n^{a_2-b} and width is n^{a_1}. Then we locate the n^b help nodes on the center of the n^b cells and every cell will has exactly one help node inside it. After that, we use the same transmission scheme as for the case $b > a_2 - a_1$. The complete transmission also consists of three steps, uplink, help node relay and downlink.

Now we begin to analyze the achievable throughput. Firstly, for Step I, following the same procedure as Lemma 3.2, we can still get an achievable throughput of $\lambda_1 = \Theta(\min\{n^{b-h}, \frac{1}{\log n}\})$. For Step II, since all the cells have the same y coordinate now, we simply let $\lambda_2 = \Theta(Wn^{-h})$ as an achievable throughput. For Step III, by following the similar procedure as Lemma 3.4, we can still get an achievable throughput of $\lambda_3 = \Theta(\max\{n^{-h}, \min\{n^{b-c-h}, \frac{1}{\log n}\}\})$. Now we get an achievable throughput for the overall network.

Theorem 3.2 *When $b \leq a_2 - a_1$, an achievable throughput for heterogeneous multicast networks with regular wireless helping networks is:*

$$\lambda = \Theta(\min\{\lambda_1, \lambda_2, \lambda_3\})$$

where

$$\lambda_1 = \min\left\{n^{b-h}, \frac{1}{\log n}\right\}$$

$$\lambda_2 = W_2 n^{-h}$$

$$\lambda_3 = \max\left\{n^{-h}, \min\left\{\frac{1}{\log n}, n^{b-c-h}\right\}\right\}$$

4 Achievable throughput of Heterogeneous Multicast Network with Random Wireless Helping Network

In this section, we study the achievable throughput of heterogeneous multicast network with random wireless helping network. We first consider the case $b > a_2 - a_1$. The analysis of the case $b \leq a_2 - a_1$ is quite similar.

Similar to [6], we first tessellate the network area with small squares (cells) whose side length is $l' = \sqrt{\frac{n^{a_1+a_2} \log m}{m}}$. The constraint $b > a_2 - a_1$ will ensure the success of this tessellation and we will have the following lemma.

Lemma 4.1. *For every cell, there exists at least one helping node inside it w.h.p.*

The proof of this lemma is just a standard application of Chernoff bound and we omit it here.

The transmission scheme of heterogeneous multicast network with random wireless helping network is just the same as that of heterogeneous multicast network with regular wireless helping network. It also consists of three steps: uplink, helping network relay and downlink. As a result, the analysis is quite similar.

Step I: From the heads (sources) to the helping network.

For tessellation with side length l', we have the following lemma which is quite similar to Lemma 3.2.

Lemma 4.2. *For every cell, there is at most $\Theta(\max\{n^{h-b} \log n, \log n\})$ heads inside it w.h.p.*

As a result, an achievable throughput for Step I is:

$$\lambda_1' = \Theta \left(\min \left\{ \frac{n^{b-h}}{\log n}, \frac{1}{\log n} \right\} \right)$$

Step II: Helping network relay.

In Step II, we use the same transmission route as that in Section 3. Similar to Lemma 3.3, we have the following lemma.

Lemma 4.3. *For every cell, the number of data flows that go across it is at most:*

$$\Theta \left(\min \left\{ n^h, \max \left\{ n^{c+h+\frac{a_1-a_2-b}{2}} \sqrt{\log n}, n^{h+\frac{a_2-a_1-b}{2}} \sqrt{\log n}, \log n \right\} \right\} \right)$$

Therefore, an achievable throughput for Step II is:

$$\lambda_2' = \Theta \left(W_2 \max \left\{ n^{-h}, \min \left\{ \frac{n^{-c-h+\frac{a_2+b-a_1}{2}}}{\sqrt{\log n}}, \frac{n^{-h+\frac{a_1+b-a_2}{2}}}{\sqrt{\log n}}, \frac{1}{\log n} \right\} \right\} \right)$$

Step III: From the helping network to clients (destinations)

Similar to Lemma 3.4, we have the following lemma:

Lemma 4.4. *For every cell, the number of cluster sessions which have at least one client inside it is no more than:*

$$\Theta(\min\{n^h, \max\{n^{c+h-b}\log n, \log n\}\})$$

Thus, an achievable throughput for Step III is:

$$\lambda_3' = \Theta\left(\max\left\{n^{-h}, \min\left\{\frac{n^{b-c-h}}{\log n}, \frac{1}{\log n}\right\}\right\}\right)$$

So we come to the following result:

Theorem 4.1 *When $b > a_2 - a_1$, an achievable throughput for heterogeneous multicast networks with random wireless helping networks is:*

$$\lambda' = \Theta(\min\{(\lambda_1', \lambda_2', \lambda_3')\})$$

where

$$\lambda_1' = \min\left\{\frac{n^{b-h}}{\log n}, \frac{1}{\log n}\right\}$$

$$\lambda_2' = W_2 \max\left\{n^{-h}, \min\left\{\frac{n^{-c-h+\frac{a_2+b-a_1}{2}}}{\sqrt{\log n}}, \frac{n^{-h+\frac{a_1+b-a_2}{2}}}{\sqrt{\log n}}, \frac{1}{\log n}\right\}\right\}$$

$$\lambda_3' = \max\left\{n^{-h}, \min\left\{\frac{n^{b-c-h}}{\log n}, \frac{1}{\log n}\right\}\right\}$$

For the case $b \le a_2 - a_1$, we can derive the following theorem in a similar way:

Theorem 4.2 *When $b > a_2 - a_1$, an achievable throughput for heterogeneous multicast networks with random wireless helping networks is:*

$$\lambda' = \Theta(\min\{\lambda_1', \lambda_2', \lambda_3'\})$$

where

$$\lambda_1' = \min\left\{\frac{n^{b-h}}{\log n}, \frac{1}{\log n}\right\}$$

$$\lambda_2' = W_2 n^{-h}$$

$$\lambda_3' = \max\left\{n^{-h}, \min\left\{\frac{n^{b-c-h}}{\log n}, \frac{1}{\log n}\right\}\right\}$$

5 Achievable throughput of Heterogeneous Multicast Network with Mobile Wireless Helping Network

In this section, we study the case the wireless helping network is mobile as described in Section 2. For heterogeneous multicast network with this kind of mobile helping network, we show a feasible transmission scheme and derive its corresponding achievable throughput. Recall that the movement of each node is within a circle centered at its home point and the radius of this circle is n^r. In the following, we will only analyze the case $b > a_2 - a_1$. One can easily analyze the case $b \leq a_2 - a_1$ in a similar manner.

Since $b > a_2 - a_1$, similar to Section 3, we can tessellate the network area into small squares (cells) whose side length is $l = n^{\frac{a_1+a_2-b}{2}}$. Then we place the home points of the $m = n^b$ helping node at the center of these m small cells. In the following, we further assume that $\frac{a_1+a_2-b}{2} < r < a_1$. Otherwise, if $r > a_1$, then the move range is larger than the network area and this is not proper. If $r \leq \frac{a_1+a_2-b}{2}$, then the movement area of each helping node is just constrained within its corresponding small cell. Then there will be no significant difference with the regular wireless helping network which is discussed in Section 3.

Since $r < a_1$, we can further tessellate the network area into big squares (cells) whose side length is $l_1 = \frac{n^r}{10}$. Then each big cell will have $(\frac{l_1}{l})^2 = \Theta(n^{2r-a_1-a_2+b})$ small cells inside it.

The transmission scheme also consists of three steps: uplink, helping network relay and downlink. In the following, we will discuss them respectively. Note that for the mobile model in this section, we will analyze problems under the Protocol Model defined in Section 2. And we will choose different transmission ranges R for the three steps. We also assume the different steps use different bandwidth, so there will be no interference between different steps.

Step I: Uplink.

In order to choose a proper transmission range for uplink, we need to know the minimum distance between any two heads. This problem is solved by the following lemma.

Lemma 5.1. *For any positive sequence d_n such that $d_n = o(n^{\frac{a_1+a_2}{2}-h})$, the distance between any two heads will be larger than d_n, w.h.p.*

Proof. One can refer to [22] for a technical proof.

With Lemma 5.1, we can get an achievable throughput for Step I. This is concluded in the following lemma.

Lemma 5.2. *An achievable throughput for Step I is:* $\lambda_1^{(m)} = \Theta(1)$ *when $b > 2h$;* $\lambda_1^{(m)} = o(n^{b-2h})$ *when $b \leq 2h$. Where $o(n^{b-2h})$ can be any small quantity compared to n^{b-2h}.*

Proof. One can refer to [22] for a technical proof.

From now on, we choose the $o(n^{b-2h})$ in Lemma 5.2 to be $\frac{n^{b-2h}}{\log n}$, hence an achievable throughput for Step I is:

$$\lambda_1^{(m)} = \Theta\left(\min\left\{1, \frac{n^{b-2h}}{\log n}\right\}\right)$$

Step II: Helping network relay

Different from the static case, now the helping nodes are mobile. So we can allow transmission between two helping nodes only when they are close enough. This will enhance the performance of achievable throughput. Besides when r tends to be $\frac{a_1+a_2-b}{2}$, the movement of the helping nodes will be restricted within its corresponding small cell, thus the throughput will be the same as the static case. All of the above assertions will be shown in the following and we will see that throughput of Step II will get a significant enhance compared to the static case in Section 3 and 4.

In order to derive achievable throughput for Step II, we first need to know the transmission ability between two adjacent big cells. This is done by the following lemma.

Lemma 5.3. *Every two adjacent big cells can support* $\mu = \Theta(W_2 n^{2r-a_1-a_2+b})$ *communication rate, where* W_2 *is the data rate for successful transmission between two help nodes.*

Proof. One can refer to [22] for a technical proof.

To derive the achievable throughput for Step II, we need to bound the number of data flows which go across every adjacent two big cells. Similar to Section 3, we have the following lemma.

Lemma 5.4. *(i)The number of data flows which go across two vertically adjacent big cells is at most w.h.p.*

$$\Theta\left(\max\{n^{h+r-a_1}, \log n\}\right)$$

(ii)The number of data flows which go across two horizontally adjacent big cells is at most w.h.p.

$$\Theta\left(\min\{n^h, \max\{n^{c+r+h-a_2}, \log n\}\}\right)$$

With the help of Lemma 5.3 and Lemma 5.4, we get an achievable throughput for Step II.

$$\lambda_2^{(m)} = \Theta\left(\min\left\{\frac{W_2 n^{2r-a_1-a_2+b}}{\max\{n^{h+r-a_1}, \log n\}}, \frac{W_2 n^{2r-a_1-a_2+b}}{\min\{n^h, \max\{n^{c+r+h-a_2}, \log n\}\}}\right\}\right)$$

$$= \Theta\left(W_2 n^{2r-a_1-a_2+b} \max\left\{n^{-h}, \min\left\{n^{-c-r-h+a_2}, n^{a_1-h-r}, \frac{1}{\log n}\right\}\right\}\right)$$

Observe this result, we can see that $\lambda_2^{(m)}$ is a monotonically increasing function with respect to r, as long as the previous assumption $\frac{a_1+a_2-b}{2} < r < a_1$ holds. Besides, when r tends to $\frac{a_1+a_2-b}{2}$ i.e., the mobility of helping nodes tends to disappear, the throughput of Step II, $\lambda_2^{(m)}$, will tend to be:

$$\Theta\left(W_2 \max\left\{n^{-h}, \min\left\{n^{-c-h+\frac{a_2-a_1+b}{2}}, n^{\frac{a_1-a_2+b}{2}-h}, \frac{1}{\log n}\right\}\right\}\right)$$

which is the exact achievable throughput for Step II in static case which has been derived in Theorem 3.1.

Step III: Downlink

Now we begin to derive an achievable throughput for downlink. Here, we will not make use of the mobility characteristic of help nodes and mobility is even a disadvantage in our transmission scheme. However, as previously said, mobility will increase the throughput of Step II, so in practice, one should make a tradeoff according to specified parameters.

For the transmission scheme, we will simply exploit a round-robin TDMA scheme. That is, we divide all the big cells into a constant number of groups such that transmissions of different big cells of the same group will not interfere with each other. Hence, each big cell gets a constant transmission rate. Now, all we need to do is to bound the number of multicast sessions which have at least one client inside a big cell. Similar to Lemma 3.4 in Section 3, we have the following lemma.

Lemma 5.5. *For every big cell, the number of multicast sessions which have at least one client inside it is no more than w.h.p.:*

$$\Theta\left(\min\left\{n^h, \max\left\{n^{h+c-a_1-a_2+2r}, \log n\right\}\right\}\right)$$

With the help of Lemma 5.5, we can get an achievable throughput for Step III:

$$\lambda_3^{(m)} = \Theta\left(\max\left\{n^{-h}, \min\left\{n^{a_1+a_2-c-h-2r}, \frac{1}{\log n}\right\}\right\}\right)$$

Now we have finished the discussion of all the three steps, and we arrive a main result:

Theorem 5.1 *When* $b > a_2 - a_1$, $\frac{a_1+a_2-b}{2} < r < a_1$, *an achievable throughput for heterogeneous multicast network with mobile wireless helping network is:*

$$\lambda^{(m)} = \Theta(\min\{\lambda_1^{(m)}, \lambda_2^{(m)}, \lambda_3^{(m)}\})$$

where

$$\lambda_1^{(m)} = \min\left\{1, \frac{n^{b-2h}}{\log n}\right\}$$

$$\lambda_2^{(m)} = W_2 n^{2r-a_1-a_2+b} \max\left\{n^{-h}, \min\left\{n^{-c-r-h+a_2}, n^{a_1-h-r}, \frac{1}{\log n}\right\}\right\}$$

$$\lambda_3^{(m)} = \max\left\{n^{-h}, \min\left\{n^{a_1+a_2-c-h-2r}, \frac{1}{\log n}\right\}\right\}$$

6 Achievable throughput of Pure Heterogeneous Multicast Network without Helping Network

In this section, we study the case that heterogeneous multicast network is not equipped with wireless helping network. The routing strategy is the same as the Step II in Section 3 and the corresponding analysis is similar.

If $h \leq a_2 - a_1$, then we simply let the achievable throughput be $\lambda_p = \Theta(n^{-h})$. This is obviously feasible by means of TDMA. Next, we focus on the case $h > a_2 - a_1$.

Firstly, as usual, we tessellate the network area with small squares (cells) whose side length is $l'' = \sqrt{\frac{n^{a_1+a_2}\log n^h}{n^h}}$. Then the following lemma holds:

Lemma 6.1. *For every cell, there is at least one head inside it w.h.p.*

Then we use the same routing strategy as Step II in Section 3. For each head-client pair, we first transmit the data flow vertically and then transmit it horizontally. By following the same procedure in Lemma 3.3, we can derive an achievable throughput and this is summarized in the following theorem:

Theorem 6.1 *An achievable throughput for heterogeneous multicast network without wireless helping network is:*
  when $h > a_2 - a_1$:

$$\lambda_p = \Theta \left(\max \left\{ n^{-h}, \min \left\{ \frac{n^{-c + \frac{a_2 - h - a_1}{2}}}{\sqrt{\log n}}, \frac{n^{\frac{a_1 - h - a_2}{2}}}{\sqrt{\log n}} \right\} \right\} \right)$$

when $h \le a_2 - a_1$:
$$\lambda_p = \Theta(n^{-h})$$

7 Discussion

In this section, we make a comparison between heterogeneous multicast network with wireless helping network and heterogeneous multicast network without wireless helping network. From Theorem 3.1, Theorem 3.2, Theorem 4.1, Theorem 4.2 and Theorem 5.1, we can see that with helping network, the achievable throughput is influenced by many parameters: the number of cluster heads, the number of clients for each session, the number of helping nodes, the length and width of the network area, the mobility radius for mobile helping network. But it is not influenced by the heterogeneity parameter ε. From Theorem 6.1, we can see that, without helping network, the achievable throughout is also influenced by a series of parameters. Now we make a comparison to see when the helping network will enhance the throughput performance significantly in the order sense and when will the mobility of helping network improve the throughput performance.

In subsection 7.1, we mainly discuss the case when the helping network is regular, but the result also holds when the helping network is random since $\log n$ factor will not influence the behavior of throughput heavily. In subsection 7.2, we use a special case to compare the performance between three kinds of networks: (i) heterogeneous multicast network without helping network, (ii) heterogeneous multicast network with regular helping network, (iii) heterogeneous multicast network with mobile helping network.

7.1 Multicast Heterogeneous Network with Regular Helping Network and Multicast Heterogeneous Network without Helping Network: A Comparison

Case I: $b - c \le 0$.

In this case, no matter the helping network is regular or random, $\lambda_3 = \Theta(n^{-h})$. Because of this bottleneck, no matter how large bandwidth the helping network has, the overall throughput can not be better than a standalone multicast network without helping network.

Case II: $b - c > 0$.

In this case, with helping network with sufficiently large W_2, λ_2 will not a bottleneck. In addition, $\lambda_3 = \min\{\frac{1}{\log n}, n^{b-c-h}\}$ and $\lambda_1 = \min\{n^{b-h}, \frac{1}{\log n}\}$. As a result, with sufficiently large W_2, the overall throughput is $\min\{\lambda_1, \lambda_3\} = \Theta(\min\{\frac{1}{\log n}, n^{b-c-h}\})$. According to Theorem 6.1, when $h \le a_2 - a_1$, this is obviously better than the standalone throughput without helping networks, $\lambda_p = \Theta(n^{-h})$.

If $h > a_2 - a_1$, we can further the situation into two cases:

If $c \le a_2 - a_1$, according to Theorem 6.1 we have $\lambda_p = \Theta(\frac{n^{a_1-h-a_2}}{\sqrt{\log n}})$. Then if $h \ge 2(b - c) + a_2 - a_1$, it is easy to see that $\min\{\lambda_1, \lambda_2\} \le \lambda_p$. So there will be no enhancement with helping network. Else if $h < 2(b - c) + a_2 - a_1$, with sufficiently large W_2, the helping network will improve the throughput significantly.

If $c > a_2 - a_1$, according to Theorem 6.1 we have $\lambda_p = \Theta(\max\{n^{-h}, \frac{n^{-c+\frac{a_2-h-a_1}{2}}}{\sqrt{\log n}}\})$. It is easy to prove that when $b \le \frac{a_2+b-a_1}{2}$, there will be no enhancement with helping network. However, when $b > \frac{a_2+b-a_1}{2}$, with sufficiently large W_2, there will be significant enhancement with helping network.

The above discussion can be summarized by the following corollary:

Corollary 7.1 *With sufficiently large W_2, helping network can enhance the throughput of heterogeneous multicast network significantly only when one of the following cases holds:*

- *(i) $b > c, h \le a_2 - a_1$*
- *(ii) $b > c, h > a_2 - a_1, c \le a_2 - a_1, h < 2(b - c) + a_2 - a_1$*
- *(iii) $b > c, h > a_2 - a_1, c > a_2 - a_1, b > \frac{a_2+h-a_1}{2}$*

Then one may ask how large W_2 can be considered as sufficiently large in Corollary 7.1? In fact, specifically, we can let $W_2 = n^x$, where x is any positive constant. Then $\lambda_2 = \Theta(n^{x-h})$ must be achievable for Step II. In order to avoid letting λ_2 as a bottleneck, we can choose x as follows:

When $c < b < c + h$, choose $x \ge b - c$, thus the achievable overall throughput is $\lambda = \Theta(n^{b-c-h})$.

When $b \ge c + h$, choose $x \ge h$, thus the achievable overall throughput is $\lambda = \Theta(\frac{1}{\log n})$.

By choosing W_2 like above, we can say W_2 is sufficiently large and Corollary 7.1 holds.

Thereby, to expect a significant enhance in the throughout performance with helping networks, one should ensure that at least one condition in Corollary 7.1 holds.

7.2 Comparison between Three Kinds of Networks: A Specified Case

Now we consider three kinds of networks:

- (i) Heterogeneous multicast network without helping network
- (ii) Heterogeneous multicast network with regular helping network
- (iii) Heterogeneous multicast network with mobile helping network

We consider a particular case as an example. The parameters are given as follows:$a_1 = 1, a_2 = 3, b = 9, h = 7, c = 5$. The bandwidth of the powerful wireless helping network is assumed to be n i.e., $W_2 = n$.

Then according to Theorem 3.1, Theorem 5.1 and Theorem 6.1, we get an achievable throughput $\lambda_p, \lambda_s, \lambda_m$ for networks (i)(ii)(iii) as follows, respectively:

$$\lambda_p = \Theta(n^{-7}), \lambda_s = \Theta(n^{\frac{-11}{2}}), \lambda_m = \Theta\left(\min\left\{\frac{n^{-5}}{\log n}, n^{2r+6}\max\left\{n^{-7}, n^{-r-9}\right\}, \max\left\{n^{-7}, n^{-8-2r}\right\}\right\}\right)$$

where $-2.5 < r < 1$ is the mobility radius exponent of the mobile helping network.

From the result of the above computation, we can see that with the help of regular helping network, the normal network can perform better. Furthermore, for some particular mobility radius exponent r, the mobility of helping network can also enhance the performance compared to static helping network. This is shown in Figure 1. In Figure 1, for simplicity, we ignore the $\log n$ term in the expression of λ_m since this will not influence the overall throughput heavily.

From Figure 1, we can see that when $-2.5 < r < -1.25$, mobile helping network performs better than regular helping network. Particularly, when $-2.5 < r < -2$, the throughput will increase as the mobility radius exponent r increases. However, when $r > -1.25$, mobile helping network performs worse than regular helping network due to the bottleneck of downlink in mobile helping network.

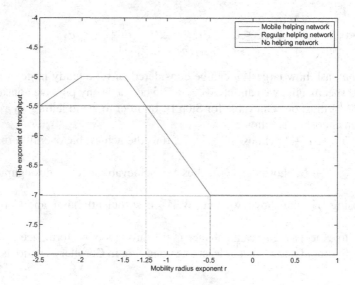

Fig. 1. Throughput Comparison between Different Helping Networks: A special case

8   Conclusion

In this paper, we study the throughput of heterogeneous multicast networks with helping networks. We discuss with quite general conditions. For instance, the network area can be a rectangle and not necessarily a square. The growing speed of every parameter is an arbitrary power of n. We discuss for three cases: helping network is regular, helping network is randomly distributed, helping network is mobile. We also discuss the case when the heterogeneous multicast network is standalone without helping network. We then make a comparison between different networks and see that under certain conditions, mobile helping network is better than static helping network, static helping network is better than having no helping network, in the sense of throughput. If the helping network is wired but not wireless, we can just let $W_2 \to \infty$ i.e. helping network relay is not a bottleneck, to get the result.

As you can see, our analysis and result provide fundamental insight to heterogeneous multicast networks with helping networks.

Acknowledgment. This paper is supported by National Fundamental Research Grant (No. 2010CB731803); NSF China (No. 60832005); China Ministry of Education New Century Excellent Talent (No. NCET-10-0580); China Ministry of Education Fok Ying Tung Fund (No. 122002); Qualcomm Research Grant; Shanghai Basic Research Key Project (No. 11JC1405100); National key project of China (2012ZX03001009, 2010ZX03003-001-01); China Postdoctoral Science Foundation Grant (No. 2011M500774).

References

1. Gupta, P., Kumar, P.R.: The capacity of wireless networks. IEEE Transactions on Information Theory 46, 388–404 (2000)
2. Franceschetti, M., Dousse, O., Tse, D.N.C., Thiran, P.: Closing the Gap in the Capacity of Wireless Networks via Percolation Theory. IEEE Transactions on Information Theory 53(3), 1009–1018 (2007)
3. Li, X.-Y.: Multicast capacity of wireless ad hoc networks. IEEE/ACM Trans. Netw. 17(3), 950–961 (2009)
4. Alfano, G., Garetto, M., Leonardi, E.: Capacity scaling of wireless networks with inhomogeneous node density: Upper bounds. IEEE J. Sel. Areas Commun. 27(7), 1147–1157 (2009)
5. Alfano, G., Garetto, M., Leonardi, E.: Capacity scaling of wireless networks with inhomogeneous node density: Lower bounds. In: Proc. IEEE INFOCOM, pp. 1890–1898 (2009)
6. Li, P., Fang, Y.: On the Throughput Capacity of Hetergeneous Wireless Networks. IEEE Transactions on Mobile Computing (2011)
7. Li, P., Fang, Y.: Impacts of topology and traffic pattern on capacity of hybrid wireless networks. IEEE Transactions on Mobile Computing 8(12), 1585–1595 (2009)
8. Liu, B., Liu, Z., Towsley, D.: On the capacity of hybrid wireless networks. In: Proceeding of the IEEE International Conference on Computer Communications (INFOCOM 2003), San Francisco, California, USA (March 2003)
9. Zemlianov, A., Veciana, G.: Capacity of ad hoc wireless networks with infrastructure support. IEEE Journal on Selected Areas in Communications 23(3) (March 2005)
10. Zhang, G., Xu, Y., Wang, X., Guizani, M.: Capacity of hybrid wireless networks with directional antenna and delay constraint. IEEE Transactions on Communications 58(7), 2097–2106 (2010)
11. Kozat, U., Tassiulas, L.: Throughput Capacity of Random Ad Hoc Networks with Infrastructure Support. In: Proc. ACM MobiCom (June 2003)

12. Li, P., Zhang, C., Fang, Y.: Capacity and Delay of Hybrid Wireless Broadband Access Networks. IEEE J. Selected Areas in Comm., Special Issue on Broadband Access Networks 27(2), 117–125 (2009)
13. Grossglauser, M., Tse, D.: Mobility increases the capacity of ad hoc wireless networks. IEEE/ACM Transactions on Networking 10, 477–486 (2002)
14. Mao, X., Li, X.-Y., Tang, S.-J.: Multicast Capacity for Hybrid Wireless Networks. In: ACM MobiHoc (2008)
15. Garetto, M., Giaccone, P., Leonardi, E.: Capacity Scaling in Ad Hoc Networks with Heterogeneous Mobile Nodes: the Sub-critical Regime. ACM/IEEE Transactions on Networking 17(6), 1063–6692 (2009) ISSN: 1063-6692
16. Garetto, M., Giaccone, P., Leonardi, E.: Capacity Scaling in Ad Hoc Networks with Heterogeneous Mobile Nodes: the Super-critical Regime. IEEE/ACM Transactions on Networking 17(5), 1522–1535 (2009)
17. Li, P., Fang, Y., Li, J., Huang, X.: Smooth Trade-offs Between Throughput and Delay in Mobile Ad Hoc Networks. IEEE Transactions on Mobile Computing 11(3), 427–438 (2012)
18. Neely, M.J., Modiano, E.: Capacity and Delay Tradeoffs for Ad-Hoc Mobile Networks. IEEE Transactions on Information Theory 51(6), 1917–1937 (2005)
19. Li, P., Zhang, C., Fang, Y.: The Capacity of Wireless Ad Hoc Networks Using Directional Antennas. IEEE Transactions on Mobile Computing 10(10), 1374–1387 (2011)
20. Zhang, G., Xu, Y., Wang, X., Tian, X., Liu, J., Gan, X., Yu, H., Qian, L.: Multicast Capacity for Hybrid VANETs with Directional Antenna and Delay Constraint. IEEE Journal on Selected Areas in Communications 30(4), 818–833 (2012)
21. Zhang, G., Xu, Y., Wang, X., Guizani, M.: Capacity of Hybrid Wireless Networks with Directional Antenna and Delay Constraint. IEEE Transactions on Communications 58(7), 2097–2106 (2010)
22. Cao, X., Zhang, J., Zhang, G., Fu, L., Wang, X.: Heterogeneous Multicast Networks with Wireless Helping Networks. Techinical Report

Enclave: Promoting Unobtrusive and Secure Mobile Communications with a Ubiquitous Electronic World

Adam C. Champion, Xinfeng Li, Qiang Zhai, Jin Teng, and Dong Xuan

Department of Computer Science and Engineering, The Ohio State University
{champion,lixinf,zhaiq,tengj,xuan}@cse.ohio-state.edu

Abstract. Thanks to smartphones' mass popularity in our society, our world is surrounded by ubiquitous electronic signals. These signals originate from static objects such as buildings and stores and mobile objects such as people or vehicles. Yet it is difficult to readily access electronic information. Current wireless communications focus on reliable transmission from sources to destinations, which entails tedious connection establishment and network configuration. This forms a virtual electronic barrier among people that makes unobtrusive communication difficult. In addition, there is concern about interacting with the electronic world due to such interactions' insecurity. To safely remove the electronic barrier, we propose Enclave, a delegate wireless device that helps people's smartphones communicate unobtrusively. We realize Enclave using two key supporting technologies, NameCast and PicComm. NameCast uses wireless device names to unobtrusively transmit short messages without connection establishment. PicComm uses the transfer of visual images to securely deliver electronic information to people's smartphones. We implement Enclave on commercial off-the-shelf smartphones. Our experimental evaluation illustrates its potential for smartphone data protection and unobtrusive and secure communication.

1 Introduction

This paper proposes Enclave, a system that provides unobtrusive and secure communication between a smartphone and the "electronic world" of prolific wireless signals that surround us.

1.1 The Concept of Enclave

With the proliferation of smartphones, our lives are increasingly "digitized." We live in a world surrounded by electronic signals. Though these signals are mainly traffic between individual users and APs or base stations, it is not difficult to imagine that, in the future, anyone can directly extract useful information from these signals just as our eyes capture visual information from the outside world. Among these electronic signals, we can discern two main categories of useful information, as Fig. 1 illustrates.

X. Wang et al. (Eds.): WASA 2012, LNCS 7405, pp. 235–247, 2012.

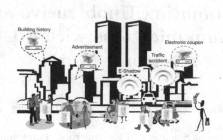

Fig. 1. The electronic world. Ubiquitous wireless signals are emitted from stationary locations like historical buildings and stores. Mobile objects like passersby or drivers broadcast personal social networking profiles [1–6], accident notifications, etc. The person at bottom right uses one wireless device to interact with the electronic world; his smartphone is private.

The first category is information from static objects. For example, government agencies can broadcast wireless bulletins near their buildings. Stores can broadcast advertisements and distribute electronic coupons to passersby who are willing to receive them wirelessly. The second category is information from mobile objects, which can be people or vehicles. A person may want to introduce himself to another for socializing or job hunting. A kind driver may want to warn others of an accident he just witnessed. In some cases, we have hybrid sources of information. Mobile users may be willing to relay bulletins containing emergency notices to others. Other drivers may also help relay the accident information to more people. People may be willing to relay coupons from stores due to incentive mechanisms [1].

However, the digital life with such wireless communications is still not a reality. In fact, it is more difficult for us to access the information in the electronic world than one might think initially. The reasons are twofold.

First, current wireless technology is designed with the goal of reliable information transmission between a sender and a receiver. Then, in most cases, network configuration and connection establishment are necessary. Complex mechanisms are enforced for reliability, such as meticulous error correction for 100% reception accuracy. However, for large-scale information dissemination, this is overkill. People cannot freely share or disseminate information to multiple people nearby without obtrusive configurations and excessive communication signaling. In some cases, 100% accuracy is not required. The aforementioned well-intentioned mechanisms actually form virtual electronic barriers among people. Second, malicious attackers prey on incautious users who dare to receive all kinds of information without filtering. Many obscenities, malicious codes, and other nefarious contents may be hidden in the exchanged wireless information. People are more willing to hide behind the electronic barriers, hardening them.

In this light, we propose Enclave to safely remove the electronic barriers and achieve unobtrusive communication. We do so via NameCast. We introduce secure communication via PicComm. Enclave is a delegate wireless device helping the *master devices* people use for wireless communication, e.g., their smartphones. We point out that Enclave is a separate mobile device that may not have a data plan and runs our software. It may seem inconvenient to separate functionality between two devices, particularly as smartphones tend to consolidate many functions on one device. While Enclave can be implemented on the smartphone used by its owner, this approach is actually too heavyweight for the smartphone. Also, it is risky: smartphones often contain much sensitive data and smartphone-based malicious code detection and information leaking attacks have not been fully studied. People can rent mobile devices when they travel to foreign countries or attend a conference; also, they can use a second device that serves as their Enclave. Such second devices can be their previously used phones without data plans. In a sense, Enclave shares a similarity to a sandbox as Enclave aims to protect the master device from attacks. However, Enclave also aims to promote unobtrusive communication with the electronic world; sandboxes do not.

The following usage scenarios illustrate typical Enclave use:

– *Tourists in a foreign country:* Suppose tourists travel to a foreign country and are eager to explore local attractions, eat at local restaurants, etc. These fixed sites broadcast location-specific information such as the history of the area and advertisements to people nearby. The tourists view the attractions, eat at the restaurants, etc. carrying their mobile devices, which receive this information and store it. When they return to their hotel, they copy some information they received to their personal phones or laptops. The mobile devices act as enclave devices and their personal phones or laptops act as master devices.

– *Conference attendees:* Suppose academics attend a conference and are eager to meet new people, explore the surroundings, etc. As they do so, their mobile devices broadcast their names, research work, etc. to people nearby and receive such information from others. They are interested in some people's information, so they connect their personal phones or laptops to their mobile devices and copy information from the latter to the former. Here, the mobile devices act as enclave devices and their personal phones or laptops act as master devices.

1.2 Our Contributions

We implement our Enclave system on commercial off-the-shelf smartphones. To enable Enclave's functionality, we propose the following two key supporting technologies that address the two challenges mentioned above:

– *NameCast:* NameCast uses wireless device names to unobtrusively transmit short messages without tedious connection establishment. As its name suggests, NameCast makes use of wireless names that are exchanged freely. For example, with a simple scan, we can see Service Set Identifiers (SSIDs) of nearby APs or the names of nearby Bluetooth devices. It is effective in opening tunnels through the electronic barriers. It makes use of erasure coding for relatively reliable communication. Besides, it enables information dissemination through via peer to peer sharing.

– *Picture Communication (PicComm):* PicComm is a type of communication based on the transfer of visual images. It is for secure delivery of collected information on the enclave device to the "backend" master device. The basic idea is that taking a picture of an image is safe from attack by malicious codes. We encode textual information to visual images on the enclave device. The master device takes a picture of the enclave device's screen, and parses the textual content there via optical character recognition (OCR). Notice this channel's characteristics help encumber information leakage as potential snoops need to be in close proximity to the devices. We incorporate a feedback channel that automatically refreshes the enclave device's textual content once the master device parses it successfully. Two options are considered for this channel: NameCast and sound. With NameCast, we transmit the feedback message via the WiFi SSID, which can hold up to 32 bytes of information. However, the master device needs to disclose its WiFi MAC address, which may be a concern to some users. Thus, we propose a second option: sound. Using sound, PicComm can achieve a higher degree of security without disclosing electronic information. The drawback is the low channel capacity: only 1 or 2 bits can be used per feedback message. PicComm divides the enclave device's screen into pieces and dynamically updates the pieces' "resolution" based on OCR performance. We design a novel OCR hash function that helps provides resolution "feedback" to the master device.

We implement Enclave with NameCast and PicComm on commercial off-the-shelf smartphones running Android 2.3. Our experimental evaluation shows Enclave's potential for reliable, secure, and unobtrusive electronic communication.

To the best of our knowledge, Enclave is the first system that interposes communication between a smartphone and the electronic world using a delegate device for the purpose of promoting unobtrusive and secure communication.

2   Related Work

There are many mobile social networking works that we classify as centralized or distributed based on the underlying system architecture. A representative centralized system is Social Serendipity [3], which detects others nearby via Bluetooth and queries a central profile database to match people based on commonalities. Nokia Sensor [4] is a representative distributed system that lets proximate users detect each other and share information via a Bluetooth connection. E-SmallTalker [7] leverages Bluetooth Service Discovery Protocol for sharing commonalities among strangers in order to initiate conversations. Existing work does not consider the "gap" between the electronic and physical worlds, i.e., when people meet each other in physical proximity, they cannot easily view related electronic profiles without connection establishment. However, strangers may not want to build up such a connection. Our work bridges this gap via NameCast, which leverages WiFi and Bluetooth names to wirelessly provide social information to nearby people without connection establishment.

Several works aim to control proximate communication using WiFi SSIDs and Bluetooth names. Beacon stuffing [8] adds information to WiFi AP beacons to realize WiFi communication without associations. Neighborcast [9] forms multicast groups among disparate WiFi clients regardless of AP association. Bluetooth device names have also been leveraged for various contexts including automatic configuration of mobile ad hoc networks [10, 11], Bluetooth device name inter-actions [12], and "proactive displays" [13]. The WiFi SSID based approach can broadcast to a wide range of nearby devices, but it can only deliver a small amount of information. The Bluetooth name based approach can deliver more information, but it only supports point-to-point communication. E-Shadow [2] uses both WiFi and Bluetooth to publish personal information; it covers a large communication range and delivers a large volume of information. However, E-Shadow does not aim for communication among neighbors. Our work differs from E-Shadow as we piggyback message delivery atop Bluetooth device discovery for rapid unobtrusive communication.

Wi-Fi Direct is an emerging technology enabling WiFi devices to detect one another, then directly establish wireless connections. This technology makes in-formation sharing easier among neighboring mobile devices. However, content made available over a Wi-Fi Direct group connection is still restricted to specific applications [14]. In this sense, the aforementioned gap between the electronic and physical world still exists. In this work, we help close it via NameCast.

Enclave and its supporting technologies can be implemented on a single smart-phone. Many smartphones support data encryption mechanisms, Bluetooth and WiFi communication, and cameras. These mechanisms can be leveraged to com-partmentalize sensitive data. Electronic communications can be leveraged to ac-cess information from physically proximate mobile devices, location information, and Internet servers. Cameras and OCR technology can be similarly leveraged to parse textual information transmitted via a visual channel. Perli et al. [15] proposed using pairs of cameras for fast information exchange. However, they do not consider it a security measure and explore its security aspects. They use two-way picture taking for feedback, requiring front cameras on both devices. Enclave can use wireless signals and sounds as feedback, which is more flexible.

3   Enclave Overview

This section describes the system architecture of Enclave, which is shown in Fig. 2. In general, Enclave has two interfaces and several parts inside shown below:

– *Interface with the electronic world:* Enclave uses NameCast as the interface with the electronic world to unobtrusively collect information from it and to send information to it on the master device's behalf. NameCast is an option for unobtrusive communication in physical proximity. Users may choose other wireless interfacing methods such as direct connection with APs.

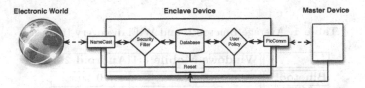

Fig. 2. Enclave system architecture and supporting technologies

– *Interface with the master device:* Enclave uses the PicComm interface with the master device to securely transmit useful requested data to it.

– *Components inside Enclave:* Enclave contains several components. It first uses the security filter to check the security of collected information from the electronic world. This component performs lightweight filtering of the received data. All received data are stored in the database. Before Enclave sends the data to the master device, they are further checked by the user policy module for security breaches. Also, Enclave has a reset module that can reset it to factory conditions, purging the system of malicious data and security threats.

The components inside Enclave are lightweight as the master often resets the enclave device. We detail in §§4–5 the two key supporting technologies, Name-Cast and PicComm, which enable Enclave's unobtrusive and secure interfaces to the electronic world and the master device, respectively.

4   NameCast: Enclave-to-Outside Communication

This section describes Enclave's unobtrusive communication between the enclave device and external information sources. We use NameCast to achieve such communication. We describe NameCast's design rationale and present NameCast's high-level framework for rapid unobtrusive communication.

4.1   Design Rationale

NameCast aims to bore tunnels through the wireless barriers by implementing unobtrusive, reliable communication of textual information among mobile devices. By *unobtrusive*, we mean that such devices should rapidly discover each other's presence electronically once they enter communication range. Mobile device users should not have to perform tedious connection establishments or network configurations in order to find nearby devices. The discovery process should be rapid and autonomous without requiring many scans to find nearby devices. NameCast's communication should work with commercial off-the-shelf mobile devices with Bluetooth and WiFi requiring minimal configuration.

To realize unobtrusive communication of textual information using Bluetooth and WiFi, NameCast needs to overcome limitations of their discovery processes. We illustrate this by examining the time incurred by such discovery processes on commodity mobile devices. Specifically, we measure Bluetooth and WiFi discovery times on two HTC Touch Diamond2s running Windows Mobile 6.1 and two Nexus phones running Android 2.3. We have one Diamond2 phone discover another Diamond2 phone and one Nexus phone discover another Nexus phone

Table 1. Average Bluetooth and WiFi discovery times

	Windows Mobile 6.1	Android 2.3
Bluetooth	18–22 s	10–20 s
WiFi	1.0–1.1 s	1.1–1.2 s

using both Bluetooth and ad hoc WiFi. The results are shown in Table 1. We find it takes 17–18 s and 1.0–1.2 s for a Nexus phone to discover a Diamond2 phone using Bluetooth and WiFi, respectively. Clearly, Bluetooth and WiFi's discovery processes need to be improved in order to achieve unobtrusive communication.

Main Ideas. At its heart, NameCast leverages the strengths of Bluetooth and WiFi's discovery processes so that they can help each other. Bluetooth can disseminate much more information at once than WiFi (248 bytes vs. 32 bytes), but Bluetooth's discovery process is much more time-consuming than WiFi's (10.24 s vs 1–2 s). We exploit WiFi's fast discovery time to guide Bluetooth's device discovery process. For this purpose, we embed information about the current state of a device's Bluetooth discovery process in its WiFi Service Set Identifier (SSID). This information is "forwarded" to nearby devices to speed up their discovery processes. Bluetooth can then discover proximate devices more quickly than if it had not received such information.

We observe that Bluetooth device names and WiFi SSIDs can transmit (short) messages without tedious network configuration or user intervention. In Name-Cast, we leverage this capability using the following 2 techniques:

– *Using WiFi to control Bluetooth:* We provide discovered Bluetooth device IDs in WiFi SSIDs, which serve to control Bluetooth device discovery. If a device discovers an SSID, it can compare the set of Bluetooth device IDs therein to its set of discovered Bluetooth devices. If there are any "matching" Bluetooth device IDs, the first device can bypass the lengthy inquiry process and directly obtain the matching Bluetooth devices' names.

– *Piggybacking message dissemination atop device discovery:* We leverage the message-carrying capability to "piggyback" message delivery on Bluetooth and WiFi discovery processes. Specifically, for a given device, we place a message and all discovered Bluetooth device IDs in this device's Bluetooth name. We also create an ad hoc network whose SSID contains (parts of) its WiFi MAC address and all discovered Bluetooth IDs. Once a second device obtains the first device's name via Bluetooth or WiFi discovery, it also receives that device's set of all discovered Bluetooth devices. We do not include each device's set of SSIDs in its Bluetooth device name or WiFi SSID since WiFi has greater range and faster discovery time than Bluetooth.

4.2   Erasure Code Based Reliable Forwarding

To achieve unobtrusive communication, NameCast forwards messages among mobile devices without connection establishment. We first describe a simple case of forwarding without reliability considerations. Then we describe how we can make forwarding more reliable using erasure codes.

Basic Forwarding. Forwarding messages to mobile devices that have not yet received these messages plays a key role in NameCast's operation. Consider Fig. 3, which depicts a simple network topology. All devices in Fig. 3 can discover each other via WiFi, but devices A and C cannot discover each other via

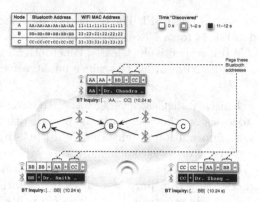

Fig. 3. Motivating topology for NameCast. Bluetooth inquiry and WiFi scanning begin at 0 s. At 2 s, nodes discover each other's SSIDs. Inquiry finishes at 10.24 s; paging 1–2 s after. Paged device names are shown in white (black background). The WiFi control frame lists each node's discovered Bluetooth addresses; double-lined ones are paged.

Bluetooth. All devices transmit control information via WiFi "control frames" and their messages in Bluetooth device names, which can store more information than SSIDs. SSIDs can be discovered within a couple seconds, whereas Bluetooth name discovery takes at least ten seconds. Such control frames contain a device's message (its Bluetooth address) along with others' messages. In the topology, B determines that A has not received C's Bluetooth address and forwards it, along with B's address, in B's control frame. Thus A can discover C's Bluetooth address and page it before Bluetooth inquiry is finished. C's message is piggybacked to A during the process. Similarly, B forwards A's address to C when it observes C has not received A's address.

This forwarding mechanism enables mobile devices to "see" each other's presence after they "meet." This surmounts the electronic barriers posed by conventional wireless protocols and achieves unobtrusive communication.

Forwarding with Reliability Enhancements. This NameCast forwarding mechanism is well suited to small-scale short message transmission without reliability. To achieve this at large scale, we enhance our mechanism to incorporate erasure coding. Our motivation is as follows. If many devices are transmitting messages to each other without connections, transmission errors are likely to occur: receivers may "miss" messages, messages may be garbled, etc. We need to enhance our forwarding mechanism so it can "recover" from these errors without substantial overhead. We use *fountain codes* to do so. In the following, we explain our rationale and coding approach.

Fountain codes are sparse graph codes for channels with erasures [16]. Such codes divide long messages into many small pieces and disseminate these pieces to receivers. Once receivers receive enough pieces, they can reconstruct the messages irrespective of the order of the pieces' delivery. Fountain codes have many desirable properties: they are simple to implement (typically using XOR operation), rateless (meaning a coding rate need not be specified in advance), and largely obviate a feedback channel. Receivers need not inform the sender about their "missing" message pieces, which can be tedious.

We use fountain codes at the MAC layer as ACKs are not present there. Acknowledging each successful channel access imposes extra overhead on protocols. Fountain codes transmit encoded messages without requiring a feedback channel. Receivers who have not received enough information need not feed this information to the message sender; as the sender keeps sending, they simply wait until they have received enough information. Our fountain coding approach uses the following concepts:

– *Bluetooth frame:* A Bluetooth frame is a message consisting of all nearby devices' Bluetooth names. Each device constructs its own frame and disseminates it to all nearby devices. Each frame has a unique two-digit ID.
– *Encoded chunk:* We encode the Bluetooth frame using fountain codes and split it into equal-size chunks, each of which fits in a Bluetooth device name. When disseminating its Bluetooth frame, each device publishes the frame's (coded) chunks in its Bluetooth name.

Devices always transmit and receive chunks. If a receiver does not receive a transmitted chunk, it gathers more chunks until it reconstructs the Bluetooth frame. This enables error recovery with low overhead, achieving reliable communication.

Protocol Details: Due to the space limit, further details are discussed in [17].

5   PicComm: Enclave-to-Master Communication

Enclave can realize secure communication between the master and enclave devices via picture communication (PicComm), a visual communication based on picture-taking without wireless communications. We detail it in this section.

Design Rationale: We need a secure communication channel between the master and enclave devices to send useful information to the master. This is challenging. Such a channel needs to be protected from eavesdropping attackers. But the master cannot totally trust the enclave, as it is exposed to the outside world in which malicious codes or data can reside. We argue that wireless connection-based communication may not be secure enough due to security problems [18] or vulnerabilities [19]. Further, some users may be concerned about disclosing their electronic identities like MAC addresses when using WiFi or Bluetooth.

We propose PicComm in Enclave to establish such secure communication. In PicComm, the master device takes pictures of the enclave device's screen, which displays textual messages, and recognizes their contents using optical character recognition (OCR). In this way, information transmission from the enclave to the master is highly secure. PicComm also needs to achieve high throughput, but a device's screen size is limited and OCR results are not 100% accurate. Intuitively, if the message on the screen has larger font size and letterspacing, OCR performs better, but the message volume on-screen decreases. Thus, we propose a dynamic resolution adjustment mechanism for PicComm to find a tradeoff between the message volume and the "resolution," i.e., font size and letterspacing. In our mechanism, the master device sends feedback to the enclave device (ACK or NAK) and a hash value indicating the OCR error amount. Based on this information, the enclave device dynamically adjusts the resolution of its on-screen message. We consider two options for the feedback channel: wireless name communication and sound. Wireless name communication is part of NameCast: we use the WiFi SSID to transmit the feedback message (up to 32 bytes). But the master device has to disclose its WiFi MAC address, which may concern some users. Thus, we propose the second option: sound. With sound, PicComm can achieve greater security without disclosing electronic information. The drawback is low channel capacity (1 or 2 bits per feedback message).

Protocol Details: Due to the space limit, further details are discussed in [17].

6   Implementation and Evaluation

We implement Enclave on Google Nexus S smartphones running Android 2.3.3. These phones have both Bluetooth and WiFi functionality. We perform factory reset using standard Android techniques [20].

6.1   Implementation

We implement NameCast on the Nexus Ss. Our prototype system is written in Java; the Android package size is 52.7 KB. Our system uses the BlueZ binary hcitool [21] for Bluetooth inquiry and paging. Our system establishes an ad hoc wireless network for each smartphone to publish WiFi SSIDs and scan for nearby networks. We implement ad hoc networking using Wireless Tools for Linux [22] and wpa_supplicant [23]. We implement erasure coding using LT codes. We set $\epsilon = 0.5$, message length $m = 20$, and chunk length $n = 60$.

We implement a similar prototype system running a *naïve version* of the NameCast protocol that publishes static Bluetooth names and WiFi SSIDs. It has no control frame information or message delivery piggybacking. We use this naïve protocol as a control in the experiments described in §6.2.

We implement PicComm on the Nexus Ss. The enclave device displays textual content of which the master device takes pictures and processes using OCR. Specifically, the enclave device displays text on the screen in a 2×2 block layout (four blocks in total). In our experiments, the enclave device displays text from *Alice's Adventures in Wonderland*. The master device processes the text using OCR Tool for Android [24], which invokes the Tesseract OCR engine [25].

6.2   Evaluation

NameCast. We test our naïve and NameCast systems in a university building with 5 Nexus Ss and 14 other mobile devices. We use 4 iPod touches, 3 laptops, and 7 mobile phones. For all experiments, we run each system ten times.

We evaluate our naïve and NameCast systems using the following metrics:
(1) *Coverage.* We measure how many devices we discover while running both

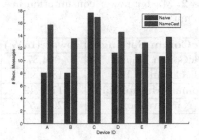

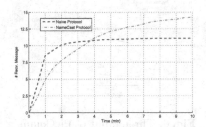

Fig. 4. Average number of received messages by each device

Fig. 5. Average time needed for devices to receive messages

systems; and (2) *Power consumption.* We measure Nexus S power consumption during each run of the naïve and NameCast systems.

Fig. 4 shows the average number of received messages for these systems. For most devices, the NameCast system discovered more devices in the network than the naïve system. This occurred because NameCast forwarded Bluetooth messages among many hops; the naïve system could only discover devices one hop away. These results are encouraging: they show the NameCast system can generally discover more Bluetooth devices in a network than a naïve system.

Fig. 5 shows the average time required for devices to receive messages with the naïve and NameCast systems. After three minutes, the number of devices the naïve system discovered levels off, whereas the number of devices the NameCast system discovers increases over time. The curves cross at about four minutes. This is unsurprising, as NameCast forwards Bluetooth messages among many hops and the naïve system can only discover messages one hop away. We see that, with enough time, the NameCast system can discover more nodes in the network than the naïve system.

Our results also illustrate NameCast's ability to achieve unobtrusive communication on a wide range of mobile devices. NameCast users need not install our software on their devices to use our protocol; they set their Bluetooth names following NameCast's format to communicate with devices running the software.

PicComm. We test PicComm using Nexus Ss. Two phones playing the roles of an enclave and a master are placed face-to-face. The following three different mechanisms are evaluated: (1) Naïve version without any feedback. The enclave device only uses a default setting and never changes its resolution setting. (2) PicComm with 1-bit feedback (via sound or NameCast). The master device only provides 1 bit of feedback, i.e., ACK or NAK, to the enclave device. The enclave device changes its resolution setting uniformly. (3) PicComm with multiple-bit feedback via NameCast. We split the enclave device's screen into four blocks and the OCRHash value for each block is 0–3, which takes 2 bits. 1 bit is reserved for a CRC check result. Totally, 9 bits of (NameCast) feedback are used.

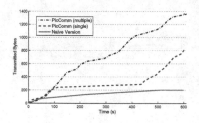

Fig. 6. Throughput of PicComm

Table 2. Master power consumption in PicComm

PicComm Setting	Power (mW)
PicComm (sound)	904.87
PicComm (1 bit)	1899.99
PicComm (Multiple bits)	1700.42
Naïve version	2027.53

We focus on the following metrics: *throughput* and *power consumption*. The results are shown in Fig. 6 and Table 2. From Fig. 6, we see that PicComm performs better with more feedback. This shows that block-based dynamic resolution adjustment helps improve PicComm's throughput. PicComm's throughput with multiple-bit feedback is almost twice that of 1-bit PicComm. We see that PicComm's throughput varies with different contents but is generally stable. The final throughput is ∼2 bytes/s, enough to transmit short messages between the master and enclave. The naïve version does not work well; only a few messages are transmitted successfully. Table 2 shows average power consumption rates of different mechanisms within a 30 minute test period. PicComm's power consumption rate is fairly low when only sound is used for feedback. With PicComm, WiFi and the camera consume the most power. With multiple-bit feedback, PicComm's power consumption rate is lower than with 1-bit feedback. We explain this as follows: fewer rounds of feedback are performed for PicComm with multiple-bit feedback, which encounters fewer OCR failures.

7   Final Remarks

We proposed *Enclave*, a delegate wireless device that helps people's smartphones communicate unobtrusively. We realized Enclave using two key supporting technologies, NameCast and PicComm. We implemented Enclave on Nexus S smartphones. Our experimental evaluation showed Enclave's potential for smartphone data protection and unobtrusive and secure communication.

References

1. Zhang, B., Teng, J., Bai, X., Yang, Z., Xuan, D.: P^3-Coupon: a Probabilistic System for Prompt and Privacy-preserving Electronic Coupon Distribution. In: PerCom (2011)
2. Teng, J., Zhang, B., Li, X., Bai, X., Xuan, D.: E-Shadow: Lubricating Social Interaction using Mobile Phones. In: ICDCS (2011)
3. Eagle, N., Pentland, A.: Social Serendipity: Mobilizing Social Software. IEEE Pervasive Computing, 28–34 (April–June 2005)
4. http://www.nokia-asia.com/support/download-software/nokia-sensor

5. Gaonkar, S., Li, J., Choudhury, R.R., Cox, L., Shmidt, A.: Micro-Blog: Sharing and Querying Content Through Mobile Phones and Social Participation. In: MobiSys (2008)
6. Miluzzo, E., Lane, N.D., Fodor, K., Peterson, R., Lu, H., Musolesi, M., Eisenman, S.B., Zheng, X., Campbell, A.T.: Sensing meets mobile social networks: the design, implementation and evaluation of the CenceMe application. In: SenSys (2008)
7. Yang, Z., Zhang, B., Dai, J., Champion, A.C., Xuan, D., Li, D.: E-SmallTalker: A Distributed Mobile System for Social Networking in Physical Proximity. In: ICDCS (2010)
8. Chandra, R., Padhye, J., Ravindranath, L., Wolman, A.: Beacon-Stuffing: Wi-Fi Without Associations. In: HotMobile (2007)
9. Chandra, R., Padhye, J., Ravindranath, L.: Wi-Fi Neighborcast: Enabling Communication Among Nearby Clients. In: HotMobile (2008)
10. Villanueva, M., Calafate, C.T., Cano, J.C., Manzoni, P.: Solving the MANET autoconfiguration problem using the 802.11 SSID field. In: MoMM (2010)
11. Reyes, J.C., Burgoa, E., Calafate, C.T., Cano, J.C., Manzoni, P.: A MANET Autoconfiguration System based on Bluetooth Technology. In: ISWCS (2006)
12. Davies, N., Friday, A., Newman, P., Rutlidge, S., Storz, O.: Using Bluetooth Device Names to Support Interaction in Smart Environments. In: MobiSys (2009)
13. McDonald, D.W., McCarthy, J.F., Soroczak, S., Nguyen, D.H., Rashid, A.M.: Proactive Displays: Supporting Awareness in Fluid Social Environments. ACM Trans. on Computer-Human Interaction 14(4), 16:1–16:31 (2008)
14. Wi-Fi Alliance: Wi-Fi CERTIFIED Wi-Fi Direct^{TM} Frequently Asked Questions, http://www.wi-fi.org/files/faq_20101021_Wi-Fi_Direct_FAQ.pdf
15. Perli, S.D., Ahmed, N., Katabi, D.: Pixnet: interference-free wireless links using lcd-camera pairs. In: MobiCom, pp. 137–148 (2010)
16. MacKay, D.: Fountain codes. IEEE Proc. Comm. 152(6), 1062–1068 (2005)
17. Champion, A.C., Li, X., Zhai, Q., Teng, J., Xuan, D.: Enclave: Promoting Unobtrusive and Secure Mobile Communications with a Ubiquitous Electronic World. Technical report, The Ohio State University (2012), http://cse.osu.edu/~champion/pubs/12_clztx_enclave_tech.pdf
18. Rowan, T.: Negotiating wifi security. Network Security 2010(2), 8–12 (2010)
19. Albanesius, C.: HTC Smartphone Vulnerability Exposes Your Personal Data, http://www.pcmag.com/article2/0,2817,2393999,00.asp
20. http://developer.android.com/guide/topics/admin/device-admin.htm
21. BlueZ, http://www.bluez.org
22. http://www.hpl.hp.com/personal/Jean_Tourrilhes/Linux/Tools.html
23. Malinen, J.: wpa_supplicant, http://w1.fi/wpa_supplicant/
24. Theis, R.M.: OCR Tool, https://github.com/rmtheis/android-ocr
25. Tesseract-OCR, http://code.google.com/p/tesseract-ocr/

Truthful Multi-unit Double Auction for Spectrum Allocation in Wireless Communications

He Huang[1], Yu-e Sun[2], Kai Xing[3], Hongli Xu[3],
Xueyong Xu[3], and Liusheng Huang[3]

[1] Computer Science and Technology, Soochow University
huangh@suda.edu.cn
[2] Urban Rail Transportation, Soochow University
[3] Computer Science and Technology, University of Science and Technology of China
kxing@ustc.edu.cn

Abstract. In this paper, we propose a truthful multi-unit double auction scheme for the scenarios that multiple buyers/sellers have different demands to buy/sell, which involves a series of bid-related buyer group construction and winner determination strategies. In the analysis, we show the correctness and effectiveness of the proposed scheme and prove that it improves the spectrum reusability and is truthful. To the best of our knowledge, it is the first multi-unit double auction approach for wireless spectrum allocation.

Keywords: spectrum allocation, multi-unit double auction.

1 Introduction

As the increasing popularity of wireless devices and applications, the ever-increasing demand of traffic poses a great challenge in spectrum allocation and usage. However, large companies and organizations occupy many spectrum resources by means of long-term and regional leases [1,2] without considering spectrum reuse, while new applicants, e.g., non-contract users, new applicant, etc., are in great shortage of spectrum resources. Therefore, it is imperative to provide an effective solution to redistribute the under-utilized spectrum resources to the ones in shortage of spectrum.

Auction, in which the spectrum owners could gain utilities to lease their idle spectrum in economic perspective [3,4] while new applicants could gain access to the spectrum, may serve as such a promising way that could better increase the efficiency, effectiveness and economic properties of the spectrum. However, in traditional one-to-many single-sided auction style (similar to FCC method) the rare resources are in centralized control of the seller/buyer, which is "resource dominant side" that has the rights to establish rule of transactions. This auction style may cause collusion or market manipulation problem.

Compared to single-sided auction [5, 6, 7], double auction mechanism is more suitable for spectrum redistribution owing to its fairness and allocation efficiency.

X. Wang et al. (Eds.): WASA 2012, LNCS 7405, pp. 248–257, 2012.

Both of the buyer and seller group will lose their relative dominant position in double auction procedure, and their relationship becomes supply and demand coordination [8]. Consequently, double auction mechanism is more likely to achieve maximum spectrum reuse under the premise of protecting the profits of buyers and sellers. TRUST [9] is regarded as the first work to tightly integrate spectrum allocation and pricing components by using double auction mechanism. However, it only considers single-unit double auction issue, and thus lacks the ability to support auction in multi-radio wireless networks, which is taken as the enabling technology of next generation wireless network communications [10,11].

However, in double auction different buyer groups stand for different purchasing power and different payoff. It is hard to ensure that all the buyers bid truthfully by using the existing clearing price rule. Besides, in spectrum auction buyers could share the same spectrum if they don't interference with each other in spectrum auction, e.g., heterogeneous geo-location could enable spectrum reuse. This requires double auction mechanism consider economic effects not only in the process of transaction set construction (just like TRUST) but also in buyer group construction section.

To solve these issues, we propose a novel multi-unit double spectrum auction which satisfies the economic properties, spectrum reuse and market clearing. Compared with existing traditional single-unit double auction approaches, the major contributions of this paper can be identified as follows:

- It jointly considers economic properties with spectrum allocation problem. It could constitute a NASH Equilibrium through the whole auction process, better improves spectrum reuse, and further leads buyers and sellers participating the auction in an honest and fair manner.
- SPRITE provides a new clearing price mechanism to assure the strategy-proof property and other essential economic properties, which is different from traditional spectrum auction methods.
- Compared with single-unit auction, it is the first work that achieves multi-unit double auction that satisfies the needs of users in multi-radio wireless networks and improves auction efficiency at the same time.

The rest of paper is organized as follows: Section2 introduces preliminaries and surveys the most related work. Section3 proposes our algorithm design. In section4, we prove the correctness, effectiveness, and evaluates the performance of our approach and Section5 concludes the paper.

2 Preliminaries and Background

2.1 Assumptions and Terminologies

We assume the double auction process is sealed-bid with no collusion. We also assume that multi-unit bids are "divisible": *A buyer/seller willing to buy/sell q units at a specified price-per-unit would also be willing to trade q' at that price, where $q' < q$. Each seller/buyer could have multi-unit homogeneous channels to sell/buy.*

We have the following notations

- I: Group of all buyers;
- J: Group of all sellers, where $I \cap J = \phi$;
- f_i: The bid of buyer i, $i \in I$, f_i can be deemed as maximum price it is willing to pay for a channel;
- K_i: Number of channels requirement for buyer i;
- g_i: The bid of seller j, $j \in J$, g_i can be deemed as minimum price it is required to sell a channel;
- K_j: Number of channels provided by seller j;
- Vf_i: For a buyer, its true valuation of the channel;
- P_{f_i}: If buyer i wins, the price it needs to pay for each channel at bid f_i;
- U_{f_i}: The utility of a buyer i, $U_{f_i} = \sum_{K_i} Vf_i - \sum_{K_i} P_{f_i}$;
- V_{g_j}: For a seller, its true valuation of the channel;
- P_{g_j}: If seller j wins, the actual payment it receives for each channel;
- U_{g_i}: The utility of a seller j, $U_{g_i} = \sum_{K_j} P_{g_i} - \sum_{K_j} V_{g_j}$

Suppose there are $|I|$ buyers and $|J|$ sellers, where $\mathbf{n} = |I| + |J|$.

(1) Strategy-proof. In a double auction, if no buyer or seller could improve its utility with an untruthful bid, the auction is called strategy-proof.

(2) Auction efficiency. The valuation of the buyers is optimized. An auction is efficient if there are no further gains from trade possible. This implies that the channels are allocated to the buyers who value them most highly. That is to say, a mechanism is efficient if it implements an allocation that maximizes welfare.

2.2   Related Research

Auction theory has been widely used for spectrum allocation, on-line business, resource allocation on computational grids and so on. In the past decades, large amount of studies have been paid on it. However, existing works often addressed single-sided auctions. TRUST can be considered as the first strategy-proof and spectrum reuse double auction method, but it only refers to one-to-one channel trading. In our opinion, this assumption makes the double spectrum auction more unreasonable.

The literature on strategy-proof mechanism design starts from the classical method by Vickrey-Clarke-Groves (VCG) mechanism (Vickrey 1961, Clarke 1971 and Groves 1973). The improved VCG double auction [12] mechanism is strategy-proof, ex-post individual-rational, and efficient, but not budget balanced with multiple buyers and sellers. Few papers deal with strategy-proof, budget-balanced double auction mechanisms. McAfee [13] proposes a strategy-proof, budget-balanced double auction mechanism for a simple exchange environment, in which all the agents exchange only one unit good. In [14], the author extended McAfee, in which all agents could exchange multi-unit goods. Wurman [15] examines a general family of auction mechanisms that admit multiple buyers and sellers, and proposes a method to transform the buyers' multi-unit

Table 1. Comparing of different double auction mechanisms

Existing auction mechanism	Strategy -proof	Ex-post budget -balanced	Individual rationality	Spectrum reuse	Multi-unit goods trading
VCG	√	×	√	×	×
McAfee	√	×	√	×	×
BC-LP	√	√	√	×	×
Wurman	√	√	√	×	√
TRUST	√	√	√	√	×
Ours	√	√	√	√	√

demand to single-unit transaction. Babaioff [16] proposes a budget-balanced and strategy-proof double auction mechanism for a bilateral exchange scenario with the simple assumption and single output restriction, where each buyer desire for a bundle of goods. Chu and Shen [17] propose an asymptotically efficient truthful double auction mechanism called BC-LP, which achieves bundle of commodities transaction for buyers. TRUST [9] is the first strategy-proof and spectrum reuse double auction method. However, it considers non-divisible one-to-one channel trading only. Table 1 shows the summarization of these existing designs using in the double spectrum auction.

3   Algorithm Design

In this section, we propose our proposed multi-unit double spectrum auction mechanism, which consists of three phases: buyer group construction; bid set and transaction set formation; and market clearing price determination.

3.1   Buyer Group Construction

Step(1): Conflict graph construction
Note that buyers within each other's communication range cannot use the same spectrum due to interference, we model the buyers' interference relationship in the network as an undirected conflict graph $G = (V, E)$, where each buyer in the network is represented by a node in the graph, V represents the node set in the graph, E represents the edge set in the graph. There is an edge $(i_1, i_2) \in E$ between nodes i_1 and i_2, if two nodes i_1 and i_2 interfere with each other. The node weight is defined as the buyer's per-channel bid price.

Step(2): Non-conflicting buyer group formation
To achieve maximum spectrum utilization/reusability, we construct buyers' *maximum independent set* to form buyer groups, where each buyer group is taken as a super buyer. The higher the total bid of a buyer group, the higher the bidding success rate for buyers in that group. The group with the highest bid could be taken as the max-weight independent set.

Note that finding maximum non-conflicting buyer bid group problem can be considered as max-weight independent set problem, which is a well-studied NP-hard combinatorial optimization problem that naturally arises in many applications. Specifically, let $C \subseteq V$ represent an independent set in $G = (V, E)$. We use $min(C)$ to denote the minimum weight of nodes in the independent set, the weight of the independent set is defined as $min(C)$ multiplied by the number of vertices in the independent set. Algorithm 1 shows the detailed procedure of Non-Conflicting Buyer group Construction (NCBC). Let $Max\_weight\_IS(i)$ denote the max-weight independent set including buyer i, and $Bid(MG_k)$ is the bid of MG_k. In the kth iteration of NCBC, we first traverse all the remaining buyers in the group, and compute the bid of each independent set formed by the remaining buyers in the buyer group I. The independent set with maximum $Bid(MG_k)$ will be chosen as the winner in this iteration. The iteration lasts until group I is empty.

Algorithm 1. Non-Conflicting Buyer Group Construction

1: $Max\_bid = 0$;
2: **for** $i = 1$ to remaining buyers in group I do **do**
3:     $Temp\_MG = Max\_weight\_IS(i)$;
4:     $Temp\_Bid = Bid(Max\_weight\_IS(i))$;
5:     **if** $(Temp\_bid > Max\_Bid)$ **then**
6:         $Max\_bid = Temp\_bid$,
7:         $MG_i = Temp\_MG$
8:     **end if**
9: **end for**
10: **for** each buyer i in MG_k **do**
11:     $|i| = |i| - \omega(MG_k)$
12: **end for**
13: delete the buyers (Satisfied $|i| - \omega(MG_k) = 0$) in set MG_k from group I
14: k increased by 1, *goto* 1 *while* group I nonempty

Theorem 1: Solution of buyer group formation game can be characterized by Nash Equilibrium (NE).

Proof: Due to page limits, the proof is referred to [18].

Step(3): Super buyer's property determination

We use $MG_1, MG_2, \ldots, MG_n$ to denote the formed non-conflicting buyer groups. A buyer group can be viewed as a super buyer. There are two parameters will be used to describe the super buyer's characteristics. One is super buyer's bid for unit commodity, $Bid(MG_k) = MinBid(MG_k) *$ *the number of buyer in MG_k*, while the $MinBid(MG_k) = min\{f_i | i \in MG_k\}$; The other is one super buyer's channel demand $\omega(MG_k)$, and the $\omega(MG_k) = min\{K_i | i \in MG_k\}$.

3.2   Bid Set and Transaction Set Formation

Without loss of generality, we assume the price-per-unit bids are arranged in descending order. We use positive quantities ($K_L > 0$) correspond to demands of buyers and negative quantities ($K_L < 0$) correspond to offers to sell from each seller. Here transaction set means the remaining super buyers and sellers at the end of a time round. Considering a scenario with M selling offers and N buying offers after bid set has been established. The $(M + 1)^{st}$-price means the $(M+1)^{st}$ highest offer among all $(M+N)$ bids. We use $rank(b_L)$ represents the position of a bid b_L in the bid set.

The $(M + 1)^{st}$-price rule is given under the following two conditions:

Condition 1: The $(M+1)^{st}$-price and M^{th}-price belong to different participants in the bid set.

If the $(M + 1)^{st}$-price comes from a seller, the transaction set construction rule can be depicted as following

$$\{K_L < 0 | rank(b_L) \geq M + 1\} \cup \{K_L > 0 | rank(b_L) < M + 1\} \tag{1}$$

If the $(M + 1)^{st}$-price comes from a buyer, the transaction set construction rule will be

$$\{K_L < 0 | rank(b_L) > M + 1\} \cup \{K_L > 0 | rank(b_L) < M + 1\} \tag{2}$$

Condition 2: The $(M + 1)^{st}$-price and M^{th}-price come from the same participant in bid set.

If the $(M + 1)^{st}$-price comes from a seller, the transaction set is the same as that in Condition 1. However, if the $(M + 1)^{st}$-price comes from a buyer, the transaction set will be different from that in Condition 1. Particularly, after initial transaction set is constructed based on rule in Condition 1, we delete the residual buyer's bid that equals to the $(M + 1)^{st}$-price in the bid set, and also delete the same number of seller's bid in descending order.

For example, if there are four sellers are willing to sell 8 channels, of which seller1 sells only one channel at price 13, seller2 sells 3 channels at price 10, seller3 sells 2 channels at price 7 and seller4 sells 1 channels at price 6. After the $(M + 1)^{st}$-rule has been executed, bid set and transaction set can be depicted as following.

$$\text{bid set:} \left\{ \underbrace{13}_{-1}, \underbrace{(12, 12)}_{2}, \underbrace{(10, 10, 10)}_{-3}, \underbrace{9}_{1}, \underbrace{(8, 8)}_{2}, \underbrace{(7, 7)}_{-2}, \underbrace{6}_{-1}, \underbrace{4}_{1}, \underbrace{(2, 2, 2)}_{3}, \right\}$$

$$\text{transaction set:} \left\{ \underbrace{(12, 12)}_{2}, \underbrace{9}_{1}, \underbrace{(7, 7)}_{-2}, \underbrace{6}_{-1} \right\}$$

3.3   Market Clearing Price Determination

To achieve the strategy-proof and market clearing aims, our algorithm charges each winning buyer the bid of the maximum weight clique it belonging to in the transaction set and pays each winning seller the maximum seller's payment in the transaction set. The primary issue in this section is to determine the clearing price which could match super buyers' channel request and sellers' channel provision. We charge all the winning buyers the same fee in the traditional auction mechanism. However, all the buyers in a winning group collaboratively pay for the designated channel in spectrum auction. Owing to correlation between buyer group construction and buyer's bid, traditional uniform clearing price strategy is hard to ensure truthful bid for each buyer. Thus, we improve the clearing price strategy, and the actual payment for each seller is the maximum bid of seller in the transaction set, which satisfied:

4   Analysis Study

In this section, we conduct analysis study to evaluate the performance of the proposed scheme under the metrics of spectrum utilization and truthfulness. Specifically, We compare the proposed scheme with the existing mechanism TRUST [9] and implement two versions of TRUST: TRUST-1 (single round auction) and TRUST-2 (multi-round auction).

Lemma 1: The proposed mechanism is truthful for buyers.

Proof: The demonstrate process is categorized into buyers respectively on the basis of case 1 to 4.

Case 1: No matter how buyer bid, it always lose in the auction in Case 1. We can conclude that the utility for buyer always goes zero.

Case 2: On the basis of observation 1, this case happens only if the buyer decreases its bid in auction process, namely $f_i' < Vf_i$. Buyer's utility is zero if it lies in this case, and the truthful action makes its utility no less than zero.

Case 3: This condition happens only if $f_i' > Vf_i$. According to lemma 1, buyers can't benefit from bidding $f_i' > Vf_i$ in case 3.

Case 4: No matter how buyer bid, it always wins the auction in Case 4. If the buyer bid $f_i' > Vf_i$, bidding truthful is the dominant strategy according to Lemma 3. Similarly, bidding truthfully is still the dominate strategy for buyers when $f_i' < Vf_i$.

Lemma 2: The proposed mechanism is truthful for sellers.

Proof:

Case 1 and Case 2: The proof procedure is the same with buyer case.

Case 3: This condition happens only if $g_j' < Vg_j$ on the basis of observation 1. We use the P_{g_j} stands for the payment to the auction winners. Owing to seller j loses in this case when it bids truthfully, we can get the conclusion that $P_{g_j} < Vg_i$. If the seller j wins the auction by bidding a lower price g_j', the payment to seller j must smaller than P_{g_j}. Thus, the payment to seller j also smaller than Vg_j, and the utility for seller j is negative when it bids untruthfully.

Case 4: the proposed mechanism pays each seller the minimum buyer group's bid in the transaction set. It is the critical value of seller group we mentioned in observation 2. According to observation 2, no matter the bidding price is f_j or f_j', the payment for seller j is all the same if it is win in the auction. That is to say, utility will not change in both conditions.

Theorem 1: The proposed mechanism is strategy-proof.

Proof: According to Lemma 1 and Lemma 2, the proposed mechanism is strategy-proof.

In the following, we conduct simulation study on the efficiency of the proposed scheme. All the simulation results are averaged over 1000 runs. All the buyers are deployed in a square 100*100 area under either random topology or clustered topology, and any two buyers within 20 unit distance are conflicting buyers and cannot bid the same channels. In the clustered topology, we set 50% of the whole buyers are distributed in a small area.

There are 30 buyers and 5 sellers in the simulations. The number of channels each buyer/seller demands/provides is in interval [1, 3]. The bidding prices for buyers are uniformly distributed in interval [10,35], and selling prices for sellers are uniformly distributed in interval [35,60].

Fig. 1 plots the degradation performance of the proposed scheme, TRUST-1 and TRUST-2 under random and clustered topologies respectively. In Fig. 1, the proposed scheme suffers less degradation than TRUST-1 and TRUST-2. This is because the proposed scheme constructs the buyer groups with each buyer's bid, thus the groups with higher bidding price are more likely to be generated. Therefore, the proposed scheme could increase the buyer groups' opportunity to successfully bid the channels.

Fig. 2 shows that SPRITE better meets the requirements of fairness principle than TRUST, which demonstrates our theoretical analysis. Fig. 3 shows that the average success rate for buyers increases from 28% up to 43% along the increase of maximum bidding price. In the clustered topology, the average success rate for sellers reaches 86% when the buyer's maximum bid equal to sellers' highest offer. In random topology, the average success rate for seller reaches 93%.

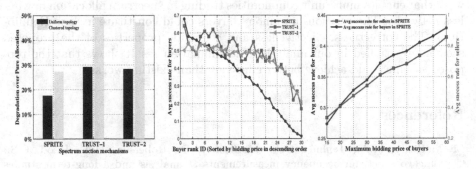

Fig. 1. Degradation   **Fig. 2.** Success rate of   **Fig. 3.** Average success
                           buyers   rate

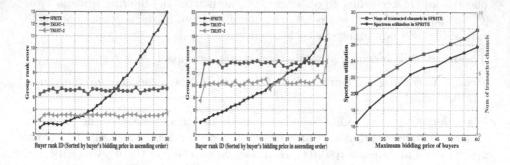

Fig. 4. Group rankings in random topology   **Fig. 5.** Group rankings in clustered topology   **Fig. 6.** Spectrum util. and # of transacted channels

Fig. 4 and Fig. 5 show the trend of group rank score corresponding to buyer's bid. We can see that in SPRITE the winning probability for a single buyer is corresponding to its bid, while in TRUST there is no such relationship. Owing to the TRUST mechanism chooses rand division method in the buyer group construction process, thus the bidding price for a buyer does not have positive connection with the rank of group it belongs to. This indicates that SPRITE provides a more reasonable solution in the realistic environment. Fig. 6 shows that the higher the maximum bidding price of buyers, the better the buyer's purchasing power, the larger the number of transacted channels, and the higher the average success rate and spectrum utilization.

5   Conclusion

In this paper, we propose a truthful multi-unit double auction framework for spectrum allocation in wireless networks. To our best knowledge, it is the first work that enables multi-unit commodities trading in spectrum allocation in wireless networks. The relationship among buyers could constitute a Nash Equilibrium. The correctness, effectiveness and economic properties of the proposed scheme are studied in our analysis. The simulation result shows that the proposed scheme could achieve better efficiency than existing works.

References

1. McHenry, M.A., Tenhula, P.A., McCloskey, D., Roberson, D.A., Hood, C.S.: Chicago spectrum occupancy measurements & analysis and a long-term studies proposal. In: Proc. TPAS (2006)
2. Jia, J.C., Zhang, Q., Zhang, Q., et al.: Revenue generation for truthful spectrum auction in dynamic spectrum access. In: Proc. of the 10th ACM Mobihoc, New Orleans, Louisiana, United States, pp. 3–12 (2009)

3. Zhu, J., Liu, K.J.R.: Multi-stage pricing game for collusion resistant dynamic spectrum allocation. IEEE Journal on Selected Areas in Communications 26(1), 182–191 (2008)
4. Kasbekar, G.S., Sarkar, S.: Spectrum auction framework for access allocation in cognitive radio networks. In: Proc. ACM Mobihoc (2009)
5. Zhou, X., Gandhi, S., Suri, S., Zheng, H.: eBay in the Sky: Strategy-Proof Wireless Spectrum Auctions. In: The Proceedings of ACM MobiCom 2008, San Francisco, CA (September 2008)
6. McAfee, R.P., McMillan, J.: Auctions and bidding. Journal of Economic Literature, 699–738 (1987)
7. Milgrom, P.R., Weber, R.J.: A theory of auctions and competitive bidding. Econometrica 1089–1122 (1982)
8. Friedman, D.: The double auction market institution: A survey. The double auction market: Institution, Theories, and Evidence, 3–25 (1993)
9. Zhou, X., Zheng, H.: TRUST: A General Framework for Truthful Double spectrum Auction. In: Proc. of IEEE Infocom 2009, Rio de Janeiro, Brazil, pp. 999–1007 (2009)
10. Dhananjay, A., Zhang, H., Li, J.Y., Subramanian, L.: Practical, Distributed Channel Assignment and Routing in Dual-radio Mesh Networks. In: Proc. of ACM SIGCOMM 2009, Barcelona, Spain, pp. 99–110 (2009)
11. Alicherry, M., Bhatia, R., Li, L.: Joint channel assignment and routing for throughput optimization in multi-radio wireless mesh networks. In: Proc. of ACM MobiCom 2005, Cologne, Germany, pp. 58–72 (2005)
12. Babaioff, M., Nisan, N.: Concurrent auctions across the supply chain. In: Proc. of Economic Commerce 2001, Tampa, Florida, United States, pp. 1–10 (2001)
13. McAfee, R.P.: A dominant strategy double auction. Journal of Economic Theory 56(2), 434–450 (1992)
14. Huang, P., Scheller-Wolf, A., Sycara, K.: Design of a multi-unit double auction e-market. Comput. Intelligence 18(4), 596–617 (2002)
15. Wurman, P.R., Walsh, W.E., Wellman, M.P.: Flexible double auctions for electronic commerce: theory and implementation. Decision Support System 24(1), 17–27 (1998)
16. Babaioff, M., Walsh, W.E.: Incentive-compatible, budget-balanced, yet highly efficient auctions for supply chain formation. In: Proc. of Forth ACM Conf. on Electronics Commerce, San Diego, United States, pp. 64–75 (2003)
17. Chu, L.Y., Shen, Z.M.: Truthful double auction mechanisms. Operation Research 56(1), 102–120 (2008)
18. Huang, H.: A Novel Strategy-proof Multi-unit Double Auction Framework for Spectrum Allocation. Tech. Report (2011),
http://staff.ustc.edu.cn/~kxing/Publications/TechReport/huang11.pdf

Joint Mobility and Heterogeneity for Connected
k-Coverage in Sparsely Deployed Wireless Sensor Nets

Habib M. Ammari

Wireless Sensor and Mobile Ad-hoc Networks (WiSeMAN) Research Lab,
Department of Computer and Information Science,
College of Engineering and Computer Science,
University of Michigan-Dearborn,
Dearborn, MI 48128, USA
hammari@umd.umich.edu

Abstract. The monitoring quality of a phenomenon depends on the *sensing coverage* provided by the sensors. Several applications require *sensing k-coverage*, where each point in the field is covered by at least k sensors. In this paper, we propose a generalized and optimized protocol for sensing k-coverage in sparsely deployed wireless sensor networks, called k-SCHEMES, using heterogeneous and mobile sensors. First, we characterize sensing k-coverage using heterogeneous sensors based on Helly's Theorem. Second, we propose an energy-efficient protocol to achieve on-demand sensing k-coverage of a region of interest in the field based on sensor group mobility. Third, we suggest two data gathering protocols on top of connected k-covered configurations for sparse and mobile heterogeneous wireless sensor networks. We corroborate our analysis with several simulation results.

Keywords: Connected k-coverage, mobility, heterogeneity, sparse sensor networks.

1   Introduction

Sensing coverage is one of the important research problems in wireless sensor networks (WSNs). Indeed, the effectiveness of any protocol is measured by its potential impact on increasing the network survivability. The latter depends on the quality of coverage provided by the network. To enhance network reliability, k-coverage is an appealing solution, where each point in a field is covered by at least k sensors.

1.1   Problem Formulation and Motivations

In this paper, we consider a generalized model to solve the mobile k-coverage problem in sparse WSNs while considering static and mobile heterogeneous sensors whose communication and sensing and ranges as well as their initial energy levels are not identical. The mobile k-coverage problem in this type of network is stated as follows, where k is the coverage degree:

X. Wang et al. (Eds.): WASA 2012, LNCS 7405, pp. 258–271, 2012.
© Springer-Verlag Berlin Heidelberg 2012

Given a region of interest (or simply region) I, a set S of heterogeneous static and mobile sensors, and a natural number k ≥ 3, select a minimum subset of sensors S' ⊆ S to remain active such that each point in I is k-covered, and the data reaches the sink while minimizing the energy consumption due to sensor mobility and communication.

Our work in this paper is motivated by the absence of such a generalized protocol for *k*-coverage in sparsely deployed WSNs, where heterogeneity and mobility coexist so the sensors could efficiently *k*-cover a region *I*. First, real-world applications may deploy heterogeneous sensors, which have a potential to extend the network lifetime and improve its reliability [21]. Second, it is important to account for sparse WSNs. Our *k*-SCHEMES protocol can accommodate these needs.

1.2 Major Contributions

We propose the first generalized protocol for *k*-coverage in sparsely deployed WSNs, called *k*-SCHEMES, which benefits from the combined advantages of sensor mobility and heterogeneity. Specifically, our *k*-SCHEMES framework considers a four-tier architecture that accounts for static and mobile heterogeneous sensors. First, we solve the *k*-coverage problem for static heterogeneous WSNs. Then, we exploit this result for *mobile k*-coverage in sparse heterogeneous WSNs using static and mobile sensors, where any region *I* in a field is *k*-covered. Also, we propose two data gathering protocols on top of mobile sensing *k*-coverage configurations in sparsely deployed heterogeneous and mobile WSNs. We corroborate our analysis with simulation results.

The rest of this paper is structured as follows. Section 2 defines key terms and presents the network model. Section 3 reviews related work on coverage. Section 4 solves the static *k*-coverage problem for heterogeneous WSNs. Section 5 solves the problem of mobile *k*-coverage in sparse heterogeneous WSNs. Section 6 gives simulation results. Section 7 concludes the paper.

2 Background

In this section, we give definitions and assumptions in the design of *k*-SCHEMES. Then, we present the energy and group mobility models we used in our study.

2.1 Background and Network Model

Definition 1: The *sensing range* of a sensor s_i is the space $SR(s_i)$ such that any event that occurs in $SR(s_i)$ will be detected by s_i. The *sensing neighbor set* of a sensor s_i consists of all the sensors located in its sensing range. ∎

Definition 2: The *communication range* of a sensor s_i is the space $CR(s_i)$ such that s_i can directly communicate with any sensor s_j in $CR(s_i)$. The *communication neighbor set* of a sensor s_i includes all the sensors located in its communication range. ∎

Definition 3: A point in a field is said to be *k-covered* if it belongs to the intersection of the sensing range of at least *k* sensors. A region *I* is said to be *k-covered* if every point in I is *k-covered*. A k-covered WSN is a WSN k-covering a field. We call *degree of coverage* of a WSN the maximum value of k such that I is k-covered.   ∎

Assumption 1: There is a single sink that is static, while the sensors could be either static or mobile. Some of these mobile sensors will act as *mobile proxy sinks* to collect data and deliver it to the sink.   ∎

Assumption 2: All the sensors are randomly and uniformly deployed in a field. Also, they are aware of their locations using a localization technique [4].   ∎

Assumption 3: The sensing range and communication range of sensor s_i are represented by disks of radii r_i and R_i, respectively.   ∎

2.2   Energy Model

We use the energy model given in [22], where the sensor energy consumption in transmission, reception, idle, and sleep modes are 60 mW, 12 mW, 12 mW, and 0.03 mW, respectively. Following [23], the energy required for a sensor to stay idle for 1 second is equivalent to *one unit of energy*. Moreover, the *energy spent in moving* is given by $E_{mv}(d) = e^{move} \times d$, where e^{move} is the energy cost for a sensor to move one unit distance, and d is the total distance traveled by a sensor [19]. As stated in [19], e^{move} is randomly selected in [0.008J, 0.012J].

2.3   Group Mobility Model

The *reference point group mobility* model (RPGM) [10] defines the mobility behavior for a group of nodes with respect to a special node, called *reference point*. The speed and motion direction of mobile nodes are derived from those of their reference point. In our experiments, we used an implementation of RPGM [10], where each sensor is supposed to move at a constant speed until it reaches its destination in the region I. We assume that a constant rate of energy drain will incur during sensor mobility [18]. Some mobile sensors, called *mobile proxy sinks*, will be selected as reference points.

3   Related Work

In this section, we describe a sample of approaches to achieve coverage in heterogeneous and mobile WSNs.

The problem of coverage and k-coverage in homogeneous WSNs has been studied well [8, 11, 20]. However, the problem of k-coverage in heterogeneous WSNs has received little attention. Duarte-Melo and Liu [6] considered two sensor deployment strategies, where the first one includes type-I sensors, while the second one includes an overlay of type-II sensors, which are more powerful but fewer in number. Then, they estimated the average network lifetime and quantified the optimal number of these type-II sensors, which act as cluster-heads. Mhatre *et al.* [15] considered a heterogeneous WSN with two types of nodes which differ by their density (λ_0, λ_1) and their battery energy (E_0, E_1). They computed the optimum node intensities (λ_0, λ_1) and node energies (E_0, E_1) to cover a surveillance area with a high probability. Wang *et al.* [17] proposed a fine analysis of coverage using two types of sensors with different capabilities and discussed the impact of heterogeneous sensing and communication ranges of the sensors on coverage and broadcast reachability. Du and Lin [5] proposed a differentiated coverage protocol for heterogeneous WSNs so different areas have different coverage degrees. Lazos and Poovendran [12] formulated the coverage problem in heterogeneous WSNs as a set intersection problem and derived analytical expressions for stochastic coverage.

Wang *et al.* [18] proposed solutions to the k-coverage problem by computing the minimum number of sensors to k-cover a field as well as their locations, and scheduling the sensors to move to these locations. In the first one, the sink computes those locations and the sensors bid for their closest locations. The second solution enables the sensors to derive the target locations. Wang *et al.* [19] generalized their solutions to the sensor selection and dispatch problems [18] for k-coverage. To the best of our knowledge, this is the only work on mobile k-coverage, which will be compared to k-SCHEMES.

In [1], we suggested a pseudo-random deployment approach for densely deployed sensors, which are distributed in different layers in a circular field based on the strength of their sensing range, communication range, and initial energy. This multi-tier architecture suffers from a few shortcomings. First, all the sensors including the sink, are static, thus suffering from the *energy sink-hole* problem [7], where all the sensors located around the sink are heavily used in forwarding data to the sink. Second, this type of pseudo-random deployment strategy is *restrictive* in the sense that the sensors should be placed in those layers with respect to their resources. Third, we assumed a densely deployed WSN to k-cover a field. Thus, our proposed pseudo-random deployment approach [1] may not be suitable for sparse WSNs. In particular, the k-coverage requirement may not be satisfied due to the lack of sensors to k-cover an entire field.

Our Proposed Work: In this paper, we propose a more general protocol, called k-SCHEMES. First, we exploit *sensor mobility* so that the neighborhood of the sink changes over time, thus solving the severe energy sink-hole problem described earlier. Second, we consider sensor *random deployment* to alleviate the restriction imposed by the pseudo-random sensor deployment strategy on the sensors' distribution in the field [1]. Third, we consider a *sparse* WSN, where the total number of sensors cannot provide full k-coverage of a field, where every point should be k-covered. But, any region I in the field could be k-covered provided that the sensors are willing to move to this region I and k-cover it. Fourth, we deal with more realistic network settings, where the sensors are generally heterogeneous. This makes our protocol more practical than existing one [2], which accounts for homogeneous sensors only.

4 k-Coverage Using Static Sensors

In this section, we analyze k-coverage in homogeneous WSNs [1]. Then, we adapt this analysis to the general case of heterogeneous WSNs.

4.1   Homogeneous k-Coverage

Helly's Theorem [3] states that if E is a family of convex sets in IR^n such that for $m \geq n + 1$, any m members of E have a non-empty intersection, then the intersection of all members of E is not empty. In [1], our characterization of k-coverage using homogeneous sensors was based on *Helly*'s Theorem [3] and the intersection of k sensing disks. The proposed k-coverage protocol assumes that each sensor selects some of its neighboring sensors to k-cover its sensing range. Thus, all the sensors are assumed to be fully cooperative when they receive queries from their sensing neighbors to stay *active* (or *on*). Next, we briefly state Theorem 1 and Theorem 2 [1] without any proof.

Theorem 1 [1]: Let $k \geq 3$. A region is k-covered with a minimum number of sensors if for any slice of width r in the region, there is an adjacent slice of width r such that their *lens* contains at least k active sensors.   ∎

Theorem 2 [1]: Let $k \geq 3$ and assume that a region I of size I_0 is sliced into overlapping Reuleaux triangles of width r. The total number of sensors required to guarantee k-coverage of this region I and denoted by $n(r, k, I)$, is given by

$$n(r, k, I) = \frac{0.8141\, k}{r^2} \times I_0$$ ∎

4.2   Heterogeneous k-Coverage

Achieving k-coverage with heterogeneous sensors is more challenging given that the sensors do not possess the same sensing range. Precisely, let us assume that a region I would be sliced into Reuleaux triangles of width r in order to k-cover it. One of the following two problems would arise.

Problem 1 (Under k-coverage): If sensors whose radii of their sensing ranges are smaller than r are to be selected to k-cover a region I, there is no guarantee that I will be k-covered. For instance, if some of those selected sensors are located on the boundary of a lens in the region I, it is impossible to k-cover the underlying lens. That is, the whole region I cannot be k-covered. Thus, the mission cannot be accomplished successfully. We refer to this problem as *under k-coverage*.

Problem 2 (Over k-coverage): If sensors whose radii of their sensing ranges are greater than r are to be selected to k-cover a region I, some parts in the region I will be more than k-covered. Thus, the sensors will not be used efficiently to extend the network lifetime. We refer to this problem as *over k-coverage*.

As can be seen, the selection of sensors to participate in the k-coverage process is the key to accomplish the mission (*i.e.*, k-coverage of a region I) for which the sensors are deployed while prolonging the network lifetime for as long as possible. Given the geometric shape of the sensing range of the sensors as well as their heterogeneous nature, it is impossible to achieve *exact k-coverage* of any region I (*i.e.*, each point in the region I is covered by exactly k sensors). In order to solve the problem of under k-coverage and alleviate the problem of over k-coverage, a sensor should select sensors to k-cover a region I using the following rule, which characterizes k-coverage in heterogeneous WSNs based on *Helly*'s Theorem [3] and Theorem 1 [1]:

k-Coverage characterization: Suppose that a region I need to be sliced into Reuleaux triangles of width r in order to be k-covered. A sensor s_i selects a sensor s_j to participate in the k-coverage of the region I only if the radius r_j of the sensing range of s_j is at least equal to r (*condition* 1) and the difference between the radii r and r_j is as small as possible (*condition* 2). As stated in Theorem 1 [1], static sensors must be selected from lenses of a slicing grid of the region I to k-cover I with a minimum number of sensors (*i.e.*, minimum k-coverage). Also, mobile sensors should move to those lenses to achieve minimum k-coverage.

Formally, **condition 1** implies $r_j \geq r$ and **condition 2** implies $r_j - r = \varepsilon$, where ε is an infinitesimal positive value, *i.e.*, $\varepsilon \to 0$. Notice that while **condition 1** helps solve the under k-coverage problem, **condition 2** helps alleviate the problem of over k-coverage. The design of our mobile k-coverage protocol for heterogeneous and mobile WSNs is based on these two conditions.

5 k-Coverage Using Mobile Sensors

In this section, we describe our solution to the problem of k-coverage using heterogeneous sensors while considering sensor mobility. First, we give the design decisions of k-SCHEMES. Second, we present our network architecture model. Third, we discuss how to achieve k-coverage of any region I based on the sensor group mobility model. Fourth, we propose two data gathering algorithms.

5.1   Four-Tier Sensor Network Architecture

Any monitoring activity, which takes place in the field and requires k-coverage, is called *mission*. Now, we propose our four-tier architecture, which consists of the following architectural elements:

- A *central gathering point* (or *static sink*). All the data generated during any mission in the field should be received by the static sink. These data is needed for a more accurate decision making process regarding the underlying mission.
- Several *mobile data collecting points* (or *mobile proxy sinks*). They collect data for any mission to which they are assigned and deliver it to the sink. Also, they are responsible for slicing a region I and determining the number of sensors needed to k-cover the region I. This helps achieve the mission goals successfully.
- A number of *static data generating points* (or *static sensors*). They are sparsely deployed in the field. Thus, they cannot ensure k-coverage of any region I. They will send their data to their corresponding mobile proxy sinks.
- A larger number of *mobile data generating points* (or *mobile sensors*). These sensors will be used to support the static sensors so that any region I in the field is guaranteed to be k-covered. They have to transmit their data to their selected mobile proxy sinks. Also, they are willing to move to any region I to k-cover it.

In other words, they are supposed to be fully cooperative with the mobile proxy sinks regarding any mission that needs to be accomplished.

5.2 k-SCHEMES Design Decisions

Now, we describe all the design decisions regarding all types of sensors that form our four-tier architecture.

- A single mission at a time will be accomplished. The case of multiple missions at the same time is left as future work.
- Each mission requires k-coverage with $k \geq 3$ so it can be done successfully.
- The static sink is aware of all the missions that will be accomplished in the field. It has an entire schedule of the regions of interest to be k-covered.
- All mobile proxy sinks and static and mobile sensors are supposed to be *randomly deployed* in the field. However, the static sink is located at the center of the field, which corresponds to optimum energy consumption for data gathering [13].
- All static sensors are *homogeneous*, *i.e.*, have the same initial energy, and sensing and communication ranges. Also, all mobile sensors are supposed to be *homogeneous*, but *more powerful* than those static sensors in terms of the above features.
- All mobile proxy sinks are *homogeneous* and *more powerful* than those static and mobile sensors with respect to all of their capabilities. Indeed, these mobile proxy sinks will be responsible to ensure k-coverage of any region I in the field. They will communicate with the static and mobile sensors to k-cover the region I. Also, they have to deliver the data to the static sink, thus, acting as data Mules [16]. It is well known that compared to processing and sensing, communication is the major source of energy consumption. This is the reason why mobile proxy sinks are more powerful than all the static and mobile sensors.
- All mobile proxy sinks and static and mobile sensors are fully cooperative. They are willing to k-cover any region I when they are requested.
- Mobile sensors will move only when they are instructed by their *leader mobile proxy sink*, which will be defined later.

5.3 Achieving Mobile k-Coverage

In this section, we propose a distributed protocol to k-cover a region I while reducing the energy consumption due to sensor communication and mobility. First, we describe how to identify a mobile proxy sink to take the lead on a mission and accomplish it. Second, we discuss how mobile sensors are selected by a mobile proxy sink so they move to the region I and participate to its k-coverage.

Mobile Proxy Sink Selection: We assume that each region I is a square area with center (x_0,y_0) and side length a. Each mobile proxy sink has a unique *id* and keeps track of the number of mobile sensors located within its communication range. Moreover, each mobile proxy sink is aware of the locations of the static sensors in the field. First, we define the *local density* of a mobile proxy sink.

Definition 4: The *local density* of a mobile proxy sink s_i, denoted by $LD(s_i)$, is the number of mobile sensors located in the communication range of s_i.   ∎

Definition 5: A mobile proxy sink s_i is said to be *denser* than a mobile proxy sink s_j if the local density of s_i is greater than that of s_j, *i.e.*, $LD(s_i) > LD(s_j)$.   ∎

The static sink specifies the region I to be k-covered. Then, it broadcasts a QUERY packet whose structure is: QUERY $= <(x_0,y_0),a>$. The selection of a mobile proxy sink, which will be responsible to carry out this mission, is determined in a distributed manner via negotiation among all mobile proxy sinks. When a mobile proxy sink s_i receives the QUERY packet, it runs the following steps whenever possible:

- *Candidacy Step:* Using its local density $LD(s_i)$ and the number of static sensors $NSS(I)$ located in the region I, s_i checks whether k-coverage of this region I can be achieved based on Theorem 2. That is, s_i determines it is a *candidate mobile proxy sink* so it can perform the mission successfully if the next inequality is satisfied:

$$LD(s_i) + NSS(I) \geq n(r, k, I)$$

  where r is the radius of the sensing range of static sensors, in case at least one static sensor would be selected by mobile proxy sink s_i to k-cover a region I. Otherwise, r is the radius of the sensing range of mobile sensors.
  - If yes, s_i is considered as a candidate mobile proxy sink for accomplishing this mission. It sends a short VOLUNTEER packet including its *id*, local density, and its current location. This packet should be received by all the mobile proxy sinks within $t_{candidate\text{-}mps\text{-}found}$ time so that they know that there is at least one candidate mobile proxy sink that has been found to carry out the mission. Then, s_i waits for some time to listen to other VOLUNTEER packets.
  - Else, s_i ignores the QUERY packet as it is unable to accomplish the mission.
- *Volunteering Step:* When a mobile proxy sink s_i receives a VOLUNTEER packet from another mobile proxy sink s_j, it checks whether it is a better candidate than s_j. Hence, s_i focuses on the energy consumption due to mobility, which depends on the distance being traveled by a sensor as stated in our energy model in Section 2.2. Given that s_i will act as a reference point, s_i estimates the average energy consumption per sensor caused by mobility as the energy consumption s_i will spend by moving to the center (x_0,y_0) of region I. Thus, s_i acts as follows:
  - If s_i is closer to (x_0,y_0) of the region I than s_j, then s_i will maintain its candidacy.
  - Otherwise, s_i will simply give up as its selection would cause higher energy consumption due to sensor mobility to the region I.
- *Leading Step:* After $t_{leader\text{-}mps\text{-}selected}$ time, a mobile proxy sink (known as *leader mobile proxy sink*) should have been selected to take the lead on accomplishing a mission. When a mobile proxy sink finds out that it is a leader mobile proxy sink, it sends out a short LEADER packet, including its *id* and the QUERY packet $<(x_0,y_0),a>$ originated from the sink.
- *Merge Step:* If after $t_{candidate\text{-}mps\text{-}found}$ time, no VOLUNTEER packet has reached the mobile proxy sinks, it means that no one of them has enough local density to ensure k-coverage of the region I. In this case, each mobile proxy sink s_i advertises a short HELLO packet including its *id*, location, and local density. When s_i receives a

HELLO packet, it compares its local density to those of all other mobile proxy sinks. Then, s_i chooses to merge its local density with the mobile proxy sink (s_j) that has the smallest local density so that the sum of the local densities of s_i and s_j is enough k-cover the region I. If s_i find more than one mobile proxy sink with the smallest local density, it breaks the tie by using the closest one to it. In case there is still tie, s_i chooses to merge with the one with the smallest id. To reduce energy consumption due to control overhead, only s_i would reply if its local density is less than that of s_j. More precisely, s_j gives up and s_i becomes a candidate mobile proxy sink. In this case, s_i is said to be a *merger mobile proxy sink*. Thus, if s_i is selected as a candidate or leader mobile proxy sink, the local density of s_j will join that of s_i. At the end of this merge operation, each candidate mobile proxy sinks broadcasts its VOLUNTEER packet to initiate the *Volunteering Step*.

Mobile Sensor Selection: The main goal in the design of k-SCHEMES is to reduce energy consumption while ensuring k-coverage of any region I. k-SCHEMES attempts to achieve this design goal by reducing the energy consumption due to several sources, such as data transmission, data reception, sensing, and sensor mobility. Knowing the number of static sensors located in the region I, say $NSS(I)$, a leader mobile proxy sink computes the necessary number of mobile sensors, denoted by $NMS(I)$, to move toward the region I and k-cover it. To this end, the mobile proxy sink randomly slice the region I into overlapping Reuleaux triangles (or slices) of radius r, where r is the radius of the sensing range of static sensors that have been selected to participate in k-covering I. In case only mobile sensors have been selected to k-cover the region I, r is the radius of the sensing range of mobile sensors. Recall that mobile sensors are more powerful than static sensors. Then, based on the distribution of lenses in the slicing grid as well as the distribution and the number of static sensors in the region I, the leader mobile proxy sink performs the next actions:

- Computes the two extreme points A and B of each lens. This pair of points will be used by the selected mobile sensors to position themselves within a lens when they move to it. This will ensure full k-coverage of the corresponding adjacent slices in the region I by exactly k sensors as stated in Lemma 1 given above.
- Computes the number of mobile sensors, $NMS(I)$, to move to the region I. This should account for the presence of $NSS(I)$ static sensors in the region I.
- Selects $NMS(I)$ mobile sensors with the highest remaining energy. There is a *threshold* for the remaining energy below which a mobile sensor cannot be selected to move to the region I. Thus, selected mobile sensors should have enough energy.
- Computes the parameters of its mobility according to the group mobility model, *i.e.*, its speed $v_{ref}(t)$, maximum speed *max_speed*, and direction deviation $\theta_{ref}(t)$.
- Assign the selected mobile sensors to the lenses and announce this assignment. The leader mobile proxy sink sends a short SELECT packet including the parameters of its mobility as stated above followed by the id's of the selected mobile sensors and the pairs of the extreme points of the lenses. Precisely, a SELECT message has one triplet $<v_{ref}(t),\ max\_speed,\ \theta_{ref}(t)>$ and $NMS(I)$ triplets, each of which has the structure $<id_i, A_j, B_j>$, where id_i is the id of mobile sensor s_i and A_j and B_j are the two extreme points of lens j in the region I. Sensor s_i can be located anywhere in the lens when it moves to the region I to be k-covered.

5.4   Data Gathering Algorithms

In this section, we describe two algorithms for data gathering in k-covered heterogeneous and sparse WSNs.

Direct Data Gathering: Each leader mobile proxy sink is responsible for delivering all collected data of a mission to the static sink. That is, once a leader mobile proxy sink collects data from the static and mobile sensors that accomplished a mission in a given region I, it moves to the center of the field to deliver the data to the static sink.

As can be seen, on the one hand, this approach does not introduce any routing overhead between a leader mobile proxy sink and any other sensor in the network. Thus, the only source of energy consumption is due to the mobility of a leader mobile proxy sink and the direct transmission of its collected data to the static sink. In order to reduce energy expenditure during data transmission, a leader mobile proxy sink would send its data to the static sink over a short distance. To reduce the amount of energy dissipated due to its mobility, a leader mobile proxy sink needs to travel as close to the shortest path between it and the static sink as possible. On the other hand, this data gathering approach incurs more delay. Indeed, if forwarded through intermediate sensors, the data would travel at a speed faster than that of a leader mobile proxy sink. Thus, this approach is not suitable for time-critical applications.

The advantages of this direct scheme are as follows:

- *Extended network lifetime:* A leader mobile proxy sink transmits its collected data to the static sink through short distances, thus consuming little amount of energy. This helps extend their lifetime, thus prolonging the operational network lifetime.
- *Alleviated data forwarding load:* Using this data gathering scheme, no sensor is needed to act as a relay node between a leader mobile proxy sensor and the static sink. Therefore, all the static and mobile sensors save their energy significantly.
- *Improved data delivery ratio:* Given that mobile proxy sinks are very powerful compared to all other sensors, the likelihood of their failure is very low. All other sensors, however, may fail. Thus, avoiding these sensors improves the ratio of successful data transmission to the static sink.

The disadvantages of this scheme are as follows:

- *High end-to-end delay:* The mobility trajectory of a leader mobile proxy sink may not coincide with the shortest path to the static sink. Also, there may be obstacles in the field, and hence, leader mobile proxy sink mobility is not straight.
- *Potential data loss:* A leader mobile proxy sink failure is crucial to the data lifetime. Indeed, data cannot reach the static sink as there is no way to regenerate them.

Chain-Based Data Gathering: Once a leader mobile proxy sink has been selected, all other mobile proxy sinks form a chain of relay nodes to forward data to the static sink. To minimize the energy consumption due to multi-hop data forwarding, the mobile proxy sinks forming the chain attempt to keep the same distance between any pair of consecutive mobile proxy sinks. Assuming there are n mobile proxy sinks, the total energy consumption required to forward a data packet from a leader mobile proxy sink to the static sink is proportional to the sum of the distances d_i, *i.e.*,

$$E_{tot} \propto \Sigma d_i^{\alpha}, \text{ for all } 1 \leq i \leq n$$

where d_i is the distance between two adjacent mobile proxy sinks s_i and s_{i+1}, $1 \le i \le n-1$, and d_n is the distance between the static sink and mobile proxy sink s_n. It is easy to prove that E_{tot} is minimum only when all those distances d_i are the same, *i.e.*,

$$d_1 = d_2 = ... = d_i = ... = d_n, \text{ for all } 1 \le i \le n$$

The data will be forwarded through the chain only until it reaches the static sink. We assume there is a sufficient number of mobile proxy sinks to form a chain between the static sink and the farthest point in a square field, which is one of its corners.

The benefits of this scheme are as follows:

- *Low delay:* These mobile proxy sinks forming the chain are powerful. Therefore, they can forward the data to the static sink through the nodes on the chain only. Hence, the data will reach the static sink in a timely manner.
- *Guaranteed data delivery:* The failure of any mobile proxy sink in the field will not affect the chain. The latter will be reorganized by the rest of the mobile proxy sink when others fail. Thus, the data is guaranteed to be delivered to the sink.

The shortcomings of this scheme are as follows:

- *Chain formation energy overhead:* There is extra energy consumption due to the chain formation and maintenance. These mobile proxy sinks need to coordinate their motion to build an efficient chain in terms of forwarding data to the static sink.
- *Chain maintenance energy overhead:* When mobile proxy sinks fail due to low energy, the chain needs to be reorganized. This requires more energy. Mobile proxy sinks should adjust their positions to forward data over the same distance.

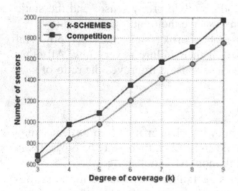

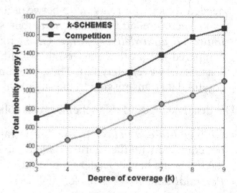

Fig. 1. k-SCHEMES vs. Competition   **Fig. 2.** *k*-SCHEMES vs. Competition

6   Performance Evaluation

In this section, we specify the simulation setup. Then, we present the simulation results of our *k*-SCHEMES protocol using a high-level simulator written in *C*.

6.1   Simulation Setup

We consider a square field. We assume that the initial energy of each static sensor is 60 Joules while that of each mobile sensor is 80 Joules. We use the energy model given in [22] (see Section 2.2). The radii of the sensing (r) and communication ranges of all static sensors are equal to $20m$ and $40m$, respectively, while those of all mobile sensors are equal to $25m$ and $50m$, respectively. All simulations are repeated 100 times and the results are averaged, where the energy consumption includes the transmission of any data and control messages exchanged for the working of k-SCHEMES.

6.2   Simulation Results

In order to fairly compare our k-SCHEMES protocol with Wang and Tseng's approach [19], we consider only homogeneous sensors. In other words, all the static and mobile sensors in our four-tier architecture are the same. Furthermore, the field is supposed to be a square of side length 600m and the region I is a square of side length 300m. Figure 1 shows that our k-SCHEMES protocol requires less number of sensors than the Competition protocol [19] to ensure k-coverage of the region I. Our characterization of k-coverage helps find a tight bound on the number of sensors for k-coverage. Also, as shown in Figure 2, the energy consumption due to mobility, which is required for the correct operation of k-SCHEMES, is less than the one needed for the Competition protocol [19]. This is due in part to the coordination between all mobile proxy sinks to select one of them as a leader to accomplish the mission. In fact, the one that will cause the least mobility energy consumption is selected as a leader mobile proxy sink. Also, this shows the effect of the group mobility model. In fact, all the selected mobile sensors form a group that follows the movement trajectory of its reference point, *i.e.*, leader mobile proxy sink.

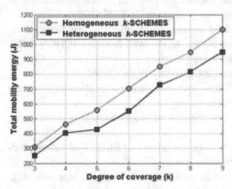
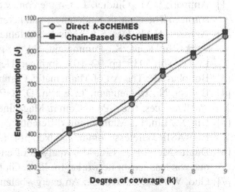

Fig. 3. k-SCHEMES   Fig. 4. Direct vs. chain-based data gathering

As expected, sensor heterogeneity helps reduce the energy consumption, thus extending the network lifetime. Figure 3 shows that our k-SCHEMES protocol using heterogeneous sensors (*Heterogeneous k-SCHEMES*) outperforms k-SCHEMES using homogeneous sensors (*Homogeneous k-SCHEMES*) as indicated in our four-tier architecture. Indeed, mobile sensors are more powerful than static ones. Hence, the number of heterogeneous static and mobile sensors to k-cover a region I is less than that of homogeneous sensors. Thus, a smaller number of mobile sensors is needed to move to the region I to k-cover it, and hence less mobility energy consumption.

Figure 4 shows that direct data gathering protocol consumes less energy than chain-based data gathering protocol. With the latter, mobile proxy sinks should communicate with each other to move to the appropriate positions in the field. This helps them form a chain in a way that they are equidistant from each other. But, the construction of this chain cost them extra energy consumption compared to the other scheme.

7   Conclusion

In this paper, we considered sparsely deployed sensors along with mobility and heterogeneity and proposed a four-tier architecture to provide k-coverage. On top of k-coverage configurations, we proposed two data gathering protocols that use mobile proxy sinks. We found that our k-SCHEMES protocol outperforms another mobile k-coverage protocol with regard to the network lifetime and the number of active sensors to ensure k-coverage. Simulation results show that k-SCHEMES has better performances for heterogeneous rather than for homogeneous WSNs.

Our future work is three-fold: Our k-SCHEMES protocol considers a single static sink and a single mission at a time. We will generalize k-SCHEMES to consider multiple static sinks and multiple missions at the same time. We plan to extend our proposed protocol to account for obstacles and mobile events in the field. We will assess the performance of k-SCHEMES in real-world sensor deployments.

References

[1] Ammari, H.M., Giudici, J.: On the connected k-coverage problem in heterogeneous sensor nets: The curse of randomness and heterogeneity. In: Proc. ICDCS (2009)

[2] Ammari, H.M., Das, S.K.: Mission-Oriented k-Coverage in Mobile Wireless Sensor Networks. In: Kant, K., Pemmaraju, S.V., Sivalingam, K.M., Wu, J. (eds.) ICDCN 2010. LNCS, vol. 5935, pp. 92–103. Springer, Heidelberg (2010)

[3] Bollobás, B.: The Art of Mathematic. Cambridge University Press (2006)

[4] Bulusu, N., Heidemann, J., Estrin, D.: GPS-less low cost outdoor localization for very small devices. IEEE Pers. Comm. Magazine 7(5) (2000)

[5] Du, X., Lin, F.: Maintaining differentiated coverage in heterogeneous sensor networks. EURASIP Wireless Comm. and Net. 5(4) (2005)

[6] Duarte-Melo, E.J., Liu, M.: Analysis of energy consumption and lifetime of heterogeneous wireless sensor networks. In: Proc. Globecom (2002)

[7] Guo, W., Liu, Z., Wu, G.: An energy-balanced transmission scheme for sensor networks. In: Proc. ACM SenSys (2003)

[8] Gupta, H., Zhou, Z., Das, S., Gu, Q.: Connected sensor cover: Self-organization of sensor networks for efficient query execution. IEEE TON 14(1) (2006)

[9] Heinzelman, W., Chandrakasan, A., Balakrishnan, H.: An application-specific protocol architecture for wireless microsensor networks. IEEE TWC 1(4) (2002)

[10] Hong, X., Gerla, M., Pei, G., Chiang, C.: A group mobility model for ad hoc wireless networks. In: Proc. MSWiM (1999)

[11] Huang, C., Tseng, Y., Wu, H.: Distributed protocols for ensuring both coverage and connectivity of a wireless sensor network. ACM TOSN (2007)

[12] Lazos, L., Poovendran, R.: Stochastic coverage in heterogeneous sensor networks. ACM TOSN 2(3) (2006)

[13] Luo, J., Hubaux, J.-P.: Joint Mobility and Routing for Lifetime Elongation in Wireless Sensor Networks. In: Proc. IEEE Infocom, pp. 1735–1746 (2005)

[14] Meguerdichian, S., Koushanfar, F., Potkonjak, M., Srivastava, M.: Worst and best-case coverage in sensor networks. IEEE TMC 4(1) (2005)

[15] Mhatre, V., Rosenberg, C., Kofman, D., Mazumdar, R., Shroff, N.: A minimum cost heterogeneous sensor network with a lifetime constraint. IEEE TMC 4(1) (2005)

[16] Shah, R.C., Roy, S., Jain, S., Brunette, W.: Data MULEs: Modeling a Three-tier Architecture for Sparse Sensor Networks. In: Proc. SNPA, pp. 30–41 (2003)

[17] Wang, G., Cao, G., Porta, T.L., Zhang, W.: Sensor relocation in mobile sensor networks. In: Proc. IEEE Infocom (2005)

[18] Wang, Y.-C., Hu, C.-C., Tseng, Y.-C.: Efficient Placement and Dispatch of Sensors in a Wireless Sensor Network. IEEE TMC 7(2) (2008)

[19] Wang, Y.-C., Tseng, Y.-C.: Distributed deployment schemes for mobile wireless sensor networks to ensure multi-level coverage. IEEE TPDS 19(9) (2008)

[20] Xing, G., Wang, X., Zhang, Y., Lu, C., Pless, R., Gill, C.: Integrated coverage and connectivity configuration for energy conservation in sensor networks. ACM TOSN 1(1) (2005)

[21] Yarvis, M., Kushalnagar, N., Singh, H., Rangarajan, A., Liu, Y., Singh, S.: Exploiting Heterogeneity in Sensor Networks. In: Proc. IEEE Infocom (2005)

[22] Ye, F., Zhong, G., Cheng, J., Lu, S., Zhang, L.: PEAS: A robust energy conserving protocol for long-lived sensor networks. In: Proc. ICDCS (2003)

[23] Zhang, H., Hou, J.: Maintaining sensing coverage and connectivity in large sensor networks. Ad Hoc & Sensor Wireless Networks 1(1-2) (2005)

LB-MAC: A Lifetime-Balanced MAC Protocol for Sensor Networks

Yang Peng, Zi Li, Wensheng Zhang, and Daji Qiao

Iowa State University, Ames, IA 50011, USA
{yangpeng,zili,wzhang,daji}@iastate.edu

Abstract. This paper presents LB-MAC, a new MAC protocol for asynchronous, duty cycle sensor networks. Different from existing sensor network MAC protocols that usually focus on reducing energy consumption and extending lifetime of individual sensor nodes, LB-MAC aims at prolonging the network lifetime through balancing the nodal lifetime between neighboring sensors. LB-MAC is lightweight and scalable as the required control information is only exchanged locally between neighbors. LB-MAC has been implemented in TinyOS and evaluated on a sensor network testbed with extensive experiments. Results show that LB-MAC is able to achieve a significantly longer network lifetime than state-of-the-art MAC protocols such as X-MAC, RI-MAC and SEESAW, while maintaining comparable levels of network power consumption, packet delay and delivery ratio.

1 Introduction

Energy conservation is perhaps the most important issue in battery-operated sensor networks. It is always desirable to extend the operational lifetime of a sensor network as much as possible. For many sensor network applications [1,2], the network lifetime is often defined as the minimal nodal lifetime among all sensor nodes in the network. This is because, the depletion of battery energy of bottleneck sensor nodes, such as the nodes close to the root node in a tree topology network, may cause network disconnection, which could render the sensor network nonfunctional. Although energy saving techniques such as energy-aware routing can be used to reduce the workload and extend the lifetime of bottleneck sensor nodes, they may still consume higher energy than other nodes in the network and thus bound the network lifetime. Besides, sensor nodes with a similar level of workload may have different nodal lifetime due to environmental or system reasons. For example, nodes with poorer-quality batteries or solar-rechargeable nodes deployed to shady locales may have shorter lifetime than their peers. Therefore, to maximize the network lifetime, it is important to extend the lifetime of individual sensor nodes or, to be more specific, the shortest nodal lifetime among all nodes.

Despite the need for a holistic approach to the energy conservation issue and to prolonging the network lifetime, most of the current MAC protocol design has been focusing on reducing the energy consumption and extending the operational

X. Wang et al. (Eds.): WASA 2012, LNCS 7405, pp. 272–291, 2012.

lifetime of individual sensor nodes. To remedy this deficiency, we investigate the MAC protocol design from the perspective of network lifetime maximization and propose a new solution, called LB-MAC (Lifetime-Balanced MAC), to achieve this goal via balancing the nodal lifetime.

1.1 Contributions

LB-MAC emphasizes the collaboration between nodes to benefit the network as a whole, even at the expense of a single node. The key idea is to allow a sensor node to adjust its MAC-layer behaviors via a few tunable parameters. The adjustment occurs in pairs between neighboring nodes; that is, each pair of neighboring sensor nodes adjust their MAC-layer behaviors together once communications between them occur.

In LB-MAC, by tuning the operational parameters, sensor nodes may operate with different *channel checking periods*, *idle listening periods* and *data retry intervals*, such that the rendezvous between sender and receiver nodes can be achieved and the communication overhead can be shifted between them. If the receiver finds itself with a longer expected lifetime than its sender, it shall attempt to take more communication overhead from the sender; otherwise, the receiver may disseminate communication overhead to the sender.

- **Shifting communication overhead from sender to receiver:** in LB-MAC, to reduce sender's energy consumption on communication, receiver may increase its channel checking period so that sender can choose a longer retry interval while the rendezvous between sender and receiver is still guaranteed.
- **Shifting communication overhead from receiver to sender:** to save energy at the receiver side, sender may attempt data transmissions more frequently with a shorter retry interval so that receiver can shorten its channel checking period and save its energy consumption on communication. Sender may also choose to keep listening idly upon a data arrival and the rendezvous between sender and receiver is then triggered solely by receiver's periodic beacons.

This way, the minimal nodal lifetime among communicating neighbors can be extended. As a result, the network lifetime may be prolonged.

We have implemented LB-MAC in TinyOS and evaluated it on a sensor network testbed. Experimental results show that, comparing with state-of-the-art MAC protocols such as X-MAC [3], RI-MAC [4] and SEESAW [5], LB-MAC achieves the design goal of significantly prolonging the sensor network lifetime through balancing nodal lifetime. Figure 1 shows the sample results with a simple tree topology; nodes 5, 6, 7, 8 are source nodes and the data rate is two packets per second. As shown in Figure 1(b), after 1.4 hours of network operation, sensor nodes running X-MAC or RI-MAC all experience severe imbalance in their nodal residual energy. In comparison, with the proposed LB-MAC protocol, all nodes have almost the same level of residual energy despite the unbalanced initial

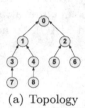

(a) Topology

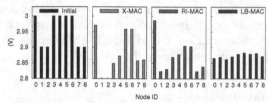

(b) Initial and residual voltage levels after the network operates for 1.4 hours with X-MAC, RI-MAC and LB-MAC, respectively. Note that, nodes 1 and 2 are bottleneck nodes in the network.

Fig. 1. A simple comparison of the proposed LB-MAC scheme with two state-of-the-art MAC protocols

nodal energy levels. As a result, the sensor network may be able to operate for a much longer time till all sensor nodes' batteries are depleted at approximately the same time. More evaluation results can be found in Section 5.

1.2   Related Work

Among MAC protocols proposed for duty cycle sensor networks [3, 4, 6, 7], S-MAC [7] and T-MAC [8] are representative synchronous protocols that require neighboring nodes to be time-synchronized and thus can align the active and sleep intervals of neighbor nodes to wake up only during the common active time periods. As the active periods usually are short, substantial energy can be saved. However, strictly synchronizing the clocks of neighboring nodes may impose high overhead.

B-MAC [6] and X-MAC [3] are representative sender-initiated asynchronous MAC protocols. In B-MAC, the rendezvous between sender and receiver is established through long preambles initiated by the sender, and X-MAC improves B-MAC by replacing the long preamble with a sequence of short, strobed preambles. A node running X-MAC may stop sending short preambles upon receiving an EarlyACK from its target receiver, thus saving more energy than B-MAC. To work under a wider range of traffic conditions, RI-MAC [4] and A-MAC [9] adopt a receiver-initiated beacon-based strategy. Each node wakes up periodically and sends out a short beacon to explicitly notify its neighbors that it is ready to receive data. When a node has data to transmit, it wakes up and waits for a beacon from its receiver. Once such a beacon is received, it starts sending the data. Compared to the sender-initiated preamble-based protocols, a receiver-initiated protocol only requires receiver to keep radio on for a short period after sending a beacon and therefore saves the receiving energy cost. Additionally, the receiver-initiated nature allows efficient collision resolution which can effectively save the transmission energy cost when channel contention is severe.

Different from [3,4,6,9], where the MAC parameters are predetermined before deployment and usually the same on all nodes in the network, MAC parameter tuning in duty cycle sensor networks has been studied in [5, 10–12]. In [11], a controller is implemented on individual sensor nodes to dynamically adjust the radio duty cycle based on network traffic condition where no collaboration exits between neighboring nodes. Authors in [12] proposed a protocol to reduce radio duty cycles by scheduling rendezvous between neighbor nodes based on the relative end-to-end delay requirement and the network traffic condition. Though these works efficiently reduce individual nodal energy consumption, they may not improve the network lifetime in general. ZeroCal [10] is a MAC layer protocol which adaptively tunes the wakeup intervals between sender and receiver to balance the energy consumption of them; however, the proposed scheme does not guarantee the end-to-end delay bound as the wakeup interval can be extended to save nodal energy. Additional, ZeroCal does not consider the adaptation of other MAC parameters such as channel checking interval and data retry interval, which can further prolong the network lifetime with proper tuning. SEESAW [5] was proposed to balance the energy consumption between sender and receiver through adapting the data retry interval at the sender side and the channel checking period at the receiver side. Though SEESAW yields longer network lifetime than B-MAC and S-MAC, the effectiveness of SEESAW is limited by several factors. Firstly, as a sender-initiated only protocol, SEESAW mandates a minimum channel checking period at the receiver side, which may incur unnecessary energy consumption under light traffic conditions. Secondly, the policies used in SEESAW for balancing nodal lifetime are empirical and not adaptive to varying network conditions.

1.3   Organization

The rest of the paper is organized as follows. Section 2 presents analytical preliminaries. Section 3 describes the design of the proposed LB-MAC protocol, which is followed by its implementation details in TinyOS in Section 4. Experimental results are presented in Section 5, and Section 6 concludes the paper.

2   Preliminaries

In this section, we first define a generic model for duty cycle MAC protocols. Based on this model, an analytical study is conducted to provide a theoretical foundation for the design of LB-MAC protocol.

2.1   A Generic Model for Duty Cycle MAC Protocols

The behaviors of sensor nodes in a duty cycle MAC protocol can be generalized as follows:

- As a receiver, a sensor node periodically wakes up to interact with potential senders. During each wakeup, the sensor node can (i) check the channel activity for incoming messages, or (ii) send out alive notifications to waiting senders, or (iii) perform both.

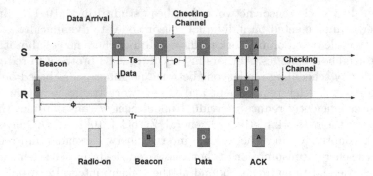

Fig. 2. A generic model for duty cycle MAC protocols

– As a sender, a sensor node turns on radio immediately after a new data packet arrives. To deliver the data packet, the sensor node can (i) send a data packet to the target receiver and wait for ACK, or (ii) wait for target receiver's alive notification to start data transmission, or (iii) perform both.

A sensor node may participate in the network activity as sender, receiver or both at the same time.

As the data packet transmission time is relatively small and can be in the same fold as a preamble in many sensor network applications, both LPL scheme in TinyOS 2.1 and UPMA-XMAC [13] protocol use data packets to replace the preambles. Similarly, in our analysis and design, we also let senders send data packets instead of preambles. Figure 2 illustrates the behaviors of sensor nodes in a generic duty cycle MAC protocol and Table 1 lists the six main parameters to characterize a MAC protocol.

Table 1. MAC protocol parameters

T_s	sender's data retry interval
ρ	sender's idle listening period
τ_s	transmission duration of a data packet
T_r	receiver's wakeup interval
ϕ	receiver's channel checking period
τ_r	transmission duration of a beacon

The above generic model can be instantiated to a certain MAC protocol with proper assignments to the parameters. For example, as shown in Table 2, the X-MAC protocol can be obtained by setting $\tau_r = 0$ (i.e., receiver does not send any beacon), $\tau_s = \tau$ (which is the data transmission duration), $T_s = \epsilon$ (which is the sum of τ and the ACK turnaround time), $\rho = T_s - \tau_s$, and $\phi = 20$ms. RI-MAC [4] can be obtained by setting $\tau_r = \tau$, $\tau_s = 0$ (i.e., sender silently waits for receiver's beacon without sending a data packet), $T_s = \infty$, $\rho = T_s - \tau_s = \infty$

Table 2. Existing MAC protocol settings

Protocol	T_s	τ_s	ρ	T_r	τ_r	ϕ
RI-MAC	∞	0	$T_s - \tau_s$	user defined	τ	7ms [4]
A-MAC	∞	0	$T_s - \tau_s$	user defined	τ	$128\mu s$ [9]
X-MAC	ϵ	τ	$T_s - \tau_s$	user defined	0	20ms [3]
SEESAW	$\frac{\phi}{1.2}$	τ	$\epsilon - \tau$	user defined	0	dynamic [5]

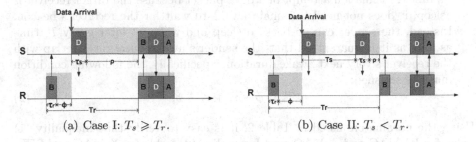

(a) Case I: $T_s \geqslant T_r$.   (b) Case II: $T_s < T_r$.

Fig. 3. Rendezvous between sender and receiver

(i.e., sender keeps listening idly as long as it has packets to send), and $\phi = 7$ms. Note that, T_r is shown as *"user defined"* for all four protocols listed in the table, as it is typically specified by the user to satisfy certain delay requirement.

2.2 Relation between Parameters

Without loss of generality, the behaviors of a sender and a receiver shown in Figure 2 are as follows.

- When a new data packet arrives, the sender sends out the packet and monitors the channel. If a receiver's beacon is received, it retransmits the data packet; if an ACK is received, it stops the transmission and goes back to sleep; if neither ACK nor beacon is received within ρ time, it goes back to sleep. After it has slept for $(T_s - \tau_s - \rho)$ time, the sender wakes up again and repeats the above procedure.
- The receiver wakes up every T_r interval, sends out a beacon, and monitors the channel for ϕ time. If a data packet is received within ϕ time, it replies with an ACK; otherwise, it goes back to sleep.

In order to deliver a data packet within user defined one-hop delay T_r, the relations between T_s, T_r, ρ and ϕ shall satisfy certain conditions, as detailed in the following two cases:

- Case I: $T_s \geqslant T_r$. Consider a scenario where a sender fails in its first transmission attempt of a data packet because the target receiver is asleep, as shown in Figure 3(a). If the sender goes to sleep before the receiver wakes up, it will retransmit the packet at T_s time after the first transmission attempt; that is, a delay of at least T_s will be incurred, which is longer than T_r. Therefore, to ensure that the data packet is delivered within delay T_r, the sender shall instead remain awake until the receiver wakes up to send a beacon, and then retransmit the packet. In other words, the following condition must be satisfied:

$$\rho \geqslant T_r - \tau_s - \tau_r - \phi. \tag{1}$$

– Case II: $T_s < T_r$. In this case, as shown in Figure 3(b), if a sender fails in its first transmission attempt of a data packet because the target receiver is asleep, it does not need to remain awake to wait for the receiver's beacon. Instead, the sender can go back to sleep and wake up later every T_s time as long as it is guaranteed that, the sender's awake durations overlap with the receiver's very next awake duration. Specifically, the following condition must be satisfied:

$$T_s \leqslant \phi + \tau_s + \tau_r + \rho. \tag{2}$$

Using the parameters listed in Table 2, it is easy to verify that Inequality (1) holds for RI-MAC and A-MAC, and Inequality (2) holds for X-MAC and SEE-SAW. In our design, we require either Inequality (1) or (2) to hold. Note that, in the above analysis, packet collisions or losses are not considered for simplicity; but they are considered in our protocol design and implementation as elaborated in Sections 3 and 4.

2.3 Lifetime Estimation

Based on the above analysis, the expected lifetime of a pair of sender and receiver, denoted as L_s and L_r respectively, can be estimated as follows:

$$L_s = \frac{e_s}{\frac{T_{r,r}}{2} \cdot \frac{(\rho_s + \tau_s)}{T_{s,s}} \cdot r_s \cdot P + g_s}, \tag{3}$$

and

$$L_r = \frac{e_r}{\frac{(\tau_r + \phi_r)}{T_{r,r}} \cdot P + g_r}, \tag{4}$$

where e_s and e_r are the amount of residual energy at sender and receiver respectively, r_s is the outgoing data rate at the sender, P is the amount of energy consumed when a node's radio is on per unit of time, and g_s and g_r are energy consumption rates of sender and receiver for other causes.

In the above estimation, the data packet outgoing rate is assumed to be low such that there is no queueing packet to be sent, which is typical in many low duty cycle applications [14, 15]. To send each data packet, the sender needs to wait for about $\frac{T_{r,r}}{2}$ time on average, with the radio duty cycle value of $\frac{\rho_s + \tau_s}{T_{s,s}}$. Therefore, it consumes about $\frac{T_{r,r}}{2} \cdot \frac{\rho_s + \tau_s}{T_{s,s}} \cdot P$ energy to deliver a packet on average.

As for the receiver, it wakes up for $\tau_r + \phi_r$ time every $T_{r,r}$ interval. Hence, its energy consumption rate can be estimated as $\frac{\tau_r + \phi_r}{T_{r,r}} \cdot P$.

More generally, a sensor node i may act as both a sender and a receiver in the network, and its expected lifetime L_i can be estimated by considering its power consumption for communicating with each of its senders (similar to the analysis in Equation (3)) and each of its receivers (similar to the analysis in Equation (4)). Details are omitted due to space limitation.

2.4   Problem Statement and Design Principle

The goal of this work is to design a MAC protocol that maximizes the lowest nodal lifetime in the network via adjustment of MAC-layer behaviors of sensor nodes. Formally, it can be described as follows:

Given:

$$P, \{\tau_{s,i}\}, \{\tau_{r,i}\}, \{T_{r,i,j} \text{ where } j \text{ is any sender of } i\},$$
$$\{r_{i,j} \text{ where } j \text{ is any receiver of } i\}, \{g_i\}, \{e_i\}.$$

Objective:

$$\max \min\{L_i\}$$

Subject to: for any sender-receiver pair (i, j),

$$T_{s,i,j} \leqslant \phi_{j,i} + \tau_{s,i} + \tau_{r,j} + \rho_{i,j}, \text{ or}$$
$$\rho_{i,j} \geqslant T_{r,j,i} - \tau_{s,i} - \tau_{r,j} - \phi_{j,i},$$

Output:

$$\{T_{s,i,j} \text{ where } j \text{ is any receiver of } i\},$$
$$\{\rho_{i,j} \text{ where } j \text{ is any receiver of } i\}, \{\phi_{i,j} \text{ where } j \text{ is any sender of } i\}.$$

Directly solving this optimization problem is impractical because it requires each node to know the residual energy levels, energy consumption rates and data arrival rates of all other nodes in the network. Acquiring these information could incur high communication overhead because of potentially large network scale and dynamic nature of the information. So instead, we approach the problem in a distributed, localized and low-cost manner. Specifically, each node only periodically coordinates with its neighboring nodes to balance the lifetime between them:

- If a node as a receiver finds itself with longer expected lifetime than its sender, it shall attempt to take more communication overhead from the sender. According to Equation (3), this can be done by increasing T_s and/or decreasing ρ at the sender side, accompanied with increasing ϕ at the receiver side to satisfy Inequality (1) or (2).
- On the other hand, if a receiver finds itself with shorter expected lifetime than its sender, it shall attempt to shift more communication overhead to the sender. According to Equation (4), this can be done by decreasing ϕ at the receiver side, accompanied with decreasing T_s and/or increasing ρ at the sender side to satisfy Inequality (1) or (2).

This way, the minimal nodal lifetime among communicating neighbors can be extended. As a result, the network lifetime may be prolonged.

3   LB-MAC Design

In LB-MAC, each pair of sender and receiver adapt their MAC-layer behaviors through tuning a few operational parameters: T_s (data retry interval) and ρ (idle listening period) for the sender and ϕ (channel checking period) for the receiver. The receiver acts in a leading role. Based on the lifetime information piggybacked in data packets from the sender, the receiver decides a proper ϕ and piggybacks it in the ACK to the sender. The receiver's behavior is elaborated in Section 3.1. Upon receiving an ACK, the sender extracts the piggybacked ϕ, based on which it adjusts its parameters T_s and ρ as elaborated in Section 3.2.

3.1   Receiver's Behavior

The operational flowchart of an LB-MAC node as receiver is shown in Figure 4. Every T_r interval (i.e., when the wakeup timer is fired), the receiver turns on radio, sends a beacon and keeps monitoring the channel for ϕ time. During the monitoring period, if a data packet is received, the following information will be extracted from the packet: *sender's estimated lifetime* and *sender's outgoing data rate*. The receiver may adjust its ϕ according to the information, and return the updated ϕ to the sender in the ACK.

When a receiver adjusts its ϕ, the adjustment scale shall be small. This is because multiple sender-receiver pairs may adjust their parameters concurrently; each pair makes the adjustment according to their current knowledge of their energy consumption rates, which can be affected by the adjustments made by

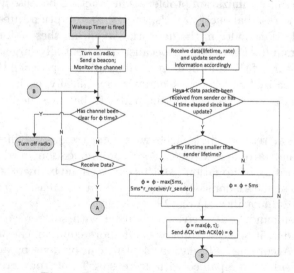

Fig. 4. Receiver's behavior in LB-MAC

other pairs. Hence, if the adjustment scale is too large, thrashing may occur and energy may be wasted. Specifically, the receiver behaves as follows, which is also shown in the flowchart:

- ϕ may be updated only when some threshold conditions are satisfied: (i) the receiver has received at least K data packets; or (ii) at least H seconds have elapsed since the last time when ϕ was updated. In our design and implementation, we empirically choose K=30 and H=60, when the difference between the two nodes' lifetime may change since the previous update of ϕ and a new update shall be necessary.
- When the receiver has a longer lifetime than the sender, it increases ϕ by 5 ms; otherwise, it decreases ϕ by the amount of $\max(5\text{ms}, \frac{r_{receiver}}{r_{sender}} \cdot 5\text{ms})$, where $r_{receiver}$ and r_{sender} are the outgoing data rates of receiver and sender, respectively. This way, the receiver's energy consumption rate could be reduced quickly; this design is based on the consideration that data collection is usually the major communication pattern in a sensor network and hence a receiver usually serves multiple senders concurrently.

3.2 Sender's Behavior

The operational flowchart of an LB-MAC node as sender is shown in Figure 5. When a data packet arrives at the sender, the buffer is checked first. If the buffer is not empty, the data packet is simply put into the buffer. Otherwise, the sender makes the first attempt of transmitting this packet, and meanwhile starting a timer that will expire every T_s time. Then, if the transmission succeeds, the sender goes to sleep; otherwise, it remains awake for ρ time and then goes to sleep. The sender also attempts transmitting data packets when it receives a beacon from the target receiver. In addition, the sender wakes up and attempts transmitting packets whenever the data retry timer expires. The timer is turned off when the buffer becomes empty.

When the sender receives an ACK to its data packet, it will adjust T_s and ρ according to the ϕ value carried in the ACK, such that (i) either Inequality (1) or (2) is satisfied to ensure data packet delivery within delay T_r, and (ii) its idle listening time is as short as possible. The adjustment is performed as follows:

- If Inequality (1) is satisfied, the average radio-on time of the sender for the successful delivery of each data packet is estimated as

$$T_s + \frac{\rho}{2}$$
$$\geqslant T_s + \frac{T_r - T_s - \tau_r - \phi}{2}, \text{ due to Inequality (1)}$$
$$= \frac{T_r + T_s - \tau_r - \phi}{2}.$$

That is, the minimum average radio-on time is

$$\frac{T_r + T_s - \tau_r - \phi}{2}, \tag{5}$$

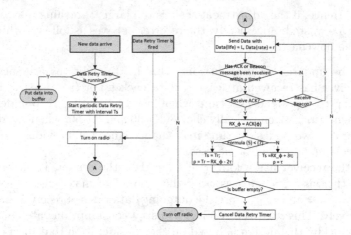

Fig. 5. Sender's behavior in LB-MAC

which can be achieved as long as

$$T_s = T_r, \quad \text{and} \quad \rho = T_r - \tau_s - \tau_r - \phi. \tag{6}$$

- If Inequality (2) is satisfied, the average radio-on time for the successful delivery of a data packet is estimated as

$$\frac{1}{2} \cdot \frac{T_r}{T_s} \cdot (\tau_s + \rho)$$

$$\geq \frac{T_r \cdot (\tau_s + \rho)}{2(\phi + \tau_s + \tau_r + \rho)}, \quad \text{due to Inequality (2)}$$

$$= \frac{T_r}{2} \cdot \left(1 - \frac{\phi + \tau_r}{\phi + \tau_r + \tau_s + \rho}\right).$$

As the transmission duration of a software ACK is similar to the transmission duration of a beacon, the minimum ρ value is τ_r. Therefore, the minimum average radio-on time is

$$\frac{T_r}{2} \cdot \left(1 - \frac{\phi + \tau_r}{\phi + \tau_r + \tau_s + \tau_r}\right), \tag{7}$$

which is achieved when

$$T_s = \phi + \tau_r + \tau_s + \tau_r, \quad \text{and} \quad \rho = \tau_r. \tag{8}$$

- If the sender's radio-on time computed by Formula (5) is less than or equal to that computed by Formula (7), T_s and τ_s are set as in Equation (6) to reduce sender's energy consumption; otherwise, T_s and τ_s are set as in Equation (8).

3.3   Robustness of the LB-MAC Design

One of the key features in LB-MAC is that, LB-MAC allows neighboring nodes to exchange additional control information and then adjust their MAC-layer behaviors together. Therefore, in order for LB-MAC to be practically useful, it is critical to ensure that LB-MAC functions properly in the presence of packet losses, route changes and multiple concurrent senders, all of which are inevitable in practical environments.

Loss of Data Packets. Loss of data packets has no effects on LB-MAC. The sender will keep retransmitting till the data is delivered successfully, or till the maximum retry limit has been reached and data is discarded. During the process, both sender and receiver operate with the previously-agreed upon MAC parameters.

Loss of ACK Packets. Loss of an ACK may cause sender and receiver to lose synchronization of their MAC behaviors, since the important decision on MAC behavior adaptation may be piggybacked in the ACK. For example, a receiver may decide to reduce ϕ and carry this decision in an ACK. Unfortunately, due to loss of this ACK, the sender never gets notified of the change and continues operating with a T_s value that is larger than the new ϕ. As a result, the Inequality (1) or (2) given in Section 2.2 may be violated, and the rendezvous between sender and receiver is lost. To deal with this issue, LB-MAC adopts a rescue mechanism. The idea is to allow a sender to change ρ to T_r when the number of data retries exceeds $\lceil T_r/T_s \rceil$, which is the maximum number of data retries during a T_r interval. This is to guarantee that sender and receiver recover from the loss of MAC behavior synchronization in at most $2T_r$ time.

Handling of Channel Contention. In LB-MAC, T_s is a tunable parameter and when it becomes too small, data messages are sent in very short intervals, which may cause severe contention to the channel and a large number of packet collisions. As a result, senders may waste energy contending for the channel. To deal with this situation, LB-MAC sets the minimum T_s value to 20ms which is specified in [3] for the same purpose.

Handling of Multiple Concurrent Senders. In LB-MAC, as the parameter tuning is made pair-wisely, a node who serves as a common receiver for multiple senders may decrease ϕ for one sender and then lose the rendezvous with other senders. To address this problem, a receiver keeps record of the ϕ value scheduled with each sender, and choose the largest ϕ value as its own channel checking period such that the rendezvous with all senders can be satisfied.

Handling of Route Changes. In practice, a sender node may switch to a new receiver due to routing updates. The receiver may waste energy on unnecessarily long channel checking period if it keeps using the ϕ value scheduled for the stale sender. In LB-MAC, the receiver node periodically checks and drops stale senders and thus the ϕ value for staled senders will not be used. Similarly, a sender node may also drop stale receivers periodically if they don't interact with each other after certain period. When the sender switches to a new receiver, it sets $\rho = T_r$ to wait for the target receiver's beacon and establish the rendezvous.

4 LB-MAC Implementation

LB-MAC has been implemented in TinyOS 2.1.0. The core scheduling component of LB-MAC is the LBMACScheduler component, which resides atop the
radio core layer and handles all operations of message processing and parameter
tuning based on the flow chart as shown in Figures 4 and 5. Some adaption
code of LB-MAC is also developed for the radio core layer which provides a
variety of low-level supports for the LBMACScheduler component. In the following, we present the message formats defined by LB-MAC and discuss some
implementation issues.

In LB-MAC, the beacon message is used by a receiver either as a beacon sent
upon its wakeup or as a software ACK sent to acknowledge the reception of a
data packet. The type field defined in a general TOS message header is reused
in the beacon messages. The same as in the implementation of RI-MAC, the
type field in a beacon message carries the backoff window size decided by the
receiver, to allow its senders to choose their backoff slots based on this value.
Different from RI-MAC and A-MAC, LB-MAC adds 2-byte fields to each beacon
message for carrying parameters ϕ. In a data packet, estimated nodal lifetime
and outgoing data rate of the sender are piggybacked to the end of the data
payload, both of which are used by the receiver when deciding MAC parameters
as discussed in Section 3.1.

In LB-MAC, estimated nodal lifetime is a key factor in determining the MAC
mode and parameters, and the capability to measure nodal residual energy level
is necessary for lifetime estimation. Though the residual energy level can be
estimated using energy meter devices [16] or monitored precisely with integrated
software and hardware support [17], only a few existing sensor motes [18,19] are
designed with the required hardware support. To cope with this constraint, the
implementation of LB-MAC adopts a software based residual energy estimation
scheme, which has also been used in existing works [20].

The basic idea is that, for each type of battery, the mapping between a battery
voltage reading and the residual energy level is found, and the information is
then input to our LB-MAC module. As an example, Figure 6 shows the mapping
that we have found for a pack of two AA Ni-Mn batteries. Particularly, we find
the mapping using the following method: A sensor mote is configured to start
working when its battery voltage reading is 3 V, in full duty cycle with sensing
activity enabled. Every a small time interval, the voltage reading is recorded
and time-stamped, until the energy is depleted. Let these records be (t_i, v_i) for
$i = 0, \cdots, n$, where $t_0 = 0$, $v_0 = 3$ and t_n is the time when the energy is found
depleted, and let the initial energy of the batteries be estimated as $e_0 = t_n \cdot v_0 \cdot I$,
where I is the current. Then, the residual energy level corresponding to battery
reading v_i can be estimated as $e_i = e_0 \cdot \frac{t_n - t_i}{t_n}$.

With the input mapping between battery readings and residual energy levels,
a sensor node can estimate its residual nodal lifetime based on its voltage reading
and consumption rate. To reduce the overhead for storing the mapping information, the whole voltage range can be divided into multiple segments such that the
mapping relation for each segment can be captured with a simple function; this

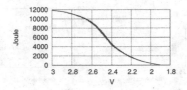

Fig. 6. Mapping between battery voltage readings and residual energy levels (for two AA Ni-Mn batteries)

way, only the functions and segment information need to be stored [21]. Though our current implementation requires extra measurement work to find out the mapping between battery readings and residual energy levels, we believe that more precise and pervasive hardware support will be available in near future due to the increasing demand of lifetime-aware services [1].

5   Performance Evaluation

Experiments have been conducted to evaluate the performance of LB-MAC and compare it with X-MAC, RI-MAC and SEESAW, in terms of network lifetime, average per-hop delay, data delivery ratio and network power consumption. Here, the network power consumption is defined as the amount of energy consumed in the whole network divided by the network lifetime.

The testbed is composed of 37 TelosB motes, organized as a 6 × 6 grid (shown in Figure 7). Node 0 is connected to PC, keeping its radio on all the time to serve as the sink. Two scenarios of event-driven sensing and data collection are emulated:

- Static events scenario, in which static events are assumed to be detected by sensors 28, 29, 32, 34, 35 and 36 only. These sensors (i.e., source nodes) generate data packets at a certain rate and forward them hop by hop to the sink.
- Dynamic events scenario, in which dynamic events are emulated to occur and be detected by sensors in one of the three dotted rectangles at a time. A sensor that detects an event generates data packets at a certain rate and forward them hop by hop to the sink.

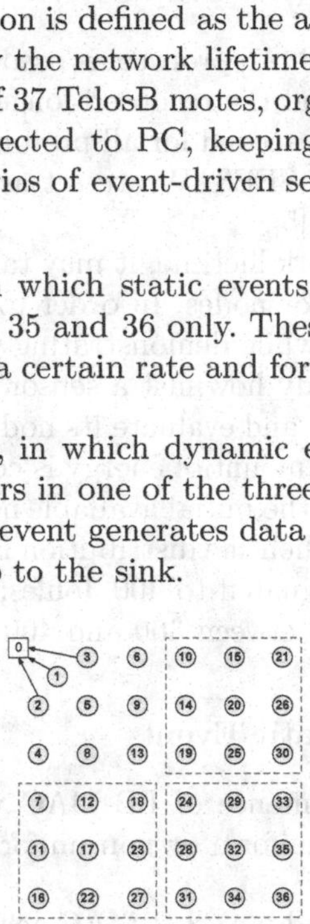

Fig. 7. Deployment of sensor nodes in testbed experiments. The routing pathes are determined by the CTP protocol.

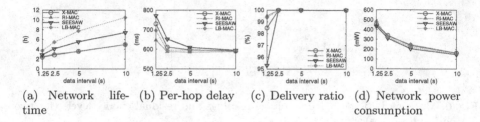

(a) Network life-time (b) Per-hop delay (c) Delivery ratio (d) Network power consumption

Fig. 8. Performance comparison with static events and uniform initial nodal energy

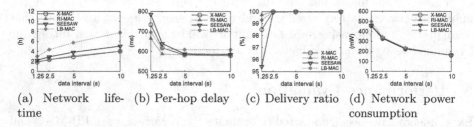

(a) Network life-time (b) Per-hop delay (c) Delivery ratio (d) Network power consumption

Fig. 9. Performance comparison with static events and non-uniform initial nodal energy

In the experiments, the CTP [22] protocol is used to form and adjust the paths for data packet forwarding, and the recorded longest hop count in the network is 8. Parameter T_r is fixed at 1 second for all protocols, and parameters ϕ, ρ and T_s for X-MAC, RI-MAC, and SEESAW are set as in Table 2 which adopt the default settings in [3], [4] and [5].

Due to the prolonged network lifetime, it may take weeks to drain completely fully-charged batteries of sensor nodes. In order to conduct the experiments in a reasonable amount of time while demonstrating the feature and performance of evaluated protocols, we study how fast a sensor node consumes a designated small portion of its full energy, and evaluate its nodal lifetime as the time period during which this designated amount of energy is consumed. Particularly, at the beginning of each experiment, the initial available nodal energy distribution may be uniform or non-uniform. When the distribution is uniform, each sensor node's initial available energy is designated to 400 Joules; when it is non-uniform, the initial available energy varies between 300 and 400 Joules.

5.1 Performance with Static Events

We first evaluated the performance of LB-MAC with static events when the initial energy distribution is uniform or non-uniform. The results are shown in Figures 8 and 9.

As shown in Figures 8(a) and 9(a), LB-MAC achieves longer network lifetime than RI-MAC, X-MAC and SEESAW do under various conditions. Particularly, when the data generation interval is 2.5 seconds, the network lifetime achieved by

LB-MAC is about 90% longer than that achieved by RI-MAC and X-MAC, and 30% longer than that achieved by SEESAW, with uniform initial nodal energy. The leading edge is even more significant (e.g., about 50% longer than SEESAW) with non-uniform initial nodal energy. This is mainly due to the following reasons. As RI-MAC and X-MAC fix MAC protocol parameters, bottleneck nodes have the heaviest workloads, consume more energy than others, and their nodal lifetime constrains the network lifetime as shown by Figure 10. Instead, LB-MAC dynamically adjusts MAC parameters to shift the communication overhead, balance nodal lifetime as shown by Figure 10, and hence significantly increases the network lifetime. SEESAW also attempts to balance nodal lifetime, but its capability of parameter adjustment is less effective than LB-MAC because its adjustments follow a set of fixed policies that are not adaptive to changes in conditions.

The evaluation results in (b), (c) and (d) of Figures 8 and 9 show that, LB-MAC does not compromise its performance in other aspects to attain longer network lifetime. Specifically, LB-MAC maintains similar packet delivery ratio, per-hop delay and network power consumption as RI-MAC, X-MAC and SEE-SAW.

A Working Trace. To further illustrate how LB-MAC adaptively changes MAC behaviors to balance nodal lifetime, Figure 11 plots changing traces of parameters T_s, ρ and ϕ at forwarding node 24, as well as the changing trace of ϕ at node 13, on path $32{\rightarrow}24{\rightarrow}13$.

At time instance 0, the estimated nodal lifetime of node 24 is higher than that of nodes 13 and 32. Hence, as the receiver of link $32{\rightarrow}24$, node 24 increases its ϕ to shift the communication overhead from 32 to itself. Meanwhile, as the receiver of link $24{\rightarrow}13$, node 13 assigns a very small value to its ϕ such that it keeps awake for only a very short duration every time it wakes up. In response, node 24 sets its T_s and ρ as in Equation (6); that is, whenever node 24 has data packets to send to node 13, it keeps awake to wait for beacon from node 13 and then transmit the packets. This way, workload associated with communication between nodes 24 and 13 is mostly shifted to node 24. As a result of the above parameter adjustment, the nodal lifetime of nodes 13, 24 and 32 is balanced gradually during the time interval [0, 0.8h]. Shortly after time instance 0.8h,

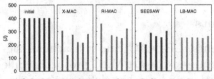

(a) Uniform initial nodal energy

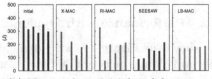

(b) Non-uniform initial nodal energy

Fig. 10. Snapshot of available remaining energy of nodes 1, 5, 13, 24, 32 and 36 after 2 hours of network operation with static events (data generation interval at source nodes is 2.5 seconds)

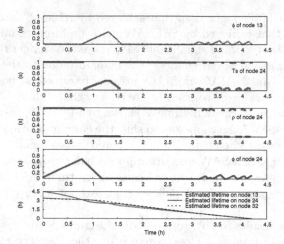

Fig. 11. Changing traces of ϕ, ρ and T_s at node 24 and ϕ at node 13 on path $32 \rightarrow 24 \rightarrow 13$

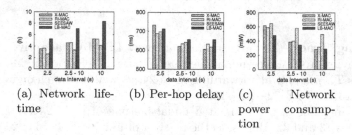

(a) Network life-
time

(b) Per-hop delay

(c)   Network
power consump-
tion

Fig. 12. Performance comparison with dynamic events and non-uniform initial nodal energy (note: data interval "2.5-10" means data packets are generated at an interval uniformly distributed in [2.5s, 10s])

node 24's nodal lifetime drops to be shorter than that of nodes 13 and 32. Adapting to the change, node 24 decreases its ϕ to shift some communication overhead to its sender node 32 on link $32\rightarrow24$, and meanwhile decreases its ρ and adjusts its T_s accordingly to shift some communication overhead to node 13 on the link $24\rightarrow13$.

5.2   Performance with Dynamic Events

As shown in Figure 12, with dynamic events, LB-MAC can still achieve significantly longer network lifetime than the state-of-the-art MAC protocols while maintaining similar network power consumption and per-hop delay as those protocols (packet delivery ratio for all protocols is close to 100% and the figures are omitted here). The results well demonstrate the robustness and good performance of LB-MAC in practical scenarios where (i) the nodal initial energy is heterogeneous, (ii) the routing paths and the traffic pattern are time-varying and (iii) the data sources are temporally and spatially dynamic. In particular, the adaptiveness and performance stability of LB-MAC under different network settings are even obvious when compared to the SEESAW protocol. In the prior experiments with static events, SEESAW attains longer network lifetime and lower network power consumption than X-MAC and RI-MAC do; however, with more dynamic routing and more time-varying traffics, the performance of SEE-SAW is degraded significantly due to its fixed and empirical polities for MAC parameter tuning. On the contrast, LB-MAC's adaptive design enables itself to overcome these practical problems and deliver good performance stably.

6   Conclusion and Future Work

In this paper, we present a new MAC protocol, called LB-MAC (Lifetime-Balanced MAC), which is designed from the perspective of network lifetime maximization. The key idea of LB-MAC is to allow sensor nodes to adjust their MAC-layer behaviors dynamically so as to extend the network lifetime through balancing nodal lifetime between communicating neighbors. The effectiveness of the proposed scheme is demonstrated via in-depth experimental results. Future work will be conducted along the following directions. As many schemes have been proposed at other layers to balance nodal lifetime or nodal energy consumption, we plan to compare LB-MAC with these schemes and study the advantage and limitations of each approach. Based on the study, we will explore the feasibility and strategy of the balancing techniques through cross-layer integration with middle layer [23], routing layer [24] or services in other network layers. We will also extend LB-MAC by adding lifetime balancing support for broadcast or multicast data services. In duty cycle sensor networks, the basic approach for broadcast or multicast is to transmit data to the destination nodes through unicast one by one [13, 25] and the advanced scheme is to delegate data transmissions to different nodes [26] so the original broadcast or multicast initiator can go to sleep earlier to save energy. Such extensions are also applicable to LB-MAC, and we believe that LB-MAC's performance may be improved further if the traffic pattern (unicast, multicast or broadcast) can be used when adjusting the MAC-layer parameters.

Acknowledgement. This work was supported partly by the NSF under Grants CNS-0831874 and ECCS-1128312.

References

1. Challen, G.W., Waterman, J., Welsh, M.: IDEA: Integrated Distributed Energy Awareness for Wireless Sensor Networks. In: MobiSys (2010)
2. Wang, W., Srinivasan, V., Chua, K.: Using Mobile Relays to Prolong the Lifetime of Wireless Sensor Networks. In: MobiCom (2005)
3. Buettner, M., Yee, G., Anderson, E., Han, R.: X-MAC: A Short Preamble MAC Protocol For Duty-Cycled Wireless. Sensor Networks. In: SenSys (2006)

4. Sun, Y., Gurewitz, O., Johnson, D.: RI-MAC: A Receiver-Initiated Asynchronous. Duty Cycle MAC Protocol for Dynamic Traffic Loads in Wireless Sensor Networks. In: SenSys (2008)
5. Braynard, R., Silberstein, A., Ellis, C.S.: Extending Network Lifetime Using an Automatically Tuned Energy-Aware MAC Protocol. In: Römer, K., Karl, H., Mattern, F. (eds.) EWSN 2006. LNCS, vol. 3868, pp. 244–259. Springer, Heidelberg (2006)
6. Polastre, J., Hill, J., Culler, D.: Versatile Low Power Media Access for Wireless Sensor Networks. In: SenSys (2004)
7. Ye, W., Heidemann, J., Estrin, D.: An Energy-Efficient MAC protocol for WirelessSensor Networks. In: INFOCOM (2002)
8. Dam, T., Langendoen, K.: An Adaptive Energy-Efficient MAC Protocol for Wireless Sensor Networks. In: SenSys (2003)
9. Dutta, P., Dawson-Haggerty, S., Chen, Y., Liang, C.J.M., Terzis, A.: Design and Evaluation of a Versatile and Efficient. Receiver-Initiated Link Layer for Low-Power Wireless. In: SenSys (2010)
10. Meier, A., Woehrle, M., Zimmerling, M., Thiele, L.: ZeroCal: Automatic MAC Protocol Calibration. In: Rajaraman, R., Moscibroda, T., Dunkels, A., Scaglione, A. (eds.) DCOSS 2010. LNCS, vol. 6131, pp. 31–44. Springer, Heidelberg (2010)
11. Merlin, C.J., Heinzelman, W.B.: Duty Cycle Control for Low-Power-Listening MAC Protocols. IEEE Transactions on Mobile Computing 9, 1508–1521 (2010)
12. Peng, Y., Li, Z., Qiao, D., Zhang, W.: Delay-Bounded MAC with Minimal Idle Listening for Sensor Networks. In: INFOCOM (2011)
13. Washington University St. Louis: UPMA Package: Unified Power Management Architecture for Wireless Sensor Networks, http://tinos.cvs.sourceforge.net/tinyos/tinyos-2.x/contrib/wustl/upma/
14. Gu, Y., He, T.: Data Forwarding in Extremely Low Duty-Cycle Sensor Networks with Unreliable Communication Links. In: SenSys (2007)
15. Wang, X., Wang, X., Xing, G., Yao, Y.: Dynamic Duty Cycle Control for End-to-End Delay Guarantees in Wireless Sensor Networks. In: IWQOS (2010)
16. Dutta, P., Feldmeier, M., Paradiso, J., Culler, D.: Energy Metering for Free: Augmenting Switching Regulators for Real-Time Monitoring. In: IPSN (2008)
17. Fonseca, R., Dutta, P., Levis, P., Stoica, I.: Quanto: Tracking Energy in Networked Embedded Systems. In: OSDI (2008)
18. Lin, K., Yu, J., Hsu, J., Zahedi, S., Lee, D., Friedman, J., Kansal, A., Raghunathan, V., Srivastava, M.: Heliomote: Enabling Long-Lived Sensor Networks. Through Solar Energy Harvesting. In: SenSys (2005)
19. Lu, G., De, D., Xu, M., Song, W.Z., Cao, J.: TelosW: Enabling ultra-low power wake-on sensor network. In: Seventh International Conference on Networked Sensing Systems, INSS (2010)
20. Lachenmann, A., Herrmann, K., Rothermel, K., Marrón, P.J.: Meeting Lifetime Goals and Providing Constant Application Quality. ACM Trans. Sen. Netw. 5, 36:1–36:36 (2009)
21. Zhu, T., Zhong, Z., Gu, Y., He, T., Zhang, Z.L.: Leakage-Aware Energy Synchronization for Wireless Sensor Networks. In: MobiSys (2009)
22. Gnawali, O., Fonseca, R., Jamieson, K., Moss, D., Levis, P.: Collection Tree Protocol. In: SenSys (2009)

23. Li, Z., Peng, Y., Qiao, D., Zhang, W.: LBA: Lifetime Balanced Data Aggregation in Low Duty Cycle Sensor Networks. In: INFOCOM (2012)
24. Li, Z., Peng, Y., Zhang, W., Qiao, D.: J-RoC: A Joint Routing and Charging scheme to prolong sensor network lifetime. In: ICNP (2011)
25. Klues, K., Hackmann, G., Chipara, O., Lu, C.: A Component Based Architecture for Power-Efficient Media Access Control in Wireless Sensor Networks. In: SenSys (2007)
26. Sun, Y., Gurewitz, O., Du, S., Tang, L., Johnson, D.B.: ADB: An Efficient Multi-hop Broadcast Protocol Based on Asynchronous Duty-Cycling in Wireless Sensor Networks. In: SenSys (2009)

Enhancing Performance and Reliability of RFID Middleware Using Mobile Agents

Jinho Ahn

Department of Computer Science, Kyonggi University
Suwon Gyeonggido, Republic of Korea
jhahn@kgu.ac.kr

Abstract. If a very large volume of data generated from the scan of RFID tags on individual items continuously flow into a single RFID middleware component with limited hardware resources, its entire data processing time for extracting necessary information from this huge amount of scanned data may become considerably longer. This paper presents mobile agent-based distributed software modules applicable to traditional RFID systems to highly alleviate a huge amount of workload of the middleware by addressing this fundamental limitation. They provide a convenient environment enabling required data to be pre-processed repeatedly in transit by transferring a mobile agent including its specified data management rules to numerous mobile readers. Simulation results verify that our proposed system performs better and more reliable than the traditional one processing the data by fixed readers after having arrived at the destination in case a large amount of RFID tag data should be processed in middlewares with RFID readers.

Keywords: distributed computing, scalability, reliability, agent mobility, RFID system.

1 Introduction

Radio Frequency IDentification(RFID) technology allows all tags physically covered by their readers to be recognized simultaneously without any human intervention unlike some other automatic identification and data capture technologies that sense objects in a serial manner[9]. If there are a certain number of tags in the coverage area of readers, they identifies all the tags in a short time and delivers them to the corresponding RFID middleware. Then, this middleware filters, transforms and aggregates tag data collected from their readers, and sends only the essential information to RFID applications executing their individual business tasks. This technical potential has RFID systems be widely used in many industrial fields such as military supply chain management, airport baggage handling and monitoring, food tracing, security and healthcare[9]. In particular, in the physical distribution industry, the introduction of RFID has enormously contributed to effectively monitoring locations and information of products in real-time.

As RFID tag prices have rapidly been decreasing, each tag is attached not only to a packing box or a pallet, but also to an individual item for managing

X. Wang et al. (Eds.): WASA 2012, LNCS 7405, pp. 292–300, 2012.

the item much more precisely. However, if a very large volume of data generated from the scan of these RFID tags on individual items continuously flow into a single RFID middleware component with limited hardware resources, its entire data processing time for extracting necessary information from this huge amount of scanned data may become considerably longer. For example, several terabytes of RFID data is expected to generate at Wal-Mart everyday[10]. This high velocity of producing electronic product codes(EPC), locations and reading time of tags may cause even modest RFID systems to generate tens of gigabytes of data daily. On the other hand, although RFID reader manufacturers attempt to raise the read rate accuracy up to 95-100%[16], the real-world observed read rate accuracy still remains on average in the 60-70% range[11]. So, due to this technological limitation, the widespread adoption of RFID technology is being delayed. Therefore, specific technologies are in great demand to handle and further to reduce the load of the middleware.

Mobile agent is an autonomous and independent software program to satisfy the corresponding user's goal on behalf of the user while visiting various target nodes through a network[1,15]. This mobile agent technology has several advantages such as reduction of network traffic, overcoming of network delay, enabling asynchronous execution and enhancement of dynamic adaptability. Thanks to these desirable features, this technology may be applicable to RFID middlewares for greatly improving their performance in several ways like in other fields such as telecommunication, ubiquitous computing, grid computing and sensor network[1,3,12,15]. A static load balancing mechanism[6] based on the min-max cost and tag count assignment was presented. Park et. al.[13] designed a decentralized load balancing mechanism by creating a connection pool between RFID middlewares and readers. Tag data are distributed to multiple middlewares from a connection pool by its manager. However, the load balancing behavior of these two mechanisms is static. So, they cannot accommodate a variety of workload patterns of incoming tag data well[4]. In order to solve this drawback, an adaptive load balancing system using mobile agents[4] was proposed. But, its centralization behavior may burden RFID middlewares with all the load sharing tasks. All these previous works mentioned above force all RFID tag data to be processed only in the middleware. Thus, different mechanisms using mobile agents are essential to highly alleviate a huge amount of workload of the middleware by addressing this fundamental limitation.

This paper presents mobile agent-based distributed software modules applicable to traditional RFID systems to satisfy this requirement efficiently. They provide a convenient environment enabling required data to be pre-processed repeatedly in transit by transferring a mobile agent including its specified data management rules to numerous mobile readers. This behavior can significantly reduce the elapsed time required for processing huge volumes of tag data at the readers and middlewares with their very high recognition rates compared with the existing ones processing the data by fixed readers after having arrived at the destination.

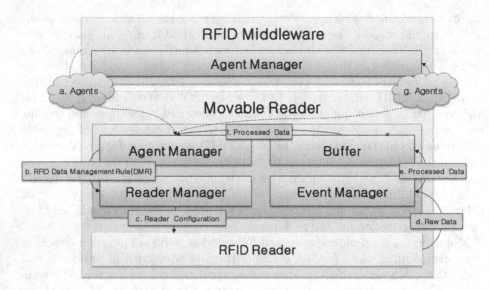

Fig. 1. Overall structure and processing steps

2   New RFID Software Modules

Like in figure 1, our proposed system consists of two parts, in-transit reader module and middleware module. First, the reader module is divided into five components, agent manager, reader manager, event manager, buffer, RFID reader. Second, the middleware module is agent manager added to the traditional RFID middleware functionality. Let us explain the entire processing steps of the system in detail using figure 1 as follows; the agent manager in the middleware part creates a mobile agent with some data management rules(DMRs) its user wants to enforce for collecting needed tag data from his or her specifying readers and then, sends the agent to the established readers. After the mobile agent has arrived at the agent manager in each reader, it gives the RFID reader the management rules it has through the reader manager. Afterwards, the reader configures its environment with the rules, and collects raw tag data from its physical sensing component accordingly and delivers them to the event manager. Next, the event manager eliminates redundant and unnecessary data from them, and makes some aggregated data complying with the DMR, which are saved into the buffer. The mobile agent continues to process all the accumulated data produced through such repetitive stages to its desired level. As the moving vehicle arrives at its appropriate place, the agent with the processed data required migrates to the agent manager in the middleware part, delivering the data to the traditional middleware module. If it is expected agent migration overhead is high because the amount of the processed data are very large, the agent attempts to establish a communication link to the agent manager in the middleware part for bringing the data to it without agent migration, disappearing after it has finished its task.

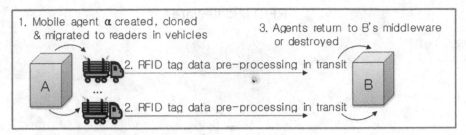

(a) In case of homogeneous environments

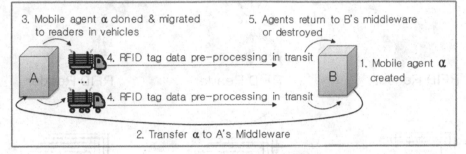

(b) In case of heterogeneous environments

Fig. 2. Applied examples

Let us show you two different examples in figure 2 for better understanding of our proposed system. The first example in figure 2(a) supposes there are agent execution and mobility enabling environments homogeneous and two different branches A and B know each other's requirements with DMRs. In this case, the agent manager in branch A's middleware part creates a mobile agent α with DMRs branch B intends to enforce and then, clones and transfers it to readers in designated vehicles. Next, the agent resumes and executes its task in the agent manager in its corresponding reader. As mentioned above, the agent makes a new configuration onto the RFID reader according to the DMR it is carrying, which allows RFID tag data coming from the reader to be pre-processed and saved into the buffer while the vehicle is in transit. As the vehicle parks at its destination, the agent with the desired pre-processed data moves to B's middleware part or is self-destroyed after having delivered the data to B's middleware.

The second example in figure 2(b) reflects heterogeneity of mobile agent execution environments and requirements with DMRs each branch assumes. This distinction forces branch B's middleware part to create a mobile agent α with DMRs in person and transfer it to A's middleware. The remaining procedure is the same as in figure 2(a).

3   Simulation

For constructing our simulation environment, we used Rifidi emulator[14], which is EPCglobal's ALE specification compliant[2,8] and implemented in java

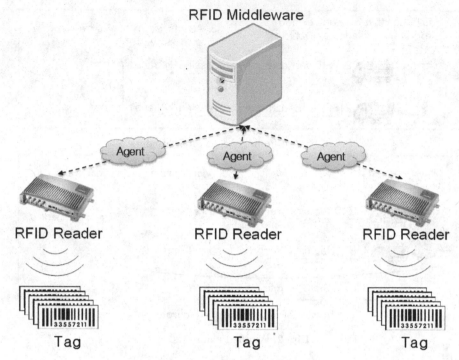

Fig. 3. Simulation model

language. Also, this emulator enables virtual RFID tags to be generated in the same environment as real-world RFID systems and supports low-level reader protocol(LLRP)[2,7]. The simulated system consists of one RFID middleware and three virtual readers like in figure 3. In order to embed our mobile agent-based modules in the emulator, we modified the software components for RFID reader and middleware like in figures 4 and 5.

In this section, we perform extensive simulations to compare our mobile agent-based RFID system (denoted by *Ours*) with the traditional one (denoted by *Prev*). Two performance indices are used; the average number of readings required until all given tags can be recognized by each RFID reader (denoted by *NORR*) and the total time required until all given tags can be recognized and their collected data, delivered to the middleware (denoted by *TTRR*). There are also two important simulation parameters as follows; the recognition rate of a RFID reader per reading (denoted by RRPR) and the number of RFID tags that each RFID reader should recognize (denoted by NORT).

Table 1 shows *NORR* of RFID readers for the various *NORT* and *RRPR* values respectively. As expected, we can see that *NORR* becomes larger as *NORT* increases, *RRPR* decreases or both. In particular, even if RRPR is up to 95%, each reader should scan tags about three times on average. Thus, if this overhead can be eliminated like in our approach, the entire tag processing time will be significantly reduced.

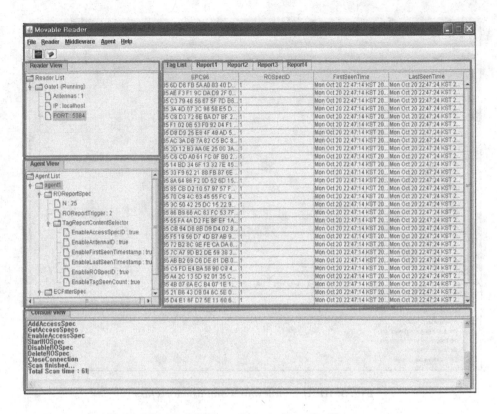

Fig. 4. RFID reader emulator for *Ours*

The left side of table 2 shows $TTRR$ of the two systems for the various $NORT$ values ranging from 100 to 800 when $RRPR$ is 95%. These simulation results indicate that $TTRR$ of *Ours* is larger than that of *Prev* if $NORT$ is less than or equal to 200 because of agent migration overhead of *Ours*. However as $NORT$ increases above 200, the effectiveness obtained from *Ours*'s pre-processing using mobile agents becomes evident. From the results, we can see that the gap between $TTRR$s of the two systems significantly increases as $NORT$ becomes larger.

The right side of table 2 illustrates their $TTRR$ for the various $RRPR$ values ranging from 80% to 99% when $NORT$ is 500. In this figure, we can see that $TTRR$ of *Ours* is much lower than that of *Prev* because $TTRR$ of *Ours* need not include the time required for RFID tag data processing of readers with the target middleware as the vehicle arrives at its destination. In particular, even if $RRPR$ is up to 99%, *Ours* reduces about 37.5% of $TTRR$ compared with *Prev*.

In conclusion, the simulation results show *Ours* significantly performs better and more reliable than *Prev* in case a large amount of RFID tag data should be processed in the middleware with RFID readers.

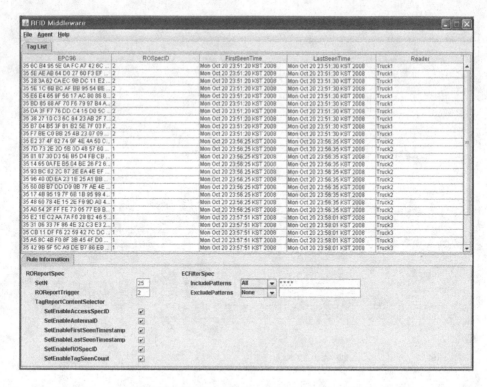

Fig. 5. RFID middleware emulator for *Ours*

Table 1. NORR

NORT	(RRPR=65%)	RRPR	(NORT=500)
200	5.9	65%	7.7
300	6.8	75%	5.3
400	7.1	85%	4.0
500	7.7	95%	2.7

Table 2. TTRR

NORT	Ours	Prev	RRPR	Ours	Prev
100	378ms	205ms	80%	627ms	1248ms
200	422ms	401ms	85%	627ms	1088ms
300	503ms	605ms	90%	627ms	1055ms
400	572ms	795ms	95%	627ms	1026ms
500	627ms	1026ms	99%	627ms	1005ms
600	698ms	1205ms			
700	735ms	1381ms			
800	804ms	1659ms			

4   Conclusion

This paper presented mobile agent-based software modules to efficiently reduce the load of the middleware by pre-processing a lot of tag data while items are in transit. This desirable feature may clearly have an effect on overcoming the low observed read rate accuracy of real-world readers and a high volume and speed of data produced from dynamic RFID environments unlike the traditional ones. Simulation results indicate that embedding our modules into RFID middlewares and readers may greatly accelerate tag data processing and provide higher level of reliability of RFID systems by raising the tag recognition rate in a short time limit. If a highly fast mobile agent transfer protocol like in [5] is used as the fundamental block of mobile agent execution environments, the agent migration latency may be considerably reduced, which makes our approach more practical.

References

1. Ahn, J.: Lightweight Fault-tolerance Mechanism for Distributed Mobile Agent-based Monitoring. In: Proc. of International IEEE CCNC Workshop on Dependable and Sustainable Peer-to-Peer Systems (January 2009)
2. Armenio, F., Barthel, H., Burstein, L., Dietrich, P., Duker, J., Garrett, J., Hogan, B., Ryaboy, O., Sarma, S.: The EPCglobal Architecture Framework Final Version 1.2, pp. 24-26 (September 2007)
3. Cimino, M., Marcelloni, F.: Autonomic tracing of production processes with mobile and agent-based computing. Information Sciences 181(5), 935–953 (2011)
4. Chae, H., Park, J., Cui, J., Lee, J.: An adaptive load balancing management technique for RFID middleware systems. Softw. Pract. Exper. 40, 485–506 (2010)
5. Cucurull, J., Marti, R., Navarro-Arribas, G., Robles, S., Borrell, J., Suades, G.: Fragment Transfer Protocol: An IEEE-FIPA based efficient transfer protocol for mobile agents. Computer Communications 33(18), 2203–2214 (2010)
6. Dong, Q., Shukla, A., Shrivastava, V., Agrawal, D., Banerjee, S., Kar, K.: Load balancing in large-scale RFID systems. Computer Networks 52(9), 1782–1796 (2008)
7. EPCglobal, Low Level Reader Protocol (LLRP), Version 1.0.1, pp. 51-92 (August 2007)
8. EPCglobal, The Application Level Events (ALE) Specification, Version 1.1 Part I: Core Specification, pp. 17-20 (2008)
9. Glover, B., Bhatt, H.: RFID Essentials, pp. 1–20. O'Reilly (2006)
10. Gonzalez, H., Han, J., Li, X., Klabjan, D.: Warehousing and Analyzing Massive RFID Data Sets. In: Proceedings of the 22nd IEEE ICDE Conference (2006)
11. Jeffery, S., Garofalakis, M., Franklin, M.: Adaptive Cleaning for RFID Large Data Bases. In: Proceeding of the 32nd International Conference on VLDB, pp. 163–174 (2006)
12. Lin, K., Chen, M., Zeadally, S., Rodrigues, J.: Balancing energy consumption with mobile agents in wireless sensor networks. Future Generation Computer Systems 28(2), 446–456 (2012)
13. Park, S., Song, J., Kim, C., Kim, J.: Load balancing method using connection pool in RFID middleware. In: Proceedings of the Fifth ACIS International Conference on Software Engineering Research, Management and Applications (SERA 2007), Busan, South Korea, pp. 132–137 (2007)

14. Rifidi Technology, Rifidi User Guide (2007),
    http://www.rifidi.org/documentation.html
15. Su, C., Wu, C.: JADE implemented mobile multi-agent based, distributed informa-
    tion platform for pervasive health care monitoring. Applied Soft Computing 11(1),
    315–325 (2011)
16. The METRO Group Future Store Initiative (1895),
    http://www.future-store.org,
    http://www.eweek.com/article2/0,1895,2152562,00.asp

An Improved Stochastic Decoding Algorithm of LTE Turbo Codes

Jiao Xianjun

Radio Systems Lab, Nokia Research Center
Beijing, 100176, P.R. China
Ryan.Jiao@nokia.com

Abstract. Turbo codes are widely used in many communication systems, and decoding algorithm is studied intensively. Most decoding algorithms are Max-Log-MAP based, which performs arithmetic computation in logarithm domain. In recent years, stochastic turbo decoding has been proposed as a potential high parallel scheme. Stochastic decoding is carried on in probability domain, and probability computations are done by logical operation of stochastic bit streams. In this paper, stochastic decoding is improved in three ways: firstly, use OR gate instead of multiplexer or Taylor expansion in exponential domain for probability adding operation, where data distribution of turbo decoding process is utilized; secondly, a direct intra parallel streams barrel shifter is used to break correlation of division results; thirdly, random initialization instead of zero initialization for flip-flop is used to shorten warming up time of decoding stages. Simulations show that these improvement methods reduce decoding complexity: it costs less hardware resources and decoding cycles/time. Stochastic decoding also shows scalable and flexible characteristics in the Software Defined Radio (SDR) scenario.

Keywords: Stochastic decoding, turbo codes, LTE, Software Defined Radio, Data parallelism.

1 Introduction

Turbo codes decoding has been studied thoroughly recent years. Most methods are Max-Log-MAP based. Max-Log-MAP convert probability multiplying to Log-Likelihood Ratios (LLR) adding and maximum [1, 2], as adder is simpler than multiplier. Stochastic turbo decoding uses original form of probability calculation, but avoids arithmetic multiplier. It converts probability to stochastic bit stream, where probability is carried by events of '1' occurrence. Then probability computation can be done by logical operation of stochastic streams. Assuming probability P is represented by a stochastic bit stream, where probability of '1' occurrence is P. Then multiplying two probabilities P_1 and P_2 can be done by put the two bit streams through AND gate. It can be proved easily that probability of '1' occurrence of output bit stream from AND gate will be $P_1 * P_2$. Adding, normalization and division operations

X. Wang et al. (Eds.): WASA 2012, LNCS 7405, pp. 301–308, 2012.

also can be done by operating stochastic bit streams [3, 4]. In [5, 6], a full stochastic decoder of LTE turbo codes is proposed.

The reset of paper is organized with five parts. probability algorithm of decoding turbo codes is described in section 2; stochastic decoding and improvement methods are described in section 3; simulation results is in section 4; considerations for SDR is described in section 5; conclusion is in section 6.

2   Probability Decoding of Turbo Codes

Fig. 1 depicts block diagram of probability turbo decoder.

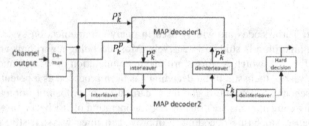

Fig. 1. Structure of turbo decoder

For every MAP decoder, channel output probability of systematic and parity bits are denoted by P_k^s and P_k^p; input priori systematic bits probability from another decoder is denoted by P_k^a; output extrinsic systematic bits probability to another decoder is denoted by P_k^e (as priori probability input of another decoder). Output posterior systematic bits probability for hard decision is denoted by P_k.

Branch metric: $\gamma_k(s', s) = P_k^a(x = i)P_k^s(x = i)P_k^p(y = j)$

The metric is for the transition from state s' to s. x and y are systematic and parity bit variable. i and j pair is the concrete input (systematic bit) and output (parity bit) of the state transition in trellis. For LTE binary turbo codes, $i, j \in \{0,1\}$.

State metric: $\alpha_{k+1}(s) = \sum_{s'} \alpha_k(s')\gamma_k(s', s)$; $\beta_k(s') = \sum_s \gamma_k(s', s)\beta_{k+1}(s)$

Forward (α) and backward (β) state metric is calculated from those states, which can be connected by transition.

Extrinsic probability: $P_k^e(x = i) = \sum_{s' \to s} \alpha_k(s') P_k^p(y = j)\beta_{k+1}(s)$

Extrinsic systematic bits probability is calculated from all states transition pairs, which generates systematic bit i and parity bit j. Notice that right side of equation doesn't include extern input P_k^a and channel native P_k^s for generating extrinsic information.

Posterior probability: $P_k(x = i) = P_k^a(x = i)P_k^s(x = i)P_k^e(x = i)$

Full information P_k is produced by new/extrinsic information P_k^e, extern input P_k^a and channel native P_k^s.

Notice that normalization should be performed to ensure $\sum_s \alpha_k(s) = 1$, $\sum_{s'} \beta_k(s') = 1$, and $\sum_{i \in \{0,1\}} P_k^e(x = i) = 1$.

3   Stochastic Decoding

A full stochastic turbo decoder is revealed in [5, 6]. Fig. 2 depicts MAP decoder structure, which is very similar with [5, 6].

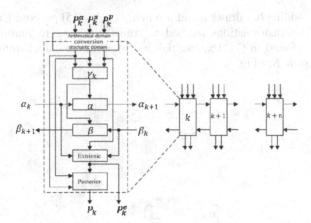

Fig. 2. Structure of MAP decoder

Unlike Max-Log-MAP decoder, stochastic decoder in Fig. 2 can run in full parallel. That means if each stage of two sub-decoders of Fig. 1 is implemented as hardware block, every part of whole turbo decoder can run every clock. In other words, all components run concurrently. The concept of iteration number is disappeared, because two sub-decoders can exchange extrinsic information every clock. So decoding cycles (DCs) is adopted to represent one cycle/iteration for stochastic decoding.

Converting probability to bit stream can be done by random number generator and comparator, detail information can be found in [3, 4]. To get probability value for hard decision, a counter can be used to count number of '1' in stream. Many cycles has to run to get enough number of '1', if reasonable precision is wanted. If multi streams run concurrently, enough number of '1' will be reached by less decoding cycles [8].

From section 2, calculations involved in each stage of MAP decoder are multiplying and normalization. Normalization will involve adding and division. Notice that multiplying can be done by AND gate [3], and it is already the simplest way. The improvement methods are mainly for normalization.

Traditional adding and division of stochastic computation are depicted in Fig. 3 (also can be found in [3]).

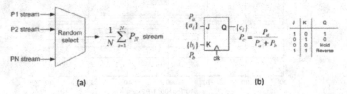

Fig. 3. (a) Stochastic adding by multiplexer. (b) Stochastic division by JK flip-flop

JK flip-flop actually performs normalization of two stochastic streams. If more than two streams need normalization, P_b should be sum of multi streams.

3.1   Improvement Method 1: Adding by OR Gate

Multiplexer for adding has drawback of too many cycles, [5] proposed an exponential and logarithmic transformations method to transfer adding to multiplying. Detail structure can be found in [7]. Exponential and logarithmic calculations are done by Taylor's expansion. See Fig. 4.

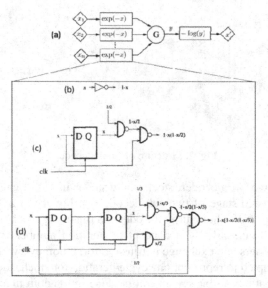

Fig. 4. (a) Principle of exponential-domain computation (Fig. 3 in [5]). (b) 1st order Taylor expansion circuit. (c) 2nd order Taylor expansion circuit. (c) 3rd Taylor expansion circuit (Fig. 3 in [7]).

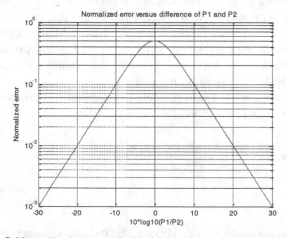

Fig. 5. Normalized error analysis of OR gate result over real adding

In this paper, adding is done by OR gate instead of prior art in turbo decoding.

If two stochastic streams (one has probability P_1, the other has probability P_2) are put through OR gate, it can be easily proved that output stream has probability P_1 + ty $P_1 + P_2 - P_1 * P_2$. Consider normalized error over real adding result $P_1 + P_2$. The error can be rewritten as $\frac{P_1 * P_2}{P_1 + P_2} = \frac{1}{(P_1/P_2) + (1/(P_1/P_2))}$. Fig. 5 plots the error versus $10 *$ sus $10 * log_{10}(P_1/P_2)$.

From Fig. 5, if difference of P1 and P2 is larger, the error will be smaller. This is the basic reason that why OR gate can be used to do adding in turbo decoding, because large difference does occur high probably among metrics in one stage. Though two streams condition is analyzed, it can be extended easily to more streams case, which is the situation of eight state metrics per stage in LTE turbo codes. Fig. 6 plots Cumulative Distribution Function (CDF) of maximum state metric and minimum state metric difference per stage before normalization. The simulation condition is first iteration, code length 6144 bits and Eb/N0 0.6dB.

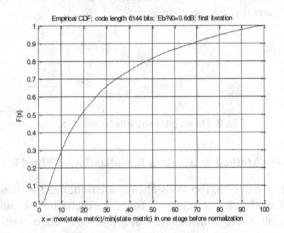

Fig. 6. CDF of differences of state metrics in one stage before normalization

From Fig. 6, 70% differences are more than 10 times, and 90% differences are more than 5 time times. Residential error is limited by normalization and code redundancy through iteration process. Simulation result in section 4 shows that the error has little impact on performance.

OR gate is much simpler than Fig. 3 (a) and Fig. 4. OR gate doesn't have warming up delay, because it is combinational logic. So it can decrease decoding cycles. Apparently, it is superior to scheme with register when consider decoding cycles.

3.2   Improvement Method 2: Direct Inter Streams Permutation

To overcome latching problem of JK flip-flop based division, [10] and [8] describe EM memory method for single bit stream and barrel shifter method for multi bits stream. See Fig. 7.

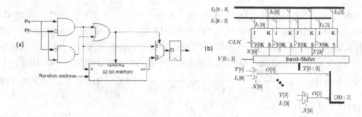

Fig. 7. (a) EM memory method for single bit stream (Fig. 6 (a) in [10]). (b) Barrel shifter method for multi bits stream (Fig. 5 (b) in [8]).

In [10] and [8], when JK flip-flop is in hold state, output stream selects bit from history memory of new born bit (known as EM memory [10]) or other stream randomly. Unlike the scheme with selection logic, multi streams are permuted directly by barrel shifter with stepping shift length every clock in this paper. Simulation shows it works, because each stream has same probability basically. Fig. 8 depicts the direct permuting method, and it is simpler than Fig. 7.

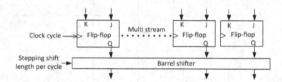

Fig. 8. Direct intra streams barrel shifter

3.3   Improvement Method 3: Random Initialization of Flip-Flop

In traditional hardware design, flip-flops always are initialized with zeros. This is not the best option for stochastic computation. Because stochastic computation counts on frequent changing bit event to achieve enough precision. Zeros initialization has to take many time to spill out those zeros in every stages. If flip-flops are initialized with random bits, warming up process and overall decoding time will be shortened.

4   Simulation Results

C language based LTE turbo codes test bench is constructed in order to test three improvement methods for stochastic decoding. Traditional Max-Log-MAP algorithm is also simulated as baseline. Shortest information length of 40 bits is chosen for rapid verification. Code rate is 1/3, which results in 3*40+12=132 bits to channel. For stochastic decoding, 32 bits width stream is used. Fig. 9 plots simulation results.

Fig. 9 shows that OR gate and direct barrel shifter work correctly. Random initialized flip-flops (curve 4) brings less number of decoding cycles than zero initialized flip-flops (curve 1~3). Random initialization with 192 decoding cycles (curve 4) has better performance than zero initialization with 320 decoding cycles (curve 3). With

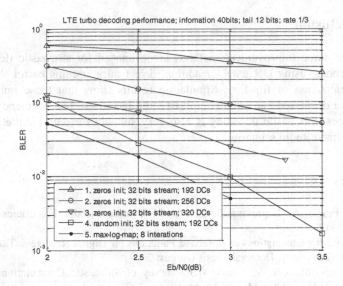

Fig. 9. Stochastic decoding BLER performance

improvement methods, 192 decoding cycles (curve 4) achieve less than 0.25dB gap with max-log-map decoding (curve 5), while 1024 decoding cycles is need in [6] to achieve the same performance. Decoding cycles in this paper has been decreased much than prior art.

5   Consideration in SDR Scenario

In SDR scenario, implementing algorithm with high parallel is a key point for utilize processor resources. Data parallelism has become more and more important in parallel computation. There are many researches on how to implement Max-Log-MAP algorithm in parallel form [9].

When Max-Log-MAP is implemented by several parallel sub decoders [9], there are some limitations. 1. The number of sub decoders can't be too big, or decoding performance will be degraded because of too short code length in each sub decoder. Parallel degree is limited. 2. The first and last decoder is a little different with other decoders. It isn't an ideal data parallelism case. An ideal case is that many same decoders process different dat. 3. If number of decoders/parallel degree is changed, parameters of overall decoder and sub decoders have to be changed accordingly.

Stochastic won't have those drawbacks. Because of native character of probability, if more quick result is desired, more same decoders/processes can be created to have more random events in unit time, which is an ideal data parallelism. If resources are limited, less decoders/streams can be used to have enough random events in longer time. Stochastic decoding has good scalable characters, every single parallel decoder maintains same implement no matter how parallel degree is changed.

6   Conclusion

In this paper, three improvement methods are proposed for stochastic decoding of LTE turbo codes: using OR gate for adding, direct intra streams barrel shifter, and random initialization of flip-flop. Simulation results show that these improvement methods have decreased hardware complexity and increased time efficiency by more than five times. Stochastic decoding is also very suitable for data parallelism in the Software Defined Radio scenario.

References

1. Vogt, J., Finger, A.: Improving the max-log-MAP turbo decoder. Electronics Letters 36, 1937–1939 (2000)
2. Salmela, P.: Implementations of Baseband Functions for Digital Receivers. Tampere University of Technology, Doctoral Thesis (August 2009)
3. Tehrani, S.S., Mannor, S., Gross, W.J.: Survey of Stochastic Computation on Factor Graphs. In: ISMVL 2007, May 13-16, pp. 54–54 (2007)
4. Brown, B.D., Card, H.C.: Stochastic Neural Computation I: Computational Elements 50(9), 891–905 (2001)
5. Dong, Q.T., Arzel, M., Jego, C., Gross, W.J.: Stochastic Decoding of Turbo Codes. IEEE Transactions on Signal Processing 58(12), 6421–6425 (2010)
6. Dong, Q.T., Arzel, M., Jégo, C.: Design and FPGA Implementation of Stochastic Turbo Decoder. In: IEEE 9th NEWCAS, June 26-29, pp. 21–24 (2011)
7. Janer, C.L., Quero, J.M., Ortega, J.G., Franquelo, L.G.: Fully Parallel Stochastic Computation Architecture. IEEE Transactions on Signal Processing 44(8), 2110–2117 (1996)
8. Arzel, M., Lahuec, C., Jego, C., Gross, W.J., Bruned, Y.: Stochastic Multiple Stream Decoding of Cortex Codes. IEEE Transactions on Signal Processing 59(7), 3486–3491 (2011)
9. Sun, Y., Cavallaro, J.R.: Efficient hardware implementation of a highly-parallel 3GPP LTE/LTE-advance turbo decoder, Integration. The VLSI Journal 44, 305–315 (2011)
10. Tehrani, S.S., Mannor, S., Gross, W.J.: Fully Parallel Stochastic LDPC Decoders. IEEE Transactions on Signal Processing 56(11), 5692–5703 (2008)

Robust Distributed Estimators for Wireless Sensor Networks with One-Bit Quantized Data

Guiyun Liu[1,*], Bugong Xu[1], and Hongbin Chen[2]

[1] College of Automation Science and Engineering,
South China University of Technology, Guangzhou 510641, China
[2] School of Information & Communication,
Guilin University of Electronic Technology, Guilin 541004, China

Abstract. In this letter, the problem of distributed estimation in a wireless sensor network with uncertain observation noise distributions is considered, where each sensor only sends one-bit quantized data to a fusion center. Two robust estimators called quantized mean estimator and trimmed mean estimator are proposed. The asymptotic relative efficiency and influence function of the proposed estimators are derived. Numerical results illustrate the performance advantages of the proposed estimators over the maximum likelihood estimator.

Keywords: Robust estimation, distributed estimation, decentralized estimation, sensor network.

1 Introduction

Sensor networks can accomplish signal processing tasks such as detection, estimation, and target tracking. The problem of distributed estimation in wireless sensor networks has been widely studied in recent years [1]–[12], where the one-bit quantized data are transmitted from sensors to a fusion center (FC). For the case where complete information about the joint distribution of observations is known, the maximum likelihood estimator (MLE) of a scalar parameter was shown to achieve the Cramér-Rao lower bound (CRLB) asymptotically [1]–[4], [12,13]. For the case where the information of the precise covariance matrix can be obtained, a one-bit adaptive quantization scheme was proposed to increase the convergence speed of iterations [8]. In addition, for the case where only the knowledge of either the observation noise range or its second-order moment is required, a universal decentralized estimation scheme was introduced [10]. Most of these works assumed that the observation noise follows a Gaussian distribution or a known non-Gaussian distribution.

However, in practice the distribution of the observation noise may not be fully known [14]. Some observations are quite atypical in that being far from the bulk

* This work was supported in part by the National Natural Science Foundation of China (61174070, 61162008), the National Natural Science Foundation of China (NSFC)-Guangdong Joint Foundation Key Project (U0735003), and the Specialized Research Fund for the Doctoral Program of Higher Education (NO.20110172110033).

X. Wang et al. (Eds.): WASA 2012, LNCS 7405, pp. 309–314, 2012.

of the data and are called outliers. Such situations can result from apparatus malfunctions and man-made impulsive activities. It is expected that a robust estimator be designed to deal with the atypical observation noise distributions. Conventional parameter estimation methods such as the most common MLE [1,2] with one-bit quantized data are inefficient in this case. Their estimation performances may degrade substantially in the presence of such outliers.

In this letter, two robust estimators are proposed under the situation that the dominant distribution of the observation noise is Gaussian but the contaminating distribution of the observation noise is not required to be Gaussian and bounded. The measures of robustness of the proposed estimators are derived. The proposed estimators have the following characteristics: firstly, they are less sensitive to minor deviations from the dominant distribution than the MLE with one-bit quantized data [1,2,12,13]; secondly, they have reasonably good (optimal or suboptimal) performances when no outliers exists.

2   Problem Formulation

Consider a wireless sensor network with a FC, where N sensors are spatially deployed to estimate an unknown parameter θ. The observation of the sensors can be represented by

$$x_k = \theta + n_k, \quad k = 1, \cdots, N, \tag{1}$$

where x_k and n_k are the k-th observation and observation noise, respectively.

Different from the traditional assumption that observation noises follow a Gaussian distribution or a bounded non-Gaussian disribution, here the distribution of n_k is modeled as

$$f(n_k) \mapsto (1 - \epsilon)G + \epsilon H, \tag{2}$$

where $G = N(0, \sigma^2)$ is the dominant Gaussian distribution, H is a contaminating distribution (outlier), ϵ is a constant fraction, and $\epsilon \in [0, 1)$. $\{f(n_k), k = 1, \cdots, N\}$ are assumed to be independently and identically distributed.

Due to the bandwidth constraint, all sensors quantize their observations into one-bit binary data by applying a common threshold τ and then transmit the quantized data directly to the FC. The channels between sensors and the FC are assumed to be orthogonal and are binary symmetric channels (BSCs) with the same crossover probability p_r.

Because the distribution of the contaminating outliers is unknown a priori and is likely unbounded, classical estimators including the exact MLE cannot be directly applied. To cope with such a situation, two robust estimators are designed to deal with the unknown distribution.

The robust estimation problem is essentially to design an estimator that has a "good" behavior in a "neighborhood" of a model [14].

3   Robust Distributed Estimators

It is observed that in the absence of outliers the MLE with raw observation is theoretically optimal in the sense that it asymptotically achieves the CRLB. Note that with one-bit quantized data, the MLEs under ideal channels and BSCs may keep the above optimality [1]–[4], [6], [12,13]. It is inferred that when the distribution of observation noise is contaminated, the MLE may not be effective without the knowledge of the distribution of observation noises. To accomplish parameter estimation without the knowledge of the distribution of observation noises, two robust distributed estimators are designed as follows.

3.1   Quantized Mean Estimator

The transmitted binary observations from the sensors $\mathbf{b} := [b(1), \cdots, b(N)]^T$ are given by the index function

$$b(k) = 1\{x_k \in [\tau, +\infty)\}, \quad k = 1, \cdots, N, \tag{3}$$

and the received binary observations in the FC $\tilde{\mathbf{b}} := [\tilde{b}(1), \cdots, \tilde{b}(N)]^T$ are given by

$$\tilde{b}(k) = \begin{cases} b(k), & \text{with probability } 1 - p_r ; \\ 1 - b(k), & \text{with probability } p_r. \end{cases} \tag{4}$$

A quantized mean estimator (QME) is adopted at the FC, which is given by

$$\hat{F}_Q(\theta) = \frac{1}{N} \sum_{k=1}^{N} \tilde{b}(k). \tag{5}$$

3.2   Trimmed Mean Estimator

A proportion of the largest and smallest observations can be discarded before being quantized. A confidence interval $[x_a, x_{1-a}]$ is defined, where x_a and x_{1-a} denote the ath and $(1-a)$th quantile, respectively. We assume that there are no information exchange between sensors and each local sensor has a prior knowledge of quantiles. Observations which are not within the interval will be ignored. In essence, such trimming results in focus on the middle proportion of a distribution. The trimmed mean estimator (TME) is defined as

$$\hat{F}_T(\theta) = \frac{1}{\tilde{N}} \sum_{k=1}^{\tilde{N}} \tilde{b}(\tilde{N}, k), \tag{6}$$

where $\tilde{b}(\tilde{N}, k)$ denotes the kth of the $\tilde{N}$ trimmed binary observations.

The above two estimators are built only on G and are robust to H. Similar to the definition of parameters of the Bernoulli random variables [13], θ is estimated by solving the following equations:

$$p_r + (1 - 2p_r)q_{(c,0)}(\tau - \theta) = \hat{F}_Q(\theta), \tag{7}$$

$$p_r + (1 - 2p_r)(q_{(c,0)}(\tau - \theta) - a) = \hat{F}_T(\theta), \tag{8}$$

where $q_{(c,\epsilon)}(\cdot)$ is the complementary cumulative distribution function (CCDF) of f. Note that $q_{(c,0)}(\cdot)$ is the CCDF of G.

4   Robustness Measure

4.1   Asymptotic Relative Efficiency

It is assumed that the contaminating distribution H is continuous in its domain of definition. The ARE of $\hat{F}_Q(\theta)$ relative to $\hat{F}_T(\theta)$ [14] is defined as:

$$ARE(\epsilon)_{Q,T} = \lim_{N \to +\infty} \frac{Var(\hat{F}_T(\theta))/[E(\hat{F}_T(\theta))]^2}{Var(\hat{F}_Q(\theta))/[E(\hat{F}_Q(\theta))]^2}, \tag{9}$$

where $E(\cdot)$ and $Var(\cdot)$ denote the mean and the variance of a variable, respectively. It is easy to obtain that [13]

$$E_Q(\epsilon) := E(\hat{F}_Q(\theta)) = p_r + (1 - 2p_r)q_{(c,\epsilon)}(\tau - \theta). \tag{10}$$

Similarly, we have

$$E_T(\epsilon) := E(\hat{F}_T(\theta)) = p_r + (1 - 2p_r)(q_{(c,\epsilon)}(\tau - \theta) - a). \tag{11}$$

Theorem 1. The ARE of $\hat{F}_Q(\theta)$ relative to $\hat{F}_T(\theta)$ can be expressed as

$$ARE(\epsilon)_{Q,T} = (1 - 2a)\frac{[1 - E_Q(\epsilon)]E_T(\epsilon)}{[1 - E_T(\epsilon)]E_Q(\epsilon)}. \tag{12}$$

Proof is omitted here.

4.2   Influence Function

Another measure of robustness of an estimator is influence function, which reflects the limiting influence of adding one more observation to a very large sample. The influence function is defined as

$$IF(x_0; T, G) = \lim_{\epsilon \to 0} \frac{T((1 - \epsilon)G + \epsilon \delta_{x_0}) - T(G)}{\epsilon}$$

$$= \frac{\partial}{\partial \epsilon} T((1 - \epsilon)G + \epsilon \delta_{x_0})|_{\epsilon \downarrow 0}, \tag{13}$$

where δ_{x_0} is the point-mass at x_0 and $\downarrow$ denotes "limit from the right". Note that T is a functional that maps every distribution into a real number. For example, the sample mean $T(f)$ may be expressed by

$$T(f) = E(x), \tag{14}$$

where $E(\cdot)$ depends on the function f. In general, the standardized sensitivity curve (SC) of samples $\{x_1, x_2, \cdots, x_N\}$ is defined as

$$SC(x_1, x_2, \cdots, x_N, x_0) = \frac{T|(x_1, x_2, \cdots, x_N, x_0) - T|(x_1, x_2, \cdots, x_N)}{1/(N + 1)}, \tag{15}$$

where $T|(\cdot)$ denotes the functional T of limited samples. $SC(x_1, x_2, \cdots, x_N, x_0)$ is expected to converge to $IF(x_0; T, G)$ with probability 1 for large samples.

Theorem 2. The SCs of $\hat{F}_Q(\theta)$ and $\hat{F}_T(\theta)$ are given by

$$SC_Q(x_1, x_2, \cdots, x_N, x_0)|_{N\downarrow+\infty} = \begin{cases} 1 - p_r - E_Q(0), & x_0 \geq \tau, \\ p_r - E_Q(0), & \text{otherwise,} \end{cases} \tag{16}$$

and

$$SC_T(x_1, x_2, \cdots, x_N, x_0)|_{N\downarrow+\infty} = \begin{cases} p_r - E_T(0), & x_0 \in [x_a, \tau), \\ 1 - p_r - E_T(0), & x_0 \in [\tau, x_{1-a}], \\ 0, & \text{otherwise,} \end{cases} \tag{17}$$

respectively.

Proof is omitted here.

5 Numerical Results

The parameters are set as $\theta = 0.96$, $\tau = 1$, $G = N(0,1)$, and $H = \frac{1}{10}e^{-\frac{1}{10}x}$ for $x > 0$. H is an exponential distribution with mean 10 and variance 100. Performance of the proposed estimators are evaluated by estimation variances, which are all averaged over 10000 independent simulation runs.

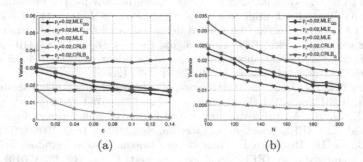

(a)   (b)

Fig. 1. Performances versus the contamination fraction ε and the number of sensors N. MLE$_{QG}$ and MLE$_{TG}$ denote performances of the proposed QME and TME, respectively. CRLB$_G$ means the CRLB by assuming the Gaussian distribution and CRLB means the CRLB by assuming the complete knowledge of the observation noise distribution. (a) Variance versus contamination fraction ε under BSC, $a = 0.02$, $p_r = 0.02$, and $\varepsilon = 0.04$; (b) Variance versus number of sensors N under BSC, $a = 0.02$, $p_r = 0.02$, and $\varepsilon = 0.04$.

Fig. 1 shows the variances of the proposed estimators as functions of the contamination fraction ε and the number of sensors N, respectively. The performances are evaluated under BSC. It is shown that performance of the QME is better than that of the TME and the MLE with known noise variance [13]. Actually, ε is unknown a prior and the CRLB by assuming the complete knowledge of the observation noise distribution is regarded as the benchmark of estimation performance. Note that the TME may trim some useful information by the thresholds ($x_{0.02}$ and $x_{0.98}$) and its performance is actually a little worse than that of the QME and the MLE [13]. The QME and the TME asymptotically achieve the CRLB with the increase of the number of sensors.

6 Conclusion

Two distributed estimators have been proposed for wireless sensor networks that are robust to uncertain observation noise distributions and outperform the classical maximum likelihood estimator. The robustness measures of the proposed estimators are derived. Performance is illustrated by numerical simulation examples, which show the effectiveness of the proposed estimators.

References

1. Ribeiro, A., Giannakis, G.B.: Bandwidth-constrained distributed estimation for wireless sensor networks—Part I: Gaussian case. IEEE Trans. Signal Process 54(3), 1131–1143 (2006)
2. Ribeiro, A., Giannakis, G.B.: Bandwidth-constrained distributed estimation for wireless sensor networks—Part II: Unknown probability density function. IEEE Trans. Signal Process 54(7), 2784–2798 (2006)
3. Xiao, J., Luo, Z., Giannakis, G.B.: Performance bounds for the rate-constrained universal decentralized estimators. IEEE Signal Process. Lett. 14(1), 47–50 (2007)
4. Aysal, T.C., Barner, K.E.: Constrained decentralized estimation over noisy channels for sensor networks. IEEE Trans. Signal Process. 56(4), 1398–1410 (2008)
5. Xiao, J., Luo, Z.: Decentralized estimation in an inhomogeneous sensing environment. IEEE Trans. Inf. Theory 51(10), 3564–3575 (2005)
6. Wu, T., Cheng, Q.: Distributed estimation over fading channels using one-bit quantization. IEEE Trans. Wireless Commun. 8(12), 5779–5784 (2009)
7. Fang, J., Li, H.: Adaptive distributed estimation of signal power from one-bit quantized data. IEEE Trans. Aero. Electron. Syst. 46(4), 1893–1905 (2010)
8. Fang, J., Li, H.: Distributed estimation of Gaussian-Markov random fields with one-bit quantized data. IEEE Signal Process. Lett. 17(5), 449–452 (2010)
9. Shen, X., Zhu, Y., You, Z.: An efficient sensor quantization algorithm for decentralized estimation fusion. Automatica 47(5), 1053–1059 (2011)
10. Chen, H., Varshney, P.K.: Nonparametric one-bit quantizers for distributed estimation. IEEE Trans. Signal Process. 58(7), 3777–3787 (2010)
11. Zherlitsyn, G., Matveev, A.S.: Min-max optimal data encoding and fusion in sensor networks. Automatica 46(9), 1546–1552 (2010)
12. Liu, G., Xu, B., Chen, H.: Decentralized estimation over noisy channels in cluster-based wireless sensor networks. Int. J. Commun. Syst. (published online, 2012)
13. Liu, G., Xu, B., Zeng, M., Chen, H.: Distributed estimation over binary symmetric channels for wireless sensor networks. IET Wireless Sensor Syst. 1(2), 105–109 (2011)
14. Huber, P.J.: Robust Statistics. Wiley, New York (1981)

Robust Energy-Efficient Power Loading for MIMO System under Imperfect CSI

Yun Rui[1], Lei Deng[2], Mingqi Li[1], Jing Li[3], and Xiangbin Yu[4]

[1] Shanghai Advanced Research Institute, Chinese Academic of Science, China
{ruiy,limq}@sari.ac.cn
[2] Department of Electronic Engineering, Shanghai Jiao Tong University, China
dl0729@sjtu.edu.cn
[3] State Key Lab. of Integrated Service Networks, Xidian University, China
jli@xidian.edu.cn
[4] Department of Electronic Engineering,
Nanjing University of Aeronautics and Astronautics, China
yxbxwy@nuaa.edu.cn

Abstract. In this paper, we will analyze the energy efficient power loading in MIMO-SVD architecture. Existing power loading schemes are developed on assumption that a scheduler possesses perfect channel state information (CSI). But we take into account the effects of channel estimation error (CEE) and propose a robust energy-efficient power loading for MIMO system under imperfect CSI. We propose two algorithms to solve the optimization problem. The simulation results show the effectiveness of our proposed power loading scheme.

1 Introduction

Multiple-input multiple-output (MIMO) technology has attracted a great attention due to its high spectral efficiency [1]. However, the application of multiple radio chains incurs a higher circuit power consumption. On the other hand, with the transmit channel side information(CSIT), singular value decomposition(SVD) can be utilized for MIMO channel to effectively create parallel independent channels, which possess different signal-to-noise ratio(SNR). Thus, by carefully performing power allocation to each subchannel, the system performance can be optimized to choose a few of the best quality channels or to use all channels to achieve the high rate [2]. Recently, due to the higher circuit power consumption, considerable research effort has been made to focus on optimizing the energy efficiency of MIMO systems, mostly considering power loading under the assumption of perfect channel state information (CSI) at the transmitter [3]. However, it is not realistic to assume transmitter always with perfect CSI in a MIMO cellular system. This paper will study the power loading under channel estimation error (CEE) for MIMO systems, which focuses on energy efficiency of the wireless link. To the best of our knowledge, there have been no studies about the impact of CEE on energy efficiency for the MIMO systems.

X. Wang et al. (Eds.): WASA 2012, LNCS 7405, pp. 315–323, 2012.

In this paper, we also consider MIMO-SVD architecture for the transceiver. By modeling CEE as an independent complex Gaussian random variable [5], we derive the effective signal-to-interference-plus-noise (SINR) at the receiver under CEE, given the availability of an estimated channel. Based on that, we can get the energy efficiency model, which is achievable rates to power consumption ratio. Different from the result in [4], the objective function after the transformation is still non-convex. Then, we further propose two method to solve this problem. One is transforming to canonical D.C.(difference of convex) programming [9], which is proved to have the only global solution. Considering the complexity, the other approximate method is proposed to relax the objective function to convex problem, which leads to the closed-form optimization solution. Simulation results show the effectiveness of the proposed two algorithms, which are fairly robust against CEE.

The rest of the paper is outlined as follows. The system model is described in Section 2. We propose two algorithms to solve the power loading problem in Section 3. Simulation results are provided in Section 4, followed by the conclusions drawn in Section 5.

2   System Model

We consider an uncorrelated flat fading MIMO system with N_t transmit and N_r receive antennas. The output signals can be modeled as

$$\mathbf{r} = \mathbf{Hs} + \mathbf{n}, \tag{1}$$

where $\mathbf{s} \in \mathbb{C}^{N_t \times 1}$ denotes transmitted signals, $\mathbf{H} \in \mathbb{C}^{N_r \times N_t}$ denotes the channel matrix, and $\mathbf{n} \in \mathbb{C}^{N_r \times 1}$ is modeled as zero-mean additive white Gaussian noise (AWGN) with variance σ_n^2. When channel estimation error occurs, we assume that the MIMO transceiver can only obtain the imperfect CSI, which is modeled as [5,6]

$$\mathbf{H} = \hat{\mathbf{H}} + \mathbf{E}, \tag{2}$$

where $\mathbf{E}$ is the estimation error matrix, and the element is with zero mean and variance σ_e^2. Then, by SVD decomposition of $\hat{\mathbf{H}}$, we can obtain

$$\hat{\mathbf{H}} = \hat{\mathbf{U}} \cdot \hat{\mathbf{D}} \cdot \hat{\mathbf{V}}^H = \hat{\mathbf{U}} \cdot diag(\sqrt{\hat{\lambda}_1}, \cdots, \sqrt{\hat{\lambda}_{N_{ss}}})\hat{\mathbf{V}}^H, \tag{3}$$

where $N_{ss} = \min\{N_t, N_r\}$ is the rank of $\hat{\mathbf{H}}$ and $\{\hat{\lambda}_i\}_{i=1}^{N_{ss}}$ is the eigenvalue of matrix $\hat{\mathbf{H}}\hat{\mathbf{H}}^H$.

Moreover, the signals sent over transmit antennas $\mathbf{s}$ are obtained by performing a transformation $\mathbf{s} = \hat{\mathbf{V}}\mathbf{Px}$, and $\mathbf{P}$ is power allocation diagonal matrix, $\mathbf{x}$ is the information symbol vector from unit-energy constellation set. Thus, the output signals can be rewritten as

$$\mathbf{r} = (\hat{\mathbf{U}} \cdot \hat{\mathbf{D}} \cdot \hat{\mathbf{V}}^H + \mathbf{E})\mathbf{s} + \mathbf{n} = \hat{\mathbf{U}}\hat{\mathbf{D}}\hat{\mathbf{V}}^H\hat{\mathbf{V}}\mathbf{Px} + \mathbf{E}\hat{\mathbf{V}}\mathbf{Px} + \mathbf{n}$$
$$= \hat{\mathbf{U}}\hat{\mathbf{D}}\mathbf{Px} + \mathbf{E}\hat{\mathbf{V}}\mathbf{Px} + \mathbf{n}. \tag{4}$$

Then, at the receiver, after the linearly processed, yield

$$\begin{aligned}
\mathbf{y} &= \hat{\mathbf{U}}^H \mathbf{r} = \hat{\mathbf{U}}^H \hat{\mathbf{U}} \hat{\mathbf{D}} \mathbf{Px} + \hat{\mathbf{U}}^H \mathbf{E} \hat{\mathbf{V}} \mathbf{Px} + \hat{\mathbf{U}}^H \mathbf{n} \\
&= \hat{\mathbf{D}} \mathbf{Px} + \hat{\mathbf{U}}^H \mathbf{E} \hat{\mathbf{V}} \mathbf{Px} + \hat{\mathbf{U}}^H \mathbf{n} \\
&= \hat{\mathbf{D}} \mathbf{Px} + \hat{\mathbf{E}} \mathbf{Px} + \hat{\mathbf{U}}^H \mathbf{n},
\end{aligned} \tag{5}$$

and the received signal on the i-th sub-channel can be expressed as

$$\begin{aligned}
y_i &= [\hat{\mathbf{D}} \mathbf{Px} + \hat{\mathbf{E}} \mathbf{Px} + \hat{\mathbf{U}}^H \mathbf{n}]_i \\
&= (\sqrt{\hat{\lambda}_i} + \hat{e}_{ii}) P_i x_i + \sum_{j=1, j \neq i}^{N_{ss}} \hat{e}_{ij} P_j x_j + \hat{n}_i \\
&= \sqrt{\hat{\lambda}_i} P_i x_i + \sum_{j=1}^{N_{ss}} \hat{e}_{ij} P_j x_j + \hat{n}_i.
\end{aligned} \tag{6}$$

Then, the SNR on the i-th subchannel can be approximated as [7]

$$SNR_i = \frac{\hat{\lambda}_i P_i}{\sigma_e^2 \sum_{j=1}^{N_{ss}} P_j + \sigma_n^2}, \tag{7}$$

where $i = 1, 2, \cdots, N_{ss}$, $N_{ss} = \min(N_r, N_t)$.

Since energy efficiency is defined as the ratio of the transmitted bit to the total energy consumptions, we can obtain the energy efficiency under imperfect CSI as

$$\max EE(\mathbf{P})\{ = \frac{\sum_{i=1}^{N_{ss}} \log(1 + SNR_i)}{\sum_{i=1}^{N_{ss}} GP_i + N_{ss} P_c} \overset{(a)}{=} \frac{\sum_{i=1}^{N_{ss}} \log(1 + SNR_i)}{\sum_{i=1}^{N_{ss}} P_i + P_c'} \} \tag{8}$$

$$s.t. \quad \sum_{i=1}^{N_{ss}} P_i \leq P_T \tag{9}$$

$$0 \leq P_i \leq P_{\max} \tag{10}$$

$$\sum_{i=1}^{N_{ss}} \log(1 + SNR_i) \geq R_{\min} \tag{11}$$

where $P_c' = \frac{N_{ss} P_c}{G}$, P_c is the average circuit power consumption in a single transmit or receiver chain, and G is defined as constant transmit power that is needed to overcome the path loss. Since it is positive constant, we can scale the objective by G, as shown in (a).

3   Proposed Algorithms

Since the optimization problem in (8) is fractional programming and the objective function, i.e., $EE(\mathbf{P})$, is non-convex and non-concave, we cannot apply convex optimization methods to solve this problem. However, according to [7], we can transform such fractional programming problem into a two-layer optimization problem. The following is the transformation process. First, we let

$$g(\mathbf{P}, q) = \sum_{i=1}^{N_{ss}} \log(1 + SNR_i) - q(\sum_{i=1}^{N_{ss}} P_i + P_c'), \tag{12}$$

$$f(q) = \{\max_{\mathbf{P} \in \mathbb{D}} g(\mathbf{P}, q)\}, \tag{13}$$

where $\mathbb{D}$ is the power constraint region consisting of (9)-(11), which is a convex set. Then from [7], we can obtain the optimal energy efficiency $EE^*(\mathbf{P}) = q^*$ when $f(q^*) = 0$. Therefore, the fraction programming problem in (8) can be solved by a two-layer algorithm as,

- *Inner Layer*: For a given q, find the maximum g^* which is also $f(q)$, i.e., $f(q) = g^* = \{\max_{\mathbf{P} \in \mathbb{D}} g(\mathbf{P}, q)\}$;
- *Outer Layer*: Find the zero point of $f(q)$, i.e., $q^* = \{q|f(q) = 0\}$.

Since the outer layer can be easily solved by bisection search algorithm [8], we focus on inner layer. Note that $g(\mathbf{P}, q)$ is still non-convex in (12), we cannot apply convex optimization solutions directly. Here we will adopt two methods to solve optimization problem in inner layer. The first is a global method using D.C. programming, and the second is a suboptimal method which can reduce the complexity.

3.1 Global Method

In this subsection, we will transform the inner layer optimization problem into a canonical D.C. programming problem. First, we rewrite (12) as

$$
\begin{aligned}
g(\mathbf{P}, q) &= \sum_{i=1}^{N_{ss}} \log(1 + SNR_i) - q(\sum_{i=1}^{N_{ss}} P_i + P_c') \\
&= \sum_{i=1}^{N_{ss}} \log(1 + \frac{\hat{\lambda}_i P_i}{\sigma_e^2 \sum_{j=1}^{N_{ss}} P_j + \sigma_n^2}) - q(\sum_{i=1}^{N_{ss}} P_i + P_c') \\
&= \sum_{i=1}^{N_{ss}} \log(\frac{\hat{\lambda}_i P_i + \sigma_e^2 \sum_{j=1}^{N_{ss}} P_j + \sigma_n^2}{\sigma_e^2 \sum_{j=1}^{N_{ss}} P_j + \sigma_n^2}) - q(\sum_{i=1}^{N_{ss}} P_i + P_c') \\
&= \sum_{i=1}^{N_{ss}} \log(\hat{\lambda}_i P_i + \sigma_e^2 \sum_{j=1}^{N_{ss}} P_j + \sigma_n^2) \\
&\quad - [\sum_{i=1}^{N_{ss}} \log(\sigma_e^2 \sum_{j=1}^{N_{ss}} P_j + \sigma_n^2) + q(\sum_{i=1}^{N_{ss}} P_i + P_c')].
\end{aligned} \tag{14}
$$

Then, we let

$$m(\mathbf{P}) = -\sum_{i=1}^{N_{ss}} \log(\hat{\lambda}_i P_i + \sigma_e^2 \sum_{j=1}^{N_{ss}} P_j + \sigma_n^2), \tag{15}$$

$$n(\mathbf{P}, q) = -[\sum_{i=1}^{N_{ss}} \log(\sigma_e^2 \sum_{j=1}^{N_{ss}} P_j + \sigma_n^2) + q(\sum_{i=1}^{N_{ss}} P_i + P_c')], \tag{16}$$

$$f_0(\mathbf{P}, q) = -g(\mathbf{P}, q) = m(\mathbf{P}) - n(\mathbf{P}, q). \tag{17}$$

Thus, the inner layer optimization problem can be rewritten as

$$f(q) = \{\max_{\mathbf{P} \in \mathbb{D}} g(\mathbf{P}, q)\} = -\{\min_{\mathbf{P} \in \mathbb{D}} f_0(\mathbf{P}, q)\} = -\{\min_{\mathbf{P} \in \mathbb{D}}[m(\mathbf{P}) - n(\mathbf{P}, q)]\}. \tag{18}$$

Then we should solve the optimization problem

$$\{\min_{\mathbf{P} \in \mathbb{D}} f_0(\mathbf{P}, q)\} = \{\min_{\mathbf{P} \in \mathbb{D}}[m(\mathbf{P}) - n(\mathbf{P}, q)]\}. \tag{19}$$

Since $m(\mathbf{P})$ and $n(\mathbf{P}, q)$ are all convex with $\mathbf{P}$, (19) is a D.C. programming problem. Next we show it can be further transformed into a canonical D.C. programming problem, which can be solved by some famous algorithms [9].

We first change the constraint region $\mathbb{D}$ consisting of (9-11) in sequence as

$$f_1(\mathbf{P}) = g_1(\mathbf{P}) - h_1(\mathbf{P}) = \sum_{i=1}^{N_{ss}} P_i - P_T \leq 0, \tag{20}$$

where $g_1(\mathbf{P}) = \sum_{i=1}^{N_{ss}} P_i$ and $h_1(\mathbf{P}) = P_T$ are convex, and $f_1(\mathbf{P})$ is a D.C. function;

$$\mathbb{D}_0 = \{\mathbf{P} \in \mathbb{R}^{N_{ss}} | 0 \leq P_i \leq P_{\max}\}, \tag{21}$$

where $\mathbb{D}_0$ is a N_{ss}-dimensional rectangle in $\mathbb{R}^{N_{ss}}$;

$$f_2(\mathbf{P}) = g_2(\mathbf{P}) - h_2(\mathbf{P}) = R_{\min} - \sum_{i=1}^{N_{ss}} \log(1 + SNR_i)$$

$$= R_{\min} - [\sum_{i=1}^{N_{ss}} \log(\hat{\lambda}_i P_i + \sigma_e^2 \sum_{j=1}^{N_{ss}} P_j + \sigma_n^2) - \sum_{i=1}^{N_{ss}} \log(\sigma_e^2 \sum_{j=1}^{N_{ss}} P_j + \sigma_n^2)]$$

$$= [R_{\min} - \sum_{i=1}^{N_{ss}} \log(\hat{\lambda}_i P_i + \sigma_e^2 \sum_{j=1}^{N_{ss}} P_j + \sigma_n^2)]$$

$$-[-\sum_{i=1}^{N_{ss}} \log(\sigma_e^2 \sum_{j=1}^{N_{ss}} P_j + \sigma_n^2)] \leq 0, \tag{22}$$

where $g_2(\mathbf{P}) = R_{\min} - \sum_{i=1}^{N_{ss}} \log(\hat{\lambda}_i P_i + \sigma_e^2 \sum_{j=1}^{N_{ss}} P_j + \sigma_n^2)$ and $h_2(\mathbf{P}) = -\sum_{i=1}^{N_{ss}} \log(\sigma_e^2 \sum_{j=1}^{N_{ss}} P_j + \sigma_n^2)$ are convex, and $f_2(\mathbf{P})$ is a D.C. function.

Therefore, the optimization problem (19) can be transformed to:

$$\{\min f_0(\mathbf{P}, q) | \mathbf{P} \in \mathbb{D}_0, f_1(\mathbf{P}) \leq 0, f_2(\mathbf{P}) \leq 0\}. \tag{23}$$

Since $f_0(\mathbf{P}, q)$, $f_1(\mathbf{P})$, $f_2(\mathbf{P})$ are D.C. functions and $\mathbb{D}_0$ is a N_{ss}-dimensional rectangle in $\mathbb{R}^{N_{ss}}$, we can transform (23) to into a canonical D.C. programming problem [9] and solve it with two types of algorithms, branch-and-bound type and outer-approximation type [9]. Therefore, we can get the global solution to optimization problem in (8).

3.2 Suboptimal Method

In this subsection, we will propose a suboptimal method to solve the inner layer optimization problem, which can reduce complexity compared to the global method in Section 3.1.

First, the following lower bound is used [10],

$$\alpha \log z + \beta \le \log(1 + z) \begin{cases} \alpha = \frac{z_0}{1+z_0} \\ \beta = \log(1 + z_0) - \frac{z_0}{1+z_0} \log(z_0) \end{cases} \tag{24}$$

That is tight with equality at a chosen value z_0 when the constants are chosen as specified above. As a result, the inner layer optimization problem can be relaxed as

$$\max g(\mathbf{P}, q) = \sum_{i=1}^{N_{ss}} [\alpha_i \log(SNR_i) + \beta_i] - q(\sum_{i=1}^{N_{ss}} P_i + P_c'). \tag{25}$$

We do the following transformation, $\tilde{P}_i = \log(P_i)$ and $P_i = e^{\tilde{P}_i}$, then we have

$$
\begin{aligned}
g(\tilde{\mathbf{P}}, q) &= \sum_{i=1}^{N_{ss}} [\alpha_i \log(SNR_i) + \beta_i] - q(\sum_{i=1}^{N_{ss}} P_i + P_c') \\
&= \sum_{i=1}^{N_{ss}} [\alpha_i \log(\frac{\lambda_i e^{\tilde{P}_i}}{\sigma_e^2 \sum_{j=1}^{N_{ss}} e^{\tilde{P}_j} + \sigma_n^2}) + \beta_i] - q(\sum_{i=1}^{N_{ss}} e^{\tilde{P}_i} + P_c') \\
&= \sum_{i=1}^{N_{ss}} [\alpha_i \log(\hat{\lambda}_i) + \alpha_i \tilde{P}_i - \alpha_i \log(\sigma_e^2 \sum_{j=1}^{N_{ss}} e^{\tilde{P}_j} + \sigma_n^2) + \beta_i] - q \sum_{i=1}^{N_{ss}} e^{\tilde{P}_i} - q P_c' \\
&= \sum_{i=1}^{N_{ss}} [\alpha_i \log(\hat{\lambda}_i) + \alpha_i \tilde{P}_i + \beta_i] - \sum_{i=1}^{N_{ss}} [\alpha_i \log(\sigma_e^2 \sum_{j=1}^{N_{ss}} e^{\tilde{P}_j} + \sigma_n^2) + q e^{\tilde{P}_i}] - q P_c' \\
&= \sum_{i=1}^{N_{ss}} [\alpha_i \log(\hat{\lambda}_i) + \alpha_i \tilde{P}_i + \beta_i] - \underbrace{[(\sum_{i=1}^{N_{ss}} \alpha_i) \log(\sigma_e^2 \sum_{j=1}^{N_{ss}} e^{\tilde{P}_j} + \sigma_n^2)}_{Convex} + \underbrace{\sum_{i=1}^{N_{ss}} q e^{\tilde{P}_i}}_{Convex}] - q P_c'
\end{aligned}
$$

$$\tag{26}$$

Since the second item is the sum of convex function, the objective is concave. Also, the constraint region is convex. Therefore, we can use Karush-Kuhn-Tucker(KKT) conditions to solve the optimization problem. Due to space limitation, we only give the final closed-form optimization solution, i.e.,

$$P_i^* = \left[\frac{\alpha_i(v^* - 1)(\sqrt{\frac{\bar{\alpha}\theta(v^*-1)}{(\lambda^*-q)} + \frac{\theta^2}{4}} + \frac{\theta}{2})}{(\lambda^* - q)(\sqrt{\frac{\bar{\alpha}\theta(v^*-1)}{(\lambda^*-q)} + \frac{\theta^2}{4}} + \frac{\theta}{2}) + \bar{\alpha}(v^* - 1)} \right]_0^{P_{\max}}, \tag{27}$$

where λ^*, v^* are KKT multipliers, $\bar{\alpha} = \sum_{i=1}^{N_{ss}} \alpha_i$, and $\theta = \frac{\sigma_n^2}{\sigma_e^2}$.

Therefore, we propose the suboptimal method as shown in Algorithm A.

A. Suboptimal Method

1: **Initialize:**
2: iteration counter $t = 0$.
3: $\alpha_i = 1$, $\beta_i = 0$, for $1 \le i \le N_{ss}$, (high SNR approximate).
4: **Repeat:**
5:    maximize: solve (25) to give solution $\mathbf{P}$.
6:    set: $\mathbf{P}^* = \mathbf{P}$.
7:    tighten: update $\alpha_i = \frac{z_i}{1+z_i}$, $\beta_i = \log(1 + z_i) - \frac{z_i}{1+z_i}\log(z_i)$, with $z_i = SNR_i(\mathbf{P})$.
8:    increment t.
9: **Until** convergence

---

4 Simulation Results

In this section, Monte Carlo simulations are used to illustrate proposed power loading algorithms to optimize EE in MIMO systems under imperfect CSI. The detailed simulation parameters are listed in Table 1. At the receiver, the ZF structure is adopted, where perfect synchronization is assumed.

Table 1. Simulation Parameters

Frame duration	0.5 ms
N_t (# of Tx antenna at user)	2
N_r (# of Rx antenna at Node-B)	2
Carrier frequency	2 GHz
Sampling frequency	7.68 MHz
Receiver	Zero forcing
Traffic model	Full buffer
σ_n^2 (Noise variance)	1
# of frames	5000

Fig. 1 shows that the energy efficiency varies on estimation error variance with both global method and suboptimal method. From this figure, we can see as the estimation error variance, i.e., σ_e^2, increases, the EE performance declines. In addition, we can compare the global method and suboptimal method in this figure. The global methods can always achieve better EE performance than suboptimal method, but the gap is very little. This substantiates the effectiveness of our proposed suboptimal method.

Fig. 2 substantiates the robustness of our proposed power loading scheme. In this figure, we use the global method to obtain the global maximal EE. We can find that when the estimation error variance $\sigma_e^2 < 10^{-2}$, the EE performance is almost flat with σ_e^2. So our proposed energy efficient power loading scheme is robust against CEE.

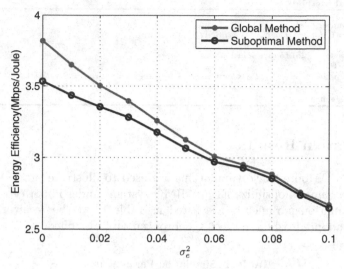

Fig. 1. EE v.s. σ_e^2

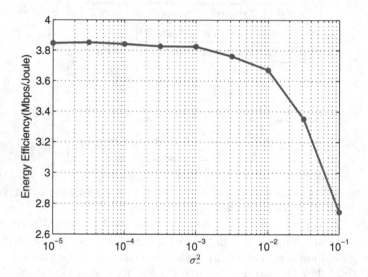

Fig. 2. EE v.s. σ_e^2

5 Conclusion

In this paper, we proposed an energy efficient power loading scheme in MIMO-SVD architecture under imperfect CSI. We first derive the close-form expression of EE in MIMO-SVD system taking into consideration of the effects of channel esti- mation error (CEE). Then we propose two algorithms to solve the optimization problem, one global method and one low-complexity suboptimal method.

The simulation results substantiate the effectiveness of our proposed EE power loading scheme. In our future work, we will try to apply our energy efficient power loading scheme to the large scale networks [11] [12].

Acknowledgement. This work was supported by National High Technology Research and Development Program (863 Program) of China under Grant No.2011AA01A105, Shanghai Committee of Science and Technology (10DZ1500700 and 11DZ1500500), Project 2011-28 from State Administration of Television, National Key Project of China (2009ZX03003-006-03), and National Science Foundation of China (61101144).

References

1. Telatar, E.: Capacity of Multi-antenna Gaussian Channels. Eur. Trans. Telecommun. 10, 585–595 (1999)
2. Dighe, P.A., Mallik, R.K., Jamuar, S.S.: Analysis of Transmit-receive Diversity in Rayleigh Fading. IEEE Trans. Commun. 51, 694–703 (2003)
3. Prabhu, R.S., Daneshrad, B.: An Energy-efficient Water-filling Algorithm for OFDM Systems. In: 2010 IEEE International Conference on Communications (2010)
4. Hassibi, B., Hochwald, B.M.: How Much Training Is Needed In Multiple-antenna Wireless Links? IEEE Trans. Inform. Theory 49, 951–963 (2003)
5. Wang, Z.Y., He, C., He, A.: Robust AM-MIMO Based on Minimized Transmission Power. IEEE Commun. Lett. 10, 432–434 (2006)
6. Song, S.H., Zhang, Q.T.: Mutual Information of Multipath Channels with Imperfect Channel Information. IEEE Trans. Commun. 57, 1523–1531 (2009)
7. Schaible, S.: Fractional Programming, II: on Dinkelbach's Algorithm. J. Manage. Sci. 22, 868–873 (1976)
8. Burden, R.L., Faires, J.D.: Numerical Analysis, 7th edn. Brooks/Core, Pacific Grove (2000)
9. Horst, R., Thoai, N.V.: DC Programming: Overview. J. Optim. Theory Appl. 103, 1–43 (1999)
10. Papandriopoulos, J., Evans, J.S.: Low-Complexity Distributed Algorithms for Spectrum Balancing in Multi-User DSL Networks. In: 2006 IEEE International Conference on Communications (2006)
11. Wang, X.B., Fu, L., Tian, X., Bei, Y., Peng, Q., Gan, X., Yu, H., Liu, J.: Converge-Cast: On the Capacity and Delay Tradeoffs. IEEE Trans. Mobile. Computing 11, 970–982 (2011)
12. Wang, X.B., Huang, W., Wang, S., Zhang, J., Hu, C.: Delay and Capacity Tradeoff Analysis for MotionCast. IEEE/ACM Trans. Networking 19, 1354–1367 (2011)

Opportunistic Channel-Hopping Based Effective Rendezvous Establishment in Cognitive Radio Networks

Yueming Duan, Guoliang Liu, and Zhipeng Cai

Department of Computer Science,
Georgia State University, Atlanta GA, USA
{yduan1,gliu6,zcai}@cs.gsu.edu

Abstract. In cognitive radio networks (CRNs), second users (SUs) exploit spectrum holes by accessing multiple channels opportunistically. In such a dynamic-spectrum-access network, the SUs equipped with cognitive radios have to establish rendezvous on a common channel before they are able to communicate with each other. Due to the intermittent appearance of primary users' signals, SUs have to access the channels opportunistically, which makes the rendezvous problem challenging. This paper focuses on blind rendezvous where neither any central controller nor common control channel is available. Under an opportunistic framework, we propose the concept of channel availability to measure the dynamic feature of channels, and we study the pairwise effective rendezvous problem systematically, for which a simple yet efficient and flexible opportunistic method is proposed. We further extend our method to the many-to-one rendezvous problem for fairness consideration. The performances of our solutions are evaluated via both theoretical analysis and extensive simulations.

1 Introduction

Spectrum is one of the most precious resources in wireless communication. Recently, numerous experimental studies [1] show that spectrum is not efficiently used in either space or time, resulting in spectrum holes. To solve the inefficient spectrum utilization problem, the research community proposed the idea of dynamic spectrum access for cognitive radio networks (CRNs), which has been proved to be a promising paradigm to take advantage of the spectrum holes [1].

In CRNs, second users (SUs) opportunistically access the spectrum (*i.e.*, channel or frequency) licensed to primary users (PUs) with the help of channel sensing technology ([2]). A SU with cognitive radio (CR) can dynamically access multiple channels provided that these channels are available to it, *i.e.*, the SU transmits data on these channels will not affect the communications of the PUs, and the SU receives data on any of these channels will not be interfered by the PUs. Due to hardware limitations of CRs, the SUs usually only transmit or receive information on one channel at a time, which results in challenges for the protocol design of CRNs. One of the most significant challenges is rendezvous

X. Wang et al. (Eds.): WASA 2012, LNCS 7405, pp. 324–336, 2012.

establishment in multi-channel communication networks. Any pair of SUs have to establish a rendezvous before they are able to communicate with each other, thus rendezvous establishment becomes a fundamental and essential operation in CRNs. Unfortunately, rendezvous establishment is nontrivial due to the fact that the available channels for each SU are usually different and dynamic. The intermittent appearance of PUs' signals prevent us using existing multi-channel communication protocols for rendezvous establishment.

In [9], some special signals are employed to facilitate the rendezvous of users. After that, the common control channel (CCC) approach ([3], [4]) is proposed to facilitate the rendezvous, in which a dedicated channel is designated as the control channel for all the SUs. Unfortunately, the CCC approach severely suffers from the problem of congestion on the common channel. Recently, channel hopping (CH) based technology ([5], [6], [7], [8]) has been proposed for rendezvous facilitation. With the CH technology, each SU selects a set of available channels and hops among these channels for a rendezvous with its potential neighbors. However, the available channels for each SU are dynamically changing, yet the existing CH based rendezvous establishments either do not consider the dynamic feature of channel availability or implicitly assume that the available channel set is stable in a long period. The work in [5] focuses on designing CH algorithm for guaranteed rendezvous of two or multiple users in time-slotted CRNs. It implicitly assumes that the available channels for each SU are stable or never change. The authors in [7] propose an optimal asynchronous channel hopping (ACH) design that maximizes the rendezvous probability between any pair of nodes, however, the imbalance traffic on different channels have not been sufficiently considered in ACH. To develop CH sequences such that any two CH sequences are able to rendezvous periodically, ETCH [6] and quorum-based channel hopping (QCH) [8] are proposed based on the overlap property of quorums in the quorum system. Since the CH sequences of the SUs are pre-determined in the design of QCH and ETCH, they still cannot adapt well enough to the dynamic spectrum environment in CRNs.

In this paper, we investigate the rendezvous problem in CRNs and aim to design flexible and effective rendezvous establishment protocols adaptive to the dynamic of spectrum resources. Opportunistic CH strategies are proposed for the SUs in the idle state, where the CH strategy is designed based on the statistic information of channel availability [10] for each SU. We also introduce the concept of effective rendezvous to distinguish existing designs from ours. By effective rendezvous, both the transmitter and the receiver have to stay on the same channel, and that channel should be available to them at the same time. The expected time-to-effective-rendezvous (TTER) is used to measure how quickly an effective rendezvous can be established. In particular, two problems are studied in this paper. We first study the opportunistic pairwise effective rendezvous problem with a systematic approach. Then, we extend the effective rendezvous into many-to-one scenario and a min-max optimization problem is proposed, for which an approximate solution is provided.

2   System Model and Problems

In this paper, we consider a static CRN with N SUs in an opportunistic spectrum sharing environment. Let $\mathcal{N} = \{s_1, s_2, \ldots, s_N\}$ denote the set of SUs in a CRN.

Channel Model: In the deployment area of a CRN, assume there exists an opportunistic spectrum sharing environment with K orthogonal frequencies (or channels) that are licensed to the PUs, and the set of channels are denoted as $\mathcal{K} = \{1, 2, \ldots, K\}$. Each SU equipped with a CR is able to access any of these K channels on the condition that the channel is available to it. For generality consideration, we assume each s_i is equipped with a single half-duplex transceiver and it can only stay or transmit over one channel at a time.

Since all SUs coexist with PUs, the transmission activities of SUs should not cause any interference to the communications of PUs, which means the SUs should access the channels in $\mathcal{K}$ opportunistically. To model the opportunistic channel accessing pattern, we propose the concept of channel availability. In particular, define μ_i^k as the probability of channel k to be available to s_i during each time slot (a duration of τ), and $0 < \mu_i^k \leq 1$ for any $s_i \in \mathcal{N}$, $k \in \mathcal{K}$. We assume each s_i has an estimation of μ_i^k for any $k \in \mathcal{K}$ based on the channel sensing history. Define $r_i(k)$ as the *rank* of channel k corresponding to node s_i, where $r_i(k)$ is a unique number from $1, 2, \ldots, K$; i.e., for any pair of $s, t \in \mathcal{K}$ that satisfies $\mu_i^s > \mu_i^t$, the inequality $r_i(s) < r_i(t)$ holds, in the case of $\mu_i^s = \mu_i^t$, $r_i(s) < r_i(t)$ if $s < t$. Intuitively, the greater the value of μ_i^k, the higher the probability that channel k is available to s_i during each time slot, and s_i should stay on channel k for more channel access opportunity.

Time-Slotted System: Similar to previous studies ([5], [6], [7], and [8]), we consider a time-slotted wireless communication system, in which the SUs are locally synchronized. A message can be successfully transmitted from s_i to s_j over channel k in time slot t iff both s_i and s_j stay on channel k, and channel k is available to both of them during time slot t. s_i can establish an effective rendezvous with s_j successfully iff during some time slot t, s_j successfully receives a *Beacon* message from s_i and s_i successfully receives an *Ack* message from s_j on some channel k, and channel k is available to both s_i and s_j during time slot t. Here we assume that one time slot is long enough to finish the *Beacon/Ack* messages exchanging process between a pair of SUs.

Channel Sensing: We say channel k is available to s_i during time slot t if the communication of the PUs will not fail due to the transmission of s_i and it can successfully receive the message aims to it. Each s_i is capable of sensing whether channel k is available to it or not. We assume perfect sensing for simplicity and SUs avoid transmitting on any channel where PUs' signals are detected. We further assume that s_i can sense a subset of channels $\mathcal{C}_i \subseteq \mathcal{K}$ at the beginning of each time slot, where the cardinal number of $\mathcal{C}_i$ is dependent on the sensing capability of s_i, the greater the value of $\mathcal{C}_i$, the higher the sensing capability of s_i. Define κ as the uniform sensing capability of SUs in a CRN, where $1 \leq \kappa \leq |\mathcal{K}|$.

A channel sensing (CS) scheme ψ determines the policy with which the SUs sense the channels. Formally, $\psi : \{(i,t) \mid s_i \in \mathcal{N}\} \mapsto \mathcal{P}(\mathcal{K})$, where $\mathcal{P}(\mathcal{K})$ is the power set of $\mathcal{K}$. Hence, $\psi(i,t)$ is the set of channels for which s_i determines to sense at the beginning of time slot t under scheme ψ, and $0 \le |\psi(i,t)| \le \kappa$.

Channel Hopping: At the beginning of each time slot, each s_i is assumed to be capable of hopping between different channels according to some specific channel hopping (CH) strategy. A CH strategy φ determines the policy according to which the SUs visit all available channels. Formally, $\varphi : \{(i,t) \mid s_i \in \mathcal{N}\} \mapsto \mathcal{K}$, where $\varphi(i,t)$ is the channel onto which s_i hops at the beginning of time slot t.

ETTER: Given the channel availabilities of all the nodes in a CRN, we use the *expected-time-to-effective-rendezvous (ETTER)* to measure the performance of our approach under the opportunistic framework. Specifically, $ETTER_{ij}$ is the number of time slots that the transmitter s_i needs to wait on average before it can establish an effective rendezvous with the receiver s_j. Given an effective rendezvous, a *Beacon/Ack* messages exchange can be successfully accomplished between a pair of SUs (s_i and s_j) during some time slot.

Problems: With the objective of minimizing *ETTER*, we investigate two problems in this paper. The first one is the *pairwise effective rendezvous* problem. In particular, given the channel availabilities of two SUs s_i and s_j, and the CH strategy of the receiver s_j, find out the optimal CS scheme ψ^* for the transmitter s_i to minimize $ETTER_{ij}$.

We further consider the *many-to-one effective rendezvous* problem, in which we assume that the forwarding scheme is predefined in a CRN, *i.e.*, the set of SUs $\mathcal{L}$ potentially employs s_j as a forwarder is predefined, where $\mathcal{L} = \{s_1, s_2, \ldots, s_L\}$. Given the channel availabilities of s_j and that of all the SUs in $\mathcal{L}$, find out the optimal CS scheme ψ^* of the transmitters in $\mathcal{L}$ and the optimal CH strategy φ^* for the receiver s_j to minimize the maximum $ETTER_{ij}$ for any $s_i \in \mathcal{L}$.

3   Opportunistic Pairwise Effective Rendezvous

In this section, we discuss the *pairwise effective rendezvous* problem. Suppose a SU s_i wants to establish an effective rendezvous with its neighbor s_j. We name s_i as the transmitter and s_j as the receiver, respectively. To solve the problem, we first provide three opportunistic CH strategies for the receiver, among which the third one is a hybrid of the first two strategies. Based on the hybrid CH strategy, we propose a greedy CS scheme for the transmitter. The performance with respect to the *ETTER* is analyzed in subsection 3.3.

3.1   Channel Hopping Strategies of Receiver

In this subsection, we discuss channel-sojourn probabilities with which the SUs stay on different channels when they are in the idle state. Under a probabilistic framework, the channel-sojourn probabilities define a particular CH scheme.

Opportunistic CH without Sensing: We first consider the opportunistic CH strategy without the help of channel sensing. For the SU s_j in the idle state at each time slot, it has to choose a channel to stay and listen to *Beacon* messages for potential data forwarding task. Intuitively, the best choice for any SU s_j in the idle state is to always stay on the channel f_j^* which has the highest channel availability, *i.e.*, $f_j^* = argmax_{k \in \mathcal{K}} \, \mu_j^k$. There are at least two reasons of not employing this simple greedy approach. Firstly, it is possible that the channel availability of channel f_j^* is extremely low for some other neighbor s_j. Secondly, for the consideration of fair channel utilization, SUs in the idle state should not always stay on the same channel. Based on these observations, we define the *channel-sojourn probabilities* as following:

$$\alpha_j^k = \frac{\mu_j^k}{\sum_{i=1}^K \mu_j^i} \tag{1}$$

In particular, s_j stays on channel k with channel-sojourn probability α_j^k at each time slot. Obviously, α_j^k is a weighted function of channel availabilities of all channels. According to the pre-determined channel-sojourn probability, the receiver s_j blindly hops to channel k with probability α_j^k at the beginning of each time slot t. This defines our first opportunistic CH strategy φ_a, where $Pr\left(\varphi_a\left(j,t\right) = k\right) = \alpha_j^k$ for any $t \geq 0$.

Greedy CH with Sensing: We further discuss CH strategy with the involvement of channel sensing. Assume a SU s_j is in the idle state at time slot t. Before it blindly hops to some channel k, it first senses the channels at the beginning of current time slot to confirm that channel is available. Define $\mathcal{S}_j$ as the set of candidate channels being chosen to be sensed by s_j, where $\mathcal{S}_j \subseteq \mathcal{K}$ and $|\mathcal{S}_j| = \kappa$. Here we employ a greedy strategy. Let s_j sense the channels with higher channel availabilities at the beginning of each time slot, *i.e.*, $\mathcal{S}_j = \{k \mid 1 \leq r_j(k) \leq \kappa\}$. Denote $\mathcal{U}_j(t)$ as the set of channels available to s_j at time slot t, where $\mathcal{U}_j(t) \subseteq \mathcal{S}_j$. Note that $\mathcal{U}_j(t)$ maybe empty.

Based on the above sensing policy, we use a greedy channel hopping strategy. If $\mathcal{U}_j(t)$ is not empty, s_j hops to channel $k_j^*(t)$, where $k_j^*(t) = argmax_{k \in \mathcal{U}_j(t)} \, \mu_j^k$; otherwise, s_j hops to the channel $\overline{k_j^*(t)}$, which is the channel belonging to $\mathcal{K}$ but not $\mathcal{S}_j$ with the highest channel availability, *i.e.*, $\overline{k_j^*(t)} = argmax_{k \in \mathcal{K} \setminus \mathcal{S}_j} \, \mu_j^k$. According to the above CH strategy with the help of channel sensing, the channel-sojourn probability is denoted as β_j^k, then

$$\beta_j^k = \begin{cases} \mu_j^k \prod_{1 \leq r_j(i) < r_j(k)} (1 - \mu_j^i) & : \quad 1 \leq r_j(k) < \kappa + 1 \\ \prod_{1 \leq r_j(i) \leq \kappa} (1 - \mu_j^i) & : \quad r_j(k) = \kappa + 1 \\ 0 & : \quad \kappa + 1 < r_j(k) \leq K \end{cases} \tag{2}$$

Similar to the CH strategy φ_1, the receiver s_j hops to channel k with probability β_j^k at the beginning of each time slot t, which defines the greedy CH strategy φ_b, where $Pr(\varphi_b(j,t) = k) = \beta_j^k$ for any $t \geq 0$.

Hybrid CH with Periodic Channel Sensing: With opportunistic CH strategy φ_a, the channels are fairly employed and it is simple to be implemented, while the disadvantage is that it cannot guarantee the SUs always stay on an idle channel with high probability. This problem can be mitigated with the help of channel sensing, in which each SU s_j senses the channels in $\mathcal{S}_j$ at the beginning of each time slot before it hops to some available channel. However, channel sensing suffers from high energy cost [10].

To find a tradeoff between energy cost and $ETTER$, we provide a hybrid CH strategy with periodic channel sensing. Let the SU s_j in the idle state perform one channel sensing every w time slots, where $1 \leq w < +\infty$. It is obvious that with the increasing of w, s_j saves more energy because of less frequent channel sensing, which in return results in higher $ETTER$ due to less channel status information. With periodic channel sensing, any s_j in the idle state randomly selects a number t_j from $0, 2, \ldots, w - 1$. At the beginning of time slots $t_j, t_j + w, \ldots, t_j + kw$, s_j employs CH strategy φ_b, where $1 \leq k < +\infty$; during other time slots, s_j employs CH strategy φ_a and hops opportunistically without channel sensing. Essentially, the hybrid CH is equivalent to opportunistic CH without sensing (φ_a) or greedy CH with sensing (φ_b), when $w = +\infty$ or 1, respectively. Denote the mixed *channel-sojourn* probability as γ_j^k, then according to Eq.1 and Eq.2,

$$
\gamma_j^k = \begin{cases}
\frac{1}{w}\mu_j^k \prod_{1 \leq r_j(i) < r_j(k)}(1 - \mu_j^i) + \frac{w-1}{w}\frac{\mu_j^k}{\sum_{i=1}^{K}\mu_j^i} & : \quad 1 \leq r_j(k) < \kappa + 1 \\[2mm]
\frac{1}{w}\prod_{1 \leq r_j(i) \leq \kappa}(1 - \mu_j^i) + \frac{w-1}{w}\frac{\mu_j^k}{\sum_{i=1}^{K}\mu_j^i} & : \quad r_j(k) = \kappa + 1 \\[2mm]
\frac{w-1}{w}\frac{\mu_j^k}{\sum_{i=1}^{K}\mu_j^i} & : \quad \kappa + 1 < r_j(k) \leq K
\end{cases}
\tag{3}
$$

Similarly, the receiver s_j hops to channel k with probability γ_j^k at any time slot t, which defines the hybrid CH strategy φ_w, where $Pr(\varphi_w(j,t) = k) = \gamma_j^k$ for any $t \geq 0$, and $1 \leq w < +\infty$.

3.2 Greedy Channel Sensing Scheme of Transmitters

In this subsection, we give a heuristic CS scheme for the transmitter given that the receiver in the idle state employs hybrid CH strategy φ_w. For simplicity, define π_j^k as the probability that s_j stays on channel k and channel k is available to s_j at time slot t, then according to Eq. 1, 2 and 3,

$$
\pi_j^k = \begin{cases}
\frac{1}{w}\mu_j^k \prod_{1 \leq r_j(i) < r_j(k)}(1 - \mu_j^i) + \frac{w-1}{w}\frac{(\mu_j^k)^2}{\sum_{i=1}^{K}\mu_j^i} & : \quad 1 \leq r_j(k) \leq \kappa + 1 \\[2mm]
\frac{w-1}{w}\frac{(\mu_j^k)^2}{\sum_{i=1}^{K}\mu_j^i} & : \quad \kappa + 1 < r_j(k) \leq K
\end{cases}
\tag{4}
$$

Considering that s_i tries to establish a rendezvous with s_j in the idle state and it employs hybrid CH strategy φ_w, to establish an effective rendezvous successfully, s_i has to hop to the same channel k, on which s_j stays. Moreover, channel k should be available to both s_i and s_j during some time slot. Here we assume s_i possesses the channel availabilities information of all its neighbors, based on which s_i can easily derive the values of γ_j^k and π_j^k for any $k \in \mathcal{K}$.

To guarantee that the *Beacon* message transmissions of s_i do not produce interference to PUs, s_i should sense the channels before each transmission. Due to the limitation of sensing capability of s_i, it is necessary for s_i to choose a subset of $\mathcal{K}$ to sense at the beginning of each time slot. Intuitively, it is better for s_i to sense the channels which make the rendezvous establishment successful with higher probability. Based on this observation, let $\lambda_{ij}^k = \mu_i^k \pi_j^k$, and $\mathcal{T}_i$ is the set of channels with top-κ highest value of λ_{ij}^k, i.e., $\mathcal{T}_i \subseteq \mathcal{K}$, $|\mathcal{T}_i| = \kappa$ and $\lambda_{ij}^x \geq \lambda_{ij}^y$ for any $x \in \mathcal{T}_i$, $y \in \mathcal{K} - \mathcal{T}_i$. Thus, our greedy CS scheme ψ_g is defined as $\psi_g(i,t) = \mathcal{T}_i$. Here λ_{ij}^k is essentially the probability that s_j stays on channel k and channel k is available to both s_i and s_j at each time slot.

Denote $\mathcal{V}_i(t)$ as the set of channels that are available to s_i at time slot t, where $\mathcal{V}_i(t) \subseteq \mathcal{T}_i$. Notice that $\mathcal{V}_i(t)$ may be empty with probability $\prod_{k \in \mathcal{T}_i}(1 - \mu_i^k)$. If $\mathcal{V}_i(t)$ is empty, s_i repeats sensing the channels in $\mathcal{T}_i$ at the beginning of time slot $t + 1$. Otherwise, s_i selects the channel $c_i^*(t)$ with the highest value of λ_{ij}^k to transmit a *Beacon* message to s_j, i.e., $c_i^*(t) = argmax_{k \in \mathcal{V}_i(t)} \lambda_{ij}^k$. Once s_j successfully receives a *Beacon* message from s_i on channel k, it senses the channel and replies with an *Ack* message if channel k is available to it. Otherwise, s_j ignores the *Beacon* message and continues the hybrid CH process. This channel sensing and *Beacon* message transmission process is repeated until s_i successfully receives an *Ack* from s_j.

3.3   Analysis

From the opportunistic perspective, we have the following results. Lemma 1 and 2 show the probability of successfully establishing an effective rendezvous between a pair of SUs. Theorem 1 shows the performance ratio of our method.

Lemma 1. *Denote $Pr(i \cdot k \cdot j)$ as the probability of transmitter s_i establishing an effective rendezvous with receiver s_j on channel k in a time slot. If s_j employs hybrid CH strategy φ_w and s_i employs CS scheme ψ_g, then,*
1. *when $k \notin \mathcal{T}_i$, $Pr(i \cdot k \cdot j) = 0$,*
2. *when $k \in \mathcal{T}_i$, $Pr(i \cdot k \cdot j) = \lambda_{ij}^k \prod_{\lambda_{ij}^l > \lambda_{ij}^k}(1 - \mu_i^l)$, where $k, l \in \mathcal{T}_i$,*

where $\mathcal{T}_i$ is defined in Section 3.2.

Proof. For the first part, since k does not belong to the candidate channel sensing set $\mathcal{T}_i$, s_i will never hop to channel k even if it is available to both s_i and s_j at some time slot, which means it is impossible for s_i to establish an effective rendezvous with s_j on channel k if $k \notin \mathcal{T}_i$.

Now consider the second part. For s_i to establish an effective rendezvous with s_j on channel k at some time slot t, three conditions should be satisfied. First, $k \in \mathcal{V}_i(t)$ (defined in Section 3.2), i.e., channel k is available to s_i at time slot t, the probability of which is μ_i^k. Second, for any $l \in \mathcal{T}_i$, $l \notin \mathcal{V}_i(t)$ if $\lambda_{ij}^l > \lambda_{ij}^k$, the probability of which is $\prod_{\lambda_{ij}^l > \lambda_{ij}^k}(1 - \mu_i^l)$. Third, s_j stays on channel k and it is available to s_j, with probability π_k^j. Thus $Pr(i \cdot k \cdot j) = \mu_i^k \pi_j^k \prod_{\lambda_{ij}^l > \lambda_{ij}^k}(1 - \mu_i^l) = \lambda_{ij}^k \prod_{\lambda_{ij}^l > \lambda_{ij}^k}(1 - \mu_l^i)$, where $k, l \in \mathcal{T}_i$. $\square$

Lemma 2. *Denote* $Pr(i \cdot j)$ *as the probability* s_i *establishing a rendezvous with* s_j *on any channel in a time slot, and* $ETTER_{ij}$ *as the expected number of time slots for an effective rendezvous establishment with the condition that* s_i *employs CS scheme* ψ_g, *then,*

1. $Pr(i \cdot j) = \sum_{k \in T_i} Pr(i \cdot k \cdot j)$.
2. $ETTER_{ij} = \frac{1}{Pr(i \cdot j)}$.

Proof. It simply follows from Lemma 1.   □

Theorem 1. *Denote* $ETTER_{ij}^*$ *as the minimum (optimal) expected number of time slots for an effective rendezvous establishment, then* $ETTER_{ij} \leq \kappa ETTER_{ij}^*$, *where* κ *is the sensing capability of SUs.*

Proof. Assume $c_1, c_2, \ldots, c_K$ is a permutation of $1, 2, \ldots, K$ satisfying $x_1 y_1 > x_2 y_2 > \cdots > x_K y_K$, where $x_k = \mu_i^{c_k}$, $y_k = \pi_j^{c_k}$ for $k \in \mathcal{K}$. For our CS scheme, $C_i = \{c_1, c_1, \ldots, c_\kappa\}$ will be chosen as the sensing set of s_i, thus the successful probability of establishing an effective rendezvous is $Pr(i \cdot j) = \sum_{k=1}^{\kappa} x_k y_k \prod_{j<k} (1 - x_j) \geq x_1 y_1$. Without loss of generality, assume $S_i^* = \{d_1, d_2, \ldots, d_\kappa\} \subseteq \mathcal{K}$ is the optimal sensing set of s_i, and $u_1 v_1 > u_2 v_2 > \cdots > u_\kappa v_\kappa$, where $u_k = \mu_i^{d_k}$, $v_k = \pi_j^{d_k}$ for $d_k \in S_i^*$, then the successful probability of establishing an effective rendezvous with optimal sensing set S_i^* is $Pr^*(i \cdot j) = \sum_{k=1}^{\kappa} u_k v_k \prod_{j<k} (1 - u_j) \leq \sum_{k=1}^{\kappa} u_k v_k \leq \sum_{k=1}^{\kappa} u_1 v_1 \leq \kappa(u_1 v_1)$. Obviously, $u_1 v_1 \leq x_1 y_1$, thus $Pr(i \cdot j) \geq \frac{1}{\kappa} Pr^*(i \cdot j)$ and $ETTER_{ij} = \frac{1}{Pr(i \cdot j)} \leq \frac{1}{\frac{1}{\kappa} Pr^*(i \cdot j)} = \kappa ETTER_{ij}^*$.   □

4   Many-to-One Effective Rendezvous

In this section, we consider the *many-to-one rendezvous establishment* problem. In such scenario, a group of nodes potentially employ a single node as forwarder. As we have shown in previous section, the channel hopping strategy of the forwarder affect the expected rendezvous delay significantly. For fairness consideration, we defined following objective function:

$$\underset{\varphi, \ \psi}{\text{minimize}} \ \underset{s_i \in \mathcal{L}}{\max} \ ETTER_{ij}. \tag{5}$$

This problem is essentially a joint optimization problem with respect to both the CH strategy of the receiver and the CS schemes of the transmitters. According to the discussion in the previous section, once the CH strategy φ of the receiver s_j is determined, we can provide a κ-approximation CS scheme for the transmitters in $\mathcal{L}$. Unfortunately, the space of the CH strategy φ is $O(2^n)$ under the opportunistic framework. Considering the hardness of the above optimization problem, we relax the constraints and derive a linear optimization problem based on which an approximate solution can be developed.

To relax the constraints, we assume the SUs in $\mathcal{L}$ can sense all the channels simultaneously. Furthermore, we assume they can transmit *Beacons* on all the channels at the same time provided that these channels are available to the transmitters. Define p_k as the probability of the receiver s_j staying on channel k, where $k \in \mathcal{K}$. Then, for $s_i \in \mathcal{L}$, $Pr(i \cdot j) = \sum_{k=1}^{K} \mu_i^k \mu_j^k p_k$ and $ETTER_{ij} = \frac{1}{Pr(i \cdot j)}$. We first solve the following optimization problem:

$$\text{minimize} \quad \max_{s_i \in \mathcal{L}} \frac{1}{\sum_{k=1}^{K} \mu_i^k \mu_j^k p_k} \tag{6}$$

$$\text{subject to} \quad \sum_{k=1}^{K} p_k = 1 \tag{7}$$

$$p_k \geq 0, \ \forall k \in \mathcal{K}. \tag{8}$$

The optimal solution of this optimization problem can be obtained with the help of *linear programming*. Denote $p^* = (p_1^*, p_2^*, \ldots, p_K^*)$ with $ETTER^*$ as the optimal solution. Since the constrains are relaxed compared to the original problem, $ETTER^*$ is a lower bound of the original problem.

Now we are ready to construct the CH strategy $\overline{\varphi}$ for the receiver s_j and the CS scheme $\overline{\psi}$ for the transmitters in $\mathcal{L}$. For the CH strategy, let $\overline{\varphi}(j, t) = k$ with probability p_k^* at each time slot, and s_j always employs the channel CH strategy $\overline{\varphi}$ in the idle state. For the CS scheme, any SU can only sense at most κ channels and transmit *Beacon* message on one channel at one time. Let the transmitter $s_i \in \mathcal{L}$ sense channels in a round-robbin manner, *i.e.*, let $\overline{\psi}(i, t) = \{t\%K + 1\}$ for $s_i \in \mathcal{L}$. Once s_i tries to establish a rendezvous with s_j, s_i sets t as 0 and starts the channel sensing process with $\overline{\psi}$. s_i transmits a *Beacon* message to s_j on that channel when it finds that the channel is available to itself, and it continues the sensing and *Beacon* message transmission process with CS scheme $\overline{\psi}$ until an *Ack* message from s_j is received successfully.

Theorem 2. *Let $ETTER_1 = max_{s_i \in \mathcal{L}} ETTER_{ij}$ with CH strategy $\overline{\varphi}$ and CS scheme $\overline{\psi}$, and $ETTER^* = max_{s_i \in \mathcal{L}} ETTER_{ij}$ with optimal CH strategy φ^* and CS scheme ψ^*, then, $\frac{1}{K} ETTER_1 = ETTER^*$, where K is the number of the available channels.*

Proof. Consider the optimal solution $ETTER^*$. We assume that all the SUs in $\mathcal{L}$ can sense all the channels simultaneously and they can also transmit *Beacon* messages on all the channels at the same time providing that these channels are available to the transmitters. With such an assumption, the probability that s_i can successfully establish an effective rendezvous with s_j is $\sum_{k=1}^{K} \mu_i^k \mu_j^k p_k^*$. Now consider that s_i employs CS scheme $\overline{\psi}$. In consecutive K time slots, s_i senses one channel at each time slot, and it can sense each of the channels k in $\mathcal{K}$ exactly once. Assume $t\%K + 1 = k$, then at time slot t, s_i senses channel k and channel k is available to it with probability μ_i^k. Thus in time slot t, the probability that s_i can successfully establish an effective rendezvous with s_j is $\mu_i^k \mu_j^k p_k^*$. Hence, in consecutive K time slots, the probability of s_i successfully establishing an effective rendezvous with s_j is $\sum_{k=1}^{K} \mu_i^k \mu_j^k p_k^*$. It follows the theorem. $\qquad \square$

According to Theorem 2, the CH strategy $\overline{\varphi}$ and the CS scheme $\overline{\psi}$ is a K-approximation of φ^* and ψ^* with respect to the optimal minimized maximum ETTER.

5 Simulation

We conduct extensive simulations to evaluate the performance of our opportunistic approach. We name our methods for the opportunistic pairwise effective rendezvous problem and many-to-one effective rendezvous problem as OPER and MOER, respectively. Three representative algorithms, JSCH [5], SYNC-ETCH [6] and ACH [7] are selected for comparison. *ETTER* and *success rendezvous ratio (SRR)* are adopted for performance measurement. Here *SRR* is defined as the ratio of successfully established rendezvous given some specific time threshold.

In the simulations, 100 nodes are randomly deployed in an area of 400m × 400m, and the transmission range of each node is set to 60m. The number of the available channels for each node varies from 3 to 27, and the channel availabilities of each channel are randomly and independently generated in an interval $[0.1, u]$, where the value of u varies from 0.6 to 1.0. Here we explicitly employ the parameter u to simulate different traffic loads of PUs. In all the simulations, each data point is an average result of 100 instances. When OPER and MOER are compared with JSCH and other rendezvous algorithms, the value of κ is set to 0 for fairness consideration, *i.e.*, the receiver does not sense the channels during a channel hopping process, and the CH strategy φ_a is employed by the receivers.

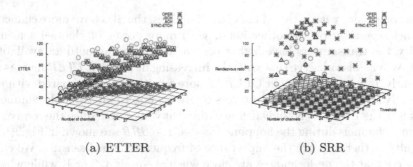

(a) ETTER   (b) SRR

Fig. 1. Performance comparison for pairwise effective rendezvous

For pairwise effective rendezvous establishment, we performed two groups of simulations. In the first one, the *ETTER* and *SRR* of our algorithms are compared with those of JSCH, ACH and SYNC-ETCH under various parameter settings, including number of channels, traffic loads of PUs (u) and time threshold (measured in terms of the number of time slots). As shown in Fig.1(a), it is clear that the *ETTERs* of the four algorithms increase with the increasing of the number of channels. Moreover, with the increasing of u (the decreasing

traffic load of PUs), the *ETTERs* of OPER decreases, which is different from
the other three algorithms. Obviously, OPER outperforms the other three algorithms significantly in various parameter settings in term of *ETTER*. Fig.1(b)
shows the *SRR* with different time thresholds and number of channels, where u
is set to 1.0. As can be seen, the *SRR* of OPER converges to 100% faster than
that of the other three algorithms, with the increasing of time threshold.

In the second group of simulations, we investigate the performance of OPER
with different settings of network parameters. In particular, we adjust the channel sensing capability of SUs (κ), traffic loads of PUs (u) and the sensing frequency of the receivers during channel hopping (w). According to Fig.2(a), the
ETTER decreases with the increasing of both u and κ.

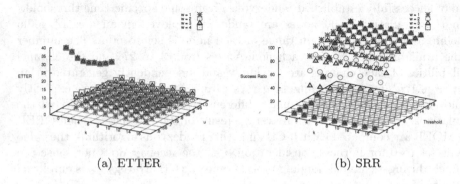

(a) ETTER   (b) SRR

Fig. 2. Performance comparison of pairwise effective rendezvous with 16 channels

On the one hand, with higher channel availabilities, the SUs have more chances
of channel accessing; on the other hand, with more power of channel sensing
capability, the transmitters have higher probability of hoping onto an available
channel. We can also observe that with the increasing of w, the *ETTER* increases
significantly. It is interesting that OPER is more sensitive to w compared with κ,
which implys it is critical for the receivers to always hop to an available channel.
When κ is 0, the *ETTERs* is equivalent for different values of w since the receivers
never sense channels during the hopping process. The *SRR* are shown in Fig.2(b).
The results further indicate the importance of frequent channel sensing. We can
also observe that the performances are close when w equals 3, 2 or 1, while when
w equals 4, the *SRR* are close to zero, which indicates the choosing of w should
be very careful because of the trade-off between energy and rendezvous delay.

For many-to-one effective rendezvous, we also compare the performance of
MOER with that of the other three algorithms. In this group of simulations,
we evaluate 100 instances and employ the average maximum *ETTER* of these
instances. Specifically, each node in the network is treated as the receiver of one
instance, and the neighbors of the corresponding receiver are the transmitting
set of the instance. According to Fig.3(a), it is obvious that the performance
of OPER is the best. Moreover, The maximum *ETTERs* increases much slower

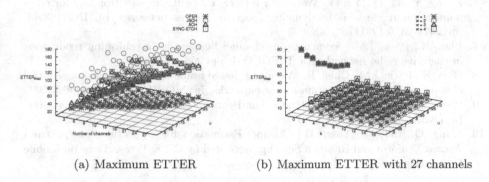

(a) Maximum ETTER   (b) Maximum ETTER with 27 channels

Fig. 3. Performance comparison of many-to-one effective rendezvous

than the other three algorithms with the increasing of the number of channels. We also consider the affect of w to maximum *ETTER*. From Fig.3(b), we obtain similar results as in the second group of simulations.

6   Conclusions

In this paper, we investigate the opportunistic channel-hopping algorithms for effective rendezvous establishment in CRNs. We consider both pairwise and many-to-one scenarios. Channel availabilities based channel hopping and sensing algorithms are proposed for efficient and effective rendezvous establishment. Our approach sufficiently considers the dynamic traffic loads of PUs and utilizes the channel sensing capability of SUs. The efficiency of our algorithms are evaluated through theoretical analysis and extensive simulations.

References

1. Akyildiz, I.F., Lee, W., Vuran, M.C., Mohanty, S.: NeXt generation dynamic spectrum access cognitive radio wireless networks: A survey. Computer Networks Journal 50(13), 2127–2159 (2006)
2. Kim, H., Shin, K.G.: Efficient Discovery of Spectrum Opportunities with MAC-Layer Sensing in Cognitive Radio Networks. IEEE Transactions on Mobile Computing 7(5), 533–545 (2008)
3. Cordeiro, C., Challapali, K., Birru, D., Sai, N.S.: IEEE 802.22: the first worldwide wireless standard based on cognitive radios. In: DySPAN, pp.328–337 (2005)
4. Jia, J., Zhang, Q., Shen, X.: HC-MAC: A Hardware-Constrained Cognitive MAC for Efficient Spectrum Management. IEEE Journal on Selected Areas in Communications 26(1), 106–117 (2008)
5. Lin, Z., Liu, H., Chu, X., Leung, Y.: Jump-stay based channel-hopping algorithm with guaranteed rendezvous for cognitive radio networks. In: INFOCOM, pp. 2444–2452 (2011)

6. Zhang, Y., Li, Q., Yu, G., Wang, B.: ETCH: Efficient Channel Hopping for communication rendezvous in dynamic spectrum access networks. In: INFOCOM, pp. 2471–2479 (2011)
7. Bian, K., Park, J.M.: Asynchronous channel hopping for establishing rendezvous in cognitive radio networks. In: INFOCOM, pp. 236–240 (2011)
8. Bian, K., Park, J.M., Chen, R.: A quorum-based framework for establishing control channels in dynamic spectrum access networks. In: MOBICOM, pp. 25–36 (2009)
9. Brent, H., Damla, T.: Link Rendezvous Protocol for Cognitive Radio Networks. In: DySPAN, pp. 444–447 (2007)
10. Liang, Q., Liu, M., Yuan, D.: Channel Estimation for Opportunistic Spectrum Access: Uniform and Random Sensing. Accepted by IEEE Transactions on Mobile Computing

The Modeling and Analysis of Context and Cardinality Constraints Role-Based Authorization Mechanism

Limin Liu[1], Yujun Liu[2], and Wei Cheng[3]

[1] Department of Optical and Electronic Engineering,
Mechanical Engineering College, Shijiazhuang, China
[2] Department of Information Engineering,
Academy of Armored Engineering, Beijing, China
[3] Department of Computer Science, University of California, Davis, CA, USA

Abstract. The Role-Based Access Control (RBAC) model, under which the users are assigned to certain roles while the roles are associated with prescribed permissions, remains one of the most popular authorization control mechanisms. Workflow is a business flow composed of several related tasks. These tasks are interrelated and context-dependent during their execution. Execution context can introduce uncertainty in authorization decisions for tasks. This paper investigates the role-based authorization model with the context constraints and dynamic cardinality constraints. The Petri-net is used to model the authorization process and the formal expression of the model is presented. The general stochastic Petri-net simplifying method is used to analyze and calculate the authorization workload of a role in the system. With this work, given the workflow load, context and role authorization system parameters, we can predict the performance of the constraints role-based authorization system on mobile devices. Based on these performance metrics, the mobile system parameters can be adjusted to achieve the optimal system performance and meet the user demand best.

Keywords: Role, Constraint, Authorization, Cardinality, Performance.

1 Introduction

Workflow is a kind of completely or partly automatic task's execution processes. These tasks are mutually dependent and are executed at a certain fashion. In order to guarantee each task to utilize the system resources under reasonable authorization, there should be an appropriate authorization mechanism in the workflow management system. When the data is flowing among the tasks of workflow, the task on execution is changing and the privilege of the task is also changing. The privilege changing of tasks is related with the context environment of the data process and the implementation of the workflow authorization depends on the procedure context too.

X. Wang et al. (Eds.): WASA 2012, LNCS 7405, pp. 337–345, 2012.
© Springer-Verlag Berlin Heidelberg 2012

Authorization constraints specify the mandatory rules that must be observed when access permissions are assigned to roles, roles are assigned to users or a user activates a role at some time. These rules are established in order to satisfy the safety control principle and business needs. In recent years, the research about constraints has becoming an important research point related to the RBAC model. These researches extend the basic constraints and some new constraint types such as relationship constraint, prerequisite constraint and cardinality constraint etc. are presented.

In this paper, the application of the role-based authorization model under context and dynamic cardinality constraint to workflow system is studied. The queuing theory is utilized to analysis and to predict the system performance.

2   Related Works

[1] has studied the TBAC (Task Based Access Control) model which was an authorization model based on tasks of a workflow instance. This model has considered the context constraints among workflow tasks, but the role organizations, role logics, the roles' relationship with system resources and the model's effect on workflow performance were not included in their studies. [2][3] introduced various constraints of the RBAC model, but they did not present the concrete scenarios of these constraints. [4] presented the simplifying methods of workflow logic model and studied the simplifying methods of workflow sub logics such as serial, parallel, selective and loop logics, but did not analyze the workflow management system's performance which contained multiple types of instances. [5] studied the relationship constraints and prerequisite constraints and also used the Petrinet to study SoD and BoD in workflow under role-based authorization mechanism. They presented the model implementation explicitly and used CTMC to study the workflow performance. The task context and cardinality constraint's implementation in a role-based authorization system was not included in their study and they did not give these constraints' effect on system performance too.

3   Authorization under Role Cardinality and Context Constraint

3.1   The Temporal Constraint Expression of Roles

The Petrinet expression of role's temporal constraint presented by [5] is utilized in this paper. Role is expressed as role place and anti-place in PN. Fig.1 illustrates the expression method.

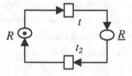

Fig. 1. Temporal constraints of the role's availability

In this figure, t_1 and t_2 are timed transitions. R is the valid place of a role and $\underline{R}$ is the invalid place of a role. $\underline{R}$ is the anti-place of R. In the current marking, the place R contains a token, which means that the role is available. After a certain time period associated with transition t_1, t_1 fires and the token is deleted from the R place and deposited into the anti-place $\underline{R}$. Then, during the next time period associated with transition t_2, the role is unavailable. The time periods associated with transition t_1 and t_2 are variables, whose values are determined by the security policy implemented in an individual organization.

3.2   Authorization under Role Cardinality Constraint

As mentioned above, this section will mainly study the dynamic cardinality constraints. Suppose that the requested role of a task is R and the active cardinality constraint of the role R is n. The authorization rule to the task under R's cardinality constraint is modeled by PN as in Fig.2.

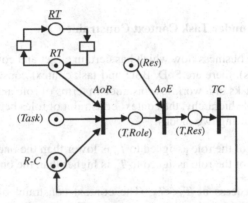

Fig. 2. Task-role assignment under active cardinality constraint

Suppose the active cardinality of role R is n. The number of the tokens in place R-C stands for the remaining available number of the role R and the maximum number is n. When Task requests the authorization of R and the active task sessions of R are fewer than n, Task can obtain the authorization successfully. The place RT, $\underline{RT}$ and the transitions between them construct the temporal constraints of the role's availability. The transition AoR is the assignment action of the role R to the task. This transition needs three input tokens: one from the place $Task$ which stands for the existence of an input task; one from the place R-C when there are remaining available active role R;

one from place RT which stands for the temporal availability of the role. The arc between the place RT and the transition AoR is bidirectional and the transition AoR will not consume the token in the place RT.

Let us take the $Trans(T)$ and $Token(P)$ as two functions which stand for the firing of the transition T and the token status of place P respectively. The output values of the function $Trans(T)$ is Boolean. The value of $Trans(T)$ is 1 if and only if the transition T is fired. The value of $Token(P)$ is integer and its value is the token number in the place P. The meaning of $\exists$ *(Expression)* is that the action will execute if and only if the *expression* is *true*. The symbols "$\&\&$" and "$\|$" stand for logic AND and OR respectively.

The formal expression of the firing of a transition or the token status in a place of the Fig.2 can be depicted as the following expressions:

$$Trans(AoR)=\exists((Token(task))\&\&(Token(R\text{-}C)>0)\ \&\&(Token(R\text{-}T)))$$

$$Trans(AoE)=\exists((Token(T,\ Role\ ))\&\&(Token(Res)>0))$$

$$Trans(TC)=\ \exists(Token(T,\ Res\ ))$$

3.3   Authorization under Task Context Constraint

Because workflow is a business flow which has certain target and composed of several related tasks (activities), there are SoD, BoD and task context constraint between the roles assigned to the tasks of a workflow instance in terms of role authorization.

From the view of role hierarchy, the context constraint of roles between tasks can be classified into the following two modes:

1) $T_a<<T_b$: the rank of the role assigned to T_a is lower than the one assigned to T_b.
2) $T_a>>T_b$: the rank of the role assigned to T_a is higher than the one assigned to T_b.

The authorization process of $T_a<<T_b$ The context constraint of task T_b to T_a is modeled in Petrinet and the authorization process of $T_a<<T_b$ is illustrated as in Fig.3.

In the figure, the rank of the role requested by task T_b is higher than that of its antecedent task T_a. R_{f1}-R_{fn} are the father roles of R which is the role assigned to the task T_a. R_{f1}-R_{fn} are sorted from low to high rank in order to observe the least privilege principle.

Add a place (T_a, R) in the Petrinet and deposit a token to it when role R is assigned to task T_a by the authorization service successfully. This place is also an input place of the authorization to the descendant task T_b, so the context constraint authorization constraint between task T_a and T_b can be guaranteed. The place ARC_{fi} is the anti-place of R_{fi}-C and the tokens in it stand for the number of active sessions of R_{fi}. n_{fi} stands for the active cardinality of R_{fi}.

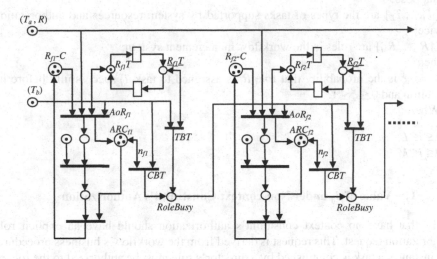

Fig. 3. Task-role assignment under task context constraint

$$Trans(AoR_{f1})= \exists((Token(T_a,R))\&\&(Token(R_{f1}\text{-}C)>0)\ \&\&(Token(R_{f1}T))$$
$$\&\&(Token(T_b)))$$
$$Trans(TBT_{f1})= \exists((Token(\underline{R_{f1}T}))\&\&(Token(T_b)))$$
$$Trans(CBT_{f1})= \exists((Token(T_b))\&\&(Boolean(Token(ARC_{f1})=n_{f1})))$$
$$Token(RoleBusy_{f1})= \exists(\ CBT_{f1}||TBT_{f1})$$
$$= \exists((Token(\underline{R_{f1}T}))\&\&(Token(T_b))$$
$$||\ (Token(T_b))\&\&(Boolean(Token(ARC_{f1})=n_{f1})))$$
$$Trans(AoR_{f2})= \exists((Token(T_a,R))\&\&(Boolean(Token(R_{f2}\text{-}C)>0))$$
$$\&\&(Token(R_{f2}T))\ \&\&(Token(RoleBusy_{f1})))$$
$$Trans(TBT_{f2})= \exists((Token(\underline{R_{f2}T}))\&\&(Token(RoleBusy_{f1})))$$
$$Trans(CBT_{f2})= \exists((Token(RoleBusy_{f1}))\&\&(Boolean(Token(ARC_{f2})=n_{f2})))$$
$$Token(RoleBusy_{f2})= \exists(\ CBT_{f2}||TBT_{f2})$$
$$= \exists((Token(\underline{R_{f2}T}))\&\&(Token(RoleBusy_{f1}))$$
$$||$$

$(Token(RoleBusy_{f1}))\&\&(Boolean(Token(ARC_{f2})=n_{f2})))$ The authorization process of $T_a>>T_b$ is same as that of $T_a<<T_b$ except that the R_{f1}-R_{fn} in Fig.3 are substituted by R_{s1}-R_{sn} which are the descendants of role R sorted from low to high ranks.

4   System Analysis under Cardinality and Workflow Context Constraints

System performance is related with processing time of role and the service time of resource. In order to know which role is requested by which task, the mapping matrix between tasks and requested roles is constructed and the value of the element d_{ij} in the matrix is:

Suppose:

$\{T_1,...,T_L\}$ are the types of tasks supported by system resources and authorization service;

$\{R_1,...,R_M\}$ are roles in the workflow management system;

then:

$d_{ij}=\xi$, ξ is the probability that role R_i is assigned to task T_j successfully before its execution and $0 \leq \xi \leq 1$.

Where:

$1 \leq i \leq L$;

$1 \leq j \leq M$.

4.1   The Value of d_{ij} under Non-context Constraint's Authorization

Tasks that have no context constraint's authorization should have an explicit role authorization request. This request is derived from the workflow's business procedure. For instance, a task accomplished by a director's role must be authorized to the role of 'director' before it can be executed. The authorization request can be obtained from the authorization request file of the workflow instance (a XACML file, for example).

The value of d_{ij} is one when the task T_j has the explicit role authorization request of R_i and zero when it has not a role authorization request of R_i. Under this circumstance, ξ can be denoted by ξ_a.

4.2   The Value of d_{ij} under Context Constraint's Authorization

The case of context constraint's authorization of a task is presented by the Fig.3. In this case, the value of d_{ij} must be obtained from the calculation of authorization probability of each dependant roles. Take the Fig.3 as the example, the model presented by Fig.3 is a General Stochastic Petri-net model, and since the time associated with each transition is exponentially distributed, the underlying stochastic process is a Continuous Time Markov Chain[6]. We can construct the Tangible Reachability Graph (TRG) of the Petri-net model and also can construct the CTMC from the TRG[5]. After the CTMC is constructed, we can calculate the infinitesimal generator (which is a two dimensional matrix, denoted by Q) of the CTMC.

Suppose there are M states in the CTMC. p_i is the probability that the CMTC stays in state s_i.

If we denote the row vector $P= [\ p_1, p_2, ..., p_i,..., p_M\ ]$, then the following linear equation system holds, where Q is the infinitesimal generator of the constructed GPSN model. P can be obtained by solving the equation system:

$$\begin{cases} PQ = 0. \\ \sum_{i=1}^{M} pi = 1 \end{cases} \tag{1}$$

The nodes in the TRG are defines by the row vector:

$$N_s=[(T_a,R), T_b, R_{f1}, \underline{R_{f1}}, R_{f2}, \underline{R_{f2}}, ..., R_{fn}, \underline{R_{fn}}]$$

In this vector, $R_{fi}=R_{fi}\text{-}C\cap R_{fi}\text{-}T$ which means the availability of role R_{fi}; $\underline{R_{fi}}$ is *RoleBusy* of R_{fi} which means the unavailability of role R_{fi}.

We suppose that the role authorization of T_b will stay at the queue of all father roles of R and wait for the first spare role if all R's father roles are busy. Though the first spare probability of all father roles of R can be calculated based on the whole workflow instances accomplished by the workflow management system, we take the uniform distribution of the father roles' spare probability in order to simplify the problem.

The following N_s state lists are the states that can lead to the successfully role authorizations of T_b:

N_s Value List	Probability
$S_1=(1,1,1,0,X,X,...,X,X)$	p_1
$S_2=(1,1,0,1,1,0,...,X,X)$	p_2
...	
$S_n=(1,1,0,1,0,1,...,1,0)$	p_n
$S =(1,1,0,1,0,1,...,0,1)$	p_{bs}

S_1-S_n are the states that can lead to the successfully role authorizations of T_b to R_{f1}- R_{fn} respectively and S is the state that all roles are busy. p_1- p_n and p_{bs} are the probability of these states.

The values of p_1-p_n and p_{bs} can be obtained by the *Eq.*1. If T_j is a context constraint's authorization task as T_b and R_i is the i_{th} father role of R, the value of d_{ij} can be expressed as following:

$$\xi_b= p_i + p_{bs}/n$$

The total probability that role R_i is assigned to task T_j successfully before its execution can be calculated as:

$$d_{ij} =\xi_a +\xi_b \tag{2}$$

4.3   Performance Analysis of a Workflow Running on Mobile Devices

Workflow on mobile devices is usually distributed to several mobile devices (Such as a mobile phone). Each mobile device accomplishes several tasks under a designated role. Suppose a workflow application composed of $T_1,...,T_L$ is running on several mobile devices, the arrival of the workflow instance is Poisson processes and its arrival rate is λ, the service time of the mobile device under role R_i is exponential distributed and the cardinality of the role is the server number. Thus the whole system can be expressed as a *M/M/C* queuing system.

$$P_0= \sum_{k=0}^{Ci-1}\frac{1}{k!}(\frac{\lambda_i}{\mu_i})^k +\frac{1}{ci!}\frac{1}{1-\rho^*}(\frac{\lambda_i}{\mu_i})^{ci}$$

Where λ_i, μ_i ,ci are the task arrival rate, mean service time and cardinality of R_i respectively. $\rho^*=\lambda_i /(\mu_i *ci)$. P_0 is the probability of no task request to R_i. Then according to queuing theory, the mean waiting time W_{qi} of the role R_i on the mobile device is:

$$W_{qi}= \frac{(ci\rho^*)^{ci} \rho^* P_0}{ci(1-\rho^*)^2 \lambda}$$

With each mobile device's the average waiting time W_{qi}, the whole system waiting time vector can be constructed as:

$$V_{Wq}=(W_{q1},\ldots W_{qi},\ldots,W_{qm})$$

With this vector, the waiting time above the require time limit can be identified. Thus the bottleneck of the workflow system running on the mobile devices can also be determined. The mobile workflow system performance can be improved by increasing the corresponding mobile device numbers or upgrading the processing ability of the mobile device under a certain role.

5   Conclusions and Future Works

In this paper, we present a role-based authorization model under task context and role cardinality constraints. We employ Petrinet to model the authorization procedure with role cardinality constraint and task dependence and also present the formal expression of this model. The authorization workload of a role in the system is analyzed and calculated by using the general stochastic Petri-net simplifying method. Based on this study, our future works will focus on the study of uncertain authorization model of roles under task context and its performance analysis. We will employ the probability, fuzzy and queuing theories to analysis and predict the more generic and complicated workflow management under cardinality and context constraints role authorization.

References

1. Thomas, R.K., Sandhu, R.S.: Task-based Authorization Controls (TBAC): A Family of Models for Active and Enterprise-oriented Authorization Management. In: IFIP TC11 WG113 11th International Conference on Database Security XI Status and Prospects, vol. 11, pp. 166–181. Chapman & Hall, Ltd.
2. Ray, I., Li, N., France, R., Kim, D.K.: Using UML to Visualize Role-based Access Control Constraints. In: Proceedings of the 9th ACM Symposium on Access Control Modelsand Technologies, Yorktown Heights, New York, USA, June 02-04, pp. 115–124 (2004)
3. Tan, K., Crampton, J., Gunter, C.: The Consistency of Task-based Authorization Constraints in Workflow Systems. In: Proceedings of 17th IEEE Computer Security Foundations Workshop, pp. 155–169 (2004)
4. Liu, S., Fan, Y.S.: Workflow Model Performance Analysis Concerning Instance Dwelling Times Distribution. In: 2009 IEEE International Symposium on Parallel and Distributed Processing with Applications, ISPA, pp. 601–605 (2009)

5. He, L., Calleja, M., Hayes, M., Jarvis, S.A.: Performance Prediction for Running Workflows under Role-based Authorization Mechanisms. In: IEEE International Symposium on Parallel and Distributed Processing, IPDPS, pp. 1–8 (2009)
6. Manolache, S.: Schedulability Analysis of Real-Time Systems with Stochastic Task Execution Times. Ph.D Thesis, Department of Computer and Information Science, IDA, Linkoping University
7. Bolch, G., Greiner, S., de Meer, H., Trivedi, K.S.: Queueing Networks and Markov Chains – Modeling and Performance Evaluation with Computer Science Applications. John Wiley and Sons, New York (1998)
8. Li, N., Tripunitara, M.V., Bizri, Z.: On Mutually Exclusive Roles and Separation-of-duty. ACM Transactions on Information and System Security (TISSEC) 10(2), 5-es (2007)

A Multiple Access Game Based MAC Protocol for Fairness Provisioning and Throughput Enhancement

Tao Jing[1], Yunqing Yang[1], Yuan Le[2], Liran Ma[3], Wei Zhou[1], and Yan Huo[1]

[1] School of Electronics and Information Engineering, Beijing Jiaotong University, China
[2] Computer Science, The George Washington University, DC, USA
[3] Computer Science, Texas Christian University, Fort Worth, TX, USA
{tjing,10120228}@bjtu.edu.cn, ppzt@gwmail.gwu.edu,
l.ma@tcu.edu, {11111032,yhuo}@bjtu.edu.cn

Abstract. This paper studies the problem of maximizing throughput under the time fairness constraint in a multi-rate wireless network using a game-theoretic approach. We model the problem as a multiple access game and propose a novel payoff function for the game. The design our proposed payoff function properly integrates throughput maximization with the time fairness constraint. Based on the design of the payoff function, we devise a novel MAC protocol named G-CSMA. In our proposed G-CSMA protocol, each station iteratively updates its transmission attempt probability according to its specific payoff function until a Nash equilibrium is reached. Our evaluation results demonstrate that our proposed G-CSMA protocol outperforms the existing mainstream MAC protocols in terms of time fairness and throughput.

Keywords: Multiple Access Game, Time Fairness, CSMA, Multi-rate Wireless Network.

1 Introduction

The primary Medium Access Control (MAC) mechanism in the IEEE 802.11 standards is called Distributed Coordination Function (DCF). The DCF mechanism uses the well-known Carrier Sense Multiple Access with Collision Avoidance (CSMA/CA) protocol to regulate the access to the medium among contending stations. Two of the major design objectives of CSMA/CA are to: i) fairly allocate the medium access opportunity to each station; and ii) effectively utilize the medium so as to maximize aggregate throughput. In general, CSMA/CA is able to provide each station with the same opportunity to access the medium in a long run. However, it has been shown that the medium utilization efficiency is seriously degraded when the contending stations have different bitrates [1]. This phenomenon is called a *performance anomaly* where the throughput of a high bitrate station falls below that of a low bitrate station. As a result, aggregate throughput is significantly decreased as well. The main cause of the performance anomaly is that it takes the low bitrate station a longer time to transmit the same size frame than that of the high bitrate station. When given the same medium access opportunity, the low bitrate station excessively occupies the medium compared to that of the high bitrate station.

X. Wang et al. (Eds.): WASA 2012, LNCS 7405, pp. 346–357, 2012.

To address this problem, many efforts have recently been made to develop different fairness criteria for a multi-rate scenario so as to improve aggregate throughout. Examples of such fairness criteria are time fairness and proportional fairness. To be specific, time fairness criterion focuses on assuring equal medium occupation time for each station. Proportional fairness criterion is closely related to time fairness criterion [2,3]. An early work of time fairness based mechanisms is introduced [4]. Another time fairness based method termed *Idle Sense* is proposed [5]. Idle sense is considered as one of the arguably best MAC protocols in the literature. A proportional fairness based throughput allocation scheme is proposed in [3]. Despite these existing efforts, there is still room for further improvements in terms of throughout and time fairness.

In this paper, we adopt a game-theoretic approach to improve the time fairness and throughput in a multi-rate wireless LAN. Game theory has recently been widely used in studying wireless networks [6,7]. Due to the nature of wireless medium access control, it can be modeled as a multiple access game [6,8]. The key element of a game is its payoff function for each player (e.g., stations in a WLAN). A payoff function describes the award that shall be given to a single player as the outcome of the game. We propose a novel payoff function that is defined as the difference between the gains obtained from a successful transmission and the costs incurred by a collision. The design of our proposed payoff function carefully incorporates throughput enhancement and the time fairness constraint. Each station's goal is to maximize its payoff benefits under the time fairness constraint by choosing an appropriate strategy. When the maximum payoff benefits are achieved, the game converges to a Nash equilibrium. Based on the design of our game, we propose a novel MAC protocol named G-CSMA. Our evaluation results demonstrate the effectiveness of our proposed G-CSMA protocol.

The rest of the paper is organized as follows. Section 2 describes the related work. Our network model is illustrated in Section 3. The design of the multiple access game is introduced in Section 4 and our proposed G-CSMA protocol is presented in Section 5. Section 6 reports our evaluation results and Section 7 draws the conclusion.

2 Related Work

We start by summarizing the related work on fairness criteria and their associated MAC protocols. There exist four widely used fairness criteria: throughput fairness, time fairness, proportional fairness, and max-min fairness. The default CSMA/CA is able to provide throughput fairness if all stations have the same bitrate and adopt the same frame size. An early work of time fairness based mechanisms is introduced [4] where a time-based regulator is adopted to balance the medium occupancy time among stations. Another time fairness based method termed *Idle Sense* is proposed [5]. Idle senses proposed improves the short-term time fairness by estimating the average number of idle slots between two transmissions. A proportional fairness based throughput allocation scheme is proposed in [3]. In this throughput allocation scheme, a station sets the initial contention window size inversely proportional to its bitrate. The max-min fairness criterion is discussed in [9]. A commonly used index for measuring fairness is developed by *Jain et al.* in [10].

There exists a significant amount of work in communication networks that makes use of game theory [6,7,11]. The framework of a generalized version of the multiple access game is introduced in [12]. The framework is used to model the selfish behavior of stations using CSMA/CA. *Jin et al.* investigate the non-cooperative game equilibria of ALOHA networks in [13]. *Lijun et al.* propose a game-theoretic model that is capable of achieving service differentiation in a distributed manner in [8, 14]. However, the existing work primarily applies the game-theoretic approach in the network consisted of homogeneous bitrate stations. In our work, we extend the game-theoretic approach to a multi-rate setting.

3   Network Model

We describe our network model in this section. We focus on a single cell multi-rate 802.11 WLAN with one AP and N stations. These stations compete for channel access by adopting the CSMA/CA protocol with no exponential backoff after a failure transmission. We assume that stations can hear each other in the network. We further assume that stations always have frames to transmit so that the network is saturated. We denote p_i as the probability of a station i that attempts to transmit a frame. If the station's contention window size is cw_i, we can approximate p_i via Eq. (1) according to [15]:

$$p_i = \frac{2}{cw_i + 1}. \tag{1}$$

When there is no station attempting to transmit, the channel can be considered as idle. Therefore, the probability of the channel being idle is:

$$p_{idle} = \prod_{i=1}^{n}(1 - p_i). \tag{2}$$

Similarly, a station can successfully transmit a frame if it is the only station in transmission. Thus, the probability of a successful transmission (referred as p_i^s) can be expressed as:

$$p_i^s = p_i \prod_{j \in N/\{i\}} (1 - p_j). \tag{3}$$

As a result, the aggregated throughput can be calculated as follows:

$$R = \frac{\Sigma_{i \in N} p_i^s E[P]}{p_{idle}\sigma + \Sigma_{i \in N} p_i^s T^s + (1 - p_{idle} - \Sigma_{i \in N} p_i^s)T^c}, \tag{4}$$

where, $E[P]$ is the average packet payload size; σ is the duration of an idle slot; T^s is the average channel occupation time of a successful transmission (i.e., $T^s = \sum_i T_i^s p_i^s$); T^s is the average channel occupation time of a collision (i.e., $T^c = E[T_i^c]$). Furthermore, T_i^s and T_i^c of station i can be calculated as:

$$T_i^s = 2\frac{ph}{br} + \frac{mh + P}{dr} + SIFS + \frac{mh + ACK}{b_{ack}} + DIFS,$$

$$T_i^c = \frac{ph}{br} + \frac{mh + P}{dr} + DIFS,$$

where, ph is PHY header size; mh is MAC header size; br is the bitrate to transmit the PHY header; b_{ack} is the bitrate to transmit an ACK frame.

4 Multiple Access Game

Game theory has been widely applied to communication networks in order to solve resource allocation problems in a competitive setting. In general, a game can be classified into two categories based on the behaviorial mode of its players: cooperative and non-cooperative [7]. In a cooperative game, players may enforce cooperative behaviour so as to exploit the possibility of common interests. On the other hand, players make decisions independently in a non-cooperative game. In this paper, we model the competition for medium among stations as a cooperative game because these stations need to jointly consider their utility gains and costs so as to improve the overall network performance. Our game is an extension of the random access game proposed in [8]. The formal definition of our game appears as follows.

Definition 1. *A multiple access game G is a cooperative game that can be defined as a triple $G = \{N, S, U\}$. $N = \{1, ..., n\}$ is a set of players (i.e., stations). $S = \{p_1, p_2, ..., p_i, ..., p_{|N|}\}$ is the strategy space that is a Cartesian product of the strategy sets of all players. The strategy set of player i is $\{p_i \in [0, \xi], \xi < 1\}$. U is the set of payoff functions of all players. The payoff function of player i is the difference between its utility function and its cost function.*

From the above definition, we can see that a strategy of station i is the choice of its transmission attempt probability p_i. The objective of game G is to maximize the payoff benefits under the time fairness constraint by selecting an appropriate strategy for each station. We detail the design of our payoff function in the following subsections.

4.1 Payoff Function Design

According to Definition 1, the payoff function of station i is composed by two parts: cost function and utility function. We denote the cost function as $c_i(\mathbf{p})$, where $\mathbf{p} = (p_1, p_2, ..., p_i, ..., p_{|N|})$. Our cost function incorporates the strategies of all stations. We denote the utility function as $v_i(p_i)$. Hence, the payoff function of station i, termed as $U_i(\mathbf{p})$, can be expressed as:

$$U_i(\mathbf{p}) = -c_i(\mathbf{p}) + v_i(p_i). \tag{5}$$

The design goal of our payoff function is to maximize throughput under the time fairness constraint. To achieve the design goal, the game needs to be to able to reach a steady state (i.e., a Nash equilibrium). We assume that there exists a Nash equilibrium. Subsequently, there also exists a vector of transmission attempt access probability $\mathbf{p}^* := (p_1^*, p_2^*, ..., p_i^*, ..., p_{|N|}^*)$ for the equilibrium. To meet the time fairness requirement, the channel occupancy time at the equilibrium shall be fairly shared between arbitrary two stations i and j:

$$T_i^s(p_i^s)^* = T_j^s(p_j^s)^*. \tag{6}$$

According to Eq. (3), we have:

$$\frac{(p_i^s)^*}{(p_j^s)^*} = \frac{p_i^* \cdot \prod_{l \neq i}(1 - p_l^*)}{p_j^* \cdot \prod_{l \neq j}(1 - p_l^*)} = \frac{p_i^*/(1 - p_i^*)}{p_j^*/(1 - p_j^*)}. \tag{7}$$

Thus, Eq. (6) can be rewritten as

$$\frac{p_i^* T_i^s}{1 - p_i^*} = \frac{p_j^* T_j^s}{1 - p_j^*}, \ 1 \leq i, j \leq N. \tag{8}$$

Next, we need to study the properties of the transmission attempt probability (i.e., the strategy) at a Nash equilibrium. Assume that at time t the transmission attempt probability of station i is $p_i(t)$ and the conditional collision probability of station i is $q_i(t)$. At the next time slot $(t+1)$, the transmission attempt probability $p_i(t+1)$ shall be adjusted based on $p_i(t)$ and $q_i(t)$. To be specific, $p_i(t + 1) = f_i(p_i(t), q_i(t))$. When station i reaches the equilibrium, p_i^* shall not change if the network remains the same. At this state, $p_i^* = f_i(p_i^*, q_i^*)$ is time independent. Assume $f_i(\cdot)$ is continuously differentiable and $\frac{\partial f_i(q_i)}{\partial q_i} \neq 0$ with $q_i \in [0, 1]$. Thus, we can represent q_i^* as a function of p_i^*:

$$q_i^* = F_i(p_i^*). \tag{9}$$

In order to maximize the payoff function $U_i(\mathbf{p})$ at a Nash equilibrium, p^* either takes the value at the boundaries of the strategy space S or satisfies $\frac{\partial U_i(\mathbf{p})}{\partial p_i} = 0$. The former case is called a trivial equilibrium, and the latter case is called a non-trivial equilibrium. In this paper, we mainly focus on the non-trivial Nash equilibrium. Hence, we have

$$c_i'(\mathbf{p}^*) = v_i'(p_i^*). \tag{10}$$

With the relationship between the cost function and the utility function defined in Eq. (10), we can illustrate the design of these two functions. Collisions can be regraded as penalties (i.e., costs) for an inappropriate strategy. As a result, the cost function of station i can be represented as

$$c_i(\mathbf{p}) = p_i q_i, \tag{11}$$

where q_i is the conditional collision probability of station i and can be expressed as

$$q_i = 1 - \prod_{j \in N/\{i\}} (1 - p_j). \tag{12}$$

We now detail the procedure to derive the utility function $v_i(p_i)$. From Eqs. (9), (10), and (11), we can have

$$v_i'(p_i^*) = q_i^* = F_i(p_i^*). \tag{13}$$

By taking the integral of Eq.(13), $v_i(p_i)$ can be expressed as

$$v_i(p_i) = \int F_i(p_i) dp_i. \tag{14}$$

To guarantee that the multiple access game G has a unique and non-trivial Nash equilibrium, we make the following three assumptions [8]:

- S1: The utility function $v_i(p_i)$ is continuously differentiable, strictly concave, and with finite curvatures that are bounded away from zero. Therefore, there exist constants α and β such that $-\beta \leq v_i''(p_i) \leq -\alpha < 0$.
- S2: Define $\Phi(\mathbf{p}) = \prod_{i \in N}(1 - p_i)$ and denote the smallest eigenvalue of $\nabla^2 \Phi(\mathbf{p})$ over $\mathbf{p}$ as γ_{min}. Thus, $-\alpha - \gamma_{min} < 0$.
- S3: Function $\Theta_i(p_i) = (1 - p_i)(1 - v_i'(p_i)), i \in N$ is strictly monotonic for all stations.

In S2, $\Phi(\mathbf{p})$ can be regarded as the channel idle probability of the network. In S3, the $\Theta_i(p_i)$ can be considered as the channel idle probability perceived by station i. If the game reaches the Nash equilibrium, according to Eqs. (12) and (13), we get

$$\Theta_i(p_i^*) = \Phi(\mathbf{p}^*). \tag{15}$$

From Eq. (15), we can see that $\Theta_i(p_i^*)$ is the same for all stations. This means that all stations perceive the same channel idle probability at the equilibrium. Based on Eq. (8), we can rewrite $\Theta_i(p_i^*)$ as a function of $\frac{p_i^* T_i^s}{(1-p_i^*)T_{max}^s}$ as follows

$$\Theta_i(p_i^*) = \chi(\frac{p_i^* T_i^s}{(1 - p_i^*)T_{max}^s}), \ 1 \leq i \leq N, \tag{16}$$

where T_{max}^s is the time that it takes the highest bitrate station to successfully transmit a packet.

We now can move to maximize the aggregated throughput. Let $\lambda = \Sigma_{i \in N} p_i$. In a reasonable large network, we can make the following two approximations: i) $\Phi(\mathbf{p}) = \prod_{i \in N}(1 - p_i) \approx e^{-\lambda}$, and ii) $P_s = \sum_{i \in N} p_i^s \approx \lambda e^{-\lambda}$. Hence, the aggregated throughput (i.e., Eq. (4)) can be expressed as

$$R = \frac{\lambda e^{-\lambda} P}{e^{-\lambda}\sigma + \lambda e^{-\lambda}T^s + (1 - e^{-\lambda} - \lambda e^{-\lambda})T^c}. \tag{17}$$

By taking the first derivative on Eq. (17), we can obtain the λ value (denoted as λ^*) that maximizes throughput R.

$$(1 - \lambda^*)e^{\lambda^*} = 1 - \frac{\sigma}{T^c}. \tag{18}$$

Note that λ^* is solely determined by σ and T^c that are constant parameters of the network. Since $\Phi(\mathbf{p}^*) = e^{-\lambda^*}$, we can turn Eq. (16) to

$$\chi(\frac{p_i^* T_i^s}{(1 - p_i^*)T_{max}^s}) = e^{-\lambda^*}. \tag{19}$$

We assume that p_i is very small when the number of stations is reasonably large. As a result, we turn Eq. (19) into

$$\chi(\frac{p_i T_i^s}{(1 - p_i)T_{max}^s}) = e^{-\lambda^*}(1 + \frac{p_i T_i^s}{(1 - p_i)T_{max}^s}). \tag{20}$$

From Eqs. (12), (13), and (20), we obtain

$$F_i(p_i) = q_i = 1 - \frac{e^{-\lambda^*}(1 + \frac{p_i T_i^s}{(1-p_i)T_{max}^s})}{1 - p_i}. \tag{21}$$

Subsequently, the utility function $v_i(p_i)$ defined in Eq. (14) can be expressed as

$$v_i(p_i) = \int F_i(p_i)dp_i = (p_i + \frac{e^{-\lambda^*}T_i^s}{(1-p_i)T_{max}^s}) + e^{-\lambda^*}(1 + \frac{T_i^s}{T_{max}^s})\ln(1-p_i). \quad (22)$$

With this utility function, we construct a multiple access game G that all stations have the same strategy set $[0, \xi]$ with $\xi < 1$. These stations make strategy decisions based on their utility functions. Note that the stations with the same bitrate shall use the same utility function and choose the same optimal strategy p_i^*. Combining Eq. (11) and Eq. (22), we get the system payoff function as

$$U_i(\mathbf{p}) = (p_i + \frac{e^{-\lambda^*}T_i^s}{(1-p_i)T_{max}^s}) + e^{-\lambda^*}(1 + \frac{T_i^s}{T_{max}^s})\ln(1-p_i) - p_iq_i. \quad (23)$$

4.2 Nash Equilibrium

With the three assumptions made in subsection 4.1, there exists a unique and non-trivial Nash equilibrium for the multiple access game G. In this section, we focus on deriving the specific strategy set of a station so as to achieve the equilibrium. Specifically, the strategy set of stations is $[0, \xi]$, and we will derive the range of ξ.

Lemma 1. *The multiple access game* G *has a unique non-trivial Nash equilibrium if* $1 - e^{-\frac{1}{2}\lambda^*} \leq \xi \leq 1 - \frac{1}{2}e^{\lambda^*}$.

Proof. We start by proving the left inequality. We organize stations into groups via their bitrates. All stations in the same group have the same bitrate, and thus, the same transmission attempt probability. Assume there are M such groups. For an arbitrary group m, suppose there are l number of stations and their transmission attempt probability is p_m. Assume $\mu = e^{-\lambda^*}(1 + \frac{p_mT_m^s}{(1-p_m)T_{max}^s})$. When $p_m = 0$ and $\mu = e^{-\lambda^*}$, we have $\Phi(\mathbf{p}) = \prod_{m\in M}(1 - \frac{\mu e^{\lambda^*}-1}{T_m^s/T_{max}^s+\mu e^{\lambda^*}-1})^l = 1 > \mu$. When $p_m = \xi$, we obtain $\mu = min\{1, e^{-\lambda^*}(1 + \frac{\xi}{1-\xi})\}$. If $\xi \geq 1 - e^{-\frac{1}{2}\lambda^*}$, we get $\Phi(\mathbf{p}) = \prod_{m\in M}(1 - \frac{\mu e^{\lambda^*}-1}{T_m^s/T_{max}^s+\mu e^{\lambda^*}-1})^l < \mu$. Since $\Phi(\mathbf{p}) = \prod_{m\in M}(1 - \frac{\mu e^{\lambda^*}-1}{T_m^s/T_{max}^s+\mu e^{\lambda^*}-1})^l$ is a continuous function of μ, there exists μ^* so as to achieve the equilibrium equation:

$$\Phi(\mathbf{p}) = \prod_{m\in M}(1 - \frac{\mu^*e^{\lambda^*}-1}{T_m^s/T_{max}^s+\mu^*e^{\lambda^*}-1})^l = \mu^*.$$

Thus, if $\xi \geq 1 - e^{-\frac{1}{2}\lambda^*}$, there exists a unique non-trivial Nash equilibrium $p_m = \frac{\mu^*e^{\lambda^*}-1}{T_m^s/T_{max}^s+\mu^*e^{\lambda^*}-1}$ for game G.

We next prove the right inequality. By calculating the maximum of $v_i''(p_i)$, we can obtain

$$diag([v_1''(p_1), v_2''(p_2), ..., v_{|N|}''(p_{|N|})]) \preceq -2e^{-\lambda^*}\mathbf{I} = -\alpha\mathbf{I},$$

where $\mathbf{I}$ is a unit matrix. Let $\zeta = (\frac{1}{1-p_1}, \frac{1}{1-p_2}, ..., \frac{1}{1-p_{|N|}})$. The Hessian matrix of $\Phi(\mathbf{p})$ can be calculated as

$$\nabla^2\Phi(\mathbf{p}) = (\zeta^T\zeta - diag^2(\zeta))\prod_i(1-p_i) \succeq \frac{-1}{1-\xi}\mathbf{I} = \gamma_{min}\mathbf{I}.$$

Because $\frac{\prod_{i\in N}(1-p_i)}{(1-p_i)^2} \leq \frac{1}{1-\xi}$ and $\zeta^T \zeta \prod_{i\in N}(1-p_i) \succeq 0$ hold for any station, if $\xi \leq 1 - \frac{1}{2}e^{\lambda^*}$, $-\alpha - \gamma_{min} < 0$, the multiple access game G has a unique Nash equilibrium.

In conclusion, the condition that the multiple access game G has a unique non-trivial Nash equilibrium is $1 - e^{-\frac{1}{2}\lambda^*} \leq \xi \leq 1 - \frac{1}{2}e^{\lambda^*}$.

5 Our MAC Protocol Design

We detail the design of our multiple access game based MAC protocol (termed as G-CSMA) in this section. In G-CSMA, a station adjusts its strategy (i.e., transmission attempt probability) in an iterative manner until a Nash equilibrium is reached. We employs a gradient play as the strategy adjustment approach [16]. In gradient play, every station adjusts a current attempt access probability gradually in a gradient direction suggested by observations of other stations actions. To be specific, at stage $(t + 1)$, station i updates its strategy according to the following equation

$$p_i(t + 1) = p_i(t) + \kappa_i(v'_i(p_i(t)) - q_i(t)), \qquad (24)$$

where κ_i is the step size and $v'_i(p_i(t)) = 1 - \frac{e^{-\lambda^*}(1+\frac{p_i(t)T_i^s}{(1-p_i(t))T_{max}^s})}{1-p_i(t)}$. The choice of κ_i determines the convergence speed to a Nash equilibrium. According to [8], we choose $\kappa_i < \frac{2}{\beta+|N|-1}$. Intuitively, the conditional collision probability q_i can be viewed as the "penalty" paid for collisions of station i. If the marginal utility $v'_i(p_i(t))$ is greater than the penalty q_i at time slot t, the station needs to increase its transmission attempt probability at the next time slot $(t + 1)$, and vice versa. When the Nash equilibrium is reached, the station's transmission attempt probability remains unchanged if the network remains the same.

However, it is difficult to calculate q_i in a distributed manner. Thus, we need to calculate q_i via approximation. Specifically, let n_i be the number of consecutive idle slots between two transmission attempts (transmission or collision). According to [5], n_i can be regraded as a geometric distribution of $\Phi(\mathbf{p})$. Hence, the average number of idle slots $\bar{n}_i = \frac{\Phi(\mathbf{p})}{1-\Phi(\mathbf{p})}$. Station i can estimate its q_i using $\bar{n}_i$ as follows:

$$q_i = 1 - \frac{\Phi(\mathbf{p})}{1 - p_i} = \frac{1 - (\bar{n}_i + 1)p_i}{(\bar{n}_i + 1)(1 - p_i)}. \qquad (25)$$

We calculate $\bar{n}_i$ via the approach proposed in [5]. Each station updates its transmission attempt probability and contention window after n_{trans} number of transmissions. Therefore, $\bar{n}_i$ needs to be updated every n_{trans} transmission as well. We denote the total idle slots during the n_{trans} transmissions as sum_{idle}. To balance the convergence speed and the estimation accuracy, we use a weighted average to estimate $\bar{n}_i$:

$$\bar{n}_i(t + 1) \leftarrow \rho\bar{n}_i(t) + (1 - \rho)\frac{sum_{idle}}{n_{trans}}, \qquad (26)$$

where ρ is a weight within the range of $[0, 1]$.

6 Evaluation

In this section, we evaluate the performance of our algorithm in terms of throughput, fairness and collision ratio.

6.1 Configuration

In our evaluation, the performance of our proposed algorithm is compared with that of the following two widely accepted algorithms: 1) the default 802.11 DCF function [17]; 2) the Idle Sense algorithm [5].

Our evaluation is performed using the INET framework package for the Omnet++ simulation environment [18]. The INET framework is shipped with the default 802.11 DCF function. In addition, we implement the Idle Sense algorithm and our G-CSMA algorithm. In our implementation, the PHY and MAC parameters are defined as described in the IEEE 802.11 standard. Specifically, the basic parameters are listed in Table 1.

Table 1. PARAMETERS IN SIMULATION

Slot Time	$20\ \mu s$	ACK Length	$112\ bits$
SIFS / DIFS	$10 / 50\ \mu s$	MAC Header	$272\ bits$
PHY Header	$192\ bits$	Bitrate of ACK	$2\ Mbps$
Bitrate of PHY Header	$1\ Mbps$	Packet Payload	$12000\ bits$

The performance comparison is conducted in two popular wireless network deployment modes: 802.11b and 802.11b/g. For each mode, we consider a scenario with fast and slow competing stations. This scenario is introduced in [5], where k slow stations compete with $n - k$ fast stations. In our evaluation, the values of n are set to 5, 10, 15, 20, 30, 40 and 50, and the values of k are set to $\frac{n}{5}$. The bitrates of slow stations are set to 1Mbps for both 802.11b and 802.11b/g modes. The bitrates of fast stations are set to 11Mbps for 802.11b mode and 54Mbps for 802.11b/g mode, respectively.

We randomly place these n stations in the simulation area. In addition, we place one AP in the center of the area. Frames are generated at each station continuously and transmitted to the AP. We assume that all stations are static, and thus the rate adaption is disabled. The bitrate of each station is defined at the initialization phase and remains the same during the entire simulation period. We further assume that all stations have the same transmission power and the same Signal-to-Interference-plus-Noise-Ratio (SINR) threshold. The initial CW value is set to 7 for all the three algorithms. For our proposed algorithm and the Idle Sense algorithm, we both use ρ and $maxtrans$ to calculate the average number of consecutive idle slots. Specifically, ρ is set to 0.5 and $maxtrans$ is set to 10 for both algorithms. Our proposed algorithm has two unique variables that are step size κ_i and λ^*. We fix the step size κ_i to 0.015. The values of λ^* are set to 0.1625 and 0.2669 for 802.11b and 802.11b/g modes, respectively.

6.2 Results

We report our performance evaluation results in terms of fairness, throughput, and collision ratio. All results are averaged over 10 runs, and each run lasts 40 seconds.

Fairness. We evaluate the fairness of channel access time using the Jain's fairness index (JFI) proposed in [10]. Ideally, if the channel access time is evenly distributed to all stations, the Jain's fairness index should equal to 1. As it is shown in Fig. 1(a) and Fig. 1(b), the fairness index of our proposed algorithm consistently approaches to 1 in both network deployment modes. Clearly, our proposed algorithm greatly outperforms the existing schemes and effectively solves the performance anomaly problem.

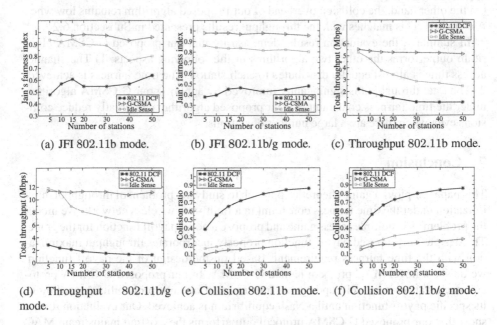

(a) JFI 802.11b mode.   (b) JFI 802.11b/g mode.   (c) Throughput 802.11b mode.

(d)   Throughput   802.11b/g   (e) Collision 802.11b mode.   (f) Collision 802.11b/g mode.
mode.

Fig. 1. Evaluation Results

Throughput. While assuring the fairness among all the stations, our objective is also to maximize the total throughput of the network. The aggregated throughput of our proposed algorithm is compared with that of the default 802.11 DCF and Idle Sense in Fig. 1(c) and Fig. 1(d). We can see that our proposed algorithm significantly outperforms the default 802.11 DCF in both modes. Such a substantial improvement is achieved by balancing the channel access time among all stations. Specifically, our proposed algorithm let fast stations transmit more frames because it takes less time for them to complete transmission compared the slow stations. As a results, slow stations are prevented from excessively occupying the channel. We also notice that our proposed algorithm outperforms the Idle Sense algorithm in most cases. Moreover, the throughput improvement of our algorithm is better when the number of stations becomes larger as shown in Fig. 1(c) and Fig. 1(d).

Collision. Collisions can severely degrade the network performance because the channel occupation time of a failure transmission (due to a collision) is almost equal to that of a successful transmission. As a result, the total throughput of the network will be greatly decreased if collisions occur frequently. Furthermore, excessive colliding frames may incur a large amount of retransmissions that flood the network, and thus, significantly increase the end to end delay. We measure the collision overhead by the ratio of the total collisions experienced by a station to its total number of transmissions. The detailed collision results are plotted in Fig. 1(e) and Fig. 1(f). We notice that when the number of competing stations n increases, the collision ratio of default 802.11 DCF approaches to 1 rapidly. That means the channel is exclusively occupied by collisions. On the other hand, the collision overhead of our proposed algorithm remains low when n increases. This matches with the throughput results presented in Subsection 6.2.

In summary, the evaluation results demonstrate that our proposed G-CSMA algorithm outperforms the other two algorithms in the following aspects: 1) The channel access time is almost equally distributed to each station. The time fairness is achieved; 2) The total throughput is significantly improved by applying our G-CSMA algorithm under the time fairness constraint; 3) Our proposed algorithm can greatly reduce collisions even when there are a large number of stations.

7   Conclusion

This paper employs a game-theoretic approach to study the problem of throughput maximization under the time fairness constraint in a multi-rate wireless network. We model the problem as a multiple access game and propose a novel payoff function for the game. The design our proposed payoff function properly incorporates throughput maximization with the time fairness requirement. Based on the design of the payoff function, we devise a novel MAC protocol named G-CSMA. In our proposed G-CSMA protocol, each station iteratively updates its transmission attempt probability according to its specific payoff function until a Nash equilibrium is achieved. Our evaluation results show that our proposed G-CSMA protocol outperforms the existing mainstream MAC protocols in terms of time fairness and throughput.

Acknowledgment. The authors would like to thank the support from the National Natural Science Foundation of China (Grant No. 61172074 and 61073160) and the National Science Foundation of the US (CNS-0831852).

References

1. Heusse, M., Rousseau, F., Berger-Sabbatel, G., Duda, A.: Performance anomaly of 802.11b. In: INFOCOM 2003, vol. 2, pp. 836–843. IEEE Press (2003)
2. Jiang, L., Liew, S.: Proportional fairness in wireless lans and ad hoc networks. In: WCNC 2005, vol. 3, pp. 1551–1556. IEEE Press (2005)
3. Banchs, A., Serrano, P., Oliver, H.: Proportional fair throughput allocation in multirate IEEE 802.11e wireless lans. Wirel. Netw. 13, 649–662 (2007)
4. Tan, G., Guttag, J.: Time-based fairness improves performance in multi-rate wlans. In: ATEC 2004. USENIX Association, Berkeley (2004)
5. Heusse, M., Rousseau, F., Guillier, R., Duda, A.: Idle Sense: an optimal access method for high throughput and fairness in rate diverse wireless lans. In: SIGCOMM 2005, pp. 121–132. ACM, New York (2005)

6. Felegyhazi, M., Hubaux, J.P.: Game theory in wireless networks: A tutorial, 1–15 (2007)
7. Saad, W., Han, Z., Debbah, M., HjØrungnes, A., Başar, T.: Coalitional game theory for communication networks: A tutorial. IEEE Signal Processing (2009)
8. Chen, L., Low, S., Doyle, J.: Random access game and medium access control design. IEEE/ACM Transactions on Networking 18, 1303–1316 (2010)
9. Bertsekas, D., Gallager, R.: Data Networks, 2nd edn. Prentice-Hall, Englewood Cliffs (1992)
10. Jain, R., Chui, D., Hawe, W.: A quantitative measure of fairness and discrimination for resource allocation in shared systems. Technical report, Digital Equipment Institution (1984)
11. Srivastava, V., Neel, J.M.: Using game theory to analyze wireless ad hoc networks. IEEE Communications Surveys Tutorials 7(4), 46–56 (2005)
12. Cagalj, M., Ganeriwalt, S., Aad, I., Hubaux, J.P.: On selfish behavior in csma/ca networks vol. 4, pp. 2513–2524 (2005)
13. Jin, Y., Kesidis, G.: Equilibria of a noncooperative game for het-erogeneous users of an aloha networks. IEEE Commun. Lett. 6(7), 282–284 (2002)
14. Chen, L., Low, S.H., Doyle, J.C.: Contention control: A game-theoretic approach. In: Proc. IEEE CDC, pp. 3428–3434 (2007)
15. Bianchi, G.: Performance analysis of the IEEE 802.11 distributed coordination function. IEEE Journal on Selected Areas in Communications 18(3), 535–547 (2000)
16. Flåm, S.D.: Equilibrium, evolutionary stability and gradient dynamics
17. IEEE: IEEE 802.11: Wireless LAN Medium Access Control (MAC) and Physical Layer (PHY) Specifications (2007)
18. OMNeT++, http://www.omnetpp.org

Forced Spectrum Access Termination Probability Analysis under Restricted Channel Handoff

MohammadJavad NoroozOliaee[1], Bechir Hamdaoui[1],
Taieb Znati[2], and Mohsen Guizani[3]

[1] Oregon State University
noroozom@onid.edu, hamdaoui@eecs.orst.edu
[2] University of Pittsburgh
znati@cs.pitt.edu
[3] Qatar University
mguizani@ieee.org

Abstract. Most existing works on cognitive radio networks assume that cognitive (or secondary) users are capable of switching/jumping to any available channel, regardless of the frequency gap between the target and the current channels. Due to hardware limitations, cognitive users can actually jump only so far from where the operating frequency of their current channel is, given an acceptable switching delay that users are typically constrained by. This paper studies the performance of cognitive radio networks with dynamic multichannel access capability, but while considering realistic channel handoff assumptions, where cognitive users can only move/jump to their immediate neighboring channels.

Specifically, we consider a cognitive access network with m channels in which a cognitive user, currently using a particular channel, can only switch to one of its k immediate neighboring channels. This set of $2k$ channels is referred to as the *target handoff channel set*. We first model this cognitive access network with restricted channel handoff as a continuous-time Markov process, and then analytically derive the forced termination probability of cognitive users. Finally, we validate and analyze our derived results via simulations. Our obtained results show that the forced access termination probability of cognitive users decreases significantly as the number k increases.

1 Introduction

Dynamic spectrum access or cognitive radio access network paradigm allows cognitive (or secondary) users (CUs) to exploit unused licensed spectrum on an instant-by-instant basis, so long as it causes no harm to primary users (PUs). That is, CUs must make sure that the licensed band is vacant before using it, and must vacate the band immediately upon the return of any PUs to their licensed band.

Cognitive radio has great potential for improving spectrum efficiency and increasing achievable network throughput of wireless communication systems. As

X. Wang et al. (Eds.): WASA 2012, LNCS 7405, pp. 358–365, 2012.

a result, it has generated significant research interests and resulted in numerous papers over this past decade. The research issues and topics that have been addressed in recent years in this regard are also numerous, ranging from fundamental networking issues to practical and implementation ones. Examples of investigated issues pertaining to cognitive networking, just to name a few, are performance modelling and characterization [3, 14, 15], spectrum access management [2, 4, 19], adaptive and learning technique development [5, 12, 16, 21], network architectures [9, 17, 18], spectrum prediction models [1, 10, 11], and protocol design [6, 13, 20]. One common shortcoming with most existing works on cognitive radio networks is that it is almost always assumed that cognitive (or secondary) users are capable of switching/jumping to any available channel, regardless of the frequency gap between the target channel and the current channel. This is not realistic [7, 8]. Due to hardware limitations, cognitive users can actually jump only so far from where the operating frequency of their current channel is, given an acceptable switching delay that users are typically constrained by [7, 8]. This paper studies the performance of cognitive radio networks, but while considering realistic channel handoff/switching assumptions, where CUs can only move/jump to channels that are immediate neighbors of their current operating channels.

The focus of this work is then on cognitive wireless networks that are enabled with dynamic multichannel access, but with limited channel handoff/switching capability. Specifically, we consider a cognitive access network with m channels in which cognitive user, currently using a particular channel and needing to vacate it due for e.g. to the return of its PUs, can only switch to one of its k immediate (from above and below) neighboring channels. This set of $2k$ channels is referred to as the *target handoff channel set*.

In this paper, we first model the cognitive access network with restricted channel handoff as a continuous-time Markov process. Then, we analytically derive the forced access termination probability of cognitive users, defined as the probability that a CU, already accessing and using a channel whose PU is returned, is forced to cease communication as a result of none of the channels in its target handoff channel set is vacant. Finally, we validate and analyze our derived results via MATLAB simulation. Our results show the impact of the channel handoff restriction in cognitive radio access on the probability of users being forced to terminate access to the system. Our obtained results show that the forced access termination probability of cognitive users decreases significantly as the number of target handoff channels increases for a fixed primary user load. The results also show that the gap between the forced termination probabilities for different numbers of target handoff channel set sizes increases with the primary user arrival rate.

To summarize, our contributions in this work are: 1) performance modelling of cognitive radio network access with limited spectrum handoff, 2) validation of our derived analytic results via simulations, and 3) study and analysis of the impact of spectrum handoff restriction on the performance behaviors of cognitive radio networks with multichannel access capability.

The rest of the paper is organized as follows. In Section 2, we state the system model. In Section 3, we model and derive analytically the forced termination probability. Section 4 validates the derived results, and analyzes the performance behaviors. Finally, in Section 5, we conclude our work.

2   Multichannel Access Model

We consider a cognitive radio multichannel access system with m primary bands, $B_1,...,B_m$, where each band is composed of n sub-bands, giving a total of mn sub-bands, termed $A_1,...,A_{mn}$. Two types of users are present in the system. Primary users (PUs) who have exclusive access rights to B_1 to B_m, and cognitive users (CUs) who are allowed to use the A_1 to A_{mn} sub-bands, but in an opportunistic manner; i.e., so long as they do not cause any harmful interference to PUs. While PUs have strict priority to use the spectrum bands, CUs are allowed to use a sub-band only when the sub-band's associated primary band is vacant; i.e., not being used by any PUs. Thus, we assume that CUs are always aware of the presence of PUs, and that as soon as any PUs reclaim their band, CUs are capable of immediately vacating the band and switch to another idle sub-band, if any exists. This is called spectrum handoff [22]. In our model, we assume that, during spectrum handoff, CUs can jump to any channel/band situated at no more than k bands away from its current operating band; the set of possible channels to which a CU is able to jump to is referred to as the *target handoff channel set*. Specifically, if an CU is currently using a sub-band belonging to primary band B_i, the CU can only jump to any sub-band from B_{i-k} to B_{i+k} when handoff is initiated. The number k is called the steps that a cognitive user is able to jump in each spectrum handoff.

3   Performance Modelling

We model the channel selection process as a continuous-time Markov process. The process is defined by its states and transition rates. In this section, we define the states and calculate the state transition rates.

As stated previously, mn sub-bands are shared by both primary and cognitive users. Thus, we define each state as an m-tuple $(i_1, ..., i_m)$ in which i_j, for $j = 1, 2, ..., m$, indicates the number of CUs in band j if $i_j > -1$, otherwise i_j is equal to -1, indicating that band j is occupied by a primary user. Note that i_j takes on values between -1 and n (i.e., $-1 \leq i_j \leq n$). Thus, the total number of states is $(n+2)^m$ and all these states are valid.

We assume that arrivals of cognitive users and primary users both follow Poisson processes with arrival rates λ_c and λ_p, respectively, and the service times are exponentially distributed with rates μ_c and μ_p, respectively.

There are four cases/events under which a state changes, and thus we only have to consider these four cases to compute the transition rate matrix, known as Q. In what follows, let $(i_1, ..., i_m)$ be the current state.

Case 1: First, consider that a cognitive user arrives to the system and selects spectrum band j. The next possible states are then $(i_1, ..., i_j + 1, ..., i_m)$ for all

$-1 < i_j < n$. Assuming that the number of these states is l, the transition rate from $(i_1, ..., i_m)$ to $(i_1, ..., i_j + 1, ..., i_m)$ is then λ_c/l. The states whose i_j value is either -1 or n do not change, because the cognitive user will be blocked and denied access to the system in this case.

Case 2: Second, consider that a cognitive user leaves spectrum band j. In this case, the next possible states are $(i_1, ..., i_j - 1, ..., i_m)$ for all $i_j > 0$. Thus, the transition rates from $(i_1, ..., i_m)$ to $(i_1, ..., i_j - 1, ..., i_m)$ is $i_j \mu_s$.

Case 3: Third, when a primary user leaves band j, the next states are $(i_1, ..., i'_j, ..., i_m)$ where $i'_j = 0$ and $i_j = -1$. Assuming that the number of occupied bands by primary users is l which means that the number of next states is l, the transition rate from $(i_1, ..., i_m)$ to $(i_1, ..., i'_j, ..., i_m)$ is then μ_p/l, where as stated earlier $i'_j = 0$ and $i_j = -1$.

Case 4: Fourth, consider that a primary user arrives to spectrum band j. Note that primary users do not select any band upon their arrivals, since they already have their predefined bands to operate on. In this case, the next states are $(i_1, ..., i'_{j-k}, ..., i'_j, ..., i'_{j+k}, ..., i_m)$ where $i'_j = -1$ and $\left(\sum_{l=j-k, l \neq j}^{j+k} i'_l = i_j \right)$ if user is not forced to terminate. User access termination occurs when none of the adjacent bands can accommodate the cognitive user that is required to vacate band j. Thus, the next states are $(i_1, ..., i'_{j-k}, ..., i'_j, ..., i'_{j+k}, ..., i_m)$ where $i'_j = -1$ and $i'_l = n$ for $i - k \leq l \leq i + k$. When the user is forced to terminate, the transition rate is λ_p, and when there is no termination, the transition rate is as follows

$$\gamma_{s'}^s = \lambda_p \left(\frac{1}{2k - \sum_{l=j-k, i'_l=-1}^{j+k} 1} \right)^{i_j} \prod_{l=0, l \neq k}^{2k} \binom{i_j}{i'_{j-k+l} - i_{j-k+l}} \tag{1}$$

where $\gamma_{s'}^s$ denotes the transition rate from state s to state s', where $s = (i_1, ..., i_m)$ and $s' = (i'_1, ..., i'_m)$. Thus far, we computed the transition rates, and we were able to determine the transition matrix Q. One can now solve the system of equations

$$\pi.Q = 0 \text{ and } \sum_{i=1}^{(n+2)^m} \pi_i = 1$$

where π_i is the stationary probability of state i and π is the stationary probability matrix.

Now, the forced termination probability P_f of a cognitive user can be defined as

$$P_f = \frac{\sum_{(s,s') \in T} \pi_s \gamma_{s'}^s}{(1 - P_b)\lambda_c}. \tag{2}$$

where T is the set that contains all state pairs (s, s') in which a user is forced to terminate when transitioning from s to s', and P_b is the blocking probability to be defined later. Formally, T can be defined as

$$T = \{(s, s') = ((i_1, ..., i_m), (i'_1, ..., i'_m)) | N_c(s) > N_c(s') \text{ and } N_p(s) < N_p(s')\}$$

where $N_c(s)$ and $N_c(s')$ are the numbers of cognitive users in state s and s', respectively, and $N_p(s)$ and $N_p(s')$ are the numbers of primary users in state s and s', respectively. The number of cognitive users in state $s = (i_1, ..., i_m)$, $N_c(s)$, can be written as

$$N_c(s) = \sum_{j=1, i_j \neq -1}^{m} i_j$$

Similarly, the number of primary users in state $s = (i_1, ..., i_m)$, $N_p(s)$, can be written as

$$N_p(s) = \sum_{j=1, i_j = -1}^{m} 1$$

When a new cognitive user arrives to the system and cannot find any empty sub-band, because the bands are occupied by primary users or any other cognitive users, the user is denied access to the system. In this case, we say that the user is blocked. The blocking probability P_b of a cognitive user trying to access the system can then be written as

$$P_b = \sum_{s \in B} \frac{\pi_s \lambda_c}{\sum\limits_{s \in S, s \neq s'} \gamma_{s'}^s} \tag{3}$$

where B is the set of all the states in which blocking occurs when a new cognitive user arrives to the system, and is defined as

$$B = \{s = (i_1, ..., i_m) | \forall j \ 1 \leq j \leq m, \ -1 < i_j < n\}$$

4   Analysis and Validation

In this section, we validate our analytic results via MATLAB simulations, and analyze the performance of cognitive radio systems with multichannel access capabilities by studying the impact of the target handoff channel set size on the forced termination probability. For this, we consider evaluating a multichannel access cognitive system with $m = 7$ primary bands, each having $n = 2$ sub-bands.

Fig.1 plots the forced termination probability of cognitive users that we analytically derived in this work as a function of the primary user arrival rate λ_p for three different values of the number of target handoff channels, k. First and as expected, observe that as the primary user arrival rate (i.e., PU load) increases, the probability that cognitive users (already using the system) are forced to leave the system due to not finding an available band in their target handoff channel set increases. Second, for a given primary user arrival rate λ_p, the greater the

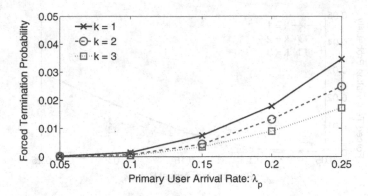

Fig. 1. Analytic results: forced termination probability as a function of the primary arrival rate λ_p for $k = 1, 2, 3$

number of target handoff channels, the lower the forced termination probability. Again, this trend of performance behavior is expected, as having more channels to switch to increases the chances of cognitive users finding available bands, which explains the decrease in the forced termination probability of cognitive users. Third, the gap between the forced termination probabilities for different numbers of target handoff channel set sizes increases with the primary user arrival rate.

Now that we investigated the performance behaviors of cognitive radio systems through the derived analytic results, we next focus on validating these derived models. For this we use MATLAB to simulate a multichannel system with primary and cognitive users arriving to the system according to Poisson process with arrival rates λ_p and λ_c, respectively. In these simulations, we compute the actual forced termination probability of cognitive users, measured as the ratio of the number of terminated users to the total number of accepted users. Fig. 2 shows the values of forced termination probabilities of the simulated cognitive network again for three values of k. Observe that the simulated performance behaviors of cognitive systems in terms of the forced termination probability match well those obtained via our analytically derived results. This validates our derived models.

To summarize, our findings in this work demonstrate the impact of the commonly made assumption of considering that cognitive users are able to handoff/switch to any available band, regardless of how far the target band is from the current band, on the performance behaviors of cognitive radio systems. Our results show the importance of considering realistic spectrum handoff (i.e., with restricted/limited target handoff channel set) when assessing the achievable cognitive radio performances. Although the performance metric investigated in this work is the forced access termination probability of cognitive users already using the system, one can easily project this analysis on other performance metrics, such as the per-user achievable throughput and user blocking probability, which are kept for future investigation.

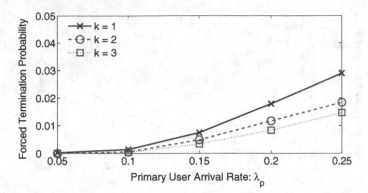

Fig. 2. Simulation results: forced termination probability as a function of the primary arrival rate λ_p for $k = 1, 2, 3$

5   Conclusion

This paper investigates the performance behaviors of cognitive radio networks enabled with dynamic multichannel access, but while considering realistic channel handoff assumptions, where cognitive users are only allowed to switch to vacant channels that are immediate neighbors of their current channels. Using Markovian analysis, we model cognitive access networks with restricted channel handoff as a continuous-time Markov process, and analytically derive the forced access termination probability of cognitive users that are already using the system. Using MATLAB, we also validate our derived results via simulations.

Our obtained results demonstrate the impact of considering realistic channel handoff restriction in cognitive radio access on the probability of cognitive users being forced to terminate access to the system, and show that the forced access termination probability decreases significantly as the number of target handoff channels increases. This work demonstrates the cognitive radio performance implications of the commonly made assumption of allowing cognitive users to switch to any available band, regardless of how far the target band is from the current band. These performance implications translate in terms of forced access termination probability as well as long-term achievable throughput and access blocking probability of cognitive users.

References

1. Ahmad, S.H.A., Liu, M., Javidi, T., Zhao, Q., Krishnamachari, B.: Optimality of myopic sensing in multi-channel opportunistic access. IEEE Transactions on Information Theory (2009)
2. Chen, L., Iellamo, S., Coupechoux, M., Godlewski, P.: An auction framework for spectrum allocation with interference constraint in cognitive radio networks. In: Proceedings of IEEE INFOCOM (2010)

3. Feng, Z., Yang, Y.: Throughput analysis of secondary networks in dynamic spectrum access networks. In: Proceedings of IEEE INFOCOM (2010)
4. Gur, G., Bayhan, S., Alagoz, F.: Cognitive femtocell networks: an overlay architecture for localized dynamic spectrum access. IEEE Wireless Communications 17(4) (2010)
5. Hamdaoui, B.: Adaptive spectrum assessment for opportunistic access in cognitive radio networks. IEEE Transactions on Wireless Communications 8(2), 922–930 (2009)
6. Hamdaoui, B., Shin, K.G.: OS-MAC: An efficient MAC protocol for spectrum-agile wireless networks. IEEE Transactions on Mobile Computing (August 2008)
7. Harada, H.: A software defined cognitive radio prototype. In: Proc. of IEEE PIMRC (2007)
8. Harada, H.: A feasibility study on software defined cognitive radio equipment. In: Proc. of IEEE DySPAN (2008)
9. Mitola III, J.: Cognitive radio: an integrated agent architecture for software-defined radio. Dissertation, Computer Comm. System Lab, Dept. of Teleinformatics, Royal Inst. Tech., Sotckholm, Sweden (2000)
10. Kim, H., Shin, K.G.: Efficient discovery of spectrum oppotunities with MAC-layer sensing in cognitive radio networks. IEEE Transactions on Mobile Computing (May 2008)
11. Li, X., Zhao, Q.C., Guan, X., Tong, L.: Optimal cognitive access of markovian channels under tight collision constraints. IEEE Journal on Selected Areas in Communications, Special Issue on Advances in Cognitive Radio Networks and Communications (to appear, 2011)
12. Liu, K., Zhao, Q.: Distributed learning in cognitive radio networks: multi-armed brandit with distributed multiple players. Submitted to IEEE Int. Conf. on Acousitcs, Speech, and Signal Processing (2010)
13. Ma, M., Tsang, D.H.K.: Joint design of spectrum sharing and routing with channel heterogeneity in cognitive radio networks. Physical Communication 2(1-2) (2009)
14. Ma, Y., Kim, D.I., Wu, Z.: Optimization of OFDMA-based cellular cognitive radio networks. IEEE Transactions on Communications 58(8) (2010)
15. Marshall, P.F.: Dynamic spectrum access as a mechanism for transition to interference tolerant systems. In: Proceedings of IEEE DySPAN (2010)
16. NoroozOliaee, M., Hamdaoui, B., Tumer, K.: Efficient objective functions for coordinated learning in large-scale distributed osa systems. IEEE Transactions on Mobile Computing (to appear)
17. Sahin, M.E., Arslan, H.: System design for cognitive radio communications. In: Proceedings of Int'l Conference on Cognitive Radio Oriented Wireless Networks and Communications (June 2006)
18. Sutton, P., et al: Iris: an architecture for cognitive radio networking testbeds. IEEE Communications Magazine 48(9) (2010)
19. Teleghan, M.A., Hamdaoui, B.: Efficiency-revenue optimality tradeoffs in dynamic spectrum allocation. In: Proc. of IEEE GLOBECOM (2010)
20. Timmers, M., Pollin, S., Dejonghe, A., der Perre, L.V., Catthoor, F.: A distributed multichannel MAC protocol for multihop cognitive radio networks. IEEE Transactions on Vehicular Technology 59(1) (2010)
21. Unnikrishnan, J., Veeravalli, V.V.: Algorithms for dynamic spectrum access with learning for cognitive radio. IEEE Transactions on Signal Processing 58(2) (August 2010)
22. Xiaorong Zhu, L.S., Yum, T.S.P.: Analysis of cognitive radio spectrum access with optimal channel reservation. IEEE Communications Letters 11(4), 304–306 (2007)

Energy-Efficient Robust Coverage under Uncertainty in Wireless Sensor Networks

Yafeng Zhao[1], Khuong Vu[2], Jiming Chen[3], Rong Zheng[2], and Chuanhou Gao[1]

[1] Department of Mathematics, Zhejiang University, China
[2] Department of Computer Science ,University of Huston, USA
[3] State Key Lab. of Industrial Control Technology, Zhejiang University, China
{yafngzh,gaochou}@zju.edu.cn,
{khuong.vu,rzheng}@cs.uh.edu,
jmchen@iipc.zju.edu.cn

Abstract. Uncertainty in the actual locations of sensors is prevalent in real deployments of wireless sensor networks (WSNs). As a result, existing algorithms and important results concerning sensor coverage need to be revisited. In this paper, we consider the issue of energy-efficient robust coverage in WSNs, where location uncertainty is modeled by bounding disks around the nominal (or intended) locations. Robust coverage is achieved by the use of a new distance metric that accounts for such uncertainty. Energy efficiency is made possible by i) judiciously selecting a set of active sensors, and ii) reduction in the sensing radii. We devise localized algorithms that are proven to ensure full coverage of region of interest while conserving energy. Extensive simulation study demonstrates the effectiveness of the proposed approach.

Keywords: WSNs, uncertainty, energy efficiency, coverage.

1 Introduction

Wireless sensor networks (WSNs) have wide applications in many areas such as military surveillance, infrastructure protection, and scientific exploration [3] [1] [7] [6]. While many implementations are limited to small-scale experiments or applications with only dozens or hundreds of sensors, recent advances in wireless communications and electronics have promoted the research of low-cost sensors [5] and large scale deployments are becoming feasible. However, due to the limitation of battery technologies, energy efficient operations in WSNs remain to be a challenging issue.

One technique to reduce energy consumption in densely deployed WSNs is through controlling the duty cycle of sensor nodes. Network lifetime can be extended by selectively putting a subset of sensors to low-power modes while maintaining the required coverage of the region of interest (RoI). In guaranteeing the sensor coverage, most existing solutions assume that sensor locations are exact. However, such an assumption rarely holds in practice. Even with on-board GPS receivers on all or selected nodes, or execution of distributed location

X. Wang et al. (Eds.): WASA 2012, LNCS 7405, pp. 366–377, 2012.
© Springer-Verlag Berlin Heidelberg 2012

algorithms, there generally exists uncertainty in sensor location. Furthermore, carefully positioned in the deployment phase, sensors may be displaced due to environmental or human factors during the course of operation.

In [8], Vu and Zheng propose the notion of robust coverage that explicitly accounts for location uncertainty. Location uncertainty is modeled by a bounding circular disk around a sensor's nominal location. The problem of determining the *common* sensing radius that ensures k-coverage of the *RoI* can be solved through the construction of order-k Voronoi diagram of disks, called order-k *max VD*. The algorithm in [8] is centralized requiring knowledge of all sensors. The use of *common* sensing radius suffers from the problem of redundant coverage. For example, as shown in Figure 1, to provide full coverage of a 500x320 field with 23 sensors, around 90% of the area is 2 or more-covered.

In this paper, we address the deficiency of the aforementioned solutions, and propose distributed energy-efficient robust algorithms that ensure full coverage of the *RoI* in presence of location uncertainty. We devise two algorithms to construct max VD and prove their accuracy. To further improve energy efficiency, a sensor selection procedure, which chooses a set of active sensors, is applied. Extensive simulation results show the correctness and effectiveness of the proposed algorithms.

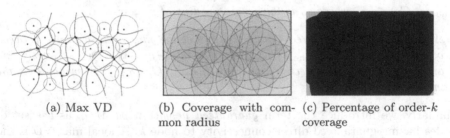

(a) Max VD   (b) Coverage with common radius   (c) Percentage of order-k coverage

Fig. 1. 23 sensors randomly deployed in the area of 500x320. Dots are sensors' nominal locations. In Figure 1a, disks are uncertainty areas, green arcs are Voronoi edges in max VDs. Solid disks in Figure 1b are coverage areas of sensors. In Figure 1c, light areas are exactly 1-covered, while the dark area is 2-or-higher covered. 90% of area is 2- or higher covered.

The rest of the paper is organized as follows. In Section 2, we introduce the network model and necessary terminologies and notations. The algorithms for constructing max VD are presented in Section 3. Theoretical analysis and design of energy-efficient robust coverage algorithm are provided in Section 4. In Section 5, we present the evaluation results followed by conclusion and future work in Section 6.

2   Preliminaries

In this section, we introduce the network model, terminologies and notations used in the rest of the paper.

2.1   Network Model

Consider n sensors $S = \{1, 2, \ldots, n\}$ in the RoI, a bounded convex 2-D polygonal region. Sensor i's *actual* location is assumed to be uniformly distributed in a disk $C_i(o_i, r_i)$ centered at its *nominal* location o_i with r_i being the uncertainty radius. Since the exact locations of sensors are unknown, some sensors may locate outside RoI. In [5], the authors categorize the sensors into internal sensors and periphery sensors. In this paper, we assume that all the sensors are intended to be deployed in RoI, i.e., $o_i \in RoI, 1 \le i \le n$. Incidents of periphery sensors are due to deployment errors. Thus, we do not make a distinction between internal and periphery nodes.

Definition 1. *(Robust point coverage) Define the maximum distance from a point p to a sensor as $d_{max}(p, C_k) = d(p, o_k) + r_k$, where $d(\cdot, \cdot)$ is the Euclidean distance. A point p in RoI is guaranteed to be covered by sensor k iff the max distance between sensor k and point p is less than k's sensing radius, i.e., $d_{max}(p, C_k) \le s_k$, where s_k is the sensing radius of sensor k.*

Definition 2. *(Robust direct connectivity) Let the maximum distance between two disks C_i and C_k as $d_{max}(C_i, C_k) = d(o_i, o_k) + r_i + r_k$. Two sensors i and k are guaranteed to be directly connected iff $d_{max}(C_i, C_k) \le T$, where T is the transmission range.*

Similarly, we introduce the term *guaranteed neighborhood* MN_k as the set of nodes having guaranteed direct connectivity to node k. A local max VD is the union of *local* Voronoi cells generated by sensors k and their respective guaranteed neighbors. Formally, let $D(C_k, C_i) = \{p | d_{max}(p, C_k) \le d_{max}(p, C_i), p \in RoI\}$. Then, $\mathcal{V}_k(S) = \bigcap_{i \in S, i \ne k} D(C_k, C_i)$ is the Voronoi cell of k in the RoI; and $\mathcal{W}_k(S) = \bigcap_{i \in MN_k, i \ne k} D(C_k, C_i)$ is the local Voronoi cell of k with respective to its guaranteed neighbors.

Consider a sensor k with sensing radius s_k. The average energy cost for sensing is modeled as $E_k = f(s_k)$ in one time slot, where $f(\cdot)$ is a (known but unspecified) function. It should be noted that our proposed algorithm is valid for other forms of energy model.

We assume that the transmission radii and the maximum sensing radii are uniform among all sensors. Furthermore, the transmission radius is at least twice the maximum sensing radius, that is, $T \ge 2s_{max}$. When the locations of sensors are exact, it has been proven that a complete coverage of a convex area implies connectivity among the set of active nodes in [10]. With uncertainty in sensor locations, a similar result will be proven. This allows us to focus on the coverage problem solely.

Finally, we consider a general placement of sensors, where a number of pathological cases are avoided. First, no two sensors locate at the same nominal location (and thus no two uncertain disks are co-circular). Second, no point is of equal distance to more than three sensors according to the d_{max} distance measure. The proposed algorithms can be generalized to handle these cases but are omitted in this paper.

2.2   Notations

Here we summarize the notations which are used throughout the paper.

S The set of sensors $\{1, 2, \ldots, n\}$.

$C_k(o_k, r_k)$ Sensor k centered at o_k with the uncertainty radius r_k. C_k is often used for simplicity.

e_{ij} The edge of the max VD corresponding to disks C_i and C_j.

$\mathcal{V}_k(S)$ The max VD region corresponding to disk C_k. MV_k is often used for simplicity.

$\mathcal{W}_k(S)$ The local max VD region for sensor k. We use $\mathcal{W}_k$ where no confusion occurs.

s_k The sensing radius of sensor k.

s_{max} The maximum sensing radius of all the sensors.

T The transmission radius of all the sensors.

RoI The region of interest. It is assumed to be a convex polygon.

2.3   Energy-Efficient Robust Coverage Problem

Consider the set of sensors $S = \{1, 2, \ldots, n\}$ in the RoI, and the locations of sensors are modeled as disks $D = \{C_1, C_2, \ldots, C_n\}$. The objective of energy-efficient robust coverage is to determine a subset of *connected* sensors $U \subseteq S$ such that every point $p \in RoI$ is *robustly* covered, and the total energy cost for sensing is minimized. Formally, we have the following optimization problem:

$$\min \sum_{i \in S} E_i$$
$$s.t. \begin{cases} \sum_{i \in S} x_i \mathbb{I}_{\{d_{max}(p, C_i) \leq s_i\}} \geq 1, \forall p \in RoI \\ E_i = x_i f(s_i) \\ x_i \in \{0, 1\}, \forall i \in S, \end{cases}$$

where x_i is a binary decision variable indicating whether sensor i is active or not. The first inequality implies that the RoI needs to be 1-covered. Even when s_i is known, the above problem is NP-hard [4]. The hardness lies in the fact that the union of coverage area is generally hard to characterize. When s_is are decision variables, the problem becomes more challenging. Next, we will first develop exact algorithms for distributed computation of max VD, and then give a heuristic algorithm for this problem.

3   Construction of Max VD

In this section, we shall introduce two methods to construct max VD. One is distributed for general settings, and the other is a localized algorithm with some restrictive assumption of the network topology.

3.1   Distributed Max VD

The distributed construction of max VD is an extension of the approach in [2] for Voronoi Diagram. We assume that each sensor knows its own nominal location and the uncertainty radius. Two sensors are Voronoi *neighbors* if they share a Voronoi edge, and are *adjacent* if they are within the transmission range of each other.

The procedure consists of two steps: *Voronoi cell refinement* and *neighbor identification*. The basic idea is to incrementally identify each sensor's Voronoi neighbors through their currently known neighbors and refine the Voronoi cells accordingly. Consider sensor i and the set of sensors M that are known to i. The max Voronoi cell of i, $\mathcal{V}_i(S)$ is contained in the intersection of $D(C_i, C_j)$, $\forall j \in M$, namely, $\mathcal{V}_i(S) \subseteq \bigcap_{j \in M} D(C_i, C_j)$.

As any new sensor becomes known to i, the estimate of $\mathcal{V}_i(S)$ is updated. Sensors do not attempt to discover their Voronoi neighbors directly. Instead, they are informed about potential neighbors by their existing Voronoi neighbors. The neighbor identification is done as follows. M is initialized to S_i's set of adjacent sensors, a refinement step is then performed for i. Next, i iterates through each Voronoi vertex (i, u, v) of its cell (created by the intersection of bisectors of $(e_{i,u}, e_{u,v}, e_{i,v})$, and informs sensor u about v, and v about u. u and v are potential neighbors of each other, and a refinement step follows at each sensor. If a change happens after the refinement at a sensor, it informs its neighbors. The process continues until no further change happens.

3.2   Localized Max VD

In a general placement, Voronoi neighbors can be outside the transmission range, in fact in the worst case can be $n - 1$ hops away (for n sensors) (Figure 2). Therefore, the worst case message complexity is $O(n)$ to identify the Voronoi neighbors of a single sensor. However, we show next when the transmission range is at least twice as much as the maximum sensing range, one-hop neighbors within the transmission range suffice to construct max VD. In other words, $\mathcal{V}_k(S) = \mathcal{W}_k(S), \forall k \in S$. This eliminates the need for neighbour identification in the distributed construction. We call it *localized max VD*.

Theorem 1. *Assume transmission radius is at least twice the sensing radius, i.e. $T \geq 2s_{max}$ and RoI is 1-covered when using the maximum sensing radius at each sensor. If sensors i and j are max VD neighbors, then $d_{max}(C_i, C_j) \leq T$.*

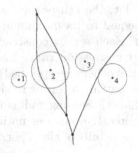

Fig. 2. Node 1 is one max Voronoi neighbor of 4. However, they are 3-hops away and node 1 is not a direct neighbor of 4.

Proof. We prove by contradiction. Assume $d_{max}(C_i, C_j) > T$. On the bisector of i and j, $e_{ij} \neq \phi$, there exists a point p, such that $d_{max}(p, C_i) = d_{max}(p, C_j)$. From the triangle inequality, we have

$$d_{max}(p, C_i) + d_{max}(p, C_j) \geq d_{max}(C_i, C_j).$$

By the definition of max VD, $d_{max}(p, C_i) = d_{max}(p, C_j) < d_{max}(p, C_k), \forall k \neq i, j$. Since p is 1-covered, there exists a sensor l such that $d_{max}(p, C_l) \leq s_{max}$. Thus, $d_{max}(p, C_i) \leq s_{max}$. Therefore, $d_{max}(C_i, C_j) \leq 2s_{max} \leq T$.

Corollary 1. *Let N_k, VN_k and MN_k be the set of neighbors within transmission range, Voronoi neighbors, and in robust direct connectivity with k, respectively. Then, we have $VN_k \subseteq MN_k \subseteq N_k$.*

Proof. From Theorem 1, we can conclude that $VN_k \subseteq MN_k$. If nodes i and j are guaranteed neighbors, i.e. $d_{max}(C_i, C_j) \leq T$, their actual distance $d(i, j) \leq d_{max}(C_i, C_j) \leq T$. Thus, $MN_k \subseteq N_k$.

From Corollary 1, we directly obtain the following results.

Corollary 2. *Under the conditions in Theorem 1, $\mathcal{V}_k(S) = \mathcal{W}_k(S)$.*

4   Energy-Efficient Robust Coverage

In this section, we introduce a heuristic algorithm to the energy-efficient robust coverage problem defined in Section 2.

The algorithm mainly consists of two parts: sensing radius refinement and active set selection. We divide time into slots. The robust coverage algorithm runs at the beginning of each slot. Sensing radius refinement adjusts the sensing radius to ensure full coverage of the *RoI* while minimizing redundantly covered area. Active set selection determines the set of sensors to be active in a slot. The remaining sensors are put to sleep mode to conserve energy. A sensor in sleep mode consumes only negligible amount of energy which we assume to be zero.

At the beginning of each slot, the sensors are all set active. For sensor k, it first set its sensing radius equal to its maximum sensing radius or the max VD cell, whichever is smaller. Each sensor constructs its local max VD based on information of sensors in transmission range and its guaranteed neighbors (shortened as "neighbors" unless otherwise specified). Active set is then decided based on the energy saving by putting a sensor to sleep (but possibly enlarging the sensing radius of its neighbors). Sensing radius is then further refined. The algorithm is carried out in an iterative manner until no further changes can be made. Next, we will present the details of the algorithm.

4.1   Sensing Radius Refinement

Given the max VD constructed by the algorithms in Section 3, the sensing radius s_k of sensor k is then determined by,

$$s_k = \max_{\{v | v \text{ is a vertice of } \mathcal{W}_k(S_a)\}} d_{max}(v, o_k), \tag{1}$$

where S_a is the set of active sensors, and the vertices of $MV_k(S_a)$ also include the intersections with RoI boundary.

4.2   Active Set Selection

We introduce *sleep benefit* as a measure to quantify the reduced energy cost by putting one sensor to sleep mode. Two factors need to be considered in determining the sleep benefit. The first is the spared energy by putting sensor k to sleep mode $f(s_k)$. The second is the additional energy consumed by other sensors to cover the Voronoi cell of the sleeping sensor. Combining these considerations, we define the following metric.

$$B_k = f(s_k) - \sum_{j \in VN_k} (f(s_j') - f(s_j)), \tag{2}$$

where E_k is the residual energy on node k, s_j and s_j' are the original and updated sensing radius of sensor j after the removal of sensor k. Not all sensors are eligible for power saving. One needs to check if the remaining sensors can still maintain full coverage. Fortunately, this can be done locally. It has been proven that the removal of a sensor results the tessellation of its Voronoi cell by its Voronoi neighbors [8]. Efficient $O(1)$ complexity algorithm exists to compute the (incremental) update to the local max VD. Consider sensor k. Upon the computation of the updated local max VD, sensor k determines the hypothetical sensing radii required for its neighbors by (1). If any of its neighbors' radius exceeds s_{max}, the sensor is not eligible to be put into sleep mode.

4.3   Energy-Efficient Robust Coverage Algorithm

Now we are in the position to present the robust coverage algorithm. The pseudo code of the algorithm is given in Algorithm 1.

The algorithm proceeds in iterations. Initially, all the sensors are active, and exchange their nominal locations and uncertainty radius information (Step 1). Each sensor computes the local max VD and determines its sensing radius by (1). It then computes its sleep benefit according to (2) and determines its eligibility for being in the sleep mode. The sensor with the highest sleep benefit becomes inactive. Ties are broken using lexical order of the node id. This process repeats until no more sensors can be put to the sleep mode. Finally, active sensors update their sensing radii by (1).

Algorithm 1. Energy-Efficient Robust Coverage Algorithm

1: Each sensor broadcasts its uncertainty information to its one-hop neighbors
2: $S_a \leftarrow S$.
3: **repeat**
4:     **for** $i \in S_a$ **do**
5:         i computes its local max VD, sensing radius and broadcasts the information
6:         **if** i is eligible **then**
7:             Compute its sleep benefit B_i
8:             **if** $B_i > \max_{j \in VN_i} B_j$ **then**
9:                 $S_a = S_a \backslash \{i\}$.
10:            **end if**
11:        **end if**
12:    **end for**
13: **until** No change in S_a

The algorithm executes in a fully distributed fashion. In each round, each sensor individually decides whether it is eligible for power saving based on its knowledge regarding its neighbors' state and sensing radius. Next we prove the correctness of the algorithm.

Lemma 1. *Sensing radius refinement does not reduce coverage. Formally, let S_a be the set of active sensors. Then,*

$$\bigcup_{i \in S_a} C(o_i, s_{max} - r_i) = \bigcup_{i \in S_a} C(o_i, s_i - r_i)$$

Proof. Consider an arbitrary point $p \in \bigcup_{i \in S_a} C(o_i, s_{max} - r_i)$, namely, p is covered by one of the active sensors. Let sensor k be the active sensor closest to p. Such a sensor exists as long as $S_a \neq \emptyset$. By (1), $d_{max}(o_k, p) \leq s_k \leq s_{max}$ (otherwise, p cannot be covered by any sensor with maximum sensing radis). Thus, p is covered by k.

Theorem 2. *Suppose the RoI is covered by the union of the maximum sensing regions of the sensors in S. The energy-efficient robust coverage algorithm ensures full coverage of the RoI.*

Proof. We know by Lemma 1 that sensing radius refinement does not decrease sensor coverage. Thus, it suffices to show that in each round, the active set selected ensures the coverage.

For any point $p \in RoI$, let $A(p)$ be the set of active sensors that can sense p, ie., $A(p) = \{k | p \in C(o_k, s_{max} - r_k), k \in S_a\}$ in the l-th round. Clearly, $A(p) \neq \emptyset$ before the first round when $S_a = S$. Let k be the sensor with the minimum sleep benefit among sensors in $A(p)$. To show that sensor k remains active in the $(l+1)$-th round and thus p is covered, we prove by contradiction.

By the criterion for active set selection, sensor k becomes inactive only when $B_k > max_{j \in VN_k} B_j$ and sensor k is eligible. Since k is eligible, $p \in \bigcup_{j \in VN_k} C(o_i, s_{max} - r_j)$. Thus $VN_k \subseteq A(p)$. Since sensor k has the highest sleep benefit among VN_k, it cannot possibly have the smallest sleep benefit among $A(p)$. Contradiction.

4.4   Handling Trivial Disks

Sensors whose uncertainty disks contains other sensors' uncertainty disks are associated with empty Voronoi cells [8] as there does not exists a point in the *RoI* that is closer to these disks than others. We call such uncertainty disks trivial disks. Given a sensor i, suppose there exists a sensor j such that $C_j \subset C_i$. The following relation holds: $d(o_i, o_j) < r_i - r_j$, or equivalently, $d(o_i, o_j) < (s_{max} - r_j) - (s_{max} - r_i)$. Therefore, $C(o_i, s_{max} - r_i) \subset C(o_j, s_{max} - r_j)$. In other words, sensor i does not contribute additional coverage region compared to sensor j. Thus, sensor i can generally be put into sleep mode. However, when sensor j's residual energy drops below ϵ, we wake sensor i up and include i in the robust coverage.

4.5   Relation between Coverage and Connectivity

It has been proven that when transmission radius is at least twice the maximum sensing radius, coverage implies connectivity [10] in absence of location uncertainty. We show this is also true when location uncertainty exists. This fact can be simply established by observing that robust coverage implies full coverage in absence of uncertainty.

5   Performance Evaluation

In this section, we perform simulation studies to evaluate the proposed algorithms. The *RoI* is a 50×50 region. The maximum sensing radius is set to be 12 and the transmission radius to be 24. The sensors are deployed in the region randomly with uniform distribution. The initial energy is 600000 units. And the energy model is given by $f(s_k) = s_k^4 + C$ [9], where s_k is the sensing radius and C is the energy cost including communication and other fixed costs set to be 20000. Though generally communication cost is dependent on the distance between the transceiver, since we assume fixed transmission radius, the cost can be approximated as a constant.

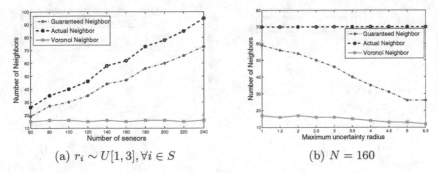

(a) $r_i \sim U[1,3], \forall i \in S$ (b) $N = 160$

Fig. 3. The number of neighbors of different types. RoI = 50x50. $T = 24$, $s_{max} = 12$.

5.1   Number of Neighbors

We first evaluate the number of sensors involved in constructing local max VD.
It has been proven in Corollary 1 that $VN_k \subseteq MN_k \subseteq N_k$. Ideally, only information among Voronoi neighbors VN_k need to be exchanged. However, since VN_k
is initially unknown, we have to resort to MN_k, the set of guaranteed neighbors.
In Figures 3a and 3b the mean number of three types of neighbors are given
with varying number of sensors in the RoI and uncertainty radius. As shown
in Figure 3a, both N_k and MN_k grow linearly with sensor density while VN_k
remains roughly constant. This is expected as more sensors are in the transmission ranges as the density increases. What is interesting is the gap between N_k
and MN_k. The size of MN_k is about 10% - 30% less than that of N_k. Thus,
consideration of MN_k reduces message complexity and storage complexity of
determining and refining local max VD structures. Similar observations can be
made in Figure 3b, which shows the impact of maximum uncertainty radius on
the number of neighbors. As the uncertainty increases, sizes of MN_k reduce as
the d_{max} distances among nodes become larger.

5.2   Reduced Redundant Coverage

Next we evaluate the reduced redundancy due to the use of sensing radius refinement and active set selection. We compare our approach with the case where
a common sensing radius is used. We apply the method in [8] to determine the
minimum common sensing radius for full coverage (also known as exposure).

To measure the redundancy, we compute the percentage of area in the RoI
that is 1-covered, 2-covered, etc. To do so, we divide the RoI into grids of width
0.01 and count the percentage of grid points that is k-covered, $k = 1, 2, \ldots$.
Figures 4 shows order-1–35 covered area with different number of sensors in the
RoI. As the sensor density grows, more area is redundantly covered when a
common sensing radius is used. This is because the exposure decreases only log-
arithmically with the number of sensors. In contrast, using the proposed energy-
efficient robust coverage algorithm, redundantly covered area is much reduced.

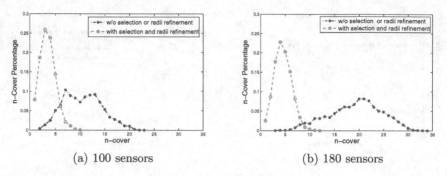

(a) 100 sensors   (b) 180 sensors

Fig. 4. Percentage of order-k coverage vs. the number of sensors. RoI = 50x50. $T = 24, s_{max} = 12$. $r_i \in [1,3], \forall i \in S$.

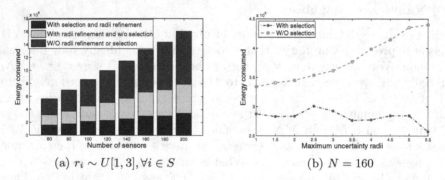

(a) $r_i \sim U[1,3], \forall i \in S$ (b) $N = 160$

Fig. 5. The energy consumed in one time slot by all the sensors

The average order of coverage remains roughly the same (around 5). Note that redundancy still exists due to the uncertainty of sensor locations.

5.3   Energy Savings

With fewer active sensors, significant energy savings can be attained. We evaluate the contribution of sensing radius refinement and active set selection. As a baseline, we include the energy consumption when all sensors are active and use maximum sensing radius. Figures 5a–5b show the energy consumed in one slot with different numbers of sensors in *RoI* and uncertainty radii. As shown in Figure 5a, sensors' energy consumption increases quickly without radius refinement and duty cycling as number of sensors increases. When radius refinement is introduced, energy consumption decreases about 50%. Furthermore, the energy consumption deliberately increases when duty cycling is performed. Figure 5b shows the energy consumption changes as the maximum uncertainty radius varies from 1 to 5.5. We observe that energy consumption with duty cycling decreases as the uncertainty radii increase. This is mainly because more and more trival disks appear and are put to sleep.

6   Conclusion

In this paper, we investigated energy-efficient robust coverage under location uncertainty in WSNs. A geometric structure corresponding to Voronoi diagram of disks was utilized to determine distributedly the minimum sensing radius needed at each sensor to maintain full coverage. Selection of the set of active sensors considered the tradeoff between putting a sensor to sleep mode and the need to possibly extend the sensing radius of its neighbors. The proposed algorithms have been shown to greatly reduce the amount of energy consumed for covering the *RoI*.

As future work, we are interested in extending the disk-based uncertainty model to account for probabilistic distribution of sensor's locations. Also of interest are efficient methods that reduce the uncertainty in sensor locations.

References

1. Al Ameen, M., Liu, J., Kwak, K.: Security and privacy issues in wireless sensor networks for healthcare applications. Journal of Medical Systems, 1–9 (2011)
2. Alsalih, W., Islam, K., Rodríguez, Y.N., Xiao, H.: Distributed voronoi diagram computation in wireless sensor networks. In: SPAA, p. 364 (2008)
3. Gungor, V., Lu, B., Hancke, G.: Opportunities and challenges of wireless sensor networks in smart grid. IEEE Transactions on Industrial Electronics 57(10), 3557–3564 (2011)
4. Gupta, H., Zhou, Z., Das, S., Gu, Q.: Connected sensor cover: self-organization of sensor networks for efficient query execution. IEEE/ACM Transactions on Networking 14, 55–67 (2006)
5. Mathur, G., Desnoyers, P., Chukiu, P., Ganesan, D., Shenoy, P.: Ultra-low power data storage for sensor networks. ACM Trans. Sen. Netw., 33:1–33:34 (2009)
6. Medina, D., Hoffmann, F., Ayaz, S., Rokitansky, C.-H.: Feasibility of an aeronautical mobile ad hoc network over the north atlantic corridor. In: 5th Annual IEEE Communications Society Conference on Sensor, Mesh and Ad Hoc Communications and Networks, SECON 2008, pp. 109–116 (June 2008)
7. Stankovic, J.A., Wood, A.D., He, T.: Theoretical aspects of distributed computing in sensor networks. Monographs in Theoretical Computer Science. An EATCS Series, pp. 835–863. Springer, Heidelberg (2011)
8. Vu, K., Zheng, R.: Robust coverage under uncertainty in wireless sensor networks. In: INFOCOM, Shanghai, China (April 2011)
9. Zhou, Z., Das, S., Gupta, H.: Variable radii connected sensor cover in sensor networks. ACM Transactions on Sensor Networks 20, 1244–1245 (2009)
10. Zhang, H., Hou, J.C.: Maintaining sensing coverage and connectivity in large sensor networks. In: Ad Hoc & Sensor Wireless Networks (2005)

Optimizing Cauchy Reed-Solomon Codes
for P2P Storage Cloud

Zhefeng Xiao[1], Zunguo Huang[1], and Yujun Liu[2]

[1] School of Computer Science,
National University of Defense Technology
Changsha 410073, China
[2] Department of Information Engineering,
Academy of Armored Forced Engineering
Beijing 100072, China
zhefeng.xiao@gmail.com, zunguo@263.net,
yjliu@nudt.edu.cn

Abstract. To overcome the drawbacks in the P2P storage clouds previously proposed, this paper designs a new P2P storage cloud, in which the erasure coding is performed on the dedicated computing nodes, rather than storage nodes. Through experiments, we find that the coding performance of the existing CRS codes has become the bottleneck of the new P2P storage cloud. Thus, we preliminarily optimize the CRS code, and confirm that the hard drive I/O performance in the computing node has caused the bottleneck in CRS coding. Therefore, we propose two buffer-based I/O minimization CRS codes and conduct a performance evaluation. The experimental results show that, on average, the preliminarily optimized CRS codes improve by 43.13%, and the coding performance of the two buffer-based I/O minimization CRS codes reach 202.282 and 275.297 MB/s, respectively, thereby meeting the performance requirements of erasure coding in the P2P storage cloud.

Keywords: erasure code, cloud storage, P2P, optimizing.

1   Introduction

With the same availability, disk utilization gained using erasure code can be higher than replication [9]. Thus, many storage clouds are transitioning from replication to erasure codes [5, 6, 8].

In the previously proposed P2P storage clouds, including Wuala [15, 16, 5], HYDRAstor [3], Tahoe-LAFS [4], etc., erasure coding is performed on the storage nodes, which also function as computing nodes. But they have some drawbacks. In Wuala and Tahoe-LAFS, erasure coding on the storage nodes occupies the user's computing resources. Moreover, they add the users into the DHT, which also occupy the user's idle hard disk space and bandwidth. Since they scale up relying on the increasing number of users, they are applied to online backup, similar to Dropbox [17], but not to data centers. In HYDRAstor, which presents saleable secondary

X. Wang et al. (Eds.): WASA 2012, LNCS 7405, pp. 378–385, 2012.
© Springer-Verlag Berlin Heidelberg 2012

storage solutions aimed at data centers, a storage node has a very high configuration [3], which increases the cost of scaling up in number. In addition, Wuala, Tahoe-LAFS, and HYDRAstor typically use a smaller fragment in the erasure coding, e.g., 64 KB in HYDRAstor, which result in more maintenance overhead.

To overcome the drawbacks, in this paper, we design a new P2P storage cloud (Fig. 1), in which the erasure coding is performed on the dedicated computing nodes. The new P2P storage cloud consists of a back-end and a front-end. The front-end includes the portal, whereas the back-end includes a cluster of computing nodes and a grid of storage nodes built around a Distributed Hash Table (DHT). The computing nodes in the cluster have so high configuration that they have to fulfill most of the computing functions in the cloud, such as erasure coding/decoding, encryption/decryption, integrity verification, access control, and compression/decompression. The storage nodes have only two functions to fulfill: data storage and reconstruction. As a result, storage nodes have lower configuration, such as servers with low power processors, e.g., Atom CPU, which can scale up in number with much lower cost. As shown in Fig. 1, only the system's storage nodes are added to the DHT storage network and not those of the users. So the cloud does not occupy the users' hard disk space and bandwidth. In addition, the cloud uses larger fixed-size fragments, e.g., 1 MB, which greatly decreases the maintenance overhead.

The P2P storage cloud is not only applied to online backup, but also data centers. We take its online backup service as an example to illustrate the workflow as follows: via PC, mobile phone or tablet PC, users store files through the portal. When uploading files, first, the portal splits the user's file into fixed-size blocks. Second, according to the principle of load balance, the block is sent to the idle computing node in the cluster of computing nodes for erasure coding. Finally, the generated data and coding fragments are distributed to the storage nodes in the DHT storage network. When downloading a file, the computing nodes obtain sufficient fragments from the DHT storage network, restore the original file, and return it to the user. Similar to HYDRAstor [3], Disp [2], the P2P storage cloud also provides user-selected choices of failure resiliency.

However, in the P2P storage cloud, erasure coding performance may become the bottleneck. Therefore, achieving high-performance erasure coding in the P2P storage cloud is of great significance for our study. The goal of this paper is to study if the erasure coding performance can meet the needs of the P2P storage cloud, and if not, how to optimize the erasure code to maximize its coding performance.

The remainder of this paper is organized as follows. Section 2 poses the problem in this paper. Section 3 introduces the preliminary optimization to the existing CRS coding and proposes two buffer-based I/O minimization CRS codes. The performance evaluation is conducted in Section 4. Section 5 discusses a blueprint for future work.

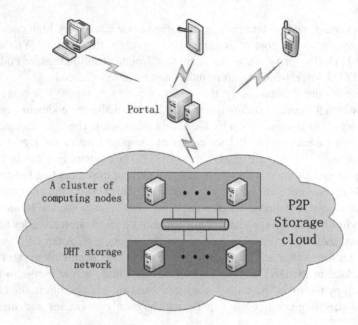

Fig. 1. P2P storage cloud architecture

2   Problem Statement

2.1   Experiment Setup

The machine for testing has an Intel i5 Core 2 4-thread processor running at 2.9 GHz, 4 GB RAM, and a 5400 RPM Serial ATA drive with an 8 MB buffer. It runs Ubuntu Linux, version 10.04.

The P2P storage cloud in our study provides user-selected choices of failure resiliency. And only the Reed-Solomon code is defined for any value of k and m. For theses reasons, we choose CRS for this paper's erasure code, which could perform much better than Vandermonde Reed-Solomon [13].

To meet the needs of the user's resilient fault-tolerance on the basis of the tradeoff between disk utilization and availability, in this paper, we set the number of data fragments, i.e., $k = 5$, and set the number of coding fragments, i.e., $m \in \{2, 5\}$. We take a large file (200 MB) and divide it into 40 data blocks with a size of 5 MB each, which are selected as the inputs of the experiment. After the data block is erasure coded, the size of each data and coding fragment generated is 1 MB. For this study, we choose the latest 1.2 version of the Jerasure Library [11] due to its best coding performance in several open-source libraries [1].

2.2   Performance of the Existing CRS Code

Based on the CRS code in the Jerasure [11] Library, the existing CRS coding performance is evaluated. The results indicate that the encoding performance of CRS codes in a variety of k and m is only 32.803 MB/S on average (Table 1).

Table 1. Existing coding performance of CRS code in the Jerasure Library

k m w	Performance (MB/S)
5 2 3	41.902
5 3 3	33.434
5 4 4	29.922
5 5 4	25.954

2.3   Problem

Through experiments, we find that the existing CRS encoding performance is very low and has become the bottleneck. This implies that for the P2P storage cloud to achieve a higher throughput, it has to deploy much more computing nodes for erasure coding, thus increasing overall costs. Thus, this paper attempts to solve the problem of optimizing the CRS coding to maximize coding performance of the computing nodes and meet the P2P storage cloud's need for erasure coding performance.

Decoding optimization is similar to the process of encoding and is closely related to the specific storage mechanism of the DHT storage network. This work concentrates on the optimization of CRS encoding and leaves the decoding for future work.

3   Optimization

3.1   Preliminary Optimization

Based on the existing CRS code, we conduct two preliminary optimizations.

- We use multi-threaded technique to generate the coding fragments in parallel.
- According to the results presented in [10, 12], we choose the optimal distribution matrix and write them into the code as constants, thereby reducing the running time of encoding.

3.2   Buffer-Based I/O Minimization CRS

3.2.1   Bottleneck in the CRS
Given that the P2P storage cloud demands the performance of CRS coding to reach 200 MB/s or higher, we calculate the write rates of a hard disk corresponding to the various code rates. When the coding performance achieves 200 MB/s, the hard disk write rate must reach at least 280 MB/S (Table 2). In fact, the ordinary hard disk write rate is far below that rate [7]. Thus, we can conclude that the I/O performance of hard disks cause the bottleneck of CRS coding.

Table 2. Hard disk write rate when CRS coding performance reaches 200 MB/S

k m	Write Rate of Data Fr.	Write Rate of Coding Fr.	Sum
5 2	200	80	280
5 3	200	120	320
5 4	200	160	360
5 5	200	200	400

3.2.2   Buffer-Based I/O Minimization CRS Code

Through the combination of experiments and theoretical analysis, we find that the I/O performance of a hard disk causes the bottleneck of erasure coding. Therefore, to improve coding performance, the data and coding fragments generated by the CRS code must be stored in the buffer of the memory (partly or in whole), rather than written to the disk, before the fragments are distributed and stored in the storage nodes. On basis of this idea, we design two buffer-based I/O minimization CRS codes, which are depicted in Figure 2.

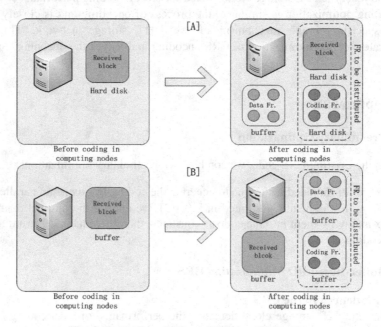

Fig. 2. Buffer-based I/O minimization CRS codes

Due to the space constraint, we briefly describe the two algorithms shown in Figure 2. In the first algorithm, the computing nodes receive the data block with the parameters k and m from the portal and save it to disk. After CRS coding, the computing nodes save the data fragments in the buffer, but save the coding fragments to disk. Finally, after the coding fragments are read from the hard disk and the data fragments are read directly from the buffer, all the fragments are sent to the storage nodes. In the second algorithm, the computing nodes receive the data block from the portal and save it to disk. After CRS coding, the computing nodes keep the data and coding fragments in the buffer. Finally, the data and coding fragments are sent directly to the storage nodes.

4   Performance Evaluation

In this section, we use the same experiment setup as Section 3.1 to evaluate the CRS optimized preliminarily and buffer-based I/O minimization CRS codes.

4.1   Experiment on Preliminary CRS Optimization

We evaluate the preliminarily optimized CRS code. The experiment results are shown in Table 3.

Table 3. Coding performance of CRS code optimization

k m w	xor	Performance (MB/S)
5 2 3	47	63.211
5 3 3	72	49.913
5 4 4	127	43.337
5 5 4	166	31.348

The average coding performance in a variety of k and m is 46.952 MB/S (Table 3). In contrast to the results in Table 1, we obtain an average of 43.13% performance improvement.

4.2   Experiments on Buffer-Based I/O Minimization CRS Codes

We conduct two simulation experiments to evaluate the buffer-based I/O minimization CRS codes. In the first experiment, the coding fragments are saved in the hard disk, but the data fragments are saved in the buffer. The experiment results are shown in Table 4. The coding performance is significantly improved for various values of k, m and w, with an average performance of 202.282 MB/s.

Table 4. Coding performance of Simulation Experiment 1

k m w	xor	Performance (MB/S)
5 2 3	47	259.067
5 3 3	72	194.175
5 4 4	127	252.844
5 5 4	166	103.040

In the second experiment, the data and coding fragments are all kept in the buffer before they are distributed to the DHT storage network. The experimental results are shown in Table 5. Compared with the first experiment, the results show that coding performance has been greatly enhanced, reaching an average of 275.297 MB/s.

Table 5. Coding performance of Simulation Experiment 2

k m w	xor	Performance (MB/S)
5 2 3	47	269.179
5 3 3	72	211.416
5 4 4	127	346.620
5 5 4	166	273.973

The experimental results show that buffer-based I/O minimization CRS codes have much higher performance than the existing CRS code and meet the P2P storage cloud's needs for coding performance, thus verifying the hypothesis that the I/O performance of a hard disk causes the bottleneck in CRS coding.

5   Future Work

Future works include: first, a detailed implementation of the prototype P2P storage cloud and a comparison of the implementation complexities and encoding performances of our proposed CRS codes; and second, the optimization of the CRS decoding.

Acknowledgements. This work is supported by the Program for Changjiang Scholars and Innovative Research Team in University under grant NO. IRT1012, the Aid Program for Science and Technology Innovative Research Team in Higher Educational Institutions of Hunan province: "Network technology" and Hunan Provincial Natural Science Foundation for China under grant 11JJ7003.

References

1. Plank, J.S., Luo, J., Schuman, C.D., Xu, L., Wilcox-O'Hearn, Z.: A performance evaluation and examination of open-source erasure coding libraries for storage. In: Proccedings of the 7th Conference on File and Storage Technologies, San Francisco, California, February 24-27, pp. 253–265 (2009)
2. Ellard, D., Megquier, J.: Disp: Practical, efficient, secure and fault-tolerant distributed data storage. Trans. The Storage 1(1), 71–94 (2005)
3. Dubnicki, C., Gryz, L., Heldt, L., Kaczmarczyk, M., Kilian, W., Strzelczak, P., Szczepkowski, J., Ungureanu, C., Welnicki, M.: HYDRAstor: A the Scalable the Secondary Storage. In: Proceedings of the Seventh USENIX Conference on File and Storage Technologies (FAST 2009), San Francisco, California, pp. 197-210 (February 2009)
4. https://tahoe-lafs.org/trac/tahoe-lafs

5. http://www.wuala.com
6. Calder, B., Wang, J., Ogus, A., Nilakantan, N., Skjolsvold, A., McKelvie, S., Xu, Y., Srivastav, S., Wu, J., Simitci, H., Haridas, J., Uddaraju, C., Khatri, H., Edwards, A., Bedekar, V., Mainali, S., Abbasi, R., Agarwal, A., Fahim ul Haq, M., Ikram ul Haq, M., Bhardwaj, D., Dayanand, S., Adusumilli, A., McNett, M., Sankaran, S., Manivannan, K., Rigas, L.: Windows Azure storage: A highly available the cloud storage service with strong consistency. In: Symposium on Operating Systems Principles (2011)
7. http://www.storagereview.com/hitachi_deskstar_5k4000_review
8. Ford, D., Labelle, F., Popovici, F.I., Stokely, M., Truong, V.-A., Barroso, L., Grimes, C., Quinlan, S.: Availability in. globally distributed the file systems. In: Operating Systems Design and Implementation (2010)
9. Weatherspoon, H., Kubiatowicz, J.: Erasure Coding Vs. Replication: A Quantitative Comparison. Revised Papers from the First International Workshop on Peer-to-Peer Systems, March 07-08, pp. 328–338 (2002)
10. Plank, J.S., Xu, L.: Optimizing Cauchy Reed-Solomon codes for fault-tolerant network storage applications. In: The NCA 2006: 5th IEEE International Symposium on from Network Computing Applications, Cambridge, MA (July 2006)
11. Plank, J.S.: Jerasure: A library in C / C + + facilitating erasure coding for storage applications.Tech. Rep. CS-07-603, University of Tennessee (September 2007)
12. Plank, J.S.: The Enumeration of optimal and good the Cauchy matrices for Reed-Solomon coding.Technical Report CS-05-570, University of the Tennessee (December 2005)
13. Blomer, J., Kalfane, M., Karpinski, M., Karp, R., Luby, M., Zuckerman, D.: An XOR-based erasure-resilient coding scheme. The Technical Report the TR-95-048, International Computer Science Institute (August 1995)
14. Plank, J.S.: A tutorial on Reed-Solomon coding for faulttolerance in RAID-like systems. Software - Practice & Experience 27(9), 995–1012 (1997)
15. Grolimund, D., Meisser, L., Schmid, S., Wattenhofer, R.: Cryptree: A Folder Tree Structure for Cryptographic File Systems. In: SRDS 2006: Proceedings of the 25th IEEE Symposium on Reliable Distributed Systems, Washington, DC, USA (2006)
16. Grolimund, D., Meisser, L., Schmid, S., Wattenhofer, R.: Havelaar: A Robust and Efficient Reputation System for Active Peer-to-Peer Systems. In: First Workshop on the Economics of Networked Systems, NetEcon 2006 (2006)
17. http://www.dropbox.com

Aerial Localization with Smartphone

Zhongli Liu, Yinjie Chen, Benyuan Liu, Jie Wang, and Xinwen Fu

Computer Science Department, University of Massachusetts Lowell
{zliu,ychen1,bliu,wang,xinwenfu}@cs.uml.edu

Abstract. This paper presents how we applied a smartphone for aerial localization. We have developed a fully functional aerial localization system *HAWK* and reported preliminary results in a related paper. In this paper, we focus on the technical details of using a smartphone Nokia N900 as a wireless sniffer on a mini helicopter and comparing the performance of three localization approaches for wireless device localization. The flight is controlled by a software controller on a laptop. The flight route can be specified in two ways: manually setting waypoints on Google map and automatically generating waypoints based on Moore space filling curve. The smartphone based sniffer captures the wireless traffic during flight and transmits the traffic dump files through a 3G network to a locator once the surveillance flight is finished. We applied three different approaches, maximum signal strength approach, centroid approach and Quasi-Newton method, for the locator on the laptop to calculate the position of the target device and compared the localization accuracy of these three localization approaches. Surprisingly, the simplest approach, maximum signal strength approach (which uses the location where the maximum signal strength is sensed as the target's location) has similar localization accuracy compared with the other two. We also provided an indoor localization approach locating the target in a recorded video.

1   Introduction

Wireless localization techniques have enjoyed great success and pervasive deployment. In a wireless localization scene, there are three participants: target, positioning infrastructure and third party. Any of these three participants can calculate the location of the target. Based on who calculates the location of the target, we can classify wireless localization technologies into three categories: self positioning, infrastructure positioning and third party localization. In self positioning, the target interacts with the positioning infrastructure such as the GPS constellation and calculates its own location. In infrastructure positioning, the infrastructure such as the cellular towers can sense the signal of an active phone and use trilateration to locate the target phone. This paper is interested in the third type of localization technique, third party localization.

In a third party localization, a third party, not the target or infrastructure, can sense the signal of the target and locate the target without the help of the positioning infrastructure and target. Third party localization has broad applications including public safety, cyber forensics, and network management.

X. Wang et al. (Eds.): WASA 2012, LNCS 7405, pp. 386–397, 2012.

For example, if travelers equipped with smartphones are lost in a forest and we want to locate them, cellular towers may not exist over there for the localization. In this scenario, we may send a mini helicopter, which is a third party, to locate the travelers via locating their smartphone through its wireless signal. For example, we can either turn on the smartphone's WiFi access point mode or develop an app for the localization purpose.

We have developed a fully functional aerial localization system *HAWK*, a mini-helicopter based aerial wireless kit, and reported preliminary results on localization in a related paper [18]. In this paper, we focus on the technical details of using a smartphone Nokia N900 as a wireless sniffer on a mini helicopter and comparing the performance of three localization approaches for wireless device localization. The contribution of this paper can be summarized as follows:

- After reporting preliminary results of HAWK in [18], we conducted intense development and analysis. The flight is controlled by a software controller on a laptop. The flight route can be specified in two ways: manually setting waypoints on Google map and automatically generating waypoints based on Moore space filling curve (Moore curve). The smartphone based sniffer captures the wireless traffic during flight and transmits the traffic dump files through a 3G network to a locator once the surveillance flight is finished. A video demo can be found at http://www.youtube.com/watch?v=ju86xnHb Eq0.
- We applied three different approaches, maximum signal strength approach, centroid approach and Quasi-Newton Method, for the locator on the laptop to calculate the position of the target device and compared the localization accuracy of these three localization approaches. Surprisingly, the simplest approach, maximum signal strength approach (which uses the location where the maximum signal strength is sensed as the target's location) has similar localization accuracy compared with the other two. An indoor localization approach is also presented, which uses the video captured by the sniffer to locate the target.

The rest of this paper is organized as follows: In Section 2, we introduce the system structure of aerial localization with smartphone. Section 3 shows three different approaches that are applied to analyze the experiments results. In Section 4, we discuss a video-based indoor localization approach. We present experimental evaluation of this system in Section 5. Section 6 discusses related work. The conclusion of this paper is in Section 7.

2   System

In this section, we first introduce the structure and basic idea of our aerial localization system, and then investigate a few challenging issues of this localization system. At last, we present our solutions to these issues.

2.1 Overview of HAWK

Figure 1 exhibits the system architecture of the aerial localization with a smartphone. There are four main components in this system: helicopter, wireless sniffer, controller and locator.

Controller   Draganflyer + Sniffer   Database   Locator

Fig. 1. Architecture of HAWK

(i) *Helicopter.* We use a mini helicopter Draganflyer X6 [15] to carry a wireless sniffer to do the aerial surveillance and localization. X6 can log its GPS coordinates during flight and transfer these GPS data to the locator. X6 can be controlled by both handheld controller and software controller.

(ii) *Wireless Sniffer.* We convert a smartphone Nokia N900 [7] to a wireless sniffer. This sniffer is attached to the mini helicopter and captures wireless traffic during a flight. The information collected by the sniffer will be transmitted to a locator through the 3G network.

(iii) *Software Controller.* The software controller runs on a Lenovo W500 laptop to autonomously maneuver the helicopter's movement while flying. The software controller is able to draw helicopter's flight route in real time, and show all the wireless devices sniffed by N900 after the flight.

(iv) *Locator.* After receiving sniffer's dump files, a software locator on the laptop will analyze the data and determine the location of the target.

2.2 Basic Idea

The basic idea of this aerial localization system is using a mini helicopter attached with a smartphone Nokia N900, which works as a wireless sniffer, to identify the location of a target wireless device. The helicopter, with the sniffer, performs the aerial surveillance over a given area while the sniffer is collecting wireless traffic such as RSSI (received signal strength indication) time series and coordinate information. When the surveillance is finished, all the collected information is transmitted to the locator. Then, these data are analyzed to calculate the target device's position.

The surveillance flight route is derived through two ways: waypoints that are generated from Moore curve and waypoints that are set from Google map as shown in Figure 2. The Moore curve approach has been discussed in [18]. The locator can draw the flight route in real time, since helicopter can log its GPS coordinates which will be transmitted to the locator simultaneously. Figure 3 shows the flight route when the helicopter is doing the surveillance according to a predefined level 2 Moore curve flight route.

 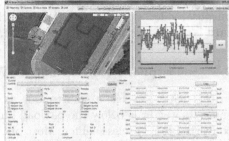

Fig. 2. Set Points on Google Map   **Fig. 3.** Flight Route in Real Time

2.3 Issues and Solutions

The aerial localization system has several issues that need to be addressed in this paper:

(i) What are the primary functions of the software controller? How to visualize the process of aerial surveillance and localization, and localization result?

(ii) Which kind of sniffer should be selected for our system to capture the wireless traffic? Since the helicopter has a payload limitation, the sniffer's weight should be considered.

(iii) How does the locator obtain the logfiles from sniffer in real time? How to find the location of target device based on these logfiles?

2.4 Functions of Software Controller

The software controller is developed in $C\#$ language, and uses a USB telemetry transceiver to communicate with the helicopter. It first sets the surveillance route for the helicopter by directly setting waypoints on Google map, or calculating a list of waypoints based on Moore Curve. Then, the helicopter with sniffer is maneuvered to fly to these waypoints sequentially to do the surveillance. [18] has discussed in details with regarding to how to control the helicopter to achieve the waypoints function. Since the helicopter can log its GPS coordinates and transmit them to software controller, we can draw the flight route on Google map in real time. After the surveillance, the target's location is calculated and is also able to be displayed on Google map.

To monitor the process of surveillance, we can also use N900's video streaming capacity. N900 is equipped with a 5.0 MP rear camera with Carl Zeiss Tessar lens and a 0.3 MP front camera. The native N900 camera application can record very decent videos and store them on its 32 GB eMMC flash. For real time video streaming, we can use bambuser [2], Qik [8], Skype and many others. We conducted experiments with these application installed on N900 to stream real time video via the 3G network, and noticed that the real time video had a severe delay of up to tens of seconds because of the 3G network. Therefore, video streaming can be used for supporting surveillance, but cannot be used for maneuvering the helicopter to avoid obstacles in a general purpose. For the later purpose, video streaming via WiFi works well. However, since our N900 WiFi card is used for monitoring WiFi traffic, it cannot be used for video streaming.

2.5   Smartphone Nokia N900 as Wireless Sniffer

In this paper, we use a smartphone as a wireless sniffer. We choose N900 because its weight is below the payload limit of the helicopter and it can be easily converted to a wireless sniffer. Most phone on market including iPhone and Android phones do not have the appropriate driver to support the necessary wireless monitor mode for full-scale sniffing.

To convert N900 into a wireless sniffer, we need to update its kernel to the latest version and install several softwares: rootsh, Enhanced Linux kernel, network-tools, and Kismet. Prior to the installation, we need to add the maemo development repository into the source list [4] by using the following commands: Menu → More → App.Manager → Application Manager → Application catalogues → New. Then, a window showing as Figure 4 pops up as below, and we fill the blanks and click "Save".

Fig. 4. Add Maemo Development Repository

Followings are the steps to install these softwares:

1. In the "Application Manager", click "Download", then type "rootsh" and "install". This helps us to gain a root shell.

2. The *enhanced Linux kernel* "kernel-power" refers to enhanced Linux kernel for power users [5], which is needed by Kismet [6]. Kernel power includes the necessary WiFi driver with monitor mode support. We install kernel-power through the Application Manager too.

3. Install wireless-tools and Kismet: First open a X Terminal, and then input commands "sudo gainroot" and "apt-get install wireless-tools kismet".

Now N900 is ready to run Kismet and work as a sniffer to collect wireless traffic. In order to let Kismet capture the wireless packets, the wireless card should work under monitor mode. Thus, we use the following commands to set the wireless card before running Kismet:

- ifconfig wlan0 down.
- iwconfig wlan0 mode monitor.
- ifconfig wlan0 up.

2.6 Downloading Logfiles and Locating the Target Device

To use the locator to derive the target device's location, we need to transmit the logfiles from sniffer to locator right after the aerial surveillance. Because the wireless card is under monitor mode when Kismet is working, we could not get these logfiles. To resolve the issue, we use 3G network to download the logfiles from sniffer to locator. However, the 3G network does not provide a public IP address to N900 and the locator can not connect to N900 directly. Therefore, we use reverse SSH, which relies on a public server (which has a public static IP address) that both N900 and locator can reach. N900 connects to the public server, waiting for the locator to connect. The locator connects to the public server, which in turn forwards that connection to N900.

[10] introduces how to set the reverse SSH in detail. There are two basic parts, on N900 and on locator.

On N900: To connect to the common server, we do the following:

1. Creating a script named as: *reverse_ssh.sh*, under the directory */usr/ share/*.

2. Setting the content of *reverse_ssh.sh* as *ssh −Nf −R* 2210 : *localhost* : 22 *root@server_ip* > */var/log/reverse_ssh.log*;.

3. Modifying the privilege of *reverse_ssh.sh* with the command: *chmod* 777 *reverse_ssh.sh*.

4. Running this script as *./reverse_ssh.sh* to connect to the server.

There is one more issue worth a brief mention here. That is, a password is required each time to connect to the server through N900. This can be resolved by SSH keys and ssh-agent which allow us to type in a passphrase only once on N900 [11].

On Locator: After a connection between N900 and server is established, we can use locator to connect to server then to N900. To establish this connection, use ssh and run the command:

$$ssh \text{ -}p \text{ } 2210 \text{ } root@localhos$$

Now the locator can download logfiles directly from N900.

After the locator obtains the logfiles, it searches these files and calculates the location of the target device. Details of these approaches used for calculation will be discussed in section 3. Figure 5 shows the flow chart of transferring data and locating process.

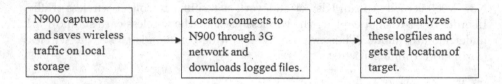

Fig. 5. Flow Chart of Transferring Data and Locating Process

3   Localization Approaches

In this section, we will introduce three different approaches that are used to calculate the location of a target device based on the logfiles collected by wireless sniffer. We also discuss advantage and disadvantage of the three approaches. In these localization approaches, we assume that the MAC address of the target device is known.

3.1   Maximum Signal Strength Approach

Kismet has the capability to log GPS coordinate where the wireless sniffer senses the maximum RSSI of each wireless device, and then saves this kind of information into *.nettxt* file automatically. Our first approach is to simply find the GPS coordinate where the sniffer receives the first maximum RSSI of the target device from *.nettxt* file, and use this coordinate as the target device's location. This approach is simple and easy to be implemented.

3.2   Centroid Approach

To improve the accuracy, we use the centroid localization approach. That is, we search and select all GPS positions where the strongest RSSIs are sensed. Then, we use the average value of these GPS positions as the target location. Among the logfiles generated from Kismet, there is a *.gpsxml* file which logs a mapping between the GPS coordinates and sensed RSSIs. Thus, we can derive the useful data from this logfile. Algorithm 1 shows the basic steps of how to calculate the location of target device based on the centroid approach. Even this approach needs a little bit more calculation than the first approach, it is more accurate.

3.3   Quasi-Newton Method

In practice, the distance between wireless sniffer and target device can be derived from RSSI values using Formulas (1) and (2). Thus, our third approach is to calculate the target device directly from the distances and RSSIs.

$$p_i = P - 10 \times r \times \log d_i + R, \tag{1}$$

$$d_i = \sqrt{(D_g)^2 + (alt_i - alt)^2}, \tag{2}$$

Algorithm 1. Centroid Approach for Localization

Require: Logfiles .gpsxml and .nettxt from sniffer
1: Set P to denote RSSI
2: Set list(x) and list(y)
3: Set t-mac as target's MAC address
4: Find the strongest RSSI from .nettxt file where the $MACaddress = t$-mac
5: Set P = strongest RSSI
6: Select all the GPS coordinates, including latitudes and longitudes, from .gpsxml
   file where $MACaddress = t$-mac and $RSSI = P$
7: Add the latitudes to x
8: Add the longitudes to y
9: Set the target's coordinate as (average(x), average(y))

---

where p_i is the RSSI that sniffer gets at GPS location (lat_i, lon_i, alt_i). We can get these four parameters and their relationship from the logfiles. P is the RSSI sensed one meter away from the target device. r is the path loss exponent that captures the rate of RSSI attenuation in the vicinity of target device. (lat, lon, alt) is the location of target device, and we assume the height for target device is 0 (alt $= 0$). R is a random variable that functions to feature the RSSI variation due to multi-path effects, asymmetries in the physical environment and other imperfections in the model itself. D_g is the great circle distance between the target device and sniffer, please refer to [14], the formula used to calculate the great circle distance.

In Formulas (1) and (2), there are four unknown parameters: P, r, lat and lon. Thus, we select four different pairs of p_i and (lat_i, lon_i, alt_i) to form four nonlinear algebraic equations.

To solve these equations, we can use a matlab function "fsolve", based on quasi-Newton method [9], to solve sets of nonlinear algebraic equations. However, to use $fsolve$ to solve the nonlinear algebraic equations, we need to supply a routine to evaluate the function vector. Different routines will result in these functions with different solutions.

4   Discussion

The localization approaches in Section 3 are all designed for outdoor environment. In this section, we will introduce an **indoor video localization approach for aerial localization**. Our mini helicopter can fly indoors although it is not safe to do this. For a safe indoor flight, we may adopt Ar Drone [1], which has a protection hulk preventing damage caused by collision. For example, Reed *et al.* [21] have developed an Ar Drone based wireless toolkit SkyNET as a 3G-enabled mobile attack drone and stealth botmaster. SkyNET can be used for indoor localization.

The challenge of the indoor environment is that we do not have a flight coordinate system like GPS used outdoor. We design a video based localization approach considering two facts: N900 can record videos and store them on its 32

GB eMMC flash, and tcpdump can collect traffic which includes RSSI time series of wireless devices. Therefore, we can try to find the image from the video at the time when N900 sensed the strongest RSSI of the target. The target should be around the scene and location displayed in this image.

To implement this approach, we need to synchronize video recording and traffic collecting. Since N900's camera application is a GUI program, we cannot use a script to start the video recording and log the starting time. The video file access time from the linux file system is too rough. To address this issue, we adopt G-Streamer [3] for N900 and use this tool to start the video recording from the command line and log the starting time with a precision of microsecond.

Algorithm 2 introduces how we do the video-based localization. We have implemented this video-based localization and are able to play the video within our software controller and fast forward the video to the right scene. The video is played with the panel displaying the RSSI time series in Figure 2.

Algorithm 2. Video-based Localization

1: Start the video recording by G-Streamer and tcpdump on N900, and log their starting time.
2: Start the indoor surveillance, and save the video and traffic on N900.
3: Transfer the saved video, saved traffic collection, and their starting time to locator.
4: Find the time when N900 senses the strongest RSSI from the target.
5: Find the image, which corresponds to the strongest RSSI, according to the saved video file, starting time of the video and the time when N900 senses the strongest RSSI from the target.
6: Locate the target device based on the image found in Step 5.

---

5   Evaluation

In this section, an introduction on how to setup the experiments is presented, followed by a discussion of the experiments results based on three different locating approaches in Section 3.

5.1   Experiment Setup

We conducted real-world field experiments to evaluate the localization capability of our aerial localization system with smartphone. We generated 3 sets of Moore curve over the campus track field as surveillance routes: level 1, level 2 and level 3 Moore curves, and another route around the track field for warwalking. The flight route is the same as [18].

In the first experiment, we configured 12 smartphones as access points (APs) and uniformly distributed them on the track field. We launched Kismet on Nokia N900 and attached N900 to the helicopter to derive location logs of these 12 smartphones. Kismet was configured to hop among all the channels with the hop velocity of 3 channels/second and total number of channels is 11. The software controller on a Lenovo W500 laptop steered the flight along the three routes to locate these APs. The warwalking experiment emulated the scene where people cannot access dead ends, such as building roofs (the field in the experiment).

In the second experiment, all 12 APs were set to one common channel, and Kismet was configured to sniff on this single channel.

5.2 Localization Results by Three Approaches

After we got the logfiles from sniffer, we used the maximum signal strength approach in Section 3.1 to analyze both experiments. That is, we selected the GPS location where the wireless sniffer received the strongest signal strength as the target device's position.

We applied the centroid approach in Section 3.2 to the second experiment. We used the Algorithm 1 in Section 3.2 to find the locations of target devices.

To evaluate the Quasi-Newton method in Section 3.3, we selected the four pairs of data, including signal strength and GPS location. Then we constructed four different equations and used matlab function "fsolve" to locate the target device. The initial value for 1 meter signal strength was -5, the path loss exponent was 4, and the target device's position was the location where we got from the second approach in Section 3.2. Figure 6 shows the localization re-

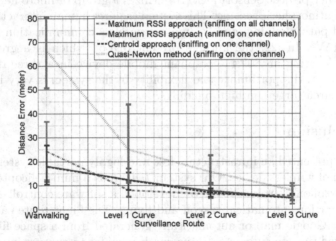

Fig. 6. Localization Error via Kismet

sults of these three approaches. This figure shows that the outcomes of both experiments are similar to the first approach. The performance of the centroid approach is slightly better. The Quasi-Newton method is the least desirable as shown in Figure 6. When solving the equations with "fsolve" function, we notice that the routine value of this function can significantly affect the localization result. We leave the theory of choosing the routine value and selecting appropriate RSSI samples for better localization accuracy as our future work.

6 Related Work

There has been considerable amount of work on device positioning in WiFi and sensor networks. Due to space limitation, we only review most related and recent work. The most related work to this paper is W.A.S.P [13] and SkyNET [21]. W.A.S.P uses a mini airplane for wireless surveillance and attacks. However, the mini airplane has to fly at a relatively high speed in order to float in the air. We have proved in [18] that W.A.S.P is not appropriate for accurate wireless localization. SketNET is designed as an aerial botmaster to exploit weak wireless devices and form a botnet. It uses Ar Drone [1] to carry a single board computer (SBC) equipped with wireless adapters for this purpose. The SBC is attached to the top of the Ar Drone since Ar Drone has its sonar ranger finder at the bottom. This design is not appropriate for wireless localization since the body of Ar Drone will disturb the received signal.

In [19], [20], the authors proposed SensorFly, an aerial sensor network, where very small helicopter can self-locate itself using anchor nodes. The authors in [17] utilized biologically inspired rules of group behavior (flocking) to enable a group of UAVs to control its own motion. This project aimed at building an indoor flocking system using small co-axial rotor helicopters. Each of the swarm members is fitted with an onboard computer and a miniature wireless video camera, so that they can gather multiple views in a single pass and analyze them. Another project SensorFlock [16] utilizes a group of micro aerial vehicles (MAVs) for atmospheric sensing. This system requires human interaction in flight control and path planning, and it supports wireless communication networking between MAVs. In [22] the authors present 3DLoc which is a ground based system for locating an 802.11-compliant mobile device in a three dimensional space. However, the portability and flexibility of the system is very limited and it cannot search targets in high buildings.

7 Conclusion

This paper presented an infrastructure free and highly portable system for aerial localization of wireless device. Our system *HAWK* is a mini helicopter attached with a smartphone - Nokia N900. We developed a software controller to control the helicopter for automatical takeoff and flying. The flight route can be either specified on Google map or automatically generated from a space filling curve. We converted the smartphone into the wireless sniffer to capture wireless traffic and applied three different approaches to evaluate the performance of our system and compared their performance. Surprisingly, the simplest approach based maximum signal strength has similar localization accuracy compared with the other two. Measurement noise and environmental noise play their roles in this observation.

Our future work includes a theoretical analysis of localization accuracy from different approaches. The practical experience of the quasi-Newton method raises many questions, e.g., how to choose the routine values and improve the localization accuracy. We also plan to use the smartphone to control the helicopter's movement and implement a fully autonomous surveillance tool. The challenge is we have to connect N900 to the helicopter with a serial cable and find/implement the right driver. Recall that we have implemented automatic takeoff and flying for HAWK. For automatical landing, the helicopter Clearly, GPS cannot provide a precise altitude measurement. We plan to equip N900 with a sonar. The SRF08 Ultra sonic range finder [12] serves this purpose well.

References

1. Ar. drone (2012), http://ardrone.parrot.com/parrot-ar-drone/usa/
2. bambuser (2012), http://bambuser.com/
3. G-streamer (2012), http://gstreamer.freedesktop.org/
4. Install chinese input on the n900 (2012), http://kenshinjeff.jp/2010/05/17/installing-chinese-input-on-the-n900/
5. Kernel power (2012), http://wiki.maemo.org/Kernel_Power
6. Kismet (2012), http://www.kismetwireless.net/
7. Nokia n900 (2012), http://en.wikipedia.org/wiki/Nokia_N900
8. Qik (2012), http://qik.com/
9. Quasi-newton method (2012), http://en.wikipedia.org/wiki/Quasi-Newton_method
10. Reverse_ssh (2012), http://wiki.maemo.org/Reverse_ssh
11. Setup ssh keys between machines (2012), http://fedoranews.org/dowen/sshkeys/
12. Srf08 ultra sonic range finder - technical specification (2012), http://www.robot-electronics.co.uk/htm/srf08tech.shtml
13. Wireless aerial surveillance platform (2012), https://rabbit-hole.org/
14. Carter, C.: Great circle distances (May 2002)
15. Draganfly Innovations, Inc. Innovative uav aircraft and aerial video systems (2012), http://www.draganfly.com
16. Hasan, A.B., Pisano, B., Panichsakul, S., Gray, P., Huang, J., Han, R., Lawrence, D., Mohseni, K.: Sensorflock: A mobile system of networked micro-air vehicles. Technical report, Department of Computer Science University of Colorado at Boulder (2006)
17. Holland, O., Woods, J., Nardi, R.D., Clark, A.: Beyond swarm intelligence: The ultraswarm. In: Proceedings of the IEEE Swarm Intelligence Symposium (2005)
18. Liu, Z., Chen, Y., Liu, B., Chao, C., Fu, X.: Hawk: An unmanned mini helicopter-based aerial wireless kit for localization. In: Inforcom 2012 (2012)
19. Purohit, A., Sun, Z., Salas, M., Zhang, P.: SensorFly: Controlled-mobile sensing platform for indoor emergency response applications. In: Proceedings of the 10th ACM/IEEE International Conference on Information Processing in Sensor Networks (IPSN) (2011)
20. Purohit, A., Zhang, P.: Sensorfly: A controlled-mobile aerial sensor network. In: The Seventh ACM Conference on Embedded Networked Sensor Systems (November 2009)
21. Reed, T., Geis, J., Dietrich, S.: Kernel power. In: Proceedings of the 5th Usenix Workshop on Offensive Technologies (WOOT) (2011)
22. Wang, J., Chen, Y., Fu, X., Wang, J., Yu, W., Zhang, N.: 3DLoc: Three dimensional wireless localization toolkit. In: Proceedings of IEEE ICDCS (2010)

A Framework of Fire Monitoring System Based on Sensor Networks*

Longjiang Guo[1,2], Yihui Sun[1], Jinbao Li[1,2],
Qianqian Ren[1,2,**], and Meirui Ren[1,2]

[1] School of Computer Science and Technology, Heilongjiang University, China
[2] Key Laboratory of Database and Parallel Computing, Heilongjiang, China
{longjiangguo,sunyihui1,wsn.qqren}@gmail.com

Abstract. Sensor networks have been widely applied in harsh environment monitoring. Fire monitoring is one of the extensive applications. But existing fire monitoring systems based on sensor networks fall into two problems. First, since sensing ability of sensor nodes is limited, the fire alarm may be delay or even fail to report. Next, because of the fire's uncertainty, it is difficult to accurately determine whether the fire break out or not. This paper proposes a new framework of fire monitoring system based on sensor networks to conquer the above two problems. The system consists of data collection mechanism adopting improved time series prediction algorithm (for short TSDC) and fire detection mechanism using neural network model. Experiment results show that our fire monitoring system can recognize the flaming fire nearly 100%, and fire warning delay can be controlled within 30s. The slow smoldering fire recognition rate can be controlled within 80%, alarm delay can be controlled within 1 minute.

1 Introduction

Traditional fire monitoring system adopts wire and the alarm information is transmitted to center with cable. In particular scenario such as old protection building, the deployment of wired fire monitoring system will influence aesthetics

* This work is supported by Program for New Century Excellent Talents in University under grant No.NCET-11-0955, Programs Foundation of Heilongjiang Educational Committee for New Century Excellent Talents in University under grant No.1252-NCET-011, Program for Group of Science and Technology Innovation of Heilongjiang Educational Committee under grant No.2011PYTD002, the Science and Technology Research of Heilongjiang Educational Committee under grant No.12511395, the Science and Technology Innovation Research Project of Harbin for Young Scholar under grant No.2008RFQXG107, 2009RFQX080 and No.2011RFXXG014, the National Natural Science Foundation of China under grant No.61070193, 60803015, Heilongjiang Province Founds for Distinguished Young Scientists under Grant No.JC201104, Heilongjiang Province Science and Technique Foundation under Grant No.GC09A109, The Natural Science Foundation of Heilongjiang Province under Grant No. F201038.
** Corresponding author.

X. Wang et al. (Eds.): WASA 2012, LNCS 7405, pp. 398–410, 2012.
© Springer-Verlag Berlin Heidelberg 2012

and function in a sense. There is no wiring requirement of fire monitoring system in WSN. The convenient installation can reduce building destruction greatly. That is a good way for fire protection of old buildings. Due to self-organization of WSN, detection system can construct network in a short time. Therefore, WSN can be applied in fire detection.

Due to sensing limitation of low-power and low-cost wireless sensor node, sensing delay occurs when get environment information such as temperature. The temperature sensing component adopted in this paper is Sensirion SHT11 digital temperature/humidity sensor. We measure heat source of 70 degree centigrade in experiment. It costs 1 minute for the ascending of temperature sensing from 25 to 70 degree centigrade. The sensing delay is the main reason for fire alarm delay. Fire is indeterminate so that fire parameter is different when fire occurs in different place, different type of fire and at different time. It is hard to judge whether fire occurs in determined algorithm. Traditional methods based on threshold produce high false positive and false negative. We mainly focus on these two problem in system.

Time series prediction algorithm is a sort of data statistical algorithm. The algorithm summarizes a series of discrete data, extracts the trend function of these data, and takes proper variable into the function to estimate corresponding value. We adopt time series prediction algorithm to process data which is collected in a certain time in sensor node, and obtain the trend function of environment parameter. Environment parameter in future time t will be forecasted when time variable is taken into the trend function. Therefore, the sensing delay of sensor node can be reduced.

Neutral network algorithm is a multiple data fusion learning algorithm. The neutral network model adapted for certain environment can be computed by training environment data samples. System with multiple data fusion neutral network algorithm detects whether fire occurs.The current fire occurring probability can be obtained when input parameters are taken into trained neutral network. Compared with system initialized threshold, the accuracy of fire alarms by using neutral network algorithm is greater than the threshold.

The rest of this paper is organized as follows: Section 2 introduces related work. Section 3 presents architecture of fire monitoring system and the design of main module in system. Section 4 describes TSDC algorithm and neutral network algorithm. Experiment and analysis are introduced in Section 5. We conclude the whole paper in Section 6.

2   Related Work

Traditional fire detection system adopts wire. Alarm information is transmitted to center with cable. Usually the components need to be connected by wiring. The installation always takes long time, even wrecks the building structure. The hardware circuitries can easily aging, and the false positive will be arise. The number of circuitries increases as the number of sensors increases. The implementation of fire protection in WSN can effectively prevent from the problems. Due to the low cost in price and the ability of adapting harsh environment, fire protection in WSN attracts widespread research.

Most researches in fire monitoring system based on WSNs focus on how to save energy of network nodes [1-4], and to extend lifetime of node. Wang Chunlei[1] proposed topology structure based on clustering to organize nodes in network. Nodes are divided into several clusters. Cluster coordinates other nodes, aggregates and forwards data to sink. Other nodes in cluster only need to monitor. Hence, the lifetime can be extended. Moreover, in order to balance energy in network, These papers use cluster electing algorithm for guaranteing the network running longer.

Multi-parameter methods on threshold are proposed in fire identification [5-8]. After collecting data in particular environment, These papers summarize a group of thresholds for fire identification. Compared with the traditional monitoring methods based on single parameter, the effect of fire detection meliorates. However, the threshold is hard to determine due to indetermination of fire. The method might be interfered by outer environment, and incurs false positive and false negative.

In order to reduce the rate of fire alarm false positive and false negative, neural network algorithm is applied in researches[9-15]. The simulate experiments show that neural network is effective for fire detection.

But all those researches do not consider that the sensing ability of wireless node is weak. Sensing delay will inevitably result in the delay of the fire alarm. So that if we deploy wireless sensor fire protection systems in museums, laboratories or offices which demand real time of fire alarm, we should reduce the sensing delay of nodes, and get real-time fire warning.

The TSDC algorithm proposed in this paper can solve node sensing delay problem. And system adopts neutral network as fire detection metric, improving the accuracy of fire alarm.

3   System Architecture

In this section, we describe the fire monitoring system architecture. Real-time fire monitoring system based on wireless sensor network consists of a large number of low-cost and low-power sensor nodes, a sink node and monitoring host computer, as shown in Fig.1. Sensor nodes are distributed in the monitoring environment and responsible for data collection, processing and transmission. In our system, nodes process the sensing data by using time series trend algorithm and the data are sent to the sink is a set of parameters describing the trend of the detection values.

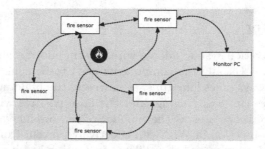

Fig. 1. Fire monitoring system architecture

Processing sensing data is divided into two parts, as shown in Fig.2. Firstly, in the sensor part, nodes collects data in a period of time, extracting the trend function. Then in the host computer part, system predicts the current values of the actual environment by using the trend function, and computers the probability of fire at this moment.

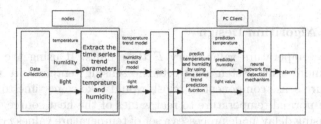

Fig. 2. Data processing model

In the sensor node part, in order to reduce the delay time of fire alarm due to the sense ability limited of wireless nodes, we propose a new node data collection method using time series prediction TSDC algorithm, processing the sense information, instead of using traditional method which nodes just send the sensing information to sink, we use TSDC algorithm processing the temperature and humidity data sensed by nodes in a period of time, extracting the trend function which there is just one time variable t in this function. Then nodes send the parameters of trend function to sink.

In the host computer part, on receiving data sent by nodes, client generates predictive function using time series trend parameters. According to different need, we set different time changing rate t' as the variable of prediction function. For example, if the fire monitoring system is set up in non-smoking area of a office building, the time variable t' set to be a fast change rate. If the system is deployed in the wild, in contrast with immediate fire alarm, we need a high success rate of fire alarm, the change rate of the time variable t' should be closed to the actual nodes sampling interval. System will get the prediction values of current temperature and humidity values in the monitoring area by taking the time variable t' into prediction function.

Finally, taking the prediction values of temperature and humidity and the actual light value into the trained neural network model to calculate the probability of occurrence of fire. If the probability value is greater than the threshold, system alerts.

4 Algorithms Design

In this section, we present the TSDC Algorithm and neural network model used in system. In our system, each node collects temperature, humidity and light sensing components. Sensing delay occurs on the temperature and humidity sensing. So we proposed a new prediction algorithm TSDC to process the temperature and humidity values sensed by nodes, reducing the sense delay.

Taking temperature sense for example, we will describe the TSDC algorithm in section 4.1. Because of the fire's an uncertainty feature, different locations, different types of combustion would affect the performance of fire. it is difficult to properly determine whether fire broking out or not. We propose a intelligent fire detection mechanism based on neural network model in fire monitoring system. We will describe the fire detection mechanism in section 4.2.

4.1   TSDC Algorithm Design

Nodes collect temperature value every Γ time units. If using the traditional method, fire monitoring system only gets the sensing temperature values. But the temperature sense component in telosb would take some time to sense temperature from normal temperature to real values of the heat source. In order to reduce the sensing delay, node processes a set of temperature values $v_1 \ldots v_i \ldots v_n$ by using time serial algorithm[16-19], extracting the temperature trend function. Then node sends the parameters of trend function to sink. System will predict the real values of heat resource by using prediction function.

There are two part in the time series trend function created by TSDC algorithm. The first part is trend component describing the trend of the sense values changing. The other part is a zero-mean weakly stationary time series model[16], indicating the trend function error. We assume that node reads temperature v_t at time t, $F(t)$ is time series trend function which denotes the real value v_t, $m(t)$ is the trend component, $X(t)$ is a weakly stationary time series model. As a result, we model the time series trend function as follows:

$$F(t) = m(t) + X(t) \tag{1}$$

TSDC algorithm is divided into three steps:(1)Create time series trend model by sensor nodes. (2)Predict values in the host computer part. (3)Update the time series prediction model by sensor nodes.

The first step is creating time series trend model by sensor nodes: We assume that each node reads temperature every Γ time units, and denotes the history of these values as $v_1 \ldots v_i \ldots v_n$, which satisfy the time serial trend function $F(t) = m(t) + X(t)$, where $m(t)$ is the trend component, $X(t)$ is a weakly stationary time series model.

In our system, in order to speed up the rate of creating the trend function, reduce the node computing complexity, we consider a linear trend component $m(t) = a + b \cdot t$, where a and b are real constants. We use least squares method to compute a and b, as shown in equation 2:

$$\sum_{t=1}^{n} (a + b \cdot t - v_t)^2 = \min \tag{2}$$

where v_t is the temperature value sensed by node.

The trend component can reflect the changing rate of values sensed by nodes in the period of detection times. But in order to improve the accuracy of the predicting time serial trend function $F(t)$, we add a error component using stationary sliding time series model, $X(t) = \alpha_1 X(t-1) + \cdots + \alpha_n X(t-n)$.

we create a serial time model where the sliding window is 3 and the standard deviation is $b(\omega)$, as shown in equation 3:

$$\begin{cases} X(t) = \alpha X(t-1) + \beta X(t-2) + \gamma X(t-3) \\ \qquad\qquad\qquad X(t) = v_t - m(t) \end{cases} \tag{3}$$

where α, β, γ are real constants. Since X(t) is stationary, then $\alpha + \beta + \gamma < 1$. Note that function $b(\omega)$ represents the standard deviation of the white noise, and as a result it provides a measurement of the quality of our prediction model.

The predicting function we want to create is $P(t)$, as shown in equation 4:

$$P(t) = m(t) + \alpha \cdot (v_{t-1} - m(t-1)) + \beta \cdot (v_{t-2} - m(t-2)) + \gamma \cdot (v_{t-3} - m(t-3)) + b(\omega) \tag{4}$$

where $m(t)$ is the trend function, α, β, γ are real constants of time serial model, $b(\omega)$ is the standard deviation.

Then we need to compute the real constants α, β, γ. We assume a queue D_v containing the difference of each sense values $v_1 \ldots v_i \ldots v_n$ with from its trend values m(i), that is $x_i = v_i - m(i)$, for each x_i, $x_i \in D_v$. Node uses the data contained in D_v to compute the coefficients α, β, γ by applying least-squares regression, and it computes the standard deviation $b(\omega)$, $b(\omega) = (\frac{\sum_{i=1}^{n}(e_i - \bar{e})^2}{n})^{-1/2}$, where $e_i = F(i) - v_i, 1 < i < n$, $\bar{e}$ is the mean of $e_1, e_2, \ldots, e_n$. Finally, nodes keep the series trend function model coefficients $a, b, \alpha, \beta, \gamma, b(\omega)$ that uniquely identify the model, and transmit them to sink.

Algorithm 1. Create time series trend model

Input: Sample time t, value v_t, total number of samples n
Output: time series trend model parameters $a, b, \alpha, \beta, \gamma, b(\omega)$
  1: event CreatModel()
  2: **while** $i < n$ **do**
  3:    collects data v_i $(t < n)$ every Γ time units
  4:    i++
  5: Calculate the parameters a, b by using equation 2
  6: Calculate the parameters α, β, γ by using equation 3
  7: Calculate error $b(\omega)$
  8: Send the time series trend model parameters to sink

The second step of TSDC algorithm is predicting data. we describe how to predict nodes monitoring values and reduce the node sense delay by using the predicting model coefficients $a, b, \alpha, \beta, \gamma, b(\omega)$ in the host computer part. When sink receives information from nodes, host computer reconstructs predicting function $P(t)$ by using the returning predicting model coefficients, as shown in equation 3. The change rate of time variable t in equation 3 is the same with node's sampling interval. In order to reduce the node sensing delay, we set variable t to be a fast change rate t' , where $t' = t + \Delta t$ or $t' = \kappa t$. Then taking the time variable t' into function $P(t)$, predict the sense values.

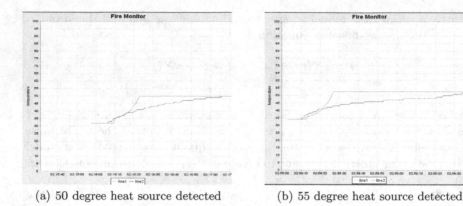

(a) 50 degree heat source detected   (b) 55 degree heat source detected

Fig. 3. Delay of temperature sensing test

Our fire monitoring system mainly focus on the timeliness fire alarm, so we set variable t to be a fast change rate t', where $t' = 1.2 \cdot t$. Firstly, we test this time serial prediction model by using single node monitoring 50 degree and 55 degree centigrade heat source, as shown in Fig.3(a) and Fig.3(b).

In Fig.3(a) and Fig.3(b), the red curve(line 2) represents monitoring values by using traditional method, the green curve(line 1) represents monitoring values by using time serial prediction method. As shown in these figures, it takes 60s and 80s to sense the heat source from 30 degree centigrade to 50 and 55 degree centigrade respectively with traditional method. But if using time serial prediction method, it can reduce the delay to 18s and 20s respectively. In this experiment, node is close to the heat source, in order to react to the changing of temperature within the shortest time. But in the real environment monitoring, the distance between fire and nodes is uncertain. If using traditional method, the monitoring delay would be more longer than experiments above. Therefore, TSDC algorithm would be meaningful in practical application.

The third step of TSDC algorithm is update the time series prediction model. System predicts the temperature values by using the prediction function $P(t)$, but the time serial trend model is not stable. When temperature trend changed, the model should be changed. Nodes that sensed the changing would update the time serial trend model and send the new model parameters to sink. In order to improve the predicting accuracy and reduce the failure probability of fire alarm, system also should send a query to network ensuring that the prediction model is valid and credible.

After sending the time serial trend model to sink, each node keeps the model parameters, and collects data v_t (t>n) every Γ time units. With these new collecting data, node creates new trend model function. Then comparing the parameter b' of trend component in new model with the parameter b kept in node, if $|b' - b| < \tau$, where τ is threshold set by system, it demonstrates that the time serial trend model working in system is still available. Otherwise, node sends new time serial trend model to sink, and sink updates its prediction function.

Algorithm 2. Predict values

Input: time variable t, sample value v_i, total number of samples n, threshold ϕ, u
Output: The prediction value $P(t)$ at time t
1: **while** sink doesn't receive new model parameters **do**
2:     Compute the value m(t) of trend model at time t, $m(t) = a + b \cdot t$
3:     Calculate the prediction value $P(t)$ at time t by using equation 3-6
4:     **if** $up = 0$ **then**
5:         Call the event function $query()$ in random manner
6:     **else**
7:         Call the event function query()
8:         $i + +$

9: **Event Query**()
10: Cink sends a query to nodes and gets the actual monitoring value v' at time t'
11: **if** $|v' - P(t')| > \phi$ **then**
12:     $up + +$
13: **else**
14:     $up - -$
15: **if** $up > u$ **then**
16:     Cink assign a task to node, and the node update time series trend model

---

In order to guarantee the difference between prediction value and real sensed value within a certain range, we use the real monitoring values feedback the system prediction model. Comparing the real monitoring value v_t with the prediction value $P(t')$ which computed in node, where $t' = t \cdot 1.2$. If the system collects u consecutive monitoring values, all of the values can make $|v_t - P(t)| \geq \phi$, and u is threshold set by system, it demonstrates that the time serial trend model working in system is not available. The node will create new model and send to sink.

4.2   Fire Detection Based on Neural Network Model

Three parameters of temperature, humidity and light intension are adopted to detect fire in our fire monitoring system. Because the fire's uncertainty feature, we propose fire detection mechanism using neural network algorithm. The fire occurring probability can be computed when the three parameters are taken into trained neutral network as input. The output of neural network algorithm is the probability p of fire. Comparing with system initialized threshold θ, system alarms when p is greater than the threshold.

Telosb node is sensitive to light intension changing, so system uses the true monitoring light values as one of the input of neural network model. And using the prediction temperature and humidity values which computed by using time serial prediction function as the other two inputs. In the system, we use three-layer feed forward neural network model. There are three neurons in the input layer, and real light values, prediction temperature and humidity values are the input respectively. There are three neurons in the hidden layer and one neuron in output layer, and the output value is the probability of the fire.

Algorithm 3. Update time series prediction model

Input: Sample time t, value v_i, model parameters $a, b, \alpha, \beta, \gamma, b(\omega)$ threshold ϕ, u, τ
Output: New time series model parameters $a', b', \alpha', \beta', \gamma', b'(\omega)$
 1: Compute the value m(t) of trend model at time t, $m(t) = a + b \cdot t$
 2: Calculate the prediction value $P(t)$ at time t by using equation 3-6
 3: **if** $|v' - P(t)| > \phi$ **then**
 4:     $up + +$
 5: **else**
 6:     $up - -$
 7: **if** $up > u$ **then**
 8:     Call event CreateModel()
 9:     $up = 0$
10: $t + +$
11: $i + +$
12: **if** $i = n$ **then**
13:     Calculate new time series trend model parameters $a', b', \alpha', \beta', \gamma', b'(\omega)$
14:     $i = 0$
15: **if** $|b' - b| > \tau$ **then**
16:     Send new model parameters to sink

Before system working, we need to collect some samples which represent the condition of normal environment and under-fire environment, then train the neural network model by using neural network learning algorithm[14,15]. Finally, we will get the parameters of neural network model, including the weight matrices ω_{ih} between input layer and hidden layer, threshold matrices b_h of hidden layer, the weight matrices ω_{ho} between hidden layer and output layer, and threshold matrices b_o of output layer. Taking the neural network model parameters into system, the fire monitoring system can work. When a set of data including light, temperature and humidity are taken into the model, system will get the probability p of fire under this condition by using equation 5.

$$p = f(\sum_{h=1}^{3} w_{ho} \cdot f(\sum_{i=1}^{3} w_{ih} x_i - b_h) - b_o) \tag{5}$$

where $f(x) = 1/(1 + e^{-x})$.

If p is greater than the preset alarm threshold, system alerts. If users require a higher accuracy of the fire alarm, the threshold should be set close to 1. If users require a immediate warning of fire, the threshold should be reduced.

5   Experiments

In this section, we present experiments results and analyse of our algorithms. We will test the TSDC algorithm, and the comprehensive performance of the system. Firstly, we compare TSDC algorithm with traditional method by using single nodes sensing heat source, and then test fire monitoring system performance including timeliness and accuracy of fire alarm by burning different materials.

5.1   System Platform Setup

System uses telosb node as monitoring node. There are temperature\humidity sense component called Sensirion SHT11, and light sense component called Hamamatsu S10871 in a single node. The client platform is developed based on java and TinyOS platform. We test the performance of system using burning material including wood, lighter, alcohol and cigarettes.

The characteristic of wood fuel is that temperature, humidity and light values will change obviously.The lighter fuel duration is shorter. Temperature and Light intension change greatly when alcohol burns. However, alcohol volatilizes greatly while it burns, so the changing of humidity is not obvious. The feature of burning cigarette is temperature, humidity and light values changing gentle. Finally, we Statistics the delay and accuracy of fire alarm according to different types of fire monitoring experiments.

Before the system works, we need to collect some samples which represent the condition of normal environment and under-fire environment, and train the neural network model by using neural network learning algorithm.

5.2   Experimental Results

Firstly, we use single nodes sensing heat source to test TSDC algorithm comparing with traditional method. The heat source is hot water which the temperature changed from 100 degree centigrade to 30 degree centigrade. We count the times that node sense temperature from 30 degree centigrade to different degree centigrade including 80,70,60,50,40,30 degree centigrade as shown in figure 4.

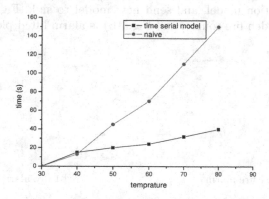

Fig. 4. Comparison of heat source monitoring time

In Fig.4, it demonstrates that the temperature sensing delay can be reduced obviously. It only takes 30s to sense temperature from 30 degree centigrade to 80 degree.

Table 1. Fire Detection Result

Material	number of samples	average alarm delay(s)	Recognition rate
wood	20	28	100%
lighter	20	24	90%
alcohol	20	21	100%
cigarettes	20	53	80%

Then by using mood, lighter, alcohol and cigarettes as fire materials respectively, we conduct 80 groups of experiments. The distance between fire and node is 15CM. The statistical of alarm delay and recognition rate of fire are shown in table 1.

Experiments demonstrate that our new fire monitoring system can recognize blaming fire(temperature, light intensity change greatly when the fire breaks out) nearly 100% and the alarm relay can be controlled in 30 seconds. The low smoldering fire can be detected in 1 minutes, and recognition rate of smoldering fire can be controlled in 80%. The fire that performs obviously, but last shortly can be detected in 30 seconds, recognition rate can be controlled in 90%.

The client interface consists of two parts. One part displays nodes distribution map. The other part displays the curves that describe the values of each node monitoring. When there is fire occurring in the monitoring area, system alerts, and the node closed to the fire will be marked red.

System can predict the monitoring values by using time serial prediction model, and Display diagram to user on client, rather than query to node online. When fire disappeared, system stop alarming, and nodes will create new time serial prediction model, and send new model to sink. Fig.5(a) shows the alarm plot of wooden fire source, and Fig.5(b) is alarm lifted plot.

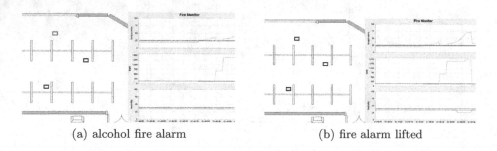

(a) alcohol fire alarm   (b) fire alarm lifted

Fig. 5. An example of alcohol fire monitoring

6   Conclusions

This paper proposes a new framework of fire monitoring system based on sensor networks in of sensor data collection mechanism uses time series prediction TSDC algorithm and fire detection mechanism using neural network model.

TSDC algorithm can greatly reduce the temperature and humidity sensing delay caused by node sensing ability limited. Neural network is a intelligent decision algorithm. Probability that fire occurs under current condition can be obtained by computing fusion of temperature, humidity and light intension. Experiment results show that the fire monitoring system can recognize the flaming fire nearly 100%, and warning delay can be controlled in the 30s. The slow smoldering fire recognition rate can be controlled in 80%, warning delay can be controlled in $1min$.

References

1. Chunlei, W., Yu, H., Qiaolin, C., Xin, L.: Design and realization of fire monitor system based on wireless sensor network. In: Proceedings of 2007 Computer Engineering and Design, vol. 28(10), pp. 2310–2320 (2007)
2. Li, Y., Qin, H., Xu, W., Zhang, L.: A WSN Based Information Acquisition System of Fire Risk. In: Proceedings of 2008 Electronics and Packaging, pp. 32–44 (2008)
3. Tu, D., Liu, S., Xie, W., Zhang, Y.: A Fire Monitoring System In ZigBee Wireless Network. In: Proceedings of IEEE WiCOM 2009, pp. 1–5 (2009)
4. Liu, S., Xie, W., Zhang, Y.: Research and implementation of WSN in fire safety Applications. In: Proceedings of IEEE WiCOM 2010, pp. 1–4 (2010)
5. da Penha Jr., O.S., Nakamura, E.F.: Fusing Light and Temperature Data for Fire Detection. In: Proceedings of IEEE ISCC 2010, pp. 107–112 (2010)
6. Liu, S., Tu, D., Zhang, Y.: Multiparameter Fire Detection Based on Wireless Sensor Network. In: Proceedings of IEEE ICIS 2009, pp. 203–206 (2009)
7. Sung, W.-T., Chen, C.-H., Chen, J.-H., Liu, Y.-F.: Multi-Sensors Data fusion for Precise Measurement based on ZigBee WSN via Fuzzy Control. In: Proceedings of 2010 3CA, pp. 156–159 (2010)
8. Liu, S., Zhang, Y., Guo, I.: Multiparameter Fire Detection Node Based on Wireless Sensor Network. Proceedings of 2010 Journal of Sensors and Actuators, 883–887 (2010)
9. Soliman, H., Sudan, K., Mishra, A.: A Smart Forest-Fire Early Detection Sensory System Another Approach of Utilizing Wireless Sensor and Neural Networks. In: Proceedings of IEEE Sensors 2010, pp. 190–194 (2010)
10. Tan, W., Wang, Q., Huang, H., Guo, Y., Zhang, G.: Mine Fire Detection System Based on Wireless Sensor Network. In: Proceedings of IEEE ICIA 2007, pp. 148–152 (2007)
11. Bahrepour, M., Meratnia, N., Paul, J.M.: HavingaSensor Fusion-based Event Detection in Wireless Sensor Networks. In: Proceedings of IEEE MobiQuitous 2009, pp. 1–9 (2009)
12. Zhang, L., Fang, G.: Design Implementation of Automatic Fire Alarm System based on Wireless Sensor Networks. In: Proceedings of IEEE ISIP 2009, pp. 410–413 (2009)
13. Ren, H., Sun, J., Tian, Z., Wang, H.: Mine fire identification method with multiparameters based on neural network. In: Proceedings of 2007 Journal of Liaoning Technical University (2007)
14. Da Penha Osman, S., Nakamura Eduardo, F.: Fusing Light and Temperature Data for Fire Detection. In: Proceedings of IEEE ISCC 2010, pp. 107–112 (2010)

15. Liu, B., Zhang, Y., Gan, F., Wang, D.: Design Intelligent Muti-sensor Fire Monitoring Based on DSP. In: Proceedings of IEEE ICEMI 2007, pp. 779–785 (2007)
16. Tulone, D., Madden, S.: PAQ: Time Series Forecasting for Approximate Query Answering in Sensor Networks. In: Römer, K., Karl, H., Mattern, F. (eds.) EWSN 2006. LNCS, vol. 3868, pp. 21–37. Springer, Heidelberg (2006)
17. Tulone, D., Madden, S.: An energy-efficient querying framework in sensor networks for detecting node similarities. In: Proceedings of IEEE MSWiM 2006, pp. 191–300 (2006)
18. Lu, C.J., Lee, T.S., Chiu, C.C.: Financial time series forecasting using independent component analysis and support vector regression. Proceedings of 2009 Decision Support Systems 47(2), 115–125 (2009)
19. Le Borgne, Y.-A., Santini, S., Bontempi, G.: Adaptive Model Selection for Time Series Prediction in Wireless Sensor Networks. Proceedings of 2007 Elsevier 87(12), 1–28 (2007)

Synchronized Flow-Based Evacuation Route Planning*

Manki Min

Dept. of EECS, South Dakota State University, Brookings, SD 57007, USA
manki.min@sdstate.edu

Abstract. When a disaster occurs, we need a routing plan to evacuate all the people in the affected area as soon as possible. For this purpose, we can model the transportation network as a graph of nodes and edges with occupancy on nodes and capacity and travel time on edges, where nodes represent places such as cities and edges represent roads. Given a transportation network graph, we can compute routes to evacuate all the people in the dangerous area by selecting paths from the source nodes (the nodes of which residents need to be evacuated) to the destination nodes (the nodes where the evacuees can be transported to). With capacity and travel time constraints on the roads (or edges), calculation of the evacuation time on the graph requires the use of time-expanded graphs. The use of time-expanded graphs, which are merely duplications of the given graph flagged with discrete time stamps, explodes the time and space complexities of the calculation of evacuation times. This drawback results in low scalability, especially when the evacuation time or the number of evacuees is relatively big compared to the size of the graph, such as the number of nodes, edges, and paths. In this paper, we present a scalable algorithm, SYNChronized FLOw Evacuation(SyncFloE), to plan the evacuation routes based on synchronized flows. The novel concept of synchronized flows replaces the use of time-expanded graphs and provides higher scalability in terms of the evacuation time or the number of evacuees. SyncFloE has computation time that only depends on the number of source nodes and the size of the graph itself, such as the number of nodes, edges, and paths. The computational results that support our claim are presented and discussed.

1 Introduction

With recently increasing occurrence of disasters such as hurricanes, tsunamis, earthquakes, and nuclear meltdowns all over the globe, the more importance is put on the efficient and effective operation of evacuation process. When such a disaster happens, the people who stay in the area that can be affected by the disaster (this area is will be different depending on the types of the disasters) need to move to safer places (often times shelters). Since there can be a lot of people that need to be evacuated, without the help of well-established evacuation routes it will be a very time-consuming and ineffective evacuation. Depending on the types of the disasters, the time that we have to compute such evacuation routes and at the same time the time that the last evacuees are evacuated, called evacuation time, can vary. Nonetheless, regardless of the type of

* Research is partly supported by NSF Award CCF-0729182.

X. Wang et al. (Eds.): WASA 2012, LNCS 7405, pp. 411–422, 2012.
© Springer-Verlag Berlin Heidelberg 2012

disasters, the algorithm must be scalable so that reasonable amount of time could be used to compute the evacuation routes and the evacuation time could be minimized.

The computation of the evacuation routes and evacuation time is based on the abstraction of the transportation network as a graph of nodes and edges with occupancy on nodes and capacity and travel time on edges, where nodes represent places such as cities and edges represent roads. Given a transportation network graph, we can compute routes to evacuate all the people in the dangerous area by selecting paths from the source nodes to the destination nodes. In this paper, we present our scalable algorithm, SYNChronized FLOw Evacuation (SyncFloE), which can compute the evacuation time without the help of time- expanded graphs. There are algorithms to compute the evacuation time in literature, but they are not scalable due to the fact that either they are based on time-expanded graphs or their computations repeat over time. SyncFloE uses the novel concept of *Synchronized Flow* to replace the use of the time-expanded graphs and/or the repetitions over time. A synchronized flow is the flow of evacuees from the source node(s) to destination node(s) that can have the same evacuation time by redistributing the evacuees over the paths along the flow from either the same source node or different source nodes. To ensure the computation of accurate evacuation times, we need to introduce *Virtual Evacuees* into the synchronized flows. Virtual evacuees are the evacuees that do not actually exist and they are added to the synchronized flow just to make the synchronized flow have the same evacuation time for all the paths.

Our contribution in this work is three-fold: firstly, our algorithm provides a new efficient way to compute the evacuation time and plan the evacuation routes. SyncFloE can compute the evacuation time extremely quickly so it can be directly used in real evacuation situation. This real-time calculation with the latest information about the roads and the cities (or places) will ensure always the most accurate evacuation routes. Secondly, our algorithm can be used in the computation of contraflow-based evacuation routes. In one of our previous work, we presented algorithms for the computation of contraflow-based evacuation routes and one of them is using the evacuation routes in its computation of contraflows. This algorithm inherits the scalability from evacuation routing algorithms and the existing evacuation routing algorithms cannot make it scalable. In addition, we are planning to extend SyncFloE to design another efficient and effective contraflow-based evacuation routing algorithm. Thirdly, the novel concept of synchronized flows will make a very powerful tool in the network flow study. In case of single packet routing, only the information of the edge such as the travel time or the capacity is required in the routing. However when we consider multiple packet routing, there's more than just the edge information in the routing computation and the synchronized flows (or time-expanded graphs as an old way) will play the key role in the routing.

The rest of this paper is as follows: Section 2 will define the problem of evacuation routing and discuss briefly the existing algorithms. In section 3, the novel concept of synchronized flows are explained and discussed. The algorithm SyncFloE is introduced in section 4 and explained. The computation results are presented and discussed in section 5 and section 6 concludes this paper.

2 Related Work

Given a transportation network graph of nodes and edges with occupancy on nodes and capacity and travel time on edges, where nodes represent places such as cities and edges represent roads, the evacuation routing problem is to find the routes, in other words a set of paths, for evacuation so that the time the last evacuees arrive the destination, called the evacuation time, become minimum. The evacuation routing problem and the traditional network routing problem are two different problems in the following reason: the traditional network routing problem considers the routing for single packet and so each edge will be used at most once for the packet and hence the attributes of the edges are enough for the routing computation. However the evacuation routing problem has multiple packets and an edge can be used more than once over time and hence the attributes of the edges are not enough for the computation. One way or another, we need to take care of this time-related attributes and the easiest way is to use the time-expanded graphs which are the duplications of the same graph tagged with discrete time-stamps with proper inter-links between them. Or one can record the usage logs for each edge and the logs become bigger as the evacuation time grows. This difference makes the use of traditional routing algorithms for evacuation routing impractical.

There isn't much work toward the evacuation routing in literature. Capacity Constrained Routing Planner (CCRP) [7–9] and its improvement CCRP++ [11] are reported in literature. CCRP is simply repeated operations of Dijkstra' shortest path algorithm in time-expanded graphs. The algorithm finds the shortest path that is available at current time repeatedly and if it cannot find a path, it increases the current time and continues finding the shortest paths until there is no more evacuees. Since CCRP is based on the time-expanded graphs, 1) it is not scalable, and 2) even worse its running time will also depend on how many duplications the time-expanded graphs have. It is not easy to have a tight estimation of the evacuation time (this number is the number of the duplications) before actually running the algorithm, and this is a kind of dilemma. CCRP++ was proposed as an improvement to CCRP and CCRP++ has much shorter running time than CCRP by reducing the number of shortest path findings. The algorithm uses the maximum capacity of each shortest path found and keeps the usage logs for each edge so that later when the same path is found, it can start from the earliest available time. Anyway CCRP++ also uses the time attributes and its computational complexity is not free from the inherent dependency to the evacuation time. As discussed in section 5, as the evacuation time increases, more precisely as the number of paths that are used grows, the running time becomes extremely higher. Even for a graph with 100 nodes and roughly 300 edges, it takes impractically long time.

We proposed our algorithm Quickest Path Evacuation Routing (QPER) in [10]. The quickest path is the path that gives the minimum evacuation time when combined with the existing paths by redistributing evacuees. QPER is using quickest paths instead of shortest paths and hence the number of paths that are used in the evacuation is much smaller in QPER than CCRP++ and the running time of QPER is more scalable than CCRP++. QPER is finding the evacuation routes for a single source node and this result became the motivation of this work, synchronized flows.

Slightly different focuses have been put on works in [1, 3, 4]. In [1], the authors discussed the problem of lane-based routing to minimize the traffic delay. The main effort of the proposed work is focused on the minimization of the crossing conflicts at the intersections of the roads. In this work, they considered maximum flow (which will give the maximum constant rate of evacuation flow) to solve the problem and hence it may not lead to an evacuation routing with minimum evacuation time. The quickest transshipment problem in [3] is the problem of minimizing the number of paths to complete the transshipment with demands that exceeds the capacity of the network capacity. By only minimizing the number of paths, we may not be able to get the minimum evacuation time, so this problem cannot be applied to our problem. [4] presents an extensive survey of the mathematical modelling of evacuation problems with different goals under different network configurations.

3   Synchronized Flows

In this section, we explain the synchronized flow that is the basis of the proposed algorithm.

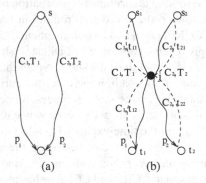

Fig. 1. Multiple paths in a synchronized flow

Let's begin with the simplest case when a source node has more than one paths as in figure 1 (a). In this case, we can freely redistribute the evacuees from one path to another to make the evacuation times of the two paths equal as in figure 2 (a). The combined evacuation time (CET) [10] is computed as follows:

$$CET = \frac{n + C_1 \cdot T_1 + C_2 \cdot T_2}{C_1 + C_2} - 1 \tag{1}$$

where n is the number of evacuees in the source node, C and T represent capacity and travel time of each path and the evacuation time of the source node is $\lceil CET \rceil$. This free redistribution of evacuees is possible at any time as long as the source node still has remaining evacuees and this separates the two cases in figure 1. In (b), the paths from different source nodes cannot have freely redistributed evacuees. In addition, the redistribution of evacuees and the resulting equalized evacuation time distinguish the evacuation routing from the traditional network routing. Figure 2 shows the arrival

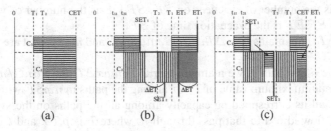

Fig. 2. Arrival Graph

graphs that represent the flows of evacuees that arrive the destination nodes and the joint node of the two paths if there's any.

Now let's consider the multiple paths from different source nodes as in figure 1 (b). In this case, unfortunately we cannot directly apply the CET calculation to equalize the evacuation times, instead we have two evacuation times. In this figure, the black colored node j is the joint node between two paths in different synchronized flows and s_1 has path p_1 and s_2 has path p_2. p_1 has capacity of C_1 and travel time of T_1 and the travel time on p_1 from s_1 to j is t_{11} and the travel time from j to t_1 is t_{12}. We can observe that the grey-shaded are in the arrival graph (figure 2 (b)) is wasted and if we could move some of the rightmost evacuees from s_1 in the upper box to this grey area, we would reduce the evacuation time of s_1. In fact, we need to look at the thick lines which shows the ending time of each path to get the same evacuation time, we call such ending time as synchronized ending time (SET). After the end time of the leftmost box (representing arrival at the joint node) until SET_2, we can put evacuees and still get the two evacuation times equal. Note that when we move the evacuees from s_1 to s_2, then SET_1 will also change and so does SET_2. As a result of this redistribution, we get figure (c) and we get CET less than ET_1 (Evacuation Time of s_1) and we can say those two paths to have synchronized flow. Still the grey-shaded area exists in (c) and this means that we need to put virtual evacuees into synchronize flows on those two paths.

The concept of virtual evacuees is the key point in synchronizing flows on the paths from the different source nodes. Next we discuss the six cases of synchronizing flows, two for the paths from the same source and four for the paths from different sources. Before we begin, let's define some notations.

- For a node n, $n.id$ means the id of n, $n.Occ$ means the occupancy (or the number of people staying) of n, $n.pSF$ means the list of SF (Synchronized Flow) that pass through n, and $n.pSF(FId)$ means the SF in $n.pSF$ with the flow id of FId.
- For a path p, $p.Cp$ means the capacity of the path p, $p.TT$ means the travel time of the path p;
  $p.Src$ means the origin node of the path p and $p.Dst$ means arrival node.
- For a synchronized flow SF, $SF.CpSum$ means the sum of capacities of paths in SF, $SF.CpTTSum$ means the sum of products of capacity and travel time; $SF.Srcs$ is the list of source nodes that evacuates along SF, $SF.FId$ is the flow id of SF;

$SF.EV$ is the number of evacuees on SF, $SF.VE$ is the number of virtual evacuees, and $SF.ET$ is the evacuation time of SF.

$n.pSF(FId)$ maintains $min\Delta T, minC, max\Delta T$, and $maxC$ that are used to calculate SETs.

For a node n in a path p, we maintain $min\Delta T/max\Delta T$ and $minC/maxC$ to be the minimum/maximum value of $T - t$ among the paths in $n.pSF$ with maximum capacity and its corresponding capacity among all the paths on the synchronized flow with flow id of FId that pass through n, where T is $p.TT$ and t is the travel time on p from $p.Src$ to n;

$n.pSF(FId)$ has SET of $n.pSF(FId).ET - n.pSF(FId).max\Delta T$ if FId is the flow id of p and $n.pSF(FId).ET - n.pSF(FId).min\Delta T$ otherwise.

- S means the set of source nodes and T means the set of destination nodes of the evacuation.
- ΔN means the number of evacuees that need to be moved from one path to another, $VirtEvac$ means the number of virtual evacuees.

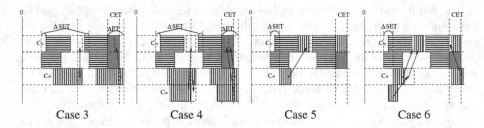

Case 3   Case 4   Case 5   Case 6

Fig. 3. Arrival graphs for cases $3 \sim 6$

Let's say p is the path that is newly added to the graph.

Case 1: If $p.Src$ does not have any synchronized flow yet and $p.Dst \in T$, we can simply make the path to have a new synchronized flow SF such that $SF.FId :=$ $p.Src.id$, $SF.CpSum := p.Cp$, $SF.CpTTSum := p.TT$, $SF.EV = p.Src.Occ$, $SF.ET = (SF.EV + SF.CpTTSum)/SF.CpSum - 1$, and $SF.Srcs := \{p.Src\}$. There is no ΔN nor $VirtEvac$.

Case 2: If $p.Src$ has the synchronized flow SF, we can add p into SF such that $SF.CpSum := SF.CpSum + p.Cp$, $SF.CpTTSum := SF.CpTTSum + p.Cp \cdot p.TT$, $SF.ET = (SF.EV+SF.VE+SF.CpTTSum)/SF.CpSum-1$, and $SF.Srcs := SF.Srcs$ $\cup\{p.Src\}$. There is no ΔN nor $VirtEvac$.

Case 3 (subcase of case 1): if p has a joint node j which has a synchronized flow SF_{old}, then $VirtEvac$ can be calculated as follows:
$jSF_N = j.PSF(SF.FId)$, $jSF_O = j.PSF(SF_{old}.FId)$,
$C_N = p.Cp$, $C_O = min(jSF_O.minC, C_N)$,
$\Delta ET = SF.ET - jSF_O.ET$,

$$\Delta SET = \Delta ET - (jSF_N.maxT - jSF_O.minT),$$
$$\Delta N_1 = \frac{C_N \cdot C_O}{C_N + C_O} \cdot \Delta ET, \ \ \Delta N_2 = C_O \cdot (\Delta ET - \Delta SET),$$
$$CS_O = SF_{old}.CpSum.$$
$$VirtEvac = \begin{cases} CS_O \cdot \frac{\Delta N_1}{C_O} - \Delta N_1, & \text{if } \Delta N_1 \geq C_N \cdot \Delta SET, \\ CS_O \cdot \left(\Delta SET - \frac{\Delta N_2}{C_N} + \frac{\Delta N_2}{C_O}\right) - \Delta N_2, & \text{o.w.} \end{cases}$$

Case 4 (subcase of case 2): if $p.Dst \in T$ and p has a joint node j which has a synchronized flow SF_{old}, then $VirtEvac$ can be calculated as follows:
$$C_N = SF.CpSum.$$
$$VirtEvac = \begin{cases} CS_O \cdot \frac{\Delta N_1}{C_O} - \Delta N_1, & \text{if } \Delta N_1 \geq C_N \cdot \Delta SET, \\ CS_O \cdot \left(\Delta SET - \frac{\Delta N_2}{C_N} + \frac{\Delta N_2}{C_O}\right) - \Delta N_2, & \text{o.w.} \end{cases}$$

The undefined variables are defined in the same way as case 3.

Case 5: If $p.Dst = j \notin T$ and $p.Src$ does not have a synchronized flow yet and j has another synchronized flow SF_{old}, then $VirtEvac$ can be calculated as follows:
$$\Delta SET = p.TT - (jSF_O.ET - jSF_O.minT).$$
$$VirtEvac = \begin{cases} CS_O \cdot p.Src.Occ \ \ p.Src.Occ, & \text{if } \Delta SET \leq 0, \\ (CS_O + \Delta SET) \cdot p.Src.Occ - p.Src.Occ, & \text{o.w.} \end{cases}$$

The undefined variables are defined in the same way as case 4.

Case 6 (subcase of case 2): If $p.Dst = j \notin T$ and $p.Src$ has a synchronized flow SF and j has another synchronized flow SF_{old}, then $VirtEvac$ can be calculated as follows:
$$\Delta SET = p.TT - (jSF_O.ET - jSF_O.minT),$$
$$\Delta N_2 = \frac{C_N \cdot C_O}{C_N + C_O} \cdot (\Delta ET \Delta SET).$$
$$VirtEvac = \begin{cases} CS_O \cdot \frac{\Delta N_1}{C_O} - \Delta N_1, & \text{if } \Delta SET \leq 0, \\ CS_O \cdot \left(\Delta SET + \frac{\Delta N_2}{C_O}\right) - \Delta N_2, & \text{o.w.} \end{cases}$$

The undefined variables are defined in the same way as case 4 or 3.

The proof of the correctness of the above formula is omitted due to the space limitation. However it is derived from the observation that the redistribution of evacuees is possible only when the evacuees are available. The condition in cases 3 ∼ 6 basically means that the SET of the old synchronized flow at the joint node is greater than the SET of the new synchronized flow so that the redistribution can happen right after the old synchronized flow ends passing by the joint node. Otherwise we need to put a pause time before redistributing the evacuees as in figure 3 case 3 or 4.

4   Synchronized Flow Evacuation (SyncFloE)

Figure 6 shows our novel algorithm SyncFloE. As we can see from the description, computation time of SyncFloE will depend on the number of shortest paths with updated available capacities of edges and it does not depend on any other factor such as the number of evacuees, capacities of the edges (and hence the capacities of the paths),

---

Initialization
1: S:= the set of source nodes, PS:= the set of poorest source nodes, T:= the set of destinations.
2: preEvactime := curEvacTime := ∞.

Iteration1 while a shortest path p from a node $s \in PS$ to a node $t \in T$ is found using available
capacities of edges:
1: if $(p.TT > \text{preEvacTime})$
2:    $PS := PS \setminus \{s\}$.
3: else
4:    (preEvactime, curEvacTime) = manipulate(p, S, PS, T, preEvacTime, curEvacTime).

Iteration2 while a shortest path p from a node $s \in PS$ to a node $t \notin T$ is found:
1: (preEvactime, curEvacTime) = manipulate(p, S, PS, T, preEvacTime, CurEvacTime).

Fig. 4. SyncFloE

and so on. This independence gives our algorithm dramatically improved scalability and
we believe that this is a lower bound for the computational complexity of evacuation
routing.

Adding a path p into a synchronized flow SF involves updating $SF.CpTTSum$,
$SF.CpSum$, $SF.EV$, $SF.VE$, and $SF.ET$. In addition, tracking all the nodes in p,
the synchronized flows passing the node n will be updated; if the flow is not already
included in $n.pSF$, then include SF into $n.pSF$, add $p.Src$ into $SF.Srcs$, update
$min\Delta T$, $minC$, $max\Delta T$, $maxC$ properly as discussed in section 3. The removal of
p from SF is almost reverse activity of the addition; rolls back the $min\Delta T$, $minC$,
$max\Delta T$, $maxC$, removes SF from $n.pSF$ if it was included by the path addition, removes $p.Src$ from $SF.Srcs$ if it was included by the path addition, and finally restores
$SF.CpSum$, $SF.CpTTSum$, $SF.EV$, $SF.VE$, $SF.ET$.

Merging two synchronized flows (SF_N into SF_O) involves adding $SF_N.CpSum$,
$SF_N.EV$, $SF_N.VE$, and $SF_N.CpTTSum$ to $SF_O.CpSum$, $SF_O.EV$, $SF_O.VE$,
and $SF_O.CpTTSum$ and adding $SF_N.Srcs$ into $SF_O.Srcs$. Split of a synchronized
flow into two flows is almost reverse activity of merging; rolls back the two synchronized flows to the ones before the merging, and removes $p.Src$ from $SF_N.Srcs$ if it
was included by the merging.

After adding/removing a path into a synchronized flow or merging/splitting two synchronized flows, we calculate the evacuation time of the whole graph by calculating
the evacuation time of each synchronized flow and updating evacuation time of the
source nodes that belong to the synchronized flow. Then curEvacTime becomes the
maximum evacuation time calculated and preEvacTime is the evacuation time of the
previous calculation. The curEvacTime and preEvacTime updated after the calculation
of evacuation time are used to determine whether or not to roll back the changes that
we introduced into the graph. When rolling back the changes, the source node of the
path will be removed from the poorest source node to give a chance to the other poorest
source nodes. If the poorest source node list becomes empty or there are no more paths,
the algorithm terminates.

```
 1: if p.Dst ∈ T,
 2:    if p.Src has a synchronized flow SF_new, // case 2
 3:       add p into SF_new.
 4:       if (curEvacTime > preEvacTime), remove p from SF_new, and PS = PS \ {p.Src}.
 5:    else if p has a joint node with another synchronized flow SF_old, // case 4
 6:          calculate VirtualEvac using Case 4, add VirtEvac to SF_old, and merge SF_new into
          SF_old.
 7:          if (curEvacTime > preEvacTime), remove VirtEvac from SF_old, and split SF_new from
          SF_old, and PS = PS \ {p.Src}.
 8:    else, // case 1
 9:       add p into a new synchronized flow SF_{p.Src.id}.
10:       if p has a joint node with another synchronized flow SF_old, // case 3
11:          calculate VirtEvac using Case 3, add VirtEvac to SF_old, and merge SF_{s.id} into SF_old.
12:          if (curEvacTime > preEvacTime), remove VirtEvac from SF_old, and split SF_{p.Src.id}
          from SF_old, and PS = PS \ {p.Src}.
13: else
14:    if s has a synchronized flow SF_new, // case 2
15:       add p into SF_new.
16:       if (curEvacTime > preEvacTime), remove p from SF_new, and PS = PS \ {p.Src}.
17:    else if p has a joint node with another synchronized flow SF_old, // case 6
18:          calculate VirtEvac using Case 6, add VirtEvac to SF_old, and merge SF_new into SF_old.
19:          if (curEvacTime > preEvacTime), remove VirtEvac from SF_old, and split SF_new from
          SF_old, and PS = PS \ {p.Src}.
20:    else, // case 5
21:       calculate VirtEvac using Case 5, add VirtEvac to SF_old, and add p into SF_old
22:          if (curEvacTime > preEvacTime), remove VirtEvac from SF_old, and remove p from
          SF_old, and PS = PS \ {p.Src}.
```

Fig. 5. Manipulate(p, S, PS, T, preEvacTime, curEvacTime)

SyncFloE repeatedly calls manipulate function (figure 5) which will have activities such as addition (or removal) of a path into a synchronized flow and merge (or split) of two synchronized flows. The computational complexity of manipulate function is bounded by the computational complexity of those activities that are bounded by the number of node because in all activities, we simply traverse the nodes at most once.

In this paper we haven't included the construction of evacuation routes but it can be obtained by storing additional information such as paths, when the path is used, etc. With the additional information we can easily reconstruct the paths and the flows that depict the evacuation routes.

5   Computational Results

We implemented two algorithms, CCRP++ and SyncFloE. For comparisons, we randomly generated n nodes in a $n \times n$ area with random occupancy for each node, with the value of n in $\{100, 200, 300, 400, 500, 1000, 5000, 10000\}$. The number of the source nodes, m_s, and the destination nodes, m_t, are randomly determined between 1 and 10 and between 1 and 5, respectively. Then the point of the disaster is randomly

generated and the m_s nodes that are closest to the disaster point are marked as source
nodes and the m_t nodes farthest from the disaster point are marked as destination nodes.
For each source node, randomly pick edges to generate at least one path. Up to $1.5 \sim$
3 times n edges are generated randomly. Each edge is assigned random capacity in between 1 and 5 and travel time proportional to the distance between two endpoint nodes.
And we ran each transportation network setting 10 times to get the average results. For
the computation we used gcc and g++ as compilers on a Linux machine with dual 2.33
GHz dual core CPU's and 4GB of RAM.

Table 1. CCRP++ VS SyncFloE

Capacity	CCRP++		SyncFloE	
Range	Evac. Time	Comp. Time	Evac. Time	Comp. Time
$1 \sim 5$	8787	12498.6	9105	0.02
$10 \sim 50$	5719	21.21	6527	0.02
$100 \sim 500$	5656	0.4	6216	0.02

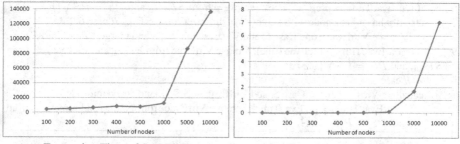

Evacuation Time of SyncFloE   Computation Time of SyncFloE

Fig. 6. Computational results of SyncFloE

CCRP++ was not run for all network settings, in fact for most settings CCRP++
took too long time, so we are just presenting one interesting results that explains why
CCRP++ is not scalable. We ran CCRP++ for a rather small sized network with 500
nodes (including 7 source nodes and 4 destination nodes) and 829 edges. To evacuate
19856 evacuees from the 7 source nodes to 4 destination nodes took 12498.6 seconds
while SyncFloE took 0.02 seconds. However when we multiplied each edge's capacity
by ten so that CCRP++ finds less paths, it took 21.21 seconds while SyncFloE took
0.02 seconds. When we multiplied the edge capacities by ten again, CCRP++ took 0.4
seconds and SyncFloE still runs in 0.02 seconds. For this network setting, the computation time has increased by at least 50 times with the decrease of the edge capacity; 50
times from 100 to 10, and 500 times from 10 to 1. The evacuation time of CCRP++ was
slightly better than that of SyncFloE and we think it might be the result of inaccurate
update of synchronized flows that pass through each node and careful investigation in
this direction is one of our future works. The evacuation time and computation time
comparison of two algorithms is given in table 1.

Table 2. Evacuation Time and Computation Time by SyncFloE

run index	n	Evac.	Comp.	n	Evac.	Comp.	n	Evac.	Comp.	n	Evac.	Comp.
1	100	887	0.01$^+$	200	2785	0.01$^+$	300	3037	0.01	400	8648	0.02
2	100	1354	0.01$^+$	200	4498	0.01$^+$	300	1420	0.01$^+$	400	10911	0.01$^+$
3	100	3069	0.01$^+$	200	4185	0.01$^+$	300	3659	0.01	400	15792	0.01$^+$
4	100	1674	0.01$^+$	200	7310	0.01$^+$	300	5695	0.01	400	3858	0.01
5	100	1901	0.01$^+$	200	2681	0.01$^+$	300	8951	0.01$^+$	400	2482	0.02
6	100	7988	0.01$^+$	200	5930	0.01$^+$	300	11213	0.01$^+$	400	5159	0.01
7	100	1775	0.01$^+$	200	2618	0.01$^+$	300	15340	0.01$^+$	400	6530	0.01
8	100	11861	0.01$^+$	200	4364	0.01$^+$	300	4936	0.01$^+$	400	8964	0.01
9	100	987	0.01$^+$	200	12413	0.01$^+$	300	4044	0.01$^+$	400	13808	0.03
10	100	1697	0.01$^+$	200	5114	0.01$^+$	300	6223	0.01	400	7206	0.02
1	500	9105	0.02	1000	7861	0.11	5000	118409	1.15	10000	136811	7.63
2	500	7431	0.02	1000	11520	0.12	5000	107008	1.51	10000	157855	7.79
3	500	7865	0.04	1000	11665	0.1	5000	86369	1.15	10000	145413	5.18
4	500	8541	0.01	1000	12399	0.11	5000	64732	1.72	10000	148794	8.61
5	500	11536	0.01	1000	13540	0.01	5000	50052	1.72	10000	137801	4.28
6	500	10387	0.02	1000	13299	0.1	5000	90902	2.22	10000	107904	8.15
7	500	2688	0.02	1000	10651	0.14	5000	67160	2.17	10000	137496	7.66
8	500	3680	0.01	1000	10025	0.12	5000	117433	2.62	10000	120094	7.69
9	500	7950	0.02	1000	20953	0.07	5000	86681	1.63	10000	137625	5.57
10	500	8028	0.03	1000	14223	0.02	5000	74652	0.93	10000	136771	7.86

$^+$ the running time was shorter than 0.01 seconds.

The results of SyncFloE is given in table 2 and the average values over 10 runs were plotted on the graphs in figure 6). The computation time of SyncFloE for smaller sized networks with up to 1000 nodes was extremely short as less than one second. The increase rate of computation time up to 1000 nodes is negligible but it starts to grow from more than 1000 nodes by at most 20 times; less than 20 times from 1000 to 5000 and four times from 5000 to 10000. This increase of computation time at large-scale networks is inevitable since with more edges, we can expect to have more paths and as a result the algorithm will run longer. This result confirms that the computational complexity of our algorithm depends on the number of paths.

The evacuation time also increases in a similar pattern as the computation time and this is because as the number of nodes grows, the graph will have more edges and longer paths. In fact, when the number of nodes was increased by ten times from 1000, the evacuation time became roughly ten times bigger. However when the number of nodes is small as 500 or less, the number of evacuees will play more important role in determining the evacuation time and hence we don't observe the similar increase pattern for the evacuation time.

6   Conclusions

In this paper, we proposed a truly scalable algorithm for evacuation routing that is not affected by factors outside of the graph itself such as the number of evacuees and the capacity of the paths used. The existing algorithms in literature, CCRP and CCRP++ were not scalable in most cases due to their dependency on the timed information such as in time-expanded graphs or in repeated computations of the same path over time. The virtual evacuees were added to the synchronized flows to equalize the evacuation times of different paths. This process gets rid of the dependency on the timed information by allowing paths from different source nodes to be grouped as a synchronized flow. We strongly believe that our novel concept of synchronized flow will play a very important · role in the evacuation routing in the future.

Our future works include the careful revision on the implementation of SyncFloE and the more thorough study on the synchronized flows and the design of contraflow evacuation routing based on the synchronized flows. We expect to improve the performance in terms of the evacuation time by carefully revising the implementation especially regarding correct logging of synchronized flows on the nodes, correct roll backs of changes, and more careful calculation of the virtual evacuees.

References

1. Cova, T.J., Johnson, J.P.: A network flow model for lane-based evacuation routing. Transportation Research Part A 37, 579–604 (2003)
2. Yang, F., Yan, X., Xu, K.: Evacuation Flow Assignment based on Improved MCMF Algorithm. In: Proc. First International Conference on Intelligent Networks and Intelligent Systems, pp. 637–640 (2008)
3. Fleischer, L.K.: Faster Algorithms For The Quickest Transshipment Problem. SIAM J. Optim. 12/1, 18–35 (2001)
4. Hamacher, H.W., Tjandra, S.A.: Mathematical Modelling of Evacuation Problems: A State of Art. Technical Report Nr. 24, Berichte des Fraunhofer ITWM (2001)
5. Kim, S., Shekhar, S.: Contraflow Network Reconfiguration for Evacuation Planning: A Summary of Results. In: Proc. Proceedings of the 13th ACM Symposium on Advances in Geographic Information Systems, pp. 250–259 (2005)
6. Kim, S., Shenkhar, S., Min, M.: Contraflow Transportation Network Reconfiguration for Evacuation Route Planning. IEEE Transactions on Knowledge and Data Engineering 20/8, 1115–1129 (2008)
7. Lu, Q., Huang, Y., Shekhar, S.: Evacuation Planning: A Capacity Constrained Routing Approach. In: Chen, H., Miranda, R., Zeng, D.D., Demchak, C.C., Schroeder, J., Madhusudan, T. (eds.) ISI 2003. LNCS, vol. 2665, pp. 111–125. Springer, Heidelberg (2003)
8. Lu, Q., George, B., Shekhar, S.: Capacity Constrained Routing Algorithms for Evacuation Planning: A Summary of Results. In: Medeiros, C.B., Egenhofer, M., Bertino, E. (eds.) SSTD 2005. LNCS, vol. 3633, pp. 291–307. Springer, Heidelberg (2005)
9. Lu, Q., George, B., Shekhar, S.: Evacuation Route Planning: Scalable Heuristics. In: Proc. 15th International Symposium on Advances in Geographic Information Systems (2007)
10. Min, M., Neupane, B.C.: An Evacuation Planner Algorithm in Flat Time Graphs. In: Proc. of ACM International Conference on Ubiquitous Information Management and Communication, ICUIMC (2011)
11. Yin, D.: A Scalable Heuristic for Evacuation Planning in Large Road Network. In: Proc. the Second International Workshop on Computational Transportation Science, pp. 19–24 (2009)

Group Multicast Capacity in Large Scale Wireless Networks

Xican Yang[1,2], Jinbei Zhang[1], and Jian Li[1]

[1] Department of Electronic Engineering, Shanghai Jiao Tong University
[2] The State Key Laboratory of Integrated Services Networks, Xidian University, China
{09420902150876,abelchina,fighting0818}@sjtu.edu.cn

Abstract. In this paper, we investigate the impact of group multicast on the capacity of large-scale random wireless networks. n nodes are randomly distributed in the networks, among which n^s nodes are selected as sources and n^d destined nodes are chosen for each. Specifically, we consider two different scenarios, i.e., (1) regular distribution scenario, and (2) random distribution scenario. The upper bound capacity of group multicast is derived for the network. Furthermore, we propose the corresponding capacity-achieving communication schemes to achieve the upper bound. Moreover, our study is the first attempt to understand how group multicast may impact on large scale network capacity from a theoretical perspective.

1 Introduction

Since the seminal work by Kumar et al. [1], which showed that the optimal unicast per-node capacity is $O(1/\sqrt{n})$, the fundamental capacity research about wireless ad hoc networks has drawn tremendous interest, such as [11], [16] and [18]. Later on, Grossglauser and Tse [2] proposed a 2-hop relaying algorithm in which nodes are allowed to move, and they demonstrated that $\Theta(1)$ capacity per source-destination is achievable but packets have to endure a larger delay of $\Omega(n)$. Since then, how to improve the network performance, in terms of the capacity and delay, has become a critical issue.

The analysis on how to improve the network performance has arised in recent years. Some works [3], [4], [5], [6], [7] investigated the improvement by introducing different kinds of mobility into the networks. Other works attempt to improve capacity by introducing base stations as infrastructure support [8], [9], [10]. Besides, there has been impressive recent works on the characterization of delay and capacity tradeoff in wireless ad hoc networks [12], [17].

However, all the above researches relay on the unicast traffic pattern. As the demand of information sharing increases rapidly, multicast traffic which genenalized both the unicast and broadcast traffic are proposed. Multicast capacity for large-scale wireless ad hoc network was first analyzed in [13]. It shows that when the number of destination nodes $k = O(n/\log n)$, the per-node multicast capacity is $\Theta(\frac{1}{\sqrt{n\log n}}\frac{W}{\sqrt{k}})$; when $k = \Omega(n/\log n)$, the per-node capacity is $\Theta(W/n)$, which is equivalent to the broadcast case. The result also implies that the per-node capacity decreases to zero as n goes to infinity. This means static ad hoc network is not scalable under unicast, multicast and

X. Wang et al. (Eds.): WASA 2012, LNCS 7405, pp. 423–437, 2012.
© Springer-Verlag Berlin Heidelberg 2012

broadcast traffic model. Wang et al. [14] generalized the result to anycast traffic pattern and Mao et al. [15] studied multicast networks with infrastructure support.

While unicast and multicast traffic pattern have been extensively studied in previous work, group multicast is still a relatively new concept and under active research. Group multicast refers to a traffic pattern in which data is delivered from a source to multiple destinations originazed in a multicast group, which differs from multicast in that its destinations are located in a more centralized area. Recently, many new applications appeared such as Introstate Television (TV), Stadium TV that impose stringent broadband services on group multicast.

In this paper, we have studied the theoretical group multicast capacity of wireless ad hoc networks. More precisely, we consider a wireless ad hoc network that consists of n nodes, among which n^s nodes are selected as sources and n^d destination nodes are chosen for each. Thus, n^s multicast sessions are formed. Furthermore, we assume that there are a set of n^{1-d} multicast groups $A = \{A_1, A_2, \ldots, A_{n^{1-d}}\}$. We study two kinds of common transmission scenarios, i.e., regular distribution scenario and random distribution scenario. The first type represents that n^{1-d} groups are regularly distributed in the network and each group covers the whole cell without intersections. While in the latter pattern these groups are randomly distributed in the network, there will inevitably be interferences due to the intersections between groups.

Our main contributions can be summarized as follows:

- Under the regular distribution scenario with group multicast, the capacity is $\Theta(\frac{1}{\sqrt{n^s}})$ when $s + d \leq 1$, and $\min\{\Theta(\frac{1}{\sqrt{n^s}}), \Theta(\frac{1}{n^{s+d-1}})\}$ when $s + d > 1$. While under the random distribution scenario, the capacity of wireless ad hoc network stays the same.
- To our best knowledge, this paper is the first work that characterizes the impact of group multicast on network capacity from a theoretical perspective.

The rest of this paper is organized as follows. In Section II, we describe the wireless network model. In Section III and IV, we investigate the capacity of regular distribution and random distribution group multicast respectively, and we give the aggregated capacity of the wireless network and analyze the results. Finally, we conclude our paper in Section V.

2   Wireless Network Model

2.1   Network Architecture

We employ the extended network model. We assume that there is a set $V = \{V_1, V_2, \cdots, V_n\}$ of n normal wireless nodes uniformly deployed in a square region with side length $\sqrt{n}$. All the wireless nodes have the same transmission power, and hence have the same transmission range r.

We further assume that there are a set of n^{1-d} multicast groups $A = \{A_1, A_2, \cdots, A_{n^{1-d}}\}$. We first study the regularly distributed networks, as shown in Figure 1, to avoid the interference among the groups. For regularly distributed networks, n^{1-d} groups divide the network region into n^{1-d} disjoint cells. Each group covers the whole cell and has n^d nodes in the group. Later on we will discuss the random-distributed situation. Note that when these groups are randomly distributed in the network, there will inevitably be interferences due to the intersections between the groups, making it difficult to schedule the model.

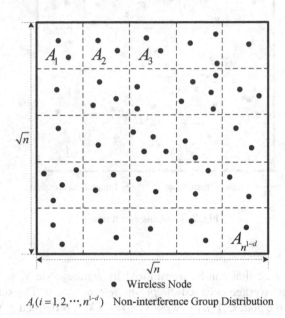

- Wireless Node
$A_i(i = 1, 2, \cdots, n^{1-d})$ Non-interference Group Distribution

Fig. 1. Network model

2.2 Multicast Traffic Pattern

Among the n wireless nodes, a total of n^s source nodes are randomly selected, and each source node chooses a distinct group which has n^d destination nodes as a multicast session. Note that a particular group may be included by different multicast sessions as destination.

2.3 Interference Model

We employ the traditional *protocol model* in [1] as the interference model. All nodes employ a common range r for all their transmissions. When node V_i transmits to a node V_j, this transmission is successfully received by V_j if

1) The distance between V_i and V_j is no more than r, i.e.,

$$|V_i - V_j| \leq r.$$

2) For every other node V_k simultaneously transmitting,

$$|V_k - V_j| \geq (1 + \Delta)r.$$

The quantity $\Delta > 0$ is a guard zone specified by the protocol to prevent a neighboring node from transmitting at the same time.

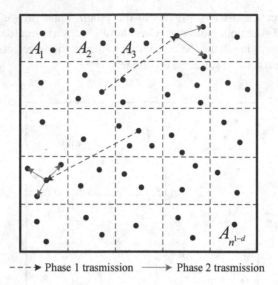

$\dashrightarrow$ Phase 1 trasmission $\longrightarrow$ Phase 2 trasmission

Fig. 2. Transmission mode

2.4   Definition of Capacity

Throughput: λ_i bits/sec that can be transmitted by source node V_i to its chosen n^d destination nodes on average is called the *per-node throughput*. The sum of per-node throughput over all the nodes, $\Lambda(n) = \lambda_1 + \lambda_2 + \cdots + \lambda_{n^s}$, is defined as the *throughput of the network.*

Feasible Throughput: A multicast rate vector $\lambda = (\lambda_1, \lambda_2, \cdots, \lambda_n)$ bits/sec is feasible if there is a spatial and temporal scheme for scheduling transmissions such that every node V_i can send λ_i bits/sec on average to its destinations. An aggregated multicast throughput $\Lambda(n)$ bits/sec is feasible if there is a feasible rate vector $\lambda = (\lambda_1, \lambda_2, \cdots, \lambda_n)$.

Capacity of The Network: The per-node throughput capacity is of order $O(f(n))$ bits/sec if there is a deterministic constant $c < +\infty$ such that

$$\liminf_{n \to \infty} Pr\left(\lambda(n) = cf(n) \text{ is feasible}\right) < 1$$

and is of order $\Theta(f(n))$ bits/sec if there are deterministic constants $c > 0$ and $c < c' < +\infty$ such that

$$\lim_{n \to \infty} Pr\left(\lambda(n) = cf(n) \text{ is feasible}\right) = 1$$

$$\liminf_{n \to \infty} Pr\left(\lambda(n) = c'f(n) \text{ is feasible}\right) < 1$$

3   Capacity of Regular Distribution Group Multicast

Any group A_i will be chosen by a certain source node as a destination with the probability $p = n^{d-1}$. Let N_i be the number of times when the group A_i is chosen as a destination, then clearly N_i follows the binomial distribution with parameters n^s and p. Easily we can derive

$$Pr(N_i = k) = \binom{n^s}{k} p^k (1 - p)^{n^s - k},$$

and the expected value of N_i is $E[N_i] = n^s p = n^{s+d-1}$. Thus we will employ different approaches to investigate the network capacity, according to the various circumstances of $s + d$.

We can randomly choose only one node inside a group as the destination node, thus the destination nodes are less than or included in the original group nodes. We define the procedure that source nodes transmit packets to destination nodes as *phase one transmission*, then we will calculate the network capacity, which is similar to the unicast capacity. When the number of destination nodes increases, just like original situation, network performance will be inevitably worse compared to phase one. We define the process that packets are transmitted from the destination node to the whole group as *phase two transmission*, and we will study capacity of phase two transmission which is similar to the broadcast capacity. We can easily know that the network capacity is upper-bounded both by the per-flow unicast capacity and the per-flow broadcast capacity. Thus, combining the two phases, we can get the upper bound of wireless network capacity. See Figure 2 for illustration.

3.1   When $s + d < 1$

The expected value of N_i diminishes to zero as the number of nodes is increased. Since the number of nodes goes to infinity while the product $n^s p$ remains fixed, the binomial distribution converges towards the Poisson distribution. Therefore the Poisson distribution with parameter $\lambda = n^s p = n^c$ can be used as an approximation to the binomial distribution here.

Capacity of Phase One Transmission.   Taking consideration of the source-destination pairs, there are totally n^s source nodes transmitting packets to their destinations. According to Kumar et al. [1], we can get the capacity of phase one transmission as

$$\lambda_1 (n) = O(\frac{1}{\sqrt{n^s}}).$$

Capacity of Phase Two Transmission.   We will take the similar approach in [19], [20], which is similar to the well-known maximum-flow and minimum-cut theorem. Considering a time interval T which is large enough, since each node can send data at $\lambda (n)$, the total amount of packets to be delivered between all source-destination pairs during T is $c_P k \lambda (n) T$, where k is the number of simultaneous transmission pairs and positive constant $1/c_P$ is the average number of bits per packet. Besides, the total wireless channel bandwidth is fixed to W bits per second, then the total number of packets the wireless network can provide is $c_p W T$. We can derive

$$c_P k \lambda (n) T \le c_p W T,$$

and thus the capacity of the wireless network is

$$\lambda(n) = O(\frac{W}{k}).$$

To determine the maximum flow, k, we derive the following lemma.

Lemma 1. *The number of times when any group is selected as a destination is at most constant when $s + d < 1$.*

Proof. Let K be a positive integer. As N_i follows the Poisson distribution with parameter $\lambda = n^s p = n^c$, then we can have

$$Pr(N_i \geq K) = \sum_{k \geq K} e^{-\lambda} \frac{\lambda^k}{k!}$$

$$\leq \sum_{k \geq K} e^{-\lambda} \lambda^k$$

$$\leq \frac{e^{-\lambda} \lambda^K}{1 - \lambda},$$

$$Pr(\max_i N_i \geq K) \leq \sum_i Pr(N_i \geq K)$$

$$\leq \frac{n e^{-\lambda} \lambda^K}{1 - \lambda}.$$

Since $c = s + d - 1 < 0$, $\lambda = n^c$ goes to zero when the number of nodes n goes to infinity. Then we can derive

$$\lim_{n \to \infty} Pr(\max_i N_i \geq K) \leq \lim_{n \to \infty} \frac{n^{cK+1} e^{-\lambda}}{1 - \lambda} = 0$$

as long as $cK + 1 < 0$. We choose $K = 1 + [\frac{1}{1-s-d}]$.

Based on Lemma 1, we can easily get the capacity

$$\lambda_2(n) = O(\frac{W}{K}) = O(1).$$

Since the network capacity is upper-bounded both by the per-flow unicast capacity and the per-flow broadcast capacity, combining phase one transmission and phase two transmission, we can derive the capacity of regular distribution scenario as

$$\lambda(n) = O(\min\{\Theta(\frac{1}{\sqrt{n^s}}), \Theta(1)\})$$

$$= O(\frac{1}{\sqrt{n^s}}).$$

Next, we will show that the bound is achievable. To achieve this goal, we design a scheduling scheme that satisfies the following two propositions.

1. For each source node V_i, we randomly and independently select a group A_i as its destination, then packets are transmitted, through ad hoc mode, from V_i to any node $V_{i,d}$ in the group A_i.
2. $V_{i,d}$ transmits the packets to all other nodes in the group A_i.

To meet the first proposition, we follow the schedule of Franceschetti et al. [21], adopting percolation theory in routing.

To meet the second proposition, we employ flooding algorithm. Flooding, where packets from a source node is delivered to all other nodes, has extensive applicability in ad hoc wireless networks. The traditional flooding scheme generates excessive packet retransmissions, resource contention, and collisions since every node forwards the packet at least once. Recently, several flooding schemes have been proposed to avoid these problems. Kim et al. [22] proposed *Priority Forwarding*, for efficient and fast flooding operations in wireless ad hoc networks. They demonstrated that with priority checking, the host closest to the coverage perimeter of a flooding packet would forward the packet immediately without delay. Obviously, the schedule can achieve the bound, and we have

Theorem 1. *The capacity of regular distribution group multicast is $\Theta(\frac{1}{\sqrt{n^s}})$, when $s + d < 1$.*

Proof. As stated above, we design a scheduling scheme which ensures the transmissions of all nodes by a time-division multi-access (TDMA) manner such that all nodes will be able to transmit at least once in every time $\sqrt{n^s} + K$ slots, thus the capacity can achieve

$$\lambda(n) = \Omega(\frac{1}{\sqrt{n^s} + K})$$
$$= \Omega(\frac{1}{\sqrt{n^s}}).$$

3.2   When $s + d > 1$

Since the expected value of N_i goes to infinity when the number of nodes increases, the methods above is not applicable anymore. Previously each group will receive information from K source nodes at most, while when $s + d > 1$ each group has to receive packets from more than constant source nodes, then the packets will be broadcast in the group. If we select a representative node similar to the previous case, it is difficult to understand the topology of the network and devise effective routing scheme since the representative node will be chosen as a destination node for many times, which is similar to the convergecast traffic pattern.

Thus we modify the transmission mode. As shown in Figure 3, we choose n^{s+d-1} nodes in each group as representatives. Firstly packets are transmitted from each source node to any representative node in a randomly selected group, and then representative nodes employ a celluar TDMA transmission scheme, broadcasting the packets to all other nodes in the group.

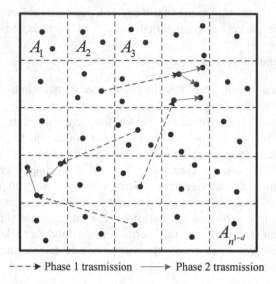

--- ▶ Phase 1 trasmission ────▶ Phase 2 trasmission

Fig. 3. Transmission mode when $s + d > 1$

Capacity of Phase One Transmission. There are totally n^s source nodes transmitting packets to their destinations and the transmission mode is the same as that of Kumar et al. [1], thus the capacity of phase one transmission is

$$\lambda_1(n) = O(\frac{1}{\sqrt{n^s}}).$$

Capacity of Phase Two Transmission. From the above derivation we have $E[N_i] = n^s p = n^{s+d-1}$, which means that every group will be chosen as a destination n^{s+d-1} times on average. In other words, $k = n^{s+d-1}$, it follows,

$$\lambda_2(n) = O(\frac{W}{n^{s+d-1}})$$
$$= O(\frac{1}{n^{s+d-1}}).$$

Combining phase one transmission and phase two transmission, we can derive the upper bound of the capacity of regular distribution scenario as

$$\lambda(n) = O(\min\{\Theta(\frac{1}{\sqrt{n^s}}), \Theta(\frac{1}{n^{s+d-1}})\}).$$

Using similar scheduling scheme as described previously, we can achieve the following theorem.

Theorem 2. *The capacity of regular distribution group multicast is* $\min\{\Theta(\frac{1}{\sqrt{n^s}}), \Theta(\frac{1}{n^{s+d-1}})\}$, *when $s + d > 1$, which is shown in Figure 4.*

Proof. We choose n^{s+d-1} nodes in each group as representatives. Firstly packets are transmitted from each source node to any representative node in a randomly selected group through ad hoc mode adopting percolation theory in routing, and then representative nodes employ the flooding scheme, broadcasting the packets to all other nodes in the group. This can be accomplished by adopting a TDMA scheme so that the time-slot is further divided into sub packet time-slots, and each node can be scheduled to transmit at least once in every $\sqrt{n^s} + n^{s+d-1}$ time-slots, thus the capacity can achieve

$$\lambda(n) = \Omega(\frac{1}{\sqrt{n^s} + n^{s+d-1}})$$

$$= \Omega(\min\{\Theta(\frac{1}{\sqrt{n^s}}), \Theta(\frac{1}{n^{s+d-1}})\}).$$

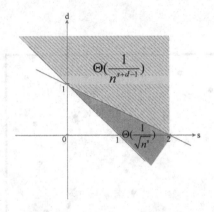

Fig. 4. Capacity of regular distribution group multicast when $s + d > 1$

3.3   when $s + d = 1$

Since $E[N_i] = n^s p = n^{s+d-1} = 1$, clearly N_i follows the Poisson distribution with parameters $\lambda = 1$ as the number of nodes goes to infinity. Thus we can get that the number of times when any group is appointed as a destination is at most $\log n^s$.

Similarly, we have

$$\lambda(n) = \min\{\Theta(\frac{1}{\sqrt{n^s}}), \Theta(\frac{1}{\log n^s})\}$$

$$= \Theta(\frac{1}{\sqrt{n^s}}).$$

4   Capacity of Random Distribution Group Multicast

In this section, we discuss the bounds for random group distribution wireless networks. As shown in Figure 5, when these groups are randomly distributed in the network, there will inevitably be interferences due to the intersections between the groups, making it difficult to schedule the model. Unlike previous analysis, we mainly discuss the random scenario capacity from the perspective of destination nodes.

Any node V_i in the network will be selected by a certain source node as its destination node with the probability $p = n^{d-1}$. Let N_i be the number of times when the node V_i is chosen as a destination node, then clearly N_i follows the binomial distribution with parameters n^s and p. Easily we can derive

$$Pr(N_i = k) = \binom{n^s}{k} p^k (1-p)^{n^s - k},$$

and the expected value of N_i is $E[N_i] = n^s p = n^{s+d-1}$. Similarly according to the various circumstances of $s + d$, we will employ different approaches to investigate the network capacity.

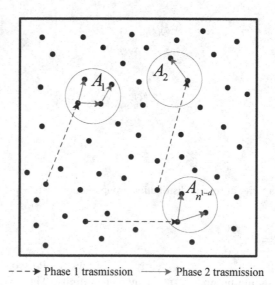

$---\blacktriangleright$ Phase 1 trasmission $\longrightarrow$ Phase 2 trasmission

Fig. 5. Transmission mode when groups are randomly distributed

4.1   When $s + d < 1$

As the number of nodes goes to infinity while the product $n^s p$ remains fixed, the binomial distribution converges towards the Poisson distribution. Therefore the Poisson distribution with parameter $\lambda = n^s p = n^c$ can be used as an approximation to the binomial distribution here. Consequently, we can derive the following lemma.

Lemma 2. *The number of times when any node is appointed as a destination node under random distribution scenario is also at most constant when $s + d < 1$.*

Proof. Let K be a positive integer. Using the same technique described previously, we can have

$$
\begin{aligned}
Pr(N_i \geq K) &= \sum_{k \geq K} e^{-\lambda} \frac{\lambda^k}{k!} \\
&\leq \sum_{k \geq K} e^{-\lambda} \lambda^k \\
&\leq \frac{e^{-\lambda} \lambda^K}{1 - \lambda},
\end{aligned}
$$

$$
\begin{aligned}
Pr(\max_i N_i \geq K) &\leq \sum_i Pr(N_i \geq K) \\
&\leq \frac{n e^{-\lambda} \lambda^K}{1 - \lambda},
\end{aligned}
$$

$$
\lim_{n \to \infty} Pr(\max_i N_i \geq K) \leq \lim_{n \to \infty} \frac{n^{cK+1} e^{-\lambda}}{1 - n^c} = 0
$$

as long as $cK + 1 < 0$. We choose $K = 1 + [\frac{1}{1-s-d}]$.

Based on Lemma 2, we have

$$
\begin{aligned}
\lambda(n) &= O(\min\{\Theta(\frac{1}{\sqrt{n^s}}), \Theta(\frac{W}{[\frac{1}{1-s-d}]+1})\}) \\
&= O(\frac{1}{\sqrt{n^s}}).
\end{aligned}
$$

Similarly, we design the following schedule to achieve the capacity bound.

1. Each source node transmits packets, through ad hoc mode, to a destination node $V_{i,d}$ in a randomly selected group.
2. $V_{i,d}$ transmits the packets to all other nodes in the group.

We follow the schedule of Franceschetti et al. [21], adopting percolation theory in routing, in order to meet the first requirement.

To meet the second requirement, we employ flooding algorithm. We should design the process such that every node acts as both a transmitter and a receiver, and each node tries to transmit packages to every one of its neighbors except the source node. In addition, the frequency that a node is transmitting should be the same as the frequency that it is receiving. Obviously, the bound can be achieved through the schedule, and we have,

Theorem 3. *The capacity of random-distribution group multicast is* $\Theta(\frac{1}{\sqrt{n^s}})$, *when* $s + d < 1$.

Proof. The proof is similar to that of Theorem 1, which employs the TDMA scheme.

4.2   When $s + d > 1$

Note that this situation is quite different from previous analysis. According to the previous derivation, we need to know the maximum times that each group can be chosen as destination. However, for randomly distributed networks, different groups may intersect and a node maybe in multiple groups. Hence, we will investigate the problem from the perspective of destination nodes instead of groups.

Let's recall some results from the appendix of Vasudevan et al. [23], as shown in Lemma 3.

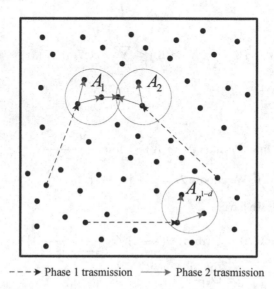

--→ Phase 1 trasmission   ──→ Phase 2 trasmission

Fig. 6. Transmission mode when groups are randomly distributed and $s + d > 1$

Lemma 3. *Let X be a Poisson random variable with parameter λ.*

 1. *If $x > \lambda$, then $Pr(X \geq x) \leq e^{-\lambda}(e\lambda)^x/x^x$.*
 2. *If $x < \lambda$, then $Pr(X \leq x) \leq e^{-\lambda}(e\lambda)^x/x^x$.*

Performing some algebraic manipulations, we obtain

Lemma 4. *The number of times when any node is appointed as a destination node under random distribution scenario is at most $2n^{s+d-1}$ when $s + d > 1$.*

Proof. As N_i follows the Poisson distribution with parameter $\lambda = n^s p = n^{s+d-1}$, then we can have

$$Pr(N_i \geq 2\lambda) \leq e^{-\lambda}(\frac{e}{2})^{2\lambda}$$
$$= (\sqrt{e})^{-2\lambda}(\frac{e}{2})^{2\lambda}$$
$$= (\frac{\sqrt{e}}{2})^{2\lambda},$$

$$Pr(\max_i N_i \geq 2\lambda) \leq \sum_i Pr(N_i \geq 2\lambda)$$

$$\leq n(\frac{\sqrt{e}}{2})^{2\lambda}.$$

Since $\frac{\sqrt{e}}{2} < 1$, $\lambda = n^{s+d-1}$ goes to infinity when the number of nodes n increases, then we have

$$\lim_{n\to\infty} Pr(\max_i N_i \geq 2\lambda) \leq \lim_{n\to\infty} n(\frac{\sqrt{e}}{2})^{2n^{s+d-1}} = 0.$$

From the above derivation we have $k = 2\lambda = 2n^{s+d-1}$, it follows,

$$\lambda(n) = O(\min\{\Theta(\frac{1}{\sqrt{n^s}}), \Theta(\frac{W}{2n^{s+d-1}})\})$$

$$= O(\min\{\Theta(\frac{1}{\sqrt{n^s}}), \Theta(\frac{1}{n^{s+d-1}})\}).$$

Using the same schedule described previously, we can then prove that the bound can be achieved, and that the capacity of the random distribution scenario is

$$\lambda(n) = \Omega(\frac{1}{\sqrt{n^s} + 2n^{s+d-1}}) = \Omega(\min\{\Theta(\frac{1}{\sqrt{n^s}}), \Theta(\frac{1}{n^{s+d-1}})\}).$$

With the above discussion, we can prove the following Theorem.

Theorem 4. *The capacity of random-distribution group multicast is* $\min\{\Theta(\frac{1}{\sqrt{n^s}}), \Theta(\frac{1}{n^{s+d-1}})\}$, *when* $s + d > 1$.

Proof. The proof is similar to that of Theorem 2, and the capacity is displayed in Figure 4.

4.3   When $s + d = 1$

This is identical to the situation when $s + d = 1$ under regular distribution scenario, and we need to establish the maximum flow of the network.

Lemma 5. *The number of times when any node is appointed as a destination node under random distribution scenario is at most* $\log n$ *when* $s + d = 1$.

Proof. When $s + d = 1$, N_i follows the Poisson distribution with parameter $\lambda = n^{s+d-1} = 1$,

$$Pr(N_i \geq \log n) \leq e^{-1}(\frac{e}{\log n})^{\log n}$$

$$\leq e^{-1}(\frac{1}{e^2})^{\log n}$$

$$= \frac{1}{en^2},$$

$$Pr(\max_i N_i \geq \log n) \leq \sum_i Pr(N_i \geq \log n)$$

$$\leq \frac{1}{en}.$$

When the number of nodes n goes to infinity , we have

$$\lim_{n \to \infty} Pr(\max_i N_i \geq \log n) \leq \lim_{n \to \infty} \frac{1}{en} = 0.$$

Thus, we have

$$\lambda(n) = \min\{\Theta(\frac{1}{\sqrt{n^s}}), \Theta(\frac{1}{\log n^s})\}$$

$$= \Theta(\frac{1}{\sqrt{n^s}}).$$

5   Conclusion

We have studied the theoretical group multicast capacity of wireless ad hoc network. In particular, we have investigated wireless networks using both regular distribution and random distribution models. Our results can well unify the previous multicast results in wireless ad hoc networks. What's more, our study is the first attempt to understand how group multicast may impact on network capacity from a theoretical perspective.

We are also interested in how to improve the throughput capacity of wireless ad hoc network by adopting multiple groups as destinations and using physical model. Although group multicast provides gain in certain wireless ad hoc network, an interesting question is what is the impact of combining group multicast and social network. And this question is also important in realistic cellular network.

Acknowledgment.   This paper is supported by National Fundamental Research Grant (No. 2010CB731803); NSF China (No. 60832005); China Ministry of Education New Century Excellent Talent (No. NCET-10-0580); China Ministry of Education Fok Ying Tung Fund (No. 122002); Qualcomm Research Grant; Shanghai Basic Research Key Project (No. 11JC1405100); National key project of China (2012ZX03001009, 2010ZX03003-001-01); China Postdoctoral Science Foundation Grant (No. 2011M500774).

References

1. Gupta, P., Kumar, P.R.: The Capacity of Wireless Networks. IEEE Trans. on Inform. Theory 46(2), 388–404 (2000)
2. Grossglauser, M., Tse, D.N.C.: Mobility increases the capacity of ad-hoc wireless networks. IEEE/ACM Trans. on Networking 10, 477–486 (2002)
3. Lin, X., Sharma, G., Mazumdar, R.R., Shroff, N.B.: Degenerate delay-capacity tradeoffs in ad-hoc networks with Brownian mobility. IEEE Trans. on Inform. Theory 52(6), 277–2784 (2006)

4. Neely, M., Modiano, E.: Capacity and Delay Tradeoffs for Ad-Hoc Mobile Networks. IEEE Trans. on Inform. Theory 51(6), 1917–1937 (2005)
5. Lin, X., Shroff, N.B.: The Fundamental Capacity-Delay Tradeoff in Large Mobile Ad Hoc Networks. In: Proc. Third Annu. Mediterranean Ad Hoc Netw. Workshop (2004)
6. Ying, L., Yang, S., Srikant, R.: Optimal delay-throughput trade-offs in mobile ad-hoc networks. IEEE Trans. on Inform. Theory 9(54), 4119–4143 (2008)
7. Li, P., Fang, Y., Li, J., Huang, X.: Smooth Trade-offs Between Throughput and Delay in Mobile Ad Hoc Networks. IEEE Trans. on Mobile Computing 11(3), 427–438 (2012)
8. Kozat, U., Tassiulas, L.: Throughput Capacity of Random Ad Hoc Networks with Infrastructure Support. In: Proc. ACM Mobicom, San Diego, CA, USA (June 2003)
9. Liu, B., Liu, Z., Towsley, D.: On the Capacity of Hybrid Wireless Networks. In: Proc. IEEE INFOCOM, San Francisco, CA, USA (March 2003)
10. Huang, W., Wang, X., Zhang, Q.: Capacity Scaling in Mobile Wireless Ad Hoc Network with Infrastructure Support. In: Proc. of IEEE ICDCS 2010, Genoa, Italy (2010)
11. Jing, T., Chen, X., Huo, Y., Cheng, X.: Achievable Transmission Capacity of Cognitive Mesh Networks With Different Media Access Control. In: Proc. IEEE INFOCOM, Orlando, Florida USA, March 25-30 (2012)
12. Fu, L., Qin, Y., Wang, X., Liu, X.: Throughput and Delay Analysis for Convergecast with MIMO in Wireless Networks. IEEE Trans. on Parallel and Distributed Systems 23(4), 768–775 (2012)
13. Li, X.-Y.: Multicast Capacity of Wireless Ad Hoc Networks. IEEE/ACM Trans. on Networking 17(3), 950–961 (2009)
14. Wang, Z., Sadjadpour, H.R., Garcia-Luna-Aceves, J.J.: A unifying perspective on the capacity of wireless ad hoc networks. In: Proc. IEEE INFOCOM, pp. 211-215 (2008)
15. Mao, X., Li, X.-Y., Tang, S.: Multicast capacity for hybrid wireless networks. In: Proc. ACM Mobihoc, New York, NY, USA, pp. 189-198 (2008)
16. Li, P., Zhang, C., Fang, Y.: The Capacity of Wireless Ad Hoc Networks Using Directional Antennas. IEEE Trans. on Mobile Computing 10(10), 1374–1387 (2011)
17. Wang, X., Huang, W., Wang, S., Zhang, J., Hu, C.: Delay and Capacity Tradeoff Analysis for MotionCast. IEEE/ACM Trans. on Networking 19(5), 1354–1367 (2011)
18. Le, Y., Ma, L., Cheng, W., Cheng, X., Chen, B.: Maximizing Throughput When Achieving Time Fairness in Multi-Rate Wireless LANs. In: Proc. IEEE INFOCOM Mini-Conference, Orlando, Florida USA, March 25-30 (2012)
19. Grossglauser, M., Tse, D.: Mobility increases the capacity of ad-hoc wireless networks. In: Proc. INFOCOM 2001, vol. 3, pp. 1360-1369 (2001)
20. Liu, J., Goeckel, D., Towsley, D.: Bounds on the Gain of Network Coding and Broadcasting in Wireless Networks. In: Proc. INFOCOM 2007, pp. 724-732 (May 2007)
21. Franceschetti, M., Dousse, O., Tse, D., Thiran, P.: Closing the Gap in the Capacity of Wireless Networks Via Percolation Theory. IEEE Trans. on Inform. Theory 53(3), 1009–1018 (2007)
22. Kim, K., Cai, Y., Tavanapong, W.: A priority forwarding technique for efficient and fast flooding in wireless ad hoc networks. In: Proc. ICCCN 2005, pp. 223–228 (October 2005)
23. Vasudevan, S., Goeckel, D., Towsley, D.F.: Security-capacity tradeoff in large wireless networks using keyless secrecy. In: Proc. ACM Mobihoc 2010, New York, USA, pp. 21–30 (2010)

Efficient Information Exchange in Single-Hop Multi-Channel Radio Networks

Weijie Shi[1], Qiang-Sheng Hua[1], Dongxiao Yu[2],
Yuexuan Wang[1], and Francis C.M. Lau[2]

[1] Institute for Theoretical Computer Science,
Institute for Interdisciplinary Information Sciences,
Tsinghua University, Beijing, 100084, P.R. China
[2] Department of Computer Science, The University of Hong Kong,
Pokfulam, Hong Kong, P.R. China
swj05652@gmail.com, {qshua,amywang}@mail.tsinghua.edu.cn,
{dxyu,fcmlau}@cs.hku.hk

Abstract. This paper studies the information exchange problem in single-hop multi-channel radio networks, which is to disseminate k messages stored in k arbitrary nodes to the entire network (with n nodes) with the fewest timeslots. By using $\Theta(\sqrt{n})$ channels, the previous best result [9] showed that this problem can be solved in $\Theta(k)$ time slots with high probability even if k is unknown and no bounds on k are given. Under the same assumptions but by using $\Theta(n)$ channels, this paper presents a novel randomized distributed algorithm called Detect-and-Drop that can solve the information exchange problem in $O(\log k \log \log k)$ time slots with high probability. Thus by allowing using more channels, our proposed algorithm contributes an exponential improvement in running time compared to that in [9]. The simulation results corroborate the analysis result.

Keywords: information exchange, single hop, multiple channels, randomized algorithm, distributed algorithm.

1 Introduction

Recent advances in wireless technology have made multi-radio multi-channel wireless networks possible practically [13]. Compared with using only one single channel, by using multiple channels, can we improve the performance of various common communication primitives such as broadcast [3] and information exchange [9,6]? The information exchange problem is to disseminate k messages stored in k arbitrary nodes to the entire network (with n nodes) with the fewest timeslots, which is also known as the multiple-message broadcasting problem [11] or the many-to-all communication problem [2]. The information exchange problem generalizes two well-known problems—broadcast ($k = 1$) and gossip ($k = n$). In this paper we restrict ourselves to single-hop networks, where each node in the network can communicate directly with every other node. The information exchange problem in single-hop networks may also take the form of the

X. Wang et al. (Eds.): WASA 2012, LNCS 7405, pp. 438–449, 2012.
© Springer-Verlag Berlin Heidelberg 2012

k-selection problem [4,14] or the contention resolution problem [18] where each of the k contenders has to exclusivly access a shared communication channel at least once.

To our best knowledge, the first study on the information exchange problem under multiple channels is due to Holzer, Pignolet, Smula and Wattenhofer [9]. In their paper, by using $\Theta(\sqrt{n})$ channels, the authors showed that the problem can be solved in $O(k)$ time slots with high probability even if k is unknown and no bounds on k are given. Since their paper restricts that each node can only receive one piece of information in each time slot, an obvious lower bound for the information exchange is $\Omega(k)$. Thus their proposed algorithm is asymptotically optimal. However, since each node can be equipped with multiple radios [13], the node can actually receive multiple messages simultaneously on multiple channels. Bearing this in mind, this paper seeks to find if there are efficient distributed algorithms that can solve the information exchange problem in $o(k)$ time slots. Our proposed algorithm answers this question affirmatively.

2 Our Contribution

In this paper, we present a randomized distributed algorithm which can complete the information exchange in $O(\log k \log \log k)$ time slots with probability at least $1 - 1/k^c$ for some constant $c > 0$ where k is the number of nodes that hold a message.[1] Our algorithm does not assume any information on the number of nodes n or the number of messages k. Although our algorithm uses more channels $(\Theta(n))$ than that $(\Theta(\sqrt{n}))$ in [9], we can exponentially reduce the time needed for accomplishing the information exchange.

3 Related Work

The information exchange problem and its variants have been extensively studied in the past decades, both for single-hop networks [18,4,14,5,9,17] and multi-hop networks [11,12,8]. By taking advantage of the collision detection ability [16] (which distinguishes between background noise and collision), Martel [15] presented a randomized adaptive protocol for the information exchange problem that works in $O(k + \log n)$ time in expectation. As argued by Kowalski in [14], this protocol can be improved to $O(k + \log \log n)$ in expectation using Willard's expected $O(\log \log n)$ selection protocol [17]. Without assuming the collision detection ability, Fernández Anta, Mosteiro, and Muñoz [5] proposed the EXP BACKON/BACKOFF algorithm which can solve the information exchange problem in $O(k)$ timeslots with high probability. Also without the collision detection ability, Yu et al. gave a randomized distributed algorithm for the dynamic version of the information exchange problem, where the messages may arrive in an adversarial pattern, in $O(k + \log^2 n)$ time slots with high probability.

---

[1] Throughout the paper, log means $\log_2$.

For multiple channels, to our best knowledge, the only efficient distributed algorithms for the information exchange problem in single-hop networks was proposed by Holzer, Pignolet, Smula and Wattenhofer in [9]. This paper gave both randomized and deterministic distributed algorithms. For the information exchange problem in multi-hop networks, there are no known efficient distributed algorithms that take advantage of multiple channels. For more references on the distributed algorithms for the information exchange problem in single-hop radio networks, please refer to [5,18,9].

The rest of the paper is organized as follows. Section 4 describes the network model and defines the the problem. Then a simple algorithm called MULTI-CHANNEL BACKON/BACKOFF which is adapted from the EXP BACKON/BACKOFF algorithm will be presented in Section 5. Our main algorithm DETECT-AND-DROP is given and analyzed in Section 6 and Section 7, respectively. The empirical evaluation result is given in Section 8 and we conclude the paper with some open problems in Section 9.

4   Model and Problem Definition

We consider a single-hop radio network consisting of n nodes and multiple channels. It is assumed that there are $4n$ available channels (later we will see that our algorithm can solve the problem with $\Theta(n)$ channels). Without loss of generality, these channels are numbered by $1, 2, \ldots, 4n$.

Initially, k $(1 \leq k \leq n)$ different messages are assigned to k arbitrary nodes, one message per node. The information exchange problem is to deliver the k messages to all nodes in the shortest time.

It is assumed that nodes have no any prior information about n or k, nor any estimates of these parameters. The only prior knowledge given to nodes is the linear relation between the number of channels and the number of nodes. So when a node selects a channel, it may actually select an unavailable channel and it will never know whether this channel is valid or not. Time is slotted into synchronous time slots. At the beginning of each time slot, a node can choose a channel and send a message via it. A message can be received if and only if there is exactly one node transmitting on a channel. If multiple nodes transmit on a channel simultaneously, a collision occurs and none of these transmissions can be correctly received. We assume that nodes are primitive and have no ability to detect collisions. At the end of the time slot, all nodes receive the successful broadcasts on multiple channels. This assumption is practical, since each node can be equipped with multiple radios [13]. It is also assumed that the sender can get feedback information from the channel on whether its transmission is successful.

5   Multi-Channel BackOn/BackOff Algorithm

In this section, we present a variant of the EXP BACKON/BACKOFF algorithm in [5] which can complete the information exchange in $O(\log^2 k)$ time with high probability. In the algorithm, nodes have two states: ACTIVE and IDLE. Nodes that have a message to transmit are in state ACTIVE initially. In the main algorithm (Algorithm 2), by estimating on the number of active nodes which increases exponentially, active nodes iteratively run a subroutine as described in Algorithm 1 trying to transmit their messages. In Algorithm 1, active nodes adopt a balls-into-bins strategy to achieve the appropriate transmission probabilities. An active node will set its state as IDLE after successfully transmitting its message.

Algorithm 1. Back-Off SubRoutine $(DROP(w))$

Require: $w > 0$
1: **while** $w \geq 1$ **do**
2:    Broadcast on channel i ($1 \leq i \leq w$) with probability $1/w$.
3:    **if** Broadcast Success **then**
4:       Set IDLE
5:    **end if**
6:    $w \leftarrow w \cdot (1 - \delta)$
7: **end while**

Algorithm 2. Multi-Channel BackOn/BackOff

1: **for** $i = \{1, 2, \ldots\}$ **do**
2:    Run: $DROP(2^i)$
3: **end for**

Using an analysis for the algorithm similar to that for the single channel case in [5], if w satisfies $k \leq w \leq 2n$, all active nodes have successfully transmitted their messages after executing subroutines $DROP(w)$ and $DROP(2w)$ for $O(\log k)$ time slots with high probability. We present the following result without giving the detailed proof.

Lemma 1. *For constant $0 < \delta < 1/e$, with probability at least $1 - 1/k^c$ for some constant $c > 0$, the information exchange can be completed in $O(\log w)$ time slots after w satisfies $k \leq w \leq 2n$.*

Since before w satisfies the condition $k \leq w \leq 2n$, in each iteration, it takes $O(\log k)$ time to execute the subroutine described in Algorithm 1. Then based on Lemma 1, the following theorem can be obtained.

Theorem 1. *For constant $0 < \delta < 1/e$, MULTI-CHANNEL BACKON/BACKOFF can complete the information exchange process in $O(\log^2 k)$ time slots with probability at least $1 - 1/k^c$ for some constant $c > 0$.*

6   Detect-and-Drop Algorithm

In this section, based on the subroutine $DROP$ given in Algorithm 1, we present a faster randomized distributed algorithm which can complete the information exchange in $O(\log k \log \log k)$ time with high probability. As shown in Algorithm 5, by doubly exponentially increasing the estimates on the value of k, active nodes iteratively execute the subroutine LDD given in Algorithm 4. The subroutine LDD consists of two parts. First, active nodes execute the subroutine $DETECT$ given in Algorithm 3 to get all possible estimates of k. Then for each obtained possible estimate, active nodes try to transmit their messages by calling the subroutine $DROP$ as described in Algorithm 1 twice. Next we will describe the algorithm in more details.

With the estimate s, in the execution of the subroutine $DETECT(s)$, active nodes broadcast on $\log s$ channels and set the transmission probabilities on these channels exponentially. In each round during the execution of the subroutine $DETECT(s)$, if on some channel i, the number of successful broadcasts exceeds $\log s$, 2^i will be seen as a possible estimate of k. If the input $s \geq k$, there is a channel i satisfying $k \leq 2^i < 2k$. In the analysis, we will show that with high probability, there will be at least $\log s$ successful broadcasts on channel i after $6 \log s$ rounds. Thus the proper estimate of k will be included in the output set $ResultSet$. Furthermore, we will also show that when $s \leq k^2$, there are at most $2 \log \log k$ channels on which more than $\log s$ successful broadcasts occur. This will ensure that the time complexity of our information exchange algorithm is at most $O(\log k \log \log k)$.

For each possible value 2^i obtained after executing the subroutine $DETECT$, all active nodes will try to transmit their messages by calling subroutines $DROP(2^i)$ and $DROP(2^{i+1})$. As discussed above, when $s \geq k$, with high probability, an estimate 2^j which locates in the interval $[k, 2k)$ is output by the subroutine $DETECT$. By Lemma 1, all active nodes can successfully broadcast their messages after executing the subroutines $DROP(2^j)$ and $DROP(2^{j+1})$ for $O(\log k)$ time slots.

Furthermore, in order to get an s as the input of $DETECT(s)$ in Algorithm 5 such that $s \geq k$, s is doubly exponentially increased instead of the traditional exponential increase. To guarantee the correctness and efficiency of the algorithm, we will show that an estimate of k in the interval $[k, k^2]$ is needed. The doubly exponential increase on one hand accelerates the estimation process; on the other hand, it ensures that there must be an estimate s in the interval $[k, k^2]$.

Algorithm 3. Detect SubRoutine ($DETECT(s)$)

Require: $s > 0$
1: **for** $j = 1$ **to** $6 \log s$ **do**
2:     Broadcast on channel i ($1 \leq i \leq \log s$) with probability $1/2^i$.
3:     Count the number of messages received on each channel
4: **end for**
5: **return** $ResultSet = \{i \mid$ more than $\log s$ messages received on channel $i\}$

Algorithm 4. A Loop of Detect-and-Drop $(LDD(s))$

Require: $s > 0$
1: Run: $DETECT(s)$, Get $ResultSet$
2: **for all** $i \in ResultSet$ **do**
3:     Run: $DROP(2^i)$
4:     Run: $DROP(2^{i+1})$
5: **end for**

Algorithm 5. Detect-and-Drop

1: **for** $i = \{1, 2, \ldots\}$ **do**
2:     Run: $LDD(2^{2^i})$
3: **end for**

---

7   Analysis

In this section, we analyse the correctness and efficiency of our information exchange algorithm. Specifically, we show that with probability $1 - \frac{1}{k^c}$ for some constant $c > 0$, the information exchange can be completed in $O(\log k \log \log k)$ time. Before starting the proof for the main theorem, some commonly used inequalities are in order.

Lemma 2. *If $0 < p \leq 1/2$, then $(\frac{1}{4})^{1/p} \leq 1 - p \leq (\frac{1}{e})^{1/p}$.*

Lemma 3. *If n is a sufficiently large natural number, $\sqrt{2\pi n}e^{n \log n - n} \leq n! \leq (\sqrt{2\pi n} + \sqrt{\pi/50n})e^{n \log n - n}$.*

By computing the differential, the following lemma can be easily proved.

Lemma 4. *If $1/2 \leq x \leq 1$, then $1/4 \leq x/4^x \leq 1/3$. If $x > 0$, then $f(x) = x/e^x$ is monotonically increasing on $(0,1)$ and monotonically decreasing on $(1, +\infty)$.*

Lemma 5. *For sufficiently large k, the following statements hold with probability at least $1 - 1/k^c$ for some constant $c > 0$.*
   (i) If $s \geq k$, there exists $i \in ResultSet$ such that $k \leq 2^i < 2k$.
   (ii) If $k \leq s \leq k^2$, the ResultSet returned by the subroutine $DETECT(s)$ satisfies: $|ResultSet| \leq 2 \log \log k$.

Proof. (i) Next we prove that if channel i satisfies $k \leq 2^i < 2k$, with large probability, at least $\log s$ broadcasts succeed in a total of $6 \log s$ broadcasts. Each node's transmitting probability on this channel is $p = 1/2^i$. So the probability that only one node transmits (and it can succeed) is:

$$P_{once} = kp(1-p)^{k-1} \geq kp(1/4)^{kp} \geq 1/4 \qquad (1)$$

The first inequality is by Lemma 2. So the probability that less than $\log s$ broadcasts succeeding is:

$$P_{fail} \leq \log s \cdot \binom{6 \log s}{\log s}(1 - P_{once})^{5 \log s} \tag{2}$$

We have the following inequality by using Lemma 3.

$$\binom{6 \log s}{\log s} \leq s^{5 \ln 5 - 4 \ln 4 + 0.01} \tag{3}$$

Thus, $P_{fail} \leq \log s / s \leq 1/k^{\frac{1}{2}}$ for large enough k.

(ii) Suppose that i is the required value in (i). We show that with high probability, for any channel j, $1 \leq j \leq i - \log \log k$ or $i + \log \log k \leq j \leq \log s$, $j \notin ResultSet$.

If $1 \leq j \leq i - \log \log k$, the transmission probability of a node on j is $p \geq \frac{\log k}{2k}$. In one round, the probability that a successful broadcast occurs is

$$P_{once} = kp(1-p)^{k-1} \leq 2kp(\frac{1}{e})^{kp} \leq \log k(\frac{1}{e})^{\log k/2} \leq \frac{\log k}{k^{3/4}} \tag{4}$$

And the probability that at least one successful broadcast occurs on these $\log \log k$ channels in $6 \log s$ rounds is

$$P_{fail} \leq 6 \log s \cdot \log \log k \cdot P_{once} \leq \frac{6 \log s \log k \log \log k}{k^{3/4}} \tag{5}$$

which is small enough to guarantee that on channel $1, 2, \ldots, i - \log \log k$, no successful transmission occurs with probability $1 - 1/k^c$ for some constant $c > 0$.

If $i + \log \log k \leq j \leq \log s$, the transmission probability of a node on j is $p \leq \frac{1}{k \log k}$; similarly,

$$P_{once} \leq \frac{2}{\log k}(1/e)^{1/\log k} \leq 2/\log k \tag{6}$$

The probability that more than $\log s$ successful transmissions occur on j is

$$P_{fail} \leq 5 \log s \cdot \binom{6 \log s}{\log s}(2/\log k)^{\log s} \tag{7}$$

Notice that $k \leq s \leq k^2$, so we get that for sufficiently large k,

$$P_{fail} \leq 10 \log k \cdot (60/\log k)^{\log k} \leq 1/k^3 \tag{8}$$

Thus, for each channel $j \geq i + \log \log k$, the probability that channel j is included in $ResultSet$ is at most $1/k^3$. Since there are at most $\log s \leq 2 \log k$ such channels, the probability that none of these channels is included in $ResultSet$ is at least $1 - \frac{1}{k^2}$.

Combining everything together, we have shown that the size of $ResultSet$ is not larger than $2 \log \log k$ with probability $1 - \frac{1}{k^c}$ for some constant $c > 0$.   □

Lemma 6. *For large enough k, the following statements hold with probability at least $1 - 1/k^c$ for some constant $c > 0$.*
(i) If $s \geq k$, $LDD(s)$ completes the information exchange.
(ii) If $s \leq k^2$, $LDD(s)$ takes $O(\log s \log \log k)$ time slots.

Proof. (i) Obviously, all nodes get the same $ResultSet$. So they run $DROP()$ at the same time. By Lemma 5, there is an i in $ResultSet$ satisfying $k \leq 2^i < 2k \leq 2n$. Then by Lemma 5, $LDD(s)$ completes the information exchange.

(ii) In the subroutine $LDD(s)$, $DETECT(s)$ takes $O(\log s)$ time. Furthermore, by Lemma 5, $|ResultSet| \leq 2 \log \log k$. And each $DROP$ subroutine takes at most $O(\log s)$ time. All together, the total time for executing $LDD(s)$ is $O(\log s \log \log k)$. □

Theorem 2. *For large enough k, with probability larger than $1 - 1/k^c$ for some constant $c > 0$, DETECT-AND-DROP completes the information exchange in $O(\log k \log \log k)$ time.*

Proof. Assume $s' = 2^{2^j}$ is the largest number satisfying $s' < k$. Then $2^{2^{j+1}} = s'^2 \leq k^2$. So there exists an integer i that satisfies $k \leq 2^{2^i} \leq k^2$. By Lemma 6, the total running time is

$$\sum_{i=1}^{\log \log k} O(\log(2^{2^i}) \log \log k) \in O(\log k \log \log k) \qquad (9)$$

which completes the proof. □

Indeed, for any known constant $c > 0$, DETECT-AND-DROP can solve the information exchange problem with cn channels in $O(\log k \log \log k)$ time. Here we use the case with n channels as an example. All nodes can split one round in the original DETECT-AND-DROP into four rounds. If a node broadcasts on Channel $4k + j$ in the lth round in the original algorithm, it broadcasts on Channel k in the $4l + j$th round now. The new algorithm takes four times that of the original time. Then we can get the following result

Corollary 1. *If the number of the channels $|C|$ is known as a function of n and $|C| = f(n) \in \Theta(n)$, then DETECT-AND-DROP can complete the information exchange in $O(\log k \log \log k)$ time.*

8   Simulation

In this section, we report our simulation of the original EXP BACKON/BACKOFF algorithm [5], the MULTI-CHANNEL BACKON/BACKOFF algorithm and the DETECT-AND-DROP algorithm. The simulation measures the average number (10 trials for each experiment) of time slots that the algorithms take until they complete the information exchange, for different values of k ($k = 10^4, 10^{4\frac{1}{3}}, 10^{4\frac{2}{3}}, 10^5, 10^{5\frac{1}{3}}, \ldots$). The constant is chosen to be $\delta = 0.366$. We set

$n = k$ and provide $2n$ and $4n$ available channels, respectively. We modify the detecting times in Algorithm 3 from $6 \log s$ to $4 \log s$ because this is actually enough to get a correct *ResultSet* in practice while not affecting the time complexity. No failure cases occur in all these simulations, which verifies that the success probabilities of these algorithms are all indeed very high.

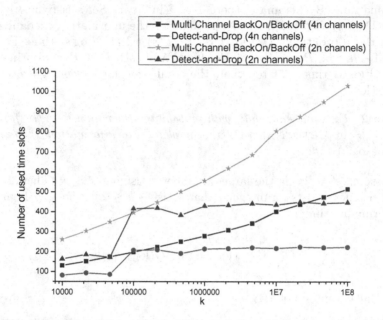

Fig. 1. Number of time slots to solve the information exchange problem

Fig. 1 and Table 1 show the result of the simulation. Table 2 reveals the hidden constant of DETECT-AND-DROP calculated by the ratio of time slots to the value of $\log k \log \log k$.

The simulation result speaks for the huge advantage of utilizing multi-channel technique. Among the five scenarios that have been simulated, the EXP BACKON/BACKOFF algorithm which uses only one channel takes the largest number of time slots, as shown in Table 1. For example, when $k = 10000$, it takes 71125 time slots to complete the information exchange with EXP BACKON/BACKOFF while our DETECT-AND-DROP algorithm only needs 82 time slots. Moreover, overall speaking, the algorithms that use $2n$ channels use more time slots than those that use $4n$ channels, as shown in Fig. 1.

Our DETECT-AND-DROP algorithm performs much faster than the MULTI-CHANNEL BACKON/BACKOFF algorithm in the simulation, as shown in Fig. 1, which verifies that our main algorithm DETECT-AND-DROP can greatly reduce the time complexity. In addition, the larger the k value, the more the number of reduced time slots. Finally, the running time of DETECT-AND-DROP increases slowly after $k \geq 10^5$, while the running time of MULTI-CHANNEL BACKON/BACKOFF increases rather rapidly.

As shown in Fig. 1, when $k \in \{10^{4\frac{2}{3}}, 10^5\}$, there is a jump in the running time of DETECT-AND-DROP. This is because for $k \geq 10^5$, Algorithm 5 needs one more execution round of Algorithm 4. With the same execution rounds of Algorithm 4, the running time grows slowly when k gets larger. (The running time is almost the same for $10^5 \leq k \leq 10^8$, as shown in Table 1.)

Table 1. Number of time slots to solve the information exchange problem

k	10^4	$10^{4\frac{1}{3}}$	$10^{4\frac{2}{3}}$	10^5	$10^{5\frac{1}{3}}$	$10^{5\frac{2}{3}}$	10^6
Exp BackOn/BackOff (single channel)	71125	1.56e+5	3.24e+5	6.58e+5	1.35e+6	2.74e+6	5.61e+6
Multi-Channel BackOn/BackOff ($2n$ channels)	262	304	350	396	448	501	556
Detect-and-Drop ($2n$ channels)	164	186	172	416	420	384	430
Multi-Channel BackOn/BackOff ($4n$ channels)	131	152	175	198	224	251	279
Detect-and-Drop ($4n$ channels)	82	93	86	208	210	192	215
k	$10^{6\frac{1}{3}}$	$10^{6\frac{2}{3}}$	10^7	$10^{7\frac{1}{3}}$	$10^{7\frac{2}{3}}$	10^8	
Exp BackOn/BackOff (single channel)	1.13e+7	2.27e+7	7.93e+7	1.68e+8	3.37e+8	7.74e+9	
Multi-Channel BackOn/BackOff ($2n$ channels)	618	686	804	876	950	1030	
Detect-and-Drop ($2n$ channels)	434	442	436	450	444	448	
Multi-Channel BackOn/BackOff ($4n$ channels)	309	343	402	438	475	515	
Detect-and-Drop ($4n$ channels)	217	221	218	225	222	224	

Table 2. Hiding Constant of Detect-and-Drop: time slots/ $\log k \log \log k$

k	10^4	$10^{4\frac{1}{3}}$	$10^{4\frac{2}{3}}$	10^5	$10^{5\frac{1}{3}}$	$10^{5\frac{2}{3}}$	10^6
Hiding Constant	1.65	1.68	1.41	3.09	2.86	2.41	2.50
k	$10^{6\frac{1}{3}}$	$10^{6\frac{2}{3}}$	10^7	$10^{7\frac{1}{3}}$	$10^{7\frac{2}{3}}$	10^8	
Hiding Constant	2.35	2.24	2.07	2.01	1.87	1.78	

Table 2 shows that the hidden constant is quite small and keeps dwindling after $k \leq 10^5$. This is because Algorithm 3 has time complexity $O(\log k)$ with a large constant coefficient, which is dominated by the time complexity of Algorithm 5 ($O(\log k \log \log k)$) which has a relatively small constant coefficient.

9 Conclusion

In this work, for the information exchange problem in single-hop multi-channel radio networks, we have proposed a novel randomized distributed algorithm called Detect-and-Drop. This algorithm uses $\Theta(n)$ channels and can solve the information exchange problem in $O(\log k \log \log k)$ time slots with high probability. Our algorithm does not need any knowledge on the number of nodes n in the network and the number of messages k. Compared with the state-of-the-art algorithm in [9] which can solve the same problem in $\Theta(k)$ time slots using

$\Theta(\sqrt{n})$ channels, our algorithm contributes an exponential improvment. There are many interesting and meaningful future work topics that are related: (1) By using multi-radio multi-channels, it would be interesting to see if we can use $o(n)$ channels (sublinear number of channels in terms of the number of nodes n) to solve the information exchange problem in $o(k)$ time slots (sublinear number of channels in terms of the number of messages k); (2) similar to the work in [18] which considers adversarial (arbitrary) arrival patterns of the messages, it is still open whether our result also holds for this dynamic version of the information exchange problem; (3) it is meaningful to extend our work to other scenarios, such as the simple multiple-access channels where the channel cannot provide any feedback information to the sender and the multi-hop networks; (4) it is still open to design a deterministic distributed algorithm that can solve the information exchange problem in sublinear time complexity under multiple-channels; (5) it will be worthwhile to see if we can apply our technique to many other related problems, such as the wake-up problem [10], the broadcast problem [1], the local broadcasting problem [19], etc.

Acknowledgements. This work was supported in part by the National Basic Research Program of China Grant 2011CBA00300, 2011CBA00302, the National Natural Science Foundation of China Grant 61103186, 61073174, 61033001, 61061130540, the Hi-Tech research and Development Program of China Grant 2006AA10Z216, and Hong Kong RGC-GRF grants 714009E and 714311.

References

1. Bar-Yehuda, R., Goldreich, O., Itai, A.: On the Time-Complexity of Broadcast in Multi-hop Radio Networks: An Exponential Gap Between Determinism and Randomization. J. Comput. Syst. Sci. 45(1), 104–126 (1992)
2. Chlebus, B.S., Kowalski, D.R., Radzik, T.: Many-to-Many Communication in Radio Networks. Algorithmica 54(1), 118–139 (2009)
3. Dolev, S., Gilbert, S., Khabbazian, M., Newport, C.: Leveraging Channel Diversity to Gain Efficiency and Robustness for Wireless Broadcast. In: Peleg, D. (ed.) DISC 2011. LNCS, vol. 6950, pp. 252–267. Springer, Heidelberg (2011)
4. Anta, A.F., Mosteiro, M.A.: Contention Resolution in Multiple-Access Channels: k-Selection in Radio Networks. In: Thai, M.T., Sahni, S. (eds.) COCOON 2010. LNCS, vol. 6196, pp. 378–388. Springer, Heidelberg (2010)
5. Fernández Anta, A., Mosteiro, M.A., Ramón Muñoz, J.: Unbounded Contention Resolution in Multiple-Access Channels. In: Peleg, D. (ed.) DISC 2011. LNCS, vol. 6950, pp. 225–236. Springer, Heidelberg (2011)
6. Gilbert, S., Kowalski, D.R.: Trusted Computing for Fault-Prone Wireless Networks. In: Lynch, N.A., Shvartsman, A.A. (eds.) DISC 2010. LNCS, vol. 6343, pp. 359–373. Springer, Heidelberg (2010)
7. Goldberg, L.A.: Design and analysis of contention-resolution protocols, EPSRC Research Grant GR/L60982, http://www.csc.liv.ac.uk/~leslie/contention.html (last modified October 2006)
8. Haeupler, B., Karger, D.R.: Faster information dissemination in dynamic networks via network coding. In: PODC, pp. 381–390 (2011)

9. Holzer, S., Pignolet, Y.A., Smula, J., Wattenhofer, R.: Time-optimal information exchange on multiple channels. In: FOMC, pp. 69–76 (2011)
10. Jurdziński, T., Stachowiak, G.: Probabilistic Algorithms for the Wakeup Problem in Single-Hop Radio Networks. In: Bose, P., Morin, P. (eds.) ISAAC 2002. LNCS, vol. 2518, pp. 535–549. Springer, Heidelberg (2002)
11. Khabbazian, M., Kowalski, D.R.: Time-efficient randomized multiple-message broadcast in radio networks. In: PODC, pp. 373–380 (2011)
12. Khabbazian, M., Kuhn, F., Kowalski, D.R., Lynch, N.A.: Decomposing broadcast algorithms using abstract MAC layers. In: DIALM-PODC, pp. 13–22 (2010)
13. Kodialam, M.S., Nandagopal, T.: Characterizing the capacity region in multi-radio multi-channel wireless mesh networks. In: MOBICOM, pp. 73–87 (2005)
14. Kowalski, D.R.: On selection problem in radio networks. In: PODC, pp. 158–166 (2005)
15. Martel, C.U.: Maximum Finding on a Multiple Access Broadcast Network. Inf. Process. Lett. 52(1), 7–15 (1994)
16. Schneider, J., Wattenhofer, R.: What Is the Use of Collision Detection (in Wireless Networks)? In: Lynch, N.A., Shvartsman, A.A. (eds.) DISC 2010. LNCS, vol. 6343, pp. 133–147. Springer, Heidelberg (2010)
17. Willard, D.E.: Log-Logarithmic Selection Resolution Protocols in a Multiple Access Channel. SIAM J. Comput. 15(2), 468–477 (1986)
18. Yu, D., Hua, Q.-S., Dai, W., Wang, Y., Lau, F.C.M.: Dynamic Contention Resolution in Multiple-Access Channels. In: Koucheryavy, Y., Mamatas, L., Matta, I., Tsaoussidis, V. (eds.) WWIC 2012. LNCS, vol. 7277, pp. 232–243. Springer, Heidelberg (2012)
19. Yu, D., Wang, Y., Hua, Q.-S., Lau, F.C.M.: Distributed local broadcasting algorithms in the physical interference model. In: DCOSS, pp. 1–8 (2011)

A Cache Based Multi-join Query Method
with Two-Phase Processing in MANET*

Yahong Guo[1], Jinbao Li[2,3], Longjiang Guo[2,3], Jinghua Zhu[2,3], and Xu Liu[2,3]

[1] School of Information Science and Technology, Heilongjiang University, Harbin,
Heilongjiang, China, 150080
[2] School of Computer Science and Technology, Heilongjiang University, Harbin,
Heilongjiang, China, 150080
[3] Key Laboratory of Database and Parallel Computing of Heilongjiang Province,
Harbin, Heilongjiang, China, 150080
jbli@hlju.edu.cn

Abstract. In this paper, we study the problem of join query in MANET and propose a new type of join query called Single-join Query Based on Caching (SQBC). This problem is proved to be a NP-hard problem and we present two polynomial approximate greedy algorithms (SOCA and MOCA) to solve the single-join query and multi-join query respectively. Both of these algorithms can ensure the low energy consumption. Moreover, MOCA can reduce the response time of query processing and minimize the energy consumption by considering the overhead of join query. Theoretical analysis and experimental results show that the algorithms proposed in this paper can effectively reduce the energy consumption, prolong the survival period of the network and enhance query efficiency.

1 Introduction

With the development of wireless communications and embedded technology, mobile ad hoc networks (MANET) are widely used in both military and civilian areas. MANET is generally organized by nodes with wireless communicating and computing ability. In many applications of MANET, the query processing techniques of data is necessary because nodes always forward and share the data. However, the characteristics of MANET including limited bandwidth, energy supply and self-configuration

* This work was partially supported by the National Natural Science Foundation of China under grant No.61070193,60803015 and 61100048, the Heilongjiang Province Founds for Distinguished Young Scientists under Grant No.JC201104, the Heilongjiang Province Science and Technique Foundation under Grant No.GC09A109, the Foundation of University Science and Technology Innovation Team Building Program of Heilongjiang Province under 2011PYTD002, the Scientific Research Found of Heilongjiang Provincial Education Department under grant No.11551343, the Harbin technological innovation found under grant No.2011RFQXG028, Program for New Century Excellent Talents in University under grant No.NCET-11-0955, Programs Foundation of Heilongjiang Educational Committee for New Century Excellent Talents in University under grant No.1252-NCET-011.

X. Wang et al. (Eds.): WASA 2012, LNCS 7405, pp. 450–461, 2012.
© Springer-Verlag Berlin Heidelberg 2012

propose challenge for the query processing technology. To conserve energy, the idea of cache is widely applied in MANET [1-4]. For the data that be queried frequently, if it can be cached in the intermediate nodes, the communication payload from intermediate nodes to source nodes and consumed energy can be reduced efficiently by storing the required data on intermediate nodes once the query incurs. Although cache scheme can reduce the overhead of transmitted data and query delay, data cache may not be sufficient to support joins query in MANET for following reasons: i) as the randomness of the data generation in MANET, the relations to be connected are distributed in large number of nodes so that it is difficult to connect these relations in low communication overhead. ii) Compared to common query processing, joins query is more complex. Meanwhile, the energy consumption of communication is much more than that of computations in MANET. Thus, it is important to design a data caching mechanism adapts to join query and minimize data traffic in MANET.

We first give the definition of single join query problem based on the cache and prove it to be a NP-complete problem. Then we propose a polynomial approximate algorithm called Sola (Single-join based on caching) which uses greedy strategy to try to minimize the energy consumption of completing the single-join query. Basing on Sola, a two-phase multi-join query method using cache is proposed and called Moca (Multi-join basing on cache). Moca uses dynamic programming to create optimal order of processing for multi-join query and divides the multi-join query into many sub queries. After that, the order will be sent to each query node which utilize Soca algorithm to execute single-join query. The Moca algorithm not only can improve the parallelism of query and reduce the latency, but also can minimize the communication cost and save energy efficiently. Theoretical analysis and experimental results indicates that Moca can make full use of the energy of nodes and fulfill the task of forwarding data well, reduce the response time of query and prolong the lifetime of the network efficiently at same time.

2   Related Work

Most applications of wireless networks are related with the data management operations[1] while a solution to maintain cache is proposed in [2] and [3] indicates that the technology of cache can be used widely. Zhou et al proposed a mechanism in which the characters and time of sensing are stored into the nodes that have sensed the target first[4]. Then the full track of the target can be computed basing on the consistency of time and track once the query appears and any node of the track can be found. Due to the important position of joins query, the joins query is gaining growing concern by researchers. In [5], a two-phase query optimization method is presented, which optimizes a query with two phases. The method takes the result of size of connection as price to get the optimal joint order so as to minimize the data transmitting. According to the order, a connection tree is built and divided into many sub queries which are sent to data node for query. The drawback of this method is that the computing complexity of creating tree is too high. Zhu et al proposed approaches the perpendicular approach (PA) in [6], the approach is able to efficiently incorporate joins with spatial constraints. In [7], the authors present SENS-Join, a general-purpose join method for sensor networks. All values of common attributes in the two connective relations are collected at first in this method. Then a filter is created to filtering the data that is not in the result set and broadcasted to the nodes in the network. Once the node receives the filter, the node sends the required tuples by using this filter. The shortcoming of this method is that it costs too much energy to create the filter.

3   Cache Based Single-Join Query Processing

3.1   Network Model

We assume that the nodes in MANET are uniform distributed in a planar area and the energy consumption of computing by the node of the network is negligible because that the transmitting of data costs most of the energy while the energy cost of computation at local disk is very low. For any two nodes i and j in the network, assume that they can communicate with each other, thus a link is existing between them. Meanwhile, suppose that the model[8] of energy consumption when node i and j are communicating is as follow:

$$cost_{ij} = \alpha + \beta d_{ij}^{n} \tag{1}$$

α and β are constant, d_{ij} is the physical distance between node i and node j, n represents the attenuation factor of path ($2 \leq n \leq 4$), $cost_{ij}$ stands for the energy consumption of sending a unit data from node i to node j.

For the network studied in this paper, following assumption is made: (1) the position of each node is known; (2) each node know the data cached in other nodes, including information about database and table; (3) the nodes of the network is classified into three categories including query nodes, cache nodes and common nodes in which query nodes are the nodes send queries and responsible for sending query message and getting the query results, cache nodes are nodes caching some data queried frequently to improve the query efficiency and common nodes are in charge of collecting and forwarding the data; (4) each node caches entire data items of one corresponding relation.

3.2   Problems Definition

In a connective network with N nodes, each node generates sensing data belong to some relations irregularly. The main study of this paper is to join these data items. However, due to the limit of energy of nodes in the network, how to design an effective processing method having low energy consumption affects the lifetime of the network and the response time of query more. As single-join is the basis of multi-join, the single-join query problem is studied at first. Then, basing on the network model proposed, a formal definition is given in this paper.

Considering the network shown in Figure 1, the square nodes represent the query nodes, the circle nodes are cache nodes, and the ellipse nodes stands for common nodes. The table near the query nodes represents the relations stored in these nodes, such as, the node A caches the relation R1 and B caches the relationR2. The table around the cache nodes stands for the relations and data items cached in these nodes. For example, in Figure 1, the node 1 caches the data items of relations R1 and R2.

For a query of R1⋈R2 sent from node A, the key problem is how to transmit the data so as to complete the query with a minimum cost of energy. The result of connection needs to be sent back to node A. Thus it is a good option to take the data items in relation R2 back to A. For a node A, many choices can be selected to collect all the data items in relation R2. For example, it is allowed to collect all the data at node B or at node 1 and node 2(all the data in relation R2 is also caching in cache node 1 and node 2). However, the longer the distance between nodes is, the higher the energy consumption in the network is, just like the equation 1 shows. Thus, choosing different way of collecting data will bring different energy consumption.

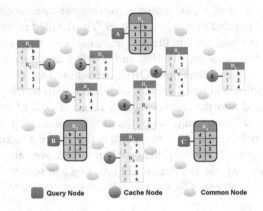

Fig. 1. Topology of networks

All in all, for a query R1⋈R2 sent form node A, the main purpose of this query is to make a connection operation to all the data items in relation R2 with the minimum cost of energy.

Definition 1: Single-join Query Based on Caching (SQBC). Suppose that the relation to be connected is R. When there are some nodes which cache parts of data item of relation R, then the problem of which several cache nodes is selected and their data is transmitted to the query node that executes connecting operation on condition that the energy consumption is low is called SQBC. The former definition of SQBC is as follows. All the data items of the relation R to be connected is given and denoted as Z, the set of relation R of all cache nodes is represented by C, and the set of data items cached is Data(C). Let Data(C) = {Data(C_i)| Data(C_i) is the data item cached in node C_i}, $Z = \cup S \in C$ Data(S). Thus, the problem of SQBC is to search for a $Q \subseteq C$, satisfying:

1. $Z = \cup_{S \in Q}$ Data(S).
2. Q is the set of nodes with the minimum cost of join query. The cost of join query is that the energy consumption of forwarding the caching data of all nodes in Q to the query node.

Theory 1: The problem of SQBC is a NP-complete problem.

Proof: If a verifiable solution of SQBC is given, then the solution can be validated whether it is correct or not in polynomial time, so the problem of SQBC is proved to be a NP problem.

We reduce a problem of set cover which is a NP-complete problem into the problem of SQBC. The formal definition of set covering problem is as follows: a finite set X is given and the set family of it is F, and $X = \cup S \in F$ S, the main goal is to get a T $\subseteq$ F and T satisfies:

1. $X = \cup_{S \in T} S$;
2. T is the minimum set family satisfied with condition 1, namely $|T|$ is smallest.

From the formal definition of SQBC and set covering, we conclude that the problem of set covering can be reduced to problem of SQB. The detailed reducing method is as follows: Z reduces to the goal set X in the problem of set covering, $Data(C)$ reduces to the set family F of problem of set covering and Q also can reduce to set family C of problem of set covering. In problem of SQBC, the solution set Q is the set of nodes that satisfies the condition and make the cost of join query to be the smallest. In other words, if a set is added into the solution set Q, then the cost of energy will be increased. However, the solution family set of the problem of set covering should be the smallest set family satisfying the condition, namely that the cost increases by 1 once a set is added into set family T. Thereby, the problem of set covering is a special example of SQBC. That is to say, the problem of set covering can reduce to the problem of SQBC. To sum up, the problem of SQBC is a NP-complete problem.

3.3   Cache Based Single Join Query Algorithm

As the problem of SQBC is a NP-complete problem, it costs large amount of energy for finding an optimal solution of the problem of SQBC in environment of resource limited MANET. Therefore, to utilize the energy efficiently and prolong the lifetime of the network, we give a polynomial approximate algorithm Soca for problem of SQBC. The algorithm can solve the problem of single-join and further reduce the energy consumption in the networks.

The algorithm Soca uses a greedy strategy, and the base idea of it is as follow: Set U is denoted as the set of the data items that is not be collected in Z. The node C_i that makes the intersection of $Data(C_i)$ and set U be maximum can be chose in a greedy way. Except for C_i, the query node r which stores all the data items of relation R also stores the data items related with $Data(C_i) \cap U$. Thus, the energy consumption in the network can be reduced when choosing a node close to query node for forwarding the data items about $Data(C_i) \cap U$. If r is closer to query node q, then q sends query messages to r directly. The messages include the name of relation which is to be connected and the set of data items needs to be forwarded by r and so on. When r receives messages from q, the $Data(C_i) \cap U$ is transmitted to q. If q is closer to C_i, then q sends query message to C_i and C_i sends the data items $Data(C_i) \cap U$ to q. The proceeding above is repeated until $Data(Q) = Z$.

For a single query shown in Figure 1, the proceeding of algorithm Soca is as follows: The query node A collects the data items $(2, 3)$ and $(3, 1)$ from the cache node 2 at first, then collects data item $(2, 2)$ from cache node 1, and finally make a join operation at A. In algorithm Soca, for cache node C_i, the energy cost of data transmitting is the multiply of the energy per unit data and the data volume, namely $E_{iq} = cost_{iq} \cdot D_i$. The definition of $cost_{iq}$ is shown in formula 1 and it is denoted as the energy consumed while sending unit data to the query node from C_i, namely the data $Data(C_i) \cap U$ sent at statement 4. Let E_{max} to be the maximum cost of energy in all cache nodes, that is to say, $E_{max} = max \{ E_{iq} \mid i \in Q \}$.

Theory 2: The algorithm Soca is a polynomial $p(n)$-approximate algorithm of SQBC in which $p(n) = E_{max} \cdot \ln(|Z| + 1)$.

Proof: Assume that Q^* is the optimal solution of problem of SQBC and the overhead of energy consumption of Q^* is E_{Q^*}.

Let C_i to be the i-th cache node selected by algorithm Soca, when C_i sends data D_i to the query node q, the energy consumption of Q is increased by E_{iq}. If the E_{iq} of choosing C_i is evenly assigned to all the data items which C_i collects at the first time, then the formal definition of energy consumption that each data item is sent to the query node can be given.

For $\forall z \in Z$, let E_z to be the overhead assigning to z. If z is collected by C_i firstly, then

$$E_z = \frac{E_{iq}}{D_i} \tag{2}$$

D_i is the first forwarded set of data items after the node C_i is selected by cache node i, thus

$$D_i = Data(C_i) - (Data(C_1) \cup Data(C_2) \cup \ldots \cup Data(C_{i-1})).$$

So, the cost of the solution Q given by algorithm Soca is $E_Q = \sum_{i \in Q} E_{iq} = \sum_{z \in Z} E_z$ and E_Q is uniformly distributed in all the data items of Z. Because Q^* is also a solution of SQBC, Q^* also has all data items include in Z. Therefore,

$$E_Q = \sum_{z \in Z} E_z \le \sum_{C_i \in Q^*} \sum_{z \in Data(C_i)} E_z \tag{3}$$

For $\forall C_j \in Q$ and $i = 1, 2, \ldots, |Q|$, let $u_j = |Data(C_j) - (Data(C_1) \cup Data(C_2) \cup \ldots \cup Data(C_i))|$, that is to say, after nodes $C_1, C_2, \ldots, C_i$ are selected and assume that C_i is selected before C_j, node C_j caches the total number of data items that are not collected. Thereby, $u_0 = Data(C_j)$, $u_{i-1} \ge u_i$, and $u_{i-1} - u_i$ is the total number of first collected data items because that the node C_i in $Data(C_j)$ is selected.

Let $k = min\{ w \mid u_w = 0 \}$, namely all data items cached in node C_i are transmitted successfully after $C_1, C_2, \ldots, C_k$ are selected. Thus,

$$\sum_{z \in Data(C_j)} E_z = \sum_{i=1}^{k} (u_{i-1} - u_i) \frac{E_{iq}}{D_i} \tag{4}$$

D_i is the set of data items after the i-th cache node is chose and the selection of C_i is to maximum the data that is not collected, thus $D_i \geq u_{i-1}$, thereby according to (4),

$$\sum_{z \in Data(C_j)} E_z \leq \sum_{i=1}^{k}(u_{i-1} - u_i)\frac{E_{iq}}{u_{i-1}} \leq E_{max}\sum_{i=1}^{k}(u_{i-1} - u_i)\frac{1}{u_{i-1}}$$

$$= E_{max}\sum_{i=1}^{k}\sum_{m=u_i+1}^{u_{i-1}}\frac{1}{u_{i-1}} \leq E_{max}\sum_{i=1}^{k}\sum_{m=u_i+1}^{u_{i-1}}\frac{1}{m}$$

$$= E_{max}\sum_{i=1}^{k}\left(\sum_{m=1}^{u_{i-1}}\frac{1}{m} - \sum_{m=1}^{u_i}\frac{1}{m}\right)$$

$$= E_{max}\sum_{i=1}^{k}H(u_{i-1}) - H(u_i) = E_{max}(H(u_0) - H(u_k))$$

$$= E_{max}H(u_0) = E_{max}H(|S|) \leq E_{max}H(|Z|)$$

$$= E_{max} \cdot \ln(|Z| + 1). \qquad\qquad \square$$

In the proceeding of derivation above, $H(\cdot)$ represents the harmonic series by which the equation of the sixth step is satisfied. According to the property of harmonic series $H(n) \leq \ln(n+1)$, the last inequality is satisfied. Therefore, theory 1 is proved completely.

4   Multi-join Query Algorithm

Multi-join query is a common query that relate to large amount of communication and data which is difficult to be collected in MANET. Therefore, basing on Soca, we propose a multi-joins query method with cache that adapt to MANET.

4.1   Query Optimization Algorithm

For a query node, although the relation sets required to be connected is known, the connection order which affects the overhead of query directly between the relations cannot be determined. The result of connection will be collected to the query node. Therefore we consider the distance between nodes as a metric to measure the cost of connection and create order of connection. For example, Relations R_1, R_2, ..., R_n are stored in query nodes q_1, q_2,...,q_n respectively and $d_{12} \leq d_{13} \leq ... \leq d_{1n}$ is a condition at the same time in which d_{12} represents the distance between query node q_1 and q_2. Assume that the user is sending the multi-join query with relations R_1, R_2, ..., R_n. Then the order of connection is $R_1 \bowtie R_2 \bowtie ... \bowtie R_n$.

For a multi-join query, not only the order of connection can affect the overhead of the query, but also the order of execution may cause different cost of query. For example, If the multi-join $R_1 \bowtie R_2 \bowtie R_3$ is sent by a user, the overhead of executing query $(R_1 \bowtie R_2) \bowtie R_3$ and $R_1 \bowtie (R_2 \bowtie R_3)$ is different because of the different overhead between single join $R_1 \bowtie R_2$ and $R_2 \bowtie R_3$. Thus, the different executing order of multi-join query will cause different overhead of query and affect the lifetime of networks and energy consumption. In order to definite the overhead of query well, we denote $R_{1 \sim n}$ as the result of $R_1 \bowtie R_2 \bowtie ... \bowtie R_n$, and $Cost(R_{1 \sim n})$ is representing the minimize cost of

$R_1 \bowtie R_2 \bowtie \ldots \bowtie R_n$. When executing $R_{1 \sim n}$, if there is disconnect at relation R_k so that the $Cost(R_{1 \sim n})$ becomes the minimum value, the cost of executing the former k relations must be the minimum cost of executing $R_{1 \sim k}$. Otherwise, there is another order of execution that make the cost of $R_{1 \sim k}$ smaller. Substituting it to query $R_1 \bowtie R_2 \bowtie \ldots \bowtie R_n$, a cost smaller than $Cost(R_{1 \sim n})$ is got, which is contradiction with definition. Therefore, the $Cost(R_{1 \sim n})$ has the character of optimal substructure. We propose a dynamic programming algorithm called Qop(Query Optimization) to determine the optimal order of multi-join query so as to make the cost of query to be minimum and further reduce the energy consumption in the network. The Qop algorithm gives the recursive definition of $Cost(R_{1 \sim n})$ at first and then create the recursive equation according to the character of optimal substructure of minimum cost so as to minimize the overhead of query. The base idea of Qop is as follows: the $Cost(R_{i \sim i})$ is only related to one relation, thus $Cost(R_{i \sim i}) = 0$. Because of the character of optimal substructure of minimum cost, we can infer that $Cost(R_{i \sim j}) = Cost(R_{i \sim k}) + Cost(R_{k+1 \sim j}) + \Delta(R_{i \sim k} \bowtie R_{k+1 \sim j})$, in which $\Delta(R_{i \sim k} \bowtie R_{k+1 \sim j})$ is the cost of $R_{i \sim k} \bowtie R_{k+1 \sim j}$ that can be solved according to the Soca proposed in part 3. Only if the minimum value of k satisfying the equation can be recursive found in section $[i, j]$, the order having the smallest cost of $Cost(R_{i \sim i})$ can be determined. In Qop, the dynamic programming selects energy consumption as the cost. Thus, the cost must be the smallest when using the order derived from the algorithm. In other word, the executing order of join query is optimized by Qop in order to get an executing scheme of costing the minimum energy.

4.2 Cache Based Multi-join Query Algorithm

When the order of multi-join query is determined, the query node sends the query message to the cache nodes to get the required data. However, if all messages are sent by this query node, the delay of query processing may be increased so that the energy of the nodes around the query node cost too fast and it lead to the breakdown of the network. To avoid the situation stated above taking place, a query tree is created basing on the set of query nodes and the result of Qop. Meanwhile, each query node executes the join query in parallel so as to solve the problem that the energy of the nodes around the query node cost too fast and reduce the delay.

Assume that the node sending the multi-join query is the main query node. A complete relation is cached in each query node, so for a multi-query with n relations, n nodes are used for caching the relations. To better determine the plan of query, n query nodes are utilized to create a query tree basing on the optimal executing order computed by Qop. Each leaf node in the tree is made up with query nodes while intermediate nodes store the results of relations connection and the root node is the main query node.

When the tree of query is built up completely, the main query node sends the query message to the other query nodes. Once the message is received at the query nodes, the query nodes execute their query plan in parallel according to the position in the query tree and cache the intermediate results into the nodes around the main query node to minimize the data transmitting in the network. The proceeding that each node executes the plan of query is as follow: Each node judges whether its brother node is a leaf node, if it is, then compares the distance from the node to the main query node with the distance from its brother node to the main query node and selects the node closer to main query node as the node which caches the intermediate results and run Soca algorithm for executing single-join operation and then replaces the parent node of it. The proceeding will be executed recursively basing on the results of Qop till all the joins accomplished. Finally, the result is sent back to the main query node.

Based on the idea above, the algorithm Moca is given in this chapter. Assumed that T_1, T_2, ..., T_n are the nodes with cache relations and T_k is the main query node. Moca creates multi-join in accordance with the distance between T_1, T_2, ..., T_n and T_k at first step. Then Qop is executed in order to get the optimal order of connection and create the tree of query. Each query node T_i makes single-join with its brother node on the basis of the position in query tree. For each single join operation, to reduce the cost of transmission, the node closer to main query node is chose as the cache node of intermediate result. Each node executes its query task in parallel and the results will be sent to T_k.

5   Performance Evaluation

Assume that the distribution of nodes is uniform in MANET and the topology using in our experiment is grid shape for simplicity although the proposed method in this paper can adapt to any topology of different distributions. The following assumption is made in the experiment: the structure of the nodes used is the same; the initial energy is 100000; the communication range of nodes is 1; each query node stores 100 records of corresponding relations because of the limited storage space of nodes; the energy consumption of sending and receiving a packet is 2 and 1 respectively.

5.1   Variation of the Connecting Relations

In this section, the impacts of the variation of the total number of connecting relations which is denoted as N_R to the performance of networks are studied.The variation of average energy consumption of different mechanisms with the increasing of N_R is shown in Figure 2. The average energy consumption is increasing when the N_R increases because that the more connecting relations involved, the more transmitting packets are transmitted and the cost of communication is, thereby the more energy consumption of each connection is. Meanwhile, the energy consumption of Moca is smallest due to that Moca uses the technology of caching and computes the optimal order of executing according to the price of energy consumption so as to ensure the cost of energy is minimum. In MOP, the technology of caching is not used and the order of execution obtained is the same as Moca, but the energy consumption is more than Moca while less than TPO and SENS. The energy consumption of SENS is more because that it costs too much energy in the step of creating the filter.

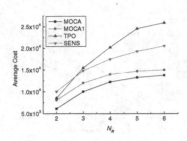
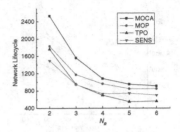

Fig. 2. NR vs. Average Cost of Energy   **Fig. 3.** NR vs. Lifetime of Networks

Figure 3 shows the variation of lifetime of networks of different mechanisms with the increasing of N_R. With the increasing of N_R, the lifetime of the network is decreasing gradually. This is because that the more the connecting relations involved, the more the energy consumption of the networks is and thereby the shorter the lifetime of networks is. In Figure 3, the cost of energy of Moca is smallest, thus the lifetime of it is longest. TPO gets the order of executing on the basis of the price which is the result of connection. Although the flows of communication are reduced, it cannot ensure the energy consumption be smallest. Therefore, the lifetime of networks of TPO is shortest.

5.2 Variation of Network Size

The impact of network size to the performance of network is studied in this section. The result of experiment is in Figure 4. The horizontal axis represents the network size, namely the length of a grid. For example, 10 in horizontal axis represents that the size of the grid in the grid topology is 10×10. Figure 4 shows that the average energy consumption is increasing with the increasing of network size. This is because that the distance between any two query nodes is increased as the network size becomes larger so that the cost of communication of connecting operation is increased, thereby the average energy consumption is increasing. As shown in figure, compared with TPO and SENS, the increasing trend of Moca and MOP is slow. This is due to that the distance between the cache node and the query node will be increased with the increasing of network size because that the cache node is selected randomly.

In Figure 5, the influence of average hops is studied. When the network size increases, the average hops of each packet transmitted is increased. This is due to that with the increasing of network size, the distance between query nodes becomes longer so that the total number of times of forwarding each packet is increasing and thereby the average hops increases. As shown in Figure 5, the average hops of forwarding each packet in Moca is the least while the average hops in TPO is the most due to that TPO choose the size of connecting result as price and is not considering the length of the path of forwarding each packet but only for reducing the communication traffic.

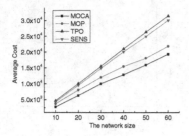
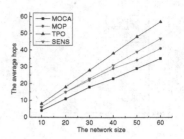

Fig. 4. Network Size vs. Average Cost of Energy

Fig. 5. Network Size vs. Average Hop

5.3 Variation of Total Number of Nodes

In this section, the performance of the network of Moca with variation of total number of nodes is studied. p_c is denoted as the percentage of the total number of cache nodes to the total number of all nodes. Figure 6 shows the variation of the average hop with the changes of the total number of nodes when N_R =2, 4, 6, 8. The horizontal axis represents the percentage of cache nodes. In Figure 6, the average hop is decreasing when the total number of nodes is increasing due to that the larger the total number of cache nodes is, the shorter the distance between the cache node and the query node is, the short the distance of the packets transmitted to query nodes is, and thereby the less the average hop is. As shown in Figure 6, when N_R =2, the average hop is less than that when N_R =8.

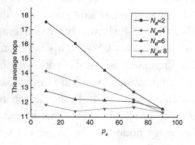
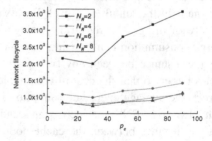

Fig. 6. The total number of cache nodes vs. Average Hop

Fig. 7. The total number of cache nodes vs. Network Lifetime

Figure 7 displays the impacts of the total number of cache nodes to the lifetime of the network. As shown in this figure, the larger the total number of cache nodes is, the less the forwarding times of the packet and energy consumption is, and the longer the lifetime of the network is. This is because that the situation in which the cache nodes are distributed randomly so that although the cache nodes store many records while they are far from the query node exists and consume too much energy. When N_R =4, 6, 8, the lifetime of the network changes slowly due to that the operation of multi-join consumes much energy.

To sum up, the performance of Moca is better than others because Moca uses the technology of caching and dynamic programming strategy. MOP does not use the technology of caching, but its order of executing is optimal, thus the performance of MOP is also good. The performance of SENS is bad due to that the energy consumption of creating filter is too much. Because TPO only considers the communication traffic and ignores the energy consumption, it is worst of all the mechanisms tested.

6   Conclusion

We propose a new type of single join cashed based query for MANET in this paper and we prove that this problem is a NP-complete problem. In order to conserve energy, a polynomial approximate algorithm Soca is proposed which uses a greedy strategy. Based on Soca, a two-phase multi-connection query algorithm (Moca) is proposed which exploits a cache mechanism. Moca first uses dynamic programming to get the optimal executing order of multi-join in order to minimum the energy consumption. Then it builds a query tree in which nodes execute the query plan in parallel according to their positions in this tree after receiving query messages. Finally the query results are sent to the main query node. Experimental results show that Soca and Moca can efficiently reduce the energy consumption, prolong the lifetime of networks and improve the query efficiency.

References

1. Ying, L., Liu, Z., Towsley, D., Xia, C.H.: Distributed operator placement and data caching in large-scale sensor networks. In: Proceedings of the IEEE INFOCOM, pp. 977–985 (2008)
2. Lim, S.H., Yu, C.S., Das, C.R.: Cooperative Cache Invalidation Strategies for Internet-Based Vehicular Ad Hoc Networks. In: Proceedings of the 18th International Conference on Computer Communications and Networks (ICCCN 2009), pp. 1–6 (2009)
3. Huang, Y., Cao, J.N., Jin, B.H., Tao, X.P., Lu, J., Feng, Y.L.: Flexible Cache Consistency Maintenance over Wireless Ad Hoc Networks. IEEE Transactions on Parallel and Distributed Systems (2009)
4. Zhou, D.P., Gao, J.: Opportunistic Processing and Query of Motion Trajectories in Wireless Sensor Networks. In: Proceedings of the IEEE INFOCOM, pp. 1197–1205 (2009)
5. Ke, H.: Two-phase query optimization in mobile Ad Hoc wireless networks. In: Proceedings of IEEE International Conference on Intelligent Computing and Intelligent Systems(ICIS 2009), pp. 515–520 (2009)
6. Zhu, X.J., Himanshu, G., Tang, B.: Join of Multiple Data Streams in Sensor Networks. IEEE Transactions on Knowledge and Data Engineering, 1722-1736 (2009)
7. Stern, M., Buchmann, E., Böhm, K.: Towards Efficient Processing of General-Purpose Joins in Sensor Networks. In: Proceedings of the 2009 IEEE International Conference on Data Engineering (ICDE 2009), pp. 126–137 (2009)
8. Shi, Y., Hou, Y.T.: Theoretical results on base station movement problem for sensor network. In: Proceedings of the IEEE INFOCOM, pp. 376–384 (2008)

Security Analysis of Opportunistic Networks Using Complex Network Properties

Srikar Mohan[1], Guangzhi Qu[1], and Fatma Mili[2]

[1] Computer Science and Engineering Department, Oakland University,
Rochester, MI 48309, USA
{smohan,gqu}@oakland.edu
[2] Department of Computer and Information Technology, College of Technology,
Purdue University, West Lafayette, IN 47907, USA
fmili@purdue.edu

Abstract. An Opportunistic Network (Oppnet) is an enhanced evolution of Mobile ad hoc network, where at any given time a route between source and destination does not exist, yet messages are routed opportunistically via intermediate contacts. We implemented two types of Oppnet deployments, an Open Oppnet and a Selective Oppnet, and analyzed both deployments by studying three Complex Network Properties, namely Average Shortest Distance, Degree Distribution, and Clustering Coefficients. In order to study the robustness of an Oppnet against network attacks, we examined Wormhole attack. According to the simulation results, severity of a Wormhole depends on the nodes location, trajectory and its neighboring nodes. When a worm tunnel was established between a popular node and an aloof node, it caused a noticeable impact on Average Shortest Distance. While in other cases Oppnet remained robust. We also observed that security in a Selective Oppnet is comparatively better than an Open Oppnet.

Keywords: opportunistic network, security, complex network.

1 Introduction

In an era of pervasive mobile computing with portable devices becoming more and more sophisticated, one might wonder if we can utilize the processing power and mobility of these devices into forming a self sustained, collaborative network. By leveraging the wireless capability and ubiquity of mobile devices we can form a temporal network that does not depend on any fixed infrastructure rather the nodes themselves take responsibility for creating and maintaining a network. The concept of Mobile ad hoc network has received a lot of attention in the recent years. An opportunistic network, also referred as Oppnet, is one of the challenging evolutions of Mobile ad hoc networks. The nodes in an oppnet move in different direction with random speed. When two or more nodes are within each others transmission range, they have an opportunity to establish a communication link and exchange data packets. A node in an Oppnet can be

X. Wang et al. (Eds.): WASA 2012, LNCS 7405, pp. 462–478, 2012.

a wireless or a wired device capable of wireless communication, example: smart phones, tablets, laptops or Wi-Fi enabled desktops. Given the plethora of such sophisticated mobile devices, an Oppnet can be almost deployed in any setting.

We categorize Oppnet deployment based on the criteria used to establish a communication link. First, a connection establishment strategy based solely on nodes being within each others transmission range can be categorized as an Open Oppnet deployment. This criterion can be deemed as a prerequisite for all Oppnet deployments. Second, in a more selective and well-informed type of Oppnet deployment, the decision to establish a communication link will also depend on certain degree of intelligence among those nodes, we categorize this deployment as a Selective Oppnet. The intelligence criteria can be based on all/any of the following parameters: nodes processing power, its memory capacity, trustworthiness based on past performance, presence of security software, compatibility, degree distribution, willingness to participate, delivery probability [17], [18], and battery life. In this research work we associate those parameters to a node with a rank. A third variation in Oppnet deployment discussed in [16], is where set of pre-defined nodes, called seed nodes, form a larger network by extending invitations to other nodes. A node that gets invited by a seed node to join the Oppnet, called helper node, may be given the privilege to invite other neighboring nodes. By granting helper nodes privilege to invite other nodes, a seed Oppnet grows into a larger Oppnet.

A prominent characteristic of an opportunistic network is that at any given point of time an end to end connection between a source node and a destination node may not always exist [18], [20]. This makes it even more challenging than Mobile ad hoc networks. Routes between source and destination node are established on the fly with the help of other intermittent nodes. Since the communication is based entirely on opportunistic contacts between nodes that are mobile with limited power supply, connections are intermittent and connection-disconnection is very common [6], this renders their communication pattern unpredictable [12]. Maintaining inter-contact time, which is the amount of time pair of nodes stays connected, and the amount of data that can be transferred during that interval of time become inevitable, especially for evaluating and predicting a nodes delivery probability. Data packets from source to destination can be broadcasted or transported via store and forward technique, where intermediate nodes (temporarily) store data packets until they find their next (suitable) opportunistic contact to forward packets in an attempt to deliver to the destination node. In any case nodes should have ample memory to hold messages from other nodes. While memory capabilities are merely an issue these days, maintaining data authenticity and integrity is challenging. Granted that there have been high-tech advancements in the advent of portable devices and smart phones, but still one must not forget that these devices posses limited and varied hardware and software resources [8].

Due to the sporadic nature of nodes in Oppnet, traditional authentication methods applicable in the presence of an infrastructure become seemingly difficult for deployment [3], [7], [8]. Any network is susceptible to be attacked by a malicious user. An Open Oppnet deployment is more likely to attract the attention of malicious nodes because nodes lack the knowledge about the authenticity of their neighbors [8]. Malicious behavior can be controlled to some extent by using the Selective Oppnet deployments because nodes form a link rationally after evaluating each others rank. Given that ranks are formulated using factors, like trustworthiness, reliability, reputation and even presence of an antivirus and antimalware software, our postulate that Selective Oppnet deployments are robust is justified.

An attacker in an opportunistic network can masquerade as a legitimate node and launch a Man In The Middle attack, since a message travels via a series of nodes, any intermediate node can read and modify the contents of the message and pass it to its neighbors and the destination node. The nodes in an Oppnet follow a store and forward method for sending messages, thus a Denial of service attack can be exploited by flooding the network with junk messages and thereby exhausting a nodes memory to store any more legitimate message. Wormhole, Blackhole, and Byzantine are other types of network exploit that can be launched by adversaries in an Oppnet.

Privacy is a big concern in an opportunistic network because nodes carry every other nodes information. Since the nodes forward packets based on opportunistic contacts they inadvertently expose their location information. Some level of privacy can be preserved if the Selective Oppnet deployment is used because in this type of Oppnet deployment a node will share a message with other nodes only if their ranks are compatible. A comprehensive study on privacy issue in Oppnet is presented by authors in [15].

In this research work we try to comprehend, using graph theory, the characteristics of an Oppnet. If we represent an Oppnet as a graph, nodes will correspond to vertices and communication links will correspond to edges. We categorize three different Oppnet deployment strategies and implement two of those strategies, namely Open Oppnet and Selective Oppnet. Nodes average shortest distance, degree distribution and clustering coefficients are the three complex network property measures we compute for both deployments under benevolent scenario. We also analyze the impact of nodes transmission range and density.

To grasp the security challenges in an opportunistic network we introduce the wormhole attack on both Oppnet deployments. After initiating the wormhole attack, we observe the changes in their complex network properties. Once we have all the data for Oppnet under benevolent and malevolent scenarios, we focus on the impact caused by wormhole by further investigating the nodes that were involved in the attack. Our aim is also to find if parameters like nodes location, trajectory or neighbors have any impact on the severity of the attack. Also, by comparing the two Oppnet deployments under malevolent scenarios, we try to find if the severity of an attack can be alleviated by shifting from an Open Oppnet deployment to a Selective Oppnet deployment. Our experimental results show that Selective Oppnet deployment is more robust against wormhole attack. Our findings can be used as an aid for designing a security measure for an Oppnet.

In Section 2 we review related work. In Section 3 we talk at length about our simulation environment, complex network properties and security impact of wormhole on Oppnet. Then in Section 4 we present our experimental results and observations and finally conclude with scope for future work.

2 Related Work

The advancements in the eternal research topic of Mobile ad hoc network have evolved the very interesting and challenging concept of Opportunistic networks. Given the ubiquity and sophistication of mobile devices these days, it is logical to imagine a collaborative network that does not rely on any fixed infrastructure and rather takes advantage of the omnipresence of these devices. Though the concept and working principle of an Oppnet is intriguing, a number of realistic applications have been deployed and tested in the past. A survey on some of those appealing applications has been conducted in [18], followed by authors proposing a taxonomy of routing technique in an Oppnet by classifying presence or absence of some form of infrastructure.

Due to the unique characteristic of decentralization in Oppnet, the security measures available for traditional networks like centralized public key distribution authorities, or certification authorities cannot be applied directly to an Oppnet [8, 3, 7]. Though access control and cryptography provide security assurance, it is important to note that nodes participating in an Oppnet may have limited processing power and battery life. So we have to be wary before putting any additional burden on a node to ensure it doesnt create any overhead that might ultimately cause a node to shut down.

Many existing security protocols in MANET cannot be applied directly to an Oppnet; in order to bolster this postulate we take Packet Leashes [11], as an example. Hu et al [11], proposed a mechanism called Packet Leashes that is capable of detecting and defending against wormhole attacks in a MANET. A wormhole attack is initiated by establishing an out of band connection between two distant nodes, which are otherwise not within each others transmission range [4]. A packet leash is tailored to restrict the maximum distance travelled by a packet. The authors define a geographical leash that ensures the senders and receivers of a packet are within certain distance, while a temporal leash restricts the distance travelled by enforcing certain upper bound on the packets lifetime. Imposing a maximum transmission distance or expiration time on a packet is impractical in an Oppnet because nodes are scattered and rely on opportunistic contacts to store and forward a message. Also, the underlying assumption that the packets sending and receiving delay are negligible contradicts with the principle of delay tolerance in an Oppnet.

The concept of oppnet is influenced from the study of delay tolerant network, also known as disruption tolerant network [18]. Burgess et al. [3] evaluate the performance of a disruption tolerant network in terms of its robustness under different attack scenarios by measuring their successful packet delivery rate. Four types of attacks are formulated, namely, dropping all packets, flooding, routing information falsification, and ack counterfeiting. Dropping of packets can be conceived as man in the middle attack, where an intermediate adversary drops all packets affecting the network performance. Presence of redundant paths from source to destination can alleviate this problem. Redundancy of messages also provides data integrity in the event a message is altered in the transit [16]. Flooding can be apprehended as an attempt to cause a denial of service. Each node stores the messages it receives from its neighbors in an attempt to forward it towards the destination node but will soon use up all its memory, thereby left with none to receive legitimate message. A wormhole can be considered a type of routing information falsification attack. Wormhole can also be considered a type of collaborative attack [21], where, either all or at least one of the nodes involved in the worm tunnel is an adversary. Details about wormhole are presented in Section 3.3. Ack counterfeiting is launched by propagating falsified acknowledgements by an adversary, indicating that a packet has reached its destination and all the intermediate nodes can delete that packet to clear their buffers. This causes intermediate victims to not receive the data packets in transit and thereby cutting a route to destination. Authors in [3] observe that even a powerful attack does not cause any severe effect on Delay Tolerant Networks and replication-based routing protocols provide robustness against these attacks even in the absence of authentication. On the contrary authors in [7], show that attacks modeled in a certain way, bolstered with certain mobility patterns and network properties can cause devastating effects in spite of using replication-based routing protocols. Our experimental results conform to [7] when we analyze the robustness of Oppnet under Wormhole attack.

3   Implementation

In this research work we implement both Open and Selective Oppnet deployments. Communication link in either deployment can be either unidirectional, bidirectional or a combination of both. The goals of an Oppnet can help in deciding the type of communication required. If nodes in an Oppnet are only required to disseminate information without having to provide any feedback to one other, then a unidirectional link will be sufficient. But say nodes in an Oppnet are collaboratively working towards solving a complex problem that requires nodes to provide feedback to one another then establishing a bidirectional link is essential. However, in this research we always assume a bidirectional link between any two connected pair of nodes. A general flow chart for analyzing Oppnet is presented in Figure 1.

In our research, we run the BonnMotion simulator to generate nodes mobility traces using Random Way Point model. The output consists of three data values for each node: a time instant t, x and y coordinates. Through the course of simulation, nodes relocate to different locations (referred as waypoints). The time instants associated with each x and y values indicate that a node, at that time instant, reached a waypoint. Since the output of BonnMotion only consists of nodes location at different time instants, we calculate their intermediate

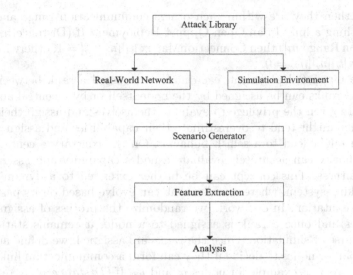

Fig. 1. Flow chart for analyzing Oppnet

locations (trajectory) to capture more refined information for each node. We define a delta time dt to find the intermediate locations for each d_t. Next we calculate the Euclidean distance between each node to every other node. Each node is assigned a transmission range which can be same or different for all nodes. For the sake of simplicity we assume all nodes to have the same transmission range. If the Euclidean distance between a node pair is less or equal to the nodes transmission range then a connection link could be established. This connection establishment scheme is suitable for the Open Oppnet deployment and serves as a primitive requirement for Selective Oppnet deployment. Once we have constructed the connectivity(adjacency) matrix for each node, we find the nodes one-hop neighbors (used in the measurement of nodes degree), multi-hop neighbors, average shortest distance and clustering coefficient. This process is repeated for each delta time d_t.

3.1   Establishing Connection

Once we have computed the intermediate location information for each node, we can construct the connectivity (adjacency) matrix by computing distance between nodes. In both deployment cases we have to determine if nodes are within each others transmission range. In order to do that we calculate the Euclidean distance between every node for each dt time instant from 0 to T. The equation to calculate the Euclidean distance between a node i and node j is given by:

$$Distance(n_i, n_j) = \sqrt{(x_i - x_j)^2 + (y_i - y_j)^2} \tag{1}$$

Once the Euclidean distance between node n_i and node n_j is calculated, we check if the distance between them is less than or equal to n_is transmission

range and if it is then they are within each others communication range and
capable of establishing a link. In an Open Oppnet Deployment If (Distance(n_i,
n_j) ¡= Transmission Range[n_i]) then ConnectionMatrix [t_l][n_i][n_j] = 1, otherwise
ConnectionMatrix [t_l][n_i][n_j] = 0.

In the Selective Oppnet deployment, each node is assigned a rank between
[Rmin, Rmax]. The ranks can be assigned by the node itself or by a central authority. If nodes are given the privilege to evaluate themselves and assign their
own rank, then they might tend to overestimate their capabilities and assign a
higher rank which might lead to a selfish behavior. On the contrary a central
rank granting authority can accurately evaluate a nodes capability and assign
it a rank in all fairness. This concept can be further extended to a dynamically evolving ranking system, where a nodes rank can evolve based on its past
performance and reputation. In our work, we randomize the process of assigning ranks to nodes and once a rank is assigned to a node, it remains static
throughout the course of simulation. Once the ranks are assigned, we define an
acceptable threshold for nodes to decide if they can form a communication link.
Going back to our previous example for nodes n_i and n_j, If ($Distance(n_i, n_j) \leq$
$TransmissionRange[n_i]$) and $|Rank[n_i] - Rank[n_j]| \leq Threshold$ then ConnectionMatrix [t_l][n_i][n_j] = 1, otherwise ConnectionMatrix [t_l][n_i][n_j] = 0.

3.2   Complex Network Properties

The study of complex network has received a lot of attention and is currently
being studied across many fields of science [23, 2]. Many systems can be described by models of complex networks, which are structures consisting of nodes
connected by links [22]. Complex network properties deal with network topo-
logical features to reveal and depict statistical properties of a complex network.
Three concepts that play an important role in the literature of complex network
properties are average shortest distance, degree distribution, and clustering coefficient.

3.3   Wormhole

A wormhole attack is launched by creating an out of band connection, also called
a worm tunnel, between nodes which are otherwise not within each others transmission range [4]. The out of band communication can be established either via
an Ethernet link or using a long range directional antenna. The nodes participating in the formation of worm tunnel could either be adversaries or could be
compromised nodes or combination of both. The scope of this research does not
cover the intentions of a node. Once a worm tunnel is established between two
distant out of range nodes, say n_i and n_j, they will tunnel packets between them.
After receiving those packets they will disseminate them among their neighbors.
When n_is neighbors receive packets from n_j or n_j's neighbors, they will assume
that nj and its neighbors are only few hops away from n_i. This will have an
impact on routing, average shortest distance, degree distribution and clustering
coefficient. To give an example, say an arbitrary neighbor (n_p) of n_i takes five

hops to reach n_j, now because of the wormhole (worm tunnel) n_p will only take two hops to reach n_j.

We implement a wormhole between a pair of nodes by forcefully establishing a connection between them for the entire course of simulation. We then reiterate this attack to cover different worm tunnel combinations between a node and every other node in the network. We then observe the difference in nodes average shortest distance, degree distribution and clustering coefficient.

4   Experimental Results

In this Section we examine, using graphs, complex network properties for Open and Selective Oppnet deployments. After analyzing graphs for both deployments under benevolent behavior, we implement the wormhole attack to observe and record the changes in complex network properties under malevolent scenario. The input parameters required for running BonnMotion are simulation time in seconds, total area in square meters, number of nodes, nodes transmission range in meters, maximum speed in m/s and maximum pause time in seconds.

4.1   Open Oppnet Deployment

All our simulations last for 500 seconds. In order to observe the impact of nodes density and nodes transmission range on complex network properties, we choose a simulation area from 500 m by 500 m, 1000 m by 1000 m or 2000 m by 2000 m, with number of nodes ranging from 100 to 850 in increments of 50 and nodes transmission range varying from 25 m to 250 m in increments of 25, the maximum speed for a node is set to 30 m/s, and the maximum pause time is set to 5 seconds.

Open Oppnet under Benevolent Scenario. Figure 2 shows the average shortest distance of nodes in an Open Oppnet with transmission range varying from 25 m to 250 m. From Figure 2 we can conclude that with higher transmission range, the nodes average shortest distance decreases and this is because with higher transmission range nodes can reach each other in fewer hops. When the transmission range is as low as 25 m, the average shortest distance is close to 0 because nodes have very low connectivity and the network is almost disconnected.

From Figure 2(b) we can see that with a high node density the average shortest distance of nodes decreases, this is because if we have large number of nodes in a smaller (simulation) area then nodes can connect to neighboring nodes in very few numbers of hops. Density of nodes is calculated as the number of nodes divided by the simulation area.

Figure 3(a) shows the impact of nodes transmission range on clustering coefficient. Higher transmission range means more nodes are capable of forming a link with their neighbors and thereby form more triangles. As the numbers of triangles amplify in comparison to triples the clustering coefficient also develops.

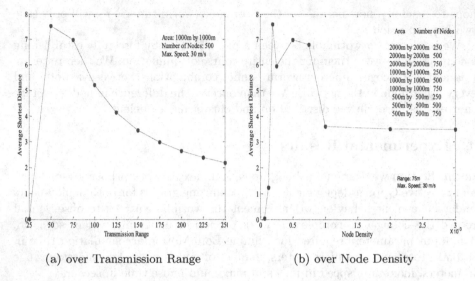

(a) over Transmission Range   (b) over Node Density

Fig. 2. Average Shortest Distance

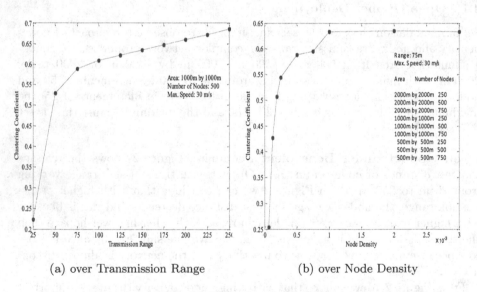

(a) over Transmission Range   (b) over Node Density

Fig. 3. Clustering Coefficient

Figure 3(b) shows the effect of nodes density on clustering coefficient. When we have a high volume of nodes in a small (simulation) area, they tend to be closely connected to one another, thereby achieving a high clustering coefficient.

Figure 4(a) shows the impact of node's transmission range on degree distribution. With the increase in transmission range nodes degree increases, meaning nodes have more one-hop neighbors; and also their degree distribution is well proportional.

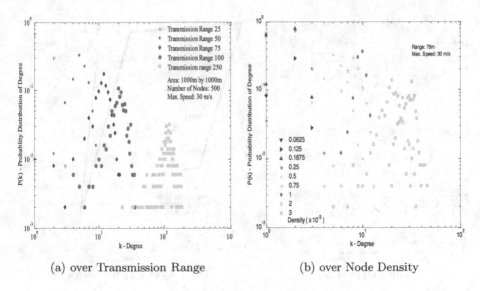

(a) over Transmission Range   (b) over Node Density

Fig. 4. Degree Distribution

From Figure 4(b), we observe that with low density, nodes have a smaller degree value and their distribution function P(k) is high. On the contrary, with high node density the nodes degree is high and its degree distribution is well proportional.

Figure 5(a) shows the average shortest distance, degree, and clustering coefficient for 500 nodes in a 1000 m by 1000 m simulation area with a transmission range of 50m. The maximum speed and maximum pause time remain unaltered as 30 m/s and 5 seconds respectively. We choose this setting as base case to study the behavior of both Oppnet deployments under benevolent and malevolent conditions. The spatial arrangement of nodes in this setting is halfway between being scarcely populated and densely populated.

Open Oppnet under Malevolent Scenario. creating a worm tunnel (physical connection) between pair of nodes. We then analyze and compare the complex network properties between benevolent and malevolent scenarios. Considering the base case, we initiate the attack by creating a worm tunnel between Node 0 and Node 1, and perform the comparison analysis. We then repeat this process with different worm tunnel combinations, such as between Node 0 - Node 2, 3 499, one at a time. Once we have all the results we cross examine them to find nodes that were most impacted by this attack.

After identifying those nodes, we further investigated to see if we can find any patterns. We analyzed nodes location, trajectory and their neighborhood and found two interesting patterns that even apply in social aspects of our lives. The first pattern suggested that, when one node has a short trajectory and is located far away from the densely populated region, we call it an aloof node, forms a

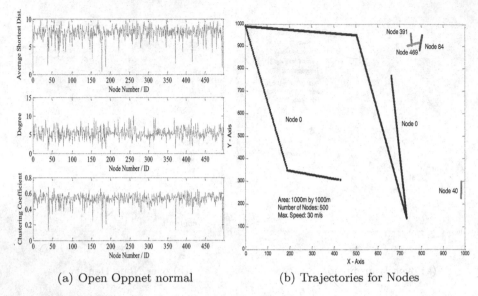

(a) Open Oppnet normal   (b) Trajectories for Nodes

Fig. 5. Open Oppnet deployment (1000 m x 1000 m Area, 500 Nodes, 50 m Transmission Range)

worm tunnel with another node which has a longer trajectory amidst the densely populated region, we call it a popular node, then that will cause a noticeable difference in average shortest distance for that aloof node, as compared to the impact by other tunnel combinations. Now in the social context if an aloof person befriends a popular person then that aloof person can meet a lot of new people through this popular person. The second pattern suggested that when an aloof node, having aloof neighbors, forms an out of band connection with a popular node then this results in a noticeable difference in the average shortest distance for the aloof node and its aloof neighbors. This is because the aloof neighbors can reach the popular node in two hops. Figure 6(a) shows the impact of wormhole attack on average shortest distance, degree and clustering coefficient when the worm tunnel is established between Node 0 and Node 40. The top most part of Figure 6(a) shows the change in the average shortest distance measure for an Open Oppnet under malevolent scenario. A negative value indicates an increase in a measure after an attack and a positive value indicates a decrease in value. So as we can see after forming a worm tunnel between Node 0 and Node 40, Node 40s average shortest distance increased. We can also see that this tunnel had a minor impact on other nodes in the network.

From Figure 5(b), we can see that Node 40 has a very small trajectory and is located very far from the center as compared to Node 0 which has a longer trajectory and is much closer to the center. So by establishing a worm tunnel with Node 0, Node 40 is able to reach many other nodes and that increases its average shortest distance measure.

The middle portion in the Figure 6(a) shows increase in degree for Node 0 and Node 40. This is because there is a physical connection, or tunnel, between them. This connection does not affect the degree measure for other nodes in the network. The bottom portion of Figure 6(a) shows decrease in the clustering coefficient for Node 40 and this is because of the new edge formed between Node 40 and Node 0. Figure 6(b), shows the impact of wormhole when a tunnel is formed between Node 0 and Node 391. From Figure 5(b), we can see that Node 391 is an aloof node and has two other aloof neighbors, Node 84 and 469. When a worm tunnel is created between Node 0 and Node 391, the average shortest distance measure increases for Node 391, 84 and 469. This is because Nodes 84 and 469 can reach Node 0 in two hops. Figure 6(b) also shows the increase in degree and decrease in clustering coefficient for Node 391.

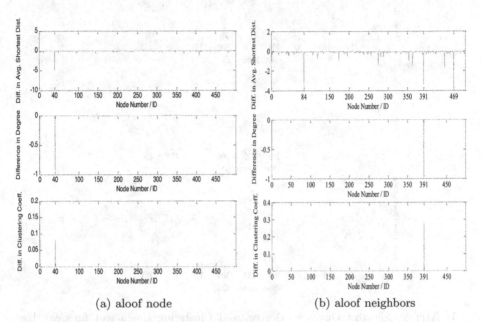

(a) aloof node   (b) aloof neighbors

Fig. 6. Difference in Average Shortest Distance, Degree, and Clustering Coefficient for Open Oppnet deployment under Wormhole (1000 m x 1000 m Area, 500 Nodes, 50 m Transmission Range)

4.2 Selective Oppnet Deployment

We choose the same base case scenario setting for Selective Oppnet deployment as we did for Open Oppnet. Here, we randomly assign a rank to all nodes between [Rmin, Rmax] and set the threshold as Rmin. Meaning if a node x has a rank Rx and another node y, which is in xs transmission range, has a rank R_y and if $|(R_x - R_y)| \leq R_{min}$ then nodes x and y can form a communication link.

Selective Oppnet under Benevolent Scenario. Figure 7 shows the average shortest distance, degree, and clustering coefficient for the Selective Oppnet deployment with a threshold of Rmin. By selecting a small threshold we see that the complex network properties have values much lower than that of an Open Oppnet deployment and this is because the criteria to form a communication is more stringent. If we increase the threshold to Rmax then the Selective Oppnet will behave like an Open Oppnet. By comparing Figure 8 and Figure 7 we can see a decrease in nodes average shortest distance, degree and clustering coefficient under benevolent scenarios.

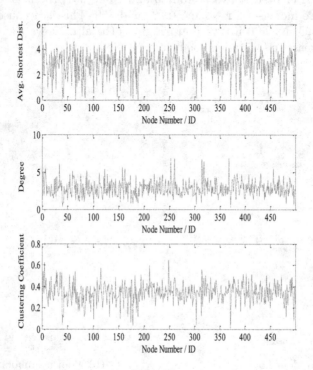

Fig. 7. Average Shortest Distance, Degree, and Clustering Coefficient for Selective Oppnet deployment (1000m x 1000m Area, 500 Nodes, 50m Transmission Range, Rmin Threshold)

Selective Oppnet under Malevolent Scenario. Figure 8(a) and 8(b) shows the complex network properties when a worm tunnel is created between Node 0 40 (aloof node) and Node 0 391 (aloof neighbors) respectively. We observe similar result patterns in both Selective Oppnet deployment and Open Oppnet deployment. The difference lies in the extent of impact caused by the wormhole on either deployment. Selective Oppnet deployment has comparatively lower impact as compared to an Open Oppnet deployment because of the stringent communication establishment criteria. Even though Selective Oppnets have lower measures as compared to Open Oppnets under benevolent scenarios yet they (Selective Oppnets) are comparatively more robust than Open Oppnets under malevolent scenarios.

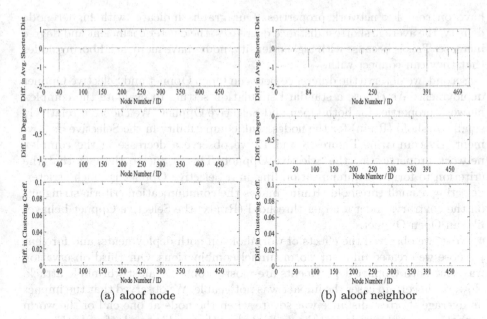

(a) aloof node   (b) aloof neighbor

Fig. 8. Difference in Average Shortest Distance, Degree, and Clustering Coefficient for Selective Oppnet deployment under Wormhole (1000m x 1000m Area, 500 Nodes, 50m Transmission Range, Rmin Threshold)

5   Observations

In this research we computed three important complex network properties, namely average shortest distance, degree distribution, and clustering coefficient for Open Oppnet and Selective Oppnet deployments. In an Open Oppnet, nodes form a communication link every time they are within each others transmission range, whereas in a Selective Oppnet the decision to establish a communication link is not only restricted to nodes being within range but also depends on evaluating a nodes rank. These measures were calculated under benevolent and malevolent scenarios. In a benevolent scenario, all the nodes in the network behave in a normal and predictable manner. However in a malevolent scenario, there are few nodes exhibiting malicious intent. In order to study the complex network properties of an Oppnet under malevolent scenario, we introduce wormhole attack.

We observed some very interesting results and patterns. First, we observed the impact of transmission range and overall node density in an Open Oppnet deployment. Figures 2, 4, and 6 displays the impact of transmission range on complex network properties. As our graphs indicate, increase in transmission range decreases the average shortest distance, increases the cluster coefficient and degree value. This is because with higher transmission range, more number of nodes falls within each others communication range and hence more nodes can connect with each other. Figures 3, 5, and 7 show the impact overall node density have on complex network properties. Our graphs indicate, with higher node density, the average shortest distance decreases, the cluster coefficient and degree increase. This is because with higher density, nodes have many neighboring nodes that they can connect with.

Second, we observe the difference between Open Oppnet and Selective Oppnet deployment. We choose a standard simulation setting to evaluate the complex network properties for both Open and Selective Oppnet. We choose a relatively small threshold (Rmin) for the nodes rank compatibility in the Selective deployment. By comparing Figures 8 and 12 we observe a decrease in the complex network properties for the Selective Oppnet. This is due to the fact that the criterion to form a communication link in a Selective Oppnet is much stricter. Selecting a small threshold (Rmin) makes the communication criteria stringent; on the contrary, under a larger threshold (Rmax) the Selective Oppnet behaves like an Open Oppnet.

Next, we observed the effects of wormhole on both deployments, and for that purpose we created different worm tunnel combinations. Our third observation was that both Oppnet deployments are mostly robust against wormhole attack. However in certain cases the impact was noticeable. We observed that the impact on average shortest distance was severe when the node at one end of the worm tunnel is a popular node and the node at the other end is an aloof node (Figures 9 and 13). A popular node is a term we use to define a node which maintains a high degree by mobilizing around densely populated areas, thereby making new connections. On the contrary an aloof node maintains a distance from rest of the nodes in the network and its motion is restricted to a limited area. From Figure 11, Node 0 is a popular node and Node 40 is an aloof node.

Our fourth observation is that when an aloof node has aloof neighbors and only one of them forms a worm tunnel with the popular node, the impact of average shortest distance affects the aloof node and its neighbors (Figures 10 and 14). This is because the neighbors are only two hops away from reaching the larger audience. From Figure 11, Nodes 391, 84 and 469 are aloof neighboring nodes. We also observed that the impacts were similar, irrespective of which aloof neighbor connected to the popular node, which leads to a possible collaborative attack.

In terms of degree and clustering coefficient, our fifth observation, the effects are mainly noticeable for nodes that are directly involved in the attack, meaning, nodes that are at either end of the worm tunnel. This can be used to pinpoint the pair of nodes involved in the worm tunnel. Finally, we observe the impact of wormhole on a Selective Oppnet deployment is much less as compare to an Open Oppnet. This is because of nodes capability to make an intelligent judgment in forming a communication link with its neighbors.

6   Conclusions

In this research work, we have laid a good foundation about Oppnet deployments and their inherent security issues. In this work we only explore, in detail, one attack scenario, that is the wormhole attack. However we would like to explore more attack scenarios to test if we could use complex network properties for detecting those attacks. Though our attack detection is based on offline observations, we could still use those observations in real time, for example observing activity of an aloof node or keeping an eye on popular nodes. In the Selective deployment we introduced the concept of assigning ranks to nodes based on various factors that will help nodes in making a more informed decision while forming a communication link with its neighbors. We would also like to propose an efficient way to compute a nodes rank by keeping into consideration various factors, like nodes processing power, memory capacity, trustworthiness, reputation, battery life and especially but not restricted to inter contact time and bandwidth because these metrics can produce a decorous metrics for computing delivery probability.

References

1. Aschenbruck, N., Ernst, R., Padella, E.G., Schwamborn, M.: BonnMotion - A Mobility Scenario Generation and Analysis Tool. In: Proc. International ICST Conference on Simulation Tools and Techniques (2010)
2. Barabasi, A.L., Albert, R.: Emergence of Scaling in Random Networks, Science Magazine. Science 286(5439), 509–512 (1999)
3. Burgress, J., Bissias, G., Corner, M., Levine, B.: Surviving Attacks on Disruption-Tolerant Networks without Authentication. In: Proc. ACM MobiHoc (2007)
4. Buttyan, L., Hubaux, J.P.: Security and Cooperation in Wireless Networks, A Graduate Textbook, Version 1.5.1. Cambridge University Press (July 2007), http://secowinet.epfl.ch/index.php?page=download.html
5. Campbell, A., Eisenman, S., Lane, N., Miluzzo, E., Peterson, R.: People-Centric Urban Sensing. In: Proc. ACM WICON (2006)
6. Chen, L.J., Yu, C.H., Sun, T., Chen, Y.C., Chu, H.H.: A Hybrid Routing Approach for Opportunistic Networks. In: Proc. ACM SIGCOMM Workshop on Challenged Networks, pp. 213–220 (September 2006)
7. Choo, F., Chan, M., Chang, E.C.: Robustness of DTN against Routing Attacks. In: Proc. IEEE COMSNETS, pp. 1 -10 (January 2010)
8. Conti, M., Kumar, M.: Opportunities in opportunistic Computing. IEEE Computer Society 43(1), 42–50 (2010)
9. Cornelius, C., Kapadia, A., Kotz, D., Peebles, D., Shin, M., Triandopoulos, N.: AnonySense: Privacy-Aware People-Centric Sensing. In: Proc. ACM MobiSys (June 2008)
10. Doria, A., Uden, M., Pandey, D.P.: Providing connectivity to the Saami nomadic community. In: Proc. International Conference on Open Collaborative Design for Sustainable Innovation (December 2002)
11. Hu, Y., Perrig, A., Johnson, D.: Packet Leashes: A Defense against Wormhole Attacks in Wireless Ad Hoc Networks. In: Proc. IEEE INFOCOM, vol. 3, pp. 1976–1986 (April 2003)
12. Huangm, C.M., Lan, K.C., Tsai, C.Z.: A survey of Opportunistic Networks. In: Proc. IEEE Advanced Information Networking and Applications - Workshops, pp. 1672–1677 (March 2008)

13. Jayakumar, G., Ganapathi, G.: Reference Point Group Mobility and Random Way-point Models in Performance Evaluation of MANET Routing Protocols. ACM Journal of Computer Systems, Networks, and Communication 2008 (January 2008)
14. Juang, P., Oki, H., Wang, Y., Martonosi, M., Peh, L.S., Rubesnstein, D.: Energy-Efficient Computing for Wildlife Tracking: Design Tradeoffs and Early Experiences with ZebraNet. In: Proc. ACM ASPLOS-X (2002)
15. Kapadia, A., Kotz, D., Triandopoulos, N.: Opportunistic Sensing: Security Challenges for the New Paradigm. In: Proc. IEEE COMSNETS, pp. 1–10 (January 2009)
16. Lilien, L., Kamal, Z.H., Bhuse, V., Gupta, A.: Opportunistic Networks: The Concept and Research Challenges in Privacy and Security. In: Proc. NSF Intl. WSPWN (2006)
17. Musolesi, M., Hailes, S., Mascolo, C.: Adaptive Routing for Intermittently Connected Mobile Ad Hoc Networks. In: Proc. IEEE WoWMoM Symposium (June 2005)
18. Pelusi, L., Passarella, A., Conti, M.: Opportunistic Networking: Data Forwarding in Disconnected Mobile Ad Hoc Networks. IEEE Communication Magazine 44(11), 134–141 (2006)
19. Petland, A., Fletcher, R., Hasson, A.: DakNet: Rethinking Connectivity in Developing Nations. IEEE Computer Society 37(1), 78–83 (2004)
20. Shikfa, A.: Security Challenges in Opportunistic Communication. In: Proc. IEEE GCC, pp. 425–428 (February 2011)
21. C. H. Vu, A. Soneye, An Analysis of Collaborative Attacks on Mobile Ad hoc Networks, Masters Thesis MCS-2009:4 (June 2009),
    http://btu.se/fou/cuppsats.nsf/all/ab24607cbd4e770ac12575d300368841/
    file/Final_Thesis_Report_hovu07_adso07.pdf
22. Wang, X.F., Chen, G.: Small World, Scale-Free and Beyond. IEEE Circuits and Systems Magazine 3(1), 6–20 (2003)
23. Watts, D.J., Stogatz, S.H.: Collective dynamics of small-world networks. Nature International Weekly Journal of Science, Nature 393, 440–442 (1998)

Joint Optimization of Interface Assignment and Channel Allocation in Cognitive Radio Mesh Networks

Jie Jia, Qiusi Lin, Jie Li, and Jian Chen

School of Information Science and Engineering, Northeastern University
110819, Shenyang, China
jiajie@ise.neu.edu.cn

Abstract. With the rapid growth of wireless networks and the increasing demand for wireless services, there will be an acute shortage of spectrum resources in the near future. A promising solution is to use the cognitive radio technology to arm the mesh nodes with opportunistic spectrum access capability, which leads to a more flexible access to spectral resources. In this paper, we investigate the joint interface assignment and channel allocation problem in cognitive radio mesh network. In order to ensure the QoS quality for each call, we propose a novel nested optimization technique based on genetic algorithm to find the optimal resource allocation. Extensive simulation results show that the proposed algorithm converges fast and approaches the global optimal solution efficiently.

Keywords: Channel allocation, interface assignment, cognitive radio, wireless mesh network.

1 Introduction

Wireless mesh networks (WMNs) usually consist of mesh routers and mesh clients, where mesh routers form the network backbone and provide access for mesh clients [1]. With the increasing number of users and a growing demand for better Quality of Service (QoS), the limited spectrum resources have become a serious obstacle to obtain high-performance data services in WMNs [2]. Moreover, traditional fixed spectrum assignment model makes this problem much worse. Fortunately, the emergence and development of the cognitive radio (CR) technology has provided a novel solution for next generation wireless communications. With its spectrum sensing, learning and adaptation capabilities, CR is able to address the heart of the problem associated with spectrum scarcity and interoperability, and it is considered as the radio platform for WMNs [3]. However, affected by the openness of the wireless frequency spectrum and the characteristics of WMN, it is of great importance to fairly and efficiently allocate the limited network resources to all users.

Recently, several channel allocation algorithms have been proposed for cognitive radio networks. In order to maximize the effective bandwidth of the whole network, a color-aware channel allocation algorithm is presented in [4]. By making channel assignments amends for the small changes locally in the network, a distributed channel

X. Wang et al. (Eds.): WASA 2012, LNCS 7405, pp. 479–487, 2012.

allocation algorithm via local bargaining is proposed in [5]. By integrating the spectrum resources into a sub-channel spectrum pool, a dynamic spectrum allocation algorithm is presented in [5]. A channel allocation algorithm based on dynamic game theory is investigated in [6], in which cognitive users can repeatedly adjust their strategic to achieve equilibrium. However, the practical flow demands on each link are not considered in the above resource allocation mechanisms, which may cause the traffic flow on the link exceeds its effective capacity when there are many end-to-end routing flows. This naturally leads to network congestion and cannot ensure the QoS level for each routing call. Recently, there has been some research on the cross-layer optimization to improve network performance. The authors in [7] investigated how to satisfy the flow demands and proposed an optimized mechanism of routing and channel allocation. However, there is a lack of routing optimization, and the routing algorithm is only used to identify flow requirements of each link. The authors in [8] present linear mixed integer programming (MILP)-based optimal algorithm to achieve a good tradeoff between fairness and throughput. By considering the dynamic variables of the spectrum availability, the authors in [9] present the robust performance for each link and proposed an optimal route selection mechanism.

In this paper, we mainly focus on the problem of channel assignment which can satisfy the QoS level of all routing flows. The rest of the paper is organized as follows. Section 3 presents the network model and describes the congestion avoidance problem. In Section 4, a nested optimization architecture based on genetic algorithm (GA) is proposed to find the optimal solution. Section 5 gives the simulation results for our algorithms, and Section 6 concludes our paper.

2   Network Model

There are M primary and N cognitive users randomly distributed in $X \times Y$ region. Assume that each node is equipped with I intelligent wireless interfaces, each of which can select its communication power intelligently, and the transmission grade Q is totally quantized into n levels. There exist k non-interfering channels $C=[c_1,c_2,...,c_k]$ used for data transmission and one common control channel used for all signal message interaction. The entire cognitive WMN can be represented as directed graph $G=\{P,S,E\}$, where $P = \{p_i \mid 1 \le i \le M\}$ is the set of primary users, $S = \{s_i \mid 1 \le i \le N\}$ is the set of cognitive users, and $E = \{e_{ij} \mid 1 \le i, j \le N\}$ is the virtual directed edge set when each cognitive user adopts the maximum communication power.

When the transmitter node i adopts the transmit power $P(e_{ij})^s$, $s \in Q$, the receiving power $P(e_{ij})^R$ of the receiving terminal node j can be calculated as,

$$p(e_{ij})^R = p(e_{ij})^s \cdot d(e_{ij})^{-\gamma} \tag{1}$$

where γ is the path loss factor, and $d(e_{ij})$ is the distance between node i and j.

Only when $p(e_{ij})^s \cdot d(e_{ij})^{-\gamma} \ge \alpha$, it can be defined as a success transmission, where α is the receiving power threshold. Apparently, the maximum transmission distance $T_i(p(e_{ij})^S)$ with transmit power $P(e_{ij})^s$ is,

$$T_i(P(e_{ij})^S) = \left(\frac{P(e_{ij})^S}{\alpha}\right)^{\frac{1}{\gamma}} \tag{2}$$

Assume the interference range $I_i(p(e_{ij})^S)$ is η ($\eta \geq 1$) times of the transmission range,

$$I_i\left(P(e_{ij})^S\right) = \eta \cdot T_i(P(e_{ij})^S) \tag{3}$$

Define x_{ij}^m as the link channel allocation variable to express the allocation of the link e_{ij} on channel m, where $x_{ij}^m = 1$ denotes that e_{ij} is assigned to the channel m, otherwise $x_{ij}^m = 0$. Since concurrent link transmission may easily cause the disorder of arriving packages, to guarantee the consistency of the routing packet, only one channel can be assigned to each directed link, namely,

$$\sum_{m=1}^{C} x_{ij}^m \leq 1 \tag{4}$$

Define y_i^m indicates the channel allocation of the node i. If $y_i^m = 1$, it denotes that the node i has the link e_{ij} or e_{ji} assigned to channel m. If $y_i^m = 0$, it means that none of the links belonging to i is assigned to channel m,

$$y_i^m = \begin{cases} 1, & \exists j \in N, e_{ij} \in E, x_{ij}^m = 1 \text{ or } e_{ji} \in E, x_{ji}^m = 1 \\ 0, & \text{otherwise} \end{cases} \tag{5}$$

The number of the channels used simultaneously by node i is limited by the number of interfaces, namely,

$$\sum_{m=1}^{C} y_i^m \leq I \tag{6}$$

For any two edges e_{uv} and e_{ij}, if node i or j is within interference range of u or v, we say that e_{uv} and e_{ij} are mutually potential interfered, and vice versa. When and only when the two potential interfered links e_{uv} and e_{ij} are assigned the same channel m, the edge e_{uv} and e_{ij} are defined as mutually interfered links. When e_{ij} selects the communication channel m and communication power q_k, the effective capacity of e_{ij} is defined as,

$$U_{ij}(m,q_k) = \frac{x_{ij}^m \cdot H_m}{1 + |N_i(m,q_k)|} \log_2\left(1 + \frac{P(e_{ij})^R}{P(e_{ij})^N}\right) \tag{7}$$

where H_m is the bandwidth of the channel m, $P(e_{ij})^R$ is the receiving power of the receiving node, $P(e_{ij})^N$ is the noise power, and $N_{ij}(m,q_k)$ is the set of the interfere links when the channel m and power level q_k is chosen. The denominator of Eq. (7) reflects the fact that all the links which interfere with each other cannot be active simultaneously. This no-interference policy leads to link capacity reduction which is captured by the scaling factor $1/(1+|N_i(m,q_k)|)$.

Define γ^{sd} as the end-to-end call requirement from node s to d. Let $a_{i,j,m}^{sd}$ express whether the flow γ^{sd} passes through link e_{ij}. If $a_{i,j,m,q_k}^{sd} = 1$, it means that flow γ^{sd} passes the link e_{ij} using channel m and power q_k. Otherwise, $a_{i,j,m,q_k}^{sd} = 0$. For any call with demand requirement γ^{sd}, all the nodes in the network should satisfy the flow conservation law. Here, we import the concept of net flow that the routing requirement γ^{sd} passes the node j. Note that the net flow is equal to the difference between the outgoing flow and the incoming flow. Namely, for $s, d, m \in N$, we have,

$$\sum_{i \in N, e_{ij} \in E} \sum_{m=1}^{C} a_{ij,m,q_k}^{sd} \gamma^{sd} - \sum_{i \in N, e_{ji} \in E} \sum_{m=1}^{C} a_{ji,m,q_k}^{sd} \gamma^{sd} = \begin{cases} \gamma^{sd}, & \text{if } s = j, \\ -\gamma^{sd}, & \text{if } d = j, \\ 0, & \text{otherwise.} \end{cases} \tag{8}$$

Let $\lambda_{i,j}^{m,q_k}$ denote the aggregate route that all the requirements pass through the link e_{ij} in the network over channel m and communication power level q_k, namely,

$$\lambda_{i,j}^{m,q_k} = \sum_{s,d \in N} a_{i,j,m,q_k}^{sd} \cdot \gamma^{sd} \tag{9}$$

In order to avoid network congestion, the aggregate traffic on link e_{ij} cannot be more than its effective capacity $U_{ij}(m, q_k)$, so,

$$\lambda_{i,j}^{m,q_k} \leq U_{ij}(m, q_k) \tag{10}$$

Let δ_{ij} be the difference between the efficient capacity $U_{ij}(m, q_k)$ and the actual carrying load $\lambda_{i,j}^{m,q_k}$,

$$\delta_{ij} = U_{ij}(m, q_k) - \lambda_{i,j}^{m,q_k} \tag{11}$$

As δ_{ij} tends to 0, the corresponding logical link e_{ij} tends to congestion. Let $\delta_{\min}$ be the congestion avoidance parameter of the network, which is defined as the minimum difference of δ_{ij} across all links that exist in the topology graph after channel allocation and power control,

$$\delta_{\min} = \min_{e_{ij} \in E} \delta_{ij} \tag{12}$$

Note that $\delta_{\min}$ represents the most congested logical link in the topology graph. In order to maximum call acceptance, we need to increase the congestion avoidance parameter of the network $\delta_{\min}$ as much as possible.

3   Nested Optimization

Interface assignment, channel allocation and congestion avoidance are interdependent sub-problems. However, all these sub-problems are NP-hard, and the integration of them for joint optimization further increases the process complexity. Genetic algorithms (GAs) are recognized to be well qualified to tackle large scale NP-hard problems [10]. In this paper, a nested optimization framework based on GA is proposed.

3.1   GA-Based Channel Allocation

To the problem of joint interface assignment and channel allocation in WMN, since the problem space corresponds to cognitive users selecting channel and communication power level for its wireless interfaces, a node based chromosome coding mechanism is designed. Each individual is represented as a two vector strings $\{\bar{a}_i, \bar{q}_i\}$. Here, $\bar{a}_i = \{a_{i,1}, \cdots, a_{i,j}, \cdots, a_{i,k}\}$ represents the set of channels to which the nodes are currently assigned, and satisfies,

$$a_{i,j} = \begin{cases} 1 & if\ node\ i\ selects\ channel\ j \\ 0 & otherwise \end{cases} \tag{13}$$

Let $\bar{q}_i = \{q_{i,1}, \cdots, q_{i,j}, \cdots, q_{i,k}\}$ represent the communication power level that the node selects in each channel,

$$q_{i,j} = \begin{cases} q_k & if\ a_{ij} = 1\ and\ q_{\min} < q_k < q_{\max} \\ 0 & otherwise \end{cases} \tag{14}$$

Note that the coding scheme discussed above also includes the mapping relationship between the channel and interface. Here, the channels are sequentially bounded to wireless interfaces of cognitive users. If j is the mth selected channel in chromosome, $1 \le m \le I$, it is used as the mth interface, and its communication power level is set to q_j. In channel selection initialization, to ensure none of the nodes uses more than I channels simultaneously, each node randomly sets I bit of its channel vector to 1. And then, the power level q_{ij} is set as q_{ij}=rand($q_{\min}$,$q_{\max}$) when a_{ij}=1, otherwise q_{ij}=0.

Each time after individual coding in the population, we can get a network topology graph and calculate effective capacity for each link according to the channel and power level allocation. Then we need to evaluate the fitness of each individual by using GA based route scheduling mechanism. Here, the individual fitness is the maximum congestion avoidance ratio with current resource allocation.

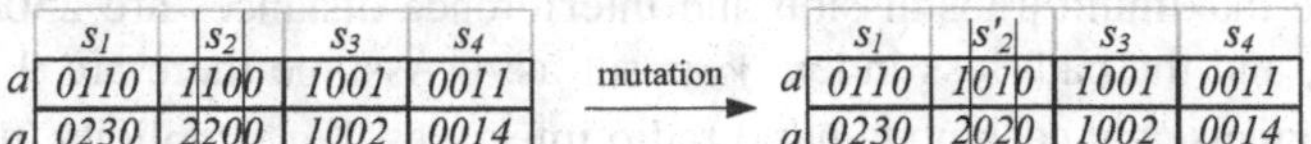

	s_1	s_2	s_3	s_4				s_1	s'_2	s_3	s_4
a	0110	1100	1001	0011	mutation	→	a	0110	1010	1001	0011
q	0230	2200	1002	0014			q	0230	2020	1002	0014

Fig. 1. The inversion variation based mutation method

Genetic evolution operations mainly include selection, recombination, mutation, and replacement. We use the roulette wheel selection method, where the chosen probability is proportional to the individual fitness-evaluation function. The recombination operator used in this paper is the single-point crossover. The mutation operator works by randomly making some minor changes in the chromosomes of the current population. In our algorithm, the mutation is conducted in an inversion variation based method. A part of the chromosome are randomly chosen and then inserted into the original location with the anti-sequenced new sub-chromosome, as shown in Fig. 1.

Only when the child's fitness is larger than its parent's, the parents are replaced by their children in the next generation. Since the duplicate individuals can constitute the same individuals gradually, the duplicate individual is kept only once in the new population and the deleted individuals are replaced by new generated ones randomly.

3.2   GA Based Routing Scheduling

Influenced by the routing scheduling order, it is necessary to work out the optimal routing scheduling order. However, searching the optimal routing schedule is also NP-hard. For this reason, we further present a GA based routing scheduling algorithm. The scheduling order is directly mapped to the solution structure. For example, in a network with 6 routing calls, an individual of the schedule is $(r_5, r_1, r_4, r_2, r_3, r_6)$, which means call r_5 is served first, and r_6 last. The improved sequential crossover method is introduced to recombine two individuals in the current generation. At first, two mating regions from its parent individual are selected randomly. Then these mating regions are swapped and added up in front of its parents. By deleting the same link number in the mating region, the offspring individuals can be obtained after recombination. With this crossover method, even if two parents are identical, new individuals can still be produced, which can maintain the population diversity. Since the generated individual after recombination has a similar structure as the channel allocation, the same mutation and replacement strategies are used to ensure the superiority of offspring individuals. As to the session in ordered routing set, the problem of finding optimal route with maximum congestion avoidance is equivalent to searching the widest bandwidth routing path. Thus the Dijkstra's routing algorithm is introduced, and we only need to replace the hop-count criteria with the effective bandwidth.

4   Simulation Results

There are 50 mesh routers randomly deployed in 1000×800 target area. The maximum transmission power is set as $20dBm$ and the transmission power levels Q is set as 16. In hence, the maximum transmission and interference distances are 250m and 500m respectively, and the path loss index γ is set as 4. Assume there are 9 available orthogonal channels, and each node has 3 radio interfaces. For simplicity, the maximum bandwidth of each channel is set to 54 Mbps. In order to ensure that SNR reaches $10dB$ when communication is successful, the noise power is set as $P_N=-85.9dBm$.

There are 20 communication sessions generated with random source, destination and equal traffic demands of 0.5Mbps. Table 1 specifies an instance for these 10 sessions in the network. The crossover probability and mutation probability is set to 0.95 and 0.05. Fig. 2 shows the network congestion avoidance degree with different genetic generations. Observing the results from the beginning to 200th generation, it is clear to see that the congestion avoidance rate directs toward the global optimal solution. After 180th generation, no better solutions can be found, which shows that our algorithm can converge to the optimal solution rapidly. We also can find the nested algorithm with routing sequence scheduling achieves a better solution than the one without scheduling, which testifies that the performance is highly influenced by the routing scheduling order. In other words, optimized orders can further improve performance of the algorithm.

Table 1. Information of the 20 sessions

Session ID	Source	Destination	Session ID	Source	Destination
1	24	8	11	1	8
2	5	18	12	2	16
3	13	9	13	3	10
4	30	19	14	4	11
5	16	10	15	30	1
6	7	23	16	6	2
7	27	29	17	21	3
8	28	21	18	27	4
9	17	25	19	1	9
10	6	20	20	14	2

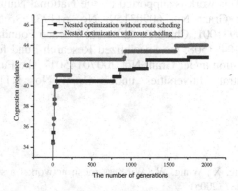

Fig. 2. Congestion avoidance ratio in different generations

We further test our algorithm in different numbers of channels and routing sessions. Fig. 3 shows the network congestion avoidance degree with different genetic generations. It is clear to see that more routing flows result lower congestion avoidance, and more channels lead to much higher congestion avoidance as expected. Although the objective value is a non-decreasing function of number of channels, when the number of channels becomes sufficiently large, further increasing the number of channels will not enhance the objective value greatly.

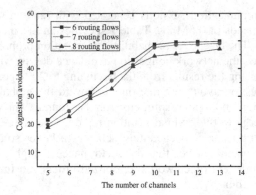

Fig. 3. Comparison of congestion avoidance in different conditions

5   Conclusion and Future Work

In this paper, we investigated the challenging problem of joint interface assignment and channel allocation for cognitive WMNs. This problem is difficult due to its large design space and the coupling relationship between resource management and upper layers. We proposed an efficient nested optimization framework based on genetic algorithm to solve this problem. Simulation results show that our algorithm can achieve the maximum network congestion avoidance very quickly.

Acknowledgments. This work is supported by the National Natural Science Foundation of China under Grant No. 60903159, No. 61173153, No. 61070162, No. 71071028 and No. 70931001; China Postdoctoral Science Foundation funded project under Grant No. 20110491508; the Specialized Research Fund for the Doctoral Program of Higher Education under Grant No. 20070145017; the Fundamental Research Funds for the Central Universities under Grant No. N110404014 and No. N110318001.

References

1. Akyildiz, I.F., Wang, X., Wang, W.: Wireless mesh networks: a survey. Computer Networks 47(4), 445–487 (2005)
2. Gupta, P., Kumar, P.R.: The capacity of wireless networks. IEEE Transactions on Information Theory 46(2), 388–404 (2000)
3. Hou, Y.T., Shi, Y., Sherali, H.D.: Spectrum sharing for multi-hop networking with cognitive radios. IEEE J. Sel. Areas Commun. 26(1), 146–155 (2008)
4. Zheng, H., Peng, C.: Collaboration and fairness in opportunistic spectrum access. In: Proceedings of the IEEE International Conference on Communications (ICC), pp. 3132–3136. IEEE Press, Seoul Korea (2005)

5. Buddhikot, M.M., Kolodzy, P., Miller, S., et al.: DIMSUMNet: new directions in wireless networking using coordinated dynamic spectrum access. In: Proceedings of the World of Wireless Mobile and Multimedia Networks (WoWMoM), pp. 78–85. IEEE Press, Taormina (2005)

6. Weiss, T.A., Jondral, F.K.: Spectrum pooling: an innovative strategy for the enhancement of spectrum efficiency. IEEE Communications Magazine 42(3), 8–14 (2004)

7. Mark, F., Mario, C., Jean-Pierre, H.: Efficient MAC in cognitive radio systems: a game-theoretic approach. IEEE Transactions on Wireless Communications 8(4), 1984–1995 (2009)

8. Ashish, R., Kartik, G., Tzi-cker, C.: Centralized channel assignment and routing algorithms for multi-channel wireless mesh networks. ACM Mobile Computing and Communications Review 8(2), 50–65 (2004)

9. Jian, T., Hincapie, R., Guoliang, X., Weiyi, Z., Bustamante, R.: Fair bandwidth allocation in wireless mesh networks with cognitive radios. IEEE Transactions on Vehicular Technology 59(3), 1487–1496 (2010)

10. Chao-Fang, S., Wanjiun, L., Hsi-Lu, C.: Joint routing and spectrum allocation for multi-hop cognitive radio networks with route robustness consideration. IEEE Transactions on Wireless Communications 10(9), 2940–2949 (2011)

11. Holland, J.: Adaptation in Natual and artificial Systems. University of Michigan Press

MPSL: A Mobile Phone-Based Physical-Social Location Verification System

Xudong Ni[1], Junzhou Luo[1], Boying Zhang[2], Jin Teng[2], and Xiaole Bai[3]

[1] School of Computer Science and Engineering, Southeast University,
Nanjing, P.R. China, 210096
{xd_ni,jluo}@seu.edu.cn
[2] Dept of Computer Science and Engineering, The Ohio State University,
OH, USA, 43210
{zhangboy,tengj}@cse.ohio-state.edu
[3] Dept of Computer and Information Science, University of Massachusetts at
Dartmouth, MA, USA, 02747
xbia@umassd.edu

Abstract. In this paper, we introduce a new concept, Physical-Social Location (PSL), and propose MPSL, a mobile phone-based system to verify users' self-report location claims for mobile social network service (MSNS). Unlike instant discrete location points, PSLs are geographic regions obtained over longer timescales and center around regularly visited locations of social significance, e.g., workplaces or neighborhoods. PSL verification can prevent the user from reporting fake locations, e.g. GPS coordinate, trajectory or geographic profile, to location-sensitive applications as well as aid online credibility in MSNS. In our MPSL system, a user's location claim is proved by a set of selective co-located people serving as "witnesses". It is composed of two parts, i.e., proof generation and verification. The former leverages a certain number of co-located people to generate co-location certificates as location proofs during their physical encounters via Bluetooth. An efficient verification scheme is proposed to make our system accurate and adaptive. Besides, incentive are taken into account to keep our distributed system applicable. We have implemented the MPSL system using real-world Nokia N82 phones. Our experimental results show that our mobile phone based system can achieve high verification accuracy and good privacy protection.

1 Introduction

As mobile phone, such as smartphones and PDAs, are becoming prevalent, Location-related Mobile Social Network Services(MSNS), e.g. Foursquare [15], Yelp [11], Google Latitude [10] and EveryTrial [13], are playing an increasingly important role in people's life. Foursquare provides a location-based social networking platform through which users can "check in " at places that are visiting and learn their friends location. Yelp allows users to post and read reviews about places. Online Social Network Services also take advantages of location

X. Wang et al. (Eds.): WASA 2012, LNCS 7405, pp. 488–499, 2012.

information, e.g., geographic profile to provide various services, like friend recommendation. All these services require user to report their current or long term location information, e.g., GPS coordinates, Trajectory or Geography Profile. Often, users can obtain rewards or benefit from being at a given location. For example, Foursquare has the user who checks in the most often at a location become the "mayor" of the location. In turn, the owner of the location (e.g., a mall) might offer a reward to this user (e.g., a coupon). Besides, Online Social Services often offer exclusive recommendation services or reviews based on users' geographic profile or previous visited places. Thus spammer and attacker may report a fake location to convince other users that he presented at some places to obtain benefits. So people do have the incentive to lie about their locations in these location-sensitive services.

Unfortunately, current mobile social network services are based on user's self-reported location claims, which make them are easily being cheated. Although most mobile users have devices capable of discovering their locations, they lack a mechanism to prove their current of past locations to applications and services. For instant, Foursquare is using GPS (and other un-reported measures) to verify a user's manually entered location [12]. Users can manipulate Smartphone's GPS-based location reporting mechanism by install malicious application [14]. Although cellular service provider have tracking services that can help verify mobile users' location in real time, the accuracy is not good enough and the location history cannot be verified. In addition, user's geographic profiles are completely based on their own typing. To solve this problem, several systems have recently been proposed [3,5,19]. However, they cannot support various location information requirements and lack feasibility. For example, [3] proposed a solution that is suitable for third-party attestation, but relies on the 802.11 access-point infrastructure, which cannot be easily deployed. [19] described a Bluetooth based distributed location proof methods, but it requires user's obtrusive operation and have no incentive mechanism.

In this paper, we firstly define physical-social location (PSL) as the geographic region that is frequently visited by people over a fairly long period of time with social significance to support MSNS. We then propose a mobile phone-based PSL verification system, called MPSL, which makes use of mobile phones to verify one's claimed PSL based on his (repeated) physical presence at that location, or disprove due to lack of such evidence. The core idea of our system is that certain people may serve as "witnesses" for one person to prove his physical presence at a PSL. The encounters with the people who frequent a locale are strong evidence that one has visited that very place. In summary, we claim the following contributions:

1. We have introduced a novel concept of Physical-Social Location, or PSL, and proposed a mobile phone-based PSL verfication system called MPSL.
2. We have proposed a new PSL verification protocol. This protocol makes use of human mobility regularity and encounter-based location proof exchange mechanism. It is light-weight, fast and accurate.

3. We have designed and implemented MPSL using real world Nokia N82 phones. Experimental results show that our MPSL system can achieve good verification accuracy.

The remainder of this paper is organized as follows. We present related work in Section 2. Section 3 illustrates the details of MPSL location proof generation and verification. Section 4 introduces the prototype system architecture and implementation. Section 5 presents the evaluation results of our system performance. Section 6 concludes the whole paper.

2   Related Work

The location based services [10,15,16] proliferate with hundreds of thousands of users in recent years. The effectiveness of these services rely on correctly reported user locations. However, some users might intentionally falsify their location information for their own sake. To prevent these malicious behavior, several creative approaches have been proposed to verify user-reported location information.Infrastructure dependent active location verification schemes infrastructure to issue and verify a dedicated location proof for nearby users[3][5]. This kind of approaches are certainly effective to verify a given location, but still have some drawbacks, such as scalability, cost and privacy issues. Another kind of infrastructure dependent approach works passively, i.e., techniques use APs to broadcast a token, only devices that are close to the AP will see this token and can automatically save it as a location proof [8]. This kind of approaches have similar issues as the approaches in the previous category. Besides, Broadcast-based approaches lack a strong binding between the location proof and the user identity, so proofs can be easily given away and used for malicious purposes.

Infrastructure independent approaches enable users to verify their random encounters at certain location via short-range communication channel and sensing based applications [2] designs a novel encounter based trust for mobile social service. It aims to provide an efficient missed-connections service using mobile devices without relying on trusted coordinating servers. Authors in [20] proposed a system that uses "integrity regions" for authentication through presence in wireless network, where "Integrity regions" are based on the verification of entity proximity through time-of-arrival ranging techniques. However, the above two approaches can not guarantee the collected proofs are really useful for location verification, because their collection process follows a random, purposeless way. Zhu et al. proposed a privacy-preserving location update system, i.e., AP-PLAUS, in [19]. Users exchange location proofs with Bluetooth in close range and update the proof to a central server with periodically changed pseudonyms. But it is lack of incentive as peer-to-peer mechanism and only supports instant location point. Our work overcomes these weaknesses as well as proposes a novel verification scheme by analyzing the proofs reported by multiple witnesses, which is resistant to perjury and other malicious attacks.

3 Mobile Physical Social Location

In this section, we present our system overview and workflow. Then we describe the detailed procedure, including location proof generation and verification.

3.1 System Overview and Workflow

MPSL is a location proof provided by a set of people, the 'witnesses', to verify that a person is physically present at a geographic region. We make use of smartphones to enable automatic 'witness' generation from 'appropriate' people we meet. There are two assumptions in our design one is each user has a uniquely public key mapped to his identity [3]; the other is collected location sensing data are trusted [8] [9].The workflow contains two parts: *location proof generation* and *location proof verification*. A concrete working example is as follows. Initially, each user prepares a PSL set L based on her daily trace. When user u_a encounters another user u_b at location c, her MPSL system will help her judge whether u_b is a "good" witness to provide location proof. If u_b is approved as a "good" witness, then u_a's MPSL system will automatically send out a request for u_b's location proof of c. Upon receiving u_a's request, u_b generates a location proof at runtime and encrypts it using his secret key. Then, u_b sends this location proof to u_a, and he also uploads the location proof to MPSL server for later use. In a similar manner, u_a collects location proofs from other users at location c. Some time later, u_a is required by an online social networking service to indicate her presence in location c, so u_a hands in all the collected location proofs at c to MPSL server. Based on u_a's submitted location proof and corresponding witnesses' submission, MPSL server can make a judgement on the authenticity of u_a's location proof of c.

3.2 Location Proof Generation

We follow a two-phase procedure to generate location proofs. In the first phase, we use a clustering method to help each user prepare a "witnessing" zone L. In the second phase, each user generates a runtime location proof based on his current locale $l \in L$ and other user's request.

To be a qualified witness for requested locales, a user needs to visit them frequently enough. [6] shows that people devote most of their time to a few locations visited with diminished regularity. Based on this fact, each user will have a few frequently visited places. We term these locales a user's *witnessing zone*, and represent it with location point sets L.To generate each user's witnessing zone, we use clustering algorithms in data mining to aggregate the user-collected GPS data. Consider that user's GPS data has large size, irregular pattern and noises, we select DBSCAN [7] as our clustering clustering algorithm. We summarize the detailed algorithm in *Algorithm 1*.

Algorithm 1. Location Set Initialization

```
1:  Input: raw GPS data set S
2:  Output: location set L
3:
4:  Parameters:
5:  Maximum radius of the neighbourhood: ε

6:  Minimum number of points within ε:
    MinPts
7:
8:  Initialization of L:
9:  ClusterID = 1
10: for each unclustered data d_i in GPS data
    set S
11:     mark d_i as clustered;
12:     N = getNeighbors(d_i, ε);
13:     if sizeof(N)< MinPts
14:         mark d_i as NOISE;
15:     else
16:         ClusterID = ClusterID+1;
17:         ExpandCluster(d_i, N, ClusterID, ε,
    MinPts)
18:     end if
19: end for
20:
21: ExpandCluster(d_i, N, ClusterID, ε,
    MinPts):
22: add d_i to the cluster numbered by Clus-
    terID;
23: for each data d_j in N
24:     if d_j is unvisitedww
25:         mark d_j as visited;
26:         M = getNeighbors(d_j, ε);
27:         if sizeof(M ≥ MinPts)
28:             N = N ∪ M;
29:     if d_j is not in any cluster
30:         add d_j to the cluster numbered by
    ClusterID
```

Algorithm 2. Location Proof Generation for User u_a

```
1:  Proof Generation:
2:  u_a finds the closest location cluster l_a for
    current location c
3:  Search nearby users and mark them as set
    U
4:  for each user u_i in set U
5:      publish closest location cluster l_i for
    current location c
6:  end for
7:
8:  u_a retrieve each l_i and store it in set S
9:  for each l_i in set S
10:     if c ∉ l_a ∪ l_i
11:         break;
12:     else if l_a ∩ l_i ≠ ∅
13:         generate shared key K_{a,i};
14:         request location proof lp_{a,i} from u_i;
15:     end if
16: end for
17:
18: for each user u_i in set S
19:     if u_i receives a request for location
    proof from u_a
20:         generate encrypted location proof
    lp_{a,i};
21:         publish lp_{a,i};
22:     end if
23: end for
24:
25: lp_{a,i} retrieved as one entry of u_a's loca-
    tion proof for l_a
26: if location c ∉ l_a
27:     add c to l_a;
28:     recalculate l_a's radius r_g and center
    (x_{cm}, y_{cm})
29: end if
```

In the second phase, user can issue a runtime location proof based on his current locale $l \in L$ and the nearby user's ID. The detailed procedure is shown in *Algorithm 2*. Suppose a user u_a meets user u_b and other users at locale c. Initially, u_a has to find the closest cluster l_a to c in her location set L. The test conditions for generating a shared key has some practical meaning as shown in Figure 2. A straightforward test condition could be $c \in l_a \cap l_b$. However, our experiment results show that the probability of generating a shared key in $l_a \cap l_b$ is fairly low. In this light, we use the combination of two test conditions. The condition $c \in l_a \cup l_b$ tests whether the current location c is a frequently visited place for u_a and u_b. The condition $l_a \cap l_b \neq \emptyset$ tests whether u_a and u_b have similarity in their visited places based on their mobility pattern. Note that we may generate a shared key in $(l_b - l_a \cap l_b)$ which is useless to prove u_a in l_a, as is the position shown by the six point star in Figure 2. To counteract this negative effect, we can ask u_a to collect multiple keys from other users. We enable this operation by calculating the Euclidean distance between c and each cluster's center, then choose the minimum value. Here, the center (x_{cm}, y_{cm}) of each cluster in location set L is determined as:

$$x_{cm} = \sum_{i=1}^{n} x_i/n, \quad y_{cm} = \sum_{i=1}^{n} y_i/n, \tag{1}$$

where (x_i, y_i) are the x and y coordinates of the ith location collected in the cluster, n is the number of location recorded in the cluster. Then u_a publishes l_a for u_b and other users to retrieve (line 4–6). After this step, u_a retrieves u_b's closest cluster l_b to locale c. Then, u_a checks whether to generate a location proof for u_b (line 9–16). u_a first tests the condition $c \in l_a \cup l_b$ is satisfied. If not, no location proof will be generated. Otherwise, u_a further tests whether the condition $l_a \cap l_b \neq \emptyset$ is satisfied. If not, he will stop generating location proof. Otherwise, he will generates a shared key $K_{a,b}$ and issues a location proof based on request for u_b and other users to retrieve (line 18–23). To test the condition $c \in l_a \cup l_b$, we define the radius r_g of a cluster centered at (x_{cm}, y_{cm}) as:

$$r_g = \sqrt{\frac{1}{n} \sum_{i=1}^{n} ((x_i - x_{cm})^2 + (y_i - y_{cm})^2)}. \tag{2}$$

Then, we check whether $r_g^{l_a}$ is less than the Euclidean distance between c and $(x_{cm}^{l_a}, y_{cm}^{l_a})$. Using formula (2), we can also test the condition $l_a \cap l_b \neq \emptyset$ by checking whether the distance between two cluster centers is no greater than the sum of $r_g^{l_a}$ and $r_g^{l_b}$. After u_a publishes the location proof, u_b will retrieve and stores it as one entry of his location proof (line 25). After certain time, u_b collects all location proofs from other users, then he encrypts the whole location proofs with his private key and uploads to the server (line 26–29).

3.3   Location Proof Verification

Here we provide the detailed process of verification. Suppose user u_a uploads a location proof for proving his past presence in location l_a. Upon receiving u_a's location proof, the server first decrypts the information by u_a's public key to check whether the requestor is u_a. Then it decrypts each proof entry in the location proof and check whether the receipt is u_a. After this step, the server gets a set of shared keys $K = \{k_1, k_2, \ldots, k_m\}$ which are generated by u_a and m different users $U = \{u_1, u_2, \ldots, u_m\}$ in l_a. If a user A wants to verify a PSL, he will send to the server a request containing the keys exchanged with appropriate witnesses. The server will check these keys to see whether they are in the witnesses' profile and decide whether the user's claim is true or not. If the key exchange only happens in l_a, the server can verify A's location proof using only one key. However, key exchange may happen outside of l_a, as was expounded in the previous section. So there is a probability for the server to make a wrong decision based on one key (Fig. 1a). We address this problem by increasing the number of keys, the probability of making decision becomes larger, as is shown in (Fig. 1b).

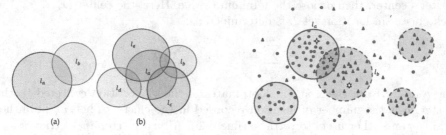

Fig. 1. Multiple Keys for PSL Verification **Fig. 2.** Effective Zones for Location Proof

Then, the server randomly selects τ keys from K to verify. Since each shared key k_i has a co-owner, the server will query the location proof uploaded by the co-owner to check whether he also has key k_i. If all τ keys pass the check, the server will accept u_a's location proof for l_a. To accurately estimate the result of location proof verification, the server needs to learn the value of τ for each user. For a preset accuracy threshold T of the server, the value of τ indicates the minimum number of shared keys that are randomly selected from key set K to ensure that the server has at least T accuracy to correctly verify u_a's location proof for l_a. Formally, suppose each shared key k_i has probability P_i to prove u_a's presence in l_a, then, τ is the minimum value of k which satisfies the following formula:

$$P[1 - \prod_{i=1}^{k}(1 - P_i) \geq T] \xrightarrow{w.h.p} 1, \qquad (3)$$

where $1 \leq k \leq m$.

In order to calculate τ, we need to decide the value of P_i. Formally, P_i is equal to the probability that u_a and u_i collocated at least once in l_a, given that u_a and u_i successfully encounter n times in a given period. If we use p_i to express the probability that a single encounter happens within l_a, then P_i can be formalized as:

$$P_i = 1 - (1 - p_i)^n = 1 - (1 - p_{a,b})^n = 1 - (1 - \frac{|\{s|s \in l_a\}|}{|\{s|s \in l_a \cup l_b\}|})^n \qquad (4)$$

n is observed encounters between two users. Using formulas (3)–(4) and sample location proofs from each user, we can train the value of τ.

4   Implementation

We have implemented a prototype of the MPSL system, including the client application and server module, as show in Figure 3. We implement our client side system with the Sun Java Wireless Toolkit on Nokia N82 smartphones, using JSR-82 and JSR-179. The size of the MIDlet application JAR file is about

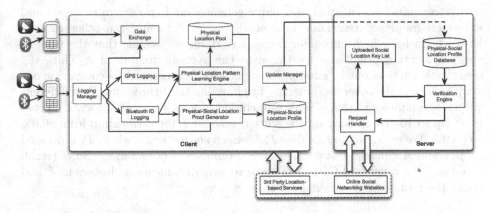

Fig. 3. Mobile-Physical-Social Location System Architecture

127KB. For the server side, we implement our verification scheme in Java. The prototype server uses Java Servlet and JSP. The location profile can be uploaded through web page and the main function of the server is to do the verification based on different trust threshold. Our system explores the Bluetooth SDP structure to publish location proofs by using the techniques introduced in [17] to publish parameters and exchange keys.

5   Evaluation

In this section, we will present our experiments details and the evaluation results.

5.1   Methodology and Experiments Setup

We evaluate our system's accuracy and efficiency. Accuracy indicates how accurate our server can prove that a person really showed up in a given place by randomly verifying τ shared keys from a user-uploaded location proof. We focus on the *true positive rate* and *false positive rate* of our location proof verification scheme with different values of τ. Recall that in real cases, a location proof can be approved if

$$1 - \prod_{i=1}^{m}(1 - P_i) \geq T. \tag{5}$$

is satisfied. While our verification scheme predicts a user's location proof can be approved if randomly selected τ keys pass its verification. Given a test location proof set, we define *true positive* to be a location proof that satisfies formula(5) and passes server verification. Thus, the *true positive rate* is the ratio of the number of true positives to the number of location proofs satisfying formula (5).

Efficiency indicates how soon our client needs to collect enough location proofs to accurately verify user-claimed location information. We compare the average number of τ that satisfies formula (3) in our location proof generation scheme with those numbers in other two naïve schemes:random-encounter based and encounter-frequency based,one randomly chooses keys and the other chooses keys whichi have high encounter frequency. Here, we assume that the time to verify a location proof is proportional to the average number of τ. Thus, the overall efficiency of our location proof generation is measured by comparing our τ with those of the other two schemes' by changing trust thresholds T to different values.The number of shared keys m included in a user-uploaded location proof is set up to 10. We also set up the trust threshold T for verification from 80.0% to 99.9%. We also need to calculate P_i for each shared key i, where P_i is decided by $p_{a,b}$ and n. Since $p_{a,b}$ is decided by the number of points in l_a and l_b (recall formula(5)), we use real GPS data trace to generate location clusters in L and count the number of points in each cluster.

Table 1. GPS Localization Time

Location	Min(s)	Max(s)	Average(s)
1	10.35	39.73	20.96
2	12.37	39.45	22.11
3	14.21	34.39	22.19
4	8.75	22.87	14.46
5	9.76	25.93	20.61
6	8.65	30.62	19.45
7	10.91	31.27	20.90
8	16.99	76.97	42.46
9	16.75	31.80	24.11
10	13.08	34.76	21.96
Overall	8.65	76.97	22.92

Table 2. Bluetooth Communication Time

# of phones	Min(s)	Max(s)	Average(s)
2	13.506	18.350	15.487
3	13.794	18.944	15.655
4	14.444	27.957	20.305
5	15.059	42.720	26.724
6	16.122	58.113	28.033
Overall	13.506	18.350	21.180

In our experiment, we use 10 mobile phones (1 iPhone 3G, 2 iPhone 4Gs, 2 Android G1s, 2 Nokia 6650s, and 3 Nokia N82s) to collect the GPS data trace from 10 people over 2 weeks. The interval between two consecutive GPS data collection is 5 minutes. The collected trace data is about 30.5M. We record the number of successful encounters over a given time period. We did 10 sets of experiment to measure the GPS localization time t_g (Table 1) and Bluetooth communication time t_b (Table 2) of our system. On average, t_g is 22.92 seconds, and t_b is 21.18 seconds. Thus, the average total time is 44.1 seconds. GPS localization time mainly depends on GPS sensor searching satellite time. It takes a long time if user locates in indoors environment, but A-GPS [18], using cellular network information can reduce the time. According to the research in [1], there are more 60% encounters greater than 1 minutes, which implies that the successful ratio of our system will be above 60%.

5.2   Accuracy

To test the overall accuracy of our location proof verification, we randomly select 1000 to 5000 location proofs with each containing 10 shared keys. We calculate $1 - \prod_{i=1}^{m}(1 - P_i)$ for each location proof to test whether it satisfies formula(6) or not. For those satisfying formula(6), we treat them as the actual "Yes" case, and

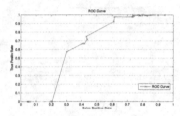
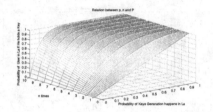

Fig. 4. ROC Curve   **Fig. 5.** Analysis of MPSL's efficiency

the rest of location proofs are treated as the actual "No" case.Next, we vary τ from 1 to 10. For a given τ, we randomly select τ keys in a given location proof to check whether it can pass server's verification. For those passing the verification, we treat them as the predicted "Yes" case, and the rest of location proofs are treated as the predicted "No" case.With the test results, we can calculate the true positive rate and false positive rate as defined previously. Based on those rates for each τ, we obtain a Receiver Operating Characteristic (ROC) curve as Figure 4.

We observe that false positive rate increases as τ becomes larger. Intuitively, this result implies that we should get a relatively small τ rather than a larger one. After repeating the experiment 10 times on another 9 sets of location proofs (1000 in each), we find that the curve shape doesn't change too much. This fact implies that given a trust threshold T for the server, our verification method can independently decide the best value of τ without concerning the probability variation in different location proofs.

5.3 Efficiency

To test the efficiency of our location proof generation method, we generate 100 sets of location proofs. In each location proof, each shared key is generated by constraining $p_{a,b} > 50\%$ and $n = 10$ in formula (4).To compare the performance, we design two other methods for generating location proof. The first method is random-encounter based. With this method, a shared key is randomly generated at a certain time when two users encounter. In our experiments, we also generate 100 sets of such location proofs. In each location proof, there is no constraints on how each shared key is generated. The second method is encounter frequency based. With this method, a shared key is generated only after two users encounter enough times. In our experiments, we generate 100 sets of such location proofs. In each location proof, each shared key is generated by constraining $n = 10$, while no constraints is put on $p_{a,b}$.By changing the value of accuracy threshold T from 80.0% to 99.9%, we obtain the performance comparison of three location proof generation methods as shown in Figure 6. From this figure, we observe that when T becomes high enough (such as 85%), the value of τ in our method is the smallest among three. In other words, our method outperforms the other two methods with less computational costs.

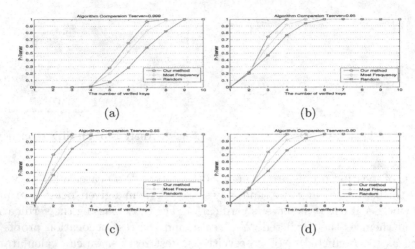

Fig. 6. (a) Efficiency comparison when Tserver=99.9%. (b) Efficiency comparison when Tserver=95.0%.(c) Efficiency comparison when Tserver=85.0%. (d) Efficiency comparison when Tserver=80.0%.

To examine the reason behind the fact we notice on the figure, we draw the curve for function $P = f(p) = 1 - (1 - p)^n$, which is the prototype of P_i's definition. From Figure 5, we can see $f(p)$ becomes larger as p becomes larger and n becomes larger. On average, the random-encounter based method has smaller p and n than our method. While the encounter-frequency based method has the same n as ours, but its p is smaller than ours. Overall, our method would have a relative high P_is among three methods.

6   Conclusion

In this paper, we introduced a new concept of Physical-Social Location (PSL). PSLs are long-term and frequently visited spots, which are normally related to one's identity. We also presented a mobile phone-based PSL verification protocol together with a sytem, called MPSL. In MPSL, a location proof uses appropriate people as "witnesses" to provide reliable evidence for an individual's physical presence. With enough number of such proofs, the PSL can be verified with accuracy. We have implemented the system and evaluated its performance on smartphones. Our experiments results show that MPSL is an accurate and efficient system to provide PSL verification.

Acknowledgement. This work is supported by National Key Basic Research program of China under Grants No. 2010CB328104, National Natural Science Foundation of China under Grants No. 61070161, No. 61070158, No. 61003257, No. 60903161 and No. 60903162, China National Key Technology R&D Program under Grants No. 2010BAI88B03, China Specialized Research Fund for the Doctoral Program of Higher Education under Grants No. 200802860031 and No. 20110092130002, Jiangsu Provincial Natural Science Foundation of China under Grants No. BK2008030, Jiangsu Provincial Key Laboratory of Network and Information Security under Grants No. BM2003201, and Key Laboratory of Computer Network and Information Integration of Ministry of Education of China under Grants No. 93K-9.

References

1. Wang, W., Srinivasan, V., Motani, M.: Adaptive Contact Probing Mechanisms for Delay Tolerant Applications. In: Proc. of ACM MobiCom (2007)
2. Manweiler, J., Scudellari, R., Cox, L.P.: SMILE: Encounter-Based Trust for Mobile Social Services. In: Proc. of ACM CCS (2009)
3. Saroiu, S., Wolman, A.: Enabling New Mobile Applications with Location Proofs. In: Proc. of ACM HotMobile (2009)
4. Karagiannis, T., Boudec, J.L., Vojnovic, M.: Power Law and Exponential Decay of Inter Contact Times between Mobile Devices. In: Proc. of ACM MobiCom (2007)
5. Luo, W., Hengartner, U.: Proving Your Location Without Giving up Your Privacy. In: Proc. of ACM HotMobile (2010)
6. Eagle, N., Pentland, A., Lazer, D.: Inferring friendship network structur by using mobile phone data. In: Proc. of PNAS (2009)
7. Ester, M., Krieger, H., Sander, J., Xu, X.: A Density-Based Algorithm for Discovering Clusters in Large Spatial Databases with Noise. In: Proc. ACM KDD (1996)
8. Lenders, V., Koukoumidis, E., Zhang, P., Martonosi, M.: Location-based Trust for Mobile User-generated Content: Applications, Challenges and Implementations. In: HotMobile (2008)
9. Gilbert, P., Cox, L.P., Jung, J., Wetherall, D.: Toward Trustworthy Mobile Sensing. In: HotMobile (2010)
10. Google Latitude, http://www.google.com/latitude/intro.html
11. Yelp, http://yelp.com/
12. Foursquare Report Attack, http://blog.foursquare.com/post/503822143/on-foursquare-cheating-and-claiming-mayorships-from
13. EveryTrail, http://www.everytrail.com/
14. FakeLocation, http://itunes.apple.com/us/app/fake-location
15. Foursquare, http://foursquare.com/
16. GeoLife, http://research.microsoft.com/en-us/downloads/b16d359d-d164-469e-9fd4-daa38f2b2e13/
17. Yang, Z., Zhang, B., Dai, J., Champion, A., Xuan, D., Li, D.: E-SmallTalker: A Distributed Mobile System for Social Networking in Physical Proximity. In: Proc. of ICDCS (2010)
18. A-GPS, http://en.wikipedia.org/wiki/Assisted_GPS
19. Zhu, Z., Cao, G.: APPLAUS: A Privacy-Preserving Location Proof Updating System for Location-based Services. In: Proc. of IEEE INFOCOM (2011)
20. Capkun, S., Cagalj, M., Karame, G.O., Tippenhauer, N.O.: Integrity Regions: Authentication through Presence in Wireless Networks. IEEE Transactions on Mobile Computing (2010)

Location Proof via Passive RFID Tags*

Harry Gao, Robert Michael Lewis, and Qun Li

The College of William and Mary

Abstract. With the surge in location-aware applications and prevalence of RFID tags comes a demand for providing location proof service with minimal cost. We introduce two protocols that provide secure and accurate location proof service using passive RFID tags. Both protocols are lightweight, adaptive and cost-effective. The first protocol assumes the connection of a user to the remote server. The second protocol does not require real time interactions with the server. Instead, it uses the self-reported time of local RFID reader (such as a cell phone), which may be biased. The user can upload the information to the server later to obtain the location proof. The paper presents a solution to derive users' actual time of presence in the absence of a reliable clock, assuming an arbitrarily large number of falsified data points from malicious users.

1   Introduction

Location proof service, which seeks to provide a means for clients to show that they are present at a particular place at a particular time, has been generated lots of interest from both companies and academia [9]. Social applications such as Foursquare, Yelp, Gowalla and Google Latitude are just some of the recent burst of location-aware services.

These applications seek to take advantage of users' location information to provide unique and personalized resources and services. Other classic examples of location proof service include location-based access control, bad player identification, creating alibi etc. It is standard to assume some preexisting certification authority (CA) [18], which would be referred to as the "server" in this paper.

In this paper we present a location proof protocol that is designed to be adaptable to different situations with respect to real-life needs. Benefits of the protocol we discuss include the possibility of replacing some of the more complicated and expensive systems in place today, providing location-based security measures, and deploying location proof services to applications previously economically prohibitive.

Passive RFID tags are distributed to where we wish to provide location proof service, so that the users can automatically scan these tags when they are present. Successful access to the tags indicates that the user is at the location. The key challenge is that accurate timekeeping is a necessity for location proof

---

* This project was supported in part by grants CNS-1117412, CAREER Award CNS-0747108, and CSUMS grant DMS 0703532.

X. Wang et al. (Eds.): WASA 2012, LNCS 7405, pp. 500–511, 2012.

service; however, a smart tag, unlike a more advanced computing devices, does not have the energy required to keep its own reliable clock. If we overcome this obstacle by assuming the proximity of a server or other powerful computational devices, such systems would not be qualitatively simpler or cheaper than existing technologies.

We present two protocols that utilize passive RFID tags to provide location proof service. The first one requires real-time server interaction, which can provide precise time of presence, and only require one remote central server. The second protocol does not require real-time server interaction, but would lose some precision due to the lack of a reliable clock. The latter is academically and practically interesting because real-time server interaction may be impossible for certain applications. For instance, if we wish to provide location proof service to subway systems in metropolitan areas, it is often the case that cell phones have little or no signal when underground. While cell phones can communicate with local RFID tags, interacting with servers become impossible in this situation. The offline server protocol broadens the field of potential applications while reduces the cost.

Both protocols require little or no user interaction, and can be fully automated. The design is a good fit for most situations location proof service may be required, such as established public locations, including shopping centers, public transportation, parking garages, offices, restaurants, hospitals etc. Our design can provide the service at a much lower cost than contemporary measures, and can help extend location proof service into sectors previously prohibited due to economic and technical concerns.

The paper first introduces two straightforward protocols for providing location proof service with and without the need for real-time communication with the server. Then we introduce an algorithm to support the offline protocol and to increase the quality of service. Due to the page limit, we have omitted the more advanced algorithms and evaluation.

2   Related Work

Considerable work has been done in the field of location proof service, primarily based on the use of sensors, computers, or other similar advanced hardware [9,11,12]. While these approaches provide a cheaper and easier means of location proof than conventional camera-based methods, the cost of deployment and maintenance is still substantial. The design we present uses RFID technology, which is significantly cheaper than other electronic devices, to achieve the same end. Unlike GPS-based or mote-based solutions, there is not a need to replace batteries, and the costs of initial deployment and hardware are significantly lower.

As noted previously, the low computational and storage capacities of RFID tags compared with sensors and computers pose a challenge. Previous work such as [3,4,8] provide important insight into designing systems and protocols that increase the reliability of the location proof service and reduce a malicious party's means to obtain location proof falsely. However, previous work tends to bypass the issue of the absence of a reliable clock by assuming the sole malicious user could not collude with others in a multi-pronged attack, or by real-time interaction with more sophisticated hardware. Without an intelligent design that derives the actual time from local information, the protocols must rely on external trusted sources such as an online server to provide the certified time. Other related work includes [14,10,13,15,7,16,5,17,1,6].

3   Problem Formulation

The overall goal is to provide location proof service using passive RFID tags. We assume the passive RFID tags can only perform simple hash functions and arithmetic calculations, and is unable to perform public encryption/decryption. We make the following assumptions about the situation in which we wish to deploy a location proof service:

1. The service is used frequently and by many users.
2. In the absence of truly malicious users, minor inexactness in the time of visit is acceptable.
3. There exists the possibility of truly malicious users who attempt to fool or disrupt the system. Assumptions concerning malicious users are discussed in Section 3.1.

3.1   Adversary Model

For the online protocol, we have an accurate clock and the malicious parties are unable to manipulate the clock to their advantage.

For the offline protocol, in the absence of malicious users, we can still determine times of presence correctly within the fluctuation range of users' clocks. At the same time, we must also be able to deal with the wickedness of malicious parties.

We assume that a malicious party has two primary goals: falsely obtaining location proof, and/or disrupting the service by making the solution wrongly record the time of presence for other users. To achieve the first goal, the malicious party may either falsely report the time at which he is present at the particular location, or report a time t at which he is not present. For example, if the malefactor Mallory attempts to demonstrate falsely that he is present at the opening ceremony of the Olympics, he can try to either show up in the Olympic stadium before or after the ceremony and obtain a location proof with a false timestamp, or simply not show up at the Olympic stadium while attempting to appear to have been present.

The malicious party is expected to have the following capabilities:

1. They can insert an arbitrarily large number of timestamps in order to contaminate the data stream, either to invalidate legitimate users' claims or corroborate malicious users' claims.

2. They can perfectly coordinate all malicious users' actions towards a common goal.
3. They can eavesdrop on legitimate users' communications.

Of the three, the first is by far most disruptive. It means that it is within the malicious party's power to submit as many timestamps as is physically feasible. Consequently, in dealing with a malicious party we must assume that in given pool of timestamps, a majority of them could be potentially malicious. While it is reasonable to argue that in certain situations the malicious party would not have enough access to dominate the data set, making an assumption on the upper bound of malicious data is difficult and unreasonable for other situations.

We have also identified two foremost weaknesses in the adversary:

1. Because of the computational intensity required to crack even short secret values via brute force and the secret values built into the RFID tags are known to the central server only, it is reasonable to assume that the malicious party cannot compromise these values. Thus, we will assume the security of timestamps reported by RFID tags to the server (as well as the security of the server itself).
2. In light of the preceding observation, the delivery of the falsified data requires the physical presence of malefactors in the proximity of an RFID tag. Marshalling a large number of malicious users in one physical location to deliver systematically falsified data would require a significant level of conspiracy and organization. For this reason it is reasonable to assume that the majority of users who report data are honest, and that there is some *a priori* upper bound on the number of malicious users present in a given span of time.

In the offline protocol, the countermeasures against a malicious party is based on a consensus of unique users, not of timestamps. This approach is based on the observation that there is no reasonable bound on the number of false time stamps, while there is a reasonable (or, at least, parameterizable) bound on the number of malicious users.

4   The Protocol

There are two protocols proposed for two different situations. The first one ultilizes a server (one can communicate with it using cellular communication, for instance), while the other requires no real time interaction from any devices other than the passive RFID tags. The latter might be necessary for specific applications where cellular signal is unaccessible or undesirable.

4.1   Symbols and Notations

Both the online and offline protocols will use the following symbols.

Reader	R
Server	S
time, adjusted time	$t, \hat{t}$
random number challenge	r
Tag's unique name	T_{id}
Secret values known to T_{id} and S	S_{id}
X encrypted by *name*'s private key	$\{X\}_{name}$

4.2   Online Protocol

The section describes a protocol that assumes the availability of a remote server to provide real time information that aid the local tags in providing the location proof service. The following protocol is designed to serve location proof, with one remote online server.

R to S	: Location Proof Service Request
S	: creates a new session for R; generates r; records r,t
S to R	: r, t
R to T_{id}	: r
T_{id}	: computes h(r, S_{id})
T_{id} to R	: h(r, S_{id}), T_{id}
R to S	: h(r, S_{id}), T_{id}, $\{T_{id}\}_R$
S	: verifies h(r,S_{id}); create the location proof: $\{T_{id}, \{T_{id}\}_R, t\}_{Server}$; end session
S to R	: $\{T_{id}, \{T_{id}\}_R, t\}_{Server}$

Pre-distribution
  Arbitrarily many RFID tags can be distributed for the purpose of providing location proof. Each should have a unique ID and secret value, and all such ID-value pairs should be known to the server and no one else.

Communication from Reader to Server
  A hello message indicating the reader's desire to obtain a location proof. The server will create a new session for this particular user, create a random challenge r, and records the time t at which the request was received.

Communication from Server to Reader
  Server sends the time of presence t and the random challenge r to the reader. The notification of time t is entirely for the reader's convenience and has no impact on the integrity of the protocol.

Communication from Reader to Tag
  The reader can then forward the challenge r to the tag. The tag uses the value r in computing a value v = $h(r, S_{id})$, where h is a one way hash function. The server can later compute the value in the same way to verify that the reader is present at the tag's location.

Communication from Tag and Reader

The tag sends the computed hash value to the reader. The tag also sends its own identification.

Communication from Reader to Server

The reader forwards both pieces of information ($v = h(r, S_{id})$ and T_{id}) to the server. The reader also signs and sends T_{id}, which allows the server to verify the user's identification. The reader does not need to send the time t because his session should still be active, so the server is aware of the value of t.

The server verifies the correctness of the hash value by carrying out the same calculation $v = h(r, S_{id})$, and if the result matches the value uploaded, the server can provide location proof to the reader.

Communication from Server to Reader

The server calculates the location proof $\{\{T_{id}\}_R, t\}_{Server}$, which encompasses four essential elements: the location, the person, the time of presence, the authenticator, in that order. The server can then terminate the session.

Note that all sessions should have a timeout threshold, and the location proof request is automatically denied if the protocol is not executed in full within the allocated time. This timeout threshold should not be too large, because an honest user with a reasonable connection would not require much time at all to complete the entire protocol. The protocol only proves that the user is present at the location some time while the location proof session is live, thus a large timeout threshold lowers the resolution of the protocol. For example, a user could take advantage of a large time out threshold by initializing the protocol prior to arrival at the desired location, then carry out the rest of the protocol later when he is actually present at the location to obtain a location proof with misleading time of presence.

4.3   Offline Protocol

The section describes a protocol that does not rely on real-time server interaction with the user. The server can be contacted at some time after users' provide timestamps to the RFID tag to provide the users to with their location proof.

The protocol contains two major components. The first component is exclusively between the reader and the tags, carried out locally in real time. The second component can be carried out at a later time, and is exclusively between the reader and the server. In the first part the reader sends the time to the tag and the tag stamps the time submitted, and provides the reader with all the information it needs upload to the server later. In the second part, the reader uploads all relevant information to the server for verification, and the server processes the information by comparing it with all the other location proof service requests. The server will consolidate the information from all the users to determine the accuracy of the readers' claims, finally infer the actual time of presence from the data available. The location proof is then sent back to the reader.

The steps of the protocol are as follows:

Pre-distribution
  Arbitrarily many RFID tags can be distributed for the purpose of providing
  location proof. Each should have a unique ID and secret value, and all such
  ID-value pairs should be known to the server and no one else.

Communication from Reader to Tag
  Because the tag has no other way of obtaining the time, the hello message
  from R to T_{id} should contain the current time t. The tag computes the
  encrypted value v using the time t, counter n (i.e., the sequence number of
  the timestamp), and secret value S_{id}:

$$v = h(t, n, S_{id}). \tag{1}$$

  The tag then increments its internal counter.

Communication from Tag to Reader
  The tag then sends v, n, and its ID back to the reader.

  The reader-tag interaction is summarized below:

R to T_{id}	: t
T_{id} computes :	v=h(t,n,S_{id}), n++
T_{id} to R	: v,n,T_{id}

The user can hold on to the information provided by the tag (v, n, T_{id}) without
any time-sensitive need to upload any information to the server. However, when
the user is ready to obtain the location proof, he can carry out the following:

1. initiate a challenge-response nonce N to verify his ID.
2. Upload N, v, n, T_{id}, t, and the public key to the server.

Upon receiving the location proof service request and all the aforementioned material, the server verifies the following information before providing the location
proof to the user:

1. *Verify that no user is using multiple pairs of keys.* A user database is queried
   to make sure the user is not using multiple public-private key pairs. Multiple
   submissions from the same user should be grouped together as such when
   calculating $\hat{t}$.
2. *Verify the tag's identication.* Carry out the same operation as the tag did in
   Eq. (1), and verify that the result matches the value v provided.
3. *Determine the time.* After checking the validity of the data point, the server
   should add it to the time-verification algorithm (described in detail in the
   following section) to calculate $\hat{t}$, the adjusted time.

Once the server obtains all three pieces of information, it can provide the location
proof by

$$\texttt{location proof} = \{\{(T_{id}), \hat{t}\}_R\}_S \qquad (2)$$

which summarily embeds the who, where and when.

Lastly, the server sends to the user the above location proof, $\hat{t}$ and the T_{id}, where the latter two serve as an readable description of the content of the location proof.

R and S	: exchange a challenge-response
	: nonce N to verify R's ID
R to S	: v, n, T_{id}, PK_R, t
S verifies	: $v == h(t, n, S_{id})$
S calculates	: $\hat{t}$
S to R	: $\{(T_{id}), \hat{t}\}_R\}_S$

4.4 Discussion

The protocols defend against many malicious attacks, and ensures that no personal or crucial information is passed back and forth when the reader communicates with the tags; therefore, an eavesdropper cannot hope to capture the radio signal and harvest users' private information. There is also little set-up, and clients can be added and removed from the system seamlessly. A malicious party cannot hope to obtain a location proof without being physically present at the location.

The online protocol needs to address denial of service attacks where a malicious user repeatedly request for a new session to be opened, hence exhausting system resources and hinder the server's capacity to aid good users. The effectiveness of this attack is limited by the timeout threshold of the session.

The offline protocol has one key difference from the online protocol: the tags receive the unreliable time of presence t from the reader, which cannot be fully trusted. Therefore the offline protocol relies heavily on the time-verification scheme from central processing and consolidation of data points.

A malicious user can report falsely the time of presence, hoping to obtain a location proof with a timestamp different from when he is actually there. He may also report a large number of data points to support his false claims and distort others time of presence. This translates to server's responsibility to sort out a large number of data points. In other words, malicious users can deliberately submit a false time t to achieve their goals outlined in the adversary model section, but behave otherwise the same as a good user to avoid detection. If a user is allowed to use multiple pairs of keys without the server's knowledge, a malicious user could create an unbounded number of phantom users and skew the $\hat{t}$ calculation, which is based on the consensus of users.

The goal of checking the uniqueness of the users is to recognize all data from one user belongs to exactly one user, but it would not allow the server to pinpoint the identity. In other words, the server is interested only in finding out how many users it is servicing, not who. This protects the users' privacy while allowing the server to correctly root out malicious inputs.

To protect users' privacy, we can segregate the tag-dispensing service from the server consolidate service. This way, the server may be aware, for example, that a particular, anonymous user travelled from point A to point B before turning to point A, it has no way of knowing exactly where points A and B are. Furthermore, all data are collected anonymously, because the server only verifies the users' uniqueness by checking the validity of the signature against a database, but the server is unable to obtain the identities or any sensitive personal information of the users. The privacy of the users is at risk only if the multiple service providers (database, consolidation service and tag-dispensing service) collude together.

5   Dealing with False Timestamps

We next turn to the problem of dealing with false timestamps, particularly those introduced into the data stream by a malicious party. Because the protocol does not make any assumptions on the delay between time of presence and the submission time, attacks such as delayed attack would have no effect on the protocol's accuracy. In general, we wish to derive from our collected data a monotonically non-decreasing series of adjusted timestamps $\hat{t}_1 \leq \hat{t}_2 \leq \cdots \leq \hat{t}_n$ that best describes the behavior of the data. From the index numbers the local tags embed in each data point we know the chronological order the data points should be in. However, there is no guarantee that the time reported at those data points are correct, or even if they are monotonically non-decreasing. If there are timestamps that are out-of-order, the central server must resolve the conflict. This means we must derive a series of adjusted timestamps, subject to the monotonicity constraint, that best resemble the data points reported in individual location proof service requests. In the following, we present our solution to this problem.

Our first step is to consider the problem of finding a monotonically non-decreasing series that minimizes an ℓ^p-norm mismatch with the observed timestamps. This solution treats all timestamps equally and attempts to find a monotonic time series that best resembles the given timestamps. This monotonicity constraint makes this approach an instance of *isotonic regression*.

The three measures of mismatch that we consider are the ℓ^1, ℓ^2, and ℓ^∞ norms, since these leads to easily solved optimization problems. The ℓ^1 fit is the least sensitive to outliers, while the ℓ^∞ fit is the most sensitive, and ℓ^2 is in-between. Thus, sporadic malicious timestamps with incorrect values affect the solution of the ℓ^1 and ℓ^2 fits less than the ℓ^∞ fit.

The ℓ^1 fit is the problem of finding a solution $t = (\hat{t}_1, \ldots, \hat{t}_n)$ of the following convex program:

$$\begin{aligned} \underset{t}{\text{minimize}} \quad & \sum_{i=1}^{n} |\hat{t}_i - t_i| \\ \text{subject to } & \hat{t}_1 \leq \hat{t}_2 \leq \cdots \leq \hat{t}_n. \end{aligned} \tag{3}$$

This problem can be transformed into the following linear program:

$$
\begin{aligned}
\underset{s,t}{\text{minimize}} \quad & \sum_{i=1}^{n} s_i \\
\text{subject to } & t_1 \leq t_2 \leq \cdots \leq t_n, \\
& -s_i \leq t_i - d_i \leq s_i, \, i = 1, \ldots, n.
\end{aligned}
\tag{4}
$$

The advantage of the linear programming formulation (4) is that linear programs can be solved very efficiently. A drawback of (4) is that there may be nonunique solutions.

The ℓ^2 fit seeks a solution of the following convex quadratic program:

$$
\begin{aligned}
\underset{t}{\text{minimize}} \quad & \sum_{i=1}^{n} | \hat{t}_i - t_i |^2 \\
\text{subject to } & \hat{t}_1 \leq \hat{t}_2 \leq \cdots \leq \hat{t}_n.
\end{aligned}
\tag{5}
$$

While this problem can be solved by standard quadratic techniques, there also exist specialized $O(n)$ algorithms for its solution (see [2] for an overview). Solutions of this problem are unique.

Finally, ℓ^∞ fit entails the solution of

$$
\begin{aligned}
\underset{t}{\text{minimize}} \quad & \max_{i=1,\ldots,n} | \hat{t}_i - t_i | \\
\text{subject to } & \hat{t}_1 \leq \hat{t}_2 \leq \cdots \leq \hat{t}_n.
\end{aligned}
\tag{6}
$$

Like the ℓ^1 fit, this problem can be transformed into a linear program:

$$
\begin{aligned}
\underset{s,t}{\text{minimize}} \quad & s \\
\text{subject to } & t_1 \leq t_2 \leq \cdots \leq t_n, \\
& -s \leq t_i - d_i \leq s, \, i = 1, \ldots, n.
\end{aligned}
\tag{7}
$$

As with the ℓ^1 fit, that there may be nonunique solutions to (7).

Unfortunately, straightforward isotonic regression is easily thwarted by a malicious party. We do not assume a bound on how many bad timestamps the malicious party can inject into the data pool, and there is no restriction on how far from the actual time the malicious data can be. As a consequence, it is not hard to see that the malicious party can take advantage of the situation by flooding the data stream with false timestamps with systematic errors (i.e., the false timestamps are all in the future or all in the past relative to the truth). With a large number of false timestamps, the malicious party can manipulate the results of any of the isotonic regression fits just described, and even a small proportion of false timestamps can cause mischief.

This point is illustrated in Fig. 1. The vertical axis denotes normalized time in the range 0 to 1. In these simulations, malicious (but self-consistent) timestamps have been introduced that are out of sync with legitimate timestamps. The results of isotonic regression for the ℓ^1, ℓ^2, and ℓ^∞ norms are indicated by the black line. We have designed more advanced approaches to resolve the problem, but they are omitted in this paper due to the page limit.

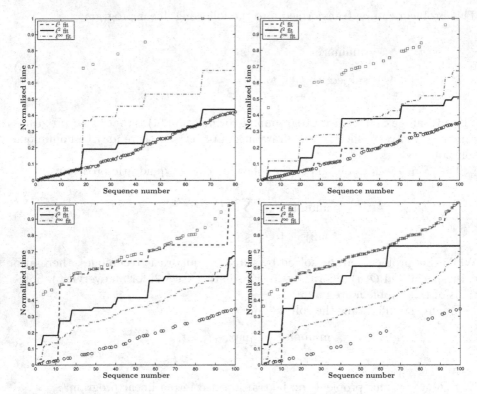

Fig. 1. The red squares are false timestamps, the blue circles are true timestamps, and the lines indicate the result of isotonic regression in the ℓ^1, ℓ^2, and ℓ^∞ norms. The four figures are for the following four cases separately: up-left (75 true, 5 false), up-right (75 true, 25 false), bottom-left (50 true, 50 false), bottom-right (25 true, 75 false).

6   Conclusions

Through two protocols and an approach to correct for incorrect user inputs, we have shown the feasibility of providing location proof service using RFID tags. While economical, the simplicity of the hardware imposes serious challenges to the central processing unit which is responsible for consolidating and verifying data from local tags.

References

1. Bai, X., Zhang, C., Xuan, D., Teng, J., Jia, W.: Low-connectivity and full-coverage three dimensional wireless sensor networks. In: Mobihoc, pp. 145–154 (2009)
2. Best, M.J., Chakravarti, N.: Active set algorithms for isotonic regression: A unifying framework. Mathematical Programming 47(1–3), 425–439 (1990)
3. Bussard, L., Bagga, W.: Distance-bounding proof of knowledge to avoid real-time attacks. In: SEC, pp. 223–238 (2005)

4. Chiang, J.T., Haas, J.J., Hu, Y.-C.: Secure and precise location verification using distance bounding and simultaneous multilateration. In: Proceedings of the Second ACM Conference on Wireless Network Security, pp. 181–192. ACM, New York (2009)
5. Ding, M., Liu, F., Thaeler, A., Chen, D., Cheng, X.: Fault-tolerant target localization in sensor networks. EURASIP Journal on Wireless Communications and Networking 2007(1), 19–19 (2007)
6. Gu, W., Bai, X., Chellappan, S., Xuan, D.: Network decoupling for secure communications in wireless sensor networks. In: 14th IEEE International Workshop on Quality of Service, IWQoS 2006, pp. 189–198. IEEE (2006)
7. Han, H., Sheng, B., Tan, C.C., Li, Q., Mao, W., Lu, S.: Counting RFID tags efficiently and anonymously. In: IEEE Infocom, San Diego, CA (March 2010)
8. Hancke, G.P., Kuhn, M.G.: An RFID distance bounding protocol. In: SECURECOMM 2005, pp. 67–73. IEEE Computer Society, Washington, DC (2005)
9. Luo, W., Hengartner, U.: Veriplace: a privacy-aware location proof architecture. In: GIS, pp. 23–32 (2010)
10. Ren, S., Li, Q., Wang, H., Chen, X., Zhang, X.: Analyzing Object Detection Quality Under Probabilistic Coverage in Sensor Networks. In: de Meer, H., Bhatti, N. (eds.) IWQoS 2005. LNCS, vol. 3552, pp. 107–122. Springer, Heidelberg (2005)
11. Saroiu, S., Wolman, A.: Enabling new mobile applications with location proofs. In: Proceedings of the 10th workshop on Mobile Computing Systems and Applications, HotMobile 2009, pp. 3:1–3:6. ACM, New York (2009)
12. Stojmenovic, I., Liu, D., Jia, X.: A scalable quorum based location service in ad hoc and sensor networks. Int. J. Commun. Netw. Distrib. Syst. 1, 71–94 (2008)
13. Tan, C.C., Sheng, B., Li, Q.: How to monitor for missing RFID tags. In: IEEE ICDCS, Beijing, China, pp. 295–302 (June 2008)
14. Wang, H., Sheng, B., Tan, C.C., Li, Q.: WM-ECC: an Elliptic Curve Cryptography Suite on Sensor Motes. Technical Report WM-CS-2007-11, College of William and Mary, Computer Science, Williamsburg, VA (2007)
15. Wang, H., Tan, C.C., Li, Q.: Snoogle: A search engine for physical world. In: IEEE Infocom, Phoenix, AZ, pp. 1382–1390 (April 2008)
16. Xie, L., Sheng, B., Tan, C.C., Li, Q., Chen, D.: Efficient tag identification in mobile RFID systems. In: IEEE Infocom, San Diego, CA (March 2010)
17. Xing, K., Ding, M., Cheng, X., Rotenstreich, S.: Safety warning based on highway sensor networks. In: Wireless Communications and Networking Conference, vol. 4, pp. 2355–2361. IEEE (2005)
18. Zhu, Z., Cao, G.: Applaus: A privacy-preserving location proof updating system for location-based services. In: INFOCOM, pp. 1889–1897 (2011)

A New Complementary Code Set with Zero Correlation Window

Lin Feng[1] and Zhenchun Wei[1,2]

[1] School of Computer and Information, HeFei University of Technology,
Hefei, Anhui, 230009, China
{wzc,fenglin}@ialab.hfut.edu.cn
[2] Research Institute of HeFei University of Technology in Changzhou,
Changzhou, Jiangsu, 213164, China

Abstract. A multiple order complementary code set with zero correlation window (ZCW) is presented in this paper. Construction method of the complementary code is inspired by that of Loose Synchronous (LS) code used in LAS-CDMA system. The complementary code is of order 4 and can provide twice number of code as the conventional LS code at the same ZCW. Therefore, the new code set will enlarge the capacity of a synchronous CDMA system. The construction method of the new code set and the proof of its relative properties are also presented in this paper.

Keywords: Zero Correlation Window (ZCW), Multiple Order Complementary Code Set, Loose Synchronous (LS) code.

1   Introduction

It is well known that the capacity of a CDMA system is tightly related to its access code design. If the aperiodic cross-correlation function (CCF) of an access code set is zero for any relative time shift and its aperiodic auto-correlation function (ACF) is zero for any relative time shift except for the origin, such access code set is ideal or perfect for a CDMA system. Consequently this CDMA system can obtain the highest capacity. Therefore, capacity of CDMA system can be mainly determined by the ACF and CCF of the access code [1]. However, Welch [3] found that there is no such ideal access code set. When there is a significant difference from distances between different mobile terminals and the base station, MAI caused by unsatisfactory CCF can bring about near-far effect in the environment of multiple path propagation, which makes the system capacity greatly reduce, and even makes the system not work [2]. What's more, imperfect ACF will result in inter-symbol interference (ISI). Subsequently Golay put forward the concept of "complementary series" [4]. Each Golay code consists of two sequences, and there exist only two Golay codes with ideal ACF and CCF as the result of cancellation between the two sequences. In 1971, Schweitzer put forward "Generalized Complementary Code Set" [9]. Each code in the set consists of $N = 2^m$ sequences ($m = 1$ is just the Golay complementary code) and there

X. Wang et al. (Eds.): WASA 2012, LNCS 7405, pp. 512–519, 2012.

exist such $N = 2^m$ access codes with ideal ACF and CCF. This code set is called complete complementary code of order N. Then D B Li constructed a complementary code set with zero correlation window [5] which called Loose Synchronous (LS) code, i.e. its CCF is zero within a certain relative time shift and its ACF is also zero within this relative time shift except on the origin. This kind of complementary code set can be regarded as a natural extent ion of Golay complementary code, and it increases the number of available complementary codes due to the relaxation of perfect ACF and CCF constraint (Golay complementary code only provide two access code). LS code set is utilized in the LAS-CDMA (Large Area Synchronous CDMA) system.

In this paper, a new complementary code of order 4 with ZCW is constructed and the construction method is inspired by that of LS code [6-8]. The motivation of this paper is to increase the number of complete complementary code of order N. Analysis and simulation results show that the new code set can double the number of complementary code of order 4 under the condition of the same ZCW compared with LS code. Therefore the new code set will increase the system capacity as well as eliminate most of the MAI and ISI within the ZCW.

This paper is organized as follows: Section II outlines the definition of complementary code set and gives two examples. In section III, it is demonstrated how the new code set is constructed. Simulation results are listed in section IV. Section V concludes the paper.

2   Introduction to Complete Complementary Code Set of Order N

K: Code number of a code set

$\{U^1, U^2, \cdots, U^K\}$: A code set consisted of K codes.

N: The number of sequences of each code in $\{U^1, U^2, \cdots, U^K\}$.

M: The length of each sequence of each code of $\{U^1, U^2, \cdots, U^K\}$. In this paper M is a power of 2, that is $M = 2^n$. n is an arbitrary positive integer.

U^i, U^k : The ith code of $\{U^1, U^2, \cdots, U^K\}$ and the jth code of $\{U^1, U^2, \cdots, U^K\}$ respectively.

$\bar{U}^i, \bar{U}^k$: The negative U^i and the negative U^k respectively.

U^i_j: The jth sequence of the ith code of $\{U^1, U^2, \cdots, U^K\}$.

$u^i_{j,m}$: The mth element of sequence U^i_j.

τ: Relative time shift

Then $\{U^1, U^2, \cdots, U^N\}$ can be expressed as

$$\begin{cases} U^1\left(U_1^1, \ U_2^1, \ \cdots\cdots, \ U_N^1\right) \\ U^2\left(U_1^2, \ U_2^2, \ \cdots\cdots, \ U_N^2\right) \\ \quad\quad\vdots \\ U^K\left(U_1^K, \ U_2^K, \ \cdots\cdots, \ U_N^K\right) \end{cases} \tag{1}$$

$$U_j^i = \left[u_{j,1}^i, u_{j,2}^i, \cdots, u_{j,M}^i\right], \quad i=1,2,\cdots,K \ , \ j=1,2,\cdots,N \ , m=1,2,\cdots,M$$

The aperiodic cross-correlation function (CCF) between U^i and U^k is defined as:

$$R_{U^i,U^k}(\tau) = \frac{1}{NM}\sum_{j=1}^{N} R_{U_j^i,U_j^k}(\tau) \tag{2}$$

Where $R_{U_j^i,U_j^k}(\tau)$ is the CCF between U_j^i and U_j^k, which is defined as:

$$R_{U_j^i,U_j^k}(\tau) = \begin{cases} \displaystyle\sum_{m=\tau+1}^{M} u_{j,m}^i u_{j,m-\tau}^{*k} & 0\leq\tau\leq M-1 \\ \displaystyle\sum_{m=1}^{M+\tau} u_{j,m}^i u_{j,m-\tau}^{*k} & -M+1\leq\tau\leq 0 \\ 0 & |\tau|\geq M \end{cases} \tag{3}$$

Where $u_{j,m-\tau}^{*k}$ is the complex conjugate of $u_{j,m-\tau}^{k}$. The aperiodic auto-correlation function (ACF) is substituting U_j^i for U_j^k.

Definition 1: A code set in form of (1) with $K = N$ is called "a complete complementary code set of order N". If ACF of arbitrary code and CCF between arbitrary two codes satisfy the following equations:

$$R_{U^i}(\tau)=0, \quad \forall\tau\neq 0 , \ \forall i=1,2,\cdots,N \tag{4}$$

$$R_{U_j^i,U_j^k}(\tau)=0 , \forall i\neq k\in\{1,2,\cdots,N\} \tag{5}$$

Here, the order N denotes the number of sequences in one code.

Definition 2: If $\exists\tau_w = \arg\min_{|\tau|}\left[R_{U_j^i,U_j^k}(\tau)\neq 0\right]$ and $R_{U_j^i}(\tau)=R_{U_j^k}(\tau)=0$, $\forall\tau\neq 0$, $\tau\leq|\tau_w|$,we define U^i and U^k as a pair of ZCW complementary codes of order N with τ_w .

τ_w is called an one-side ZCW.

3   Construction Method of a ZCW Complementary Code Set of Order 4

L :   The sequence length of initial codes of A^n ,here $L = 4$.

A^n :   A ZCW complementary code set of order 4 with $M = 2^{n-1}L$.

A_i^n :   The ith code of A^n .

$C1^n$:   The LS code set of order 2 with $M = 2^n$,which is $\left\{ C_1^2, C_2^2, C_3^2, C_4^2 \right\}$ when $n = 2$.

$C1_i^n$:   The ith code of $C1^n$.

$C2^n$:   The LS code set of order 2 with $M = 2^n$,which is $\left\{ C_4^2, C_3^2, C_2^2, C_1^2 \right\}$ when $n = 2$.

$C2_i^n$:   The ith code of $C2^n$.

3.1   Construction Method

Each sequence of a ZCW complementary code set of order 4 still has the length of 2^n , but each code contains 4 sequences.

Step1: The initial codes of the ZCW complementary code set of order 4 are $A^1 = \left\{ A_1^1, A_2^1, A_3^1, A_4^1 \right\}$. Each code has four sequences. The first two sequences of A_i^1 are the two sequences of C_i^2 , which denotes the ith code in C^2 .The last two sequences of A_i^1 are the two sequences of C_{5-i}^2 , which denotes the $(5-i)th$ code in C^2 .That is $A_i^1 \left(C_i^2, \ C_{5-i}^2 \right), i = 1,2,3,4$ when $n = 1$.

$$A^1 = \begin{cases} A_1^1 \left(C_1^2, \ C_4^2 \right) \\ A_2^1 \left(C_2^2, \ C_3^2 \right) \\ A_3^1 \left(C_3^2, \ C_2^2 \right) \\ A_4^1 \left(C_4^2, \ C_1^2 \right) \end{cases} \quad \begin{cases} A_1^1 \left(U_1^1 U_1^2, \ U_2^1 U_2^2, \ U_1^2 \bar{U}_1^1, \ U_2^2 \bar{U}_2^1 \right) \\ A_2^1 \left(U_1^1 \bar{U}_1^2, \ U_2^1 \bar{U}_2^2, \ U_1^2 U_1^1, \ U_2^2 U_2^1 \right) \\ A_3^1 \left(U_1^2 U_1^1, \ U_2^2 U_2^1, \ U_1^1 \bar{U}_1^2, \ U_2^1 \bar{U}_2^2 \right) \\ A_4^1 \left(U_1^2 \bar{U}_1^1, \ U_2^2 \bar{U}_2^1, \ U_1^1 U_1^2, \ U_2^1 U_2^2 \right) \end{cases}$$

, that is

Step2:

For arbitrary $n \geq 2$, every four codes of A^n can be generated by the four kinds of concatenation mentioned in definition 4 of every two codes of A^{n-1} . Similar to the step 2 in section 2.2 the concrete rule is

$$A_{4i-3}^n = A_{2i-1}^{n-1} A_{2i}^{n-1}$$

$$A_{4i-2}^n = A_{2i-1}^{n-1} \overline{A}_{2i}^{n-1}$$

$$A_{4i-1}^n = A_{2i}^{n-1} A_{2i-1}^{n-1}$$

$$A_{4i}^n = A_{2i}^{n-1} \overline{A}_{2i-1}^{n-1}, \quad i = 1, 2, \cdots, Q, \quad Q \text{ is quarter the code numbers of } A^n.$$

With the method A_i^α can be expressed as

$$A_i^n \left(C1_i^{n+1}, \quad C2_i^{n+1} \right), i = 1, 2, \cdots, 2^{n+1} \tag{6}$$

What is more, $C1_i^n$ and $C2_i^n$ are LS codes with the same property about ZCW.

3.2   General Properties

Property 3: Suppose that code A and code B are a pair of ideal complementary codes of order 4 with sequence length of M. Then the cascading code AB and $A\overline{B}$ are a pair of ideal complementary codes as well as BA and $B\overline{A}$. The cascading code AB and BA are a pair of ZCW complementary codes of order 4 with $\tau_w = M$ as well as AB and $B\overline{A}$, $A\overline{B}$ and BA, $A\overline{B}$ and $B\overline{A}$.

Proof : Applying (2), the ACF of AB can be calculated.

$$R_{AB}(\tau) = R_A(\tau) + R_{B,A}(\tau - M) + R_B(\tau) + R_A(M + \tau) = 0, \forall \tau \neq 0$$

It is easy to prove that the ACF of $B\overline{A}$, $A\overline{B}$ and BA are the same value.

Applying (4), the CCF between AB and $A\overline{B}$ can be calculated

$$R_{AB,A\overline{B}}(\tau) = R_A(\tau) + R_{B,A}(\tau - M) + R_{B,\overline{B}}(\tau) + R_{A,\overline{B}}(M + \tau)$$

$$= R_A(\tau) - R_B(\tau) = 0$$

Similarly, the CCF between AB and $A\overline{B}$ can be calculated

$$R_{AB,BA}(\tau) = R_{A,B}(\tau) + R_B(\tau - M) + R_{B,A}(\tau) + R_A(M + \tau) = 0, \tau < |M|$$

The CCF between other codes can be calculated in the same way, and it is easy to prove this property.

Property 4: If $\{A, B, C, D\}$ is a complete complementary code set of order 4, arbitrary code in cascading code set $\{AB, A\overline{B}, BA, \overline{B}A\}$ and arbitrary code in cascading code set $\{CD, C\overline{D}, DC, D\overline{C}\}$ are a pair of ideal complementary codes of order 4. The CCF is always zero for any τ relative time shift.

Proof: Just calculate the CCF between AB and CD as an example

$$R_{AB,CD}(\tau) = R_{A,C}(\tau) + R_{B,C}(M - \tau) + R_{B,D}(\tau) + R_{A,C}(M + \tau)$$

Because code set $\{A, B, C, D\}$ is a complete complementary code set of order 4, applying (7) , we can easily get the following result:

$$R_{A,C}(\tau) = R_{B,C}(M - \tau) = R_{B,D}(\tau) = R_{A,C}(M + \tau) = 0$$

That is

$$R_{AB,CD}(\tau) = 0$$

As the proof in Property 3 has proved

$$R_{AB}(\tau) = R_{CD}(\tau) = 0, \forall \tau \neq 0$$

So AB and CD are a pair of complete complementary codes of order 4. The property between other codes can be proved in the same way.

Property 5: $\forall n$, there are $K = 2^{n+1}$ codes in A^n with $M = 2^{n-1}L$. Among these codes , code subset

$$\left\{ A^n_{\gamma i-(\gamma-1)}, A^n_{\gamma i-(\gamma-2)}, \cdots, A^n_{\gamma i}, A^n_{\gamma k-(\gamma-1)}, A^n_{\gamma k-(\gamma-2)}, \cdots, A^n_{\gamma k} \right\} \quad i = 1, 2, \cdots, 2^{n-\log_2 \gamma}$$,

$\gamma = 2, 2^2 \cdots; 2^n$, $k = 2^{n-\log_2 \gamma} + 1, \cdots, 2^{n-\log_2 \gamma+1}$ of 2γ codes is a ZCW complementary code set of order 4 with $\tau_w = 2^{n-\log_2 \gamma}L$.

4   Simulation

Taking $n = 3$ for example, there are totally $K = 2^{n+1} = 16$ codes generated by the method of section 3.1 with each sequence which has the length of 16. A part of simulation results are given as follows:

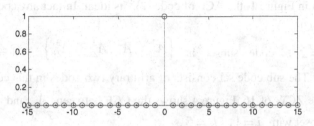

Fig. 1. ACF of code A_1^3

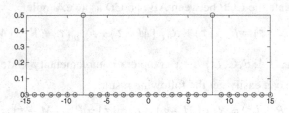

Fig. 2. CCF between code A_1^3 and code A_3^3

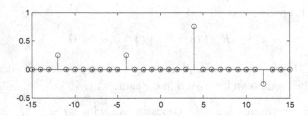

Fig. 3. CCF between code A_1^3 and code A_6^3

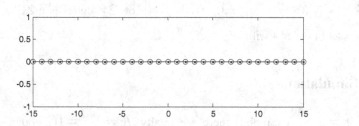

Fig. 4. CCF between code A_1^3 and code A_9^3

As is shown in Figure 1, the ACF of code A_1^3 is ideal. In fact any code in the code set has ideal ACF.

When $\gamma = 2$, code subset is $\left\{ A_{2i-1}^3, A_{2i}^3, A_{2k-1}^3, A_{2k}^3 \right\}$, $i = 1,2,3,4$, $k = 5,6,7,8$. The sub code set consists of arbitrary two codes in this code set which has an one-side ZCW of 16. Figure 4 shows the CCF between A_1^3 and A_9^3, which is in the code subset with $i = 1$, $k = 5$.

5   Conclusion

In this paper, a method of constructing a ZCW complementary code set of order 4 has been proposed. The new constructed code set has more number of codes than the traditional LS code with the same one-side ZCW. At the same time, the use of the new code set can do favor to reduce most of the MAI and ISI, and increase the capacity of the communication system.

Acknowledgments. This paper is funded by the following projects: International science and technology cooperation project of Anhui , China (10080703001), Industry-Academic-Research project of Guangdong, China (2010B090400305, 2010B090400332, 2011B090400457), Research Fund for the Doctoral Program of Higher Education of China (20090111120004, 20100111110004), Jiangsu natural science foundation project (BK2011236), Anhui natural science foundation project (1208085QF113).

References

[1] Li, D.B.: The perspectives of large area synchronous CDMA technology for the fourth-generation mobile radio. IEEE Communication Magazine 43, 114–118 (2003)

[2] Viterbi, A.J.: CDMA: Principles of Spread Spectrum Communications. Addison-Wesley, Reading (1995)

[3] Welch, L.R.: Lower bounds on the maximum cross-correlation of signals. IEEE Trans Inform. Theory 20, 397–399 (1974)

[4] Golay, M.J.E.: Complementary series. IRE Trans. Inform. Theory IT-7, 82–87 (1961)

[5] Fan, P.Z., Suehiro, N., Kuroyanagi, N., Deng, X.M.: A class of binary sequences with zero correlation zone. Electronics Letters 35, 777–779 (1999)

[6] Li, D.B.: A spread spectrum multiple access coding method with zero correlation window. PCT/CN00/00028 (2000)

[7] Yang, X., Mo, Y., Li, D., Bian, M.: New Complete Complementary Codes and Their Analysis. In: Global Telecommunications Conference, November 26-30, pp. 3899–3904 (2007)

[8] Yu, Z., Yang, X., Li, D.: A New Scheme for Constructing High Code Efficiency LS ZCW Multiple Access Codes. In: First International Conference on Communications and Networking in China, ChinaCom 2006, October 25-27, pp. 1–4 (2006)

[9] Schweitzer, B.P.: Generalized Complementary Code sets, Ph.D. Thesis, University of California, Los Angeles (1971)

Real-Time Data Aggregation
for Contention-Based Sensor Networks
in Cyber-Physical Systems

Qin Liu[1], Yanan Chang[1], and Xiaohua Jia[2]

[1] School of Computer, Wuhan University, Hubei 430072, China
{qinliu,ynchang}@whu.edu.cn
[2] Department of Computer Science, City University of Hong Kong,
Tat Chee Avenue, Kowloon, Hong Kong
csjia@cityu.edu.hk

Abstract. Wireless sensor network plays an important role in information collection and data gathering in cyber-physical systems. We study
real-time data aggregation problem for wireless sensor networks that use
CSMA/CA MAC layer protocols. The problem is, for a given sink, a set
of sensor nodes and a delay bound, to maximize the average transmission success probability of all sensor nodes within the delay bound. In
CSMA/CA protocols, the success probability and the expected transmission delay are highly sensitive to node interference, and the node interference is often very high in the large scale cyber-physical systems. We
divide the system time into time-frames with fixed size and schedule the
transmission of nodes into time-frames. The size of time-frame is much
larger than the time-slot in pure TDMA protocols. The transmissions of
all child nodes under the same parent are scheduled in the same time-
frame and they compete the channel access in CSMA/CA fashion. In this
system model, the construction of data aggregation trees becomes very
important in maximizing the success probability of data collection. We
solve the joint routing and scheduling problem by first constructing an
aggregation tree that minimizes the node interference. Then, we propose
an efficient greedy scheduling method to assign time-frames to sensor
nodes. Extensive simulations have been done and the results show that
our proposed method can improve the success probability significantly.

Keywords: Data aggregation tree, real-time, wireless sensor networks,
cyber-physical systems.

1 Introduction

Wireless sensor network is a major component in cyber-physical systems and
it plays an important role in information collection and data gathering in the
systems. Data aggregation is a common method for collecting data in wireless
sensor networks. Many applications of sensor networks require real-time data
collection. That is, a data packet must arrive at the sink node within a specified delay bound. However, almost all the products of sensor nodes available

X. Wang et al. (Eds.): WASA 2012, LNCS 7405, pp. 520–531, 2012.

on the market conform with IEEE 802.15.4 or IEEE 802.11 standard and use CSMA/CA-based protocols. The CSMA/CA protocols are notorious for guaranteeing real-time data transmissions. On one hand, if we want to guarantee the success probability of data transmission, we have to leave sufficient time for each node to sense the channel and retry in CSMA/CA model and the real-time requirement can hardly be met; on the other hand, if we want to guarantee the delay-bound for data collection, nodes may not be able to successfully transmit the data out within a delay-bound due to signal interference or collision.

In this paper, we study the real-time data aggregation problem for wireless sensor networks that use CSMA/CA MAC layer protocols. Our aim is to maximize the average success probability of data transmission of all sensor nodes for a given delay-bound. We divide the system time into fixed size time-frames. We let all child nodes under the same parent compete the channel access in CSMA/CA fashion in the same time-frame and try to schedule the transmissions of parent nodes in different time-frames to avoid collision. This is the combination of CSMA and TDMA models. But, the size of time-frame used in our method is much larger than the time-slot in pure TDMA protocols, which does not need stringent clock synchronization among the sensor nodes.

The success probability of data transmission in CSMA/CA model is highly sensitive to the level of interference [1,2]. In our method, the interference of a node comes from two sources: a) the transmissions of sibling nodes, because all child nodes under the same parent are scheduled in the same time-frame; b) the transmissions of nodes under other parents but are scheduled in the same time-frame. This is because we have limited time-frames within a delay-bound and there are concurrent transmissions scheduled in the same time-frame. Therefore, the overall success probability of data transmission heavily depends on the structure of the data aggregation tree and the transmission schedule in time-frames. In this paper we study the joint optimization issue of data aggregation routing and transmission scheduling. We first propose an algorithm for data aggregation tree construction, which minimizes the overall interference of all sensor nodes. Then, we propose an efficient greedy scheduling algorithm to assign transmissions of nodes into time-frames such that the interference among concurrent transmissions is minimized. Extensive simulations have been done and the results show that our proposed method can improve the success probability significantly.

The rest of the paper is organized as follows. The related work is reviewed in Section 2. The problem is formulated in Section 3. Our proposed solution is presented in Section 4. The simulation is reported in Section 5 and the conclusion is drawn in Section 6.

2   Related Work

In wireless sensor networks, CSMA/CA-based MAC layer protocols are widely used due to their simplicity. Lu et. al presented a real-time communication architecture based on IEEE 802.11 protocols for large-scale sensor networks [3]. It uses heuristic information to prioritize the packets, but it does not give performance analysis. Zhang et al. investigated the problem of maximizing information collection under a delay bound constraint for CSMA/CA-based protocols in sensor networks [1]. They proposed an optimal algorithm and a distributed algorithm to allocate the maximal allowable transmission delay at each sensor node.

TDMA-based protocols are regarded as an ideal technology for real-time applications. Li et al. studied the time complexity, message complexity, and energy complexity of data collection, algebraic data aggregation, and data selection in wireless sensor networks [4]. Although TDMA-based protocols are good for real-time applications, they are not suitable to be employed in low-cost sensor nodes, because the requirement of tight synchronization is too expensive to be met in low-cost sensor networks in practice. We proposed a hybrid method of CSMA/CA and TDMA for the real-time data aggregation in wireless sensor networks [2].

There are many works on the construction of routing trees [5,6]. Ghosh et al. investigated throughput-delay tradeoff for fast data collection in sensor networks. They designed an (α, β) -bicriteria approximation algorithm to produce a bounded-degree minimum-radius spanning tree, with the radius of the tree at most β times the minimum possible radius for a given degree bound Δ^*, and the degree of any node at most $\Delta^* + \alpha$, where α and β are positive constants [5]. However, the property of low-degree does not necessarily imply low interference.

3   System Model and Problem Formulation

We are given a sensor network $G = (V, E)$, where V consists of N sensor nodes $v_1, v_2, \ldots, v_N$ and one sink v_0. There is an edge $(v_i, v_j) \in E$ if and only if v_i and v_j are within the communication range of each other. We consider the real-time data aggregation. Suppose the end-to-end delay bound for a data aggregation query is Δ. That is, the data from any sensor node should reach the sink within a delay of Δ. A data aggregation tree T is a tree rooted from the sink node v_0 and containing all nodes in V. For data aggregation, a non-leaf node in the tree must wait for data packets from all its child nodes before it aggregates them together with its own data and forwards the aggregated data to its parent node. We assume data packets sent by all nodes have the same size due to data aggregation. The traffic is assumed to be saturated that a sensor node always has one packet to send.

We adopt protocol interference model in this paper. That is, node v_i is said to be interfered by node v_j if v_i is within the interference range of v_j. Let I_i denote the set of nodes that v_i is interfered by (including v_i itself), and $I(v_i)$ denote the number of nodes in this set. We call $I(v_i)$ the node interference of v_i. The success probability $p_s(v_i)$ for node v_i to transmit a packet to its parent depends on the interference $I(v_i)$ and the maximal allowed transmission time for v_i, denoted by $\delta(v_i)$. Thus, the success probability $p_s(v_i)$ can be calculated by a function f with the variables $I(v_i)$ and $\delta(v_i)$ as in equ. (1). The details of the calculation can be found in [1,7].

$$p_s(v_i) = f(I(v_i), \delta(v_i)). \qquad (1)$$

In CSMA/CA protocols, it is not possible to 100% guarantee a success transmission for a node, given the node interference and the maximal allowed transmission time. With a real-time constraint, there are some nodes whose data packets cannot get through. What we can do is to maximize the success probability of transmissions. With high success probability of data transmission, the sink node can receive data from more nodes. Therefore, our objective is to maximize the average success probability of all sensor nodes:

$$\bar{p}_s = 1/N \sum_{i=1}^{N} p_s(v_i). \qquad (2)$$

By achieving the above goal, the information collected at the sink can be maximized.

In our method, we divide the system time into time-frames with fixed size τ and let all nodes under the same parent to transmit in the same time-frame in CSMA/CA fashion. Note the size of time-frame used here is much larger than the size of time-slot in pure TDMA models. For a node $v_i \in V \setminus \{v_0\}$, let $p(v_i)$ denote the parent node of v_i, and $t(v_i)$ is the time-frame scheduled to v_i for data transmission, $1 \leq t(v_i) \leq L = \lceil \Delta/\tau \rceil$. For each parent node, all its child nodes use CSMA/CA protocols compete for transmission within the same time-frame, which is:

$$\forall v_i, v_j \in V \setminus \{v_0\} \text{ and } p(v_i) = p(v_j) : t(v_i) = t(v_j). \qquad (3)$$

Since a parent node cannot transmit data until it receives all of data packets from its child nodes, this time sequence constraint requires that any $v_i \in V \setminus \{v_0\}$ should always be assigned with a time-frame earlier than $p(v_i)$, which is:

$$\forall v_i \in V \setminus \{v_0\} : t(v_i) < t(p(v_i)). \qquad (4)$$

As the nodes that transmit in the different time-frames do not interfere with each other, the interference of node v_i only comes from the nodes transmitting in the same time-frame, that is:

$$I(v_i) = \left| \{v' | v' \in I_i \text{ and } t(v') = t(v_i)\} \right|. \qquad (5)$$

Given the size of time-frame τ for node v_i to transmit a data packet to its parent, the success probability $p_s(v_i)$ can be maximized when $I(v_i)$ is minimized [1,7]. Thus, we convert the original objective of maximizing equ. (2) to minimizing the average interference of all nodes, which is:

$$\bar{I}(v) = 1/N \sum_{i=1}^{N} I(v_i). \qquad (6)$$

The problem of our concern can be formally stated as follows. Given a set of sensor nodes, one sink and a number of time-frames, the problem is how to construct a data aggregation tree and assign time-frames to sensor nodes, such that the average node interference defined in equ. (6) is minimized. Since the scheduling problem alone is already NP-hard [2], our joint routing and scheduling is also NP-hard.

4   Our Proposed Solution

The real-time data aggregation problem we study aims at maximizing the average transmission success probability of all sensor nodes. This a complicated problem, because aggregation tree construction and time-frame assignment are interdependent with each other. To construct the aggregation tree and route traffic for the maximum success probability, we need to know the interference of each node; however, the interference of nodes cannot be determined before time-frame assignment is known. Our solution breaks this interdependent cycle by first constructing a data aggregation tree that minimizes the average node interference assuming the use of a simple scheduling method. Then, we propose a greedy scheduling to assign the time-frames to sensor nodes. Before going to the details of the proposed algorithm, we start with analyzing the relationship between the data aggregation tree and the maximum k-cut problem.

4.1   Relationship between Data Aggregation Tree and Maximum k-Cut

We consider a special case of our problem where a simple scheduling method is used. We first give the definitions of node height and tree height. Let $h(v_i)$ be the height of node v_i in the aggregation tree T, which is:

$$h(v_i) = \begin{cases} 0 & \text{if } v_i = v_0 \\ h(p(v_i)) + 1 & \text{otherwise} \end{cases}.$$

The height of tree T is the maximum node height in T:

$$h(T) = \max_{v_i \in T}\{h(v_i)\}.$$

The simple scheduling method (SS) assigns the time-frame to a sensor node based on its hop distance to the sink along the aggregation tree. The child nodes of the sink are assigned with the last time-frame (time-frame L). The nodes that are two hops away from the sink are assigned with time-frame $L - 1$. This operation goes on until all the leaf nodes having their time-frames assigned. Specifically, node v_i is assigned with time-frame $L + 1 - h(v_i)$. It is clear that SS satisfies the constraints in (3) and (4).

Since SS assigns the same time-frame to the nodes with the same height, we use H_l to denote the set of nodes with the height l, which are scheduled to transmit data during time-frame $L + 1 - l$. We also define $H_0 = \{v_0\}$. Notice that $H_{L-h(T)}, \ldots, H_L$ are empty. A more efficient scheduling method is proposed in section 4.4. Let $I(H_l)$ be the total interference of the nodes in H_l. The average node interference of equ. (6) for the special case can be rewritten as:

$$\bar{I}_{SS}(v) = 1/N \sum_{l=1}^{L} I(H_l), \tag{7}$$

because interference only occurs among the nodes that are scheduled for transmission in the same time-frame.

We will prove that problem of minimizing the average node interference $\bar{I}_{SS}(v)$ defined in equ. (7) is a constrained maximum k-cut problem. We introduce the interference graph $G_I(V_I, E_I)$ as follows. The vertex set V_I is the set of sensor nodes $\{v_1, v_2, \ldots, v_N\}$. For a pair of vertices v_i and v_j in V_I, there is an edge $(v_i, v_j) \in E_I$ if and only if v_i and v_j interfere with each other. For any subset $S \subseteq V_I$, let $G_I(S)$ denote the induced subgraph of $G_I(V_I, E_I)$ whose vertex-set is S and $E_I(S)$ its edge-set.

Given the set of sensor nodes, the concerned special case of our problem is then transformed into that of partitioning the node set V_I into disjoint set $H_1, \ldots, H_L$, such that the average node interference in equ. (7) is minimized, while for any set H_l, $1 \leq H_l \leq L$, the nodes in H_l can be covered by the nodes in H_{l-1}, which is:

$$\forall v_i \in H_l, 1 \leq l \leq L : \exists v_j \in H_{l-1}, (v_i, v_j) \in E. \tag{8}$$

This node cover constraint guarantees that the data packet transmitted by any node in H_l can be received by at least one node in H_{l-1}. We now see the relationship between this minimizing $\bar{I}_{SS}(v)$ and the *maximum k-cut problem*.

Definition 1. *For a graph $G(V, E)$ and a partitioning of V into k disjoint sets $V_1, \ldots, V_k$, a k-cut is a subset of E consisting of edges whose two endpoints are in two different sets V_i and V_j, $i \neq j$. The weight of a k-cut is the number of edges in the cut. The maximum k-cut problem is to find a partitioning of V that produces the maximum k-cut.*

Theorem 1. *Given a set of nodes $\{v_1, v_2, \ldots, v_N\}$, a partitioning of the set of nodes into disjoint sets $H_1, \ldots, H_L$, is the optimal solution to the problem of minimizing $\bar{I}_{SS}(v)$ if and only if it is the optimal solution to the maximum k-cut problem in $G_I(V_I, E_I)$ with $k = L$, while the node cover constraint specified in (8) is satisfied.*

Proof. Since minimizing $\bar{I}_{SS}(v)$ is transformed into the problem of partitioning V into L subsets such that equ. (7) is minimized, we need to prove the finding a partitioning of V_I which minimizes equ. (7) is equivalent to finding the optimal solution to the maximum k-cut problem in $G_I(V_I, E_I)$ with $k = L$, subject to the node cover constraint (8).

Consider $H_1, \ldots, H_L$ as a partitioning of V_I, subject to the constraint (8). Let $w(H_1, \ldots, H_L)$ denote the weight of k-cut and $|E_I|$ the total number of all edges in E_I. From the definition of a k-cut, we have:

$$w(H_1, \ldots, H_L) = |E_I| - \sum_{l=1}^{L} |E_I(H_l)|. \tag{9}$$

From equ. (7), it yields:

$$|E(H_l)| = 1/2 \cdot \sum_{v_i \in H_l} I(v_i)$$
$$= 1/2 \cdot I(H(l)).$$

Then equ. (9) is turned into:

$$w(H_1, \ldots, H_L) = |E_I| - 1/2 \cdot \sum_{l=1}^{L} I(H_l)$$
$$= |E_I| - 1/2 \cdot \sum_{i=1}^{N} I(v_i)$$
$$= |E_I| - N/2 \cdot \bar{I}_{SS}(v). \tag{10}$$

Therefore, minimizing $\bar{I}_{SS}(v)$ in $G(V, E)$ is equivalent to maximizing the constrained weight k-cut in $G_I(V_I, E_I)$ with $k = L$, subject to the node cover constraint (8). □

We construct the data aggregation tree in two major steps. The first step is to partition the network into layers of tree nodes such that the average interference of all layers is minimized. The second step is to select parent nodes for all nodes in the layers. The two steps are explained in the following subsections respectively.

4.2   Partition Network into Tree Layers

We transform the problem of minimizing average node interference for SS to the constrained maximum k-cut problem, which is NP-complete [8]. The best known approximation algorithm was proposed in [9] that could produce a k-cut whose weight is at least $1/(1 - 1/k + 2 \ln k/k^2)$ times of the weight of the maximum k-cut. However, this method is based on solving a semidefinite programming relaxation, leading to a high complexity. In the following, we present an efficient heuristic algorithm.

Our algorithm is a generalization of a local search method for solving the maximum cut problem where $k = 2$ [10]. The algorithm first generates a valid partitioning of V_I into L disjoint set $H_1, \ldots, H_L$. A valid partitioning is the one that satisfies the node cover constraint (8). Then, for any $v_i \in V_I$, v_i is moved from partition H_l to $H_{l'}$ if the weight of the k-cut is strictly increasing and the move is valid in terms of preserving the node cover constraint. This move operation is repeated until no further improvement can be made.

When we move a node $v_i \in V_I$ from H_l to $H_{l'}$, we need to check the validity of a partitioning (i.e., whether the node cover constraint (8) is preserved or not). The move is not valid if 1) H_{l+1} cannot be covered by $H_l \setminus \{v_i\}$; or 2) $H_{l'} \cup \{v_i\}$ cannot be covered by $H_{l'-1}$. We assume the number of time-frames available is always larger than or equal to $h(T)$, i.e., $L \geq h(T)$.

We use the breadth-first search (BFS) tree for the initial valid partition of V_I. Given the BFS tree T_B, it assigns the nodes with the height $h(T_B)$ to $H_{L-h(T_B)+1}$. These are the leaf nodes in T_B that are the furthest away from the sink. Then, the nodes with height $h(T_B) - 1$ are allocated to $H_{L-h(T_B)+2}$. Repeat this process until the nodes are the child nodes of the sink. The initial empty sets $H_{h(T_B)+1}, \ldots, H_L$ will be gradually filled up as the algorithm moves nodes to them to increase the weight of k-cut. The details of the algorithm to partition network into tree layers (PNTL) are in Algorithm 1.

Algorithm 1. Partition Network into Tree Layers (PNTL)

Input: $G_I = (V_I, E_I)$ and $k(= L)$
Output: $H_1, \ldots, H_L$
Begin
   Generate an initial valid partitioning of V_I: $H_1, \ldots, H_L$ that satisfies constraint (8).
   Repeat
     For any node $v_i \in H_l$
       For any node set $H_{l'}$ and $v_i \notin H_{l'}$
       Move v_i to $H_{l'}$ if
         (I) The weight of k-cut is strictly increased; and
         (II) The move is valid in terms of preserving node cover constraint.
       End-For
     End-For
     Until no such a move of any v_i that increases the weight of k-cut.
End

4.3 Parent Selection in Tree Construction

After the first step, we obtain a set of partitions $H_1, \ldots, H_L$. It divides the sensor nodes into different layers according to their distance with the sink and guarantees that the data packet transmitted by a node in the lower layer can be received by at least one node in the next higher layer. But it does not assign parent for nodes. It is important to select the right parent for a node, because different parent selection may lead to different performance if considering the general case of our problem.

Now, we need to select a parent for each node. The parent selection is done in a top-down fashion. For the nodes in H_1, all of them have the sink as their parent. For the nodes in the sets $H_l, 2 \leq l \leq L$, parent assignment is done in two steps. In the first step, some nodes in H_l are connected to the tree (having their parents assigned). These nodes can be covered by solely one node in H_{l-1}. In the second step, for the rest of unconnected nodes in H_l that have multiple parent candidates, we always assign them parents to minimize the node interference (and the potential node interference) on the tree constructed so far. For node $v_i \in H_l$ and v_i's parent candidate $v_j \in H_{l-1}$, the in-tree nodes (those having their parent assigned) that are within the interference area of v_i can be classified into three categories if v_i is connected to v_j:

- the nodes that are interfered with v_i, denoted by $V_C(v_i, v_j)$. These nodes have the same parent v_j as v_i.
- the nodes that are not interfered with v_i. These nodes cannot transmit data at the same time with v_i, whose parents are either the ancestors of v_j or the descendants of v_j.
- the rest of nodes that are possibly interfered with v_i, denoted by $V_{PC}(v_i, v_j)$. The interference caused by these nodes can be decided only when the time-frame is assigned.

For all parent candidates of v_i, we connect v_i to the parent that leads to the minimum node interference $|V_C(v_i, v_j)|$; if there is a tie, the one with the minimum potential node interference $|V_{PC}(v_i, v_j)|$ is selected. The details of algorithm for parent selection (PS) are in Algorithm 2.

Algorithm 2. Parent Selection (PS)

Input: $H_1, \ldots, H_L$
Output: T
Begin
    Each node in H_1 is assigned with v_0 as their parent node.
    For $2 \le l \le L$
        Assign parents for the nodes in H_l that are covered by only one node in H_{l-1}.
        For each of the unassigned nodes v_i in H_l
            Compute $|V_C(v_i, v_j)|$ and $|V_{PC}(v_i, v_j)|$ for each parent candidate v_j.
            Select the parent for v_i that leads to the least node interference
            (and the potential node interference).
        End-For
    End-For
End

4.4 Greedy Scheduling Algorithm for Time-Frame Assignment

Given the aggregation tree T, we propose a more efficient greedy scheduling algorithm (GS) than SS to assign time-frames to the sensor nodes. GS works in the bottom-top fashion along T. We first introduce some notations. For a parent node $v_j \in V$, we use $tc(v_j)$ to denote the time-frame assigns to the child nodes of v_j. For a parent node v_j whose child nodes have not been assigned with a time-frame, $ec(v_j)$ denotes the earliest eligible time-frame for the child nodes of v_j to transmit data packets to v_j, and $lc(v_j)$ is the latest eligible time-frame. The initialization of $ec(v_j)$ and $lc(v_j)$ is discussed later. Let U be the set of parent nodes whose child nodes are ready to be assigned with a time-frame, and M the set of nodes that are assigned with time-frames so far. Following the definition of $\bar{I}_{SS}(v)$ in equ. (7) under SS, we define the average node interference for set M under the GS scheduling in equ. (11).

The basic idea of GS is as follows. Set U is initialized to contain only the parents whose child nodes are all leaf nodes. Each time, for all parents in U, find the node and the time-frame for its child nodes that minimizes $\bar{I}_{GS}(v)$ in equ. (11). Suppose the chosen node is v^* and the time assigned to its child nodes is $tc(v^*)$, $tc(v^*) \in [sc(v^*), lc(v^*)]$. Then v^* is removed from U. Its parent node $p(v^*)$ will be added to U when $p(v^*)$ has no more child node in U. This operation is repeated until U becomes empty, where all nodes in the network are now assigned with time-frames.

$$\bar{I}_{GS}(v) = 1/|M| \sum\nolimits_{v_i \in M} \left| \{v'|v' \in I_i \text{ and } t(v') = t(v_i)\} \right|. \tag{11}$$

Now, we look at the initialization of $ec(v_j)$ and $lc(v_j)$ for all parent nodes $v_j \in V$. The latest eligible time-frame for the child nodes of v_j, i.e., $lc(v_j)$, depends on

$h(v_j)$. Starting from the top of the tree, for a parent node v_j with height 0 (sink v_0), i.e., $h(v_0) = 0$, $lc(v_0) = L$. For a parent node v_j with height 1, $lc(v_j) = L-1$. We keep on this operation to assign values to $lc(v_j)$ for all parent nodes v_j in the top-down fashion along the tree. The values of $lc(v_j)$ for all parent nodes do not change during the execution of the algorithm. The earliest eligible time-frame for the child nodes of v_j, i.e., $ec(v_j)$, is determined starting from the parent of leaf nodes all the way up to the root of the tree. The initialization of $ec(v_j)$ is:

$$ec(v_j) = \begin{cases} 1 & \text{if all child nodes of } v_j \text{ are leaf nodes} \\ \max_{p(v_i)=v_j}\{tc(v_i)\} + 1 & \text{otherwise} \end{cases}.$$

Due to space limitation, the details of algorithm GS are omitted.

5   Simulations

The purpose of the simulations is to evaluate the performance of our proposed algorithm under various parameter settings. We examine four combinations of data aggregation trees and scheduling methods, namely BFST+SS, BFST+GS, PNTL+SS and PS+GS.

In the simulation setting, 100 sensor nodes are randomly distributed in a $1000 \times 1000m^2$ square region. The sink node is located in the center of the region. The packet size is fixed as 128 bytes. In the MAC layer, the size of contention window is fixed as 32 [1]. We vary the delay bound from $50ms$ to $150ms$. We set the transmission range and interference range to $150m$ and $300m$ for all nodes, respectively. All the results reported in the following are averaged over 100 runs.

For each combination of data aggregation tree and scheduling method, it has a pair of parameters $(h_{\max}, L)$. The parameter $h_{\max}$ is the maximum allowed height of the aggregation tree and L is the number of available time-frames. We have $h_{\min} \leq h(T) \leq h_{\max} \leq L$, where $h_{\min}$ is equal to the height of the BFS tree. Given the delay bound Δ, a larger L means the more number of time-frames are available, but each time-frame has a smaller size.

We first evaluate the average success probability by fixing $L = h_{\min}$. Fig. 1(a) shows the average transmission probability of sensor nodes versus delay bound for different algorithms. From Fig. 1(a), we can make the following observations: 1) The average success probability increases as the delay bound increases. This trend is more significant when the delay bound is tight. 2) As the delay bound reaches a certain value, the curves of PNTL+SS and PS+GS become flat, because each sensor node has already had sufficient time to compete with other sensor nodes for transmission and their success probability is close to 1. 3) The maximum k-cut based algorithms PNTL+SS and PS+GS perform much better than the BFS tree based algorithms BFST+SS and BFST+GS. 4) When the aggregation tree is not good, scheduling method has great impact on the result, because BFST+GS is much better than BFST+SS. However, if the aggregation tree is well formed, it leaves little optimization space for scheduling.

We then evaluate the average success probability by fixing $L = h_{\min} + 2$ in Fig. 1(b). We can find the top four curves are the maximum k-cut based

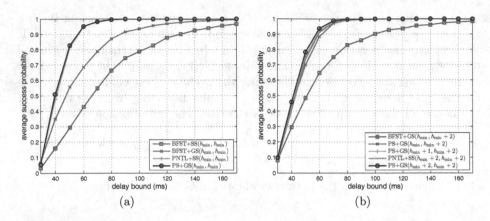

Fig. 1. The average success probability versus delay bound (a) $L = h_{min}$ (b) $L = h_{min} + 2$

algorithms, and they show great superiority to BFST+GS. Although the top four curves stay very close, we can still see PNTL+SS($h_{min} + 2, h_{min} + 2$) performs between PS+GS($h_{min}, h_{min} + 2$) and PS+GS($h_{min} + 1, h_{min} + 2$), and PS+GS($h_{min} + 2, h_{min} + 2$) is the best one. It indicates that our tree construction method can distribute the node interference into different time-frames effectively.

Since we convert the original objective of maximizing the average success probability to minimizing the average interference of all nodes, we show the average node interference for different algorithms under varying parameters in Fig. 2. We can see from Fig. 2 that minimizing the average node interference is confirmed to be consistent with maximizing the average success probability (for a given size of time-frame). For example, the comparison of the average success probability in Fig. 1(a) is validated by bar (1), (2), (5) and (6) in Fig. 2.

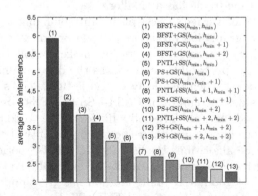

Fig. 2. The average node interference of different algorithms with varying parameters

6   Conclusion

We have studied real-time data aggregation problem for wireless sensor networks that use CSMA/CA MAC layer protocols in cyber-physical systems. Our goal is to maximize the average transmission success probability of all sensor nodes. We divided the system time into time-frames with fixed size and scheduled the transmission of each senor into time-frames. The transmissions of all child nodes under the same parent are scheduled in the same time-frame and they compete the channel access in CSMA/CA fashion. In this system model, the construction of data aggregation trees becomes very important. We first proposed an algorithm for data aggregation tree construction, which minimizes the overall interference of all sensor nodes. Then, we proposed an efficient greedy scheduling algorithm to assign transmissions of nodes into time-frames. Extensive simulations have been done and the results show that our proposed method can improve the success probability significantly.

Acknowledgments. This work was supported by grants from National Natural Science Foundation of China (No. 61103217, 61173137, and 60970117).

References

1. Zhang, J., Jia, X., Xing, G.: Real-time data aggregation in contention-based wireless sensor networks. ACM Transactions on Sensor Networks 7(1), 1–25 (2010)
2. Liu, Q., Chang, Y., Jia, X.: Real-time data aggregation with high success probability in contention-based wireless sensor networks. In: International Conference on Mobile Ad-hoc and Sensor Networks (MSN), pp. 60–67 (2011)
3. Lu, C., Blum, B., Abdelzaher, T., Stankovic, J., He, T.: Rap: A real-time communication architecture for large-scale wireless sensor networks. In: IEEE Real-Time and Embedded Technology and Applications Symposium (RTAS), pp. 55–66 (2002)
4. Li, X., Wang, Y.: Complexity of data collection, aggregation, and selection for wireless sensor networks. IEEE Transactions on Computers 60(3), 386–399 (2011)
5. Ghosh, A., Incel, O., Kumar, V., Krishnamachari, B.: Multichannel scheduling and spanning trees: Throughput–delay tradeoff for fast data collection in sensor networks. IEEE/ACM Transactions on Networking (99), 1731–1744 (2011)
6. Hu, X.D., Shuai, T., Jia, X., Zhang, M.: Multicast routing and wavelength assignment in wdm networks with limited drop-offs. In: IEEE INFOCOM, vol. 1. IEEE (2004)
7. Barowski, Y., Biaz, S., Agrawal, P.: Towards the performance analysis of IEEE 802.11 in multi-hop ad-hoc networks. In: IEEE Wireless Communications and Networking Conference (WCNC), vol. 1, pp. 100–106 (2004)
8. Hochba, D.S.: Approximation algorithms for NP-hard problems. PWS Publishing Company (1997)
9. Erlebach, T., Jansen, K., Kaklamanis, C., Persiano, P.: An optimal greedy algorithm for wavelength allocation in directed tree networks. DIMACS Series in Discrete Mathematics and Theoretical Computer Science, vol. 40, pp. 117–129. American Mathematical Society (1998)
10. Schäffer, A.: Simple local search problems that are hard to solve. SIAM Journal on Computing 20(1), 56–87 (1991)

On the Performance of TDD and LDD Based Clone Attack Detection in Mobile Ad Hoc Networks

Dapeng Wang[1], Pei Li[2], Pengfei Hu[3,4], Kai Xing[3,4], Yang Wang[3,4],
Liusheng Huang[3,4], and Yanxia Rong[5]

[1] Alcatel-Lucent Shanghai Bell,
No.388, Ningqiao Road, Shanghai, 201206, China
[2] College of Information Systems and Management, National Univ. of Defense Tech.,
Changsha, Hunan 410073, China
[3] School of Computer Science and Technology, Univ. of Sci. and Tech. of China,
P.O. Box 4, Hefei, Anhui 230027, China
[4] Suzhou Institute for Advanced Study, Univ. of Sci. and Tech. of China,
166 RenAi Road, Suzhou, Jiangsu 215123, China
[5] Worldquant, LLC.,
650 5th Avenue, New York, NY 10103 USA
{pfhu,kxing,lshuang,angyan}@ustc.edu.cn, peili@nudt.edu.cn
Dapeng.Wang@alcatel-sbell.com.cn, yxrong@gmail.com

Abstract. Clone attack detection is envisioned as a promising problem in distributed networking environments, e.g., wireless sensor networks, mobile ad hoc networks [5,2,9,3,7,1,8,4] . In this paper, we analyze the performance of Time domain based detection (TDD) and Space domain based detection (SDD) [6] of clone attacks in mobile ad hoc networks in terms of detection ratio and time. The study shows that TDD and SDD utilizes network resource efficiently and achieves great scalability and robust detection performance compared with existing schemes. In particular, the storage overhead of sensors is independent of the network size, and is evenly distributed across the network. Moreover, it only takes limited communication overhead to verify the validity of any node. In addition to the analysis, we also propose simulation study for clone attack detection. According to our proved theorems, TDD and SDD enable users to detect clones in an efficient and effective manner in the network.

1 Introduction

So far, various clone attack detection methods have been proposed for sensor networks and mobile ad hoc networks. In *centralized* detection methods, every node's information is periodically collected by the base station in order to detect clone nodes. In *distributed* detection methods, clones nodes are detected by witness nodes in the network. In *localized* detection methods, clone nodes are detected by its neighbors. The performance of these methods has been studied [5,2,9,3,7,1] in static networks. But few of them target the performance of these

X. Wang et al. (Eds.): WASA 2012, LNCS 7405, pp. 532–539, 2012.

methods in mobile environments. In this paper, we study existing clone detection methods that are designed for mobile ad hoc networks, TDD, and SDD, and compare them with XED [8]. Our major contributions are summarized as follows.

- We analyze the performance of TDD and SDD on storage and communication overhead. The results indicate the fairness of TDD and SDD on storage and communication, therefore no storage hot spots will be generated. In addition, the storage consumption at each sensor is independent of the network size, thereby TDD and SDD scales well to large networks.
- We theoretically study the communication overhead for a user to detect clone nodes. The study shows that the overhead of SDD is comparable with the light communication overhead of XED, and the overhead of TDD is relative low compared with existing distributed and centralized schemes.
- We also propose extensive simulation study to verify the effectiveness and efficiency in clone nodes detection in terms of detection accuracy, detection time, scalability, etc. Our results indicates that TDD and SDD outperforms existing localized detection schemes XED in various aspects.

The rest of the paper is organized as follows. First we briefly overview the TDD and SDD schemes in Section 2. We then conduct theoretical performance analysis on storage and communication overheads in Sections 3. We then study their performance and simulation results are reported in Section 4. The paper is concluded in Section 5.

2   Overview of TDD and SDD

In this section, we briefly overview the basic concept of time domain based detection (TDD) and space domain based detection (SDD) of clone attacks.

We consider a mobile ad hoc network comprised of N nodes, with each having the minimum and maximum communication ranges of R_{min} and R_{max}, respectively. We assume that the clocks of all nodes are loosely synchronized and every node is able to obtain its location information and verify the locations of its neighbors. We also assume that each node stores a public location generation function H_{loc} and a public time generation function H_{time}.

Each node u has a unique one-way hash chain. Whenever two nodes u and v meet each other, they issue a challenge from their one-way hash chain to each other and exchange the following authenticated messages:

$$Message_{u \to v} : (u||v||t^u||loc^u||ch_i^u||Sig^u),$$

$$Message_{v \to u} : (v||u||t^v||loc^v||ch_j^v||Sig^v),$$

where t and loc represent the time and the location at which they meet each other, ch_i^u (ch_j^v) represents u's $(v$'s) challenge whose index is the smallest among all unissued challenges in u's $(v$'s) challenge chain, and Sig^u (Sig^v) is the signature signed by u (v) with u's $(v$'s) public key for $Message_{u \to v}$ $(Message_{v \to u})$. These information will be kept by $v(u)$ in a fixed time duration $2D$.

The basic idea of TDD is sketched as follows: At each time interval T_{k-1} of duration T, v computes a time $t \in T_{k-1}$ for each node u in the network using the time generation function H_{time} taking the identity u, the challenge ch_k^{TN}, and T_{k-1} as inputs. If u and v did meet each other at a time interval $t \pm \Delta$, where Δ is a system-defined parameter, v reports the information that it has obtained from u during $t \pm \Delta$ to the location $H_{loc}(u,t)$. Otherwise v stops its reporting procedure on u. At the location $H_{loc}(u,t)$, the node closest to $H_{loc}(u,t)$ is responsible for receiving these reports and launching a check on them. Messages from different reporters should have consistent location and challenge claims on u. Any violation would signal clone attack on identity u.

The basic idea of SDD is sketched as follows:

– SDD-LC: Local Check
  When two nodes v and u meet each other, they exchange information. After v receives from u $Message_{u \to v}$: $(u||v||t_i^u||loc_i^u||ch_{i_k}^u||Sig_i^u)$, v first verifies the authenticity of this message by the public key of u. If the message fails to pass the authenticity check, v reports an external attack on u (namely the message is faked). Otherwise, v records this message in its table, and check whether the newly received information of u is consistent with the information it has recorded for u in its table. If $Message_{u \to v}$ violates any history records of u^1, there must be a node replication attack on identity u.
– SDD-LWC: Local Witness Check
  Given a node u and its replica u_r, u and u_r inevitably generate information contradicting with each other in the network. This information may be recorded by the witness nodes of u and u_r during the information exchange. Once the witness nodes meet each other and exchange their recorded information about identity u, they may find the contradictory information breaking the violation rules defined in [6]. Thus the node replication attack on identity u can be detected.

3   Storage and Communication Overheads Analysis

Due to the simple structure, TDD and SDD have several well-defined properties that lead to promising performance. The following theorems provide the analysis.

Lemma 1. *Let λ denote the number of nodes a node u meets in unit time, the storage overhead of TDD at each node is $O(\lambda T)$*

Proof. Given a node u, it is easily seen that at each time interval t, the node stores the messages exchanged from the nodes it meets. Therefore the storage overhead is $O(\lambda T)$ ■

Lemma 2. *Let λ denote the number of nodes a node u meets in unit time, the message overhead of TDD at each node during each time interval is $O(2\lambda\delta\sqrt{N})$*

---

^{1} the violation is defined in [6]

Proof. Given a node u, the number of nodes it reports during each time interval is $2\lambda\delta$, Therefore the message overhead incurred by each node during each interval is $2\lambda\delta\sqrt{N}$ ∎

Lemma 3. *Let λ denote the number of nodes a node u meets in unit time, the storage overhead of SDD at each node is $O(2\lambda D)$*

Proof. Given a node u, it is easily seen that the node stores the messages exchanged from the nodes it meets and keeps these messages for $2D$ time duration. Therefore the storage overhead is $O(2\lambda D)$.   ∎

Lemma 4. *Let λ denote the number of nodes a node u meets in unit time, the message overhead of SDD at each node in unit time is $O(\lambda)$*

Proof. Given a node u, it is easily seen that the number of nodes it exchanges messages with in unit time is λ.   ∎

4   Performance Evaluation

In this section, we evaluation the detection performance of TDD and SDD, and compare them with XED [8], a localized clone attack detection scheme.

Our simulation study is conducted based on MATLAB. In the simulation settings, we randomly deploy $N = 1000$ nodes randomly moving in an area of 100×100 area. The number of clone nodes is selected in $[10, 50]$. The communication radius is set between $[2, 5]$. All simulation results are averaged over 100 runs.

Fig. 1 provides the comparison results of TDD, SDD, and XED in terms of the time cost to detect all clone nodes given communication radius equals to 5.0. In the figure, we can see that TDD takes the least time to detect all replicas since it launches detection procedure every time interval in a distributed manner. For localized detection, SDD outperforms XED due to its effective design of one-way hash chain.

Fig. 2 provides the comparison results of TDD and SDD in terms of the time cost to detect all clone nodes at different communication radii. In the figure, we can see that TDD takes the least time to detect all replicas than SDD at the same communication radius due to the difference of their detection manner (distributed/localized).

Fig. 3 and Fig. 4 show the detection time of TDD and SDD at various communication radii. In the two figures, we can see that the larger the communication radius, the less the detection time, the more the clone nodes, the longer the detection time.

Fig. 5 and Fig. 6 provides the comparison results of XED with TDD/SDD in terms of detection ratio when TDD/SDD detects all clone nodes at different communication radii. In the figures, we can see that both TDD and SDD outperforms XED. The larger the communication radius, the better the detection ratio, the more the clone nodes, the smaller the detection ratio.

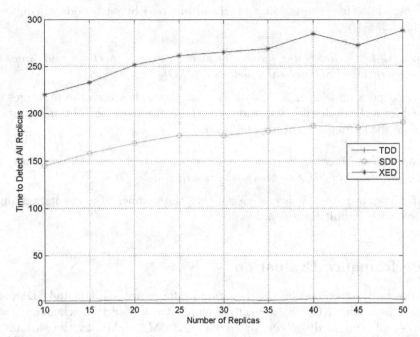

Fig. 1. Time cost to detect all clone nodes given communication radius equals to 5.0

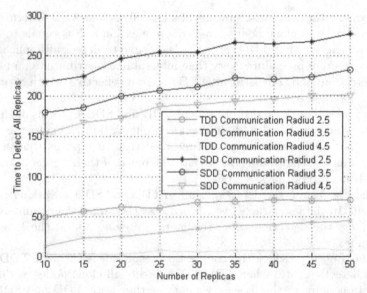

Fig. 2. Time cost to detect all clone nodes at various communication radii

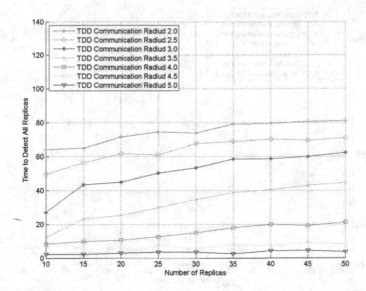

Fig. 3. Detection Time of TDD at various communication radii

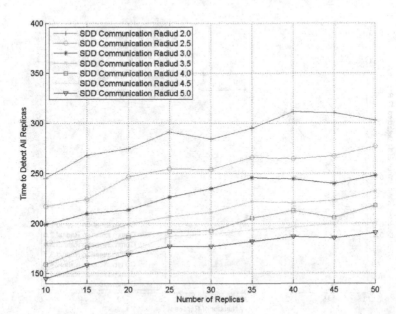

Fig. 4. Detection Time of TDD at various communication radii

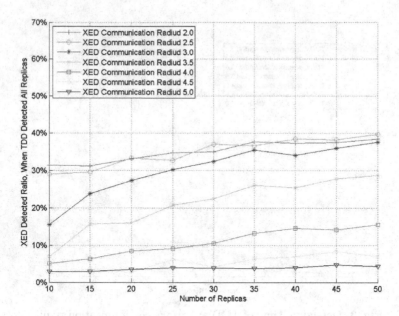

Fig. 5. Detection ratio of XED when TDD detects all clones

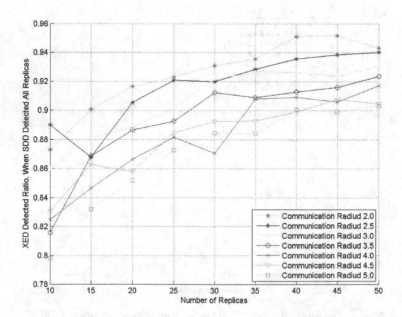

Fig. 6. Detection ratio of XED when SDD detects all clones

5   Conclusion

Previous node replication detection schemes depend primarily on a stationary network model. To address these fundamental limitations, we provide a study of clone detection methods in MANETs. Specifically, we analyze three schemes, XED, TDD, and SDD. Our analysis studies their overhead, detection accuracy and detection time. Results indicate that in distributed detection schemes, TDD could achieve the best detection accuracy and least detection time at the cost of communication overhead. In localized detection scheme, SDD achieves much better detection accuracy and least detection time than that of XED, but incurs more storage overhead. Both TDD and SDD could provide a robust detection accuracy disregarding node collusion and the number/distribution of replicas/compromised nodes.

References

1. Brooks, R.R., Govindaraju, P.Y., Pirretti, M., Vijaykrishnan, N., Kandemir, M.T.: On the detection of clones in sensor networks using random key predistribution. IEEE Transactions on Systems, Man, and Cybernetics, Part C 37(6), 1246–1258 (2007)
2. Choi, H., Zhu, S., Laporta, T.: Set: Detecting node clones in sensor networks. In: SecureComm 2007, pp. 341–350 (2007)
3. Conti, M., Di Pietro, R., Mancini, L.V., Mei, A.: A randomized, efficient, and distributed protocol for the detection of node replication attacks in wireless sensor networks. In: MobiHoc 2007, pp. 80–89 (2007)
4. Ho, J.-W., Wright, M., Das, S.: Fast detection of replica node attacks in mobile sensor networks using sequential analysis. In: IEEE INFOCOM, pp. 1773–1781 (2009)
5. Parno, B., Perrig, A., Gligor, V.: Distributed detection of node replication attacks in sensor networks. In: IEEE SP 2005, pp. 49–63 (2005)
6. Xing, K., Cheng, X.: From time domain to space domain: Detecting replica attacks in mobile ad hoc networks. In: IEEE INFOCOM 2010, pp. 1595–1603 (2010)
7. Xing, K., Liu, F., Cheng, X., Du., D.H.C.: Real-time detection of clone attacks in wireless sensor networks. In: IEEE ICDCS 2008, pp. 3–10 (2008)
8. Yu, C.-M., Lu, C.-S., Kuo, S.-Y.: Mobile sensor network resilient against node replication attacks. In: IEEE SECON 2008, vol. 16, pp. 597–599 (2008)
9. Zhu, B., Addada, V.G.K., Setia, S., Jajodia, S., Roy, S.: Efficient distributed detection of node replication attacks in sensor networks. In: ACSAC, pp. 257–267 (2007)

Active User Authentication for Mobile Devices

Yan Sui[1], Xukai Zou[1], Feng Li[2], and Eliza Y. Du[3]

[1] Department of Computer and Information Science,
Indiana University Purdue University Indianapolis, Indianapolis, IN 46202
ysui@iupui.edu, xkzou@cs.iupui.edu
[2] Department of Computer and Information Technology,
Indiana University Purdue University Indianapolis, Indianapolis, IN 46202
fengli@iupui.edu
[3] Department of Electrical and Computer Engineering,
Indiana University Purdue University Indianapolis, IN 46202
yidu@iupui.edu

Abstract. Enterprises today are dealing with the challenges involved in enabling secure and remote access for mobile device users. People often bring their personal mobile devices into works and use them to access corporate resources, and also store their private information on personal mobile devices. This has prompted investigation of new security policies and techniques. Authentication is the first gate for protecting access to personal mobile devices or access remote resources through personal mobile devices. Conventional authentication does not require user re-authentication for continuous usage of the devices. And attackers can target at a post-authentication session. In this paper, we study the active authentication for personal mobile devices and propose a biometrics based active authentication system. The proposed system is secure, effective and user-friendly. Our experimental results also show the feasibility of the proposed system.

Keywords: User authentication, biometrics, active authentication, mobile devices.

1 Introduction

The emergence of personal mobile devices (e.g., smart phones, PDA, tablet PCs) has changed people's way of working, studying and entertaining. And people are using their personal mobile devices to access remote resources, e.g., e-banking, working documents, and more and more sensitive and private information are stored in personal mobile devices, e.g., contacts, calendars. The popularity of personal mobile devices and the criticality of information they are dealing with prompt investigation and development of new security policies and technologies. User authentication is the first gate for protecting access to personal mobile devices or access to resources through personal devices [11]. Current authentication system does not make differentiation between the initial log-in user and the intruder as long as the session remains active, and typical systems incorporate

X. Wang et al. (Eds.): WASA 2012, LNCS 7405, pp. 540–548, 2012.

no mechanisms to verify that the user originally authenticated is the user still in control of the personal mobile devices. Thus, unauthorized individuals can improperly obtain access to the personal mobile devices if a user leaves an open session.

The active authentication system (AAS) is proposed to address this problem by developing ways to continuously sample credentials from a user to validate the user's identity. Besides the requirements of conventional authentication, there are several additional requirements for the continuous authentication, e.g., non-intrusive [13]. The continuous authentication should be transparent to users and do not cause additional burdens. According to the non-intrusiveness, username/password is not suitable for continuous authentication since it is not feasible to require users to input a password periodically, e.g., every second. A promising direction emerging from this effort is biometrics [12]. Biometrics binds users to their biological traits. Some commonly used biometrics are iris, face, fingerprint, etc. A typical biometric authentication system includes two stages: registration and verification. For registration, the authentication system samples user biometrics (e.g., iris image), pre-processes biometric data (e.g., remove noise, segment interested biometric part), extracts biometric features and generates a biometric template to quantitatively represent the biometrics. The biometric template is stored in the system database. For any future verification, the user biometrics is sampled again, and through the same processes a query template is generated and matched against the stored template for authentication. Biometrics is suitable for the AAS, since biometrics is both intrinsically linked with users and (for some of them) is non-intrusively collectable. However, there are several obstacles of applying biometrics in the AAS for personal mobile devices:

- Data Input: biometrics acquisition is a fuzzy process, and due to this reason biometric samples from the same person are not exact matchable. A matching mechanism for biometric authentication or biometrics based active authentication is needed.
- System/Credential security and user privacy: while existing works focus on the performance (authentication accuracy and detection accuracy of intrusion), they ignore one important aspect of active authentication, that is, security of the system and and user privacy. It is possible that authentication credentials be replaced or lost, which can cause system security risks. Also it is possible that the user credential sent from user (client) to the authentication server be intercepted and later replayed. User credentials (e.g., biometrics) may directly link to user personal information. Lost of users' credentials may infringe user privacy.

In this paper, we identify the possible attack model for active authentication and propose a biometrics based active authentication system. The proposed system can be used in personal mobile device for effective user authentication. The following of the paper is organized as follows. Section 2 reviews the related works. Section 3 proposes the new biometrics active authentication system and also presents security analysis. Section 4 shows our experimental results and proves the feasibility of the proposed system. Section 5 concludes the paper and proposes our future work.

2   Related Work

Conventional user authentication on personal mobile devices (e.g., mobile phones) provides only a one-time authentication upon switch-on; and top five vendors of mobile phones do not have automatic locking as default setup [12]. According to [12], users are willing to see that biometrics becomes an option used for authentication.

Biometrics based active authentication has been studied in the application of protecting PCs and workstations. Niinuma et. al. proposed using soft biometrics (user face color, clothing color at log-in time) and hard biometrics (face eigen-features) for active authentication [9]. The system registered a user template at password log-in, thus if the password is stolen the system will always think the impostor is the legitimate user. The system only uses soft biometrics for continuous authentication. Users can dress similar clothes (e.g., uniforms) and have similar face color. Physiological biometrics has been used a lot in active authentication [13,8,16,3]. Sim et. al. proposed to use face and fingerprint for authentication [13]. They use holistic score fusion to integrate face and fingerprint observations over time. However, the system requires training. There are efforts using behavior biometrics (e.g., keystrokes, mouse movement) for active authentication [7,4,2]. Monrose et. al. proposed to use keystroke dynamics for active authentication [7]. They collected timing information (e.g., duration and latency) through training and found those keys and key combinations that are used often by the user and typed in a stable way. There are many challenges in using keystrokes for active authentication. First, users are using their devices on free text, thus finding those stable "features" is difficult. Second, the way user using their devices can be highly dynamic and easily affected by their mood, health situations, etc. Finally, training can be a burden to users.

From the review of related work, it is observed even though these active authentication researches are proposed to enhance the security of the system, the usage of the technique itself may introduce some security and privacy issues. The credentials used in the techniques (i.e., biometrics) may cause risks, and it may involve more user-privacy leakage.

3   Proposed Biometrics Based Active Authentication System

In this section, we first present the authentication model and identify potential attacks of such a model, and then propose a biometrics based active authentication system. Through our security analysis, the proposed system is secure against these attacks.

3.1   Attack Model

The distributed authentication model (Fig. 1) consists of personal mobile devices (e.g., PDA, smart phones) and an authentication server. The authentication server periodically receives biometric samples of the user who is using the device and authenticates if he/she is legitimate or not. Since the user biometrics will be collected and calculated continuously on user's devices and transmitted through the networks to be verified on the server side, the network attacks such as eavesdropping attack and replay attack need to be considered and addressed. Different from one-time authentication, the attacker can accumulate a larger amount of evidences towards user biometrics by using the common network attacks if a vulnerability in the network has been exploited.

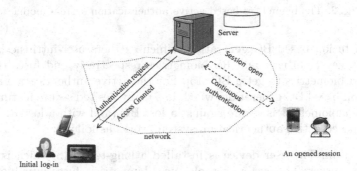

Fig. 1. The system model

We also consider the server database can be compromised such that attackers obtain user credentials and further try to derive user biometrics from compromised credentials. It is also possible that adversaries acquire physical access to the devices, such as a co-worker or a family member attempting to access the device, or a stranger who steals the device and tries to get the information on the device.

3.2   Biometrics Based Active Authentication Model

The proposed biometrics based active authentication system (Fig. 2) contains three stages: registration, verification and continuous authentication. Initially, the system samples the user biometrics and generates a BioCapsule (BC) which is stored in the system database. During log-in (verification), the user is sampled again and the derived BC is compared with the stored BC. If the log-in verification is successful, the session is open. And during the open session, the user biometrics is sampled periodically and the derived BCs are sent to the authentication server for continuous authentication.

In this system, we propose to use BC for authentication. The BC concept was first proposed in [14]. The BC in [14] was based on the difference of the user biometrics and that of a so-called reference subject (RS). After that, we

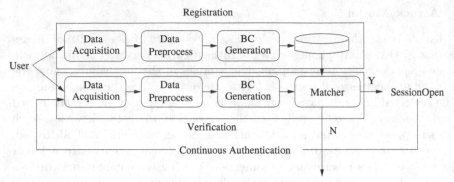

Fig. 2. The biometrics based active authentication system model

proposed a fusion based BC generation, which extracts user-intrinsic key and RS-intrinsic key from user and RS biometrics respectively and fuses the key-transformed biometrics to get a BC [15]. For the active authentication system, we use fusion based BC generation, which has many desired secure features such that the user biometrics is secure against a lost BC (and with a lost RS).

The proposed active authentication system works as follows:

- Registration: The user device is installed a long-term RS which is shared with the server. The system samples user biometrics, fuses user biometrics and the long-term RS biometrics. The derived long-time BC is stored in the server. By sharing a seed RS, the user device and the server implicitly agree upon a set of short-term RSs $RS_1, RS_2, \cdots, RS_n$. Generating the short-term RSs utilizes a one-way hash chain such that given RS_i it is not feasible to derive RS_{i+1}.
- Log-in (verification): The device samples user's biometrics, along with the long-term RS generates the long-term BC. The long-term BC is fused with a one-time short-term RS to generate a one-time BC, e.g., BC_1, which is sent to the server. The server uses the long-term BC it stores and the agreed short-term RS_1 to generate the one-time BC_1'. BC_1 and BC_1' are matched for log-in authentication.
- Continuous authentication: Periodically the device samples user's biometrics, generates the long-term BC and then a one-time BC_i through fusion of the long-term BC with a short-term RS_i. And the server matches BC_i against one-time BC_i' generated through fusion of the long-term BC stored in its database and the short-term RS_i. If the authentication fails, the device is locked out.

3.3   Security Analysis

The proposed active authentication system is secure against attacks raised in subsection 3.1, which is analyzed as follows.

- Security against eavesdropping: thanks to the secure feature of our BC mechanism that given BC the user biometrics is hard to obtain. From the one-time BC_i', attackers can not obtain long-term BC and user biometrics. Thus, the system will be secure against eavesdropping.
- Security against replay: for each authentication request, the authentication credential (i.e., one-time BC) is generated from long-term BC and a changing RS. Thus, the old one-time BCs are not matchable against new ones, thus replay attack is not feasible.
- Security against information accumulation: the one-time BCs are generated using various RSs, and it is like one-time key. Accumulation of one-time BCs will not help to recover long-term BC or user biometrics.
- Security against long-term BC lost: the long-term BC is generated by a fusion of the long-term RS and user biometrics, and the proposed fusion is secure such that in face of a compromised fusion result (i.e., long-term BC), user biometrics is not revealed [15].
- Security against device lost: from the device, attackers can obtain long-term RS and short-term RSs, but no user biometrics. Even attackers obtain BCs (e.g., long-term BC or one-time BCs), the fusion is designed to be secure against lost of both RSs and BCs, thus the user biometrics will not be compromised.

4   Experimental Results

We evaluate the performance of the system by testing the authentication accuracy of the one-time BC. We used the iris as a test case. Iris is considered to be the most reliable biometrics [5], and mobile devices equipped with particular cameras can capture iris images effectively. The experiment was simulated using the ICE database which is provided by National Institute of Standards and Technology for the Iris Challenge Evaluation (ICE) 2005 [1]. The ICE database

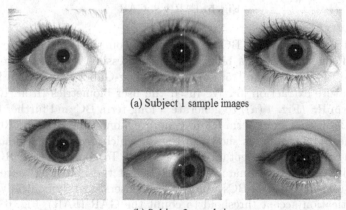

(a) Subject 1 sample images

(b) Subject 2 sample images

Fig. 3. ICE sample images

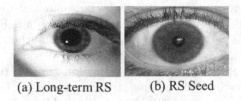

(a) Long-term RS   (b) RS Seed

Fig. 4. RS images

contains 2953 images in which 1,426 images from the right eye from 132 subjects, and 1,527 images from the left eye from 132 subjects (Fig. 3). We used the right set images for test. We chose one iris image from ICE as our long-term RS (Fig. 4 (a)) and one iris image from UBIRIS [10] as the RS seed (Fig. 4 (b)) to generate a set of short-term RSs.

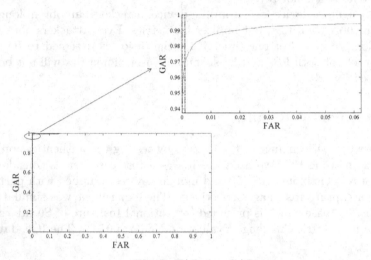

Fig. 5. FAR v.s. GAR

We constructed a one-time BC for each image from the ICE database. We used circle-based edge detection for biometrics preprocessing, and for BC generation, we used the BC proposed in [15] in which 1D Log-Gabor is used as a bandpass filter for feature extraction [6]. We fused the user biometrics (from ICE) with the long-term RS (Fig. 4 (a)) to generate a long-term BC and further fused the long-term BC with a short-term RS to generate a one-time BC. The ROC curve for one-time BC matching is shown in Fig. 5, which gives the false acceptance rate (FAR) v.s. genuine acceptance rate (GAR). To generate each ROC curve for a set of BCs, we cross-matched the BCs, got the matching scores of BCs from same user and that of BCs from different users, and dynamically changed the authentication accept threshold to count the GAR (FAR). Fig. 6 gives the inter-class and intra-class distribution. The EER (i.e., equal error rate when FAR equals to FRR) of the system is 0.011, and the authentication accuracy

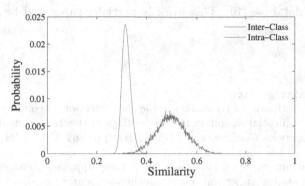

Fig. 6. Inter-class and intra-class distribution

is around 99%. These results indicate that the one-time BC mechanism is good for identity-bearing. Moreover, instead of using a same short-term RS (as the experiment setting), each one-time BC generation actually is using a changing (different) short-term RS, which will gives a higher BC accuracy and better system performance. Due to the identity bearing of the one-time BC and desired security features, the iris based BC can be used as identity credentials for secure authentication.

It is evident that due to biometric identity-bearing, the solid design criteria of BC, and the introduction of one-time BCs, the proposed biometrics based active authentication is practical, effective and secure.

5   Conclusion

In this research, we proposed a secure and practical biometrics based active authentication system. The proposed system considers potential attacks in distributed mobile devices - server authentication model and design effective mechanisms to defeat them. Our experimental results on the key component of the system (i.e., one-time BC) show the feasibility of the system. The proposed system has many desired features: 1) the system is secure and able to defeat various attacks; 2) the security of the user biometrics is guaranteed and the user privacy is preserved; 3) experimental results prove the feasibility of the proposed approach; 4) it supports "one-click sign on" across multiple systems by using a distinct RS on each system; and 5) the system does not require user training, and is both easy to use and transparent to end-users since they are not required to remember a password. We will continue to work on this research and extend our existing work. We will implement the proposed approach in a real system and test its performance (e.g., computational cost).

Acknowledgment. The authors would like to thank the National Institute of Standards and Technology (NIST) for the Iris Challenge Evaluation (ICE) 2005 [1] and Department of Computer Science at the University of Beira Interior for UBIRIS database [10]. This work is partially supported by IU CACR research grant.

References

1. http://iris.nist/gov/ice/
2. Ahmed, A.A.E., Traore, I.: Dynamic sample size detection in continuous authentication using sequential sampling. In: Proceedings of the 27th Annual Computer Security Applications Conference, ACSAC 2011, pp. 169–176. ACM, New York (2011)
3. Azzini, A., Marrara, S., Sassi, R., Scotti, F.: A fuzzy approach to multimodal biometric continuous authentication. Fuzzy Optimization and Decision Making 7(3), 243–256 (2008)
4. Brosso, I., La Neve, A., Bressan, G., Ruggiero, W.V.: A continuous authentication system based on user behavior analysis. In: International Conference on Availability, Reliability and Security, pp. 380–385 (2010)
5. Daugman, J.: How iris recognition works. IEEE Transactions on Circuits and Systems for Video Technology 14(1), 21–30 (2004)
6. Libor, M.: Recognition of human iris patterns for biometric identification. Technical report, University of Western Australia (2003)
7. Monrose, F., Rubin, A.D.: Keystroke dynamics as a biometric for authentication. Future Gener. Comput. Syst. 16(4), 351–359 (2000)
8. Niinuma, K., Jain, A.K.: Continuous user authentication using temporal information. In: Society of Photo-Optical Instrumentation Engineers (SPIE) Conference Series. Society of Photo-Optical Instrumentation Engineers (SPIE) Conference Series, vol. 7667 (April 2010)
9. Niinuma, K., Park, U., Jain, A.K.: Soft biometric traits for continuous user authentication. IEEE Transactions on Information Forensics and Security 5(4), 771–780 (2010)
10. Proença, H., Alexandre, L.A.: UBIRIS: A Noisy Iris Image Database. In: Roli, F., Vitulano, S. (eds.) ICIAP 2005. LNCS, vol. 3617, pp. 970–977. Springer, Heidelberg (2005)
11. Dimensional Research Report. The impact of mobile devices on information security: a survey of it professionals. Technical report (2012)
12. Sieger, H., Kirschnick, N., Moller, S.: User preferences for biometric authentication methods and graded security on mobile phones. In: Symposium on Usability, Privacy and Security, SOUPS (2010)
13. Sim, T., Zhang, S., Janakiraman, R., Kumar, S.: Continuous verification using multimodal biometrics. IEEE Transactions on Pattern Analysis and Machine Intelligence 29(4), 687–700 (2007)
14. Sui, Y., Zou, X., Du, E.: Biometrics-based authentication: A new approach. In: 2011 Proceedings of 20th International Conference on Computer Communications and Networks (ICCCN), pp. 1–6 (August 2011)
15. Sui, Y., Zou, X., Du, Y., Li, F.: Design and analysis of a highly user-friendly, secure, privacy-preserving, and revocable authentication method. IEEE Transactions on Computers (submitted, 2012)
16. Xiao, Q., Yang, X.D.: A facial presence monitoring system for information security. In: IEEE Workshop on Computational Intelligence in Biometrics: Theory, Algorithms, and Applications, CIB 2009, March 30-April 2, pp. 69–76 (2009)

Adaptive Power Controlled Routing
for Underwater Sensor Networks

Manal Al-Bzoor, Yibo Zhu, Jun Liu, Ammar Reda,
Jun-Hong Cui, and Sanguthevar Rajasekaran

Department of Computer Science and Engineering
University of Connecticut , Storrs, CT 06269-2155
{mbzoor,yiz09005,jul08003,reda,jcui,rajasek}@engr.uconn.edu

Abstract. Energy efficiency and mobility robustness are two of the
main performance metrics to be addressed when designing any routing protocol for underwater sensor network (UWSN). Energy efficiency
leads to a prolonged network life time, while mobility robustness ensures
high and stable delivery ratio. Most of the routing strategies designed
for UWSN require a full knowledge of the three dimensional location of
nodes. In this paper, we introduce an energy efficient routing schema
that does not require any location information, and achieves high packet
delivery ratio for both static and mobile scenarios in sparse or dense
networks. In our routing strategy, nodes assign themselves to concentric layers. A node to layer assignment is determined by signal power of
a received interest packet broadcast by sink nodes. Routing paths are
determined on the fly, and a forwarder is chosen based on its layer number and residual energy. Nodes are assumed to be able to adjust their
transmission power to a finite set of values. Low power level is most
likely selected by nodes when the network is dense, whereas a higher
power level is selected when the network is sparse or when nodes at layers closer to the sink has more residual energy. Simulation results shows
that our routing protocol achieves a high delivery ratio and a low energy
consumption while reducing the delay when compared with other routing
strategies for both sparse and dense networks.

1 Introduction

Underwater Sensor Networks (UWSN) can be used for monitoring, navigation,
surveillance and tracking applications in various environmental, industrial and
military domains [1,2]. Recent years has witnessed a tremendous increase of
interest in such applications. This motivates more research for an efficient deployment strategies and protocol stack design of UWSN. In this paper we are
concerned with the design of routing protocols. However, the intrinsic condition
of underwater environment raises many challenges for the design of an efficient
and reliable routing protocol.

Acoustic communication technology is used for communication at the physical layer of UWSN. However, acoustic waves suffer from limited bandwidth,

X. Wang et al. (Eds.): WASA 2012, LNCS 7405, pp. 549–560, 2012.
© Springer-Verlag Berlin Heidelberg 2012

high attenuation, and long propagation delays [3]. Similar to terrestrial sensor nodes, underwater sensor nodes are battery operated and hence energy efficiency poses another challenging design factor. Furthermore, UWSN nodes suffer from voluntary and involuntary movement that causes an unpredictable mobility in the network. This further raises the challenges to an efficient data transfer from source nodes to sink nodes in underwater environment. To cater for those challenges, we propose a multihop routing protocol to reduce power consumption and ensure a high delivery ratio. In Our routing routing strategy, nodes needs only to know to which layer they belong according to the power level of an interest packet sent by sink nodes. We use adaptive power control to send at high power level to ensure connectivity between nodes when the nodes gets sparse due to mobility and at low power level when the network is dense and static. We use concentric layering of nodes where forwarders are selected from layers closer to sink. Furthermore, using the concentric layering ensures the packets are flying towards the sink nodes using shortest end to end paths.

By using adaptive power control over concentric layered network architecture, our work achieves a good balance among multiple performance metrics. Our routing protocol switches between shorter links to reduce energy consumption and longer links to maintain a high delivery ratio for sparse or dense network in a static or mobile mode.

This paper is organized as follows. In section 2, we summarize the related work. In section 3, we describe our routing technique, review the underwater acoustic channel and analyze energy and delay performance metrics. In section 4, we present and discuss the simulation results. Finally in section 5, we conclude this work and discuss future work.

2   Related Works

A large number of routing techniques have been proposed for terrestrial ad hoc networks. However, due to the characteristics of underwater environment, most of these techniques are not suitable for UWSN [4]. Only few distinctive routing algorithms were designed specifically for underwater networks, most of which are categorized under geographic routing protocols [5,6].

Vector Based Forwarding (VBF) [7] is a trajectory based routing protocol for UWSN. VBF forms a virtual pipe between a source and a destination. The pipe width and the density of nodes in the pipe determine the successful delivery of data. Potential forwarders hold the packet based on a desirableness factor. This factor is large for a forwarder closer to the vector formed by source to destination pair. Unlike our proposed schema, VBF assumes that nodes have full knowledge of their locations and nodes have fixed transmission range.

Focused Beam Forwarding (FBR) [8] assumes each node is capable of knowing its three dimensional location, senders has full knowledge of the sink location and is capable of sending at a finite set of power levels. In FBR, a sender sends a route request packet with the first lowest power level and waits for route reply packet from all potential nodes within a cone of a specified angel. If no forwarder replies, the sender resends at higher power level. If no node replies within maximum power level, the sender starts shifting its cone left and right of the main cone. Like FBR we use multiple power levels to establish routes dynamically. In addition to assuming full dimensional location information, which itself a challenge left to be solved, FBR assumes sink location is fixed which reduces the flexibility of the network. FBR also does not specify the criteria for selecting the forwarder node which might cause unbalanced energy consumption.

In Depth Based Routing (DBR) [6] only depth information is required. Sender nodes broadcast a message with header information about its depth relative to the sink node. A receiving node forwards the message if its depth is less than the sender's depth. The process is repeated until data packet reaches one of the sink nodes. Depth threshold is the major design parameter that affects the performance of DBR drastically. DBR has only a greedy mode, which alone is not able to achieve high delivery ratio in sparse areas. DBR has a good delivery ratio in dense networks, but forwarding the data packets in a broadcast fashion can decrease the performance of the network by increasing energy consumption and prolonging end to end delay due to retransmission.

Path Unaware Layered Routing Protocol (PULRP) [9] uses a layering architecture that is formed around the sink. Sink node builds the first layer using a probing energy of a certain threshold. One node in each layer is selected to send a probing energy to form the next layer. The way the layers are assumed to be formed is not clear and nothing is being said about how a node is selected to send the probing energy. Routing is then determined in a greedy fashion to choose nodes from next layers. Our routing differs from PULRP by the approach we use to assign nodes to layers, selecting the forwarding nodes, adaptively controlling power level for packet transmission, and supporting multisink architecture.

3   Adaptive Power Controlled Routing Protocol (APCR)

In this section we start by describing the protocol design, and then we show a mathematical representation of the major design metrics that affects the protocol operation.

3.1   Protocol Design

We assume Q nodes are deployed randomly on a three dimensional topology of volume V. Nodes can tune their power level $p_1, p_2, ..p_N$ per packet transmission, where N is the number of power levels used. Our routing strategy consists of two phases, layer assignment phase and data transmission phase. During layer assignment phase, nodes are assigned to M layers each of width l. Packet forwarding or delivery is determined per packet in the transmission phase.

Layer Assignment Phase: Surface sinks are equipped with acoustic modem of higher power capabilities than underwater sensor nodes and could reach distances up to few kilometers in range. For example using a WHOI Modem, a

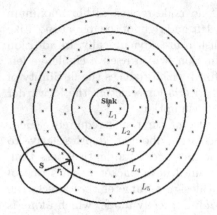
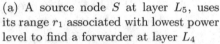

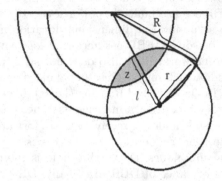

(a) A source node S at layer L_5, uses its range r_1 associated with lowest power level to find a forwarder at layer L_4

(b) Intersection between two spheres of radius R and r respectively, volume of intersection is shown by the shaded area

Fig. 1. Layering Architecture and Volume of Intersection

distance of up to 5 kilometers can be reached under highest power level [10]. All nodes are initially assigned a default layer id equal to maximum layer id. If we set number of layers to 6, then all nodes are assigned to layer id L_6 initially. After setting the network, the layer assignment phase starts by surface sink sending an interest packet at its lowest power level. Each interest packet carries a layer id number based on the power level used. For example, and interest packet sent at minimum power level, will have a layer Id of L_1. Nodes receiving the interest packet will compare their current layer id by the layer id carried by the interest packet and will set their layer id to the lower of the two. Repeatedly, surface sinks send with the next power level, each time incrementing the layer id number in the interest packet. Accordingly, nodes compare the layer id in the received packet by their assigned id and choose the least of them. The layering phase is repeated at spaced intervals depending on the degree of mobility and packet delivery ratio. Fig. 1a shows the layering architecture that is formed in our routing strategy with 5 layers that corresponds to the power level of sink node's interest packets.

Communication Phase: In the layer assignment phase, nodes assign themselves to layers according to signal power of an interest packet received from a sink node. When the layers are first formed all nodes will set their transmission power to the highest level. When a node wants to send data to the sink, it will send a forwarder discovery packet. Neighbors receiving this packet and who are at layers closer to the sink will reply with (layer id, residual energy, node id). Sender will then reduce its transmission power to the range that covers the closest neighbor replied. Fig. 1a shows a source node S, using its lowest range, tries to find a forwarder in the intersection of the sphere formed by its range radius r_1 and the sphere formed by the radius of layer L_4.

During network operation, nodes send at the assigned minimum transmission power. Nodes keep track of their forwarded packets. Acknowledgment is being sent when a data packet is received by a forwarder or by sink nodes. The acknowledgment packet carries information about the forwarder layer id and its residual energy. If the sender does not get acknowledgment, or if the residual energy of the forwarder is low, then the sender tries to find a forwarder using the next power level. To summarize, nodes adaptively increase or decrease their transmission power according to information received during packet transmission, if no neighbor is found, power is increased, if forwarders are found at multiple layers then the power is decreased to cover only the layer closest to the sender's layer. For maximizing the delivery ratio in the mobile case scenario, a forwarder discovery message is sent for each packet transmission that increases the delay for each packet by the round trip time of the control packet. However, we will show in section 4 this does not pose a considerable delay increase. To overcome the possible interference, we reduce number of exchanged control packets by selectively sending forwarder discovery message only when acknowledgments are not received.

3.2 Power Level, Energy Consumption and End to End Delays in APCR

Acoustic Power and Electrical Power: The electrical power $P_t(l)$ in watt of an acoustic modem depends solely on the transducer efficiency and the power level $P(l)$ covering a distance l. The transducer is responsible for converting electrical power to acoustic power. Since no transducer is 100% efficient, the transducer efficiency η considerably affect the generated acoustic power. The relationship between electrical power and acoustic power needed to cover a distance l is defined by

$$10log(\eta P_t(l)) = 170.8 - 10logP(l) + D_I . \tag{1}$$

Where 170.8 is a conversion factor between electric power and power level and D_I is the directivity index of the antenna. The power level is estimated using the signal level $S(l)$ over the frequency bandwidth $B_3(l)$ such that $P(l) = \int_{B_3(l)} S(l)$. In our work we adopted the design of acoustic physical layer as in [3] for calculating signal level $S(l)$, attenuation $A(l, f)$ and noise $N(f)$. For a signal to noise ratio required to be greater than a specified threshold SNR_0 at the receiver side with a narrow-band bandwidth $B_3(l)$, the power level is approximated by

$$P(l) \approx SNR_0 B_3(l) \frac{N(f)}{A^{-1}(l, f)} . \tag{2}$$

It can be clearly noted that, power is decreased by decreasing the distances, so we conclude that using shorter distances would surely reduce the power level needed, although the propagation delay will be slightly longer.

Energy Consumption and Path Delays: Assuming a transmission rate B, a data packet length L, speed of sound c and a transmission range r_i, . The energy consumed and the delay per hop for each data packet is approximated as in [11].

$$E_{hopD}(r_i) = \frac{(P_r + P_t(r_i))L}{B}, \quad \Delta_{hopD}(r_i) = \frac{L}{B} + \frac{r_i}{c}. \tag{3}$$

Delay and energy are strictly related to actual distance traveled by the acoustic signal from sender to a receiver. However we are interested in finding an approximation of these values and hence we are assuming that receivers are located at the maximum distance covered by each range r_i. In addition to the data packet in APCR, a sender may send a forwarder discovery packet. A number of neighbors $n(r_i)$ covered by range r_i replies back for the sender to establish its potential forwarder list. Assuming the exchanged control packet length is L_c, the delay and energy consumed is approximated by

$$E_{hopC}(r_i) = \frac{2\,n(r_i)L_cP_r + (1 + n(r_i))L_cP_t(r_i)}{B}, \quad \Delta_{hopC}(r_i) = 2(\frac{L_c}{B} + \frac{r_i}{c}). \tag{4}$$

Forwarder discovery messages are sent depending on the network scenario. For a static network this is done once before sending the first data packet and later when the forwarders in the current forwarder list consume their energy. For a highly mobile network, this is done more frequently when acknowledgments are not received. We add a condition c_h for hop h such that

$$c_h = \begin{cases} 1 & , \ Discovery\ packet\ sent\ for\ hop\ h \\ 0 & , \ Otherwise \end{cases}. \tag{5}$$

The per hop h total delay and total energy consumed using range r_i are

$$E_h = E_{hopD}(r_i) + c_h\,E_{hopC}(r_i), \quad \Delta_h = \Delta(r_i) + c_h\,\Delta_{hopC}(r_i). \tag{6}$$

For k number of hops, the total energy consumed per data packet and the total per path delay are

$$E_{path} = \sum_{h=1}^{k} E_h, \quad \Delta_{path} = \sum_{hop=1}^{k} \Delta_h. \tag{7}$$

In APCR number of hops k depends on number of layers M, transmission range r_i, and Layer Width l.

Case 1. $c_h = 0$, When the network is static, a forwarder discovery message is not needed for each data packet. We assume the sender is located at the border of the furthest layer so the maximum number of hops is $k \approx \frac{Ml}{r_1}$. If each sender and forwarder on the path from source to sink find a potential forwarder at its lowest transmission power and its range $r_1$then the total energy consumed and the end to end delay are

$$E_{path} = \frac{Ml}{r_1} E_{hopD}(r_1), \quad \Delta_{path} = \frac{Ml}{r_1} \Delta_{hopD}(r_1). \tag{8}$$

If nodes along the forwarding path used their maximum range Nr_1, then number of hops is $k \approx \frac{Ml}{Nr_0}$, the per hop range is $r_i = Nr_1$ for all hops and the per path end to end delay and energy are

$$E_{path} = \frac{Ml}{Nr_1} E_{hopD}(Nr_1), \quad \Delta_{path} = k = \frac{Ml}{Nr_1} \Delta_{hopD}(r_1). \tag{9}$$

Case 2. $c_h = 1$, When the network is highly dynamic, sender and forwarders will send forwarder discovery packet for each data packet. If each finds forwarder at lowest power level with a corresponding ranger_1 then

$$E_{path} = \frac{Ml}{r_1}(E_{hopD}(r_1) + E_{hopC}(r_1)), \quad \Delta_{path} = \frac{Ml}{r_1}(\Delta_{hopD}(r_1) + \Delta_{hopC}(r_1)). \tag{10}$$

If a sender finds next hop forwarder at its maximum transmission power, then number of hops is $k \approx \frac{Ml}{Nr_1}$ but number of discovery packets and replies will be proportional to number of power levels N such that

$$E_{path} = \frac{Ml}{Nr_1}(E_{hopD}(Nr_1) + \sum_{j=1}^{N} E_{hopC}(j\,r_1)). \tag{11}$$

$$\Delta_{path} = \frac{Ml}{Nr_1}(\Delta_{hopD}(Nr_1) + \sum_{j=1}^{N} \Delta_{hopC}(j\,r_1)). \tag{12}$$

To evaluate equations 8,9,10,11 and 12, we need to find number of neighboring nodes involved in the exchange of discovery packet for each power range used.

Relationship between Range and Number of Forwarding Nodes: In APCR, Q nodes are uniformly distributed in the network of volume V, node density ρ is defined as $\rho = \frac{Q}{V}$. We need to find an approximate value of possible forwarding nodes $n(r_i)$ for each node using power range level r_i. For a node at layer i, $n(r_i)$ represents number of nodes residing in volume of intersection v_i between the node range r_i and the layer $i-1$. So that $n(r_i) = \rho v_i$. The normalized intersection volume v can be obtained by solving the sphere-sphere Intersection equation. To find the volume of intersection between two spheres of radius r and R respectively and the distance between the two spheres centers is d, we use equation 13 [12].

$$v = \frac{\pi}{12d}(r + R - d)^2(d^2 + 2dr - 3r^2 + 2dR + 6rR - 3R^2). \tag{13}$$

To find the volume occupied by the intersection of the communication spheres of a node at layer i a layer $i-1$, we set the radius of layer $i-1$ as $R = (i-1)l$, where l is the layer width as defined earlier. Let's assume the sender is at the outer border of its layer i then the distance between the node and the sink is $d = R = i\,l$. In order for a sender to find a potential forwarder at lower layers, the minimum communication range should be selected so that it exceeds the layer width l by a distance z, so we set $r = l + z$. Increasing z will result in an increase of the volume of intersection represented by shaded area in Fig. 1b. This will increase the probability of finding forwarder nodes at the given transmission range r. Applying these parameters in equation 13 and reducing we get

$$v_{(i,l,z)} = \pi z^2 \left(\left(1 - \frac{1}{i} \right) l + \left(\frac{2}{3} - \frac{1}{i} \right) z - \frac{z^2}{4 i\, l} \right). \tag{14}$$

The probability of finding a neighbor in the volume of intersection v assuming a uniform distribution of nodes is $P_{(n=1)} = 1 - e^{-\rho v_{(i,l,z)}}$. We assume a low node density ρ, hence for a small z associated with lowest power level, the probability of finding one neighbor in the intersection area is very small, while this value is much higher when we use the maximum range. We will leave the investigation for the effect of varying z for a future work. For a network with node density of 0.1×10^{-6} per cubic meter, a sender at $1200m$ away from sink node, number of layers $M = 6$, layer width $l = 200$, number of ranges $N = 3$ and minimum range $r_1 = 250m$. The probability of finding a neighbor for r_1 is small, so we assume that only one neighbor is present at the minimum range. For ranges 500 and 750 the probability is almost 1 and we approximate number of neighbors as $n(r_i) = \rho v_{(i,l,z)}$, evaluated to 8 nodes for $r_2 = 500$ and 48 nodes for $r_3 = 750$. For calculating power consumption for each power level used, we fixed the frequency at $14\,kHz$, the corresponding bandwidth at $17.72\,kHz$, the target signal to noise ratio SNR_0 at $20dB$, and the attenuation unit normalizing factor A_0 at $30dB$. We used $90mWatt$ for P_r regardless of the distance, $P_t(250)$ is $1.3watt$, $P_t(500)$ is $2.15watt$ and $P_t(750)$ is $4.41watt$. The data packet size is set to $64byte$ and the control packet is set to $4bytes$ with a transmission rate of $10kbps$. Approximates of per path end to end delay in seconds (s) and energy consumption in joule (j) are found by applying the above values in equations 8,9,10,11 and 12. For $c = 0$;$Epath(250) = 0.37\,j$, $Epath(750) = 0.46\,j$, $\Delta_{path}(250) = 1.09\,s$, and $\Delta_{path}(750) = 1.11\,s$. For $c = 1$;$Epath(250) = 0.40\,j$, $Epath(750) = 2.05\,j$,$\Delta_{path}(250) = 2.80\,s$, and $\Delta_{path}(750) = 5.13\,s$. Exchanging control packets to find a forwarder for each packet transmission $c = 1$ is favorable for maintaining high delivery ratio. However our analytical results show the cost of using per packet forwarder discovery on energy and delays, therefore we limit the frequency of forwarder discovery packets to cater to the network robustness and hence sacrifice a slight reduction in delivery ratio as will be shown next.

4   Performance Evaluations

To evaluate our work, we conducted extensive simulations of the proposed routing strategy. We used Aqua-Sim, an ns2 based simulator for underwater sensor networks [13]. We modified the design of Aqua-Sim so that we can set per packet transmission power and range.

4.1   Simulation Settings

In all simulation scenarios, nodes are uniformly distributed in a $1km \times 1km \times 1km$ three dimensional topology. Surface sinks are deployed at the topology surface. We allow each node to set its transmission power to cover ranges $250m$, $500m$, and $750m$ respectively. The distance from the furthest node to the sink node at the center of the surface area is 1.224 km using Pythagorean Theorem, hence we set number of layers to be 6 layers. For DBR we fixed the transmission range at 250m. For mobile scenario, we made all the nodes move randomly in a random way point model with speed of 1-4 m/s. We used underwater broadcast MAC as the underlying MAC protocol. We adopted the physical layer parameters used in [14], we fixed the frequency at $14\,kHz$, the corresponding BW at $17.72\,kHz$, the target signal to noise ratio SNR_0 at $20dB$, and the attenuation unit normalizing factor A_0 at $30dB$. We measured the average end to end delay of all packets generated throughout the whole simulation time. Total energy consumption is the sum of all energy dissipated by all nodes. Per bit energy consumption is defined by total energy consumed over the total number of delivered data bits. Delivery ratio is calculated as total number of packets submitted successfully to sink node over total number of packets generated by all source nodes.

4.2   DBR vs. APCR

We compared our routing strategy with DBR, a multihop routing protocol that was proved to outperform VBF routing and was tested for static, mobile and multisink scenarios. We monitored the three performance metrics, energy consumption, end to end delay and delivery ratio by varying number of nodes from 20 to 400. In Fig. 2a, we measured the energy as per successful delivered bit. DBR nodes forward multiple copies of the same data packet and this consumes more energy than APCR which only forwards one copy of the data packet while keeping the size and count of the control packets small. Fig. 2b shows the average end to end delay. DBR has a higher delay because of the hold off time used to limit number of forwarded copies. In addition, forwarding multiple copies of a data packet in a dense network may result in an interference and triggers retransmission which accounts for larger delays. DBR has a very low delivery ratio when the network is sparse that falls below 35% when number of nodes is less than 100. DBR achieves a good delivery ratio above 65% for number of nodes above 200 and around 80% for a highly dense network of more than 400 nodes. On the other hand, results show that APCR has a high and stable delivery ratio above 85% for both dense and sparse networks. Delivery ratio can be further increased by limiting number of control packets exchanged and limit the interference at the MAC layer.

4.3   Mobility Handling

We tested our protocol for both static and mobile cases. Fig. 3a shows that energy consumption are almost the same for static and mobile case when number

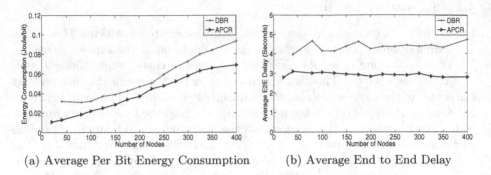

(a) Average Per Bit Energy Consumption   (b) Average End to End Delay

Fig. 2. Adaptive Power Controlled Routing vs. Depth Based Routing

of nodes is less than 150 and the total consumed energy starts to increase when the network becomes more dense. For sparse network, APCR will need to send at higher power levels to maintain connectivity and maximize delivery ratio. When the network becomes more dense, APCR favors shorter links which in turns reduces the per path energy consumption while for mobile case, nodes are moving and control packets are sent more frequently to discover neighbors which consumes more energy. Average end to end delay is shown in Fig. 3b. Referring to the end to end delay equations shown in section 3, one can conclude that delay is reduced using longer links. In APCR mobile scenario, nodes tend to increase their transmission power to guarantee a higher delivery ration and hence the delay is less than that of static case. The delivery ratio and other performance metrics are highly affected by the underlying MAC protocol and hence for the used broadcast MAC protocol delivery ratio is usually less than 1. Delivery ratio is reduced by a fraction of around 25% for mobile case and this is an expected but still accepted loss due to nodes mobility.

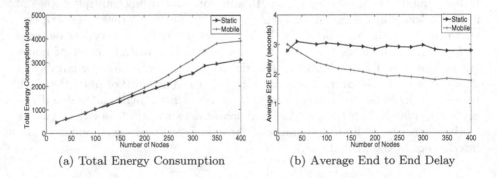

(a) Total Energy Consumption   (b) Average End to End Delay

Fig. 3. Adaptive Power Controlled Routing, Static Topology vs. Mobile Topology

4.4   Multiple Sink Architecture

Not only APCR supports sparse and dense networks, but also supports multiple sink architecture. Here we tested the performance of our protocol using one sink and compared that with a four sink scenario. Total energy consumption was reduced slightly as shown in Fig. 4a. Delivery ratio was maintained above 0.82 for both cases. The major enhancement over one sink architecture is in average end to end delay as shown in Fig. 4b. Using multiple sink architecture can reduce the delay by a factor of almost 0.25%. Delay reduction is a result of distance reduction between source nodes and sink nodes.

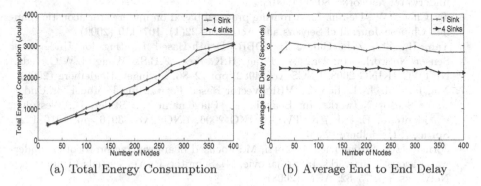

(a) Total Energy Consumption   (b) Average End to End Delay

Fig. 4. APCR: One sink and 4 Sinks, a. End to End Delay and b. Delivery ratio

5   Conclusions and Future Work

In this paper, we proposed an adaptive power controlled routing (APCR) protocol that scales with network size and handles mobility with a slight reduction in performance. Unlike other geographical routing protocols, APCR require no location information. APCR uses hierarchical layering of nodes based on the power level of interest packets sent by sink nodes. Nodes in APCR are assumed to be able to adjust per packet transmission power to maintain high delivery ratio, reduce energy and lower end to end delay for various network conditions. The concentric layering architecture in APCR ensures the directivity of data toward the sink nodes. Furthermore, APCR works well with multiple sink UWSN architecture, maintains fixed delivery ratio while noticeably enhancing end to end delay and slightly reducing total energy expenditure. Extensive simulation results show that APCR has a higher delivery ratio, lower delay and lower energy expenditure when compared to DBR. Furthermore, results show that mobility is well handled in APCR, and the reduction in performance due to mobility affects only the delivery ratio with a reasonable measure.

To further support our protocol, a future work will discuss the impact of various underlying MAC protocols on the performance of APCR. Furthermore, we will conduct further investigation on the effect of protocol parameters specifically the step size between the used power levels.

References

1. Cui, J.H., Kong, J., Gerla, M., Zhou, S.: The challenges of building scalable mobile underwater wireless sensor networks for aquatic applications. IEEE Network 20(3), 12–18 (2006)
2. Akyildiz, I.F., Pompili, D., Melodia, T.: Challenges for efficient communication in underwater acoustic sensor networks 1(2), 3–8 (2004)
3. Lucani, D.E., Stojanovic, M., Médard, M.: On the relationship between transmission power and capacity of an underwater acoustic communication channel. CoRR, abs/0801.0426 (2008)
4. Harris III, A.F., Zorzi, M.: On the design of energy-efficient routing protocols in underwater networks, 80–90 (2007)
5. Jin-Cheng, W., De-Shi, L.: A routing protocol based on underwater acoustic channel. Chinese Journal of Sensors and Actuators 22(1), 107–110 (2009)
6. Yan, H., Shi, Z.J., Cui, J.-H.: DBR: Depth-Based Routing for Underwater Sensor Networks. In: Das, A., Pung, H.K., Lee, F.B.S., Wong, L.W.C. (eds.) NETWORKING 2008. LNCS, vol. 4982, pp. 72–86. Springer, Heidelberg (2008)
7. Xie, P., Cui, J.-H., Lao, L.: VBF: Vector-Based Forwarding Protocol for Underwater Sensor Networks. In: Boavida, F., Plagemann, T., Stiller, B., Westphal, C., Monteiro, E. (eds.) NETWORKING 2006. LNCS, vol. 3976, pp. 1216–1221. Springer, Heidelberg (2006)
8. Jornet, J.M., Stojanovic, M., Zorzi, M.: Focused beam routing protocol for underwater acoustic networks. In: Stojanovic, M., Schniter, P., Ye, W. (eds.) Underwater Networks, pp. 75–82. ACM (2008)
9. Gopi, S., Kannan, G., Chander, D., Desai, U.B., Merchant, S.N.: Pulrp: Path unaware layered routing protocol for underwater sensor networks, pp. 3141–3145 (2008)
10. Freitag, L., Grund, M., Singh, S., Partan, J., Koski, P., Ball, K.: The whoi micromodem: an acoustic communications and navigation system for multiple platforms. In: OCEANS, 2005. Proceedings of MTS/IEEE, vol. 2, pp. 1086–1092 (2005)
11. Zorzi, M., Casari, P., Baldo, N., Harris III, A.F.: Energy-efficient routing schemes for underwater acoustic networks. IEEE Journal on Selected Areas in Communications 26(9), 1754–1766 (2008)
12. Kern, W.F., Bland, J.R.: Solid Mensuration with Proofs, 2nd edn. Wiley, New York (1948)
13. Xie, P., Zhou, Z., Peng, Z., Yan, H., Hu, T., Cui, J.-H., Shi, Z., Fei, Y., Zhou, S.: Aqua-sim: An ns-2 based simulator for underwater sensor networks. In: OCEANS 2009, MTS/IEEE Biloxi - Marine Technology for Our Future: Global and Local Challenges, pp. 1–7 (October 2009)
14. Jornet, J.M., Stojanovic, M., Zorzi, M.: On joint frequency and power allocation in a cross-layer protocol for underwater acoustic networks. IEEE Journal of Oceanic Engineering 35(4), 936–947 (2010)

Aqua-OS: An Operating System
for Underwater Acoustic Networks

Haining Mo, Son Le, Zheng Peng, Zhijie Shi, and Jun-Hong Cui

Department of Computer Science and Engineering, University of Connecticut,
Storrs, CT, USA, 06269
{haining.mo,sonle,zhengpeng,zshi,jcui}@engr.uconn.edu

Abstract. Underwater acoustic networks have recently emerged as a promising approach for oceanic applications such as exploration and surveillance. This new type of networks differs from terrestrial wireless sensor networks in that the network nodes are powerful and well equipped with many resources for diverse applications in challenging environments. Existing operating systems for terrestrial wireless sensor networks may not be able to fully utilize the resources available in underwater networks or work efficiently in the underwater environment with diverse application requirements. This calls for a new operating system design for underwater acoustic networks. Motivated by this, we propose a plan to implement an operating system for underwater acoustic networks: Aqua-OS. Aqua-OS is going to be robust, highly customizable and energy efficient to tackle the harsh underwater environment, fully utilize the hardware resources and meet the diverse application requirements.

Keywords: Underwater networks, Operating systems.

1   Introduction

As a water planet, the vast yet unexplored water resources on the earth have fascinated human being for thousands of years. In recent years, there has been a rapidly growing interest in monitoring and exploring the aqueous environments. Underwater acoustic networks (UANs), as an emerging technology, have attracted more and more researchers and become a promising solution for a large amount of applications in the underwater environment . UANs can be employed to monitor the underwater environment, which is crucial for preventing pollution and detecting climate change. It provides a method to allow network nodes, gateways and surface buoys to communicate with each other and therefore makes the data transmission more efficient and effective. Other applications of UANs include undersea exploration and tactical surveillance like detecting and classifying submarine, underwater vehicles and divers. Compared with the traditional technologies, UANs are more flexible, real-time, low cost and accurate.

UAN is a completely new type of network with unique characteristics. First, the harsh underwater environment makes communications in UANs very challenging. Since acoustic channel instead of radio is employed as the medium for signal transmission in the water, the data propagation delay is extremely long for UANs due

X. Wang et al. (Eds.): WASA 2012, LNCS 7405, pp. 561–573, 2012.

to the low propagation speed of the acoustic signals (1500m/s). The absorption, multipath and fading of the acoustic channels lead to a very limited bandwidth in UANs. Also the UAN nodes are highly dynamic due to the current and fish movement leading to unstable communication links and intermittent connectivity. All these factors make UAN communications very difficult. Second, different from terrestrial wireless sensor network nodes, UAN nodes are much more powerful in terms of processing and computation capability and equipped with more resources and devices. But meanwhile, UAN nodes still have limited power supply and therefore low power design is always a concern for UANs. Third, UAN applications are highly diverse and may involve a lot of advanced algorithms imposing intensive computation and high energy consumption.

As a result, fundamental changes have to be made and significant efforts need to be put into every layer of the UANs, including the hardware, the operating system, the protocols and the application software. Among these layers, the operating system is indispensable and of critical importance for UANs. It serves as the interface between the hardware and the software and bridges the specific underwater applications with the physical system of the UAN nodes. It is also responsible for the management of shared resources including processor time and memory as well as for the coordination and scheduling of multiple tasks. Despite its importance, there has been little work on the operating systems for UANs. In fact, the aforementioned characteristics call for a shift in the design philosophy for the operating systems of UANs. An OS for UANs needs to work reliably to survive the challenging underwater environments. It also has to fully utilize the resources in UAN nodes and meanwhile achieve energy efficiency to save the limited power. Moreover, a UAN OS needs to fit the computation intensive nature and the diverse requirements of the UAN applications.

In this paper, we are going to investigate the operating systems for UANs and propose a plan to design and implement a dedicated operating system for UANs: Aqua-OS. Aqua-OS is different from other operating systems in three aspects. It is going to take robustness as the top priority given the harsh underwater environment which makes both the hardware and software prone to failures. Aqua-OS is also going to be highly customizable to meet the diverse requirements in UAN applications. An OS Components Toolbox and an optimizer are going to be provided to tailor Aqua-OS in a way optimally fitting the specific application requirements and user preferences. Further, Aqua-OS will take energy efficiency into account since power consumption is always a big issue in UANs where all the devices are usually equipped with limited power supplies.

The rest of the paper is organized as follows. In Section II, we study some related works. In Section III, we discuss the motivation and goal of Aqua-OS. A detailed description on the features Aqua-OS is going to provide is presented in Section IV and we conclude the paper in Section V.

2   Related Works

Operating System has always been a subject attracting tremendous attention from researchers. For OSes running on servers, desktops and laptops, Windows and Linux have been in the dominant position for a long time. With the development of the micro-controllers and micro-processors, OSes for embedded systems including Embedded

Linux, Windows CE and μC/OS-II have emerged as a big success over the last several decades. For Terrestrial Wireless Sensor Networks (TWSNs), it has become a hot research topic and a couple of OSes have been implemented to serve the TWSN nodes.

MANTIS OS is an embedded multithread operating system for wireless sensor platforms. MANTIS achieves a very small RAM footprint, which is less than 500 bytes. It also allows users to reprogram the entire operating system, a single thread or a set of variants within a thread on the fly. Besides, it reduces the power consumption of the system by switching to sleep mode when all the active threads have called the sleep function. MANTIS is designed for the TWSNs. It does not take into consideration the special characteristics of the underwater environment and the diverse requirements of the underwater applications and therefore cannot be directly applied to UANs.

TinyOS is specifically designed for TWSNs, which is characterized by limited resources, low power supply and event-centric applications. It employs an event-driven scheduling mechanism. TinyOS also allows users to build applications from a large number of very fine-grained components. It takes into account the low power design by allowing a subsystem to go to an idle state. However, TinyOS is designed for sensor nodes with quite limited processing capability and resources and therefore does not fit the UAN nodes. In addition, the event-driven scheduling method of TinyOS is not suitable for underwater applications.

eCos, which is an embedded operating system, provides a configuration system for application software to allow more customizability and configurability. This configuration system provides application programmers with a way to impose their functionality and implementation requirements on the run-time components of eCos. In another word, eCos allows the application programmers to tailor the operating system to fit their specific requirements and preferences. This configuration system also allows developers to extend the functionality of eCos by adding new run-time components. Considering the very diverse application requirements in UANs, the configuration system in eCos could be adopted by the UAN OSes to enhance their flexibility and configurability.

There exist other embedded operating systems. Contiki is an OS for networked embedded systems or wireless sensor networks. It supports IP communication, both IPV4 and IPV6, by providing its own uIP stack. It also provides a software-based power profiling scheme to track the power consumption of each sensor node. μC/OS-II is an embedded OS which provides a preemptive real-time multitask kernel for micro-processors. It achieves a very small memory footprint and supports all types of micro-processors from 8 bit to 64 bit. However, none of these OSes is designed for applications in UANs. To better serve the applications in UANs, a dedicated operating system which takes into consideration the special characteristics of the UAN applications is highly desired.

3 Motivation and Goal

3.1 Examining Existing Operating Systems

There have been a lot of researches on operating systems for servers, desktop computers, laptops and embedded systems. Since a UAN node is typically considered as an embedded system, we focus on investigating the embedded operating systems.

Generally speaking, there are two types of embedded operating systems. Some operating systems are tailored for low-end micro-controllers or micro-processors. They usually have limited capability for multi-task scheduling and coordination. Instead of providing dynamic memory allocation, these operating systems usually only support static memory management. One example falling into this category is TinyOS. TinyOS is dedicated for TWSN nodes which are equipped with micro-controllers with quite limited processing power. To fit the limited processing capability and power supply of the sensor network nodes, TinyOS employs a non-preemptive event-driven scheduling method as well as a static memory management scheme. Other operating systems like embedded Linux are targeted for powerful micro-processors. These operating systems can support some advanced features including multi-task scheduling and virtual memory management. An example is the Autonomous Underwater Vehicles (AUVs) which are usually equipped with very powerful multi-task processors. Therefore embedded Linux or even Windows can be installed on AUVs to fulfill multiple tasks. Due to the special characteristics of the UANs, both of these two types of operating systems are not suitable for underwater applications, as will be discussed in details below.

3.2   Why Not TinyOS

The operating systems for low-end processors are not suitable for UANs which provide much more powerful hardware resources. Also different from TWSNs, applications in UANs are more diverse and complicated ranging from data acquisition to data processing and compression. Some applications may even involve complex algorithms which are both time and energy consuming. In this context, low-end hardware platforms and OSes like TinyOS are not good fits for UANs due to the lack of strong computation capability and the energy inefficiency. To validate this conclusion, we tested the performance of UAN applications running on low-end hardware platforms and OSes as well as on more powerful hardware platforms and the corresponding OSes. Given the computation intensive nature of the UAN applications, we employ Fast Fourier Transform (FFT) as the representative for UAN applications due to its computation complexity. T-Mote and TinyOS are employed to represent the low-end hardware platforms and OSes due to their popularity in TWSNs. Gumstix, which is a powerful embedded processor and a promising candidate to work as the controller for UAN nodes, as well as the embedded Linux are selected as the representative for more powerful hardware platforms and OSes.

Both the execution time and the energy consumption of FFT running on these two platforms are compared with varying numbers of points in FFT. The result of the execution time is shown in Fig. 1 and that of the energy consumption is shown in Fig. 2. We can see that the combination of Gumstix and embedded Linux achieves a much smaller execution time and energy consumption than that of T-Mote and TinyOS. Also as the number of points in FFT increases, the execution time and energy consumption of T-Mote and TinyOS grow much faster. This preliminary investigation proves that OSes for low-end hardware platforms like TinyOS are not good candidates for UAN applications.

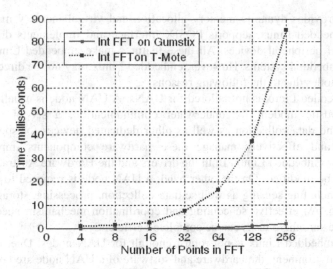

Fig. 1. Execution Time of FFT on T-Mote and Gumstix

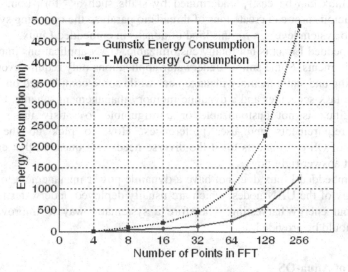

Fig. 2. Energy Consumption of FFT on T-Mote and Gumstix

3.3   Why Not Embedded Linux

In the above section, we prove that embedded Linux outperforms TinyOS in terms of both execution time and energy consumption when running computation intensive UAN applications. In this section, we study whether embedded Linux can be directly applied to UANs. Embedded Linux is a multi-task operating system usually employing time-sharing schemes to schedule multiple tasks. There are also some variants of embedded Linux like RTLinux which uses preemptive scheduling mechanism to guarantee the real-time performance of embedded systems. Embedded

Linux also provides dynamic memory allocation and virtual memory management. Besides, embedded Linux supports POSIX interface and implements drivers for a wide range of peripheral devices. All these features make embedded Linux an ideal choice for embedded systems. However, embedded Linux may not be directly applied to the UAN nodes due to the following reasons.

First, embedded Linux is not tailored for UANs. A UAN node is usually equipped with an acoustic modem for underwater communication, a set of sensors for monitoring and data collection as well as other dedicated devices for specific tasks. To reliably and effectively manage these hardware components imposes great challenges for embedded Linux. Both the drivers and the Hardware Abstraction Layer may need to be modified. On the other hand, a UAN node is required to complete a set of tasks including sensing as well se data collection, processing, storage, sending and receiving. An effective scheduling and coordination mechanism needs to be in place to make sure these tasks can be completed efficiently.

Second, embedded Linux is not robust enough for UAN nodes. Due to the harsh underwater environment, the hardware and software of a UAN node are both prone to failures. Embedded Linux is not capable of handling these failures. Besides, embedded Linux can be easily undermined by skills such as "fork bomb", which means a malicious user can create tons of threads to paralyze the operating system. So far there is no system level fix for this kind of attacks in embedded Linux.

Third, embedded Linux is not totally customizable. UAN applications impose very diverse requirements. Some simple underwater applications only require event-driven task scheduling and static memory management while some complicated ones call for a preemptive task scheduler and a dynamic memory management scheme. Currently, embedded Linux is not customizable or configurable to satisfy these different application requirements and user preferences. How to pick up the optimal combination of OS components to fit the diverse needs is a question that embedded Linux cannot answer right now.

Finally, embedded Linux does not have a dynamic power management to save the limited energy of the UAN nodes, which are usually deployed underwater for a long period without energy harvesting. Therefore a systematic way to improve energy efficiency should be provided.

3.4   Goal of Aqua-OS

Motivated by the disadvantages of the current existing operating systems when being applied to UANs, we propose a plan to design and implement a new operating system dedicated for UANs: Aqua-OS. Aqua-OS is going to realize the following features to fit the applications in the UANs.

First, Aqua-OS is going to provide robustness to underwater applications. Based on the aforementioned underwater environment characteristics, we take the robustness as the highest priority. To handle the hardware and software failures as well as the malicious user attacks, Aqua-OS will provide a system status updating component that runs periodically and an emergency handling component that can be activated regardless of current system status, e.g. CPU usage, disk space or task property. This emergency handling component will handle the exceptions caused by either failures or attacks and reset the affected hardware or software components if needed.

Second, Aqua-OS is going to be customizable and reconfigurable. Applications in UANs pose very diverse demands. In order to meet these demands, Aqua-OS is going to be highly customizable before deployment and highly reconfigurable after deployment. In another word, a system designer can pick different components e.g. a specific scheduling method, a memory management scheme, a set of drivers and a tailored protocol stack from a component warehouse of Aqua-OS to generate a dedicated operating system specifically fitting his or her application requirements. Even after the deployment of the network node, the system designer can still dynamically load and unload components in Aqua-OS on the fly. To achieve this goal, Aqua-OS provides an OS Components Toolbox which serves as the component warehouse. An OS optimizer is in place to take the application requirements and user preferences as inputs and pick up the optimal combination of components from the OS Components Toolbox.

In addition, Aqua-OS will take into consideration the energy efficiency of the UANs, which means it will provide a dynamic power management system to save energy. Aqua-OS will also smartly balance the performance and energy consumption of the system to maximize the usability of the system under various constrains.

Finally, Aqua-OS is going to provide some features users usually desire from an embedded OS. These include a fast boot-up time and a small memory footprint. Aqua-OS will also try to reduce the OS overhead including the task context switch time and the memory usage.

4   Aqua-OS

In this section, we propose the plan to design and implement Aqua-OS and describe the two key features in Aqua-OS: the OS Components Toolbox and the optimizer.

4.1   Aqua-OS Overview

Aqua-OS is composed of two major modules: the OS Components Toolbox (OCT) and the optimizer. The OCT consists of a set of essential system components for the OS from which the OS users can select their needed components based on the application requirements and their preferences. For instance, OCT provides both event-driven based scheduler and preemptive scheduler and users can choose either one based on the specific application scenario. The preemptive scheduler provides better processor utilization while the event-based scheduler generally uses less energy. Another example is the scheme for failure detection and recovery. There can be many options for this purpose from the OCT, and they are different in their performances: a more sophisticated method enhances the reliability of the UAN system but will most probably use more resources and energy while a simple scheme only provides limited reliability but consumes less resources and energy. Therefore, an appropriate failure detection and recovery scheme needs to be chosen based on a specific UAN application. Sometimes, even the choice of the file systems determines the system performance. For example, the FAT16/32 is simple and suitable for application operating on a small set of data while NTFS or ext2/3 allows application with larger data.

The best combination of the components is picked from the OCT by the Aqua-OS optimizer. This module takes application requirements and user preferences as the inputs and then selects the set of components from the OCT that best matches the inputs to generate the customized Aqua-OS.

4.2   OS Components Toolbox

OCT provides a set of components for task scheduling, memory management, power management as well as failure detection and recovery. Therefore the optimizer of Aqua-OS can choose the optimal combination of the system components from OCT based on the application requirements and user preferences.

4.3   Task Management and Process Scheduling

Depending on how tasks are managed, OSes can be classified into two categories: event-based and thread-based. In event-based operating systems, non-preemptive scheduling is usually adopted: a task runs to completion and is not preempted by other tasks; therefore, there is no context-switching between tasks. In this regard, event-based OSes introduce less overhead than thread-based ones. A typical example of an event-based OS is TinyOS which is popularly used TWSNs. In such networks, each node is usually equipped with limited hardware capability, powered by batteries. Due to this hardware limitation, the design of TinyOS aims at simplicity to improve energy efficiency.

In contrast to event-based OSes, thread-based OSes usually employ preemptive task scheduling. In this scheme, a task can be preempted by others. This scheme generally improves system performance in terms of processor utilization and system responsiveness, especially when tasks in sensor networks are I/O intensive. Nevertheless, this task scheduler is more complex and involves context-switching overhead, which can shorten battery lifetime. Most modern generic operating systems such as Windows or Linux are preemptive.

In the context of UANs, the networks are usually sparser than TWSNs, but have more powerful network nodes. Some of them are powered by solar panels or fuel cells; therefore, energy efficiency is not as critical as in TWSNs, although still important. A more powerful processor can allow a node to preprocess the acquired data before sending it to reduce network traffic, which means tasks in UANs will include more computation than TWSNs. With these remarks in mind, we plan to implement a hybrid approach for Aqua-OS. Specifically, the OS is event-based to maintain its responsiveness to events and a task can be preempted by another using customizable policies. We are also going to provide users with pure event-based or preemptive scheduling methods and therefore the Aqua-OS optimizer can choose the best scheduling method for the specific applications.

4.4   Memory and Storage Management

Memory management is an important issue for every OS. It has great influence on the performance of the OS and applications running on it. The choice of memory management techniques depends on application requirements and hardware capability. Many OSes used in TWSNs have very simple memory management methods because typical terrestrial nodes have a small amount of memory. TinyOS, for example, does not support dynamic memory management; the size of memory allocated to each component is determined at the compilation phase.

In underwater networks, the assumption of small memory no longer holds because the systems (e.g. underwater sensor nodes or AUVs) often consist of more advanced hardware. Additionally, because underwater applications are complicated and diverse, they have quite different requirements on memory size and memory access patterns from terrestrial ones. In order to facilitate more complicated applications, Aqua-OS will provide dynamic memory allocation. Along with this feature, Aqua-OS will also support virtual memory (VM) management, which brings about better main memory utilization from preventing memory fragmentation. Another advantage of VM is the robustness of the OS since each process has its own address space separated from the others'. Moreover, VM offers applications more memory than actually available main memory. Also static memory management is provided by OCT to fit applications requiring a very simple memory management scheme.

Besides memory management, file systems are needed in underwater systems to store large amount of data or applications. File systems will allow for a flexible and convenient way to manage large storage space. For example, since communications over the acoustic link are error-prone and energy consuming, a data set is usually held for some period of time, after which it will be processed (e.g. compressed) and then transmitted. If that data set is large, it should be stored in external memory rather than the main memory. Without a file system, an application will have to handle the storage device by itself, which is error prone and may corrupt data of other applications. Aqua-OS will support multiple file systems to facilitate different requirements or preferences. The Aqua-OS optimizer is responsible for picking up the file system that optimally balances the file system performance and the resource consumption.

As the cost of flash memory keeps falling, a large flash memory module can be included into the hardware platform in which it plays the role of storage for the file system and/or swap space for the VM. Without a swap space, we can save some energy, but the number of programs that can be loaded simultaneously will be limited by the capacity of the main memory.

4.5   Adaptive Power Management

Some underwater systems can be powered by solar panels or fuel cells, and as such, their batteries can be recharged. However, efficient usage of the batteries is still an important issue because the alternative power sources will not work during a particular time frame, e.g. daytime for solar panels. Most existing OSes for TWSNs take design simplicity as a factor in reducing power consumption. A few of them consider dynamic power adjustment. TinyOS allows for hardware power management, but it is up to applications to decide when to put a device into a sleep state. MANTIS simply shuts down the scheduler when no task is to be scheduled. Contiki has a software-based online energy estimation mechanism for sensor nodes.

A limitation of existing OSes for TWSNs is that they mainly focus on power saving at the processor or controller. In UANs, other devices, for example acoustic modems or sensors usually consume more energy than the processor; therefore, in order to optimize energy efficiency, it is necessary to consider other components.

Aqua-OS will implement some adaptive dynamic power management (DPM) algorithms which utilize run-time information to reduce power consumption when systems are serving light workload or idle. Aqua-OS manages the power at three different levels: the component level, the node system level, and the network system level. At each level, Aqua-OS provides a particular sub-DPM algorithm to supervise and control the state of the "components", and together, the three algorithms can reduce energy consumption of the system. At the component level, there are three candidate mechanisms: clock gating, supply shutdown and multiple and variable power supplies . The sub-DPM algorithm controls these mechanisms and makes decision on when and which mechanism to be selected for which device. At the node system level, power management can be considered as a constrained optimization problem when components and requests are modeled as stochastic processes and it provides the flexibility to tradeoff between power and performance . At the network system level, the customized DPM algorithm can be in cooperation with some energy-conscious communication protocols, and by increasing the predictability of communication patterns (predict the arrival time of messages/packets), idle times can be exploited to force communication devices into a low-power inactive state . The Aqua-OS optimizer is going to select one or a combination of power management schemes based on different application requirements and user preferences.

4.6   Failure Detection and Recovery

For the hardware failure detection and recovery, Aqua-OS maintains a hardware dependency structure to keep track of the threads that depend on specific hardware components. This structure is updated by a Hardware Monitoring Thread (HMT) running in the kernel space. If an application thread detects a hardware component failure, via an incorrect return value following a system call, for example, it reports this event to HMT. After confirmation of the failure occurrence, HMT notifies all threads using the hardware component of the failure. After these threads have handled this failure, HMT blocks all of them and starts the Hardware Exception Handler to recover the hardware failure. Finally, HMT resumes these threads. HMT requires little resource usage because of its limited functions; therefore, it can reside in the main memory all the time to survive hardware failures. This hardware failure detection and recovery mechanism strengthens both energy efficiency by blocking relevant threads and system robustness by handling hardware component failures.

For the software failure detection and recovery, Aqua-OS separates kernel address space and user address space to prevent malfunctioning application threads from tampering with kernel code or data. Also for critical threads e.g. AUV flight control thread, they can register their important memory ranges to the kernel. In this way, instead of direct access, other threads trying to access these memory ranges need to perform a system call to request the kernel to access for them, which can avert malicious threads from modifying critical thread data. On processors supporting the hierarchical protection domain scheme e.g. IA32 architecture, Aqua-OS can also utilize this feature to implement different privilege modes which are assigned different permissions. To further enhance protection against malicious software, Aqua-OS maintains a lightweight security rule database which defines the illegal or dangerous software behaviors including accessing kernel or protected memory addresses, fork bomb and attempts to deplete system resources. Also different illegal software behavior has different damage weight. Once the total weight of illegal behaviors performed by a thread exceeds a threshold, kernel can terminate this specific thread. By the aforementioned software failure detection measures, Aqua-OS effectively protects the OS kernel as well as the critical threads and meanwhile prevents the malicious threads from undermining system reliability and security. Based on the application requirements and user preferences, the Aqua-OS optimizer will choose a couple of failure detection and recovery schemes to balance the system reliability and resource consumption.

4.7   Aqua-OS Optimizer

The Aqua-OS optimizer is illustrated in Fig. 3. The optimizer is composed of three components: OS Component Combination, objectives and metric evaluation. Aqua-OS will pick a couple of hardware drivers from the hardware abstraction based on the specific hardware platform of a UAN node. In addition, a component will be chosen from each of the four categories of the OCT as listed in Section 4.2. For instance, preemptive scheduler is chosen as the scheduling method and component level and node system level power management schemes are selected as the power management strategy. The selected hardware drivers and components from OCT form an OS Component Combination. Aqua-OS defines a uniform set of metrics to evaluate the performance of an individual OS Component Combination. Currently we have four metrics: OS overhead, P_o (the additional processing time incurred by the OS itself), OS footprint, P_f (the memory usage by the OS), real-time performance, P_r and OS energy consumption, P_e. For each specific OS Component Combination, we obtain a performance metric vector $V_p = \{P_o, P_f, P_r, P_e\}$. The application requirements and user preferences form the Objectives and create an objective vector $V_o = \{\alpha_o, \alpha_f, \alpha_r, \alpha_e\}$, where α_o is the weight for P_o, α_f is the weight for P_f and so on. Different application requirements and user preferences lead to different V_o. For instance, a real-time application has a larger α_r while a long-term non time sensitive application has a larger α_e to emphasize on energy efficiency. For each OS Component Combination, Aqua-OS calculates its performance score $S = \alpha_o P_o + \alpha_f P_f + \alpha_r P_r + \alpha_e P_e$. The OS Component Combination that achieves the highest performance score S is selected to generate an Aqua-OS version which is optimal for the given application requirements and user preferences.

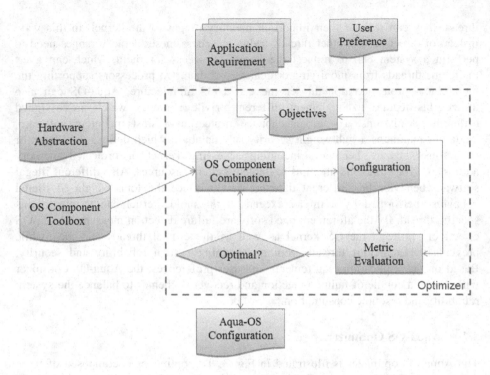

Fig. 3. Aqua-OS Optimizer

5   Conclusions and Ongoing Work

The significant difference in hardware configuration between TWSNs and UANs suggests that existing operating systems for TWSNs will not fully utilize the more powerful hardware if used in the underwater settings. In conjunction with more powerful hardware, underwater software is more complicated and diverse which needs to be supported by a more advanced operating system. Aqua-OS is designed to meet this requirement by offering applications robustness, customizability and energy efficiency.

Aqua-OS is very much a work in progress. We will not try to develop a completely new operating system from scratch. Instead, we will construct the Aqua-OS based on the popular embedded Linux, which already provides preemptive multitask scheduler, dynamic and virtual memory management, a variety of file systems and drivers for a wide range of devices. For the first step, we are going to integrate all these components into the Aqua-OS Components Toolbox. In addition, we will add more components including event-driven task scheduler, static memory management, dynamic power management as well as failure detection and recovery mechanisms into the OS Components Toolbox. For the second step, we will implement the Aqua-OS Optimizer, which can pick up the optimal component combination based on application requirements and user preferences. In this way, we can reduce the workload of the development of Aqua-OS and make sure the applications running on embedded Linux can be ported to Aqua-OS without changes.

References

[1] Cui, J.-H., Kong, J., Gerla, M., Zhou, S.: Challenges: Building Scalable Mobile Underwater Wireless Sensor Networks for Aquatic Applications. IEEE Network 20(3), 12–18 (2006)

[2] Heidemann, J., Ye, W., Wills, J., Syed, A., Li, Y.: Research Challenges and Applications for Underwater Sensor Networking. In: WCNC, Las Vegas, NV (2006)

[3] Bhatti, S., Carlson, J., Dai, H., Deng, J., Rose, J., Sheth, A., Shucker, B., Gruenwald, C., Torgerson, A., Han, R.: MANTIS OS: An Embedded Multithreaded Operating System for Wireless Micro Sensor Platforms. Mobile Networks and Applications 10(4), 563–579 (2005)

[4] Levis, P., Madden, S., Polastre, J., Szewczyk, R., Woo, A., Gay, D., Hill, J., Welsh, M., Brewer, E., Culler, D.: TinyOS: An Operating System for Sensor Networks. In: Ambient Intelligence, pp. 115–148. Springer, Heidelberg (2005)

[5] http://ecos.sourceware.org/

[6] http://www.contiki-os.org/p/about-contiki.html

[7] Levis, P., Gay, D.: TinyOS Programming. Cambridge University Press, New York (2009)

[8] Cao, Q., Abdelzaher, T., Stankovic, J., He, T.: The LiteOS Operating System: Towards Unix-Like Abstractions for Wireless Sensor Networks. In: IPSN (2008)

[9] http://www.tinyos.net/tinyos-2.x/doc/html/tep115.html

[10] Dunkels, A., Gronvall, B., Voigt, T.: Contiki - A Lightweight and Flexible Operating System for Tiny Networked Sensors. In: LCN (2004)

[11] Benini, L., Bogliolo, A., De Micheli, G.: A Survey of Design Techniques for System-level Dynamic Power Management. IEEE Transactions on VLSI Systems 8(3), 299–316 (2000)

[12] Sinha, A., Chandrakasan, A.: Dynamic Power Management in Wireless Sensor Networks. IEEE Design and Test of Computers 18(2), 62–74 (2001)

[13] Paleologo, G., Benini, L., Bogliolo, A., De Micheli, G.: Policy Optimization for Dynamic Power Management. IEEE Transactions of Computer Aided Design 18(6), 813–833 (1999)

[14] Lu, Y.-H., De Micheli, G.: Comparing System-level Power Management Policies. IEEE Design and Test of Computers 18(2), 10–19 (2001)

Spectrum Efficiency of Nested Sparse Sampling

Junjie Chen[1], Qilian Liang[1], Jie Wang[2], and Hyeong-Ah Choi[3]

[1] Department of Electrical Engineering
University of Texas at Arlington
Arlington, TX 76019-0016 USA
junjie.chen@mavs.uta.edu, liang@uta.edu
[2] Department of Computer Science
University of Massachusetts Lowell
Lowell, MA 01854 USA
wang@cs.uml.edu
[3] Department of Computer Science
George Washington University
Washington, DC 20052 USA
hchoi@gwu.edu

Abstract. This paper addresses the spectrum efficiency study of nested sparse sampling in the estimation of power spectral density for QPSK signal. The authors proposed nested sampling only showed that this new sub-Nyquist sampling algorithm could achieve enhanced degrees of freedom, but did not consider its spectrum efficiency performance. Spectral efficiency describes the ability of a communication system to accommodate data within a limited bandwidth. In this paper, we provide the procedures of using nested sampling structure to estimate the QPSK signal's autocorrelation and power spectral density (PSD) using a set of sparse samples. From our simulation results, we show that by making N_1 and N_2 large enough, the main lobe of PSD obtained from nested sparse sampling is much narrower than the original QPSK signal. That is, the bandwidth B occupancy of the sampled signal is smaller, which improves the spectrum efficiency. Besides the smaller average rate, the enhanced spectrum efficiency is a new advantage of nested sparse sampling.

Keywords: Spectrum Efficiency, Nested Sampling, Autocorrelation, PSD.

1 Introduction

In recent years, spectrum efficiency has gained renewed interest in wireless communication system. From [1], we know that the performance of a particular communication system is often measured in terms of spectral efficiency (or bandwidth efficiency). Spectral efficiency describes the ability of a communication system to accommodate data within a limited bandwidth. It reflects how efficiently the allocated bandwidth is utilized and defined as the ratio of the throughput data rate

X. Wang et al. (Eds.): WASA 2012, LNCS 7405, pp. 574–583, 2012.
© Springer-Verlag Berlin Heidelberg 2012

per Hertz in a given bandwidth. Letting R to be the data rate in bits per second, and B the bandwidth occupied, the bandwidth efficiency η is expressed as

$$\eta = \frac{R}{B} bit/s/Hz \tag{1}$$

If we apply shannon's capacity to AWGN non-fading channel, i.e., $C = B \log_2(1 + \frac{S}{N})$, and with the knowledge that all communication rates are below channel capacity $R \leq C$ [10], we can get the fundamental upper bound [1] on achievable spectrum efficiency, for an arbitrarily small probability of error, where $\frac{S}{N}$ is the signal to noise ratio.

$$\eta_{max} = \frac{C}{B} = \log_2(1 + \frac{S}{N}) \tag{2}$$

From (1), if we hope to improve the spectrum efficiency, we should either increase the data rate R or efficiently use the bandwidth B. Lots of efforts have been made to increase the spectrum efficiency. For example, power and spectral efficient family of modulations for wireless communication systems were introduced in [2]. The author in [3] proposed a high spectrum efficient multiple access code. Cognitive radios have been proposed as a method to efficiently reuse the licensed limited spectrum. And in general, the spectral efficiency can be improved [4] by frequency re-use, spatial multiplexing, OFDMA, or some radio resource management techniques such as efficient fixed or dynamic channel allocation, power control, link adaptation etc.

A new approach to super resolution spectral estimation using nested sparse sampling is provided by [5] and [6]. The authors has already proved that this new sub-Nyquist sampling algorithm could achieve enhanced degrees of freedom. While in this paper, we will show that this nested sparse sampling is much more spectrum efficiency, i.e., it occupies a much narrower bandwidth than the original non-sampled signal.

Traditional sampling methods are based on Nyquist rate sampling, which will have poor efficiency in terms of both sampling rate and computational complexity. Nowadays, more and more techniques are proposed to overcome the Nyquist sampling. Compressive sensing [9] provides us a new point of view, which could only use much less samples to perfectly recover the original signal at a high compression ratio. The authors give a new idea of co-prime sampling in [6], which uses two uniform sampling to estimate the autocorrelation for all lags.

Differently, nested sparse sampling is an non-uniform sampling, using two different samplers in each period. Although the signal is sampled sparsely and nonuniformly at $1 \leq l \leq N_1 T$ and $(N_1 + 1)mT, 1 \leq m \leq N_2$ for one period, the autocorrelation $R_c(\tau)$ of the signal $x_c(t)$ could be estimated at all lags $\tau = kT$, k, l, and m are all integers. Hence, nested sparse sampling can be used to estimate power spectrum even though the samples in the time domain can be arbitrarily sparse [6].

In this paper, we give the principle of nested sparse sampling and provide the procedures of using nested sampling structure to estimate the QPSK signal's autocorrelation and power spectral density (PSD). From our simulation results, we also show that with if we choose N_1 and N_2 larger, the main lobe of PSD obtained from nested sampling is much narrower than the original QPSK signal. That is, the occupied bandwidth B in expression (1) is smaller, which makes the spectrum efficiency higher. Besides the smaller average rate, the increased spectrum efficiency is a new advantage of nested sparse sampling.

The rest of this paper is organized as follows. In section 2, we give a brief overview of nested sparse sampling. Spectrum estimation based on the difference sets obtained in nested sampling structure is detailed in section 3. In Section 4, we provide the numerical results of the power spectrum density estimation. Conclusions are presented in Section 5.

2   Nested Sparse Sampling

The nested array was introduced in [5] as an effective approach to array processing with enhanced degrees of freedom [8]. The time domain autocorrelation could also be obtained from sparse sampling with nested sampling structure [7]. And the samples of the autocorrelation can be computed at any specified rate, although the samples from this nested sparse sampling are sparsely and nonuniformly located.

In the simplest form, the nested array [7] has two levels of sampling density, with the level 1 samples at the N_1 locations and the level 2 samples at the N_2 locations.

$$1 \leq l \leq N_1, \text{for level 1}$$

$$(N_1 + 1)m, 1 \leq m \leq N_2, \text{for level 2}$$

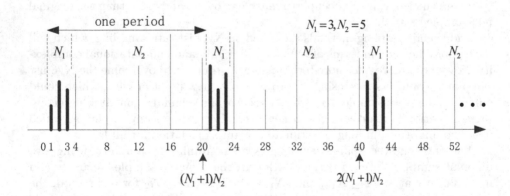

Fig. 1. Nested sampling with $N_1 = 3, N_2 = 5$

Fig. 1 shows an example of periodic sparse sampling using nested sampling structure with $N_1 = 3$ and $N_2 = 5$. The cross-differences are given by

$$k = (N_1 + 1)m - l, 1 \leq m \leq N_2, 1 \leq l \leq N_1 \qquad (3)$$

The cross-differences [7] are in the following range with the maximum value $(N_1 + 1)N_2 - 1$, except the integers and the corresponding negated versions shown in (5).

$$- [(N_1 + 1)N_2 - 1] \leq k \leq [(N_1 + 1)N_2 - 1] \tag{4}$$

$$(N_1 + 1), 2(N_1 + 1), \cdots, (N2 - 1)(N_1 + 1) \tag{5}$$

For example, consider the example in fig. 1, where $1 \leq m \leq 5$ and $1 \leq l \leq 3$, the cross differences $k = (N_1 + 1)m - l$ will achieve these values

$$1, 2, 3, (), 5, 6, 7, (), 9, 10, 11, (), 13, 14, 15, (), 17, 18, 19$$

with $4, 8, 12, 16$ missing.

Besides these integers, the difference 0 is also missing, for the reason that m and l are nonzero. While, we notice that the self differences among the second array could cover all of the missing differences, as shown

$$(N_1 + 1)(m_1 - m_2), 1 \leq m_1, m_2 \leq N_2 \tag{6}$$

The difference-co-array could be obtained from the cross-differences and the self-differences, which is a filled difference co-array as shown in (4). This means that using nested array structure, with sparse samples, we could obtain the degrees of freedom as

$$2[(N_1 + 1)N_2 - 1] + 1 = 2(N_1 + 1)N_2 - 1 \tag{7}$$

Using the above principle, we could get a sparse sampling using nested sampling structure as shown in fig. 1. We have two levels of nesting, with N_1 level-1 samples and N_2 level-2 samples in each period, with period $(N_1 + 1)N_2$. This shows that nested sampling is non-uniform and the samples obtained are very sparse.

Therefore, in $(N_1 + 1)N_2T$ seconds, there are totally $N_1 + N_2$ samples. The average sampling rate is

$$f_s = \frac{N_1 + N_2}{(N_1 + 1)N_2} \approx \frac{1}{N_1 T} + \frac{1}{N_2 T} \tag{8}$$

Here, $T = 1/f_n$, $f_n \geq 2f_{max}$ is the Nyquist sampling frequency, which is greater than twice of the maximum frequency. As the Nyquist sampling rate is $1/T$, the average sampling rate of nested sampling is smaller than the conventional Nyquist sampling rate.

If we set N_1 and N_2 larger, the average sampling rate f_s would be arbitrarily smaller. In the numerical results section, we will show that with N_1 and N_2 becoming larger, the bandwidth of the power spectrum density goes narrower, i.e., the spectrum gets more efficiently used.

3   Power Spectral Density Estimation Based on Nested Sparse Sampling

In this part, we will detail the estimation of PSD using nested sampling structure. In signal and systems analysis, the autocorrelation plays a very important role. The autocorrelation function of a random signal describes the general dependence of the values of the samples at one time on the values of the samples at another time.

The autocorrelation [11] of a real and stationary signal $x_c(t)$ is defined by this averaging

$$R_c(\tau) = E[x_c(t)x_c^*(t - \tau)] \tag{9}$$

Where T is the period of observation. $R_c(\tau)$ is always real-valued and an even function with a maximum value at $\tau = 0$.

For sampled signal, define $x(n) = x_c(nT)$, for some fixed spacing T. For the autocorrelation samples, $R(k) = R_c(kT)$, where R_c as shown in (9). Therefore,

$$R(k) = E[x_c(nT)x_c^*((n - k)T)] = E[x(n)x^*(n - k)] \tag{10}$$

$R(k)$ can be computed from samples of $x_c(t)$ taken at an arbitrarily lower rate using nested sparse sampling. The power spectral density (PSD) describes how the power of a signal or time series is distributed with frequency. The PSD is the Fourier transform of the autocorrelation function of the signal if the signal is treated as a wide-sense stationary random process [12]. Therefore, the Fourier transform of $R_c(\tau)$ is the PSD $S(f)$,

$$S(f) = \int_{-\infty}^{\infty} R_c(\tau)e^{-2\pi i f \tau} d\tau \tag{11}$$

$S(f)$ is a real-valued, nonnegative function. Definition (11) shows that $S(-f) = S(f)$, i.e., the PSD is an even function of frequency f.

For the samples obtained from nested sparse sampling, consider the product $x(n_1)x^*(n_2)$, with n_1 and n_2 belong to the first period in fig. 1. We will get the samples at the following locations

$$1, 2, \ldots, N_1, (N_1 + 1), 2(N_1 + 1), \cdots, N_2(N_1 + 1) \tag{12}$$

The set of differences $n_1 - n_2$ are exactly the difference-co-array described in (4, that is, $n_1 - n_2$ will achieve all integer values in (4.

we can see that although the signal is sampled sparsely and nonuniformly at $1 \leq l \leq N_1$ and $(N_1 + 1)m, 1 \leq m \leq N_2$ for one period, the autocorrelation $R_c(\tau)$ of the signal $x_c(t)$ could be estimated at all lags $\tau = k$.

An estimate of the autocorrelation samples for all k could be obtained [7] by averaging the products $x(n_1)x^*(n_2)$ over L periods,

$$\hat{R}(k) = \frac{1}{L} \sum_{l=0}^{L-1} x(n)x^*(n - k) \tag{13}$$

Taking the Fourier transform of the estimated autocorrelation $\hat{R}(k)$, we could obtain the power spectral density of the samples got from the nested sparse sampling.

4 Numerical Results

This section presents some numerical results for the autocorrelation and power spectrum density estimation using nested sampling structure. We use QPSK modulated signal with carrier frequency $f_c = 400Hz$, which could be expressed as [1]

$$s_{QPSK}(t) = \sqrt{\frac{2E_s}{T_s}}cos[2\pi f_c t + (i-1)\frac{\pi}{2}] \tag{14}$$

where T_s is the symbol duration. In our simulation, we set $E_s = 1$ and $T_s = 1/50$.

The power spectrum density [1] of a QPSK signal using rectangular pulses can be expressed as

$$P_{QPSK}(f) = \frac{E_s}{2}[(\frac{sin\pi(f-f_c)T_s}{\pi(f-f_c)T_s})^2 + (\frac{sin\pi(-f-f_c)T_s}{\pi(-f-f_c)T_s})^2] \tag{15}$$

Fig. 2 shows the PSD of a QPSK signal for rectangular and raised cosine filtered pulses. The x-axis refers to the frequency in Hz, and the y-axis are the normalized power spectral density in dB. It can be observed the PSD centers at $f_c = 400Hz$ with symmetric sidelobes on both sides.

If we zoom in fig. 2, as shown in fig. 3, we could notice bandwidth for the original QPSK signal is about $416 - 384 = 32Hz$.

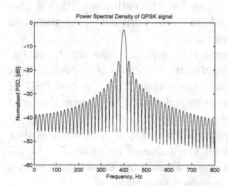
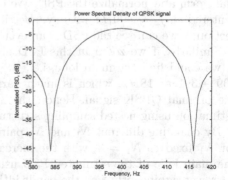

Fig. 2. PSD of the QPSK signal   **Fig. 3.** Zoom in the main lobe of PSD for QPSK signal

The estimated autocorrelation using nested sampling structure is plotted in fig. 4. In the simulation, we use $N_1 = 7$, $N_2 = 11$, and $L = 10$. Therefore, $\hat{R}(k)$ can be estimated for $\mid k \mid \leq (N_1 + 1)N_2 - 1$. For each period, we totally get $(N_1 + 1)N_2 = (7+1) \times 11 = 88$ samples.

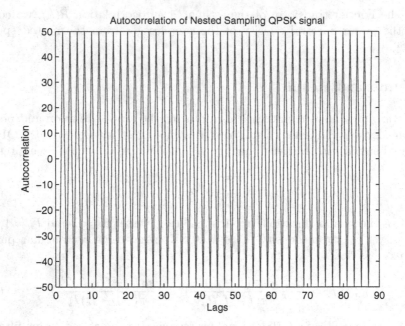

Fig. 4. Nested Sampling Estimated Autocorrelation of the QPSK Signal

Using the relationship of autocorrelation and the PSD described in section 3, we could obtain the estimated PSD using nested sampling structure for this QPSK signal as shown in fig. 5. In the simulation, we use 1024 point fast Fourier transform and normalize the PSD. We can see that the estimated PSD is also centered at $f_c = 400Hz$ with symmetric sidelobes on both sides. As stated in section 3, we can see the PSD is an even function.

Similarly, if we zoom in this PSD around the central frequency f_c, in fig. 6, we could find the main lobe, i.e., the bandwidth occupied is approximately $409 - 391 \approx 18Hz$, which is much narrower than that $32Hz$ of the PSD of the original QPSK signal. Hence, the spectrum efficiency is improved in the estimation using nested sampling structure.

By changing different N_1 and N_2 pairs, as shown in fig. 7, it is obvious that for N_1 fixed to $N_1 = 3$, with the increase of the value of N_2 from $5, 7$ to 13, the main lobe of the estimated PSD using nested sampling structure becomes narrower significantly, i.e., the bandwidth occupied gets smaller.

Similarly, fig. 8 shows that with the increase of N_1 from $N_1 = 3, 5$ to $N_1 = 11$, while N_2 fixed to $N_2 = 13$, the main lobe also gets narrower, which also results in the increase of spectrum efficiency. From the results got from figures 7 and 8, we conclude that in the nested sparse sampling process, besides its advantage of less samplers, with N_1 and N_2 chosen larger, the bandwidth of the PSD occupied will becomes narrower, which increases the spectrum efficiency.

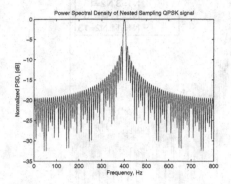

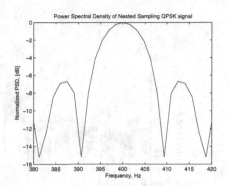

Fig. 5. PSD of Nested Sampling QPSK signal (N1=7,N2=11)

Fig. 6. Zoom in the main lobe of PSD for Nested Sampling QPSK signal(N1=7,N2=11)

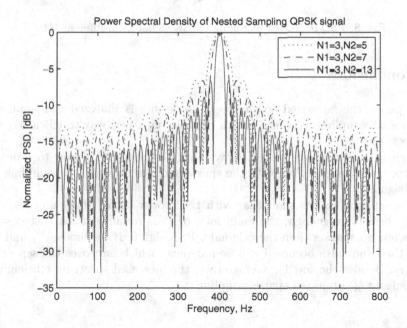

Fig. 7. PSD of Nested Sampling QPSK signal with different N2

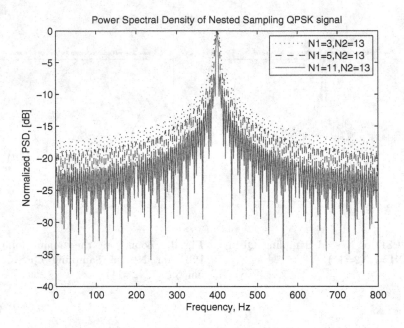

Fig. 8. PSD of Nested Sampling QPSK signal with different N1

5   Conclusions

In this paper, the estimated power spectrum density is analyzed and simulated using nested sampling structure, which provides us a new way to efficiently use the spectrum.

We give the principle of nested arrays and the procedure of how to estimate the autocorrelation and PSD with the sparse samples using nested sampling for QPSK signal.

Our simulation results show that with the proper choice of N_1 and N_2, i.e., making them large enough, the main lobe of PSD obtained from nested sampling is much narrower than the original QPSK signal. If we choose N_1 and N_2 larger, the bandwidth occupied will be narrower, which improves the sepctrum efficiency. Besides the smaller average rate, the increased spectrum efficiency is a new advantage of nested sparse sampling.

References

1. Rappaport, T.S.: Wireless Communications: Principles and Practice, 2nd edn., pp. 278–302. Prentice Hall PTR
2. Mehdi, H., Feher, K.: FQPSK, Power and Spectral Efficient Family of Modulations for Wireless Communication Systems. In: IEEE Vehicular Technology Conference, pp. 1562–1566 (June 1994)

3. Li, D.: A High Spectrum Efficient Multiple Access Code. In: APCC/OECC, pp. 18–22 (October 1999)
4. Alouini, M.-S., Goldsmith, A.J.: Area Spectral Efficiency of Cellular Mobile Radio Systems. IEEE Transactions on Vehicular Technology 48(4), 1047–1066 (1999)
5. Pal, P., Vaidyanathan, P.P.: Nested Arrays: A Novel Approach to Array Processing With Enhanced Degrees of Freedom. IEEE Transactions on Signal Processing 58(8), 4167–4181 (2010)
6. Pal, P., Vaidyanathan, P.P.: Coprime Sampling and the MUSIC Algorithm. In: Digital Signal Processing Workshop and IEEE Signal Processing Education Workshop, pp. 289–294 (January 2011)
7. Vaidyanathan, P.P., Pal, P.: Sparse Sensing with Co-Prime Samplers and Arrays. IEEE Transactions on Signal Processing 59(2), 573–586 (2011)
8. Pal, P., Vaidyanathan, P.P.: A Novel Array Structure for Directions-of-Arrival Estimation with Increased Degrees of Freedom. In: Acoustics Speech and Signal Processing, pp. 2606–2609 (March 2010)
9. Candes, E.J., Wakin, M.B.: An Introduction To Compressive Sampling. IEEE Signal Processing Magazing, 21–30 (March 2008)
10. Cover, T.M., Thomas, J.A.: Elements of Information Theory, 2nd edn. John Wiley & Sons, Inc., Hoboken (2006)
11. Ricker, D.W.: Echo Signal Processing, pp. 23–26. Springer, ISBN 1-4020-7395-X
12. Stoica, P., Moses, R.L.: Introduction to Spectral Analysis, 1st edn., pp. 1–13. Prentice Hall, Upper Saddle River (1997)

HMPR: Forwarding Based on History Meeting Prediction Routing in Opportunistic Networks

Yun Li[1,2,*], Meng Xu[1], Qilie Liu[1,3], and Jihong Yu[1]

[1] Key lab of Mobile Communication technology, Chongqing University of Posts and
Telecommunications, Chongqing 400065, China
[2] National Mobile Communications Research Laboratory,
Southeast University of China, Nanjing 210096, China
[3] Key lab of OptoElectronics Technology and System, Ministry of Education,
Chongqing University, Chongqing 400044, China
liyun@cqupt.edu.cn, xumengzk@163.com

Abstract. Opportunistic networks are challenging networks characterised by frequency disconnections and partitioning. The data propagation process follows a "store-carry-and-forward" transmission manner, instead of the usual "hop-by-hop" forwarding model. In view of the impact of history information of nodes on whether messages are successfully delivered to destination, the scheme based on history meeting predictability routing(HMPR) is put forward. The scheme is primarily based on the contact duration and the meeting frequency of history information of network nodes, and predicts the utility of messages successfully delivered to the destination. Through comparing the utility value, nodes can determine messages whether to be forwarded. The simulation results show that, compared this scheme with traditional Epidemic routing and Prophet routing, the proposed routing scheme has the higher delivery ratio of packets, the lower overhead ratio and the less average buffer time.

Keywords: opportunistic networks, epidemic, prophet, utility value, routing.

1 Introduction

Opportunistic Networks [1] have the unique feature of intermittent connectivity, which makes routings quite different from other wireless networks. There are some characteristics of no existing end-to-end paths, unknown network topology, and higher network delay and so on. The opportunistic networks take full advantage of the communication opportunity by the movement of the mobile devices. The data is propagated in a store-carry-and-forward paradigm, which

* The authors would like to thank the anonymous reviewers and editor for their valuable comments and suggestions. And thank the support by the National Science Foundation of China, the Science and Technology Research Project of Chongqing Municipal Education Commission of China, the Natural Science Foundation Project of CQ CSTC.

X. Wang et al. (Eds.): WASA 2012, LNCS 7405, pp. 584–594, 2012.

overcomes the shortage of no end-to-end connections, and is not essential to link with the full-connected of the network. As previously pointed out, opportunistic networks are widely used in special conditions networks environment [2], pocket switched networks [3], sensor networks [4], and industrial production application [5]. So far, more and more researchers have mainly focused on routing protocols issues of opportunistic networks, such as Epidemic Routing [6], Context-Aware Routing [7] and Prophet Routing [8], etc.

In this paper, we put forward the history meeting prediction routing (HMPR), the routing protocol based on HMPR, which intends to achieve the following targets: make sure the optimal paths to destination nodes and ensure more messages successfully delivered from source node or relay nodes to destination node. The proposed HMPR uses mainly two parameters, namely, the contact time and the meeting frequency of history information of network nodes, to prioritize messages for transmission that are stored in their buffer. According to these parameters, the utility value of successful delivered messages to the destination can be predicted in the opportunistic networks. Compared the utility value with the neighbor node, the relay nodes can determine whether messages in their buffer can be forwarded. We detailedly compare HMPR with other exiting routing algorithms of the opportunistic networks. The simulation results also show, HMPR has a better performance in the term of delivery ratio of packets, overhead ratio and average buffer time.

The remainder of this paper is structures as follows. In section 2 of this paper introduces the related works. In section 3 gives the detail of our proposed HMPR. In section 4 describes the simulation environment and ananlyses the results. The conclusion is discussed in section 5.

2   Related Works

A large number of routing protocols, which make good performances in the special networks environment, have been proposed for opportunistic networks. In opportunistic networks, the node density is much lower, the transmission range of nodes is much smaller and is only a small part of the networks. Obviously, end to end paths can be established hardly, it gives rise to some bad performances of the networks. However, the routing scheme research has been paid much more attention in opportunistic networks. As we all know, the simplest strategy to deliver messages in opportunistic networks is called single-hop transmission or direct transmission [9]. In this paper [10], the major idea is to develop appropriate data forwarding metrics, by exploiting the transient node contact pattern, for more accurate prediction of node contact capability within the given time constraint.The LocalCom scheme[11], which achieves three main steps: neighboring graph construction, community detection and forwarding plan determination, utilizes the inherent social communities to facilitate packet forwarding. Obviously, the disadvantages of some exiting routing schemes can take arbitrarily long time and inducing that more messages could not be successfully delivered. Therefore, it is necessary to devise some strategies to solve the existing issues which can influence the performance in the opportunistic networks. Some routings which are involved in our research have been proposed in the following.

Epidemic routing [6] is an early sparse network flooding routing protocol which had been proposed in delay tolerant networks (DTN) [12]. In the flooding, every node forwards no-duplicated packets to the nodes it meets. Each node has maintained a summary vector. When two nodes randomly meet, they exchange their respective summary vector to each other, and then exchange only messages that its peer nodes does not have in its buffer. Epidemic is a pragmatic strategy only in case of small size messages and very sparse network. At the same time, the routing is based on assumption that each node has fixed bandwidth and buffer space, and stores some messages from each contact with other nodes. If storage space is finite, the messages will overflow when the buffer is full. Otherwise, as long as storage space is infinite, all of the messages from the sending nodes can be stored in the buffer.

Prophet routing [8, 13] is mainly used in the intermittent networks, and is also presented in other DTN protocols of early generation, like Epidemic routing. It uses history of previous encounters with neighbor nodes to estimate probabilistic metric, which is called delivery predictability. If the two nodes often encounter, they will have a higher delivery predictability, and they exchange delivery predictability, which is updated after each contact. On the basis of history information, each node can select messages that have higher possibility to reach the intended destinations, and decides to transfer them to its contact node. However, this routing scheme does not work well in opportunistic networks where the nodes movements are not predictable.

3 HMPR Design

In this section, we first introduce the design of network model, then discuss our utility value computation and updating, and finally give a forwarding scheme.

3.1 Network Model

For the scenario shows in the figure 1, dashed line arrow illustrates the comparison information of utility value of message forwarding between relay nodes and the destination node. The source node or relay node S, which intends to send messages to the destination node D, encounters random relay nodes A, B and C in the transmission range. It is very necessary to select a better relay node from the nodes A, B and C to deliver messages to the destination node D. In the following, we also mainly define three variables: utility value, contact opportunity and reliable transmission efficiency.

3.2 The Utility Value Computation

Definition 1. The utility value ω_{ij} of successfully delivered messages to the destination is the product of contact opportunity β_{ij} and messages reliable

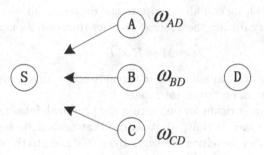

Fig. 1. Relay Selection Scheme

transmission efficiency η_{ij} between a random relay node i and the destination node j as follows:

$$\omega_{ij} = \beta_{ij} \times \eta_{ij} \tag{1}$$

Definition 2. The contact opportunity β_{ij} is that the total history contact duration between a random relay node i and the destination node j, divided by the total history contact duration of the relay node i that has contacted with the other nodes, i.e.,

$$\beta_{ij} = \frac{\sum\limits_{n=1}^{\infty} T[i(n),\ j(n)]}{\sum\limits_{m} \sum\limits_{n=1}^{\infty} T[i(n),\ k(n,\ m)]} \tag{2}$$

where the extent of β_{ij} is $0 \le \beta_{ij} \le 1$, n is the meeting frequency between two nodes, m is the number of nodes, and $T[\cdot]$ is the each history contact duration between two nodes.

Definition 3. The reliable transmission efficiency η_{ij} is that by predicting the practical data transmission quantity M', divided by predicting the data transmission quantity M in theory, i.e.,

$$\eta_{ij} = \frac{M'}{M} \tag{3}$$

where M' indicates by predicting the practical data transmission quantity of waiting for being delivered in buffer of relay nodes, M shows by predicting the data transmission quantity in theory during the average contact duration $\overline{T}$.

When the two nodes meet in the transmission range, they can exchange some messages for an arbitrary time interval. The computation of the history average contact duration $\overline{T}$ between the nodes is following:

$$\overline{T} = \frac{\sum\limits_{n=1}^{\infty} T[i(n),\ j(n)]}{n} \tag{4}$$

According to the (4), we can also compute the data transmission quantity of the prediction in theory during the average contact duration $\overline{T}$, i.e.,

$$M = R \times \overline{T} \tag{5}$$

where R is the data transmission rate in the network, which is randomly deployed in the mobile network environment model.

We use a simple algorithm for predicting the practical data transmission quantity M'. The main idea is that, we presume that each node has the number of packets N in its buffer to deliver messages from this node to the destination node. And each packet is set a deadline, which is also called "time to live" (TTL). It is obvious that, if and only if the messages is completely delivered to next node before the deadline, the node will gain an optimum transmission value $p'_j > 0$, and these value is summed up by the practical data transmission quantity, i.e.,

$$M' = \sum_{j \in J} p'_j \tag{6}$$

where J is the packet set of practical delivery packets and $J \subseteq N$, and p'_j is the each size of successfully delivered packets in the node set J.

What follows in the passage shows the pseudo code of our proposed the practical data transmission quantity M' between relay nodes and the destination. Initially, in the algorithm the packet set J is an empty set, P_r and m_r respectively indicate the rth packet and itself size in buffer of the relay node. where $\{P_r\}$ indicates a set of all waiting delivered packets, and $\cup$ shows union in set. Messages waiting to being delivered are queuing in the buffer according to the delivered message size as a descending order. Specifically, the main ideas can be summarized in the above algorithm as follows.

Algorithm 1. The pseudo code of computing M'

Input:
　　Input:$M' = 0$; $J \in \emptyset$; $m_1 \geq m_2 \geq m_3 \geq \cdots\cdots \geq m_N$.
Iteration:
　1: label:
　2: **for all** $(r = 1; r <= N; r + +)$ **do**
　3:　　**if** $M' + m_r \leq M$ **then**
　4:　　　$M' = M' + m_r$;
　5:　　　$M = M - m_r$;
　6:　　　$J = J \cup \{P_r\}$;
　7:　　**end if**
　8:　　**if** $M' + m_r > M$ **then**
　9:　　　goto label;
　10:　**end if**
　11:　**if** $M = 0$ **then**
　12:　　break out;
　13:　**end if**
　14:　output the value of M' ;
　15: **end for**

3.3   The Utility Value Updating

The main thought of the utility value updating of delivery messages in each node is that, a list of utility value is owned by each node, and is updated constantly. The list shows how to deliver messages by the utility value in each node. Once they come into the communication range, the list would be exchanged to each other between two nodes. The utility value is updated as follows: we assume that k is some relay node. When the messages are delivered from another relay node i to the destination node j, if the relay node k has never encountered the destination node j, the utility would holds $\omega_{kj} = 0$. If the utility value of the nodes between the relay node k and the destination node j is greater than the utility value of between the relay node i and the destination node j, in other words, $\omega_{kj} > \omega_{ij}$, the utility value of the node k will update in the following:

$$\omega_{kj} = \omega'_{kj} + \alpha \times (\omega_{kj} - \omega_{ij}) \tag{7}$$

where ω_{ij} and ω_{kj} respectively indicate utility value of the nodes between the relay node i and the destination node j, and utility value of the nodes between the relay node k and the destination node j. ω'_{kj} indicates the latest updating utility value of the nodes k, and $\alpha(\alpha \in (0, 1))$ is the zoom coefficient, which reflects the transitivity of forwarding utility [14].

3.4   Forwarding Scheme

The main points of the forwarding scheme are that, the comparisons of delivery utility value will occur among the relay nodes of carrying messages and others relay nodes as they encounter in the communications range. There are two cases in the HMPR forwarding scheme in the following.

- If the delivery utility value of the relay nodes of carrying messages is less than the delivery utility value of the others relay nodes, then the relay nodes of carrying messages will deliver messages to the others relay nodes.
- If the delivery utility value of the relay nodes of carrying messages is greater than or equal to the delivery utility value of the others relay nodes, then the relay nodes of carrying messages will not deliver the messages to the other relay nodes, in other words, the buffer of the nodes will store them all the time until the relay nodes of carrying messages will encounter the destination node or the relay nodes with a larger utility value than themselves.

4   Performance Evaluations

In this section, we evaluate the performance of HMPR with other two existing routing protocols, such as Epidemic and Prophet. We choose the ONE (Opportunistic Network Environment) [15] simulator for performance evaluations. ONE is a power tool that is designed to simulate and evaluate routing protocols for specific DTN environment, and it is also bundled some popular DTN protocol implementations. All those evaluation results of these protocols show in this paper were using the shipped protocols in ONE, without any modifications. And we also use the Helsinki city scenario in our simulation.

4.1   Simulation Settings

For our simulation, we assume interpersonal communication between mobile users in a city using modern mobile phones or similar devices, using Bluetooth at 2Mbit/s net data rate with 10m radio range and the high speed mobile device at 10Mbit/s net data rate with 100m radio range. In the simulation environment, we deploy three node types: pedestrians, cars and trams. Meanwhile, we use three node mobility models: Random Way Point (RWP), Shortest Path Map (SPM) and Map Route Movement (MRM). All messages are randomly generated with different sizes at source nodes, and intended destinations during initialization of the simulation. Message size is randomly selected from 200KB to 500KB, and the TTL value is also randomly set from 1 hour to 5 hours in the network. The mobile devices have up to 10MB and 50MB of free buffer space for storing and forwarding messages. We have 126 mobile nodes, and these nodes move in a terrain of 4500 × 3400m. We set very sparse network parameters (see Table I for detail). We also define parameters for the Prophet routing following the recommendation in the paper, where P_{init}=0.75, β=0.25 and γ=0.98.

Table 1. Simulation Environment

PARAMETER	Pedestrians	Cars	Trams
Number of nodes	80	40	6
Waiting time(s)	$0 \sim 120$	$0 \sim 60$	$0 \sim 120$
Speed(m/s)	$0.5 \sim 1.5$	$2.7 \sim 13.9$	$7 \sim 10$
Transmission range(m)	10	50	100
Mobility model	RWP	SPM	MRM
Simulation time(Ks)	45	45	45

4.2   Analysis of Simulation Results

In this paper, we consider four metrics of the routing performance evaluations [16] as follows:

- Delivery ratio is that the number of messages delivered to the destination divided by the number of messages which the source had been created. It reflects the integrity and reliability of the routing protocols.
- Overhead ratio is that the number of messages in relay nodes subtracts the number of successful delivery messages to the destination, and then divided by the number of successful delivery messages. It reflects the message delivery overhead of the performance in the network.
- Average delay time indicates that the average value of delay time which is created by the successful delivery messages to the destination. It affects the total average communication time of the source and destination and is one of the indicators reflecting the network performance.

- Average buffer time shows that the average value of the buffer time which is created by storage messages stayed in the node buffer in the network. It affects the total average time of storage messages which stayed in the node buffer and is also one of the indicators reflecting the network performance.

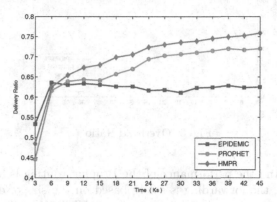

Fig. 2. Delivery Ratio

Impact of Delivery Ratio. From the figure 2, we find that delivery ratio of the HMPR scheme is better than Epidemic and Prophet routing. And the performance becomes well with the growth of simulation timeframe among these routings. Epidemic is a flood routing scheme, which suffers from the inability to deliver messages to recipients that are in other transmission range when message are sent. Before 6 Ks the performance of Epidemic is better, and with the growth of time the network congestion emerges due to excessive duplicates in the network, so that most of the messages would not be successfully delivered. The Prophet routing can be considered as a better routing in term of the messages delivery ratio, but the performance is worse than the HMPR with the growth of the transmission cost. The proposed HMPR is not only to be considered that the messages can be delivered by means of relay nodes, but also to achieve delivery messages to the destination for an optimal transmission. In the HMPR scheme, we take into account some main factors that meeting frequency, contact duration and message size and so on.

Impact of Overhead Ratio. Figure 3 shows message overhead ratio with different simulation timeframe. From the figure, we can learn about the performance of HMPR outperforms the Epidemic and Prophet routing. The reason of the advantages comes from some factors that messages are successfully delivered to the destination in HMPR scheme. Each forwarding node is selected optimally, instead of blind determining relay nodes for messages delivery. So HMPR can avoid some cost of some unnecessary forwarding process. With the same environment, the more overhead ratio is, the worse the performance is in the network. Epidemic routing has a larger overhead is that a large number of messages are only to be relayed in forwarding process, but not to be delivered to

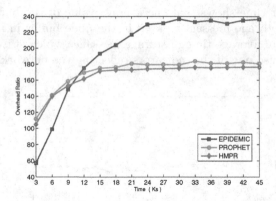

Fig. 3. Overhead Ratio

the destination. And the performance of the Prophet routing is better than the Epidemic routing, the forwarding is solely based on the size of delivery probability between the meeting nodes, message size and TTL value are not discussed in the protocol.

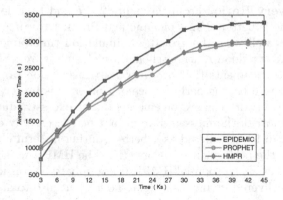

Fig. 4. Average Delay Time

Impact of Average Delay Time. In the figure 4, we will realize average delay of the HMPR scheme is almost the same with the Prophet routing, but they are better than Epidemic routing. The average delay time is increasing with the growth of the simulation timeframe, and most of messages enter the forwarding queue in node buffer. The main reason why the average delay is higher is coupled to the fact that more message are delivered in the networks. The advantage of HMPR scheme is that much more messages can be delivered from relay nodes to the destinations. These extra messages to be delivered are messages that were dropped at smaller queue sizes, but now are able to reside in the queues long enough to be delivered to their destinations. This incurs a longer delay time for these messages, so that the average delay is much larger.

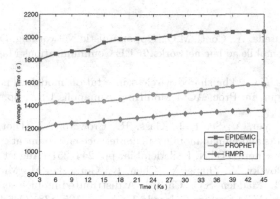

Fig. 5. Average Buffer Time

Impact of Average Buffer Time Figure 5 shows us the performance of average buffer time among three routings in different simulation timeframe. See as the figure, in the finite storage space, the average buffer time of HMPR scheme is clearly less than Epidemic and Prophet routing, and the HMPR makes use of the scheme of the contact duration and meeting frequency to deliver messages to the destination, so that the messages can traverse the networks effectively. In this paper, we consider that the message size and the TTL value of each message are important for network performance of message delivery to the destination. However, the Prophet routing waits for the companies of destination passively and wastes lots of time. After the TTL reaches some value, the forwarding capacity of the network becomes the performance bottleneck. In Epidemic routing, although a node forwards the messages to each node it meets, what the large cost of the average buffer time is that the phenomenon of network congestion often occurs to the extent that the performance is not better than other routings.

5   Conclusion

In this paper, we have proposed the routing scheme based on history meeting prediction routing (HMPR) for the opportunistic networks against the existing problems. We have compared HMPR with the classic Epidemic and Prophet through the ONE simulation. The results demonstrate that the involved performances of the HMPR scheme are much better than any other in the above routings. As for the average delay, HMPR and Prophet are roughly similar. However, HMPR has higher delivery ratio and lower overhead ratio. In finite storage space, the average buffer time makes a signal improvement, because we consider that the message size and TTL value are two key factors for effective data transmission. Network delay can bring some extra expenses in metrics of data transmission and storage. We will do future works for complying with the reality need in the network to enhance the protocol's performance.

References

1. Pelusi, L., Passarella, A., Conti, M.C.: Opportunistic Networking: Data forwarding in disconnected mobile ad hoc networks. IEEE Communications Magazine 44, 134–141 (2006)
2. Small, T., Haas, Z.C.: The shared wireless infestation model: A new ad hoc networking paradigm. In: Proc. ACM MobiHoc, Annapolis USA, pp. 233–244 (June 2003)
3. Hui, P., Chaintreau, A., Scott, J., Gass, R., Crowcroft, J., Diot, C.C.: Pocket switched networks and human mobility in conference environments. In: Proc. ACM SIGCOMM Workshop WDTN, Philadelphia, pp. 244–251 (August 2005)
4. Hull, B., Bychkovsky, V., Zhang, Y., Chen, K., Goraczko, M., Miu, A., Shih, E., Balakrishnan, H., Madden, S.C.: CarTel: A distributed mobile sensor computing system. In: Proc. ACM SenSys, Colorado USA, pp. 125–138 (October 2006)
5. Pentland, A., Fletcher, R., Hasson, A.J.: DakNet: Rethinking connectivity in developing nations. IEEE Journals and Magazines, Computer 37, 78–83 (2004)
6. Vahdat, A., David Becker, S.: Epidemic routing for partially connected ad hoc networks. In: Technical Report CS2000, Department of Computer Science, Duke University, USA, pp. 1–14 (2000)
7. Musolesi, M., Hailes, S., Mascolo, C.: Adaptive routing for intermittently connected mobile ad hoc networks. In: IEEE WoWMoM, Italy, pp. 183–189 (June 2005)
8. Lindgren, A., Doria, A., Schelen, O.: Probabilistic Routing in Intermittently Connected Networks. In: Proc. ACM MobiHoc, vol. 7, pp. 239–254, Annapolis USA (June 2003)
9. Wang, C., Liu, J., Kuang, J.: Performance Analysis on Direct Transmission Scheme under RWP Mobility Model in DTMSNs. In: E Wireless Communications, Networking and Mobile Computing(WiCOM), Turkey, pp. 23–25 (September 2011)
10. Gao, W., Cao, G.: On Exploiting Transient Contact Patterns for Data Forwarding in Delay Tolerant Networks. In: IEEE ICNP, USA, pp. 193–202 (October 2010)
11. Li, F., Wu, J.: LocalCom: A Community-based Epidemic Forwarding Scheme in Disruption-tolerant Networks. In: IEEE SECON, Rome Italy, pp.1–9 (June 2009)
12. Masood, S.H., Raza, S.A., Coates, M.J.: Content Distribution Strategies in Opportunistic Networks. Technical Report CS 2011, Montreal, Canada, McGill University, Canada, pp. 1–65 (December 2011)
13. Li, Q., Zhu, S., Cao, G.: Routing in Socially Selfish Delay Tolerant Networks. In: IEEE INFOCOM, Shanghai, China, pp. 1–6 (April 2010)
14. Fujihara, A., Ono, S., Hiroyoshi Miwa, C.: Optimal Forwarding Criterion of Utility-based Routing under Sequential Encounters for Delay Tolerant Networks. In: IEEE INCoS, Fukuoka Japan, pp. 279–286 (December 2011)
15. Keranen, A., Ott, J., Karkkainen, T.: The ONE Simulator for DTN Protocol Evaluation. In: SIMUTools, Proceedings of the 2nd International Conference on Simulation Tools and Techniques, Rome, pp. 1–10 (March 2009)
16. Yan, X., Huang, X., Peng, W.: Simulation based performance evaluation of DTN routing protocols. Computer Technology and Development, vol 20, 1–4 (2010)

Bloom Filter-Based Ad Hoc Multicast Communication in Cyber-Physical Systems and Computational Materials

Homa Hosseinmardi, Nikolaus Correll, and Richard Han

Department of Computer Science
University of Colorado at Boulder, Boulder, CO, USA
{homa.hosseinmardi,nikolaus.correll,rhan}@colorado.edu

Abstract. This article presents an efficient ad hoc multicast communication protocol for next-generation cyber-physical systems and computational materials. Communication with such systems would be gestural, and when cells within such materials detect a motion, they would share that information with each other. We want to achieve efficient communication among only the group of nodes that sense a particular (gestural) event. Our approach is to employ a Bloom filter-based approach to label the multicast group with an approximate error-resilient multicast tag that captures the temporal and spatial characteristics of the sensor group. A Bloom filter is a space-efficient probabilistic data structure that is used to test whether an element is a member of a set. We describe our Bloom filter-based multicast communication (BMC) protocol, and report simulation results.

1   Introduction

This paper explores the issue of establishing efficient multicast communication amongst an ad hoc group of cells or nodes that comprise next-generation cyber-physical systems and/or computational materials. We envision that future cyber-physical systems may resemble a computational wall, or amorphous computing façade, as shown in Fig. 1. Such a system would be comprised of many individual cells that sense the environment and communicate with each other. For example, in the case of an amorphous computing façade, the individual nodes may contain pressure, light, infrared and perhaps even simple vision sensors, and actuators that can change the translucency of each cell in the wall to admit more/less light, and/or "open/close" the cell to admit/shut off outside air flow. We further imagine that communicating with such cyber-physical systems will be gestural in nature, i.e. opening a window or set of cells would be done by making one gesture such as drawing an "O" shape in mid-air or on the wall that is recognized by the wall, while making another gesture would close the window or set of cells, such as drawing a "C" shape. The sensors on the cells would detect the motion, and those affected cells would share information with each other. They would collectively compute and decide which pattern was detected, and then actuate accordingly. The cells themselves are assumed to have fairly limited computational and communication resources.

X. Wang et al. (Eds.): WASA 2012, LNCS 7405, pp. 595–606, 2012.

Fig. 1. An artist's rendering of a future cyber-physical system, namely an amorphous computing façade consisting of many communicating sensor/actuator cells

Our system model does not require that these amorphous facades be networked to a powerful back-end server, and permits them to be installed as independent stand-alone units. We only assume that each cell is provided sufficient power by some means, either wired or even wirelessly via RF energy. In addition, we don't assume that all nodes are necessarily wired together, and allow wireless communication between cells. As a result, we must tolerate packet loss. With this more general system model, we are able to admit broader scenarios for next-generation cyber-physical systems. For example, smart e-clothing is being explored, and we imagine that in the future clothing will become a computational material. Communication with such a smart shirt would involve sketching a gesture over the cloth, such as a "B" to indicate that the shirt should self-button, or "L" to light an LED embedded in the clothing. The individual cells in the shirt would sense the gesture, communicate with each other to determine the gesture, and then actuate accordingly. Similarly, wireless sensor networks could benefit from the ad hoc multicast routing approach that we develop here. Our model also is flexible enough to accommodate non-uniformity of cells.

Our goal is to achieve efficient communication among only the group of nodes that sense a particular (gestural) event, and limit the overhead involved in establishing such ad hoc multicast communication. Our approach is to employ a Bloom filter-based approach to label the multicast group with an approximate error-resilient multicast tag that captures the temporal and spatial characteristics of the sensor group. A Bloom filter is a space-efficient probabilistic data structure that is used to test whether an element is a member of a set. We describe our Bloom filter-based multicast communication (BMC) protocol in the following, and report simulation results.

2   Related Work

Demand for growth in the size of ad-hoc networks has led to many researches done on scalable multicast routing. Also an important aspect in cyber-physical systems is bandwidth, space and computational efficiency [1]. Bloom Filter main characteristic is membership query [2], and they have several applications in networks [3-8] like security [4-5], duplicate packet and loop detection [6-7], and anonymous routing [8]. Also in-network-element and in-packet Bloom Filter based forwarding uses membership query property that encodes the routing path to a small hashed stream [4, 9]. The drawback of Bloom filters is the probability of false positives, which in general causes inefficiency in networks. Data leakage to neighbors that are not part of a multicast group problem that is introduced by false positive and [10] has addressed methods to reduce the drawbacks of Bloom Filter false positives.

In [11] a multicast forwarding scheme has been proposed that Bloom filter of interfaces exist in network elements. Upon arriving a packet, decision will be made on the forwarding interface. The authors in [12] propose a DSR protocol to find the routing path and source node will compute the Bloom filter of the path that is replied back to it and put it in packets. When each node receives a packet, it will first check if it is the destination. If the receiver node was not the destination then it will check the membership of its neighbors in the Bloom filter of the packet, i.e. hash the ID of each neighbor to see if the correct bits are set in the Bloom filter of the packet, and forward the packet for each neighbor that is a member of the Bloom filtered set. We use in packet Bloom filter too, but a thresholding algorithm with bitwise comparing of packet's Bloom filter decide on forwarding of the packet.

The previous approaches assume that the sender has complete knowledge of the members of either the path or multicast group, when computing the Bloom filter (BF) tag, and relies on an exact match at each hop as the tagged packet is forwarded. Our approach permits the sender to know only a subset of the multicast group when computing the Bloom filter, yet still allows the packet to reach most of the other members of the multicast group. This is because at each hop, rather than having each node compare its (or its neighbor's) BF hash (ID) to the BF packet tag, our Bloom filter is computed based on the event packets flooded (this is limited by a TTL) in response to the motion sensing event. Each node who has seen the same event caches all such seen packets, creating a group of IDs seen at each node for an event. A node '1' will send data packets to the multicast group by appending its BF tag hash (group IDs seen at '1'). Intermediate nodes '2' will compare their BF tag hash (group IDs seen at '2') to the packet's BF tag, and if the comparison is within a threshold number of bits, then the packet is accepted for further forwarding. Our approach is therefore also error-resilient, since it can tolerate the loss of some packets, and we seek only an approximate match, rather than an exact match.

3   BMC Protocol

We describe the design of a Bloom-filter based Multicast Communication (BMC) protocol including three Phases. Phase. I is member discovery through data-driven message broadcasting after detecting a motion. Phase. II is setting up a multicast routing path that will be done through assigning a multicast tag to each node based on members stored in its table. In Phase. III data will be shared among the multicast group, using the multicast tag.

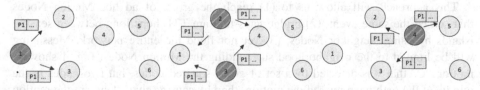

Fig. 2. Phase. I, event broadcasting. Nodes detecting a motion (dashed), will broadcast an Event-Packet to all their neighbors, which will propagate the information hop-by-hop.

3.1   Phase. I: Discovering Members

During the data-driven discovery process each node builds a multicast group member list by forwarding and storing Event-Packets. Upon detecting a motion, all nodes that detected the motion, called Motion-Nodes, will broadcast an Event-Packet to all

$$\text{Event-Packet} = \text{< Node-ID, X, Y, Motion-Order>}$$

their neighbors, including their ID, location and possibly additional metadata that we classify as "Motion-Order" data, e.g. an optional timestamp. Each event packet gets forwarded hop by hop as shown in Fig. 2. If a Motion-Node receives another node's event packet within some time bound D of its own detection of a motion event, then it accepts the event packet as an indication that the message sender is part of the same motion sensing event, adds the sender (contents of its event packet) to its multicast table, and forwards the message by broadcasting it again. In the absence of message loss and sensing loss, such a simple approach will allow all contiguous nodes that sensed an event to quickly learn all other nodes that sensed the same event, and thus establish an ad hoc multicast group. We assume that different sensing events are separated by at least D seconds, e.g. each separate gesture might take a second, so D would be less than one second.

However, sensor nodes in the middle of a motion may fail to detect that event for any number of reasons, e.g. different calibrations, insufficient local stimuli, flaky electromechanical/chemical sensors, etc. This can result in disconnected islands of Motion Nodes that sensed the same event. To bridge these islands, the event packets must be forwarded through nodes that may not have detected the event. To deal with this issue, we institute a TTL for event packets. When a Motion Node first broadcasts its event packet, the TTL is set to some default. A node that receives this packet with TTL>0 and has not detected the motion is nonetheless a candidate for participating as a bridging node between two islands. We call such nodes Neighbor Nodes of the Motion Nodes. A Neighbor Node will decrement the TTL, record the event packet into its potential multicast table, and re-broadcast the packet. When TTL become zero, the message will not be forwarded any more. Note also that Motion Nodes that accept an event message will reset the TTL to its initial default value on each re-broadcast and do not decrement the TTL. Fig. 3 depicts the flowchart of the BMC algorithm. Broadcasting in Phase I will be stopped when there is not any message to be forwarded by Motion Nodes and Neighbor Nodes.

This approach will allow us to (1) reach the group of ad hoc Motion Nodes that sensed the same event, (2) bridge gaps that are TTL hops long between sensing islands by using Neighbor Nodes, (3) yet not flood the entire network. Messaging will be limited to the neighborhood surrounding the Motion Nodes. Fig. 4 shows a motion "C" that was detected by a set of green squared nodes, but two nodes in the middle of the path have missed the motion, thereby causing two islands in the motion group.

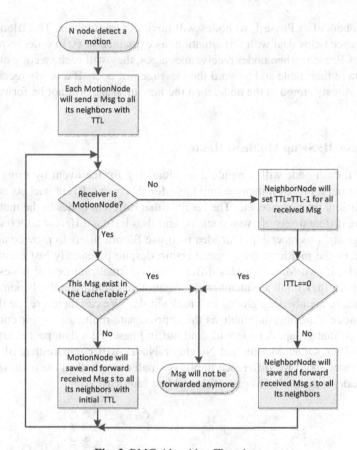

Fig. 3. BMC Algorithm Flowchart

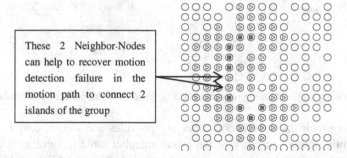

These 2 Neighbor-Nodes can help to recover motion detection failure in the motion path to connect 2 islands of the group

Fig. 4. Neighbor-Nodes in 3 hops have BF tag of the motion group "C". All motion events (filled nodes) are considered to belong to the same cluster as the TTL is set to 3 in this example

Nodes marked with blue triangles are Neighbor Nodes by TTL=3, and are candidates for connecting two islands. All Motion Nodes and Neighbor Nodes will have a table of multicast group members after Phase I. When considering the probability of message loss, it is possible that all nodes do not receive all the event packets hence group members after Phase I, so nodes will have different tables. The Bloom filter's error resilience helps deal with this situation, as explained next. In order to reduce the overhead of Phase I, when nodes receive messages, they will cache a copy of received information in their table and forward the message just once. If a newly received message is previously stored in the node, then the new message will not be forwarded any further.

3.2   Phase. II: Setup Multicast Route

In Phase. II, each node will compute a multicast tag for the event by using a Bloom Filter operating on its own membership table for this event. Event packets can be lost due to collision, interference, etc. The result is that different nodes in the motion event will receive different sets of event packets, and thus have a different table/view of the multicast group's membership. Our idea is to use Bloom filters to provide an approximate label of the multicast group membership despite potentially lost event packets. For example, if two Motion Nodes differ in only a small number of nodes with respect to whom they think are members in the motion event, then the Bloom filters of their respective membership groups will look similar. We can therefore use the Bloom filter of a node's membership table as the approximate multicast tag for communication amongst that group. A node will send out in Phase. III a data packet tagged with its Bloom filter. Other Motion and Neighbor Nodes will compare that Bloom filter with their own, and if the difference in bits is small enough, then the node will accept and re-broadcast the packet as part of this ad hoc multicast group.

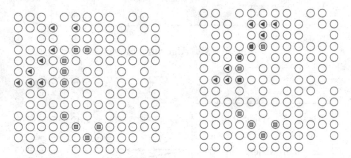

Fig. 5. 2 motion with overlapping neighborhood (left) and overlapping group members (right)

For sending their data, the Bloom filter tag provides a compact, easy to compute, and sufficiently unique summary of the group member table for multicast communications in the presence of packet loss. Imagine motions "C" and "Z" have happened in different times, but involve each others' neighborhoods, so there may be some common nodes to both motions, as shown in Fig. 5. If nodes of group "Z" use a Bloom Filter (BF) tag to send out their data, because it has been produced by the members of its group, then it has a low correlation with the BF tag of group "C" and nodes can recognize it is not data from members of group "C". Even if groups "C" and "Z" have some common nodes, correlation of BF tags within a group member is bigger than correlation between BF tags of two different groups. A Bloom Filter array is initially a stream of M zero bits, mapping each member of the group $G=$ {a, b,...,d} with N members using a hash function to one bit of its stream and setting it to one as it has been shown in the upper figure of Fig. 6. Each member x can be hashed K times, $h_i(x)$ where $i=1, 2...K$. If we label nodes in Fig. 5 right-hand with Node-ID, group "C" has 9 Motion Nodes with the set "C"={43, 44,58,70,82,119,132,146,133} and group "Z" has 10 Motion Nodes with set "Z"={17,18,19,30,43,58,69,80,81,82}. They have 3 Motion Nodes {43, 58, 82} in common and these nodes will have 2 group tables and therefor 2 BF tags. Fig. 6 shows 2 different BF tags assigned to a Motion Node with Node-ID=82 for groups "C" and "Z". In a Bloom Filter with length $M=48$, each member of the table "C" and table "Z" of Node "82" is hashed two times and create the tags showed in Fig. 6 for Node "82". BF tag in each received data packet would be compared bitwise; for example the bitwise XOR of "C" BF tag with data packet BF tag is 2 "one" bits and the bitwise XOR of "Z" BF tag with data packet BF tag is 20 "one" bits. For a threshold T less than 20 and more than 2, Node "82" can discriminated data packets of group "C" and "Z" from each other. Similarly, for the Motion Nodes that are not common between motions, each node will have one group table and compares a received packet's tag to the BF tag of its table. By $T<20$ bits, node accepts the packet as being part of its multicast group.

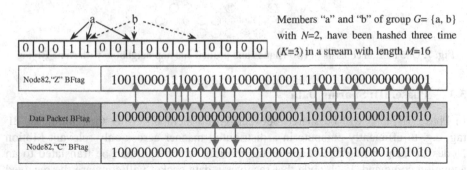

Members "a" and "b" of group $G=$ {a, b} with $N=2$, have been hashed three time $(K=3)$ in a stream with length $M=16$

Fig. 6. The upper one shows how bloom filter works- Lower ones show Bloom Filter tag assigned to Motion Node "82", a common node of 2 different groups shown in Figure 5-righ hand

But we cannot set threshold T too small because packet loss means that the members of a group will have similar but not necessarily identical BF tags. However we can see from Fig. 6 the correlation between Motion Nodes inside a group is bigger than correlation with another group member tags and choosing a proper threshold T can both exclude non-group members while including the vast majority of legitimate group members.

Each Neighbor Node in Phase II will compute its BF tag using received event packets with TTL>0 from Phase I. This will allow it to decide whether a data packet received with some multicast tag in Phase. III should be forwarded or re-broadcast using the thresholding similarity scheme above. We observe from Fig. 4 that even though the TTL substantially limited the number of nodes participating in the ad hoc multicast group, there is still considerable inefficiency in the large number of Neighbor Nodes that re-broadcast data, yet serve not useful bridging function between two islands. A simple and yet efficient way to reduce the number of Neighbor Nodes participating in Phase III is elimination using data location. Each node knows its location and also knows the location of group members based on the event packets that it has received and stored in its table. Therefore Neighbor Nodes that are more than TTL/2 hops from Motion Nodes can be pruned and will remove their table and will not participate in forwarding data. The radius of neighborhood with BF tag can be chosen, considering the sparsity of the network or environmental conditions like message loss probability. Fig. 7 illustrates a case where we have substantially pruned the set of Neighbor Nodes for TTL=3.

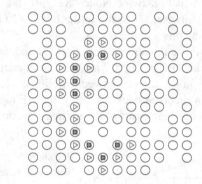

Fig. 7. One motion consists of two islands and pruned one hop neighbors with same BF tag

3.3   Phase. III: Sharing Data

In Phase. III, data will be shared between group members using their multicast BF tag, e.g. to efficiently compute in a distributed manner across only relevant Motion Nodes the sequencing and shape of the motion, which can then be translated to an actuation command. Each node that receives a data packet will compare the received packet BF tag with its BF tag. If their correlation was big enough, each node will save a copy and broadcast the data packet for its neighbors. Determining the proper threshold for correlation between BF tags, will be essential to prevent data leakage between two different groups and data loss inside a group. Note that the data shared in this phase can be used to communicate temporal ordering information, which is important for determining the directionality of a gesture, not just its shape. One way to accomplish this is to share time stamps, either in Phase. I or III. However, we do not need to assume that all cells have globally synchronized time stamps, or even locally synchronized time stamps, in order to extract ordering. One approach would be to establish local ordering in Phase. I, i.e. each node that detects an event simply records the order in which it hears event packets from its neighbors, then shares that local ordering information in phase III with the other nodes in the multicast group. Each node can then reconstruct an approximate ordering, which should be sufficient to differentiate gestures.

4   Results

We have proposed a distributed computing algorithm for bloom filter based multicast communication in an Ad Hoc network. Nodes in the multicast group use their Bloom Filtered member table as their multicast tag. Using bloom filter help the network being resilient in the case that all members do not have all the group members in their table. It means even if 10 percentages of even packets during Phase I be lost, and if some of group member do not receive all the even packets, data can be delivered to them. The BMC algorithms is evaluated based the Ratio of Membership Discovery (RMD) metric. It shows the ratio of node pairs of the group that can recognize they are in the same multicast group to the total number of node pairs in the motion group.

Number of pairs in the group = (number of Motion Nodes)^2- number of Motion Nodes

For the Motion Nodes inside a group, it is desired that RMD reached one. It means that each Motion Node can recognize received data packet that belongs to its multicast group members. Imagine nodes (Motion or Neighbor) that have BF tags of different groups. The desired RMD between different groups is zero. It means in each node comparing its BF tag with received data packet BF tag, node should know that it is a data form its group members or not, and the membership between two different groups should be zero. In this case even when two groups have common members, data packets can find their proper group members comparing their BF tags.

Consider a non-homogenous network in Fig. 4 that is sparse and in average each node have less than three neighbors. After detecting a motion "C", Motion Nodes start Phase I to share their information in event packets and compute their multicast tag. In this special motion, 9 nodes have detected the motion and 2 nodes have missed the motion and cause 2 islands in the group as shown in Fig. 4. The probability of event packet loss during Phase. I is 5%. It may cause some group members to not receive all packets from other group members. After exchanging event packets, in Phase. II each node will compute its Bloom Filter for the list of group nodes in its own table. In Phase. III each node will send out a data packet with its BF tag attached as the multicast group tag. Each node belong to the group will decide based on the correlation between its BF tags and the received packet BF tag.

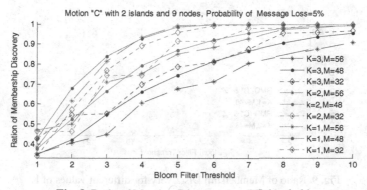

Fig. 8. Ratio of Member Discovery vs. BF threshold

We will evaluate our algorithm considering different Probability of packet loss, Threshold, Filter size, Number of hashing. Fig. 8 shows ratio of node pairs of the group "C" that can catch they are in the same group to the total number of node pairs in the group. For a typical group size 9, Filter size 32, 48 and 56 with K=1, 2, 3 in a Probability of packet loss 5% group RMD is evaluated. It can be seen that with lower K and higher threshold, the ratio of group pairs that catch each other will increase.

In order to figure out the cost of low K, low M and bigger threshold consider the case that nodes may have BF tag form different groups at the same time. In this situation higher threshold may mislead nodes to assign other groups Motion Nodes as their group member. Consider Fig. 5 with right hand motion, where motion "Z" has happened after motion "C" and has 3 nodes in common with motion group "C". BF tag of each group member is produced by its table, but 3 common nodes out of 10 nodes will increase the correlation of different groups Bloom Filter tags. Fig. 9 shows that different K just changes the threshold parameter and does not affect BMC algorithm performance.

From Fig. 8 it can be inferred that BMC algorithm approximately works same in different Filter size for group membership discovery when there is only one motion. However if more than one motion exist, Fig. 10 shows that for small filter length in order to discriminate groups, small threshold should apply. This small threshold can lead some pairs in the same group can recognize each other as one motion group. For example in Fig. 11 for M=24 in threshold 4 RMD between "C" and "Z" reaches zero, when the RMD inside group "C" is still below one. Vertical dash line determine a threshold for which RMD inside group is one and RMD between groups is zero. We can conclude the Size of Bloom Filter tag will affect ratio of false membership discovery when there are overlapping motions and this limit us in the lower bound of Bloom filter size. Also for M=48 it is obvious that the cost of increasing threshold can be increasing false membership discovery and nodes cannot discriminate the two group form each other.

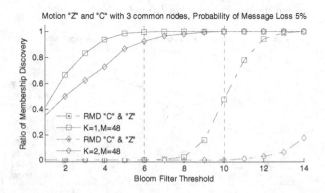

Fig. 9. Ratio of Membership Discovery for different values of K

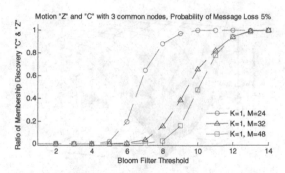

Fig. 10. Ratio of Member Discovery between groups "C" and "Z"

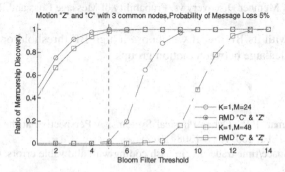

Fig. 11. Ratio of Member Discovery in group "C" (solid lines) and Ratio of Member Discovery between groups "C" and "Z" (marked lines)

As we mentioned before, Probability of packet loss cause motion nodes do not receive all group members message and have different tables and different Bloom Filter tags. Fig. 12-left hand shows even with Probability of message loss up to 12%, with a Bloom filter size M=48 and K=1, threshold 8 can reach RMD one. This Figure implies that higher threshold will be needed to recover group membership inside a group when the Probability of packet loss increases. However the cost of higher threshold is increasing RMD between groups as it is shown in the Fig. 12- right hand. Fig. 13 shows RMD of motion "C" for M=48 and K=1 versus Bloom filter size and Probability of packet loss. After Phase. I and constructing BF tags in Phase. II, each node will

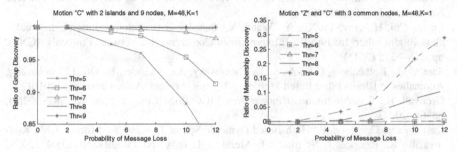

Fig. 12. Ratio of Member Discovery vs. Probability of Message Loss

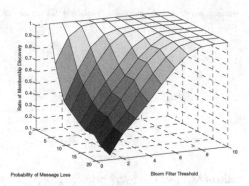

Fig. 13. Ratio of Member Discovery vs. Probability of Message Loss and BF Threshold

send out its data with its BF tag. If we choose a high BF threshold or low filter size, we will have data leakage between motion groups.

References

1. Kim, K.D., Kumar, P.R.: Cyber–Physical Systems: A Perspective at the Centennial. Proceedings of the IEEE 100, 1287–1308 (2012)
2. Bloom, B.H.: Space/time trade-offs in hash coding with allowable errors. Commun. ACM, 422–426 (1970)
3. Tarkoma, S., Rothenberg, C.E., Lagerspetz, E.: Theory and Practice of Bloom Filters for Distributed Systems. IEEE Communications Surveys & Tutorials 14(1) (2012)
4. Broder, A., Mitzenmacher, M.: Network applications of bloom filter: a survey. Internet Mathematics 1(4), 485–509 (2003)
5. Särelä, M., Esteve Rothenberg, C., Zahemszky, A., Nikander, P., Ott, J.: BloomCasting: Security in Bloom Filter Based Multicast. In: Aura, T., Järvinen, K., Nyberg, K. (eds.) NordSec 2010. LNCS, vol. 7127, pp. 1–16. Springer, Heidelberg (2012)
6. Deng, F., Rafiei, D.: Approximately detecting duplicates for streaming data using stable Bloom filters. In: SIGMOD 2006: Proceedings of the 2006 ACM SIGMOD International Conference on Management of Data, pp. 25–36. ACM, New York (2006)
7. Whitaker, A., Wetherall, D.: Forwarding without Loops in Icarus. In: Proceedings of Open Architectures and Network Programming (OPENARCH), pp. 63–75 (2002)
8. Dong, Y., Wing Chim, T., Li, V.O.K., Yiu, S.M., Hui, C.K.: ARMR: Anonymous routing protocol with multiple routes for communications in mobile ad hoc networks. Ad Hoc Network, 1536–1550 (2006)
9. Li, D., Cui, H., Huy, Y.: Xia, Y., Wang, X.: Scalable data center multicast using multiclass Bloom Filter. In: 19th IEEE International Conference on Network Protocols (ICNP), pp. 266 – 275 (2011)
10. Särelä, M., Rothenberg, C.E., Aura, T., Zahemszky, A., Nikander, P., Ott, J.: Forwarding Anomalies in Bloom Filter Based Multicast. Technical report, Aalto University (2010)
11. Grönvall, B.: Scalable multicast forwarding. SIGCOMM Comput. Commun. Rev. 32(1), 68–68 (2002)
12. Castelluccia, C., Mutaf, P.: Hash-Based Dynamic Source Routing. In: Mitrou, N.M., Kontovasilis, K., Rouskas, G.N., Iliadis, I., Merakos, L. (eds.) NETWORKING 2004. LNCS, vol. 3042, pp. 1012–1023. Springer, Heidelberg (2004)

On Wireless Network Infrastructure Optimization for Cyber-Physical Systems in Future Smart Buildings

Jia Liu[1], Tianyou Kou[1], Qian Chen[2], and Hanif D. Sherali[3]

[1] Dept. of ECE, The Ohio State University, Columbus, OH 43210
[2] Dept. of FABE, The Ohio State University, Columbus, OH 43210
[3] Dept. of ISE, Virginia Tech, Blacksburg, VA 24061

Abstract. Today, most cyber-physical systems (CPS) in smart buildings require a wireless-based network infrastructure for sensing, communication, and actuation. In such CPSs, the energy expenditure and hence battery lifetime of the wireless network infrastructure depend heavily upon the placement of the base stations (BS). However, in indoor environments, BS placement is particularly challenging due to the impact of building structures and floors/walls separations. In this paper, we study the problem of jointly optimizing BS placement and power control in buildings to prolong the battery lifetime of sensors in the CPS network infrastructure. We first show that the joint BS placement and power control problem can be formulated as a mixed-integer non-convex program (MINCP), which is NP-hard and difficult to solve especially when the network size is large. To address this difficulty, we propose a novel efficient algorithm called ECPC that targets at large-sized network infrastructures in buildings. Our theoretical analysis and numerical results show that ECPC achieves competitive solutions compared to the true optimal solutions obtained by the branch-and-bound method.

1 Introduction

Today, most cyber-physical systems (CPS) in smart buildings require a wireless network infrastructure for sensing, communication, and actuation. However, studies show that the poor battery lifetime performance of current wireless sensors is becoming a critical factor that affects the future prospect of these emerging CPSs in smart buildings. To prolong battery lifetime, there are two complementary approaches. The first one is to increase battery capacity, which had proved to be difficult over the years: The second approach is to reduce the energy expenditure. Since a wireless sensor's energy expenditure depends heavily on the distance from its associated base station (BS), BS placement optimization has become one of the most effective methods to address the battery lifetime issue.

In the literature, BS placement optimization has been studied for various types of wireless networks (see, e.g., cellular networks [1,2], sensor networks [3–5], and references therein). However, the focus of these existing work is *not* on CPS in building environments. Indeed, when the unique physical features of building

X. Wang et al. (Eds.): WASA 2012, LNCS 7405, pp. 607–618, 2012.
© Springer-Verlag Berlin Heidelberg 2012

environments are taken into consideration, BS placement optimization becomes much more challenging. In addition to the obvious change from 2-D planes to 3-D spaces, building environments have a complex impact on wireless channels: Different interior spaces (e.g., atrium, office, hallway, or basement) with different wall/floor separations yield different signal path losses and fading patterns. Also, building safety codes may impose further physical restrictions to the BS locations, which is unseen in the conventional BS placement literature. So far, it is unclear how to construct good mathematical models and optimization algorithms to capture these unique physical factors for CPS network infrastructure.

In this paper, we address the above challenges by studying the joint optimization of BS placement and power control to minimize the *uplink* transmission power of wireless sensors for CPSs in building environments. The main results of this work are as follows: i) we show that the joint BS placement and power optimization is a challenging *mixed-integer non-convex* optimization problem (MINCP), which is NP-hard and no off-the-shelf optimization methods can be readily applied; ii) to address this difficulty, we propose an efficient algorithm called ECPC (abbreviation for expansion-clustering-projection-contraction) that incorporates several novel ideas specifically designed for CPSs in buildings; and iii) we perform complexity and approximation ratio analysis for the proposed ECPC algorithm. Both our theoretical and numerical results indicate that ECPC yields competitive solutions compared to the global optimal solutions.

The remainder of this paper is organized as follows. In Section 2, we review the related work reported in the literature, putting our work in a comparative perspective. We then present our network model and problem formulation in Section 3. The proposed ECPC solution procedures, along with their numerical results, are presented in Section 4. Section 5 concludes this paper.

2   Related Work

In the literature, there has been a large body of work on BS placement for cellular networks (see e.g., [1,2]) and sensor networks (see, e.g., [3–5]). In contrast, results on BS placement in buildings remains limited and most work in this area considered performance metrics different from ours (e.g., minimum number of BSs to ensure network coverage [6–11], channel assignment/load balancing [12,13], bit error rate minimization [14,15], and throughput maximization [16–18]). Most of these efforts, except [18], considered problems in 2-D planes (i.e., single floor). The focus of [18], however, was on indoor propagation model evaluations and little effort was made in developing optimization algorithms to optimize BS placement. Moreover, a common problem formulation approach in [8–11,19] is to discretize the coverage region into a set of finite candidate locations. As a result, BS placement problems were usually modeled as a mixed-integer linear programming problem (MILP), which can be readily solved by off-the-shelf integer programming solvers (e.g., CPLEX). In contrast, our model allows the region to be continuous. This leads to a much more challenging problem because there are an infinite number of BS candidate locations, implying that off-line path loss

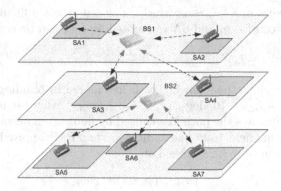

Fig. 1. An illustration of a CPS wireless infrastructure with multiple BSs and SAs in a multi-floor building

computation is no longer feasible. In our previous related works [20,21], we have proposed two non-trivial reformulation approaches to transform the problem into a mixed-integer convex program (MICP) and a mixed-integer linear program (MILP), respectively, thus enabling the use of branch-and-bound method (BB) to find a global optimal solution. However, due to the NP complexity nature of BB, the global optimization algorithms in [20,21] do not scale well as the network size increases.

3   Network Model and Problem Formulation

1) Indoor Wireless Channel Modeling. We consider a wireless CPS network infrastructure in a multi-floor building with M BSs and N sensing areas (SA), as shown in Figure 1. We use $\mathcal{N}$ to denote the set of all SAs. Here, an SA could be any subregion in the building where wireless sensors of the CPS are installed. For simplicity, we assume in this paper that M is large enough to ensure network coverage. We denote the BSs and SAs as BS1, ..., BSM and SA1,..., SAN, respectively. We further assume that co-channel interference among all BSs is negligible under a proper channel assignment and reuse scheme. The case where co-channel interference exists will be left for our future study. We use (u_i, v_i, w_i), $i = 1, \ldots, N$, to denote coordinates of the center of SA i. The length and width of SA i are denoted as L_i and W_i, respectively. Similarly, (x_m, y_m, z_m), $m = 1, \ldots, M$, denotes the coordinates of BS m, which are to be determined. Due to the practical use of building space, the BSs of a CPS network infrastructure are usually required to be mounted on the ceiling of each floor. Also, in buildings, a wireless sensor could be installed on each floor. As a result, the vertical coordinates w_i and z_m cannot be arbitrary and can only take on integer values: $1, 2, \ldots, F$, where F is the maximum number of floors.

To ensure that BS m can cover every point in SA i, we define the distance as the straight line between BS m and the point in SA i that is *furthest* away from BS m. We let h and ρ_i denote the height of each floor and the average installation height of the sensors in SA i, respectively. Then, it is not difficult to show that the distance between BS m and SA i, denoted as d_{im}, can be computed as:

$$d_{im} = [(|x_m - u_i| + \frac{1}{2}L_i)^2 + (|y_m - v_i| + \frac{1}{2}W_i)^2 + |(z_m - w_i + 1)h - \rho_i|^2]^{\frac{1}{2}}. \quad (1)$$

In this paper, we adopt the following path loss model in building environments [22]: $P_{R_m} = P_{T_i} - L_{d_0} - 10\alpha \log_{10}(d_{im}/d_0) - L_{FAF}$, where α is the path loss index and L_{FAF} denotes the path loss caused by floor attenuation factor (FAF). Moreover, numerous field tests had indicated that FAF approximately follows the following relationship [22, Table 4.4]:

$$L_{FAF} = \begin{cases} \Lambda_1 + (\varphi - 1)\Lambda_a, & \text{if } \varphi \geq 1, \\ 0, & \text{if } \varphi = 0, \end{cases} \quad (2)$$

where Λ_1 represents the FAF for a single floor separation, Λ_a represents the FAF for each additional floor, and φ denotes the number of separating floors. Combining all the earlier discussions and after converting P_{R_m}, P_{T_i}, and L_{d_0} from dB scale to a linear scale, it is not difficult to derive the following result for path loss modeling in building environments:

$$P_{R_m} = \frac{P_{T_i}}{H(z_m, w_i)\Lambda^{|z_m - w_i|}d_{im}^\alpha}, \quad \forall i, m. \quad (3)$$

Here, $H(z_m, w_i)$ is a step function that depends on z_m and w_i and has the following structure:

$$H(z_m, w_i) = \begin{cases} H_0, & \text{if } z_m = w_i, \\ H_1, & \text{if } z_m \neq w_i, \end{cases}$$

where $H_0 = L_{d_0}d_0^{-\alpha}$, $H_1 = L_{d_0}d_0^{-\alpha}10^{(\Lambda_1 - \Lambda_a)/10}$, and $\Lambda = 10^{\Lambda_a/10}$.

2) QoS Requirement Constraints. To maintain the transmission data rate that satisfies a sensor's QoS requirement, a necessary condition is that the received power at the BS should be greater than a certain threshold value. We let $P_{\min}$ denote the minimum threshold value. According to (3), we have: $\frac{P_{T_i}}{H(z_m, w_i)\Lambda^{|z_m - w_i|}d_{im}^\alpha} \geq P_{\min}, \forall i, m$. After rearranging and letting $B_i(z_m, w_i) = H_0 P_{\min}$ if $z_m = w_i$ or $H_1 P_{\min}$ if $z_m \neq w_i$, we have

$$B_i(z_m, w_i)\Lambda^{|z_m - w_i|}d_{im}^\alpha - P_{T_i} \leq 0, \forall i, m. \quad (4)$$

3) BS Association Modeling. Unlike conventional wireless networks, in building environments, the channel to the nearest BS may not be the best because the nearest BS could be separated by floors, which leads to an inferior channel due to FAF. Rather than specifying a BS association rule, we model BS association as a part of the overall joint BS placement and power control optimization. For this purpose, we define the following set of binary variables:

$$\gamma_{im} = \begin{cases} 1 & \text{if SA } i \text{ is associated with BS } m, \\ 0 & \text{otherwise.} \end{cases}$$

Then, the BS association can be modeled as:

$$\sum_{m=1}^{M} \gamma_{im} = 1, \quad \forall i = 1, \ldots, N. \tag{5}$$

Considering BS association, we modify the QoS constraint in (4) as:

$$B_i(z_m, w_i)\gamma_{im}\Lambda^{|z_i - w_i|}d_{im}^{\alpha} - P_{T_i} \leq 0, \quad \forall i, m. \tag{6}$$

4) Problem Formulation. To prolong the sensor battery lifetime and ensure fairness among all SAs, we can minimize the total transmission power from all SAs. Incorporating all constraints, the joint BS placement and power optimization (BSPO) can be formulated as:

$$\textbf{BSPO:} \text{ Minimize} \sum_{\forall i} P_{T_i}$$

subject to Constraints in (1), (5), and (6).

Since (1) and (6) are non-convex and involve integer variables, BSPO is a *mixed-integer non-convex program* (MINCP), which is NP-hard in general [23]. Further, since Problem BSPO is highly unstructured, no off-the-shelf optimization method can be readily applied. As mentioned earlier, in [20,21], we have proposed two novel reformulation strategies to transform BSPO into a mixed-integer convex program (MICP) and a mixed-integer linear program (MILP), respectively, both of which enabled the use of branch-and-bound (BB) approach to solve the problem to global optimality. The major benefit of using BB is that, upon its convergence, it *guarantees* finding a global optimal solution to the BSPO problem. However, we note that due to the NP nature of the mixed-integer problems, the convergence time of BB increases exponentially as the network size gets large. Therefore, in this paper, we focus on designing an efficient algorithm that offers competitive solutions for large-sized building networks.

4   ECPC: An Efficient Solution Approach

In this section, we propose an algorithm called ECPC (abbreviation for "expansion–clustering–projection–contraction") for large-sized building networks. In what follows, we will first present the basic idea of ECPC. Then, from Section 4.1 to Section 4.3, we present the details of each component in ECPC.

Basic Idea of ECPC: The basic idea of ECPC is motivated by the observation that the main difficulty in solving BSPO stems from: i) the FAF effect, and ii) the integrality constraints on the vertical coordinates. This observation leads us to the following idea: First, suppose that we can expand the network from the original space to an *equivalent virtual 3-D space* without floors and yet the path loss effect after expansion is equivalent, then the problem becomes much easier. This is because we can partition the SAs into M clusters in the virtual space, where SAs in each cluster are "close" to each other. Since there is no FAF effect within each cluster, it is easy to determine the optimal BS placement for each cluster. Next, we project the BS placement to the locations corresponding to the nearest floor in the virtual space and then shrink the virtual space back to the original one. As a result, we arrive at a solution to the original problem.

Clearly, the solution quality of the ECPC approach hinges heavily on the details in carrying out the expansion, clustering, projection, and contraction. As will be seen later, the expansion subtask is non-trivial and care must be taken to obtain a satisfactory performance. In the remainder of this section, we will develop these key components of ECPC.

4.1   Expansion

Let $\mathcal{S}$ and $\hat{\mathcal{S}}$ represent the original space and the expanded space, respectively. We let $e(p_i) \in \hat{\mathcal{S}}$ denote the image of the expansion mapping of point $p_i \in \mathcal{S}$. The concept of *equivalent distance* is defined as follows:

Definition 1. *For two points $p_i, p_j \in \mathcal{S}$, if the path loss effect between $e(p_i) \in \hat{\mathcal{S}}$ and $e(p_j) \in \hat{\mathcal{S}}$ is the same as that between p_i and p_j, then we call the distance $\hat{d}_{ij}$ between points $e(p_i)$ and $e(p_j)$ the equivalent distance for p_i and p_j.*

For ease of algebraic manipulations, we consider $s_{ij} \triangleq d_{ij}^2$ and $\hat{s}_{ij} \triangleq \hat{d}_{ij}^2$ rather than d_{ij} and $\hat{d}_{ij}$ directly. Under Definition 1 and the discussions in Section 3, it is not difficult to derive the following expression (details are omitted here due to space limitation):

$$\hat{s}_{ij} = \begin{cases} s_{ij}, & \text{if } w_i = w_j, \\ s_{ij}G(w_i, w_j), & \text{if } w_i \neq w_j, \end{cases} \qquad (7)$$

where the term $G(w_i, w_j)$ is defined as $G(w_i, w_j) \triangleq 10^{\frac{\Lambda_1 + (|w_i - w_j| - 1)\Lambda_a}{20\alpha}}$.

Next, we need to determine the new coordinates of the SAs in $\hat{\mathcal{S}}$. A natural choice is to find a new set of coordinates $(\tilde{u}_i, \tilde{v}_i, \tilde{w}_i) \in \hat{\mathcal{S}}$, $i = 1, \ldots, N$, such that the pair-wise distance $\tilde{d}_{ij}$ is as close to $\hat{d}_{ij}$ as possible. Notice that $\tilde{w}_i$ is no longer integer-valued in $\hat{\mathcal{S}}$. This problem is closest in spirit to the classical multidimensional scaling (MDS) problem that often arises in statistics and information visualization [24]. However, we point out that classical MDS techniques cannot be applied here due to the "arbitrariness" of the MDS solutions. That is, for an optimal MDS solution, any rotation or reflection is also a valid optimal solution. This poses a problem to our ECPC approach since we not only need to determine the optimal BSs locations in $\hat{\mathcal{S}}$, but also need to recover the corresponding locations in $\mathcal{S}$. The arbitrariness of an MDS solution makes such a reversed mapping difficult. In this paper, we propose the following approach to circumvent the above MDS limitations.

We first note that in $\mathcal{S}$, there is no floor separation between SAs on the same floor. As a result, $\hat{s}_{ij} = s_{ij}$ for any two SAs i and j on the same floor. From this observation, a natural approach is to retain the horizontal coordinates of

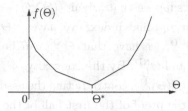

Fig. 2. An illustration of the structure of the objective function in Problem (9).

all SAs to preserve the distances between same-floor SAs. This also means that the expansion will *only* occur along the vertical direction. However, due to the nonlinear FAF effect, it is difficult to precisely model the appropriate expansion along the vertical direction. To simplify the problem, we propose to use the following linear expansion rule:

$$(\tilde{u}_i, \tilde{v}_i, \tilde{w}_i) = (u_i, v_i, w_i h\theta), \tag{8}$$

where $\theta > 1$ is a linear vertical scaling factor. Under this rule, we have $\tilde{d}_{ij}^2 = (u_i - u_j)^2 + (v_i - v_j)^2 + (w_i - w_j)^2 h^2 \theta^2$, $\forall i, j \in \{1, \ldots, N\}, w_i \neq w_j$. Next, we want to find the optimal θ such that the total difference between $\tilde{d}_{ij}^2$ and the equivalent squared distance $\hat{s}_{ij}$ is minimized. This can be formulated as the following minimization problem after some algebraic manipulations (details are omitted due to space limitation):

$$\underset{\Theta \geq 0}{\text{Minimize}} \sum_{i,j \in \Omega} |a_{ij}\Theta + b_{ij}|, \tag{9}$$

where $a_{ij} \triangleq (w_i - w_j)^2 h^2$, $b_{ij} \triangleq (u_i - u_j)^2 + (v_i - v_j)^2 - \hat{s}_{ij}$, $\Theta \triangleq \theta^2$, and $\Omega \triangleq \{i, j \in \{1, \ldots, F\} : i < j, w_i \neq w_j\}$. In (9), Θ is the decision variable.

For convenience, let $f(\Theta)$ denote the objective function of Problem (9). Since $f(\Theta)$ is convex and piece-wise linear, $f(\Theta)$ has a structure as depicted in Figure 2. Due to this special structure, we can devise a *polynomial-time* line search algorithm. First, it is easy to see that the minimizer of Problem (9) must be located at the non-differentiable points of $f(\Theta)$ because all other points have non-zero derivatives. The non-differentiable points of $f(\Theta)$, denoted as Θ_{ij}^{ND}, can be easily computed as $\Theta_{ij}^{\text{ND}} = -b_{ij}/a_{ij}$, for all $(i, j) \in \Omega$. Also, noting that $\Theta \geq 0$, we only need to consider the set of non-negative Θ_{ij}^{ND}. Let the set Ω_+ be defined as $\Omega_+ = \{(i, j) \in \Omega : \Theta_{ij}^{\text{ND}} \geq 0\}$. For convenience, we re-index the elements in Ω_+ such that $\Theta_1 \leq \ldots \leq \Theta_{|\Omega_+|}$. Then, solving Problem (9) becomes finding the optimal index, denoted as I^*, from Ω_+. Let $\mathcal{I} = \{I_1, \ldots, I_2\}$ be the initial index set, where $I_1 = 1$ and $I_2 = |\Omega_+|$. Then, our algorithm is based on the following result:

Proposition 2. *Let I_1' and I_2' be two indices with $I_1 \leq I_1' < I_2' \leq I_2$. If $f(\Theta_{I_1'}^{\text{ND}}) > f(\Theta_{I_2'}^{\text{ND}})$, then $I_1' \leq I^* \leq I_2$. On the other hand, if $f(\Theta_{I_1'}^{\text{ND}}) < f(\Theta_{I_2'}^{\text{ND}})$, then $I_1 \leq I^* \leq I_2'$.*

Proof. By contradiction, suppose that when $f(\Theta_{I_1'}^{\mathrm{ND}}) > f(\Theta_{I_2'}^{\mathrm{ND}})$, we have $I_1 \leq I^* < I_1'$. Since I^* is the optimal index, we have $f(\Theta_{I^*}^{\mathrm{ND}}) < f(\Theta_{I_2'}^{\mathrm{ND}})$. Also, since $\Theta_{I^*}^{\mathrm{ND}} \leq \Theta_{I_1'}^{\mathrm{ND}} < \Theta_{I_2'}^{\mathrm{ND}}$, we have that $\Theta_{I_1'}^{\mathrm{ND}}$ can be represented as a convex combination of $\Theta_{I^*}^{\mathrm{ND}}$ and $\Theta_{I_2'}^{\mathrm{ND}}$. By the convexity of $f(\cdot)$, we have $f(\Theta_{I_1'}^{\mathrm{ND}}) < \max\{f(\Theta_{I^*}^{\mathrm{ND}}), f(\Theta_{I_2'}^{\mathrm{ND}})\} = f(\Theta_{I_2'}^{\mathrm{ND}})$, contradicting the assumption that $f(\Theta_{I_1'}^{\mathrm{ND}}) > f(\Theta_{I_2'}^{\mathrm{ND}})$. This completes the proof of the first half of the lemma. The other half of the lemma can also be proved similarly. □

Proposition 2 implies that we can reduce the index set by ignoring either the indices that are larger than I_2' or smaller than I_1', depending on the comparison between $f(\Theta_{I_1'}^{\mathrm{ND}})$ and $f(\Theta_{I_2'}^{\mathrm{ND}})$. Thus, we can choose I_1' and I_2' in the following *dichotomous* way: for $\mathcal{I} = \{I_1, \ldots, I_2\}$, we let $I_1' = \lfloor \frac{I_1+I_2}{2} \rfloor$ and $I_2' = \lfloor \frac{I_1+I_2}{2} \rfloor + 1$. This process continues until there are only two elements left in the index set. Then, the optimal index I^* can be found by simply comparing the objective values at these two indices. In finding I^*, the computation complexity is dominated by the evaluation of $f(\cdot)$. Since we reduce the size of the index set by approximately half in each iteration, we only need $O(\log_2(|\Omega_+|))$ objective value evaluations, which is evidently polynomial-time.

4.2   Clustering

To perform clustering, we first construct a matrix $\tilde{\mathbf{D}}$ in $\hat{\mathcal{S}}$, where the entry $[\tilde{\mathbf{D}}]_{ij}$ in the i-th row and the j-th column represents the distance between SA i and SA j. Initially, we treat each SA in $\mathcal{S}$ as an individual cluster. Then, the clustering proceeds in the following "bottom-up greedy" fashion. In each iteration, we merge two closest clusters (could be two SAs, two clusters, or a cluster and an SA) into a new cluster. Next, update the new distances of the remaining clusters to the new cluster. In the next iteration, we repeat the merging based on the updated $\tilde{\mathbf{D}}$. After each iteration, the number of clusters in $\hat{\mathcal{S}}$ is reduced by 1. This process continues until there are M clusters remaining.

Different strategies could be employed in updating $\tilde{\mathbf{D}}$ in each iteration. For example, the distance between an existing cluster E_1 and a new cluster E_2 could be computed using the maximum distance between the elements of each cluster, i.e., $d(E_1, E_2) = \max\{d(p_1, p_2) : p_1 \in E_1, p_2 \in E_2\}$, or the average distance between the elements of each cluster, i.e., $d(E_1, E_2) = \frac{1}{|E_1||E_2|} \sum_{p_1 \in E_1} \sum_{p_2 \in E_2} d(p_1, p_2)$. We refer to these two strategies as "updating with maximum distance" (UMD) and "updating with average distance" (UAD), respectively.

After clustering, we need to determine the optimal BS location for each cluster. Since there is no floor separation in $\hat{\mathcal{S}}$, each SA's power is solely determined by the distance to the BS in the cluster. Thus, we only need to find an optimal BS location to minimize a certain metric related to the distance from the BS to the SAs. Let $\mathcal{C}_m$ denote the m-th cluster. Let $(\tilde{x}_m, \tilde{y}_m, \tilde{z}_m) \in \hat{\mathcal{S}}$ denote the location of the m-th BS for the m-th cluster. Then, the optimal BS location can be formulated as the following optimization problem (details are omitted due to space limitation):

$$
\begin{aligned}
\text{Minimize } & \sum_{i=1}^{|\mathcal{C}_m|} s_{im}^{-\frac{\alpha}{2}} \\
\text{subject to } & s_{im} \geq (\tilde{x}_m - \tilde{u}_i)^2 + (\tilde{y}_m - \tilde{v}_i)^2 \\
& + (\tilde{z}_m - \tilde{w}_i)^2, \; \forall(\tilde{u}_i, \tilde{v}_i, \tilde{w}_i) \in \mathcal{C}_m.
\end{aligned}
\tag{10}
$$

The decision variables in (10) are $(\tilde{x}_m, \tilde{y}_m, \tilde{z}_m)$ and s_{im}. It can be easily verified that (10) is a standard second-order cone program (SOCP), which can be efficiently solved by standard convex programming solvers.

4.3   Projection and Contraction

Since the expansion in ECPC occurs only along the vertical direction, the projection of the m-th BS can be easily done by fixing $\tilde{x}_m$ and $\tilde{y}_m$ and changing the value of $\tilde{z}_m$ to the vertical coordinate of the nearest floor. Then, the contraction of the m-th BS location back to the $\mathcal{S}$ can be done by simply letting $x_m = \tilde{x}_m$, $y_m = \tilde{y}_m$, and $z_m = \tilde{z}_m / h\theta^*$. Here, θ^* is the optimal expansion factor obtained earlier by solving Problem (9).

4.4   Complexity and Approximation Ratio Analysis

In this section, we first analyze the computational complexity of the ECPC algorithm. As mentioned earlier, in ECPC, to determine the expansion ratio Θ, we need $O(\log_2(|\Omega_+|))$ times of objective function evaluations. Note that $|\Omega_+|$ is on the order of $O(N^2)$. For partitioning the N SAs into M clusters, exactly $N - M$ times of groupings and updates are needed. The complexity of solving M SOCP in the form of (10) is $O(M\sqrt{N/M}) = O(\sqrt{NM})$ [25]. Finally, we need exactly $2M$ iterations in performing projection and contraction. Thus, combining all the above discussions, we have the following result, which clearly shows that the ECPC scheme is a polynomial-time algorithm:

Proposition 3. *The computational complexity of the proposed ECPC scheme is* $O(2\log_2 N + 2M + \sqrt{NM})$.

Next, we analyze the approximation ratio of the ECPC algorithm. First, we note that the dominant source error comes from the expansion step, in which we only use a linear expansion factor to model the complex relationship in the equivalent space, which is obviously nonlinear. The inexact expansion will in turn lead to erroneous group in the clustering stage, which may associate an SA with a BS that has an inferior channel quality. However, a nice feature of the ECPC scheme is that all the inexact expansions only occur between SAs in different floors. Based on this insight, we can derive the following approximation ratio bound for the ECPC algorithm:

Theorem 4. *The approximation ratio of the proposed ECPC scheme is upper bounded by*

$$
1 + \frac{|\Omega|}{N} \left(\frac{F^2 h^2 + x_{\max}^2 + y_{\max}^2}{\min_{(i,j) \in \mathcal{N}} d_{ij}} \right)^{\alpha}.
\tag{11}
$$

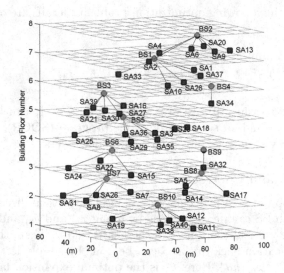

Fig. 3. The solution for a 40-SA 10-BS network under the ECPC approach

Due to space limitation, we relegate the proof details of Theorem 4 to [26]. It is worth pointing out that the approximation ratio bound in (11) is a worst case upper bound. In practice, the ECPC algorithm usually works much better than the bound in (11), as evidenced by the numerical examples presented in the next subsection.

4.5   Numerical Results

To see the efficiency of ECPC, we use a network with 40 SAs in a 7-story building as an example. The building's length, width, and per-floor height are 100, 60, and 3 meters, respectively. We use 10 BSs to serve the entire network. The maximum transmission power for each sensor is 1 W. The minimum received power threshold for each sensor is −90 dBm. The path loss exponent is 4. Note that the BB approach in [20, 21] is not a practical choice for such a large-sized network. Under ECPC, however, it only takes 9.98 seconds to find a solution, which shows the efficiency of ECPC. The BSs placement and the BS-SA associations are illustrated in Figure 3 (for better visibility, we only plot the centers of the SAs in Figure 3).

To compare the gap between ECPC solutions and the objective values obtained under the BB approach in [20, 21], we randomly generated 50 networks with 3 BSs, 10 SAs, in a 3-story building. As mentioned earlier, a major feature of BB is that it guarantees finding an optimal solution to the original problem. For these 50 examples, the mean objective value of ECPC and the mean of the true optimal values are 0.4181 W and 0.2073 W, respectively. The standard deviation are 0.3252 and 0.1313 W, respectively. Further, there are 36 (72%) examples where the ECPC objective value is less than twice of the true optimal objective value, including 8 examples (16%) where two solutions coincide . The mean of normalized objective values (ECPC divided by true optimum) is 1.995 (with a standard deviation of 0.7261). Thus, we can see that ECPC offers competitive results compared to true optimal solutions.

5 Conclusion

In this paper, we investigated the joint BS placement and power control optimization to prolong the sensor battery lifetime for cyber-physical systems (CPS) in building environments. We show that the joint BS placement and power control problem can be formulated as a mixed-integer non-convex program, which is difficult to solve to global optimality for large-sized networks even after convexification and linearization. To address this difficulty, we developed an efficient algorithm called ECPC that incorporates several novel ideas specifically designed for CPSs in building environments. We conducted both theoretical and numerical analysis for the ECPC scheme. Our numerical results showed that ECPC provides competitive solutions compared to the true optimal solutions obtained by the branch-and-bound based approach used in our previous work. We note that CPS network infrastructure in smart buildings is an important and yet under-explored area. Possible future directions include to study the trade-off between power and other performance metrics, such as throughput, delay, etc.

References

1. Hurley, S.: Planing effective cellular mobile radio networks. IEEE Trans. Veh. Technol. 51(2), 243–253 (2002)
2. Mathar, R., Niessen, T.: Optimum positioning of base stations for cellular radio networks. Wireless Networks 6, 421–428 (2000)
3. Hou, Y.T., Shi, Y., Sherali, H.D., Midkiff, S.F.: On energy provisioning and relay node placement for wireless sensor networks. IEEE Trans. Wireless Commun. 4(5), 2579–2590 (2005)
4. Efrat, A., Har-Peled, S., Mitchell, J.: Approximation algorithms for two optimal location problems in sensor networks. In: Proc. IEEE Conference on Broadband Networks (BroadNets), Boston, MA, October 3-7, pp. 767–776 (2005)
5. Shi, Y., Hou, Y.T.: Optimal base station placement in wireless sensor networks. ACM Transactions on Sensor Networks 5(4) (November 2009)
6. Lu, J.-L., Jaffrès-Runser, K., Gorce, J.-M., Valois, F.: Indoor wLAN planning with a QoS constraint based on a Markovian performance evaluation model. In: Proc. IEEE International Conference on Wireless and Mobile Computing, Networking and Communications, Montreal, QC, June 19-21, pp. 152–158 (2006)
7. Jaffrès-Runser, K., Gorce, J.-M., Ubéda, S.: Multiobjective QoS-oriented planning for indoor wireless LAN. In: Proc. IEEE VTC Fall, Montreal, QC, September 25-28, pp. 1–5 (2006)
8. Sherali, H., Pendyala, C., Rappaport, T.: Optimal location of transmitters for micro-cellular radio communication system design. IEEE J. Sel. Areas Commun. 14(4), 662–673 (1996)

9. Wong, J., Mason, A., Neve, M., Sowerby, K.: Base station placement in indoor wireless systems using binary integer programming. IEE Proceedings – Communications 153(5), 771–778 (2006)
10. Adickes, M.D., Billo, R.E., Norman, B.A., Banerjee, S., Nnaji, B.O., Rajgopal, J.: Optimization of indoor wireless communication network layout. IIE Transactions 34(9), 823–836 (2002)
11. Bahri, A., Chamberland, S.: On the wireless local area network design problem with performance guarantees. Computer Networks 48, 856–866 (2005)
12. Lee, Y., Kim, K., Choi, Y.: Optimization of AP placement and channel assignment in wireless LANs. In: Proc. IEEE Local Computer Networks (LCN), Tampa, FL, November 6-8, pp. 831–836 (2002)
13. Bejerano, Y., Han, S.-J., Li, L.E.: Fairness and load balancing in wireless LAN using association control. In: Proc. ACM MobiCom, Philadelphia, PA, September 26–October 1, pp. 2326–2330 (2004)
14. Kobayashi, M., Haruyama, S., Kohno, R., Nakagawa, M.: Optimal access point placement in simultaneous broadcast system using OFDM for indoor wireless LAN. In: Proc. IEEE PIMRC, London, UK, September 18-21, pp. 200–204 (2000)
15. Jiang, T., Zhu, G.: Uniform design simulated annealing for optimal access point placement of high data rate indoor wireless LAN using OFDM. In: Proc. IEEE PIMRC, Beijing, China, September 7-10, pp. 2302–2306 (2003)
16. Ling, X., Yeung, K.L.: Joint access point placement and channel assignment for 802.11 wireless LAN. IEEE Trans. Wireless Commun. 5(10), 2705–2711 (2006)
17. So, A., Liang, B.: Efficient wireless extension point placement algorithm in urban rectilineal WLANs. IEEE Trans. Veh. Technol. 57(1), 532–547 (2008)
18. Butterworth, K., Sowerby, K., Williamson, A.: Base station placement for in-building mobile communication systems to yield high capacity and efficiency. IEEE Trans. Commun. 48(4), 658–669 (2000)
19. Stamatelos, D., Ephremides, A.: Spectral efficiency and optimal base placement for indoor wireless networks. IEEE J. Sel. Areas Commun. 14(4), 651–661 (1996)
20. Liu, J., Kou, T., Chen, Q., Sherali, H.D.: Femtocell base station deployment in commercial buildings: A global optimization approach. IEEE J. Sel. Areas Commun. 30(3), 652–663 (2012)
21. Liu, J., Chen, Q., Sherali, H.D.: Algorithm design for femtocell base station placement in commercial building environments. In: Proc. IEEE INFOCOM, Orlando, FL, March 25-30, pp. 3233–3237 (2012)
22. Rappaport, T.S.: Wireless Communications: Principles and Practice. Prentice Hall, Upper Saddle River (2002)
23. Nemmhauser, G.L., Wolsey, L.A.: Integer and Combinatorial Optimization, 2nd edn. Wiley-Interscience Publication, New York (1999)
24. Cox, T.F., Cox, M.A.A.: Multidimensional Scaling, 2nd edn. Chapman and Hall/CRC, Boca Raton (2000)
25. Boyd, S., Vandenberghe, L.: Convex Optimization. Cambridge University Press, Cambridge (2004)
26. Liu, J., Chen, Q., Kou, T., Sherali, H.D.: On wireless network infrastructure optimization for cyber-physical systems in future smart buildings. Technical Report, Dept. of ECE, Ohio State University (July 2011),
http://www2.ece.ohio-state.edu/~liu/publications/CPS_Bldg_TR.pdf

Building a Microscope for the Data Center

Nuno Pereira, Stefano Tennina, and Eduardo Tovar

CISTER/INESC-TEC, ISEP, Polytechnic Institute of Porto, Porto, Portugal
{nap,sota,emt}@isep.ipp.pt

Abstract. Managing the physical and compute infrastructure of a large
data center is an embodiment of a Cyber-Physical System (CPS). The
physical parameters of the data center (such as power, temperature, pressure, humidity) are tightly coupled with computations, even more so in
upcoming data centers, where the location of workloads can vary substantially due, for example, to workloads being moved in a cloud infrastructure hosted in the data center. In this paper, we describe a data collection
and distribution architecture that enables gathering physical parameters
of a large data center at a very high temporal and spatial resolution
of the sensor measurements. We think this is an important characteristic to enable more accurate heat-flow models of the data center and
with them, find opportunities to optimize energy consumption. Having
a high resolution picture of the data center conditions, also enables minimizing local hotspots, perform more accurate predictive maintenance
(pending failures in cooling and other infrastructure equipment can be
more promptly detected) and more accurate billing. We detail this architecture and define the structure of the underlying messaging system that
is used to collect and distribute the data. Finally, we show the results of
a preliminary study of a typical data center radio environment.

1   Introduction

Data centers are a central piece of today's Internet infrastructure and have become critical for many medium and large organizations. A data center is a facility
(one or more rooms, floors or buildings) custom built to house large computing
systems, including networking, storage systems and also power distribution and
cooling.

The operation of a data center is an instantiation of a Cyber-Physical System
(CPS) in the sense that it requires managing physical parameters, such as power
and environmental variables of the data center (e.g., temperature, humidity,
pressure), that are coupled with computations. This is especially true in future
data centers, where we can expect that management of cloud-related workload
will be performed more aggressively. This workload management includes distributing or consolidating workloads throughout data center machines, and this
impacts physical parameters (power and environmental) of the data center in a
very dynamic manner.

This paper reports the progress being developed towards energy-efficient operations and the integrated management of cyber and physical aspects of data

X. Wang et al. (Eds.): WASA 2012, LNCS 7405, pp. 619–630, 2012.

centers. We are developing an integrated system composed by wired and wireless sensors which monitor power consumptions of the servers and environmental conditions, with the goal of achieving an overall reduction of data centers' energy consumptions. The architecture we propose here is intended to be hierarchical, modular and flexible enough to achieve high temporal and spatial resolution of the sensor measurements, with negligible latencies of sensors' reports to the data center management control station.

Overall, the advantage of having fine-grained power and environmental measurements in this application scenario is twofold: (i) measuring the power consumption at the single server level has enormous benefits for the business logic of data centers' owners, since they can offer services and billing to their customers based on the actual consumption[1], and (ii) although there are in literature models to predict heat-flows used in commercial Computer Room Air Cooling (*CRAC*) systems, those models often lack of spatial resolution, so the availability of micro-climate conditions would help improving those models as well as continue feeding them with real data will improve the reliability and accuracy of their forecasts.

Fine-grained measurements are also the basis to provide different views of the system, each of them customized to different users. Our architecture allows to set the desired resolution of the readings upon user's requests, for example to investigate some problems in a specific area (row, room or floor) of the data center building. Every single sensor can be configured by setting user defined alarms and trigger measurements reports adaptively, by changing or (re-)configuring specific thresholds at run-time.

In this paper, we describe the data collection and distribution architecture. We will detail how the environmental and power data will be collected from the data center and initial deployment experiments. The remaining of this paper is organized as follows. Section 2 describes related work in the same topic of monitoring data center conditions. Section 3 overviews our proposed hierarchical and modular system architecture by focusing on its data gathering part, while Section 4 presents the way data collected are exposed to the end users using the publish-subscriber paradigm. Section 5 deals with preliminary results on wireless sensor network (WSN) deployment we did in a real data center in Lisbon, Portugal, in November 2011. Section 6 concludes this paper with an overview on the on-going future work.

2   Related Work

Thermal management and green data centers have received considerable attention in recent research literature. Two main approaches can be identified: mechanical design-based and software-based [1]. The former approaches aim at studying the airflow models, data centers layout and cooling system design in

---

[1] This project is being carried out in conjunction with a medium/large service provider in the area (Portugal Telecom), which defined this as an important goal of the system.

order to optimize the location of the racks and CRAC units. On the other hand, the latter approaches focus on minimizing the cooling costs by distributing or migrating jobs among the servers. The result of this study is the design of thermal-aware scheduling mechanism to distribute the workload where the power budget (i.e., the product of power and temperature [2]) is more favorable. However, in the current data center thermal management systems, the mechanical- and software-based approaches are usually independent on each other [1].

A closely related problem, power management in data centers, has been an important concern for some time now [3–7]. Dynamic voltage scaling [3, 5] in QoS-enabled web-servers can minimize energy consumption subject to service delay constraints. On/off power management schemes [4–7] have also been studied in the context of data centers.

Few very recent approaches rely on building software models through a joint coordination of cooling and load management [8, 9]. However, the complexity of data center airflow and heat transfer is compounded by each data center facility having its own unique layout, so achieving a general model is difficult [10]. In fact, in [8], authors stress that their model has several parameters that need to be determined for specific applications. Then, acquiring data at a fine enough resolution to validate models is a considerable undertaking and current research issue concerning the type and placement of sensors need to be addressed [10].

Along this line, some recent work [11, 12] pushed in the direction of deploying wireless sensor nodes and monitor the thermal distribution, to figure out how to avoid hot-spots and overheating conditions. In [12], for example, 108 wireless sensor nodes were deployed in a floor of the IBM data center in Geneva. We differ from these works in the sense that we want very fine-grained (in space and time) gathering of power and environmental parameters and including other physical quantities other than only temperature. Our goal is also to build a representation of the data center through which administrators and designers can rigorously identify problems and solutions.

Our approach has similarities to [1], where authors propose a (proactive) thermal management system built upon an air flux mathematical model, which leads to a formulation of a minimization of cooling energy problem. Moreover, in [13], the same authors developed a joint communication and coordination scheme that enables self-organization of a network of external heterogeneous sensors (thermal cameras, scalar temperature and humidity sensors, airflow meters) into a multi-tier sensing infrastructure capable of real-time data center monitoring. Differently from [1, 13], our proposed system is based on a hierarchical, modular, flexible and fine-grained sensor network architecture, where data collected from heterogeneous sensors (including power data) and the analysis of their inter-correlations will enable closer examination and a better understanding of the flow and temperature dynamics within each data center [14]. To our knowledge, no previous work enables correlating power and environment characteristics on a per rack or per-server granularity.

Multiple long-wavelength infrared image sensors can be used to capture thermal maps of an environment [15]. While thermal cameras are an interesting approach, we find that they suffer from several practical issues: (i) the current cost of thermal cameras is substantial, and, due to field-of-view limitations (data centers are typically organized in narrows rows), a high number of them can be required to cover a data center; (ii) mapping the view of the camera with the infrastructure being monitored is more challenging than with point sensors, and it is especially difficult to manage when changes are made to the layout of the data center (e.g., addition/removal of servers and racks). However, as in [13], our system has provisions to support thermal image sensors as a smart sensor that can provide point temperature readings with a configurable resolution.

The data collection and distribution architecture described in this paper builds upon previous work in SensorAndrew [16], which defined an Internet-scale infrastructure for sensing and actuation, using the XMPP protocol (more details about XMPP are given later) at its core, providing both point-to-point and publish-subscribe communication, confidentiality, access control, registration, discovery, event logging and management of sensor/actuator devices.

There are a number of other efforts, which address some of these functionalities. The MQ Telemetry Transport (MQTT) [17] is a publish-subscribe messaging protocol, designed for constrained devices. While it is very lightweight and as been successfully applied in several areas [18–20], it does not provide any flexible mechanism to define messaging format and has also no built-in security features. The Global Sensor Networks (GSN) [21] supports the flexible integration and discovery of sensor networks and sensor data. It is a service-oriented architecture, where sensors can be accessed using SQL queries and web services. GSN is substantially single-application centric and does not support security features. Pachube [22] recently gained increased visibility with its real-time data collection infrastructure that enables sensor-derived data to be distributed at Internet scale. Pachube, however, focuses on much larger time scales for the data collection than we are interested in.

3   Architecture Overview

The architecture of our system can be divided into three main sections. (i) The data-producing entities such as the sensor networks, which gather environmental data, IT equipment or building equipment, which gather the data from the environment, and also power consumption data. The data from these sensor networks is delivered to a (ii) data distribution system that acts as a broker between the (iii) data producing entities and the consuming applications (e.g., logger applications, alarm monitor, user interface applications).

At the core of the architecture depicted in Figure 1 there is a data distribution middleware, which will take care of handling the data coming from different sources such as the environmental and power sensors and deliver this data to the applications interested in this data. The applications can be a data logger that gathers historical information, visualization tools, alarms monitors or any other application that can be developed in the future.

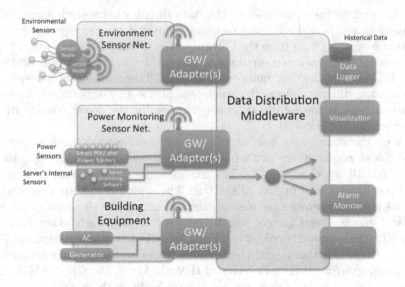

Fig. 1. Architecture Overview

In the following subsections, our proposed system architecture will be described in more detail, highlighting each component of the data gathering and data distribution system.

3.1   Environment and Power Data Collection

In order to trade-off among (i) fine-grained sensors' measurement (spatial) resolution, (ii) system flexibility and modularity and (iii) low-latency reporting of the measurements, the proposed architecture for the data collection is a mix of wired and wireless technologies.

The WSN is a stacked multi-tier architecture, where each level represents a network tier with the corresponding devices and communication technology used. The lower level, *level-0* consists of sensor nodes, i.e., computational units with several physical sensors attached, which perform sensing tasks and deliver data to the devices at the next level in the hierarchy through a wired bus. At *level-1*, cluster heads are responsible for querying the sensor nodes within their respective cluster. A cluster is composed by one cluster head (bus master) and several sensor nodes (bus slaves) attached to the wired bus. Then, these cluster heads are responsible for data aggregation and sensor fusion. They communicate using IEEE 802.15.4 with devices at the next level in the hierarchy. At the *level-2* of the network hierarchy, (environment) gateways are present. These devices have the highest computational capabilities among the devices present in the sensor network field. Gateways provide the data gathered from the sensor network to the data distribution system in a standard format. Finally, in *level-3*, the data distribution provides means to deliver the data gathered from the sensor network to the applications. The data distribution system supports any number of gateways and applications in a distributed and transparent way.

Sensor Nodes: starting from the bottom of the network architecture, a Sensor Node is a communication/computation enabled device physically linked (e.g., over a I2C bus) to a given number of sensors. These sensors are responsible for measuring different physical parameters like, e.g., temperature, humidity, pressure, as well as several power sensors to monitor the power consumption of each server in the rack.

To keep the complexity low, at this tier of the Network Architecture, the Sensor Nodes communicate with one Cluster Head over a bus, e.g., using a RS485/MODBUS technology [23]. In particular, the Cluster Head node acts as a local coordinator and master of the bus. The sensor nodes are deployed one each rack and their sensors get measurements from all the elements of the rack.

Cluster Heads: the Clusters will be connected with each other in a Zig-Bee/IEEE802.15.4 mesh topology to form a WSN Patch, where a common Gateway is in charge of gathering data and sending them over long range communication technology (e.g., WiFi). In terms of HW platforms, the Cluster Head node will be the same platform as a generic Sensor Node, with an on-board ZigBee radio.

Gateways: the sensor network can have one or more Gateways. Gateways maintain representations of the data flows from the sensor network to the data distribution system. They perform the necessary adaptation of the data received from the WSN. The gateways can be deployed as one per room serving all the rows of racks in that room; more gateways can also be deployed to improve radio coverage, for load-balancing or for redundancy.

3.2   Data Distribution

The data distribution middleware is a central part of the proposed architecture. This system is in charge of distributing the data from the source to the interested applications. We leverage on the previous experience of SensorAndrew [16] and employ the eXtensible Messaging and Presence Protocol (XMPP) [24] as the core protocol for managing sensor data collection and distribution. In this architecture, sensors (and actuators) are modeled as XMPP event nodes in a push-based publish-subscribe architecture. The loosely coupling between publisher and subscribers allows a higher scalability and more dynamism in the network topology. Moreover, this architecture supports the following features [16, 24]: (i) standard messaging protocol; (ii) extensible message types; (iii) point-to-point and multicast messaging; (iv) data tracking and/or event logging; (v) security, privacy and access control; (vi) registration and discovery services (vii) redundancy and Internet-scale.

The XMPP [24] is the basis for the messaging of our system. XMPP is an open-standard communications protocol for message-oriented middleware based on Extensible Markup Language (XML). Unlike most instant messaging protocols, XMPP uses an open systems approach of development and application, by which anyone may implement an XMPP service and interoperate with other organizations' implementations. The architecture of an XMPP network is run in a fully distributed fashion, i.e., there is no central master server. XMPP has extensions for several models, including one-to-one communication and publish-subscribe model, and can be location-aware. It has built-in authentication with support for secure channels (SSL and TLS) and supports storage of messages for later delivery. XMPP applications include network management, content syndication, collaboration tools, file sharing, gaming, and remote systems monitoring. Finally, XMPP is implemented by a large number of clients, servers, and code libraries, and most of this software is distributed as free and open source.

4   Mapping The World

We have defined a hierarchy, adapted to the environment of a data center, that structures the messaging system. As we will describe in this section, this hierarchy reduces the number of data items (event nodes) that a user application needs to subscribe to and also allows for the user applications to zoom-in the data center in a flexible manner.

The hierarchy is defined through an XML schema that models the world. This model includes 3D geographical and logical information of all elements, including sensors, servers, racks, rooms and even buildings or cities. The model includes hierarchical links: servers can be placed *logically* inside a room, racks can be placed inside a room, and a room can be connected to a building and so on. The logical organization makes it simpler to organize the hierarchy without depending on the geographical / 3D information of the model. These levels in a data center context are shown in Figure 2. This is a logical hierarchy reflected on the XMPP event nodes, which lives in the XMPP servers. In this way, this hierarchy can be replicated and load-balanced by using the common mechanisms implemented by the XMPP server.

With this hierarchical arrangement, for example, when an administrator wants to have data from a given room, the user application only needs to subscribe to that room and automatically he will be subscribed to all the sensors in that room. This could however result in a single client subscribing to a large number of event nodes, which can be a problem for clients with limited processing, memory and battery life capacities, such as, e.g., a mobile phone.

To address this issue, we took advantage of the fact that our messaging system can have XMPP event nodes which are direct representations of physical nodes (e.g., a real sensor node on a rack), but it can also have XMPP event nodes which can represent a category or a set of nodes with some common logical characteristics (e.g., belonging to a given room). In this way, a room might have a representation in the messaging system as a virtual logical XMPP node, and, for example, the temperature values of a room will be published as a trace over time of the aggregated (e.g., average, minimum or maximum) values of all the measurements from the sensor nodes belonging to that room, while all those readings will be published on virtual physical XMPP nodes to be available later for different views. Figure 3 represents a possible configuration of this mechanism.

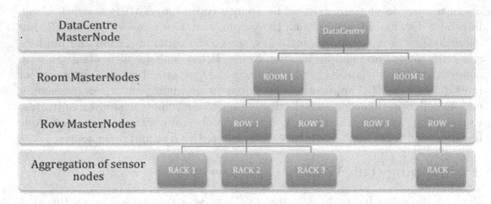

Fig. 2. Hierarchy of the nodes

It is important to note that this architecture supports several clients. For example, we can simultaneously have the following: (i) a logger application that subscribes to all nodes and simply logs all the data; (ii) an application that subscribes to specific events nodes that deliver alarm notifications; (iii) an application that is only interested in the data for a particular row of the data center; (iv) an application that, for management and configuration purposes, only needs to know when a new device is added to the system; (v) an application that is only interested in power readings. We also built a graphical user interface (GUI) application that can run in both desktops and mobile devices that provides an overview of the data center conditions. It is a simple and clean interface that gathers all relevant data, allowing the user to navigate trough a representation of the data center and observe the data collected.

5   The Data Center Radio Environment

This section presents a first step toward enabling a large installation of wireless communicating devices. It is often assumed that the presence of lots of metallic surfaces (such as racks) and power cables suspended on the ceiling, makes a data center room a harsh environment in terms of radio signal propagation. Therefore, we conducted an analysis of the radio conditions of a typical data center, to assess the validity of that assumption and evaluate its impact. The measurements were performed in a data center (located in Lisbon, Portugal) owned by the largest Portuguese telecommunications operator, Portugal Telecom (PT), which also provides hosting and cloud-based services. The objective of such measurement campaign has been twofold: (i) evaluate the available IEEE 802.15.4 channels for the monitoring network to be deployed in the data center, and (ii) test the connectivity among IEEE 802.15.4 radios in the field, in order to identify the requirements for the formation of the network topology.

Background Noise: We first acquired the background noise level, i.e., the possible interference on the monitoring network due to external IEEE 802.11/WLANs.

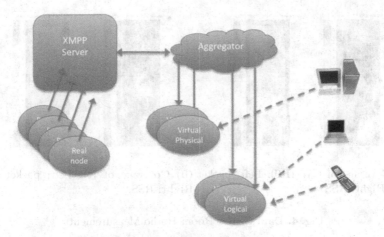

Fig. 3. Node Distribution Proposal

To do this, we used a frequency spectrum analyzer [25]. As expected, we observed that there are only few IEEE 802.15.4 channel in the 2.4 GHz band available. Channel 26, as it shown a negligible interference from 802.11, was the preferred channel for our measurements. In general, these background noise measurements show that the number of available channels in a typical data center might be low.

WSN Connectivity: For the connectivity measurements, we used 9 TelosB [26] nodes (a GW and 8 routers) running on batteries and 3 TelosB power by USB, acting as sniffers. The routers were placed at the top of the center rack of 9 rows on a data center.

First, we checked the connectivity between routers. For this, we placed the GW on a corner of the data center and the routers (R1-R8) were left on the center of the rows. This experiment tested that the chain among the GW and all the routers was working, i.e., the GW started emitting beacons, R1 gets these beacons, associates to the GW and start emitting its own beacons. Then R2 gets R1's beacons, associates with R1 and starts emitting its own beacons, and so on until R8. At run time, all routers were able to emit non-interfering beacons, on a time-division fashion.

Then, we started taking measurements with the 3 sniffer nodes as follows. First, we placed the 3 nodes on one half of the row and then on the other half of the row (the 3 nodes were spaced about 1.5 meters from each other, where the one furthest from the middle was 5 meters from the center), then we collected packets for 5 minutes in each half section of the row and repeated this procedure for 9 rows.

The measurements were performed by looking at a counter in the beacon payload that was incremented each time a beacon was transmitted. By extracting the source address and the counter in the beacons from the sniffers' logs we could measure the packet loss probability on each measurement point and with respect

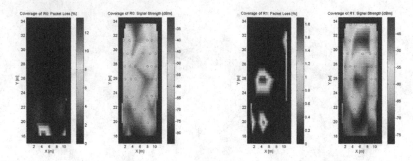

(a) Coverage of GW (R0). Left: packet (b) Coverage of R1. Left: packet loss.
loss. Right: RSS.   Right: RSS.

Fig. 4. Data Center Room Radio Measurements

to each router, as well as information about the Received Signal Strength (RSS)
of each received packet. By combining these data, it was possible to build maps of
the coverage for each beacon emitter. Figure 4 shows such results for the GW and
the cluster head R1. The packet loss is better than what one could have expected:
in general the majority of the routers was able to cover half of the room with
negligible losses (i.e., *packetloss* < 2%). Only spots of connectivity loss areas
were evidenced, e.g., in proximity of a pillar in the room: these conditions can
be resolved by planning accurately the position of the routers (cluster heads).

6   Conclusion

Instrumenting data centers with very fine spatial and temporal granularity has
a twofold advantage in terms of business logic of data centers owners and have
a better control on the micro-climate conditions in the rooms.

We have defined an efficient, hierarchical and modular system architecture,
and we are developing specialized hardware to enable it. Moreover, we made a
study on the radio performance in a real data center. This study enabled us to
understand better the radio conditions. Our findings confirm reports by previous
work [11, 12]: even in a data center room of reasonable dimensions, each wireless
node could interfere with up to 65% of the nodes. Then, having too many nodes
interfering with each other is an obstacle towards gathering sensor readings with
high temporal resolution, and this needs to be considered in our design.

Overall, we believe that our architecture, which mixes wired and wireless technologies in a modular and flexible fashion, enables interesting trade-offs between
fine-grained monitoring and low-latency.

Acknowledgement. We would like to acknowledge (in alphabetical order)
the help by Bruno Saraiva, João Loureiro, Manuel Santos, and Ricardo Severino during the implementation of this work. This work was supported by the

SENODS project, ref. SENODS - FCOMP-01-0124-FEDER-012988, co-funded by National Funds through the FCT-MCTES (Portuguese Foundation for Science and Technology) and by ERDF (European Regional Development Fund) through COMPETE (Operational Programme 'Thematic Factors of Competitiveness'), the CMU-PT Program, by National Funds through the FCT-MCTES (Portuguese Foundation for Science and Technology), under the Carnegie Mellon Portugal Program with Grant ref. FCT-CMU-PT/0012/2006 and the NoE CONET, funded by the European Commission, with grant nr. FP7-ICT-224053.

References

1. Lee, E.K., Kulkarni, I.S., Pompili, D., Parashar, M.: Proactive thermal management in green datacenters. Journal of Supercomputing 51(1), 1–31 (2010)
2. Heath, T., Centeno, A.P., George, P., Ramos, L., Jaluria, Y., Bianchini, R.: Mercury and freon: temperature emulation and management for server systems. SIGOPS Oper. Syst. Rev. 40(5), 106–116 (2006)
3. Bohrer, P., Elnozahy, E.N., Keller, T., Kistler, M., Lefurgy, C., McDowell, C., Rajamony, R.: The case for power management in web servers. In: Power Aware Computing, pp. 261–289. Kluwer Academic Publishers, Norwell (2002)
4. Xu, R., Zhu, D., Rusu, C., Melhem, R., Mossé, D.: Energy-efficient policies for embedded clusters. In: Proceedings of the 2005 ACM SIGPLAN/SIGBED Conference on Languages, Compilers, and Tools for Embedded Systems, LCTES 2005, pp. 1–10. ACM, New York (2005)
5. Horvath, T., Abdelzaher, T., Skadron, K., Liu, X.: Dynamic voltage scaling in multitier web servers with end-to-end delay control. IEEE Trans. Comput. 56(4), 444–458 (2007)
6. Meisner, D., Gold, B.T., Wenisch, T.F.: Powernap: eliminating server idle power. In: Proceedings of the 14th International Conference on Architectural Support for Programming Languages and Operating Systems, ASPLOS 2009, pp. 205–216. ACM, New York (2009)
7. Wang, S., Chen, J.-J., Liu, J., Liu, X.: Power saving design for servers under response time constraint. In: Proceedings of the 2010 22nd Euromicro Conference on Real-Time Systems, ECRTS 2010, pp. 123–132. IEEE Computer Society, Washington, DC (2010)
8. Parolini, L., Sinopoli, B., Krogh, B.H.: Reducing data center energy consumption via coordinated cooling and load management. In: Proceedings of the 2008 Conference on Power Aware Computing and Systems, HotPower 2008, p. 14. USENIX Association, Berkeley (2008)
9. Zhou, R., Wang, Z., Bash, C.E., McReynolds, A.: Data center cooling management and analysis – a model based approach. In: 28th Annual Semiconductor Thermal Measurement, Modeling and Management Symposium (SEMI-THERM 2012), San Jose, California, USA (March 2012)
10. Rambo, J., Joshi, Y.: Modeling of data center airflow and heat transfer: State of the art and future trends. Distrib. Parallel Databases 21(2-3), 193–225 (2007)
11. Liang, C.-J.M., Liu, J., Luo, L., Terzis, A., Zhao, F.: Racnet: a high-fidelity data center sensing network. In: Proceedings of the 7th ACM Conference on Embedded Networked Sensor Systems, SenSys 2009, pp. 15–28. ACM, New York (2009)

12. Weiss, B., Truong, H.L., Schott, W., Scherer, T., Lombriser, C., Chevillat, P.: Wireless sensor network for continuously monitoring temperatures in data centers. In: IBM RZ 3807 (2011)
13. Viswanathan, H., Lee, E.K., Pompili, D.: Self-organizing sensing infrastructure for autonomous management of green datacenters. IEEE Network 25(4), 34–40 (2011)
14. Schmidt, R.R., Cruz, E.E., Iyengar, M.: Challenges of data center thermal management. IBM Journal of Research and Development 49(4.5), 709–723 (2005)
15. Fredrik Karlsson, J., Moshfegh, B.: Investigation of indoor climate and power usage in a data center. Energy and Buildings 37(10), 1075–1083 (2005)
16. Rowe, A., Berge, M.E., Rajkumar, R.: Sensor andrew: Large-scale campus-wide sensing and actuation. International Business 55(1), 1–14 (2011)
17. Locke, D.: Mq telemetry transport (mqtt) v3.1 protocol specification (2010)
18. Stanford-Clark, A.J., Wightwick, G.R.: The application of publish/subscribe messaging to environmental, monitoring, and control systems. IBM J. Res. Dev. 54(4), 396–402 (2010)
19. Wilson, S., Frey, J.: The smartlab: Experimental and environmental control and monitoring of the chemistry laboratory. In: Proceedings of the 2009 International Symposium on Collaborative Technologies and Systems, CTS 2009, pp. 85–90. IEEE Computer Society, Washington, DC (2009)
20. Ganev, V., Chodos, D., Nikolaidis, I., Stroulia, E.: The smart condo: integrating sensor networks and virtual worlds. In: Proceedings of the 2nd Workshop on Software Engineering for Sensor Network Applications, SESENA 2011, pp. 49–54. ACM, New York (2011)
21. Aberer, K., Hauswirth, M., Salehi, A.: A middleware for fast and flexible sensor network deployment. In: Proceedings of the 32nd international conference on Very large data bases, VLDB 2006, pp. 1199–1202. VLDB Endowment (2006)
22. About us - Pachube (2007), http://community.pachube.com/about
23. Modbus over serial line - specification & implementation guide - v1.0 (February 2002), http://www.modbus.org/docs/Modbus_over_serial_line_V1.pdf
24. Xmpp standards foundation, http://xmpp.org
25. Metageek's WiSpy, http://www.metageek.net/products/wi-spy/
26. Memsic's TelosB, http://www.memsic.com/products/wireless-sensor-networks/wireless-modules.htm

Probabilistic Bandwidth Assignment in Wireless Sensor Networks[*]

Dawood Khan[1], Bilel Nefzi[2], Luca Santinelli[3], and YeQiong Song[2]

[1] LAAS-CNRS, 7 avenue du Colonel Roche - 31077 Toulouse France
khan@laas.fr
[2] Université de Lorraine - LORIA,
615 Jardin Botanique - 54600 Villers-les-nancy France
{bilel.nefzi,song}@loria.fr
[3] INRIA, 615 Jardin Botanique - 54600 Villers-les-nancy France
luca.santinelli@inria.fr

Abstract. With this paper we offer an insight in designing and analyzing wireless sensor networks in a versatile manner. Our framework applies probabilistic and component-based design principles for the wireless sensor network modeling and consequently analysis; while maintaining flexibility and accuracy. In particular, we address the problem of allocating and reconfiguring the available bandwidth. The framework has been successfully implemented in IEEE 802.15.4 using an Admission Control Manager (ACM); which is a module of the MAC layer that guarantees that the nodes respect their probabilistic bandwidth assignment as well as the bandwidth assignment policy applied. The proposed framework also aims to accurately analyze the behaviors of communication protocols for energy-consumption and reliability purposes. We evaluate the probabilistic bandwidth assignment methods using CSMA/CA access protocol of IEEE 802.15.4. Furthermore, we analyze the behavior of the ACM and compare the performance of the network using the ACM against the original standard. The simulation results show that the use of ACM increases the overall performance of the network.

1 Introduction

Wireless Sensor Network (WSN) is considered as one of the key technologies for building the future Cyber-Physical Systems (CPS) as it allows today's information systems to monitor and control the physical environment. Often, monitoring and acting through the WSN forms feedback loops within which the control decision should be made in real-time. So the QoS (Quality of Service) of the existing WSNs must be enhanced since most of them mainly focus on the energy efficiency without performance guarantees in terms of bandwidth allocation and end-to-end delay. Designing and analyzing the QoS of WSNs is challenging because of the highly dynamic behavior of WSNs. Moreover, the WSNs need to

[*] This work has been partially supported by the ANR Quasimodo project under grant ANR 2010 INTB 0206 01.

X. Wang et al. (Eds.): WASA 2012, LNCS 7405, pp. 631–647, 2012.
© Springer-Verlag Berlin Heidelberg 2012

operate with energy saving policies (e.g., duty-cycled nodes), which further complicates the design and analysis. In general, WSN analysis aims to evaluate the performance limits of a WSN deployment and to guarantee certain QoS. Therefore, it is essential to determine the *performance bounds* for end-to-end latency, energy, node buffer size, and reliability with respect to the network density, communication protocols, and network topology.

For preserving scalability, most of existing low-power WSNs adopt contention-based MAC. Providing guaranteed resource is even more challenging due to the random nature of channel access method and radio channel behavior; which can be described by a random probability distribution function. In addition, the node reliability/failure is probabilistic due to sudden sensor loss or decay of battery [1]. Therefore, it is often impossible to provide the deterministic QoS in WSNs.

Furthermore, in WSNs the event/packet (packet generating process) inter-arrivals follow also probabilistic distribution, for example due to the random back-offs in contention based protocols. Jung et al. [2] have shown that the protocols like Carrier Sense Multiple Access with Collision Avoidance (CSMA/CA), modeled using Markov chain, can only provide probabilistic resource guarantees.

Complexity and uncertainty makes WSNs intrinsically probabilistic. Thus, we require analysis methodologies for WSNs which provide the performance guarantees (QoS) with the probabilistic bounds.

In contrast to some recent probabilistic end-to-end delay analysis works [3], [4] which focus on the performance evaluation methods, the probabilistic approach developed in this paper offers a degree of flexibility, while allowing to cope with the dynamics of the environment (channel) and the applications in WSNs. The approach developed can be divided into two parts: i) the analysis, which is a theoretical framework for the analysis of WSNs based on probabilistic network calculus; ii) the Admission Control Manager (ACM), it is a MAC level implementation which ensures that the performance guarantees provided by the analysis part are met. This is achieved in the ACM by actively droping the packets based on the availability of bandwidth (considered probabilistic in this paper) and accepted performance guarantee (QoS) by a node (at the time of composition of the network); in a probabilistic manner.

1.1   Related Work

The IEEE 802.15.4 protocol is the popular standard for WSNs and specifies the Medium Access Control (MAC) sub-layer and the physical layer of Low-Rate Wireless Personal Area Networks (LR-WPANs) [5]. Some works in WSNs [6,7], analyze the system with deterministic Network Calculus (NC) [8] to provide worst-case performance bounds for end-to-end latency and per-hop node buffer size. These frameworks rely on deterministic MAC protocols such as Time Division Multiple Access (TDMA) and deterministic routing protocols with worst-case analysis. Most often this contention free communication requires cluster tree topology [9] since the mesh topology uses contention based MAC for its reliability and robustness, thus limiting the mesh topologies to provide deterministic worst-case bounds.

WSNs are also required to be adaptive. Most of the approaches over the IEEE 802.15.4, tackle the problem of point-to-point communication within the star with a deterministic model. Relevant time guaranteed communication examples are iGAME [10] where the authors propose, using network calculus, a methodology to study the bandwidth allocation problem, and GSA [11] that tries to minimize the total number of unallocated time-slots by applying a scheduling-based strategy. WSNs have to cope with reactive paradigms, i.e. change the bandwidth allocation according to the events appearing in the environment. Examples of adaptive systems are [12] and [13], where the authors propose an adaptive solution designed to satisfy real-time constraints and maximize event detection efficiency under variable network load conditions. Focusing on adaptive WSNs, [14] advances on the analysis providing a component-based abstraction of WSNs wherein they apply QoS analysis with no strict timing constraints concerns. All these approaches tend to assume or guarantee a worst-case behavior of the WSN application. Instead, recent trends depicts the probabilistic approach, using stochastic network calculus [15,16], as flexible enough to cope with the requirements of complex and adaptive WSNs application.

Contributions of the Paper
We propose a probabilistic methodology to dimension a WSN which is modeled with network components. Each network component is identified by a probabilistic arrival stream of data and a probabilistic communication resource guaranteed to it. By hierarchically composing components and probabilistic resource guarantees, it is possible to ease the overall analysis of the system and appropriately configure the network. In particular, we address the problem of allocating and reconfiguring the bandwidth assigned to each node using a MAC level ACM, and we do analysis of MAC-level protocols. The ACM avoid unnecessary transmissions when the bandwidth is not sufficient, which helps to reduce the number of collisions, thus saving energy. Our flexible methodology enables WSN designer to analyze different communication protocols either contention-based like CSMA/CA or contention-free, such as TDMA.

2 Component Based WSN Modeling

Component based design envisions the system as a composition of components. Each component abstracts a process or a physical entity into a black box with interfaces to observe and drive its behavior. We model the WSN nodes as basic computational units which implement functions with temporal or QoS requirements [14]. Therefore, WSN nodes can be abstracted as components and the communication (and associated requirements) between nodes representing the link among components. This abstraction makes it easy to analyze and design a WSN; since we can abstract multiple components as one component resulting from their composition. Moreover, component-based approach to the network modeling decomposes the complexity of WSN systems into parts; which can be individually analyzed, thus reducing the overall complexity.

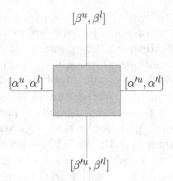

Fig. 1. A model of a component with its interface abstracting a part of a system

The component has an interface associated with it that describes the functional and non-functional behaviors of the component. The interface plays a central role in the component-based design of complex systems such as WSNs; because it defines the notion of composability: *two or more components are compatible if they work together properly.* Figure 1 depicts a generic WSN component and its component interface abstraction.

2.1 System Model

We consider a WSN-based CPS for monitoring application where the system consists of a set of sensor nodes collecting data; which is then sent towards collection points (sinks) with bounded transmission delays. We also consider the hierarchical cluster-tree topology for its flexibility and scalability[1]. At the lowest level there are star topologies where a Coordinator (C) manages End-Devices (EDs) to form a leaf cluster. We can obtain a large scale network by extending and interconnecting the star topology clusters in a hierarchical manner creating the so called cluster-tree topology as shown is Figure 2. In the cluster-tree topologies coordinators manage either EDs (nd_i) or other coordinators C_k.

Without the loss of generality we assume that coordinators C_i do not sense (i.e., their assigned bandwidth is entirely redistributed to the children) and their main function is to maintain the topology and to hierarchically allocate the bandwidth.

2.2 Node Component Model

Following the reasoning of Network Calculus and Real-Time Calculus [8,17] we define abstraction for WSN components.

Workload and Bandwidth Abstraction. The cumulative functions R and S represent the amount of workload and bandwidth respectively; $R(t)$ and

---

[1] The assumptions are merely considered for the ease of explanation. However, the approach is valid for other application scenarios and network architectures.

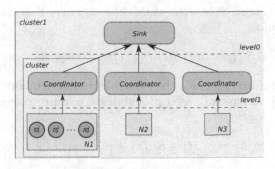

Fig. 2. WSN hierarchical architecture with end devices, control coordinators and clusters elements. Our simulation applies this architecture with $N_1 = 5$, $N_2 = 15$ and $N_3 = 10$.

$S(t)$ give respectively the amount of workload required and bandwidth available/requested in the time interval $[0, t)$. While $R(t)$ describes a concrete trace of an event/packet stream; the arrival curve α, [8] provides an abstract model which provides an upper-bound on any admissible trace of event/packets in any time interval of length Δ. The same reasoning is applicable to the service $S(t)$ and its service curve β in the interval domain.

Generic aperiodic events are more appropriately modeled with a distribution function (hence a random variable) and its Cumulative Distribution Function (CDF) X, corresponding to the arrival distribution of workload/events (of packet arrival). With probability distributions it is possible to better capture the aperiodicity of aperiodic events. We do not consider any particular CDF in our framework for the packet generating process (simulations most of the time consider a Poisson process) as it is not in the scope of this paper.

Definition 1 (Bounded Workload $R^+(t)$). *The "largest" cumulative work function such that the probability of CDF X having event count larger than or equal to $R^+(t)$ is lower than a threshold value of Ω.*

$$R^+(t) = \sup\{R(t)|P[X(t) \geq R(t)] \leq \Omega\}, \tag{1}$$

The extension of the NC to the aperiodic events results in the probabilistic bound where

$$\alpha(\Delta) \ : \ R^+(t) - R^+(s) \leq \alpha(t - s) \ \forall s < t, \tag{2}$$

with $\alpha(0) = 0$ and $\Delta = t - s$. The probabilistic arrival curve is the couple *curve, probability threshold* $\langle \alpha, \Omega \rangle$, where the probability threshold Ω represents the accuracy of α being the upper bound: *the probability that the events are upper bounded is $1 - \alpha$.*

Definition 2 (Bounded Bandwidth $S^-(t)$). *The "smallest" cumulative bandwidth function such that the probability of CDF Y having bandwidth smaller than* *or equal to $S^-(t)$ is lower than a threshold value Λ, where Y is the distribution for bandwidth availability.*

$$S^-(t) = \inf\{S(t)|P[Y(t) < S(t)] \leq \Lambda\}. \tag{3}$$

The service curve β lower bounds the available resources in any time interval of length Δ. Therefore, interval based probabilistic resource provisioning curve is represented as:

$$\beta(\Delta) \; : \; S^-(t) - S^-(s) \geq \beta(t-s) \; \forall s < t. \tag{4}$$

The probabilistic bandwidth provisioning curve is the couple $\langle \beta, \Lambda \rangle$ where the probability thresholds Λ gives the probability to find bandwidth provisioning below the lower bound β. The model is capable of modeling any possible bandwidth supply in the interval domain, including the bandwidth provisioning by the control coordinators in WSNs. Figure 3 shows the upper and lower bounds applied for building interfaces; in this work we are only interested in lower bounds on bandwidth and upper bounds on workload, which are sufficient to guarantee schedulability among components. In practice, finding the arrival function may be easy as usually the work-arrivals follow the Poisson distribution function for which there is a closed form expression. However, we can also model some other CDFs with the numerical-approximation for count models of the CDF or based on simulations, see [18]; again this is not the goal of the current work.

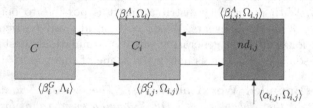

Fig. 3. WSN Component composition

Component Interfaces. To model interfaces of WSN components we make use of an approach similar to the real-time calculus [17] and to the assume/guarantee interfaces [19] tailored towards guarantees on the bandwidth-availability, and requests. *An interface of a generic network component has input and output variables related to event streams (the arrivals) and resource availability (the services).* We refer our interface model to *Probabilistic WSNs Interface* (PWI) with the intention of describing component behaviors in terms of curves and their threshold bounds, outlining its probabilistic nature and behavior.

In our framework, the input interface $\langle \alpha_{i,j}, \Omega_{i,j} \rangle$ (the node's bounded sensing rate) describes the j-th ED component $nd_{i,j}$ of the i-th cluster. The input event/packet stream translates[2] into a resource demand $\langle \beta_{i,j}^A, \Omega_{i,j} \rangle$; which defines

---

[2] That is α_i and β_i^A have same distribution function.

the probabilistic bandwidth requested from the coordinator, *assumed* to transmit properly the messages resulting from the event sensing. This is the upper bounded bandwidth requested by a node from its coordinator, based on the nodes constraints such as QoS, deadline, end-to-end delay etc. The ED receives the bandwidth from its parent as $\langle \beta_{i,j}^G, \Lambda_{i,j} \rangle$, which is the lower bound bandwidth *guaranteed* by the coordinator. The tuple $(\langle \alpha_{i,j}, \Omega_{i,j} \rangle, \langle \beta_{i,j}^A, \Omega_{i,j} \rangle, \langle \beta_{i,j}^G, \Lambda_{i,j} \rangle)$ forms the PWI of an ED $nd_{i,j}$.

Similarly, the component link between the coordinator C_i and its parent coordinator is given by $\langle \beta_i^A, \Omega_i \rangle$ and $\langle \beta_i^G, \Lambda_i \rangle$ (in terms of bandwidth). These are the assumed (i.e. requested from parent coordinator) and the guaranteed bandwidth (i.e. by the parent coordinator) respectively. Similarly, the coordinator C_i's PWI formed with child nodes is given by $\langle \beta_i^G, \Lambda_i \rangle$ and $\langle \beta_{i,j}^G, \Lambda_{i,j} \rangle$. The Figure 3 depicts the network components, their interfaces and their composition. Moreover, ED components may also have outputs representing residual resource $(\langle \beta_{i,j}', \Lambda_{i,j}' \rangle)$ and output-arrivals $(\langle \alpha_{i,j}', \Omega_{i,j}' \rangle)$, see [20]. We do not discuss the residual resource and output-arrivals in this paper as the analysis here is resource-oriented.

3   WSN Modeling

With a probabilistic model for WSN components, the bandwidth assignment problem become a probabilistic problem. The bandwidth is allocated in accordance to the requests from the nodes. Each node communicates the tuple $\langle \beta^A, \Omega \rangle$ to its parent node; that is the probability of demand/request is bound by Ω. In other words it is going to ask for a service greater than β^A in $1 - \Omega$ percent of the cases.

3.1   Bandwidth Assignment

With the probabilistic model, we can guarantee that a coordinator will provide β^G in Λ percent of the cases. For the remaining cases the resource provisioning is less than β^G with probability of $1 - \Lambda$. The coordinator then, computes the resource share for the nodes it manages (lower layer nodes) by normalizing the available resource (allocated to the coordinator by its parent coordinator) with respect to the resource demand from its nodes.

The i-th coordinator of a cluster asks for the resource from its parent node; which guarantees a resource $\langle \beta_i^G, \Lambda_i \rangle$. The resource demand of C_i $\langle \beta_i^A, \Omega_i \rangle$ (requested by cluster coordinator C_i from its parent), comes form the combination of the resource requests of the nodes underneath, $\beta_i^A = \sum_{j=1}^{N_i} \beta_{i,j}^A$ with probability $\Omega_i = min_i\{\Omega_{i,j}\}$. Finally, the resource that C_i provides to its ED nodes $nd_{i,j}$ $\langle \beta_{i,j}^G, \Lambda_{i,j} \rangle$ is

$$\beta_{i,j}^G = \frac{\beta_i^G}{\beta_i^A} \beta_{i,j}^A$$

$$\Lambda_{i,j} = \Lambda_i - \Omega_{i,j} - \Lambda_i \cdot \Omega_{i,j} \tag{5}$$

where $\Lambda_{i,j}$ is the probabilistic of the interface.

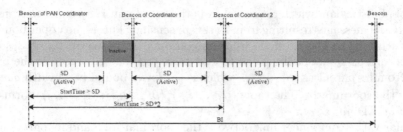

Fig. 4. The `superframe` structure of the PAN coordinator and an example of beacon scheduling of three coordinators

For the bandwidth allocation among the coordinators; the parent coordinators normalize the available resource using the accumulated resource requests $\sum \beta_i^A$ of its children cluster C_is. The normalized resource is then distributed among children cluster nodes with a probabilistic guarantee computed using the probability guarantee of the resource-request, and the probabilistic guarantee of the coordinators resource availability. The resource guarantee for cluster coordinators follows the same principle as in Equation (5) where instead of nodes $nd_{i,j}$ is applied to the coordinators C_i.

3.2   Bandwidth Based Component Composability

The probabilistic model allows us to a define flexible relationship among the curves; consequently, this results in the notion of probabilistic composability.

Definition 3 ("Greater than or Equal to "($\succeq$). *We define the greater than or equal to operator*[3] *($\succeq$) over two probabilistic curves $\langle \omega, \Omega \rangle$ and $\langle \lambda, \Lambda \rangle$ with ω and λ the curves and Ω and Λ their respective bounding probabilities, as $\langle \omega, \Omega \rangle \succeq \langle \lambda, \Lambda \rangle \iff \omega \geq \lambda \wedge \Omega \geq \Lambda$*

The following lemma provides the probabilistic guarantees for the composition of two WSN components; wherein one component is assuming a service and the second component is guaranteeing some service. The Lemma 1 is the probabilistic bound on the service that a component will offer to its workload after the composition, i.e. after a cluster coordinator guarantees some service.

Lemma 1 (Resource Reliability). *Given two probabilistic curves $\langle \beta^A, \Omega \rangle$ and $\langle \beta^G, \Lambda \rangle$ respectively an upper and lower bounding probabilistic curves, then $\min\{1, \Omega + \Lambda - \Omega \cdot \Lambda\}$ is the service-reliability probability.*

Proof. The output response of the component depends on two inputs, which are β^A and β^G. We know that probability of β^A being larger is Ω and the probability of β^G being smaller is Λ. Therefore, probability of the components service reliability depends on, $P[\beta^A \wedge \beta^G]$. This probability for the independently

---

[3] Based on the concept of stochastic dominance and stochastic ordering used in decision theory and decision analysis.

distributed random variables can be found as $P[\beta^A] + P[\beta^G] - P[\beta^A] \cdot P[\beta^G] = \Omega + \Lambda - \Omega \cdot \Lambda$, and since probability can never be larger than one, we have $\min\{1, \Omega + \Lambda - \Omega \cdot \Lambda\}$.

With this premise, it is possible to define the probabilistic composability for WNSs.

Theorem 1 (Probabilistic Composability). *Given two components i and j and two probabilistic curves $\langle \beta_i^G, \Omega_i \rangle$ and $\langle \beta_j^A, \Lambda_j \rangle$ being respectively the probabilistic lower bound to the resource provisioning (the guarantee) of the i-th component and the probabilistic upper bound to the resource demand (the assumption) of the j-th component; then i and j are composable with a probability p iff*

$$\langle \beta_i^G, \Omega_i \rangle \succeq \langle \beta_j^A, \Lambda_j \rangle \ \wedge \ p \le \min\{1, \Omega_i + \Lambda_j - \Omega_i \cdot \Lambda_j\} \tag{6}$$

Proof. The theorem follow as a consequence of Lemma 1.

4 Application to IEEE 802.15.4

4.1 CSMA/CA Using IEEE 802.15.4 superframe Structure

In the beacon-enabled mode of IEEE 802.15.4, a coordinator in a Personal Area Network (PAN) periodically sends beacon frames to synchronize the associated nodes. The standard defines a superframe structure between two successive beacon transmissions. The superframe structure is divided into an active portion and a low power inactive portion. Figure 4 shows an example of the superframe structure. The superframe structure is specified by two values; the superframe duration (SD) which defines the active portion and the beacon interval (BI) which defines the interval between two consecutive beacons. The SD and BI periods are defined using two parameters; the superframe order (SO) and the beacon order (BO), respectively. Equation (7) gives the definition of SD and BI as a function of SO and BO, respectively. In this equation, aBaseSuperframeDuration is a constant value defined by the standard which is equal to $15.36ms$

$$\left.\begin{array}{l} BI = aBaseSuperframeDuration \cdot 2^{BO} \\ SD = aBaseSuperframeDuration \cdot 2^{SO} \end{array}\right\} \tag{7}$$

$$1 \le SO \le BO \le 14$$

The standard supports the cluster tree topology wherein the coordinators form a multi-hop tree. The root coordinator is called PAN coordinator. Every coordinator provides synchronization (through beacon transmissions) to other devices or other coordinators. Therefore, to avoid beacon collision a beacon scheduling scheme has to be used among coordinators. The IEEE 802.15.4 standard imposes that BO and SO have to be equal for all superframes on a PAN and suggests the scheduling of beacons so that active periods of neighbor coordinators and

Table 1. Maximum number of messages that can be transmitted to the PAN coordinator

SO	2	3	4
MaxNbMsgs	80	120	220

two-hop neighbor coordinators do not overlap. Figure 4 gives an example of beacon scheduling of three coordinators.

Each child forwards data only during its parents active period. In particular, to transmit data to the PAN coordinator, the child coordinators and the EDs must transmit their data during the active period of the PAN coordinator. Therefore, the maximum bandwidth to be assigned by the PAN coordinator is defined as the maximum number of messages (noted MaxNbMsgs hereafter) that can to be transmitted to the PAN coordinator during the SD of every BI. We have done some preliminary simulations to determine suitable values of MaxNbMsgs. MaxNbMsgs depends on the duration of the SD period. Table 1 shows the values of MaxNbMsgs as a function of SO.

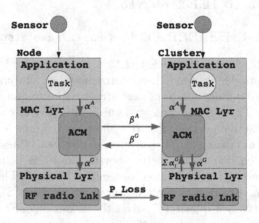

Fig. 5. System view and ACM

4.2   Admission Control Manager

The ACM, Figure 5, is a component of the MAC layer in every node of WSN. The ACM ensures that the *bandwidth assignment* policy is respected. The network has two working stages; a setup stage and a normal working stage. The setup stage works as follows. First, the PAN coordinator gathers service requests from all the nodes of the network. Then, it runs the bandwidth assignment algorithm (Based on the implementation of Equation 5). Finally, the bandwidth determined by the algorithm for each node is assigned as the guaranteed service to cluster coordinators and EDs. During the normal working stage the ACM becomes active. We note that the PAN coordinator can decide to re-execute the setup stage sometime later. The decision can be based on the reception of new service requests or changes in the network; like node mobility or death.

The ACM constantly monitors all the packets received by the MAC layer (from upper and lower layers) and decides which ones are accepted or dropped, exercising admission control tests. The decision to drop packets is based on the assigned guaranteed service to the node, $\langle \beta^G, \Lambda \rangle$. However, the ACM of the ED and the ACM of the cluster coordinators work in a different manner. For EDs, it monitors only the packets received from the application layer and ensures that the number of forwarded packets to the parent node does not exceed β^G. The Λ^G is not taken into consideration in the packet dropping process of the EDs' ACM. For cluster coordinators, the ACM monitors the packets received from children EDs and the application layer. The dropping of the packets received from children EDs is based on Λ^G of the transmitting ED; while it is based on the β^G of the cluster coordinator for the packets it receives from its application layer. We note that the ACM of the PAN coordinator monitor all received packets but does not drop any of them in case it is the destination. We can now define a metric based on the packets dropped by the ACM, called as packet-loss ration as:

Definition 4 (Packet-Loss-Ratio(PLR)). *The packet-lost-ratio (PLR) for* i^{th} *node is defined as* $l_i(t) = \frac{L_i(t)}{R_i(t)}$, *where* $L_i(t)$ *gives the packets lost in an interval* $(0, t]$.

This is be achieved by keeping two counter in an ACM; that is to count L and R. This gives us an estimate of PLR at each event (i.e. packet dropped or packet arrived). Therefore, intuitively for a given bandwidth assignment higher PLR means lower energy usage by a node; since the unnecessary transmission due to limited bandwidth were avoided. Simply put, the ACM tries to ensure that energy is only consumed for potentially successful transmissions. Although, higher PLR may seem to indicate a noticeable performance issue (QoS); however, it is important to note that the packets are dropped in an ACM based on the agreed level loss indicated by the probabilistic bounds. Moreover, higher PLR does not always indicate a problem; for example when high PLR at the PAN node is acceptable (as it may be within required QoS level).

Let us take the example of an ED which has obtained $\langle \beta^G = 2$ `packets/`
`superframe`, $\Lambda^G = 50\% \rangle$ from its parent, named C_F. The ACM of ED is responsible for ensuring that no more than two packets are transmitted to its parent C_F every `superframe`. For example, if the application generates four packets during the actual `superframe`, two of them will be dropped. The ACM of the C_F transmits the two received packets to its own parent only 50% of the time; for other 50% of the time the ACM can transmit zero or one packet to its own parent (i.e. 50% of the time, it may drop one or both packets).

4.3   Simulation Setup

As a test case we consider the network shown in Figure 2. It is composed of one PAN coordinator (Network Coordinator), three cluster coordinators and 30 EDs, five EDs attached to the first coordinator, 15 EDs attached to the second coordinator and 10 EDs attached to the third coordinator.

All coordinators, including the PAN coordinator, have a non overlapping active periods. The network uses the ZigBee [21] tree routing protocol. The simulation is performed using OPNET simulator [22], and Table 2 summarizes all the simulation parameters.

Table 2. General simulation parameters

Application parameters		
Packet length		100 bits
Service Request $\langle \alpha_i^A(p/s), \Omega_i^A \rangle$ first set of sim		variable
Service Request $\langle \alpha_i^A(p/s), \Omega_i^A \rangle$ second set of sim		$\langle 2\,p/s, 1 \rangle$
Inter-arrival distribution		constant
Destination		PAN coordinator
P_G		0.9
Network parameters		
Cm, Rm and Lm		20, 3 and 2
MAC parameters		
superframe	BO	8
	SO	2, 3 and 4
Beacon Start Time	C_1, C_2 and C_3	0.49s, 1s and 1.7s
CSMA/CA	Minimum Back-off Exponent	3
	Maximum Back-off Number	4
Acknowledgment		disabled
PHY parameters		
Data rate		250 kb/s
P_{loss}		0.1
Other parameters		
Simulated duration		900s
Energy model		Micaz

We performed two sets of simulations. The first one illustrates the behavior of the ACM. The second one compares the results of our bandwidth allocation scheme using the ACM against the original IEEE 802.15.4 standard. The simulations and the results are described next.

4.4   The Behavior of the ACM

We fix the value of SO to three and varied the EDs service request. The duration of the active period is constant and $\beta^G = 120$ `packets/superframe`, see Table 1. We also note that coordinators do not transmit messages. We report the bandwidth assigned by the PAN coordinator to each ED; the total number of packets sent; the total number of packets received by the PAN coordinator (which is the destination); the total number of packets dropped by the ACM; and the total number of packets dropped due to CSMA/CA failure or collision.

Table 3 illustrates the obtained results. We observe that if the total service request is less than the guaranteed bandwidth, cases of $\langle \alpha_i^A = 0.5(pkts/s), \Omega_i^A = 0.8 \rangle$ and $\langle \alpha_i^A = 1(pkts/s), \Omega_i^A = 0.8 \rangle$, the ACM drops few packets. In fact, the ACMs of EDs do not drop any packets, since the guaranteed service is higher

Table 3. Results of the first set of simulations. pkts, sf, and Nb designate packets, **superframe**, and number respectively.

$\langle \alpha_i^A(pkts/s), \Omega_i^A \rangle$	$\langle 0.5, 0.8 \rangle$	$\langle 1, 0.8 \rangle$	$\langle 2, 0.8 \rangle$
$\langle \beta_i^A(pkts/sf), \Omega_i^A \rangle$	$\langle 1.96, 0.8 \rangle$	$\langle 3.96, 0.8 \rangle$	$\langle 7.86, 0.8 \rangle$
Total service requests	58.98	117.96	235.92
$\langle \beta^G(pkts/sf), \Lambda^G \rangle$	$\langle 4, 0.98 \rangle$	$\langle 4, 0.98 \rangle$	$\langle 4, 0.98 \rangle$
Nb of created pkts	13500	26970	53940
Nb of received pkts	5462	8252	8337
Nb of dropped pkts by the ACM	114	243	26694
Nb of dropped pkts due to CSMA/CA failure or collision	7924	18475	18909

than the requested service and the packet inter-arrival distribution is constant. However, since the guaranteed probability is not equal to one, some of the packets will be dropped by the ACMs of cluster heads. When the total service request exceeds the guaranteed bandwidth the ACMs of EDs drop the packets to respect the allocated bandwidth; that is $\langle \alpha_i^A = 2(pkts/s), \Omega_i^A = 0.8 \rangle$. We also notice that the admission of packets by ACM for transmission does not guarantee the packets successful transmission. This is illustrated by the number of dropped packets due to CSMA/CA failure or collisions. In fact, multiple nodes may try to transmit accepted packets at the same time which results in a collision. We recall also that transmissions are not acknowledged and the duty cycle is equal to 3.125%. Nevertheless, the use of ACM minimizes the number of dropped packets due to collision or CSMA/CA failure as we will see in the next subsection.

4.5   Comparison with the Original Standard

In this simulation set, we fixed the service request of EDs and varied the SO. We measure the number of packets received by the PAN coordinator, the number of packets dropped either due to CSMA/CA failure or due to collisions, and the average end-to-end delay of the received packets. We compare the results of our bandwidth allocation scheme using the ACM against the original IEEE 802.15.4 standard (without the use of any bandwidth allocation scheme and control). For comparison we have set the service request probability (Ω_i^A) of each ED to 1.

Figure 6 shows the simulation results. Figure 6(a) corresponds to the number of the received packets by the PAN coordinator. We can notice that when using ACM and bandwidth-allocation: the number of received packets increases as SO increases. In fact, increasing SO means increasing the guaranteed bandwidth as pointed out in Table 1; therefore, each ED receives higher allocated bandwidth. We also observe that we obtain similar results for the number of received packets with and without the use of the ACM. However, both versions (with and without the ACM) do not follow the same path to obtain these similar results. Indeed, without using the ACM, dropped packets are caused by collisions or CSMA/CA failure. However, when the ACM is used, packets are dropped mainly by the ACM (though some packets are dropped by collisions or CSMA/CA failures). Figure 6(b) and figure 6(c) illustrates this result. The use of the ACM, therefore,

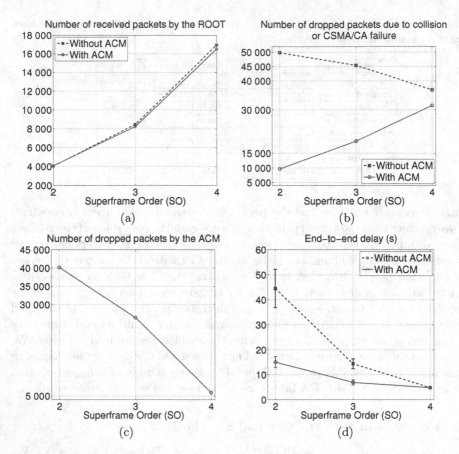

Fig. 6. Results of the second simulation set. "Without ACM" corresponds to the standard IEEE 802.15.4.

avoids useless transmissions; as the chance of failure/collision increases due to the limited bandwidth. The ACM ensures that the allocated bandwidth is respected by dropping the packets before they attempt their transmission; which can reduce the number of collisions. Consequently, this decreases the end-to-end delay. Figure 6(d) shows the end-to-end delays of the received packets with and without the use of the ACM. Indeed, the results show that the use of the ACM decreases the end-to-end delay of the received packets.

Figure 7 shows coordinators' average life-time in days. We used the Micaz [23] energy consumption model for the analysis. We observe that actively dropping overloaded packets by ACM ensures higher life-times for coordinators. Nevertheless, the results look similar. This is for two reasons. First, most of the consumed energy is due to the active period not traffic transmission and reception. Second, the active period in IEEE 802.15.4 does not depend on the traffic. The results will be different in the case of a dynamic mac protocol like B-MAC [24] or X-MAC [25] since active period lengths depend on traffic load. Hence, applying our

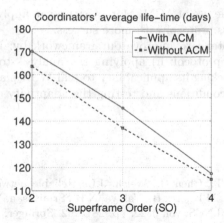

Fig. 7. Energy consumption

framework (through the use of the ACM) will ensure a better performance than the original protocols and more importantly will guarantee a lower bound on the network life-time. In fact, when the nodes send all the received packets from the application layer without exercising packet admission control and the available bandwidth is not enough to handle them all, a lot of packets will collide. This results in an energy waste since it is used to transmit packets which will not be received by the sink. Our bandwidth assignment policy is based on the available bandwidth. Hence, active packet dropping ensures that the admitted packets will be transmitted to the sink with a higher probability of success.

5   Conclusions

In this paper we proposed an approach which applies a component based and hierarchical cluster-tree topologies for WSNs by modeling and analyzing such distributed systems in a probabilistic approach. We also proposed a MAC level Admission Control Manager (ACM) which does bandwidth assignment and control for the required performance guarantees (QoS) in a probabilistic manner using the probabilistic bounds. Our framework offers flexibility of a probabilistic approach, therefore, we are able to provide probabilistic guarantees for the system functionality, or degradation; in harsh environments and complex systems.

The probabilistic bandwidth assignment approach has been successfully implemented in IEEE 802.15.4 through the admission control manager. The simulation results showed that the ACM drops packets to respect the bandwidth assigned by the PAN coordinator (to every device in the network). Consequently, we were able to decrease the number of useless transmissions while providing the same performance; that is the number of received packets. Which ensures that the energy is conserved by avoiding useless transmissions. Moreover, we were able to ameliorate the end-to-end delay. Nevertheless, because of the inherent behavior of CSMA/CA, the dropping of packets due to the collisions cannot be totally prevented by the use of ACM. Moreover, we can apply our framework to a contention-free access protocol with more success.

In the future we intend to improve our framework by: i) applying it to a contention-free access protocol; ii) applying the analysis to different network topologies; and iii) checking its applicability to real WSN platforms/testbeds in the dynamic network conditions and testing the adaptivity of the probabilistic approach.

References

1. Sastry, S., Radeva, T., Chen, J., Welch, J.L.: Reliable networks with unreliable sensors. In: Aguilera, M.K., Yu, H., Vaidya, N.H., Srinivasan, V., Choudhury, R.R. (eds.) ICDCN 2011. LNCS, vol. 6522, pp. 281–292. Springer, Heidelberg (2011)
2. Jung, C., Hwang, H., Sung, D., Hwang, G.: Enhanced markov chain model and throughput analysis of the slotted csma/ca for ieee 802.15.4 under unsaturated traffic conditions. IEEE Transactions on Vehicular Technology 58(1), 473–478 (2009)
3. Wang, Y., Vuran, M., Goddard, S.: Cross-layer analysis of the end-to- end delay distribution in wireless sensor networks. In: 30th IEEE Real-Time Systems Symposium, pp. 138–147. IEEE Computer Society (2009)
4. He, W., Liu, X., Zheng, L., Yang, H.: Reliability calculus: A theoretical framework to analyze communication reliability. In: 30th International Conference on Distributed Computing Systems, ICDCS 2010, pp. 159–168. IEEE Computer Society (2010)
5. LAN-MAN Standards Committee of the IEEE Computer Society: Wireless Medium Access Control (MAC) and Physical Layer (PHY) Specifications for Low-Rate Wireless Personal Area Networks (LR-WPANs). IEEE Press (2006)
6. Schmitt, J.B., Roedig, U.: Sensor Network Calculus – A Framework for Worst Case Analysis. In: Prasanna, V.K., Iyengar, S.S., Spirakis, P.G., Welsh, M. (eds.) DCOSS 2005. LNCS, vol. 3560, pp. 141–154. Springer, Heidelberg (2005)
7. She, H., Lu, Z., Jantsch, A., Zheng, L.R., Zhou, D.: Deterministic worst-case performance analysis for wireless sensor networks. In: International Wireless Communications and Mobile Computing Conference, IWCMC 2008, pp. 1081–1086 (August 2008)
8. Le Boudec, J.Y., Thiran, P.: Network calculus: A Theory of Deterministic Queuing Systems for the Internet. Springer-Verlag New York, Inc. (2001)
9. Jurcík, P., Koubaa, A., Severino, R., Alves, M., Tovar, E.: Dimensioning and worst-case analysis of cluster-tree sensor networks. ACM Transactions on Sensor Networks 7 (2010)
10. Koubâa, A., Alves, M., Tovar, E., Cunha, A.: An implicit gts allocation mechanism in IEEE 802.15.4 for time-sensitive wireless sensor networks: theory and practice. Real-Time Syst. 39(1-3), 169–204 (2008)
11. Na, C., Yang, Y., Mishra, A.: An optimal gts scheduling algorithm for time-sensitive transactions in IEEE 802.15.4 networks. Comput. Netw. 52(13), 2543–2557 (2008)
12. Huang, Y.-K., Pang, A.-C., Hung, H.-N.: An adaptive gts allocation scheme for IEEE 802.15.4. IEEE Transactions on Parallel and Distributed Systems 19(5), 641–651 (2008)

13. Nastasi, C., Marinoni, M., Santinelli, L., Pagano, P., Lipari, G., Franchino, G.: BACCARAT: a Dynamic Real-Time Bandwidth Allocation Policy for IEEE 802.15.4. To appear in the Proceedings of IEEE Percom 2010, International Workshop on Sensor Networks and Systems for Pervasive Computing (PerSeNS 2010), Mannheim, Germany, March 29-April 2. IEEE (2010)
14. Santinelli, L., Chitnis, M., Nastasi, C., Checconi, F., Lipari, G., Pagano, P.: A component-based architecture for adaptive bandwidth allocation in wireless sensor networks. In: IEEE Symposium on Industrial Embedded Systems, SIES (2010)
15. Jiang, Y.: A basic stochastic network calculus. SIGCOMM Comput. Commun. Rev. 36(4), 123–134 (2006)
16. Xie, J., Jiang, Y.: Stochastic network calculus models under max-plus algebra. In: Proceedings of the Global Communications Conference, GLOBECOM 2009, Honolulu, Hawaii, USA, November 30 - December 4, pp. 1–6 (2009)
17. Thiele, L., Chakraborty, S., Naedele, M.: Real-time calculus for scheduling hard real-time systems. In: ISCAS, vol. 4, pp. 101–104 (2000)
18. Khan, D., Navet, N., Bavoux, B., Migge, J.: Aperiodic traffic in response time analyses with adjustable safety level. In: 14th IEEE International Conference on Emerging Techonologies and Factory Automation - ETFA (2009)
19. Wandeler, E., Thiele, L.: Interface-based design of real-time systems with hierarchical scheduling. In: RTAS, pp. 243–252 (2006)
20. Santinelli, L., Meumeu Yomsy P., Maxim, D., Cucu-Grosjean, L.: A component-based framework for modeling and analysing probabilistic real-time systems. In: 16th IEEE International Conference on Emerging Technologies and Factory Automation (2011)
21. Zigbee Specification Document 053474r17 (January 2008), http://www.zigbee.org
22. OPNET, OPNET Simulator, v 15.0, http://www.opnet.com
23. Micaz: Micaz datasheet (2011), http://www.memsic.com/
24. Polastre, J., Hill, J., Culler, D.: Versatile low power media access for wireless sensor networks. In: SenSys 2004: Proceedings of the 2nd International Conference on Embedded Networked Sensor Systems, pp. 95–107. ACM, New York (2004)
25. Buettner, M., Yee, G.V., Anderson, E., Han, R.: X-mac: a short preamble mac protocol for duty-cycled wireless sensor networks. In: SenSys 2006: Proceedings of the 4th International Conference on Embedded Networked Sensor Systems, pp. 307–320. ACM, New York (2006)

Secondary User Monitoring in Unslotted Cognitive Radio Networks with Unknown Models

Shanhe Yi[1], Kai Zeng[2], and Jing Xu[1]

[1] Department of Electronics and Information Engineering
Huazhong University of Science and Technology, Wuhan 430074, China
{yishanhe@smail,xujing@mail}.hust.edu.cn
[2] Department of Computer and Information Science
University of Michigan - Dearborn, Michigan 48128, USA
kzeng@umich.edu

Abstract. Cognitive radio networking (CRN) is a promising technology to improve the spectrum utilization by allowing secondary users (unlicensed users) to opportunistically access white space (spectrum holes) in licensed bands. Monitoring the detailed characteristics of an operational cognitive radio network is critical to many system administrative tasks. However, very limited work has been done in this area. In this paper, we study the passive secondary user monitoring problem in an unslotted cognitive radio network, where the users' traffic statistics are unknown in priori. We formulate the problem as a multi-armed bandit (MAB) problem with weighted virtual reward. We propose a dynamic sniffer-channel assignment policy to capture as much as interested user data. Simulation results show that the proposed policy can achieve a logarithmic regret with relative scalability.

Keywords: secondary user monitoring, cognitive radio networks, multi-armed bandit.

1 Introduction

The proliferations of wireless communication and ever-increasing wireless traffic demand have put significant pressure on spectrum utilization. On the one hand, the unlicensed spectrum has become over crowded. On the other hand, a large portion of licensed bands are underutilized [1]. The un-balanced spectrum allocation and usage lead to the so-called "spectrum scarcity" problem. The concept of opportunistic spectrum access (OSA) has emerged as a way to dramatically improve spectrum utilization, thus solve this problem. In OSA, the unlicensed users can dynamically access to the licensed band (white space) without interfering the communication among primary users. Cognitive radio [2, 3] is a promising technology to realize OSA, where the secondary users (cognitive radios) can sense the absence or presence of the primary users and opportunistically access to or evacuate from the primary spectrum/channels. A variety of

X. Wang et al. (Eds.): WASA 2012, LNCS 7405, pp. 648–659, 2012.

emerging applications, including smart grid, public safety, broadband cellular, and medical applications, are expected to be supported by OSA and cognitive radio networking [4].

Monitoring the detailed characteristics of an operational cognitive radio network is critical to many system administrative tasks, such as spectrum policy enforcement, wireless advisory, fault diagnosis, anomaly detection, attack detection, forensics, resource management, and critical path analysis for network upgrades. However, very limited work has been done in this area [5].

In this paper, we study the passive monitoring problem in cognitive radio networks. Our goal is to capture as much as interested secondary user data. Different from the monitoring in traditional wireless networks [6–8], monitoring a cognitive radio network faces unique challenges: 1) Secondary users' activities are unknown in priori. Due to the agility of the cognitive radio and the activity of the primary user, the secondary users may jump among different channels to seek the best spectrum and communication opportunity or stay in the same channel, lowering its transmission power level or alerting modulation scheme to avoid interference. Furthermore, different secondary users may have different traffic patterns. 2) Cognitive radio networks usually have much wider spectrum than traditional wireless networks. Due to the limitation of hardware technology, each sniffer can only monitor one channel at a time. It becomes difficult or infeasible to deploy a large amount of sniffers to monitor all the channels at all the times.

To solve the above two challenges, we need to learn the characteristics of the primary and secondary users' traffic, meanwhile dynamically assign the limited number of sniffers to the most profit channels where the concerned secondary users may reside in. There exists an interesting tradeoff between assigning sniffers to channels which are already known as the most beneficial based on the current knowledge, versus exploring the channels which are under-observed. This category of learning and decision making under uncertainty defined by a classical tradeoff between exploration and exploitation fits into the multi-armed bandit (MAB) framework [9].

In this paper, we study the secondary user monitoring problem in an unslotted cognitive radio networks without prior knowledge of the user traffic statistics. The objective is to maximize the expected captured data of interested secondary users. The problem appears to be much more complicated than a slotted system due to the arbitrary starting and ending times of the transmissions of primary or secondary users. The challenge comes from capturing data of interested secondary users coexisting with primary users and unconcerned secondary users in a highly dynamic wireless network. Sniffers are dynamically assigned to operate on different channels to perform data capturing. During the capture, a sniffer must make a decision whether to keep operating on the current channel or switch to another channel. We formulate the problem as a MAB problem with weighted virtual reward. We propose a dynamic sniffer-channel assignment policy to capture as much as interested user data. Simulation results show that the proposed policy can achieve a logarithmic regret with relative scalability. To the best of our knowledge, we are the first to work on the secondary user monitoring in unslotted cognitive radio networks with unknown models.

The rest of this paper is organized as follows. Related work is discussed in Section 2. Section 3 formulates the problem. Then we present our policy for optimal data capturing in Section 4. In Section 5, simulation results and performance analysis are presented. Finally, we conclude this paper and discuss future works in Section 6.

2   Related Work

2.1   Multichannel Wireless Network Monitoring

Most recently, Arora *et al.* [8] applied MAB to study the optimal sniffer-channel assignment (OSCA) problem in multichannel wireless networks. It considers *sniffer-centric* monitoring [7] that aims to monitor the busiest channels. The core difference between our work and the multichannel wireless network monitoring is that we differentiate secondary users from primary users. When a primary user is found in a channel, our sniffer will switch to other channels to capture the interested secondary user data.

2.2   Cognitive Radio Network Monitoring

Very limited work has been done on secondary user monitoring in cognitive radio networks. Chen *et al.* proposed a secondary user data capturing mechanism applying machine learning technology [5]. The basic idea is to estimate the packet arrival time of interested user data and reuse the sniffer in the time domain. A sniffer can switch to other channels to capture interested data and switch back if it has enough time to do so without missing the next interested packet in the current channel. Dedicated sniffers are used to explore interested packets on different channels. Different from [5], this paper more focuses on the strategy and decision-making study of sniffers to capture data efficiently. We formulate the problem as a MAB problem and no dedicated sniffers are used to sweep channels.

2.3   Opportunistic Spectrum Access

MAB framework has been adopted to study opportunistic spectrum access (OSA) in cognitive radio networks. Liu *et al.* applied UCB1 method proposed in [10] to single user-channel selection in [11]. Liu and Zhao formulated the second user spectrum access problem as decentralized MAB problem and gave logarithmic regret policies in [12, 13]. These works are based on slotted systems. Recent work [14] applied MAB to an unslotted primary user system. Our work has fundamentally different objective from OSA. We aim to capture as much as interested secondary user data, while OSA aims to find the channels with least primary user activity or better spectrum access opportunity. Therefore, we cannot directly apply the OSA methods to secondary user monitoring. When a primary emerges, our sniffer will switch to other channels since we are only interested in secondary user data. We also need to learn the statistics of secondary user data in order to make decisions for sniffers, while OSA does not have this component and only concerns the statistics of primary users.

3 Problem Formulation

3.1 System Model

We consider a cognitive radio network with K channels. Each channel is used by one primary user. There are N secondary users and S sniffers. We are interested in the data of M secondary users. We have $M \leq N$ and $S < K$. Multiple secondary users can be in the same channel but they transmit at different times without collision. We assume each secondary user only stays in one channel and they will keep silent when the primary user shows up in the same channel. However, we do not know which secondary users stay in which channels or their traffic statistics in priori. Each sniffer can only monitor one channel at a time, but it can switch channels at any time. The sniffers are assumed to be able to identify the secondary and primary users by examining the packet header or signal feature.

The traffic of PUs is modeled as an on-off renewal process [15]. Similar to [16], Markovian assumption is relaxed on the primary traffic and we assume that the busy period may be arbitrarily distributed while the idle period has an exponential distribution. During the idle period of PU, we also model the traffic of SUs with different on-off renewal processes. Therefore the whole traffic on each channel is actually a combinational on-off renewal process with multi-states indicating which user is occupying the channel at the moment. Note that the channels are occupied temporally from primary users to secondary users. The states of each channel are firstly split into *PU-on* state and *PU-off* state where *on* means the PU is working in the channel and *off* means that PU is absent. Then, the *PU-off* state is split into separately *SU-on* state and *SU-off* state of different SUs since secondary user will use these idle channels for communication.

The occupancy duration (the *on* state) of PUs and SUs in every appearance follow the corresponding distributions denoted by the following random variables

$$Y_{pu} = \{Y_{pu_1}, \cdots, Y_{pu_k} \cdots, Y_{pu_K}\}$$
$$Y_{su} = \{Y_{su_1}, \cdots, Y_{pu_j} \cdots, Y_{su_N}\}$$

where $k \in [1, K]$ and $j \in [1, N]$.

We denote the interested secondary user set as T_{su} which is a subset of all the secondary users. Fig. 1 gives an example of $T_{su} = \{su_1, su_3, su_4, su_5, su_7\}$ out of seven SUs ($M = 5, N = 7, K = 3$), where both su_3 and su_4 access to channel 2 and both su_5 and su_7 access to channel 3.

According to the statistical characteristics of network traffic, a categorical distribution is introduced to portray the appearance frequency of a set of secondary users in channel k with a probability set P_k which is defined as follows:

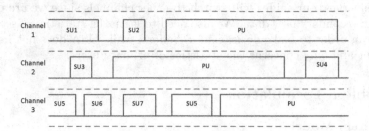

Fig. 1. Traffic Model

$$\boldsymbol{P}_k = \{p_1, \cdots, p_{j_k}, \cdots, p_{n_k}\}$$

$$\forall k \in [1, K], \sum_{j_k=1}^{n_k} p_{j_k} = 1$$

$$\sum_k n_k = N, k \in [1, K]$$

where n_k is the index of secondary users in channel k.

Since the information of appearance probability of SUs is not known in priori, we utilize the observation of SU appearance times to estimate the appearance probability. During the data capture, sniffers collect information to build up a statistical appearance probability of secondary users in channel k denoted by $\boldsymbol{P}_k^o$.

We assume a centralized system where a decision center is used to gather all the information collected from sniffers and make dynamic online sniffer-channel assignment decisions in order to capture interested secondary user data as much as possible.

3.2   MAB Problem Formulation

A typical Multi-Armed Bandit problem consists of a series of components including *player, arm, reward, regret* and *policy* [9, 17, 18]. By mapping sniffers to players and channels to arms, channel assignment of sniffers for data capture without prior knowledge falls into a multi-player multi-armed bandit problem naturally.

Since there is no prior information about secondary user traffic characteristics, sniffers have to identify and monitor the channels which have potential for the most beneficial reward to fulfill the goal of capturing transmission data of interested users as much as possible. To deal with this challenge, we keep recording the length of observed complete idle and busy period length of interested users appeared in channel k in vectors denoted by $\boldsymbol{x}_k^o$, $\boldsymbol{y}_k^o$, respectively. Both $\boldsymbol{x}_k^o$ and $\boldsymbol{y}_k^o$ are updated after each valid capture which succeeds to capture corresponding interested user data. Note that for the need to evaluate the accessibility of channel, the history of $\boldsymbol{x}_k^o$ and $\boldsymbol{y}_k^o$ are recorded. We also count the number of records and keep calculating the average of all the observation values of $\boldsymbol{x}_k^o$ and $\boldsymbol{y}_k^o$ and average them up to the current time (sample mean) which are denoted by $\hat{\boldsymbol{x}}_k^o$ and $\hat{\boldsymbol{y}}_k^o$, respectively.

The total captured data of sniffers is summed up by the length of every captured data of all the interested secondary users denoted by

$$V_o(t - t_0) = \sum_{n(t_0)}^{n(t)} \sum_k \sum_m y_{k,m}^o(n) \tag{1}$$

where $y_{k,m}^o$ is the element in $\boldsymbol{y}_k^o$, $k \in [1, K]$ is the index of channel and $m \in [1, M]$ is the index of interested user. t_0 and t are the start time and end time, respectively. $n(t)$ is the count number of $\boldsymbol{y}_k^o$ history from time t_0 to t.

Different interesting secondary users appear in different channels with different probabilities and their occupancy durations have different distributions. Take these two influential factors into consideration, a virtual reward of channel k is proposed as a weighted length of captured data which is given by

$$V_k = \sum_m \frac{\hat{y}_{m,k}^o}{\hat{y}_{m,k}^o + \hat{x}_{m,k}^o} p_{m,k}^o \tag{2}$$

where $\hat{y}_{m,k}^o$ and $\hat{x}_{m,k}^o$ is the average length of busy/idle period recorded in vector $\hat{\boldsymbol{y}}^o$ and $\hat{\boldsymbol{x}}^o$ and m is the index of interested secondary users. $p_{m,k}^o$ is the estimation of interested secondary user appearance probability which is the element in $\boldsymbol{P}_k^o$.

In order to measure the performance of strategies or policies dealing with MAB problems, *regret* is introduced as a key metric. If the reward model, user traffic parameters, and other useful prior knowledge are known, it is easy to infer that sniffers should always make the right decision to capture interested user data as much as possible by utilizing these prior knowledge. The total data captured by a "genie" is denoted by $V^*(T)$ which is similar to $V_o(T)$ in Eq. (1) but using prior knowledge. Thus the regret is given as a difference of expected value of gained reward between the "genie" and the proposed method:

$$\mathbb{E}V^*(T) - \mathbb{E}V_o(T)$$

4   Optimal Data Capture Policy

In this section, we introduce an optimal strategy for sniffers to perform efficient data capture. Our proposed policy is centralized, which can be divided into two parts: monitor policy and decision policy.

4.1   Monitor Policy

We modify the sensing and transmission scheme for single secondary user in [14] into our monitor policy for multiple sniffers to fulfill our goal.

Similar to [14], when a sniffer is assigned to a given channel, it is required to keep working for at least two successive complete idle or busy period before leaving. However, there is an exception when a sniffer senses that the assigned channel is occupied by a primary user. Since the duration of a primary user occupation is usually longer than the secondary users' and we are interested in secondary user monitoring, when a sniffer encounters such a situation, it switches to another channel immediately to perform monitor policy again. Thus the utilization of sniffers is improved and the tensity of limited monitoring resource gets relieved to some extent. As mentioned above, during the busy period of interested users, sniffers capture the data, collect the complete periods information, and then send it to the decision center, which will decide if the sniffer should stay on the current channel or switch to another one according to the decision policy which will be proposed in Section 4.2.

As to the initialization, sniffers follow the same rule to capture data of each channel in sequence in order to generate initial estimations of unknown parameters. Initialization process with a single sniffer abiding the monitoring rule is illustrated in Fig. 2.

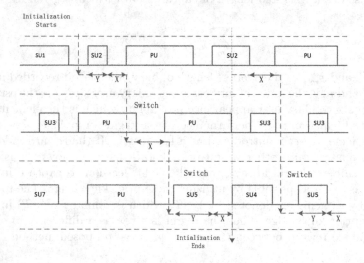

Fig. 2. Initialization and Monitor Rule

As shown in the figure, since the first idle/busy period is incomplete and the following user is an interested secondary user, three consecutive idle/busy periods are monitored of which the latter two are complete. Then the sniffer switches to the next channel to perform initialization monitoring. After finding the user in this channel is a primary user, the sniffer switches to the next channel immediately. When it comes to a multi-sniffer case, each sniffer chooses a random but different sequence of channels to conduct initialization separately as shown above. The initialization is finished after gaining information from every channel and followed by regular monitoring.

4.2 Decision Policy

We adopt the policy named UCB1 (Upper Confidence Bound) proposed in [10], which is able to achieve logarithmic regret for reward distribution with finite support. In UCB1, a decision index denoted by $I(t)$ is computed for each arm before making decisions. In our system model, $I(t)$ can be calculated from observations x^o, y^o and observed appearance probabilities $\hat{P}^o$. The index has the following form:

$$I_k(t) = \overline{V_k}(t) + \sqrt{\frac{2\log(t)}{\sum_m n_{k,m}(t)}}$$

where $\overline{V_k}(t)$ is the sample mean of virtual reward defined in Eq. (2) up to time t and $\sum_m n_{k,m}(t)$ is a counting number of successful capture of interested users in channel i.

The update rule follows

$$\overline{V_k}(t + \Delta t) = \begin{cases} \frac{\overline{V_k}(t) + V_k(t,t+\Delta t)}{n_{k,m}(t)+1} & \text{if SU m is captured at channel k;} \\ \overline{V_k}(t) & \text{else} \end{cases}$$

$$n_{k,m}(t + \Delta t) = \begin{cases} n_{k,m}(t) + 1 & \text{if SU m is captured at channel k;} \\ n_{k,m}(t) & \text{else} \end{cases}$$

where $V_k(t, t + \Delta t)$ is the incremental virtual reward from time t to time $t + \Delta t$.

The index is updated after each valid capture and available channel(arm) k with the highest index is chosen for available sniffer:

$$k = \arg\max_k I_k(t)$$

As proved in [10], there exists an optimal logarithmic regret in UCB1 method.

5   Performance Analysis

In order to evaluate the performance of our proposed policy, we developed a simulator using MATLAB. We examine the performance under different number of channels, sniffers and users. In the simulation, the number of channels K is set from 4 to 6 and the number of interesting users M is set from 4 to 12. We consider both single sniffer and multiple sniffer cases. In all the cases, the busy/idle periods of users follow exponential distributions. The busy/idle periods of primary users are much longer than those of secondary users. Both $\mathbb{E}Y_{pu}^{on}$ and $\mathbb{E}Y_{pu}^{off}$ is set as 1. The busy periods of secondary users follow different exponential distributions while the idle periods follow the same. $\mathbb{E}Y_{su}^{on}$ is random selected from 0.2 to 0.4 and $\mathbb{E}Y_{su}^{off}$ is set as 0.1. The appearance probabilities of SUs in channels are also randomly generated. The simulation results shown in each figure are the averages over 200 runs.

Fig. 3 gives the regret in which the logarithmic regret order of the proposed policy can be observed. Due to the monitor rule, as more sniffers participate in the monitoring, the information about the interested user traffic characteristics

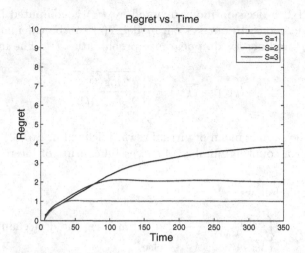

Fig. 3. Regret *vs.* Time (S=[1,2,3] M/N=8/12 K=4)

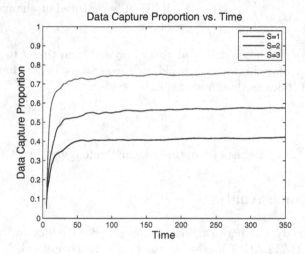

Fig. 4. Data Capture Proportion *vs.* Time (S=[1,2,3] M/N=8/12 K=4)

can be estimated more accurately and the regret converges more quickly. Therefore, the regret is diminished and converges faster when the number of sniffers increases.

Fig. 4 shows the proportion of captured interested user data under different number of sniffers. The proportion increases asymptotically which indicates that under the proposed policy, the data captured by the limited number of sniffers is able to catch up with the "genie" as long as the time goes on. The more sniffers we have, the higher ratio of data is captured.

Fig. 5 gives the reward of using different number of sniffers which is positively correlated to the number of sniffers More involved sniffers result in more data captured. The accumulated gain increases linearly against time.

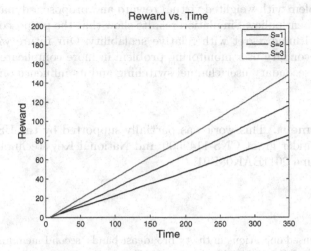

Fig. 5. Reward *vs.* Time (S=[1,2,3] M/N=8/12 K=4)

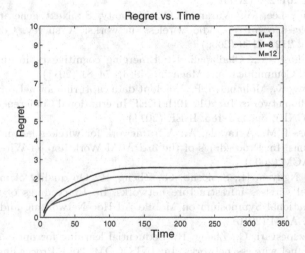

Fig. 6. Regret *vs.* Time (S=2 M/N=[4,8,12]/12 K=4)

In Fig. 6, we vary M, the number of interested users. The simulation result of *regret* shows that our proposed policy is relatively scalable against the number of interested secondary user. While halving or doubling the number of interested users, the increment or decrement percentage of regret is about 25%.

6   Conclusions and Future Work

In this paper, we study secondary user monitoring problem in unslotted cognitive radio networks with unknown user traffic statistics. We formulate the problem as a MAB problem with weighted virtual reward and propose a dynamic sniffer-channel assignment policy. Simulation results show that the proposed policy can achieve a logarithmic regret with relative scalability. Our future work will be to study the secondary user monitoring problem in more complicated scenarios by considering secondary user channel switching and its influence on our policy design.

Acknowledgement. This work was partially supported by the US NSF CA-REER award under grant CNS-1149500 and National Key Technologies R&D Program of China 2011BAK08B01.

References

1. FCC: Unlicensed operations in the tv broadcast bands, second memorandum opinion and order. FCC 10-174 (September 2010)
2. Haykin, S.: Cognitive radio: Brain-empowered wireless communications. IEEE JSAC 23(2), 201–220 (2005)
3. Akyildiz, I.F., Lee, W., Vuran, M.C., Mohanty, S.: Next generation/dynamic spectrum access/cognitive radio wireless networks: A survey. Computer Networks 50(13), 2127–2159 (2006)
4. Wang, J., Ghosh, M., Challapali, K.: Emerging cognitive radio applications: A survey. IEEE Communications Magazine 49(3), 74–81 (2011)
5. Chen, S., Zeng, K., Mohapatra, P.: Efficient data capturing for network forensics in cognitive radio networks. In: 2011 19th IEEE International Conference on Network Protocols (ICNP), pp. 176–185. IEEE (2011)
6. Yeo, J., Youssef, M., Agrawala, A.: A framework for wireless lan monitoring and its applications. In: Proceedings of the 3rd ACM Workshop on Wireless Security, pp. 70–79. ACM (2004)
7. Chhetri, A., Nguyen, H., Scalosub, G., Zheng, R.: On quality of monitoring for multi-channel wireless infrastructure networks. In: Proceedings of the Eleventh ACM International Symposium on Mobile Ad Hoc Networking and Computing, pp. 111–120. ACM (2010)
8. Arora, P., Szepesvari, C., Zheng, R.: Sequential learning for optimal monitoring of multi-channel wireless networks. In: INFOCOM, 2011 Proceedings IEEE, pp. 1152–1160. IEEE (2011)
9. Robbins, H.: Some aspects of the sequential design of experiments. Bulletin of the American Mathematical Society 58(5), 527–535 (1952)
10. Auer, P., Cesa-Bianchi, N., Fischer, P.: Finite-time analysis of the multiarmed bandit problem. Machine Learning 47(2), 235–256 (2002)
11. Lai, L., El Gamal, H., Jiang, H., Poor, H.: Cognitive medium access: Exploration, exploitation, and competition. IEEE Transactions on Mobile Computing 10(2), 239–253 (2011)
12. Liu, K., Zhao, Q., Krishnamachari, B.: Decentralized multi-armed bandit with imperfect observations. In: 48th Annual Allerton Conference on Communication, Control, and Computing (Allerton), pp. 1669–1674. IEEE (2010)
13. Liu, K., Zhao, Q.: Distributed learning in multi-armed bandit with multiple players. IEEE Transactions on Signal Processing 58(11), 5667–5681 (2010)

14. Tehrani, P., Zhao, Q., Tong, L.: Multi-channel opportunistic spectrum access in unslotted primary systems with unknown models. In: 2011 4th IEEE International Workshop on Computational Advances in Multi-Sensor Adaptive Processing (CAMSAP), pp. 157–160. IEEE (2011)
15. Zhao, Q., Sadler, B.: A survey of dynamic spectrum access. IEEE Signal Processing Magazine 24(3), 79–89 (2007)
16. Chen, S., Tong, L.: Low-complexity distributed spectrum sharing among multiple cognitive users. In: Military Communications Conference, 2010-MILCOM 2010, pp. 2274–2279. IEEE (2010)
17. Lai, T., Robbins, H.: Asymptotically efficient adaptive allocation rules. Advances in Applied Mathematics 6(1), 4–22 (1985)
18. Agrawal, R.: Sample mean based index policies with o (log n) regret for the multi-armed bandit problem. Advances in Applied Probability, 1054–1078 (1995)

Design and Spectrum Efficiency
of a New Waveform

Lei Xu[1], Qilian Liang[1], Jie Wang[2], and Hyeong-Ah Choi[3]

[1] Department of Electrical Engineering,
University of Texas at Arlington, Arlington, TX 76019-0016
xu@wcn.uta.edu, liang@uta.edu
[2] Department of Computer Science,
University of Massachusetts Lowell, Lowell, MA 01854
wang@cs.uml.edu
[3] Department of Computer Science,
George Washington University, Washington, DC 20052, USA
hchoi@gwu.edu

Abstract. With the rapid deployment of new wireless devices and applications in cellular systems and wireless local area networks (WLAN), there is a growing demand for wireless radio spectrum in last several decades. Spectrum efficiency attracts more and more attention. In this paper, we try to improve the spectrum efficiency from the view of waveform design. Based on the zero correlation zone (ZCZ) concept, we present the definition and properties of a set of new triphase coded waveforms –ZCZ sequence-pair set (ZCZPS) in this paper and propose a method to use the optimized punctured sequence-pair along with Hadamard matrix in the zero correlation zone to construct the optimized punctured ZCZ sequence-pair set (optimized punctured ZCZPS). According to property analysis, the optimized punctured ZCZPS has good autocorrelation and cross correlation properties. Encoding the proposed codes on the frequency domain, we obtain that the proposed codes have narrower mainlobe and lower sidelobes comparing with Gold codes.

Keywords: spectrum efficiency, zero correlation zone, optimized punctured sequence-pair.

1   Introduction

The usage of radio spectrum resources and the regulation of radio emissions are coordinated by national regulatory bodies like the Federal Communications Commission (FCC). The FCC assigns spectrum to licensed holders on a long-term basis for large geographical regions, however, a large portion of the assigned spectrum might be not efficiently used by these holders during some period of time. Hence, spectrum efficiency is attracting more and more attentions.

Spectrum efficiency is referred to as information rate that can be transmitted over a given bandwidth in a specific communication system. Sometimes, the energy allocation of a given bandwidth is also used as a metric for spectrum

X. Wang et al. (Eds.): WASA 2012, LNCS 7405, pp. 660–669, 2012.

efficiency. Hence, spectrum efficiency is a measure of how efficiently a limited frequency spectrum is utilized by protocols on different layers. Innovative communication technologies that can exploit the wireless spectrum in a more intelligent and flexible way are studied to improve the spectrum efficiency. On one hand, the cognitive radio which equips wireless users the capability to optimally adapt their operating parameters according to the interactions with the surrounding radio environment has been receiving an increasing attention in recent years [1] [2] [3]. On the another hand, PN sequences, such as Gold codes are widely used in the modern cellular system as reference signals for channel estimation, hence, the spectrum efficiency of the GOLD codes is of great importance. It is ideal to obtain the spectrum performance as narrower mainlobe and higher Peak mainlobe to sidelobe ratio which could assure spectrum efficiency. In this paper, we would like to find a set of codes which have better spectrum efficiency.

Based on the ZCZ [4] concept, we propose triphase coded waveforms called ZCZ sequence-pair set (ZCZPS), which can reach zero autocorrelation sidelobe during ZCZ and zero mutual cross correlation peaks during the whole period. We also present and analyze a method to construct the triphase coded waveforms and subsequently apply them to a radar detection system. The method is that optimized punctured sequence-pair joins together with Hadamard matrix to construct optimized punctured ZCZ sequence-pairs set (optimized punctured ZCZPS). We encode the proposed codes on the frequency domain which is similar to OFDM technique. We obtain that the spectrum efficiency of the proposed codes is better than that of the Gold codes.

The rest of the paper is organized as follows. Section 2 gives the definition and properties of ZCZPS. In Section 3, the optimized punctured ZCZPS is provided, and a method using optimized punctured sequence-pair and Hadamard matrix to construct ZCZPS is given and proved. In Section 4, the properties of an exaple of the optimized punctured ZCZPS are simulated and analyzed. In section 5, encoding the proposed codes on the frequency domain and better spectrum efficiency is achieved. In Section 6, final conclusions and future works are provided on optimized punctured ZCZPS.

2 The Definition and Properties of ZCZ Sequence-Pair Set

Zero correlation zone is a new concept provided by Fan [4] in which the autocorrelation and cross correlation sidelobes are zero while the time delay is kept within the value τ instead of the whole period of time domain.

We consider ZCZPS($\mathbf{X}, \mathbf{Y}$), $\mathbf{X}$ to be a set of K sequences of length N and $\mathbf{Y}$ to be a set of K sequences of the same length N:

$$\mathbf{x}^{(p)} \in \mathbf{X} \ p = 0, 1, 2, ..., K - 1 \tag{1}$$
$$\mathbf{y}^{(q)} \in \mathbf{Y} \ q = 0, 1, 2, ..., K - 1 \tag{2}$$

The autocorrelation function for sequence-pair $(\mathbf{x}^p, \mathbf{y}^p)$ is defined by:

$$R_{\mathbf{X}^{(p)}\mathbf{y}^{(p)}}(\tau) = \sum_{i=0}^{N-1} x_i^{(p)} y_{(i+\tau)modN}^{(p)*}, 0 \leq \tau \leq N-1 \tag{3}$$

The cross correlation function for sequence-pair $(\mathbf{x}^p, \mathbf{y}^p)$ and $(\mathbf{x}^q, \mathbf{y}^q), p \neq q$ is defined by:

$$C_{\mathbf{X}^{(p)}\mathbf{y}^{(q)}}(\tau) = \sum_{i=0}^{N-1} x_i^{(p)} y_{(i+\tau)modN}^{(q)*}, 0 \leq \tau \leq N-1 \tag{4}$$

$$C_{\mathbf{X}^{(q)}\mathbf{y}^{(p)}}(\tau) = \sum_{i=0}^{N-1} x_i^{(q)} y_{(i+\tau)modN}^{(p)*}, 0 \leq \tau \leq N-1 \tag{5}$$

For pulse compression sequences, some properties are of particular concern in the optimization for any design in engineering field. They are the peak side-lobe level, the energy of autocorrelation sidelobes and the energy of their mutual cross correlation [5]. Therefore, the peak sidelobe level which represents a source of mutual interference and obscures weaker targets can be presented as $\max_K |R_{\mathbf{X}^p\mathbf{y}^p}(\tau)|, \tau \in Z_0$ (zero correlation zone) for ZCZPS. Another optimization criterion for the set of sequence-pair is the energy of autocorrelation sidelobes joined together with the energy of cross correlation. By minimizing the energy, it can be distributed evenly, and the peak autocorrelation level can be minimized as well [5]. Here, the energy of ZCZPS can be employed as:

$$E = \sum_{p=0}^{K-1} \sum_{\tau=1}^{Z_0} R_{\mathbf{X}^{(p)}\mathbf{y}^{(p)}}^2(\tau) + \sum_{p=0}^{K-1} \sum_{q=0}^{K-1} \sum_{\tau=0}^{N-1} C_{\mathbf{X}^{(p)}\mathbf{y}^{(q)}}(\tau) \tag{6}$$

$$(p \neq q)$$

According to (6), it is obvious to see that the energy can be kept low while minimizing the autocorrelation and cross correlation of the sequence-pair set.

Then, the ZCZPS can be constructed to minimize the autocorrelation and cross correlation of the sequence-pair set, and the definition of ZCZPS can be expressed:

Definition 2-1. Assume $(x_i^{(p)}, y_i^{(p)})$ to be a sequence-pair of set (X, Y) of length N and the number of sequence-pairs K, where $p = 0, 1, ..., N-1, i = 0, 1, ..., K-1$. If sequences in the set satisfy the following equation:

$$R_{\mathbf{X}^{(p)}\mathbf{y}^{(q)}}(\tau) = \sum_{i=0}^{N-1} x_i^{(p)} y_{(i+\tau)mod(N)}^{(q)*} = \sum_{i=0}^{N-1} y_i^{(p)} x_{(i+\tau)mod(N)}^{(q)*}$$

$$= \begin{cases} \lambda N, & \text{for } \tau = 0, p = q \\ 0, & \text{for } \tau = 0, p \neq q \\ 0, & \text{for } 0 < |\tau| \leq Z_0 \end{cases} \tag{7}$$

where $0 < \lambda \leq 1$, then $(x_i^{(p)}, y_i^{(p)})$ is called a ZCZ sequence-pair, $ZCZP(N, K, Z_0)$ is an abbreviation, and $(\mathbf{X}, \mathbf{Y})$ is called a ZCZ sequence-pair set, $ZCZPS(N, K, Z_0)$ is an abbreviation.

3   Optimized Punctured ZCZ Sequence-Pair Set

3.1   Definition of Optimized Punctured ZCZ Sequence-Pair Set

Matsufuji and Torii have provided some methods of constructing ZCZ sequences in [6] [7]. In this section, a novel triphase coded waveform, namely the optimized punctured ZCZ sequence-pair set, is constructed through applying the optimized punctured sequence-pair [8] to the zero correlation zone. . In other words, optimized punctured ZCZPS is a specific kind of ZCZPS.

Definition 3-1 [8]. Sequence $\mathbf{u} = (u_0, u_1, ..., u_{N-1})$ is the punctured sequence for $\mathbf{v} = (v_0, v_1, ..., v_{N-1})$,

$$u_j = \begin{cases} 0, & \text{if } u_j \text{ is punctured} \\ v_j, & \text{if } u_j \text{ is Non-punctured} \end{cases} \tag{8}$$

Where the number of punctured bits in sequence $\mathbf{v}$ is p. Then, suppose $v_j = (-1, 1)$, $\mathbf{u}$ is p-punctured binary sequence, $(\mathbf{u}, \mathbf{v})$ is called a punctured binary sequence-pair.

Definition 3-2 [8]. The autocorrelation of punctured sequence-pair $(\mathbf{u}, \mathbf{v})$ is defined

$$R_{\mathbf{uv}}(\tau) = \sum_{i=0}^{N-1} u_i v_{(i+\tau) mod N}, 0 \leq \tau \leq N-1 \tag{9}$$

If the punctured sequence-pair has the following autocorrelation property:

$$R_{uv}(\tau) = \begin{cases} E, & \text{if } \tau \equiv 0 \bmod N \\ 0, & \text{otherwise} \end{cases} \tag{10}$$

the punctured sequence-pair is called optimized punctured sequence-pair [8]. Where, $E = \sum_{i=0}^{N-1} u_i v_{(i+\tau) mod N} = N - p$, is the energy of punctured sequence-pair.

If $(x_i^{(p)}, y_i^{(p)})$ in Definition 2-1 is constructed by optimized punctured sequence-pair and a certain matrix, such as Hadamard matrix or an orthogonal matrix, where

$$x_i^{(p)} \in (-1, 1), \quad i = 0, 1, 2, ..., N-1$$

$$y_i^{(q)} \in (-1, 0, 1), \quad i = 0, 1, 2, ..., N-1$$

$$R_{\mathbf{x}^{(p)}\mathbf{y}^{(q)}}(\tau) = \sum_{i=0}^{N-1} x_i^{(p)} y_{(i+\tau)mod N}^{(q)*} = \sum_{i=0}^{N-1} y_i^{(p)} x_{(i+\tau)mod N}^{(q)*}$$

$$= \begin{cases} \lambda N, & \text{for } \tau = 0, p = q \\ 0, & \text{for } \tau = 0, p \neq q \\ 0, & \text{for } 0 < |\tau| \leq Z_0 \end{cases} \tag{11}$$

where $0 < \lambda \leq 1$, then $(x_i^{(p)}, y_i^{(p)})$ can be called optimized punctured ZCZ sequence-pair set.

3.2 Design for Optimized Punctured ZCZ Sequence-Pair Set

Based on odd length optimized punctured binary sequence pairs and a Hadamard matrix, an optimized punctured ZCZPS can be constructed from the following steps:

Step 1: Considering an odd length optimized punctured binary sequence-pair (u, v), the length of each sequence is N_1

$$\mathbf{u} = u_0, u_1, ..., u_{N_1-1}, u_i \in (-1, 1),$$
$$\mathbf{v} = v_0, v_1, ..., v_{N_1-1}, v_i \in (-1, 0, 1),$$

Step 2: A Hadamard matrix B of order N_2 is considered. The length of the sequence of the matrix is N_2 which is equal to the number of the sequences. Here, any Hadamard matrix order is possible and $\mathbf{b}^i$ is the row vector.

$$\mathbf{B} = [\mathbf{b}^0; \mathbf{b}^1; ...; \mathbf{b}^{N_2-1}],$$
$$\mathbf{b}^i = (b_0^i, b_1^i, ..., b_{N_2-1}^i),$$
$$R_{\mathbf{b}^i \mathbf{b}^j} = \begin{cases} N_2, & \text{if } i = j \\ 0, & \text{if } i \neq j \end{cases}$$

Step 3: Doing bit-multiplication on the optimized punctured binary sequence-pair and each line of Walsh sequences set B (Hadamard matrix), then sequence-pair set (X, Y) is obtained,

$$\mathbf{b}^i = (b_0^i, b_1^i, ..., b_{N_2-1}^i), i = 0, 1, ..., N_2 - 1,$$
$$x_j^i = u_{jmodN_1} b_{jmodN_2}^i, 0 \leq i \leq N_2 - 1, 0 \leq j \leq N - 1,$$
$$\mathbf{X} = (\mathbf{x}^0, \mathbf{x}^1, ..., \mathbf{x}^{N_2-1}),$$
$$y_j^i = v_{jmodN_1} b_{jmodN_2}^i, 0 \leq i \leq N_2 - 1, 0 \leq j \leq N - 1,$$
$$\mathbf{Y} = (\mathbf{y}^0, \mathbf{y}^1, ..., \mathbf{y}^{N_2-1})$$

Since most of optimized punctured binary sequence-pairs are of odd lengths and the lengths of Walsh sequence are $2^n, n = 1, 2, ...$, most of $GCD(N_1, N_2) = 1$, common divisor of N_1 and N_2 is 1, $N = N_1 * N_2$. If $GCD(N_1, N_2) \neq 1$, N should be the least common multiple $lcm(N_1, N_2)$. The construction method for the case of $GCD(N_1, N_2) \neq 1$ should be similar to $GCD(N_1, N_2) = 1$, so we would only consider the case of $GCD(N_1, N_2) = 1$ in this paper. The sequence-pair set $(\mathbf{X}, \mathbf{Y})$ is optimized punctured ZCZPS and $N_1 - 1$ is the zero correlation zone

Z_0. The length of each sequence in optimized punctured ZCZPS is $N = N_1 * N_2$ that depends on the product of length of optimized punctured sequence-pair and the length of Walsh sequence in Hadamard matrix. The number of sequence-pair in optimized punctured ZCZPS rests on the order of the Hadamard matrix. The sequence $\mathbf{x}^i$ in sequence set $\mathbf{X}$ and the corresponding sequence y^i in sequence set Y construct a sequence-pair $(\mathbf{x}^i, \mathbf{y}^i)$ that can be used as a pulse compression code. The correlation property of the sequence-pair in optimized punctured ZCZPS is:

$$R_{\mathbf{x}^i \mathbf{y}^j}(\tau) = R_{\mathbf{x}^j \mathbf{y}^i}(\tau) = R_{\mathbf{uv}}(\tau mod N_1) R_{\mathbf{b}^i \mathbf{b}^j}(\tau mod N_2)$$
$$= R_{\mathbf{uv}}(\tau mod N_1) R_{\mathbf{b}^j \mathbf{b}^i}(\tau mod N_2)$$
$$= \begin{cases} EN_2, & \text{if } \tau = 0, i = j \\ 0, & \text{if } 0 < |\tau| \le N_1 - 1, i = j \\ 0, & \text{if } i \ne j \end{cases} \tag{12}$$

where $N_1 - 1$ is the zero correlation zone Z_0.

Proof

1) When $i = j$,

$$\tau = 0, R_{\mathbf{uv}}(0) = E, R_{\mathbf{b}^i \mathbf{b}^j}(0) = N_2,$$
$$R_{\mathbf{x}^i \mathbf{y}^j}(0) = R_{\mathbf{uv}}(0) R_{\mathbf{b}^i \mathbf{b}^j}(0) = EN_2;$$
$$0 < |\tau| \le N_1 - 1, R_{\mathbf{uv}}(\tau) = 0,$$
$$R_{\mathbf{x}^i \mathbf{y}^j}(\tau) = R_{\mathbf{uv}}(\tau mod N_1) R_{\mathbf{b}^i \mathbf{b}^j}(\tau mod N_2) = 0;$$

2) When $i \ne j$,

$$\tau = 0, R_{\mathbf{b}^i \mathbf{b}^j}(0) = 0,$$
$$R_{\mathbf{x}^i \mathbf{y}^j}(0) = R_{\mathbf{x}^j \mathbf{y}^i}(0) = R_{\mathbf{uv}}(\tau mod N_1) R_{\mathbf{b}^i \mathbf{b}^j}(\tau mod N_2) = 0;$$
$$0 < |\tau| \le N_1 - 1, R_{\mathbf{uv}}(\tau) = 0,$$
$$R_{\mathbf{x}^i \mathbf{y}^j}(\tau) = R_{\mathbf{x}^j \mathbf{y}^i}(\tau) = R_{\mathbf{uv}}(\tau mod N_1) R_{\mathbf{b}^i \mathbf{b}^j}(\tau mod N_2) = 0.$$

According to Definition 2-1, the sequence-pair set constructed by the above method is a ZCZPS.

4 Properties of Optimized Punctured ZCZ Sequence-Pair Set

Considering the optimized punctured ZCZPS that is constructed by the method mentioned in the last part, the autocorrelation and cross correlation properties can be simulated and analyzed. For example, the optimized punctured ZCZPS (X, Y) is constructed by 31-length optimized punctured binary sequence-pair $(\mathbf{u}, \mathbf{v})$, $\mathbf{u} = [+++--+-]$, $\mathbf{v} = [+++00+0]$ (using $'+'$ and $'-'$ symbols for $'1'$ and $'-1'$) and Hadamard matrix H of order 4. We follow the three steps presented in Section **B** to construct the 124-length optimized punctured ZCZPS. The number of sequence-pairs here is 4, and the length of each sequence is $7 * 4 = 28$. The first row of each matrix $\mathbf{X} = [\mathbf{x}_1; \mathbf{x}_2; \mathbf{x}_3; \mathbf{x}_4]$ and $\mathbf{Y} = [\mathbf{y}_1; \mathbf{y}_2; \mathbf{y}_3; \mathbf{y}_4]$ constitute a certain optimized punctured ZCZP $(\mathbf{x}_1, \mathbf{y}_1)$. Similarly, the second row of each matrix $\mathbf{X}$ and $\mathbf{Y}$ constitute another optimized punctured ZCZ sequence-pair $(\mathbf{x}_2, \mathbf{y}_2)$ and so on.

$$\mathbf{x}_1 = [+ + + - - + - + + + - - + - + + + - - + - + + + - - + -];$$
$$\mathbf{y}_1 = [+ + + 00 + 0 + + + 00 + 0 + + + 00 + 0 + + + 00 + 0];$$
$$\mathbf{x}_2 = [+ - + + + - - - - + - - + + + + - + + - - - - + - - + + +];$$
$$\mathbf{y}_2 = [+ - - + 00 - 0 - + - 00 + 0 + - + 00 - 0 - + - 00 + 0];$$
$$\mathbf{x}_3 = [+ + - + - + + - + + + + + - - - + - + - - + - - - - - +];$$
$$\mathbf{y}_3 = [+ + - 00 + 0 - + + 00 + 0 - - + 00 - 0 + - - 00 - 0];$$
$$\mathbf{x}_4 = [+ - - - - - + + + - + - + + - + + + + + - - - + - + - -];$$
$$\mathbf{y}_4 = [+ - - 00 - 0 + + - 00 + 0 - + + 00 + 0 - - + 00 - 0];$$

Optimized punctured ZCZ sequence-pairs $(\mathbf{x}_1, \mathbf{y}_1)$ and $(\mathbf{x}_2, \mathbf{y}_2)$ are the two example pairs which are simulated and investigated in the following parts.

Autocorrelation and Cross Correlation Properties. The autocorrelation property of 28-length optimized punctured ZCZ sequence pair set $(\mathbf{X}, \mathbf{Y})$ and 31-length Gold codes are shown in Fig. 1.

From the Fig. 1, the sidelobe of autocorrelation of ZCZPS can be as low as 0 when the time delay is kept within $Z_0 = N_1 = 7$. The peak sidelobes of autocorrelatoin of Gold codes are no more than 0.3 but not zero.

The cross correlation property of 28-length optimized punctured ZCZ sequence pair set $(\mathbf{X}, \mathbf{Y})$ and 31-length Gold codes are shown in Fig. 2.

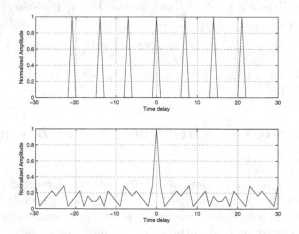

Fig. 1. Autocorrelation property: optimized punctured ZCZPS (Upper) and Gold sequences (Under)

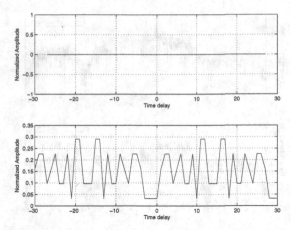

Fig. 2. Cross correlation property: optimized punctured ZCZPS (Upper) and Gold sequences (Under)

The cross correlation value of ZCZ codes is 0 during the whole time domain. The cross correlation values of Gold codes are no more than 0.3 but never be 0.

Based on the above figures, it is always true that employing this construction method, the cross correlation is zero over the whole period and the sidelobe of autocorrelation of ZCZPS could be kept as low as 0 among ZCZ.

It is also known that a suitable criterion for evaluating code of length N is the ratio of the peak signal divided by the peak signal sidelobe (PSR) of their autocorrelation function, which can be bounded by [9]

$$[PSR]_{dB} \leq 20log_2N = [PSR_{max}]_{dB} \qquad (13)$$

The only uniform phase codes that can reach the PSR_{max} are the Barker codes whose length is equal or less than 13. The sidelobe of the new codes shown in Fig. 1 and Fig. 2 can be as low as 0, and the peak signal divided by the peak signal sidelobe can be as large as infinite. Besides, the length of the new code is various and much longer than the length of the Barker code.

5   Spectrum Efficiency of the Proposed Codes

We also study and compare the spectrum properties of the proposed codes and the Gold codes. The power spectrum density (PSD) of the two codes are shown in Fig. 3.

From Fig. 3, it is easy to see that the PSD of the proposed codes assembles the PSD of GOLD codes except for several high sharp pulses. As is known that PSD is the fourier transform of the autocorrelation on time domain, here, the sharp pulses are corresponding to the multiple peaks of the autocorrelation of the proposed codes, which are caused by the codes constructing methods.

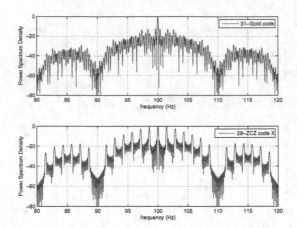

Fig. 3. Power Spectrum Density: optimized punctured ZCZPS (Upper) and Gold sequences (Under)

If we apply our codes in time domain directly, the PSD performance of our codes is not better than the PSD of Gold codes indicating no gain from the view of spectrum efficiency. In some other words, the main lobe of the proposed codes is not narrower, and the sidelobe is not lower than the Gold codes.

However, if we apply the proposed codes and Gold code on the frequency domain, we will obtain some gain on spectrum efficiency. Take OFDM for example, a large number of closely spaced orthogonal sub-carrier signals carried data. And it is well known that Gold codes are widely used as reference signal in LTE system which employed the OFDM techniques. Hence, for the sake of simplicity but not losing the generality, we assume that we assign the proposed codes and Gold codes on the frequency domain and to study their performances. We know that autocorrelation and PSD are always a set of fourier transform pair. It is straightforward to obtain that the frequency domain performance of this assignment could be very alike the Fig. 1 by exchanging the parameter of X axis from 'Time' into 'Frequency'. Since bandpass filter is usually used to obtain the useful period bandwidth, the frequency shift should be successfully limited within the ZCZ. If the frequency shift is within the ZCZ, according to Fig. 1 the performance of the proposed codes is better than that of the Gold codes by having a narrower main lobe and zero side lobes. Correspondingly, the time domain performance of the proposed codes and the Gold codes are similar to Fig. 3 by exchanging the parameter of X axis from 'Frequency' into 'Time'. Accordingly, the time domain performance of the proposed codes are comparable to that of the Gold codes.

6   Conclusions

In this paper, we study the spectrum efficiency from the view of waveform design aspect. We provide the definition and properties of a set of triphase coded waveforms–ZCZ sequence-pair set. Based on optimized punctured sequence-pair and Hadamard matrix, we have investigated a constructing method for the triphase coded waveform–optimized punctured ZCZPS made up of a set of optimized punctured ZCZPs along with studying its properties. The significant advantage of the optimized punctured ZCZPS is that it considerably reduces the sidelobe as low as zero in the ZCZ, and also zero mutual cross correlation value in the whole time domain. Comparing with the widely used Gold codes, the proposed codes have narrower mainlobe and much lower sidelobe. Encoding the proposed codes on the frequency domain, we obtain better spectrum efficiency of the proposed codes than that of the Gold codes. Hence, the proposed codes could be a good candidate for the scenario using Gold codes if more effective usage of radio spectrum is required. In the future, we will study how to use the proposed codes in the real scenarios. Some simulations of cellular systems using different codes may be implemented to study the spectrum efficiency improvements.

References

1. Mitola, J.: Cognitive radio: An integrated agent architecture for software defined radio, Ph.D. dissertation, KTH Royal Inst. of Technol., Stockholm, Sweden (2000)
2. Haykin, S.: Cognitive radio: Brain-empowered wireless communications. IEEE J. Sel. Areas Commun. 23(2), 201–220 (2005)
3. Akyildiz, I.F., Lee, W.-Y., Vuran, M.C., Mohanty, S.: Next generation/ dynamic spectrum access/cognitive radio wireless networks: A survey. Comput. Netw. 50, 2127–2159 (2006)
4. Fan, P.Z., Suehiro, N., Kuroyanagi, N., Deng, X.M.: A class of binary sequences with zero correlation zone. IEE Electron. Letter 35(10), 777–779 (1999)
5. Somaini, U.: Bianry sequences with good autocorrelation and cross correlation properties. IEEE Transactions on Aerospace and Electronic Systems AES-11(6), 1226–1231 (1975)
6. Matsufuji, S., Suehiro, N., Kuroyanagi, N., Fan, P.Z.: Two types of polyphase sequence set for approximately synchronized CDMA systems. IEICE Trans. Fundamentals E862A(1), 229–234 (2003)
7. Torii, H., Nakamura, M., Suehiro, N.: A new class of zero correlation zone sequences. Tran. Inform. Theory 50, 559–565 (2004)
8. Jiang, T.: Research on Quasi-Optimized Binary Signal Pair and Perfect Punctured Binary Signal Pair Theory, Ph.D Dissertation: Yanshan University (2003)
9. Richards, M.A.: Fundamentals of Radar Signal Processing. McGraw-Hill (2005)

Exploiting Spectrum Spatial Reusability for Routing in Multi-hop Wireless Networks*

Tong Meng and Fan Wu**

Shanghai Key Laboratory of Scalable Computing and Systems,
Department of Computer Science and Engineering,
Shanghai Jiao Tong University, China
{mengtong,fan-wu}@sjtu.edu.com

Abstract. Routing metrics are essential to achieve a good end-to-end throughput on a min-cost path in multi-hop wireless networks. Originally, most routing algorithms were based on min-hop count metric. Then link-quality aware metrics, ETX and ETT, are proposed. After that, the emergence of opportunistic and any-path routing, leads to metrics such as EOTX and EAX. But almost all the previous routing metrics take the sum of all the link weights when choosing a min-cost path. They ignore that a pair of links on a path might be able to transmit at the same time without interference and hence it is inappropriate to include both of their weights in the whole path. In this work, we suggest exploiting such spatial reusability when designing routing metric to improve end-to-end throughput. We propose Spatial Reusability Aware Routing Metric (SAR) with the corresponding Spatial Reusability Aware Routing Algorithm. Our simulation results have shown good improvement in throughput.

Keywords: Spatial Reusability, Routing, Multi-hop, Wireless Network.

1 Introduction

In wireless network, it is essential to find the best path between data source and destination to achieve high end-to-end throughput, which is the task of routing algorithms. Originally, most routing algorithms were based on min-hop count metric, which is a metric that assumes perfect wireless links and tends to minimize the number of hops on the path. However, in the face of lossy links in wireless environment, protocols using min-hop metric does not perform well because they may include some poor links with high loss ratios. Then taking link quality into consideration, a lot of link-quality aware metrics have been designed. De Couto et al. [1] proposed the Expected Transmission Count (ETX)

---

* This work was supported in part by China NSF grant 61170236 and 61133006. The opinions, findings, conclusions, and recommendations expressed in this paper are those of the authors and do not necessarily reflect the views of the funding agencies or the government.

** Corresponding author.

X. Wang et al. (Eds.): WASA 2012, LNCS 7405, pp. 670–676, 2012.

that weights the links by the expected number of retransmissions depending on their loss ratios. With link quality measured more precisely, ETX-based routing algorithms improves the end-to-end throughput significantly. Inspired from ETX and by adding the factor of link bandwidth, Draves et al. [2] developed the Expected Transmission Time (ETT) and got even better performance. After that, the emergence of new ideas of routing, namely opportunistic and any-path routing, leads to metrics such as EOTX [3] and EAX [4].

We notice that almost all the previous routing metrics, ETX as an example, simply take the sum of all the link weights when choosing a min-cost path. This method seems reasonable when all links on a path are in each other's interference range. Yet for a long path, a pair of links on it might be able to transmit at the same time without interference and hence it is inappropriate to include both of their weights in the whole path. We regard this phenomenon as a form of spatial reuse.

In this work, we suggest exploiting spatial reusability of wireless communication media in multi-hop wireless networks to improve end-to-end throughput. We also propose a simple routing metric called Spatial Reusability Aware Routing Metric (SAR) taking spectrum spatial reusability into account and develop corresponding Spatial Reusability Aware Routing Algorithm to implement SAR-metric. Our main contributions are that we introduce a new idea in designing routing metric which is exploiting spectrum spatial reusability, and bring chance to further improve end-to-end throughput of multi-hop wireless networks.

Our simulations on ns-2 have shown strong evidence of the existence and effect of "spatial reuse" on a path. We test our algorithm in a 80-node network with a modified AODV protocol and compare the throughputs achieved with our metric on different paths with that with the original ETX metric. The results show that about 10% of all the source-destination pairs achieve apparent improvement with an average of nearly 400 (kbps).

2   System Model and Motivating Example

In this section, we illustrate the network model we employ and provide motivating example to demonstrate the necessity of considering "spatial reusability" in routing metric.

2.1   System Model

As most of the other works in routing metrics, we consider a static multi-hop wireless network, in which each of the nodes has a single radio interface and works on the same channel. In this preliminary work, we focus on deterministic single-path routing. In our following works, we will consider the case of opportunistic any-path routing.

We assume the loss ratio of the link is determined by SINR/BER model. As in (1), the SINR value is the received signal strength ratio between the packet that's being accessed P, and the addition of noise N and interference packets I.

$$SINR = \frac{P}{N + I}. \tag{1}$$

According to the SINR/BER table, we can get the bit error rate of the packet from its SINR value. The loss ratio r is calculated by (2) using the packet size l. In that way, whether a packet can be successfully received by a node is determined by the packet's SINR.

$$r = 1 - (1\text{-}BER)^{\,l}. \tag{2}$$

We also assume every transmission is independent with identical distribution of loss ratio. To exploit the spatial reusability, two hops in a network can transmit free of interference if their source and destination nodes are at least out of each other's interference range (IR). With the network model we explain in the above, we show an inspiring example that demonstrates the power of spatial reusability as follows.

Because we only consider single-rate, single-radio case currently, ETX is applied to evaluate the weight of each wireless link. The ETX of a link is calculated from the loss ratios in the forward and reverse directions. Denote by r_f and r_r, the forward and reverse delivery ratios of a link is the probabilities that a data packet and an ACK packet can be successfully received, respectively. The expected number of transmissions is [1]:

$$\text{ETX} = \frac{1}{(1\text{-}r_f) \times (1\text{-}r_r)}. \tag{3}$$

The equation (3) is based on the assumption that the transmission of a packet can be regarded as a Bernoulli trial.

2.2   Motivating Example

To show the effect of spatial reusability in wireless routing, let's consider two paths as shown in Fig. 1. In Fig. 1, there're two routes between source node 1 and destination node 6. They are route I with 5 hops and route II with 4 hops. The ETX value of each hop is indicated beside the links in the figure. Note that the first and the last hop on route I can work at the same time without interfering each other, while there're no such link pair on route II. For convenience, we define such kind of link pair to be a *reuse pair*.

By the ETX metric, route II is preferred because its ETX sum, which is 10.1, is smaller than the value 11.1 of route I. However, considering the fact that link (1-2) and (5-6) can work in the meanwhile, they together do not need to consume as much bandwidth as two consecutive hops. Thus if we subtract the weight of link (5-6) from route I's ETX, it will get smaller ETX than route II instead; and by estimation, route I can achieve a 10% higher throughput than route II because the first four hops on route I have better quality compared with the hops on route II.

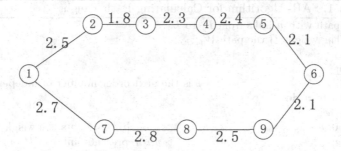

Fig. 1. A motivating example showing the effect of spatial reuse

Fig. 1 demonstrates the raw ETX metric's drawback of ignoring the possibility of "spatial reusability" between links. Taking such reusability into consideration, we give our simple metric in the next section.

3   SAR Algorithm

In this section, we explain our SAR Metric and present the SAR Algorithm based on the metric. Different from ETX which simply sums up the ETX values of all the links on a path, in SAR metric we consider the combination of *independent units* (IUs), which is a group of links where every two of them can make up a reuse pair. An IU can also contain only one single link which does not belong to any reuse pairs. We use W_i to denote the weight of the i-th IU whose value is equal to the largest weight among all the links of an IU. In our Metric, the weight of the path, represented by W_{path}, is calculated by equation (4).

$$W_{path} = \sum_i (W_i). \tag{4}$$

We only count the weight of IUs in our metric. So those hops from the same IU will be counted only once. In that way, spatial reusability between links in wireless networks can be synthesized in the design of routing metric. Now the main task of the metric will be deciding the combination method of independent units on a path. Because find an optimal combination of IUs, which is similar to the problem of determining the chromatic number of a graph in graph-coloring field, is known to be NP-complete, we suggest finding sub-optimal routes using one of the many existing polynomial time graph-coloring algorithms. We apply a simple first-fit algorithm to decide IU combination and calculate the weight of a path shown as below.

The SAR Algorithm goes through all the links from source to destination, and judges if a link is in the same independent unit with some link before it on the path. If so, add this link to that unit and update the IU's weight to be the biggest weight among all its links. Otherwise, create a new IU consisting of this single link. Hence the algorithm is in $O(n^2)$ and ends in polynomial time.

Algorithm 1. SAR-Algorithm for Calculating Path Weight

Input: A path with n links from L_1 to L_n.
Output: The weight of the path W_{path}.

$W_{path} = 0$;
$p = 1$;   ▷ p is the next order number of independent unit
for i from 1 to n **do**
    $IU[i] \leftarrow \phi$;
    $\omega[i] \leftarrow 0$ ▷ $\omega[i]$ represents the weight of ith IU
    $u[i] \leftarrow i$;   ▷ $u[i]$ represents link i's IU order number
end for
for i from 1 to n **do**
    if $i < 3$ **then**
        $W_{path} \leftarrow W_{path} + W_i$;
        $IU[p] \leftarrow \{i\}$; $\omega[p] \leftarrow W_i$;
        $p \leftarrow p + 1$;
        $continue$;
    end if
    $\delta \leftarrow W_i$;
    $flag \leftarrow 0$;   ▷ $flag$ is 0 means link i is in a new IU
    for j from 1 to i-2 **do**
        $reuse\_flag \leftarrow reuse\_judge(u[j], i)$;
        if $reuse\_flag = 1$ **then**
            $\delta \leftarrow max\{0, W_i - \omega[u[j]]\}$;
            $flag \leftarrow 1$;
            $u[i] \leftarrow u[j]$;
            $\omega[u[i]] \leftarrow max\{\omega[u[i]], W_i\}$;
            $IU[u[i]] \leftarrow IU[u[i]] \cup \{i\}$;
            $break$;
        end if
    end for
    $W_{path} \leftarrow W_{path} + \delta$;
    if $flag = 0$ **then**
        $u[i] \leftarrow p$;
        $IU[p] \leftarrow \{i\}$; $\omega[p] \leftarrow W_i$;
        $p \leftarrow p + 1$;
    end if
end for

Plus the number of links on a path won't be quite huge, our SAR algorithm won't bring too much overhead to the routing process. Note that the function $reuse\_judge(x, y)$ on the above is to judge whether link y belongs to independent unit x. If the link can reuse with all the links from the unit, the function returns 1; or it returns 0.

4 Implementation

In this preliminary work, a modified AODV protocol with additional reuse information header is implemented to integrate SAR Algorithm. What's more, we take the real scene of transmitting in wireless environment into consideration and add an interference factor to SAR Metric. This is because in the original design of our metric, the weight of a IU is the largest weight among all links in that unit and the other links' weights are then omitted, whereas that's in the case where the links of the same IU can actually work at the same time. Without link-level synchronization, two links from the same unit may not transmit simultaneously sometimes. That results in interference between IUs and may lead to more transmissions before a packet is successfully received by the destination. So we add the interference factor to counteract the phenomenon whose value is 10% of the unit's weight. Every time a new hop is grouped into an independent unit, we add such a factor to the weight of the whole path. We calculate the factor that way to reflect the fact that the kind of interference is related to the weight of the IU to which the new hop belongs.What's more, because we only consider single rate case currently, ETX is stilled applied to evaluate the weight of each wireless link.

5 Simulation

In this section, we compare SAR implemented as in the above section with the original ETX-based AODV using simulations on ns-2. We build a network with 80 nodes within an 2000m×2000m area. RTS/CTS is turned off and CBR is used to generate 1500-byte packets under a 11M bandwidth. For simulations, 150 source and destination pairs are chosen, all of which are at least 900m and at most 1200m away. Furthermore, for every single source destination pair, we choose to use the original path found by ETX if weight of the best path under SAR is smaller than that of the original one by less than 10%.

Fig. 2 plots all these paths' throughputs. The x value of all the points is the throughput from ETX-based AODV. The y value is the result of the same pair of source and destination from SAR. Those nodes above link y=x correspond to those paths where SAR outperforms original ETX. From the figure, we can see that about 10% of all the simulated pairs achieve apparent throughput improvement compared with original ETX. The average improvement of them is calculated to be 375.98 (kbps), and we notice that there're several nodes that get almost 100% higher throughput among them and one data point shows even 200% improvement. There're still a larger part of all the source-destination pairs that performs equally under the two metrics. Some of those pairs use the same path because of our "at least 10% better" restriction. Still there are groups that choose different paths from the two metrics. That can also prove that integrating spatial reusability in the design of routing metric does not impair the network's performance.

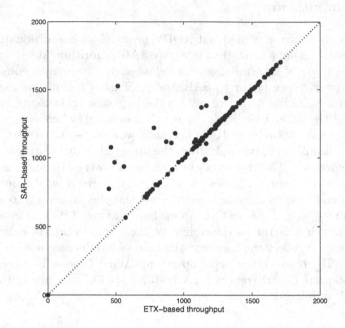

Fig. 2. Throughput comparison of two metrics

6   Conclusion

In this work, we have proposed to exploit the spatial reusability in wireless multi-hop routing and design a simple routing metric called SAR and an algorithm as well. Our simulation results demonstrate the possibility of improving the throughput by exploiting spectrum spatial reusability in wireless networks. In the future, we intend to investigate effective algorithms for counting reuse pairs. Opportunistic any-path routing is to be extended, too.

References

1. De Couto, D., Aguayo, D., Bicket, J., Morris, R.: A High-throughput Path Metric for Multi-Hop Wireless Routing. In: ACM MOBICOM (2003)
2. Draves, R., Padhye, J., Zill, B.: Routing in Multi-radio, Multi-hop Wireless Mesh Networks. In: ACM MOBICOM (2004)
3. Chachulski, S.: Trading Structure for Randomness in Wireless Opportunistic Routing. M.S. Thesis (2007)
4. Zhong, Z., Wang, J., Nelakuditi, S., Lu, G.-H.: On Selection of Candidates for Opportunistic Opportunistic Anypath Forwarding. In: ACM SIGMOBILE (2006)

Human Tracking for Daily Life Surveillance Based on a Wireless Sensor Network

Sen Zhang and Wendong Xiao

School of Automation and Electrical Engineering,
University of Science and Technology Beijing,
30 Xueyuan Road, Haidian District, Beijing 100083, P.R. China
zhangsen1989@hotmail.com, wendongxiao68@gmail.com

Abstract. This paper proposes a human motion tracking approach for daily life surveillance in a distributed wireless sensor network using ultrasonic range sensors.Because the human target often moves with high non linearity, the proposed approach applies the unscented Kalman filter (UKF) technique. Experimental results in a real human motion tracking system show that the proposed approach can perform better tracking accuracy compared to the most recent human motion tracking scheme in the real test-bed implementation.

1 Introduction

Human motion tracking is receiving increasing attention from researchers of different fields of study nowadays. The interest is motivated by a wide range of applications, such as wireless healthcare, surveillance, human-computer interaction, and so on. A complete model of human consists of both the movements and the shape of the body. Many of the available systems consider the two modeling processes as separate even if they are very close. In our study, the movement of the body is the target.

Most of the human motion tracking systems are based on vision sensors. Recently, there has been a significant amount of work in tracking people trajectory across multiple image views. Some of the proposed approaches present systems that are capable of segmenting, detecting and tracking people using multiple synchronized surveillance cameras located far from each other. But they try to hand off image-based tracking from camera to camera without recovering real-world coordinates [7]. Some other work has to deal with large video sequences involved when the image capture time interval is short [4]. The most recent work on vision based people tracking systems develop wireless sensor networks with low resolution camera to predict the trajectory of human movement [8]. However, most vision-based approaches to moving object detection is computationally intensive and costly expensive [6]. They often involve intensive real-time computations, such as image matching, background subtraction, and overlapping identification [6]. In fact, in many cases, due to the availability of prior knowledge on target motion kinematics, the intensive and expensive imaging detector array appears

X. Wang et al. (Eds.): WASA 2012, LNCS 7405, pp. 677–684, 2012.

inefficient and unnecessary. For example, a video image consisting of 100×100 pixels with 8-bit gray level contains 80 kbits of data, while the position and velocity can be represented by only a few bits [3].

Instead of the centralized processing tracking system based on vision, a promising alternative system named distributed wireless sensor network (WSN) has been quickly developed recently. It consists of many low cost, spatially dispersed position sensor nodes. Each node can compute and process information that it received and transfer the information among the sensor nodes that are placed within its communication range or to its leader node. Although there are many applications on WSN on target tracking problems [1] [2] [3], few papers can be found on human motion tracking in real time systems [5]. We will develop such a system by WSN in this paper.

From our point of view, human tracking with multiple sensors is an intrinsic multi-sensor data fusion problem. Multi-sensor data fusion is such a process through which we combine readings from different sensor nodes, remove inconsistencies, and pull all the information together into one coherent structure. Although some work of multi-sensor data fusion in WSN has been proposed [1], the tracking accuracy is still limited because of the high non linearity property of the human target. In this paper, a UKF filter is employed to estimate the velocity and position of the human trajectory in WSN. UKF filter has the ability to switch between a high process noise (or alternatively, higher order or turn) model in the presence of maneuvers and a low process noise model in the absence of maneuvers. This point gives the UKF filter its advantage over simpler estimators like the Kalman filter and EKF. Compared to the existing work based on EKF [1], the proposed algorithm can give more accurate estimation by using multiple models for human motion in a real time tracking system developed in this paper.

The layout of the paper is as follows: Sect. 2 presents the multiple models for human motion tracking. Sect. 3 presents the UKF estimator for our application. Sect. 4 proposes the sensor node selection method for our framework. Sect. 5 presents the simulation results and experimental results. Conclusions and future work are drawn in Sect. 6.

2   Problem Formulation

In this section we formulate the human motion tracking as a distributed multi-sensor data fusion problem. We consider the human moving in a 2-D Cartesian coordinate system. The target state includes the human velocity, the human position in the coordinate and the turn rate when the trajectory is along a curve. We can build up the system models as follows.

2.1   Coordinated Turn Model

In order to describe the human's more complex trajectory, such as turn left or turn right, here we apply the coordinated turn model similar to that in [3]:

$$\mathbf{x}_2(k+1) = \mathbf{F}_2(\mathbf{x}_2(k)) + \mathbf{G}_2 \mathbf{v}_2(k) \tag{1}$$

where $\mathbf{x}_2(k+1) = [P_x(k+1) \quad V_x(k+1) \quad P_y(k+1) \quad V_y(k+1) \quad \omega]^T$,

$$\mathbf{F}_2(\mathbf{x}_2(k)) = \begin{bmatrix} P_x(k) + \frac{\sin\omega T}{\omega} \cdot V_x(k) - \frac{1-\cos\omega T}{\omega} \cdot V_y(k) \\ \cos\omega T \cdot V_x(k) - \sin\omega T \cdot V_y(k) \\ P_y(k) + \frac{1-\cos\omega T}{\omega} \cdot V_x(k) + \frac{\sin\omega T}{\omega} \cdot V_y(k) \\ \sin\omega T \cdot V_x(k) + \cos\omega T \cdot V_y(k) \\ \omega \end{bmatrix}$$

$$\mathbf{G}_2(K) = \begin{bmatrix} \frac{1}{2}T^2 & T & 0 & 0 & 0 \\ 0 & 0 & \frac{1}{2}T^2 & T & 0 \\ 0 & 0 & 0 & 0 & T \end{bmatrix}^T$$

Where ω is the assumed unknown constant turn rate and $\mathbf{v}_2(k)$ is the process noise. Although the actual turn rate is not exactly a constant, we can assume that it is not changed in a very short time interval. For convenience, we assume that $\mathbf{v}_2$ is a zero mean Gaussian white noise with variance $\mathbf{Q}_2(k)$.

2.2 System Observation Model

In order to build up the estimation scheme using UKF, the sensor observation model is needed. If sensor j is used, $Z_j(k)$ is applied to denote the k-th measurement of the target at time step t_k. The measurement model is given by

$$Z_j(k) = h_j(x(k)) + v_j(k) \tag{2}$$

where h_j is a (generally non-linear) measurement function depending on sensor j's measurement characteristic and parameters (e.g., its location). $v_j(k)$ is a variable representing measurement noise in sensor j. It is independent and assumed to be zero-mean Gaussian distribution white noise. The covariance of $v_j(k)$ is $R_j(k)$.

2.3 UKF Filter

Based on the above the coordinated constant turn model and the system observation model, the interacting multiple model filter is applied to estimate the system state variable which includes the target's position coordinate and velocity.

Given the estimate $\hat{\mathbf{x}}(k \mid k)$ of $\mathbf{x}(k)$ and its estimation error covariance $\mathbf{P}(k \mid k)$, in order to avoid the linearization involved in the EKF, the UKF works by generating a set of points whose sample mean and sample covariance are $\hat{\mathbf{x}}(k \mid k)$ and covariance $\mathbf{P}(k \mid k)$, respectively. The nonlinear function is applied to each of these points in turn to yield a transformed sample, and the predicted mean and covariance are calculated from the transformed samples. The samples are deterministically chosen so that they capture specific information about the Gaussian distribution.

For highly nonlinear systems, the UKF has advantages over the EKF. It avoids the linearization that causes substantial errors in the EKF for nonlinear systems and possible singular points in Jacobian matrices. The basic UKF algorithm (one cycle) can be seen in [10].

3   Sensor Node Selection

In the sensor selection scheme, it is assumed that each sensor is able to detect the target and determine it's range. Another assumption is that the locations of all the sensors are known. One of the approaches simply selects the nodes closest to the predicted target location as estimated by the tracker. The drawback of the "closest" node approach is that it only roughly selects the sensor nodes and does not consider the contribution to the tracking accuracy and the energy consumption quantitively and simultaneously. In this paper, we propose an adaptive sensor selection scheme under UKF filter by jointly selecting the next tasking sensor and determining the sampling interval at the same time based on both of the prediction of the tracking accuracy and tracking energy cost under the UKF filter based tracking system. The details of this scheme is similar to the method in paper [11].The only difference is that the IMM filter will be replaced by the UKF in the selection process.

4   Experimental Results

Our test-bed is shown in Fig. 1. All the hardwares in the test-bed are supplied by Crossbow Technology. The test-bed consists of the following hardwares: MicaZ (processor with on-board ZigBee radio), MDA100CA, MIB510 (USB programmer), and SRF02 (active ultrasonic sensor with I2C bus).

Fig. 2shows the MicaZ mote, which operates in the 2400 MHz to 2483.5 MHz band, and uses the Chipcon CC2420, IEEE 802.15.4 compliant, ZigBee ready radio frequency transceiver integrated with an Atmega128L micro-controller. It has an integrated radio communication transceiver working at 2.4 GHz frequency with a transmission data rate of 250K bps and indoor transmission range of 20 to 30 meters. It runs TinyOS and is programmed on nesC.

The MDA100CA series sensor boards have a precision thermistor, a light sensor/photocell, and general prototyping area. The prototyping area supports connection to all eight channels of the Mote's analog to digital converter (ADC 0 to 7), both USART serial ports and the I2C digital communications bus. The prototyping area also has 45 unconnected holes that are used for breadboard of circuitry. See Fig. 3.

Fig. 1. The Test-bed

Fig. 2. The MicaZ mote

Fig. 3. The MDA100CA Sensor Board

The MIB510 interface board (See Fig. 4) is a multi-purpose interface board used with the MicaZ. It supplies power to the devices through an external power adapter option, and provides an interface for a RS-232 Mote serial port and reprogramming port. The MIB510 has an on-board in-system processor (ISP) to program the Motes. Code is downloaded to the ISP through the RS-232 serial port. The ISP programs the code into the mote. The ISP and the Mote share the same serial port. The ISP runs at a fixed baud rate of 115.2 kbaud. The ISP continually monitors incoming serial packets for a special multi-byte pattern. Once this pattern is detected, it disables the Mote's serial RX and TX (two legs), then takes control of the serial port.

The SRF02(See Fig.5) is a single transducer ultrasonic range sensor. It features both I2C and a Serial interfaces. I2C interface is used in this project.

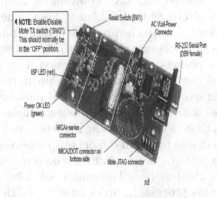

Fig. 4. MIB510 programmer board

Fig. 5. The SRF02 Ultrasonic Sensor

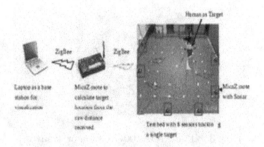

Fig. 6. The Human Tracking System

We use only 8 sensors in the test-bed. New commands in the SRF02 include the ability to send an ultrasonic burst on its own without a reception cycle, and the ability to perform a reception cycle without the preceding burst. SRF02's minimum measurement range is around 15cm (6 inches). This sensor has a detection angle of 15 degree and a maximum range of 6m.

The developed target tracking system, see Figs. 1 and 6, is made up of 8 ultrasonic sensor nodes. These 8 ultrasonic sensors located along the edge of the area respectively with coordinates (200, 0), (250, 170), (50, 300), (0, 110), (100, 0), (250, 60), (150, 300), (0, 230). The orientations of the sensors (clockwise from the positive x-axis) are respectively 65°, 90°, 50°, 75°, 100°, 110°, 90°, 120° such that the sound waves are not reflected from nearby walls/ obstacles. Each node is allocated with an ID number and a XY coordinate. Their locations are shown in Fig. 1 to cover a monitoring area of 2.5m x 3.0m. The tracking target is a human. A MicaZ mote will be attached to each sensor node.

On the base station, a laptop is connected to the network through a MicaZ mote for receiving data packets via USB connection. Fig. 6 shows the tracking system deployed in the test bed. Upon receiving an initial time synchronizing beacon from processing mote, all sensor nodes will initialize their starting time for sensor nodes. These sensor nodes will broadcast their sensor readings with one sensor reading at a time to the processing mote to avoid sensors' interference. The processing mote will also program the default measurement for each sensor.

The real time data is collected from a human who is moving around within the sensor coverage area of the test-bed. The sensor selection scheme is performed during the data collection process. In order to simplify the sensor selection algorithm, we selected one sensor at each time step in the experiments. The data

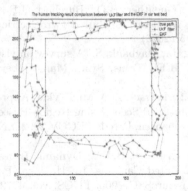

Fig. 7. The Human Tracking System Experimental Result with UKF and EKF

collected is run by UKF filter based tracking approach proposed in Sect. 2 and we compared the experimental results with the method in [12]. Fig. 7shows the comparison of the result with UKF and EKF respectively. We can see that the result from UKF is better than the results from EKF in the real test bed.

5   Conclusions

This paper presents an UKF filter based adaptive sensor scheduling scheme for human tracking in wireless sensor networks. It uses cheap range sensor nodes in wireless sensor networks by jointly selecting the next tasking sensor and determining the sampling interval based on predicted tracking accuracy and tracking cost under the UKF filter frame. Simulation results show that the new scheme can achieve significant energy efficiency without degrading the tracking accuracy. There are still many issues remaining for future study. Multi-step, multi-sensor selection based adaptive sensor scheduling and sensor scheduling for multi-target tracking are both challenging problems for further investigations.

References

1. Mazor, E., Averbuch, A., Bar-Shalom, Y., Dayan, J.: Interacting Multiple Model Methods in Target Tracking: A Survey. IIEEE Trans. on Aerospace and Electronic Systems 34(1), 103–123 (1998)
2. Lu, D., Yao, Y., He, F.: Sensor management based on cross-entropy in interacting multiple model Kalman filter. In: Proceedings of the 2004 American Control Conference, Boston, USA, July 2004, pp. 5381–5386 (2004)
3. Mallick, M., La Scala, B.F.: IMM Estimator for Ground Target Tracking with Variable Measurement Sampling Intervals. In: Proceedings of the 9th International Conference on Information Fusion(ICIF 2006), Florence, Italy, pp. 1–8 (July 2006)
4. Cai, Q., Aggarwal, J.K.: Tracking human motion in structured environments using a distributed-camera system. IIEEE Transactions on Pattern Analysis and Machine Intelligence 21(12), 1241–1247 (1999)

5. Hao, Q., Brandy, D.J., Guenther, B.D., Burchett, J.B., Shankar, M., Feller, S.: Human Tracking with Wireless Distributed Pyroelectric Sensors. IIEEE Sensors Journal 6(6), 1683–1696 (2006)

6. Hu, W., Tan, T., Wang, L., Maybank, S.: A survey on visual surveillance of object motion and behaviors. IEEE Trans. Syst., Man, Cybern. C, Appl. Rev. 34(3), 334–352 (2004)

7. Mittal, A., Davis, L.S.: M2Tracker: A Multi-view Approach to Segmenting and Tracking People in a Cluttered Scene Using Region-Based Stereo. In: Heyden, A., Sparr, G., Nielsen, M., Johansen, P. (eds.) ECCV 2002. LNCS, vol. 2350, pp. 18–33. Springer, Heidelberg (2002)

8. Zajdel, W., Cemgil, A.T., Kröse, B.J.A.: Dynamic Bayesian Networks for Visual Surveillance with Distributed Cameras. In: Havinga, P., Lijding, M., Meratnia, N., Wegdam, M. (eds.) EuroSSC 2006. LNCS, vol. 4272, pp. 240–243. Springer, Heidelberg (2006)

9. Bar-Shalom, Y., Li, X.R., Kirubarajan, T.: Estimation with Applications to Tracking and Navigation. John Wiley and Sons, INC. (2001)

10. Xiong, K., Zhang, H., Chan, C.: Performance evaluation of UKF-based nonlinear filtering. Automatica 42(2), 261–270 (2006)

11. Zhang, S., Xiao, W., Ang Jr., M.H., Tham, C.K.: IMM Filter based Sensor Scheduling for Maneuvering Target Tracking in Wireless Sensor Networks. In: Proceedings of the Third International Conference on Intelligent Sensors, Sensor Networks and Information Processing (ISSNIP 2007), Melbourne, December 3-6, pp. 751–756 (2007)

12. Toh, Y., Xiao, W., Xie, L.: A Wireless Sensor Network Target Tracking System with Distributed Competition based Sensor Scheduling. In: Proceedings of the Third International Conference on Intelligent Sensors, Sensor Networks and Information Processing (ISSNIP 2007), Melbourne, December 3-6, pp. 257–262 (2007)

The Node Movement Models Based on Lagrange Motion for 3-D Underwater Acoustic Sensor Network[*]

Zhaohua Yang[1], Shaobin Cai[2, 3], Nianmin Yao[2], Haiwei Pan[2], and Qilong Han[2]

[1] College of Instrumentation and Opto-electronics Engineering,
Beijing University of Aeronautics & Astronautics, Beijing, China, 100191
[2] College of Computer, Harbin Engineering University, Harbin, China, 150001
[3] College of Acoustic Engineering, Harbin Engineering University, Harbin, China, 150001
Caishaobin@hrbeu.edu.cn

Abstract. UWASN (UnderWater Acoustic Sensor Network) is a kind of WSN (Wireless Sensor Network) consisting of underwater acoustic sensor nodes. In its studies, the simulation is a key tool for the research of UWASN. However, the existing node movement models can not reflect the motion characteristics of nodes in a 3-D space, caused by the sea current. So, a new node movement model, based on Lagrange motion, is proposed in this paper to describe the movement of nodes in a 3-D oceanic current. It is proved that the new model can more really describe the 3-D movements of nodes in the current by the performance analysis.

Keywords: UnderWater Acoustic Sensor Network, Movement, Model, Lagrange, 3-D.

1   Overview

UWASN (UnderWater Acoustic Sensor Network) is a kind of WSN (Wireless Sensor Network) consisting of underwater acoustic sensor nodes, which can be deployed for real-time warship monitoring, oceanographic data collection, environmental monitoring, disaster prevention, etc. There are two ways for the performance analysis of UWASN. One of them is the sea test, the other is the simulation. However, the fee of the sea test is so huge that it can't be used frequently. Therefore, the simulation is a key tool for the research of UWASN. In the performance simulation analysis of underwater acoustic sensor network, a movement model, which can reflect the real movement of the nodes in the ocean, is the base of the performance analysis. Now, simple model and model based on Lagrange motion is the classic movement model of UWASN. However, the existing node movement models can not reflect the motion characteristics of nodes in a 3-D space, caused by the sea current.

[*] The work is supported by National Science foundation of China (41176082, 61073182, 40827003, and 61073183), the Fundamental Research Funds for the Central Universities (HEUCF100607), and Young backbone teacher project of Heilongjiang province (1155G15).

X. Wang et al. (Eds.): WASA 2012, LNCS 7405, pp. 685–693, 2012.

In this paper, a new node movement model based on Lagrange motion is proposed, which can reflect the sea current movement. Compared with the old movement model based on Lagrange motion, the new model has the following characters: (1) the impact of unexpected events on the movement of the nodes is considered; (2) the states of seawater are different under the different pressure.

The rest of the paper is arranged as following: firstly, the simple movement model is introduced in chapter 2; secondly, the model based on Lagrange is introduced in chapter 3; thirdly, a 3-D underwater mobility model based on Lagrange is proposed in chapter 4; fourthly, the performance of the new model is analyzed by mathematics and simulations in chapter 5; finally, a conclusion is drawn in chapter 6.

2   Simple Movement Model

The static model is the simplest one [1]. In a static model, the positions of all nodes do not change. The static model can not reflect the node movement characters of UWASN. Hence, a simple movement model was proposed [1]. In this model, the nodes of the same layer do not change, and their movements are caused by the powers, which have the same direction. Now, the model is described as following:

$$x(t) = x(t-1) + v_{cx}$$
$$y(t) = y(t-1) + d_t v_{cy} \tag{1}$$

In the above formula, $d_t = \begin{cases} -1 & if \quad d(t-1)=1 \quad \delta \quad y(t-1))l_{cy} \\ 1 & if \quad d(t-1)=-1 \quad \delta \quad y(t-1)(-l_{cy} \end{cases}$, v_{cx} and v_{cy} are two

random numbers in the interval $[0 , v_{max}]$, l_{cy} is the threshold of nodes oscillatory movement. Therefore, in this model, the nodes move slowly with a state of swing. The model is simple, easy to control, and suitable for the anchored UWASN. This kind of movement model with AUV nodes, whose movement trajectories are sine curve, was used in the performance analysis [1].

Now, in the marine surveying and mapping, Euler and Lagrange methods are mainly used for independent fundamental measurement research [2]. In the Euler method, the collected data don't change with time; In Lagrange method, the data are collected by the underwater equipments, which move with the ocean current. Hence, a unique description of the ocean current can be given by Lagrange method.

In shallow water area, the water depth is normally between 100m~300 m. The speed of current is relatively slow; the movement is not very complicated. Hence, a motion model based on the Euler method is proposed [3]. In this model, all nodes do swing movement in a certain area, or do clockwise or counterclockwise rotation movement in other areas. The movement is described as following:

$$\begin{cases} V_x = k_1\lambda\sin(k_2 x)\cos(k_3 y) + k_1\lambda\cos(2k_1 t) + k_4 \\ V_y = -\lambda v\cos(k_2 x)\sin(k_3 y) + k_5; \end{cases} \qquad (2)$$

In the above formula, V_x is the speed of x direction, V_y is the speed of y direction. k_1、k_2、k_3 and λ are the coefficient closely related to environment, such as, the tide and the depth, which change with the environment; k_4、k_5 are random variables related with environment. Therefore, in the model, described in the above formula, the speed of the node is related with time t and the coordinates (x, y) of node [2] (shown in fig.1).

3 Models Based on Lagrange motion

The movements of ocean current particles based on curve model are studied in a miles-long current [4] [5] [6]. The influence of vertexes and flows and of all layers is considered in this model.

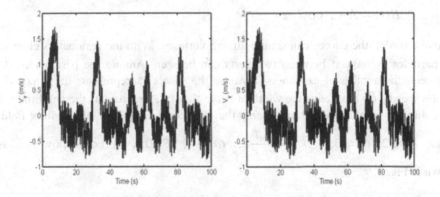

Fig. 1. The relationship between speed and time

In oceanic surveying, it is usually assumed that movements of particles in the vertical direction normally are floating movement [7]. In other words, the nodes do not initiatively accelerate their movement. In this case, the floating movements of nodes are related to the environmental density. So, their movement is usually like-Damped movement because of the resistance of sea water.

The water of deep or shallow sea area is pushed by strong winds; the up and down stream are formed. So, the internal fluctuations are created in the current. However, according to oceanic models, the phenomenon above can be ignored. In the 70's of last century, a nodes movement model, which can effectually reflected the main characteristics of two-dimensional ocean currents (flow and vortex) is proposed by Dr

Bower[reference]. In this model, if any two-dimensional incompressible currents is represented by φ, then the speed of a node $U = (u, v)$ is be described as following:

$$u = -\frac{\partial \varphi}{\partial y}; \qquad v = \frac{\partial \varphi}{\partial x} \tag{3}$$

In the above formula, u presents x axis direction speed, and v presents y axis direction speed. Now, the Lagrange movement trajectories of a node can be described as following:

$$\dot{x} = -\partial_y \varphi(x, y, t), \dot{y} = -\partial_x \varphi(x, y, t) \tag{4}$$

Furthermore, the model also defined the curved injection flow as following:

$$\varphi(x, y, t) = -\tanh\left[\frac{y - B(t)\sin(k(s - ct))}{\sqrt{1 + k^2 B(t)^2 \cos^2(k(x - ct))}}\right] + cy \tag{5}$$

$$B(t) = A + \varepsilon\cos(\omega t)$$

In above model, the curves can shuttle among vortexes. With the parameters change, the particles exchanged between two parts can be seen. Among the parameters, k represents the number of exchanged flows in the space; c represents the y axis direction speed; B represents the width of curve flows; ε represents the amplitude of the entire flow field; and ω represents the movement frequency of the flow field. When $A = 1.2$, $c = 0.12$, $k = \frac{2\pi}{7.5}$, $\omega = 0.4$, $\varepsilon = 0.3$, the ocean flow field is shown in Fig. 2.

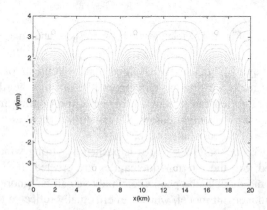

Fig. 2. Environment of flow-field

Fig. 3 depicts the movement of particles (represents nodes) in curved flow model. In Figure 4.3,   a cycle is 0.03 days, the size of a curved flow is 7.5 km, the speed of a peek is 0.3m/s, and a simulation cycle is a half day. In Fig. 3, it can be seen that the movement of nodes is a Lagrange movement. In this flow field, particles not only can move from vortex to curve, but also can move from curve to vortex.

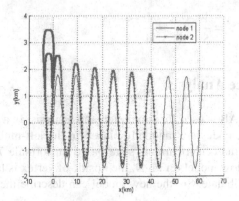

Fig. 3. The movement of particles in flow-field

Compared with the simple model, this model based on Lagrange motion can reflect the 2-D movement characters of a node in currents can. However, it still can not simulate the movements of nodes in a complicate 3-D space.

4   The 3-D Underwater Mobility Model Based on Lagrange

In order to describe the 3-D movement of the sensor nodes, the formula 3 is improved in this section. Firstly, the impact of unexpected events on the movement of the nodes is considered. So, the speed of a node $U = (u, v)$ is described as following:

$$u = -\frac{\partial \varphi}{\partial y} + \sigma u(t)$$

$$v = \frac{\partial \varphi}{\partial x} + \sigma v(t)$$

(6)

In the above formula $\sigma u(t)$ is the variance of the Gaussian noise of X-axis direction speed, $\sigma v(t)$ is the variance of the Gaussian noise of Y-axis direction speed. Their mean value is 0 and their variance is σ^2 □

Secondly, the model is modified according to that the states of seawater are different under the different pressure. That is, in the normal movement law of ocean current, the speed of the deep flow is lower than speed of the surface flow. So, the new model is defined as following:

$$\phi(x', y', t) = -(0.7 + \frac{1}{|z|+10}) \tanh \left[\frac{y' - B(t)\sin(k(s-ct))}{\sqrt{1 + k^2 B(t)^2 \cos^2(k(x'-ct))}} \right] + cy' \quad (7)$$

$$B(t) = A + \varepsilon \cos(\omega t)$$

In the above formula, $x' = \frac{1}{5}x$, $y' = \frac{1}{4}y$.

5   Performance Analysis

In the section, MATLAB is used for simulation and analysis. In a 30km×120km×5km 3D underwater space, nodes are randomly placed in the left-middle 2km×4km×5km area. Fig.4 describes the ocean currents state based on formula 7, which has an improved the curve jet flow model. In Fig.4, the upside of vertex is larger than the lower of it, just likes infundibulate. So, the new model can describe the inherence of ocean current better.

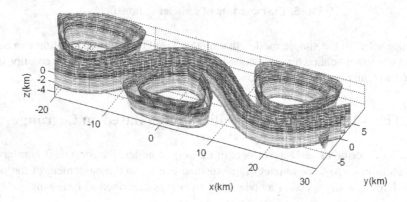

Fig. 4. Sketch of flow field

In Fig.5 the 2-D node movement trajectories of the original model and the improved model are compared when 6 $\sigma u(t)$ =0.002, $\sigma v(t)$ =0.008. From Fig.5, it can be seen that not only the node shuttle between vertex and curves but also the influence of unexpected events on nodes movement are reflected in the improved model. So, the improved model can describe the ocean current better.

Fig.6 describes the movement track of a DNR (Dive "N" Rise) node in 3D space. In Fig.6, the bounder is set $\pm \varphi = \frac{|Z|+10}{7|Z|+80} \times 0.536$ to divide the area. If the

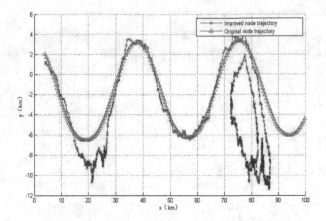

Fig. 5. Track of speed model of changed

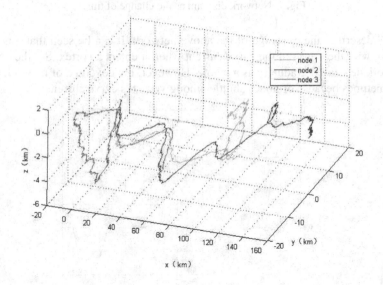

Fig. 6. Track of node with current movement

calculation result of formula (7) is in $[-\varphi, +\varphi]$, the node is in the vortexes, otherwise, the nodes in the jet stream. So, formula (6) can be used to calculate the real speed of a DNR node in the flow field.

Fig.7 describes the normal stochastic swing in vertical direction of 100 nodes, which are randomly placed in 8×2×5km area (shown in Fig.7 (a)). In Fig.7, red'+' represents AUV node, blue '*' represents the common node. After 3 hours, nodes move with the current, and their final states are shown as Fig.7 (b). From the figures, it can be seen all normal nodes move as a whole.

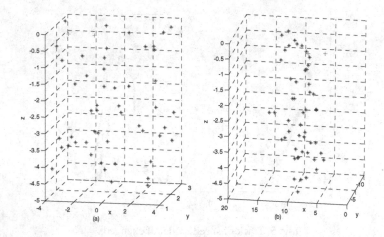

Fig. 7. Network diagram as the change of time

Fig. 8 describes the coverage of the above network. It can be seen that a node can not move with the others in the curve current when it enters a vortex. So, the coverage of network decreased gradually as a whole. However, the coverage of network regression sometimes because of nodes shuttle among vortexes curve current.

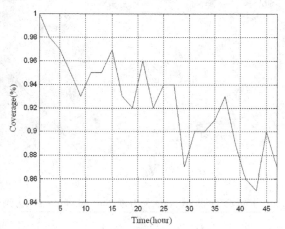

Fig. 8. Coverage of node

6   Conclusion

As a key tool for the research of UWASN, the simulation plays an important role in the studies of UWSAN. On the basis of analyzing existed models for UWSAN, a modified node movement model based on Lagrange motion for 3-D space is proposed in this paper. The performance analyses show that the new model is better than the existing ones. It can more closely simulate the movements of nodes in a 3-D oceanic current.

References

1. Jaffe, J., Schurgers, C.: Sensor, networks of freely drifting autonomous underwater explorers. In: WUWNet 2006, Los Angeles, CA, pp. 93–96 (2006)
2. Sybrandy, A., Niiler, P.: Woce/toga Lagrangian drifter construction manual. San Diego, California, Scripps Institution of Oceanography, Tech. Rep. SIO REF 91/6, WOCE Report 63, 58 (1991)
3. Zhou, Z., Jun-Hong, C., Amvrossios, B.: Scalable Localization with Mobility Prediction for Underwater Sensor Networks. In: NFOCOM 2008. The 27th Conference on Computer Communications, pp. 2198–2206. IEEE (2008)
4. Rossby, T., Dorson, D., Fontaine, J.: The rafos system. J. Atmos. Oceanic Tech. 3(4), 672–679 (1986)
5. Caruso, A., Paparella, F., Vieira, L.F.M., Erol, M., Gerla, M.: The Meandering Current Mobility Model and its Impact on Underwater Mobile Sensor Networks. In: Proc. of the IEEE INFOCOM, pp. 2198–2206 (April 2008)
6. http://kepu.ccut.edu.cn/100k/read-htm-tid-9517.html
7. M.Talha Isik, Student Member, and ed. A: Three Dimensional Localization Algorithm for Underwater Acoustic Sensor Networks. IEEE Transactions on Wireless Communications 8(9), 4457–4463 (2009)

Performance Analysis of Aloha for String Multi-hop Underwater Acoustic Sensor Networks

Yao Nianmin, Yu Hongyang, Cai Shaobin, and Han Qilong

College of Computer Science and Technology, Harbin Engineering University, Harbin, China
{yaonianmin,yuhongyang,caishaobin,hanqilong}@hrbeu.edu.cn

Abstract. Underwater acoustic sensor networks, characterized by long propagation delays and limited channel bandwidth, have drawn significant attentions and plentiful work has been done on the analysis of media access control protocols, including the contention-based ones for multi-hop underwater acoustic sensor networks. However, these existing models have not been validated by the simulations or the experiments. Moreover, we find that the models are inaccurate since they implicitly assume that a node can transmit two packets at the same time which is impractical. In order to improve the model, in this paper we continually focus on the performance analysis of Aloha for a string multi-hop network. We also conducted simulations via NS-3 using Thorp attenuation model to validate the proposed model, and we found that our model can better coincide with the simulation results. In underwater sensor networks, moreover, we found another factor need to be considered which is the influence of the nodes outside of the transmission radius.

Keywords: Underwater acoustic sensor networks, performance analysis, Aloha, multi-hop.

1 Introduction

Underwater sensor networks is becoming an important research topic. It has a wide range of collaborative applications, such as navy military surveillance, oceanographic data collection, ocean resource exploration, disaster prevention and so on. Since both radio signal and optical signal suffer significant attenuation in salt water [4], acoustic technology is the typical physical layer communication method adopted by the underwater sensor networks, namely, Underwater Acoustic Sensor Networks (UASNs). The speed of acoustic waves in water is approximately 1500 m/s, which is 2×10^5 times lower than the radio waves. Thus, compared with wireless sensor networks (WSNs), UASNs are featured by long propagation delay and limited bandwidth.

Similar to the WSNs, medium access control (MAC) protocols play a very important role in UASNs, which significantly impact the performance. Currently, the research efforts for UASNs have almost been devoted to single-hop networks, which are summarized in surveys [1], [2]. In particular, Ref. [5] presents some theoretical analyses of contention-based protocols such as Aloha for UASNs. However, multi-hop networks, which can provide a wider area coverage, are usually employed in

X. Wang et al. (Eds.): WASA 2012, LNCS 7405, pp. 694–704, 2012.

practical [3]. Therefore, in this paper we focus on the performance of theory and simulation for underwater multi-hop scenarios.

Pure Aloha is one of the contention-based MAC protocols, which allows nodes to transmit at will. And Aloha has been the basis of many wireless MACs since its proposal in the 1970s [7]. Based on a computation-efficient physics-based underwater channel model is available, it shows that the contention-based protocols based on the pure Aloha protocol may be effective for UASNs [6].

In [8], the first analytical model is proposed for the contention-based protocols in a string multi-hop network. The model provides a method for computing the expected network utilization and the probability of packet delivery to the gateway from an arbitrary sensor. As a follow-up work, p-persistent Aloha is analyzed in multi-hop string UASN [9]. In addition, a summary of these models are provided in [10].

In fact, there are two disadvantages of in work in [8]. First, since the node cannot transmit two packets at the same time, there is no collision among the packets sent by the same node. However, the model includes the corresponding probability, and thus the collision probability of a packet reception must be higher than the actual one. Second, the models are not validated by the simulations or experiments.

In this paper we propose a new model with the consideration of no packets from the same node simultaneously to improve the models. In order to validate the proposed model, we also simulated Aloha in a string multi-hop network via NS-3 using Thorp attenuation model, which is ignored by the existing works. The simulation results show that our analysis is more accurate than the original one. However, there is another factor need to be considered which is the influence of the nodes outside of the transmission radius. We will focus more on this factor in future research.

The rest of the paper is organized as follows. Section 2 gives a brief overview of the string multi-hop network model, and proposes the new model of Aloha for multi-hop UASNs. Section 3 validates the proposed method via simulations and analyzes the differences between the model evaluation results and the simulation results. Finally, Section 4 concludes the work.

2   Performance Analysis of Multi-hop Aloha

In this section, we first briefly describe the multi-hop string network model [8]. Based on it, then we develop an analytical model of the performance of Aloha protocol for multi-hop UASNs.

2.1   Multi-hop String Network Model

Same as that in [8], in the analysis we adopt the string multi-hop topology as depicted in Fig. 1. In the network, each node generates packets following an independent identical Poisson distribution with parameter λ, i.e., on average each node generates λ packets per second. Whenever receiving a packet from its upstream neighbor, a node immediately forwards the packet to the downstream one.

We notice the fact that a packet cannot be transmitted when the node is busy with sending, so our network model considers this point while it has not ignored by the existing models. In order to ensure the expected packet transmission rate of each node is equal to the theoretical one λ, a packet will be retried to be sent after a backoff following an exponentially distribution with λ if the node is busy with sending when this packet arrives. In this way, a packet behaves like a new packet when it cannot be transmitted. As a result, in simulation the packet transmission rate of each node will be same as the one defined in the theory model.

We also assume that the transmission range of each node is only sufficient to reach its 1-hop neighbors and the interference range is less than the distance to any 2-hop neighbor. We further assume a constant packet size and uniform transmission rate for all nodes, which result in a constant packet transmission time T. Therefore, the offered load (original packets) of each node is λT.

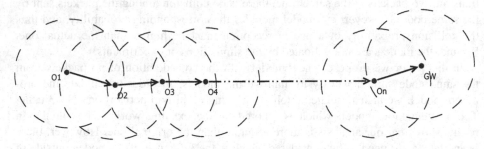

Fig. 1. String Topology

As mentioned in [8], the string topology of Fig.1 favors the downstream traffic over the upstream traffic, as the packet from the downstream will only be lost if it collides with a packet at a node further downstream.

2.2 Aloha Analysis for Multi-hop UASNs

In order to analyze the performance of Aloha for UASNs, we should address the success rate of packet reception at each hop. The success probability of O_i's transmission, P_i, is the success probability that O_{i+1} receives its packet, which is given as below [8]:

$$P_i = \Pr\{successful\ reception\ at\ O_{i+1}|\ packet\ transmitted\ by\ O_i\} \qquad (1)$$

Before going further, let us first figure out the accumulative packet transmission rate λ_i at O_i. Specifically, given that each node originates packets at the same rate λ, we have [8]:

$$\lambda_i = \lambda\left(1 + \sum_{k=1}^{i-1} \prod_{h=k}^{i-1} P_h\right), \quad i = 1, ..., n. \qquad (2)$$

The successful reception of a packet from O_i at node O_{i+1} depends on the state of O_{i+1}. The reception of a packet will fail while O_{i+1} is currently overhearing the transmission of a packet from its downstream neighbor O_{i+2}, or currently sending a packet to O_{i+2}. And the reception of packet will success only if O_{i+1} is idle in twice the packet's reception time, i.e., $2T$. These constraints are independent.

Therefore, the probability that no traffic is generated by O_j during a packet's reception period is[8]:

$$\frac{e^{-(2T)(\lambda_j)}(2T\lambda_j)^0}{0!} = e^{-(2T)(\lambda_j)} \tag{3}$$

As shown in Fig. 2, the work in [8] assumes that the interference range is less than the distance between any 2-hop neighbor-pairs, and thus only the traffic generated by 1-hop neighbors of the recipient of interest should be considered. Thus, they determine the likelihood that any node in the contending node set $C_i = \{O_i, O_{i+1}, O_{i+2}\}$ will inject traffic such that it arrives at the reception point at any time during the reception of the packet of interest.

Recall that the arrival follows the Poisson process, so the probability of a successful reception of a packet from O_i is dependent upon C_i and is [8]:

$$P_i = e^{-2T(\lambda_i + \lambda_{i+1} + \lambda_{i+2})}, i = 1, \dots, n-2$$
$$P_{n-1} = e^{-2T(\lambda_{n-1} + \lambda_n)} \tag{4}$$
$$P_n = e^{-2T(\lambda_n)}$$

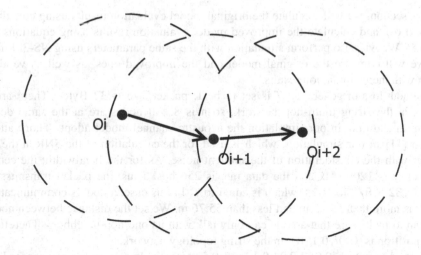

Fig. 2. Contending Node Set

However, equation (4) is inaccurate. Considering the reception of a packet from O_i at node O_{i+1}, since the time that O_i takes to transmit a packet is equal to the duration O_{i+1} takes to receive a packet as well as that O_i cannot transmit two packets at the same time, there should be no collision at O_{i+1} caused by the packets from the same node O_i. That is, the probability of successful receiving has nothing to do with whether or not O_i is sending packets when O_{i+1} is receiving a packet from O_i. Therefore, equation (4) is updated as,

$$P_i = e^{-2T(\lambda_{i+1}+\lambda_{i+2})}, i = 1, \ldots, n-2$$
$$P_{n-1} = e^{-2T(\lambda_n)} \tag{5}$$
$$P_n = 1$$

Combining equations (2) and (4), as well as (2) and (5) respectively, we can obtain n nonlinear equations with respect to n variables, $\lambda_1, \lambda_2, \ldots, \lambda_n$. These n variables can be obtained by solving the following minimization problem [8]:

$$\min_{\lambda_1, \lambda_2, \ldots, \lambda_n} \sum_{i=1}^{n}[F_i(\Lambda) - \lambda_i]^2 \tag{6}$$

where
$\Lambda = (\lambda_1 \ \lambda_2 \ \ldots \ \lambda_n)$, and
$F_i(\Lambda) = \lambda(1 + \sum_{k=1}^{i-1} \prod_{h=k}^{i-1} P_h)$, where P_h is a function of Λ as given by equations (4) or (5).

The Nelder-Mead simplex method has been quite effective to solve this minimization problem [14]. In the next section, we will calculate above equations using this method via matlab.

3   Experiments

In this section, we will calculate the original model evaluation results using equations (2) and (4), and calculate the improved model evaluation results using equations (2) and (5). We will also perform simulation with the same parameters using NS-3. Finally, we will compare the original model and the improved ones, as well as validate them with them simulation results.

Without loss of generality, T is set to be 1, packet size is 32 Bytes. There are 9 nodes in the string multi-hop network, so n is 8. All nodes are at the same depth 100m. In addition, in our simulation the acoustic channel model adopts Thorp attenuation [11] in our simulation, which is used for the calculation of the SNR at the receiver with the consideration of the ambient noise. As for the bandwidth, the center frequency is 12000 Hz and the data rate is 256 bps. Thus, the packet transmission time is $32 \times 8/256 = 1s$, which is equal to T. In this case, a node's communication range is more than 55.75 m and less than 55.76 m. We set the distance between nodes as 50m to make sure that a node can only talk with its one-hop neighbors. Therefore, O_i's position is $(50i, 0, 100)$ in the string topology network.

First, λ is set as $0.002, 0.01, 0.1$, and 0.5 respectively to vary the per-sensor load like [8]. Fig. 3 shows the original, improved and simulation results of the aggregate traffic load of each node $(\lambda_i, i = 1, \ldots, n)$. Same as stated in [8], we can see that λ_i increases when i increases, regardless of n. We can also observe that the improved model can better match the simulation results than the original one, except for $\lambda = 0.5$.

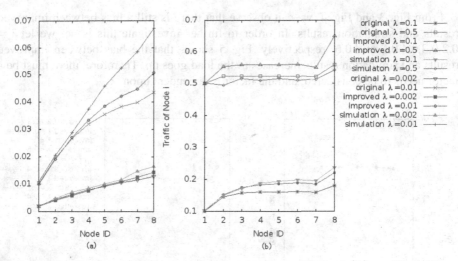

Fig. 3. Original, improved and simulation results of Node Traffic Load (λ_i) vs. Node ID at $\lambda = 0.002, 0.01, 0.1$ *or* 0.5

Fig. 4 shows that P_i deceases except at the last two nodes due to their smaller contending node sets. When the load exceeds $\lambda = 0.5$ each node has reached its saturation status and P_i becomes stable. In particular, no matter what load is chosen, simulation results of P_n is always approaching to 1, and therefore equations (5) is more accurate than equations (4).

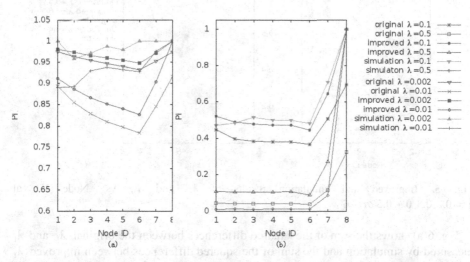

Fig. 4. Original, improved and simulation results of P_i vs. Node ID at $\lambda = 0.002, 0.01, 0.1$ *or* 0.5

From Fig. 3 and Fig. 4, we can observe that there is still a bias between improved results and simulation results. In order to further investigate this issue, we let $\lambda = 0.2, 0.3, 0.4, 0.5$ and 0.6, respectively. Fig. 5 shows that the bias between improved results and simulation results increases as the load goes up. Therefore, there must be a factor needs to be considered, and the factor is dependent upon λ.

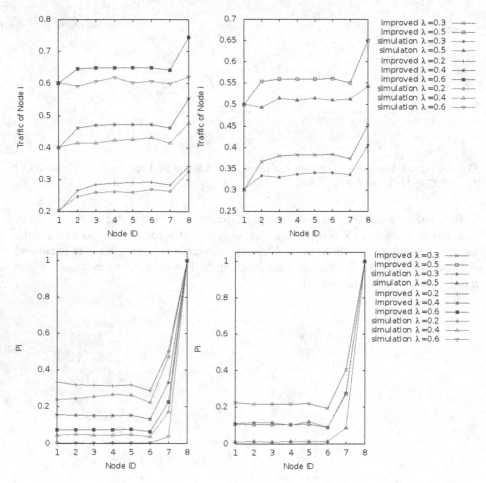

Fig. 5. Improved and simulation results of λ_i and P_i vs. Node ID at $\lambda = 0.2, 0.3, 0.4, 0.5$ or 0.6

Fig. 6(a) shows the sum of the squared differences between the original λ_i and λ_i measured by simulation and the sum of the squared differences between improved λ_i and the λ_i measured by simulation versus the λ. We can observe that the improved model can better match the simulation results than the original one when $0 < \lambda < 0.2$. However, the original model is more accurate than the improved one when $\lambda > 0.2$.

Fig. 6(b) shows the sum of the squared differences between original P_i and simulation P_i and the sum of the squared differences between improved P_i and simulation P_i versus the λ. We can observe that the improved model is always more coincident with the simulation results than the original model. Considering P_n significantly impacts the results, we compute the sum of the squared differences of P_i expect P_n, again. We can observe that the bias of improved model evaluation results are larger than the original one when $\lambda > 0.2$. These match the results in Fig. 6(a).

In the rest part we will explore the possible reasons for the bias between improved model and the simulation results. One possible reason of the bias could be that nodes

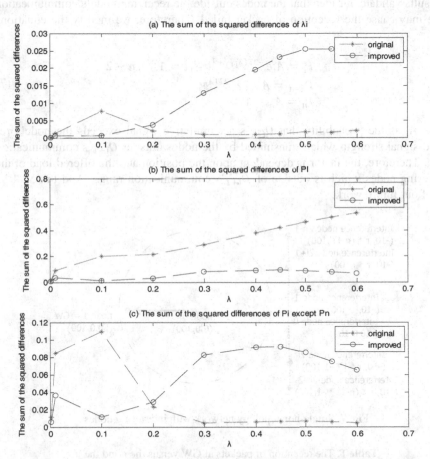

Fig. 6. In (a) the sum of the squared differences between original λ_i and simulation λ_i and the sum of the squared differences between improved λ_i and simulation λ_i versus the λ. In (b) the sum of the squared differences between original P_i and simulation P_i and the sum of the squared differences between improved P_i and simulation P_i versus the λ. In (c) the sum of the squared differences between original P_i and simulation P_i except P_n and the sum of the squared differences between improved P_i and simulation P_i except P_n versus the λ.

outside the receiving node's communication range may transmit their packets and their accumulative signals may result in an error of the receiving packet. This has been considered by WSNs research community [15].We further performed simulation on single-hop topology network with interfering nodes, as depicted in Fig. 7. In this simulation, node 0 randomly generate packets at an average rate of $\lambda = 0.1$. Node 1 is the only receiver, i.e., gateway (GW). Each node outside the GW's communication range is an interfering node. We set the distance between interfering nodes as r, and the simulation time is 10000s. We still use the similar simulation settings as above. Table 1 shows the reception of packets at GW versus the r and the n. The experimental results validate our idea that the nodes outside the receiving node's communication range may cause the reception of packet failed. Therefore, we modify the equations (5) as:

$$P_i = A_i e^{-2T(\lambda_{i+1}+\lambda_{i+2})}, i = 1, \ldots, n-2$$
$$P_{n-1} = A_{n-1} e^{-2T(\lambda_n)} \tag{7}$$
$$P_n = A_n \approx 1$$

where A_i is the probability that O_{i+1}'s accumulative signal exceeds the node's required signal strength which transmitted by the nodes outside O_{i+1}'s communication range. Therefore, the factor is dependent upon the position and the offered load of the interfering nodes which is outside of O_{i+1}'s communication range. And this will be part of our future work.

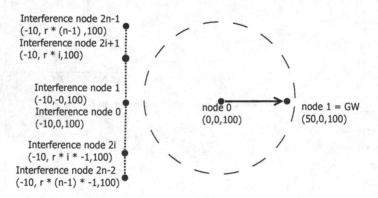

Fig. 7. Single-hop topology network with interfering nodes

Table 1. The reception of packets at GW versus the r and the n

Interfering node's number	r	Node 0 Send	Node 1 Received
20	2	1036	0
10	3	1036	497
10	10	1036	1036
0	-	1036	1036

4   Conclusion

In this paper, we propose a new performance analytical model of aloha for Multi-hop UASNs. The simulation results justifies that our model is more accurate.

We also explore a new factor needs to be considered in UASNs, which is dependent upon the position and offered load of the interfering nodes which are outside of the receiver's communication range. And this would be our future work.

Acknowledgment. This work is supported by the National Natural Science Foundation of China under Grant No. 61073047, Fundamental Research Funds for the Central Universities HEUCFT1007, HEUCF100607 and Harbin Special funds for Technological Innovation Talents, 2012RFLXG023.

References

1. Akyildiz, I.F., Pompili, D., Melodia, T.: State of the art in protocol research for underwater acoustic sensor networks. SIGMOBILE Mobile Computing Communication Review 11(4), 11–22 (2007)
2. Heidemann, J., Ye, W., Willis, J., Syed, A.A., Li, Y.: Research challenges and applications for underwater sensor networking. In: Proceedings of the IEEE Wireless Communications and Networking Conference, WCNC 2006, Las Vegas, NV, April 3–6, pp. 229–235 (2006)
3. Chitre, M., Shahabudeen, S., Stojanovic, M.: Underwater acoustic communications and networking: Recent advances and future challenges. Marine Technology Society Journal 42(1), 103–116 (2008)
4. Schill, F., Zimmer, U.R., Trumpf, J.: Visible Spectrum Optical Communication and Distance Sensing for Underwater Applications. In: Proc. Australasian Conf. Robotics and Automation (2004)
5. Xie, P., Cui, J.: Exploring Random Access And Handshaking In Large Scale Underwater Wireless Acoustic Sensor Networks. In: Proc. MTS/IEEE Oceans Conference (September 2006)
6. Xie, G.G., Gibson, J., Diaz-Gonzalez, L.: Incorporating Realistic Acoustic Propagation Models in Simulation of Underwater Acoustic Networks: A Statistical Approach. In: Proc. MTS/IEEE Oceans Conference, Boston (September 2006)
7. Abramson, N.: The ALOHA system. In: Proceedings of AFIPS 1970 Fall Joint Computer Conference, vol. 37, pp. 281–285 (1970)
8. Gibson, J., Xie, G., Xiao, Y., Chen, H.: Analyzing the Performance of Multi-hop Underwater Acoustic Sensor Networks. In: IEEE Oceans 2007, Aberdeen, Scotland (2007)
9. Xiao, Y., Zhang, Y., Gibson, J.H., Xie, G.G.: Performance Analysis of p-persistent Aloha for Multi-hop Underwater Acoustic Sensor Networks. In: International Conference on Embedded Software and Systems, pp. 305–311 (2009)
10. Xiao, Y., Zhang, Y., Gibson, J.H., Xie, G.G., Chen, H.: Performance analysis of ALOHA and p-persistent ALOHA for multi-hop underwater acoustic sensor networks. In: Cluster Computing, vol. 14(1), pp. 65–80 (2011)

11. Harris, A.F., Zorzi, M.: Modeling the underwater acoustic channel in ns2. In: Proceedings of the 2nd International Conference on Performance Evaluation Methodologies and Tools, ValueTools, Nantes, France, October 22 - 27, pp. 1–8. ICST (Institute for Computer Sciences Social-Informatics and Telecommunications Engineering), Belgium (2007)
12. Berkhovskikh, L., Lysanov, Y.: Fundamentals of Ocean Acoustics. Springer (1982)
13. Urick, R.: Principles of Underwater Sound. McGraw-Hill (1983)
14. Olsson, D.M., Nelson, L.S.: The Nelder-Mead Simplex Procedure for Function Minimization. Technometrics 17(1), 45–51 (1975)
15. Yang, Y., Hou, J.C., Kung, L.-C.: Modeling the Effect of Transmit Power and Physical Carrier Sense in Multi-hop Wireless Networks

Two Connected Dominating Set Algorithms for Wireless Sensor Networks

Najla Al-Nabhan[1], Bowu Zhang[2], Mznah Al-Rodhaan[1], and Abdullah Al-Dhelaan[1]

[1] Department of Computer Science, King Saud University, Riyadh, Saudi Arabia
[2] Department of Computer Science, The George Washington University, Washington DC, USA
{nalnabhan,rodhaan,dhelaan}@ksu.edu.sa,
bowuzh@gwmail.gwu.edu

Abstract. In this work, we present the design of two novel algorithms for constructing connected dominating set (CDS) in wireless sensor networks (WSNs). Both algorithms are intended to minimize CDS size. The first algorithm has a performance factor of 5 from the optimal solution, which outperforms the best-published results (5.8+ ln 4) in [1]. The second algorithm is an improved version of the first one. We included the theoretical analysis and simulation results showing the effectiveness of both algorithms.

Keywords: Connected Dominating Set, Wireless Sensor Networks, Maximal Independent Set, Unit Disk Graph, Approximation Algorithm.

1 Introduction

Wireless sensor networks are gaining more interest in a variety of applications. Of their different characteristics and challenges, network management and lifetime are the most considered issues in WSN based systems. Connected dominating set (CDS) is known to be an efficient strategy to control network topology, reduce overhead, and extend network lifetime. Using Minimum Connected Dominating Set (MCDS), minimum number of nodes is participating in routing and management tasks.

Designing a CDS algorithm for WSNs is very challenging. Various techniques were developed in the literature to tackle this problem. Unfortunately, finding an MCDS is an NP-hard problem and approximation is required. There are quite a few existing approximation techniques with different performance ratios and design perspectives. For a survey of the existing CDS construction techniques, we refer the readers to [2] and the references therein.

The concept of the connected dominating set (CDS) comes from graph theory [3]. It defines a set of nodes for a given connected graph. The definition of a CDS can be described as follows: For a given connected graph (network) $G = (V, E)$, where V is the set of vertices (nodes) and E is the set of edges (an edge or link exists between any two nodes if they are within the transmission range of each other) that provides the available communications, a dominating set (DS) is a subset V' of V, where for each vertex u of V, u is either in V' or at least one neighbor vertex of u is in V'. A DS is called a CDS if the sub-graph induced by the vertices in the DS is connected [4].

X. Wang et al. (Eds.): WASA 2012, LNCS 7405, pp. 705–713, 2012.
© Springer-Verlag Berlin Heidelberg 2012

The heuristics for CDS construction can be divided into two sets. The first set of heuristics strives to find disconnected, Maximal Independent Set (MIS) of nodes that are joined through a minimum spanning tree or a Steiner tree. The second type of heuristics concentrates on evolving a CDS by growing a small trivial CDS [5][6]. An MIS is a dominating set that satisfies the following conditions: i) nodes in the MIS are pairwise nonadjacent, and ii) no more nodes can be added to maintain the non-adjacency property of this set. Each node, which is not in the MIS, is adjacent to at least one node in MIS. If we connect the nodes in the MIS through some nodes not in the MIS, a CDS is then constructed [1].

This work proposes a design of two connected dominating set construction algorithms that provide better approximations compared to the existing state-of-the-art MCDS. In both approaches, we used a Unit Disk Graph (UDG) to model a WSN. We simplified the CDS construction by first finding a special independent set S_1 with the following property: the hop-distance between any two complementary subsets S1 and S2 of S_1 is exactly three. Second, we tried to find a small set of nodes S_2 to dominate the multiple disconnected components resulted from constructing S_1 in the first step. Then, the introduced nodes S_2 in the second step are connected with the nodes in S_1 to form a dominating set, which will yield the final CDS after adding more connecting nodes. We provided performance analysis of the first approach. Moreover, we simulated our algorithms and compared them to the S-MIS algorithm proposed in [1]. The results showed an improved performance of our proposed approaches when employed for large-scale networks and completely randomly deployed networks.

2   The Proposed Algorithms

2.1   Approach-I

From a top view, Approach-I constructs a CDS via four main steps. For illustration purpose, we employed a coloring scheme to differentiate node states during the CDS construction. S_1 (dominators) nodes are marked black. The nodes used to cover the disconnected regions in phase-2 are marked red (the set of nodes in S_2). Connectors are marked blue and dominatee nodes are marked gray. Other colors (white, orange and yellow) are temporarily introduced to make the elaboration of the algorithm easier: white is used for initialization, orange to mark nodes at a certain distance to a black node, and yellow to mark disconnected regions after S_1 construction.

- **Phase-1: S_1 Construction.** The definition of independent sets guarantees that any pair of nodes in an independent set is separated by at least two hops. The S_1 constructed in this phase guarantees that the hop-distance between any pair of its complementary subsets is exactly three. We extend the Method in [7] to construct S_1 that satisfies the exact-three-hop property. The scenario of S_1 construction goes through the following steps: first, given an arbitrary rooted spanning tree T spanning all nodes, we define the tree level of a node u as the number of hops in T between u itself and i, where i is the root of T. All nodes are initially undominated and are colored white. Nodes will be eventually marked with different colors during the execution of the algorithm. The root node (i) initiates the S_1 construction by coloring itself black. Then, it broadcasts a *"BLACK"* message to its 1-hop neighbors. Upon receiving i's "BLACK" message by a white neighbor, the white node changes its current color from white to gray and broadcasts a "GRAY" message to its 1-hop neighbors. When a white neighbor receives a "GRAY" message, it changes its color from white to yellow, and broadcasts a "YELLOW" message to its 1-hop neighbors. Consequently, upon receiving a "YELLOW" message by a white node, a white node colors itself orange. The orange color is a temporary color. Next, the algorithm repeats the following steps until no orange/white nodes left in the graph:

1. Selects an orange node u to color it black. The selected orange node satisfies the following two conditions: i) its level is the lowest (closes to the root) among all orange nodes, and ii) it has the maximum number of 3-hop black neighbors. The selected node u is colored black.
2. Node u broadcasts a "BLACK" message in order to dominate its 1-hop yellow, orange, and white nodes by coloring them gray. Then a newly colored grey node broadcasts a "GRAY" message.
3. Upon receiving a "GRAY" message, a white or orange node colors itself yellow and broadcasts a "YELLOW" message. Upon receiving a "YELLOW" message, a white node colors itself orange.

After the algorithm terminates, any gray node is definitely 1-hop from a black node that dominates it, and any yellow node is 2-hop from a black node; nodes are either black (S_1), gray (dominated nodes), or yellow (disconnected components).

The figure below shows an example of a graph G containing 40 nodes after S_1 construction initiated by node 1. Each yellow node is at least two hops away from any black node. Thus, yellow nodes form multiple connected components of the network graph. It is shown that these disconnected regions represent a small portion of the network. The algorithm described in Phase-2 handles these connected components.

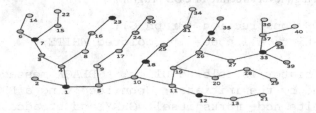

Fig. 1. G After constructing S_1

- **Phase-2: Covering Disconnected Regions (CDC).** After Phase-1 completes, we have two types of connected components (yellow), with each being a disconnected region: i) the vertical one with nodes at the same tree level separated by one hop or disconnected, and ii) the horizontal one containing only some leaf nodes of the spanning tree. In this phase, we compute a minimum dominating set for each connected component by the following procedure. All the dominators computed from this phase are colored by red and they form the set S_2.

1. For each vertical connected component, let l be the lowest level of the nodes. If the component contains only nodes in l, choose one yellow node and color it red and its neighbors gray. In this case, one red node can cover the whole connected component. If nodes at level $l+1$ exist, select the minimum number of yellow nodes from level l or $l+1$ to cover all yellow nodes in l and maximum number of yellow nodes in $l+1$. Color these nodes red and all their yellow neighbors gray. Repeat this procedure until no yellow node left in the connected component.
2. For each horizontal connected component, we start from the left-most node u and color the right-most node v that covers u and the maximum number of yellow nodes in the component. Color v red and its neighbors gray. Repeat this procedure until no yellow node left in the horizontal connected component.

- **Phase-3: Connecting S_2 Nodes to S_1 Nodes.** Each red node has at least one black node that is only two hops away. Hence, we need to include at most one gray node in order to connect a red node i to its nearest black node. However, multiple red nodes can be connected to a node in S_1 using one connector. Having small number of connectors is preferred. Thus in this phase, we change some gray nodes to blue using a similar approach in [1]. A gray node that has the maximum number of red neighbors is included as a connector and marked blue. When a gray node u is colored blue, all its one hop black/red neighbors are combined together to form one region. On completion of this phase, each connected component dominated by red node is linked and combined into a region with at least one black node using some blue connectors.
- **Phase-4: Connecting S_1 Nodes all Together.** We apply the fourth algorithm to connect all black nodes to form the final CDS. Each black node has at least a black neighbor that is only three hops away. To connect the nodes in S_1, we need to include at most two gray nodes to connect an S_1 node to its nearest S_1 node. The final CDS is obtained after this forth step, when S_1-to-S_1 connectors are found. The union of the black, red and blue sets produces the final CDS. The below pseudo code represents a high level structure of CDS program.

```
Program CDS Construction (Graph G){
Initialization: all nodes are colored WHITE;
begin:
1: the initiator is colored black; a BLACK message is
broadcasted by the initiator; Upon receiving a BLACK mes-
sage, a white node marks itself GRAY and broadcasts a
GRAY message; Upon receiving a GRAY message, a white node
marks itself YELLOW and broadcasts a YELLOW message; Upon
receiving a YELLOW message, a white node marks itself
ORANGE;
2: while (Exist Orange node){Select one orange node that
has the lowest level among all orange nodes, and has the
maximum number of 3-hop black neighbors; color it BLACK,
and broadcasts a BLACK message; Upon receiving a BLACK
message by a white, orange or yellow message it marks it-
```

self Gray; Upon receiving a GRAY message by a white or
orange node, it marks itself YELLOW and broadcasts a
YELLOW message; Upon receiving a YELLOW message, a white
node marks itself ORANGE;};
3: While(Exist a yellow node in a vertical connected component v){ l:=lowest level in v; If (all nodes in v are
in l){ choose a yellow node u color it red and its neighbors gray;}else{find the minimum set S of yellow nodes
from level l or l+1 to cover all yellow nodes in l and
maximum number of yellow nodes in l+1; Color nodes in S
red and all their yellow neighbors gray}};
4: While (Exist a yellow node in a horizontal connected
component h){x:=left-most node in h; y:= right-most node
in h that covers x and the maximum number of yellow nodes
in h; Color y red and its neighbors gray};
5: While (Exist DISCONNECTED RED node){Find a GRAY node u
that has the maximum number of RED neighbors and at least
one BLACK neighbor. Then mark u BLUE, and all its RED
neighbors as CONNECTED};
6: While (Exist a GRAY node x that is adjacent to at
least i BLACK nodes in different BLACK-RED-BLUE components){FIND a GRAY node u that has the maximum i, mark u
BLUE, combines u's different adjacent components into one
component};
7: If (Exist a BLACK node r, r is 3 hops from any BLACK-
RED-BLUE components){Mark r's GRAY neighbor, which has
the maximum degree, as BLUE; combines u's different adjacent components into one component};end.

2.2 Approach-II

The second proposed approach has four phases. Most of these phases are similar to those in Approach –I except phase-2.

- **Phase-1.** Construct S_1 using the same algorithm that was used in Approach-I.
- **Phase-2.** We defined the *coverage factor* of a yellow node x as the number of its yellow neighbors. A gray/yellow node x that has the highest coverage factor is marked red and a "RED" message is broadcasted by x in order to dominate its 1-hop yellow neighbors by coloring them gray. On completion of this phase, all yellow nodes are marked red or gray.
- **Phase-3.** In this phase we connect CDC nodes to S_1 nodes. If a gray node u was marked red in Phase-2 of this approach, u is already connected to an S_1 node and we do not need to introduce any connectors for u.
- **Phase-4.** To find S_1-to-S_1 connectors by employing the same algorithm that was used in Phase-4 of Approach-I.

The performance enhancement in this approach comes from two sources. The first is having a smaller set of red nodes than in approach-I, when a gray node with a higher coverage factor than any yellow node within its 1-hop region is selected. The second scenario is by having a smaller number of connectors for CDC nodes, since gray nodes marked red do not need to be connected to S_1 nodes. One or both scenarios can occur during the execution of Approach-II.

3   Performance Analysis

In this subsection we analyze the performance of approach-I, which is our main introduced approach in this work.

Theorem 1. *Let D be any MCDS of a unit-disk graph G. If ∀ two complementary subsets u and v of S_1, u and v are three hops away from each other, then* $|S_1| \leq |D|$. *Proof.* We claim that $\forall u \in D$ is either in S_1 or adjacent to at most one node in S_1. Otherwise, there exist two nodes in S_1 that are two hops away, a contradiction. On the other hand, because D is an MCDS, $\forall u \in S_1$ is either in D or adjacent to at least one node in D. Therefore $|S_1| \leq |D|$.

Theorem 2. *Let S_2 be any CDC and D be any MCDS of a unit-disk graph G, then* $|S_2| \leq |D|$. *Proof. This theorem follows from the geometric structure of the horizontal and vertical connected components and the determination of the red nodes for each connected component.*

Theorem 3. *Number of CDC connectors $\leq 1. |MCDS|$. Proof.* Let S_2 be any CDC and D be any MCDS of a unit-disk graph G. For $\forall u \in S_2$, there exist at least one gray node i that is 1-hop distance from a node $v \in S_2$. i is selected to connect u to v. Hence, we need at most one connector node to connect each node in S_2 to a node in S_1. Then, the number of the required CDC connectors $\leq$ number of red nodes. From Theorem 1, $|S_2| \leq |MCDS|$, therefore, number CDC connectors $\leq |MCDS|$.

Theorem 4. *Number of S1 connectors $\leq 2. |MCDS|$. Proof.* S_1 satisfies that: for any two complementary subsets *S1* and *S2*, then $|S1-S2| = 3$. Hence, there exist two nodes *u*, and *v* that can connect *S1* and *S2*. And we know from Theorem 1 that $|S_1| \leq |MCDS|$. Connect all subsets we need at most $2. |MCDS|$. Hence, if at most two nodes are used to connect each S_1 node, then the total number of required S_1 connectors is $\leq 2. |MCDS|$.

Theorem 5. *Approach-I produces a CDS with a size bounded by 5opt, where opt is the size of the MCDS. Proof. This theorem follows from the previous four theorems.*

4   Simulation Results

In order to verify our proposed algorithms, we evaluated their performance using simulation and compared them to the S-MIS algorithm. In this simulation, we focused on CDS size as a main and most important performance measure. We generated a total of N nodes in a fixed 1000*1000 2D square. The transmission range of each node is R. We considered R values that keep network connected. For $R \in$ [200, 800], we changed N from 36 to 400. We included two deployment schemes: the uniform random deployment model and the partial random deployment model [8][9]. In uniform random deployment, for each node both coordinates are generated independently using a random number generator delivering uniformly distributed values. Thus, each of the N sensors has equal probability of being placed at any point inside the deployment field. The uniform random deployment is considered as a completely random model and preferred by many applications. Besides, the partial random deployment model strives to achieve a grid layout of the sensor node. It provides desirable characteristics (i.e. coverage). In partial random deployment (or grid-based deployment), we divided the deployment model into cells, each cell hosts a sensor. A sensor is randomly placed inside the cell. The size of a cell is calculated as a function of the number of nodes N and the deployment area A [8][9]. Fig. 2 and Fig. 3 illustrate the relationship between our two proposed approaches and the S-MIS algorithm, for N= 70 and 225, respectively, and $R \in$ [300, 700]. In Fig. 4, we evaluated the performance of the three algorithms for different values of N ranging from 36 to 225. The y-axis shows CDS size and the x-axis presents the average number of nodes per unit area. The sizes of CDSs generated by Approach-I and Approach-II are smaller than S-MIS as the network size increases. They perform comparably for small and low dense network. However, Approach-II always outperforms both Approach-I and S-MIS in uniform random and grid-based deployments, and for small and large-scale networks. This improvement is gained from minimizing the number of S1 and CDC connectors, which usually affects CDS size as well as MIS size.

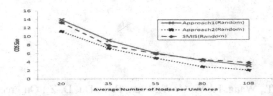

Fig. 2. CDS size for a random network of 70 nodes

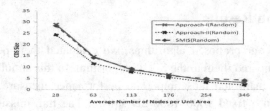

Fig. 3. CDS sizes for a random network of higher node density

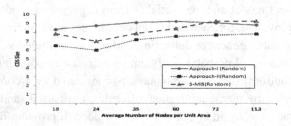

Fig. 4. CDS size for variable $N \in [36, 225]$, $R=400$

5   Conclusion

In this work, we proposed two novel approaches for CDS construction in wireless sensor networks. Both approaches target to minimize CDS size. For the first approach, we theoretically analyzed its performance ratio. Throughout the simulation, we studied the impact of our proposed approaches compared to the S-MIS algorithm. Results showed an improved performance of both proposed algorithms over S-MIS for large scale networks. Approach-II always outperforms Approach-I and S-MIS as a result of minimizing the number of connectors when dominated nodes are used to dominate disconnected components of the network. For future work, we plan to implement the distributed versions of the proposed approaches. Additionally, a number of improvements can be added to the proposed approaches in order to minimize CDS size.

References

1. Li, Y., Thai, M.T., Wang, F., Yi, C.-W., Wan, P.-J., Du, D.-Z.: On greedy construction of connected dominating sets in wireless networks. Wireless Communications & Mobile Computing - RRM for Next-Generation Wireless and Mobile Communication Systems 5(8) (December 2005)
2. Blum, J., Ding, M., Thaeler, A., Cheng, X.: Connected Dominating Set in Sensor Networks and MANETs. In: Handbook of Combinatorial Optimization, vol. 5, pp. 329–369. Kluwer Academic Publishers (2005)

3. West, D.B.: Introduction to Graph Theory. Prentice Hall, Upper Saddle River (2001)
4. Liang, O.: Multipoint Relay and Connected Dominating Set Based Broadcast Algorithms for Wireless Ad Hoc Networks. Monash University, Melbourne (2007)
5. Rai, M., Verma, S., Tapaswi, H.: A Power Aware Minimum Connected Dominating Set for Wireless Sensor Networks. Journal of Networks 4(6), 511–519 (2009)
6. Rai, M., Verma, S., Tapaswi, S.: A Heuristic for Minimum Connected Dominating Set with Local Repair for Wireless Sensor Networks. In: Eighth International Conference on Networks, ICN 2009, pp. 106–111 (2009)
7. Wan, P., Alzoubi, K., Frieder, O.: Distributed construction of connected dominating set in wireless ad hoc networks. Mobile Networks and Applications 9, 141–149 (2004)
8. Bondorf, S., Jens, B.: Statistical Response Time Bounds in Randomly Deployed Wireless Sensor Networks. In: LCN 2010 Proceedings of the 2010 IEEE 35th Conference on Local Computer Networks, Washington, DC, USA., pp. 340–343 (2010)
9. Poe, W., Schmitt, B.: Node deployment in large wireless sensor networks: coverage, energy consumption, and worst-case delay. In: AINTEC 2009 Asian Internet Engineering Conference, New York, USA, pp. 77–84 (2009)

A Cross-Layer Approach for Congestion Control in Real-Time Transmission in Wireless Sensor Networks

Aihua Fan[1], Yu Tang[2,*], and Changqin Bu[2]

[1] School of Computer Science, Xi'an Polytechnic University, Xi'an, China
fanaihua@xpu.edu.cn
[2] School of Computer Science and Engineering,
University of Electronic Science and Technology of China, Chengdu, China
yutang@uestc.edu.cn

Abstract. Congestion detection and control is considered as major challenge to implementation of real-time transmission in wireless sensor network, particularly under the situations where both the total packet loss and the real-time packet deadline are required to take care of. The demand of congestion detection and control is hard, if not impossible at all, to meet in a single transmission protocol layer in wireless sensor network due to its hop-by-hop transmission pattern. The work presented in this paper shows that the cross-layer approach combining a performance-differentiated scheduling in routing layer and a priority-based packet dropping policy at control layer can provide a key support to congestion control in implementation of real-time transmission in wireless sensor networks. Simulation experiments on TinyOS/TOSSIM platform shows an encouraging result from the proposed approach in providing congestion detection and control in a wireless sensor network with real-time support.

Keywords: Wireless sensor network, real-time transmission, cross-layer, congestion control.

1 Introduction

The Collection Tree Protocol (CTP) [1-2] demonstrates to be an efficient network topology used to collect field sensor data in a wireless sensor network with a hierarchical architecture, particularly for the applications such as battlefield situational awareness, environmental monitoring, and homeland security control. Under such a tree topology the distributed sensor nodes are grouped into various segments, namely clusters, with each cluster having a head, shown in Fig. 1. The cluster head serves as the sink node for the cluster it is responsible for, and eventually routs the packets to the designated root (base station) under certain transmission protocol. When implementing a real-time transmission under such a collection tree topology, packet jamming and congestion control at the cluster head play a key role in providing quality service for packet routing and transmission. Two major issues may cause packet jamming in transmission. First is that the packet arrival rate exceeds the

X. Wang et al. (Eds.): WASA 2012, LNCS 7405, pp. 714–721, 2012.
© Springer-Verlag Berlin Heidelberg 2012

node processing rate, which lead to a congestion in the packet waiting queue, mostly, at the cluster head where the data convergence is performed. Service quality at routing and transmission layers is the second key to the packet congestion issue, in which the packet dispatching and transmission policy may eventually impose an impact on the performance in upper layers of wireless sensor network.

Since packet jamming may lead to problems of buffer overflow and packet loss at the sensor nodes on transmission path and transmission delay due to queuing latency, the congestion control is considered as an essential feature in protocol design that is needed for implementation of real-time transmission in wireless sensor network. Congestion detection and control are two major research topics in this field. Different from traditional TCP/IP wired network, wireless sensor network uses the queue length in waiting buffer [3-4] or the packet processing time [5] to estimate the probability of congestion. Other researches on congestion detection include the buffer utilization ratio [6], channel load monitoring [7], and congestion ratio [8]. Congestion control in wireless sensor network is mainly enforced by adjusting the packet forwarding rate at sensor node according to the network congestion status it receives from adjacent nodes [6-8]. If the CN bit is used to report congestion information, normally the adding-increment-multiplying-decrement type algorithm is applied to tune the sending speed. A fine-grained scheduling on transmission rate may be achieved with more network status information embedded in congestion report [9].

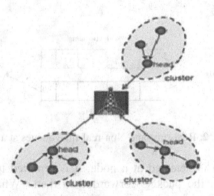

Fig. 1. Clustered architecture and packet routing path

In this paper we propose a cross-layer approach that implements a performance-differentiated scheduling schema in packet dispatching so that a congestion control is enforced at each node when the network is under high workload, and the packets with various transmission latency bounds are routed in differentiated speed. This cross-layer design is aiming at providing a congestion control mechanism in real-time transmission in wireless sensor networks. The rest of paper is organized as: Section 2 presents the implementation of congestion control in real-time transmission, and in Section 3, a simulation experiment on TinyOS 2.0 platform [10-11] to evaluate the performance of the cross-layer approach. Section 4 summarizes our work and discusses further researches in future.

2   Congestion Control through Performance-Differentiated Dispatching

In this section, we propose a queue length ratio method to detect congestion detection at each intermediate node and a performance-differentiated packet dispatching algorithm to apply congestion control when congestion happens.

2.1   Congestion Detection

In the real-time transmission scenario we discuss here, at each sensor node, two packet queues are used for real-time (RT) packets and non-real-time (NRT) packets, respectively, shown in Fig. 2. The two classes of packets arriving at the node are classified into above two queues and dispatched from the head of each queue for transmission under a performance-differentiated algorithm. The congestion detection criterion is defined as: the congestion is considered happening when the queue length (the number of waiting packets in a queue) reaches the half of the queue size in either queue, i.e. the queue length ratio reaches 1/2. The ratio of RT queue length to NRT queue length at a moment can also be used as a threshold to detect the congestion, since a high RT/NRT ratio may indicate that the network is slow down in forwarding the RT packets, which can be considered as a congestion condition for the RT packets.

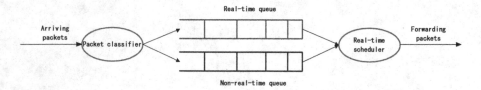

Fig. 2. Real-time and Non-real-time queues at a node

When congestion is detected at a node, it is reported to its adjacent nodes by setting the C/N bit in the packets forwarded to them. When a node receives the packets from other nodes, it updates its routing table with the information carried by the packets. For instance, node A received a packet from node B with the CN bit set to 1, so it updates its routing table with the CN bit for node B set, shown in Fig. 3. When node A needs to select a node as next hop to forward its packets, it disqualifies node B even it has a smaller number of hops from the sink, since node B's CN bit is set, indicating the congestion happens on node B.

Neighbor ID	ATT(ms)	CN
B(2)	320	1
C(3)	451	0
D(4)	551	0
--	--	--

Fig. 3. Node A's routing table

2.2   Congestion Control Approach

The RT packets are more sensitive to congestion situations for they have a transmission deadline, and a delay in transmission due to packet jamming may cause a packet loss. With being said, the packet receiving ratio, i.e. the packet arrival ratio for the RT packets that arrives at the sink prior to their deadline, is considered as a measurement on the transmission reliability of wireless sensor network, presented as below.

$$\eta = \frac{N_r}{N_s} \times 100\%$$

where η is the receiving ratio for RT packets, N_r the number of receiving packets, and N_s the total number of sending packets.

Upon the congestion being detected, the congestion control can be implemented through a performance-differentiated dispatching algorithm at sensor node, in which the arriving packets are classified into two waiting queues and dispatched for forwarding based on the queue length ratio of the two waiting queues. This queue length ratio based dispatching algorithm can be described as:

1) Initialization: RT_counter = 0, NRT_flag = FALSE, RT_window = N;
2) Check condition (RT queue is empty), if yes, switch to 3); otherwise, switch to 4);
3) Check condition (NRT queue is empty), if yes, go back to 2); otherwise, switch to 5);
4) Check condition (RT_counter > RT_window), if yes, set NRT_flag = TRUE; otherwise, switch to 6);
5) If (NRT_flag = TRUE) switch to 7); otherwise switch to 2);
6) Dispatch an RT packet for transmission and increment RT_counter, then switch to 2);
7) Dispatch an NRT packet for transmission, set RT_counter to 0, set NRT_flag to FALSE, and then switch to 2).

The queue length ratio based algorithm is coarse-grained scheduling schema under which the RT class packets are favored such that, when workload at a node is high, in every scheduling window, N RT packets are transmitted before one NRT packet gets dispatched. Obviously, this algorithm is not appropriate for the scenarios where we need to leverage resources among packets with various priority values, but cannot be simply classified into two classes.

To improve the drawback of above coarse-grained dispatching algorithm, we propose another priority-based dispatching algorithm that implements a performance-differentiated packet dispatching and packet dropping strategy when congestion happens. Two basic operations are performed by this algorithm: first, select a packet with the highest priority value from the queue for dispatching; second, when congestion happens and packet dropping is needed, select a packet with the lowest priority in the queue for dropping. The queue model for the priority-based dispatching algorithm is shown in Fig. 4, in which a circular queue with a default size of 12 is implemented, and the queue size can be dynamically allocated in offset in runtime. When selecting a packet from the queue for dispatching, the dispatcher traverses the queue to identify the packet with the highest priority for transmission, thus the time complexity of the algorithm is $O(L)$, with L is the length of queue.

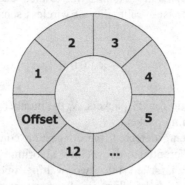

Fig. 4. Queuing model for priority-based algorithm

3   Performance Assessment

In order to assess the performance of the proposed cross-layer design in packet congestion control, we performed a simulation experiment on TinyOS/TOSSIM platform [10-11]. The simulation uses various sensor network topology consists of 40, 60, 80, or 100 nodes. Fig. 5 shows the predefined routing map of a 40-node topology. To evaluate the performance of proposed RCTP protocol under various work conditions, we compare RCTP with CTP in two reliability tests, i.e. Launching Interval Test and Topology Size Test.

The Launching Interval Test is designed to assess the reliability of RCTP under various launching speed. The RT packet receiving percentile is used as the reliability measurement, and is displayed versus the launching interval time in Fig. 6, in which an 80-node topology is used. The comparison on reliability numbers between RCTP and CTP shows, among 6 interval values tested, RCTP equals or outperforms CTP at 4 values, yet slightly underperforms at two values. The results indicate that RCTP performs better in supporting real-time packets under a dynamic environment.

Figure 7 displays the results of Topology Size Test, in which we evaluate the reliability of RCTP against CTP under an increasing topology size from 40-node to 100-node. The comparison between the reliability numbers of RCTP and CTP indicates that CTP performs slightly better than RCTP does before the topology size reaches 100. This may verify that RCTP trades the total reliability for supporting real-time transmission by dropping more NRT packets under congestion conditions, which causes an increase in total packet loss. Yet the result of the 80-node topology shows RCTP may adapt to large-scale network and deliver a better performance than CTP does.

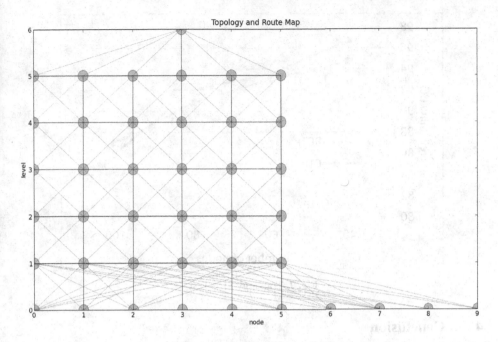

Fig. 5. Experimental topology with 40 sensor nodes

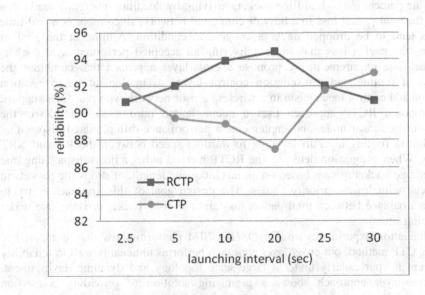

Fig. 6. Launching interval test (80-node)

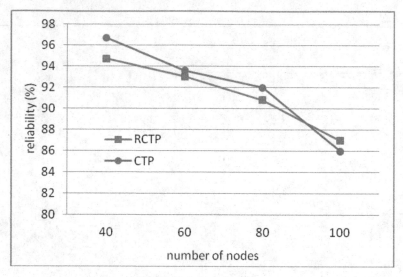

Fig. 7. Topology Size Test

4   Conclusion

Congestion detection and control demonstrates to be a major challenge to implementation of real-time transmission in wireless sensor network, in the sense that lifting the percentage of real-time packets arriving by deadline inherently leads to a rise in the total packet loss in a busy or congested network, since more non-real-time packets tend to be dropped under a congestion condition. Aiming at the goal of reducing the packet loss rate while delivering an accepted performance to packets with real-time requirement, we propose a cross-layer approach that combines the features at routing and transmission control layers to implement the congestion detection and control mechanism in a wireless sensor network with real-time support. The proposed RCTP approach uses a queue length ratio method to detect the congestion at sensor node, and implements a performance-differentiated dispatching algorithm in routing layer to leverage forwarding speed between the RT and NRT packets. When congestion detected, the RCTP method either adjusts dispatching rate between two packet queues based on an instant queue length, or drops the packets in the queue with lowest priority values. The design goal of this approach is try to achieve a balance between total packet loss and real-time packet arriving rate under congestion situations.

Simulation experiments on TinyOS/TOSSIM platform show that, compared to existing CTP method, our cross-layer approach performs noticeably well in reliability measurement, particularly under a large-scale topology and dynamic environment. The cross-layer approach shows a promising solution to providing congestion detection and control function and supporting real-time transmission in wireless sensor networks.

References

[1] Network Working Group, The Collection Tree Protocol Draft (2006)

[2] Gwanali, O., Fonseca, R., Jamieson, K., Moss, D., Levis, P.: Collection tree protocol. In: Proceedings of the 7th ACM Conference on Embedded Networked Sensor Systems (SenSys), Berkeley, CA (November 2009)

[3] Wan, C.-Y., Eisenman, S.B., Campbell, A.T.: CODA: Congestion detection and avoidance in sensor networks. In: SenSys Proc. First Int. Conf. Embedded Networked Sensor Syst., pp. 266-279 (2003)

[4] Hull, B., Jamieson, K., Balakrishnan, H.: Mitigating congestion in wireless sensor networks. In: Proc. Second Int. Conf. Embedded Networked Sensor Syst., pp. 134–147 (2004)

[5] Iyer, Y.G., Gandham, S., Venkatesan, S.: STCP: A generic transport layer protocol for wireless sensor networks. In: Proc Int Conf. Comput. Commun. Networks, ICCCN, vol. 2005, pp. 449–454 (2005)

[6] Sankarasubramaniam, Y., Akan, O.B., Akyildiz, I.F.: ESRT: Event-to-sink reliable transport in wireless sensor networks. In: Proc. Int. Symp. Mobile Ad Hoc Networking Comput., pp. 177–188 (2003)

[7] Wan, C.-Y., Eisenman, S.B., Campbell, A.T.: CODA: Congestion detection and avoidance in sensor networks. In: SenSys Proc. First Int. Conf. Embedded Networked Sensor Syst., pp. 266–279 (2003)

[8] Chonggang, W., Sohraby, K., Lawrence, V., Bo, L., Yueming, H.: Priority-based congestion control in wireless sensor networks. In: Proc. IEEE Int. Conf. Sensor Netw. Ubiquitous Trustworthy Comput., pp. 22–29 (2006)

[9] Ee, C.T., Bajcsy, R.: Congestion control and fairness for many-to-one routing in sensor networks. In: Proceedings of the 2nd International Conference on Embedded Networked Sensor Systems Baltimore. ACM, Baltimore (2004)

[10] TinyOS website, http://www.tinyos.net/

[11] Levis, P., Lee, N., Welsh, M., Culler, D.: TOSSIM: Accurate and Scalable Simulation of Entire TinyOS Applications. In: Proceedings of the First ACM Conference on Embedded Networked Sensor Systems (SenSys 2003), Los Angeles, CA (November 2003)

A Theoretical Study on the Orientation Problem in Linear Wireless Sensor Networks[*]

Jianghong Han[1,2], Xu Ding[1,2], Lei Shi[1,2], Dong Han[3], and Zhenchun Wei[1,2]

[1] School of Computer Science and Information,
Hefei University of Technology, Hefei 230009, China
[2] Engineering Research Center of Safety Critical Industrial Measurement
and Control Technology, Ministry of Education, Hefei 230009, China
[3] Department of Computer Science, University of Houston, Houston, TX 77004, USA

Abstract. A theoretical approach of acquiring arrival angles of signals sensed by sensor nodes in linear wireless sensor networks is introduced. The arrival angles of signals can be obtained by the estimation of signal covariance matrices. In this article, firstly, the existence of the solution to the estimation problem is studied intensively. Later on, the solution to this problem of estimating real-valued covariance matrices is discussed by the approach of maximum-likelihood estimation. Finally, this approach is expanded to the realm of complex-valued covariance matrices.

Keywords: arrival angles of signals, estimation of covariance matrices, maximum-likelihood estimation.

1   Introduction

Wireless sensor networks (WSNs) consisted of huge amount of sensor nodes and base station(s) are capable of performing numerous unmanned tasks in extreme environments, such as volcano areas, toxic areas, underwater and underground etc. WSNs play a very important role in many aspects of our modern society. For instance, with the aid of wireless sensor network, we can make our weather forecast more precise. In situations involving emergency services, such as poisonous gas leaks, wireless sensor networks will reduce our costs on locating and rescuing persons in danger.

Linear wireless sensor networks (LWSNs) are a special family of wireless sensor networks with regard to linear network topology. Compared with normal wireless sensor networks, LWSNs exhibit lower complexity. Even though simple in topology, LWSNs possess numerous practical applications, such as monitoring public transportations, oil pipes, factories and plants. Nowadays, intensive researches in the field of WSNs focus on Network protocols, such as routing protocols, MAC protocols and cross-layer protocols, etc., which aim to alleviate the energy overhead of sensor nodes

---

[*] This paper is sponsored by National Natural Science Foundation of China(NSFC) with Grant No. 60873003, No.60873195 and Ph. D. Programs Foundation of Ministry of Education of China with Grant No. 2010JYBS0762.

X. Wang et al. (Eds.): WASA 2012, LNCS 7405, pp. 722–732, 2012.

and meet the real-time requirements in data transmission[1-6]. However, this article will primarily introduce a theoretical study of the estimation of signal covariance matrix in linear sensor networks which will be helpful in dealing with determining the direction of events popping up in the inspecting field of a LWSN.

The remainder of this article is organized as follows: in section 2, the covariance matrix estimation problem will be briefly introduced as well as the mathematical modeling of the signal covariance matrix of LWSNs. What is more, the underlying relationship between the direction determination problem and the estimation of signal covariance matrix is also revealed given this model. Section 3 will look into the existence of solutions to the estimation problems referring to the maximum-likelihood estimation. In section 4, the attention will be paid to how to obtain such a solution to the estimation problem. Additionally, the result of the estimation problem with respect to real-valued covariance matrices will be broaden into the realm of complex-valued covariance matrices which have a close relationship to orientation problems in LWSNs. Section 5 will conclude this article.

2   Brief Introduction to the Estimation of Covariance Matrix

In the area of statistics, the estimation of a covariance matrix[7-10] is to approximately determine the unknown covariance matrix C of an M-dimension multivariate random variable R given a series of $x_1, x_2, ..., x_N$. Each x_i is an M-dimension vector drawn from the multivariate distribution of which the probability density function is $p(x_i)$. And the covariance matrix C in calculated by $E[(R - E(R))(R - E(R))^H]$, where $E(\cdot)$ is an expectation, and $(\cdot)^H$ denotes the conjugate transpose of a matrix.

Assume that N events of interest burst out in the deploying area of the LWSN, and are sensed by M sensor node. Recall that these sensors are arranged in a linear fashion as shown in fig.1.

Suppose that the signals are narrow-banded with certain known frequency f in advance, and the sensors are equally spaced with respect to each other. It   is also assumed that these signals propagate over the distance long enough to make sure that the N received signals by all M sensors are parallel to each other as shown in fig.2.

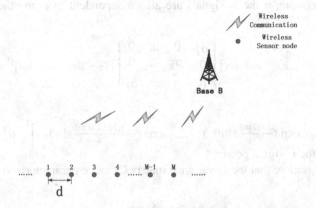

Fig. 1. Wireless Sensor Networks deployed in a linear fashion

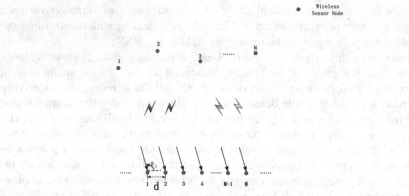

Fig. 2. N events of interest sensed by M sensor nodes

The N signals can be expressed by a M-by-N array manifold matrix G of the form

$$G = \begin{bmatrix} 1 & 1 & \cdots & 1 \\ \exp\left(-\dfrac{j2\pi d}{\lambda}\sin\theta_1\right) & \exp\left(-\dfrac{j2\pi d}{\lambda}\sin\theta_2\right) & \cdots & \exp\left(-\dfrac{j2\pi d}{\lambda}\sin\theta_N\right) \\ \cdots & \cdots & \cdots & \cdots \\ \exp\left(-\dfrac{j(M-1)2\pi d}{\lambda}\sin\theta_1\right) & \exp\left(-\dfrac{j(M-1)2\pi d}{\lambda}\sin\theta_2\right) & \cdots & \exp\left(-\dfrac{j(M-1)2\pi d}{\lambda}\sin\theta_N\right) \end{bmatrix}_{M\times N}$$

where λ denotes the wavelength of the signal, d denotes the distance between two sensor nodes, and θ_i denotes the arrival angle of the ith event with respect to the line of sensor nodes. If the received signals are interfered by some additive noise with zero mean and σ_n^2 variance Gaussian distribution which is uncorrelated with signals, the covariance matrix C of the received signals is of the form:

$$C = C_N + GPG^H \tag{1}$$

where C_N denotes the covariance matrix of M-dimension additive noise with zero mean and σ_n^2 variance Gaussian distribution, P denotes the correlation matrix between signals. Furthermore, it the N signals are also independent to each other, (1) can be cast as

$$C = \sigma_n^2 I_M + \begin{bmatrix} g_1 & g_2 & \cdots & g_N \end{bmatrix} \begin{bmatrix} \sigma_1^2 & 0 & \cdots & 0 \\ 0 & \sigma_2^2 & \cdots & 0 \\ \cdot\cdot & & \cdots & \\ 0 & 0 & \cdots & \sigma_N^2 \end{bmatrix} \begin{bmatrix} g_1 & g_2 & \cdots & g_N \end{bmatrix}^H = \sigma_n^2 I_M +$$

$$\sum_{i=1}^N \sigma_i^2 g_i g_i^H \tag{2}$$

where $g_i = \begin{bmatrix} 1 & \exp\left(-\dfrac{j2\pi d}{\lambda}\sin\theta_1\right) & \cdots & \exp\left(-\dfrac{j(M-1)2\pi d}{\lambda}\sin\theta_N\right) \end{bmatrix}^T$, σ_n^2 is the noise power, σ_i^2 is the ith signal power.

Till now, it is clear that the covariance matrix C can be parameterized by σ_n^2, $\{\sigma_i^2\}$, and $\{\theta_i\}$, i.e.,

$$C = C(\sigma_n^2, \{\sigma_i^2\}, \{\theta_i\}) \tag{3}$$

From (3), it is obvious that the covariance matrix conveys knowledge about the arrival angle θ_i of the ith signal in that C is a function of $\{\theta_i\}$ which will help us determine the direction of this signal. In the following sections, our discussion is mainly focused on how to estimating covariance matrices with certain special structure which is also possessed by C.

3   Estimation of Real-Valued Covariance Matrices with Certain Structure

The covariance matrix C is a complex valued toeplitz (please refer to the appendix for detailed information) matrix as is shown in (2). What is more, C is also a hermitian matrix since C is equal to C^H. However, even if C is such a structured matrix, it is still not easy to estimate C in that C is complex valued. Therefore, we first introduce the method which can be used to estimate some structured real valued matrices, and then the result will be extended to the realm of complex valued matrices.

3.1   Estimating the Covariance Matrices through Maximum-Likelihood Method

Suppose that the N real valued samples $x_1, x_2, ..., x_N$ are drawn from an M-dimension Gaussian distribution with zero mean and covariance matrix C. Therefore, the probability density function for each x_i is

$$p(x_i) = (2\pi)^{-\frac{M}{2}} \det(C)^{-\frac{1}{2}} exp\left(-\frac{x_i{}^T C^{-1} x_i}{2}\right) \qquad (4)$$

If all these samples are independent to each other, the joint probability density function of these N samples is

$$p(x_1, x_2, ..., x_N) = (2\pi)^{-\frac{MN}{2}} \det(C)^{-\frac{N}{2}} exp\left(-\sum_{i=1}^{N} \frac{x_i{}^T C^{-1} x_i}{2}\right) \qquad (5)$$

In (4) and (5), the covariance matrix C is unknown and to be estimated, however, we presume that C is with certain structure.

The log-likelihood function of C is

$$\ln\left(L(C; \{x_i\})\right) = \ln\left(p(x_1, x_2, ..., x_N)\right) = -\frac{MN}{2}\ln 2\pi - \frac{N}{2}\ln\det(C) - \frac{1}{2}\sum_{i=1}^{N} x_i{}^T C^{-1} x_i$$

$$= \frac{MN}{2}\ln 2\pi - \frac{N}{2}\ln\det(C) - \frac{1}{2}tr\left(C^{-1}\sum_{i=1}^{N} x_i x_i{}^T\right) \qquad (6)$$

The proof of the second equation can be found in Appendix.

Instead of maximizing the log-likelihood function stated in (6), it is equivalent to maximize the function

$$L'(C; \{x_i\}) = -\text{lndet}(C) - \text{tr}\left(C^{-1} \frac{1}{N} \sum_{i=1}^{N} x_i x_i^T\right) \tag{7}$$

Our estimator of C is $\hat{C} = \text{argmax}(L'(C; \{x_i\}))$.

3.2   The Existence of the Solution to the Maximum-Likelihood Problem of Certain Structured Covariance Matrices

In previous section, we have pointed out the estimation problem we are about to solve. In this section, a further study on the existence of solutions to this estimation problem will be carried out before discussing how to obtain such solutions. The real valued nonnegative-definite symmetric matrices will be taken into consideration because the observed samples will form such structured matrices.

Let $S = \frac{1}{N} \sum_{i=1}^{N} x_i x_i^T$, and substitute S into (7), we have

$$L'(C; S) = -\text{lndet}(C) - \text{tr}(C^{-1}S) \tag{8}$$

Obviously, S is a nonnegative definite symmetric matrix, and our estimation problem can be formulated as a optimization problem

Maximize: $L'(C; S) = -\text{lndet}(C) - \text{tr}(C^{-1}S)$

Subject to: C belongs to the set of nonnegative definite matrices

Before discussing the optimization problem, it is presumed that S is a positive definite matrix for every sample x_i we acquire only possesses zero valued entries if S is nonnegative definite but not positive definite, which will make the problem extremely difficult to deal with.

To prove the existence of solutions, we first look into the value of the objective function. We can prove that the objective function has an upper bound, and when det(C) goes to zero, the value of the function tends to be minus infinity. To prove this, we need a lemma first.

Lemma 1: if A and B are two positive definite symmetric matrices, there exists one unitary matrix U which will shoe these two matrices into diagonal matrices simultaneously through congruent transformation. (The proof of this lemma can be found in Appendix)

Theorem 1: the value of the objective function in above optimization problem has an upper bound, and tends to be minus infinity while det(C) goes to zero.

Proof: Firstly, suppose that C is positive definite, which means that det (C) is greater than zero. Because C and S are both real valued positive definite symmetric matrices, we know from Schur Theorem that there exists unitary matrices U_1 and U_2 which will make C and S congruent to two diagonal matrices. Moreover, from lemma 1, there will be one unitary matrix U which could shape C and S congruent to diagonal matrices simultaneously, i.e.,

$$U^T CU = \Lambda_C = \begin{bmatrix} c_1 & \cdots & 0 \\ \vdots & \ddots & \vdots \\ 0 & \cdots & c_M \end{bmatrix}, \text{and } U^T SU = \Lambda_S = \begin{bmatrix} s_1 & \cdots & 0 \\ \vdots & \ddots & \vdots \\ 0 & \cdots & s_M \end{bmatrix}$$

Therefore, $tr(C^{-1}S)$ can be rewritten as

$$tr(C^{-1}S) = tr(U(U^T CU)^{-1}U^T SUU^T) = tr(U\Lambda_C^{-1}\Lambda_S U^T) = tr(\Lambda_S\Lambda_C^{-1}) = \sum_{i=1}^M \frac{s_i}{c_i} \quad (9)$$

For arbitrary positive number a, $det(C) = a$, we can calculate the minimum value of $tr(C^{-1}S)$ via Lagrange Multiplier. If $tr(C^{-1}S)$ has a minimum value, then it means the value of (8) has an upper bound. The optimization problem here is

Minimize: $tr(C^{-1}S)$

Subject to: $det(C) = \prod_{i=1}^M c_i = a$

The Lagrange function is

$$F(\{c_i\}, \lambda) = tr(C^{-1}S) + \lambda[det(C) - a] \quad (10)$$

when $\begin{cases} c_i = \frac{s_i}{\lambda a} \\ \lambda = \frac{det(S)^{\frac{1}{M}}}{a^{\frac{1}{M}}} \frac{1}{a} \end{cases}$, $tr(C^{-1}S)$ will achieve its minimum value $\frac{det(S)^{\frac{1}{M}}}{det(C)^{\frac{1}{M}}} M$, and

$L'(C; S) \leq -\ln det(C) - \frac{det(S)^{\frac{1}{M}}}{det(C)^{\frac{1}{M}}} M$, which means that $L'(C; S)$ has an upper bound when C is positive definite.

If C is singular, i.e., $det(C) = 0$, the value of $L'(C; S) = -\ln det(C) - tr(C^{-1}S)$ tends to be minus infinity, which means $p(x_1, x_2, \ldots, x_N)$ tends to be zero, thus, trivial.

Therefore, we proved that $L'(C; S)$ has an upper bound when C is positive definite, and tends to be minus infinity when C is singular.

Form this theorem, we know that for any nonnegative definite matrix C, the value of $L'(C; S)$ will be less or equal to $-\ln det(C) - \frac{det(S)^{\frac{1}{M}}}{det(C)^{\frac{1}{M}}} M$.

In the following part of this section, we will prove that the solution to the maximum-likelihood problem does exist. However, before starting proving, one definition and one lemma need to be introduced.

Definition: For a positive number e, there is a set of es $M_e = \{M \in R^{M \times M} | |m_{ij}| \leq e\}$, where M is a $M \times M$ matrix, and m_{ij} is the entry lying in the ith row and j^{th} column of the matrix.

Lemma 2: If a matrix A a real valued nonnegative definite symmetric matrix, a_{mn} is the largest element among all entries in A with respect to magnitude, then we have $tr(A) \geq |a_{mn}|$. (The proof of this lemma can be found in Appendix.)

Now we start to prove the existence of the solution:

The set of nonnegative definite symmetric matrices is denoted as M_S. The intersection of M_e and M_S is shown in fig.3. It is clear that M_S is closed, and the boundary of M_S is the set of singular nonnegative definite symmetric matrices. The boundary of $M_e \cap M_S$ contains two parts: one is the set of singular nonnegative definite symmetric matrices (drawn in solid line), and the other is the set of positive definite symmetric matrices with one element on the main diagonal equal to e (drawn in the dash line). Moreover, from theorem 1, it is clear that the finite values of $L'(C; S)$ can only be obtained in the interior of M_S.

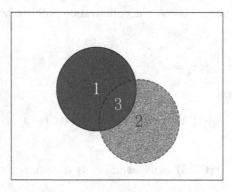

Fig. 3. The intersection of M_S and M_e. The area 1 denotes the set of M_S. The area 2 denotes the set of M_e, and the area 3 denotes the intersection of them.

To prove the existence of such a solution, we want to prove that for a large enough positive number e, the solution lies in the intersection of M_S and M_e. It is proved by contradiction. If such an e does not exist, it means for any e, there will always be an e' larger than e, and the optimal value of $L'(C; S)$ in $M_S \cap M_{e'}$ will be greater than that in $M_S \cap M_e$. Intuitively, the value of $L'(C; S)$ will be maximized when e goes to positive infinity. From lemma 1, we know there is a unitary matrix U which will transform C and S into diagonal matrices Λ_C and Λ_C simultaneously. Without losing generality, assume that c_k and s_l are the largest and smallest diagonal elements in Λ_C and Λ_C respectively. Form (9), $L'(C; S)$ can be cast as

$$L'(C; S) = -\sum_{i=1}^{M} (\ln c_i + \frac{s_i}{c_i}) = -\left(\ln c_k + \frac{s_k}{c_k}\right) - \sum_{i=1,i\neq k}^{M} (\ln c_i + \frac{s_i}{c_i})$$
$$\leq -\left(\ln c_k + \frac{s_l}{c_k}\right) - \sum_{i=1,i\neq k}^{M} (\ln c_i + \frac{s_i}{c_i})$$

(11)

The inequality holds for c_k and s_l are the largest and smallest diagonal elements in Λ_C and Λ_C respectively. From lemma 2, if the largest element in C is c_{mn} which is equal to e, it is obvious that

$$Mc_k \geq \text{tr}(C) \geq c_{mn} = e$$

(12)

Therefore, $c_k \geq \frac{e}{M}$, which indicates that when e goes to positive infinity, c_k will also go to positive infinity. What is more, when c_k tends to positive infinity, the value of $L'(C; S)$ will be minus infinity. Hence, it contradicts the hypothesis that when e goes to positive infinity, $L'(C; S)$ will be maximized. So, the solution to the estimation problem must exist and can be found in the intersection of M_S and M_e with certain large e.

4   The Method of Solving the Estimation Problem

In this section, the method of solving the estimation problem is acquired through total differential of a function. Recall the objective function is

$$L'(C; S) = -\ln\det(C) - \operatorname{tr}(C^{-1}S)$$

when this function achieves its maximum, the total differential of this function will be zero.

Note that the objective function is the function with matrix parameter. The total differential of a $F(M)$, where M is a matrix parameterized by $m_1, m_2, \ldots, m_k$, is

$$d(F(M)) = \sum_{i=1}^{k} \frac{\partial(F(M))}{\partial m_i} dm_i \qquad (13)$$

For example, if $F(M) = M$, and M is parameterized by all its elements, then the total differential of $F(M)$ is

$$dF(M) = \begin{bmatrix} 1 & \cdots & 0 \\ \vdots & \ddots & \vdots \\ 0 & \cdots & 0 \end{bmatrix} dm_{11} + \cdots + \begin{bmatrix} 0 & \cdots & 0 \\ \vdots & \ddots & \vdots \\ 0 & \cdots & 1 \end{bmatrix} dm_{NN} = \begin{bmatrix} dm_{11} & \cdots & dm_{1N} \\ \vdots & \ddots & \vdots \\ dm_{N1} & \cdots & dm_{NN} \end{bmatrix}$$

The total differential of the first part of (8) is

$$d(\det(C)) = \sum_{i=1}^{M} \frac{\partial \sum_{j=1}^{M} c_{ij} C_{ij}^*}{\partial c_{ij}} dc_{ij} = \operatorname{tr}(C^{-1}dC) \qquad (14)$$

where the C_{ij}^* denotes the adjoint matrix of c_{ij}.

The total differential of the second part of (8) is

$$d(\operatorname{tr}(C^{-1}S)) = -\operatorname{tr}(C^{-1}dCC^{-1}S) \qquad (15)$$

Therefore, the total differential of (8) is

$$d(L'(C; S)) = \operatorname{tr}(C^{-1}dCC^{-1}S - C^{-1}dC) = \operatorname{tr}[(C^{-1}SC^{-1} - C^{-1})dC] \qquad (16)$$

For any feasible direction of variation of C, the total differential must be zero, i.e., $\operatorname{tr}[(C^{-1}SC^{-1} - C^{-1})dC]$ must be zero. Especially, when dC meets the structure requirements of C, and since (16) is always zero for arbitrary direction of variation of C, we can substitute dC by C, which leads to

$$\operatorname{tr}(C^{-1}S) = M \qquad (17)$$

From this, it is clear that if there are no further constraints on C, the best estimator of C is S itself.

Till now, only the real valued covariance matrices estimation is taken into consideration. However, from the form of array manifold matrix, we know that the matrices of interest are complex valued matrices. Nevertheless, we can alter the estimation problem of complex valued matrices to the estimation of real valued matrices via reconstructing S.

Recall that in the real valued scenario, $S = \frac{1}{N}\sum_{i=1}^{N} x_i x_i^T$. Similarly, when the elements of x_i are complex valued, $S = \frac{1}{N}\sum_{i=1}^{N} x_i x_i^H$. We can struct $S^R = \frac{1}{N}\sum_{i=1}^{N} \begin{bmatrix} Re(x_i) \\ Im(x_i) \end{bmatrix} [Re(x_i)^T \quad Im(x_i)^T]$ which is obviously real valued, and positive definite symmetric as well. We can use the real valued and positive definite symmetric matrix S^R to estimate C^R.

Let $\quad O = \frac{1}{N}\sum_{i=1}^{N} Re(x_i)Re(x_i)^T$, $\quad P = \frac{1}{N}\sum_{i=1}^{N} Im(x_i)Im(x_i)^T$, and $Q = \frac{1}{N}\sum_{i=1}^{N} Re(x_i)Im(x_i)^T$, thus, $S^R = \begin{bmatrix} O & Q \\ Q^T & P \end{bmatrix}$. The estimation of C is acquired by averaging the outer product of N sensed data. What is more, the relationship between C^R and C is one-to-one mapping, i.e., $c_{ij} = o_{ij} + p_{ij} - jq_{ij} + jq_{ji}$.

Therefore, we can acquire the estimation of a complex valued matrix via estimation of a corresponding real values matrix. It is shown in the following example that how to acquire the arrival angels.

Suppose there are N events of interest and M sensor in the field. $x_1, x_2, ..., x_N$ are N samples we acquired, and each sample x_i is a M-dimension vector with each element equal to the signal of the ith event acquired by a sensor. Each vector is complex valued. The matrix $S = \frac{1}{N}\sum_{i=1}^{N} x_i x_i^H$ is used to estimate the covariance matrix C.

From above discussion the estimator of C can be obtained from the estimation of a real valued matrix $S^R = \begin{bmatrix} O & Q \\ Q^T & P \end{bmatrix}$ via Maximum-likelihood approach. Denote C' as the estimator of C. From section 2, the covariance matrix has the form of (1). Suppose that the received signals are interfered by some additive noise with zero mean and σ_n^2 variance Gaussian distribution, and the ith power of received signals is σ_i^2. We can acquire the array manifold matrix G through the following equation:

$$C' = \sigma_n^2 I_M + \sum_{i=1}^{N} \sigma_i^2 g_i g_i^H \tag{19}$$

Every g_i is with the form $\left[1 \quad exp\left(-\frac{j2\pi d}{\lambda}\sin\theta_1\right) \quad ... \quad exp\left(-\frac{j(M-1)2\pi d}{\lambda}\sin\theta_N\right)\right]$, which means the each arrival angle θ_i is now available to us.

5   Conclusion

In this article, intensive study has been made in order to estimate the angles of arrival of signals sensed by sensor nodes in linear wireless sensor networks. In dealing with this problem, we use signal covariance matrix estimation techniques after the discussion of the relationship between arrival angles and signal covariance matrices. The maximum-likelihood estimation approach is adopted to solve the estimation problem. In future researches, the relationship between arrival angles and covariance matrices needs to be further studied, which will reveal a much more explicit insight into the relationship between these subjects. Studies of other methods, such as parameter estimation, which will give us a direct way to acquire the arrival angles, and minimum entropy estimation, will also be carried out successively.

References

1. Zimmerling, M., Dargie, W., Reason, J.M.: Energy-Efficient Routing in Linear Wireless Sensor Networks. In: 2007 IEEE International Conference on Mobile Ad-hoc and Sensor Systems, vol. 1-3, pp. 210–212 (2007)
2. Gibson, J., Xie, G.G., Yang, X.: Performance Limits of Fair-Access in Sensor Networks with Linear and Selected Grid Topologies. In: GLOBECOM 2007: 2007 IEEE Global Telecommunications Conference, vol. 1-11, pp. 688–693 (2007)
3. Noori, M., Ardakani, M.: Characterizing the traffic distribution in linear wireless sensor networks. IEEE Communication Letters 12(8), 554–556 (2008)
4. Hong, L., Xu, S.: Energy-Efficient Node Placement in Linear Wireless Sensor Networks. In: International Conference on Measuring Technology and Mechatronics Automation (ICMTMA), vol. 2, pp. 104–107 (2010)
5. Ahmed, A.A., Shi, H., Shang, Y.: A survey on network protocols for wireless sensor networks. In: Proceedings of the International Conference on Information Technology: Research and Education, pp. 301–305 (August 2003)
6. Ye, W., Heidemann, J., Estrin, D.: Medium access control with coordinated adaptive sleeping for wireless sensor networks. IEEE/ACM Transactions on Networking 12(3), 493–506 (2004)
7. Werner, K.: Kronecker: structured covariance matrix estimation. In: Proceedings of 2007 IEEE International Conference on Acoustics, Speech, and Signal Processing, vol. 3, pts. 1-3, pp. 825–828 (2007)
8. Richter, A.: ML estimation of covariance matrix for tensor valued signals in noise. In: 2008 IEEE International Conference on Acoustics, Speech and Signal Processing, vol. 1-12, pp. 2349–2352 (2008)
9. Jansson, M.: ML Estimation of Covariance Matrices with Kroneckor and Persymmetirc Strucure. In: Proceedings of 2009 IEEE 13th Digital Signal Processing Workshop & 5th IEEE Proessing Education Workshop, vol. 1, 2, pp. 298–301 (2009)
10. Werner, K.: On Estimation of Covariance Matrices With Kronecker Product Structure. IEEE Transactions on Signal Processing 56(2), 478–491 (2008)

Appendix

Toeplitz Matrix

A matrix T is a toeplitz matrix if arbitrary element t_{ij} in T is equal to t_{i-j}, i.e.,

$$T = \begin{bmatrix} t_0 & \cdots & t_{1-M} \\ t_1 & \cdots & t_{2-M} \\ \cdots & \cdots & \cdots \\ t_{M-1} & \cdots & t_0 \end{bmatrix}$$

$$\sum_{i=1}^{N} x_i^T C^{-1} x_i = \sum_{i=1}^{N} \text{tr}(x_i^T C^{-1} x_i) = \sum_{i=1}^{N} \text{tr}(C^{-1} x_i x_i^T) = \sum_{i=1}^{N} C^{-1} \text{tr}(x_i x_i^T)$$

Lemma 1

Proof: if A and B are positive definite symmetric, the matrix A+B is also positive definite symmetric. It is obvious that a positive definite symmetric matrix is congruent to identity matrix I. Therefore, A+B is congruent to I, and the congruence matrix is U1, i.e., $U_1^T(A + B)U_1 = I$. It is clear that the matrix $U_1^T A U_1$ is positive definite symmetric as well, hence, there exists one unitary matrix U_2 which will change $U_1^T A U_1$ into a diagonal matrix Λ_A, i.e., $U_2^T U_1^T A U_1 U_2 = \Lambda_A$. Hence,

$$U_2^T U_1^T(A + B)U_1 U_2 = \Lambda_A + U_2^T U_1^T B U_1 U_2 = I.$$

Therefore, $U_2^T U_1^T B U_1 U_2 = I - U_2^T U_1^T A U_1 U_2$, which means that $U_2^T U_1^T B U_1 U_2$ is also a diagonal matrix. So, there exists one unitary matrix $U_1 U_2$ which can shape A and B into diagonal matrix simultaneously.

Lemma 2

Proof: if a_{mn} is positive, we construct a vector with mth and nth entries equal to 1 and -1. Then we have

$$x^T A x = a_{mm} + a_{nn} - a_{mn} - a_{nm} = a_{mm} + a_{nn} - 2a_{mn} \geq 0$$

Because A is nonnegative definite, it elements on the main diagonal are all greater than or equal to zero. Therefore, we have $\text{tr}(A) \geq 2a_{mn} \geq a_{mn}$.

If a_{mn} is negative, we construct a vector with mth and nth entries both equal to 1. Then we have

$$x^T A x = a_{mm} + a_{nn} + a_{mn} + a_{nm} = a_{mm} + a_{nn} + 2a_{mn} \geq 0$$

Therefore, we have $\text{tr}(A) \geq -2a_{mn} \geq -a_{mn} = |a_{mn}|$.

Leveraging Cloud Computing for Privacy Preserving Aggregation in Multi-domain Wireless Networks

Chengxin Xiao, Weiwei Jia, Haojin Zhu, Suguo Du, and Zhenfu Cao

Shanghai Jiao Tong University, Shanghai 200240, P.R. China
{xcjack,jlss,zhu-hj,sgdu,zfcao}@sjtu.edu.cn

Abstract. Enabling privacy preserving outsourced data aggregation is regarded as an important issue for multi-domain wireless networks. In this paper, we present a novel hybrid cloud based privacy preserving outsourced data aggregation framework. To achieve this, we introduce a hybrid storage cloud and aggregator cloud architecture, in which both of the storage clouds and aggregator cloud are assumed to be untrusted but they cannot collude with each other. Based on this security assumption, we propose two novel protocols, including the pro-active privacy preserving data aggregation and passive privacy preserving data aggregation schemes, which are based on the idea of secret sharing. The pro-active scheme allows the user to pro-actively split their data to multiple storage clouds to avoid data leaking while the passive scheme allows the users to store their encrypted data in storage cloud and aggregator to finish the data aggregation based on the encrypted data. The detailed performance simulations are given to demonstrate the security, effectiveness and efficiency of the proposed scheme.

Keywords: Privacy Aggregation, Cloud Computing, Participatory Sensing.

1 Introduction

Data aggregation is regarded as an important research topic in wireless networks. For example, participatory sensing is an emerging paradigm that targets the seamless collection of data from a large number of user-carried devices. By equipping a sensor to a mobile phone, participatory sensing enables harvesting dynamic information about environmental trends by aggregating the information from any individual sensors. The potential applications of participatory sensing include ambient air quality, urban traffic patterns, health-related information, parking availabilities, sound events, etc [1]. Different from conventional wireless sensor networks, in which the sensors may be owned by the same network operator, mobile devices are tasked to participate into gathering and sharing local knowledge; thus, different entities co-exist and might not trust each other. In this work, we coined such kind of wireless networks which are comprised of various trust domains as multi-domain wireless networks.

Privacy issue is arising as an important issue for data aggregation in wireless multi-domain networks. We consider individuals of the communities with generated private data for personal or confidential reasons. These data could also be of value if shared with the community for fusion purposes to compute aggregate metrics of mutual interest. One main problem in such applications is privacy. This problem will be more serious

X. Wang et al. (Eds.): WASA 2012, LNCS 7405, pp. 733–744, 2012.

if the individuals come from various domains, which makes it lack a centralized and trusted aggregator to make the privacy preserving data aggregation.

The existing privacy preserving aggregation approaches use either a trusted third party, peer-to-peer techniques, or adding some noises to each data for data aggregation and face a delicate privacy versus utility tradeoff [1–3]. However, applying the existing solutions to the considered wireless multi-domain networks faces the following challenges. Firstly, the existing proposals normally assume a static system topology or a trusted aggregator for the privacy preserving data aggregation. This assumption is not suitable for wireless multi-domain networks which are characterized as multiple trust domains and thus lack a centralized aggregator. Secondly, the existing solutions only consider the data aggregation while fail to consider the data storage issues, while, in practice, the ideal aggregation scheme should only require the individuals to submit their data for once but allow the flexible aggregation queries for multiple times to meet the diversified aggregation goals. Therefore, it is desirable to design a new privacy preserving architecture to allow the flexible and efficient privacy preserving data aggregation.

On the other hand, cloud computing is envisioned to enable on-demand access to computing and data storage resources [4], which can be configured to meet unique constraints of the clients and utilized with minimal management overhead. The recent rapid growth in availability of cloud services makes such services attractive and economically sensible for clients with limited computing or storage resources who are unwilling or unable to procure and maintain their own computing infrastructure. Leveraging cloud in data aggregation has the advantage of expertise consolidation, since cloud can potentially offer the service with much lower cost and also with better scalability, performance, and availability guarantees. Therefore, not surprisingly, outsourcing data stream and the desired computations to a third party server becomes a practical alternative to many companies. Such outsourcing of data and computation has received a lot of attention in recent years, partly due to the increasing availability of cloud computing [5, 6].

In this study, we propose a novel Cloud based Privacy Preserving Aggregation Architecture (CPPA), which aims to jointly consider data storage and aggregation in the same framework. Different from existing solutions which consider a trusted third party, we will introduce two kinds of untrusted clouds, coined as storage clouds (SC) and the aggregation cloud (AC), which are responsible for data storage and data aggregation, respectively. In the multi-domain networks, the users will submit their encrypted data to their SC for once and SCs allow the aggregation cloud to make the data aggregation for multiple times. To enable the untrusted aggregator for privacy preserving data aggregation, we propose two novel schemes, including proactive privacy preserving aggregation scheme (PPPA) and reactive privacy preserving aggregation (RPPA), which allow the aggregator to compute the aggregation result without obtaining any individual value. Specifically, PPPA allows privacy preserving data aggregation without any encryption protocols by enabling the users proactively to split their data into multiple shares, which are stored at different SCs and will be recovered at the AC as long as all of there data is collected by AC. Different from PPPA, RPPA allows data encrypted in the SCs and could be aggregated at the aggregator as long as all of the aggregation data is received by AC. In both of schemes, CPPA supports the privacy preserving aggregation while only requires the users to provide data for once, which achieves the maximum flexibility for users.

The remainder of this paper is organized as follows. Section 2 introduces the system model and some preliminaries. Section 3 presents our protocol, Section 4 analyzes the security. Section 5 presents the experiments on our protocol and Section 6 concludes this paper.

2   System Model and Preliminaries

In this section, we introduce some motivating applications, and then define the system models and design goals.

2.1   Motivating Applications

We envision three distinct aggregation scenarios using CPPA. The first scenario is aggregating information coming from multiple domains of mobile social networks (Twitter, Youtube, Douban, or Renren). The task is often performed by a social network aggregator, which pulls together information into a single location, such as the average rating on a specific movie. This aggregation is presently not always possible due to privacy concerns and heterogeneous jurisdiction. The second scenario is analyzing private data owned by independent organizations with a mutual benefit in collaborating. Participatory sensing belongs to this category [1–3]. The last scenario is financial aggregation [7] for mobile payments. In financial aggregation, a user may have multiple accounts usually held at various providers and the third party aggregator will provide the various aggregation services for single user (e.g., balance forecasting, long-term investment projections) or multiple users (e.g., aggregating real estate data from external companies). In the current financial aggregation model, the users were very concerned that having all their information in one place, and accessing other bank accounts, would lead to a lack of privacy and security and expose them to unwanted marketing. So there is the dilemma of the need to provide the information necessary to have a useful outcome but then risking misuse of this information.

2.2   Network Model

To achieve privacy guaranteed outsourced aggregation, we consider the following cloud based aggregation model, in which four parties participate in the data storage and aggregation, including *trusted server*, *the users*, *Storage Cloud* (or *SC*) and *Aggregator Cloud* (or *AC*). Under this model, the users stores their encrypted data by using the parameters from *trusted server* before they store their outsourced data in the storage clouds. Note that, the users may upload their data to multiple storage clouds corresponding to multiple financial service providers (e.g., banks) in reality. Then users submit their data to *aggregator* . When an aggregation request is triggered, *aggregator cloud* sends a request to the *storage cloud*. *Storage cloud* thus transform users' data then send to *aggregator cloud*. Finally the *aggregator cloud* can compute the result.

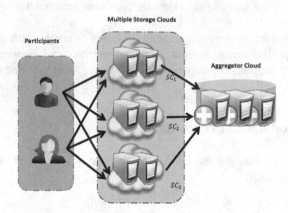

Fig. 1. System Model

2.3 Threat Model and Security Assumptions

In the system, we assume that *trusted server* is a trusted third party, who will be responsible for generating the secret keys for users. Both of the *storage cloud* and *aggregator cloud* are curious but honest, which means that they are curious about the users' data but will honestly to follow the protocols. In particular, we consider the following two privacy attack models:

- *Storage Privacy Cheating Model*: An untrusted cloud server (or a cloud server hacked by attackers) may compromise the cloud users privacy by accessing or even misusing their sensitive data (e.g., leaking their confidential information to their business competitors), which may incur serious consequences.
- *Aggregation Privacy Cheating Model*: An untrusted data aggregation cloud may compromise the cloud users privacy by accessing or even misusing their sensitive data.

However, we do not assume that the storage cloud and aggregator cloud collude to launch the attack. This assumption has been supported by the recent research [8].

2.4 Design Goals

The proposed scheme is expected to achieve the following security and performance goals:

- Secure Data Storage: Our scheme could resist Storage Privacy Cheating attacks launched by the untrusted SC.
- Privacy Preserving Aggregation: Our scheme could resist Aggregation Privacy Cheating attacks launched by the untrusted AC.
- Efficiency: The computation and transmission overhead of secure cloud computing auditing should be minimized.

3   Overview of the Protocols

CPPA is comprised of two protocols, *Proactive Privacy Preserving Aggregation Protocol* (or *PPPA*) and the *Reactive Privacy Preserving Protocol* (or *RPPA*). PPPA corresponds to the case that the user could arbitrarily split the data into multiple shares and thus take advantage of secret sharing to hide the data. In stead, RPPA could be employed in the case that the user's data is pre-determined and thus cannot be changed. In this case, RPPA allows the user to store their data encrypted in homomorphic encryption and the aggregation result will be recovered by the AC. Specifically, we have a more detailed description on PPPA and RPPA, which are shown in Fig. 2 and Fig. 3.

PPPA is based on the idea of the secret sharing, which is implemented at the data uploading phase. When users upload their data to SCs, the users actively and randomly divide their data into shares, and distribute these shares into the SCs. Since we do not assume the collusion attack between the SCs, the randomly dividing and the independently data storage ensures the privacy of users' data. On the other hand, to prevent AC from obtaining the data storage information from SCs, we propose a novel linear equation based aggregation scheme, which enables AC to obtain the aggregation results without knowing the individual data from each SC.

Different from PPPA, RPPA does not assume the data splitting in the data uploading phase. In stead, users use Paillier homomorphic encryption and the aggregator's public key $P(pk_{agg}, \cdot)$ to encrypt their data shares before uploading [9]. Since every user uses the same (aggregator's) public key to encrypt their shares, it is feasible to aggregate on the ciphertext by employing the homomophic properties of Paillier encryption. To prevent partial sum information for each SC, we propose the second protocol which is based on the homomorphic encryption and data sharing idea, which also enables the AC to obtain the aggregation results without knowing the individual data from each SC or each user.

Note that, the proposed CPPA scheme is a general framework, which could allow the diversified aggregation applications. It could support the case of a single user with multiple domain aggregation, in which a user may have different accounts in different domains (or SCs). RPPA could naturally support multiple users in a single domain. Hence, both PPPA and RPPA could support multiple users in multiple domains. In the next section, we will present the protocol details.

4   Concrete Protocols

In this section, we propose two protocols to realize the privacy-preserving storage and privacy-preserving aggregation. Our first protocol, called the *proactive protocol*, offers the privacy-preserving storage based on data owners randomly dividing their data before storing. Moreover, we present the corresponding aggregation protocol to efficiently realize the privacy-preserving data aggregation. Our second *passive protocol* is based on the Paillier encryption to provide the privacy for each shares stored in the cloud. The security of the second protocol is built on the security of Paillier encryption and CDH problem.

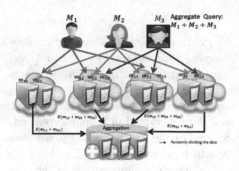 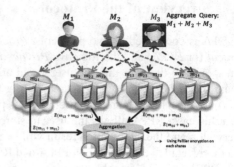

Fig. 2. Proactive Privacy Preserving Aggregation Protocol

Fig. 3. Reactive Privacy Preserving Aggregation Protocol

4.1 Protocol I: Proactive Privacy Preserving Aggregation (PPPA) Protocol

In our first protocol, we allow the user initiatively and randomly divide his true values into shares. A storage cloud is responsible for storing one share. Since the randomness of each share, the storage cloud is ignorant of the user's true values. In the following, we design a novel protocol to realize the privacy-preserving aggregation on the partial summation which is the sum of different users' shares stored in one storage cloud. Let u_i denote the partial summation for cloud i. Our basic idea is to permit the storage cloud randomly dividing his partial summation into m shares. That is, for storage cloud i's data u_i which has $u_i = c_{i1} + c_{i2} + \cdots + c_{im}$. To clearly describe our idea, we use a matrix (1) to represent the n storage clouds' data shares. Each row represents a cloud's data shares. For example, u_i is represented by the ith row $(c_{i1}, c_{i2}, \cdots, c_{im})$.

$$\begin{pmatrix} c_{11} & c_{12} & \cdots & c_{1m} \\ c_{21} & c_{22} & \cdots & c_{2m} \\ \cdots & \cdots & \cdots & \cdots \\ c_{n1} & c_{n2} & \cdots & c_{nm} \end{pmatrix} \tag{1}$$

Thus the desired result of the data aggregation is $\sum_{i=1}^{n} u_i = \sum_{i=1}^{n} \sum_{j=1}^{m} c_{ij} = \sum_{j=1}^{m} \sum_{i=1}^{n} c_{ij}$. The only way by which the aggregator can get the results is to collect the $\sum_{i=1}^{n} c_{ij}$ for each column while have no idea about the shares value c_{ij}. In order to achieve this goal, we design a novel mechanism to regard the $\sum_{i=1}^{n} c_{ij}, j = 0, 1, \cdots, m$ as a uniqueness solution of linear equations.

4.2 Protocol Description

We explain our protocol from two aspects: the secure storing and the privacy preserving aggregation.

– **Secure Storing.** The user randomly divides their data into shares and distributes these shares into cloud. One cloud is responsible for storing one share.

– **Privacy Preserving Aggregation**

Step 1. For n storage clouds, a trusted server needs to distribute keys to each storage cloud. To generate those keys, the trusted server generate n random numbers $r_1, r_2, ..., r_n$ and ensure that $\sum_{i=1}^{n} r_i = 0$, where n is the number of storage clouds. Then the trusted server distributes these random numbers to the storage clouds, each storage cloud get one number. We use c_{im} to denote the random value.

$$c_{im} \longleftarrow r_i \tag{2}$$

where c_{im} is the random number from trusted server and the sum of c_{im} is zero. $\sum_{i=1}^{n} c_{im} = 0$

– **Step 2.** The aggregator cloud launches the aggregation query to the storage cloud. Each storage cloud will do aggregation locally first to get the partial summation of the queried users. We use R_i to present the local result.

Then each storage cloud split the local result R_i into m parts, where m is the security parameters. Storage device split the local result combining with its key c_{im} distributed by trusted server in step 1.

$$R_i = c_{i1} + c_{i2} + ... + c_{im} \tag{3}$$

– **Step 3.** Then the aggregator generates a matrix M with m dimensions. we use a matrix (4) to represent the nonsingular matrix M.

$$\begin{pmatrix} x_{11} & x_{12} & \cdots & x_{1m} & x_{1m+1} \\ x_{21} & x_{22} & \cdots & x_{2m} & x_{2m+1} \\ \cdots & \cdots & \cdots & \cdots \\ x_{m1} & x_{m2} & \cdots & x_{mm} & x_{mm+1} \end{pmatrix} \tag{4}$$

Then the aggregator sends matrix M to all storage clouds. After receiving this matrix, storage cloud transform $c_{i1}, c_{i2}, c_{i3}, ..., c_{im}$ to $y_{i1}, y_{i2}, ..., y_{im}$. For each storage cloud, the process is as below:

$$\begin{cases} y_{i1} = c_{i1} + c_{i2}x_{12} + ... + c_{im}x_{1m} + s_{i1}x_{1m+1} \\ y_{i2} = c_{i1} + c_{i2}x_{22} + ... + c_{im}x_{2m} + s_{i2}x_{2m+1} \\ ... \\ y_{im} = c_{i1} + c_{i2}x_{m2} + ... + c_{im}x_{mm} + s_{im}x_{mm+1} \end{cases} \tag{5}$$

Then storage cloud send $y_{i1}, y_{i2}, ..., y_{im}$ to the aggregator.

– **Step 4.** To get the aggregation value, the aggregator adds all y_{ij} together and gets a new equation set, the equation set is as follows:

$$\begin{cases} \sum_{i=1}^{n} y_{i1} + s_{01}x_{1m+1} = \sum_{i=1}^{n} c_{i1} + \sum_{i=1}^{n} c_{i1}x_{11} + ... + \sum_{i=1}^{n} c_{im}x_{1m} \\ \sum_{i=1}^{n} y_{i2} + s_{02}x_{2m+1} = \sum_{i=1}^{n} c_{i1} + \sum_{i=1}^{n} c_{i1}x_{21} + ... + \sum_{i=1}^{n} c_{im}x_{2m} \\ ... \\ \sum_{i=1}^{n} y_{im} + s_{0m}x_{mm+1} = \sum_{i=1}^{n} c_{i1} + \sum_{i=1}^{n} c_{i1}x_{m1} + ... + \sum_{i=1}^{n} c_{im}x_{mm} \end{cases} \tag{6}$$

By solving the above equation matrix, AC can get $\sum_{i=1}^{n} c_{i1}, \sum_{i=1}^{n} c_{i2}, ..., \sum_{i=1}^{n} c_{im}$. Then the final result is the sum of all c_{ij}.

$$Result = \sum_{i=1}^{n} \sum_{j=1}^{m} c_{ij} \tag{7}$$

4.3   Protocol II: Passive Protocol

In this section we introduce our second protocol.

- **Secure Storing.** As the setup, each user encrypt their data with the public key of aggregator. We use Paillier homomorphic encryption here so that the aggregator can compute the sum of users' data. Then users upload their data to any storage clouds. For each user i, we denote the user's data by u_i and denote the encrypted data by $P(u_i)$.
- **Privacy Preserving Aggregation**
  Step 1. The trusted server generates n random numbers $r_1, r_2, ..., r_n$ and ensures that $\sum_{i=1}^{n} r_i = 0$, where n is the number of storage clouds. Then the trusted server distribute these random numbers to storage clouds. Each storage cloud get one number. We use sk_i to denote the random number.

$$sk_i \longleftarrow r_i \tag{8}$$

  where sk_i is the random number from trusted server and the sum of sk_i is zero. $\sum_{i=1}^{n} sk_i = 0$.
- **Step 2.** When the aggregator needs to do aggregation, it sends a request package to each storage cloud, including the ID of participated users. After receiving the request, each storage cloud finds the participated users' data and do aggregation locally first. For each storage cloud i, the process is as below:

$$R_i \longleftarrow \prod_{j=1}^{k} P(u_j) \tag{9}$$

$$A_i \longleftarrow R_i H(t)^{sk_i} \tag{10}$$

  where t is time slot, H is a hash function, sk_i is the key generated by trusted server. Then the storage cloud sends A_i to aggregator.
- **Step 3.** After receiving $A_1, A_2, ..., A_n$ from the storage clouds. The aggregator compute the result is as below:

$$EncryptedResult = \prod_{i=1}^{n} A_i = \prod_{i=1}^{n} R_i H(t)^{sk_1 + sk_2 + ... + sk_n} \tag{11}$$

  where n is the number of storage clouds. Note that $\sum_{i=1}^{n} sk_i = 0$, so the result is computed as:

$$EncryptedResult = \prod_{i=1}^{n} R_i H(t)^{sk_1 + sk_2 + ... + sk_n} = \prod_{i=1}^{n} R_i \tag{12}$$

We use Paillier homomorphic encryption here, so the final result is like below:

$$Result = D(EncryptedResult) = D(\prod_{i=1}^{n} R_i) = \sum_{j=1}^{m} u_j \qquad (13)$$

where m is the total number of participated users.

5 Security Analysis

In this section, we will discuss the correctness and the robustness of the proposed scheme as follows.

5.1 The Security Analysis of Protocol I

The correctness of protocol I is obvious and the aggregator get the desired result after implementing the protocol. In the following, we will discuss the robustness of our protocol.

Theorem 1. Based on the security of the Paillier encryption scheme and the CDH difficult problem, our protocol II is secure under the storage privacy cheating model and the aggregation privacy cheating model.

In the data storage phase, the user, using the Paillier and the aggregator's public key, encrypt his data shares before uploading. The privacy of data shares is based on the security of the Paillier encryption. For the aggregation, the aggregator cloud receive the encrypted partial summation $R_i H(t)^{sk_i}$ from each cloud. With the ignorant of the secret key sk_i for ith cloud storage, the aggregator can not recover the $R_{(i)}$ which is based on the CDH problem. Therefore, the protocol I achieves the privacy-preserving aggregation for each cloud's partial summation.

5.2 The Security Analysis of Protocol II

Correctness. In the advanced protocol, the data aggregator can correctly get the sum of the users' data. By decrypting the received data from the storage cloud, the aggregator obtains the linear equations set as in the basic protocol. Moreover, Since that the different chosen of $x_1, x_2, \cdots, x_m$, the equation set has the unique solution. So the aggregation result is correct.

Robustness. We also discuss how to prevent the storage privacy leaking attack in terms of storage privacy leaking and aggregation privacy leaking.

1. **Preventing Storage Privacy Leaking:** Since our data storage is based on the homomorphic encryption. Therefore, the security of the data storage is based on the security of the adopted homomorphic encryption.
2. **Prevent Aggregation Privacy Leaking:** In our protocol, the participant i use x_1, $x_2, \cdots, x_m$ to construct an equation set which has $m + 1$ variables and m equations. Moreover, the aggregator has no information on the data shares. Therefore our protocol guarantees the privacy-preserving data aggregation.

6   Performance Evaluation

In this section we presents a detailed implementation and evaluation of the proposed protocol. We chose different parameters and evaluate the performance the proposed scheme.

6.1   Experimental Testbed Setup

In the experiment, we implement the program in Java and run the program in a computer with 2.26GHz dual-core CPU and 2G memory. The data set we used is the usage information of CPU cluster from Morgan Stanley. We use Paillier homomorphic encryption in our experiment, Paillier instance we used here is constructed with 512 bits of modulus. We tested both of our protocol I and protocol II.

6.2   Experimental Result

In this section we do experiment to evaluate our protocol I and protocol II. Then we compare and analyze these two protocols.

6.3   Protocol I

We tested the number of security parameters ranged from 5 to 55, the number of users ranged from 10000 to 50000 and the number of storage clouds ranged from 10 to 30 in our experiment. We tested cost of users, cost of storage clouds and cost of aggregator in our experiment.

The result shown in Fig.4 is the cost of storage clouds. We tested different security parameters, where the definition of security parameter is the dimension of the matrix M. It is also the same as the number of split shares in each storage clouds. We use Vandermonde matrix here when the storage cloud transform the users' data, so the main cost of storage cloud mainly depends on the construction of Vandermonde matrix we chosen. We can see in those graphs the cost of storage clouds increased with the number

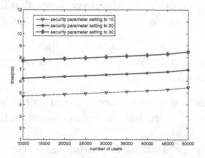
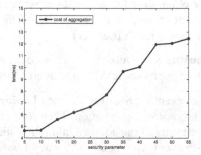

Fig. 4. Cost of storage clouds with different security parameter

Fig. 5. Cost of aggregator with different security parameter

of users increasing and also the value of security parameter (the same as dimension of Vandermonde matirx) increasing.

The result shown in Fig.5 is the cost of aggregator. Aggregator's responsibility in our protocol is to generate matrix M for storage clouds and to solve the equation set and get the final result. So the cost of aggregator is the cost of solving equation set and the construction of matrix M. It is increased with the increasing of the dimension of the matrix.

6.4 Protocol II

For protocol II, we also tested the number of security parameters ranged from 5 to 55, the number of users ranged from 10000 to 50000 and the number of storage clouds ranged from 10 to 30 in our experiment. We tested cost of users, cost of storage clouds and cost of aggregator in our experiment.

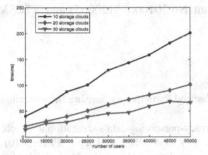
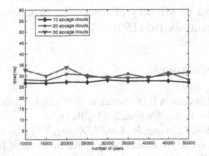

Fig. 6. Cost of storage clouds with different number of storage clouds and different number of users

Fig. 7. Cost of aggregator with different number of storage clouds and different number of users

The result shown in Fig.6 is the cost of storage devices. In our protocol, the users needs to encrypt their data and store in the storage devices, each user store data in one device. Then for aggregation, storage device needs to aggregate the participated users locally before it sends data to aggregator. So the cost of storage devices is mainly depends on the local participated data. We can see as the number of storage devices increasing, the cost of each storage device decreased. And the cost of each storage device as the number of users increasing.

Fig.7 is the result of cost of aggregator. In our protocol II, the aggregator needs to do aggregation on the encrypted data and needs to decrypt and get the final result, so the main cost here is the cost of decryption. As we can see in the graph, the cost of aggregator almost the same when the number of users increasing. That's because the storage device will do aggregation locally first, then send the local result to the aggregator. As the number of storage devices increasing, the cost of aggregator increased slightly because the main cost is decryption but not multiplication.

7 Conclusion

In this paper, we have proposed a new privacy preserving architecture to support flexible outsourced data aggregation in multi-domain wireless networks by leveraging hybrid cloud computing. The basic idea of the proposed scheme is allowing multiple clouds to share only a part of the secret while the collaboration of them allows the users could achieve privacy preserving data aggregation for inputting the data for once. Our future work includes implement it on a large scale testbed and evaluate the performance of the proposed scheme.

Acknowledgement. The work described in this paper was partially supported by Morgan Stanley. Morgan Stanley and Shanghai Jiao Tong University Innovation Center of Computing in Financial Services have entered into Collaboration Agreement No.CIP-A20110324-3. This research was also supported by National Natural Science Foundation of China (Grant No.61003218, 70971086, 61161140320, 61033014), Doctoral Fund of Ministry of Education of China (Grant No.20100073120065) and STCSM (Grant No. 10511501503).

References

1. Cristofaro, E.D., Soriente, C.: PEPSI: Privacy-Enhanced Participatory Sensing Infrastructure. In: Proc. of WiSec 2011 (2011)
2. Shi, J., Zhang, R., Liu, Y., Zhang, Y.: PriSense: privacy-preserving data aggregation in people-centric urban sensing systems. In: Proc. of IEEE INFOCOM 2010, San Diego. IEEE (2010)
3. Zhang, F., He, L., He, W., Liu, X.: Data Perturbation with State-Dependent Noise for Participatory Sensing. In: Proc. of INFOCOM 2012, Orlando, FL (2012)
4. Yu, S., Wang, C., Ren, K., Lou, W.: Achieving secure, scalable, and fine-grained data access control in cloud computing. In: Proc. of IEEE INFOCOM 2010 (2010)
5. Popa, R.A., Zeldovich, N., Balakrishnan, H.: CryptDB: A practical encrypted relational DBMS, Technical Report MIT-CSAIL-TR-2011-005. MIT (2011)
6. Shi, E., Chan, T., Rieffel, E., Chow, R., Song, D.: Privacy-preserving aggregation of time-series data. In: Proc. NDSS 2011 (2011)
7. Singh, S., Fleischmann, K., Ponton, T., Bellamy, S.: Alleviating Privacy and Security Concerns in Financial Aggregation Programs. Communications Policy & Research Forum 2009 (2009)
8. Duan, Y., Canny, J., Zhan, J.: P4P: Practical Large-Scale Privacy-Preserving Distributed Computation Robust against Malicious Users. In: Proc. of USENIX Security 2010 (2010)
9. Paillier, P.: Public-Key Cryptosystems Based on Composite Degree Residuosity Classes. In: Stern, J. (ed.) EUROCRYPT 1999. LNCS, vol. 1592, pp. 223–238. Springer, Heidelberg (1999)

Author Index